DISABILITY LAW COMPLIANCE MANUAL

GARY S. MARX

Member of the Alabama, District of Columbia, and Maryland Bars

GARY G. GOLDBERGER

Member of the California and Maryland Bars

WARREN, GORHAM & LAMONT
Boston ● New York

DEDICATION

to our wives
Julie Rabinowitz Marx and Deborah Goldberger
and our children
Jacob Marx, Jennifer Goldberger, and Stephanie Goldberger
with love

Preface

This volume presents a comprehensive analysis of the Americans With Disabilities Act of 1990 (ADA) and provides practical advice on compliance. It includes a thorough study of the legislative history of the ADA, as well as the case law under predecessor statutes. Statutory language and administrative regulations are carefully examined, and areas of uncertainty are indicated.

For convenience, four appendixes are included following the text: case summaries, the complete text of the Americans With Disabilities Act of 1990, regulations under the ADA, and a list of resources on employing persons with disabilities.

The authors wish to thank Robin Stutman and Julie Vaughan for their contributions to Chapters 2 and 3, respectively, and Wendy Fink for her assistance in the preparation of the case summaries. Thanks also to the editorial staff of WG&L for their guidance, good humor, and patience in shaping this work.

GARY S. MARX
GARY G. GOLDBERGER

May 1991

Summary of Contents

Table of Contents

3 Reasonable Accommodation

4 ADA Title II: Public Accommodations and Services Operated by Public Entities

5 ADA Title III: Public Accommodations and Services Operated by Private Entities

6 ADA Title IV: Telecommunications

7 Tax Considerations

TABLE OF CONTENTS

CHAPTER 1

Introduction to the Americans With Disabilities Act of 1990

¶ 1.01 NEED FOR THE ADA

On July 26, 1990, President George Bush signed into law the Americans With Disabilities Act of 1990 (the ADA).[1] Congress's goals in passing the ADA were to provide a clear and comprehensive mandate to end discrimination against individuals with disabilities and to bring them into the economic and social mainstream of American life.[2] The purpose of the ADA is "to provide clear, strong, consistent, enforceable standards addressing discrimination against individuals with disabilities."[3]

There are over 43 million Americans with one or more physical or mental disabilities.[4] As the nation's population increases, so does the number of disabled.[5] Historically, our society has tended to isolate and segregate these people.[6] Census data, national polls, and studies have all shown that the disabled, as a whole, "occupy an inferior status in our society and are severely disadvantaged socially, vocationally, economically, and educationally."[7]

In considering the ADA, Congress found that discrimination against the disabled is a "serious and pervasive social problem."[8] Disabled individuals encounter both outright intentional discrimination and unintentional discrimination arising from "architectural, transportation, and communication barriers, overprotective rules and policies, failure to make modifications to existing facilities and practices, exclusionary qualification standards and criteria, segregation, and relegation to lesser ser-

---

[1] Americans With Disabilities Act of 1990, Pub. L. No. 101-336, 104 Stat. 327 (hereinafter cited as ADA) (signed into law July 26, 1990).

[2] Congressional Statement of Purpose, ADA § 2(b)(1); Report of the House Comm. on Education and Labor on the Americans With Disabilities Act of 1990, HR Rep. No. 485, 101st Cong., 2d Sess., pt. 2 (1990) (hereinafter cited as H. Comm. on Educ. and Lab. Rep.) at 22.

[3] Congressional Statement of Purpose, ADA § 2(b)(2).

[4] ADA § 2(a)(1).

[5] Id.

[6] ADA § 2(a)(2).

[7] ADA § 2(a)(6).

[8] ADA § 2(a)(2).

vices, programs, activities, benefits, jobs or other opportunities."[9]

Prior to the ADA's passage, there was only limited protection against such discrimination.[10] The Rehabilitation Act of 1973[11] legislation that is now nearly two decades old, only applies to certain federal contractors and grantees. Other statutes in the area, such as the Fair Housing Act Amendments of 1988,[12] are of similarly limited scope.[13] Moreover, while every state and the District of Columbia has a law addressing the issue of discrimination against the handicapped, most of these statutes fail to provide the breadth of protection found in the ADA.[14]

¶ 1.02 SCOPE OF THE ADA—GENERALLY

The ADA provides protection and benefits to the disabled in the areas of employment, public services (including transportation), public accommodations and services provided by private entities (including private transportation services), and telecommunication. The term "disability" is broadly defined: Disabled individuals are all individuals with a physical or mental impairment that substantially limits a major life activity, as well as individuals who have a record of such impairment or who are regarded as having such an impairment even though they do not.[15]

Title I of the ADA sets forth the provisions relating to the employment of the disabled. It applies to employers, employment agencies, labor organizations, and joint labor-manage-

---

[9] ADA § 2(a)(5).

[10] ADA § 2(a)(4); H. Comm. on Educ. and Lab. Rep. at 47.

[11] 29 USC § 701–796i.

[12] 42 USC § 3601–3619.

[13] The Fair Housing Act Amendments of 1988 provide the disabled with protection from discrimination in the sale, rental, and accessibility of housing.

[14] H. Comm. on Educ. and Lab. Rep. at 47.

[15] ADA § 3(2).

ment committees.[16] In addition to prohibiting discrimination against the disabled by such entities, it incorporates many of the standards and obligations contained in the regulations implementing Section 504 of the Rehabilitation Act, including the key requirement that covered entities provide reasonable accommodations for the disabled unless doing so would impose an undue hardship.[17] Title I also regulates the use of medical examinations and drug testing. It incorporates by reference the enforcement provisions contained in Title VII of the Civil Rights Act of 1964.[18]

Title II of the ADA concerns public services provided by public entities. It generally states that no qualified individual with a disability may be discriminated against by a department, agency, special purpose district, or other instrumentality of a state or local government.[19] It also includes specific requirements relating to public transportation provided by public authorities.[20] For example, Title II requires all new fixed route buses to be accessible unless a transit authority can demonstrate that no lifts are available from a qualified manufacturer.[21] Similarly, a public transit authority must provide paratransit for disabled individuals who cannot use mainline accessible transportation unless doing so would impose an undue financial burden.[22] Title II incorporates the enforcement mechanisms set forth in Section 505 of the Rehabilitation Act.[23]

Title III of the ADA concerns public accommodations and services provided by private entities. Its basic principle is that no individual may be discriminated against on the basis of disability so as to prevent his full and equal enjoyment of goods, services, facilities, privileges, advantages, and accommodations of any place of public accommodation operated by a private

---

[16] ADA § 101(2).

[17] ADA § 102.

[18] ADA § 107.

[19] ADA § 202.

[20] ADA §§ 221–246.

[21] ADA § 222.

[22] ADA § 223.

[23] ADA § 203.

entity.[24] Public accommodations include restaurants, hotels, doctors' offices, pharmacies, grocery stores, shopping centers, and similar establishments.[25] Under Title III, all existing facilities covered by the ADA must be made accessible to the disabled if the changes are "readily achievable"—able to be accomplished without significant difficulty or expense.[26] New construction and major modifications of such facilities must be designed and constructed to be readily accessible and usable by the disabled.[27] Title III also includes specific prohibitions regarding discrimination in public transportation services provided by private entities.[28] Title III is enforced by pattern and practice cases brought by the U.S. Attorney General and by private actions comparable to those brought under Title II of the Civil Rights Act of 1964.[29]

Title IV of the ADA requires that telephone services offered to the general public include telecommunication relay services such that the disabled who use nonvoice terminal devices are provided service comparable to that offered individuals who use voice telephones.[30]

Finally, Title V contains miscellaneous provisions relating to the construction and application of the ADA.

¶ 1.03 PRE-ADA FEDERAL STATUTES

The ADA is derived from pre-1990 federal statutes designed to protect the disabled from discrimination and mandating affirmative action on their behalf under certain circumstances. Of these pre-ADA laws, the most important for interpreting the ADA is the Rehabilitation Act of 1973 as amended.[31] Knowledge of the Rehabilitation Act is critical in two respects.

---

[24] ADA § 302.

[25] ADA § 301(7); H. Comm. on Educ. and Lab. Rep. at 23.

[26] ADA § 301(9).

[27] ADA § 303.

[28] ADA §§ 302(b)(2), 304.

[29] ADA § 308.

[30] ADA § 401.

[31] 29 USC §§ 701–796i.

First, the ADA provides that in interpreting its provisions, the principles established under Section 504 of the Rehabilitation Act are to be followed except where the new statute expressly adopts a different standard.[32] In the legislative history of the ADA, the point is repeatedly made that Congress was building on principles developed by courts and federal agencies in interpreting the Rehabilitation Act. For example, the definition of a disabled individual under the ADA is derived from the Rehabilitation Act's definition of "handicapped" and the enforcement agencies' interpretation of that term.[33] Similarly, Rehabilitation Act cases are often cited in the Committee Reports to explain the principles underlying ADA provisions.[34] Moreover, parts of the ADA itself were derived from Rehabilitation Act regulations.[35] Therefore, unless the language of the ADA requires a contrary result, precedent developed under the Rehabilitation Act, especially cases under Section 504 of that act, should be assumed to be good law under the ADA.

Second, knowledge of the Rehabilitation Act is important because it is to remain in force after the effective date of the ADA. This is significant because the Rehabilitation Act, unlike the ADA, places affirmative action obligations on covered employers. It is also important because the penalties for violating the Rehabilitation Act are potentially greater than those imposed by the ADA. Therefore, although the ADA supplants the Rehabilitation Act in many respects, the older act must be considered in evaluating the rights of the disabled.

---

[32] Report of the House Comm. on the Judiciary on the Americans With Disabilities Act of 1990, HR Rep. No. 485, 101st Cong., 2d Sess., pt. 3 (1990) (hereinafter cited as H. Comm. on Jud. Rep.) at 69.

[33] See Report of the Senate Comm. on Labor and Human Resources on the Americans With Disabilities Act of 1989, S. Rep. No. 116, 101st Cong., 1st Sess. (1989) (hereinafter cited as S. Comm. on Lab. and Hum. Resources Rep.) at 21; H. Comm. on the Jud. Rep. at 29; the Equal Employment Opportunity Commission's (EEOC's) Interpretive Guidelines at 56 Fed. Reg. 8592 (1991) ("Congress intended the relevant caselaw developed under the Rehabilitation Act be generally applicable to the term 'disability' as used in the ADA").

[34] S. Comm. on Lab. and Hum. Resources Rep. at 24, 27; H. Comm. on Jud. Rep. at 41.

[35] S. Comm. on Lab. and Hum. Resources Rep. at 30.

[1] Rehabilitation Act of 1973

Careful consideration should be given to the differences, often subtle, between Sections 501, 503, and 504 of the Rehabilitation Act, since Congress opted to follow the slightly more liberal approach of Section 504 in drafting the ADA. Similarly, in evaluating precedent under the Rehabilitation Act for the purpose of interpreting the ADA, careful attention must be paid to which provision of the older act was involved.

Section 501 of the Rehabilitation Act mandates affirmative action in employment by every federal agency, department, and instrumentality, including the U.S. Postal Service.[36] Affirmative action plans must cover hiring, placement, and promotion of handicapped employees. The regulations make clear that Section 501 also prohibits discrimination on the basis of handicap,[37] and that it encompasses a duty to provide reasonable accommodation for an applicant or employee's handicap.[38]

Section 503 of the Rehabilitation Act applies to contractors and subcontractors with federal contracts or subcontracts for the procurement of personal property or nonpersonal services (including construction) exceeding $2,500. It requires that such contractors take affirmative action in hiring and promoting "qualified individuals with handicaps."[39] In addition, such contractors must not discriminate in employment against such handicapped individuals.[40]

Section 504 of the Rehabilitation Act prohibits discrimination against the handicapped in any program or activity receiving federal financial assistance or conducted by an executive agency of the federal government or the U.S. Postal Service.[41] Specifically, Section 504 provides, in relevant part, that

---

[36] 29 USC § 791.

[37] 29 CFR §§ 1613.701, 1613.703.

[38] 29 CFR § 1613.704.

[39] 29 USC § 793.

[40] 41 CFR § 60-741.4.

[41] 29 USC § 794.

[n]o otherwise qualified individual with handicaps . . . shall, solely by reason of her or his handicap, be excluded from the participation in, be denied the benefits of, or be subjected to discrimination under any program or activity receiving Federal financial assistance or under any program or activity conducted by any Executive agency or by the United States Postal Service.[42]

"Federal financial assistance" includes "any grant, loan, contract (other than a procurement contract or a contract of insurance or guaranty), or any other arrangement . . . which . . . makes available assistance in the form of (1) Funds; (2) Services of Federal personnel; or (3) Real and personal property or any interest in or use of such property . . . ."[43]

The U.S. Supreme Court, in *Consolidated Rail Corp. v. Darrone*,[44] ruled that Section 504 of the Rehabilitation Act does not apply only to programs whose primary purpose is to promote employment.[45] However, the Court held that Section 504's non-discrimination provision is limited "to the specific program or activity receiving federal funds."[46] Congress overruled the latter holding by passing the Civil Rights Restoration Act of 1987. Under this legislation, Section 504's ban on discrimination applies to the entire entity receiving federal assistance.

[a] Defining the Scope of Statutory Protection

Generally, the Rehabilitation Act protects "handicapped" individuals in the employment settings that have been described. Whether a particular applicant or employee is handicapped is a determination that must be made on a case-by-case basis; parties cannot rely on generalized or abstract views of a disability in issue.[47]

---

[42] Id.

[43] 45 CFR § 84.3(h).

[44] Consolidated Rail Corp. v. Darrone, 465 US 624 (1984).

[45] See id. at 632–633.

[46] Id. at 635–636.

[47] See Perez v. Philadelphia Hous. Auth., 677 F. Supp. 357 (ED Pa.), aff'd per curiam, 841 F2d 1120 (3d Cir. 1987).

The Rehabilitation Act defines "an individual with handicaps" as

> any person who (i) has a physical or mental impairment which substantially limits one or more of such person's major life activities, (ii) has a record of such an impairment, or (iii) is regarded as having such an impairment.[48]

As discussed in detail in Chapter 2, the ADA adopts the same definition for the term "individual with a disability."

A "physical or mental impairment" is defined by regulations under the Rehabilitation Act as

> (1) any physiological disorder or condition, cosmetic disfigurement, or anatomical loss affecting one or more of the following body systems: neurological; musculoskeletal; special sense organs; cardiovascular; reproductive; digestive; genito-urinary; hemic and lymphatic; skin; and endocrine; or (2) any mental or psychological disorder, such as mental retardation, organic brain syndrome, emotional or mental illness, and specific learning disabilities.[49]

"Major life activities" are defined by the regulations under the Rehabilitation Act to include "caring for one's self, performing manual tasks, walking, seeing, hearing, speaking, breathing, learning, and working."[50] In a manner more restrictive than that suggested by cases under Section 504 of the Rehabilitation Act, Section 503 of that act has been interpreted to require that in order to be considered "substantially limited," one must be "likely to experience difficulty in securing, retaining or advancing in employment because of a handicap."[51]

The definition of a handicapped individual also includes an individual with a "record" of a covered impairment or who is "regarded as having such an impairment." Thus, under the Rehabilitation Act, one could be completely recovered or not substantially impaired, and still be included in the definition of

---

[48] 29 USC § 706(8)(B).

[49] 29 CFR § 1613.702(b).

[50] 29 CFR § 1613.702(c).

[51] 41 CFR § 60-741.2.

a handicapped individual.[52]

Under Section 501 of the Rehabilitation Act, a "'qualified handicapped person' means with respect to employment, a handicapped person who, with or without reasonable accommodation, can perform the essential functions of the position in question without endangering the health and safety of [himself] or others . . . ."[53] Under Section 503 of the Rehabilitation Act, a "qualified handicapped individual" is defined as a handicapped individual "who is capable of performing a particular job, with reasonable accommodation to his or her handicap."[54] Under Section 504 of the Rehabilitation Act, a "qualified handicapped person" means "[w]ith respect to employment, a handicapped person who, with reasonable accommodation, can perform the essential functions of the job in question . . . ."[55]

[i] Contagious diseases. The Rehabilitation Act excludes from protection under Section 503 or Section 504, as those sections relate to employment,

> an individual who has a currently contagious disease or infection and who, by reason of such disease or infection, would constitute a direct threat to the health or safety of other individuals or who, by reason of the currently contagious disease or infection, is unable to perform the duties of the job.[56]

However, a person with a contagious disease, who does not present such a health or safety risk, may be covered by the Rehabilitation Act if he is "otherwise qualified" to perform the duties of the job in question.[57] Under the Rehabilitation Act, courts must look to the medical evidence and particular job in each case to determine whether the risk of contagion can be eliminated by reasonable accommodation.[58]

---

[52] See id.

[53] 29 CFR § 1613.702(f).

[54] 41 CFR § 60-741.2.

[55] 28 CFR § 41.32.

[56] 29 USC § 706(8)(C).

[57] See School Bd. of Nassau County, Fla. v. Arline, 480 US 273 (1987).

[58] See 134 Cong. Rec. H584 (Mar. 2, 1988).

The U.S. Department of Justice (DOJ) has taken the position in a memorandum that an individual infected with the human immunodeficiency virus (HIV) is protected under Section 504 of the Rehabilitation Act, so long as he can perform the duties of his job, and so long as he does not pose a direct risk to the health or safety of others.[59] The Office of Federal Contract Compliance Programs (OFCCP) follows the DOJ memorandum in resolving complaints involving HIV-related discrimination that are filed against government contractors and subcontractors under Section 503 of the Rehabilitation Act.[60] Both agencies have concluded that a person infected with the HIV virus presents little risk of contagion in most employment settings.[61] The OFCCP has declared that because medical evidence shows that the AIDS virus is not transmitted by casual physical contact, federal contractors or subcontractors attempting to justify adverse employment decisions based on infection with the AIDS virus will have a heavy burden to bear.[62] However, since there may be situations where the risk is substantial, employers should make a case-by-case determination as to whether the particular employee is "otherwise qualified" for the position, notwithstanding his infection with the AIDS virus.[63]

[ii] Limitations on employers—individualized inquiry. In most instances, evaluation of the risks posed by a particular handicap in a specific employment setting will require an individualized inquiry; however, there may be instances where blanket exclusion of a class of handicapped individuals will be permitted.[64]

Generalized medical or physical standards or criteria that

---

[59] See U.S. Department of Justice Memorandum on Application of Section 504 of the Rehabilitation Act to HIV-Infected Individuals (Sept. 27, 1988) (hereinafter cited as DOJ Memo).

[60] OFCCP Federal Contract Compliance Manual Ch. 6, App. D, § 4.C. (hereinafter cited as OFCCP Manual).

[61] See id. at § 5.B.; DOJ Memo, supra note 59.

[62] See OFCCP Manual at § 5.B.

[63] See DOJ Memo, supra note 59.

[64] See Davis v. Meese, 692 F. Supp. 505 (ED Pa. 1988) (because of lack of reliable test to determine which insulin-dependent diabetics pose significant

exclude handicapped individuals from consideration, irrespective of their qualifications to perform the particular job in question, are proscribed under the Rehabilitation Act. Instead, an employer must examine *each* applicant's qualifications and abilities in conjunction with the specific requirements of *each* position.[65] Medical or physical standards used to place employees in a particular position must exclude only those individuals who are not qualified to perform that job. Categorical disqualification based on disability is prohibited. In addition, regulations under the Rehabilitation Act provide that when an employer seeks to impose physical or mental job requirements that screen out otherwise qualified handicapped workers, the burden is on the employer to demonstrate that any such requirements are related to the specific job at issue and are consistent with business necessity and the safe performance of that job.[66] These principles were followed by the Congress in drafting the ADA and are discussed in Chapter 2.

An employer may conduct a medical examination or inquire into an applicant's mental or physical condition when screening applicants for employment.[67] However, such inquiries must be limited to an individual's ability to perform a particular job; in other words, they must be job-related.[68] Finally, when employers choose to conduct such medical examinations or inquiries, any information gleaned therefrom must be kept strictly confidential, except that (1) supervisors may be notified of restrictions or accommodations pertaining to the handicapped individual's job; (2) first aid and safety personnel may be notified where emergency treatment may be required; and (3) government compliance officials must be informed.[69] As discussed in Chapter 2, a similar result is now mandated by the ADA.

---

risk of hypoglycemic attack while on duty, blanket exclusion from employment as Federal Bureau of Investigation (FBI) special agents permitted).

[65] See 41 CFR § 60-741.6(c).

[66] 41 CFR § 60-741.6(c)(2).

[67] 41 CFR § 60-741.6(c)(3).

[68] 41 CFR § 60-741.6(c).

[69] 41 CFR § 60-741.6(c)(3).

[iii] Limitations on employees—"substantial." In order to establish a covered handicap under the definition set forth in the Rehabilitation Act, a person must show that he "has a physical or mental impairment which substantially limits one or more of such person's major life activities." Accordingly, it has been held that where an individual's impairment is of a transitory nature, without permanent effect on his health, that individual is not protected under the Rehabilitation Act as a "qualified handicapped person."[70] As discussed in Chapter 2, it is less clear how temporary conditions are to be treated under the ADA.

It has also been held that traits that merely prevent an individual from performing a specific job do not qualify as "handicaps."[71] Therefore, a trait that impedes a person from performing a specific job, but that does not generally interfere with his employability, is not a handicap under the Rehabilitation Act because it is not substantially limiting. There was much litigation of this issue under the Rehabilitation Act, and the question is left unclarified by the ADA.

[b] Statutory Obligations of Employers

[i] Nondiscrimination. The Rehabilitation Act prohibits discrimination against qualified handicapped workers by covered federal contractors, government agencies, or programs receiving federal assistance. This includes discrimination in hiring, firing, promotion, or terms and conditions of employment.[72]

[ii] Affirmative action. Under Section 503 of the Rehabilitation Act, a covered contractor or subcontractor is required to do outreach, recruit, hire, and promote handicapped applicants or employees.[73] A similar obligation is imposed on the federal

---

[70] See Stevens v. Stubbs, 576 F. Supp. 1409 (ND Ga. 1983).

[71] See Jasany v. US Postal Serv., 755 F2d 1244 (6th Cir. 1985); accord EE Black, Ltd. v. Marshall, 497 F. Supp. 1088, 1100 (D. Haw. 1980) (if disqualifying characteristic unique to only one specific job, it is not substantially limiting, and individual would not be protected under Act).

[72] 41 CFR § 60-741.4(a).

[73] See 41 CFR § 60-741.4.

government by Section 501 of the Rehabilitation Act.[74] The U.S. Supreme Court has held that Section 504 of the Rehabilitation Act does not impose affirmative action requirements on recipients of federal financial assistance.[75] In making this determination, the Court relied on the difference in language between Section 504 (which refers to nondiscrimination) and Sections 501 and 503 (which refer to affirmative action).

Affirmative action under the Rehabilitation Act involves recruiting employees through employment agencies or organizations that refer handicapped workers. It does not entail the use of goals, timetables, or numerical quotas.[76]

Contractors are required to examine their personal practices and procedures to "assure careful, thorough and systematic consideration of the job qualifications of known handicapped applicants and employees for job vacancies."[77] For example, job applications, interviews, hiring criteria, or tests (physical or otherwise) cannot systematically screen out or place handicapped applicants at a disadvantage because of their disabilities. Instead, the entire hiring process should be accessible to individuals with perceptual or physical disabilities. In addition, personnel "procedures must be designed so as to facilitate a review of the implementation of this requirement by the contractor or the Government."[78] Contractors should also evaluate whether handicapped employees can take part in training, educational, social, and recreational programs.[79]

The regulations require large contractors (those with fifty or more employees and contracts of $50,000 or more) to invite all applicants and employees to identify themselves voluntarily as

---

[74] See 38 USC § 2012(a).

[75] See Southeastern Community College v. Davis, 442 US 397, 410 (1979).

[76] Compare Exec. Order No. 11,246 (Sept. 24, 1965), as amended by Exec. Order No. 11,375 (Oct. 13, 1967) and Exec. Order No. 12,086 (Oct. 8, 1978).

[77] 41 CFR § 60-741.6(b).

[78] Id.

[79] 41 CFR § 60-741.6(h)(3)(iv).

handicapped.[80] Affirmative action obligations under the Rehabilitation Act apply only to individuals so identified or otherwise known by the employer to be handicapped. The contractor is not required to search applicant or employee medical files to ascertain whether or not an individual is handicapped.[81] Where an applicant or employee provides such identifying information, the employer is required to keep the information confidential. Finally, the employer is prohibited from treating adversely any individual who refuses to provide such information.[82]

All covered contractors must include a standard affirmative action clause in their government contracts.[83] In addition, an employer who has fifty or more employees and a contract of $50,000 or more must create and maintain a written affirmative action plan.[84] These written affirmative action plans must be annually updated, and any significant revisions to them must be internally publicized by the employer.[85]

[iii] Reasonable accommodation. Under the Rehabilitation Act, an employer must provide "reasonable accommodation" for the known disabilities of an applicant or employee, unless such accommodation would entail "undue hardship" for the business or agency.[86] Reasonable accommodation may include

---

[80] See 41 CFR § 60-741.5.

[81] See 41 CFR § 60-741.5(c)(3).

[82] See 41 CFR § 60-741.5(c)(1).

[83] 41 CFR § 60-741.4.

[84] See 41 CFR § 60-741.5.

[85] See 41 CFR § 60-741.5(b).

[86] The regulations promulgated under Section 503 define a "qualified handicapped individual" as someone "capable of performing a particular job, with reasonable accommodation to his or her handicap." 41 CFR § 60-741.2. The U.S. Supreme Court in Southeastern Community College v. Davis, 442 US 397 (1979), found the reasonable accommodation requirement applicable to both Sections 503 and 501, relying upon the "affirmative action" obligations contained therein. 442 US at 410. However, because of the lack of affirmative action language in Section 504, the Court held that recipients of federal aid do not have an affirmative action duty to accommodate. Instead, their duty is limited to not discriminating. Nonetheless, the Court suggested that in certain situations, refusal to accommodate could amount to discrimination under Section 504. See *Davis*, supra, at 412–413.

altering facilities for accessibility to the handicapped, modifying job schedules, or providing special equipment, devices, or personnel to assist individuals with perceptual impairments.[87]

Whether a specific accommodation is reasonable or would constitute an undue hardship is determined on a case-by-case basis.[88] The burden of demonstrating that a particular accommodation would impose an undue hardship is on the employer.[89]

The regulations under the Rehabilitation Act set forth a number of factors to be used in determining whether an accommodation would entail undue hardship. For example, under Section 501, the size of the agency program, the type of agency operation, the type of accommodation proposed, and its cost should all be considered.[90] Under Section 503, business necessity and expense may be considered.[91]

Rehabilitation Act cases suggest that an employer may be justified in refusing to accommodate a handicapped individual where providing such accommodation would violate a collective-bargaining agreement.[92] An accommodation is also not reasonable if its provision requires an employer to eliminate an essential job function[93] or to reassign many of the job's duties to other workers.[94]

Courts have also held that the Rehabilitation Act does not require an employer to place an applicant in or transfer an employee to a different job if that individual is unable to per-

---

[87] See 29 CFR § 1613.704(b).

[88] See, e.g., Redmond v. GAF Corp., 574 F2d 897, 902–903 (7th Cir. 1978).

[89] See, e.g., Hall v. US Postal Serv., 857 F2d 1073, 47 Fair Empl. Prac. Cas. (BNA) 1540 (6th Cir. 1988).

[90] See 29 CFR § 1613.704(c); 45 CFR § 84.12(c).

[91] See 41 CFR § 60-741.6(d).

[92] See Shea v. Tisch, 870 F2d 786 (1st Cir. 1989); Carter v. Tisch, 822 F2d 465 (4th Cir. 1987).

[93] See Jasany v. US Postal Serv., 755 F2d 1244, 1250 (6th Cir. 1985).

[94] See Treadwell v. Alexander, 707 F2d 473 (11th Cir. 1983).

form the essential functions of his present job.[95] Currently, the regulations governing federal employment do not impose such a requirement.[96] However, the Equal Employment Opportunity Commission (EEOC) has proposed in new regulations that an agency be required under its Section 501 affirmative action duties to transfer handicapped employees who are no longer able to perform the essential functions of their jobs. Because this requirement would fall under an agency's affirmative action duty, not its reasonable accommodation duty, it would not be subject to the undue hardship defense.[97]

The ADA's treatment of the concept of "reasonable accommodation" generally follows the foregoing principles and is discussed in detail in Chapter 2.

[c] Enforcing the Statute

[i] Government agencies. The EEOC is charged with enforcing Section 501 of the Rehabilitation Act.[98] In carrying out this charge, the EEOC uses the same enforcement mechanisms as those provided under Title VII of the Civil Rights Act of 1964, namely, filing of charges, investigations, administrative hearings, and so on.

The OFCCP enforces Section 503 of the Rehabilitation Act through compliance reviews and complaints.[99]

In order to assess whether a contractor is fulfilling his affirmative action obligations under the statute, the OFCCP

---

[95] See, e.g., Carty v. US Postal Service, 623 F. Supp. 1181, 1188 (D. Md. 1985).

[96] 29 CFR §§ 1613.702(f), 1613.704.

[97] 54 Fed. Reg. 45748–45749 (1989) (to be codified at 29 CFR § 1614.203(g)).

[98] Regulations implementing Section 501 are published at 29 CFR §§ 1613.701–1613.709. Complaints presenting both discrimination and nondiscrimination claims fall within the jurisdiction of the Merit Systems Protection Board (MSPB). See 5 USC § 7702; see also 5 CFR § 1201.151.

[99] Regulations setting forth Section 503 enforcement procedures can be found at 41 CFR §§ 60-741.1–60-741.54 . The OFCCP regulations for enforcing Section 402 of the Vietnam-Era Veterans Readjustment Act are set forth at 41 CFR §§ 60-250.1–60-250.54.

may conduct a compliance review. In the course of a compliance review, the OFCCP will examine such things as the employer's affirmative action plan, the accessibility of the employer's facilities, and the employer's attempts to recruit qualified handicapped workers.

In addition, where an individual who is protected by the statute believes he has been discriminated against by a covered contractor, he may file a complaint with the Director of the OFCCP.[100] The complaint must be filed within 180 days of the alleged discrimination, unless this time is extended upon a showing of good cause.[101] If a contractor has an internal review procedure, the agency will defer action on a complaint for sixty days.[102] Complaints not resolved internally after sixty days will be investigated by the OFCCP.[103] Where the OFCCP finds no discrimination, or otherwise declines to seek administrative relief against the employer, it will notify the complainant of its decision. The complainant then has the right to seek review of this determination by the Director of the OFCCP.[104]

Where the OFCCP determines that an employer is not in compliance with the statute, it may seek resolution through conciliation.[105] After conciliation proceedings are successfully concluded, the noncomplying contractor will be required to execute a written commitment to cure the violation.[106] If conciliation attempts fail, the OFCCP may commence administrative enforcement proceedings.[107] To remedy the violation, the agency may seek to terminate the contract, debar the contractor

---

[100] 41 CFR § 60-741.26(a).

[101] See id. The Department of Labor has held that there is no time limit on the filing of an OFCCP administrative complaint. See OFCCP v. Ozark Airlines, No. 80-OFCCP-24, 40 Fair Empl. Prac. Cas. (BNA) 1859 (June 13, 1986).

[102] 41 CFR § 60-741.26(b).

[103] Id.

[104] 41 CFR § 60-741.26(g)(1).

[105] 41 CFR § 60-741.26(g)(2).

[106] Id.

[107] See 41 CFR §§ 60-741.26(g)(3), 60-741.28, 60-741.29.

from obtaining federal contracts, or withhold contractual payments.[108]

Individuals may seek judicial review of OFCCP determinations under Section 503 of the Rehabilitation Act.[109] However, the Secretary of Labor's decision not to bring a handicap discrimination action has been held to be a nonreviewable exercise of agency discretion.[110] Similarly, at least one court of appeals has held that the Secretary of Labor's decision not to bring an enforcement action under Section 402 of the Vietnam-Era Veterans Readjustment Act (VEVRA) is nonreviewable as a decision committed to agency discretion under the Administrative Procedures Act.[111]

Enforcement responsibility for Section 504 of the Rehabilitation Act is delegated to the federal agency providing the financial assistance at issue in a particular dispute. Coordination of Section 504 implementation and enforcement is the responsibility of the U.S. Attorney General.[112] When a recipient of federal financial assistance is found to be in violation of the Rehabilitation Act, the agency with enforcement responsibility may seek termination of the recipient's funding after the recipient has been accorded the opportunity for a hearing.[113] Agency action under Section 504 is reviewable under the "arbitrary and capricious" standard.[114]

---

[108] 41 CFR § 60-741.28.

[109] See Communications Workers v. Donovan, 37 Fair Empl. Prac. Cas. (BNA) 1362 (SDNY 1985).

[110] See Andrews v. Conrail, 40 Fair Empl. Prac. Cas. (BNA) 492, 495 (SD Ind. 1986); but see Moon v. Secretary, US Dep't of Labor, 747 F2d 599 (11th Cir. 1984), cert. denied, 471 US 1055 (1985).

[111] 5 USC §§ 551–559. See Clementson v. Brock, 806 F2d 1402 (9th Cir. 1986); cf. Healy v. Bergman, 609 F. Supp. 1448 (D. Mass. 1985) (decision of OFCCP Regional Director that employee was not a "qualified handicapped individual" reviewable under arbitrary and capricious standard).

[112] Exec. Order No. 12,250, 45 Fed. Reg. 72995 (1980).

[113] See, e.g., 45 CFR § 84.61; 45 CFR § 80.8 (Department of Health and Human Services).

[114] See NAACP v. Wilmington Medical Center, Inc., 453 F. Supp. 280, 304 (D. Del. 1978).

[ii] Private right of action. The majority view is that there is no private right of action against a covered contractor to enforce Section 503 of the Rehabilitation Act.[115]

On the other hand, both Section 501 and Section 504 of the Rehabilitation Act do provide for a private right of action against covered employers.[116] The Rehabilitation Act explicitly states that the remedies, procedures, and rights set forth in Section 717 of Title VII of the Civil Rights Act of 1964 shall be available under Section 501 of the Rehabilitation Act.[117] Similarly, it provides that the remedies, procedures, and rights set forth in Title VI, shall be available under Section 504.[118] Section 794a(b) provides for reasonable attorney fees to a prevailing party, other than the United States, in any action or proceeding to enforce or charge a violation of the Rehabilitation Act.[119]

Actions filed under Section 501 of the Rehabilitation Act must name the head of the federal agency or department that

---

[115] See, e.g., Davis v. United Air Lines, Inc., 662 F2d 120 (2d Cir. 1981); Beam v. Sun Shipbuilding & Dry Dock Co., 679 F2d 1077 (3d Cir. 1982); Painter v. Horne Bros., Inc., 710 F2d 143 (4th Cir. 1983); Rogers v. Frito-Lay, Inc., 611 F2d 1074 (5th Cir. 1980); Hoopes v. Equifax, Inc., 611 F2d 134 (6th Cir. 1979); Simpson v. Reynolds Metals Co., 629 F2d 1226 (7th Cir. 1980); Simon v. St. Louis County, Mo., 656 F2d 316 (8th Cir.), cert. denied, 455 US 976 (1981); Fisher v. City of Tucson, 663 F2d 861 (9th Cir. 1981); Hodges v. Atchison, Topeka & Santa Fe Ry. Co., 728 F2d 414 (10th Cir.), cert. denied, 469 US 822 (1984).

[116] See 29 USC §§ 794a(a)(1), 794a(a)(2). For cases recognizing a private right of action under Section 504, see Leary v. Crapsey, 566 F2d 863 (2d Cir. 1977); NAACP v. Medical Center, Inc., 599 F2d 1247 (3d Cir. 1979); Davis v. Southeastern Community College, 574 F2d 1158 (4th Cir. 1978), rev'd on other grounds, 442 US 397 (1979); Jennings v. Alexander, 715 F2d 1036 (6th Cir. 1983); Lloyd v. Regional Transp. Auth., 548 F2d 1277 (7th Cir. 1977); Miener v. Missouri, 673 F2d 969 (8th Cir. 1982); Kling v. County of Los Angeles, 633 F2d 876 (9th Cir. 1980). For a discussion of whether a plaintiff must exhaust his administrative remedies prior to suit, see Boyd v. US Postal Serv., 752 F2d 410 (9th Cir. 1985); Smith v. US Postal Serv., 766 F2d 205 (6th Cir. 1985); Johnson v. Orr, 747 F2d 1352 (10th Cir. 1984).

[117] See 29 USC § 794a(a)(1).

[118] See 29 USC § 794(a)(2).

[119] See 29 USC § 794a(b).

allegedly discriminated.[120] Based on the incorporation of Title VII rights, remedies, and procedures, courts have held that certain defendants falling within Title VII's exemptions may not be sued under Section 501.[121] Courts have also applied other Title VII special exceptions to Section 501.[122]

In order to bring suit under Section 504 of the Rehabilitation Act, a plaintiff must have been the intended beneficiary of, an applicant for, or a participant in a federally funded program.[123] In addition, an action may be brought under Section 504 even when the primary purpose of the federal assistance is not to promote employment.[124] There is some disagreement among the courts as to whether compensatory damages are recoverable under Section 504.[125]

[2] Vietnam-Era Veterans Readjustment Act

Although of more limited applicability than the Rehabilitation Act, mention should be made of Section 402 of VEVRA, prohibiting discrimination against individuals in the protected class[126] and placing additional affirmative obligations on covered employers.[127] This statute, which is also enforced by the

---

[120] See, e.g., Desroches v. US Postal Serv., 631 F. Supp. 1375 (DNH 1986).

[121] See, e.g., Reardon v. American Postal Workers Union, 43 Fair Empl. Prac. Cas. (BNA) 1348 (DNJ), appeal dismissed without opinion, 480 US 927, 107 S. Ct. 1559 (1986) (federal employees union).

[122] See, e.g., Skillern v. Bolger, 725 F2d 1121 (7th Cir.), cert. denied, 469 US 835 (1984) (veteran's preference exception); Hurst v. US Postal Serv., 653 F. Supp. 259 (ND Ga. 1986) (bona fide seniority system exception).

[123] See Simpson v. Reynolds Metals Co., 629 F2d 1226 (7th Cir. 1980).

[124] See Consolidated Rail Corp. v. Darrone, 465 US 624 (1984).

[125] Compare Recanzone v. Washoe County School Dist., 696 F. Supp. 1372 (D. Nev. 1988) and Gelman v. Department of Educ., 544 F. Supp. 651 (D. Colo. 1982) (compensatory damages recoverable) with Shuttleworth v. Broward County, 649 F. Supp. 35 (SD Fla. 1986) and Boxall v. Sequoia Union High School Dist., 464 F. Supp. 1104 (ND Cal. 1979) (compensatory damages not recoverable).

[126] See 41 CFR § 60.250.4.

[127] 38 USC § 2012.

OFCCP, requires federal contractors and subcontractors with contracts for the procurement of personal property and nonpersonal services (including construction) in excess of $10,000 to take affirmative action to hire and promote qualified disabled veterans and veterans of the Vietnam era.[128] Covered contractors must also list employment opportunities with their state employment service.[129] Qualified disabled veterans include those entitled to disability compensation for a 30 percent or more disability, or those veterans released or discharged for a disability incurred or aggravated in the line of duty.[130]

VEVRA explicitly provides that a protected veteran who believes that a covered contractor has violated its contractual obligation relating to the employment of veterans, or has discriminated against him because of his handicap, may file a complaint with the Veteran's Employment Service of the Department of Labor.[131] The Secretary of Labor then must investigate and take such action as warranted under the contract and applicable laws and regulations.[132]

VEVRA applies to all operations and facilities of a covered contractor, not merely to those involved in work on the contract.[133] There is no private cause of action under VEVRA.[134]

¶ 1.04 STATE LAWS

Although a detailed analysis of state laws is beyond the scope of this book, it should be noted that almost every state has a law proscribing discrimination on the basis of disability. These laws differ, however, with respect to the scope of their coverage. For example, in some states, mental illness is a covered disability,

---

[128] Id.

[129] 41 CFR § 60-250.4.

[130] 38 USC 2011(1).

[131] 38 USC § 2012(b).

[132] Id.

[133] See 38 USC § 2012(a).

[134] See Barron v. Nightingale Roofing, Inc., 842 F2d 20 (1st Cir. 1988); De Leon Cruz v. Loubriel, 539 F. Supp. 250 (DPR 1982).

while, in others, only physical disabilities are covered. States also differ as to the types of mental and physical disabilities covered. Moreover, state laws vary as to whether accommodation is required and, if so, how much accommodation. Limitations on coverage also differ, especially with respect to cases where the health or safety of the individual or others is endangered, where the essential functions of the position cannot be performed, or where the individual suffers from a contagious disease or drug or alcohol addiction.

¶ 1.05 CONSTRUING THE ADA

In drafting the ADA, Congress was aware that confusion would arise over how to construe the new act in light of preexisting federal and state statutes protecting the disabled. Accordingly, Title V of the ADA contains a number of provisions explaining how the new law is to be applied in light of these statutes. Title V of the ADA also amended the Rehabilitation Act to bring it into accord with the new law.

[1] Relationship to Rehabilitation Act

Section 501(a) of the ADA provides in part that "except as otherwise provided in the [ADA]" nothing in the legislation "shall be construed to apply a lesser standard than the standards applied under title V of the Rehabilitation Act of 1973 (29 U.S.C. 790) or the regulations issued by the Federal agencies pursuant to such title." The House Committee Report on the ADA states that "the standards of title V of the Rehabilitation Act shall apply for purposes of the ADA to the extent the ADA does not explicitly adopt a different standard than Section 504 of the Rehabilitation Act."[135] Thus, under Section 501(a) of the ADA, "in those instances where the ADA explicitly provides a different standard from Section 504 of the Rehabilitation Act, the ADA standard applies to the ADA, but not to Section 504."[136]

---

[135] H. Comm. on Jud. Rep. at 69.
[136] Id.

EXAMPLE: Eastern A&M receives a large grant from the federal government for one of its programs. The program is run out of a building that is not accessible to the disabled and that cannot be modified without considerable expense. Section 504 of the Rehabilitation Act might require Eastern A&M to make major structural changes in the facility if the program could not be made accessible by other means. On the other hand, if Eastern A&M did not receive federal funds and was only subject to the ADA, that legislation's lower standard regarding access to public accommodations in existing buildings would apply. Under Title III of the ADA, access need only be provided if this can be done in a "readily achievable" manner (i.e., if it can be accomplished without much difficulty or expense in light of the factors set forth in Section 301 of the ADA).

The DOJ analysis of the relationship between the Rehabilitation Act and the ADA states that

[T]he ADA is not intended to apply lesser standards than are required under title V of the Rehabilitation Act of 1973, as amended (29 U.S.C. 790–794), or the regulations implementing that title. The standards of title V of the Rehabilitation Act apply for purposes of the ADA to the extent that the ADA has not explicitly adopted a different standard than title V. Where the ADA explicitly provides a different standard from section 504, the ADA standard applies to the ADA, but not to section 504. For example, section 504 requires that all federally assisted programs and activities be readily accessible to and usable by persons with handicaps, even if major structural alterations are necessary to make the program accessible. The ADA, in contrast, only requires alterations to existing facilities if the modifications are "readily achievable," that is, able to be accomplished easily and without much difficulty or expense. An entity that is covered under both section 504 and the ADA is still required to meet the "program accessibility" standard in order to comply with section 504, but would not be in violation of the ADA unless it failed to make "readily achievable" modifications. On the other hand, an entity covered by the ADA is required to make "readily achievable" modifications even if the program can be made accessible without any architectural modifications. Thus, an entity covered by both section 504 and the ADA must meet both the "program accessibility" and the "readily achievable requirement."[137]

The EEOC has published Interpretive Guidelines stating that

[T]he existence of a lesser standard of protection to individuals with disabilities under the ADA will not provide a defense for failing to meet a higher standard under another law. Thus, for example, title I of the ADA would not be a defense to failing to collect information required to satisfy the affirmative action requirements of Section 503 [of the Rehabilitation Act].[138]

For the most part, the ADA provides the same or greater protection for the disabled than the Rehabilitation Act, except that the Rehabilitation Act arguably provided greater protections for drug users.

Section 512 of the ADA provides that for purposes of programs and activities under Titles I, II, and III of the Rehabilitation Act, "an individual shall not be excluded from the benefits of such program or activities on the basis of his or her current illegal use of drugs if he or she is otherwise entitled to such services."[139] With regard to educational programs and activities,

local educational agencies may take disciplinary action pertaining to the use or possession of illegal drugs or alcohol against any handicapped student who is currently engaging in the illegal use of drugs or in the use of alcohol to the same extent that such disciplinary action is taken against non-handicapped students.[140]

In such cases, the education agency may impose disciplinary

---

[137] Department of Justice Proposed Regulations, Section-by-Section Analysis at 7, 56 Fed. Reg. 7456 (1991).

[138] EEOC's Interpretive Guidelines at 56 Fed. Reg. 8592 (1991).

[139] ADA § 512(a), adding § 7(8)(C)(iii).

[140] ADA § 512(a), adding § 7(8)(C)(iv).

action without providing the due process otherwise applicable under the Rehabilitation Act.[141]

Regarding alcohol use, Section 512 of the ADA clarifies that under the Rehabilitation Act, the term "individual with handicaps" does not include any individual who is an alcoholic whose current use of alcohol prevents him from performing the duties of the job in question or whose employment, by reason of his current alcohol abuse, would constitute a direct threat to property or the safety of others.[142]

[2] Other Federal and State Laws

Section 501(b) of the ADA provides that "[n]othing in [the ADA] shall be construed to invalidate or limit the remedies, rights and procedures of any Federal law or law of any State or political subdivision of any state or jurisdiction that provides greater or equal protection for the rights of individuals with disabilities than are afforded under [the ADA]." As stated by the House Committee on the Judiciary Report, "the basic principle underlying this provision is that Congress does not intend to displace any of the rights or remedies provided by other federal laws or other state laws (including common law) which provide greater or equal protection to individuals with disabilities."[143] This result is consistent with other federal civil rights legislation.[144]

> EXAMPLE: Employee Jones lives in a jurisdiction where a statute prohibits discrimination against the disabled and

---

[141] ADA § 512(a), adding § 7(8)(C)(iv). 34 CFR Section 104.36 would have required certain procedures to have been followed by educational agencies disciplining users of illegal drugs and alcohol had Section 512(a) not been added to the Rehabilitation Act. 34 CFR Section 104.36 requires notice, an opportunity for the parents or guardian of the person to examine relevant records, an impartial hearing with opportunity for participation by the person's parents or guardian, and representation by counsel and review procedure.

[142] ADA § 512(a), adding § 7(8)(C)(v).

[143] H. Comm. on Jud. Rep. at 70.

[144] H. Comm. on Educ. and Lab. Rep. at 135.

allows for punitive damages. State courts have also recognized the tort of wrongful discharge in violation of a local statute. If Jones were discharged because he developed a disability, he would be able to seek relief, including punitive damages, both under the state statute and for the common-law tort even though he would only be able to recover back pay if he sought relief under the ADA.

There was some concern that the language of Section 501(b) of the ADA might prohibit restrictions on smoking in public places or at worksites. As a result, language was added to Section 501(b) from the House version of the bill providing that "nothing in the Act is to be construed to preclude legislation prohibiting or restricting smoking in places of employment, in transportation provided by public and private entities and places of public accommodation." [145]

Section 501(b) allows a disabled individual to seek relief under both the ADA and any other applicable federal law. In addition, if a state statute provides fewer remedies in one context but more rights in another, the state statute is not preempted, and a disabled individual can seek relief under the state statute when it is to his benefit. The legislative history contains the following illustration:

> The California Fair Employment and Housing Act (FEHA) does not cover persons with mental disabilities. However, the FEHA has been construed to provide compensatory and punitive damages. Because the ADA covers mental disabilities, the FEHA could be construed as not covering equal or greater rights than the ADA. However, a person with a physical disability may choose to sue under the FEHA, as well as under the ADA, because of the availability of [greater] damages under the FEHA. Section 501(b) ensures that the FEHA is not preempted by the ADA. [146]

Congress recognized that there may be circumstances in which the ADA conflicts with other federal legislation. For

---

[145] HR Rep. No. 596, 101st Cong., 2d Sess. (1990) (hereafter cited as Conference Report) at 84.

[146] H. Comm. on Jud. Rep. at 70.

example, the ADA may be construed to be in conflict with certain Occupational Safety and Health Administration (OSHA) requirements. [147] According to the House Committee on Education and Labor, Congress expects "the Attorney General to exercise coordinating authority to avoid and eliminate such conflicts." [148]

There was concern that Section 501(b) would affect the right of employers under the food-handling provision of Section 103(d) of the ADA. The Conference Report made two points concerning this issue. First, the report concludes that "if a state or locality has a disease control law, or any other public health law, which places certain requirements on certain employees, employers or businesses, but which does not discriminate against people with disabilities, such laws would not be affected or preempted in any way by the ADA." [149]

> EXAMPLE: A disease control law requires that all employees who handle food wash their hands every half hour and wear gloves while preparing meals. Such a law would not be affected or preempted by the ADA.

Second, the Conference Report states that "if a state or locality has a disease control law or any other public health law, which applies to certain people with disabilities . . . that law would also not be preempted by the ADA as long as the requirements of that state or local law were designed to protect against individuals who pose a direct threat to the health and safety of others." [150] A "direct threat" for purposes of this provision is one that poses a significant risk to the health and safety of others that cannot be eliminated by reasonable accommodation. [151]

The EEOC's Interpretive Guidelines state that

The ADA does not preempt medical standards or safety requirements established by Federal law or regulations. It

---

[147] H. Comm. on Educ. and Lab. Rep. at 135–136.

[148] Id.; S. Comm. on Lab. and Hum. Resources Rep. at 84.

[149] Conference Report at 84.

[150] Id.

[151] Id., incorporating Section 101(3) of the ADA into Section 501(b).

does not preempt State, county, or local laws, ordinances or regulations that are consistent with this Part, and are designed to protect the public health from individuals who pose a direct threat which cannot be eliminated by reasonable accommodation to the health and safety of others. However, the ADA does preempt inconsistent requirements established by state or local law for safety or security sensitive positions. [152]

EXAMPLE: If a state has a law that requires people with certain contagious diseases, such as tuberculosis, to take specified precautions to prevent the spreading of the disease, the state law would not be preempted. Similarly, if a state or locality requires that certain precautions be taken by carriers of sexually transmitted diseases (or that the risk be disclosed to partners), the state law would not be preempted.

A covered entity allegedly in violation of the ADA cannot successfully defend its action by relying on the obligation to comply with the requirements of any state or local law that imposes prohibitions or limitations on the eligibility of qualified persons to practice any occupation or profession. [153]

The EEOC's Interpretive Guidelines give the following example:

[S]uppose a municipality has an ordinance that prohibits individuals with tuberculosis from teaching school to children. If an individual with dormant tuberculosis challenges a private school's refusal to hire him or her because of the tuberculosis, the private school would not be able to rely upon the city ordinance as a defense under the ADA. [154]

---

[152] EEOC's Interpretive Guidelines at 56 Fed. Reg. 8592 (1991).

[153] Id.

[154] Id.

CHAPTER 2

ADA Title I: Employment

¶ 2.01 DEFINITIONS AND COVERAGE

Title I of the ADA contains the employment provisions. Title I protects all individuals with disabilities who are in the United States—regardless of their national origin and regardless of their status. Thus, whether an applicant or employee is in fact a U.S. citizen is not a consideration under the ADA.[1] The ADA likely does not apply to individuals employed abroad by U.S. employers.[2]

Generally, the employment title incorporates the definitions of such terms as "persons," "employer," and "commerce" contained in Title VII of the Civil Rights Act of 1964.[3] The ADA's employment coverage parallels that of Title VII.[4] Under Section 101(5), Title I of the ADA applies to all employers engaged in an industry affecting commerce who have fifteen or more employees for each working day in each of twenty or more calendar weeks in the current or preceding calendar year.

In determining who is an employee for purposes of the fifteen-employee threshold, the courts will evaluate the economic realities of the relationship between the business and the

---

[1] EEOC Interpretive Guidelines, 56 Fed. Reg. 8592 (Feb. 28, 1991).

[2] See EEOC v. Arabian Am. Oil Co., 113 L. Ed. 2d 274 (1991).

[3] ADA § 101(7); EEOC Interpretive Guidelines, 56 Fed. Reg. 35,740 (July 26, 1991).

[4] 42 USC § 2000e (1985).

individual viewed in light of common-law principles of agency.[5] Generally, the term "employee" will be broadly construed to provide coverage.[6] Officers and family members may be considered employees even though they do not receive a salary.[7]

In ascertaining whether a parent corporation will be considered the employer of its subsidiary's employees, the courts will generally consider the degree of (1) interrelated operations; (2) common management; (3) centralized control of labor relations; and (4) common ownership.[8]

As under Title VII, the Age Discrimination in Employment Act (ADEA), and other labor legislation, the term "industry affecting commerce" allows for the ADA to have the fullest jurisdictional breadth constitutionally permissible under the commerce clause.[9] Although the use of industry affecting commerce may suggest a limitation to for-profit enterprises, the ADA covers enterprises operated for nonprofit or charitable purposes (except where expressly excluded), as well as commercial enterprises.[10]

The ADA applies to private employers, employment agencies, labor organizations, joint labor-management committees, governments, governmental agencies, and political subdivi-

---

[5] See, e.g., EEOC v. Zippo Mfg. Co., 713 F2d 32 (3d Cir. 1983); Cobb v. Sun Papers, Inc., 673 F2d 337 (11th Cir. 1982).

[6] See, e.g., Armbruster v. Quinn, 711 F2d 1332 (6th Cir. 1983). An individual may be entitled to the protections of the civil rights laws even though they would not be counted in determining whether the employer employs the requisite number of employees for purposes of determining coverage under the statutes. See Graves v. Women's Professional Rodeo Ass'n, 49 Fair Empl. Prac. Cas. (BNA) 731 (WD Ark 1989).

[7] EEOC v. Pettegrove Truck Serv., Inc., 49 Fair Empl. Prac. Cas. (BNA) 1452 (SD Fla. 1989).

[8] See, e.g., Radio Union v. Broadcast Serv., 380 US 255 (1965); Armbruster v. Quinn, 711 F2d 1332 (6th Cir. 1983).

[9] See, e.g., Martin v. United Way of Erie County, 829 F2d 445 (3d Cir. 1987).

[10] See, e.g., Martin v. United Way of Erie County, 829 F2d 445 (3d Cir. 1987); see also 56 Fed. Reg. 35,547 (July 26, 1991).

sions.[11] Section 502 of the ADA sets forth the necessary language for judicial enforcement of the ADA against the states. The section provides that:

A state shall not be immune under the eleventh amendment to the Constitution of the United States from an action in Federal or State court of competent jurisdiction for a violation of the act. In any action against a state for a violation of the requirement of this Act, remedies (including remedies both at law and in equity) are available for such a violation to the same extent as such remedies are available against any public or private entity other than a state.

This provision was necessary to comply with the U.S. Supreme Court's standards for removing state immunity as set forth in *Atascadero State Hospital v. Scanlon.*[12] The reference to allowing state court actions was added by the House and receded to by the Senate in Conference.[13]

Title I does not, however, cover the federal government, Indian Tribes, or bona fide private membership clubs (other than labor organizations) who are exempt from taxation under Section 501(c) of the Internal Revenue Code (IRC).[14] The private club exemption is based on a similar exemption in Title II of the Civil Rights Act of 1964.[15] In determining whether a private entity qualifies as a private club for purposes of Title II, courts have considered such factors as the degree of member control of club operations, the selectivity of the membership selection process, whether substantial membership dues are charged, whether the entity is operated on a nonprofit basis, the

---

[11] ADA § 101(7). Section 502 of the ADA expressly addresses the question of state immunity.

[12] Atascadero State Hosp. v. Scanlon, 473 US 234 (1985). See Report of the House Comm. on the Judiciary on the Americans With Disabilities Act of 1990, HR Rep. No. 485, 101st Cong., 2d Sess., pt. 3 (1990) (hereinafter cited as H. Comm. on Jud. Rep.) at 72.

[13] HR Rep. 596, 101st Cong., 2d Sess. (1990) (hereinafter cited as Conference Report) at 85.

[14] ADA § 101(5). The ADA contains specific rules as to its applicability to Congress. ADA § 509.

[15] 42 USC §§ 2000a-1–2000a-6.

extent to which the facilities are open to the public, the degree of public funding, and whether the club was specifically created to avoid compliance with civil rights laws.[16] The proposed Justice Department's regulations under the ADA indicate that a similar test will be applied to the new act and the Equal Employment Opportunity Commission (EEOC) is likely to follow the Justice Department's guidelines. [17]

Agents of covered entities (such as officers and supervisors of an employer) are subject to the ADA's requirements and may be held personally liable for their violations of the ADA.[18]

Title VII's exception for elected officials and their employees and appointees was intentionally deleted from the ADA.[19]

The employment provisions become applicable to employers in stages:[20]

- For employers with twenty-five or more employees, the ADA becomes effective on July 26, 1992.
- For employers with more than fifteen employees (but less than twenty-five), the ADA becomes effective on July 26, 1994.

While the ADA applies to religious organizations, Section 103(c) provides that a religious organization (including religious corporations, associations, educational institutions, or societies) may give a preference to individuals of a particular religion to perform work connected with the organization. This provision parallels similar language in Section 702 of Title VII of the

---

[16] See, e.g., Tillman v. Wheaton-Haven Recreation Ass'n, 410 US 431 (1973); Daniel v. Paul, 395 US 298 (1969); Olzman v. Lake Hills Swim Club, Inc., 495 F2d 1333 (2d Cir. 1974).

[17] 56 Fed. Reg. 35,552–35,553 (July 26, 1991).

[18] ADA § 101(5) (the term "employer" means "any agent of such person").

[19] Report of the House Comm. on Education and Labor on the Americans With Disabilities Act of 1990, HR Rep. No. 485, 101st Cong., 2d Sess. pt. 2 (1990) (hereinafter cited as H. Comm. on Educ. and Lab. Rep.) at 54; 56 Fed. Reg. 35,740 (July 26, 1991).

[20] ADA §§105, 108.

Civil Rights Act of 1964[21] and is construed in a consistent manner.[22] Section 702 has generally been interpreted to allow employers to base relevant hiring and promotion decisions on religious preferences but not other characteristics protected by Title VII.[23]

A religious organization may require that all applicants and employees comply with the tenets of such organization (whether such tenets are written or oral).[24] This provision is based on similar language in Title IX of the Educational Amendments of 1972[25] and should be consistently interpreted.[26]

> EXAMPLE: A Mormon organization wishes to hire only Mormons to perform certain jobs. If a person with a disability applies for the job, but is not a Mormon, the organization can refuse to hire him. However, if two Mormons apply for a job, one with a disability and one without a disability, the organization cannot discriminate against the applicant with the disability because of that person's disability.[27]

> EXAMPLE: Assume that Desiard Country Club, an exempt organization under IRC Section 501(c), wishes to hire only nondisabled individuals to work in its dining rooms. If two individuals apply for a job, one with a disability and one without a disability, the country club can discriminate against the applicant with the disability because of that person's disability even if he is the more qualified person.

---

[21] 42 USC § 2000e-1 (1985).

[22] H. Comm. on Jud. Rep. at 46. The constitutionality of Section 702 was upheld in Amos v. Corporation of the Presiding Bishop of Church/Latter-Day Saints, 44 Fair Empl. Prac. Cas. (BNA) 20 (US 1987).

[23] See, e.g., EEOC v. Fremont Christian School, 781 F2d 1362 (9th Cir. 1986).

[24] EEOC Regs. 29 CFR § 1630.16(a); EEOC Interpretive Guidelines, 56 Fed. Reg. 35,752 (July 26, 1991).

[25] 20 USC § 1681(a)(3) (1985).

[26] H. Comm. on Jud. Rep. at 46.

[27] H. Comm. on Educ. and Lab. Rep. at 76.

¶ 2.02 WHAT CONSTITUTES A DISABILITY?

A threshold question under the ADA is what constitutes a disability. Section 3(2) of the ADA gives a three-prong definition, providing that disability means, with respect to an individual:

- Prong 1—A physical or mental impairment that substantially limits one or more of the major life activities of such individual
- Prong 2—A record of such an impairment
- Prong 3—Being regarded as having such an impairment

This definition is comparable to the definition of an individual with handicaps in Section 7(8)(B) of the Rehabilitation Act of 1973. Congress intended the relevant case law under the Rehabilitation Act generally to be applicable to the term "disability" in the ADA.[28]

Congress's use of disability, rather than an individual with handicaps, was not a substantive change but rather an attempt to use more currently acceptable terminology.[29] Efforts to substitute a specific list of disabilities were repeatedly rejected in favor of Section 3(2)'s broad definition.[30]

However, the analysis of what is meant by an individual with handicaps by the Department of Health, Education, and Welfare in its regulations implementing Section 504 and the analysis by the Department of Housing and Urban Development in its regulations implementing the Fair Housing Amendments Act of 1988 apply to the construction of what a disability is under the ADA.[31] Generally, these regulations are more

---

[28] EEOC Interpretive Guidelines, 56 Fed. Reg. 35,740 (July 26, 1991); Report of the Senate Comm. on Labor and Human Resources on the Americans With Disabilities Act of 1989, S. Rep. No. 116, 101st Cong., 1st Sess. (1989) (hereinafter cited as S. Comm. on Lab. and Hum. Resources Rep.) at 21; H. Comm. on Educ. and Lab. Rep. at 50; H. Comm. on Jud. Rep. at 27.

[29] EEOC Interpretive Guidelines, 56 Fed. Reg. 35,740 (July 26, 1991); H. Comm. on Jud. Rep. at 26–27; S. Comm. on Lab. and Hum. Resources Rep. at 50–51.

[30] 136 Cong. Rec. E1914 (June 13, 1990) (Congressman Hoyer).

[31] H. Comm. on Educ. and Lab. Rep. at 55.

favorable to the disabled than those issued pursuant to Section 503 of the Rehabilitation Act.

For the ADA's coverage to apply in an employment situation, other factors than the existence of a disability must be applicable. The individual also must be otherwise qualified at the time of the job action in question.[32] Then, it must be considered whether the employer can reasonably accommodate the individual's disability in performing the job. Thus, if an applicant or employee cannot perform the essential functions of the job in question at the time of hiring or promotion, the employer has no duty to reasonably accommodate.

> **EXAMPLE:** John Smith is currently disabled and scheduled for surgery. He applies for a position as a machine operator. Although Smith cannot perform the essential functions of the job at the time he applies, he will be able to perform those duties after the surgery. Under these facts, the prospective employer need not accommodate Smith's disability because Smith is not otherwise qualified at the time he applied for the position.

A significant issue under the ADA is whether an employer has an obligation to attempt to reasonably accommodate when an employee becomes unable to perform the essential functions of his job at a date subsequent to his hiring. The question this raises is whether the employer must offer the employee reassignment or permanent light duty.

Cases under the Rehabilitation Act generally held that an employer had no duty to reassign an employee in such circumstances because he is no longer otherwise qualified.[33]

However, there is indication in the legislative history of the ADA that the duty to accommodate attaches at hiring (or on

---

[32] 136 Cong. Rec. E1914 (June 13, 1990) (Congressman Hoyer).

[33] See Jasany v. US Postal Serv., 33 Fair Empl. Prac. Cas. (BNA) 1115, 1117 (ND Ohio 1983), aff'd, 755 F2d 1244, 1250 (6th Cir. 1985); Black v. Frank, 52 Fair Empl. Prac. Cas. (BNA) 1059 (SD Ala. 1990); Wimbley v. Bolger, 642 F. Supp. 481 (WD Tenn. 1986); Carty v. Carlin, 623 F. Supp. 1181 (D. Md. 1985); Alderson v. Postmaster Gen., 598 F. Supp. 49 (WD Okla. 1984).

promotion), and, therefore, the fact that the employee becomes unqualified would not deprive him of his right to reasonable accommodation, including reassignment.[34] This result is supported by the fact that the ADA lists reassignment as one of the accommodations that must be considered by an employer. Some courts under the Rehabilitation Act reached a similar conclusion.[35]

> EXAMPLE: Employee Jones becomes disabled during employment. As a result of his disability, Jones can no longer perform all the essential functions of his job. Jones therefore asks his employer to transfer the functions that he cannot perform to other employees. Jones's employer may have an obligation to grant this request as a reasonable accommodation even though it would have had no duty to modify the essential functions of the job if Jones were only an applicant for employment.

Recognizing the possibility that employers might discriminate against individuals who have characteristics indicating an increased possibility of disability in the future, the House Committee on Education and Labor stated in its report on the ADA that "the possibility of future incapacity does not by itself render the person not qualified."[36] However, precedent under the Rehabilitation Act suggests that in some circumstances, the possibility of future injury may, in light of other factors, warrant a refusal of job opportunities to a disabled individual.

For example, in *E.E. Black, Ltd. v. Marshall*,[37] an often cited Rehabilitation Act case likely to be followed in interpreting the ADA, the court held "that in some cases a job requirement that screens out qualified handicapped individuals on the basis of possible future injury, could be both consistent with necessity and safe performance of the job" and, therefore, not be illegal

---

[34] H. Comm. on Educ. and Lab. Rep. at 55.

[35] See Rhone v. US Department of Army, 655 F. Supp. 734 (ED Mo. 1987). The issue of "reassignment" as an accommodation is discussed at ¶ 2.07[5].

[36] H. Comm. on Educ. and Lab. Rep. at 55.

[37] EE Black, Ltd. v. Marshall, 497 F. Supp. 1088 (D. Haw. 1980).

discrimination.[38] The court described a hypothetical case of a person with a 90 percent chance of suffering a heart attack within one month of beginning a new job. The court concluded that in such a case an employer would be justified in refusing to hire the individual.

Generally, the courts indicated under the Rehabilitation Act that more than a remote possibility of future injury is required.[39] The proper standard under the Rehabilitation Act, and likely under the ADA, was stated by the Ninth Circuit in *Mantolete v. Bolger:*[40]

> [W]e hold that in order to exclude such individuals, there must be a showing of a reasonable probability of substantial harm. Such a determination cannot be based merely on an employer's subjective evaluation or, except in cases of a most apparent nature, merely on medical reports. The question is whether, in light of the individual's work history and medical history, employment of that individual would pose a reasonable probability of substantial harm.[41]

Cases under the Rehabilitation Act suggest that the following factors must be considered in deciding whether a possibility of future injury can be a basis for not hiring or promoting an individual:[42]

- The likelihood of injury
- The seriousness of the possible injury
- The imminence of the injury

The EEOC has adopted this approach as part of its proposed regulations on an employer's right not to hire an applicant who is

---

[38] Id. at 1104.

[39] See, e.g., Mikucki v. US Postal Serv., 41 Fair Empl. Prac. Cas. (BNA) 1503 (D. Mass. 1986); Bentivegna v. US Department of Labor, 694 F2d 619 (9th Cir. 1982); Department of Labor v. Texas Indus., 47 Fair Empl. Prac. Cas. (BNA) 18 (DOL 1988).

[40] Mantolete v. Bolger, 767 F2d 1416 (9th Cir. 1985).

[41] Id. at 1422.

[42] See Department of Labor v. Texas Indus., 47 Fair Empl. Prac. Cas. (BNA) 18 (DOL 1988).

considered a direct threat. [43]

As under the Rehabilitation Act, an employer will likely be justified in finding an employee unqualified if he does not meet its moral requirements. For example, a police officer who uses illegal drugs [44] or an individual who violates the employer's prohibitions against criminal convictions [45] may both be subject to discharge. Violations of moral requirements may be an acceptable basis for denying employment opportunities to a disabled individual even if the misconduct is related to a disability. [46]

[1] Specific Impairments

The first prong of the ADA Section 3(2) definition of disability includes any individual who has (1) a physical or mental impairment that (2) substantially limits a major life activity.

The ADA does not specify all the covered disabilities. Congress determined that

> it is not possible to include in the legislation a list of all the specific conditions, diseases or infections that would constitute physical or mental impairments because of the difficulty of ensuring the comprehensiveness of such a list, particularly in light of the fact that new disorders may develop in the future. [47]

The determination of whether an individual has a disability is based on the effect of an impairment on the life of the individual and not on the name or diagnosis of the impairment. As stated in the EEOC's Interpretive Guidelines: "Some impairments may be disabling for particular individuals but not for

---

[43] See EEOC Regs. at 29 CFR § 1630.2(r); EEOC Interpretive Guidelines, 56 Fed. Reg. 35,730 (July 26, 1991).

[44] Copeland v. Philadelphia Police Dep't, 840 F2d 1139 (3d Cir. 1988).

[45] Huff v. Israel, 573 F. Supp. 107 (MD Ga. 1983), vacated, 732 F2d 943 (11th Cir. 1984); Swann v. Walters, 620 F. Supp. 741 (DDC 1984); McGarvey v. District of Columbia, 468 F. Supp. 687 (DDC 1979).

[46] See id.

[47] S. Comm. on Lab. and Hum. Resources Rep. at 22.

others, depending on the stage of the disease or disorder, the presence of other impairments that combine to make the impairment disabling or any number of other factors."[48] Other impairments, such as HIV infection, are inherently substantially limiting.[49]

[a] Physical

The ADA generally adopts the definition of the term "physical and mental impairment" found in the regulations implementing Section 504 of the Rehabilitation Act.[50] The legislative history to the ADA indicates that the term means, at a minimum:[51]

- Any physiological disorder or condition including, but not limited to conditions, diseases, and infections, such as orthopedic, visual, speech and hearing impairments, cerebral palsy, epilepsy, muscular dystrophy, multiple sclerosis, cancer, heart disease, and diabetes
- Cosmetic disfigurement
- Anatomical loss affecting one or more of the following body systems: neurological, musculoskeletal, special sense organs, respiratory, speech organs, cardiovascular, reproductive, digestive, genito-urinary, hemic and lymphatic, skin, and endocrine

The legislative history also makes clear that a person carrying the human immunodeficiency virus (HIV) is covered by the ADA.[52]

After receiving comments to its proposed regulations, the EEOC added to its comments on the final regulations a state-

---

[48] EEOC's Interpretive Guidelines, 56 Fed. Reg. 8594 (Feb. 28, 1991).

[49] Id.

[50] EEOC Interpretive Guidelines, 56 Fed. Reg. 8592 (Feb. 28, 1991).

[51] EEOC Regs. § 1630.2(h), at 56 Fed. Reg. 8587 (Feb. 28, 1991); H. Comm. on Educ. and Lab. Rep. at 50. See Fair Housing Act Regulation definition at 24 CFR § 100.201.

[52] H. Comm. on Educ. and Lab. Rep. at 52; S. Comm. on Lab. and Hum. Resources Rep. at 22. 136 Cong. Rec. S9697 (July 13, 1990) (Comments of Senator Kennedy).

ment that the term "impairment" does not include characteristic predisposition to illness or disease.[53] The final regulations also added a statement that pregnancy is not an "impairment."[54]

Cases under the Rehabilitation Act applied similar language in that statute to such conditions as diabetes,[55] back conditions,[56] cerebral palsy,[57] blindness,[58] learning disabilities (including dyslexia),[59] epilepsy,[60] asthma,[61] multiple sclerosis,[62] deafness,[63] alcoholism,[64] allergies,[65] cancer,[66] heart condi-

---

[53] 56 Fed. Reg. 35,727, 35,741 (July 26, 1991).

[54] Id.

[55] Davis v. Meese, 692 F. Supp. 505 (ED Pa. 1988); Bentivegna v. US Department of Labor, 694 F2d 619 (9th Cir. 1982); Brown v. County of Genesee, 37 Fair Empl. Prac. Cas. (BNA) 1595 (WD Mich. 1985); Brown v. American Home Prods. Corp., 520 F. Supp. 1120 (D. Kan. 1981).

[56] Thornhill v. Marsh, 816 F2d 1182 (9th Cir. 1989); Perez v. Philadelphia Hous. Auth., 46 Fair Empl. Prac. Cas. (BNA) 1385 (ED Pa. 1987), aff'd, 841 F2d 1120 (3d Cir. 1988); Daubert v. US Postal Serv., 31 Fair Empl. Prac. Cas. (BNA) 459 (D. Colo. 1982); EE Black, Ltd. v. Marshall, 497 F. Supp. 1088 (D. Haw. 1980); Department of Labor, OFCCP v. Texas Indus., Inc., 47 Fair Empl. Prac. Cas. (BNA) 18 (DOL 1988).

[57] Bruegging v. Burke, 48 Fair Empl. Prac. Cas. (BNA) 140 (DDC 1987).

[58] Carter v. Bennett, 840 F2d 63 (DC Cir. 1988); Brown v. Sibley, 650 F2d 760 (5th Cir. Unit A 1981); Gurmankin v. Costanzo, 411 F. Supp. 982 (ED Pa. 1976), aff'd, 556 F2d 184 (3d Cir. 1977); Upshur v. Love, 474 F2d 332 (ND Cal. 1979); McNutt v. Hills, 426 F. Supp. 990 (DDC 1977). See also Doherty v. Southern College of Optometry, 659 F. Supp. 662 (WD Tenn. 1987) (retinitis pigmentosa); Kampmeier v. Nyquist, 553 F2d 296 (2d Cir. 1977) (vision in one eye); Wright v. Columbia Univ., 520 F. Supp. 789 (ED Pa. 1981) (vision in one eye).

[59] Stutts v. Freeman, 694 F2d 666 (11th Cir. 1983); DiPompo v. West Point Military Academy, 708 F. Supp. 540 (SDNY 1989).

[60] Reynolds v. Brock, 815 F2d 571 (9th Cir. 1987); Duran v. City of Tampa, 430 F2d 75 (MD Fla. 1977); Drennon v. Philadelphia Hosp., 428 F. Supp. 809 (ED Pa. 1977).

[61] Carter v. Tisch, 822 F2d 465 (4th Cir. 1987).

[62] Carter v. Case Central, 849 F2d 1048 (7th Cir. 1988); Pushkin v. Regents of Univ. of Colo., 658 F2d 1372 (10th Cir. 1981).

[63] Strathie v. Department of Transp., 716 F2d 227 (3d Cir. 1983); Camenisch v. University of Tex., 616 F2d 127 (5th Cir. 1980), remanded on other grounds, 451 US 390 (1981); Shirey v. Devine, 670 F2d 1188 (DC Cir. 1982); Bonner v. Lewis, 857 F2d 559 (9th Cir. 1988); Crane v. Lewis, 551 F.

tions,[67] high blood pressure,[68] paraplegia,[69] repeated shoulder dislocation,[70] loss of leg,[71] dwarfism,[72] spina bifida,[73] cystic fibrosis,[74] osteoarthritis,[75] strabismus,[76] hepatitis B carrier,[77] and Crohn's disease.[78]

In its Interpretive Guidelines, the EEOC states that impairment does not include physical characteristics such as eye color, hair color, left-handedness, or height, weight, or muscle tone that are within normal range and are not the result of a physio-

---

Supp. 27 (DDC 1982), further proceedings, Crane v. Dole, 617 F. Supp. 156 (DDC 1985); Jones v. Illinois Dep't of Rehabilitation Servs., 504 F. Supp. 1244 (ND Ill. 1981); Crawford v. University of NC, 440 F. Supp. 1047 (MDNC 1977); Greater Los Angeles Council on Deafness v. Zolin, 607 F. Supp. 175 (CD Cal. 1984), aff'd in part and rev'd in part and remanded on other grounds, 812 F2d 1103 (9th Cir. 1987).

[64] Simpson v. Reynolds Metals Co., 629 F2d 1226 (7th Cir. 1980); Athanas v. Board of Educ. of School Dist. 111, 28 Fair Empl. Prac. Cas. (BNA) 569 (ND Ill. 1980); Whitaker v. Board of Higher Educ., 461 F. Supp. 99 (EDNY 1978).

[65] Vickers v. Veterans Admin., 549 F. Supp. 85 (WD Wash. 1982).

[66] Harrison v. Marsh, 46 Fair Empl. Prac. Cas. (BNA) 971 (WD Mo. 1988).

[67] Treadwell v. Alexander, 707 F2d 473 (11th Cir. 1983).

[68] Bey v. Bolger, 540 F. Supp. 910 (WD Mo. 1988).

[69] Simon v. St. Louis County Police Dep't, 14 Fair Empl. Prac. Cas. (BNA) 363 (ED Mo. 1977), aff'd in part and rev'd in part, 656 F2d 316 (8th Cir. 1981); Smith v. Fletcher, 559 F2d 1014 (5th Cir. 1977).

[70] Mahoney v. Ortiz, 645 F. Supp. 22 (SDNY 1986).

[71] Ward v. Massachusetts Bay Transp. Auth., 550 F. Supp. 1310 (D. Mass. 1982).

[72] Dexler v. Tisch, 660 F. Supp. 1418 (D. Conn. 1987).

[73] Harrison v. Drosick, 423 F. Supp. 180 (SD W. Va. 1976).

[74] Gerben v. Holsclaw, 692 F. Supp. 557 (ED Pa. 1988).

[75] Coley v. Secretary of the Army, 689 F. Supp. 519 (D. Md. 1987).

[76] Jasany v. US Postal Serv., 33 Fair Empl. Prac. Cas. (BNA) 1115, aff'd, 755 F2d 1244 (6th Cir. 1985).

[77] New York Ass'n for Retarded Children v. Carey, 612 F2d 644 (2d Cir. 1979); Kohl by Kohl v. Woodhaven Learning Center, 672 F. Supp. 1221 (WD Mo. 1987).

[78] Kling v. County of Los Angeles, 633 F2d 876 (9th Cir. 1980).

logical disorder.[79]

The existence of an impairment is determined without regard to mitigating measures, such as medicines or prosthetic devices.[80] As the EEOC's Interpretive Guidelines explain

> For example, an individual with epilepsy would be considered to have an impairment even if the symptoms of the disorder were completely controlled by medicine. Similarly, an individual with hearing loss would be considered to have an impairment even if the condition were correctable through the use of a hearing aid.[81]

When the relevant agencies were drafting their regulations under the Rehabilitation Act, there was an attempt by commentators to restrict the use of the word "handicap" to conditions generally understood to be contemplated by that word. However, the agencies tended to reject this approach.[82] In contrast, the EEOC, in its Interpretive Guidelines, suggests that under the ADA, it may be inclined to apply the legislation only to conditions that are traditionally considered as being disabling. For example, the EEOC has indicated that it will generally not consider obesity as covered by the ADA although the condition would otherwise fall within the ADA's literal definition of the term disability.[83]

---

[79] EEOC Interpretive Guidelines, 56 Fed. Reg. 35,741 (July 26, 1991).

[80] Id.; S. Comm. on Lab. and Hum. Resources Rep. at 23; H. Comm. on Educ. and Lab. Rep. at 52; H. Comm. on Jud. Rep. at 28.

[81] EEOC Interpretive Guidelines, 56 Fed. Reg. 35,741 (July 26, 1991).

[82] See the comments of the Department of Health and Human Services:

Comments suggested narrowing the definition [of handicap] in various ways. The most common recommendation was that only "traditional" handicaps be covered. The Department believes, however, that it has no flexibility with the statutory definition to limit the term to persons who have severe, permanent, or progressive conditions that are most commonly regarded as handicaps.

45 CFR Subtitle A, App. A, § 3. The Department of Health and Human Services went on to state, however, that "[t]he Department intends, however, to give particular attention in its enforcement of section 504 [of the Rehabilitation Act] to eliminating discrimination against persons with severe handicaps that were the focus of concern in the Rehabilitation Act of 1973."

[83] EEOC Interpretive Guidelines, 56 Fed. Reg. 35,741 (July 26, 1991).

Consistent with this view, and in contrast to the agencies' approach, courts under the Rehabilitation Act generally rejected claims under that statute when the "disabling" condition was not of the type typically considered a handicap.[84] For example, the court in *Forrisi v. Bowen*[85] held:

> The Rehabilitation Act assures that truly disabled, but genuinely capable, individuals will not face discrimination in employment because of stereotypes about the insurmountability of their handicaps. It would debase this high purpose if the statutory protections available to those truly handicapped could be claimed by anyone whose disability was minor and whose relative severity of impairment was widely shared. Indeed, the very concept of an impairment implies a characteristic that is not commonplace and that poses for the particular individual a more general disadvantage in his or her search for satisfactory employment.

[b] Mental

The legislative history to the ADA and the regulations under the Rehabilitation Act indicate that the term "mental impairment" means any mental or psychological disorder, such as mental retardation, organic brain syndrome, emotional or mental illness, and specific learning disabilities.[86] It does not include, however, common personality traits, such as poor judgment or a quick temper, where these are not symptoms of a mental or psychological disorder.[87]

---

[84] See, e.g., de la Torres v. Bolger, 781 F2d 1134 (5th Cir. 1986) (being left-handed is not an "impairment" cognizable under the Rehabilitation Act); Tudyman v. United Airlines, 608 F. Supp. 739 (CD Cal. 1984) (obesity not a handicap).

[85] Forrisi v. Bowen, 794 F2d 931 (4th Cir. 1986).

[86] H. Comm. on Educ. and Lab. Rep. at 51. See Fair Housing Act Regulations definition at 24 CFR § 100.202(a)(2); Rehabilitation Act Regulation definition at 29 CFR § 1613.702 (1987); EEOC Regs. § 1630.2(h)(2). The term "specific learning disabilities" is used "to describe such conditions as perceptual handicaps, brain injury, minimal brain dysfunction, dyslexia and developmental aphasia." (42 Fed. Reg. 22685 (May 4, 1977).)

[87] EEOC Interpretive Guidelines, 56 Fed. Reg. 35,741 (July 26, 1991).

Under the Rehabilitation Act, conditions such as apraxia,[88] schizophrenia,[89] manic depression,[90] and anxiety disorders[91] were found to be covered.[92]

In determining what constitutes a mental impairment, courts typically look to the American Psychiatric Association's *Diagnostic and Statistical Manual of Mental Disorders*, the latest version being typically referred to as DSM-III-R.[93] Senator Armstrong stated in the ADA debate that "[a] private entity that wished to know what the act might mean with respect to mental impairments would do well to turn to DSM-III-R because that is the one reputable place where mental disorders are listed category-by-category, name-by-name."[94]

There was concern in the Congress that the term "mental impairment" could be applied in too loose a manner. While the term is broad, experience under the Rehabilitation Act indicates that the courts will limit its application by focusing on other limitations contained in the ADA:

- *Acrophobia.* In *Forrisi v. Bowen*,[95] the U.S. Court of Appeals for the Fourth Circuit held that the plaintiff had

---

[88] Arneson v. Heckler, 879 F2d 393 (8th Cir. 1989).

[89] Doe v. Colautti, 592 F2d 704 (3d Cir. 1979); Bolthouse v. Continental Wingate, 656 F. Supp. 620 (WD Mich. 1987).

[90] Matzo v. Postmaster Gen., 46 Fair Empl. Prac. Cas. (BNA) 869 (DDC 1987), aff'd, 861 F2d 1290 (DC Cir. 1988); Gardner v. Morris, 752 F2d 1271 (8th Cir. 1985).

[91] Shea v. Tisch, 870 F2d 786 (1st Cir. 1989).

[92] See also Forrisi v. Bowen, 794 F2d 931 (4th Cir. 1986); Doe v. Region 13 Mental Health-Mental Retardation Comm'n, 704 F2d 1402 (5th Cir. 1983); Franklin v. Postal Serv., 687 F. Supp. 1214 (SD Ohio 1988); Guerriero v. Schultz, 557 F. Supp. 511 (DDC 1983); Doe v. Syracuse School Dist., 508 F. Supp. 333 (NDNY 1981).

[93] See, e.g., Doe v. New York Univ., 666 F2d 761, 768 (2d Cir. 1981); Rezza v. US Department of Justice, 46 Fair Empl. Prac. Cas. (BNA) 1366 (ED Pa. 1988); Drew P. v. Clarke Co. School Dist., 676 F. Supp. 1559, 1561 n.3 (MD Ga. 1987); Schmidt v. Bell, 33 Fair Empl. Prac. Cas. (BNA) 839 (ED Pa. 1983).

[94] 135 Cong. Rec. S11174 (Sept. 14, 1989) (Statement by Senator Armstrong).

[95] Forrisi v. Bowen, 794 F2d 931 (4th Cir. 1986).

failed to show that his acrophobia (fear of heights) was a covered handicap because there was no evidence that it substantially limited a major life activity.[96]

- *Depressive Neurosis.* Depressive neurosis has been held to be a handicap within the meaning of the Rehabilitation Act but the plaintiff was found not "otherwise qualified."[97]

- *Paranoid Schizophrenia.* A person who suffers from the condition of paranoid schizophrenia, which is controllable by medication, and who does not take such medication, has been found not to be an "otherwise qualified" handicapped person.[98]

- *Manic Depression.* A manic depressive employee has been held not to be "otherwise qualified" because of an inability to report for work and remain on duty.[99]

- *Borderline Personality Disorder.* A medical school was not required to admit a student who had a long history of medical problems and was diagnosed as having a borderline personality disorder.[100]

- *Schizoid Personality Disorder.* A foreign service officer was not "otherwise qualified" because he could not accept an overseas assignment because of his therapy for a schizoid personality disorder.[101]

---

[96] For a state law case involving "carbon monoxide phobia," see Barnes v. Barbosa, 494 NE2d 619 (Ill. App. Ct. 1986).

[97] Doe v. Region 13 Mental Retardation Comm'n, 704 F2d 1402 (5th Cir. 1983). However, a jury verdict for the plaintiff was overturned because the plaintiff, a health worker, was found not to be "otherwise qualified."

[98] Franklin v. Postal Serv., 687 F. Supp. 1214 (SD Ohio 1988). For another case involving paranoid schizophrenia, see Swann v. Walters, 620 F. Supp. 741 (DDC 1984).

[99] Matzo v. Postmaster Gen., 46 Fair Empl. Prac. Cas. (BNA) 869 (DDC 1987). For a state court decision applying local law and the Rehabilitation Act, see Balzac v. Columbia Univ. Press, 39 Fair Empl. Prac. Cas. (BNA) 830 (NY App. Div. 1985), holding that an employer was not entitled to summary judgment when it fired a manic depressive employee upon his return from treatment.

[100] Doe v. New York Univ., 666 F2d 761 (2d Cir. 1981). See also Fields v. Lyng, 44 Fair Empl. Prac. Cas. (BNA) 1036 (D. Md. 1988), where a district court found a disabled individual not otherwise qualified after the EEOC had held that the employee was disabled by a borderline personality disorder.

[101] Guerriero v. Schultz, 31 Fair Empl. Prac. Cas. (BNA) 196 (DDC 1983).

- *Stress Disorders.* An employee who suffered from post-traumatic stress disorder (post-Vietnam syndrome) was not "otherwise qualified" within the meaning of the Rehabilitation Act because of his record of violence. [102]

[c] Other

The legislative history shows the intent of Congress to define a disability to include alcoholism and drug addiction, provided that the individual is not currently using a controlled substance or alcohol. [103] However, special considerations apply to these conditions. [104]

Advanced age, in and of itself, is not an impairment within the meaning of the ADA. However, the EEOC's Interpretive Guidelines note that the "various medical conditions commonly associated with age, such as hearing loss, osteoporosis or arthritis, would constitute impairments within the meaning of [the EEOC's proposed] regulations." [105]

Most cases under the Rehabilitation Act placed the burden

---

[102] Schmidt v. Bell, 33 Fair Empl. Prac. Cas. (BNA) 839 (ED Pa. 1983).

[103] H. Comm. on Educ. and Lab. Rep. at 51. Alcoholism is a covered disability under the Rehabilitation Act. See, e.g., Simpson v. Reynolds Metals Co., 629 F2d 1226 (7th Cir. 1980); Athanas v. Board of Educ. of School Dist. 111, 28 Fair Empl. Prac. Cas. (BNA) 569 (ND Ill. 1980); Whitaker v. Board of Higher Educ., 461 F. Supp. 99 (EDNY 1978). Although alcoholism was a covered disability under the Rehabilitation Act, the courts tended not to be receptive to claims based on this disability. For example, in LeMere v. Burnley, 683 F. Supp. 275 (DDC 1988), the U.S. District Court for the District of Columbia held that the termination of a federal employee due to ongoing attendance and performance problems linked to alcoholism did not violate the Rehabilitation Act. The court found that the Federal Aviation Administration's previous attempts at accommodation (which primarily focused on detoxification programs) were more than reasonable and determined that the plaintiff's erratic conduct had become an "undue hardship" to the agency's operations.

[104] See infra ¶ 2.14.

[105] EEOC Interpretive Guidelines, 56 Fed. Reg. 8592 (Feb. 28, 1991); S. Comm. on Lab. and Hum. Resources Rep. at 22–23; H. Comm. on Educ. and Lab. Rep. at 51–52; H. Comm. on Jud. Rep. at 28–29.

of proof on the plaintiff to establish the existence of a handicap; it is likely that the same rule will apply under the ADA. [106]

[2] Substantial Limitations on Life Activities

Congress clearly intended to have the term "disability" construed broadly. However, the definition includes neither simple physical characteristics, nor limitations based on environmental, cultural, or economic disadvantages. [107]

Merely having an impairment is not sufficient for protection under the ADA. The impediment must be to such a degree that it substantially limits a major life activity. [108] A major life activity includes one or more of the following:

- Walking
- Seeing
- Hearing
- Speaking
- Breathing
- Learning

---

[106] See Jasany v. US Postal Serv., 755 F2d 1244 (6th Cir. 1985); Treadwell v. Alexander, 707 F2d 473 (11th Cir. 1983).

[107] EEOC Interpretive Guidelines, 56 Fed. Reg. 35,741 (July 26, 1991).

[108] See Jasany v. US Postal Serv., 755 F2d 1244 (6th Cir. 1985), in which the U.S. Court of Appeals for the Sixth Circuit held that a postal service employee who could no longer perform an essential function of his position due to his crossed-eyes was not a "qualified handicapped individual" entitled to the protection of the Rehabilitation Act. The district court found that Jasany's strabismus impaired his ability to work on the mail-sorting machine and that this qualified as a major life activity for purposes of the Rehabilitation Act's definition of a handicapped person. However, the district court held that Jasany nevertheless failed to establish that he was a "qualified" handicapped person as defined by the statute. On appeal, the Sixth Circuit affirmed the decision of the lower court, but found that the district court erred in concluding that Jasany was a "handicapped" person. The Sixth Circuit reasoned that Jasany's strabismus never had any effect on any of his activities, including his past work history and ability to carry out other duties at the office apart from the operation of the mail-sorting machine. Thus, his impairment did not substantially limit one or more of his major life activities, and Jasany did not qualify to bring a cause of action under the Rehabilitation Act.

- Working
- Participating in community activities[109]
- Caring for one's self
- Performing manual tasks[110]

[a] Defined by EEOC

According to the EEOC's Interpretive Guidelines and proposed regulations, major life activities refers to those "basic activities that the average person in the general population can perform with little or no difficulty."[111] Thus, it covers such activities as "sitting, standing, lifting, and reaching."[112]

Multiple impairments that combine to limit substantially one or more life activities also constitute a disability, according to the EEOC.[113]

According to the legislative history to the ADA, a wide variety of restrictions will be found to limit substantially one or more major life activities. The Department of Labor regulations under the Rehabilitation Act state that the term "life activities" includes such items as "communication, ambulation, selfcare, socialization, education, vocational training, employment, transportation, adapting to housing. . . ." The Department of Health and Human Services regulations under the Rehabilitation Act and the Housing and Urban Development regulations under the Fair Housing Act are similar, defining major life activities as "functions such as caring for one's self, performing

---

[109] Participating in community activities is only included in the House Committee on Education and Labor Report. H. Comm. on Educ. and Lab. Rep. at 52. The legislative history does not define the term "participate in community activities."

[110] H. Comm. on Educ. and Lab. Rep. at 52; H. Comm. on Jud. Rep. at 28; S. Comm. on Lab. and Hum. Resources Rep. at 22. See also 29 CFR § 1630.2(i).

[111] EEOC Interpretive Guidelines, 56 Fed. Reg. 35,741 (July 26, 1991); EEOC Regs. 29 CFR § 1630.2(i).

[112] EEOC Interpretive Guidelines, 56 Fed. Reg. 35,741 (July 26, 1991). See also S. Comm. on Lab. and Hum. Resources Rep. at 22; H. Comm. on Educ. and Lab. Rep. at 52; H. Comm. on Jud. Rep. at 28.

[113] EEOC Interpretive Guidelines, 56 Fed. Reg. 35,741 (July 26, 1991).

manual tasks, walking, seeing, hearing, speaking, breathing, learning, and working."[114] The scope of what is considered a major life activity under the ADA is at least as broad as these definitions, if not broader.

The EEOC's regulations set forth the following factors to be considered in determining whether an individual is substantially limited in a major life activity:[115]

- The nature and severity of the impairment
- The duration or expected duration of the impairment
- The permanent and long-term impact, or expected permanent or long-term impact of or resulting from the impairment

The EEOC Interpretive Guidelines state that:

> The term "duration" as used in this context, refers to the length of time an impairment persists, while the term "impact" refers to the residual effects of an impairment. Thus, for example, a broken leg that takes eight weeks to heal is an impairment of fairly brief duration. However, if the broken leg heals improperly, the "impact" of the impairment would be the resulting permanent limp. Likewise, the effect on cognitive functions resulting from a traumatic head injury would be the impact of that impairment.[116]

Ultimately, the determination of whether an individual is substantially limited in a major life activity must be made on a case-by-case basis.[117]

Whether a person suffers from a restriction that substantially limits one or more major life activities is a comparative test. A person is considered "an individual with a disability which substantially limits one or more major life activities" only when the individual's important life activities are restricted as to the conditions, manner, and duration under which they can be

---

[114] 45 CFR § 84.3(j)(2)(ii)(1988); 24 CFR § 100.201(b)(1990).

[115] 29 CFR § 1630.2(j)(2).

[116] EEOC Interpretive Guidelines, 56 Fed. Reg. 35,741 (July 26, 1991).

[117] Id.

performed in comparison to most people. If the individual's limitations are comparable to that of most people, the disability is not covered.[118] As stated by the EEOC's proposed regulations, the term "substantially limits" means "significantly restricted as to the condition, manner, duration under which an individual can perform a particular major life activity as compared to the condition, manner, or duration under which the average person in the general population can perform the same major life activity."[119]

In discussing the comparative nature of this part of the definition, the House Committee on Education and Labor uses the example of a person who can walk ten miles continuously but suffers pain during the eleventh mile. The committee stated that such a person would not be covered by the ADA because "most people would not be able to walk eleven miles without experiencing some discomfort."[120]

> EXAMPLE: An individual who was once able to walk at an extraordinary speed would be substantially limited in the major life activity of walking if, as a result of a physical impairment, he were only able to walk at an average speed or even a moderately below average speed.[121]

The EEOC Interpretive Guidelines further illustrate this principle:

> [A]n individual who uses artificial legs is substantially limited in the major life activity of walking because the individual can perform that major life activity in a significantly restricted manner i.e., only the use of prosthetic devices. An individual is also substantially limited in the major life activity of walking if the individual can only walk for a very brief period of time. Similarly, a diabetic who without insulin would lapse into a coma would be substantially limited

---

[118] H. Comm. on Educ. and Lab. Rep. at 23.

[119] EEOC Regs., at 29 CFR § 1630.2(j)(ii).

[120] H. Comm. on Educ. and Lab. Rep. at 52.

[121] 56 Fed. Reg. 35,741 (July 26, 1991).

because the individual can only perform major life activities with the aid of medication.[122]

The evaluation of whether a restriction limits a major life activity must be made without regard to mitigating measures, such as auxiliary aids. For example, a person suffering from a hearing limitation is limited in a major life activity even though the restriction is fully corrected by use of a hearing aid. Similarly, persons with impairments such as epilepsy or diabetes are covered by the ADA even though the effects of their illness are controlled by medication. The EEOC's proposed regulations were amended to make clear that "the determination of whether an impairment substantially limits one or more major life activities is to be made without regard to the availability of medicines, assistive devices, or other mitigating measures.[123]

[b] Case Law

In *School Board of Nassau County v. Arline*,[124] the U.S. Supreme Court discussed what the term "substantial limitation of one or more major life activities" means for purposes of the Rehabilitation Act. A similar construction will likely apply under the ADA.

In *Arline*, tuberculosis was considered a handicap under the record of disability prong of the "disability" definition. The *Arline* Court held that the fact that the plaintiff's "impairment was sufficient enough to require hospitalization [was] more than sufficient to establish that one or more of her major life activities were substantially limited by her impairment."[125]

Among many examples under the Rehabilitation Act of conditions that were found to cause a substantial limitation are: ankylosing spondylitis (which causes stiffening of the joints),[126]

---

[122] EEOC Interpretive Guidelines, 56 Fed. Reg. 35,741 (July 26, 1991). S. Comm. on Lab. and Hum. Resources Rep. at 23; H. Comm. on Educ. and Lab. Rep. at 52.

[123] 56 Fed. Reg. 35,727 (July 26, 1991).

[124] School Bd. of Nassau County v. Arline, 480 US 273 (1987).

[125] Id. at 281.

[126] Sisson v. Helms, 751 F2d 991 (9th Cir. 1985).

permanent osteoarthritis of the knee joints,[127] the amputation of the leg below the kneecap,[128] heart conditions,[129] and even hypersensitivity to tobacco smoke.[130] On the other hand, conditions such as left-handedness,[131] varicose veins,[132] and an undisclosed nonpermanent disease[133] were held not to be disabilities under the Rehabilitation Act and are not likely to be covered by the ADA.

Under the ADA, the limitations do not have to be related to the disabled person's ability to perform job duties. For example, regarding HIV-positive individuals, the House Committee on Education and Labor concluded that such persons were covered because of a "substantial limitation to procreation and intimate sexual relationships."[134]

[c] Temporary Conditions

A question left open by the ADA is the treatment of injuries that are not permanent, but nevertheless constitute a physical impairment that substantially limits the individual's life while the impairment lasts. The EEOC's regulations specifically list the duration of an impairment as a factor in determining whether a disability substantially limits a major life activity.

A number of courts concluded under the Rehabilitation Act that there is no coverage for transitory illnesses that have no permanent effect on a person's health.[135] However, the ADA potentially covers such conditions, provided that they last more

---

[127] Guinn v. Bolger, 598 F. Supp. 196 (DDC 1984).

[128] Longoria v. Harris, 554 F. Supp. 102 (SD Tex. 1982).

[129] Bento v. ITO Corp. of RI, 599 F. Supp. 731 (DRI 1984).

[130] Vickers v. Veterans Admin., 549 F. Supp. 85 (WD Wash. 1982).

[131] de la Torres v. Bolger, 610 F. Supp. 593 (ND Tex. 1985), aff'd, 781 F2d 1134 (5th Cir. 1986).

[132] Oesterling v. Walters, 760 F2d 859 (8th Cir. 1985).

[133] Stevens v. Stubbs, 576 F. Supp. 1409 (ND Ga. 1983).

[134] H. Comm. on Educ. and Lab. Rep. at 52. This conclusion was supported by the Department of Justice's report on the "Application of Section 504 of the Rehabilitation Act to HIV-Infected Individuals" (Sept. 27, 1988).

[135] See, e.g., Stevens v. Stubbs, 576 F. Supp. 1409 (ND Ga. 1983); Doss v. General Motors Corp., 25 Fair Empl. Prac. Cas. (BNA) 419 (CD Ill. 1980);

than a short period. The question left open by the ADA is how long the condition must last (or be expected to last) until the individual is entitled to protection.

The Preamble to the Department of Justice's proposed Interpretive Guidelines stated as follows regarding temporary conditions:

> An impairment is not necessarily excluded from the definition of "disability" simply because it is temporary. The duration, or expected duration, of an impairment is, however, one factor that may properly be considered in determining whether the impairment substantially limits a major life activity. Temporary impairments, such as a broken leg, are not commonly regarded as disabilities, but in rare circumstances the degree of the limitation and its expected duration may be substantial. . . . It must be emphasized that each case must be evaluated on its own merits.[136]

Similarly, the EEOC's final Interpretive Guidelines state that: "[T]emporary, non-chronic impairments of short duration, with little or no long term or permanent impact, are usually not disabilities. Such impairments may include, but are not limited to, broken limbs, sprained joints, concussions, appendicitis and influenza."[137]

> EXAMPLE: Assume an employee suffers a bad back injury while skiing. Her family doctor suggests three months in bed and surgery if the pain does not lessen. In the event of surgery, the employee will be off work for a year. Since the injury is a physical impairment substantially limiting a major life activity, the ADA arguably applies if, in fact, the employee is unable to work for a year.

Perez v. Philadelphia Housing Authority[138] illustrates that

---

Advocates v. Sears, Roebuck & Co., 21 Fair Empl. Prac. Cas. (BNA) 506 (Ill. App. Ct. 1978).

[136] 56 Fed. Reg. 35,549 (July 26, 1991).

[137] EEOC's Interpretive Guidelines, 56 Fed. Reg. 35,741 (July 26, 1991).

[138] Perez v. Philadelphia Hous. Auth., 677 F. Supp. 357 (ED Pa. 1987), aff'd, 841 F2d 1120 (3d Cir. 1988).

whether a temporary illness constitutes a disability is to be decided on a case-by-case. In *Perez*, the plaintiff had injured her back in 1984 and was discharged after a year on disability. By 1986, however, she had recovered, and she brought suit alleging handicap discrimination. The defendant contended that the plaintiff's condition was not covered by the Rehabilitation Act because it was only "temporary." In rejecting this contention, the court held:

> PHA [Philadelphia Housing Authority] contends that plaintiff was not handicapped under the Rehabilitation Act because she suffered from transitory back pain and not from a commonly recognized handicap. This generalized approach is not well taken. "The question of who is a handicapped person under the Act is best suited to a case-by-case determination."[139]

[d] Certain Types of Employment

A substantial issue under the Rehabilitation Act, and one left unclarified by the ADA, is whether a condition is covered by the ADA when it limits the individual's access to one or two types of employment but otherwise does not limit the person's employability or otherwise impair a major life activity. Arguably, such a condition is covered, because working is considered a major life activity.

[i] Case law. The Rehabilitation Act case most often cited in support of the proposition that working is a major life activity is *E.E. Black, Ltd. v. Marshall.*[140]

In *Black*, the employee was a member of a carpentry apprenticeship program. The program required 8,000 hours of field work to achieve journeyman status. During an employer medical examination, it was discovered that the applicant had a congenital back problem. This condition did not prevent the employee's performance of his apprentice duties but did indicate a risk of future problems. Based on this risk, the government

---

[139] Id. 677 F. Supp. at 360–361.

[140] EE Black, Ltd. v. Marshall, 497 F. Supp. 1088 (D. Haw. 1980).

contractor/employer refused to hire the employee. The contractor contended that the Rehabilitation Act only covered individuals who encounter difficulty with obtaining employment in general and not those persons who are merely denied a particular job or type of job.

A complaint was filed with the Department of Labor alleging handicap discrimination under Section 503 of the Rehabilitation Act. The administrative law judge (ALJ) required the employee to show that his impairment "impeded activities relevant to many or most jobs" and held for the contractor. Reversing, the Assistant Secretary of Labor held that an individual is "substantially limited" if the impairment is a current bar to the individual's own choice of employment. The contractor brought suit in federal district court to overturn the secretary's decision.

The federal District Court for Hawaii rejected both the ALJ's and the assistant secretary's definition. The court held that the ALJ's reasoning was overly restrictive and would undercut the purposes of the Rehabilitation Act. The court noted that the act would be of little comfort to a chemist rejected for a job because of an impairment even though he could find work as a streetcar conductor. On the other hand, the court rejected the assistant secretary's definition as overly broad, allowing for a claim by a person with acrophobia who was denied a job on a high floor of a building but was offered ten comparable jobs on a lower floor by the same employer.[141] The court chose a middle

---

[141] See Forrisi v. Bowen, 794 F2d 931 (4th Cir. 1986), in which the U.S. Court of Appeals for the Fourth Circuit held that a utility systems repairer who suffered from a fear of heights was not "handicapped" as defined under the Rehabilitation Act and, thus, not entitled to the act's protection. Forrisi had been terminated when he told his supervisor he would be unable to climb ladders beyond a certain height. When Forrisi brought suit under the Rehabilitation Act, the district court held that he had failed to satisfy the threshold requirement of being a "handicapped individual" as defined by the Rehabilitation Act. The court noted that Forrisi did not maintain that his acrophobia substantially limited his major life activities or that he had a history of an impairment that so limited him. To the contrary, Forrisi testified that his fear of heights "never affected [his] life at all on any job or anything" before the job at HHS. The Fourth Circuit, on appeal, affirmed the summary judgment against Forrisi. The court found that Forrisi was not a "handicapped individual," and that even had he been genuinely perceived by his employer to be

ground, reasoning that the focus should not be solely on the individual or the impairment.

The *Black* court listed the following factors, to be applied on a case-by-case basis, for determining whether a person's impairment substantially limits employment opportunities:[142]

- The number and types of jobs from which the impaired individual is disqualified
- The geographic area to which the applicant has reasonable access
- The applicant's own job expectations and training
- The criteria or qualifications in use generally
- The types of jobs to which the rejection would apply

Under the *Black* test, a court assumes that all employers offering the same job or similar jobs would use the same requirement or screening process.

An example of the application of the *Black* test is the decision in *Tudyman v. United Airlines*,[143] where a flight attendant claimed he was handicapped because he was denied a job with an airline as a result of his failure to meet the airline's weight restriction. The plaintiff argued that because the weight restriction prevented him from obtaining a job for which he was otherwise qualified, the requirement transformed him into a handicapped individual. The court in *Tudyman* rejected this argument, reasoning that

> [t]here is no authority for the proposition that failure to qualify for a single job because of some impairment . . . constitutes being limited in a major life activity. The regulations define major life activity as, *inter alia*, "working," 45 C.F.R. Section 84.3(j)(2)(ii), but not "working at the specific job of plaintiff's choice."[144]

---

handicapped, the Rehabilitation Act offered him no protection from termination because his life activities were not "substantially limited" as required by the act.

[142] EE Black, Ltd. v. Marshall, supra note 134, at 1100–1101.

[143] Tudyman v. United Airlines, 608 F. Supp. 739 (CD Cal. 1984).

[144] Id. at 745. See also State of Minn. v. Hennepin County, 51 Fair Empl.

The U.S. Court of Appeals for the Second Circuit decision in *Daley v. Koch*[145] further illustrates this point. In *Daley*, the applicant had passed the written examination required of applicants for the police department. As a result, he was certified for placement on a list of eligible candidates for appointment. Subsequently, he was examined by police department psychologists, who determined that he showed "poor judgment, irresponsible behavior and poor impulse control." Based on these findings, he was determined to be "unsuitable to be a police officer." The applicant sued under Section 504 of the Rehabilitation Act.

On appeal from the dismissal of the plaintiff's action, the Second Circuit concluded that the applicant was not an individual with a handicap within the meaning of Section 504. According to the court: "Being declared unsuitable for the particular position of police officer is not a substantial limitation of a major life activity."[146]

Black was also followed in *Forrisi v. Bowen*,[147] in which the U.S. Court of Appeals for the Fourth Circuit held that a utility system repair man was properly dismissed from his employment after he stated that his acrophobia prevented him from climbing on high ladders. The court reasoned that merely because the plaintiff was "unsuited for one position in one plant" did not mean that there was a substantial limitation on a major life activity.[148]

In drafting the ADA, Congress agreed with the rationale of cases such as *Black, Tudyman, Daley,* and *Forrisi.* For example, the House Committee on the Judiciary Report on the ADA states as follows:

Prac. Cas. (BNA) 166 (Minn. 1989) (holding that the fact that applicant was denied employment with sheriff's department because he could not meet job qualification of 20/100 uncorrected vision did not make the individual disabled).

[145] Daley v. Koch, 892 F2d 212 (2d Cir. 1989).

[146] Id.

[147] Forrisi v. Bowen, 794 F2d 931 (4th Cir. 1986).

[148] Id. at 935.

A person with an impairment who is discriminated in employment is . . . limited in the major life activity of working. However, a person who is limited in his or her ability to perform only a particular job, because of circumstances unique to that job site or the materials used, may not be substantially limited in the major life activity of working. For example, an applicant whose trade is painting would not be substantially limited in a major life activity of working if he has a mild allergy to a specialized paint used by one employer which is not generally used in the field in which the painter works. [149]

[ii] EEOC regulations. The EEOC's regulations also follow the *Black* line of cases. Under those regulations, an individual is substantially limited in his ability to work if he is significantly "restricted in the ability to perform either a class of jobs or a broad range of jobs in various classes as compared to the average person having comparable training, skills and abilities." [150] According to the regulations, however, "the inability to perform a single job does not constitute a substantial limitation in the major life activity of working." [151]

The regulations state that in determining whether a limitation on working is a disability, the following factors "may" be considered:

- The geographical area to which the individual has reasonable access
- The job from which the individual has been disqualified because of an impairment, the number and types of jobs utilizing similar training, knowledge, skills or abilities, within that geographical area, from which the individual is also disqualified because of the impairment (class of jobs)
- The job from which the individual has been disqualified because of an impairment, and the number and type of other jobs not utilizing similar training, knowledge, skills or abilities, within that geographical area, from which the

---

[149] H. Comm. on Jud. Rep. at 29.

[150] 29 CFR § 1630.2(j)(3)(i).

[151] Id.

individual is also disqualified because of the impairment (broad range of jobs in various classes)

The EEOC's Interpretive Guidelines to the proposed regulations actually stated the foregoing factors "should" rather than "may" be considered. The EEOC changed this language in the final guidelines to clarify "that the factors are relevant to, but are not required elements of a showing of a substantial limitation on working." [152]

In addition, the Interpretive Guidelines to the final regulations also added language clarifying that the "number and types" of jobs do not require significant technical data. [153] The added language states:

> The terms "numbers and types" of jobs and "number and types of other jobs" as used in the factors . . . are not intended to require an onerous evidentiary showing. Rather, the terms only require the presentation of evidence of general employment demographics and/or of recognized occupational classifications that indicate the approximate number of jobs (e.g. "few", "many", "most") from which an individual would be excluded because of an impairment. [154]

Under this regulation, an individual is not substantially limited in working just because he is unable to perform a particular job for a single employer or because he is unable to perform a specialized job or profession requiring extraordinary skill or prowess or talent. [155]

The EEOC proposed Interpretive Guidelines provided the following example:

> [A] surgeon who is no longer able to perform surgery because of an impairment that results in slightly shaky hands would not be substantially limited in working merely because of the inability to perform this chosen specialty.

---

[152] 56 Fed. Reg. 35,728 (July 26, 1991).

[153] Id.

[154] 56 Fed. Reg. 35,742 (July 26, 1991).

[155] EEOC Interpretive Guidelines, 56 Fed. Reg. 35,741–35,742 (July 26, 1991).

This is so because the surgeon would be excluded from a narrow range of jobs, and would still be able to perform various other positions, in the same class, utilizing his training as a physician.[156]

The final Interpretive Guidelines deleted this example because the EEOC found it to be confusing to some commentators.[157] The final guidelines state, instead:

For example, an individual who cannot be a commercial airline pilot because of a minor vision impairment but who can be a commercial airline co-pilot or a pilot for a courier service, would not be substantially limited in the major life activity of working. Nor would a professional baseball pitcher who developed a bad elbow and could no longer throw a baseball be considered substantially limited in the major life activity of working. In both of these examples, the individuals are not substantially limited in the ability to perform any other major life activity and, with regard to the major life activity of working, are only unable to perform either a particular specialized job or a narrow range of jobs.[158]

On the other hand, the EEOC's regulations recognize that an individual does not have to be totally unable to work to be considered substantially limited in the major life activity of working. Under the regulations, an individual is substantially limited in the life activity of working if he is restricted in his ability to perform a class of jobs or a broad range of jobs in various capacities as compared to an average person of similar qualifications.

The EEOC Interpretive Guidelines contain the following example:

[A]n individual who has a back condition that prevents the individual from performing any heavy labor would be sub-

---

[156] 56 Fed. Reg. 8593 (Feb. 28, 1991), citing Forrisi v. Bowen, 794 F2d 931 (4th Cir. 1986); Jasany v. US Postal Serv., 755 F2d 1244 (6th Cir. 1985); EE Black, Ltd. v. Marshall, 497 F. Supp. 1088 (D. Haw. 1980).

[157] 56 Fed. Reg. 35,728 (July 26, 1991).

[158] 56 Fed. Reg. 35,742 (July 26, 1991).

stantially limited in the major life activity of working because the individual's impairment eliminates his or her ability to perform a class of jobs. This would be so even if the individual were able to perform jobs in another class, e.g. the class of semi-skilled jobs.[159]

The EEOC Interpretive Guidelines also give a second example:

[A]n individual has an allergy to a substance found in most high rise office buildings but seldom found elsewhere, that makes breathing difficult. Since the individual would be substantially limited in the ability to perform a broad range of jobs in various classes that are conducted in high rise office buildings within the geographical area to which he or she has reasonable access, he or she would be substantially limited in working.[160]

[3] Excluded Conditions Under Section 511

Some members of Congress expressed their concern that sexual preferences could be perceived as a protected characteristic under the ADA. Others were concerned that plaintiffs' attorneys, through the use of psychiatric experts, would expand the ADA to cover conditions beyond Congress's intent. Accordingly, Section 511(b) of the ADA contains an expansive list of conditions not within the ADA's definition of disability. The list includes:

- Homosexuality and bisexuality[161]
- Transvestism, transsexualism, pedophilia, exhibitionism, voyeurism, gender identity disorders not resulting from physical impairments or other sexual behavior disorders[162]

---

[159] EEOC Interpretive Guidelines, 56 Fed. Reg. 35,742 (July 26, 1991).

[160] Id.

[161] ADA § 511(a).

[162] ADA § 511(b)(1).

- Compulsive gambling,[163] kleptomania,[164] or pyromania[165]
- Psychoactive substance use disorders resulting from current use of illegal drugs[166]

The EEOC's regulations have incorporated these exceptions.[167] Obviously, an individual is not automatically covered by the ADA simply because he does not fall within one of the listed exclusions.[168]

The House and Senate both expressed the conclusion that homosexuality and bisexuality are not "impairments" or "disabilities."[169] As stated in the House Committee on Education and Labor Report, "[h]omosexuality and bisexuality were never considered impairments under this Act and therefore were never covered as disabilities."[170] As to the other listed conditions, they would have arguably fallen within the ADA's protections absent

---

[163] There is some indication that compulsive gambling might have been considered a covered handicap under the Rehabilitation Act. See Rezza v. US Department of Justice, 46 Fair Empl. Prac. Cas. (BNA) 1366 (ED Pa. 1988). See also 135 Cong. Rec. S10773 (Sept. 7, 1989) (Comments of Senator Armstrong).

[164] See Fields v. Lyng, 48 Fair Empl. Prac. Cas. (BNA) 1037 (D. Md. 1988), a case under the Rehabilitation Act in which kleptomania was analyzed as a disability.

[165] ADA § 511(b)(2).

[166] ADA § 511(b)(3). The list of eleven items contained in Section 511(b) was taken from a longer list proposed by Senator Armstrong. 135 Cong. Rec. S10753 (Sept. 7, 1989) (Comments of Senator Armstrong). Under a compromise, Senator Armstrong agreed not to ask for a roll-call vote on his entire list in return for having the eleven items included in the ADA by voice vote. Id. at 10785–10786.

[167] 29 CFR § 1630.3.

[168] 56 Fed. Reg. 35,730 (July 26, 1991).

[169] The exclusion of homosexuality and bisexuality is consistent with the Department of Health, Education, and Welfare regulations and judicial decisions under the Rehabilitation Act. 42 Fed. Reg. 22686 (May 4, 1977); Blackwell v. US Department of Treasury, 830 F2d 1183 (DC Cir. 1987).

[170] H. Comm. on Educ. and Lab. Rep. at 142; see Blackwell v. US Department of Treasury, 830 F2d 1183 (DC Cir. 1987), in which the U.S. Court of Appeals for the District of Columbia held that the Rehabilitation Act does not encompass sexual orientation or preference.

an express exclusion. Transvestism is excluded by both Section 511 and Section 508.[171]

Interestingly, one of the prime sponsors of the ADA, Senator Harkin, argued that even the abbreviated list contained in Section 511(b) was not necessary because, in his opinion, the ADA already excluded conditions such as exhibitionism, pedophilia, voyeurism, and kleptomania.[172] Such a statement may support an argument that conditions such as those listed in Section 511(b) are not exclusive and that other conditions of a similar nature fall outside the ADA's definition of "disability."

However, it is important to note that a person with one of the listed conditions may also have another disability, which is covered by the ADA. If the person is discriminated against on the basis of the covered disability, that discrimination is still prohibited.[173]

> EXAMPLE: Employee Smith has a sexual behavior disorder. He decides to seek psychiatric help that would require him to miss an extended period of work. Employee Smith's employer would not have to accommodate the employee's request for leave. If, however, Employee Smith's psychiatrist concludes that the sexual behavior disorder is related to another non–sexually related mental condition, the employer would have to accommodate the request.

The current use of drugs is also an excluded disability.[174]

[4] Record of Disability

The second prong of the definition of disability includes an individual who has a record of having had a condition such as

---

[171] H. Comm. on Educ. and Lab. Rep. at 142. Section 508 was an amendment added by Senator Helms. 135 Cong. Rec. S10776 (Sept. 7, 1989). A similar exclusion exists under the 1988 Fair Housing Act, also as a result of the efforts of Senator Helms. 42 USC § 3602 (1988).

[172] 135 Cong. Rec. S10754, 10765 (Sept. 7, 1989) (Comments of Sen. Harkin).

[173] H. Comm. on Educ. and Lab. Rep. at 142.

[174] See infra ¶ 2.14.

described under part one of the test. [175] Under this second prong, the ADA protects persons who have a history of, or who have been misclassified as having, a mental or physical impairment that substantially limits one or more major life activities.

According to the House Committee on Education and Labor, "[t]his provision is included in the definition in part to protect individuals who have recovered from a physical or mental impairment which previously substantially limited them in a major life activity." [176]

There are many types of records that could potentially contain information regarding disabilities, including, but not limited to, education, medical, and employment records. [177]

The most common examples of individuals protected by this prong of the definition are: [178]

- Persons who have recovered from mental or emotional illness, heart disease, or cancer (e.g., individuals with a history of an impairment)
- Persons who have been misclassified as mentally retarded (e.g., individuals who have been misclassified as having an impairment)

The EEOC's regulations under the ADA state: "'Has a record of such impairment' means has a record of, or has been misclassified as having, a mental or physical impairment that substantially limits one or more major life activities." [179]

Guidelines under the Rehabilitation Act give the following description of the phrase:

"Has a record of such impairment" means that an individual may be completely recovered from a previous physical or mental impairment. It is included because the attitude of employers, supervisors and coworkers toward the previous impairment may result in an individual experiencing diffi-

---

[175] See supra ¶ 2.02.

[176] H. Comm. on Educ. and Lab. Rep. at 52.

[177] EEOC Interpretive Guidelines, 56 Fed. Reg. 35,742 (July 26, 1991).

[178] Id.

[179] 24 CFR § 100.201(c).

culty in securing, retaining, or advancing in employment. The mentally restored, those who have experienced heart attacks or cancer often experience such difficulty. Also this part of the definition would include individuals who may have been erroneously classified and may experience discrimination based on this misclassification. This group may include persons such as those who have been misclassified as mentally retarded or mentally restored.[180]

In order for this section to apply, the record relied upon by an employer must indicate that the individual has had a substantially limiting impairment within the meaning of the ADA. The fact that an individual has a record of being a disabled veteran, or of disability retirement, or is classified as disabled for other purposes, does not guarantee that the record discloses a disability for purposes of this prong of the ADA's definition.[181]

The most significant case under the Rehabilitation Act relating to this prong of the disability definition is *School Board of Nassau County v. Arline*,[182] in which a person who had previously been hospitalized for tuberculosis was held to be disabled. This prong was also found applicable to former patients of a psychiatric hospital,[183] as well as individuals suffering from cardiovascular disease,[184] shoulder dislocations,[185] and hepatitis B.[186]

---

[180] 29 CFR pt. 60-741, App. A.

[181] EEOC Interpretive Guidelines, 56 Fed. Reg. 35,742 (July 26, 1991). See supra ¶ 2.02.

[182] School Bd. of Nassau County v. Arline, 480 US 273 (1987).

[183] Allen v. Heckler, 780 F2d 64, 66 (DC Cir. 1985) ("[a]lthough plaintiffs are no longer institutionalized, the [Rehabilitation] Act recognizes that discrimination also occurs against those who at one time had a disabling condition. The handicap that these people face is the continuing stigma of being a former psychiatric patient; this disability does not disappear on discharge from the hospital. . . ."); Sites v. McKenzie, 423 F. Supp. 1190 (ND W. Va. 1976), Doe v. Syracuse School Dist., 508 F. Supp. 333 (NDNY 1981); Pridemore v. Legal Aid Soc'y of Dayton, 625 F. Supp. 1171 (SD Ohio 1985).

[184] Bey v. Bolger, 540 F. Supp. 910 (ED Pa. 1982).

[185] Mahoney v. Ortiz, 645 F. Supp. 22 (SDNY 1986).

[186] Kohl by Kohl v. Woodhaven Learning Center, 672 F. Supp. 1221 (WD Mo. 1987).

The burden of proof of showing that an applicant or employee has a record of impairment should be on the plaintiff. Similarly, the applicant or employee should be required to produce evidence that the employer knew of the record.

[5] Regarded as Having Disability

The third prong of the definition of disability includes an individual who is regarded as having a covered disability even though such person would not otherwise fall within either the first or second parts of the test.[187]

Under the EEOC's regulations, this third prong covers three classes of individuals:

- Persons who have physical or mental impairments that do *not* limit a major life activity *but* who are nevertheless perceived by covered entities (employers, places of public accommodation) as having such limitations (for example, an employee with controlled high blood pressure that is not, in fact, substantially limiting, is reassigned to less strenuous work because of his employer's unsubstantiated fear that the individual will suffer a heart attack if he continues to perform strenuous work. Such a person would be "regarded" as disabled).[188]

- Persons who have physical or mental impairments that substantially limit a major life activity only because of a perception that the impairment causes such a limitation (for example, an employee has a condition that periodically causes an involuntary jerk of the head, but no limitations on his major life activities. If his employer discriminates against him because of the negative reaction of customers, the employer would be regarding him as disabled and acting on the basis of that perceived disability).[189]

---

[187] See supra ¶ 2.02.

[188] EEOC Interpretive Guidelines, 56 Fed. Reg. 35,742 (July 26, 1991).

[189] Id. S. Comm. on Lab. and Hum. Resources Rep. at 24; H. Comm. on Educ. and Lab. Rep. at 53; H. Comm. on Jud. Rep. at 30–31.

- Persons who do not have a physical or mental impairment but are treated as having a substantially limiting impairment (for example, a company discharges an employee based on a rumor that the employee is HIV-positive. Even though the rumor is totally false and the employee has no impairment, the company would nevertheless be in violation of the ADA).[190]

This part of the ADA's definition of "disability" is based on the Rehabilitation Act's protection provided persons "regarded as having an impairment." The Rehabilitation Act's regulations define this term to mean

> those individuals who are perceived as having a handicap, whether an impairment exists or not, but who, because of attitudes or for any other reason, are regarded as having a handicap by employers or supervisors who have an effect on the individual securing, retaining or advancing in employment.[191]

Similarly, the regulations under the Fair Housing Act state that the term includes someone who does not have a mental or physical disability "but is treated by another person as having such an impairment."[192]

As stated in the legislative history of the Rehabilitation Act

> This subsection includes within the protections of Sections 503 and 504 those persons who do not in fact have the condition which they are perceived as having, as well as those persons whose mental or physical condition does not substantially limit their activities and who are thus not technically within the [first or second prong of the definition of a "disability"]. Members of both these groups may

---

[190] 29 CFR § 1630.2(1). Interestingly, the Interpretive Guidelines use the term "perceived," while the final regulations use the term "treated." It appears, however, that no substantive difference is intended. S. Comm. on Lab. and Hum. Resources Rep. at 23; H. Comm. on Educ. and Lab. at 53; H. Comm. on Jud. Rep. at 29. See also EEOC Interpretive Guidelines, 56 Fed. Reg. 35,742 (July 26, 1991).

[191] 41 CFR pt. 60-741, App. A.

[192] 24 CFR § 100.201(d).

be subject to discrimination on the basis of their being regarded as handicapped.[193]

Similarly, Representative Steny Hoyer, chief House sponsor of the ADA, stated during the debate on the bill that the protections of this prong of the definition prohibit discrimination, whether or not the person's impairment actually limit a major life activity.[194]

The key factual determination to be made under this section is whether the employer treats the applicant or employee as disabled.[195] Among examples of individuals found protected under the Rehabilitation Act were an applicant for employment with diabetes,[196] an employee with an asymptomatic congenital back problem,[197] a man who refused employment because of epilepsy despite the fact that he had not had a seizure in eighteen years,[198] a police officer who had suffered multiple shoulder dislocations,[199] an individual with an abnormal electrocardiogram,[200] and a person who walked with a limp.[201] This prong of

---

[193] S. Rep. No. 1297, 93d Cong., 2d Sess., reprinted in 1974 US Code Cong. and Admin. News 6373, at 6389–6390.

[194] 136 Cong. Rec. E1914 (June 13, 1990) (Statement of Rep. Hoyer).

[195] 29 CFR § 1630.2(1); 56 Fed. Reg. 35,742 (July 26, 1991). See, e.g., Pridemore v. Legal Aid Soc'y of Dayton, 625 F. Supp. 1171 (SD Ohio 1985); Diaz v. US Postal Serv., 658 F. Supp. 484 (ED Cal. 1987). But see Alderson v. Postmaster Gen. of the US, 598 F. Supp. 49 (WD Okla. 1984), in which the U.S. District Court for the Western District of Oklahoma held that the termination of a probationary Postal Service employee for performing duties at a rate below that expected of him was not violative of the Rehabilitation Act, even though the employee was perceived to be handicapped by an injury sustained on the job. The court reasoned that no accommodation is required when there is only a "perceived handicap" rather than an actual disability.

[196] Brown v. County of Genesee, 37 Fair Empl. Prac. Cas. (BNA) 1595 (WD Mich. 1985).

[197] OFCPP v. EE Black, Ltd., 19 Fair Empl. Prac. Cas. (BNA) 1624 (DOL 1979), aff'd, 23 Fair Empl. Prac. Cas. (BNA) 1254 (D. Haw. 1980).

[198] Duran v. City of Tampa, 430 F. Supp. 75 (MD Fla. 1977).

[199] Mahoney v. Ortiz, 645 F. Supp. 22 (SDNY 1986).

[200] Bey v. Bolger, 540 F. Supp. 910 (ED Pa. 1982).

[201] 42 Fed. Reg. 22686 (May 4, 1977).

the disability definition of the Rehabilitation Act also covers individuals are HIV-positive[202] or who have hepatitis B.[203]

This protection is particularly important for individuals with stigmatic conditions that are viewed as physical impairments but do not in fact result in a substantial limitation of a major life activity. The ADA makes illegal discrimination premised upon such negative reactions or attitudes. For example, if a restaurant refuses to hire a severe burn victim based on a feared negative reaction of customers, the ADA would be violated.[204]

However, the mere fact that the general population perceives a condition as disabling is insufficient by itself to include an affected individual under this prong of the definition. There must be proof that the particular employer perceived the individual as disabled.

In including this provision in the ADA, Congress was clearly motivated by the U.S. Supreme Court's decision in *School Board of Nassau County v. Arline*,[205] in which the Court discussed the "regarded as having an impairment" language of the Rehabilitation Act. The Court noted that Congress had included this language in the Rehabilitation Act because it was expressly concerned with protecting individuals who do not have impairments that substantially limit their functioning.

According to the *Arline* Court, which is quoted favorably throughout the ADA's legislative history, "[s]uch an impairment might not diminish a person's physical or mental capabilities, but could nevertheless substantially limit the person's ability to work as a result of the negative reaction of others to the impairment."[206]

---

[202] Doe v. Centinela Hosp., 57 USLW 2034, No. CV87-2514 PAR (CD Cal. June 30, 1988); 56 Fed. Reg. 35,742 (July 26, 1991).

[203] Kohl by Kohl v. Woodhaven Learning Center, 672 F. Supp. 1221 (WD Mo. 1987).

[204] See Note, "Facial Discrimination, Extending Handicap Laws to Employment Discrimination Based on Physical Appearance," 100 Harv. L. Rev. 2035 (1987).

[205] School Bd. of Nassau County v. Arline, 480 US 273 (1987).

[206] Id. at 283; H. Comm. on Educ. and Lab. Rep. at 53.

In *Arline*, the Court gave examples of individuals who would fall within the third prong of the disability definition, including a cerebral palsied child and a woman crippled by arthritis. According to the Court, both these individuals would possess physical characteristics that an employer may perceive as limiting the individual's ability even though both such persons would be qualified to perform a particular job.

The original enactment of the Rehabilitation Act did not contain this protection. In discussing Congress's amendment of that legislation in 1974 to include such coverage, the *Arline* Court reasoned that Congress had "acknowledged that society's accumulated myths and fears about disability and diseases are as handicapping as are the physical limitations that flow from the actual impairment."[207] The purpose of the amendment was to "combat the effects of erroneous but nevertheless prevalent perceptions about the handicapped."[208]

Under the Rehabilitation Act, applicability of this aspect of the test more commonly arose when pre-employment medical examinations indicated a potential problem. For example, the Rehabilitation Act was applied to an employee whose back x-ray showed some abnormalities but who was asymptomatic and capable of performing the essential functions of the position in question.[209] The limitation on pre-employment medical examinations should reduce such litigation.[210]

Even if an individual has a disease—for example, cerebral palsy—he will not automatically be entitled to the protections of the ADA as long as (1) the disease has not resulted in a substantial limitation of a major life activity and (2) the employer can establish that it does not "regard" the person as disabled despite the condition.[211]

Some cases under the Rehabilitation Act suggest that the "regarded as" prong is applicable where an applicant or

---

[207] School Bd. of Nassau County v. Arline, supra note 205, 480 US at 284.

[208] Id. at 279.

[209] EE Black, Ltd. v. Marshall, 497 F. Supp. 1088 (D. Haw. 1980).

[210] See infra ¶ 2.13.

[211] See Pridemore v. Legal Aid Soc'y of Dayton, 625 F. Supp. 1171 (SD Ohio 1985).

employee disputes an employer's contention that he cannot meet a physical requirement of a position.[212] Theoretically, this third prong is broad enough to cover any physical limitation, even the need for glasses to correct moderate vision problems. For example, if a job description requires 20/100 uncorrected vision, a person requiring glasses could be said to be perceived as disabled by the employer.

Although most courts under the Rehabilitation Act rejected such a broad construction,[213] an argument can be made from the legislative history of the ADA that the new act expands the protection provided by this third prong of the disability definition. This view is supported by statements of the Senate Committee on Labor and Human Resources,[214] and the Committee on Education and Labor Report of the ADA.[215] Both groups cited *Thornhill v. Marsh*[216] and *Doe v. Centinela Hospital,*[217] a potentially significant factor, because neither decision suggests a need for the plaintiff to establish an impact on employability beyond the particular job in question.

On the whole, however, given the state of the law at the time of the passage of the ADA, if Congress had intended to reject the majority rule under the Rehabilitation Act, it would have done

---

[212] See Thornhill v. Marsh, 49 Fair Empl. Prac. Cas. (BNA) 6 (9th Cir. 1989).

[213] See, e.g., de la Torres v. Bolger, 781 F2d 1134 (5th Cir. 1986).

[214] S. Comm. on Lab. and Hum. Resources Rep. at 24. The report also cites as examples of covered individuals "people who are rejected for a particular job for which they apply because of findings of a back abnormality in an x-ray, notwithstanding the absence of symptoms, or people who are rejected for a particular job solely because they wear hearing aids." Id.

[215] H. Comm. on Educ. and Lab. Rep. at 53–54.

[216] Thornhill v. Marsh, 866 F2d 1182 (9th Cir. 1989). In *Thornhill,* the U.S. Court of Appeals for the Ninth Circuit held that an employee discharged on the basis of an erroneous interpretation of a congenital spine abnormality fell within the "regarded as" prong of the term "disability" under the Rehabilitation Act.

[217] Doe v. Centinela Hosp., 57 USLW 2034, No. CV87-2514 PAR (CD Cal. June 30, 1988). In *Centinela,* the district court ruled that an individual who had been excluded from a drug and alcohol rehabilitation program because of seropositivity to the AIDS virus fell within the third prong of the disability definition under the Rehabilitation Act.

so in clearer language. The EEOC appears to have adopted this approach by incorporating the *Black* test discussed previously into the "regarded as disabled" prong. In discussing the situation where an individual is excluded from a particular job because he was regarded as disabled, the EEOC's Interpretive Guidelines state "the determination of whether there is a substantial limitation in working is contingent upon the number and types of jobs from which the individual is excluded because of an impairment."[218]

A theoretical problem raised by application of the *Black* test to the "regarded as" prong is how one determines whether other employers will make the same assumptions as the employer charged with discrimination. The EEOC's proposed Interpretive Guidelines state the following on this issue:

> In determining whether or not an individual is regarded as substantially limited in the major life activity of working, it should be assumed that all similar employers would apply the same exclusionary qualification standard that the employer charged with discrimination used. The determination of whether there is a substantial limitation in working is contingent upon the number and types of jobs from which the individual is excluded because of an impairment. An assessment of the number and types of jobs from which an individual "regarded as" disabled in working would be excluded can only be achieved if the qualification standard of the employer charged with discrimination is attributable to all similar employers. Were it otherwise, an employer would be able to use a discriminatory qualification standard as long as the standard was not widely followed.[219]

> EXAMPLE: Suppose Employee Kahn has a heart murmur that has gone undetected and has not caused any limitations on the individual's activities. In the course of a routine medical examination given to all newly employed heavy machine operators, the murmur is discovered. Kahn's employer withdraws the offer of employment because it believes Kahn cannot operate a heavy machine safely. By

---

[218] EEOC Interpretive Guidelines, 56 Fed. Reg. 35,742 (July 26, 1991).
[219] Id.

assuming that all employers hiring heavy machine operators would use this same standard, Kahn would be excluded
from a broad range of jobs, and, therefore, there would be a
substantial limitation on his life activity of working.[220]

Under the EEOC's initial approach, the rule under the ADA
would have been that where a plaintiff's only claim is that he is
regarded as disabled because of his exclusion from a particular
job, the plaintiff would have had to establish the proof required
in *Black* and the EEOC regulations under the first prong of the
"disability" definitions.

Generally, in cases under the third prong, the burden of
proof should be on the applicant or employee to introduce evidence showing that he has been regarded as having an impairment and that this perception resulted in an adverse decision
being made by the employer. When such proof is shown, the
burden then would switch to the employer to establish that its
decision was not motivated in whole or in part by the alleged
perception.[221]

¶ 2.03 COVERED EMPLOYMENT ACTIONS

Section 102(a) of the ADA sets forth its general rule. That section provides: "No covered entity shall discriminate against a
qualified individual with a disability because of the disability of
such individual in regard to job application procedures, the
hiring, advancement, or discharge of employees, employee compensation, job training, and other terms, conditions, and privileges of employment."[222]

---

[220] Id.

[221] 56 Fed. Reg. 35,743 (July 26, 1991). See Bibbs v. Block, 778 F2d 1318
(8th Cir. 1985); but see Price Waterhouse v. Hopkins, 109 S. Ct. 1775 (1989),
in which plurality held that an employer may escape liability when adverse
action based on illegal motive provided that it can show that it would have
made the same decision even if it had not had improper motive. Section 5 of
the Civil Rights Act of 1990 would have rejected *Price Waterhouse*.

[222] This was essentially the same "general rule" contained in the original
bills introduced in the House (HR 2273) and in the Senate (S. 933).

The legislative history to the ADA indicates that the broadest possible construction is to be given to the type of employment decisions covered by Section 102(a). Relying on regulations issued under the Rehabilitation Act, the House Committee on Education and Labor Report states that the ADA applies to the following matters:[223]

- Recruitment, advertising, and processing of applications for employment
- Hiring, upgrading, promotion, award of tenure, demotion, transfer, layoff, termination, right of return from layoff, and rehiring
- Rates of pay or any other form of compensation and changes in compensation
- Job assignment, job classification, organizational structures, position descriptions, lines of progression, and seniority lists
- Leaves of absence, sick leave, or any other leave
- Fringe benefits available by virtue of employment, whether or not administered by the covered entity
- Selection and financial support for training, including apprenticeships, professional meetings, conferences, and other related activities, and selection for leaves of absence to pursue training
- Employer-sponsored activities, including social or recreational programs

A few examples illustrate the possible breadth of Section 102(a). In each instance, however, liability would depend upon all the facts and circumstances of the case.

In the first instance, a company function is held in a private home.

EXAMPLE: Widget Company has a Christmas party each year at its president's home, which is not disabled-accessible. Holding the party at this home would likely violate the ADA unless some accommodation could be made such that

---

[223] H. Comm. on Educ. and Lab. Rep. at 54–55.

the disabled workers could attend the party on an equal basis with other employees.

In the second situation, two types of discrimination could come into play.

EXAMPLE: Rubber Ball, Inc., has season tickets to its home town minor league baseball team. The team plays in a stadium that is not disabled-accessible. The tickets are available to the company's factory workers based upon seniority. In the past, the company had a policy of not hiring the disabled for factory positions based upon its own assumptions concerning employee safety. After the effective date of the ADA, however, the company hires a disabled person as a factory foreman. The company may be in violation of the ADA in two respects. First, the tickets may be deemed a "fringe benefit" not equally available to the new disabled employee because he cannot attend the game. Second, there is a question of whether the use of seniority to distribute the benefit has a disparate impact on newly hired disabled workers. [224]

In another example, an employment screening practice may put disabled candidates at a disadvantage.

EXAMPLE: Widget America recruits its employees primarily through one well-known employment agency. That agency's primary means of seeking candidates is by on-campus interviews. The agency does not interview at any colleges predominately for the disabled (e.g., a school for the deaf). Moreover, it only interviews candidates who have played varsity sports. Although these criteria do not exclude all disabled individuals, the practices may tend to screen out disabled individuals, and, therefore, the company may be held in violation of the ADA. [225]

A final situation deals with company programs held off-site.

_____

[224] See infra ¶ 2.05[4].
[225] See infra ¶ 2.10.

EXAMPLE: Westward, Inc., has a voluntary after-hours program whereby senior management holds seminars on various topics affecting Westward's industry. The seminars have traditionally been held in the back room of a local restaurant. If that restaurant is not disabled-accessible, Westward will be in violation of the ADA should it continue to hold its seminars at that location to the detriment of its disabled employees.

¶ 2.04 NO PREFERENCE FOR DISABLED IN HIRING

Under the ADA, an employer has no obligation to prefer applicants with a disability over other applicants. Rather, the employer's duty is to consider applicants and make employment decisions without regard to an individual's disability or the employer's obligation to reasonably accommodate the disabled.

The House Committee on Education and Labor noted that by including the phrase "qualified individual with a disability," it intended to

> reaffirm that this legislation does not undermine an employer's ability to choose and maintain qualified workers. The legislation simply provides that employment decisions must not have the purpose or effect of subjecting a qualified individual with a disability on the basis of his or her disability.

According to the Committee, the employer has no obligation under the ADA to prefer applicants with disabilities over other applicants on the basis of disability.

The committee provides the following illustrations:[226]

EXAMPLE: Suppose an employer has an opening for a typist, and two persons apply for the job. One applicant, who has a disability, can type fifty words per minute. The other applicant, who does not have a disability, can type seventy-five words per minute. The employer is permitted to choose the

---

[226] H. Comm. on Educ. and Lab. Rep. at 55.

applicant with the higher typing speed provided that typing speed is an essential function of the job.

EXAMPLE: Suppose in the previous example that the applicants could both type at the same speed but that one of them suffered from a hearing impairment that could be accommodated by the purchase of a telephone headset with an amplifier. In such a case, the employer could not reject the disabled applicant solely on the basis of the cost of purchasing the headset.

As said by Representative Owen during the House debate on the ADA

> The employer is free to select the most-qualified applicant, and is under no obligation to prefer applicants with disabilities over other applicants. But if two applicants are equally qualified, an employer is not permitted to select the nondisabled applicant solely due to the other applicant's disability, even if the disability means the employer would have to provide some kind of accommodation. [227]

Similarly, Representative Edwards, the Chairman of the Subcommittee on Civil and Constitutional Rights of the Committee on the Judiciary, stated: "Like other civil rights laws, the ADA does not require employers to hire unqualified persons, nor does it require employers to give preference to persons with disabilities. The ADA simply states that a person's disability should not be an adverse factor in the employment process." [228]

One example of the foregoing under the Rehabilitation Act is *Bruegging v. Burke*. [229] The employee in that case had cerebral palsy and was employed as a GS-9 legal publications specialist at the Office of the Federal Register. After being denied promotion to GS-11 on a number of occasions, the employee brought suit alleging handicap discrimination. Although the court found that the employee was qualified for the GS-11 position, it concluded

---

[227] 136 Cong. Rec. H2632 (May 22, 1990) (Comments by Rep. Owen).

[228] 136 Cong. Rec. H2638 (May 17, 1990) (Comments by Rep. Edwards).

[229] Bruegging v. Burke, 48 Fair Empl. Prac. Cas. (BNA) 140 (DDC 1987).

that he was not the most qualified candidate and that the government had no duty to lower its accuracy standards to accommodate the employee's disability.

As under the Rehabilitation Act, a disabled individual is still required under the ADA to meet his employer's standards of appropriate conduct.[230] Similarly, if a disabled individual fails to meet the employer's policies due to reasons unrelated to his impairment, no accommodation is required.[231]

¶ 2.05 SPECIFIC PROHIBITED ACTS OF DISCRIMINATION

[1] In General

Section 102(b) of the ADA lists the acts of "discrimination" made illegal by Section 102(a):

Prohibited are the limiting, segregating, or classifying of a job applicant or employee, in a way that adversely affects that applicant's or employee's opportunities or status because of that individual's disability. Also illegal is participating in a contractual or other arrangement or relationship that has the effect of subjecting a covered entity's qualified applicant or employee with a disability to the discrimination prohibited by the ADA. Such a relationship includes that with an employment or referral agency, labor union, an organization providing fringe benefits to an employee or the covered entity, or an organization providing training and apprenticeship programs.

Utilizing standards, criteria, methods of administration

---

[230] See, e.g., Dowden v. Tisch, 52 Fair Empl. Prac. Cas. (BNA) 93 (ED Tex. 1989), in which the U.S. District Court for the Eastern District of Texas held that a U.S. Postal Service mail carrier who suffers from diabetes and arthritis was not "otherwise qualified" for his job, where he refused to obey his supervisor's orders and, thus, was properly dismissed.

[231] See Thomas v. General Servs. Admin., 49 Fair Empl. Prac. Cas. (BNA) 1602 (DDC 1989), in which the U.S. District Court for the District of Columbia held that a paraplegic employee was not "otherwise qualified" because his poor performance and poor attitude disqualified him from the protections of the Rehabilitation Act.

that have the effect of discrimination on the basis of disability, or that perpetuate the discrimination of others who are subject to common administrative control is considered discrimination. Other acts of discrimination involve excluding or otherwise denying equal jobs or benefits to a qualified individual because that individual has an association or relationship with someone having a known disability.

Not making reasonable accommodations to the known physical or mental limitations of an otherwise qualified individual with a disability who is an applicant or employee is prohibited, unless the covered entity can demonstrate that the accommodation would impose an undue hardship on the operation of its business. Also discriminatory is denying employment opportunities to a job applicant or employee who is an otherwise qualified individual with a disability, if that denial is based on the need of such covered entity to make reasonable accommodation to the physical or mental impairments of the employee or applicant.

Qualification standards, employment tests, or other selection criteria that screen out or tend to screen out an individual with a disability or a class of individuals with a disability cannot be used unless the standard, test, or other selection criteria is shown to be job-related for the position in question and is consistent with business necessity. Failing to select and administer tests concerning employment in the most effective manner is prohibited. An employer must ensure that a test administered to a job applicant or employee who has a disability that impairs sensory, manual, or speaking skills must yield test results that accurately reflect the skills, aptitude, or other factor that the test purports to measure (rather than reflecting the impaired sensory, manual, or speaking skills of that individual, except where such skills are the factors the test purports to measure).

The scope of each of these prohibitions is discussed in the following sections.

[2] Disparate Treatment

Section 102(b)(1) outlaws intentional discrimination against the disabled. For example, it would be a violation of this section for an employer to exclude an employee with a severe facial disfigurement from staff meetings because the employer did not like to look at him.[232] It would also be illegal under this section to refuse to hire individuals with AIDS who were otherwise qualified.[233]

This section of the ADA is essentially the disparate treatment theory developed under Title VII of the Civil Rights Act of 1964, and the analysis developed by the U.S. Supreme Court under that statute is applicable.[234] Under this theory, an employment action may not be taken based on the individual's race, color, religion, sex, or national origin. Therefore, in actions under Section 102(b)(1), the plaintiff has the ultimate burden of proving by a fair preponderance of the evidence that the defendant discriminated against him on the basis of his disability. He may establish a prima facie case by proving that he applied for a position for which he was qualified and was rejected under circumstances indicating discrimination on the basis of an impermissible factor. The burden then shifts to the defendant to rebut the presumption of discrimination by coming forward with evidence that the plaintiff was rejected for a legitimate reason, whereupon the plaintiff must prove that the reason was not true but a pretext for impermissible discrimination.

The key to a successful defense against a disparate impact claim is that the disabled individual was treated differently not because of his disability but for some other legitimate nondiscriminatory reason. In its final Interpretive Guidelines, the EEOC made clear that the fact that an individual's disability is not covered by insurance or would cause the employer's insurance premiums or workers' compensation costs to rise is not a

---

[232] EEOC Interpretive Guidelines, 56 Fed. Reg. 35,742, 35,751 (July 26, 1991).

[233] Id.

[234] EEOC Regs. at 29 CFR § 1630.15. See also EEOC Interpretive Guidelines, 56 Fed. Reg. 35,751 (July 26, 1991), stating that the U.S. Supreme Court's disparate treatment analysis developed in McDonnell Douglas Corp.v. Green, 411 US 792 (1973), and Texas Dep't of Community Affairs v. Burdine, 450 US 248 (1981), applies to the ADA.

legitimate nondiscriminatory reason.[235]

In enacting the ADA, Congress did not address directly the issue of "dual motives," where the disability of the applicant or employee is only part of the motivation for the employer's adverse decision. However, the Civil Rights Act of 1990, vetoed by President George Bush, would have answered this question, providing that if the complaining party demonstrated that race, color, religion, sex, or national origin was a contributing factor for any employment practice, even though other factors also contributed to the practice, an unlawful employment practice would be shown.[236] This provision was intended to reverse the U.S. Supreme Court's decision in *Price Waterhouse v. Hopkins*.[237] It remains to be seen whether the civil rights bill introduced in 1991 will ultimately resolve this issue.

Besides discrimination based upon a malevolent motive, Section 102(b)(1) will also be violated when the employer acts solely on the basis of unsupported presumptions, even if the belief is held in good faith. A common law theme throughout the ADA is that an employer must make employment decisions based on facts applicable to individual applicants or employees and not on the basis of presumptions as to the limitations of individuals with disabilities.

As stated in the House Committee on Education and Labor Report:

> The Act is premised on the obligation of employers to consider people with disabilities as individuals and to avoid prejudging what an applicant or employee can or cannot do on the basis of that individual's appearance or any other

---

[235] 56 Fed. Reg. 35,751 (July 26, 1991).

[236] Civil Rights Act of 1990 § 5(a).

[237] Price Waterhouse v. Hopkins, 49 Fair Empl. Prac. Cas. (BNA) 954 (1989). In *Price Waterhouse*, which lacked a majority opinion, the Court held that when there was sufficient direct evidence of discrimination, the burden of persuasion would shift to the defendant to prove that its decision was not affected by an improper motive. Under *Price Waterhouse*, an employer can escape liability by demonstrating that it would have made the same decision even without the improper motive. This decision was contrary to most lower court precedent. See, e.g., Bibbs v. Block, 778 F2d 1318 (8th Cir. 1985).

easily identifiable characteristic, or on a preconceived and often erroneous judgment about an individual's capabilities based on "labeling" of that person as having a particular kind of disability.[238]

Thus, for example, it would be a violation of Section 102(b)(1) for an employer to limit the duties of an individual with a disability based on[239]

- A presumption of what was in the best interest of that individual
- A presumption of the ability of the individual to perform a particular task
- A presumption that persons with disabilities would not be interested in moving into a particular type of job

Where employers were found to have acted on the basis of such presumptions, the courts under the Rehabilitation Act were particularly likely to have found in favor of a disabled applicant or employee.[240]

Section 102(b)(1) also prohibits actions or circumstances that tend to segregate the disabled from other workers. Under the ADA, all employment activities must take place in an integrated manner.[241] This prohibition applies to both work and nonwork areas offered by the employer, including break rooms or lunch rooms.

Congress did appear to recognize, however, that in some circumstances, separate accommodations may be appropriate. For example, the House Committee on Education and Labor Report indicates that if a break room is located on the second

---

[238] H. Comm. on Educ. and Lab. Rep. at 58.

[239] EEOC Interpretive Guidelines, 56 Fed. Reg. 35,746 (July 26, 1991).

[240] For example, in Pushkin v. Regents of Univ. of Colo., 658 F2d 1372 (10th Cir. 1981), the U.S. Court of Appeals for the Tenth Circuit held that a medical residency program applicant suffering from multiple sclerosis was qualified for the program apart from his handicap and that the reasons articulated by the program's examining committee for rejecting the applicant were based on incorrect assumptions or inadequate factual grounds.

[241] EEOC Interpretive Guidelines, 56 Fed. Reg. 35,746 (July 26, 1991).

floor of an existing building that is inaccessible, the ADA will not be violated so long as comparable amenities (e.g., a coffee pot, table, chairs for co-workers, or refrigerator) are available to a worker who uses a wheelchair on the first floor. According to the report, the actual size of the alternative break room does not have to be comparable so long as the employee who uses a wheelchair has equivalent opportunities to other workers, including the opportunity to take a break and eat lunch with a co-worker.[242] The EEOC apparently recognized this distinction when it changed the proposed regulations' requirement that reasonable accommodations be made to ensure that disabled individuals enjoy the "same" benefits to a requirement that the accommodation provided ensure "equal" benefits.[243]

[3] Contractual and Other Arrangements or Relationships

Section 102(b)(2) of the ADA specifies that discrimination includes participating in a contractual or other arrangement or relationship that results in discrimination against the disabled. This provision is derived from the Rehabilitation Act.[244] It does not, however, affect the determination of whether one is a "covered entity" or "employer" within the meaning of the ADA.[245]

The ADA lists the following examples of situations that entail this type of relationship:

- Use of an employment or referral agency
- Membership in a labor union
- Existence of an organization providing fringe benefits to an employee of a covered entity
- Use of an organization providing training and apprenticeship programs

The intent of Congress, according to the legislative history, is for this section to apply to a situation where a covered entity

---

[242] H. Comm. on Educ. and Lab. Rep. at 58.

[243] 56 Fed. Reg. 35,729 (July 26, 1991).

[244] See 45 CFR Subtitle A, § 84.11.

[245] 56 Fed. Reg. 35,731, 35,746 (July 26, 1991).

enters into a contractual relationship with another entity and, because of that relationship, the covered entity's own employees or applicants are subject to discrimination. The basic premise of the section is that an entity may not do through a contractual relationship that which it may not do directly. In other words, the ADA is to be applied to the employer "as if" it were doing directly that which was being done by the party with whom it has the contractual relationship.[246] It is not intended to add any additional obligations on employers.[247]

Under the EEOC's regulations, Section 102(b)(2) applies "whether the [covered] entity offered the contract or initiated the relationship, or whether the entity accepted the contract or acceded to the relationship."[248] According to the EEOC's Interpretive Guidelines, the section is violated even if the employer did not intend for the contract to have a discriminatory effect.[249]

Congress cited specific situations that would violate this provision:

- If the training company contracted by the employer intended to hold its instructions in a physically inaccessible location, the employer would have a duty to consider methods of reasonable accommodation for its employees who use wheelchairs.[250]
- If an employer contracted with a hotel for a conference for the employer's employees (or for its customers, but employees were required to attend), the employer has an affirmative obligation to ensure that the hotel is accessible by its employees.[251]
- If a disabled person wanted to apply for a position in a store in an inaccessible mall, the store would have an affirmative obligation to deliver to the disabled individual an application for employment or to interview the

[246] H. Comm. on Educ. and Lab. Rep. at 60.

[247] 56 Fed. Reg. 35,731 (July 26, 1991).

[248] EEOC Regs. at 29 CFR § 1630.6.

[249] EEOC Interpretive Guidelines, 56 Fed. Reg. 35,746 (July 26, 1991).

[250] H. Comm. on Educ. and Lab. Rep. at 60; see also EEOC Interpretive Guidelines, 56 Fed. Reg. 35,746 (July 26, 1991).

[251] H. Comm. on Educ. and Lab. Rep. at 60.

person at an accessible location. If the applicant is otherwise qualified, the store would then be required to determine whether a reasonable accommodation could be made, without undue hardship, such that the person could get to the worksite.[252]

Other situations, not explored by Congress, may raise more difficult questions but appear nevertheless to violate the ADA:

- If a property manager retained a subcontractor to provide services at an inaccessible building, where the property manager did not want disabled employees working at the site because of unsubstantiated safety concerns, the subcontractor's disabled employees might have a cause of action against their employer as well as the property manager.
- If an employer hired most of its temporary employees from a particular employment agency, which was located in a building that is not disabled-accessible, the employer might have to ensure that the agency is attempting to reasonably accommodate disabled applicants.

The EEOC's proposed Interpretive Guidelines had an example indicating that if a copier company provided its customers service contracts for its machines, it would have a duty to ensure the availability of any reasonable accommodation necessary to enable its employees with disabilities to service the machines of the company's customers.[253]

Many employers filed comments with the EEOC arguing that this example could be interpreted as meaning that employers are required to make their customers' premises accessible. As a result, the final guidelines significantly narrow the employer's obligation. The final guidelines state:

For example, a copier company whose service representative is a dwarf could be required to provide a stepstool as a reasonable accommodation to enable him to perform the necessary repairs. However, the employer would not be

---

[252] Id. at 61.

[253] EEOC Interpretive Guidelines, 56 Fed. Reg. 8598 (Feb. 28, 1991).

required, as a reasonable accommodation, to make structural changes to its customer's inaccessible premises.[254]

Some members of Congress were concerned that Section 102(b)(2) could be construed to subject an employer to liability merely on the basis of contractual relationships with another entity even though there was no impact on the employer's own employees or applicants. For example, what if the property manager in the aforementioned scenario would not hire disabled individuals itself, but place no restrictions on its subcontractors? In addressing this issue, the House Committee on Education and Labor Report states that Section 102(b)(2) would not apply to such a situation, where the covered entity contracts with another entity, which discriminates against its own employees or applicants.[255] The covered entity would have no liability for the discrimination of the second entity.[256]

[4] Disparate Impact

Section 102(b)(3) incorporates a disparate impact standard into the ADA.[257] This standard involves making decisions that, although neutral on their face, have the practical result of discriminating on the basis of race or other covered classifications.

[a] Legislative History

The House Committee on Education and Labor stated that the availability of the disparate impact theory in cases under the ADA was necessary in order "to ensure that the legislative man-

---

[254] 56 Fed. Reg. 35,746–35,747 (July 26, 1991).

[255] H. Comm. on Educ. and Lab. Rep. at 59.

[256] Id.

[257] Section 102(b)(3) is closely related to Section 102(b)(6). The discussion in this chapter relating to disparate impact under Section 102(b)(3) is equally applicable to Section 102(b)(6). To some degree, Sections 102(b)(3) and 102(b)(6) appear to be redundant. One possible way to distinguish the two provisions would be to apply Section 102(b)(3) to practices and policies and Section 102(b)(6) to selection criteria.

date to end discrimination does not ring hollow."[258]

In drafting the ADA, Congress stated that Section 102(b)(3) is derived "from general forms of discrimination that were set out in regulations implementing section 504 of the Rehabilitation Act of 1973 (see 45 CFR Part 84)."[259] Appendix A to those regulations states as follows regarding the appropriate disparate impact analysis:

> [Section 504] prohibits employers from using tests or other selection criteria that screen out or tend to screen out handicapped persons unless the test or criterion is shown to be job related and alternative tests or criteria that do not screen out or tend to screen out as many handicapped persons are not shown . . . to be available. This paragraph is an application of the principles established under Title VII of the Civil Rights Act of 1964 in *Griggs v. Duke Power Company.*[260]

Section 102(b)(3) essentially means that individuals protected by the ADA may make out a prima facie case by providing evidence showing that an employment procedure involved in actions such as hiring or promotion tends to screen out the disabled unless the employer shows that the practice is job-related and justified by business necessity. Under Section 103(a) of the ADA, an employer is not liable if the challenged criteria are job-related and required by business necessity.[261] The EEOC's Interpretive Guidelines give the following example:

> [A]n employer interviews two candidates for a position, one of whom is blind. The employer decides that while it is not essential to the job it would be convenient to have an employee who has a driver's license and so could occasionally run errands by car. The employee hires the individual who is sighted because the individual has a driver's license. This is an example of a uniformly applied criterion, having

---

[258] H. Comm. on Educ. and Lab. Rep. at 61.

[259] Id.

[260] Griggs v. Duke Power Co., 401 US 424 (1971).

[261] EEOC Regs. at 29 CFR § 1630.163015(b); EEOC Interpretive Guidelines, 56 Fed. Reg. 35,751–35,752 (July 26, 1991).

a driver's permit, that screens out an individual who has a disability that makes it impossible to obtain a driver's permit. The employer would, thus, have to show that this criterion is job-related and consistent with business necessity.[262]

The EEOC's regulations provide that it is unlawful for a covered entity to use standards, criteria, or methods of administration that are not job-related and consistent with business necessity. These standards, criteria, or methods may not have the effect of discriminating on the basis of disability or perpetuate the discrimination of others who are subject to common administrative control.

The regulations indicate that employees or applicants suing on a disparate impact theory under the ADA do not have to produce the statistical proof required in cases under Title VII. This is the approach adopted by the EEOC in its Interpretive Guidelines on the ADA.[263]

Second, the reference to *Griggs v. Duke Power Co.* suggests that courts facing the issues of disparate impact and business necessity under the ADA should follow that opinion rather than the U.S. Supreme Court's more recent decision in *Wards Cove v. Atonio,*[264] a case that significantly undercut the holding in *Griggs.*[265]

Congress was aware of the *Wards Cove* decision at the time of enacting the ADA and was equally aware that the regulations under the Rehabilitation Act had adopted the *Griggs* approach. Therefore, regardless of the continued validity of *Griggs* in the Title VII context, it appears that Congress intends the courts and

---

[262] EEOC Interpretive Guidelines, 56 Fed. Reg. 35,751–35,752 (July 26, 1991).

[263] EEOC Interpretive Guidelines, 56 Fed. Reg. 35,749 (July 26, 1991).

[264] Wards Cove v. Atonio, 490 US 642 (1989).

[265] Id. at 657–658. For example, in *Wards Cove,* the Court held that an employer prevails once it demonstrates that a practice having a disparate impact is justified by business necessity, even if the employee or applicant shows that their employer could have utilized practices with a less disparate impact. The *Wards Cove* decision also lessened the standard for what justifications constitute a "business necessity." Id. at 660–661.

the enforcement agencies to follow *Griggs* (and not *Wards Cove*) in addressing the issue of disparate impact and business necessity under the ADA.

Even without the Rehabilitation Act regulations' reference to *Griggs*, Congress, in drafting the ADA, suggested that the *Wards Cove* standard should not be applied under the new act.

[b] EEOC Interpretation

The EEOC has adopted the approach of Congress in its Interpretive Guidelines:

> [E]ven if [a] criterion is job-related and consistent with business necessity, an employer could not exclude an individual with a disability if there is a less discriminatory criterion that meets the legitimate needs of the business, or if the criterion could be met or job performance accomplished with a reasonable accommodation. [266]

The EEOC Interpretive Guidelines use as an example the possibility of an employer that required as part of its application process an interview that was job-related and consistent with business necessity. According to the EEOC, the employer would not be able to refuse to hire a hearing-impaired applicant because he could not be interviewed, because an interpreter could be provided as a reasonable accommodation that would allow the individual to be interviewed.

One area in which the disparate impact analysis may be particularly important is with job qualifications, an area also addressed in Section 102(b)(6). It may occur that employers will define a job in such a way that it has two components, one of which the disabled individual can perform and the other which he cannot. Assuming that both components constitute "essential functions" of the job as defined, the question becomes whether the combining of the tasks is justified. Analysis developed under the Rehabilitation Act indicates that an employee could challenge the employer's criteria under such circumstances.

For example, the Department of Labor regulations under

---

[266] EEOC Interpretive Guidelines, 56 Fed. Reg. 35,752 (July 26, 1991).

Section 504 of the Rehabilitation Act state that the covered entity

> (a) shall provide for, and shall adhere to, a schedule for the review of the appropriateness of all job qualifications to ensure that to the extent job qualifications tend to exclude handicapped individuals because of their handicap, they are related to the performance of the job and are consistent with business necessity and safe performance.

> (b) Whenever [a covered entity] applies job qualifications in the selection of applicants, employees or participants for employment or training or other change in employment status such as promotion, demotion or training, which would tend to exclude handicapped individuals because of their handicap, the qualifications shall be related to the specific job or jobs for which the individual is being considered and shall be consistent with business necessity and safe performance. The burden will be on [the covered entity] to demonstrate that it has complied with the requirement of this paragraph. [267]

The EEOC has rejected this approach. Rather, according to the EEOC's Interpretive Guidelines, "[a]n employer or other covered entity is not required to reallocate essential functions." [268] The EEOC's rationale is that "[t]he essential functions are by definition those that the individual who holds the job would have to perform, with or without reasonable accommodation, in order to be considered qualified for the position." [269]

The EEOC's Interpretive Guidelines also state that not all uniformly applied policies or practices are subject to challenge under the disparate impact analysis. It provides the example of a no-leave policy (e.g., no leave during the first six months of employment). According to the EEOC, such practices are to be

---

[267] 29 CFR § 32.14.

[268] 56 Fed. Reg. 35,744 (July 26, 1991).

[269] Id. Since the EEOC rejected similar logic when it concluded that an employer may be required to reassign employees as a reasonable accommodation even though they could not perform the essential functions of the job, greater justification should have been expressed in rejecting the rule established under the Rehabilitation Act.

contested, if at all, on the basis of whether a modification of the policy would be a reasonable accommodation.[270] The guidelines provide no insight into which practices are precluded from disparate impact analysis.

[c] U.S. Supreme Court Ruling in *Choate*

Employers wishing to limit the use of the disparate impact theory under the ADA may find support in the legislative history's statement that Section 102(b)(3) is consistent with the principles announced in *Alexander v. Choate.*[271] Although the U.S. Supreme Court in *Choate* indicated that the disparate impact theory may be applicable to the Rehabilitation Act, the overall tenor of the decision is not as broad as that indicated by the language of Section 102(b)(3).

Challenged in *Choate* was a state's proposal to impose a limitation on the number of annual in-patient hospital days for which state Medicaid would reimburse hospitals on behalf of Medicaid recipients. A class of disabled Medicaid recipients argued against the fourteen-day limitation, asserting that the proposal's implementation would have a disproportionate impact on the disabled in violation of Section 504 of the Rehabilitation Act who often require more in-patient care.

In resolving this issue, the Court first held that it is not always necessary to find a discriminatory intent in order for there to be a violation of the Rehabilitation Act. The Court reasoned that much

> of the conduct that Congress sought to alter in passing the Rehabilitation Act would be difficult if not impossible to reach were the Act construed to proscribe only conduct fueled by a discriminatory intent. For example, elimination of architectural barriers was one of the central aims of the act, [cite omitted], yet such barriers were clearly not erected with the aim or intent of excluding the handicapped. . . . [272]

---

[270] EEOC Interpretive Guidelines, 56 Fed. Reg. 35,752 (July 26, 1991).

[271] Alexander v. Choate, 469 US 287 (1985).

[272] Id. at 297.

The Court said that statements in the legislative history to Section 504 indicating Congress's intent to eliminate barriers to the disabled would ring hollow if the resulting legislation could not rectify the harms resulting from action that discriminated by effect as well as design.

However, the U.S. Supreme Court did not hold in *Choate* that the disparate impact analysis was generally available under the Rehabilitation Act. The Court actually stated that it believed there was reason to question whether Congress intended Section 504 to embrace claims of disparate impact discrimination.[273] In fact, the *Choate* Court held that it was rejecting "the boundless notion that all disparate-impact showings constitute prima facie cases under Section 504" and stated that it was merely assuming "without deciding that Section 504 reaches at least some conduct that has an unjustifiable disparate impact upon the handicapped."[274]

While some federal agencies have construed *Choate* as merely an elaboration of the undue hardship standard,[275] the overall language of the opinion suggests that the U.S. Supreme Court viewed the disparate impact analysis as appropriate in only the exceptional case. In fact, the case could be construed to hold that an employer or program generally has no duty to accommodate a disabled individual as long as it is not motivated by an improper animus against the disabled and provided that the disabled are not wholly excluded from job opportunities.[276] Thus, employers wishing to limit Section 102(b)(3) scope (as well as that of Section 102(b)(6)) could contend that the reference to *Choate* by Congress in the ADA's legislative history suggests a narrower applicability of the disparate impact theory than might be otherwise indicated from the literal language of the statute.

---

[273] Id. at 295.

[274] Id. at 299.

[275] See Final Rulemaking of Department of Transportation at 51 Fed. Reg. 18,996 (1986).

[276] See American Disabled for Accessible Public Transp. v. Skinner, 881 F2d 1184 (3d Cir. 1989).

[5] Relationship to Disabled Covered

Section 102(b)(4) significantly expands the Rehabilitation Act by providing that discrimination includes excluding or otherwise denying jobs or benefits to a qualified individual because of a known disability of an individual with whom the qualified individual is known to have a relationship or association. [277] Harassment or other discrimination against such an individual is equally prohibited. [278]

The protection provided by Section 102(b)(4) is to be broadly construed and is not limited to family relationships. It includes family, friends, and persons who provide care for persons with disabilities. The House Committee on the Judiciary and the House Committee on Education and Labor both rejected amendments that would have limited protection to relatives by blood, marriage, adoption, or guardianship. [279] An attempt to obtain a floor vote on such an amendment was not allowed by the House Rules Committee. [280]

The following examples illustrate possible violations of Section 102(b)(4):

- An applicant applies for a job and discloses to the employer that his spouse has cancer. The applicant is qualified for the job but the employer fears that the applicant will be frequently required to miss work or to leave work early in order to care for his spouse. Based on this assumption, the employer decides not to hire the applicant. [281]
- A qualified applicant applies for a job and discloses that a close friend has AIDS. Based on an irrational fear that the

---

[277] H. Comm. on Jud. Rep. at 38. See also EEOC Regs. at 29 CFR § 1630.8. Although the Rehabilitation Act did not contain such protection, the Fair Housing Amendments Act of 1988 contained a provision prohibiting discrimination against a buyer or renter because he "associated with" a handicapped person. 42 USC §§ 3604(f)(1)(C), 3604(f)(2)(C).

[278] 56 Fed. Reg. 35,731, 35,747 (July 26, 1991).

[279] H. Comm. on Jud. Rep. at 38.

[280] Cong. Rec. H2629 (May 22, 1990) (Comments of Cong. DeLay).

[281] EEOC Interpretive Guidelines, 56 Fed. Reg. 35,747 (July 26, 1991).

applicant may expose his work force to the HIV virus, the employer rejects the applicant.

- A qualified applicant is offered a job subject to a post-offer psychological examination. During that examination, it is revealed that one or more of the applicant's family members are alcoholics or drug users. The employer would violate the ADA should it rescind the offer on this basis.

To illustrate that this section applies to all benefits and privileges of employment, the final Interpretive Guidelines added the following example to the proposed guidelines:

For example, an employer that provides health insurance benefits to its employees for their dependents may not reduce the level of those benefits to an employee simply because that employee has a dependent with a disability. This is true even if the provision of such benefits would result in increased health insurance costs for the employer. [282]

The burden of proof is on the individual claiming discrimination to prove that the employer's adverse action was motivated by the individual's relationship with a person with a disability. [283] An employer will not be liable under this section if it establishes that it did not know of the relationship or association. [284]

The protection provided by Section 102(b)(4) is not as broad as that provided to the disabled themselves. In particular, there is no obligation on an employer to reasonably accommodate the person who is in a relationship with a disabled individual. The EEOC's Interpretive Guidelines state that "an employee would not be entitled to a modified work schedule as an accommodation to enable the employee to care for a spouse with a disability." [285]

---

[282] 56 Fed. Reg. 35,747 (July 26, 1991).

[283] H. Comm. on Jud. Rep. at 38.

[284] Id. at 39.

[285] EEOC Interpretive Guidelines, 56 Fed. Reg. 35,747 (July 26, 1991).

¶ 2.06　OTHERWISE QUALIFIED INDIVIDUAL

Section 102(b)(5)(a) of the ADA requires that reasonable accommodation be made for "an otherwise qualified individual who is an applicant or employee. . . ." The section applies to all employment decisions, not just hiring and promotion.

[1]　Definition

Following the regulations developed under the Rehabilitation Act, qualified individual is defined in Section 101(8) to mean "an individual with a disability who, with or without reasonable accommodation, can perform the essential functions of the employment position that such individual holds or desires."[286]

The EEOC's regulations state that qualified individual with a disability means "an individual with a disability who satisfies the requisite skill, experience and education and other job related requirements of the employment position such individual holds or desires, and who, with or without reasonable accommodation, can perform the essential functions of the job."[287]

In the EEOC's final Interpretive Guidelines, the EEOC added language to the proposed guidelines clarifying that the determination of whether a person is qualified must be made at the time the employment action is taken and cannot be based on speculation that the individual will become unable to perform the job in the future or may cause increased health insurance or workers' compensation costs.[288]

The first step in the analysis under Section 102(b)(5)(A) is to determine if an applicant or employee is a qualified individual with the requisite skill, experience, and education.[289] The

---

[286] As noted in Brennan v. Stewart, 834 F2d 1248, 1262 (5th Cir. 1988), the question of "reasonable accommodation" becomes part of the otherwise qualified analysis.

[287] EEOC Regs. 29 CFR § 1630.2(m). The final regulations added the words "and other job related" requirements, terminology not contained in the proposed regualtions. 56 Fed. Reg. 35,728 (July 26, 1991).

[288] 56 Fed. Reg. 35,728, 35,743 (July 26, 1991).

[289] EEOC Interpretive Guidelines, 56 Fed. Reg. 35,743 (July 26, 1991).

EEOC's Interpretive Guidelines give the example of determining whether an accountant is qualified for a certified public accountant (CPA) position. The first step is to examine the individual's credentials to determine whether the individual is a licensed CPA.[290] The second step is to determine whether or not the individual can perform the essential functions of the position desired, with or without reasonable accommodation.[291]

[2] Essential Functions

The term "essential functions" is used to ensure that persons with disabilities are not disqualified because they cannot perform duties incidental to the job. The concept was derived from cases under the Rehabilitation Act.[292] The legislative history cites with approval regulations of the Department of Health, Education, and Welfare under the Rehabilitation Act stating that the disabled "should not be disqualified simply because they may have difficulty in performing tasks that bear only a marginal relationship to a particular job."[293]

Under the EEOC's proposed regulations, essential functions was defined to mean the primary job duties that are intrinsic to the employment position the individual holds or desires.[294] Because of employer comments, the final regulations state instead that "[t]he term essential functions means the fundamental job duties of the employment position the individual holds or desires."[295]

The term does not include the marginal or peripheral functions of the position that are incidental to the performance of the

---

[290] Id.

[291] Id.

[292] See School Bd. of Nassau County v. Arline, 480 US 273 (1987); Jasany v. US Postal Serv., 755 F2d 1244, 1251 (6th Cir. 1985); Simon v. St. Louis County, 656 F2d 316 (8th Cir. 1981).

[293] S. Comm. on Lab. and Hum. Resources Rep. at 26; H. Comm. on Educ. and Lab. Rep. at 54, citing 42 Fed. Reg. 22686 (1977).

[294] EEOC Prop. Regs. at 29 CFR § 1630.2(n); 56 Fed. Reg. 35,743 (Feb. 28, 1991).

[295] 56 Fed. Reg. 35,729 (July 26, 1991); 29 CFR § 1630.2(n)(1).

primary job functions.[296] Typically, the determination of the "essential functions" of a position will be a question of fact.[297]

For example, employers often require applicants to have valid drivers licenses for nondriving jobs because of the convenience of having an employee who drives to do an occasional errand or because of concern that employees who rely on public transportation are likely to be late for work or unable to work overtime. However, under the essential function aspect of determining who is a qualified individual, these concerns would not be valid reasons for excluding a person with a disability who could not drive.[298]

Another step in the analysis of essential functions is determining whether the employer actually requires the person holding the position at issue actually to perform the purported essential function. For example, an employer may state that typing is an essential function of a job. If, in fact, the employer has never required any particular employee in that position to type, this would be evidence that typing is not an essential function of the position.[299]

The next step of the analysis is to determine, if the employee is required to perform the particular function, would the removal of that function fundamentally alter the position.[300]

[a] What Makes a Job Function Essential

The EEOC's regulations set forth three key factors that, among others, must be considered in determining whether a job function is essential:

- The reason the position exists is to perform that function.[301] For example, if an individual is hired to proofread

---

[296] Id.

[297] See, e.g., Hall v. US Postal Serv., 857 F2d 1073 (6th Cir. 1988).

[298] H. Comm. on Educ. and Lab. Rep. at 55.

[299] EEOC Interpretive Guidelines, 56 Fed. Reg. 8595 (Feb. 28, 1991).

[300] Id.

[301] EEOC Regs. at 29 CFR § 1630.2(n)(2)(i).

documents, therefore, the ability to read documents would then be an essential function. [302]

- The limited number of employees available among whom the performance of that job function can be distributed. [303] This may be a factor either because the total number of available employees is low or because of the fluctuating demands of business operations. [304] In that type of situation, each employee must perform a multitude of different functions; therefore, the performance of those functions by each employee becomes more critical and the options for reorganization more limited. [305] Or, in a larger work force, the workflow may shift between heavy demand and low-demand periods, creating a situation where performance of each function during the peak periods becomes critical. [306] In evaluating this factor, employers need to consider only "available employees" and not all employees regardless of their current job or level. [307]

- The task function is highly specialized, so that the incumbent in the position is hired for his expertise or ability to perform the particular function. [308]

[b] Evidence That Shows a Job Function Is Essential

The proposed regulations list four categories of evidence that may indicate whether a particular function is essential. In a change from the proposed regulations to the final EEOC rules, the EEOC clarified that all the following evidence is relevant and must be considered when available. [309]

---

[302] EEOC Interpretive Guidelines, at 56 Fed. Reg. 35,743 (July 26, 1991).

[303] EEOC Regs. at 29 CFR § 1630.2(n)(2)(ii).

[304] 56 Fed. Reg. 35,743 (July 26, 1991).

[305] EEOC Interpretive Guidelines, 56 Fed. Reg. 35,743 (July 26, 1991). See Treadwell v. Alexander, 707 F2d 473 (11th Cir. 1983).

[306] EEOC Interpretive Guidelines, 56 Fed. Reg. 35,743 (July 26, 1991). See Drexler v. Tisch, 660 F. Supp. 1418 (D. Conn. 1987).

[307] 56 Fed. Reg. 35,729 (July 26, 1991).

[308] EEOC Regs. at 29 CFR § 1630.2(n)(2)(iii).

[309] 56 Fed. Reg. 35,729 (July 26, 1991).

[i] Employer's judgment and job descriptions. The first two evidentiary statements relating to determining a position's essential functions are:[310]

- The employer's judgment as to which functions are essential
- Written job descriptions prepared before advertising or interviewing applicants for jobs

Although the original bills in the House and Senate did not have the evidentiary provisions now contained in Section 101(8), even before the amendments, Congress intended the courts to give some consideration to the employer's judgment as to what functions of a job are essential.[311]

However, no more weight should be given to the employer's judgment and written job descriptions than any other factor. Such evidence *does not* create an evidentiary presumption in favor of the employer (in fact, an amendment to create such a presumption was defeated in the House Judiciary Committee).[312] The EEOC expressly rejected the creation of a rebuttable presumption in considering comments to its proposed regulations.[313]

The legislative history to the Judiciary Committee amendments indicates that the committee was concerned that as originally drafted, Section 101(8) could be read to mean that the employee alone could define the essential functions and that the employer's judgment could be disregarded. Therefore, the amendment was added to clarify that the employer's judgment should be considered with all other evidence.[314] Similarly, the history to the floor amendment indicates that it should be read as being neutral as to the weight to be given to the employer's judgment as to which functions are essential.[315]

---

[310] EEOC Prop. Regs. at 29 CFR §§1630.2(n)(3)(i), 1630.2(n)(3)(ii).

[311] H. Comm. on Educ. and Lab. Rep. at 64.

[312] H. Comm. on Jud. Rep. at 33. See also Cong. Rec. H2623 (May 22, 1990); 56 Fed. Reg. 35,729 (July 26, 1991).

[313] 56 Fed. Reg. 35,729 (July 26, 1991).

[314] 136 Cong. Rec. H2623 (May 22, 1990).

[315] Id. (Comments of Rep. Fish); see also 136 Cong. Rec. E1914 (June 13,

Job descriptions were also relevant under the Rehabilitation Act. In *Guinn v. Bolger*,[316] the U.S. District Court for the District of Columbia held that an employer is responsible for the content of its standard position description and that an employee is entitled to rely on such description as a statement of the essential functions of her job when bringing a claim under the Rehabilitation Act. The court in *Guinn* rejected the employer's attempt to take adverse action against the plaintiff because of her inability to perform job duties not included in the relevant job description. The *Guinn* decision is consistent with numerous other cases under the Rehabilitation Act.[317]

In addition to the job description itself, employers should be able to introduce into evidence internal studies and reviews relating to the description as well as reports from outside experts. Obviously, the conclusions of human resource personnel, job evaluators, consultants, and attorneys prepared in the normal course of business should be given weight as to a particular position's essential functions.

The proposed EEOC's Interpretive Guidelines were clarified to make clear that covered entities are not required to develop and maintain written job descriptions.[318]

[ii] Time spent performing the function. The regulations state that the time spent performing a function is another indication of whether the function is essential.[319] For example, if an employee spends the vast majority of his time working at a cash register, this would be evidence that operating a cash register is an essential function. However, the mere fact that a function is not frequently performed should not, by itself, establish that a duty is not essential. Each job must be judged on a case-by-case

---

1990) (Comments of Rep. Hoyer); 136 Cong. Rec. S9686 (July 13, 1990) (Comments of Sen. Harkin).

[316] Guinn v. Bolger, 598 F. Supp. 196 (DDC 1984).

[317] See Treadwell v. Alexander, 707 F2d 473, 476 n.5 (11th Cir. 1983); Prewitt v. US Postal Serv., 662 F2d 292, 298 (5th Cir. 1981); Coleman v. Darden, 595 F2d 533, 535 (10th Cir. 1979).

[318] 56 Fed. Reg. 35,729 (July 26, 1991).

[319] EEOC Regs. at 29 CFR § 1630.2(n)(3)(iii).

basis, and there may be circumstances in which job functions only occasionally performed are nevertheless essential.

[iii] **Consequences of not requiring function to be performed.** Another factor that may be considered under the regulations is the consequence of failing to require an employee to perform the function.[320] For example, the EEOC's Interpretive Guidelines state that although a firefighter may not regularly have to carry an unconscious adult out of a burning building, the consequences of failing to require the firefighter to be able to perform this function would be so serious that it should be deemed essential.[321]

[iv] **Work experience of incumbents.** The EEOC's regulations state that the work experience of past incumbents in the job and the current work experience of incumbents in similar jobs may be evidence of whether a job function is essential.[322]

[v] **Collective-bargaining agreement.** Finally, after receiving comments to the proposed regulations, the EEOC added to the list of factors "the terms of a collective bargaining agreement."[323]

[vi] **Other evidence.** The Interpretive Guidelines make clear that the list is not exclusive and that the types of evidence on the list will not be given greater weight than the types of evidence not listed.[324]

One of the other facets of whether an essential function exists focuses on whether the disabled individual can accomplish the desired results and not how the employee accomplishes such results.[325] The following examples illustrate this point:

EXAMPLE: Northern Company has a rule that its warehouse workers be able to carry packages with both arms. Applicant

---

[320] EEOC Regs. at 29 CFR § 1630.2(n)(3)(iv).

[321] EEOC Interpretive Guidelines, 56 Fed. Reg. 35,743 (July 26, 1991).

[322] EEOC Regs. at 29 CFR §§ 1630.2(n)(3)(v), 1630.2(n)(3)(vi).

[323] 56 Fed. Reg. 35,729, 35,743 (July 26, 1991).

[324] EEOC Interpretive Guidelines, 56 Fed. Reg. 35,743 (July 26, 1991).

[325] See H. Comm. on Jud. Rep. at 33.

Smith cannot meet this requirement because of his disability but he, in fact, has the ability to lift and carry most packages with one arm. With some accommodation, he can move all the packages between locations. Under Section 101(8), the applicant would be a "qualified individual." [326]

EXAMPLE: Northern Company seeks to hire a computer operator. The "essential function" of such a position is the ability to access, input, and retrieve information from the computer. Applicant Jones is blind but has the ability to access, input, and retrieve information from the computer by means of adaptive equipment. Such an applicant would be deemed "qualified" under the ADA. [327]

Once the "essential functions" of a particular job are determined, the burden of proof is on the plaintiff to establish that he is qualified for the position with or without accommodation as was generally the case under the Rehabilitation Act. [328]

Some commentators have argued that the term "essential function" should include a requirement that the applicant or employee perform the function in a reasonable time and a reasonable manner. Such factors, however, are more properly considered in connection with whether the individual is otherwise qualified and not part of the essential function analysis.

---

[326] See, e.g., Prewitt v. US Postal Serv., 682 F2d 292 (5th Cir. 1981).

[327] H. Comm. on Jud. Rep. at 33.

[328] See Prewitt v. US Postal Serv., 662 F2d 292 (5th Cir. 1981), citing McDonnell Douglas Corp. v. Green, 411 US 792 (1973) and Texas Dep't of Community Affairs v. Burdine, 450 US 248 (1981); Nisperos v. Buck, 720 F. Supp. 1424, 1427 (ND Cal. 1989); Anderson v. University of Wis., 665 F. Supp. 1372, 1391 (WD Wis. 1987); cf. Pushkin v. Regents of Univ. of Colo., 658 F2d 1372, 1385–1387 (10th Cir. 1981) (rejecting disparate treatment analysis in action under Section 504 and outlining elements of prima facie case) and Doe v. New York Univ., 666 F2d 761 (2d Cir. 1981) (distinguishing suits in which defendant acknowledges relying on plaintiff's handicap from those in which defendant denies reliance). In attempting to carry this burden, attorneys representing applicants and employees should review all prior job descriptions of the employer created before the passage of the ADA. Inconsistency may indicate that the new job description was developed for the sole purpose of creating an "essential function" defense.

[c] With or Without Accommodation

A key aspect of Section 101(8)'s definition is that the disabled applicant must be able to perform the essential functions with or without accommodation by the employer. Thus, for example, one might contend that an ability to hear or see might preclude an individual from performing the essential functions of a profession such as law. However, the fact that such an individual could perform such functions with the assistance of an aide who spoke sign language or a reader would require the conclusion that the disabled attorney was otherwise qualified.

An example of the foregoing under the Rehabilitation Act is *Davis v. Frank*,[329] in which a federal district court held in favor of a deaf plaintiff who was denied the position of a time and attendance clerk on the ground that she could not answer a telephone. The evidence at trial demonstrated that the plaintiff could perform all the duties of the position she sought except answering the telephone, a job function that had not been included in earlier job descriptions for this position. While the job required an ability to communicate with employees, there was evidence at trial that the plaintiff could perform this role by reading lips, use of written notes, and expansion of the existing TTY keyboard telephone system. In holding for the plaintiff, the court found that an "ability to hear conversational voice" was not a necessary and legitimate physical requirement required by business necessity.[330] The court next reviewed and found reasonable a number of accommodations ranging from laminating cards containing common phrases the plaintiff might need to use frequently to preparing a list of phrases that individuals could point to when communicating with the plaintiff.[331]

---

[329] Davis v. Frank, 50 Fair Empl. Prac. Cas. (BNA) 1188 (ND Ill. 1989).

[330] Id. at 1193, citing Bentivegna v. US Department of Labor, 694 F2d 619, 622 (9th Cir. 1982) and Carter v. Casa Central, 849 F2d 1048, 1053 (7th Cir. 1988).

[331] Other cases under the Rehabilitation Act in which employees were found not otherwise qualified include Simon v. St. Louis County, Mo., 735 F2d 1082 (8th Cir. 1984); Treadwell v. Alexander, 707 F2d 473 (11th Cir. 1983); Fields v. Lyng, 705 F. Supp. 1134 (D. Md. 1988); Harris v. Adams, 49 Fair Empl. Prac. Cas. (BNA) 1036 (6th Cir. 1989).

Of course, if an employee cannot perform the essential functions of the position with or without reasonable accommodation, no further obligation is placed on the employer.[332]

[d] Case Law

A seminal case interpreting the term "otherwise qualified" under Section 504 of the Rehabilitation Act is the U.S. Supreme Court's decision in *Southeastern Community College v. Davis*.[333] In that case, Davis, who suffered from a serious hearing disability, applied for admission into Southeastern's nursing program, but was rejected. She sued under Section 504 of the Rehabilitation Act, alleging that she was an otherwise qualified handicapped individual and that her application was rejected solely by reason of her handicap. The U.S. Supreme Court disagreed, finding that nothing in the Rehabilitation Act prohibited an educational institution from requiring reasonable physical qualifications for admission to a clinical training program. The Court thus refused to order the school to hire someone to follow the applicant around daily to interpret speech for the applicant whenever necessary. It disputed the appeals court's belief that the otherwise qualified standard under Section 504 includes those who would be able to meet the requirements of a particular program in every respect except as to limitations imposed by their handicap. Instead, it accepted the rationale of the district court as closer to the plain meaning of the statutory language — an otherwise qualified person is one who is able to meet all of a program's requirements in spite of his handicap.[334]

Thus, under *Davis*, a disabled individual is otherwise qualified only if he demonstrates that he is able to perform all the requirements of the job, with or without accommodation, and that even then he may be rejected for the position solely on the basis of his handicap.[335]

---

[332] See, e.g., Treadwell v. Alexander, 707 F2d 473 (11th Cir. 1983); Schmidt v. Bell, 33 Fair Empl. Prac. Cas. (BNA) 839 (ED Pa. 1983); Caylor v. Alexander, 29 Fair Empl. Prac. Cas. (BNA) 727 (MD Ala. 1981).

[333] Southeastern Community College v. Davis, 442 US 397 (1979).

[334] Id. at 405–406.

[335] See Pushkin v. Regents of Univ. of Colo., 658 F2d 1372 (10th Cir.

The *Davis* Court's construction of the term "otherwise qualified" is likely narrower than Congress intended for purposes of the ADA. The failure of the committee reports to cite *Davis* in this regard, coupled with the overall tenor of the reports on this issue, indicate that Congress intended a less stringent standard under the new act. At a minimum, the ADA requires more of a focus on the essential functions of the job than indicated by *Davis*, and there is no requirement under the ADA that the employer be motivated by an animus against the disabled as might have been suggested by the U.S. Supreme Court. Under the ADA, the focus is not on whether the plaintiff is otherwise qualified as analyzed by the *Davis* Court, but rather on whether there is a reasonable accommodation (e.g., an interpreter) that could be provided without undue hardship to the employer so that the disabled individual is able to perform the essential functions of the job.

It should also be noted that most courts applying *Davis* under the Rehabilitation Act have read the decision more broadly than its literal language by blending the requirement of "reasonable accommodation" with the question of whether the employee is qualified.[336] *Davis* also appears inconsistent with the Department of Justice regulations under the Rehabilitation Act.[337]

[e] Medical Releases and Physician Reports

A question that arose under the Rehabilitation Act was whether a disabled applicant or employee can be required to provide a medical release indicating that he can safely perform the essential functions of a position. This was suggested in *Walker v. Attorney General of the United States*,[338] which

---

1981); Cook v. US Department of Labor, 688 F2d 699 (9th Cir. 1982); Doe v. New York Univ., 666 F2d 761 (2d Cir. 1981); Prewitt v. US Postal Serv., 662 F2d 292 (5th Cir. 1981).

[336] See, e.g., Doe v. Region 13 Mental Health-Mental Retardation Comm'n, 704 F2d 1402 (5th Cir. 1983); Prewitt v. US Postal Serv., 662 F2d 454 (5th Cir. 1981); Hall v. US Postal Serv., 857 F2d 1073 (6th Cir. 1983).

[337] 29 CFR § 1613.704.

[338] Walker v. Attorney Gen. of the US, 572 F. Supp. 100 (DDC 1983).

involved an incorrect diagnosis of a serious cardiac condition restricting the plaintiff to nonstressful work. The court concluded that where the available facts showed that the plaintiff was not otherwise qualified, the employer did not violate the Rehabilitation Act by firing the employee who, as it turned out, was capable of performing the essential functions of the job. Other Rehabilitation Act cases indicate that the employer cannot place the burden on the applicant or employee to produce a medical release, and these holdings appear more in line with Congress's intent under the ADA.[339]

A related question, however, is whether an employer is required to accept an opinion from a disabled individual's physician stating that the individual can safely perform all essential job functions. This issue was addressed in *Carter v. Casa Central*,[340] in which the U.S. Court of Appeals for the Seventh Circuit held that a director of nursing services who suffered from multiple sclerosis was otherwise qualified to perform the essential functions of her job, based on her treating physician's findings to that effect. However, the court did not suggest that an employer must unquestionably accept the employee's doctor's view in all circumstances.[341] In fact, according to the court, an employer may, in an appropriate situation, require its own independent medical exam. The employer here erred because it lacked adequate support for its assumptions concerning the plaintiff's ability. The court found that an employer's concerns about the abilities of a handicapped employee must be based on more than "reflexive reactions"—no matter how well-intentioned—about a handicapped individual's ability to do the job.[342]

¶ 2.07 REQUIRED REASONABLE ACCOMMODATIONS

The second component of Section 102(b)(5) is a requirement that the employer provide a disabled employee or applicant with

---

[339] See Carter v. Casa Central, 849 F2d 1048 (7th Cir. 1988).

[340] Id.

[341] Id. at 1056.

[342] Id.

those "reasonable accommodations," if any, which will allow the disabled individual to perform the essential functions of the job. The obligation to make reasonable accommodations is a form of nondiscrimination that applies to all employment decisions, including the job application process. [343]

[1] Equal Employment Opportunity Commission Regulations and Guidelines

The EEOC's regulations define reasonable accommodation to mean: [344]

- Any modification or adjustment to a job application process that enables a qualified individual with a disability to be considered for the position such qualified individual desires
- Any modification or adjustment to the work environment, or the manner or circumstances under which the position held or desired is customarily performed, that enables a qualified individual with a disability to perform the essential functions of that position
- Any modification or adjustment that enables a covered entity's employee with a disability to enjoy equal (not necessarily the "same") benefits and privileges of employment as are enjoyed by its other similarly situated employees without disabilities

The proposed EEOC regulations contained identical language with the addition of the phrase "that will not impose an undue hardship on the covered entity's business" after each component. This language was deleted from the final regulations to clarify that "undue hardship is a defense to, rather than an aspect of, reasonable accommodation." [345] Regarding the third

---

[343] EEOC Interpretive Guidelines, at 56 Fed. Reg. 35,744 (July 26, 1991); see also 56 Fed. Reg. 35,729, discussing changes in proposed regulations to clarify that an individual with a disability who requests a reasonable accommodation to participate in the application process must be eligible only with respect to the application process.

[344] EEOC Regs. at 29 CFR § 1630.2(o)(1).

[345] 56 Fed. Reg. 35,729 (July 26, 1991).

component, the final regulations changed the words "enjoy the same benefit" to the current language of "enjoy equal benefits," thus emphasizing that benefits need not be identical.[346]

Section 101(9) of the ADA states that reasonable accommodation includes two aspects. First, there is an accessibility component set forth in Section 101(9)(A). Under this part of the definition, the employer has a duty to make physical changes in the workplace such that existing facilities used by employees are readily accessible to and usable by individuals with disabilities.[347]

According to the EEOC's Interpretive Guidelines, this component "includes both those areas that must be accessible for the employee to perform essential job functions, as well as non-work areas used by the employer's employees for other purposes."[348] Thus, for example, accessible break rooms, lunch rooms, training rooms, auditoriums, transportation, gymnasiums, rest rooms, and the like may be required as reasonable accommodations.[349]

Second, there is a modification component. Section 101(9)(B) sets forth the following examples of modifications that an employer must consider:[350]

- Job restructuring
- Part-time or modified work schedules
- Reassignment to a vacant position
- Acquisition or modification of equipment or devices
- Appropriate adjustment or modification of examinations, training materials, or policies
- Providing of qualified readers or interpreters

The EEOC's Interpretive Guidelines list other examples,

---

[346] Id.

[347] "Readily accessible" for purposes of Title I should have the same meaning as that term under Title III.

[348] EEOC Interpretive Guidelines, 56 Fed. Reg. 35,744 (July 26, 1991).

[349] EEOC Interpretive Guidelines, 56 Fed. Reg. 35,744 (July 26, 1991).

[350] See also EEOC Regs. at 29 CFR § 1630.2(n)(2) (listing similar examples).

including: permitting the use of accrued paid leave or providing additional unpaid leave for necessary treatment; making employer-provided transportation accessible; providing personal assistants, such as a page turner or travel attendant; providing additional handicap-accessible parking spaces; and allowing a disabled individual to himself provide an accommodation that the employer may not be obligated to provide.[351] After the proposed regulations were issued, many commentators requested clarification regarding whether the provision of daily attendant care is a form of reasonable accommodation. The EEOC modified the final regulations only to state that it may be a reasonable accommodation to provide personal assistants to help with specified duties related to the job.[352] The modifications listed in Section 101(9)(B) and the EEOC's Interpretive Guidelines are of the type often considered under the Rehabilitation Act.[353]

The accommodations set forth in the statute, proposed regulations, and the Interpretive Guidelines are not meant to be exhaustive.[354] Rather, they are intended to provide general directions about the nature of the obligations imposed upon employers. Conversely, employers are not required to implement each of the modifications set forth in the section. What constitutes a reasonable accommodation depends upon the facts of each case.[355]

---

[351] EEOC Interpretive Guidelines, 56 Fed. Reg. 35,744 (July 26, 1991).

[352] 56 Fed. Reg. 35,729, 35,744 (July 26, 1991).

[353] See, e.g., Carter v. Bennett, 840 F2d 63 (DC Cir. 1988); Ackerman v. Western Elec. Co., 48 Fair Empl. Prac. Cas. (BNA) 1354 (ND Cal. 1986); Trimble v. Carlin, 633 F. Supp. 367 (ED Pa. 1986); Vickers v. Veterans Admin., 549 F. Supp. 1197 (WD Wash. 1982); Crane v. US Department of Transp., 551 F. Supp. 27 (DDC 1982).

[354] H. Comm. on Educ. and Lab. Rep. at 62; EEOC Interpretive Guidelines, at 56 Fed. Reg. 35,744 (July 26, 1991).

[355] H. Comm. on Educ. and Lab. Rep. at 62. The U.S. Commission on Civil Rights attempted to develop a more precise definition. It defined "reasonable accommodation" for purposes of the Rehabilitation Act to mean the "providing or modifying devices, services, or facilities or changing practices or procedures in order to match a particular person with a particular program or activity. Individualizing opportunities is this definition's essence." U.S. Com-

As stated by the House Committee on the Judiciary Report: "A reasonable accommodation should be tailored to the needs of the individual and the requirements of the job."[356] This is consistent with the conclusion of the U.S. Commission on Civil Rights that "individualizing opportunities is [the] essence" of reasonable accommodation.[357] There must be, however, a nexus between an individual's disability and the need for accommodation.[358]

The facts and circumstances aspect of what constitutes reasonable accommodation was the subject of a colloquy between Senators Hatch and Harkin, two major proponents of the bill in the Senate:

MR. HATCH: It is my understanding that a reasonable accommodation as required in section 102(b)[5] would take into consideration the nature of a particular industry for the purpose of determining what type of accommodation would or would not, constitute an undue hardship. In other words, the Americans With Disabilities Act would not require that a specific accommodation, which could be easily made in a traditional office setting, be implemented in a nontraditional setting, such as construction worksite, if it imposed an undue hardship. Would my colleague please comment on whether or not my interpretation of the language and intent of this legislation is correct, with regard to different industries employing different types of accommodation.

MR. HARKIN: I would say to my friend from Utah that he has correctly interpreted the "reasonable accommodation" requirement of title I of the ADA bill. Just as each person with a disability is unique in his or her requirements for accommodation to help meet their potential in the workplace, each industry, indeed each separate business, may be unique in the type accommodation employers are able to

---

mission on Civil Rights, Accommodating the Spectrum of Individual Abilities (US Gov't Printing Office: Washington, D.C. 1983) at 102.

[356] H. Comm. on Jud. Rep. at 39.

[357] U.S. Commission on Civil Rights, Accommodating the Spectrum of Individual Abilities (US Gov't Printing Office: Washington, D.C. 1983) at 102.

[358] 56 Fed. Reg. 35,731 (July 26, 1991).

provide without significant difficulty or expense. As is outlined in the Committee report, no action on the part of an employer that is "unduly costly, extensive, substantial, disruptive, or that will fundamentally alter the nature of the program" is required under [the ADA]. This is the basic framework that is to apply in all types of different covered industries and workplaces under the bill. [359]

Such statements are consistent with the interpretation of reasonable accommodation that courts applied under the Rehabilitation Act. [360]

The accommodation offered the employee or applicant does not have to be the "best" accommodation possible. Rather, the offered accommodation is sufficient if it allows the disabled individual to meet the job-related demands of his position. For instance, the EEOC's Interpretive Guidelines give the following example:

An employer would not have to provide an employee disabled by a back impairment with a state-of-the-art mechanical lifting device if it can provide a less expensive and more readily available device that enables the employee to perform the essential functions of the job. [361]

The ADA requires employers to undertake more than a minimal effort to find reasonable accommodations. [362] Thus, an employer

---

[359] 135 Cong. Rec. S10735 (Sept. 7, 1989) (Comments of Sens. Harkin and Hatch).

[360] See Rosiak v. US Department of the Army, 679 F. Supp. 444 (MD Pa. 1987) (multiple transfers of new employee who was found to be unusually sensitive to certain compounds held reasonable accommodation); Carter v. Bennett, 840 F2d 63 (DC Cir. 1988) (blind employee's request that all written material be provided in braille held not a reasonable accommodation); Gardner v. Morris, 752 F2d 1271 (8th Cir. 1985) (manic depressive's request that employer supply a physician for him while he was on foreign assignment not reasonable accommodation).

[361] EEOC's Interpretive Guidelines at 56 Fed. Reg. 35,744 (July 26, 1991); S. Comm. on Lab. and Hum. Resources Rep. at 35; H. Comm. on Educ. and Lab. Rep. at 66; Carter v. Bennett, 840 F2d 63 (DC Cir. 1988).

[362] An example under the Rehabilitation Act is Harrison v. Marsh, 691 F. Supp. 1233 (WD Mo. 1988), in which the U.S. District Court for the Western

cannot presume that no accommodation is possible.[363] Although the failure to receive technical assistance is not a defense for failing to resonably accommodate, the prudent employer should, at a minimum, seek (and document) technical assistance.[364]

Under the guidelines, an employer is obligated to make reasonable accommodations only to the physical and mental limitations known to the employer. Thus, an employer is not expected to accommodate disabilities of which it is unaware.[365] If an employee with a known disability is having difficulty performing his job, an employer may inquire whether the employee is in need of reasonable assistance. In general, however, it is the responsibility of the disabled individual to inform the employer that an accommodation is needed. When the need for accommodation is not obvious, an employer may require the disabled individual to provide documentation of the need for the accommodation as a prerequisite to the providing of the assistance.[366]

In the absence of a request by the employee, it would be inappropriate for an employer to provide an accommodation.[367] The House Committee on Education and Labor Report states, for example, that "it would be unlawful to transfer unilaterally a

---

District of Missouri held that the Department of the Army failed to meet its accommodation duty when it told a clerical employee who was unable to type continuously after a radical mastectomy that she would have to take the one position they offered, or leave.

[363] For example, in Fitzgerald v. Green Valley Area Educ. Agency, 589 F. Supp. 1130 (SD Iowa 1984), the U.S. District Court for the Southern District of Iowa held that an education agency had an obligation under the Rehabilitation Act to consider alternatives that would have eliminated a bus-driving requirement for a handicapped job applicant. The critical facts to the court in this case were that the defendant gave the plaintiff the impression that coming for an interview would be futile, and that the defendant neither considered whether the accommodation was possible or suggested to the plaintiff that it might be.

[364] See 29 CFR § 1630.9(c) and 56 Fed. Reg. 35,731 (July 26, 1991), on the effect of failure to receive technical assistance.

[365] 56 Fed. Reg. 35,748 (July 26, 1991).

[366] Id.

[367] EEOC Regs. at 29 CFR § 1630.9(d); EEOC Interpretive Guidelines, at 56 Fed. Reg. 35,744 (July 26, 1991); H. Comm. on Educ. and Lab. Rep. at 65.

person with HIV infection from a job as teacher to a job where such person has no contact with students."[368] The report also cites with approval *Chalk v. U.S. District Court Central District of California,*[369] in which the U.S. Court of Appeals for the Ninth Circuit held that when a state department of education barred a teacher from his classroom duties, and subsequently reassigned him to an administrative position after he was diagnosed as having AIDS, it violated Section 504 of the Rehabilitation Act. However, if the disabled individual refuses a necessary reasonable accommodation, that individual may not be considered qualified.[370] The EEOC's Interpretive Guidelines give the following example:

> [A]n individual with a visual impairment that restricts his or her field of vision but who is able to read unaided would not be required to accept a reader as an accommodation. However, if the individual were not able to read unaided, and reading was an essential function for the job, the individual would not be qualified for the job if he or she refused a reasonable accommodation that would enable him or her to read.[371]

An employer must consider allowing a disabled individual to provide his own accommodation if the disabled individual chooses to do so.[372]

One issue likely to arise under the ADA is co-worker resentment of an accommodation being made for an individual, when the disability may not be known. Unfortunately, the legislative history of the ADA suggests that it would be inappropriate for an employer to inform the co-workers as to the individual's disability or the reasons why the accommodation was made.

---

[368] H. Comm. on Educ. and Lab. Rep. at 65.

[369] Chalk v. US District Ct. Cent. Dist. of Cal., 840 F2d 701 (9th Cir. 1988).

[370] EEOC Prop. Regs. at 29 CFR § 1630.9(d); EEOC Interpretive Guidelines, 56 Fed. Reg. 35,744 (July 26, 1991).

[371] EEOC Interpretive Guidelines, 56 Fed. Reg. 35,744 (July 26, 1991); S. Comm. on Lab. and Hum. Resources Rep. at 34; H. Comm. on Educ. and Lab. Rep. at 65; H. Comm. on Jud. Rep. at 71–72.

[372] 56 Fed. Reg. 35,731, 35,748 (July 26, 1991).

[2] Job Restructuring

Job restructuring within the meaning of Section 101(9)(B) means modifying a job such that a disabled person can perform its essential functions. It does not mean, however, that the essential functions themselves must be modified.[373] Examples of restructuring include:[374]

- Eliminating nonessential elements of the job
- Redelegating assignments
- Exchanging assignments with another employee
- Redesigning procedures for task accomplishment
- Modifying the means of communication that are used on the job

Such alternatives were generally considered under the Rehabilitation Act.[375]

The EEOC's Interpretive Guidelines give the following example:

[A]n employer may have two jobs, each of which entails the performance of a number of marginal functions. The employer hires a qualified individual with a disability who is able to perform some of the marginal functions of both jobs but not all the marginal functions of either job. As an accommodation, the employer may redistribute the marginal functions so that all the marginal functions are made part of the position to be filled by the qualified individual with a disability. The remaining marginal functions that the

---

[373] See Bruegging v. Burke, 48 Fair Empl. Prac. Cas. (BNA) 140 (DDC 1987); Bento v. ITO Corp., 599 F. Supp. 731 (DRI 1984).

[374] EEOC's Interpretive Guidelines, 56 Fed. Reg. 35,744 (July 26, 1991).

[375] See, e.g., Harrison v. Marsh, 46 Fair Empl. Prac. Cas. (BNA) 971 (WD Mo. 1988) (a clerk-typist recovering from a mastectomy allowed to mix filing with typing rather than prolonged straight typing); Wallace v. Veteran Admin., 683 F. Supp. 758 (D. Kan. 1988) (a nurse recovering from drug problem allowed to exchange duties involving handling and administration of drugs with other nurses); Ackerman v. Western Elec. Co., 48 Fair Empl. Prac. Cas. (BNA) 1354 (ND Cal. 1986); Trimble v. Carlin, 633 F. Supp. 367 (ED Pa. 1986); Vickers v. Veterans Admin., 549 F. Supp. 1197 (WD Wash. 1982).

individual with a disability cannot perform would then be transferred to the other position.[376]

There is no requirement that essential functions of a position be reallocated.[377]

EXAMPLE: Suppose a security guard position requires the individual holding the job to inspect identification cards. An employer would not have to provide an individual who is legally blind with an assistant to look at the cards. In this instance, the assistant would be performing the job, not assisting the disabled individual.[378]

[3] Modified Schedules

There was significant testimony before the Congress concerning the need for flexibility in scheduling in particular circumstances. Two examples of such accommodation cited in the legislative history to Section 101(9)(B) are:

- Persons with epilepsy, who may require constant shifts rather than rotation from day to night shifts
- Persons with mobility impairments who depend on a public transportation system that is not currently fully accessible

A difficult question will arise when several individuals request modified schedules. While an employer may be able to reasonably accommodate the first individual who requests an accommodation, it may become increasingly difficult as the employer is requested to allow modified schedules for subsequent disabled applicants and employees. The legislative history suggests that situations are to be judged on a case-by-case basis, indicating that a request that was "reasonable" for the first person requesting it may become "unreasonable" when sought by the second or third applicant or employee.[379]

---

[376] EEOC Interpretive Guidelines, 56 Fed. Reg. 35,744 (July 26, 1991).

[377] Id.

[378] Id., citing Coleman v. Darden, 595 F2d 533 (10th Cir. 1979).

[379] Similar issues are likely to arise with respect to other accommodations. For example, what if an employer can accommodate the request of one

[4] Unpaid Leave

Section 101(9)(B) does not specifically address the question of whether an employer must reasonably accommodate a disabled individual by allowing unpaid leave beyond that offered other employees. The legislative history to that section suggests that such an accommodation must be offered. For example, the House Committee on Education and Labor Report states that "reasonable accommodation may also include providing additional unpaid leave days, if such provision does not result in an undue hardship for the employer."[380] This language further suggests that the disabled must be given some leeway with respect to an employer's rule against tardiness if the lateness results from the disability.[381] However, the ADA does not require an employer to provide the disabled with more paid leave than nondisabled employees.[382]

[5] Reassignment

There was much litigation under the Rehabilitation Act over whether a disabled individual had the right to demand permanent light duty work or reassignment if he became disabled while employed. Employers successfully argued that an employee who could no longer perform the essential functions of the job was no longer otherwise qualified, and, therefore, there was no duty to

---

hearing-impaired individual at a particular workstation but not two such individuals. Similarly, what if there is enough room at a workspace for an individual in a wheelchair but not two such individuals (e.g., behind a restaurant counter or a bar). Again, the reasonableness of the second applicant's or employee's needed accommodation should be judged with recognition of the restraints caused by the initial accommodation.

[380] H. Comm. on Educ. and Lab. Rep. at 63.

[381] But see Wimbley v. Bolger, 642 F. Supp. 481 (WD Tenn. 1986), in which the U.S. District Court for the Western District of Tennessee held that a former postal employee who was dismissed for excessive unscheduled absenteeism was not automatically "handicapped" because of his 30 percent service-connected disability and, thus, not entitled to the protection of the Rehabilitation Act.

[382] S. Comm. on Lab. and Hum. Resources Rep. at 31.

accommodate the handicap.[383]

This logic appears to have been rejected by the Congress in drafting Section 101(9)(B), which specifically lists reassignment as a possible accommodation. This new language, not contained in the Rehabilitation Act, suggests that cases rejecting such an accommodation under that statute are not to be followed under the ADA. Thus, if because of a disability an employee can no longer perform the essential functions of the job, a transfer to another vacant job for which the employee is qualified may be required. Reassignment is not available to applicants for employment.[384]

Bumping another employee—moving that individual out of a position to create a vacancy—is not required under the ADA.[385] Nor is an employer required to promote an individual with a disability as a means of accommodation.[386]

As a general rule, reassignment should be considered an option only if there is no other accommodation that would allow the employee to continue in his present position. The EEOC's Interpretive Guidelines view reassignment, in general, as some-

---

[383] See, e.g., Shea v. Tisch, 870 F2d 786 (1st Cir. 1989); Carter v. Tisch, 822 F2d 465 (4th Cir. 1987); Black v. Frank, 52 Fair Empl. Prac. Cas. (BNA) 1061 (SD Ala. 1990) ("[t]he courts, however, have found that 'reassignment' is not required under the Rehabilitation Act and that an employee is properly fired if he can perform the essential functions of his given position"); Jasany v. US Postal Serv., 33 Fair Empl. Prac. Cas. (BNA) 1115, 1117, aff'd, 775 F2d 1244 (6th Cir. 1985) ("[t]he requirement of accommodation refers to adjustment with the job for which the handicapped employee was hired"); Wright v. Tisch, 45 Fair Empl. Prac. Cas. (BNA) 151 (ED Va. 1987); Wimbley v. Bolger, 642 F. Supp. 481, 486 (WD Tenn. 1986) ("the duty to reasonably accommodate only contemplates accommodation of a qualified handicapped employee's present position"); Carty v. US Postal Serv., 623 F. Supp. 1181 (D. Md. 1985); Alderson v. Postmaster Gen., 598 F. Supp. 49, 55 (WD Okla. 1984) ("[t]he regulation clearly refers to making the particular job, not another job for the handicapped person who was not hired, accessible to handicapped persons").

[384] EEOC Interpretive Guidelines, 56 Fed. Reg. 8596 (Feb. 28, 1991).

[385] H. Comm. on Educ. and Lab. Rep. at 63. See also Daubert v. US Postal Serv., 733 F2d 1367 (10th Cir. 1984); Hurst v. US Postal Serv., 653 F. Supp. 259 (ND Ga. 1986).

[386] EEOC Interpretive Guidelines, 56 Fed. Reg. 35,744 (July 26, 1991).

thing that should be considered only when accommodation within the individual's current position would pose an undue hardship on the employer. [387]

On the other hand, employers may not utilize reassignments as a means for limiting, segregating, or otherwise discriminating against the disabled by forcing them to take less desirable positions, designated offices, or facilities. Whenever possible, employers must reassign individuals with disabilities to equivalent positions in terms of pay, status, benefits, and the like. According to the EEOC's Interpretive Guidelines, "an employer may reassign an individual to a lower graded position if there are no accommodations in the current position and there are no vacant equivalent positions for which the individual is qualified with or without accommodation." [388]

[6] Modification of Equipment

Disability rights advocates repeatedly testified that most disabilities could be accommodated by modest modifications to equipment or devices. As discussed more fully in Chapter 3, the Job Accommodation Network (JAN) operated by the President's Committee on Employment of People With Disabilities has accumulated nearly 17,000 available solutions on which employers may draw in investigating methods of accommodating disabled applicants and employees.

Reasonable accommodation does not extend to provision of adjustments or modifications that are primarily for the personal benefit of the individual with a disability. [389] In discussing this aspect of the ADA, the proposed EEOC Interpretive Guidelines indicated that if an adjustment or modification assisted the individual throughout his daily activities, on and off the job, it would be considered a personal item that the employer is not required to provide. [390] The final Interpretive Guidelines expand and slightly modify the proposed guidelines by indicating that

---

[387] Id.

[388] Id.

[389] 56 Fed. Reg. 35,747 (July 26, 1991).

[390] 56 Fed. Reg. 8596 (Feb. 28, 1991).

an employer may have to provide personal items where they are specifically designed or required to meet job-related needs.[391] The final guidelines state:

> Thus, if an adjustment or modification is job-related, e.g. specifically assists the individual in performing the duties of a particular job, it will be considered a type of reasonable accommodation. On the other hand, if an adjustment or modification assists the individual throughout his or her daily activities, on and off the job, it will be considered a personal item that the employer is not required to provide.

For example, an employer would not be required to provide an employee with a disability with a prosthetic limb, wheelchair, or eyeglasses.[392] Nor would an employer have to provide as an accommodation an amenity or convenience that is not job-related, such as a private hot plate, hot pot, or refrigerator that is not provided to employees without disabilities.[393] On the other hand, an employer may have to provide a visually disabled individual with eyeglasses that specifically enable the individual to use the office computer monitors, but that are not otherwise needed by the individual outside the office.[394]

[7] Supported Employment

The EEOC's Interpretive Guidelines note that the term "supported employment" is often used to describe a wide variety of programs to assist the disabled. The guidelines stress, however, that the term includes many programs that may, or may not, be reasonable accommodations depending on the facts of a particular case. Among those accommodations that the guidelines suggest may be reasonable accommodations are the providing of modified training material and the providing of a temporary "job coach" to assist in the training of a qualified individual with a disability.

---

[391] 56 Fed. Reg. 35,731, 35,747 (July 26, 1991).

[392] 56 Fed. Reg. 35,747 (July 26, 1991).

[393] Id.

[394] 56 Fed. Reg. 35,744 (July 26, 1991).

EXAMPLE: Employee Smith suffers a disabling injury. With the aid of an occupational therapist, Smith will be able to perform the job he held prior to his injury. Under such circumstances, the hiring of an outside professional to assist Smith in resuming his position might be a reasonable accommodation.

[8] Examples From Legislative History

The legislative history to the ADA reveals numerous examples of the accommodations that Congress envisioned, many of which could be provided at minimal cost.

- For blind individuals, such accommodations include adaptive hardware and software for computers, electronics visual aids, braille devices, talking calculators, magnifiers, audio recordings, and braille material. For example, a $45 light probe could be provided for a receptionist who is legally blind, allowing her to determine which lines on a telephone were ringing, on hold, or in use.
- For individuals with hearing impairments, accommodations may include providing telephone handset amplifiers, telephones compatible with hearing aids, and telecommunication devices for the deaf (TDDs). In such a situation, a medical technician who is deaf may need a $26.95 timer with an indicator light to perform required lab tests.
- For individuals with limited physical dexterity, accommodations may include gooseneck telephone headsets, mechanical page turners, and raised or lowered furniture. For example, a salesperson with cerebral palsy could be provided a $49.95 headset for a phone that allowed him to write while talking.

[9] Cost

Under the Rehabilitation Act and comparable state statutes, the courts tended to require the purchase of equipment for the disabled applicant or employee when the items were of minimal cost.[395]

---

[395] For example, in Ackerman v. Western Elec. Co., 48 Fair Empl. Prac.

A question that arose throughout the debate on the ADA is whether the employee may be required to bear any of the cost of such accommodation. The answer appears to be no. If an accommodation will constitute an undue hardship, the employer should ask (or employee may offer) to pay the difference between the amount that would not be an undue hardship and the total cost of the accommodation. If the employee is willing to pay the cost of the accommodation, no undue hardship will be found to exist. When an employee pays any of the cost of the accommodation, the employer should check with the relevant wage and hour agencies to determine whether the amount of the contribution will be considered for overtime or other purposes.

The legislative history is clear that an employer is not required to purchase exclusively personal use items for disabled employees, such as hearing aids or glasses, even if the cost is minimal.[396]

[10] Collective-Bargaining Agreements

There may be times in which the provisions of a collective-bargaining agreement conflict with the ADA. Under the Rehabilitation Act, the collective-bargaining agreement would not protect the employer; that rule has been incorporated into the ADA.[397] Thus, for example, physical criteria specified in collective-bargaining agreement that causes a disparate impact on the disabled and that are not job-related and consistent with business necessity would be illegal under the ADA.[398]

Cas. (BNA) 1354 (ND Cal. 1986), a case under the California Fair Employment and Housing Act, the U.S. District Court for the Northern District of California held that an employer had illegally discriminated against an asthmatic employee because she could perform the essential functions of her job and reasonable accommodations were available, such as the purchase of paper masks.

[396] H. Comm. on Educ. and Lab. Rep. at 64.

[397] The regulations under the Rehabilitation Act provide that "a recipient's obligation to comply with this subpart [employment] is not affected by any inconsistent term of any collective bargaining agreement to which it is a party." 45 CFR § 84.11(c).

[398] H. Comm. on Educ. and Lab. Rep. at 63.

A more difficult question is whether an employer can be required to take an action to accommodate a handicapped employee when such accommodation would violate a labor agreement. For example, if a collective-bargaining agreement reserves certain jobs for employees with a given amount of seniority, can an employer be required to place a disabled employee in such a position in order to accommodate the disability? The legislative history to Section 101(9)(B) indicates that the answer is yes, although the presence of the labor agreement may be considered by a court in determining whether the accommodation would be an undue hardship.[399] This represents a change from the Rehabilitation Act.[400]

As a result of the ADA, it is suggested that new collective-bargaining agreements should include a provision permitting the employer to comply with the ADA.

The one area where a collective-bargaining agreement may assist an employer is in determining the essential functions of a position. If a labor agreement lists the job duties associated with a particular job, the legislative history to the ADA and the EEOC's Interpretive Guidelines indicates that it could be used as evidence of the essential functions of the position for purposes of Section 101(8).[401]

[11] Alternative Accommodations

In the event there are two effective accommodations, the employer may choose the accommodation that is less expensive or easier for the employer to implement as long as the elected

---

[399] Id.; 56 Fed. Reg. 35,752 (July 26, 1991).

[400] See, e.g., Daubert v. US Postal Serv., 733 F2d 1367 (10th Cir. 1984) (court held that the Postal Service's contractual obligations to its employees and their union under the collective-bargaining agreement represented a legitimate business reason in the discharge of a disabled employee); Hurst v. US Postal Serv., 653 F. Supp. 259 (ND Ga. 1986) (court held that the rights afforded a qualified handicapped individual under the Rehabilitation Act do not prevail over seniority rights established within an applicable collective-bargaining agreement).

[401] H. Comm. on Educ. and Lab. Rep. at 63; 56 Fed. Reg. 35,743 (July 26, 1991).

accommodation is effective.[402] Consideration must be given, however, to the employee's or applicant's expressed choice.[403]

The Senate Committee on Labor and Human Resources Report states that the expressed choice of the disabled individual should be given primary weight unless it would cause an undue hardship or another reasonable accommodation is available.[404] This view is inconsistent with other report language suggesting that the employer may choose between two accommodations unless it is construed to apply only when two accommodations are not equally effective.[405]

[12] Burden of Proof

The ADA continues to follow the rule under the Rehabilitation Act that while the plaintiff must show that he is capable of performing the essential functions of the job at issue (with or without accommodation), the burden of proof is on the employer on the issue of whether a reasonable accommodation is available.[406] The House Committee on Education and Labor cited with approval the federal agency regulations on this issue.[407]

As stated by the U.S. Court of Appeals for the Fifth Circuit in *Prewitt v. U.S. Postal Service*[408]

---

[402] H. Comm. on Jud. Rep. at 40; S. Comm. on Lab. and Hum. Resources Rep. at 35; H. Comm. on Educ. and Lab. Rep. at 66.

[403] H. Comm. on Educ. and Lab. Rep. at 67.

[404] S. Comm. on Lab. and Hum. Resources Rep. at 35.

[405] H. Comm. on Jud. Rep. at 40; S. Comm. on Lab. and Hum. Resources Rep. at 35; H. Comm. on Educ. and Lab. Rep. at 66.

[406] H. Comm. on Educ. and Lab. Rep. at 71; Arneson v. Heckler, 879 F2d 393 (8th Cir. 1989), on remand, 53 Fair Empl. Prac. Cas. (BNA) 965 (ED Mo. 1990) (an example of the application of the burdens of proof under the Rehabilitation Act).

[407] See, e.g., 45 CFR § 84.13 (Department of Health and Human Services); 29 CFR § 1613.705 (EEOC); 28 CFR § 42.512 (Department of Justice); 29 CFR § 32.14 (Department of Labor).

[408] Prewitt v. US Postal Serv., 662 F2d 292 (5th Cir. 1981).

> [T]he burden of proving inability to accommodate is on the employer. . . . The employer has greater knowledge of the essentials of the job than does the handicapped applicant. The employer can look to its own experience, or, if that is not helpful, to that of other employers who have provided jobs to individuals with handicaps similar to those of the applicant in question. Furthermore, the employer may be able to obtain advice concerning possible accommodations from private and government sources.[409]

While the burden of persuasion in proving inability to accommodate always remains with the employer, once the employer presents credible evidence that accommodation would not be reasonably possible, the plaintiff has the burden of coming forward with evidence concerning his individual capabilities and suggestions for possible accommodations to rebut the employer's evidence.[410]

[13] Known Disabilities Only

An employer's duty to reasonably accommodate only applies to known physical or mental disabilities of an applicant or employee. Thus, an employer's obligations under the ADA are only triggered once an employee or applicant asks for an accommodation.[411] This result is consistent with cases under the Rehabilitation Act.[412]

One question this raises is the obligation of the employer when the disability is obvious but the issue of accommodation is not raised by the applicant or employee himself. While portions of the legislative history may indicate that the employer is to ignore the disability if not raised by the disabled individual, the

---

[409] Id. at 292, 308.

[410] Id.; but see Pushkin v. Regents of Univ. of Colo., 658 F2d 1372 (10th Cir. 1981) (rejecting traditional disparate treatment analysis).

[411] EEOC Interpretive Guidelines, 56 Fed. Reg. 35,744, 35,748 (July 26, 1991).

[412] Lutter v. Fowler, 41 Fair Empl. Prac. Cas. (BNA) 1227 (DDC), aff'd, 808 F2d 137 (1986), Walker v. Attorney Gen. of the US, 32 Fair Empl. Prac. Cas. (BNA) 1857 (DDC 1983).

impracticality of this approach suggests that prudent employers will initiate the discussion regarding the disability and possible accommodations that may be required.[413] As noted, the EEOC's Interpretive Guidelines provide that if an employee with a known disability is having difficulty performing a job, an employer may inquire whether the employee is in need of a reasonable accommodation.[414] Such discussions should include a review with the applicant or employee of the employer's obligations under the ADA and the employer's willingness to discuss possible accommodations with disability experts. This approach is supported by precedent under the Rehabilitation Act.[415] On the other hand, where the disability of the applicant or employee is not obvious, the employer should not inquire into whether there is a disability or a need for accommodation.

[14] Physical or Mental Impairments

Section 102(b)(5)(B) makes it illegal to deny employment opportunities to a qualified job applicant or employee if such denial is based on the need to make reasonable accommodation to the physical or mental impairment of such individual. Originally, this prohibition was set forth as Section 102(b)(6).[416] There was some concern, however, that this provision could be applied even when the accommodation would constitute an undue hardship on the employer. To avoid this result, this provision was made a subpart of Section 102(b)(5) in order to clarify that the undue hardship language applied to both sections.[417] Thus, this

---

[413] H. Comm. on Educ. and Lab. Rep. at 65.

[414] 56 Fed. Reg. 35,748 (July 26, 1991).

[415] See Ferguson v. US Department of Commerce, 46 Fair Empl. Prac. Cas. (BNA) 241 (MD Fla. 1988), in which the U.S. District Court for the Middle District of Florida held that a Department of Commerce employee's excessive absenteeism, frequent failure to return to work on the dates promised, and failure to obtain appropriate leave slips, occurring after twenty years of exemplary service, should have signaled an underlying problem requiring further investigation rather than the employee's dismissal.

[416] Section 102(b)(5)(B) was originally Section 102(b)(6) of S. 933 and HR 2733.

[417] HR Conf. Rep. No. 101-596, Conf. Rep. on S. 933, Americans With

change provides that if an employer discriminates against a disabled individual solely on the basis of the need to reasonably accommodate an impairment, the employer would nevertheless not be in violation of the ADA if it could show that all reasonable accommodations would constitute an undue hardship.[418]

An employer could argue, using the legislative history of Section 102(b)(5)(B), that the section is not violated even if the employer performed no analysis of the costs of accommodation prior to its denial of job opportunities (provided that the employer were able to demonstrate undue hardship at trial). However, such a result would be inconsistent with other parts of the legislative history showing that Congress was particularly concerned with prohibiting generalizations concerning the disabled; instead, it required case-by-case analysis on issues under the ADA. It is also supported by the legislative history's inclusion of a recommended procedure for determining whether reasonable accommodations are available.[419] Therefore, as was typically the case under the Rehabilitation Act, it is likely that the courts will evaluate the employer's efforts in determining what accommodations were available and their cost in deciding whether Section 102(B)(5)(b) was violated.[420]

¶ 2.08 NO ACCOMMODATION IF UNDUE HARDSHIP RESULTS

According to Section 101(10)(A) of the ADA, undue hardship means an action that requires significant difficulty or expense,

---

Disabilities Act of 1990, Joint Explanatory Statement of the Committee on Conference at 59.

[418] EEOC Prop. Regs. at 29 CFR § 1630.9(b); EEOC Interpretive Guidelines, 56 Fed. Reg. 8600 (Feb. 28, 1991).

[419] 56 Fed. Reg. 35,748 (July 26, 1991).

[420] See, e.g., Trimble v. Carlin, 633 F. Supp. 367 (ED Pa. 1986). In *Trimble*, the U.S. District Court for the Eastern District of Pennsylvania held that the U.S. Postal Service had discriminated against a handicapped employee by dismissing him from duty without establishing that reasonable accommodation for his physical limitations was impractical.

when considered in light of certain factors.[421] Furthermore, it is an "action that is unduly costly, extensive, substantial, disruptive, or that will fundamentally alter the nature" of a job.[422] The legislative history indicates that this provision derives from interpretations by the federal agencies that applied the term as it was set forth in regulations implementing Sections 501 and 504 of the Rehabilitation Act, and should be consistently applied with those interpretations.[423] As under the Rehabilitation Act, the burden of proving undue hardship is on the employer.[424]

Although the term "undue hardship" has been used in other legislation, Congress decided to add a definition to the ADA for two reasons. First, a definition of undue hardship was thought necessary to distinguish it from the definition of readily achievable in Title III of the ADA governing the requirement to alter existing public accommodations. As discussed in Chapter 5, readily achievable means an action that is able to be easily accomplished and that can be carried out without much difficulty or expense. The duty to provide reasonable accommodation under Title I of the ADA, including the duty to make a workplace accessible as required by Section 101(9)(A), is a much higher standard than the duty to remove barriers in existing buildings and creates a more substantial obligation on the employer.[425]

Second, a definition was included in order to distinguish the duty to reasonably accommodate under the ADA from the U.S. Supreme Court's interpretation of that duty under Title VII of the Civil Rights Act of 1964 in *TVA v. Hardison*.[426] In that case, the Court held that an employer has an obligation to reasonably accommodate an employee's religious beliefs only if the cost to the employer is de minimis. Unlike the *Hardison* definition,

---

[421] See infra ¶ 2.08[1].

[422] S. Comm. on Lab. and Hum. Resources Rep. at 35.

[423] H. Comm. on Educ. and Lab. Rep. at 67.

[424] EEOC Regs. at 29 CFR § 1630.15(d); EEOC Interpretive Guidelines, 56 Fed. Reg. 35,752 (July 26, 1991); H. Comm. on Jud. Rep. at 42.

[425] H. Comm. on Jud. Rep. at 40. The term "readily accessible" should be interpreted the same for purposes of both Title I and Title III.

[426] TVA v. Hardison, 432 US 63 (1977).

undue hardship under the ADA is intended to convey a significant, as opposed to a de minimis or insignificant, obligation on the part of the employer.[427]

[1] What Constitutes Undue Hardship?

Section 101(10)(B) sets forth the factors to be considered in determining whether an accommodation would impose an undue hardship:

- The nature and cost of the accommodation needed under the ADA
- The overall financial resources of the facility or facilities involved in the provision of the reasonable accommodation, the number of persons employed at the facility, the effect on expenses and resources or the impact otherwise of the accommodation on the operation of the facility
- The overall financial resources of the covered entity, the overall size of the business of a covered entity with respect to the number of its employees, and the number, type, and location of its facilities
- The type of operation or operations of the covered entity, including the composition, structure, and functions of the work force of such entity; the geographic separateness, administrative, or fiscal relationship of the facility or facilities in question to the covered entity

The factors set forth in Section 101(10)(B) are not intended to be an exhaustive list.[428] Among other factors that might be considered are the impact of the accommodations on co-workers, the effect of accommodations already provided other employees, and modifications that would fundamentally alter the nature of the job in question. In addition, the final Interpretive Guidelines of the EEOC state that the terms of a collective-bargaining agreement may be relevant in determining whether a requested

---

[427] EEOC Interpretive Guidelines, 56 Fed. Reg. 35,744–35,745 (July 26, 1991); H. Comm. on Jud. Rep. at 40; S. Comm. on Lab. and Hum. Resources Rep. at 36; H. Comm. on Educ. and Lab. Rep. at 68–69.

[428] H. Comm. on Educ. and Lab. Rep. at 69.

accommodation would pose an undue hardship.[429]

Thus, as stated by the EEOC in its Interpretive Guidelines, the concept of undue hardship is not limited to financial realities but "refers to any accommodation that would be unduly costly, extensive, or disruptive or that would fundamentally alter the nature or operation of the business."[430]

The EEOC's Interpretive Guidelines give the following example:

> [A]n individual with a disabling visual impairment that makes it extremely difficult to see in dim lighting applies for a position as a waiter in a nightclub and requests that the club be brightly lit as a reasonable accommodation. Although the individual may be able to perform the job in bright lighting, the nightclub will probably be able to demonstrate that particular accommodation, though inexpensive, would be an undue hardship if the bright light would destroy the ambience of the nightclub and/or make it difficult for the customers to see the stage show.[431]

An accommodation is not unduly disruptive if it results from co-workers' or patrons' fears and prejudices toward the individual with a disability and not from providing the accommodation.[432] Similarly, an employer cannot establish undue hardship by showing only that a requested accommodation would affect employee morale.[433]

> **EXAMPLE:** Northeastern Company hires Jones, an individual who is HIV-positive. Jones's co-workers threaten to quit unless he is terminated. Northeastern will violate the ADA should it accede to its employees' demand.

---

[429] 56 Fed. Reg. 35,733 (July 26, 1991).

[430] EEOC Interpretive Guidelines, 56 Fed. Reg. 35,744–35,745 (July 26, 1991); S. Comm. on Lab. and Hum. Resources Rep. at 35; H. Comm. on Educ. and Lab. at 67.

[431] EEOC Interpretive Guidelines, 56 Fed. Reg. 35,744–35,745 (July 26, 1991).

[432] EEOC Interpretive Guidelines, 56 Fed. Reg. 35,752 (July 26, 1991).

[433] 56 Fed. Reg. 35,733 (July 26, 1991).

The legislative history indicates that the number of employees or applicants potentially benefiting from an accommodation may be a relevant consideration in determining undue hardship —if more than one person with a disability uses the accommodation, the relative financial impact of the accommodation is reduced.[434] For instance, if a ramp is installed for a new employee who uses a wheelchair, but that will benefit mobility-impaired applicants and employees in the future, the accommodation may be reasonable, even though it might not have been so if installed for a single individual. In another case, assistive devices for hearing or visually impaired persons that may be shared by more than one employee may be reasonable, even though they might not have been so if only one employee needed such a device.

Although use by more than one disabled individual would support a finding that no undue hardship was present, the House Committee on Education and Labor Report makes clear that "the fact that an accommodation is used by only one employee should not be used as a negative factor in favor of a finding of undue hardship."[435]

A second additional factor included in the legislative history is the availability of outside funding to pay for accommodations.[436] For example, if funds are available from a state vocation rehabilitation agency, or if federal, state, or local tax deductions or credits are available, such facts must be considered in determining whether an undue hardship exists. Conversely, the lack of outside funding is not considered a defense to the obligation to provide a reasonable accommodation.[437]

If an employer determines that an accommodation would impose an undue hardship, it should permit the disabled individual to provide his own accommodation.[438] In such circumstances, the employer should provide the employee or applicant

---

[434] H. Comm. on Educ. and Lab. Rep. at 69.

[435] Id.

[436] EEOC Interpretive Guidelines, 56 Fed. Reg. 35,745 (July 26, 1991).

[437] H. Comm. on Educ. and Lab. Rep. at 69.

[438] EEOC Interpretive Guidelines, 56 Fed. Reg. 35,745 (July 26, 1991).

with as much accommodation and support as it can without incurring an undue hardship. [439]

[2] Weight Given to Various Factors

The standard for determining undue hardship is relative. [440] Thus, the weight given to each factor set forth in Section 101(10)(B) varies depending on the facts of a particular situation and turns on the nature and costs of the accommodation in relation to the employer's resources and operation.

The order of the factors within Section 101(10)(B) do not reflect any priority as to the weight to be given them. [441] Similarly, the fact that an employer is a large entity should not be construed to negate the importance of other factors. [442]

The fact that an accommodation was found not to be a hardship for an employer in one industry would not mean that a similar accommodation would be required in a different industry. [443] Conversely, as stated in the EEOC's Interpretive Guidelines, "an accommodation that poses an undue hardship for one employer at one particular time may not pose an undue hardship for another employer, or even the same employer at another time." [444]

The House Committee on Education and Labor quoted with approval the Department of Health, Education, and Welfare regulations explaining the use of undue hardship in the Rehabilitation Act:

> Thus, a small day-care center might not be required to expend more than nominal sum, such as that necessary to equip a telephone for use by a secretary with impaired

---

[439] S. Comm. on Lab. and Hum. Resources Rep. at 36; H. Comm. on Educ. and Lab. Rep. at 69.

[440] H. Comm. on Jud. Rep. at 41.

[441] Id.

[442] H. Comm. on Educ. and Lab. Rep. at 68.

[443] See 135 Cong. Rec. S10735 (Sept. 7, 1989) (Comments of Sens. Hatch and Harkin).

[444] EEOC Interpretive Guidelines, 56 Fed. Reg. 8602 (Feb. 28, 1991).

hearing, but a large school district might be required to make available a teacher's aide to a blind applicant for a teaching job. Further, it might be considered reasonable to require a state welfare agency to accommodate a deaf employee by providing an interpreter, while it would constitute an undue hardship to impose that requirement on a provider of foster home care services. [445]

This principle is further illustrated by *Nelson v. Thornburgh*, [446] which was cited with approval by the House Committee on Education and Labor. In *Nelson*, a group of state income maintenance employees who were blind requested several accommodations, including the use of readers, braille forms, and a computer that stores and retrieves information in braille. The cost of these accommodations was substantial. However, the court ordered the accommodations to be made on the ground that the additional dollar burden was only a small fraction of the state agency's personnel budget. [447]

Repeated efforts were made during congressional consideration of the ADA to limit the employer's obligation to 10 percent of the disabled employee's pay as a per se rule of undue hardship. However, these efforts were defeated as being contrary to the flexible approach intended by Section 101(10). It was also argued that such an amendment would discriminate against employees with lower salaries. [448] Similarly, the EEOC rejected comments to its proposed regulations seeking to add as a factor the relationship of an accommodation's cost to the value of the position at issue, as measured by the compensation paid the holder of the position. [449]

[3] Multiple Facilities

The original version of Section 101(10) did not include any reference to the treatment of covered entities with multiple

---

[445] 42 Fed. Reg. 22,676 et seq. (May 4, 1977).

[446] Nelson v. Thornburgh, 567 F. Supp. 369 (ED Pa. 1983).

[447] See also 136 Cong. Rec. E1915 (June 13, 1990) (Remarks of Rep. Hoyer).

[448] See also id. on reasons why this 10 percent limit was rejected.

[449] 56 Fed. Reg. 35,730 (July 26, 1991).

facilities.[450] Concerns were expressed, however, that a court would look only at the resources of the local facility involved, or only at the resources of the parent company, in determining whether a particular accommodation constituted an undue hardship. Thus, the original bill was amended such that the resources of both the local facility involved and that of the parent company would both be taken into account.

If an employer contends that only the financial resources of the site where the individual will be employed should be considered, there must be "a factual determination of the relationship between the employer and the site that will provide the accommodation."[451] The EEOC's Interpretive Guidelines give the following example:

> [A]n independently owned fast food franchise that receives no money from the franchisor refuses to hire an individual with a hearing impairment because it asserts that it would be an undue hardship to provide an interpreter to enable the individual to participate in monthly staff meetings. Since the financial relationship between the franchisor and the franchise is limited to payment of an annual franchise fee, only the financial resources of the franchisee would be considered in determining whether or not providing the accommodation would be an undue hardship.[452]

In evaluating whether the parent's resources should be attributable to the local facility, the following factors should be considered:[453]

---

[450] Original HR 2273 provided at Section 101(9)(B) (later became Section 101(10)(B)) for consideration of only:

> (i) the overall size of the business of the covered entity with respect to the number of employees, number and type of facilities, and the size of the budget;
> (ii) the type of operation maintained by the covered entity, including the composition and structure of the workforce of such entity; and
> (iii) the nature and cost of the accommodation needed under this Act.

[451] EEOC Interpretive Guidelines, 56 Fed. Reg. 35,745 (July 26, 1991).

[452] Id.

[453] EEOC Regs. at 29 CFR § 1630.2(p)(2).

- The functions of the work force
- Geographic separateness
- The administrative relationship of the local facility to the parent, such as whether the parent provides to the local facility resources in connection with employee benefits, services, and hiring

The Committee on the Judiciary concluded that courts are to consider whether, as a result of compliance with the ADA's requirements, the local plant is threatened with closure by the parent company or faced with job loss.[454]

> EXAMPLE: The parent company is located in New Jersey. It has a local facility in rural Alabama that is only marginally profitable. The local facility lacks the funds to perform the accommodations required for disabled accessibility. Although the parent company has the resources to pay for the accommodation, the local facility would be operating at a loss if the cost of accommodation were included in the local plant's cost structure. On this basis, the parent company, in good faith, would determine to close the plant rather than make the accommodation. Under these facts, an undue hardship would likely be found.[455]

[4] Type of Operation

Congress appeared to be concerned primarily with the construction industry and temporary worksites in adding the type of operation as a consideration. The Reports of the House Committee on Education and Labor and the Committee on the Judiciary both illustrate the intent of this provision by stating that it might fundamentally alter the nature of a construction site or be unduly costly to implement or maintain physical accessibility for an applicant or employee who uses a wheelchair if, for example, the site's terrain and building structure change daily as

---

[454] H. Comm. on Jud. Rep. at 41.

[455] See also 136 Cong. Rec. E1915 (June 13, 1990) (Remarks of Rep. Hoyer).

construction progresses. [456] According to the committee reports, such temporary worksites should be held to a lesser standard than more permanent places of employment (e.g., an office building). [457]

A colloquy between Senators Hatch and Harkin, managers of the bill in the Senate, further illustrate concern over application of the ADA at construction sites:

> MR. HATCH: I have heard from several contractors who do not wish to exempt themselves from doing their part in assisting people with disabilities find meaningful employment in the construction industry [but] who are confused as to what latitude they will have under the ADA. To state the obvious, construction is physically demanding work. The construction site is a place of employment where permanence and consistency are virtually unknowns. From the digging and pouring of foundations, to painting and decorating, a project undergoes metamorphosis in which a point of land may be transformed. . . . Points of accessibility for the workers may change daily as a project enters different stages of completion.
>
> [W]ould having to make constant different accommodations at different points on the site as would often be the case on temporary worksites be a factor taken into consideration in assessing which accommodations would pose an "undue hardship" for an employer?
>
> MR. HARKIN: . . . To quote the committee report language, the factors [in determining undue hardship] include . . . "the type operation maintained by the covered employer." . . . [T]his would include consideration of the special circumstances incurred on the temporary worksite for purposes of determining whether or not an accommodation would impose an undue hardship for the employer. Construction is unlike manufacturing, and most other types of industry, in that [a construction] employer is usually confronted with monitoring multiple worksites at remote

---

[456] H. Comm. on Educ. and Lab. Rep. at 70; H. Comm. on Jud. Rep. at 41. See also 136 Cong. Rec. H2623 (May 22, 1990) (Comments of Cong. Staggers).

[457] Id.; see also 56 Fed. Reg. 35,752 (July 26, 1991).

locations, and this would be taken into account under [the undue hardship] factors. [458]

¶ 2.09 FOUR-STEP ACCOMMODATION PROCESS

Congress, as evidenced by the legislative history, as well as the EEOC's Interpretive Guidelines, suggests a four-step process in determining whether and how a disability may be reasonably accommodated. [459] According to the Report of the House Committee on Education and Labor, a problem approach should be utilized to identify the particular tasks or aspects of the work environment that limit performance and to identify possible accommodations that will result in meaningful equal opportunity. [460]

After a request for accommodation has been made, an indepth interview should be held with the disabled individual. The disabled individual should be encouraged not only to discuss the limitation involved but his own recommendations for accommodations. According to disability rights advocates, most problems can be resolved at this stage by means of candid discussions between the employer and the disabled employee or applicant.

If such informal discussions do not result in a resolution, a more formal analysis is required.

[1] Analysis of Job Tasks

Step 1 involves a determination of the essential and nonessential functions of the job in question and any barriers existing in the work environment. With the assistance of the disabled individual, an analysis should be made of the employee's or applicant's

---

[458] 135 Cong. Rec. S10735 (Sept. 7, 1989) (Comments of Sens. Harkin and Hatch).

[459] S. Comm. on Lab. and Hum. Resources Rep. at 34–35; H. Comm. on Educ. and Lab. Rep. at 65; EEOC Interpretive Guidelines, 56 Fed. Reg. 35,748 (July 26, 1991).

[460] H. Comm. on Educ. and Lab. Rep. at 65.

abilities and limitations. The employer should then identify the job tasks or work environment that limit the individual's effectiveness or prevent performance.

[2] Investigation of Accommodation Methods

In step 2, based on the analysis of step 1, the employer should investigate possible methods of accommodations with the disabled individual and such groups as the State Vocational Rehabilitation Service Agency, local or national organizations representing individuals with the particular handicap, and other employers.

[3] Determination of Whether Undue Hardship Would Result

Once possible accommodations are determined, in step 3, the employer should perform its own internal analysis as to whether the accommodation is reasonable and whether it would result in undue hardship. Larger companies should consider establishing a committee composed of employees from different backgrounds—human resources, financial, production—to make this determination. The disabled employee should be consulted as part of this process. If the company determines that the cost is prohibitive, it should evaluate whether public or charitable support is available or whether tax credits apply. The disabled individual may also be consulted concerning bearing part of the cost if the employer determines that the accommodation would be an undue hardship.

[4] Implementation of Accommodation

Finally, in step 4, the accommodation is implemented. Progress should be closely monitored and internal reports prepared. The individual who established the accommodations pursuant to steps 2 and 3 should evaluate the situation on a monthly basis until both the employee and the employer are comfortable with the result.

For example, an employer has open a sack handler position requiring the employee to pick up fifty-pound sacks and carry them from the company loading dock to the storage room; a sack handler who is disabled by a back impairment requests a reasonable accommodation.

- *Step 1.* Upon receiving the request, the employer analyzes the sack handler job and determines that the essential function and purpose of the job is not the requirement that the job holder physically lift and carry the sacks, but the requirement that the job holder cause the sack to move from the loading dock to the storage room.

- *Step 2.* The employer meets with the sack handler to ascertain precisely the barrier posed by the individual's specific disability to the performance of the job's essential function of relocating sacks. At this meeting, the employer learns that the individual can, in fact, lift the sacks to waist level but is prevented by his disability from carrying the sacks from the loading dock to the storage room. The employer and the individual agree that any of a number of potential accommodations, such as the provision of a dolly, hand truck, or cart, could enable the individual to transport the sacks that he has lifted.

- *Step 3.* Upon further consideration, however, it is determined that the provision of a cart is not a feasible effective option. No carts are currently available at the company, and those that can be purchased by the company are the wrong shape to hold many of the bulky and irregularly shaped sacks that must be moved. Both the dolly and the hand truck, on the other hand, appear to be effective options. Both are readily available to the company, and either will enable the individual to relocate sacks that he has lifted.

- *Step 4.* The sack handler indicates his preference for the dolly. In consideration of this expressed preference, and because the employer feels the dolly will allow the individual to move more sacks at a time and be more efficient than the hand truck, the employer ultimately provides the sack handler with a dolly in fulfillment of the obligation to make reasonable accommodations.

The inclusion in the legislative history of a process for determining whether and how a disability may be reasonably accommodated creates an argument that Congress intended this approach to be a "safe harbor" for employers. If so, an employer who follows in good faith each of the specified four steps should arguably be free from liability.

> **EXAMPLE:** Employee Jayne Jones is disabled and works for Widget, Inc. She applies for a machine operator position she has seen posted on Widget's bulletin board. After reviewing Widget's job description for the machine operation position, Jones informs Widget's Human Resources Department that she cannot perform the functions of the job without some form of accommodation. After meeting with Jones and determining that she is unable to perform an essential function of the position (the operating of the machine itself), Widget contacts JAN and various relevant state agencies to determine whether accommodations are available. These entities are unable to suggest any modifications to Widget's machine that would allow Jones to operate it, although one suggests that Widget could purchase a different type machine that Jones could operate. Human Resources asks Widget's Financial Department to evaluate the feasibility of purchasing the new machine and is told that the cost is prohibitive. There are no tax credits available for the machine, and Jones lacks the resources to help defray the cost. Under these facts, if the recommended process creates a "safe harbor," then Jones cannot prevail in an action against Widget.

While there is no safe harbor under the Rehabilitation Act, cases under that statute suggest that employers following the recommended process are more likely to find their actions upheld.[461]

---

[461] See Solomon v. Secretary, Smithsonian Inst., 50 Fair Empl. Prac. Cas. (BNA) 387 (DDC 1989), in which the U.S. District Court for the District of Columbia rejected an employee's claim that she was denied a promotion because of her stuttering primarily because it was impressed with her supervisor's candor and his "care and sensitivity" in addressing plaintiff's handicap.

¶ 2.10 CRITERIA PROHIBITED TO SCREEN OUT DISABLED

Congress was impressed by extensive testimony that "[e]very government and private study on the issue has shown that employers disfavor hiring persons with disabilities because of stereotypes, discomfort, misconceptions, and unfounded fears of decreased productivity."[462] Witnesses testified that employers often justified their discrimination by reliance on standards, examinations, and tests that unfairly screened the disabled but that, in fact, do not accurately predict a disabled individual's abilities. To counter this situation, Section 102(b)(6) mandates employment selection procedures that ensure that the disabled are not excluded from job opportunities unless they are actually unable to do the essential functions of the job at issue. The provision is applicable to all types of selection criteria, including requirements that an employee not pose a direct threat to self or others, vision or hearing requirements, walking requirements, lifting requirements, or employment tests.[463] The EEOC's proposed regulations under this section also included a requirement that an employee not pose a direct threat to himself or others, but this language was deleted in the final version to clarify that the "direct threat" factor can only be raised as a defense.[464]

Under Section 102(b)(6), a disabled individual cannot be denied employment because of a failure to meet a particular "standard, test, or selection criteria," unless the employer can show that the standard, test, or selection criteria is

- Job-related for the position in question
- Consistent with business necessity
- Cannot be modified to reasonably accommodate the disability in question

Job criteria that violate this three-part test are illegal, even if the employer acts unintentionally.[465]

---

[462] H. Comm. on Educ. and Lab. Rep. at 71.

[463] EEOC Interpretive Guidelines, 56 Fed. Reg. 8600 (Feb. 28, 1991).

[464] 56 Fed. Reg. 35,731 (July 26, 1991).

[465] Id.

[1] Business Necessity Standard

As stated by the EEOC's regulations:

> It is unlawful for a covered entity to use qualification standards, employment tests, or other selection criteria that screen out or tend to screen out an individual with a disability or a class of individuals with disabilities on the basis of disability unless the standard, test or other selection criteria, as used by the covered entity, is shown to be job-related for the position in question and is consistent with business necessity. [466]

The EEOC added the phrase "on the basis of disability" to the final regulations to clarify that a selection criterion that is not job related and consistent with business necessity violates the ADA only when it screens out an individual with a disability (or a class of such persons) on the basis of disability. According to the EEOC, there must be a nexus between the exclusion and the disability. A selection criterion that screens out a disabled individual for reasons not related to the disability does not violate the law. [467]

Business necessity as used in the ADA has the same meaning as the concept of business necessity under Section 504 of the Rehabilitation Act. [468] As discussed previously, this means that the *Griggs* standard of business necessity applies under the ADA and not the more lenient standard set forth by the U.S. Supreme Court in *Wards Cove*. [469] Under the *Griggs* standard, selection criteria may not be used to exclude an individual with a disability if that individual could satisfy the criteria with the provision of a reasonable accommodation, including the adoption of an alternative, less discriminatory criterion. [470]

> EXAMPLE: A person with a disability applies for a job and meets all the selection criteria except one that he cannot

---

[466] EEOC Regs. at 29 CFR § 1630.10.

[467] 56 Fed. Reg. 35,731 (July 26, 1991).

[468] EEOC Interpretive Guidelines, 56 Fed. Reg. 35,749 (July 26, 1991).

[469] See supra ¶ 2.05[4].

[470] EEOC Interpretive Guidelines, 56 Fed. Reg. 35,749 (July 26, 1991).

meet because of a disability. In that situation, the criterion must concern an essential, nonmarginal aspect of the job, be carefully tailored to the job, and be justified by business necessity. If the criterion meets this test, it is nondiscriminatory on its face and is otherwise lawful under the legislation. However, the criterion may not be used to exclude an applicant with a disability if the criterion can be excluded by reasonable accommodation. A reasonable accommodation may entail adopting an alternative, less discriminatory criterion.[471]

According to the EEOC's Interpretive Guidelines, the Uniform Guidelines on Employee Selection Procedures[472] do not apply to the Rehabilitation Act and are similarly inapplicable to the ADA's provisions. The most significant aspect of this rule is that individuals with disabilities do not have to produce the statistical proof required in actions under Title VII of the Civil Rights Act of 1964. On the other hand, it also suggests that employers do not have to produce formal validation studies in order to show business necessity and job relatedness.

EXAMPLE: Midwest Company has a requirement that its loading dock workers be able to lift bags weighing 100 pounds and carry them 50 yards. Sally Smith and John Jones—an individual disabled by a bad back—both apply for a loading dock position and both are rejected when they fail the lifting requirement. If Smith challenged her non-selection alleging sex discrimination under Title VII, she would have to establish the statistical proof of disparate impact on women required by *Wards Cove* and could not allege that there are less restrictive alternatives. On the other hand, if Jones sued under the ADA, he could prevail without introduction of any statistical evidence showing that the requirement had a disparate impact on handicapped individuals. All Jones would need to establish was that there were reasonable accommodations available that

---

[471] S. Comm. on Lab. and Hum. Resources Rep. at 37–38.
[472] 29 CFR pt. 1607; 56 Fed. Reg. 35,749 (July 26, 1991).

would not constitute an undue hardship on Midwestern (e.g., allowing him to use a cart, dolly, or hand truck).

[2] Administration of Tests

In discussing Section 102(b)(6), Congress cited with approval the case of *Stutts v. Freeman*.[473] In that case, the plaintiff was dyslexic. He was denied the job of heavy equipment operator because he could not pass a written test used by the employer for entering a training program, a prerequisite for the job in question. The written test had a disparate impact on persons with dyslexia. The legal issues presented were whether the written test for admission to the training program, and the reading requirements of the training program, were necessary criteria for the heavy equipment operator job. If the answers to both those questions were yes, the question would then become whether a reasonable accommodation could enable the person with a disability to meet the employment criteria at issue.

The record in *Stutts* reflected that the plaintiff could perform the heavy equipment operator position. In fact, the court found that everyone involved in the case conceded that Stutts would have no problem doing the actual job, but that he might experience difficulty with the outside reading requirements of the training program. If selected, Stutts could overcome this obstacle by obtaining the assistance of someone to act as a reader. Therefore, the company failed to comply with the statute by eliminating him without implementing an alternative (oral) test or by failing to adjust the entry requirements to accommodate his dyslexia.[474]

The EEOC's regulation on the administration of tests states as follows:

> It is unlawful for a covered entity to fail to select and administer tests concerning employment in the most effective manner to ensure that, when a test is administered to a job

---

[473] Stutts v. Freeman, 694 F2d 666 (11th Cir. 1983).

[474] Id. at 669, n.3; H. Comm. on Jud. Rep. at 72; S. Comm. on Lab. and Hum. Resources Rep. at 38.

applicant or employee who has a disability that impairs sensory, manual or speaking skills, the test results accurately reflect the skills, aptitude, or whatever other factor of the applicant or employee that the test purports to measure, rather than reflecting the impaired sensory, manual or speaking skills of such employee or applicant [except where such skills are the factors that the test purports to measure].[475]

The intent of this regulation is to "further emphasize that individuals with disabilities are not to be excluded from jobs that they can actually perform because a disability prevents them from taking a test or negatively influences the results of a test."[476] In essence, the regulation provides that an employer must make reasonable accommodations regarding testing as it would any other employment matter.

As with other reasonable accommodations, the employer is not required to give an alternative test where the usual format is designed to measure a skill considered essential for the position. For example, an employer can require that an applicant with dyslexia take a written test for a particular position if the ability to read is essential to the effective performance of the job (e.g., proofreader) and there would be no reasonable accommodation that would allow the applicant to perform the job.[477] Similarly, an employer could require that an applicant complete a test within established time frames if speed were one of the skills being tested.[478] However, as with all such tests, the test results could not be used to exclude disabled individuals unless the skill was necessary to an essential function of the job and no reasonable accommodation was available that would not impose an undue hardship.[479]

The EEOC's Interpretive Guidelines set forth the following examples of accommodations in the contexts:[480]

---

[475] EEOC Regs. at 29 CFR § 1630.11.

[476] EEOC Interpretive Guidelines, 56 Fed. Reg. 35,749–35,750 (July 26, 1991).

[477] 56 Fed. Reg. 35,750 (July 26, 1991).

[478] Id.

[479] Id.

[480] Id.; see also Crane v. Dole, 617 F. Supp. 156 (DDC 1985).

- Giving a written test instead of an oral one if the applicant or employee has a disability that impairs speaking skills or auditory information
- Giving an oral test instead of a written one if the applicant or employee has a disability affecting his ability to read
- Providing a reader or sign interpreter for a disabled applicant or employee
- Giving written tests in large print or braille
- Allowing the disabled individual greater time to take the test

Of course, all examinations must be given in accessible locations or a comparable alternative must be arranged for the disabled individual.

As is generally the case under the ADA, the employer is obligated to make such reasonable accommodations only if it is aware that the employee or applicant is disabled and that the disability impairs sensory, manual, or speaking skills.[481] Similarly, Section 102(b)(6) and the EEOC's proposed regulation do not require the employer to offer the applicant or employee a choice of test formats. Rather, it merely requires the employer to provide, upon request, alternative, accessible tests to a disabled individual needing such an accommodation.

An employer may invite applicants to request accommodations for taking tests and may further request that documentation be provided verifying the need for the accommodation.[482] Generally, the disabled individual should request an alternative testing format or other testing accommodation prior to the administration of the test or as soon as the individual with a disability becomes aware of the need for the accommodation.[483]

[3] Burden of Proof

According to the legislative history, Congress intends that the courts apply the burden of proof in the same manner as federal

---

[481] EEOC Interpretive Guidelines, 56 Fed. Reg. 8600 (Feb. 28, 1991).

[482] 56 Fed. Reg. 35,732, 35,750 (July 26, 1991).

[483] 56 Fed. Reg. 35,750 (July 26, 1991).

agencies have under Section 504 of the Rehabilitation Act.[484] Thus, the burden of proof will be on the employer to show each of the elements required by Section 102(b)(6). For example, Department of Labor Regulation Section 32.14 states that the covered entity has the burden to demonstrate that its job qualifications are job-related and consistent with business necessity.[485]

A question that arises under Section 102(b)(6), as well as Section 102(b)(3), is how an employer will be able to demonstrate the validity of any standard, test, or criteria. Traditional validity studies of the type developed under Title VII of the Civil Rights Act of 1964 and required by the Uniform Guidelines on Employee Selection Procedures are not conclusive under the Rehabilitation Act and, therefore, not likely to be found decisive under the ADA.[486] There is also the difficulty of proving the validity of tests or criteria that relate only to the essential functions of a job rather than to all its components. This suggests that a more flexible approach to proving business necessity (or the lack thereof) will be developed under the ADA as compared to Title VII.

[4] Combination of Tasks

Apart from employment tests, Section 102(b)(6) will apply whenever an employer defines a job in such a way that it has two components, one of which the disabled individual can perform and the other which he cannot. Assuming that both components constitute essential functions of the job as defined, the question becomes whether the combining of the tasks is justified. Since the EEOC's Interpretive Guidelines state that an employer has

---

[484] See, e.g., 45 CFR § 84.13 (Department of Health and Human Services); 29 CFR § 1613.705 (EEOC); 28 CFR § 42.512 (Department of Justice); 29 CFR § 32.14 (Department of Labor).

[485] 29 CFR § 32.14. As to judicial decisions discussing the issue of burden of proof generally, see Prewitt v. US Postal Serv., 662 F2d 292, 307–310 (5th Cir. 1981); Doe v. New York Univ., 666 F2d 761, 776 (2d Cir. 1981); Stutts v. Freeman, 694 F2d 666, 669 (11th Cir. 1983); Bey v. Bolger, 540 F. Supp. 910, 924–925 (ED Pa. 1982).

[486] EEOC Interpretive Guidelines, 56 Fed. Reg. 35,749 (July 26, 1991); see also 45 CFR Subtitle A, App. A, § 17.

no duty to reallocate essential functions, it would appear that combining essential functions in such a way that disabled individuals are excluded, will not violate the ADA absent discriminatory intent. [487]

Section 103(a) of the ADA restates Section 102(b)(6) in the form of a defense, and the two provisions are likely to be construed consistently.

¶ 2.11 DISABLED WORKER'S DIRECT THREAT TO OTHERS

In enacting the ADA, Congress was particularly concerned about the treatment of the disabled who, as a matter of fact or employer prejudice, were believed to be a direct threat to others. To address this issue, Section 103(b) provides that an employer may have a requirement that "an individual not impose a direct threat to the health and safety of other individuals in the workplace." Direct threat, for purposes of Section 103(b), means "a significant risk to the health and safety of others that cannot be eliminated [or reduced] by reasonable accommodation." [488]

The concept behind Section 103(b) stems from the Civil Rights Restoration Act of 1988, [489] the Fair Housing Amendments Act, [490] as well as the Rehabilitation Act as interpreted. It applies to all individuals with disabilities and not simply those with contagious diseases or infections. [491]

In order to meet Section 103(b)'s standard, the employer must prove that the "person poses a significant risk to the safety of others or property, not a speculative or remote risk, and that no reasonable accommodation is available that can remove that risk." [492] The particular aspect of the disability causing the threat

---

[487] 56 Fed. Reg. 35,744 (July 26, 1991).

[488] ADA § 101(3); 29 CFR § 1630.2(r).

[489] Pub. L. No. 100-259, 29 USC § 706(8)(C).

[490] Pub. L. No. 100-430, 42 USC § 3604(f)(9).

[491] H. Comm. on Jud. Rep. at 45.

[492] H. Comm. on Educ. and Lab. Rep. at 56; 29 CFR § 1630.2(r).

must be identified.[493] The burden of proof is not on the applicant or employee to prove that he poses no risk.[494]

As stated in the EEOC's Interpretive Guidelines regarding the "direct threat" regulation:

> [If] an individual poses a direct threat as a result of a disability, the employer must determine whether a reasonable accommodation would either eliminate the risk or reduce it to an acceptable level. If no accommodation exists that would either eliminate the risk or reduce the risk, the employer may refuse to hire an applicant or may discharge an employee who poses a direct threat.[495]

The legislative history to the ADA provides that an employer must make its decision on a case-by-case basis, and not have a general policy barring a particular class of individuals. Congress's intent was that determinations not be based upon "generalizations, misperceptions, ignorance, irrational fears, patronizing attitudes or pernicious mythologies."[496]

Despite this language, an across-the-board rule was found acceptable in limited circumstances under the Rehabilitation Act. For example, in *Davis v. Meese*,[497] the primary issue was whether insulin-dependent persons could not safely perform the essential functions of special agents and investigative specialists, a finding that could justify an across-the-board rule prohibiting such persons from holding these positions.[498] In discussing the propriety of an across-the-board rule, the court held:

---

[493] 56 Fed. Reg. 35,745 (July 26, 1991).

[494] H. Comm. on Jud. Rep. at 46, citing Chalk v. US District Court, 840 F2d 701, 707 (9th Cir. 1988).

[495] 56 Fed. Reg. 35,745 (July 26, 1991).

[496] H. Comm. on Educ. and Lab. Rep. at 56.

[497] Davis v. Meese, 692 F. Supp. 505 (ED Pa. 1988).

[498] The district court found that the only substantial danger of an insulin-dependent diabetic serving as a special agent or investigative specialist would be the danger that such person will have a sudden and unexpected hypoglycemic episode while on an assignment that would render such person temporarily unable to function physically and/or mentally without assistance from some other person or persons. According to the court, such an occurrence could have dire consequences, endangering completion of the assignment, the safety of coworkers, the public, and the diabetic. Id. at 516.

Although blanket exclusions are generally unacceptable, legitimate physical requirements are proper even though such requirements may, in effect, exclude an entire class. If the requirements are directly connected with and substantially promote safety and job performance concerns, then such requirements may be held valid notwithstanding that they effect a group or a class rather than a single individual. [499]

The court concluded that the rule excluding these individuals was justified because there was no method of testing that could reliably determine whether certain individual insulin-dependent diabetics were at little or no risk of a severe hypoglycemic occurrence while on assignment.

A conclusion that an applicant or employee would cause a direct threat to others must be founded on "well-informed judgment grounded in a careful and open-minded weighing of the risks and alternatives." [500] The House Committee on Education and Labor cited with approval *Hall v. U.S. Postal Service,*[501] regarding whether a direct threat exists. There, the court, agreeing also with the Eleventh Circuit, said that while legitimate physical qualifications may be essential to the performance of certain jobs, both that determination and the determination of whether accommodation is possible are fact-specific issues. Therefore, the court said that it was obligated to scrutinize the evidence before determining whether the defendant's justification reflected a well-informed judgment grounded in a careful and open-minded weighing of the risks and alternatives, or whether they were simply conclusory statements that were being used to justify reflexive reactions grounded in ignorance or capitulation to public prejudices.

---

[499] Id. at 517.

[500] Hall v. US Postal Serv., 857 F2d 1073 (6th Cir. 1988), quoting School Bd. of Nassau County v. Arline, 480 US 273 (1987); see also Mantolete v. Bolger, 757 F2d 1416 (9th Cir. 1985); Strathie v. Department of Transp., 716 F2d 227 (3d Cir. 1983).

[501] Hall v. US Postal Serv., 857 F2d 1073 (6th Cir. 1988).

[1] Contagious Diseases

The direct threat language is most important in the area of contagious diseases. In drafting Section 103(b), Congress cited with approval the U.S. Supreme Court's opinion in *School Board of Nassau County v. Arline.*[502]

Arline involved a school teacher who was discharged after contracting tuberculosis. She sued the school authorities, claiming unlawful discrimination under Section 504 of the Rehabilitation Act. The trial court held that although Arline suffered a handicap, she was not a handicapped person within the meaning of the act because it could not "conceive that Congress intended contagious diseases to be included within the definition of a handicapped person."[503] Alternatively, the trial court held that even if Arline fell within the definition, she was not qualified to teach elementary school because of the disability. The Court of Appeals for the Eleventh Circuit reversed, holding that persons with contagious diseases were within the Rehabilitation Act's coverage.

The U.S. Supreme Court granted certiorari and affirmed the court of appeals in an opinion by Justice Brennan. Chief Justice Rehnquist, joined by Justice Scalia, dissented. The Court concluded that "a person who poses a significant risk of communicating an infectious disease to others will not be otherwise qualified for his or her job if reasonable accommodation will eliminate that risk."[504] The Court remanded the case to the district court for a determination on whether such a risk existed. Applying this test on remand, the district court in *Arline* held that the plaintiff was "otherwise qualified" and was entitled to reinstatement and back pay under the Rehabilitation Act.[505]

Under *Arline*, a trial court is required to make findings regarding four factors:[506]

---

[502] School Bd. of Nassau County v. Arline, 480 US 273 (1987).

[503] Id.

[504] Id.

[505] School Bd. of Nassau County v. Arline, 692 F. Supp. 1286 (MD Fla. 1988).

[506] School Bd. of Nassau County v. Arline, 480 US 273 (1987).

- The nature of the risk—how the disease is transmitted
- The duration of the risk—how long the carrier is infectious
- The severity of the risk—what the potential harm is to third parties
- The probabilities the disease will be transmitted and will cause varying degrees of harm

These factors are incorporated into the EEOC's regulations' definition of the direct threat.[507]

Findings on these factors must be based "on reasonable medical judgment given the state of medical knowledge," and the courts are required to give particular deference to the judgment of public health officials.[508]

[2] Special Case of Food Handlers

One of the few issues of contention in the House Senate Conference on the ADA related to food handlers. The House wanted to specify that it would not be a violation of the ADA for an employer to refuse to assign or continue to assign any employee with an infectious or communicable disease of public health significance to a job involving food handling. The only proviso to this rule was that the employer had to offer an alternative employment opportunity for which the employee would sustain no economic damage. No such amendment existed in the Senate bill. A compromise was reached by the House and Senate conferees, so that Section 103(d)(1) of the ADA gives the Secretary of Health and Human Services the authority to publish a list of infectious and communicable diseases transmitted through handling of food.[509] This list is to be updated annually. If an individ-

---

[507] EEOC Regs. at 29 CFR § 1630.2(r); 56 Fed. Reg. 35,745 (July 26, 1991).

[508] Id.; School Bd. of Nassau County v. Arline, 480 US 273 (1987).

[509] There was an unsuccessful effort to expand the list to include diseases that "may be" transmitted by food handling instead of "are" transmitted. See 136 Cong. Rec. S9540–9543 (July 11, 1990) (Comments of Sens. Dole and Helms).

ual has a disease contained on the list, an employer may refuse to assign the individual to a job involving food handling if no other reasonable accommodation exists that would avoid the risks associated with food handling by such individual. Section 103(d)(3) further states that it does not preempt state, county, or local laws applicable to food handling that are designed to protect the public health. [510]

According to the Conference Report, the goal of this provision was to ensure that accurate information is conveyed to the public regarding infectious and communicable diseases. It was the conferees' intent that unsupported fears concerning certain diseases, AIDS in particular, would be diminished by a list based on accepted public health methodologies and statistical practices. The conferees stated that the lack of public awareness regarding which diseases are and which are not transmitted through the handling of food contributes to false impressions on the subject. [511] In addition, by updating the list annually, changes in medical views could be quickly taken into account.

Section 103(d) follows the basic concept of reasonable accommodation as used throughout the ADA.

In the case where an individual has an infectious disease that can be eliminated by taking medication for a specified period, the employer would have to accommodate the individual by offering the time off to take such medication, unless that accommodation would constitute an undue hardship for the employer. On the other hand, if an applicant for employment has a disease contained on the list, and no accommodation is available that would not cause an undue hardship, the employer does not have to hire the applicant. But, if the individual with the disease is an employee, the employer must attempt to reassign him to a non–food-handling position as an accommodation. [512]

A person with a disease contained on the list prepared

---

[510] See EEOC Regs. at 29 CFR § 1630.16(e); EEOC Interpretive Guidelines, 56 Fed. Reg. 35,727, 35,753 (July 26, 1991).

[511] Joint Explanatory Statement of the Committee of Conference at 62.

[512] EEOC Interpretive Guidelines, 56 Fed. Reg. 35,753 (July 26, 1991).

pursuant to Section 103(d) is not necessarily an individual with a disability for purposes of Section 3(2) of the ADA. Therefore, it is possible for an individual to be entitled to the limited protection provided by Section 103(d) regarding a food-handling position but otherwise not entitled to any other safeguards under the ADA. However, the legislative history to the ADA states repeatedly that a person who is HIV-positive–the type of individual that prompted the addition of Section 103 to the ADA—is an individual with a disability.

The anti-preemption language of Section 103(d)(3) requires that the local law meet two conditions. First, the law must be specifically designed to protect the public health or safety of others that cannot be eliminated by reasonable accommodation. This is comparable to the direct threat requirement of Section 103(b). [513] Second, the laws must pertain to the secretary's list of infectious and communicable diseases. [514]

[3] Mental Disabilities

Section 103(b) applies to both physical and mental disabilities that may cause a direct threat to others. However, the legislative history makes clear that when dealing with mental disabilities, the employer must identify the individual's specific behavior that would pose the anticipated threat. [515] The employer cannot rely on generalization relating to the particular mental disability involved. Rather, "there must be objective evidence from the person's behavior that the person has a recent history of overt acts or making threats which caused harm or which directly threatened harm." [516]

---

[513] Joint Explanatory Statement of the Committee of Conference at 63.

[514] Id.; see also 136 Cong. Rec. S9532 et seq. (July 11, 1990) (Comments of Sen. Hatch and others on Food Handling Amendment).

[515] H. Comm. on Educ. and Lab. Rep. at 57; 56 Fed. Reg. 35,745 (July 26, 1991).

[516] H. Comm. on Jud. Rep. at 46. See also Adams v. US General Serv. Admin., 51 Fair Empl. Prac. Cas. (BNA) 647 (DDC 1989), in which the U.S. District Court for the District of Columbia held that a former U.S. General Services Administration employee suffering from "maladaptive reactions to psychological stressor" condition was not otherwise qualified to perform his

An employer would violate the ADA if it discharged (or refused to hire) an individual solely on the basis that such person has mental retardation or has sought treatment for a mental disorder.[517] However, the employer would not violate the ADA by suspending such an employee if the treatment was the direct result of a violent act and the employer has a good faith belief, based on a credible medical basis, that the employee currently poses a direct threat to co-workers or customers.

Section 103(b) cannot be used to circumvent the ADA's prohibition against pre-employment inquiries into a person's disabilities or as a basis for generalized requests for medical records. It is clear that the prohibition against pre-offer medical examinations also applies to psychological exams.[518]

As in other areas of the ADA, the determination of whether a direct threat exists must be based on the current condition of the applicant or employee. The decision to exclude cannot be based on a fear that a direct threat of injury to the applicant, employee, or others may arise in the future.[519]

> EXAMPLE: Applicant Young was hospitalized at one time for violent behavior. His treating physicians have indicated that he is currently fine although there will always be some likelihood of a problem in the future. Congress indicated that it would be a violation of the ADA for the employer not to hire Young, based solely on his prior treatment, even though there is a possibility that he may be a direct threat to others in the future.

A colloquy between Representatives Hoyer and Bartlett, the Democratic and Republican leaders on the legislation in the House, illustrates the interplay between the direct threat provision and the qualification standard.

---

job in spite of his handicap where the employee was unable to refrain from using physical violence on his supervisor.

[517] H. Comm. on Jud. Rep. at 46 n.37.

[518] H. Comm. on Jud. Rep. at 46. See infra ¶ 2.14 for further discussion.

[519] H. Comm. on Jud. Rep. at 46, citing Mantolete v. Bolger, 767 F2d 1416, 1422 (9th Cir. 1985); see also 136 Cong. Rec. H2623 (May 22, 1990) (Comments of Cong. Fish).

BARTLETT: [S]ection 103(b) . . . permits a requirement that an individual with a disability not pose a direct threat to the health and safety of other individuals in the workplace if reasonable accommodation will not eliminate the direct threat. . . . As I understand it, this qualification standard is intended to spell out clearly the right of an employer to take action to protect the right of its employees and other individuals in the workplace, including not assigning an individual to a job if such assignments would pose a direct threat to those individuals. Is my understanding correct?

HOYER: [T]he gentleman's understanding is correct, assuming the employer cannot eliminate the direct threat by making reasonable accommodation.

BARTLETT: [I]t is also my understanding that in determining what constitutes a significant risk, the employer may take into consideration factors such as the magnitude, severity, or likelihood of the risk to other individuals in the workplace, again assuming that such factors could not be eliminated by reasonable accommodation.

HOYER: The gentleman's understanding is correct. Of course, the burden will be on the employer to show the relevance of such factors in relying on the qualification standard.[520]

¶ 2.12 DISABLED WORKER'S DIRECT THREAT TO SELF

The literal language of Section 103(b) indicates that the direct threat must be to other workers and not to the disabled individual himself. This construction is supported by the legislative history's admonition that employers should not act in a paternalistic way towards the disabled.[521] Nevertheless, the EEOC has construed Section 103(b) more broadly.

[1] Equal Employment Opportunity Commission Guidelines

The EEOC's final regulations state that an employer may require, as a qualification standard, that an individual not pose a

---

[520] 136 Cong. Rec. H2428 (May 17, 1990) (Comments by Reps. Bartlett and Hoyer).

[521] H. Comm. on Educ. and Lab. Rep. at 56.

direct threat to his own health or safety. The guidelines further say that if performing the particular functions of a job would result in creating a high probability of imminent substantial harm to the individual, the employer could reject or discharge that individual, unless a reasonable accommodation that would not cause an undue hardship would prevent the harm. [522]

For example, an employer would not be required to hire an individual disabled by narcolepsy, who frequently and unexpectedly loses consciousness, for a carpentry job where essential functions require the use of power saws and other dangerous equipment, and where no accommodation exists that will reduce or eliminate the risk.

There is legislative history in the ADA supporting the EEOC's interpretation. For example, the House Committee on Education and Labor Report states that if a doctor performing a postconditional offer examination were to determine that there was a high probability of substantial harm if the candidate performed the particular functions of the job in question, the applicant could be rejected. [523] However, too broad a reading of such language would undermine the same committee's conclusion that an employer cannot use its paternalistic concerns for the safety of the disabled to disqualify otherwise qualified applicants. [524] Although many disability rights groups challenged the EEOC's definition of direct threat when the proposed regulations were issued, the EEOC refused to delete the direct threat to self component. [525]

As a general rule, where an employer intends to reject an applicant due to an increased risk of injury to himself or others,

---

[522] 29 CFR § 1630.15(b); EEOC Interpretive Guidelines, 56 Fed. Reg. 35,745 (July 26, 1991). The EEOC's Interpretive Guidelines are consistent with regulations and cases under the Rehabilitation Act. 29 CFR § 1613.702(f); see also Dexler v. Tisch, 660 F. Supp. 1418 (D. Conn. 1987); Prewitt v. US Postal Serv., 662 F2d 292, 310 n.25 (5th Cir. 1981); Mantolete v. Bolger, 96 FRD 179 (D. Ariz. 1982).

[523] H. Comm. on Educ. and Lab. Rep. at 73. There is also some indication in the House Committee on Education and Labor Report that a significant risk to property might be sufficient to justify a rejection of an applicant. Id. at 56.

[524] H. Comm. on Educ. and Lab. Rep. at 56.

[525] 56 Fed. Reg. 35,730 (July 26, 1991).

both the risk and the likelihood of imminent harm must be considerable and supported by substantial evidence.[526] As previously stated, such evidence must consist of individualized factual data, rather than stereotypical or patronizing assumptions.[527]

> EXAMPLE: A candidate, undergoing a post-offer, pre-employment medical examination has an abnormality that shows up on an x-ray. While the candidate may not be excluded solely on that basis, if the examining physician concludes that there is a high probability of reasonably imminent harm if the candidate performed the particular functions of the job in question, the employer could reject the candidate. This is so unless the employer could make a reasonable accommodation to the candidate's condition that would avert such harm and such accommodation would not cause an undue hardship.[528]

There are three key points from the legislative history and the EEOC's Interpretive Guidelines[529] that must be stressed regarding the foregoing example:

- An assessment must be made that there exists a high probability of imminent substantial harm, based on valid medical analysis.[530]
- Any determination by a company physician can be challenged by evidence from the complainant's physician — an employer is not shielded from liability merely by a

---

[526] See, e.g., Mantolete v. Bolger, 767 F2d 1416 (9th Cir. 1985); Department of Labor v. Texas Instruments, 47 Fair Empl. Prac. Cas. (BNA) 1573 (OFCCP 1988).

[527] EEOC Interpretive Guidelines, 56 Fed. Reg. 35,745 (July 26, 1991).

[528] H. Comm. on Educ. and Lab. Rep. at 73.

[529] EEOC Interpretive Guidelines, 56 Fed. Reg. 8597 (Feb. 28, 1991).

[530] H. Comm. on Educ. and Lab. Rep. at 73. For example, in Department of Labor, OFCCP v. Texas Indus., Inc., 47 Fair Empl. Prac. Cas. (BNA) 18 (DOL 1988), the Department of Labor held that an employer had violated the Rehabilitation Act by rejecting an applicant for a cement-truck-driving position because of a possibility that she may have a spasm (caused by a problem with her lower back) while driving.

statement from its physician that a threat of imminent, substantial harm exists by hiring an applicant with a particular disability. [531]

- Employment decisions must not be based on paternalistic views about what is best for a person with a disability—a physical or mental employment criterion can be used to disqualify a person with a disability only if it has a direct impact on the ability of the person to do the actual jobs without imminent substantial threat of harm. [532]

[2] Case Law

Bentivenga v. U.S. Department of Labor [533] is cited with approval in the legislative history in support of the proposition that an employer cannot use a generalized fear about risks from the employment environment—such as exacerbation of the disability caused by stress—to disqualify a person with a disability. [534] In *Bentivenga*, the City of Los Angeles had hired the plaintiff as a building repairer, a position for which, as a condition of employment, all applicants had to pass a physical examination. Applicants with diabetes were required to demonstrate "control," meaning blood sugar test results consistently below a certain level. The city determined that the plaintiff could not meet this test, and discharged him.

In evaluating the city's regulation, the court found that, because of the importance of preserving job opportunities for the handicapped, a high standard applies to job qualifications that adversely affect the handicapped. If a job qualification acts to exclude handicapped individuals, it must be directly connected with, and must substantially promote, both business necessity and safe performance. Therefore, the city has the burden of demonstrating that its job qualifications meet this stan-

---

[531] H. Comm. on Educ. and Lab. Rep. at 73–74.

[532] Id. at 74.

[533] Bentivenga v. US Department of Labor, 694 F2d 619 (9th Cir. 1982).

[534] H. Comm. on Educ. and Lab. Rep. at 74.

dard, according to the court.[535] Applying this standard, the court found that the city's evidence was insufficient to prove an increased risk of injury to the plaintiff because of his diabetes or the possibility that he would suffer long-term health problems. Thus, it concluded that the city's rejection of the plaintiff on the basis of the medical examination was unlawful.

In *Chiari v. City of League City*,[536] the court held that the defendant did not violate Section 504 of the Rehabilitation Act when it fired a construction inspector who suffered from Parkinson's disease. Almost a majority of the plaintiff's job tasks in *Chiari* required him to walk around construction sites, climb into buildings under construction, and enter ditches to inspect pipes. After the plaintiff had stumbled on one occasion and fallen on another, the defendant had him examined by two neurosurgeons. Both doctors determined that he was not fit to be an inspector. Based on this conclusion, and an inability to accommodate the employee's condition, the defendant terminated him. In upholding the defendant's action, the court reasoned that a "genuine substantial risk" of injury to oneself is enough to render an employee not otherwise qualified.

Another example of the application of this requirement under the Rehabilitation Act's Office of Federal Contract Compliance Programs (OFCCP) regulations is *OFCCP v. E.E. Black, Ltd.*[537] There, the OFCCP brought an action against an employer who had withdrawn an offer of employment after a medical examination revealed the applicant had a congenital back problem. There was no evidence, however, that the condition would have prevented the individual from performing the job for which he was hired. Under these facts, the employee was found to be handicapped within the meaning of the Rehabilitation Act (as he would be under the ADA) and the employer had violated that statute.

---

[535] Bentivenga v. US Department of Labor, supra note 477, 694 F2d at 622.

[536] Chiari v. City of League City, 920 F2d 311 (5th Cir. 1990).

[537] OFCCP v. EE Black, Ltd., 19 Fair Empl. Prac. Cas. (BNA) 1624 (DOL 1979), aff'd, 23 Fair Empl. Prac. Cas. (BNA) 1254 (D. Haw. 1980).

¶ 2.13 RESTRICTIONS ON EMPLOYER'S USE OF MEDICAL EXAMS, INQUIRIES

Section 102(c)(1) of the ADA provides that the prohibition against discrimination referred to in Section 102(a) includes medical examinations and inquiries. The rest of Section 102(c) defines the scope of this prohibition—regarding pre-offer of employment inquiries, postoffer examinations, and allowable inquiries during the course of employment. Underlying Section 102(c)(1) was Congress's conclusion that information obtained from employment applications and interviews "was often used to exclude individuals with disabilities—particularly those with so-called hidden disabilities such as epilepsy, diabetes, emotional illness, heart disease and cancer—before their ability to perform the job was even evaluated."[538] This provision expanded regulations issued under the Rehabilitation Act relating to pre-employment inquiries.[539]

[1] Pre-Employment Inquiries Prohibited

Section 102(c)(2) generally prohibits pre-employment examinations or inquiries to determine whether such applicant is an individual with a disability or the nature or severity of such a disability.[540]

To ensure that Section 102(c)(2) is not read to prohibit inquiries into an applicant's capabilities to perform the essential aspects of a job, the section also provides that the covered employer may make pre-employment inquiries into the ability of an applicant to perform job-related functions. Therefore, employers remain free to ask questions that relate to the applicant's ability to perform job-related acts, as long as the questions

---

[538] S. Comm. on Lab. and Hum. Resources Rep. at 38; H. Comm. on Jud. Rep. at 42.

[539] See OFCCP Reg., 41 CFR § 60-741.6(c). For a case discussing the application of this regulation, see OFCCP v. EE Black, Ltd., 19 Fair Empl. Prac. Cas. (BNA) 1624 (DOL 1979), aff'd, 23 Fair Empl. Prac. Cas. (BNA) 1254 (D. Haw. 1980).

[540] EEOC Regs. at 29 CFR § 1630.13(a); EEOC Interpretive Guidelines, 56 Fed. Reg. 35,750 (July 26, 1991); H. Comm. on Educ. and Lab. Rep. at 73.

are not phrased in terms of the applicant's disability.[541] In fact, Section 102(c)(4) expressly provides that a covered employer may make inquiries into the ability of an employee to perform job-related functions. Such valid inquiries include:

- For a messenger position—the employer may not ask an applicant if he has any visual disabilities that would limit her capacity to drive, but may, of course, ask the employee if she has a valid driver's license.[542]
- For a construction job—an employer may ask an applicant whether he can climb a scaffolding, but cannot ask if he has any restrictions on his mobility.[543]
- For a manufacturing job—an employer may ask the individual if she will be able to perform the function of assembling small parts.[544]

Under the EEOC's final regulations, an employer "may ask an applicant to describe or to demonstrate how, with or without reasonable accommodation, the applicant will perform job-related functions."[545] However, the employer may not inquire as to the nature or severity of the disability.[546]

EXAMPLE: An employer may ask an individual with one leg who applies for a position as a home washing machine repairman to demonstrate or explain how, with or without reasonable accommodation, he would be able to transport himself and his tools down basement stairs. The employer could not ask the individual how he lost the leg or whether the loss of the leg is indicative of an underlying impairment.[547]

---

[541] H. Comm. on Educ. and Lab. Rep. at 73.

[542] S. Comm. on Lab. and Hum. Resources Rep. at 39; EEOC Interpretive Guidelines, 56 Fed. Reg. 35,750 (July 26, 1991).

[543] See 136 Cong. Rec. H2632 (May 22, 1990) (Comments of Rep. Owens).

[544] EEOC Interpretive Guidelines, 56 Fed. Reg. 35,750 (July 26, 1991).

[545] 29 CFR § 1630.14(a); 56 Fed. Reg. 35,750 (July 26, 1991).

[546] Id.

[547] 56 Fed. Reg. 35,750 (July 26, 1991).

An employer may not, however, use an application form that lists a number of potentially disabling impairments and ask the applicant to check any of the impairments he may have.[548] Nor may an applicant be asked how he became disabled or his prognosis.[549]

Interestingly, the EEOC's Interpretive Guidelines state that while an employer cannot ask how often a disabled individual may require leave for treatment or other reasons, it may state the attendance requirements of the job and inquire whether the applicant can meet them.[550] This language could be read to suggest that an employer could reject a disabled applicant who expresses an inability to satisfy attendance requirements. However, if an employer were to rely on such a basis for rejecting a disabled applicant, it would run the risk of being held liable for failing to attempt to reasonably accommodate the individual by offering a more flexible schedule.

Many employer groups urged the EEOC to allow employers to inquire about an employee's workers' compensation history at the pre-employment stage. They argued that such inquiries were job-related and justified by business necessity. Disability rights groups, on the other hand, argued that any such inquiries would illegally compel the disclosure of disabilities. Based on the comments, the EEOC's final Interpretive Guidelines state that an employer cannot inquire about an individual's workers' compensation history at the pre-offer stage.[551]

Section 102(c)(2) parallels the requirements set forth in the implementing regulations under Section 504 of the Rehabilitation Act.[552] It is more favorable to the disabled than the Rehabilitation Act's protection under Section 503.

One question likely to arise under Section 102(c)(2) is whether an employer is precluded from inquiring into an individual's limitations when the disability is obvious. For example,

---

[548] Id.

[549] Id.

[550] Id.

[551] 56 Fed. Reg. 35,732, 35,750 (July 26, 1991).

[552] H. Comm. on Educ. and Lab. Rep. at 72.

it would seem contrary to the purposes of the ADA if an employer were precluded from initiating a discussion of possible accommodations for a blind applicant or one who uses a wheelchair. An employer should be allowed to make inquiries in such circumstances, and Section 102(c)(2) should be construed only to limit inquiries into nonobvious disabilities.

A number of police and safety-related organizations sought clarification from the EEOC as to whether physical agility tests were precluded pre-offer. The final guidelines state that a physical agility test is not a medical test and may be given at any time in the application or employment process, provided that the test is given to all similarly situated applicants and employees regardless of disability and provided the test meets the other requirements of the ADA, namely, job relatedness and business necessity.[553]

Finally, the final Interpretive Guidelines state that Section 102(c) does not restrict employers from collecting information and inviting individuals to identify themselves as individuals with disabilities as required to satisfy the affirmative action obligation of those entities covered by Section 503 of the Rehabilitation Act.

[2] Limited Exception for Conditional Job Offers

Once a conditional offer of employment has been made, the ADA allows an exception from the prohibition against pre-employment examinations and inquiries. Section 102(c)(3) provides that a covered employer may require a medical examination and/or inquiry after the offer of employment has been made to a job applicant and before the start of employment. The employer may condition an employment offer on the results of such examination, if three requirements are met:[554]

- All entering employees are subject to such an examination, regardless of disability.

---

[553] 56 Fed. Reg. 35,750 (July 26, 1991).

[554] Id. at 73.

- Information obtained regarding the applicant's medical condition or history is collected and maintained on separate forms and in separate medical files and is treated as a confidential medical record.
- The results of such an examination are used only in accordance with the ADA.

The legislative history demonstrates a clear congressional intent that this provision be narrowly construed.[555] The confidentiality requirement of Section 102(c)(3) contains three exceptions that are expressly set forth in the ADA. They parallel regulations issued by the Department of Labor under the Rehabilitation Act.[556] These exceptions provide that:

- Supervisors and managers may be informed regarding the necessary restrictions on the work or duties of the employee and necessary accommodations.
- First aid and safety personnel may be informed, when appropriate, if the disability might require emergency treatment.
- Government officials investigating compliance with the ADA shall be provided relevant information on requests.

Medical information obtained in an examination pursuant to Section 102(c)(3) may also be used by the employer as baseline data to assist the employer in measuring physical changes attributable to on-the-job exposure to potentially hazardous substances.[557]

Consistent with the purpose of the ADA, the results of the postoffer medical examination cannot be used to exclude an individual from an employment opportunity unless (1) the disability is such that the person is no longer qualified to perform the essential functions of the job with or without reasonable accommodation[558] or (2) pursuant to Section 103(b) and the

---

[555] Id.

[556] 41 CFR § 60-741.6(c).

[557] H. Comm. on Educ. and Lab. Rep. at 74.

[558] H. Comm. on Jud. Rep. at 43; S. Comm. on Lab. and Hum. Resources Rep. at 39.

EEOC's regulations under that section, the individual has a currently contagious disease, infection, or other medical condition that poses a direct threat to the health or safety of himself or other individuals in the workplace that cannot be avoided by reasonable accommodation.[559]

According to the EEOC's Interpretive Guidelines, these permitted medical examinations are not required to be job-related and consistent with business necessity. However, should the employer elect not to hire the applicant or take any other adverse action on the basis of the examination, that decision must comply with the ADA.

As stated in the guidelines

> [I]f an employer withdraws an offer of employment because the medical examination reveals that the employee does not satisfy certain employment criteria, either the exclusionary criteria must not screen out or tend to screen out individuals with disabilities, or they must be job related and consistent with business necessity. As part of the showing that an exclusionary criteria is job related and consistent with business necessity, the employer must also demonstrate that there is no reasonable accommodation that will enable the individual with a disability to perform the essential functions of the job.[560]

The EEOC's Interpretive Guidelines contain the following example:

> [A]n employer makes a conditional offer of employment to an applicant, and it is an essential function of the job that the incumbent be available to work every day for the next three months. An employment entrance examination then reveals that the applicant has a disabling impairment that, according to reasonable medical judgment that relies on the most current medical knowledge, will require treatment that will render the applicant unable to work for a portion of the three month period. Under these circumstances, the

---

[559] ADA § 103(b); EEOC Interpretive Guidelines, 56 Fed. Reg. 35,751 (July 26, 1991).

[560] EEOC Interpretive Guidelines, 56 Fed. Reg. 35,751 (July 26, 1991).

employer would be able to withdraw the employment offer without violating the [ADA].[561]

One question that arises is whether the medical examination has to be given to all new employees, as literally required by the ADA, or just to employees desiring the position sought by the disabled individual. For example, if an employer requires warehouse personnel to take postoffer medical examinations but not secretaries, is the ADA violated? The legislative history indicates that medical examinations may be required so long as they are given to all entering employees in a particular category.[562] For example, "an entity can test all police officers rather than all city employees, or all construction workers rather than all construction company employees."[563] Similarly, all entering employees within the same job category must be subject to the examination.[564] Accordingly, despite the breadth of the language of Section 102(c)(3), all employees should be construed to mean all those within a particular category or all similarly situated employees. This is the position adopted by the EEOC.[565]

Another issue that arises under Section 102(c)(3) is whether it applies to all employees or just those with a disability as defined in Section (3)(2) of the ADA. For example, what if an employee has an abnormality in his back that is shown on an x-ray, but the applicant himself is unaware of the condition and has not had his life restricted by it in any way. In such circumstances, an argument could be made that the individual does not have a disability within the meaning of the ADA because the abnormality does not limit one or more of the individual's major life activities.[566] If the individual does not have a disability, he

---

[561] Id.

[562] H. Comm. on Educ. and Lab. Rep. at 73; S. Comm. on Lab. and Hum. Resources Rep. at 39.

[563] Id.

[564] H. Comm. on Jud. Rep. at 43.

[565] EEOC Regs. at 29 CFR § 1630.14(b); EEOC Interpretive Guidelines, 56 Fed. Reg. 35,751 (July 26, 1991).

[566] Most courts under the Rehabilitation Act reasoned that the fact that an applicant was disqualified from a particular job did not constitute a substantial limitation on a major life activity provided that other employment

may not have a cause of action under the ADA because the ADA's general rule is that discrimination is prohibited only against a qualified person with a disability.

Language in the House Committee on Education and Labor Report, however, suggests that the postoffer restrictions on medical examinations would apply regardless of whether the tested individual has a disability within the meaning of Section (3)(2). In discussing the requirement that decisions to reject applicants based upon postoffer exams must be based on valid medical analysis, the committee referred to such back x-rays revealing anomalies in asymptomatic persons as usually having low predictive value. Therefore, employers should be diligent in ensuring that their examining physicians make assessments based on testing measures that actually and reliably predict the substantial, imminent degree of harm required.[567] That the committee indicates that the prohibitions of Section 102(c)(3) apply to asymptomatic conditions suggests that the section prohibits discrimination based on postoffer examinations even if the affected individual is not substantially limited in a major life activity.

The legislative history indicates also that more leeway should be given in pre-employment medical examinations with regard to safety and security-sensitive positions than with other types of employment. The Conference Report states as follows regarding safety and security-sensitive positions:

> [I]n certain industries, such as air transportation, applicants for security and safety related positions are normally chosen on the basis of many competitive factors, some of which are identified as a result of post-offer pre-employment medical examinations. Thus, after the employer receives the results of the post-offer medical examinations for applicants for safety or security sensitive provisions, only those applicants who meet the employer's criteria for the job must receive confirmed offers of employment, so long as the employer does not use the results of the exam to screen out qualified individuals with disabilities on the basis of disability.[568]

---

opportunities were available. See, e.g., Forrisi v. Bowen, 794 F2d 931 (4th Cir. 1986); Tudyman v. United Airlines, 608 F. Supp. 739 (CD Cal. 1984).

[567] H. Comm. on Educ. and Lab. Rep. at 73.

[568] Conference Report at 59.

The conference concluded that limitations on postoffer medical exams should not "override any legitimate medical standards or requirements established by Federal, state or local law, or by employers for applicants for safety or security sensitive positions, if the medical standards are consistent with this Act."[569] The reference to employers suggests that Congress intended that more deference should be given to employers regarding security and safety positions than might be the case under Section 102(c)(3) generally.[570] However, the disabled individual may still challenge the legitimacy of any requirement.[571] Section 102(c)(3) also raises the question of whether an employee or applicant can be excluded when the medical examination reveals that although the individual can currently perform the essential functions of the job, that individual would be unable to do so within a short period. For example, an examining physician might find that the applicant or employee had a degenerative condition that would within a short time preclude working or that the disabled individual's exposure to work conditions would rapidly cause the person's condition to deteriorate. Neither the language of the ADA nor its legislative history provide a clear answer on the issue. However, the ADA's focus on the qualifications of the individual at the time of the job action in question, as well as the emphasis in the legislative history of Section 102(c)(3) on imminent risks, suggests that

---

[569] Id. at 60. For example, in Mahoney v. Ortiz, 645 F. Supp. 22 (SDNY 1986), the U.S. District Court for the Southern District of New York held that a city department of personnel medical standard that required automatic disqualification of any police officer applicant who had suffered two or more dislocations of the same shoulder, regardless of surgical repair, was reasonable and not violative of the Rehabilitation Act.

[570] See Davis v. Meese, 692 F. Supp. 505 (ED Pa. 1988), in which the U.S. District Court for the Eastern District of Pennsylvania upheld a policy of the Federal Bureau of Investigation that precluded insulin-dependent persons from being employed in certain positions.

[571] The House Committee on Education and Labor Report at 74 cites with approval the case of Strathie v. Department of Transp., 716 F2d 227 (3d Cir. 1983), in which the U.S. Court of Appeals for the Third Circuit held that the Department of Transportation's dismissal of a hearing-impaired school bus driver was improper, as the reasons stated in support of its hearing requirement did not advance the essential purpose of the program.

unless the physician concludes that the individual will be unable to work almost immediately, such future problems could not be the basis for an adverse action.

Another area not addressed by the ADA is the need for employers to notify state workers' compensation boards of an employee disability for purposes of ensuring coverage under second-injury funds. These funds typically provide part of the compensation when a disabled or previously injured worker suffers a second injury. However, under the literal language of Section 102(c)(3), the employer could not notify the fund of the results of its examination revealing the initial disability.

The final Interpretive Guidelines state on this point that employees and other covered entities may submit information to state workers' compensation offices or second-injury funds in accordance with state workers' compensation law without violating the ADA. [572]

In addition, the final Interpretive Guidelines state that information obtained from an examination permitted by the ADA may be used for insurance purposes allowed by the ADA. [573]

[3] Examinations During Employment Restricted

Section 102(c)(4)(A) of the ADA prohibits certain examinations and inquiries during the course of employment. The section provides that a covered employer may not require a medical examination and may not make inquiries of an employee as to whether such employee is an individual with a disability or as to the nature or severity of the disability, unless that examination or inquiry is shown to be job-related and consistent with business necessity. [574] The proposed regulations of the EEOC adhere to this language. [575]

Senator Edward Kennedy, a primary sponsor of the legisla-

---

[572] 56 Fed. Reg. 35,751 (July 26, 1991).

[573] Id.

[574] H. Comm. on Jud. Rep. at 43.

[575] EEOC Prop. Regs. at 29 CFR § 1630.13(b).

tion, called Section 102(c)(4)(A) a strict standard.[576] The test is not merely whether there exists a business purpose for the examination or inquiry but "whether the alleged purpose is so essential to the safe and efficient operation of the business as to override any" adverse impact on the disabled.[577] Generally, "necessity connotes an irresistible demand"[578] and a "compelling need . . . to maintain the practice" beyond routine business consideration.[579] Thus, if the legitimate goals of safety and efficiency can be served by reasonably available alternatives to the medical examination or inquiry, with less discriminatory effect, the employer will be required to pursue that option. This will typically place a heavy burden on the employer.[580]

According to the EEOC's Interpretive Guidelines, Section 102(c)(4) permits employers to make inquiries and to require medical examinations—fitness for duty exams—when there is a need to determine whether an employee is still able to perform the essential functions of the job.[581] The EEOC further concluded that this section permits periodic physicals to determine fitness for duty or monitoring if such physicals or monitoring are required by medical standards or requirements established by a federal, state, or local law, provided such laws are consistent with the ADA's requirement of job-relatedness and business necessity.

---

[576] 136 Cong. Rec. S9697 (July 13, 1990) (Comments of Sen. Kennedy). Senator Edward Kennedy was especially interested in the medical examination limitations as it relates to AIDS. The Senator stated:

> Employees on the job also receive significant protection with regard to medical examination. They must be subjected to an examination or inquiry only if such examinations and inquiries are "job related and consistent with business necessity." This is a strict standard. Again, current medical and scientific judgments, including current CDC guidelines, do not call for HIV-testing as necessary for virtually any job in the work force. Again, paid blood and semen donors would be an exception.

Id.

[577] Robinson v. Lorillard Corp., 444 F2d 791 (4th Cir. 1971).

[578] United States v. Bethlehem Steel, 446 F2d 652 (2d Cir. 1971).

[579] Hawkins v. Anheuser-Busch, Inc., 697 F2d 810 (8th Cir. 1983).

[580] See, e.g., Dothard v. Rawlinson, 433 US 321 (1977); Hawkins v. Anheuser-Busch, Inc., 697 F2d 810 (8th Cir. 1983).

[581] EEOC Interpretive Guidelines, 56 Fed. Reg. 35,751 (July 26, 1991).

The legislative history to Section 102(c)(4) demonstrates that Congress was primarily concerned with examinations and inquiries that unfairly stigmatize persons with a disability who are otherwise fully capable of performing the essential functions of their job. For instance, under Section 102(c)(4), it would be illegal for the employer to require an employee who starts to lose a significant amount of hair to be tested for cancer, unless both job-relatedness and business necessity could be shown. [582] This conclusion was premised upon testimony in Congress that there still exists widespread irrational prejudice against persons with cancer and that even though the employer may have no intent to penalize the affected employee, the individual with the disability may legitimately object "to merely being identified, independent of the consequences." [583]

The following list illustrates medical examinations that are acceptable under the ADA:

- Biennial medical examinations of bus and truck drivers that are required by federal safety regulations. [584]
- Examinations in certain industries where employees must possess particular physical qualifications (e.g., pilots may have to meet medical standards established by federal, state, or local law or regulation, or otherwise fulfill requirements for obtaining a medical certificate). [585]
- Medical exams where a particular job function has a direct public safety aspect (e.g., the physical condition of a flight attendant), even if a medical certificate is not required by law. [586]
- Employees exposed to certain toxic and hazardous substances must be medically surveyed at specific intervals (e.g., employees exposed to lead), under several health standards promulgated under the Occupational Safety

---

[582] H. Comm. on Jud. Rep. at 44; H. Comm. on Educ. and Lab. Rep. at 74; S. Comm. on Lab. and Hum. Resources Rep. at 39.

[583] H. Comm. on Educ. and Lab. Rep. at 75.

[584] Id. at 74.

[585] Id.

[586] Id.

and Health Act of 1970,[587] the Federal Coal Mine Health Safety Act of 1979, as amended,[588] and various state laws. Medical examinations may be conducted to determine whether the exposure to such substances has had any negative effect on the employees.[589]

In addition, the EEOC's final Interpretive Guidelines state that employers are permitted to make inquiries and require medical examinations if necessary to the reasonable accommodation process.[590]

However, the mere fact that an employer complies with a safety and health regulation does not mean that the employer is insulated from liability. For example, the House Committee on Education and Labor Report in its discussion of Section 102(C)(4) cited with approval *Strathie v. Department of Transportation.*[591] In that case, the court held that a Department of Transportation's dismissal of a hearing-impaired school bus driver based on a state regulation was improper because the regulation did not advance the essential purpose of the school bus program. The court reasoned that a bus driver who wears a hearing aid does not create any more of an appreciable risk to the safety of passengers than does a driver who wears glasses; therefore, the standard was unenforceable.[592]

[4] Wellness Programs Remain Legal

Many groups active in the legislative process leading to the passage of the ADA were concerned that the ADA could be read to prohibit wellness programs. As a response to these concerns, the ADA was amended expressly to allow for such activity.[593] These programs often include medical screening of such things

---

[587] 29 USC § 655.

[588] 30 USC §§ 801 et seq.

[589] H. Comm. on Educ. and Lab. Rep. at 74.

[590] 56 Fed. Reg. 35,751 (July 26, 1991).

[591] Strathie v. Department of Transp., 716 F2d 227 (3d Cir. 1983).

[592] Id. at 232.

[593] H. Comm. on Jud. Rep. at 43; 136 Cong. Rec. E1915 (June 13, 1990) (Comments of Rep. Hoyer).

as high blood pressure, weight problems, glaucoma, cancer detection, exercise programs, and psychological health. They can also be used to provide treating physicians with x-rays and lab tests that help reduce the cost of medical care.[594]

These activities are acceptable under Section 102(c)(4) as long as the programs are voluntary and the medical records are kept in a confidential manner; they may not be used to limit health insurance eligibility or to prevent occupational advancement.[595] Also, such programs cannot be used to circumvent the prohibition against medical examinations that are not job-related and not consistent with business necessity.[596]

Where practicable, an employer should have such programs run by independent outside parties who are under a contractual obligation not to disclose to the employer any information learned during the process unless the contractor makes a good faith decision that there is an imminent danger to the employer's work force or customers. Disclosures required under Section 102(c)(3) should also be permissible.

[5]　Voluntary Self-Identification of the Disabled

The legislative history to Section 102 indicates a congressional intent not to prohibit employers from inviting disabled applicants to identify themselves voluntarily if the employer's purpose is to further employment opportunities for the disabled.[597]

Thus, consistent with the regulations implementing the Rehabilitation Act, employers may solicit indications from applicants as to whether and to what degree a disability exists, under any of the following limited circumstances:[598]

---

[594] EEOC Prop. Regs. at 29 CFR § 1630.14(c); H. Comm. on Jud. Rep. at 44.

[595] H. Comm. on Educ. and Lab. Rep. at 75.

[596] H. Comm. on Jud. Rep. at 44.

[597] H. Comm. on Educ. and Lab. Rep. at 75; H. Comm. on Jud. Rep. at 44; S. Comm. on Lab. and Hum. Resources Rep. at 40.

[598] Id.

- When the employer is taking remedial action to correct the past effects of past discrimination against the disabled
- When the employer is taking voluntary action to overcome the effects of conditions that resulted in limited employment opportunities for persons with disabilities
- When the employer is taking affirmative action required by Section 503 of the Rehabilitation Act

If an employer seeks information under these circumstances, Section 102 will not be violated, provided that the employer takes the following two steps:[599]

- The employer must state clearly on any written questionnaire used to solicit the information or make clear orally (if no written questionnaire is used) that the information requested is intended for use solely in connection with its remedial action obligations or its voluntary or affirmative action efforts.
- The employer must clearly communicate to the applicants and employees from whom the information is sought that the information is being requested on a voluntary basis, that it will be kept confidential, that refusal to provide the information will not subject the applicant or employee to any adverse treatment, and that the information will not be used in any manner inconsistent with the requirements of the ADA.

¶ 2.14 ILLEGAL DRUG OR ALCOHOL USE

One of the longest sections of Title I of the ADA is Section 104 on the illegal use of drugs and alcohol. Sections 104(a) and 104(b) address the issue of how current and former drug abusers are to be regarded with respect to the term "individual with a disability." Sections 104(c) and 104(d) discuss the use of drug testing at the workplace in relationship to Section 103's restrictions on examinations and inquiries. Finally, Section 104(e) concerns the relationship between the ADA and Department of Transportation drug-testing requirements.

---

[599] H. Comm. on Educ. and Lab. Rep. at 75–76; H. Comm. on Jud. Rep. at 44; S. Comm. on Lab. and Hum. Resources Rep. at 40.

[1] Current vs. Former Drug Users

Section 104(a) of the ADA states that, for purposes of Title I of the ADA, the term "qualified individual with a disability" does not include any employee or applicant who currently engages in the illegal use of drugs, when the covered employer acts based on such use.

The terms "illegal use of drugs" and "drugs" are defined in Section 101(6) of the ADA as follows:

(A) In general—The term "illegal use of drugs" means the use of drugs, the possession of which is unlawful under the Controlled Substances Act (21 U.S.C. 812). Such term does not include the use of a drug taken under the supervision by a licensed health care professional, or other uses authorized by the Controlled Substances Act or other provisions of Federal law.

(B) Drugs—The term "drug" means a controlled substance, as defined in schedules I through V of section 202 of the Controlled Substances Act.

This language is incorporated into the EEOC's regulations.[600]

The basic principle of Section 104(a) is that a person who is currently using an illegal substance under federal law is not disabled within the meaning of the ADA and, therefore, may be denied employment opportunities on the basis of such drug use.[601]

Section 104(a) is virtually identical to Section 510(a) of the ADA, which states that: "For purposes of this Act, the term 'individual with a disability' does not include an individual who is currently engaged in illegal use of drugs, when the covered entity acts on the basis of such use." The two sections are to be construed in a consistent fashion.[602]

Referring to the actions of the covered employer, Section

---

[600] EEOC Regs. at 29 CFR § 1630.3(a).

[601] EEOC Regs. at 29 CFR § 1630.16(b); EEOC Interpretive Guidelines, 56 Fed. Reg. 35,745–35,746 (July 26, 1991); H. Comm. on Educ. and Lab. Rep. at 77.

[602] H. Comm. on Jud. Rep. at 47.

104(a) makes clear that if an adverse action is taken against a current user of illegal drugs who is otherwise disabled, to the extent the adverse action is taken on the basis of the disability still covered by the ADA, the covered employer must comply with the ADA and may not unjustly discriminate.[603]

The comments of Senator Harkin, a leader in the Senate's passage of the ADA, further explains the purpose of Section 104(a)'s language that prohibits an employer from discriminating on the basis of disability, even if the applicant or employee also happens to be a drug user:

> Of course, if the [employer's] action were taken on the basis of the current use of illegal drugs, the disabled person would not have special protection simply by virtue of his or her disability. In other words, current users of illegal drugs, disabled or not, are not protected by this act from actions based on their current use of illegal drugs. At the same time, the fact that a disabled person is a current user of illegal drugs does not mean that the person is not protected under the act when actions are taken against that individual, not on the basis of the current use of illegal drugs, but on the basis of the disability.[604]

The Conference Report's discussion of Section 104(a) indi-

---

[603] H. Comm. on Educ. and Lab. Rep. at 77. As stated by Senator Harkin:

That agreement . . . reflected in a new section 104 dealing with drugs and alcohol . . . was offered as an amendment on the floor. As originally drafted, subsection (a) of that section read, "For purposes of this title, the term 'qualified individual with a disability' shall not include any employee or applicant who is a current user of illegal drugs when the covered entity acts on the basis of such use." The last phrase of the subsection was added to make clear that if the covered entity discriminated against a person on the basis of a disability covered under this act, not on the basis of current use of illegal drugs, that action is still prohibited.

135 Cong. Rec. S11224–11225 (Sept. 15, 1989).

[604] Id. (Statement by Sen. Tom Harkin). Senator Harkin's statement was in the context of clarifying that while there had been multiple amendments to Section 104(a) on the issue of disabled individuals who were also current drug users, the original amendment and the subsequent amendments had the same meaning and intent. The original amendment was actually used in the final version of the ADA.

cates that it was Congress's intent that employers be free to discharge or deny employment opportunities to persons who illegally use drugs without fear of being held liable for discrimination. It is important to note that there does not have to be any connection between the illegal drug use and deficient work performance.

As set forth in the Conference Report, the critical inquiry is whether the test shows a reasonable likelihood of current drug use:

> The provision is not intended to be limited to persons who use drugs on the day of, or within a matter of days or weeks before, the employment action in question. Rather, the provision is intended to apply to a person whose illegal use of drugs occurred recently enough to justify a reasonable belief that a person's drug use is current.[605]

The EEOC's Interpretive Guidelines state that the term "currently engaging" is not intended to be limited to the use of drugs on the day of or within a matter of days or weeks before the employment action in question.[606]

The language used in both the Conference Report and the EEOC guidelines clearly expresses an intent that an employer may refuse to hire an individual who has used drugs during a period prior to the employment action in question. However, when prior use is too long ago to be considered current is left unanswered by the ADA, its legislative history, and the EEOC. For example, what if an applicant fails the employer's drug test and a short period later requests retesting and passes? The legislative history leaves open the question of whether the passing of the second test negates a finding of current use. Such cases will have to be decided on a case-by-case basis, with the employer evaluating all the facts and circumstances to indicate whether the second test shows that the individual is no longer a current drug user.

The issue of when drug use is no longer current is particu-

---

[605] Conference Report at 64.

[606] 56 Fed. Reg. 35,746 (July 26, 1991).

larly important in the case of an employee who voluntarily notifies his employer that he has in the recent past used illegal drugs but is no longer doing so and has enrolled in a rehabilitation program. Since one of the purposes of Section 104 is to provide an incentive for persons with a drug problem to seek treatment, the legislative history to the ADA suggests that an employee should be protected under such circumstances even if drug testing reveals the presence of illegal drugs taken prior to the employee's entry into the rehabilitation program.[607] This result is also suggested by Section 104(b)(ii), which states that a person participating in a rehabilitation program and no longer using illegal drugs is entitled to the ADA's protection. Although the ADA does not define what a rehabilitation program is, the EEOC's Interpretive Guidelines state that term includes both in-patient and out-patient programs, as well as other employee assistance programs that provide professional assistance and counseling for persons who illegally use drugs.[608] The final Interpretive Guidelines added to this list the term "professionally recognized self-help programs."[609]

An individual cannot demonstrate that he is no longer a current illegal drug user simply by showing treatment in a rehabilitation program. The burden of proof is on the individual to offer evidence, such as drug test results, indicating that there is no current use of illegal drugs if the employer requests such proof.[610]

The legislative history fails to address adequately the issue of whether an employer can consider the applicant's or employee's likelihood of recidivism in determining whether the individual is a current drug user. This fact is arguably relevant to determining the reasonableness of an employer's determination that the employee or applicant is a current user. However, there was an effort in the House to add a provision to Section 104 that would have expressly allowed employers to consider an individ-

---

[607] H. Comm. on Educ. and Lab. Rep. at 77, 80; 136 Cong. Rec. H2443 (May 17, 1990) (Comments by Rep. Rangel).

[608] EEOC Interpretive Guidelines, 56 Fed. Reg. 35,746 (July 26, 1991).

[609] 56 Fed. Reg. 35,730, 35,746 (July 26, 1991).

[610] Id.

ual's former drug use in making employment decisions. This provision, which was rejected, would have provided that

> [an employer] may take into consideration an individual's history of drug addiction or alcoholism, the period of time the individual has been free of drugs or alcohol, and whether the individual has successfully completed treatment for such condition before assigning or continuing to assign such individual to safety sensitive positions.[611]

Opponents of this amendment successfully argued that the concerns underlying the measure were addressed by the ADA's direct threat provision[612] and that the amendment was contrary to the ADA's intent to protect individuals who have overcome their disabilities.[613]

[a] Limited Protection of Former Drug Abusers

Section 104(b) extends the protection of the ADA to rehabilitated drug abusers. The section states that a qualified individual with a disability cannot be excluded who:

- Has successfully completed a supervised drug rehabilitation program and is no longer engaging in the illegal use of drugs, or has otherwise been rehabilitated successfully and is no longer engaging in such use
- Is participating in a supervised rehabilitation program and is no longer engaging in such use
- Is erroneously regarded as engaging in such use, but is not engaging in such use

However, it is not violation of the ADA for a covered employer to adopt or administer reasonable policies or procedures, including but not limited to drug testing, designed to ensure that an individual is no longer engaging in the illegal use of drugs. This section is virtually identical to Section 510(b) of the ADA, and

---

[611] 136 Cong. Rec. H2636 (May 22, 1990) (Motion by Rep. DeLay).

[612] 136 Cong. Rec. H2637 (May 22, 1990) (Comments by Rep. Edwards).

[613] Id. (Comments by Rep. Hoyer).

the two sections are to be construed consistently.[614]

To be afforded the ADA's protection, the employee must do more than just demonstrate participation in a drug treatment program. As is spelled out in each of the three parts under Section 104(b), the employee must not be currently using an illegal drug. To support this condition, employers are expressly permitted to conduct drug tests or take reasonable actions to ensure that an individual is no longer using illegal drugs. This right is spelled out more specifically in Section 104(d), which entitles employers to seek reasonable assurances that no illegal use is occurring or has occurred recently enough so that continuing use is a real and ongoing problem.[615]

Congress recognized that many people continue to participate in drug treatment programs long after they have stopped using illegal drugs. It concluded that these persons should be allowed the protection of the ADA. Thus, the reference to those employees who have otherwise been successfully rehabilitated is to be interpreted to include participation in in-patient or out-patient programs, as well as appropriate employee assistance programs that provide professional (not necessarily medical) assistance and counseling.[616]

Section 104(b) was deemed necessary once Congress removed current drug use from the definition of a disability.[617] Under the standard Rehabilitation Act analysis, an individual with a past or perceived disability is protected only if the actual physical or mental condition at issue is itself a disability. Since the condition of drug use is no longer a disability within the meaning of Section 3(2) of the ADA, it was necessary to provide the express protection set forth in Section 104(b).[618]

Curiously, Congress felt it necessary also to find that, as with all other disabilities, such individuals must prove that they are disabled, have a record of a disability, or are regarded as

---

[614] H. Comm. on Jud. Rep. at 47.

[615] Conference Report at 64.

[616] Id.

[617] H. Comm. on Educ. and Lab. Rep. at 77.

[618] Id.

having a disability, defined under Section 504 of the Rehabilitation Act and the ADA (i.e., a physical or mental impairment that substantially limits a major life activity).[619] This language suggests that an employer may be able to refuse to offer a position to a former drug abuser whose use neither substantially limited his life nor caused him to be regarded as having such a limitation.

> EXAMPLE: Applicant Jones occasionally smoked marijuana in social settings without any impact on his career. If Jones's prospective employer can demonstrate that Jones was not substantially limited in a major life activity because of such drug use, and that such a social user is not typically regarded as disabled, the employer may legitimately discriminate against the individual under the literal interpretation of the legislative history. On the other hand, if Jones had been addicted to heroin, the prospective employer could not discriminate, since that drug use likely caused a substantial limitation on a major activity of Jones's life.

A conflict might arise between Section 104(b)(2) and Section 104(a) when an employee or applicant informs his employer that he is participating in a supervised rehabilitation program and is no longer engaging in drug use but, in fact, a drug test reveals the presence of an illegal substance taken prior to the rehabilitation effort. Under such circumstances, the legislative history would support an argument that the employee could be terminated, despite his entry into the rehabilitation program.[620]

[b] Employer Actions to Combat Drug Use

Section 104(c) of the ADA sets forth procedures that an employer may implement to ensure a drug-free workplace. That section lists four employer actions that apply to all employers, regardless of whether they are subject to specific federal regulations. The employer may:

- Prohibit the illegal use of drugs and alcohol at the workplace by all employees

---

[619] Id.

[620] Id.

- Require that employees shall not be under the influence of alcohol or be engaging in the illegal use of drugs at the workplace
- Require that employees behave in conformance with the requirements established under the Drug-Free Workplace Act of 1988[621]
- Hold an employee who engages in the illegal use of drugs or who is an alcoholic to the same qualification standards for employment or job performance and behavior that such entity holds all of its other employees, even if unsatisfactory performance or behavior is related to the drug use or alcoholism of such employee

Out of concern for the need to test individuals in the transportation industry, Section 104(e) of the ADA provides that

Nothing in this title shall be construed to encourage, prohibit, restrict or authorize the lawful exercise by entities subject to the jurisdiction of the Department of Transportation of authority to—

(1) test employees of such entities in, and applicants for, positions involving safety-sensitive duties for the illegal use of drugs and for on-duty impairment by alcohol; and

(2) remove such persons who test positive for illegal use of drugs or on-duty impairment by alcohol pursuant to paragraph (1) from safety-sensitive duties in implementing subsection (c) [of Section 104].

The EEOC regulations adopt this language.[622]

The House Committee on Education and Labor clarified the purpose of Section 104(e) by stressing three points in its report.

First, the committee expressed its approval of the current practice of considering alcohol and drug-related driving convictions (as recorded by the individual states and made available to employers through the National Drivers Register at the Depart-

---

[621] 41 USC 701 et seq.

[622] EEOC Regs. at 29 CFR §§ 1630.16(b), 1630.16(c).

ment of Transportation) for the licensing of motor carrier drivers and railroad engineers, and the certification of airline pilots.[623] The committee also stated its conclusion that violation of state or federal drug and alcohol laws may be considered as indicators of fitness for duty for safety-sensitive transportation positions.[624]

Second, the committee stated that Section 104(e) could be used as a defense by an employer where disciplinary action is taken against an employee for drug or alcohol use away from the workplace (e.g., an air crew member who, in violation of Federal Aviation Administration rules, drinks alcohol within eight hours of going on duty).

Finally, the committee reasoned that Section 104(e) should be available to an employer who takes disciplinary action against an employee who fails a drug or alcohol test administered in accordance with federal and state laws (e.g., the suspension of a truck driver who tests positive for illegal drugs or who refuses to take a drug test mandated by the Department of Transportation).[625]

During the course of the House consideration on Section 104(e), it was determined that the same principles should be applied in other areas and expanded in the transportation context. Thus, Section 104(c)(5) was added to apply to employers subject to federal regulations, including

- Department of Defense regulations
- Nuclear Regulatory Commission regulations
- Department of Transportation regulations

Under Section 104(c)(5), a person who tests positive on an employment-related drug test conducted and verified in conformity with federal regulations or guidelines is deemed to be currently engaging in illegal use of drugs and may not invoke the ADA's protections (subject to the employee's right to show that he is being erroneously regarded as engaging in such use as

---

[623] H. Comm. on Educ. and Lab. Rep. at 78.

[624] Id.

[625] Id.

provided in Section 104(b)(3)). [626] By implication, the same rule should apply in determining whether an employee is a current user of drugs for purposes of Section 104, in general.

[2] Current Alcohol Use

Regarding alcoholics, Congress addressed the issue by amending the Rehabilitation Act to make it consistent with the ADA. Section 512(a) of the ADA adds the following to the Rehabilitation Act:

> For purposes of Section 503 and 504 as such sections relate to employment, the term "individual with handicaps" does not include any individual who is an alcoholic whose current use of alcohol prevents such individual from performing the duties of the job in question or whose employment, by reason of such current alcohol abuse, would constitute a direct threat to property or safety of others. [627]

This rule will be applied under the ADA and, in fact, merely restates the law as existing under the Rehabilitation Act. [628]

¶ 2.15 DISCRIMINATION PROHIBITED IN GIVING DISABLED HEALTH INSURANCE

The ADA prohibits the denial of health insurance coverage to an individual based solely on that person's disability. In addition,

---

[626] Conference Report at 64–65 ("[t]he conferees intend that the authority for transportation entities to remove persons who test positive includes authority for dismissal or disqualification, consistent with the provisions of this title. The conferees do not intend to prevent individuals covered by the employment provisions of the Act, from challenging a positive test by invoking the protection of section 104(b)(3)").

[627] ADA § 512(a). Even without this amendment, Section 7(7) of the Rehabilitation Act had similar language relating to alcoholics. 29 USC § 706(b).

[628] See Garrison v. District of Columbia, 51 Fair Empl. Prac. Cas. (BNA) 94 (DDC 1989), in which the U.S. District Court for the District of Columbia held that an alcoholic government employee is not "otherwise qualified," and thus may not claim protection under the Rehabilitation Act.

an employer cannot deny a qualified applicant a job because the employer's current insurance plan does not cover the person's disability or because of the increased cost of purchasing insurance that would cover such person.[629]

As stated by Senator Edward Kennedy

> An employer may not refuse to hire an applicant because of a feared increase in insurance costs. This is necessary because otherwise a huge loophole would be created in the employment protections of the ADA. It can certainly be anticipated that people with disabilities will incur some higher health costs than those without disabilities. If that could be used as a justification for employment discrimination, however, the employment protections of the ADA would, in practice, be more theory than reality.[630]

All people with disabilities must have equal access to the health insurance coverage that the employer provides to all other employees. In other words, an employee with a disability must receive health insurance if the employer is offering health insurance to other employees.[631]

Similarly, any limitations in insurance coverage must be limitations that are placed on all employees equally.[632]

[1] No Special Treatment Required

The ADA does not require, however, special treatment for persons with a disability. Accordingly, it is permissible for an employer to offer insurance policies that limit coverage for certain procedures or treatments even though this might have a disparate impact upon certain disabled individuals.[633]

---

[629] H. Comm. on Educ. and Lab. Rep. at 136.

[630] 136 Cong. Rec. S9697 (July 13, 1990) (Comments of Sen. Kennedy).

[631] EEOC Interpretive Guidelines, 56 Fed. Reg. 8597 (Feb. 28, 1991); H. Comm. on Educ. and Lab. Rep. at 136; S. Comm. on Lab. and Hum. Resources Rep. at 85; 136 Cong. Rec. S9697 (July 13, 1990) (Comments of Sen. Kennedy).

[632] 136 Cong. Rec. H2632 (May 22, 1990) (Comments of Rep. Owens).

[633] H. Comm. on Educ. and Lab. Rep. at 59. See also supra ¶ 2.05[4].

As the House Committee on Education and Labor stated regarding employee benefits in general

[T]he Committee wants to clarify that in its view, as is stated by the Supreme Court in *Alexander v. Choate*, 469 U.S. 287 (1985), employee benefit plans should not be found to be in violation of this legislation under a disparate impact analysis simply because they do not address the special needs of every person with a disability, e.g., additional sick leave or medical coverage.[634]

This principle was echoed by the EEOC's Interpretive Guidelines, which state that activities permitted by Section 501 do not violate the EEOC's regulations—even if they result in limitations on individuals with disabilities—provided that these activities are not used as a subterfuge to evade the purposes of these regulations.[635]

For example, an employer may have coverage that limits the number of blood transfusions per employee per year without violating the ADA; however, an employee who is a hemophiliac and who has exceeded this limit may not be denied coverage for other conditions, such as a broken leg or heart surgery, merely because of the existence of hemophilia. Or, a limitation may be placed on the number of x-rays or certain categories of drugs without violating the ADA so long as the limitation applies to disabled and nondisabled employees alike.

The EEOC's Interpretive Guidelines give the following example:

[A]n employer that reduces the number of paid sick leave that it will provide to all employees, or reduces the amount of medical insurance coverage that it will provide to all employees, is not in violation of the [EEOC's] regulations, even if the benefits reduction has an impact on employees with disabilities in need of greater sick leave and medical coverage.[636]

---

[634] H. Comm. on Educ. and Lab. Rep. at 137.

[635] EEOC Interpretive Guidelines, 56 Fed. Reg. 35,753 (July 26, 1991).

[636] EEOC Interpretive Guidelines, 56 Fed. Reg. 35,746 (July 26, 1991).

[2] Preexisting Condition Clauses Allowed

The ADA does not prohibit preexisting condition clauses included in insurance policies offered by employers.[637] Employers may continue to offer insurance containing such clauses, even though the exclusion adversely affects people with disabilities, so long as such clauses are not used as a subterfuge to evade the purposes of the legislation.[638]

The insurance and employee benefits industries played an active role in the debate on the ADA. As a result, Section 501(c) was added to the ADA to define the impact of the ADA on insurance. This section establishes that the ADA is not to interfere with the right of insurers and employers to design and administer insurance products and benefit plans, provided that such products and plans are based upon established principles of insurance risk classification. Thus, under Section 501(c), insurers and employers may continue the practices they followed prior to the ADA's enactment, provided that such practices are in accordance with accepted principles of insurance risk classification. However, where the insurance of persons with disabilities is not based upon bona fide risk classification, the ADA remains applicable.[639] Moreover, Section 501 does not apply to those entities that establish, sponsor, observe, or administer plans not involving benefits, such as liability insurance plans.

Section 501(c)(1) provides that nothing in the legislation is to be construed to prohibit or restrict "an insurer, hospital or medical service company, health maintenance organization, or any agent, or entity that administers benefit plans, or similar organizations from underwriting risks, or administering such risks that are based on or not inconsistent with State law." The purpose of this provision was to make clear that insurers may continue to sell and underwrite life, health, and other insurance on an individually underwritten basis and that other entities can continue to service such insurance.[640]

---

[637] Id.

[638] H. Comm. on Educ. and Lab. Rep. at 59, 137.

[639] Id. at 138.

[640] Id. at 137.

Section 501(c)(2) states that nothing in the legislation is to be construed to prohibit or restrict "a person or organization covered by this Act from establishing, sponsoring, observing or administering the terms of a bona fide benefit plan that are based on underwriting risks, classifying risks, or administering such risks that are based on or not inconsistent with State law." According to the House Committee on Education and Labor, this provision recognizes the need for employers and their agents to establish and observe the terms of employee benefit plans, so long as these plans are based on underwriting classification of risks.[641]

There was some concern expressed that Sections 501(c)(1) and 501(c)(2) could be read to affect the preemption of state insurance laws on employee benefit plans by the Employee Retirement Income Security Act (ERISA). To answer these concerns, Section 501(c)(3) was added to the ADA, providing that nothing in the legislation is to be construed to prohibit or restrict "a person or organization covered by this Act from establishing, sponsoring, observing or administering the terms of a bona fide benefit plan that is not subject to State laws that regulate insurance." This provision merely clarifies that self-insured plans currently protected from state law by ERISA's preemption provisions remain exempt from state insurance laws.[642]

[3] Benefit Plans Cannot Be Used as Subterfuge to Evade the ADA

The breadth of Sections 501(c)(1), 501(c)(2), and 501(c)(3) is limited by a final clause in Section 501(c) providing that the rights granted insurers and employers in those three paragraphs are not to be used as a subterfuge to evade the purposes of Titles I and III. Language in Section 501 stating that reliance on sound actuarial principles or experience shall not be used as a subterfuge to evade the purposes of Titles I and III is not helpful, because no definition of actuarial principles is contained in the

---

[641] Id.

[642] Id. at 136.

ADA's legislative history.[643] Also, subterfuge is not defined in the statute or its legislative history.

Congress's use of the subterfuge language is potentially significant in two respects. First, the U.S. Supreme Court ruled in *Public Employees Retirement System of Ohio v. Betts*[644] that benefit plans in existence before the passage of the ADEA could not be a subterfuge to evade the purpose of that legislation.

In *Betts*, the Court considered whether an employee benefit plan that limited disability benefits to those under the age of 60 constituted a subterfuge to evade the purposes of the ADEA.[645] The Court held that a benefit plan adopted prior to the enactment of the ADA could not be a subterfuge to evade the purposes of the ADEA.

Although Congress overruled *Betts* in the Older Workers Benefit Protection Act (OWBPA), it did so in part by removing from the ADEA the word "subterfuge." Since subterfuge remains in Section 501(c) of the ADA, employers may contend that the rationale announced in *Betts* applies and that pre-ADA benefit plans cannot be challenged as a subterfuge.

However, despite the ADA's use of the subterfuge language, Congress's rejection of the U.S. Supreme Court's interpretation of that term in the OWBPA suggests that the courts should not exempt pre-ADA plans from scrutiny. This conclusion is supported by the legislative history, which states that the subterfuge language applies "regardless of the date the insurance plan or employer benefit plan was adopted."[646] The EEOC has adopted this approach in its Interpretive Guidelines.[647]

Second, the language of Section 501(c)(3) raises the question of what constitutes a subterfuge in general. For example, if

---

[643] ADA § 501(c).

[644] See Public Employees Retirement Sys. of Ohio v. Betts, 109 S. Ct. 2854 (1989), 50 Fair Empl. Prac. Cas. (BNA) 104 (US 1989); see also McMann v. United Air Lines, Inc., 434 US 192 (1977).

[645] 29 USC § 623 (1988).

[646] H. Comm. on Educ. and Lab. Rep. at 137; S. Comm. on Lab. and Hum. Resources Rep. at 85.

[647] EEOC Interpretive Guidelines, 56 Fed. Reg. 35,753 (July 26, 1991).

an employer's decision to limit coverage is based on good faith assumptions unrelated to the disabled, is the plan protected by Section 501(c)(3) if it meets the other requirements of the section?[648] In *Betts*, the U.S. Supreme Court held that in order for a benefit plan to be found to be a subterfuge for evading the ADEA, the plaintiff must demonstrate that the plan was adopted for the purpose of discriminating against older workers with respect to some aspect of the employee's employment, independent of the challenged benefit program.[649] Because Congress was aware of this definition of subterfuge at the time of the passage of the ADA, the *Betts* definition is arguably appropriate in this context; therefore, an actuarially based plan should be protected under Section 501(c) absent proof of intent to discriminate against the disabled and discriminatory effect.

Another possible definition of subterfuge can be derived from the legislative history's endorsement of *Alexander v. Choate*.[650] That case suggests that a plan will be upheld unless it will deprive a disabled individual of any meaningful participation in the program. Thus, under *Choate*, a plan could be upheld provided that the disabled individual receives some benefit from the plan and there is no evidence of intentional discrimination.

In addition to confusion over the ADA's subterfuge language, the legislative history also fails to address clearly how the interplay among the various rules relating to insurance and the duty to reasonably accommodate will actually work in practice.

---

[648] See McGann v. H&H Music Co., 742 F. Supp. 392 (SD Tex. 1990). An argument could be made that a plan is not protected where it is based on stereotypes regarding the disabled. Support for this position can be found in the legislative history to the OWBPA that suggests that early retirement benefit plans that are based on certain stereotypical assumptions concerning older workers may be illegal. See "Final Substitute Statement of the Managers" of S. 1511. However, if the "stereotypical assumptions" are actuarially based, Section 501(c)'s protection would appear to be available.

[649] See also EEOC v. Westinghouse, 53 Fair Empl. Prac. Cas. (BNA) 493 (3d Cir. 1990); Mitchell v. Mobil Oil Corp., 896 F2d 463, 471 n.3 (10th Cir. 1990); Garbarczyk v. Board of Educ., 53 Fair Empl. Prac. Cas. (BNA) 843 (SDNY 1990).

[650] Alexander v. Choate, 469 US 287 (1985).

However, the legislative history indicates that the following results are intended:

> **EXAMPLE:** Eastern Company's insurance plan excludes coverage for employees with major back injuries. Applicant Young has such a back injury and, therefore, would not be available for health insurance under Eastern's policy if he were hired. Eastern would be in violation of the ADA if it were to hire Young and not provide him with health coverage. It would also be in violation of the ADA if Eastern were not to hire Young because of the increased cost of having to purchase insurance to cover him.

> **EXAMPLE:** New Company's health insurance plan excludes coverage for preexisting back injuries. Applicant Smith has such an injury. The company must offer its plan to Smith. However, the fact that Smith would not receive coverage for expenses associated with his back injury would not be a violation of the ADA (provided that the insurance meets the requirements of Section 501). If New Company's insurance plan allowed for coverage of preexisting back injuries provided that increased premiums were paid, New Company would be required to provide Smith the insurance and pay the increased rates (subject to the undue hardship defense).

¶ 2.16 REQUIRED NOTICE TO APPLICANTS, EMPLOYEES

Section 105 of the ADA provides that every covered employer, employment agency, labor organization, or joint labor-management committee must post notices in a format accessible to applicants, employees, and members describing the obligations imposed by the ADA. Consistent with this provision, the EEOC is modifying its EEO poster to include a description of the ADA. The legislative history to this section indicates, however, that Congress's intent went beyond merely requiring the posting of a notice.

The House Committee on Education and Labor Report states that an employer "must notify applicants and employees of its obligations under the legislation to make reasonable accommodation."[651] There may be instances where merely posting a notice will be insufficient, such as when a disabled person receives an application by mail or is interviewed over the phone. Similarly, employers may make job offers during on-campus interviews or at job fairs. Since a posted notice will be ineffectual in such circumstances, the intent of Section 105 would be frustrated unless the employer implements alternative means of communicating its obligations to the applicant beyond merely posting a notice. Therefore, it is suggested that a statement of obligations be placed on all employment applications, in brochures on the employer provided prospective employees or otherwise directly communicated to an applicant. Recruiters should incorporate into their presentation a standard statement of the employer's EEO policy, including a description of the company's ADA obligations. A statement concerning the rights of the disabled should also be included in the employer's personnel manual.

¶ 2.17 PROTECTION OF EXERCISE OF RIGHTS UNDER THE ADA

Following the pattern of most civil rights legislation, Section 503(a) provides that "no person shall discriminate against any individual because such individual has opposed any act or practice made unlawful by this Act or because such individual made a charge, testified, assisted, or participated in any manner in an investigation, proceeding or hearing under the Act." Similarly, Section 503(b) provides that "[i]t shall be unlawful to coerce, intimidate, threaten, or interfere with any individual in the exercise or enjoyment of, or on account of his or her having aided or encouraged any other individual in the exercise or enjoyment of, any right granted or protected by this Act." The language of Sections 502(a) and 502(b) is incorporated into the EEOC's regulations, which also include "harassment" as unlawful conduct.[652]

---

[651] H. Comm. on Educ. and Lab. Rep. at 64.

[652] EEOC Regs. at 29 CFR § 1630.12.

Section 502(c) provides for the same remedies and procedures for victims of retaliation and coercion as are available in the underlying title. For example, an individual who was retaliated against in an employment discrimination complaint would have the same remedies and procedures available under Section 107 of the ADA as an individual alleging employment discrimination itself.[653]

> **EXAMPLE:** Smith is a nonsupervisory employee of the Northern Company. Smith has read about the ADA and has taken it upon himself to assist a number of employees in filing requests for various forms of accommodations that Smith believes are required under the ADA. Under Section 503(a), Smith cannot be disciplined for this activity provided that he is acting in good faith and otherwise performing his job to acceptable standards—even though he has no official personnel function.

As under the Civil Rights Act of 1964, these provisions are likely to be construed broadly.[654]

¶ 2.18 ENFORCEMENT PROCEDURES AND REMEDIES UNDER TITLE VII

Under Section 107(a) of the ADA, the remedies and procedures set forth in Sections 706, 707, 709, and 710 of the Civil Rights Act of 1964, as amended, are available with respect to actions by the EEOC, the Attorney General, or any private individual who believes that he has been discriminated against in violation of the ADA. As to state and local governments, the Attorney General will have authority to bring pattern and practice cases. Although the EEOC is required to provide technical assistance to employers, the EEOC's failure to provide such advice is not a defense.[655]

---

[653] H. Comm. on Jud. Rep. at 72.

[654] See, e.g., Hart v. JT Baker Chem. Corp., 598 F2d 829 (3d Cir. 1979); Silver v. KCA, Inc., 586 F2d 138 (9th Cir. 1978).

[655] EEOC Reg. § 1630.1(a); 56 Fed. Reg. 35,727 (July 26, 1991).

[1] Judicial Relief

The final version of Section 107(a) contains two significant changes from the original House and Senate bills. First, the original bill also incorporated the remedies available under Section 1981 of the Civil Rights Act of 1866. Under court decisions construing that statute, plaintiffs would have been entitled to remedies such as punitive damages and damages for emotional distress. Also, jury trials would have been available. However, the final version of the ADA provides for back pay and judge trials only. [656]

As a result of negotiations, an amendment was adopted to the original ADA language providing that people with disabilities would be entitled to the same remedies available under Title VII, including any subsequent amendments to that legislation. This amendment shifted the debate from the ADA to the more controversial Title VII bill. An attempt to amend the original bill in the House to freeze (limit) the ADA remedies to those in Title VII at the time of the ADA's enactment was rejected. [657] Thus, should the remedy provisions of Title VII be amended, such an amendment would apply to the ADA.

The second major change was that the original bill provided protection to individuals who are "about to be subject to discrimination." This provision was deleted on the basis that Title VII already provides protection against discrimination in those circumstances; thus, a specific provision in this title was unnecessary. [658] Congress cited with approval the U.S. Supreme Court's decision in *International Brotherhood of Teamsters v. United States*, [659] in which the Court articulated the futile gesture doctrine. The Court in *Teamsters* held: "When a person's desire for a job is not translated into a formal application solely

---

[656] Although the Civil Rights Act of 1990 passed both houses of Congress by substantial margins, President George Bush vetoed the legislation. The veto was sustained by one vote in the Senate. A renewed effort to pass similar legislation is expected in the 102d Congress.

[657] H. Comm. on Jud. Rep. at 48.

[658] H. Comm. on Educ. and Lab. Rep. at 82; S. Comm. on Lab. and Hum. Resources Rep. at 43.

[659] International Bhd. of Teamsters v. United States, 431 US 324 (1977).

because of his unwillingness to engage in a futile gesture he is as much a victim of discrimination as is he who goes through the motions of submitting an application."[660]

A question that arose regarding Section 107(a) was whether a disabled employee would have standing to file a charge of discrimination on the discovery that the employer is about to redesign or build new office space in such a way that it will be inaccessible. Recognizing that an employer may be able to create an undue hardship defense if an employee were required to delay filing a charge until after construction were completed, Congress concluded that "the employee is allowed to bring a suit to stop the illegal construction or restructuring before it begins."[661]

Under Title VII, an individual who believes he has been discriminated against must first file a charge of discrimination with the EEOC. There was some concern that language in the ADA could be read to allow the disabled to seek judicial relief without initially seeking resolution through the EEOC. The House Committee on the Judiciary Report makes clear, however, that the disabled must follow the same procedures as minorities and other protected individuals must follow under Title VII.[662]

Section 107(b) mandates that the EEOC must issue regulations to enforce the provision of Title I no later than one year after the date of the enactment of the ADA. Therefore, final regulations were issued on July 26, 1991 (the EEOC's final regulations are set forth in Appendix C).

[2] Alternative Dispute Resolution

In an effort to minimize litigation and to encourage the use of alternative dispute resolution procedures, Section 513 of the ADA states: "Where appropriate and to the extent authorized by

---

[660] Id. at 324, 365–367.

[661] H. Comm. on Educ. and Lab. Rep. at 83; S. Comm. on Lab. and Hum. Resources Rep. at 43.

[662] H. Comm. on Jud. Rep. at 48–49.

law, the use of alternative dispute resolution, including settlement negotiations, conciliation, factfinding, minitrials, and arbitrations, is encouraged to resolve disputes under the Act."

One of the questions this provision raised was whether the results of an arbitration would be binding on an applicant or employee. In language that is likely to undercut the use of alternative procedures, the House Committee on the Judiciary stated regarding Section 513 that

> The Committee wishes to emphasize, however, that the use of alternative dispute resolution mechanisms is intended to supplement, not supplant, the remedies provided by the Act. Thus, for example, the Committee believes that any agreement to submit disputed issues to arbitration, whether in the context of collective bargaining or in an employment contract, does not preclude the affected person from seeking relief under the enforcement provisions of the Act. [663]

The committee cited with approval the U.S. Supreme Court's decision in *Alexander v. Gardner-Denver.* [664] There, the Court held that a unionized employee who submits a grievance to arbitration under a collective-bargaining agreement raising claims of discrimination actionable under Title VII of the Civil Rights Act of 1964 does not give up the right to file a lawsuit under Title VII based on the same discriminatory conduct. The Court reasoned that a union submitting a grievance to arbitration on behalf of its member seeks to vindicate contractual rights under a collective-bargaining agreement, while a Title VII action is premised on a statutory right created by Congress. Congress expressly acknowledged its concurrence with this view in formulating the ADA. [665]

An issue arising under *Gardner-Denver*, and not addressed in the legislative history to Section 513, is the weight, if any, that should be given to a prior arbitration award in a judicial action under the ADA. The courts faced with the issue after *Gardner-Denver* have not reached a uniform result. While some courts

---

[663] Id. at 76–77.

[664] Alexander v. Gardner-Denver, 415 US 36 (1974).

[665] Conference Report at 89.

have held that arbitrators' awards should be given considerable weight,[666] others have indicated that they are entitled to no weight.[667] The U.S. Supreme Court in *Gardner-Denver* merely stated that the award should be "accorded such weight as the court deems appropriate."[668]

The significance of the legislative history's cite to *Gardner-Denver* is, however, thrown into doubt by the U.S. Supreme Court's more recent decision in *Gilmer v. Interstate/Johnson Lane Corp.*[669] In that case, the U.S. Supreme Court ruled that its decision in *Gardner-Denver* only applied to arbitrations under a collective-bargaining agreement and that an employee in a non-union context is bound by his agreement to arbitrate. This interpretation of *Gardner-Denver* was a departure from the common reading of that case and clearly a narrower construction than Congress had in mind in its discussion of the case in the ADA's legislative history. As a result, courts interpreting the ADA will be faced with a clear conflict between what Congress apparently intended by its cite to *Gardner-Denver* and what the U.S. Supreme Court now has held in *Gilmer*.

Where private litigation is pursued under the ADA, reasonable attorney fees, including litigation expenses (such as expert witness fees and travel expenses) and court costs, are available to the prevailing party under Section 505 of the ADA.[670] The ADA expressly provides that attorney fees can be awarded for time spent during the administrative process as well as in court. Section 505 is to be interpreted in a manner consistent with the Civil Rights Attorney's Fee Act,[671] including that statute's defi-

---

[666] See Becton v. Detroit Terminal, 687 F2d 140 (6th Cir. 1982).

[667] See Rubin v. State Farm Mut. Ins. Co., 26 Fair Empl. Prac. Cas. (BNA) 1519 (SDNY 1981).

[668] Alexander v. Gardner-Denver, supra note 664, 415 US at 60.

[669] Gilmer v. Interstate/Johnson Lane Corp., No. 90-18 (US May 13, 1991).

[670] The Judiciary Committee expressly included litigation expenses in response to the U.S. Supreme Court's decision in Crawford Fitting Co. v. JT Gibbons, 482 US 437 (1987), which held that expert witness fees and the like are not recoverable without express statutory authority.

[671] 42 USC § 1988.

nition of prevailing party as construed by the U.S. Supreme Court. The legislative history to Section 505 makes clear that attorney fees should be awarded against an unsuccessful plaintiff only under the standard set forth in *Christianburg Garment Co. v. EEOC*,[672] a case in which the Court held that a plaintiff should not be assessed fees unless a court finds the plaintiff's claim to be "frivolous, unreasonable or groundless."[673]

¶ 2.19 APPLICATION TO CONGRESS AND LEGISLATIVE AGENCIES

Although the ADA applies to Congress and the agencies of the legislative branch, Congress elected to enact special rules regarding its enforcement. In the Senate, Section 509(a) provides that claims under the ADA (as well as the Civil Rights Act of 1964 and the ADEA) are to be adjudicated before the Senate Select Committee on Ethics. In the House, Section 509(b) provides that the remedies and procedures of the Fair Employment Practices Resolution are to be followed.[674] Sections 509(a)(6) and 509(b)(3) further provide that the Architect of the Capitol is to develop procedures for enforcing the ADA with regard to nonemployment matters. As to the Architect of the Capitol, the Congressional Budget Office, the General Accounting Office, the Library of Congress, the Office of Technology Assessment, and the U.S. Botanic Garden, the chief official of each instrumentality is to establish remedies and procedures for enforcement of the ADA. Section 509(c)(5) provides that regarding instrumentalities of the legislative branch, nothing in the section alters the enforcement procedures for individuals with disabilities provided in the General Accounting Office Personnel Act of 1980 or the regulations issued thereunder.

---

[672] Christianburg Garment Co. v. EEOC, 434 US 412, 422 (1978).

[673] H. Comm. on Jud. Rep. at 73. The report also cites Hughes v. Rowe, 449 US 5 (1980), which reaffirmed *Christianburg*.

[674] House Resolution 558 of the 100th Congress as agreed to October 4, 1988.

CHAPTER 3

Reasonable Accommodation

Background information on the practical aspects of making reasonable accommodations and interacting with individuals with specific disabilities was provided, in part, by Mainstream, Inc. Established in 1975, Mainstream is a private, nonprofit organization that works with employers and rehabilitation professionals around the country to move greater numbers of persons with disabilities into the workplace. For further information, write Mainstream, Inc., PO Box 65183, Washington, D.C. 20035-5183.

This chapter discusses several common disabilities identified during congressional consideration of the ADA legislation and provides advice about how employers may comply with their reasonable accommodation obligations under Title I. While the focus of this chapter is on the reasonable accommodation obligations of employers, the principles discussed can be applied by entities subject to the reasonable accommodation provisions of other titles of the ADA.

¶ 3.01 WHAT IS REASONABLE ACCOMMODATION?

Title I of the ADA provides that if an employer does not make reasonable accommodation for the known limitations of a qualified individual with disabilities, it is considered to be discrimination. Only if the employer can show that providing the accommodation would place an undue hardship on the operation of the employer's business can discrimination be disproved.

The ADA does not define the term "reasonable accommodation." Rather, it provides a list of examples of types of accommodations designed to ensure that a person with a disability will be able to perform the essential functions of a job, as follows:

- Physical or structural changes (i.e., making existing facilities readily accessible, or acquiring or modifying equipment or devices)
- Modifications to the job itself (i.e., job restructuring, part-time or modified work schedules, or reassignment to vacant positions)
- Modifications to examinations and training materials, provision of qualified readers and interpreters, and other similar accommodations

Since necessary accommodations may only be determined after considering the individual and the tasks involved, reasonableness also may only be determined on a case-by-case basis. The necessity of an accommodation is determined by considering a person's actual abilities and limitations and how they fit actual work requirements.

Through court decisions interpreting the Rehabilitation Act

of 1973 and other previous legislation, precedents have been set in some areas regarding those accommodations that are reasonable for various types of disabilities. In addition, experts on the different disabilities have recommended types of accommodations. For many disabilities then, the courts and experts have provided what amounts to a general format for compliance with the provisions of the ADA when an employer is considering hiring a disabled individual.

¶ 3.02 THE COST OF ACCOMMODATING THE DISABLED

Employers are necessarily concerned about the expense involved in meeting the ADA's requirements. A study done by the Job Accommodation Network (JAN will be further explained in a later section) found that 31 percent of the accommodations suggested by the ADA could be made at no cost, 19 percent of the accommodations suggested could be made at a cost of between $1 and $50, 19 percent of the accommodations suggested could be made at a cost of between $50 and $500, 19 percent of the accommodations suggested could be made at a cost of between $500 and $1,000, 11 percent of the accommodations suggested could be made at a cost of between $1,000 and $5,000, and only 1 percent of the accommodations suggested cost more than $5,000. In other words, 50 percent of the suggested accommodations cost less than $50, and 69 percent cost less than $500.

Examples of types of accommodations suggested by JAN are a device attached to a personal computer that allows a deaf person to make and receive phone calls and a computer that is equipped to read out loud virtually anything appearing on its screen. It was reported that accommodations such as these would cost only about $200.

A study done by the Berkeley Planning Association for the Department of Labor in 1982 reported that one half of the suggested accommodations cost nothing, and more than two thirds cost less than $100. The Berkeley study compared the costs of the accommodations to the benefits accumulated by the company (e.g., productivity) and found that the benefits surpassed the costs of the accommodations. The study also found that only 22 percent of the employees with disabilities in the companies surveyed needed special accommodations.

¶ 3.03 MAKING THE PROPER ACCOMMODATION

Employers must bear in mind that each individual will have different requirements and will need to be evaluated on an individualized basis. This process of placement and accommodation can be successful if the following four-step approach is taken.

1. *Determine the fundamental job tasks.* Analyzing the fundamental job tasks means simply making a list of each task that will need to be performed by the employee.

2. *Determine the individual's abilities.* The applicant should be analyzed on an individual basis to determine his abilities and limitations, such as his ability to lip-read or hear the telephone ring.

3. *Determine conflicts between fundamental job tasks and the individual's abilities.* The results of the first and second steps should be compared in order to determine whether any incompatibilities exist.

4. *Determine and evaluate solutions to those conflicts.* If any conflicts are found, accommodations (i.e., solutions) should be considered and made.

A clearinghouse for information on accommodations is the Job Accommodation Network, West Virginia University, 809 Allen Hall, PO Box 6122, Morgantown, West Virginia 26507-9984. JAN is an international information network and consulting resource to enable qualified workers with disabilities to be hired and retained. When an employer requires information regarding possible accommodations, a consultant at JAN will search its computer records for information based on the functional requirements of the specific job, the functional limitations of the worker, environmental factors, and other relevant information. The consultant will then provide the employer with information about similar situations that have arisen in the past and suggest proposed accommodations. JAN is a service of the President's Committee on Employment of People With Disabilities, and there is no cost to an employer for its use. However, employers using the service are asked to make a commitment to provide JAN with information regarding its accommodation efforts. JAN can be reached by telephone at 1-800-526-7234 or 1-304-293-7186.

¶ 3.04 ACCOMMODATING SPECIFIC DISABILITIES

As discussed in detail in Chapter 2, under the ADA, a disabled individual means an individual with "a physical or mental impairment that substantially limits one or more of the major life activities of such individual,"[1] as well as an individual with a record of such an impairment or one who is regarded as having such an impairment. It is not possible to cover all the specific conditions that may be considered physical or mental impairments under the ADA. However, several common disabilities will be discussed in this chapter, including hearing and visual impairment, arthritis, heart disease, cancer, diabetes, epilepsy, cerebral palsy, mental illness, and paraplegia and quadriplegia.

To help employers better understand all that is involved in employing a disabled individual and making reasonable accommodations if necessary, the remainder of this chapter will examine these selected disabilities by

- Discussing the disability itself
- Covering issues arising when interviewing and/or considering a disabled individual for a position
- Considering accommodations that may need to be made for the disabled in the workplace

[1] Hearing Impairment

Hearing impairment may be caused by disease, accident, or a birth injury or congenital defect that affects one or more parts of

---

[1] ADA § 3(2)(A).

the ear. A hearing-impaired person may be able to communicate through sign language, finger spelling (i.e., use of hand positions to represent the letters of the alphabet), and writing, as well as through lipreading, though it is reported that even the most skilled lip-readers can only comprehend about 35 percent of what is being said. A deaf individual whose hearing loss arose after language skills were acquired may also communicate through speech, but it is generally hard to understand until the listener is used to it. The ability of a hearing-impaired individual to communicate varies with the degree of hearing loss and when it occurred.

It is clear from the legislative history to the ADA that hearing impairment is a covered disability.[2] Similarly, a number of cases under the Rehabilitation Act held that hearing impairments constitute a handicap.[3] For example, in *Crane v. Dole*,[4] the plaintiff was denied a position with the Federal Aviation Administration (FAA) as an aeronautical information specialist due to his hearing impairment. The court held that the FAA should have tested the plaintiff and, if he failed the hearing test, the agency should have considered reasonable accommodations, such as phones designed to amplify voices.

It is a common belief that a hearing-impaired individual is a safety hazard on the job. But, because deaf individuals are usually more visually alert than their co-workers, they are less susceptible to common hazards in the work environment. If the buddy system and signaling devices are used, problems involving hearing-impaired individuals during emergency situations are also reduced.

---

[2] HR Conf. Rep. No. 485, pt. 2, 101st Cong., 2d Sess. (1990) (hereinafter cited as H. Comm. on Educ. and Lab. Rep.) at 51.

[3] Strathie v. Department of Transp., 716 F2d 227 (3d Cir. 1983); Camenisch v. University of Tex., 616 F2d 127 (5th Cir. 1980), remanded on other grounds, 451 US 390 (1981); Shirey v. Devine, 670 F2d 1188 (DC Cir. 1982); Bonner v. Lewis, 857 F2d 559 (9th Cir. 1988); Jones v. Illinois Dep't of Rehabilitation Servs., 504 F. Supp. 1244 (ND Ill. 1981); Crawford v. University of NC, 440 F. Supp. 1047 (MDNC 1977); Greater Los Angeles Council on Deafness v. Zolin, 607 F. Supp. 175 (CD Cal. 1984), aff'd in part and rev'd in part and remanded on other grounds, 812 F2d 1103 (9th Cir. 1987).

[4] Crane v. Dole et al., 617 F. Supp. 156 (DDC 1985).

When considering a hearing-impaired individual for employment, two of the issues to examine are the noise factor and what is called recruitment. Contrary to the popular belief that a hearing-impaired individual is an ideal employee to place in a loud environment, certain consistent loud noises can cause further damage to an individual who already has damaged hearing. Recruitment is a condition in which noises at certain frequencies sound much louder to an individual who is hearing impaired than they would to an individual with normal hearing. This not only causes frustration and/or pain, but can also cause further hearing damage. These loud noises and vibrations can distort and interfere with the sound amplification of an individual's hearing aid. Thus, the noise factor is an important issue to consider when deciding to employ a hearing-impaired individual.

If it is decided that an individual who is hearing impaired would be able to complete the tasks required and can be placed in a noise-safe environment, the next step is the interview. Preparation prior to the interview can avoid awkward communication problems. When responding to an application and/or résumé, an employer should respond in writing and should inquire into what kind of accommodation the individual believes should be made, if any. One of the accommodations commonly requested for the interview is a sign language interpreter. Under Rehabilitation Act regulations and some state and local laws, employers may be required to obtain and pay for the services of the interpreter. When an interpreter is used for the interview, the interviewer should always maintain eye contact with the applicant and speak directly to him. Because the interpreter will be a few words behind the interviewer, the interviewer should not rush, but speak in a normal manner. If no interpreter is present,

- The applicant should sit directly across from the interviewer in a well-lighted room.
- The interviewer should remember to speak normally, trying to articulate the words carefully.
- The interviewer should use facial expressions and body language when it is appropriate.

- The interviewer should remember always to maintain good eye contact.
- The interviewer should always watch the applicant's face to catch signs that the individual does not understand. When something is not understood, the interviewer should rephrase the sentence rather than repeat it.

Individuals who are hearing impaired are relatively easy to orchestrate into the work environment, first, because of the nature of the disability and, second, because of the advanced technology available to assist them, such as the telecommunication device for the deaf (TDD). Another common accommodation for deaf individuals is a sign language interpreter at meetings and during training programs. To facilitate further the adjustment of a hearing-impaired individual in the workplace, supervisors and co-workers should all be aware of how best to communicate with him. Most deaf individuals have developed preferred methods of communicating with the "hearing world."

Three examples of actual accommodations made for hearing-impaired individuals follow:[5]

1. A plant worker who is hearing impaired was able to retain his job and avoid transfer to a lower-paying job within the company by the use of a telephone amplifier designed to work in conjunction with his hearing aid. The cost of this accommodation was $23.95.

2. A medical technician who is deaf was able to perform the laboratory tests required for her job by the use of a timer with an indicator light. The cost of this accommodation was $26.95.

3. A laboratory worker who is hearing impaired was able to perform crucial laboratory procedures that required a timer by the use of a vibrating wrist alert system. This system also alerted her to emergency alarms. The cost of this accommodation was between $500 and $1,000.

[2] Vision Impairment

Blindness may result from an accident or disease or may be present at birth. Vision may also be impaired by color blindness, tunnel vision, and other such disabilities.

---

[5] Examples provided by JAN.

Vision impairments are among those covered by the ADA.[6] Cases under the Rehabilitation Act also found vision impairments to be covered handicaps.[7] For example, in *Carter v. Bennett*,[8] the plaintiff alleged that her termination was caused by her employer's failure to reasonably accommodate her blindness. While the court held that blindness was a disability, it found the defendant had made reasonable accommodation by providing part-time readers, special equipment, and a reduced work load.

Many people believe that blind individuals are a considerable safety risk at the worksite. As a general rule, blind and visually impaired individuals may actually be less of a safety risk than sighted employees, because their disability may make them more attentive. To facilitate the interview process, an employer should do the following:

- Always offer assistance before giving it.
- Remember to avoid the common behavior of talking loudly to a blind individual. The interviewer should be sure to use a normal speed and tone of voice, keeping in mind that it is not necessary to avoid words like "see," and "look," as blind individuals use them also.
- Review the job tasks and their limitations with the applicant. Ask the applicant to offer ideas about accommodations he feels will be necessary.

Individuals who are blind or visually impaired are reasonably easy to mainstream into the work environment, not only because of the nature of the disability, but because of the number of devices that have become available in recent years to assist them. Many of these devices are quite inexpensive. The

---

[6] H. Comm. on Educ. and Lab. Rep. at 51.

[7] Brown v. Sibley, 650 F2d 760 (5th Cir. Unit A 1981); Gurmankin v. Costanzo, 411 F. Supp. 982 (ED Pa. 1976), aff'd, 556 F2d 184 (3d Cir. 1977); Upshur v. Love, 474 F2d 332 (ND Cal. 1979); McNutt v. Hills, 426 F. Supp. 990 (DDC 1977). See also Doherty v. Southern College of Optometry, 659 F. Supp. 662 (WD Tenn. 1987) (retinitis pigmentosa); Kampmeier v. Nyquist, 553 F2d 296 (2d Cir. 1977) (vision in one eye); Wright v. Columbia Univ., 520 F. Supp. 789 (ED Pa. 1981) (vision in one eye).

[8] Carter v. Bennett, 840 F2d 63 (DC Cir. 1988).

employer should keep in mind that the visually impaired individual will probably own one or more of the devices already.

The adaptation of the work place for a visually impaired individual can involve making sure that fixtures, supplies, and so on, are imprinted with braille or raised graphics. When introducing a blind employee to co-workers, do so on an individual basis, as it makes it easier for the disabled individual to associate names with voices. Three examples of actual accommodations made for visually impaired individuals follow:[9]

1. A blind receptionist was given a light probe that let her determine which lines on the telephone were ringing, on hold, or in use at her company. The cost of this accommodation was $45.

2. A visually impaired data entry operator was allowed to change her desk layout from the right side to the left. The cost of this accommodation was $0.

3. An anti-glare screen that minimizes glare was given to an individual with an eye disorder in which glare causes increased fatigue.

[3] Arthritis

Arthritis encompasses over 100 different rheumatic conditions that cause aches and pain in joints and connective tissues throughout the body. Rheumatoid arthritis is one of the most commonly recognized types of arthritis. Its symptoms are pain, swelling, and stiffness in the joints, causing the joints' motion to become limited. The disease is progressive and sometimes results in deformity of the affected joints. Arthritis may be caused by injury, such as the dislocation of a joint.

The degrees of disability caused by arthritis vary widely, depending upon the part of the body affected and the extent to which the arthritis has accelerated. Some arthritis sufferers are able to work, but experience excessive absences due to their conditions. Others must simply work at a reduced pace because of the stiffness or pain they suffer. A conscientious employer should keep in mind the arthritis sufferer's physical capabilities

---

[9] Examples provided by JAN.

and limitations when hiring or creating work assignments and should suggest that the arthritis sufferer receive continuous medical care in order to keep the arthritic condition from becoming progressively worse and causing deformity. A person suffering from arthritis can usually stay at work by remaining under medical care.

Arthritis is among the many disabilities identified in the legislative history of the ADA [10] as a covered disability. There are also cases under the Rehabilitation Act holding that arthritis is a handicap. [11] For example, in *Guinn v. Bolger*, [12] the plaintiff, an employee of the U.S. Postal Service (USPS), was given time off without pay from her light-duty position. The court held that arthritis of the knee constituted a handicap under the Rehabilitation Act and warranted reasonable accommodation for a qualified individual.

Essential to placing persons with arthritis in the job market is the completion of a job analysis. That is, an employer should analyze how tasks are accomplished, the physical movements and mental processes involved in the work activity, duration of total time involved in performing each work activity, as well as the frequency with which work activities are performed. In this way, possible incompatibilities may be examined and the need for accommodation explored.

Joint-preservation therapy is a means by which the impact of arthritis is reduced by teaching the sufferer how to work around his pain and stiffness. One kind of joint-preservation technique involves modifying the arthritis sufferer's use of his joints in daily activity. The first step is to reduce the exertion of force on the joints, such as by using an electric device rather than a manual one, or by moving a computer programmer's monitor to a spot where turning of the head and upper body is not necessary. Another technique involves modifying the method by which the arthritis sufferer performs an activity. This could involve simply creating a work schedule such that heavy activities are mixed with lighter activities, or arranging rest periods

---

[10] H. Comm. on Educ. and Lab. Rep. at 51.

[11] E.g., Coley v. Secretary of the Army, 692 F. Supp. 557 (ED Pa. 1988).

[12] Guinn v. Bolger, 598 F. Supp. 196 (DDC 1984).

throughout the course of the workday. A third joint-preservation technique involves the use of equipment, such as a finger splint, to prevent the complete outstretching of the fingers for a worker who needs to write for long periods, or seating appropriate to the arthritis sufferer's body size so that good leverage is available for sitting and rising.

An example of an accommodation that could be made for a clerk with limited use of his hands would be the provision of a "lazy susan" file holder for his desk, to prevent him from having to reach across the desk. The cost of this accommodation would be approximately $85.

[4] Heart Disease

Heart disease encompasses a wide variety of heart ailments, of which hypertensive heart disease is the most common. Hypertensive heart disease results when the heart becomes enlarged from prolonged high blood pressure and the arteries of the heart become narrowed or hardened. Hypertension increases the risk of heart attacks and strokes but may be controlled by drugs. Coronary heart disease occurs when the coronary arteries are narrowed and the heart muscle receives less oxygen than it should. Hypertension, diabetes, and high cholesterol levels can contribute to coronary heart disease. Congenital heart disease is yet another kind of heart impairment, with varying degrees of severity. Surgical treatment for serious congenital heart defects can often restore normal health.

About 85 percent of those who have experienced a mild-to-moderate heart attack return to work. A person suffering from hypertension can work if the hypertension is being effectively controlled by medication and if he reduces the stress in his life. A person suffering from congenital heart defects that have been surgically corrected should experience no work-related problems.

The legislative history of the ADA includes heart conditions among covered disabilities.[13] Cases under the Rehabilitation

---

[13] H. Comm. on Educ. and Lab. Rep. at 51.

Act also held that heart conditions constitute a covered handicap.[14] For example, in *Carty v. Carlin*,[15] the plaintiff held a position with the USPS as a part-time mail collector. After he suffered a heart attack, he was transferred to a laborer-custodian position. Ultimately, he was terminated for failure to perform the job duties of the new position. The court held that although a heart condition was a disability and warranted reasonable accommodation, in this case, the reasonable accommodation did not require a further transfer or reassignment.

Most jobs tend to involve varied activities, and most periods of strenuous activity tend to be of short duration. Even people with low physical capacities can often tolerate surprisingly high work loads, provided that the strenuous activities are of short duration and adequate rest periods are interspersed. Those suffering from chest pain or exercise-induced irregular heartbeats should not, however, be exposed to even short periods of strenuous activity. Alternatively, they should have no difficulty working at nonstrenuous activities for a full eight-hour workday, including rest periods. An employer should categorize the activities of a particular position as strenuous or nonstrenuous and take this into account when assessing an individual's qualifications. An applicant's or employee's physician should complete a medical examination and determine his functional capabilities and limitations.

Employers may request that cardiac patients coming back to work provide written recommendations from their personal physicians regarding job restrictions. They may also permit such employees to return to work on a graduated work schedule. For instance, an employee may return to work for only four hours a day, five days a week, for the first few weeks, and thereafter increase his daily work hours until a full eight-hour day is achieved. It is usually not advisable for cardiac patients to work overtime for the first six months after their return. If the employee performed a strenuous job prior to suffering the heart problem, it may be advisable to reassign him to a less strenuous position upon his return to work. A reevaluation of the

---

[14] E.g., Treadwell v. Alexander, 707 F2d 473 (11th Cir. 1983).

[15] Carty v. Carlin, 623 F. Supp. 1181 (D. Md. 1985).

employee's physical limitations should be made and approval by the company's medical director should be obtained before permitting him to resume strenuous activities.

Employers may want to consider various types of health promotion programs, including the following:

- Information programs where pamphlets and films are shown on nutrition and health care subjects
- Exercise and weight-reduction programs
- Detection and screening programs with referral to community health care providers
- Cafeteria programs aimed at healthier eating habits for those trying to reduce the salt in their diets, the overweight, and those with elevated cholesterol levels

The type of accommodation that may be made for an individual returning to work after suffering heart problems is shown by the case of a grounds keeper who, after a stroke, had limited use of one of his arms. He wanted to return to work but was unable to complete some of the requirements of his position, such as raking grass. The use of an arm extension on his rake allowed him to control it with his good arm, and the man was able to resume his work.[16]

[5] Cancer

Cancer covers many diseases characterized by uncontrolled growth and spread of abnormal cells. While cancer can result in death if uncontrolled, some forms of cancer may be cured if detected and treated promptly.[17] Breast cancer is the leading form of cancer and cause of death among women between the ages of 40 and 44. The five-year survival rate for localized breast cancer was 96 percent in 1985. Risk factors for lung cancer include cigarette smoking and exposure to certain industrial substances, such as asbestos. The survival rate of patients with diagnosed lung cancer is not very high—only 13 percent live

---

[16] Example provided by JAN.

[17] A discussion of all the various types of cancer is beyond the scope of this chapter. Only three leading types will be noted.

five or more years after diagnosis. Skin cancer affects more than 400,000 people each year. The majority of cases are easily curable. Excessive exposure to the sun, having a fair complexion, and occupational exposure to coal tar, pitch, and arsenic compounds are thought to be risk factors.

Cancer is among the several disabilities mentioned during legislative deliberations regarding the ADA as a covered handicap.[18] Some cases under the Rehabilitation Act have also held that cancer is a covered disability. For example, in *Harrison v. Marsh*,[19] a clerk-typist was diagnosed as having breast cancer and underwent a mastectomy. When her employer failed to provide a less strenuous job to accommodate her loss of strength, a court held that cancer was a covered disability under the Rehabilitation Act and that the employer was required to provide reasonable accommodation for her condition.

Most people who have been treated for cancer want to go back to their jobs and are encouraged to do so by their physicians. Because cancer can affect so many parts of the body, and in differing levels of severity, there is a wide range of possible employment problems to be considered. Problems facing the cancer patient who is returning to work may include coping with changes in functional abilities and the attitudes of supervisors and co-workers.

[6] Diabetes

A diabetic's pancreas cannot produce sufficient insulin to utilize correctly the sugar and starches that are obtained through consumed food. Diabetes can usually be controlled through a combination of insulin intake, exercise, and diet. Exercise is important to a diabetic because it helps to keep his weight and blood sugar at normal levels. Many diabetics are able to control their condition through a diet low in sugar and starch. Diabetics should be encouraged to maintain a balance of prescribed insulin, if any, as well as a proper diet and exercise.

---

[18] H. Comm. on Educ. and Lab. Rep. at 51.

[19] Harrison v. Marsh, 691 F. Supp. 1223 (WD Mo. 1988).

Not only do diabetics have to cope with the condition itself, but the diabetes makes them more susceptible to other impairments as well, such as arteriosclerosis and eye troubles, such as blurred vision and cataracts. Susceptibility to these other impairments is greatly lessened by maintaining a proper diet and exercise regimen, and being under the care of a physician.

It is clear from the legislative history of the ADA that diabetes is a covered handicap,[20] and there are cases under the Rehabilitation Act that hold it is covered under that legislation as well.[21] One example is *Serrapica v. City of New York*,[22] in which the plaintiff applied for a position with the City of New York as a sanitation worker. After undergoing a medical examination, the plaintiff's blood sugar level was found to be very high, and he was disqualified. The court held that diabetes is a covered disability but that in this case, the plaintiff was in poor control of his disease, and he constituted a possible danger to himself and co-workers and was, therefore, not qualified for the position he was seeking.

When considering a diabetic for employment, one of the major issues the employer should investigate during the interview is the severity of the condition and how often an insulin reaction occurs. Applicants able to treat their diabetes with diet or with oral agents to maintain their blood sugar level are typically able to perform any job for which they are otherwise qualified because they rarely suffer these reactions. However, it may be inappropriate to place an individual using insulin to treat a more severe case of diabetes in a position where it would be dangerous for him to stop what he is doing to treat a reaction, or where a sudden insulin attack could cause him or a co-worker harm. Again, the employer must consider the severity and frequency with which these reactions occur. For example, if, for one year, the individual has not had a reaction in which uncon-

---

[20] H. Comm. on Educ. and Lab. Rep. at 51.

[21] Davis v. Meese, 692 F. Supp. 505 (ED Pa. 1988); Bentivegna v. US Department of Labor, 694 F2d 619 (9th Cir. 1982); Brown v. County of Genesee, 37 Fair Empl. Prac. Cas. (BNA) 1595 (WD Mich. 1985); Brown v. American Home Prods. Corp., 520 F. Supp. 1120 (D. Kan. 1981).

[22] Serrapica v. City of NY, 708 F. Supp. 64 (SDNY 1989).

sciousness has occurred, many medical professionals would find it acceptable for that individual to drive passenger vehicles.

Typically, diabetics are no more likely to suffer from excess absenteeism than the general population. Moreover, after placement has been made, it is relatively easy to accommodate the diabetic in the workplace. The most common accommodation for a diabetic involves his work schedule. Diabetics should generally be allowed to work the day shift. Because split shifts and shift changes can interfere with a diabetic employee's control of his diabetes (by interfering with his insulin, exercise, eating schedule), these assignments must be carefully evaluated before being given.

[7] Epilepsy

Epilepsy is a disability that is as common as diabetes and more common than cancer, cerebral palsy, multiple sclerosis, muscular dystrophy, and tuberculosis combined. About 75 percent of those with epilepsy acquired the disorder before the age of 18, but it can affect anyone at any age. Despite being widespread, it is one of the most feared disabilities.

Contrary to general belief, epilepsy is not an emotional or psychological disturbance. It is a symptom of a central nervous system disorder. Various events can cause it, including a blow to the brain, an infection, a clogged blood vessel, lack of oxygen, impaired circulation, prenatal or birth injuries, infectious diseases, tumors, and so on.

Petit mal seizures usually occur when an individual is between the ages of 6 and 14. These seizures range from just one or two to fifty or more in a single day and are characterized by rapid blinking or twitching of the eyes and/or awkward arm and head movements. The individual having a seizure is not aware of the event and only experiences short periods of memory loss. Petit mal continues on into adulthood, usually with decreased severity, although sometimes this type of seizure disappears at puberty.

Grand mal is the type of seizure most commonly associated with epilepsy in adults. Convulsions may last from one to twenty minutes and are characterized by lack of oxygen in the blood, foaming at the mouth, rigidity of the body, and jerking movements. A psychomotor seizure, on the other hand, may last between fifteen and twenty minutes and is characterized by abrupt mental confusion followed by the repetition of uncoordinated random movements.

Epilepsy is one of the disabilities identified in the legislative history of the ADA as a disability,[23] and several cases under the Rehabilitation Act held that epilepsy constitutes a covered handicap under that act as well.[24] In *Mantolete v. Bolger*,[25] for example, the plaintiff, an epileptic, was denied a machine distribution clerk position with the USPS based on a medical officer's recommendation that her disability posed a risk to the plaintiff and others. In finding that the plaintiff had been discriminated against, the court in *Mantolete* held there is a duty to reasonably accommodate epileptic individuals.

Although there is no cure for epilepsy, 50 percent of those with the condition can completely control their seizures with anticonvulsant drugs, while another 30 percent can partially control their seizures with these drugs. There are four major disability-related issues that should be addressed during the interview:

1. *Whether or not the seizures are under control.* If the seizures have been under control for at least one year, the epilepsy should not restrict the individual in the workplace.

2. *The frequency and predictability of the seizures and the recovery time after a seizure.* This will have a bearing on what type of position the applicant is able to fill. The applicant's performance or productivity would not be affected, for instance, if the seizures only occurred while he was sleeping.

3. *The type and characteristics of the applicant's seizures.* Does the individual lose consciousness or fall during a seizure? Exactly what occurs when the individual is having a seizure?

---

[23] H. Comm. on Educ. and Lab. Rep. at 51.

[24] Reynolds v. Brock, 815 F2d 571 (9th Cir. 1987); Duran v. City of Tampa, 430 F2d 75 (MD Fla. 1977); Drennon v. Philadelphia Hosp., 428 F. Supp. 809 (ED Pa. 1977).

[25] Mantolete v. Bolger, 767 F2d 1416 (9th Cir. 1985).

This will determine the kind of situation in which the applicant can be placed. For example, an individual with petit mal seizures that occur fairly often may not be appropriate for a position where constant concentration is necessary.

4. *The presence of any "indicators" to the onset of an applicant's seizures.* Certain elements, such as specific odors, flickering or flashing lights, emotional distress, certain sounds, tastes, or other sensations, can be catalysts for an individual's seizures. These catalysts vary from person to person, and, therefore, knowledge of an applicant's "indicator," if there is one, can assist the interviewer in determining whether any accommodations might help to prevent the seizures.

Proper placement of an individual with epilepsy is crucial. For example, an individual who does not have complete control through medication over his seizures may not be appropriate for a position where he will be next to moving machinery that could cause potential injury in the instance of a seizure. Because in most cases no adjustments to the work environment are necessary in order to employ an individual with epilepsy, adaptation of such an individual into the work situation is usually simple.

[8] Cerebral Palsy

Cerebral palsy describes a host of muscular dysfunctions that result from injury to, or malformation of, the areas of the brain that control the motor functions of the body. Manifestations of cerebral palsy include: stiff movement of the arms and legs, staggering gait, involuntary or uncontrolled motion of the arms and legs, difficulty in speaking, difficulty in chewing and swallowing, drooling, tremors in the extremities, and lack of coordination in body movement. The condition may be caused by infectious diseases or poor health in the expectant mother. In some people, cerebral palsy may be accompanied by convulsive seizures and intellectual or sensory deficiencies.

Cerebral palsy is a physical impairment that is identified as a covered disability in the legislative history of the ADA.[26] Case law under the Rehabilitation Act has also held that cerebral

---

[26] H. Comm. on Educ. and Lab. Rep. at 51.

palsy is a handicap. For example, in *Bruegging v. Burke*,[27] the plaintiff had cerebral palsy and held a position in a federal office. He brought suit after he was denied a promotion on five occasions. The court held that cerebral palsy was a disability warranting reasonable accommodation but that the defendant had met them by requiring him to perform less volume of work than his counterparts, not assigning tasks requiring difficult mental reasoning, and giving him a special typewriter and telephone.

When assessing a job applicant with cerebral palsy, a supervisor should not make assumptions about his capabilities. People with cerebral palsy may be highly intelligent even though they may not appear so because of their disorders and behavior. A job applicant with cerebral palsy has usually gone through an extensive rehabilitation process that enables him to function using alternate methods to perform routine tasks. In many cases, a person with cerebral palsy can perform activities at the rate of a healthy individual due to these adaptive movements.

There is a relatively high incidence of communication problems among those with cerebral palsy. During an interview, an employer should allow the speaker to talk at his own pace and should inform the speaker when he is not being understood.

The capabilities of an afflicted person must be ascertained on an individual basis. The disabled person should always be consulted as the primary source for understanding his abilities and limitations with respect to the functional requirements of a job. The employer should compare the requirements of a position with the abilities and limitations of a person with cerebral palsy, and appropriate accommodations that can be made. The employer should examine how tasks are accomplished, the physical movements and/or mental processes involved in the work activity (such as pulling, pushing, lifting, carrying, sitting, hearing, reasoning, and remembering), the time involved in performing each work activity, as well as the frequency of performing each task.

Limitations vary among people affected by the disability,

---

[27] Bruegging v. Burke, 696 F. Supp. 674 (DDC 1987).

but some of the following are common: difficulty in handling and fingering, inability to use upper extremities, limitation in speech, lack of coordination, susceptibility to seizures, difficulty in interpreting information, and difficulty in hearing and seeing. The possibility of successful employment for cerebral-palsied individuals is enhanced by early medical treatment and physical therapy, realistic vocational planning, and appropriate education and vocational training.

[9] Mental Illness

Mental illness encompasses many personality and social disorders, and often results in a substantially diminished capacity for coping with the ordinary demands of life. Those who have a mental illness are usually of normal intelligence and are often only temporarily afflicted. It is important to note that a "former" mentally ill person is always susceptible to a relapse. For this reason, it is important to recognize the symptoms of the disease in order to keep them under control. The causes of mental illness are not well understood, although many factors may contribute to it, including heredity, stress, and recreational drugs and alcohol. In addition, sometimes physical problems, such as brain damage, venereal disease, and encephalitis, can cause mental illness.

Schizophrenia is the name given to a large group of disorders. It generally lasts longer than six months, and the schizophrenic often experiences deterioration in work productivity, social relationships, and self-care. The symptoms of schizophrenia are varied, including: delusions, hallucinations, thought disorders (manifested by disconnected speech), withdrawal from the outside world, and abnormal psychomotor activity (rocking back and forth, pacing, or immobility). Affective disorders, such as severe depression and mania, are often characterized by cycles of depression and elation, with the depression lasting for long periods. During a major depressive episode, the individual may harbor feelings of hopelessness and worthlessness, thoughts of dying, or even suicide. During a period of elation (manic episode), the individual often exhibits symptoms such as hyperactivity, decreased need for sleep, inflated self-esteem, and increased loud speech. Other forms of mental illness include anxiety disorders, which can be manifested in irrational fears (such as agoraphobia), anxiety, or panic attacks, and personality disorders, which involve an incapability to form healthy social relationships or behave in a socially acceptable manner.

Treatment for mental illness may involve medication, such as tranquilizers and antidepressant drugs, psychotherapy, and hospitalization.

Mental illness is a covered disability under the ADA, according to the legislative history of the act.[28] Cases under the Rehabilitation Act have also held that mental illness is a handicap. For example, in *Matzo v. Postmaster General,*[29] the plaintiff, a manic depressive employee of the USPS, was terminated after a period of continuous absences. The court determined that mental illness was indeed a handicap and held that reasonable accommodation should be made to those who are afflicted. In this case, the court said that the USPS had already made the required reasonable accommodations in light of the plaintiff's condition, such as allowing him to take leave twice weekly for therapy and permitting numerous absences.

One of the most common misconceptions about job applicants with a history of mental illness is that recovered mental patients are potentially dangerous and can "break" at any time. This is a fallacy—those who have suffered mental illness are more likely to be depressed and withdrawn than aggressive. In addition, most relapses of mental illness occur gradually, and symptoms can be detected early and dealt with before becoming too severe.

Often, a mentally ill person who is ready to face the job market will be referred to an employer for a job opening by a local vocational rehabilitation agency. The potential employer should inquire about the nature of the person's illness and its symptoms. Some important questions that should be asked are:

- What symptoms indicate that the job candidate is becoming ill?

---

[28] H. Comm. on Educ. and Lab. Rep. at 51.

[29] Matzo v. Postmaster Gen., 685 F. Supp. 260 (DDC 1987).

- What is the job candidate doing to keep the illness under control so that it will not interfere with work?
- Does the job candidate believe he is mentally capable of dealing with the demands of the work load?

Employers should watch for indications that the employee is suffering the onset of an episode of mental illness. Such clues include a habitual increase in lateness or absences, increasing accidents, inattention to duties, change in physical appearance, uncontrolled crying, staring into space, and mood swings.

[10] Paraplegia and Quadriplegia

Paraplegia is some degree of paralysis occurring approximately from the waist down. A paraplegic may be able to walk with a cane or crutches, or it may be necessary for a paraplegic to use a wheelchair for mobility. Many paraplegics are able to drive a car. Quadriplegia is some degree of paralysis from the neck down. A quadriplegic may rely on a respirator for breathing, or may have the use of his upper body except for finger grasp.

Generally, people who are paraplegic or quadriplegic are in that state due to a spinal cord injury, most often caused by an automobile accident.

In the legislative history of the ADA, paraplegia and quadriplegia are both identified as covered disabilities.[30] Cases under the Rehabilitation Act have also held that both paraplegia and quadriplegia are handicaps.[31] One of these cases is *Smith v. Fletcher*,[32] in which the plaintiff, a paraplegic, held a position with the National Aeronautics and Space Administration. Two employees with the same qualifications as the plaintiff were promoted two levels above the plaintiff while the plaintiff was downgraded. The court held that paraplegia is a covered disability and found that the plaintiff had been discriminated against

---

[30] H. Comm. on Educ. and Lab. Rep. at 51.

[31] Simon v. St. Louis County Police Dep't, 497 F. Supp. 41, 14 Fair Empl. Prac. Cas. (BNA) 363, (ED Mo. 1977), aff'd in part and rev'd in part, 656 F2d 316 (8th Cir. 1981).

[32] Smith v. Fletcher et al., 559 F2d 1014 (5th Cir. 1977).

on the basis of her impairment by being denied positions whose functions she could physically perform.

Before hiring a paraplegic or quadriplegic, an employer must analyze the position available and the skills necessary to complete the job and consider the disabled individual's skills in light of these tasks and the accommodations that would be necessary if the disabled candidate is hired. Interview facilities should be accessible to the disabled candidate according to specifications set out in regulations issued by the Architectural and Transportation Barriers Compliance Board. (See Appendix C.) During the interview, the employer should do the following:

- Make maneuvering easier for the applicant by removing unnecessary furniture that might obstruct his path
- Ask the applicant if he would like help before giving it, so the applicant can explain exactly how to help
- Get on the same eye level as the applicant and try to maintain that level throughout the interview

The interviewer should present to the applicant the duties that are required for the position and ask if he thinks he would be able to accomplish them and what accommodations would need to be made. It is also often a good idea to take the applicant on a tour of the worksite when discussing necessary accommodations. Since many paraplegics and quadriplegics have dexterity and/or coordination problems, accommodations may be necessary at the pre-employment testing stage, such as individual testing, extended time limits, assistance with turning pages, or enlarged blocks on answer sheets.

Employee disabilities must be analyzed on a case-by-case basis. Accommodations for paraplegics and quadriplegics can range from putting books on lower shelves to providing automatic door openers.

The following are three examples of accommodations that have been made for individuals who are paraplegic or quadriplegic. These examples illustrate the point that accommodations can allow a disabled individual to become a productive employee, with little or no inconvenience to the employer.[33]

---

[33] Examples provided by JAN.

1. A systems analyst was able to access high-security areas by the use of a light installed at the door to the secured area that alerted the security guard that an individual in a wheelchair was approaching and needed assistance with the door. The cost of this accommodation was $50.

2. A secretary was able to use the desk in her office when wood blocks placed under the desk raised its height so the wheelchair could fit under it. The cost of this accommodation was $0.

3. A sales agent who had lost the use of his arms and hands due to a neck injury was able to review files and give dictation by using an automatic page turner and a voice-activated tape recorder. The cost of these accommodations was between $500 and $1,000.

CHAPTER **4**

ADA Title II: Public Accommodations and Services Operated by Public Entities

¶ 4.01 INTRODUCTION AND EFFECTIVE DATES

Title II of the ADA is designed to prohibit discrimination against the disabled by public entities. It covers the provision of services, programs, activities, and employment by public entities. Generally speaking, if a government or governmental unit provides services, programs, or activities to the public—such as financial assistance or grants, emergency telephone services, educational programs, or licensing—the same access to and opportunities to participate and derive benefit that are afforded to persons without disabilities must be afforded to the disabled. Any reasonable modification or aid necessary to afford access to the disabled must be made or furnished.

Subtitle A of Title II states the general rule against discrimination applicable to all public entities, while Subtitle B sets forth specific prohibitions against discrimination that, while falling within the general prohibition of Subtitle A, apply just in the context of public transportation provided by public entities.

A public entity to which Title II applies includes:[1]

a) a state or local government;

b) any department, agency, special purpose district or other instrumentality of a state or local government; and

c) the National Railroad Passenger Corporation (Amtrak), and any commuter authority as this term is defined in section 103(8) of the Rail Passenger Service Act.[2]

Section 504 of the Rehabilitation Act of 1973[3] and the

---

[1] ADA § 201(1).

[2] Section 103(8) of the Rail Passenger Service Act (45 USC 502(8)) defines commuter authority as

any State, local, or regional authority, corporation, or other entity established for purposes of providing commuter service, and includes the Metropolitan Transportation Authority, the Connecticut Department of Transportation, the Maryland Department of Transportation, the Southeastern Pennsylvania Transportation Authority, the New Jersey Transit Corporation, the Massachusetts Bay Transit Authority, the Port Authority Trans-Hudson Corporation, any successor agencies, and any entity created by one or more such agencies for the purpose of operating, or contracting for the operation of, commuter service.

[3] 29 USC § 794.

regulations promulgated thereunder already prohibit discrimination against the disabled by state and local governments— and agencies or instrumentalities thereof—that are receiving federal assistance. Given this, Title II has two primary purposes. First, it extends the prohibitions against discrimination in the Rehabilitation Act to state and local governments, and agencies or instrumentalities thereof, regardless of whether the government, agency, or instrumentality is receiving any federal funds or assistance. Second, it clarifies the requirements of Section 504 for public transportation entities that receive federal assistance, particularly with respect to commuter railroads, and also prohibits discrimination by all public entities that provide public transportation regardless of whether the entity receives federal assistance.[4]

The purpose of Title II is to continue the Rehabilitation Act's goal of breaking down "barriers to the integrated participation of people with disabilities in all aspects of community life."[5] Title II will work in the same manner as Section 504 of the Rehabilitation Act, and many of the same general guidelines that have developed with respect to Section 504 will also apply to Title II. For example, a public entity must provide equal opportunity and access to the disabled, but not if doing so will be an "undue hardship" or "undue burden."[6] In this context, though, an undue hardship or burden must be more than just substantial; Congress has recognized that compliance with Section 504 of the Rehabilitation Act and Title II of the ADA may

---

[4] Report of the House Comm. on Education and Labor on the Americans With Disabilities Act of 1990, HR Rep. No. 485, 101st Cong., 2d Sess., pt. 2 (1990) (hereinafter cited as H. Comm. on Educ. and Lab. Rep.) at 84; Report of the Senate Comm. on Labor and Human Resources on the Americans With Disabilities Act of 1989, S. Rpt. No. 116, 101st Cong., 1st Sess. (1989) (hereinafter cited as S. Comm. on Lab. and Hum. Resources Rep.) at 44; Report of the House Comm. on Energy and Commerce on the Americans With Disabilities Act of 1990, HR Rep. No. 485, 101st Cong., 2d Sess., pt. 4 (1990) (hereinafter cited as H. Comm. on Energy and Com. Rep.) at 26.

[5] Report of the House Comm. on the Judiciary on the Americans With Disabilities Act of 1990, HR Rep. No. 485, 101st Cong., 2d Sess., pt. 3 (1990) (hereinafter cited as H. Comm. on Jud. Rep.) at 50.

[6] Id. See also discussion of these terms in connection with Titles I and III of the ADA.

place a substantial burden on public agencies, but has determined that the goal of integrating the disabled into society merits incurring substantial burden.[7]

The standards for interpreting Section 504 of the Rehabilitation Act are generally made applicable to Title II. Similarly, the provisions of Titles I and III of the ADA as they relate to provide equal employment opportunity and access to facilities and services are incorporated into Title II to the extent they are not inconsistent with the regulations implementing Section 504.[8]

Therefore, in determining whether a particular accommodation necessary to afford employment by a Title II public entity to a disabled person is an undue hardship, the factors to be considered, such as the size and budget of the employer, are the same ones set forth in regulations interpreting Section 504 of the Rehabilitation Act, and basically the same as those to be applied in connection with Title I of the ADA.[9] The appendix accompanying Section 504 regulations, quoted with approval by the House Judiciary Committee in its report on Title II of the ADA, states by way of an example:

> [A] small day-care center might not be required to expend more than a nominal sum, such as that necessary to equip a telephone for use by a secretary with impaired hearing, but a large school district might be required to make available a teacher's aide to a blind applicant for a teaching job. Further, it might be considered reasonable to require a state welfare agency to accommodate a deaf employee by providing an interpreter, while it would constitute an undue hardship to [impose] that requirement on a provider of foster home care services.[10]

---

[7] Id. See also Dopico v. Goldschmidt, 687 F2d 644 (2d Cir. 1982); New Mex. Ass'n for Retarded Citizens v. New Mex., 678 F2d 847 (10th Cir. 1982); Nelson v. Thornburgh, 567 F. Supp. 369 (ED Pa. 1983); Bentivegna v. Department of Labor, 694 F2d 619 (9th Cir. 1982); Rhone v. US Dep't of Army, 665 F. Supp. 734 (ED Mo. 1987).

[8] H. Comm. on Jud. Rep. at 51.

[9] For more detailed discussion of these standards, see discussion of Title I in Chapter 2.

[10] 42 Fed. Reg. 22,688 (May 4, 1977).

Similarly, with respect to access to facilities and services, what constitutes an undue burden for the public entity can be determined by reference to relevant regulations implementing Section 504 of the Rehabilitation Act[11] and to the standards set forth in Title III of the ADA.[12] Again, the totality of the factors concerning the public entity, such as its size, budget, available resources, and whether the inherent nature of the facility or service would be altered if access to a particular disabled person is provided, must be considered. As is also the case with Title III of the ADA, if it is determined that providing full and complete access to a facility or program does constitute an "undue burden," the public entity still must do as much as it can that is not as burdensome to provide the maximum benefit possible to the disabled.[13]

Separate but equal facilities or services are not a permissible way of complying with Title II, regardless of the quality of the facilities or services provided to the disabled. While specialized facilities or services for persons with disabilities—such as special recreation programs—are not in any way prohibited by Title II, "the existence of such programs can never be used as a basis to exclude a person with a disability from a program that is offered to those without disabilities, or to refuse to provide an accommodation in a regular setting."[14] This same approach is taken in Title III.

Generally, the provisions of Title II take effect either on the day of enactment of the ADA (July 26, 1990) or eighteen months thereafter (January 26, 1992). The provisions that take effect on the day of enactment are the following:

- Subtitle A's provisions directing the Department of Justice to issue regulations
- Subtitle B, Part I, Sections 222, 223(b) through 223(f), 224, 225, 227(b), 228(b), and 229
- Subtitle B, Part II, Sections 242 and 244

---

[11] See, e.g., 28 CFR pt. 39.

[12] See discussion of "undue burden" in the Title III context in Chapter 5.

[13] H. Comm. on Jud. Rep. at 51.

[14] Id. at 50.

The provisions that take effect eighteen months after the date of enactment are the following:

- All of Subtitle A except those sections relating to the issuance of regulations by the Department of Justice
- Subtitle B, Part I, Sections 221, 223(a), 226, 227(a), 228(a), and 230
- All of Subtitle B, Part II, except Sections 242 and 244

¶ 4.02 PROHIBITIONS: PUBLIC ACCOMMODATIONS AND SERVICES GENERALLY

Title II's general, broad prohibition against discrimination is set forth in Section 202. This provision provides that, subject to other provisions of Title II, no "qualified individual with a disability" shall by reason of such disability be excluded from participation in or be denied the benefits of the services, programs, or activities of a public entity, or be subjected to discrimination by any such entity. It is a broad, wide-sweeping command that applies without regard to whether any federal funding or assistance is involved. Essentially, it is an extension and clarification of the prohibitions against discrimination included in Section 504 of the Rehabilitation Act.

Though Section 202 of the ADA is meant just to incorporate Section 504 of the Rehabilitation Act, it does not contain the language in Section 504 that prohibits denial of benefits to an individual "solely by reason of her or his handicap." This was a conscious omission, for two main reasons, based primarily on the word "solely." First, Congress recognized that the Rehabilitation Act's language created confusion since it could conceivably be read not to prohibit a denial of benefits that was based on several impermissible grounds, just one of which was disability-related (another ground used could be race-related, for example); in such instances, the disability would not be the sole reason for the denial of benefits, and the strict letter of the Rehabilitation Act would not have been violated. Second, perhaps recognizing this confusion, the regulations issued by most executive branch agencies to implement the Rehabilitation Act already track the language used in Section 202 of the ADA.[15] Congress agreed with the approach taken by the executive branch agencies and adopted this language in Title II to reinforce that a denial of benefits where one—but not necessarily the sole—reason for the denial was the presence of a disability is a violation of both Section 504 of the Rehabilitation Act and Section 202 of the ADA.[16]

The forms of discrimination prohibited by Section 202 are identical to the discrimination prohibited in Titles I and III of the ADA.[17] The descriptions of types of prohibited discrimination set forth in Sections 102(b), 102(c), and 302(b) of the ADA, and the construction of these passages in regulations, guidelines, and case law, for example, would apply equally to Section 202.[18]

[1] Qualified Individual With a Disability

No qualified individual with a disability can be discriminated against by a public entity under Section 202. "Qualified individual with a disability" as defined in Section 201(2) means

an individual with a disability who, with or without reasonable modifications to rules, policies, or practices, the removal of architectural, communication, or transportation barriers, or the provision of auxiliary aids and services, meets the essential eligibility requirements for the receipt of services or the participation in programs or activities provided by a public entity.

Auxiliary aids and services in this context include, but are not limited to, the following:

---

[15] H. Comm. on Educ. and Lab. Rep. at 85; S. Comm. on Lab. and Hum. Resources Rep. at 44.

[16] H. Comm. on Educ. and Lab. Rep. at 85, 86; S. Comm. on Lab. and Hum. Resources Rep. at 45.

[17] H. Comm. on Educ. and Lab. Rep. at 84; S. Comm. on Lab. and Hum. Resources Rep. at 44.

[18] H. Comm. on Educ. and Lab. Rep. at 84.

(1) Qualified interpreters, notetakers, transcription services, written materials, telephone handset amplifiers, assistive listening devices, assistive listening systems, telephones compatible with hearing aids, closed caption decoders, open and closed captioning, telecommunication devices for deaf persons (TDD's), videotext displays or other equally effective methods of making aurally delivered materials available to individuals with hearing impairments;

(2) Qualified readers, taped texts, audio recordings, Brailled materials, large print materials, or other effective methods of making visually delivered materials available to individuals with visual impairments;

(3) Acquisition or modification of equipment or devices; and

(4) Other similar services and actions.[19]

A person has a disability for purposes of all titles of the ADA if the person has a physical or mental impairment that substantially limits one or more of the person's major life activities, a record of such an impairment, or is regarded as having such an impairment.[20]

The term "individual with a disability" does not include an individual who is currently engaging in the illegal use of drugs, when the public entity acts on the basis of such use.[21] In such an instance, the public entity may discriminate because of the drug use, unless the services involved relate to drug rehabilitation. However, if an individual who formerly used illegal drugs is not currently engaging in illegal drug use and has successfully been rehabilitated or is currently participating in a supervised rehabilitation program, the public entity may not discriminate against that individual on the basis of the former drug use.[22]

An individual is not a qualified individual if no reasonable amount of accommodation will enable the person to meet the eligibility requirements for the service requested; if, however, a

---

[19] See Department of Justice regulation 28 CFR § 35.104.

[20] See ADA § 3(2).

[21] See Department of Justice regulation 28 CFR § 35.104.

[22] See Department of Justice regulation 28 CFR § 35.131(2).

reasonable modification of some kind to rules or procedures, or the providing of reasonable auxiliary aids or services, would enable the individual to meet eligibility requirements, the individual would be qualified. This is similar to the approach taken in the Rehabilitation Act to the extent that

> the manifestations of a person's disability prevent that person from meeting the basic eligibility requirements of the program—for example, by causing substantial interference with the operation of the program or by posing a significant risk to the health or safety of others that cannot be eliminated by reasonable accommodation—that manifestation of the person's disability may be taken into account by the operator of the program in denying service to the person with the disability.[23]

[2] Relief Available for Violation

Since Title II is closely related to Section 504 of the Rehabilitation Act, the relief available to redress a violation by a public entity of the antidiscrimination provisions of Section 202 of the ADA is the same relief that can be had for a violation of Section 504. Section 203 of the ADA incorporates by reference the enforcement provisions of Section 505 of the Rehabilitation Act.[24] Section 505 of the Rehabilitation Act, in turn, incorporates the remedies, procedures, and rights set forth in Section 717 and Title VI of the Civil Rights Act of 1964.[25] The incorporation of Section 717 is for purposes of employment discrimination—covered by Section 501 of the Rehabilitation Act—while the incorporation of Title VI is for a violation of Section 504 of the Rehabilitation Act.

Section 502 of the ADA eliminates immunity of a state in state or federal court under the Eleventh Amendment for violations of the ADA. A state will be liable in the same manner, and subject to the same remedies at law and equity, as any private or public entity other than a state.

---

[23] H. Comm. on Energy and Com. Rep. at 38.

[24] 29 USC § 794(a).

[25] 42 USC §§ 2000e-16, 2000d.

Attorney fees may be awarded to a prevailing party (other than the federal government) in an administrative or court proceeding pursuant to Section 505 of the ADA.

The Department of Justice's regulations prohibit both a public and a private entity from discriminating against an individual just because that individual opposed a practice or procedure that is unlawful under Title II.[26]

The Department of Justice's regulations also require that any public entity with fifty or more employees designate at least one employee to coordinate efforts to comply with Title II.[27] The public entity must adopt grievance procedures, and the designated employee will be responsible for investigating any complaints filed.

A procedure for instituting complaints against a public entity without going to court is provided in the regulations.[28] An individual who believes he is the victim of discrimination in violation of Title II may file a complaint with the federal agency designated in the regulations as the "responsible agency" for the public entity against whom the discrimination is alleged. The complaint must be filed within 180 days after the act of discrimination is alleged to have occurred, unless the agency extends such time for good cause. If the responsible agency finds a violation to have occurred, the violation will be corrected— either voluntarily through negotiations with the public entity, or through the intervention of the Attorney General.

This procedure is a totally voluntary one. An individual may file suit in court without filing an administrative complaint, or an individual may file suit at any time while an administrative complaint is pending. No exhaustion of remedies is required.[29]

---

[26] See Department of Justice regulation 28 CFR § 35.134.

[27] See Department of Justice regulation 28 CFR § 35.107.

[28] See Department of Justice regulations 28 CFR §§ 35.170–35.176. The agencies to whom complaints should be directed, and area of jurisdiction, are listed at 28 CFR § 35.190.

[29] H. Comm. on Educ. and Lab. Rep. at 98; S. Comm. on Lab. and Hum. Resources Rep. at 57–58.

[3] Regulations

Except with respect to matters that are dealt with specifically in Subtitle B, the Department of Justice was given the responsibility for issuing, and has issued, regulations in an accessible format to implement Subtitle A of Title II of the ADA.[30] The Secretary of Transportation has issued regulations to implement the provisions of Subtitle B.[31]

The Department of Justice's regulations include specific standards for facilities and vehicles to which Subtitle A applies in the regulations, except that these standards are not applicable to facilities, stations, rail passenger cars, and vehicles that are covered more specifically in Subtitle B.[32] These standards incorporate the accessibility standards of the Architectural and Transportation Barriers Compliance Board's (ATBCB) Accessibility Guidelines for Buildings and Facilities (with the exception of the elevator exemption) and the Uniform Federal Accessibility Standards (UFAS), for new construction.[33] The requirements of ADA Title I and the Equal Employment Opportunity Commission regulations issued pursuant thereto, and the Rehabilitation Act regulations if applicable, are incorporated for Title II employment matters.[34]

With three exceptions, the Department of Justice's regulations are required to be consistent with the ADA (not just Title II) and with regulations that implement Section 504 of the Rehabilitation Act—specifically the coordination regulations under Part 41 of Title 28, Code of Federal Regulations issued by the Department of Health, Education, and Welfare on January 13, 1978, applicable to recipients of federal financial assistance. The exceptions are that with respect to regulations concerning the terms "program accessibility," "existing facilities," and "communications," the regulations must be consistent with regulations and analysis contained in Part 39 of Title 28 of the Code of

---

[30] ADA § 204(a). See 28 CFR pt. 35.

[31] See 49 CFR pt. 37.

[32] ADA § 204(c).

[33] See 28 CFR § 35.151.

[34] See 28 CFR § 35.140(b).

Federal Regulations, applicable to federally conducted activities under Section 504 of the Rehabilitation Act.

Where there is a conflict between the general Department of Justice regulations and the more specific Department of Transportation regulations in the area of public transportation, the Department of Transportation's regulations prevail.[35]

[a] Standards and Guidelines

The Department of Justice's regulations governing Subtitle A set forth numerous standards and guidelines for compliance by public entities with the subtitle. Reducing them to their essence, it can be generally stated that the regulations require public entities to abide by the ADA Title I requirements in connection with employment issues,[36] and to abide by the ADA Title III ideas in connection with accessibility issues.

The proposed regulations prohibit a public entity from, among other things:

- Denying the disabled an equal opportunity to participate in its activities, services, or programs
- Discriminating indirectly by entering into contractual relationships or licenses with others who then discriminate against the disabled
- Insisting that the disabled be treated separately or differently from the nondisabled unless necessary to provide an equal level of benefits
- Providing any aid or assistance to an organization that discriminates against the disabled
- Denying a qualified disabled person an opportunity to be a member of a planning or advisory board
- Insisting that a disabled person participate in a separate but equal program

---

[35] See Department of Justice regulation 28 CFR § 35.102(b).

[36] See Department of Justice regulation 28 CFR § 35.140. See also Equal Employment Opportunity Commission regulations at 29 CFR pt. 1630; Department of Justice regulations at 28 CFR pt. 41.

- Using criteria or methods of administration that have the effect of discriminating against the disabled[37]

A public entity must personally modify its practices or procedures as necessary to avoid such discrimination.[38] Moreover, if providing equal treatment and opportunity to the disabled, such as through auxiliary aids, costs the public entity additional money, the public entity is prohibited from recovering this cost by levying a surcharge just on the disabled; to do so would constitute discrimination.[39]

The regulations state that a qualified disabled person cannot be excluded from participation in a program, service, or activity of a public entity because the entity's facilities are inaccessible to or unusable by the disabled (a Title III concept)— although if a program, service, or activity, when viewed as a whole, is readily accessible to and usable by individuals with disabilities, it is not a violation if one portion of the program service or activity is not accessible or usable.[40] While a public entity must operate programs, services, or activities that are accessible when viewed as a whole, a public entity does not have to

- Take action to make every one of its existing facilities accessible
- Take action to provide access that would pose an undue financial or administrative burden
- Take action that would fundamentally alter the nature of the service, program, or activity
- Take action that would impair the significant historic features of a historic preservation building[41]

There are many ways that a public entity can choose to modify its programs, services, and activities to provide access to the disabled. Some examples include redesign of equipment,

---

[37] See Department of Justice regulation 28 CFR § 35.130.

[38] See Department of Justice regulation 28 CFR § 35.130(b)(7).

[39] See Department of Justice regulation 28 CFR § 35.130(f).

[40] See Department of Justice regulation 28 CFR §§ 35.149, 35.150.

[41] See Department of Justice regulation 28 CFR § 35.150(a).

reassignment of services to accessible buildings, assignment of aides to users, home visits, delivery of services at alternate accessible sites, alteration of existing facilities, construction of new facilities, and use of accessible rolling stock.[42] Where other methods of compliance are effective, a public entity is not required to alter an existing facility or construct a new one. If the public entity does undertake alterations or new construction (if the alteration or new construction was commenced after January 26, 1992), though, the work must be accessible and must meet either the accessibility requirements of the UFAS or the ATBCB's ADAAG.[43] When features or equipment are added to promote accessibility, the public entity's obligation is not thereby discharged. It has a continuing obligation to maintain such features or equipment in good working condition.[44]

When a historic property is involved, and a physical alteration is not required because it would significantly alter the historic nature of the property, the public entity must still, to the greatest extent feasible, endeavor to provide as much access as possible to the disabled. The proposed regulations provide two ways of how this could be done: by using audiovisual means to show sections of the building that cannot be made accessible, or by assigning guides to take the disabled through otherwise inaccessible portions of the building, if practical.[45] Innovative solutions in these situations are encouraged by the regulations.[46]

The effective date of the Department of Justice's regulations is January 26, 1992. However, where structural changes in facilities are undertaken, they must be made no later than three years after this effective date (but as expeditiously as possible).[47] When a public entity that plans to undertake structural changes to comply with the regulations has fifty or more employees, a transition plan must be developed by the entity (unless such a

---

[42] See Department of Justice regulation 28 CFR § 35.150(b)(1).

[43] Id.

[44] See Department of Justice regulation 28 CFR § 35.151.

[45] See Department of Justice regulation 28 CFR §§ 35.150(b)(2), 35.151(d).

[46] Id.

[47] See Department of Justice regulation 28 CFR § 35.150(c).

plan was already developed pursuant to a regulation implementing Section 504 of the Rehabilitation Act). This plan must be developed, within six months after January 26, 1992, in consultation with representatives of the disabled community, and tell how the facility involved will be made accessible.[48]

[i] **New construction and alterations.** The regulations require that any new construction of a facility by, on behalf of, or for the use of a public entity that is started after January 26, 1992, be designed and constructed so that the facility is accessible to and usable by the disabled.[49] Similarly, a facility that is altered by, on behalf of, or for the use of a public entity after January 26, 1992, in a manner that affects or could affect the usability of part or all of the facility, must be altered to the maximum extent feasible so that the altered portion is readily accessible to and usable by individuals with disabilities.[50] Again, this is a concept taken from Title III of the ADA.

[ii] **Communications.** One type of service provided by most state and local governments is the availability of an emergency telephone number, often 911, that individuals can call in case of fire, sudden illness, or other life-threatening situations. According to the House Committee on Education and Labor, most of the 911 systems nationwide are not hooked up to telecommunication devices for the deaf (TDDs) and cannot therefore be accessed by persons with speech or hearing disabilities who use TDDs. Though the broad mandate to make telephone communications accessible to the disabled is provided in Title IV of the ADA, Title II requires that where telephone emergency systems are provided to the public, the systems must be equipped with technology to enable persons using TDDs (or computer modems, under the proposed regulations) to call 911 directly and get an immediate response.[51]

Where a public entity communicates with applicants and the people it services by telephone, it must use TDDs or other

---

[48] See Department of Justice regulation 28 CFR § 35.150(d).

[49] See Department of Justice regulation 28 CFR § 35.151(a).

[50] See Department of Justice regulation 28 CFR § 35.151(b).

[51] H. Comm. on Educ. and Lab. Rep. at 85.

equally effective telecommunication to communicate with hearing- or speech-impaired individuals. [52]

A public entity must ensure that the disabled can obtain information from it as to the existence and location of accessible services, facilities, and activities. Additionally, at all inaccessible entrances to public facilities, signage must be posted telling where an accessible entrance can be found or where information about access can be obtained. [53]

These communications requirements must be complied with unless compliance would either alter the nature of the activity or program or cause an undue financial or administrative burden. Such a conclusion can only be reached by a public entity if good reason exists, and if the reason is put into writing. In these cases, the public entity still must provide the disabled with access or equal treatment to the maximum extent feasible under the circumstances. [54]

[b] Self-Evaluation

The Department of Justice regulations provide a procedure for self-evaluation by a public entity of the public entity's services, policies, and practices that may not meet the requirements of Subtitle A of Title II. [55] Comments should be solicited from interested persons, including individuals with disabilities and organizations representing such individuals, as part of this evaluation process. This self-evaluation must be conducted within one year of January 26, 1992.

To the extent that services, policies, and practices do not comply with Subtitle A, they must be corrected. This evaluation procedure need not be followed if the public entity has already conducted a self-evaluation pursuant to a regulation implementing Section 504 of the Rehabilitation Act, except as to services, policies, and practices that were not included in the self-evaluation that was previously conducted.

---

[52] See Department of Justice regulation 28 CFR § 35.161.

[53] See Department of Justice regulation 28 CFR § 35.163.

[54] See Department of Justice regulation 28 CFR § 35.164.

[55] See Department of Justice regulation 28 CFR § 35.105.

¶ 4.03 PROHIBITIONS: TRANSPORTATION GENERALLY

Subtitle B applies to prohibit specific instances of discrimination under Section 202 of the ADA by public entities that provide public transportation services. It does not create new prohibitions beyond what is covered in Subtitle A; it just gets more specific about transportation issues. Subtitle B is drafted so that the discriminatory actions set forth therein are violations not only of Section 202 of the ADA, but also of Section 504 of the Rehabilitation Act.

There are several reasons why, having already expanded the antidiscrimination umbrella to cover all public entities and all types of services offered by public entities in Subtitle A, Congress wanted also to address the area of public transportation specifically in Subtitle B. The reasons relate primarily to the clarification or correction of misunderstandings that have arisen in the implementation of Section 504 of the Rehabilitation Act with respect to public transportation services provided by public entities. Congress wanted to make it clear that the regulations promulgated by the Department of Transportation to implement Section 504 in the transportation area[56] apply to commuter railroads and not just to Amtrak. It also wanted to direct and guide the Department of Transportation, the Federal Railroad Administration, and the ATBCB to develop accessibility regulations and guidelines that recognize the differences between Amtrak and commuter railroads. Further, Congress felt it was important to ensure that regulations applicable to Amtrak intercity trains recognize and take into account the practical reality that accessibility requirements can vary from one type of passenger car to another (such as from a one-level car to a bi-level car). Finally, Congress needed to modify the way accessibility is to be achieved by Amtrak, and the timetable for achieving it, in light of the reality that Amtrak's congressionally mandated budget in the last several years has been lower than what has been needed to carry out Congress's original intent in this area.[57]

---

[56] See 49 CFR § 27.73.

[57] H. Comm. on Educ. and Lab. Rep. at 26, 27.

Subtitle B is divided into two parts—Part I covers public transportation by means other than aircraft or certain rail operations, and Part II deals with public transportation by intercity and commuter rail. As indicated earlier, Title II of the ADA, and therefore Subtitle B, only applies to services, programs, or activities provided by public entities. Public transportation that is provided by a private entity, therefore, does not fall within Title II (it is covered by Title III, which applies to public services and accommodations provided by private entities).

Congress did not include travel by air within the scope of any part of the ADA because of the passage of the Air Carrier Access Act,[58] a measure designed to address discrimination by air carriers. The expectation is that regulations will be issued pursuant to that law to carry out adequately congressional intent to prohibit discrimination by air carriers.[59] However, Title II does apply to fixed facilities, such as airports, provided or operated by public entities that are used in connection with air travel and with related services provided or operated by public entities, such as ground transportation.[60]

Congress recognized that transportation vehicles are occasionally donated by a private entity to a public entity—through a bequest, for example. It did not want to stop this practice by imposing a requirement that the accessibility requirements of Title II be met in order for the public entity to accept and use a donated vehicle, so Title II is not intended to apply to such donated vehicles. At the same time, though, Congress also did not intend for public entities to go out and arrange to have vehicles donated to them just to get around the provisions of Title II; this would be contrary to the intent of the ADA, and a violation of Title II.[61]

The prohibitions against discrimination contained in Subti-

---

[58] Pub. L. No. 99-435, amending 49 USC App. 1301, 1374 (1986).

[59] H. Comm. on Educ. and Lab. Rep. at 87, 121; S. Comm. on Lab. and Hum. Resources Rep. at 46, 72.

[60] Id.

[61] H. Comm. on Educ. and Lab. Rep. at 87; S. Comm. on Lab. and Hum. Resources Rep. at 46.

tle B apply generally not just to the design of vehicles and facilities but to their operation as well:

> Thus, new fixed route buses must have lifts, and new and key stations must have elevators or other means to ensure accessibility as necessary components for a transit authority to be in compliance with the provisions of this title of the legislation. Merely installing the access equipment is never sufficient by itself, however; the lifts and elevators must also operate, be in good working order, and be available when needed for access in order for an entity to be in compliance with the law.[62]

Public entities, in purchasing, leasing, remanufacturing, or altering transportation vehicles covered by Subtitle B, and in constructing or altering stations covered by the subtitle, would be well advised to obtain a warranty from the vendor or contractor with whom they are dealing that the vehicle or work done complies with the standards of Title II of the ADA and all regulations and guidelines thereunder. Additionally, these public entities should ask for an agreement from such vendor or contractor to indemnify them against any loss stemming from a failure of the vehicle or work done to comply with Title II and the regulations and guidelines. Doing so will offer some protection to public entities because, for the most part, if there is a violation of Title II, the public entity will bear liability — even if it acted in good faith to comply with Title II and the error was by one of its vendors or contractors.

¶ 4.04 BUSES, RAPID RAIL, AND LIGHT RAIL

[1] Definitions

Part I of Subtitle B covers public transportation other than by aircraft or certain rail operations. Section 221 of the ADA defines the following terms used in Part I to make clear the scope of Part I's applicability.[63]

---

[62] Id.

[63] The statute skips from Section 205 at the end of Subtitle A to Section 221 at the start of Subtitle B.

1. *Designated public transportation.* Transportation, other than public school transportation, by bus, rail, or any other conveyance (other than aircraft, since the ADA does not cover aircraft travel, or intercity or commuter rail transportation, since Part II of Subtitle B covers them) that provides the general public with general or special service, including charter service, on a regular and continuing basis.

2. *Fixed route system.* A system of providing designated public transportation on which a vehicle is operated along a prescribed route according to a fixed schedule—such as a municipal bus system. This is similar to the definition of fixed route system in Section 301 of Title III.

3. *Demand responsive system.* Any system of providing designated public transportation that is not a fixed route system (i.e., one that does not operate along a prescribed route or according to a fixed schedule). Demand responsive system has virtually the same definition for Part I of Subtitle B as it does in Section 301 of Title III.

4. *Operates.* Used in connection with either of the afore-mentioned systems, the term includes operation of such system by a person under a contractual or other arrangement with a public entity—so if a public entity subcontracts with a private firm to run its municipal bus service, the requirements of Title II still apply to the bus service.

5. *Secretary.* The Secretary of Transportation, who is charged with issuing the regulations implementing Subtitle B.

6. *Public school transportation.* Transportation by school bus vehicles of schoolchildren, personnel, and equipment to and from a public elementary or secondary school and school-related activities. School bus operations by public entities are considered demand responsive systems.

[2] Vehicles

[a] Fixed Route Systems

Section 222 of the ADA generally prohibits a public entity that operates a fixed route system from purchasing or leasing vehicles of any kind, including buses, rapid rail, and light rail vehicles,[64] that are not readily accessible to and usable by individuals

---

[64] Proposed Department of Transportation regulations 49 CFR §§ 37.51,

with disabilities, including individuals who use wheelchairs. Though individuals who use wheelchairs are specifically referenced in all parts of the section, access must be afforded and equal attention devoted to persons with all types of disabilities.

The public entity's obligation is to make sure its newly acquired or remanufactured vehicles are readily accessible to and usable by the disabled. This means that the disabled, no matter what their disability, must be able "to enter into and exit and safely and effectively use a vehicle used for public transportation."[65]

Among the features necessary to make a vehicle readily accessible and usable are for persons in wheelchairs, lifts or ramps and other equipment to be able to take them into a vehicle, and for there to be fold-up seats or other wheelchair spaces with appropriate securement devices inside the vehicle.[66] These features and equipment must be kept in good working order, though; providing lifts that do not work would still be considered discrimination.[67] The lifts or ramps should also be made available to individuals who have mobility impairments but who do not use wheelchairs, such as persons using crutches or walkers.

More specific guidance in this area is provided in the proposed regulations issued by the Secretary of Transportation.[68] The proposed regulations contain standards that a vehicle must meet to be considered accessible under the ADA. These standards, however, will be replaced in the final regulations by the standards set out in the ATBCB's guidelines for Title II.

How many wheelchair spaces must be provided in a vehicle depends upon the vehicle, the number of vehicles in the fleet, the vacancy rate, and the usage of the vehicle by persons with wheelchairs. The number of wheelchair spaces, then, is a determina-

---

37.53, 37.55, and 37.57 relate to the purchase, lease, and remanufacture of rapid and light rail vehicles.

[65] H. Comm. on Educ. and Lab. Rep. at 88.

[66] Id.

[67] S. Comm. on Lab. and Hum. Resources Rep. at 46.

[68] See proposed Department of Transportation regulation 49 CFR § 37.

tion to be made by the public entity that provides the transportation.[69] Technical specifications and guidelines for the lifts, ramps, wheelchair spaces, and the like, however, will be provided in the final supplemental minimum guidelines issued to implement the ADA and Title II and incorporated into the Department of Transportation's final regulations.

[i] **New vehicles.** Section 222(a) applies to the purchase or lease of a new vehicle. It labels it as discrimination for a public entity that operates a fixed route system to purchase or lease a new bus, a new rapid rail vehicle, a new light rail vehicle, or any other new vehicle to be used on such system, if the solicitation for such purchase or lease is made after August 26, 1990 (the thirtieth day following the July 26, 1990, enactment of the ADA), and if such vehicle is not readily accessible to and usable by individuals with disabilities, including individuals who use wheelchairs. "New" in this context means that it is the first sale or lease of the vehicle, and there has been no prior use.[70]

If a new vehicle is purchased or leased for which the solicitation was made within the thirty days following July 26, 1990, the purchase or lease is not covered by Title II's accessibility requirements. The key date in this regard is when the public entity asks for bids from manufacturers to build buses, or when the public entity begins to offer to purchase or bid for the purchase or lease.[71]

[ii] **Used vehicles.** Small and rural communities frequently buy used buses because they do not have the money to buy new ones but still want to provide transportation to residents; the ADA is not intended to prevent these communities from continuing to provide such transportation. Section 222(b) applies specifically to the purchase or lease of a used vehicle, other than one that has been remanufactured. It makes it discrimination for a public entity that operates a fixed route system to purchase or lease, at any time after August 26, 1990, a used vehicle for such

---

[69] H. Comm. on Educ. and Lab. Rep. at 48.

[70] Id. at 47.

[71] S. Comm. on Lab. and Hum. Resources Rep. at 47.

system unless the public entity makes a demonstrated good faith effort to purchase or lease a used vehicle that is readily accessible to and usable by individuals with disabilities, including persons in wheelchairs.

A used vehicle is one that was purchased or leased by its original owner earlier than June 26, 1990.[72] The demonstrated good faith effort referred to must be a nationwide—not a local or regional—search to locate a used accessible vehicle, such as a bus, with advertisements in national magazines and inquiries to national trade associations.[73] If, after making such a good faith effort, the public entity cannot find an accessible used vehicle for purchase or lease, it is then not discrimination for it to purchase or lease a used vehicle that is not fully accessible. (The ADA does not force the public entity to purchase a new bus.) Even so, to the extent that it does not constitute an undue burden to do so, any aids or assistance that the public entity can provide to make the vehicle accessible to as many disabled individuals as possible must be provided. For instance, if a bus with a lift or ramp cannot be found, and the bus purchased is not accessible to individuals in wheelchairs, the public entity can still train its bus drivers to furnish assistance to enable persons with other mobility impairments, such as crutches or walkers, to board and be comfortably seated.

A public entity that cannot in good faith locate an accessible used vehicle is not required to obtain a waiver from the Urban Mass Transit Administration (UMTA) in order to purchase or lease a used, not-fully-accessible vehicle, contrary to what proposed regulations require in connection with a new vehicle. However, if a public entity purchases or leases a used vehicle that is not readily accessible to and usable by the disabled, it must retain documentation evidencing its good faith efforts to locate an accessible used vehicle for two years, and must make

---

[72] H. Comm. on Educ. and Lab. Rep. at 90; S. Comm. on Lab. and Hum. Resources Rep. at 49. See also proposed Department of Transportation regulation 49 CFR Section 37.5, which indicates that the date of purchase or lease is the date on which the public entity becomes legally obligated to obtain the vehicles, such as the time of contract execution.

[73] Id.

such documentation available on request to the public and the UMTA.[74]

With the passage of the ADA, the number of buses available that will be fully accessible to the disabled will become increasingly greater. Accordingly, as time goes by, it will become harder and harder for a public entity to prove that it was unable to locate such a used vehicle.

[iii] Remanufactured vehicles. Section 222(c) applies to remanufactured vehicles where the remanufacture extends the vehicles' usable life by five years or more. "Remanufacture" means to strip a vehicle to its frame and rebuild it, or structurally to restore a vehicle and install new or rebuilt components to extend its service life.[75] The general rule is that it is an act of discrimination for a public entity that operates a fixed route system to remanufacture a vehicle, or to purchase or lease a vehicle that is remanufactured so as to extend the usable life of the vehicle for five years or more, for use on the fixed route system, unless the vehicle is, after remanufacture, readily accessible to and usable by individuals with disabilities (including individuals in wheelchairs) to the maximum extent feasible. This rule applies in two instances:

1. When the remanufacture or the solicitation for the remanufacture occurs after August 26, 1990
2. When the purchase or lease of a vehicle that has already been remanufactured (to extend the usable life for five or more years) is made after August 26, 1990, but during the usable life of the vehicle, as extended

Generally, when a vehicle is remanufactured, the burden to rebuild it so as to include accessibility features is no greater than

---

[74] See proposed Department of Transportation regulation 49 CFR § 37.23.

[75] Report of the House Comm. on Public Works and Transportation on the Americans With Disabilities Act of 1990, HR Rep. No. 485, 101st Cong., 2d Sess., pt. 4 (1990) (hereinafter cited as H. Comm. on Pub. Works and Transp. Rep.) at 28; H. Comm. on Educ. and Lab. Rep. at 90; S. Comm. on Lab. and Hum. Resources Rep. at 50. See also proposed Department of Transportation regulation 49 CFR § 37.5.

putting these features in a new vehicle; since accessibility is required in new vehicles purchased, it is only logical to require it in remanufactured vehicles to accomplish Title II's purpose of providing accessible transportation for all persons.

The caveat provided that a remanufactured vehicle need be made accessible only to the maximum extent feasible means that the remanufactured vehicle need be modified to make it accessible only to the extent that the modifications made "do not adversely affect the structural integrity of the vehicle in a significant way."[76] The proposed regulations state that it shall be considered feasible to remanufacture a bus or other vehicle so as to make it readily accessible unless an engineering analysis indicates that including accessibility features would have a significant adverse effect on the structural integrity of the vehicle.[77]

One exception is made to the accessibility requirement in remanufacturing, to protect the historical character of a vehicle operated by a public entity *solely* on a route segment that is included on the National Register of Historic Places. Title II does not require that structural changes be made that would significantly alter the historic character of a vehicle that fits this description. With such a remanufactured vehicle, accessibility features must be included that do not significantly alter the vehicle's historic character, but features that would destroy the historic character need not be included—and the public entity may purchase or lease it after remanufacturing without it being considered discrimination.

Neither the statute nor the legislative history provides any definition for what is meant by a vehicle of historic character. Rather, the statute leaves this definition for the Secretary of Transportation, to be included in the secretary's implementing regulations. The proposed regulations leave the determination of whether a vehicle is of historic character to the UMTA, but final regulations will change this and provide a definition.[78]

---

[76] H. Comm. on Pub. Works and Transp. Rep. at 28.

[77] See proposed Department of Transportation regulation 49 CFR § 37.25(c).

[78] See proposed Department of Transportation regulation 49 CFR § 37.25(e).

Section 222 applies to a public entity regardless of the size of the community in which it operates the fixed route system. An amendment to provide for the possibility of a waiver of the section's applicability for a fixed route system operated by a public entity in an urbanized area with a population of 200,000 or less was defeated on the floor of the House of Representatives.[79]

[b] Demand Responsive Systems

Some communities operate transportation systems where an individual must call to request transportation service before it is rendered—demand responsive systems. This is different from a fixed route system, where vehicles run regularly scheduled routes and no advance call need be made by an individual in order to board a vehicle at a scheduled location.

Section 224 of the ADA labels it as discrimination, under both Section 202 of the ADA and Section 504 of the Rehabilitation Act, for a public entity that operates a demand responsive system to purchase or lease a new vehicle for use on such system if the vehicle is not readily accessible to and usable by individuals with disabilities, including individuals who use wheelchairs. This section only applies, though, to a purchase or lease for which a solicitation is made after August 25, 1990, thirty days after the July 26, 1990, effective date of Section 224.

There is an exception to this provision, in recognition of the fact that many smaller communities cannot afford to purchase or lease only the more expensive accessible vehicles. If the overall level of service provided by the entire demand responsive system to the disabled is equivalent to the level of service provided to individuals without disabilities, every vehicle purchased or leased by the public entity need not be fully accessible. The legislative history indicates that equivalent service is provided if the operator of the system has, or has access to, a vehicle (including a vehicle operated in conjunction with a portable boarding device) that is readily accessible to and usable by individuals with disabilities on an "on-call" basis—so that if an

---

[79] See 136 Cong. Rec. at H2606–H2611 (May 22, 1990).

individual with a mobility impairment calls for service, a vehicle that is accessible to that person is available to be dispatched.[80]

The Department of Transportation's proposed regulations elaborate upon this by stating that equivalent service is provided by a demand responsive system if the service available to the disabled, including wheelchair users, is provided in the most integrated setting feasible and is equivalent to that provided other individuals with respect to the following:

- Response time;
- Fares;
- Geographic area of service;
- Hours and days of service;
- Restrictions based on trip purpose;
- Availability of information and reservations capability; and
- Any constraints on capacity or service availability.[81]

Prior to purchasing an inaccessible vehicle, though, the public entity operating the demand responsive system must file a certification that it meets these standards contained in the regulations.[82]

In a demand responsive system, the time delay between a disabled individual's call for transportation and the arrival of an accessible transportation vehicle should be no greater than the waiting period for a nondisabled individual.[83]

The prohibitions against discrimination applicable to operators of fixed route systems under Section 222 apply to the purchase or lease of both new and used vehicles. Section 224

---

[80] H. Comm. on Pub. Works and Transp. Rep. at 32.

[81] See proposed Department of Transportation regulation 49 CFR § 37.27(c). See also proposed regulations 49 CFR §§ 37.51, 37.53, 37.55, and 37.57 for regulations dealing with rapid and light rail vehicles.

[82] See proposed Department of Transportation regulation 49 CFR § 37.27(d). The form of the certification required is set out in an appendix to 49 CFR pt. 37.

[83] H. Comm. on Educ. and Lab. Rep. at 94; S. Comm. on Lab. and Hum. Resources Rep. at 53, 54.

only applies to demand responsive systems in connection with the purchase or lease of new vehicles. The more general antidiscrimination provisions of Title II, Subtitle A, however, would still apply to the purchase or lease of used vehicles by a demand responsive system.

[c] One Car Per Train Rule

If a public entity puts two or more cars on a train in a light or rapid rail system, with the exception of certain historic trains, at least one car must be accessible to persons with disabilities, including persons who use wheelchairs.[84] This must be complied with as soon as practicable, but at the latest by July 25, 1995, five years after the effective date of the section. This requirement does not apply to one-car trains, such as streetcars. Again, failure to do this is discrimination for purposes of both Section 202 of the ADA and Section 504 of the Rehabilitation Act.

With a vehicle of historic character that is to be used on a segment of a light or rapid rail system included on the National Register of Historic Places, if remanufacturing the vehicle to make it accessible would significantly alter the historic character of the vehicle, the public entity that operates the system need only make those modifications—or purchase or lease a remanufactured vehicle with those modifications—that, to the maximum extent feasible, make the vehicle accessible without significantly altering the historic character of the vehicle.

[d] Temporary Exemption: Lifts Unavailable

Section 225 of the ADA gives the Secretary of Transportation the authority to relieve temporarily a public entity that operates either a fixed route system or a demand responsive system from its obligation under Section 222(a) or Section 224 to purchase new buses that are readily accessible to and usable by individuals with disabilities, when lifts are not available.[85]

---

[84] ADA § 228(b).

[85] Department of Transportation proposed regulations empower the UMTA administrator to exercise such authority. See 49 CFR §§ 37.21(b)–37.21(h), 37.27(e).

This relief, or exemption, is not available for other types of vehicles and is not even available for used buses.

To qualify for this temporary relief, the public entity must establish the following to the satisfaction of the secretary:

1. The public entity's initial solicitation for new buses specified that the buses were to be equipped with lifts and were to be otherwise accessible to and usable by individuals with disabilities;

2. Hydraulic, electromechanical, or other lifts are unavailable from any qualified manufacturer thereof for use or installation on the buses;

3. The public entity has made good faith efforts to locate a qualified manufacturer to supply the lifts to the manufacturer of the buses in sufficient time to comply with the solicitation; and

4. Further delay in purchasing the buses in order to wait for lifts to become available and installed would significantly impair transportation services in the community served by the public entity.

The secretary cannot grant temporary relief if these factors are not established. Even if they are established, the secretary still does not have to afford relief—the decision is discretionary. For example, if the factors are present but a substitute model of bus with a lift is available that would largely perform the same function as the one solicited, the secretary may not be willing to grant an exemption; the public entity may have to purchase the accessible substitute.

If the secretary chooses to grant an exemption from Section 222(a) or Section 224 to permit a public entity to purchase a new bus that is not equipped with a lift, the exemption must be limited in duration by a specified date; once that date passes, the public entity is again subject to the Title II sections previously waived. Anytime relief is granted by the secretary, the appropriate committees of Congress must be notified by the secretary. The statute does not specify whether these committees are just the House and Senate committees with jurisdiction over the Department of Transportation, or the respective labor committees as well.

The statute empowers the secretary to take such action as may be appropriate in the event it is determined either before or after relief is granted that a public entity fraudulently applied for the relief. If relief is still in effect, the secretary must cancel the relief.

[e] Exception: Public School Transportation

By excluding public school transportation from the definition of designated public transportation, Congress has exempted public school bus service from the requirements of Title II. This was done because discrimination in public school bus service is already amply covered in and prohibited by Section 504 of the Rehabilitation Act,[86] and Congress did not intend for school systems that receive federal assistance to be subject to any different requirements under the ADA than they already are under the Rehabilitation Act.[87] Under the Rehabilitation Act, public agencies that provide school bus transportation must provide service to children with disabilities equivalent to that provided nondisabled children.[88] There is no requirement that all school buses be disabled-accessible, only that if a disabled child requires transportation the particular bus that services the child's route must be accessible.

Interpretation of the school bus exemption from the ADA through regulations is meant to take into account special arrangements that are currently made with school districts in the providing of transportation. As the House Committee on Public Works and Transportation stated:

> For example, although the definition speaks to transportation "to and from a public elementary or secondary school and school-related activities," it is the Committee's intent to include in the scope of this exemption from the provisions of the Act, transportation of pre-Kindergarten children to Head Start or special education programs which

---

[86] 29 USC § 794.

[87] H. Comm. on Pub. Works and Transp. Rep. at 26.

[88] S. Comm. on Lab. and Hum. Resources Rep. at 45; see also 34 CFR pt. 104.

receive Federal assistance. Similarly, it is the Committee's intent to include in this exemption transportation arrangements which permit pre-school children of school bus drivers to ride a school bus, or special arrangements allowing pre-school children of teenage mothers to be transported to day care facilities at a school or along the school bus route so that these mothers may continue to attend school.[89]

[3] Paratransit Services

Some disabled individuals will, because of the severe nature of their disability, be unable to use the public transportation services that are available to the general public. For them, transportation by a special transportation system that may consist of special small buses or vans and that is available at the request of a disabled individual—called paratransit service—has sometimes been provided by public entities that operate fixed route systems.

Section 223 of the ADA, which takes effect eighteen months after the July 26, 1990, enactment of the ADA, compels public entities that operate fixed route transportation systems to provide paratransit or special transportation service to those who, because of their disabilities, cannot otherwise use the fixed route transportation systems. Failure to provide such service at a level comparable to that provided on the fixed route system to the nondisabled will generally be considered discrimination under both Section 202 of the ADA and Section 504 of the Rehabilitation Act. Similarly, the failure to provide such service to the disabled who qualify for it with a response time that is as comparable as practicable to what exists in the public entity's fixed route system for the nondisabled is likewise considered discrimination.

Comparable as used in Section 223 does not mean identical[90] or equivalent, and it must be interpreted with a degree of

---

[89] H. Comm. on Pub. Works and Transp. Rep. at 26, 27.

[90] H. Comm. on Pub. Works and Transp. Rep. at 28.

flexibility.[91] It is clearly more difficult and expensive to provide paratransit service than regular scheduled transportation service, and this can be taken into account by a public entity.

Similarly, "comparable to the extent practicable," used in connection with response time, requires even more flexibility. It must be recognized that the shorter the response time is, the more expensive the service. A response time for paratransit service close to that of the general transportation system that habitually operates on short notice will not be feasible for most public entities. Advance notice will usually be necessary to achieve a comparable response time. It would be permissible, therefore, for regulations to require an eligible disabled person to give twenty-four hours' notice to the provider of paratransit service in order to get the same response time as in the general transportation system.[92]

Not all the disabled qualify for paratransit service. Paratransit service must be provided only for those persons whose disability is such that it prevents them from using the normal transportation provided by the public entity. This is not inconsistent with the general Title II mandate that vehicles be accessible to persons with disabilities. Rather, Section 223 is a recognition that there are some mental and physical disabilities whose nature and severity are such as to prevent individuals with these disabilities from gaining access to and using mainline transportation vehicles—vehicles that would still be considered fully accessible to most disabled, including persons in wheelchairs, under the ADA. One example of such a disability might be a mental impairment that renders a person so disoriented that he is unable to use normal public transportation without getting lost and missing the correct stop.

An exception to Section 223 is that its obligation to provide paratransit service does not extend to a public entity that operates a fixed route system that just provides commuter bus service.

---

[91] 136 Cong. Rec. at H2446 (May 17, 1990) (Statement of Cong. J.P. Hammerschmidt).

[92] Id. at H2447.

Regulations will be issued under Section 223 by the Secretary of Transportation within one year after the ADA's enactment to implement the section's mandate and provide more specifically exactly what paratransit service must be provided. The statute does include some minimum levels and requirements that must be included in the guidelines.

[a] Eligibility

Public entities must be required to provide paratransit or other special transportation services to any disabled person who is unable, as a result of the disability, to board, ride, or disembark without help from anyone else with the exception of an operator of a wheelchair lift or other boarding assistance device, from any vehicle on the system that is fully accessible and usable by individuals with disabilities. All types of disabilities are covered, including vision impairment, as long as the impairment is sufficiently severe to limit substantially one or more major life activities. [93]

Paratransit or special service must also be provided to a disabled individual who, with a wheelchair lift or other boarding assistance device, is able to board and travel on one of the fixed route system's fully accessible vehicles, if the individual wants to travel on a route of the system during regular operating hours but at a time (or within a reasonable period of such time) when a fully accessible vehicle is not being used to provide transportation on the particular route the individual wishes to travel.

In general, for purposes of Section 223 and the regulations, the concepts of boarding or disembarking are limited to getting on and off a vehicle once a person is already at the stop. The obligation of the fixed route system does not generally include getting a disabled individual to and from the stop. There is a narrow exception to this, however. If a disabled individual has a specific impairment-related condition that prevents the individual from traveling to and from a location where he can board or exit the vehicle—a condition such as chronic fatigue, blindness, lack of cognitive ability to remember and follow directions, or

---

[93] H. Comm. on Pub. Works and Transp. Rep. at 29.

special sensitivity to temperature[94]—paratransit service must be provided from where the individual is located.

Persons who use wheelchairs are often aided in their mobility by the presence of curb cuts placed by the local government. There could be some disagreement about whether the lack of curb cuts, coupled with an individual's mobility impairment, constitutes a barrier to that individual's ability to leave the sidewalk and board a transportation vehicle that would trigger the right to paratransit services. The House Committee on Education and Labor and the Senate Committee on Labor and Human Resources, both of which had broad legislative jurisdiction over the entire ADA, have said that an architectural barrier, such as the lack of a curb cut that prevents access, could trigger the public entity's obligation to provide paratransit.[95] The House Committee on Public Works and Transportation, however, which had specific legislative jurisdiction over only the transportation-related provisions of the ADA, and which added the amendment containing the narrow exception relating to travel to and from a stop, stated that:

> The Committee does not intend for the existence of architectural barriers to trigger eligibility for paratransit under this section if these barriers are not the responsibility of the fixed route operator to remove. In particular, no eligibility for paratransit exists due simply to a lack of curb cuts in the path of travel of an individual with a disability since, in the short term, such barriers can often be navigated around and, more importantly, pressure to eliminate these architectural barriers must be maintained on the state and local governmental entities responsible for eliminating them.[96]

On this issue, the view of the Committee on Public Works and Transportation should carry greater weight, for two primary reasons. First, it is the committee of greatest expertise on transportation-related issues. Second, the enacted version of Part I,

---

[94] Id.

[95] H. Comm. on Educ. and Lab. Rep. at 91; S. Comm. on Lab. and Hum. Resources Rep. at 51.

[96] H. Comm. on Pub. Works and Transp. Rep. at 29.

Subtitle B in Title II is more similar to the Committee on Public Works and Transportation-passed legislation than to the versions passed by the two labor committees.

When a disabled individual qualifies for paratransit services, the public entity must also provide a seat on the vehicle to enable one person to travel along with the disabled person. If the disabled person wishes to have others travel along as well, they must be permitted to ride if there are seats available that would not otherwise be used by other individuals with disabilities and their accompanying one person and if they are going to the same destination as the disabled person with whom they are traveling.[97]

[b] Service Areas

Regulations must require that paratransit and special transportation services be provided throughout the entire area served by a particular fixed route system, except for any area in which the public entity provides only commuter bus service. In areas where the fixed route system provided by one public entity overlaps with a similar system operated by another entity, or serves an area contiguous to it, cooperation between the entities is encouraged. They may work out a joint plan for providing paratransit service, or they may even agree that one public entity will provide all of the paratransit service in the area. All that is required is for the service provided to meet the requirements of Section 223 and regulations thereunder without regard to who is providing the service. Similarly, each public entity bears responsibility for making sure the service provided in its area meets ADA requirements regardless of who is providing it.

If paratransit services are already provided by someone else in the public entity's service area, the public entity is not required to provide duplicate services—as long as the services already being provided meet the requirements of Section 223 and the regulations. The public entity is still accountable for making sure that acceptable paratransit or other special transportation services are provided, though. If the service provided

---

[97] Id. at 30.

falls below ADA-required level, therefore, the public entity has committed an act of discrimination even though the services are actually provided by another.

[c] Service Criteria

Regulations must establish criteria for determining the minimum level of paratransit or special transportation service that a public entity must provide in order to comply with Section 223. At a minimum, the following criteria should be met:

1. All persons with disabilities who are unable to use the vehicles servicing the fixed route system, and at least one companion for each such person, must be eligible for the paratransit or special transportation services.
2. The length of time a user of the paratransit or other transportation must wait for transportation must be comparable to the extent practicable to the time a user of the normal fixed route system vehicle over the same route would have to wait for service.
3. There can be no priorities or restrictions established that are based on the purpose of the trip.
4. The fare charged for the paratransit or special transportation service must be comparable to the fare charged for the same route at the same time of day on the regular fixed route system vehicles. Comparable, however, does not mean identical; in recognition of the higher costs incurred in providing paratransit service, the paratransit fare can be higher than the regular fare.[98]
5. The paratransit or special transportation service must be available during the same hours and days as the fixed route system, and must be provided for the same geographical area that the fixed route system serves.[99]

Regulations may set forth additional minimum requirements for the providing of paratransit or special transportation

---

[98] 136 Cong. Rec. at H2446 (May 17, 1990) (Statement of Cong. J.P. Hammerschmidt).

[99] H. Comm. on Educ. and Lab. Rep. at 92; S. Comm. on Lab. and Hum. Resources Rep. at 51, 52.

service, so a public entity that only complies with the criteria listed above may not be insulated from committing an act of discrimination. But a public entity that does not meet these criteria is clearly guilty of discrimination.

[d] Public Participation in Development of Plan

Each public entity that operates a fixed route system must develop a plan for providing the level of paratransit and special transportation services required by Section 223, and must submit its plan for approval to the Secretary of Transportation by January 26, 1992, eighteen months after the enactment of the ADA. Thereafter, the plan must be annually revised and sent to the Secretary of Transportation.

Regulations must require a public entity to hold a public hearing, provide an opportunity for public comment, and consult with the disabled as part of the process of developing a plan.

If the plan submitted meets the requirements of Section 223 and the regulations issued thereunder, the Secretary of Transportation will approve it, and the public entity will begin to implement it (though nothing prevents the public entity from beginning implementation earlier on its own, subject to the secretary's approval). If the requirements are not met, the secretary will disapprove the plan and tell the public entity the reasons for disapproval. Within ninety days of the date of disapproval, the public entity must resubmit the plan with modifications to eliminate the reasons for disapproval and must begin implementing the plan.[100]

A public entity's failure to timely submit a plan, failure to timely submit or implement a modified plan, failure to submit a modified plan that complies with the statute and regulation, or failure to follow the plan or modified plan will constitute discrimination.[101]

In addition to the items mentioned, the Secretary of Transportation may include in the regulations any other requirements

---

[100] ADA § 233(d).

[101] ADA § 223(e).

that are deemed necessary to carry out the purpose of Section 223.

[e] Compliance Steps

By statute, the Secretary of Transportation had until July 26, 1991, to promulgate the regulations implementing Section 223. As of August 9, 1991, however, these final regulations had not been issued. It will be difficult for public entities to complete their implementation plans before this date, since the plans cannot provide for full compliance with the regulations before the regulations are issued. Substantial groundwork can be done before the regulations are issued, though, because of the mandates and suggestions provided in the statute and legislative history; the period from July 26, 1991, until January 26, 1992, when the plans must be filed with the Secretary of Transportation, can then be used for putting in the details necessary to comply with the regulations.

The effective date for Section 223's general prohibition against discrimination, January 26, 1992,[102] is the same as the deadline for submission of plans to the Secretary of Transportation. It is unlikely, therefore, that public entities will know by the effective date whether their plans have been approved. Public entities may not have this knowledge for some time, moreover, because the statute sets no deadline for the secretary's approval or disapproval of a plan.

The best course of action for public entities is to put into effect as of January 26, 1992, at the latest, the steps they believe are necessary to comply with Section 223 and the regulations issued thereunder. These steps would presumably be what the entity provided for in the plan it submitted to the Secretary of Transportation. Providing no paratransit service, or a grossly inadequate level of such service after January 26, 1992, with the excuse that the public entity had not yet received a response concerning its plan from the Secretary of Transportation, is not likely to be a sufficient defense to a charge of discrimination.

To help it provide some level of paratransit service in the

---

[102] ADA § 231(a).

interim before an approved plan becomes fully operational, or before an approved plan can be fully implemented, public entities should consult with groups representing the disabled for suggestions.

Section 223 is not meant to prevent a public entity from providing a level or type of paratransit service greater than the minimum level required, or from providing service to more individuals than required.

[f] Exception: Undue Financial Burden

There is an exception to the statutory mandate on a public entity to comply fully with Section 223 and regulations issued thereunder. If a public entity can demonstrate to the satisfaction of the Secretary of Transportation that providing the paratransit and special transportation services required by this section and the regulations would impose an undue financial burden on it, the public entity need only provide such services to a level that would not be an undue financial burden.

The undue financial burden limitation, while meant to permit a public entity to provide less than the full services required, is not meant to permit a public entity to provide no such services at all—even if providing even the most basic level of service still constitutes an undue financial burden for the public entity. The statute does not itself require basic service, but rather permits the regulations issued by the Secretary of Transportation to require some basic level of service despite the financial burden this may place on a public entity. Congressional intent on this point is clear, though. As stated by the House Committee on Public Works and Transportation, "the Committee expects the regulations issued by the Secretary under this section to require a basic level of paratransit service to be provided by the fixed route operator." [103]

Although the regulations will provide more detail as to how the determination of whether an expense constitutes an undue financial burden is made, some general guidelines can be set forth. This determination will vary according to the specific

---

[103] H. Comm. on Pub. Works and Transp. Rep. at 31.

situation of the fixed route system and public entity involved. Factors that can be considered, however, include such matters as the financial constraints within which the public entity operates the fixed route system, the population and population density of the area served, the level of paratransit service already being provided in the area, the residential patterns, the interim degree of accessibility of fixed route transit services, the amount of fare increases necessary—if any—to provide paratransit services, and the reduction necessary—if any—in the overall level of transportation provided by the system.[104] The regulations may permit using a flexible numerical formula of some kind to make this determination.[105]

The criteria developed by the Secretary of Transportation for determining when compliance constitutes an undue financial burden must balance promoting the goals of the statute against not imposing an overly severe burden on operators. Imposition of a fixed percentage spending requirement beyond which an operator need not go is not proper where this level would not ensure adequate compliance with the statute's aims.[106]

[4] Facilities

Sections 226 and 227 of the ADA are aimed at making as many facilities as possible used in the provision of designated transportation by a public entity—such as a bus station or bus stop—accessible to and usable by individuals with disabilities.

[a] New Construction

Section 226 provides that if a public entity constructs a new facility for use in the providing of designated public transportation services, the facility must be readily accessible to and usable

---

[104] Id.; H. Comm. on Educ. and Lab. Rep. at 91; S. Comm. on Lab. and Hum. Resources Rep. at 50.

[105] H. Comm. on Pub. Works and Transp. Rep. at 31.

[106] As an example of such an improper fixed spending requirement, see ADAPT v. Skinner, 881 F2d 1184 (3d Cir. 1989).

by individuals with disabilities, including individuals who use wheelchairs. If a new facility is not so accessible and usable, it constitutes discrimination for purposes of both Section 202 of the ADA and Section 504 of the Rehabilitation Act. This would apply to facilities—as long as the facility is constructed by a public entity—such as bus stations, bus stops, rail stations (other than intercity or commuter stations), parking facilities at bus and rail stations, and boat terminals that provide designated public transportation services. The obligation in Section 226 becomes effective on January 26, 1992, eighteen months after the enactment of the ADA.

[b] Alterations

Section 227(a) provides two general rules that apply with respect to alterations made to an existing facility used in connection with the provision of designated transportation services by a public entity. This section does not require a public entity to make any alterations to its facilities. It only applies once the public entity decides on its own to make alterations.

First, if a public entity voluntarily chooses to make alterations to an existing facility, and the alterations affect or could affect the usability of the facility or part thereof, the public entity must make such alterations (either on its own or through others that it supervises) in a manner so that to the maximum extent feasible the altered portions of the facility are readily accessible to and usable by individuals with disabilities, including individuals who use wheelchairs. Failure to do so constitutes discrimination under Section 202 of the ADA and under Section 504 of the Rehabilitation Act. As an example, if a public entity knocks down a covered bus stop that contains benches under the covering to put up a new seating facility, the new facility should be configured so that there is room under cover for persons in wheelchairs.

Second, where the public entity voluntarily undertakes an alteration that affects or could affect usability of or access to an area of the facility containing a primary function, the entity must make the alterations in such a manner that, to the maximum extent feasible, the path of travel to and from the altered area and the bathrooms, telephones, and drinking fountains serving the altered area are readily accessible to and usable by individuals with disabilities once the alterations are completed, including individuals who use wheelchairs—unless the cost and scope of alterations that would be necessary to the path of travel, bathroom, telephones, and drinking fountains would be disproportionate to the overall alterations being made, under criteria established by the Attorney General.[107] Failure to follow this mandate constitutes discrimination as above. For example, if the ticket counter in a bus station operated by a public entity has alterations made to it, as part of the alterations, the entity must make sure that the bathrooms, telephones, and drinking fountains that serve the ticket counter are accessible to the disabled, and that the disabled can go from the ticket counter to these locations. Not every bathroom, telephone, and fountain in the bus station needs to be accessible, though. It is sufficient if one of each that serves the ticket counter area (if there is one of each—if there is no water fountain in the station, the public entity is not required by the ADA to install one) is accessible.

These rules are the same as the rules that apply to alterations of existing public accommodations and commercial facilities in Title III of the ADA.[108]

[c] Special Rule for Key Stations

Section 227(b) applies only to stations used in rapid rail and light rail systems operated by a public entity, and only to "key" stations in such systems. Unlike Section 227(a), it requires public entities to undertake affirmatively to make changes, including structural changes if necessary, in order to render the key stations accessible to and usable by individuals with disabilities,

---

[107] See ¶ 5.05[2][c] for a discussion of these criteria. Basically, if the cost of alterations to provide access would exceed 20 percent of the costs of alterations to the primary function area, it will be considered disproportionate under the Attorney General's criteria.

[108] For more detailed discussion of the meaning and impact of these rules, and elaboration on the meaning of phrases such as "to the maximum extent feasible" and "disproportionate to the overall alterations in terms of cost and scope," see the discussion of Section 303(a) at ¶ 5.05.

including individuals who use wheelchairs, as soon as practicable but not later than July 26, 1993 (three years after the effective date of the section).

The statute gives the Secretary of Transportation the power to extend the July 26, 1993, deadline for some key stations in a system if these systems need extraordinarily expensive structural changes to, or replacement of, existing facilities in order to render them accessible. The secretary has the authority to extend the deadline for a system to as long as thirty years after the section's effective date, or July 26, 2020, but if the deadline is extended by more than twenty years, by the end of the twentieth year (July 25, 2011) at least two thirds of the key stations in the system must be readily accessible to and usable by individuals with disabilities. The determination of what constitutes an "extraordinarily expensive structural change" is left to the Secretary of Transportation.

The failure of a public entity to meet the July 26, 1993, deadline if no extension is granted, to meet an extended deadline, or the failure to have at least two thirds of the key stations accessible by July 25, 2011, if longer than a twenty-year extension is granted, will be discrimination for purposes of Section 202 of the ADA and Section 504 of the Rehabilitation Act.

The Secretary of Transportation will, in regulations, establish criteria for determining which stations in rapid rail and light rail systems are key stations. The criteria

> will include characteristics such as high ridership, transfer points (including "feeder" points of transfer from other fixed route systems), and high ridership, end-of-the-line stations. When high ridership is the sole factor in determining a key station, consideration should be given to the proximity of that station to other key stations. Each of several closely grouped, high volume stations need not be designated a key station solely due to a high volume of ridership.[109]

Local settlement agreements that are the product of good faith negotiations between public entities and representatives of

---

[109] H. Comm. on Pub. Works and Transp. Rep. at 33, 34.

the disabled community and that identify which stations on the system are key are encouraged.[110] These type of agreements should fully meet the requirements of Section 227(b).

Public entities are required to draw up a plan for making their key stations accessible to and usable by the disabled, and to submit this plan to the Secretary of Transportation. The public entity must consult with the disabled affected by the plan, and must hold a public hearing and solicit public comment on the plan. The final plan submitted to the secretary must take into account such consultations and public input.

The plan must contain milestones for achieving the goals of Section 227(a). These will set forth the timetable by which significant events will occur that will enable the public entity to reach these goals—such as the actions that will be taken to make particular key stations accessible and dates by which each such station will be accessible.

[d] Exception

Section 228(a) of the ADA provides rules applicable to existing nonkey stations.[111] It requires that if a public entity operates a designated transportation program or activity in existing facilities, the program or activity, when viewed in its entirety, must be readily accessible to and usable by individuals with disabilities. This requirement takes effect eighteen months after enactment of the ADA, or January 26, 1992. The standard is the same one that currently applies to facilities that receive federal funds under regulations issued by the Department of Transportation to implement Section 504 of the Rehabilitation Act.[112] A failure to meet the requirement in Section 228(a) constitutes discrimination under Section 202 of the ADA and under Section 504 of the Rehabilitation Act.

-----

[110] Id.

[111] HR Conf. Rep. No. 101-596, Conf. Rep. on S. 933, Americans With Disabilities Act of 1990, Joint Explanatory Statement of the Comm. of Conference (1990) at 33.

[112] H. Comm. on Educ. and Lab. Rep. at 96; S. Comm. on Lab. and Hum. Resources Rep. at 55.

There is an exception to the obligation in Section 228(a). Unless otherwise required either because alterations are being made[113] or because structural changes are required to make a key light or rapid rail station accessible,[114] a public entity is not required to make structural changes to existing facilities just to make the facilities accessible to individuals who use wheelchairs. At a facility covered by this exception, the public entity additionally does not have to provide individuals in wheelchairs with services provided to persons not in wheelchairs if the individuals in wheelchairs could not use or benefit from these services.

[e] Accessibility Standards

Section 230 of the ADA provides guidelines and protection to public entities who engage in new construction or alterations to facilities covered by Part I of Subtitle B before final regulations containing standards are issued. It applies to new construction or alterations that meet all three of these tests:

1. A valid and appropriate state or local building permit for the construction or alterations is obtained prior to the issuance of final regulations.
2. The construction or alteration authorized by the permit begins within one year of receipt of the permit.
3. The work authorized is completed under the terms of the permit.

In such a case, if the construction or alterations meet the UFAS in effect at the time the permit is issued, this will satisfy the accessibility requirements of Sections 226 (new facilities) and 227 (alterations to existing facilities). There is, however, one exception. If the Secretary of Transportation's regulations have not been issued by one year after the ATBCB has issued its minimum guidelines under Section 504 of the ADA, compliance with the ATBCB's minimum guidelines will instead be neces-

---

[113] ADA § 227(a).

[114] ADA § 227(b).

sary for a facility to be considered accessible to and usable by persons with disabilities until final regulations are issued.

¶ 4.05 INTERCITY AND COMMUTER RAIL

Part II of Subtitle B, Title II prohibits discrimination against the disabled on Amtrak intercity rail transportation and commuter rail transportation, and in stations used in connection therewith.

Section 242 of the ADA sets forth some specific conduct by persons providing intercity rail service—Amtrak—and persons providing commuter rail service that would be discrimination under both Section 202 of the ADA and Section 504 of the Rehabilitation Act. By so doing, it also tells these persons the minimum level of what must be provided to accommodate the disabled in intercity rail transportation and commuter rail transportation, including accommodations necessary in used rail cars, remanufactured rail cars, and rail stations.

In connection with rail transportation here, the use of the term "readily accessible to and usable by individuals with disabilities, including individuals who use wheelchairs" refers to the "ability of individuals with disabilities, including individuals who use wheelchairs, to enter into, exit from, and safely and effectively use a rail passenger car or station used in public transportation."[115] Because the ADA is not intended to supersede the Federal Railroad Safety Act of 1970,[116] any modifications made to rail cars or stations because of the ADA cannot exceed what is permitted by this act or any rules, regulations, or standards issued thereunder.

Though wheelchair users are specifically mentioned in the statute, "accessibility" and "usability" encompass more than just making a rail car or station accessible to these persons. Accessibility and usability must be for individuals with the full range of disabilities, including but not limited to mobility impairments, visual impairments, hearing impairments, and cognitive impairments such as mental retardation. Some fea-

---

[115] H. Comm. on Energy and Com. Rep. at 44.
[116] 45 USC § 421.

tures that would promote accessibility and usability in rail cars include braille signs denoting restrooms, water fountains and exits, loudspeaker systems in the cars, nonslip surfaces on steps and floors, and bright lighting in boarding and exiting areas. The statute does not specify exactly what must be included in the rail cars and stations, though. This is left to regulations to be issued by the Secretary of Transportation under Section 244 of the ADA.

Despite the specific reference to persons in wheelchairs, in most of Section 242, the installation of ramps, lifts, or other equipment is not required in any *particular* circumstance. This is because of the wide variance in design characteristics of rail cars and rail stations. Some stations have high passenger platforms, some have low platforms, and some service freight trains as well as passenger trains. Entrances on rail cars are similarly of varying heights. Mandating installation of one uniform-sized lift would not be feasible, therefore, because what worked for one car at one particular station might not work at the next station. All that is required is that equipment—such as portable lifts— be available and used, regardless of whether it is permanently affixed to the car or station, and that such equipment permit persons with mobility impairments, including those in wheelchairs, to get on and off the trains.[117]

With one exception relating to food service cars, the ADA is not intended in any way to sanction or encourage traveling between cars by persons in wheelchairs (other than by exiting from a car onto the station platform and then entering another car from the platform). This was seen by Congress as an unsafe practice that could put the wheelchair passenger in danger and, in turn, subject railroads to lawsuits. In the food service area, however, the right to eat in an integrated setting was seen as outweighing safety concerns. Other than with respect to food service, the ADA does not require Amtrak or commuter railroads to provide access to persons in wheelchairs between rail cars.[118]

---

[117] H. Comm. on Energy and Com. Rep. at 44, 45.

[118] Id. at 48, 49.

[1] Definitions

Section 241 of the ADA sets out the definition of terms used in Part II.

1. *Intercity rail transportation.* For purposes of Part II, this is transportation provided by Amtrak.

2. *Commuter rail transportation.* Short-haul rail passenger service operated in metropolitan and suburban areas, whether within or across the geographic boundaries of a state, usually characterized by reduced fare, multiple ride, and commutation tickets and by morning and evening peak period operations.[119]

3. *Commuter authority.* Any state, local, or regional authority, corporation, or other entity established for purposes of providing commuter service, and includes the Metropolitan Transportation Authority, the Connecticut Department of Transportation, the Maryland Department of Transportation, the Southeastern Pennsylvania Transportation Authority, the New Jersey Transit Corporation, the Massachusetts Bay Transit Authority, the Port Authority Trans-Hudson Corporation, any successor agencies, and any entity created by one or more such agencies for the purpose of operating, or contracting for the operation of, commuter service.[120]

4. *Rail passenger car.* With respect to intercity rail transportation, these are single-level and bi-level coach cars, single-level and bi-level dining cars, single-level and bi-level sleeping cars, single-level and bi-level lounge cars, and food service cars.

5. *Station.* This includes the portion of a property located appurtenant to a right-of-way on which intercity or commuter rail transportation is operated, where such portion is used by the general public and is related to the provision of such transportation, including passenger platforms, designated waiting areas, ticketing areas, restrooms. Where a public entity providing rail transportation owns the property, the station also includes concession areas, to the extent that such public entity exercises control over the selection, design, construction, or alteration of the property. A mere flag stop, however, is not considered a station. Among the obligations mandated by Part II is the obligation to make certain rail passenger stations accessible to the

---

[119] See Section 103(9) of the Rail Passenger Act, 45 USC § 502(9).

[120] See Section 103(8) of the Rail Passenger Act, 45 USC § 502(8).

disabled. As a matter of policy, though, Congress did not want to impose this obligation on private parties that might own stations in cases where such private parties have little or no business interest in the continuation of rail passenger service at these stations—such as where the private party owner is a freight railroad that enters into an agreement to let Amtrak have some use of the station. [121] Accordingly, only the parties that actually operate the intercity or commuter rail service being provided to passengers at a station or, where applicable, the public entities that own all or some of the station bear responsibility for making the station accessible.

6. *Responsible person.* For each station, this is:

- The public entity, where the public entity owns more than half of the station.
- The persons who actually are providing intercity or commuter rail transportation to the station, when more than half of the station is owned by a private party. The Secretary of Transportation will, by regulations, allocate responsibility for ensuring access among the several persons when there are multiple persons providing the transportation.
- The persons who actually are providing intercity or commuter rail transportation to the station, *and* any public entities that own any part of the station, when no one party owns more than half of the station. Where more than one party qualifies as a responsible party, the division of responsibility will be allocated equitably in regulations issued by the Secretary of Transportation.

[2] Intercity Rail Cars

Generally speaking, Amtrak cannot purchase or lease a rail car for which the solicitation is made after August 25, 1990 (thirty days after the effective date of Section 242), unless the car is readily accessible to and usable by all types of disabled persons. Although Congress intended for most of the requirements concerning what is accessible and usable to be spelled out in regula-

---

[121] H. Comm. on Energy and Com. Rep. at 43.

tions issued by the Secretary of Transportation[122] rather than by statute, it did include some specific instructions in Section 242(a)(2) for what must be in certain types of new cars, or what does not need to be included, for the car to be considered accessible to and usable just by persons who use wheelchairs. It is important to recognize that these specific mandates have no bearing on disabilities other than wheelchair usage. They do not in any way lessen Amtrak's obligation to make sure that new cars are accessible to and usable by persons with other disabilities. Similarly, they do not lessen Amtrak's obligation to provide access to persons in wheelchairs except as specifically stated.

In cases where no special rules or requirements are included in the statute with respect to persons in wheelchairs, the relevant accessibility found in Federal Railroad Administration regulations[123] should apply and should provide guidance for regulations and standards to be issued by the Secretary of Transportation and the ATBCB.[124]

Neither the Secretary of Transportation nor the ATBCB has the power under the ADA to require that Amtrak widen aisles or passageways in rail cars to accommodate persons in wheelchairs. Given the general disapproval in the ADA of any car-to-car movement by such persons, no valid purpose was seen in forcing Amtrak to the expense and possible lower revenues of narrowing seats, bedrooms, and kitchens, all of which would inconvenience the nondisabled.[125]

[a] Single-Level Coaches

New single-level coaches must be able to be entered by a person in a wheelchair, there must be space in the coach for the wheelchair to be parked and secured, there must be a seat in the coach to which such person can transfer, there must be a space to

---

[122] Until final regulations implementing Section 244 are issued by the Department of Transportation, proposed regulation 49 CFR Section 37.87 provides interim accessibility standards for intercity rail passenger cars.

[123] 49 CFR § 27.73(b)(2).

[124] H. Comm. on Energy and Com. Rep. at 46.

[125] Id. at 46, 47.

fold and store the wheelchair after the person is seated, and the coach must have a restroom usable by such individual.

For all single-level coaches, new or used, regardless of when they were purchased, Section 242(a)(3) sets forth numerical requirements for the number of wheelchair spaces that must be provided on any train that includes one or more single-level passenger coaches. These requirements are phased-in over a ten-year period. The wheelchair spaces are to be included in the single-level passenger coaches, as well as in food service cars. Even if no new cars are purchased, existing cars must comply with these requirements.

Two types of wheelchair spaces are included—spaces to park and secure wheelchairs for people who wish to remain in them while on the train, and spaces to fold and store wheelchairs for people who wish to transfer to regular seats in the coach. Each type of space is considered separately. For each type, by as soon as practicable but no later than July 25, 1995 (five years after enactment), the train must have at least half as many spaces as there are single-level passenger coaches on the train. By no later than July 25, 2000, or sooner if practicable, the train must have as many spaces as single-level passenger coaches on the train.

Only two of either type of space per car count towards the numerical requirement here. The idea is to spread accessible spaces throughout the train, rather than concentrate them in any one car. Any car that has either type of space on it must also have a restroom that is accessible to persons in wheelchairs, and the car must be able to be entered directly from the station platform —whether by just rolling in or by a lift or similar device—by a person in a wheelchair.

[b] Single-Level Dining Cars

For new single-level dining cars, the statute sets out what features the car does *not* need to have. Failure to have these features will not render the car inaccessible, therefore. A single-level dining car is not required to be configured so that it can be directly entered from the station platform by a person in a wheelchair. As long as the person in a wheelchair can enter the dining car from another car on the train, this is sufficient. Additionally, if the single-level dining car does not contain a restroom for other passengers, it is not required to put in a restroom usable by a person in a wheelchair; if the car does have a restroom, though, it should be accessible to persons in wheelchairs.

A special requirement is included mandating that table service be provided in a single-level dining car to persons in wheelchairs if the following specific conditions are all met:

1. The car was purchased after July 26, 1990, the date of enactment of the ADA.
2. The car next to the end of the dining car through which a wheelchair may enter is itself accessible to a wheelchair.
3. The person in the wheelchair is able to exit the car in which he is seated onto the station platform, move along the station platform, and enter the accessible car referred to in condition (2), above, that is next to the dining car— all without the train having to move within the station.
4. There is space in the dining car to park and secure the wheelchair at the time the passenger wishes to eat, if the passenger wishes to remain in the wheelchair, or there is space in the dining car to store and fold the wheelchair if the passenger wishes to transfer from the wheelchair to a seat.

Where these requirements are otherwise met, Amtrak is required to place an accessible rail car into which persons in wheelchairs may enter next to the dining car, unless not practicable to do so. From this car, such persons will be able to enter the dining car without exiting onto the platform. This situation represents the only time the ADA permits a person in a wheelchair to travel through the train between cars.

One other requirement is set forth relating to single-level dining cars on trains used to provide intercity transportation. Unlike the requirement discussed earlier, this one applies to dining cars regardless of whether they were purchased before or after enactment of the ADA. Additionally, it covers all the disabled, not just those in wheelchairs. It is designed to afford them access to food service on intercity trains that is equivalent to what is provided the nondisabled, except for any possible lack of physical access to the dining car. On a train that has a single-level dining car that is used to provide food service, appropriate aids and services, including a hard surface on which to eat at their seat, must be provided to the disabled and to persons who are traveling with them. Included in this would be aids such as a braille menu or a reader to assist persons with vision impairments, writing pads to assist persons with certain speaking or hearing disorders, and service to the disabled person and the person's companion at their seats if they are unable to easily travel to the dining car.[126]

[c] Bi-Level Dining Cars

For dining cars with two levels of seating, the statute again tells what does not have to be included, rather than what has to be included, to permit accessibility and usability. It allows Amtrak to omit the accommodations that are required for persons in wheelchairs in single-level passenger cars. Therefore, bi-level dining cars do not have to permit entry by persons in wheelchairs, they do not have to have space in which a wheelchair can be parked and secured, they do not have to have a seat to which a passenger in a wheelchair can transfer, they do not have to have space for a wheelchair to be stored if the passenger does so transfer, and they do not have to have a restroom accessible to and usable by persons in wheelchairs.

There are two requirements, however, that could apply to an intercity train in which a bi-level dining car is used to provide food service.[127] The first applies only if such train also includes a bi-level lounge car (this is different from the dining car) that was purchased after July 26, 1990. If it does, table service in this lounge car must be provided "to individuals who use wheelchairs and to other passengers."[128] The primary purpose of this is to enable persons in wheelchairs who cannot climb to the top level of a bi-level dining car to still dine with their companions in an alternate location. The statutory language is drafted so that it

---

[126] Id. at 49.

[127] ADA § 242(a)(4)(B).

[128] ADA § 242(a)(4)(B)(i).

is actually much broader than this. Read literally, any passenger could conceivably demand food service in the lounge car. But, stated the House Committee on Energy and Commerce, which drafted this provision:

> The Committee notes that the requirement to provide table service to other passengers in such a lounge car does not require that Amtrak, in effect, treat the table area of the lounge car as though it were itself a dining car. Although the Committee expects Amtrak in most instances to provide table service in the lounge car as a matter of course to passengers dining with a disabled individual, Amtrak has discretion to establish reasonable conditions for the availability to other passengers of table service in the lounge car.[129]

The second requirement applies on all trains on which a bi-level dining car is used to provide food service, regardless of the date on which any car on the train was purchased. Similar to what is required on a train with a single-level dining car, appropriate auxiliary aids and services, including a hard surface on which to eat at their seats, must be provided to ensure that all individuals with disabilities, and passengers traveling with them, have food service equal to that afforded the nondisabled (with the exception, to some disabled persons, of access to the bi-level dining car).

[d] One Car Per Train Rule

Amtrak is required to have at least one passenger car per train that is readily accessible to and usable by individuals with disabilities, including individuals who use wheelchairs, as soon as practicable but not later than July 26, 1995, five years after enactment of the ADA. This is the same requirement that also applies to light or rapid rail systems operated by public entities.[130]

---

[129] H. Comm. on Energy and Com. Rep. at 49.

[130] See ADA § 228(b).

[3] Commuter Cars

[a] New

Any new car purchased or leased for use in commuter rail transportation, for which the solicitation to buy or lease is made after August 25, 1990, must be accessible to individuals with disabilities, including persons in wheelchairs, to the extent required in regulations to be issued by the Secretary of Transportation. This provision does not by itself force any commuter authority to purchase or lease a new car. If such a purchase or lease is made, however, the car purchased or leased must be accessible.

Though most requirements for what commuter rail cars must contain in order to be considered accessible will be set out in the regulations, there are some items the regulations cannot compel: [131]

1. If a car has no restroom for any person on it, regulations cannot compel inclusion of a restroom to be used by a person in a wheelchair.
2. Regulations cannot require that there be space on the car to fold and store a wheelchair.
3. Regulations cannot require that there be a seat on the car to which a person can transfer from a wheelchair.

As is the case with Amtrak trains, regulations cannot compel the widening of aisles to accommodate wheelchairs, because of the impact of doing so on other passengers and on the commuter authority's revenues and costs. [132]

Generally, except where there is a conflict with anything set forth above, Congress expressed approval of the regulations that deal with accessibility and wheelchairs issued by the Federal Railroad Administration [133] and suggested that the additional Department of Transportation regulations incorporate the guidelines in them. [134]

---

[131] ADA § 242(b)(1)(B).

[132] H. Comm. on Energy and Com. Rep. at 50.

[133] These regulations are codified at 49 CFR § 27.73(b)(2).

[134] H. Comm. on Energy and Com. Rep. at 50.

[b] Used

As discussed separately in an earlier section, new intercity or commuter rail cars for which the solicitation to purchase or lease is made after August 25, 1990, must be accessible. It is not always financially possible for an operator to purchase or lease a new car, though, and used cars are often procured instead; not all of these used cars, however, are currently accessible to the disabled. Because of this, a slightly lower requirement is set out for the purchase or lease of a used intercity or commuter rail car than for a new car. The purchaser or lessee must only make a demonstrated good faith effort to purchase or lease an accessible used car. If such an effort locates an acceptable, available, accessible used car, then if any used car is purchased or leased, it must be accessible. If, after demonstrated good faith efforts, including a national search, no acceptable, available, accessible car can be found, then a car that is not accessible to the disabled may be purchased or leased and such purchase or lease will not be considered discrimination.[135] Documentation evidencing the good faith efforts taken to locate an accessible car must be retained for two years after the purchase date of a not-fully-accessible car and must be made available upon request to the UMTA administrator or Federal Railroad Administration administrator.[136]

Nothing in the statute prevents the Secretary of Transportation from promulgating different requirements for accessibility in used cars than in new ones, if a legitimate basis exists for so doing. The proposed regulations, however, do not do this.

[c] Remanufactured

It is considered discrimination for a person to remanufacture an intercity or commuter rail car so as to extend its usable life for ten years or more, unless the car is made readily accessible to and usable by individuals with disabilities (including

---

[135] ADA § 242(c). See also proposed Department of Transportation regulation 49 CFR § 37.83.

[136] See proposed Department of Transportation regulation 49 CFR § 37.83(d).

individuals in wheelchairs) to the maximum extent feasible. [137] As in other instances in the ADA involving remanufacturing, [138] the words "to the maximum extent feasible" are used to make it clear that accessibility in this context does not require doing anything that would destroy the structural integrity of a vehicle. [139] This could be interpreted to mean that an accessibility feature must be implemented in the remanufacturing process unless an engineering analysis shows that including accessibility features required by the regulations would have a significant adverse effect on the structural integrity of the car.

Similarly, if a person purchases or leases an intercity or commuter rail car that has been remanufactured to extend its useful life for ten years or more, the car after remanufacture must be readily accessible to and usable by individuals with disabilities (including individuals in wheelchairs) to the maximum extent feasible. [140] Failure to comply with this constitutes discrimination for purposes of Section 202 of the ADA and Section 504 of the Rehabilitation Act. Therefore, both those who remanufacture and those who purchase or lease remanufactured cars must ensure the accessibility of those cars.

[d] One Car Per Train Rule

This rule applies to commuter trains just as it does to Amtrak trains. At least one passenger car per commuter train must be accessible to individuals with disabilities, including people in wheelchairs, as soon as practicable, but at the latest by July 25, 1995. Details as to what is needed on a commuter train for it to be considered accessible will be provided in regulations to be issued by the Secretary of Transportation. [141] The regulations should require, though, that the accessible car stop at a clearly marked location on the train station platform level with

---

[137] ADA § 242(d)(1).

[138] ADA § 222(c).

[139] H. Comm. on Energy and Com. Rep. at 51.

[140] ADA § 242(d)(2).

[141] Until final regulations implementing Section 244 are issued by the Department of Transportation, proposed regulation 49 CFR Section 37.89 provides interim accessibility standards for commuter rail cars.

the car so that a person in a wheelchair can easily board.[142]

To the extent that its accessible rolling stock is limited, a commuter authority does have the discretion during the five-year phase-in period to decide where and how this stock is to be deployed, taking into account ridership levels and predicted usage by the disabled on different routes. Such action would be consistent with the mandate to comply with the rule "as soon as practicable."[143] Commuter authorities must either modify or remanufacture existing cars to make them accessible, or purchase or lease new cars that will be accessible in sufficient numbers to meet the one-car-per-train standard by the deadline imposed.

[4] Stations

[a] New Construction

Any new station built for use in intercity or commuter rail transportation must be accessible to the disabled or it constitutes discrimination.[144] The Secretary of Transportation will issue regulations providing the requirements for what is necessary for a station to be considered accessible to and usable by the disabled. This provision took effect on July 26, 1990, the day of enactment of the ADA.[145]

[b] Alterations

The "responsible person," as this term is defined in Section 241(5),[146] must make all Amtrak stations accessible to and usable by the disabled as soon as practicable, but not later than

---

[142] H. Comm. on Educ. and Lab. Rep. at 97; S. Comm. on Lab. and Hum. Resources Rep. at 56.

[143] H. Comm. on Energy and Com. Rep. at 49, 50.

[144] ADA § 242(e).

[145] The guidelines that should be followed for making a new station accessible until the secretary's regulations are issued are discussed in infra ¶ 4.05[5][b].

[146] See supra ¶ 4.05[1].

twenty years after the ADA's July 26, 1990, enactment.[147] As part of regulations issued by the Secretary of Transportation concerning accessibility requirements for existing stations, a plan must be developed by the appropriate party for making the existing stations accessible that both reflects consultation with the disabled affected and establishes milestones for achieving accessibility.

In commuter rail systems, only the key stations are required to be made accessible to and usable by the disabled.[148] Accessibility must be attained within three years after the ADA's enactment, with one exception: The Secretary of Transportation is given the authority to extend the three-year deadline to up to twenty years for particular stations where the only means of providing accessibility is to raise the entire passenger platform or carry out some other extraordinarily expensive structural change. Again, the person charged by the statute with making the changes to a station is the person who qualifies as the responsible person under Section 241(5). Failure to make required changes constitutes discrimination by the responsible person for purposes of Section 202 of the ADA and Section 504 of the Rehabilitation Act.

Regardless of whether it is the responsible person for all or any of the stations in its commuter rail system, each commuter authority must disclose which stations in its system are the "key stations."[149] Before making this disclosure in final form, though, the commuter authorities are required to consult with the disabled and organizations representing them as part of the process of deciding which stations are key, and must hold a public hearing on the issue to receive input from the local community. Among the factors to be taken into account in determining which stations are key are the level of ridership at a station (the higher the ridership, the more likely the station is key) and whether the station serves as a transfer or feeder system (if it does, it is more likely to be key).

---

[147] ADA § 242(e)(2)(A).

[148] Id.

[149] ADA § 242(e)(2)(A)(iii).

As is the case with Amtrak, the regulations issued by the Secretary of Transportation will also require the appropriate person to develop a plan for implementing the transformation of existing key commuter stations to accessible stations. The plan must reflect consultation with the disabled affected by it and must establish milestones for achieving accessibility.

The time frame for making existing stations accessible on both Amtrak and commuter systems is "as soon as practicable" but in no event later than twenty or three years, respectively. The use of the term "as soon as practicable" is meant to make it clear that the intent is for accessibility to be created earlier than either three or twenty years. If funds and other resources necessary to make a station or part of it accessible are available before the end of the period, the work must be done at the time the funds and resources are available. Amtrak, the commuter authority, or other responsible party cannot in such situations put off the work that could otherwise be done until the three- or twenty-year deadline arrives; this would not be "as soon as practicable."[150]

Some stations may be used to provide intercity or commuter rail service and also some other form of rail transportation. At the very least, those parts of such stations used for purposes of furnishing intercity or commuter rail transportation, including paths of travel to these parts, must comply with the requirements set out above.

[i] Requirements. Section 242(e)(2)(B) sets forth the rules for when an alteration is made to an existing station in an intercity or commuter rail system. It applies to alterations that are undertaken voluntarily as well as to alterations undertaken in order to comply with the statutory obligation to make certain existing stations accessible.

The standard is similar to what is generally imposed for the making of alterations to other structures by the ADA.[151] If an alteration is made to any part of an existing station that could affect the usability of all or part of the station, the responsible

---

[150] H. Comm. on Educ. and Lab. Rep. at 97; S. Comm. on Lab. and Hum. Resources Rep. at 56.

[151] See, e.g., ADA §§ 227, 303.

person, owner, or person in control of the station must make the alteration in such a manner that, to the maximum extent feasible, the altered portions of the station are readily accessible to and usable by the disabled upon completion. Failure to meet this requirement constitutes discrimination under both Section 202 of the ADA and Section 504 of the Rehabilitation Act. Unlike the rest of Section 242, this requirement applies to the person who is actually having the alteration done, rather than just to the "responsible person."

Similarly, if alterations affect or could affect the usability of or access to an area of the station containing a primary function, the responsible person, owner, or person in control of the station must normally make the alterations so that, to the maximum extent feasible, the path of travel to the altered area, and to the bathrooms, telephones, and drinking fountains serving the altered area are readily accessible to and usable by the disabled. As is the case elsewhere in the ADA,[152] there is an exception: If such alterations to the path of travel, bathrooms, telephones, and drinking fountains are disproportionate to the overall alterations in their cost and scope, they do not need to be done. The Attorney General's regulations provide guidelines for determining when such alterations can be considered disproportionate in cost and scope. Whatever can be done to promote access without crossing the line of disproportionality, however, must be done. Again, failure to comply with this requirement constitutes discrimination.[153]

[ii] Cooperation of responsible person. The statutory framework, as previously mentioned, places the obligation to make certain stations accessible on the responsible person. The responsible person will not always be the owner of the station or even the one in control of the station. To prevent an owner or other person in control from thwarting the intent of the ADA or the efforts of the responsible person, Section 242(e)(2)(C) was added to require an owner, or other person in control of a

---

[152] See ADA § 303(a)(2).

[153] See ¶ 5.05[2][c] for a discussion of disproportionality in these regulations.

station, to cooperate, within reason, with a responsible person in the responsible person's efforts to comply with Section 242(e)(2)(A) and 242(e)(2)(B). Failure to so cooperate constitutes discrimination.

One example of a failure to cooperate would be a demand by a station owner that the responsible person provide an unreasonably high insurance bond before commencing alterations. [154]

Even if an owner or other person in control fails to provide cooperation, though, and this failure causes the responsible person to be unable to comply with the statute, the responsible person would still be guilty of discrimination. The failure to receive cooperation is not an acceptable defense. The owner or other person in control is also guilty of discrimination, but just for their lack of cooperation, not for the responsible person's noncompliance.

The owner or other person would, however, be liable to the responsible person for any harm or loss suffered by the responsible person as a result of the owner or other person's violation of the duty to cooperate. This liability could be in the form of damages caused by delay, indemnification for damages the responsible person has to pay a disabled person because of discrimination caused by the lack of cooperation, or injunctive relief to force cooperation. [155]

[5] Accessibility Requirements

Section 243 of the ADA requires that accessibility standards included in regulations issued by the Secretary of Transportation to implement Part II of Subtitle B be consistent with the supplemental guidelines issued by the ATBCB under Section 504(a) of the ADA.

Section 244 of the ADA requires that the secretary's regulations be promulgated, in an accessible format, by July 25, 1991, one year after enactment of the ADA. [156]

---

[154] H. Comm. on Energy and Com. Rep. at 53.

[155] Id.

[156] The regulations had not yet been issued by August 9, 1991.

The statute permits reference to existing guidelines and standards for efforts to make intercity and commuter rail stations and rail passenger cars accessible before the Secretary of Transportation's final regulations have been issued.[157] Compliance with the interim accessibility requirements during the periods indicated in the following sections will immunize the person complying from being guilty of discrimination—even if the final regulations differ from the interim requirements. The interim requirements also provide guidance until the Secretary of Transportation's regulations are issued.

[a] Rail Cars

The interim guidelines provide a frame of reference to determine when a rail passenger car is considered accessible to and usable by the disabled under Sections 242(a) through 242(d) before final regulations are issued. Until these regulations come out, a rail passenger car will be considered accessible to and usable by the disabled if the design for the car complies with the laws and regulations, including guidelines and supplemental guidelines of the ATBCB, governing accessibility of such a car—as long as these laws and regulations do not conflict with Part II of Subtitle B and are in effect at the time the design for the car is substantially completed.

A rail car owner who meets these interim requirements during the appropriate period will not be guilty of discrimination for the work covered, even if subsequent regulations contain requirements that were not met by the design. The key point in time here is the time at which the design for the car is substantially completed—not the time at which construction or alteration of the car is substantially completed. If the design is finished before regulations are issued, but regulations come out before construction starts, then compliance with the interim standards would still provide insulation against a charge of discrimination.

[b] Stations

A two-tiered reference system exists for work done to intercity or commuter rail stations. First, if a valid and appropriate

---

[157] ADA § 245.

state or local building permit is obtained prior to the issuance of the final regulations for either new construction or alterations to an existing station, if the work authorized by the permit begins within one year of receipt of the permit, and if such work is completed under the terms of the permit, then except as mentioned in the second tier, compliance with the UFAS in effect at the time the permit is issued will be viewed as meeting the requirements for accessibility and usability in Section 242(e).

Second, if the Secretary of Transportation has not issued final regulations by one year after the supplemental guidelines are promulgated by the ATBCB, then instead of complying with the UFAS, the person in control of the work must comply with such supplemental guidelines in order to meet requirements for accessibility and usability.

[6] Paratransit Services Not a Requirement

The ADA imposes no obligation on a public entity to provide paratransit or special transportation services as part of an intercity or commuter rail transportation system.[158] If Amtrak or commuter rail authorities also provide other modes of transportation that fall within Part I of Subtitle B, though, such as certain bus service or light rail transportation, the paratransit obligation in Part I would apply but only to the modes covered therein. If, however, Amtrak or a commuter rail authority just associates or does business with any provider of transportation who does have an obligation to provide paratransit service—such as by arranging with a public entity to make bus transportation available at Amtrak stations—Amtrak or the commuter authority would have no paratransit obligation.[159]

¶ 4.06 FEDERAL WILDERNESS AREAS

Both environmentalists and advocates for the disabled were concerned with the application of the ADA to wilderness areas.

---

[158] H. Comm. on Energy and Com. Rep. at 53.

[159] Id.

As a result, Section 507 of the ADA was added, which directs the
National Council on Disability to conduct a study on the effect
wilderness designations and wilderness land management practices have on the ability of the disabled to use and enjoy the
National Wilderness Preservation System as established under
the Wilderness Act. [160]

Some members of Congress expressed apprehension that
the Wilderness Act could be construed to limit the rights of
individuals who use wheelchairs. Thus, Section 507(c) of the
ADA was added during the House-Senate Conference to reaf-
firm Congress's intent that the Wilderness Act does not prohibit
the use of a wheelchair in a wilderness area by a disabled individual. The Conference Report expands upon this by indicating
that federal agencies, and their private subcontractors, may have
some affirmative duty to assist the disabled in certain instances
in wilderness areas:

> Consistent with this section and the Wilderness Act of
> 1964, the Conferees intend that, where appropriate and
> consistent with management objectives and maintenance of
> the wilderness characteristics of the area, the land manage-
> ment agencies charged with management responsibilities
> for wilderness areas designated under the authority of the
> Wilderness Act of 1964 should, when constructing or recon-
> structing a trail, bridge or facility, comply with the intent of
> this Act. In cases where the Agencies have delegated or
> subcontracted their responsibilities, the intent of this sec-
> tion shall apply to the designee or contractor. [161]

Despite this language in the Conference Report, though,
Section 507(c) also states that, consistent with the Wilderness
Act, no agency is required to provide any form of special treatment or accommodation, or to construct any facilities or modify
any conditions of lands within a wilderness area in order to
facilitate use by persons in wheelchairs. In order to construe this

---

[160] 16 USC § 1131.

[161] H. Conf. Rep. No. 101-596, Conf. Rep. on S. 933, Americans With
Disabilities Act of 1990, Joint Explanatory Statement of the Comm. of Conference (1990) at 86.

statutory language in a manner consistent with the Conference Report, it should be interpreted to mean that no accommodation is required if such accommodation would be inconsistent with the Wilderness Act.

CHAPTER 5

ADA Title III: Public Accommodations and Services Operated by Private Entities

¶ 5.01 BACKGROUND

Title III of the ADA expands protection for the disabled that was first afforded by the Architectural Barriers Act of 1968 and the Rehabilitation Act of 1973.[1]

[1] Architectural Barriers Act of 1968

The Architectural Barriers Act of 1968[2] required that buildings constructed by, leased in whole or in part to, or financed by, the federal government be made accessible to the disabled. It charged four federal agencies—the General Services Administration (GSA), U.S. Postal Service, Department of Defense, and Department of Housing and Urban Development (HUD)—with the responsibility for developing their own standards for the construction of disabled-accessible facilities and for the alteration of existing facilities.

The Department of Defense issues standards for construction and alteration of defense installations, HUD issues standards for residential structures covered by the Architectural Barriers Act except those funded or constructed by the Department of Defense, the U.S. Postal Service deals with postal facilities, and the GSA covers all buildings included within the Architectural Barriers Act that are not within the purview of the other three agencies. These four agencies ultimately adopted uniform standards—the Uniform Federal Accessibility Stan-

---

[1] Some of the other pieces of legislation that Congress has enacted to help provide equal rights and opportunities for the disabled include:

1. Urban Mass Transportation Act of 1970 (49 USC § 1612), requiring eligible jurisdictions to provide accessibility plans for mass transportation;
2. Surface Transportation Assistance Act of 1982 (49 USC App. 1612(d)), which required the Department of Transportation to issue minimum criteria for providing service to the disabled via surface transportation;
3. Education for All Handicapped Children Act of 1973 (20 USC § 1401 et seq.), providing that each handicapped child is entitled to a free appropriate education in the least restrictive environment; and
4. National Housing Act Amendments of 1975 (12 USC § 1701 et seq.), providing for barrier removal in federally supported housing.

[2] 42 USC §§ 4151–4157.

dards (UFAS)—designed to minimize the differences that had previously existed in the four separate sets of standards.

[2] Rehabilitation Act of 1973

The Rehabilitation Act of 1973[3]—primarily in Section 504[4]—prohibited federal agencies and recipients of federal funds from discriminating against the disabled. To ensure and promote compliance with the standards developed by the four agencies, the Rehabilitation Act additionally created the Architectural and Transportation Barriers Compliance Board (ATBCB), also known as the Access Board. The ATBCB was later given the responsibility, by a 1978 amendment to the Rehabilitation Act, to develop minimum guidelines and requirements for these standards relating to the design, construction, or alteration of facilities that are federally funded or constructed. The ATBCB is composed of twenty-two members—eleven representing different federal agencies plus eleven members appointed by the president from the general public.[5]

The ATBCB has carried out its mandate by developing Minimum Guidelines and Requirements for Accessible Design (MGRADs),[6] which set out its minimum guidelines and requirements for the standards dealing with the construction and alteration of facilities that fall within the scope of the Architectural Barriers Act and the Rehabilitation Act. In developing the UFAS, the four standard-setting agencies (GSA, Postal Service,

---

[3] 29 USC § 701 et seq.

[4] Section 504 of the Rehabilitation Act (29 USC Section 794) reads, in pertinent part:

No otherwise qualified individual with handicaps in the United States . . . shall, solely by reason of her or his handicap, be excluded from the participation in, be denied the benefits of, or be subjected to discrimination under any program or activity receiving Federal financial assistance or under any program or activity conducted by any Executive agency or by the United States Postal Service.

[5] The eleven agencies represented are: GSA, U.S. Postal Service, Veterans Administration, and the Departments of Housing and Urban Development, Defense, Education, Health and Human Services, Justice, Labor, Interior, and Transportation.

[6] 36 CFR pt. 1190.

Defense, HUD) have made sure that the technical requirements therein meet or exceed the comparable provisions in the ATBCB's guidelines.

[3] American National Standards Institute: Standards

Voluntary technical standards for providing accessibility to the disabled in the design of buildings and facilities in the private sector have been developed by the American National Standards Institute (ANSI). A committee was appointed by the ANSI —the Accredited Standards Committee on Architectural Features and Site Design of Public Buildings and Residential Structures for Persons With Handicaps, more easily referred to as Committee A117—made up of disability groups, design professionals, rehabilitation specialists and services, building owners and management associations, building product manufacturers, building code developers and administrators, senior citizen organizations, and federal standard-setting departments. The current version of the standards developed—ANSI A117.1-1986—is similar, by design, to the UFAS. As indicated, the ANSI standards are purely voluntary but serve as guidance for private entities to adopt and follow as they wish. The ATBCB's guidelines, though, which are binding on federal agencies and entities receiving federal aid, incorporate and refer to many of the technical standards adopted by the ANSI.

[4] ADA Title III

[a] In General

Title III builds upon the foundation established by the Architectural Barriers Act and the Rehabilitation Act. It basically extends the prohibitions that currently exist against discrimination in facilities constructed or financed by the federal government to apply to all privately operated public accommodations. With the passage of the ADA, the determinative factor in whether a structure must accommodate the disabled is no longer federal government funding or involvement. Now, with few exceptions, all public accommodations, including transportation provided to the public by private entities, must be accessible to the disabled.

Section 504 of the Rehabilitation Act is a very brief, general statute that takes most of its meaning from regulations enacted pursuant to it.[7] The ADA is substantially more detailed than Section 504, but will be further explained by regulations that will likely be given great weight by courts called upon to determine whether an entity has complied with the ADA.

Both Section 504 of the Rehabilitation Act and Title III of the ADA require that new construction, and substantial alterations to existing structures, be accessible to the disabled. The Rehabilitation Act, through regulations, also requires that a covered entity (a recipient of federal aid) take at least modest steps to make existing facilities accessible.[8] Title III on its face clearly imposes certain obligations on an owner/operator of existing public accommodations to make them accessible. These

---

[7] In one case, Atlantis Community, Inc. v. Adams, 453 F. Supp. 825 (D. Colo. 1978), the court even refused to grant the plaintiffs relief because it felt Section 504 was so general that the section failed to provide a sufficient definition of duties expected of the defendant—even though the defendant, a regional transportation district, was planning to purchase buses that did not have hydraulic lifts and wheelchair-securing devices available.

In Rhode Island Handicapped Action Committee v. Rhode Island Pub. Transit Auth., 718 F2d 490, 494 (1st Cir. 1983), the court also found Section 504 to be "both ambiguous and lacking in specifics." Because of this, the court felt that it would be inappropriate for it to determine what was required to accommodate the disabled under the statute. Instead, the court deferred to the regulations issued pursuant to the statute by the Department of Transportation as furnishing the appropriate guidelines for what the statute required.

Though Title III of the ADA is more detailed than Section 504, these cases may indicate that courts will give great weight to the guidelines set out in regulations issued under the ADA in determining whether a defendant has complied with the ADA.

[8] See Dopico v. Goldschmidt, 687 F2d 664, 652 (2d Cir. 1982), a case involving public transportation and handicapped individuals, quoting from American Pub. Transit Ass'n v. Lewis, 655 F2d 1272 (DC Cir. 1981): "[B]ecause the barriers to equal participation are physical rather than abstract, some sort of action must be taken to remove them, if only in the area of new construction or purchasing." Lewis does indicate that an action that imposes an extremely heavy financial burden is beyond what Section 504 requires, though, and need not be undertaken.

owner/operators must provide auxiliary aids to assist the disabled in their use of the public accommodations (such as a braille menu or a reader to assist a blind person in a restaurant), unless it is an undue burden to do so, and they must remove structural architectural, communications, and transportation barriers that hinder use of facilities by the disabled, where readily achievable to do so.

Testimony before congressional committees considering the rights of the disabled focused in part on the fact that "an overwhelming majority of individuals with disabilities lead isolated lives and do not frequent places of public accommodation."[9] Three primary reasons for this isolation were offered to the Senate Committee on Labor and Human Resources:

1. People with disabilities do not feel that they are welcome and can participate safely in places of public accommodation.

2. They experience fear and self-consciousness about their disability stemming from degrading experiences they or their friends with disabilities have experienced.

3. The existence of architectural, communication, and transportation barriers in places of public accommodation prevents people with disabilities from going to these places.[10]

Title III of the ADA is meant to "bring individuals with disabilities into the economic and social mainstream of American life" by removing the barriers in places of public accommodation and by making it clear that the disabled are as welcome as all other persons in these places.[11]

---

[9] Report of the Senate Comm. on Labor and Human Resources on the Americans With Disabilities Act of 1989, S. Rep. No. 116, 101st Cong., 1st Sess. (1989) (hereinafter cited as S. Comm. on Lab. and Hum. Resources Rep.) at 10.

[10] Id. at 11.

[11] Report of the House Comm. on Education and Labor on the Americans With Disabilities Act of 1990, H. Rep. No. 485, 101st Cong., 2d Sess., pt. 2 (1990) (hereinafter cited as H. Comm. on Educ. and Lab. Rep.) at 99; see also S. Comm. on Lab. and Hum. Resources Rep. at 10, 20.

Title III applies generally to privately owned public accommodation facilities and to the rights of the disabled to use these facilities. It does not apply to private clubs, to public entities such as governments or government agencies, or to religious entities. Title III does not govern any terms or conditions of employment offered by the owners of public accommodations, as these employment practices are covered in Title I of the ADA.

[b] Effective Dates

The general effective date for the provisions of Title III is eighteen months after enactment. Enactment was on July 26, 1990, so most of Title III takes effect on January 26, 1992.

There are several instances where the effective date for certain specific provisions of Title III is the July 26, 1990, date of enactment. The provisions that went into effect upon enactment are the following:

- Those that deal with discrimination in the transportation area by a private entity that is not primarily in the business of providing transportation for people, that operates a fixed route system or a demand responsive system[12]
- Those that deal with discrimination in the transportation area by a private entity that is primarily in the business of providing transportation for people, that purchases or leases a new vehicle (other than an automobile, a van with less than eight seats, or an over-the-road bus)[13]
- The direction that the Office of Technology Assessment (OTA) undertake a study concerning accessibility and over-the-road buses[14]
- The direction that the Secretary of Transportation and Attorney General issue regulations to carry out Title III[15]

---

[12] Section 302(a) for purposes of Sections 302(b)(2)(B) and 302(b)(2)(C) only.

[13] Section 304(a) for purposes of Section 304(b)(3) only, and Section 304(b)(3).

[14] ADA § 305.

[15] ADA § 306.

Congress wanted small businesses to have time in addition to the effective aforementioned dates to learn the requirements of the ADA and to come into compliance with it before they will be subject to a civil action for a violation.[16] An amendment was added to Title III during the House of Representatives' floor debate on the bill to delay enforcement of the bill's provisions against small businesses because of the

> potential costs [to small businesses] and unfamiliar require-
> ments that compliance with the ADA will entail . . . no one
> wants a small business to fail because complying with or
> defending oneself under the ADA requires costly and time-
> consuming lawsuits or because regulations have not been
> issued informing businesses about the ADA's requirements.
> [The] amendment responds to these concerns without alter-
> ing the scope or the substance of the ADA. Although we
> recognize that final regulations are often issued long after
> laws are in effect, we do not seek to delay the effective date
> of the public accommodations title or tie the effective date
> to the issuance of final regulations.[17]

The amendment delayed enforcement against small businesses as follows:

1. Other than for actions under Section 303, no civil action may be brought against a business that employs twenty-five or fewer employees and has gross receipts of $1 million or less alleging that a discriminatory act occurred during the first six months after Title III's effective date.
2. Other than for actions under Section 303, no civil action may be brought against a business that employs ten or fewer employees and has gross receipts of $500,000 or less alleging that a discriminatory act occurred during the first year after Title III's effective date.

---

[16] See HR Conf. Rep. No. 596, 101st Cong., 2d Sess. (1990), Conf. Rep. on S. 933, Americans With Disabilities Act of 1990, Joint Explanatory Statement of the Committee on Conference, at ¶ 61(a).

[17] 136 Cong. Rec. at H2464 (May 17, 1990) (Statement of Cong. John LaFalce, chairman of the House Committee on Small Business, one of the two co-sponsors of the amendment).

The gross receipts test is presumably meant to be gross receipts within the business's most recent fiscal year. This is not certain, however, as both the statute and accompanying legislative history are silent on this point. It is clear, though, that in order for an action to be brought against a small business, the violation of the ADA must have occurred after either the six-month or the one-year period, whichever is applicable, has expired.[18]

The amendment does not delay applicability of the ADA to small businesses; it just delays enforcement. As Congressman Steny Hoyer, the House floor manager for the ADA, stated during debate on the amendment, "I want to make it clear, and I think we all do understand this, that the law itself will be in effect and they [small businesses] will be under an obligation, of course to make the accommodations."[19] Small businesses should still begin to accommodate the disabled, therefore, as of the effective date of the ADA.

¶ 5.02 ADA: TERMS AND CONCEPTS

[1] Public Accommodation

[a] Existing Statutory Use

The use of the words "public accommodation" or "place of public accommodation" is not completely new with the ADA.

---

[18] This point is made in the following colloquy (136 Cong. Rec. at H2464 (May 17, 1990)) between the amendment's two sponsors, Cong. LaFalce and Cong. Tom Campbell:

> Mr. Campbell: Whereas the amendment states that during the first 6 months after the effective date no civil action shall be brought against businesses that fit these specifications, and similarly during the first year, I think the question should be made very clear that for actions or failures to take action during that period a lawsuit could not be brought once the 6 months is over.

> Mr. LaFalce: Mr. Chairman, that is absolutely correct. No action could be brought for any action or inaction during either the 6 months or the 1-year period respectively.

[19] 136 Cong. Rec. at H2465 (May 17, 1990) (Statement of Cong. Steny Hoyer).

Section 201 of Title II of the Civil Rights Act of 1964[20] prohibits discrimination by any place of public accommodation on grounds of race, color, religion, or national origin.[21] As defined in Section 201, place of public accommodation is, to the extent its operations affect interstate commerce

> 1. Any inn, hotel, motel, or other establishment which provides lodging to transient guests, other than an establishment located within a building which contains not more than five rooms for rent or hire and which is actually occupied by the proprietor of such establishment as his residence;
>
> 2. Any restaurant, cafeteria, lunchroom, lunch counter, soda fountain, or other facility principally engaged in selling food for consumption on the premises, including, but not limited to, any such facility located on the premises of any retail establishment; or any gasoline station;
>
> 3. [A]ny motion picture house, theater, concert hall, sports arena, stadium or other place of exhibition or entertainment; and
>
> 4. [A]ny establishment (A)(i) which is physically located within the premises of any establishment otherwise covered by this subsection, or (ii) within the premises of which is physically located any such covered establishment, and (B) which holds itself out as serving patrons of such covered establishment.[22]

Title III of the ADA incorporates much of the Civil Rights Act's definition of a place of public accommodation, but adds more and broader examples to the definition.

[b] Covered by the ADA

Title III of the ADA prohibits discrimination in all places of public accommodation. Central to the purpose of Title III is the

---

[20] 42 USC § 2000a.

[21] Section 201 reads: "All persons shall be entitled to the full and equal enjoyment of the goods, services, facilities, privileges, advantages, and accommodations of any place of public accommodation, as defined in this section, without discrimination or segregation on the ground of race, color, religion, or national origin."

[22] 42 USC § 2000a(b).

description in Section 301(7) of what constitutes a public accommodation.

Two tests must be satisfied for an establishment to be considered a public accommodation: "[I]ts operations must affect commerce, and it must be operated by a private entity but be held open to the public."

The word "commerce" as used in this test really means matters affecting interstate commerce, since the federal government only has regulatory power over such matters. Section 301(1) defines "commerce" for purposes of Title III as

> travel, trade, traffic, commerce, transportation, or communication—
>
> (A) among the several States;
>
> (B) between any foreign country or any territory or possession and any State; or
>
> (C) between points in the same State but through another State or foreign country.

Title III also applies to privately owned or operated commercial facilities that are not held open to the public, but only with respect to new construction and alterations undertaken by these commercial facilities.[23]

[i] Twelve categories. There are twelve categories of private entities set forth in Section 301(7) that are to be considered public accommodations for purposes of Title III. No other category of privately owned entity falls within the scope of Title III, but the listing of specific types of entities within each of the twelve categories is not exhaustive. In most categories, after a listing of specific types of places included, words like "or other place" are included. Congress very clearly intended that within each category the listed types of places were merely representative, and that other similar types of places within the same category that were not specifically listed would, nevertheless, be considered as a public accommodation. Both the House Com-

---

[23] H. Comm. on Educ. and Lab. Rep. at 100; S. Comm. on Lab. and Hum. Resources Rep. at 59.

mittee on Education and Labor and the Senate Committee on Labor and Human Resources included the following language in their legislative reports:

> The Committee intends that the "other similar" terminology should be construed liberally, consistent with the intent of the legislation that people with disabilities should have equal access to the array of establishments that are available to others who do not currently have disabilities. [24]

The legislative histories list several examples of what is meant by this language. A "golf course" is mentioned in the category dealing with places of recreation, as is the broadly stated "other place of exercise or recreation." While such other place of exercise or recreation would include such golf-related areas as a driving range, putting course, or miniature golf course, such non–golf-related places of recreation as tennis courts, baseball fields, basketball courts, dance halls, playgrounds, aerobic facilities, video arcades, swimming pools, beaches, camping areas, fishing and boating facilities, and amusement parks would also fall within the category as a covered place of public accommodation. [25]

The twelve categories and examples of the "other similar" language are provided in the following list.

1. An inn, hotel, motel, or other place of lodging, except for an establishment located within a building that contains not more than five rooms for rent or hire and that is actually occupied by the proprietor of such establishment as the residence of such proprietor.

The key words here are "other place of lodging." Guesthouses, hostels, pensions, resorts, campgrounds, and trailer parks whose purpose is short-term stay rather than residential would fall under this category. If a place of lodging contains part residential and part nonresidential facilities—such as a large hotel that has a residential wing—only the nonresidential

---

[24] Id.

[25] Id.

accommodations would be public accommodations covered by the ADA.[26]

The definition here excepts from the ADA small, traditional "mom-and-pop" guesthouses where no more than five rooms are available for rent and where the proprietor occupies the premises as the proprietor's residence. The ADA does not require that the "owner" live on the premises, only the proprietor, so that if a nonresident owner of one of these small guesthouses hires a proprietor who lives on the premises, the guesthouse would be excepted from the ADA.

2. A restaurant, bar, or other establishment serving food or drink.

Many establishments that would not normally be considered restaurants or bars serve food or drink, such as stadiums hosting athletic contests and motion picture theaters. The language of this category would seem to include these types of entities, though it is not important that it do so since other categories specifically enumerate these places.

3. A motion picture house, theater, concert hall, stadium, or other place of exhibition or entertainment.

4. An auditorium, convention center, lecture hall, or other place of public gathering.

These categories are similar to each other. For instance, a convention center that is a place of public gathering can be used to hold indoor sporting events, making it also a place of exhibition or entertainment. And, generally, a place of exhibition or entertainment also involves a public gathering. Other places that would fall within these categories include a circus, classroom in a private school, outdoor performance stage, amphitheater, temporary outdoor facility, and meeting room.

5. A bakery, grocery store, clothing store, hardware store, shopping center, or other sales or rental establishment.

This category encompasses the vast array of private stores that exist. Though only a few types are listed, all others are included, ranging from pet stores to sporting goods stores to

---

[26] H. Comm. on Educ. and Lab. Rep. at 100; S. Comm. on Lab. and Hum. Resources Rep. at 59. The residential portion of a hotel would be covered under the Fair Housing Act (42 USC §§ 3601 et seq.), though.

specialty stores to department stores. No size limitation is included, so both very large and very small stores are included. This category covers stores that sell goods, regardless of what the goods are—perishable and nonperishable goods, food, large stores, small stores, stores selling only expensive items and stores selling low-priced merchandise. A realtor's office, an on-site sales office at a housing development, a rental office at an apartment building, and a car rental office all would be covered.

6. A laundromat, dry cleaner, bank, barber shop, beauty shop, travel service, funeral parlor, gas station, office of an accountant or lawyer, pharmacy, insurance office, professional office of a health care provider, hospital, or other service establishment.

This category is similar in its broad scope to the previous category, but instead of focusing on providers of goods, it focuses on providers of service. All private entities that provide some sort of a service to the public fall within this definition. Included would be such businesses as a tailor's shop, architect's office, real estate appraiser's office, veterinarian's office, engineer's office, physical therapist's office, and other offices visited by the public. The automatic teller machines located inside or outside bank offices fall into this category.

7. A terminal, depot, or other station used for specified public transportation.

This would include a bus terminal, train station, airport, subway station, passenger shipping or boating point of embarkation, and monorail terminal. Because the word "station" is used, it is doubtful that a mere bus stop or taxicab stand that is not actually a station would be considered a public accommodation. "Specified public transportation" is a defined term[27] meaning transportation by bus, rail, or any other conveyance (other than by aircraft) that provides the general public with general or special service (including charter service) on a regular and continuing basis.

8. A museum, library, gallery, or other place of public display or collection.

This category is meant to include those places where people

---

[27] See ADA § 301(10).

go to view or browse through materials. It would include permanent displays and collections, as well as portable collections, such as traveling libraries or bookmobiles, and traveling displays of artwork housed in mobile facilities, such as trailers. Privately owned houses that are open to the public for tours, such as homes of famous persons or former presidents, would fit into this category. Likewise, privately owned restored areas that include many old houses and shops kept open for public display would be covered. Reading rooms also fall within this category.

9. A park, zoo, amusement park, or other place of recreation.

This category is oriented toward outdoor places of recreation that are privately owned and held open to the public. Municipal parks and the like are not covered by Title III since they are publicly rather than privately owned. The words "place of recreation" are also used in the last category, so there is some overlap between the categories, but the last category is aimed more at places of exercise and sport than is this category—and, again, any overlap is immaterial. A carnival or entertainment park such as Disneyland would be included in this category.

10. A nursery, elementary, secondary, undergraduate, or postgraduate private school, or other place of education.

In addition to the range of private schools specified, places where private lessons are given would fall within this category. Thus, places such as music schools, art schools, martial arts schools, and language schools would be covered by Title III. Because of the exemption of religious entities from the ADA, though, a place of education operated by a religious organization would not be included as a place of public accommodation.

11. A day-care center, senior citizen center, homeless shelter, food bank, adoption agency, or other social service center establishment.

This category encompasses the range of social service providers, but only to the extent the providers are private entities rather than public agencies. Private counseling centers of all sorts, youth centers, soup kitchens, and immigrant assistance centers would come under this category.

12. A gymnasium, health spa, bowling alley, golf course, or other place of exercise or recreation.

This category is very broad and brings under the ADA all privately owned places of exercise or recreation. Private tennis and other racquet sport courts, weight and exercise rooms, fitness clubs, baseball batting cages, swimming pools, saunas, steamrooms, jacuzzis, ice hockey rinks, and roller-skating arenas would fall within this category as long as they are held open for public use. Not only would the actual exercise part of the facility be covered by Title III, but also any locker room and other facilities on the same premises.

For ease of referral, the Attorney General's regulations label the facilities that fall within the twelve categories listed in Section 301(7) as places of public accommodation. A public accommodation, in these regulations, is the "private entity that owns, leases (or leases to), or operates a place of public accommodation." [28] However, the regulations make it clear that if a private entity owns, operates, or leases two facilities, one of which is a place of public accommodation and one of which is not, Title III only applies to the facility that is a place of public accommodation. [29]

A public accommodation does not lose this status just because it may receive some federal financial assistance, though this assistance subjects the public accommodation to Section 504 of the Rehabilitation Act, as well as to Title III of the ADA. [30]

The ADA is not meant to apply to residential facilities, but if a facility has residential and nonresidential uses, the ADA is applicable to the portion that is used for nonresidential purposes. [31] Additionally, to the extent that a home or part thereof is used as a facility that falls within one of the twelve enumerated categories—such as a doctor's or dentist's office within a home—it is covered by the ADA. [32]

---

[28] 28 CFR § 36.104.

[29] 28 CFR § 36.102(b)(2).

[30] H. Comm. on Educ. and Lab. Rep. at 100; S. Comm. on Lab. and Hum. Resources Rep. at 59.

[31] H. Comm. on Educ. and Lab. Rep. at 100; S. Comm. on Lab. and Hum. Resources Rep. at 59.

[32] 28 CFR § 36.207.

While by definition the ADA applies to private schools, compliance with the ADA does not require

> a private school to provide a free appropriate education or develop an individualized education program in accordance with regulations implementing section 504 of the Rehabilitation Act of 1973 (34 CFR Part 104) and regulations implementing part B of the Education of the Handicapped Act (34 CFR Part 300). Of course, if a private school is under contract with a public entity to provide a free appropriate public education, it must provide such education in accordance with section 504 of the Rehabilitation Act and part B regulations of the Education of the Handicapped Act.[33]

The ADA does not limit the private entities that can qualify as public accommodations to those that are for-profit or commercial facilities (the term "commercial facilities" is defined in Section 301(2) of the ADA but this term is not used in connection with the definition of "public accommodation") or that charge for their services or product. Privately operated social service programs, which are often free to participants, are specifically included as public accommodations. Other charitable activities could also be public accommodations, then, if they fall within one of the twelve categories.

There is overlap among the categories, and a single entity might fall within several categories. This is not important, though, for entities in the different categories are all treated the same by the ADA as long as they are public accommodations. Attention need not be paid to which category an entity falls within as long as it falls within a category.

An entity that otherwise qualifies under one of the twelve categories can still only be a public accommodation if it affects interstate commerce. A backyard tennis court, pool, or garden that is not held open to the public would not affect commerce, and would not therefore be a public accommodation.

---

[33] H. Comm. on Educ. and Lab. Rep. at 100; S. Comm. on Lab. and Hum. Resources Rep. at 59, 60.

[ii] **Entity otherwise not a public accommodation.** An entity that is not otherwise a public accommodation, such as a trade association or a performing artist, may become a public accommodation when it leases space for a meeting or a performance at a hotel, convention, stadium, or similar facility. While under the regulations the specific responsibilities for compliance can be allocated between the lessor and lessee by contract, generally, the lessee should be responsible for complying with Title III insofar as making auxiliary aids available to the disabled attending the meeting or performance, and making sure that all displays erected by the lessee are accessible to the disabled.[34] If the entity was a private club leasing space for a private function, though, no obligation under the ADA would be created. Nor would an obligation arise if the space was donated to the non-public accommodation, rather than leased.[35]

[c] Exemption: Private Clubs and Religious Organizations

Section 307 exempts from the coverage of the ADA private clubs or establishments that are also exempted from coverage under Title II of the Civil Rights Act of 1964.[36] The ADA is not to apply to religious organizations or entities controlled by religious organizations, including places of worship. A church sanctuary would not have to make its facilities accessible to the disabled, and would not have to ensure that any new construction or alteration is accessible.[37] A school operated by a religious organization would fall within this exception.[38]

This exemption also applies to events sponsored by a relig-

---

[34] See 28 CFR § 36.201 and Department of Justice section-by-section analysis accompanying 28 CFR § 36.201 of the Department of Justice's regulations.

[35] See section-by-section analysis accompanying 28 CFR § 36.201.

[36] 42 USC § 2000-a(e).

[37] Report of the House Comm. on the Judiciary on the Americans With Disabilities Act of 1990, HR Rep. No. 485, 101st Cong., 2d Sess., pt. 3 (1990) (hereinafter cited as H. Comm. on Jud. Rep.) at 66.

[38] H. Comm. on Educ. and Lab. Rep. at 125; S. Comm. on Lab. and Hum. Resources Rep. at 76; see also ¶ 3.02[2].

ious organization or an entity controlled by a religious organization, held on its own property, that are open to nonmembers of the organization or entity.[39]

The use of the phrase "entities controlled by religious organizations" is modeled after and meant to be construed similarly to that of the Education Amendments of 1972, Title IX, as amended by the Civil Rights Restoration Act of 1988.[40] The phrase is also meant to be construed consistently with how this wording in Title IX has been interpreted in the Attachment that accompanied the Assurance of Compliance with Title IX required by the U.S. Department of Education.[41]

A purely private facility not open to the public, such as a private club, is not a public accommodation. Neither is a facility operated by a government agency or other public entity a public accommodation, though such a facility would be governed by Title II of the ADA and could also be covered by the Rehabilitation Act.[42]

A question arose under the Civil Rights Act as to whether a club was public or private. If it was public, it was covered by the Act, but if it was purely private in a way that the general public was not welcomed, it was outside the Act's scope. A similar issue could arise under Title III of the ADA, and the case law that developed under the Civil Rights Act may provide guidance on when a club is public or private for purposes of the ADA. If a club is purely private, it would not accommodate the public and would not therefore be a place of public accommodation, so that Title III of the ADA would not apply to it—though, importantly, Title I of the ADA would still apply to the club in the employment context.

---

[39] Id.

[40] See 20 USC § 1681(a)(3), which says "this section shall not apply to an educational institution which is controlled by a religious organization if the application of this subsection would not be consistent with the religious tenets of such organization."

[41] H. Comm. on Educ. and Lab. Rep. at 125; S. Comm. on Lab. and Hum. Resources Rep. at 76; H. Comm. on Jud. Rep. at 66.

[42] See section-by-section analysis accompanying 28 CFR § 36.104 of the Department of Justice's regulations.

As indicated, under Section 201 of the Civil Rights Act, a genuinely private club is not a public accommodation.[43] In determining whether an organization is a private club, the following factors are considered:

- The selectivity of the group in admission of members. The more selective, the more likely the group is private.
- The existence of formal membership procedures.
- The degree of membership control over internal governance, particularly with regard to new members.
- The organization's history.
- The ability of nonmembers to use club facilities.
- The substantiality of dues.
- The presence of advertising for the organization.
- The predominance of the profit motive in the organization's operations.[44]

If a private facility conducts public tours of its facility, such as a tour of an otherwise private movie studio or plant, only the tour route is considered a public accommodation subject to Title III, according to the Department of Justice's regulations.[45]

[2] Commercial Facility

A "commercial facility" is defined by Section 301(2) of the ADA as one that is intended for nonresidential use and whose operations will affect commerce. Title III applies to a commercial facility only to the extent new construction or alterations are undertaken. This term does not include a railroad locomotive, railroad freight car, railroad caboose, intercity railroad car, com-

---

[43] See, e.g., Cornelius v. Benevolent Protective Order of Elks, 382 F. Supp. 1182 (D. Conn. 1974); Wesley v. Savannah, Ga., 294 F. Supp. 698 (SD Ga. 1969).

[44] Id; see also Tillman v. Wheaton-Haven Recreation Ass'n, 410 US 431 (1973); Daniel v. Paul, 395 US 298 (1969); Solomon v. Miami Woman's Club, 359 F. Supp. 41 (SD Fla. 1973); Nesmith v. YMCA of Raleigh, NC, 397 F2d 96 (4th Cir. 1968).

[45] See section-by-section analysis accompanying 28 CFR § 36.104 of the Department of Justice's regulations.

muter railroad car or railroad car owned by a private entity (that is treated elsewhere in Title III,[46]) railroad right-of-way, or facility that is covered or expressly exempted from coverage under the Fair Housing Act of 1968[47](since a facility covered by the Fair Housing Act is already under an obligation not to discriminate against a person with a disability).

Many commercial facilities will also be public accommodations, such as a retail department store or any other building that contains a facility meeting the description of public accommodations provided in Section 301(7). But other commercial facilities, such as office buildings that do not contain any of the entities listed in Section 301(7), factories, and warehouses, would not be public accommodations; these types of commercial facilities are not held open to the general public. Since Congress intended for the obligation of nondiscrimination in new construction or alterations to apply to all commercial establishments, and not just public accommodations, the new term "commercial facilities" was created and included along with public accommodations within Section 303.[48]

The use of the term "facility" includes all or any portion of buildings, structures, sites, complexes, equipment, roads, walks, passageways, parking lots, or other real or personal property or interest in such property, including the site where the building, property, structure, or equipment is located.[49] This is consistent with the definition of this term included in both the UFAS and the accessibility standards published by the ANSI.[50] Both indoor

---

[46] Section 304 applies to private operators of public transportation systems who are primarily in the business of providing transportation.

[47] 42 USC § 3601 et seq.

[48] In earlier versions of the ADA, the term "potential places of employment" was used in Title III instead of "commercial facilities." To avoid confusion between Title I, which deals with employment practices, and Title III, the original term was replaced by "commercial facilities" even though the definition and scope remains the same as with the earlier term. See H. Comm. on Educ. and Lab. Rep. at 117.

[49] H. Comm. on Educ. and Lab. Rep. at 114.

[50] Section 3.5 of both the UFAS (Apr. 1, 1988) and the voluntary ANSI standards (ANSI A117.1-1986) define facility as "all or any portion of a building, structure, or area, including the site on which such building, structure

and outdoor areas where man-made improvements, structures, equipment, or property have been added to the natural environment are included. Since a building's parking lot is part of the facility, where access is required, curb cuts must be made.

[3] Readily Achievable

Section 301(9) introduces and defines the concept of "readily achievable," used by Title III[51] in connection with barrier removal. This concept will determine if the failure of a public accommodation to remove architectural barriers and structural communication barriers in existing facilities, or to remove transportation barriers in certain existing vehicles and rail passenger cars, constitutes discrimination under the ADA. A failure to remove such barriers is considered discrimination if the removal would have been readily achievable. Conversely, if removal is not readily achievable, failure to remove is not discriminatory.

If removal itself is not readily achievable, though, the public accommodation still has an obligation under the ADA to make its goods, services, facilities, privileges, advantages, or accommodations available to the disabled through alternative methods—such as furnishing aids—as long as these alternative methods are themselves readily achievable.[52]

The concept of what is readily achievable is vital to the ADA's aim of promoting access for the disabled without unduly and unfairly burdening owners of existing places of public accommodation.

Section 301(9) defines readily achievable as "easily accomplishable and able to be carried out without much difficulty or expense." What is readily achievable varies from situation to situation, and is determined on a case-by-case basis by taking into account the following factors set out in Section 301(9):

---

or area is located, wherein specific services are provided or activities performed."

[51] See ADA §§ 302(b)(2)(A)(iv), 302(b)(2)(A)(v).

[52] See ADA § 302(b)(2)(A)(v).

1. The nature and cost of the action needed in order to remove structural barriers in existing facilities and vehicles;
2. The overall financial resources of the facility or facilities involved in the action, the number of persons employed at the facility or facilities, and the effect on expenses and resources or the impact otherwise of the retrofitting upon the operation of the facility or facilities;
3. The overall financial resources of the covered entity, the overall size of the business of a covered entity with respect to the number of its employees, and the number, type, and location of its facilities; and
4. The type of operation or operations of the covered entity, including the composition, structure, and functions of the work force of such entity, and the geographic separateness, administrative or fiscal relationship of the facility or facilities in question to the covered entity.

The Department of Justice in its regulations declined to establish any numerical formula for determining whether a change is readily achievable. Rather, it chose to implement the flexible case-by-case approach chosen by Congress, by reiterating the statutory factors with several minor additions.[53] For instance, the regulations permit an entity to take safety requirements, including those necessary for crime prevention, into account in ascertaining whether a change is readily achievable, and make it clear that the line of inquiry starts with the site involved in the action and only includes a parent company if applicable.[54]

Readily achievable is different from "readily accessible," a term also created by the ADA. "Readily accessible to and usable by individuals with disabilities" is used in connection with accessibility requirements for alterations and new construction[55] and focuses on the person with a disability and addresses the degree of ease with which an individual with a disability can

---

[53] See 28 CFR § 36.104 and section-by-section analysis accompanying this section.

[54] 28 CFR § 36.104.

[55] See ADA § 303.

enter and use a facility; it is access and usability that must be ready. The readily achievable standard, however, focuses on the entity that operates the business and is concerned with the degree of ease or difficulty the entity would have in removing the barrier.[56]

Both the House Committee on Education and Labor and the Senate Committee on Labor and Human Resources state in their reports on the ADA:

> It is important to note that readily achievable is a significantly lesser or lower standard than the "undue burden" standard used in this title and the "undue hardship" standard used in title I of this legislation. Any changes that are not easily accomplishable and are not able to be carried out without much difficulty or expense when the preceding factors [this refers to the factors set out in Section 301(9)] are weighed are not required under the readily achievable standard, even if they do not impose an undue burden.[57]

The regulations issued by the Department of Justice adopt this position as well, but recognize that the factors used in determining whether an action is readily achievable or would result in an undue hardship are identical.[58]

Although both committees make this statement, no further elucidation is provided concerning what each believed the "significant difference" between the two standards to be. From the description of each standard, there may not be a tremendous *practical* difference between the two. This conclusion is bolstered by the comments of the House Committee on the Judiciary, which stated in its report on the legislation, contrary to the two labor committees, that the analysis in determining what is readily achievable

> is the same as in title I, when considering whether a reasonable accommodation in the employment context will

---

[56] H. Comm. on Educ. and Lab. Rep. at 109, 110; S. Comm. on Lab. and Hum. Resources Rep. at 65, 66.

[57] H. Comm. on Educ. and Lab. Rep. at 109; S. Comm. on Lab. and Hum. Resources Rep. at 65.

[58] See section-by-section analysis accompanying 28 CFR § 36.304.

impose an undue hardship. The same factors adopted during Committee consideration of the bill for "undue hardship" were adopted for "readily achievable."[59]

Interestingly, the statutory readily achievable definition adopted and reported on by the Judiciary Committee—and this definition was included in the enacted ADA in Section 301(9)—was virtually identical to what was adopted by both labor committees, with the addition by the judiciary committee of language to protect businesses in depressed or rural areas that may be operating at the margin or at a loss.

The test used to determine whether a change is readily achievable is largely a balancing test. The readily achievable standard can be described as a

> significantly lesser or lower standard than the "undue burden" standard used in this title and the "undue hardship" standard used in title I . . . . Any changes that are not easily accomplishable and are not able to be carried out without much difficulty or expense when the preceding factors [listed previously] are weighed are not required under the readily achievable standard, even if they do not impose an undue burden.[60]

The floor manager for the House of Representatives debate on the ADA, Congressman Hoyer, stated that readily achievable "is clearly intended to ensure that what is expected of business is reasonable and proper, and that businesses are not threatened by this legislation."[61]

The factors included in the legislation for determining whether a change is readily achievable are not given different weights by either the ADA itself or the legislative history. Each public accommodation must make its own determination of whether a change is readily achievable based upon its own application of the specific factors to its particular circumstances.

---

[59] H. Comm. on Jud. Rep. at 55.

[60] H. Comm. on Educ. and Lab. Rep. at 109; S. Comm. on Lab. and Hum. Resources Rep. at 65.

[61] 136 Cong. Rec. at H2426, 2427 (May 17, 1990) (Statement of Cong. Steny Hoyer).

The key in applying the factors is to recognize that readily achievable only means modest changes. If a major change or restructuring is required, it is not readily achievable.

The barriers dealt with by Title III are those features, or the lack thereof, that prevent the disabled from enjoying access to buildings, facilities, or vehicles. For example, a restroom contains a barrier if there are no grab bars or the like to enable persons in wheelchairs to move from the wheelchair to the toilet. A building or restaurant presents a similar barrier if the only way to enter is by climbing stairs and there is no ramp to afford access to wheelchairs. An elevator contains a barrier to the blind if there are no braille markings for the different floors, or if there is no way for them to know the floor at which the elevator is stopping.

The type of barrier removal to which the readily achievable standard is intended to be applied includes the addition of grab bars, simple ramping of a few steps, lowering of telephones, addition of raised letter and braille markings on elevator control buttons, addition of flashing alarm lights, and similar modest adjustments.[62] Barriers can be removed by the addition of these items with little difficulty or expense.

The more expensive a change is, the less likely it is that the change is readily achievable. Similarly, if a change hinders the efficient operation of the entity, it would likely not be readily achievable. If a change is not expensive and would not significantly adversely affect the operations of the entity, though, it should be readily achievable even if it is not certain how many disabled persons will benefit from the change. The ATBCB minimum guidelines provide technical standards for making certain facilities and elements accessible. Not all of these standards will be readily achievable in the context of existing facilities, but if a change is readily achievable, the standards applicable to it will provide guidance.

An example cited during floor debate in the House of Representatives on the ADA is illustrative:

---

[62] H. Comm. on Educ. and Lab. Rep. at 110; S. Comm. on Lab. and Hum. Resources Rep. at 66.

Must all the aisles in a store be widened to accommodate wheelchairs?

No. The ADA does not require that aisles be widened. It does require access to shopping services, if making such services accessible is readily achievable; that is, easily accomplishable and able to be carried out without much difficulty or expense. Thus, widening aisles is one way of providing access, but there are others: reorganizing the placement of frequently purchased items at the front or front end of aisles; making customer assistants willing to retrieve items for those with disabilities; taking phone orders for mailing or pick up at curb side, and providing catalogs and flyers.[63]

¶ 5.03 DISCRIMINATION

Section 302 guarantees to the disabled the right to full and equal enjoyment of goods, services, facilities, privileges, advantages, or accommodations offered by a place of public accommodation. To accomplish this, it is not sufficient for a place of public accommodation merely to provide accessible features; these features must also be usable by the disabled. To this end, equipment that provides access—such as elevators and automatic doors—must be regularly maintained and kept in working condition.[64] While isolated instances of equipment failure by itself does not violate the ADA, repeated failure of equipment necessary to afford access due to improper or inadequate maintenance would be a violation.[65] Being usable also means that an accessible path of travel cannot be regularly blocked by furniture, file cabinets, plants, or other obstructions.[66]

Section 302(a) sets forth the general rule of Title III applica-

---

[63] 136 Cong. Rec. at H2420 (May 17, 1990) (Statement of Cong. Steve Bartlett, a member of the House Committee on Education and Labor).

[64] See 28 CFR § 36.211.

[65] Id. See also section-by-section analysis accompanying 28 CFR § 36.211.

[66] Id.

ble to public accommodations prohibiting them from discriminating against the disabled. It is a simple, broad-sweeping rule:

> No person who owns, leases (either as lessor or lessee), or operates a place of public accommodation may discriminate against anyone because of a disability so as to deny the disabled person the full and equal enjoyment of the goods, services, facilities, privileges, advantages, or accommodations of the place of public accommodation.

The rest of Title III just fleshes out this rule by providing more specific definition of the types of conduct that constitute discrimination under Section 302(a).

Full and equal enjoyment does not mean that the disabled must actually achieve the exact same result or level of achievement as the nondisabled. It does mean, though, that the disabled must be afforded an equal opportunity to be able to obtain the same result or level of achievement as the nondisabled.[67]

Title III does not require that the disabled be preferred over the nondisabled, or be given more opportunities than the nondisabled. As Congressman Hoyer, the lead sponsor and House floor manager of the ADA, made clear, all that is guaranteed by the legislation is a "level playing field" on which the disabled can compete and enjoy opportunities just as the nondisabled can.[68] The disabled are just guaranteed equal status.

Sections 302(a) and 302(b)(1) both speak in terms of generalized types of conduct that is prohibited. In Section 302(b)(2), and elsewhere in Title III, there are descriptions of specific types of prohibited conduct, including exceptions and limitations to what is prohibited. To the extent there is any apparent conflict between the general descriptions and the specific language, the specific language is meant to prevail.[69]

---

[67] H. Comm. on Educ. and Lab. Rep. at 101; S. Comm. on Lab. and Hum. Resources Rep. at 60.

[68] 136 Cong. Rec. at H2427 (May 17, 1990) (Statement of Cong. Steny Hoyer).

[69] H. Comm. on Educ. and Lab. Rep. at 104; S. Comm. on Lab. and Hum. Resources Rep. at 61.

The prohibition against discrimination applies to the owner of the building that houses the public accommodation, as well as to the public accommodation itself (or the operator thereof). The owner must make such changes to promote accessibility as are within its control and readily achievable, and the tenant must do the same. Any actions of the owner that affect the ability of the disabled to use the public accommodation are covered by the nondiscrimination provisions of Section 302. For example, the owner of a shopping center could not refuse to modify a "no pets" policy that prohibits blind persons from using seeing-eye dogs to gain access to individual stores in the shopping center.

Importantly, an organization that leases or rents public accommodation space is prohibited from leasing or renting this space from an entity that discriminates against the disabled in violation of the ADA. If a hotel has not made the changes to a meeting room that are readily achievable, it is in violation of the ADA and so, consequently, is an organization that might lease or rent this room for a meeting. This provision does not necessarily require organizations to lease only fully accessible facilities, but it does require them to lease facilities that are in compliance with the ADA. Therefore, leased facilities should be within the readily achievable standard where full accessibility is *not* required.[70]

However, the issue is raised of whether the employer can lawfully hold a meeting or functions for employees in a hotel or other meeting room that is not fully accessible but that does contain all readily achievable barrier removal and auxiliary aids. For example, the hotel would satisfy its obligations under Title III of the ADA by removing architectural barriers and providing auxiliary aids; it does not have an obligation to make its meeting room fully accessible unless the room is the product of new construction or a major alteration. The employer, however, has an obligation under Title I of the ADA not to discriminate against disabled employees. If a meeting is held in a room that is not fully accessible to disabled employees, the employer could

---

[70] 136 Cong. Rec. at H2624 (May 22, 1990) (Statement of Cong. Hamilton Fish, ranking minority member of the House Committee on the Judiciary).

be in violation of Title I of the ADA even though the hotel that leased the employer the room is in compliance with Title III.

Though a public accommodation may offer a disabled person an accommodation, aid, service, opportunity, or benefit, under Section 501(d) of the ADA, this person is not required to accept such offerings if he does not wish to. This provision was added "to clarify that nothing in the ADA is intended to permit discriminatory treatment on the basis of disability, even when such treatment is rendered under the guise of providing an accommodation, service, aid or benefit to the individual with disability."[71]

Three types of general conduct or activities are prohibited and are considered discriminatory by Section 302(b)(1)(A). First, the denial of any opportunity to participate to a disabled person or class is prohibited. This includes subjecting an individual or class of individuals on the basis of disability directly, or through contractual, licensing, or other arrangements, to a denial of the opportunity of the individual or class to participate in or benefit from the goods, services, facilities, privileges, advantages, or accommodations of an entity. The denial of an opportunity to participate that is equal to that afforded a non-disabled person is the second prohibited conduct. This conduct includes affording an individual or class of individuals, on the basis of disability, directly or through contractual, licensing, or other arrangements with the opportunity to participate in or benefit from a good, service, facility, privilege, advantage, or accommodation that is not equal to that afforded to other individuals. The third prohibited conduct is providing a benefit to a disabled person that is separate and not as effective as the benefit afforded a nondisabled person.

This is further defined as providing an individual or class of individuals, on the basis of disability directly, or through contractual, licensing, or other arrangements with a good, service, facility, privilege, advantage, or accommodation that is different or separate from that provided to other individuals, unless such action is necessary to provide the individual or class of individuals with a good, service, facility, privilege, advantage, or

---

[71] H. Comm. on Jud. Rep. at 72.

accommodation, or other opportunity that is as effective as that provided to others.

These provisions contain part of the basic thrust of the public accommodation section of the ADA. They make it a violation of the ADA if the disabled are not given the same opportunities as persons who are not disabled to use and benefit from what a public accommodation has to offer. If, for legitimate practical reasons, such use, benefit, and opportunity cannot be identical, then a different use, benefit, or opportunity can be provided if this different use, benefit, or opportunity is equally as effective as that which is extended to the nondisabled.

Section 302(b)(1)(iv) clarifies that a public accommodation is not permitted to do indirectly via contractual relationship what it cannot do directly. It provides that the "individual or class of individuals" phrase included in the three types of prohibited general activities of Sections 302(b)(1)(i), 302(b)(1)(ii), and 302(b)(1)(iii) is intended to refer to and include the clients or customers of the covered public accommodation that enters into the contractual, licensing, or other arrangement. For example, a department store cannot without being guilty of discrimination itself subcontract out space in its store to an operator of a shoe boutique if it knows the boutique will ignore the requirements of Title III—this would deny disabled customers in the department store access to the independently operated shoe section.

A public accommodation, however, is not liable for discriminatory practices of other entities it has contractual relationships with as long as this discrimination is not passed through by the public accommodation to its own customers.[72] Therefore, for instance, a department store would not be guilty of discrimination just because it purchases shirts from a manufacturer whose own factory is in violation of the ADA.

[1] Segregation

Sections 302(b)(1)(B) and 302(b)(1)(C), taken together, "are intended to prohibit exclusion and segregation of individuals

---

[72] H. Comm. on Educ. and Lab. Rep. at 101.

with disabilities and the denial of equal opportunities enjoyed by others based on, among other things, presumptions, patronizing attitudes, fears, and stereotypes about individuals."[73] Section 302(b)(1)(B) requires that goods, services, facilities, privileges, advantages, and accommodations be afforded to a disabled person in the most integrated setting appropriate to the needs of the individual, while Section 302(b)(1)(C) states that notwithstanding the existence of separate or different programs or activities that might be legitimately provided to a disabled person under Section 302, that person still cannot be denied the opportunity to participate in the programs or opportunities that are not different or separate.

Though an important principle of the ADA is to affirm and guarantee the right of the disabled to participate in programs that are not separate and different

> the ADA should not be construed to jeopardize in any way the continued viability of separate private schools providing special education for particular categories of children with disabilities, sheltered workshops, special recreational programs, and other similar programs.[74]

The provisions in Sections 302(b)(1)(B) and 302(b)(1)(C) obviously require an assessment of the facts on a situation-by-situation basis. Public accommodations are not permitted to generalize or presume about what persons with a given disability can do; rather, public accommodations must make their decisions based upon the facts and circumstances of the particular individual or individuals before them or likely to come before them.[75]

Two examples serve to illustrate the concept of affording the disabled the opportunity to participate in a way equal to that afforded the nondisabled, while at the same time maintaining the existence of meaningful separate or different programs.

---

[73] Id. at 102; S. Comm. on Lab. and Hum. Resources Rep. at 60.

[74] H. Comm. on Educ. and Lab. Rep. at 102; S. Comm. on Lab. and Hum. Resources Rep. at 61.

[75] H. Comm. on Educ. and Lab. Rep. at 102; S. Comm. on Lab. and Hum. Resources Rep. at 60, 61.

EXAMPLE: A museum offers a special tour that permits blind persons to touch sculptures on display. There is nothing wrong with this, but blind persons cannot be prohibited from touring the exhibit on their own with the museum's regular recorded tour if they so choose. They are entitled to have the choice of either the separate tour or touring on their own in the same manner as nondisabled persons.[76]

EXAMPLE: It would not be a violation of the ADA for an establishment to offer recreational programs specially designed for children with mobility impairments. These children would still have the right, though, to decline to participate in such special programs in favor of participating in other recreational services that are made available to nondisabled children (assuming their participation does not unduly interfere with the service provided). The recreational establishment could neither exclude disabled children from these other services nor require them to attend only the specially designed programs.[77]

The idea of providing goods, services, opportunities, and benefits to the disabled in the most integrated setting is a way of guaranteeing access to the disabled equal to that afforded the nondisabled in a manner that is reasonable for the place of public accommodation to provide under the circumstances. For example, persons in wheelchairs are entitled to access to an auditorium that is equal to the nondisabled to the extent possible. This means that persons in wheelchairs must be afforded access superior to merely placing them in the back of the hall, away from other persons in their party, in the worst seats, as has historically been the only access provided them. Safety concerns have often been offered as a rationalization for doing this, the argument being that the disabled need to be where they can exit the building quickly in the event of fire or other emergency.

Safety is a valid point to consider. However, a key tenet underlying the enactment of the ADA is that this rationalization

---

[76] H. Comm. on Educ. and Lab. Rep. at 102; S. Comm. on Lab. and Hum. Resources Rep. at 61.

[77] Id.

and others like it are inaccurate stereotypes based on incorrect assumptions, in this case about the ability of a person in a wheelchair to exit quickly a public hall. The legislative history points out that some people in wheelchairs can move more quickly than people who are not in wheelchairs and that, in these cases, the slow-moving nondisabled person presents more of a safety hazard in case of fire or other emergency than does the person in the wheelchair.[78] Areas closer to the front of the auditorium must be made available for seating persons with mobility impairments, including persons in wheelchairs, and they must also be able to sit with their nondisabled friends in these areas.

As indicated, the ADA requires places of public accommodation to do only what is reasonable but that will still afford equal access wherever possible to the disabled. In the example of the auditorium and theater seating, it is proper to consider safety concerns, but they must be balanced against the rights of the disabled to equal access.

The balance struck under the UFAS for dealing with wheelchair seating in general is an example of a proper way of handling wheelchair seating.[79] UFAS 4.33.3, which deals with the placement of wheelchair locations, states:

> Wheelchair areas shall be an integral part of any fixed seating plan and shall be dispersed throughout the seating area. They shall adjoin an accessible route that also serves as a means of egress in case of emergency and shall be located to provide lines of sight comparable to those for all viewing areas, except that accessible viewing positions may be clustered for bleachers, balconies, and other areas having sight lines that require slopes of greater than 5 percent. Equivalent accessible viewing positions may be located on levels having accessible egress.[80]

The Appendix to UFAS 4.33.3 (A4.33.3) states: "The location of wheelchair areas can be planned so that a variety of positions within the seating area are provided. This will allow choice in

---

[78] H. Comm. on Educ. and Lab. Rep. at 103.

[79] Id.

[80] UFAS (Apr. 1, 1988).

viewing and price categories."[81]

The key point in UFAS 4.33.3 and its Appendix is the mandate that the wheelchair areas be dispersed throughout the seating area so that the disabled can have views—and choices—as good as the nondisabled. This concept is retained by Section A4.33.3 of the ATBCB Americans With Disabilities Act Accessibility Guidelines for Buildings and Facilities (ADAAG),[82] and is formalized by the Department of Justice regulations (which mirror the UFAS on this point).[83] The legitimate aspects of the safety concern are satisfied by placing the wheelchair areas next to accessible entrance and exit routes.

For purposes of the ADA, it is important that seating for the disabled, such as persons in wheelchairs, be available in a way that they are able to sit with their nondisabled companions. New construction must ensure that seats for the disabled are integrated into the overall seating plan so as to ensure this. Existing auditoriums, theaters, and similar facilities should make every effort to integrate equal seating for the disabled into their floor arrangement, to the extent that it is readily achievable to do so.[84] If it is not readily achievable to modify seating arrangements in existing facilities—e.g., if it is too difficult or expensive to do so—then a next best solution should be sought. For example, if a person in a wheelchair cannot be given seating as good as the nondisabled, then at the very least they must be afforded the opportunity to sit with the other members of their party; temporary seating, such as folding chairs, could be set up next to where a wheelchair is placed.[85]

Similarly, for persons with hearing or visual impairments, an auditorium or theater should make seats available up front—whether or not these individuals are also in wheelchairs—so these patrons can hear or see the performance.[86]

---

[81] Id.

[82] 36 CFR pt. 1191, 56 Fed. Reg. 35,540, 35,541 (July 26, 1991).

[83] 28 CFR § 36.308.

[84] See supra ¶ 5.02[3] for discussion of the term "readily achievable."

[85] H. Comm. on Educ. and Lab. Rep. at 103. See also 28 CFR § 36.308.

[86] Id.

Importantly, regardless of whether the readily achievable option for a particular existing facility is some form of retrofitting or redesign, or merely a lesser accommodation, such as providing folding chairs, the facility should have a plan developed for how they will best integrate persons with disabilities and provide them with equal opportunities. With a plan in place, when the disabled visit the facility, they will be able to be seated quickly in the same fashion as the nondisabled. The facility should not put itself in the position of having to develop a method of handling each situation involving a disabled person as it occurs, thereby singling out the disabled person for special treatment and possible public embarrassment. If that person is treated differently from others, it will be discrimination.

[2] Administrative Methods

Section 302(b)(1)(D) prohibits an entity from using standards, criteria, or methods of administration that either have the effect of discriminating on the basis of a disability or perpetuate the discrimination of others who are subject to common administrative control. It is identical to Section 102(b)(3), except that Section 102(b)(3) applies the prohibition to the employment process.

Section 302(b)(1)(D) incorporates a disparate impact standard to ensure that the legislative mandate to end discrimination is clear and effective. It is aimed at prohibiting conduct that may not be intended to be discriminatory towards the disabled but is discriminatory in effect, and is derived in part from the general forms of discrimination that were set out in regulations implementing Section 504 of the Rehabilitation Act.[87]

Cited with approval in the legislative history is *Alexander v. Choate*,[88] a U.S. Supreme Court case decided under Section 504 of the Rehabilitation Act. Although Section 504 does not on its

---

[87] See H. Comm. on Educ. and Lab. Rep. at 61.

[88] Alexander v. Choate, 469 US 287 (1985). Among other things, the U.S. Supreme Court also said in this case that the objectives of Section 504 of the Rehabilitation Act must be balanced with the need to impose reasonable boundaries to accomplish them, that accommodations necessitating funda-

face make any reference to discrimination by effect as opposed to direct discrimination, the Court said that Congress's purpose of eliminating discrimination in enacting the Rehabilitation Act would be frustrated if the legislation was interpreted in such a way that it did not prohibit discrimination by effect as well as design.

[3] Disability of Associate

Section 302(b)(1)(E) labels it a discriminatory practice to exclude or otherwise deny equal goods, services, facilities, privileges, advantages, accommodations, or other opportunities to an individual or entity—without regard to whether this particular individual is disabled—because of the known disability of another individual with whom the individual or entity is known to have a relationship or association. This section is similar in concept to Section 102(b)(4), except that Section 102(b)(4) is concerned with hiring practices. Since an entity that provides service to or is associated with the disabled can be discriminated against by a public accommodation, it is included in Section 302(b)(1)(E) though absent from Section 102(b)(4).

For example, a nondisabled person goes to an indoor arena to buy two tickets to an event being held there, and tells the arena management that the second ticket is for a friend who is infected with the human immunodeficiency virus (HIV). The management decides not to sell the person any tickets because it holds the mistaken impression that other patrons will become infected by the friend. If the person is someone to whom the arena would otherwise sell tickets, Section 302(b)(1)(E) makes it discriminatory for the arena to choose not to do so now. However, if there are other legitimate reasons not related to any disability of the friend for not selling tickets to the person—such as that the person has a track record of creating disturbances at events—the arena still may properly refuse to sell the person the tickets. Title III is triggered only where there is a refusal because of the disability of the other person.

---

mental changes to the nature of a program were not required by Section 504, and that expenditures that were unduly burdensome did not have to be made.

As another example, it would be a violation of Section 302(b)(1)(E) for a day-care center to refuse admission to a child whose brother has HIV disease.[89]

There are no limitations in Section 302(b)(1)(E) on the meaning of "an individual with whom the individual or entity is known to have a relationship or association." Clearly, the relationship or association is not limited to familial relationships, and an amendment that would have restricted the relationships or associations to which Section 302(b)(1)(E) applied was rejected by the House Committee on Education and Labor.[90]

¶ 5.04 AVOIDING PROHIBITED DISCRIMINATION

After the general prohibition contained in Section 302(b)(1), Section 302(b)(2) sets forth certain specific acts of conduct that are prohibited and are considered discrimination by the ADA. The purpose of this section is to reinforce the ADA's overall goal of affording the disabled effective and meaningful opportunity to participate equally with the nondisabled in society's offerings.

Should there be any conflict between any of the general prohibitions of Section 302(b)(1) and the specific prohibitions described in Section 302(b)(2), the specific prevail over the general.[91]

Where the statute specifically prohibits certain acts of conduct if done directly by an entity, the conduct is still prohibited if the entity engages in this conduct indirectly—whether intentionally or not. A public accommodation cannot enter into a contract with a third party that has the effect of discriminating against a disabled person if the public accommodation is prohibited from so discriminating against the disabled person directly. It cannot use a contractual provision to reduce any of its obligations under the ADA.[92]

---

[89] See section-by-section analysis accompanying Department of Justice regulation Section 36.205.

[90] H. Comm. on Educ. and Lab. Rep. at 62.

[91] Id. at 104.

[92] Id.

At the same time, however, a public accommodation is only responsible for conduct it can control. It is not responsible for the conduct of a third party, even if this conduct affects the disabled who are customers of both the public accommodation and the third party. For example, a retail store that is a tenant in a mall must comply with the ADA and make its premises accessible to the disabled. But, if the store is a tenant in a mall that does not provide access to the disabled, so that the disabled cannot get through the mall to the store, the store is not responsible for this discrimination — the owner of the mall would be the guilty party, since the lack of access is within its control and dominion, not the store's. The store is not at fault for doing business with the mall owner; the store only has control over, and is therefore responsible for, what happens once someone comes in, or tries to come in, its door.

[1] Equal Access

[a] Obligation to Provide

The legislation makes it clear that it is not enough just to afford the disabled access. The participation in and access of the disabled to the benefits of public accommodations is to be equal to that of the nondisabled wherever possible. Accordingly, it would be violation of this section for a restaurant to permit entry by persons with Down's syndrome but to require them to sit in a special section away from the main body of tables. Similarly, the restaurant cannot adopt a policy that permits entry by persons in wheelchairs only if these disabled persons are accompanied by a nondisabled attendant. The enjoyment of a public accommodation by the disabled cannot without good reason be made more burdensome or subject to more requirements than the enjoyment of the nondisabled.

A public accommodation is likewise prohibited from trying unnecessarily to establish that a person has a disability. For example, a credit application cannot ask whether the applicant has ever had a disability, or has ever been hospitalized for mental illness. These factors are not a valid part of the credit decision, so there is no justification for inquiring about them.

Section (b)(2)(A)(i) does not just prohibit conduct that actually does screen out the disabled from equal participation. By its language, it also prohibits conduct that could *tend to* limit participation. This idea is taken from regulations implemented under Section 504 of the Rehabilitation Act,[93] and is aimed at prohibiting conduct that is not a direct, total bar to participation but still diminishes the opportunity for participation by the disabled. For instance, if a drugstore refuses to accept a check in payment for a prescription unless a valid driver's license is offered but will accept no other forms of identification, the blind and other disabled who are unable to drive will effectively be barred from cashing a check — for no legitimate business reason. The store's policy makes no mention of limiting participation by the disabled, but the policy has the effect of disproportionately excluding them, and is therefore discriminatory. The disabled can easily be accommodated in this situation, and the store's interest protected as well, if the store changes its policy to allow other forms of picture identification also to be used to cash a check.

[b] Exception: Threat to Health or Safety

Section 302(b)(3) sets forth an exception to the general rule of Section 302 that it is discrimination to deny a disabled person equal access to public accommodations. Added as an amendment to the ADA by the House Committee on the Judiciary, Section 302(b)(3) excuses an entity from having to provide an individual with equal access and enjoyment if the individual poses a direct threat to the health or safety of others. The term "direct threat" is defined as a significant risk to the health or safety of others that cannot be eliminated by a modification of policies, practices, or procedures or by the provision of auxiliary aids or services.[94] This concept is also included in Title I dealing with employment practices[95] — and the reasoning behind its

---

[93] See, e.g., 45 CFR § 84.13.

[94] HR Conf. Rep. No. 596, 101st Cong., 2d Sess. (1990), Conf. Rep. on S. 933, Americans With Disabilities Act of 1990, Joint Explanatory Statement of the Committee on Conference at ¶ 50.

[95] See ADA §§ 101(3), 103(b).

inclusion in Title I is also applicable to the inclusion in Section 302[96] — and is contained as well in the Civil Rights Restoration Act[97] and the Fair Housing Amendments Act of 1988.[98]

This idea is not meant to imply that people with disabilities automatically pose any risks to others. Rather, its purpose is to address any concerns that may arise in this area and to establish clearly the strict standard that must be met before services, goods, or access may be denied to a disabled person based on the fear that such individual poses a risk to others.[99]

The definition used of "direct threat" is a codification of the standard articulated by the U.S. Supreme Court in *School Board of Nassau County v. Arline*.[100] In this case, the Court held that a "person who poses a significant risk of communicating an infectious disease to others in the workplace will not be otherwise qualified for his or her job if reasonable accommodation will not eliminate that risk."[101]

Whether or not there is a risk of transmitting the infection to others must be determined based on objective and accepted public health guidelines, not based on stereotypes, fears, and misimpressions. Each decision must also be based on the particular facts of the individual case. The Department of Justice regulations explain this as follows:

> In determining whether an individual poses a direct threat to the health or safety of others, a public accommodation must make an individualized assessment, based on reasonable judgment that relies on current medical knowledge or on the best available objective evidence, to ascertain: the nature, duration, and severity of the risk; the probability that the potential injury will actually occur; and

---

[96] H. Comm. on Jud. Rep. at 62.

[97] Pub. L. No. 100-259, 29 USC § 706(8)(C).

[98] Pub. L. No. 100-430, 42 USC § 3604(f)(9).

[99] H. Comm. on Jud. Rep. at 62.

[100] School Bd. of Nassau County v. Arline, 480 US 273 (1987).

[101] Id. at 287, n.16.

whether reasonable modifications of policies, practices, or procedures will mitigate the risk.[102]

The direct threat standard was added to the legislation to eliminate the possibility that the disabled would be denied equal access, goods, or services based on reasoning that had nothing to do with an objective evaluation of the facts and circumstances concerning the particular disabled person involved.

Should there be litigation involving this issue (by analogy to the use of the direct threat standard in the Title I employment context), the disabled person is not required to prove that he poses no risk to others.[103] To prove this with certainty would be extremely difficult, if not impossible.[104]

Denial of access to the disabled person can only be made if the person poses a significant risk of injury to others. A "significant" risk is meant to be higher than merely an "elevated" risk, and must be based on the current condition of the disabled person, not a condition that occurred in the past. In addition, in order to exclude a disabled person based on this standard, the public accommodation must have actual proof that the disability presents a significant risk to others; the burden of proof in subsequent litigation would rest first on the public accommodation.[105]

[2] Eligibility Criteria

Section 302(b)(2)(A)(i) includes as discrimination the imposition or application of eligibility criteria that screen out or tend to screen out an individual with a disability or any class of individuals with disabilities from fully and equally enjoying any goods, services, facilities, privileges, advantages, or accommodations, unless such criteria can be shown to be necessary for the provi-

---

[102] See 28 CFR § 36.208(c).

[103] H. Comm. on Jud. Rep. at 46.

[104] See Chalk v. U.S. Dist. Court, 840 F2d 701, 707 (9th Cir. 1988), which discusses Section 504 of the Rehabilitation Act in connection with an employment decision.

[105] H. Comm. on Jud. Rep. at 46.

sion of the goods, services, facilities, privileges, advantages, or accommodations being offered. It would be a violation of this section for a restaurant to refuse to serve the blind or deaf or for a food store to refuse to allow the blind in, for example, because these disabilities are irrelevant to being served food in a restaurant or buying food in a store.

Eligibility criteria that limits participation of the disabled would not be considered a violation of Section 302(b)(2)(A)(i) if such criteria was necessary to the providing of goods, services, facilities, privileges, advantages, or accommodations by the entity that adopted the criteria. This is an important defense to a charge of discrimination. A crucial balance sought by Congress in the ADA was the guaranteein3 of equal rights for the disabled without unduly burdening businesses. As is stated in the House Committee on Education and Labor report:

> A public accommodation may . . . impose neutral rules and criteria that are necessary for the safe operation of its business. For example, a height limit for certain rides at an amusement park will screen out certain adults of short stature, but may still be a legitimate safety criterion. Safety criteria, however, must be based on actual risks and not on speculation, stereotypes, or generalizations about disability.[106]

If the effects of a person's disability prevent the person from meeting the basic eligibility requirements of a public accommodation (a person in a wheelchair being unable to skydive) or cause substantial interference with the operation of the public accommodation (the nature of the disability requires that so much attention be paid to the disabled person by the facility operator that other users of the facility are ignored), these effects may properly be taken into account by the public accommodation in denying services. Prejudice or stereotypes, however, cannot be the basis for a public accommodation's conclusion that a disabled person fails to meet its eligibility requirements. Individuals with disabilities can similarly not be excluded from participation or access just to cater to the tastes or preferences of

---

[106] H. Comm. on Educ. and Lab. Rep. at 105.

other users of a public accommodation. [107]

The decision-making calculus must also consider whether the facility operator can make any minor changes or alterations that would enable the disabled person to meet the eligibility criteria. If it can, it must. It may not, however, levy a surcharge for doing so, or for providing auxiliary aids, on a particular individual or class of individuals with a disability. [108] A refundable deposit would not be considered as such a surcharge, however. [109]

[3] Modifications in Policies

A form of discrimination prohibited in Section 302(b)(2)(A) is a failure to make reasonable modifications in policies, practices, or procedures, when such modifications are necessary to afford such goods, services, facilities, privileges, advantages, or accommodations to individuals with disabilities, unless the entity can demonstrate that making such modifications would fundamentally alter the nature of such goods, services, facilities, privileges, advantages, or accommodations. A service provider cannot refuse to provide service to an individual just because the individual has a disability. If the service provider, however, would in the normal course of business not provide service to the disabled person for reasons unrelated to the disability, Title III does not force the entity to provide service.

For example, a physician specializing in treating burn victims could not refuse to treat a deaf person's arm burns just because the person was deaf, as long as the doctor would have treated the burns if the person was not deaf. A foot doctor, however, who would not normally treat any person, disabled or not, for burns, would not have to treat this person. The foot doctor could properly refer the patient to another physician who regularly handled this type of work. Even if the injury was to the foot, if the doctor would not normally treat such injury regard-

---

[107] See section-by-section analysis accompanying Department of Justice regulation 28 CFR § 36.301.

[108] See Department of Justice regulation 28 CFR § 36.301(c).

[109] See section-by-section analysis accompanying 28 CFR § 36.301(c).

less of the patient's disability, referral is proper. If the disability itself presents specialized complications relating to the patient's health that the doctor is not equipped to handle, again, referral is proper.[110]

The same reasoning can be applied to a drug rehabilitation clinic. A clinic that would accept a patient but for the fact that the patient has a disability, such as the presence of the HIV virus, cannot refuse this patient admittance. The clinic, however, has no obligation to accept a disabled person who has no drug problem, since it would not have accepted a similar nondisabled person. It can refer this person elsewhere, assuming it would do the same for a nondisabled person. As is the case with the foot doctor above, if the mere presence of a disability in and of itself presents complications that the clinic or doctor is not qualified to handle, referral elsewhere is proper.[111]

The common thread in these examples is the fact that if action or inaction in denying service or care to a disabled person is arbitrarily related to the existence of a disability, the conduct is discriminatory. If, however, there is a legitimate reason for the denial unrelated to the disability, or if the mere presence of the disability renders the service provider unable to provide competent service, refusal is not discriminatory. If some action would occur after refusal with a nondisabled person — such as referring a patient to another doctor — it must also occur after refusal with a disabled person.

Modifications may be necessary to afford access to the disabled. For example, an entity that normally does not allow dogs on the premises would need to modify this rule to permit entry of a seeing-eye dog accompanying a blind person, a hearing-eye dog accompanying a deaf person, or a service dog accompanying a person with some other disability.[112] Since refusal to admit the dog in these circumstances has the effect of denying meaningful access to the disabled person, failure to modify the policy would

---

[110] H. Comm. on Educ. and Lab. Rep. at 106; S. Comm. on Lab. and Hum. Resources Rep. at 62, 63.

[111] H. Comm. on Educ. and Lab. Rep. at 106; S. Comm. on Lab. and Hum. Resources Rep. at 63.

[112] 28 CFR § 36.302(c).

be discrimination under Section 302(b)(2)(A)(ii). Similarly, the public accommodation must permit the disabled person to be accompanied by the dog while using the facility.

Other situations would also require modifications. A parking lot that bars vans with raised roofs could modify this rule to permit wheelchair-accessible vans with raised roofs if such vans can indeed fit into the lot. A department store could modify a one-person-per-dressing-room rule to permit a disabled individual to receive assistance from a friend.[113] A store with check-out aisles must keep enough accessible aisles open to ensure a level of service to the disabled equivalent to that provided other persons.[114] At no time should every accessible aisle be closed while other inaccessible aisles are open.

As is the case under Section 302(b)(2)(A)(i), Section 302(b)(2)(A)(ii) does not require a modification to be made if it would be unreasonable to do so, or if the fundamental nature of what is being offered would be altered by the modification. For example, if a seeing-eye dog communicated with a blind person by barking, a public accommodation at which complete silence was essential would not be discriminating if it failed to modify its no-dog policies to admit the seeing-eye dog.

[4] Auxiliary Aids and Services

[a] Obligation to Provide

Auxiliary aids and services is defined in Section 3(1) to include:

(A) [Q]ualified interpreters or other effective methods of making aurally delivered materials available to individuals with hearing impairments;

(B) [Q]ualified readers, taped texts, or other effective methods of making visually delivered materials available to individuals with visual impairments;

---

[113] See section-by-section analysis accompanying Department of Justice regulation 28 CFR § 36.302.

[114] 28 CFR § 36.302(d).

(C) [A]cquisition or modification of equipment or devices; and

(D) [O]ther similar services and actions.

An important part of providing auxiliary aids and services is the public accommodation's obligation to communicate effectively with the disabled.

Section 302(b)(2)(A)(iii) specifies as discrimination the failure to take such steps as may be necessary to ensure that no individual with a disability is excluded, denied services, segregated, or otherwise treated differently than other individuals because of the absence of auxiliary aids and services, unless the entity can demonstrate that taking such steps would fundamentally alter the nature of the good, service, facility, privilege, advantage, or accommodation being offered or would result in an undue burden.[115] The entity is given the obligation of providing auxiliary aids and services to accommodate the persons where it is not burdensome to do so.

Section 302(b)(2)(A)(iii) addresses the situation in which, for example, a blind person patronizes a restaurant. If the restaurant simply gives the blind person the same non-braille menu it would give a sighted person, and offers no assistance in reading it, this would be discriminatory conduct under Section 302(b)(2)(A)(iii). The section would require that the restaurant provide assistance so that the blind person is able to understand the menu in the same manner as a sighted person. Providing a braille menu would be sufficient, but not mandatory. Providing someone to read the menu out loud to the blind person would be simple and also sufficient.

By including "other similar services and actions" in Section 3(1)(d), Congress has made it clear that the list of auxiliary aids and services is meant only to provide general guidance and illustration, not to be exhaustive. Additional, more specific examples and guidance are provided in a Department of Justice regulation, which says in part:

---

[115] These limitations are present in regulations and cases under Section 504 of the Rehabilitation Act as well. See Southeastern Community College v. Davis, 442 US 397 (1979); see also 28 CFR § 39.160(d).

(b) Examples. The term "auxiliary aids and services" includes—

(1) Qualified interpreters, notetakers, computer-aided transcription services, written materials, telephone handset amplifiers, assistive listening devices, assistive listening systems, telephones compatible with hearing aids, closed caption decoders, open and closed captioning telecommunication devices for deaf persons (TDD's), video text displays, or other effective methods of making aurally delivered materials available to individuals with hearing impairments;[116]

(2) Qualified readers, taped texts, audio recordings, Brailled materials, large print materials, or other effective methods of making visually delivered materials available to individuals with visual impairments;[117]

(3) Acquisition or modification of equipment of devices; and

(4) Other similar services and actions.

(c) Effective communication. A public accommodation shall furnish appropriate auxiliary aids and services where necessary to ensure effective communication with individuals with disabilities.

(d) Telecommunication devices for the deaf (TDD's).[118]

(1) A public accommodation that offers a customer, client, patient, or participant the opportunity to make outgoing telephone calls on more than an incidental convenience basis shall make available, upon request, a TDD for the use of an individual who has impaired hearing or a communication disorder.

(2) This part does not require a public accommodation to use a TDD for receiving or making telephone calls incident to its operations.

---

[116] "Aurally delivered materials" are meant to include nonverbal sounds and alarms and computer-generated speech, as well as oral materials, according to the Department of Justice section-by-section analysis accompanying 28 CFR § 303.

[117] Other examples would be signage or mapping, audio description services, secondary auditory programs (SAP), telebraillers, and reading machines.

[118] TDDs means the same as the phrase "text telephone" used in the ATBCB's ADAAGs.

(e) Closed caption decoders. Places of lodging that provide televisions in five or more guest rooms and hospitals that provide televisions for patient use shall provide, upon request, a means for decoding captions for use by an individual with impaired hearing.

(f) Alternatives. If provision of a particular auxiliary aid or service by a public accommodation would result in a fundamental alteration in the nature of the goods, services, facilities, privileges, advantages, or accommodations being offered or in an undue burden, i.e., significant difficulty or expense, the public accommodation shall provide an alternative auxiliary aid or service, if one exists, that would not result in such an alteration or such burden but would nevertheless ensure that, to the maximum extent possible, individuals with disabilities receive the goods, services, facilities, privileges, advantages, or accommodations offered by the public accommodation.

The Department of Justice's regulations do not require a public accommodation to provide its customers, clients, or participants with individually prescribed devices, such as prescription eyeglasses or hearing aids, or with services of a personal nature including assistance in eating, toileting, or dressing.[119]

Because of the fact that telecommunications relay services will become widespread because of Title IV of the ADA, Congress did not intend for Title III to require (and the regulations do not so require) a public accommodation to use a TDD in receiving or making calls incident to its operations.[120] Hearing-disabled persons will be able to communicate with retail establishments, doctors' offices, restaurants, and other places of public accommodation via the relay services implemented by Title IV. A public accommodation, however, that provides an opportunity for individuals to make outgoing calls on a more than incidental basis, such as a hotel or a hospital, must provide a TDD upon request.[121] Similarly, a hotel should also provide a

[119] See Department of Justice regulation 28 CFR § 36.306.

[120] H. Comm. on Educ. and Lab. Rep. at 107; S. Comm. on Lab. and Hum. Resources Rep. at 64.

[121] H. Comm. on Educ. and Lab. Rep. at 107, 108; S. Comm. on Lab. and Hum. Resources Rep. at 64.

TDD or similar device at its front desk to be able to receive calls from guests who use TDDs in their rooms. Where a security telephone is required to gain entry to a place of public accommodation, though, a TDD or other effective means of communication for hearing- or speech-disabled persons must be provided. [122]

An example of a simple equipment modification that would aid certain disabled persons would be for a museum that provides an audiotaped tour to add braille adhesive labels to the buttons of a select number of tape players so that the tape players can be operated by blind persons.

An example of an auxiliary aid that is not required is the open-captioning of feature films playing in movie theaters, although Congress wants to both encourage filmmakers to make open-captioned versions of films and to encourage theaters to have at least some preannounced screenings of open-captioned feature films. [123] If a public accommodation provides film or slide shows for the purpose of imparting information to the public, however—such as a health clinic that communicates information about an illness through a slide presentation or a travel agency that uses videotapes to impart information about travel destinations—the public accommodation is required to make such information accessible to the disabled, by closed-captioning or other means. [124]

[b] Exception: Undue Burden

The obligation to provide auxiliary aids or services to ensure equal access and enjoyment by the disabled is not meant to place an undue burden—a "significant difficulty or expense" [125]—upon public accommodations. "Undue burden" as used in Section 302(b)(2)(A)(iii) is meant to be analogous to

---

[122] See section-by-section analysis accompanying Department of Justice regulation 28 CFR § 36.303.

[123] H. Comm. on Educ. and Lab. Rep. at 108; S. Comm. on Labor and Hum. Resources Rep. at 64.

[124] Id.

[125] See Department of Justice regulation 28 CFR § 36.303(a).

the phrase "undue hardship" used in Title I of the ADA, and is derived from Section 504 of the Rehabilitation Act and regulations promulgated thereunder.[126] By analogy to the definition of undue hardship in Section 101(10), then, an undue burden would be one that requires significant difficulty or expense,[127] taking the following four factors into consideration:

1. The nature and cost of the auxiliary aid or service
2. The overall financial resources of the facility or facilities involved in providing the aid or service; the number of persons employed at such facility; the effect on expenses and resources, or the impact otherwise of the provision of such aid or service upon the operation of the facility
3. The overall financial resources of the covered entity; the overall size of the business of a covered entity with respect to the number of its employees; the number, type, and location of its facilities
4. The type of operation or operations of the covered entity, including the composition, structure, and functions of the work force of the entity; the geographic separateness, administrative, or fiscal relationship of the facility or facilities in question to the covered entity

The determination of whether the provision of an auxiliary aid or service is an undue burden is meant to be made on a case-by-case basis, based upon the facts of the specific situation.[128]

The types of auxiliary aids and services that are to be provided to the disabled is not a static category. As technology improves and new aids and services are developed over time, Title III requires that these new aids and services be provided, subject to the undue burden limitation of Section 302(b)(2)(A)(iii). An aid or service that is available now, but that

---

[126] H. Comm. on Educ. and Lab. Rep. at 106, 107; S. Comm. on Lab. and Hum. Resources Rep. at 63.

[127] Department of Justice regulation 28 CFR § 36.303 reflects this. See also regulation 28 CFR § 36.104, which defines undue burden as "significant difficulty or expense," and incorporates and expands on the statutory factors to consider in determining whether something is an undue burden.

[128] H. Comm. on Educ. and Lab. Rep. at 106, 107; S. Comm. on Lab. and Hum. Resources Rep. at 63.

is an undue burden to provide—perhaps because of the current expense of providing it—may, because of technological advances, become easily providable in the future. If it does, it must be furnished at that time in the future.

Just because one way of meeting this obligation may be unduly burdensome, however, does not automatically relieve the public accommodation of its obligation under the ADA. It must still seek out other ways to try and meet its obligation. For example, if a retail store determined that it is an undue burden for it to put all of its price tags and aisle markers in braille to assist blind persons, or to lower its shelves of merchandise to assist persons in wheelchairs, it must still attempt to seek out other, less burdensome ways of guaranteeing the disabled equal access and enjoyment. It can do this by providing an employee who can perform functions such as reading prices to a blind person or guiding that person through the store and describing merchandise on the shelves. That employee could also bring down merchandise from upper shelves for the person in a wheelchair who is unable to reach it.

Only if there are no effective auxiliary aids or services that are not unduly burdensome would the public accommodation be relieved of its obligation under this section. In most situations, however, even if equal access cannot be guaranteed by a reasonable auxiliary aid or service, a nonburdensome aid or service should be available that would at least *improve* the access available to the disabled. Since some access is better than no access, in situations where providing equal access is overly burdensome, the public accommodation must strive to provide at least some reasonable access up to the limits of where it is not an undue burden to do so.

In most situations, the auxiliary aid or service needed to provide meaningful access to the disabled will be a simple, inexpensive matter to provide, a small adjustment.[129] Before providing an aid or service to a disabled person, though, the

---

[129] H. Comm. on Educ. and Lab. Rep. at 107; S. Comm. on Lab. and Hum. Resources Rep. at 63.

public accommodation should try to consult with the persons affected.[130]

[5] Special Goods and Purchase of Furniture and Equipment

A public accommodation is not required to alter its inventory to carry accessible or special goods designed for individuals with disabilities. Examples of these goods would include brailled versions of books, books on audiocassettes, closed-captioned videotapes, special sizes or lines of clothing, and special foods to meet particular dietary needs. If the public accommodation normally accepts special orders for unstocked goods, though, it must accept a special order for an accessible good or good designed to assist individuals with disabilities as long as the good can be obtained from a supplier from whom the public accommodation customarily does business.[131]

[6] Barrier Removal

Section 302(b)(2)(A)(iv) deals with discrimination that takes place because of a public accommodation's failure to remove a barrier that prevents access to the disabled when the barrier could be removed without great difficulty and expense. It labels as discriminatory conduct the failure by a public accommodation to remove architectural barriers, and communication barriers that are structural in nature,[132] in existing facilities, and transportation barriers in existing vehicles and rail passenger cars used by an establishment for transporting individuals where such removal is readily achievable—but this obligation does not include barriers that can only be removed through the retrofitting of vehicles or rail passenger cars by the installation of a hydraulic or other lift.

It is important to note that this section only deals with

---

[130] Id.

[131] See Department of Justice regulation 28 CFR § 36.307.

[132] The Department of Justice interprets the statute to mean that communications barriers that are not structural in nature, i.e., that are not part of the physical structure of the facility, are auxiliary aids and services.

existing facilities or vehicles, not requirements for facilities or vehicles that have not yet been constructed. In crafting this section, Congress specifically rejected both the idea that all existing facilities or vehicles should be grandfathered out of the ADA—that there would be no obligation by an owner of an existing facility or vehicle to make it accessible to the disabled—and the opposite idea that every existing facility or vehicle had to be retrofitted to make them disabled-accessible by their owner.[133] Instead, Congress adopted the middle-ground position that changes must be made by owners in order to make a facility or vehicle more accessible to the disabled only if these changes are readily achievable.

Readily achievable, as applied to barrier removal, means a structural change or alternative method that is easily accomplished and able to be carried out without much difficulty or expense.

What is readily achievable will vary based on the facts and circumstances of a particular case. If barrier removal is not easily accomplishable, then removal is not readily achievable. The type of barriers to which this section can apply ranges from steps that persons in wheelchairs cannot get down to elevator panels or similar public displays that cannot be read by the blind. The kind of barrier removal that is anticipated to be readily achievable "includes the addition of grab bars, the simple ramping of a few steps, the lowering of telephones, the addition of raised letter and braille markings on elevator control buttons, the addition of flashing alarm lights, and similar modest adjustments."[134] Again, though, judgment must be made on a case-by-case basis. It might be easy to put up a wheelchair ramp near or over one set of stairs, where a simple ramp is all that is needed, while it might be difficult to do the same thing for another set where ramping would be more extensive or the slope of the incline more severe. The first barrier removal would be readily achievable, while the second would not be. Accordingly,

---

[133] H. Comm. on Educ. and Lab. Rep. at 109; S. Comm. on Lab. and Hum. Resources Rep. at 65.

[134] H. Comm. on Educ. and Lab. Rep. at 110; S. Comm. on Lab. and Hum. Resources Rep. at 66.

the second barrier would not have to be removed. Installing an elevator where none exists would likewise be considered difficult and expensive to do, and would not be readily achievable.

An establishment that uses vehicles or rail passenger cars to transport individuals is not guilty of discrimination if it does not retrofit the vehicles or rail passenger cars with hydraulic lifts to provide access for the disabled when the only way fully to remove existing barriers to access is to install these lifts. If some access can be afforded without installing hydraulic lifts, though, barriers must be removed to the extent possible if readily achievable.

A public accommodation may be required to remove or relocate temporary or movable structures that act as barriers to the disabled if removal or relocation is readily achievable. For example, a restaurant may need to rearrange its tables or seating arrangements so that persons in wheelchairs can dine there, or a retail store may need to rearrange its shelves and displays to permit access by the disabled. Not all of the seating in a restaurant or all of the shelves and displays in a store need to be rearranged, though, even if it is readily achievable to move them. Enough must be rearranged to provide the disabled with access to a representative selection of what is available in the public accommodation, but physical access to every table or display is not required. In the retail store, the disabled customer in a wheelchair should be able to get close enough to the merchandise to see what the store offers. From there, it is sufficient if the store provides an individual who will get and bring over specific merchandise that the customer identifies (though the store can adopt other procedures that achieve the same result). If rearranging or moving furniture, tables, equipment, or display racks results in a significant loss of selling or serving space, though, it would not be considered to be readily achievable. [135]

The Department of Justice regulations contain considerable illustrations of steps that can be taken to eliminate barriers. These are not meant to be an exhaustive listing, but include:

- Installing ramps
- Making curb cuts in sidewalks and entrances

---

[135] See Department of Justice regulation 28 CFR § 36.304(f).

- Repositioning shelves
- Rearranging tables, chairs, vending machines, display racks, and other furniture
- Repositioning telephones
- Adding raised markings on elevator control buttons
- Installing flashing alarm lights
- Widening doors
- Installing offset hinges to widen doorways
- Eliminating a turnstile or providing an alternative accessible path
- Installing accessible door hardware
- Installing grab bars in toilet stalls
- Rearranging toilet partitions to increase maneuvering space
- Insulating lavatory pipes under sinks to prevent burns
- Installing a raised toilet seat
- Installing a full-length bathroom mirror
- Repositioning the paper towel dispenser in a bathroom
- Creating designated accessible parking spaces
- Installing an accessible paper cup dispenser at an existing inaccessible water fountain
- Removing high-pile low-density carpeting
- Modifying vehicle hand controls[136]

In recognition of the fact that a place of public accommodation may not have the money to eliminate all barriers at once, the regulations set out a suggested (not mandatory) order of priority for a public accommodation to follow in removing barriers. Whatever is readily achievable should be done, in this order:

1. Access should first be provided to the place of public accommodation from public sidewalks, the parking lot or parking facilities, or public transportation stops.

---

[136] See Department of Justice regulation 28 CFR § 36.304(b).

2. Next, access should be provided to those areas of a public accommodation where goods and services are made available to the public, through rearranging displays, for example.

3. Access should then be provided to restroom facilities.

4. Next, any other measures necessary to provide access to goods, services, facilities, privileges, advantages, or accommodations should be taken.[137]

Normally under the ADA, when alterations are done to a public accommodation, they must be made so as to make the altered area accessible, to the maximum extent feasible. However, the Department of Justice regulations provide that an alteration undertaken solely to remove a barrier need not comply with the accessible "path of travel" requirements of Section 303(a)(2) and 28 CFR Section 36.403.[138]

Providing a portable ramp to remove a barrier is permitted only if it is not readily achievable to install a permanent ramp.[139] If a portable ramp is used, it must be safe in light of its projected users.

Section 302(b)(2)(A)(v) reiterates by statute a point already mentioned earlier. It states that when barrier removal under Section 302(b)(2)(A)(iv) is not readily achievable, it is still considered discriminatory conduct if the public accommodation does not provide its goods, services, facilities, privileges, advantages, or accommodations to the disabled through alternative methods, if such alternative methods are readily achievable.

The alternative methods envisioned by Section 302(b)(2)(A)(v) include such easily accomplished accommodations as coming to the door to receive dry cleaning from or returning it to a person in a wheelchair who is unable to come through the cleaner's door; permitting a disabled patron who is unable to sit at a bar to have just a drink to sit at a table when the restaurant otherwise requires that patrons having only beverages sit at the bar, providing assistance in retrieving items for a

---

[137] See Department of Justice regulation 28 CFR § 36.304(c).

[138] See Department of Justice regulation 28 CFR § 36.304(d).

[139] See Department of Justice regulation 28 CFR § 36.304(e).

disabled person from a location that the disabled person is unable to reach, providing curb service or home delivery, providing refueling service at inaccessible self-service gas stations, and rotating the movies shown at a multifloor or multiscreen theater where not all screens are accessible and advertising this fact so that all movies play at some reasonable time in the accessible first-floor theater.[140]

[7] Examinations and Courses

Section 309 sets forth the obligation of a person who offers examinations or courses related to applications, licensing, certification, or credentialing for secondary or postsecondary education, professional, or trade purposes either to offer these examinations or courses in settings that are accessible to the disabled or to offer alternative accessible arrangements to persons with disabilities. Unlike other parts of Title III, Section 309 is not limited in its applicability to a public accommodation or a commercial facility. It applies to any private entity that offers the exams or courses covered.

This section was added to Title III by the House Committee on the Judiciary in order to fill a perceived gap created when licensing, certification, and other testing authorities are not covered by either Section 504 of the Rehabilitation Act or by Title II of the ADA.[141] Section 504 applies to such an authority if it receives federal money, and Title II applies if the authority is operated by a state or local government; an authority covered under either of these provisions is already under an obligation to make all of its programs accessible to the disabled.

The Judiciary Committee noted, however, that states often require an individual to have licensing or certification provided by authorities not covered by either the Rehabilitation Act or Title II in order for the individual to practice a particular profes-

---

[140] H. Comm. on Educ. and Lab. Rep. at 110, 111; S. Comm. on Lab. and Hum. Resources Rep. at 66. See also Department of Justice regulation 28 CFR § 36.305.

[141] H. Comm. on Jud. Rep. at 68.

sion or trade.[142] Examples would be, depending upon the particular state, bar examinations that license persons to practice law, as well as examinations to license beauticians, realtors, real estate appraisers, and accountants. Other types of exams that would be covered by Section 309 if given by a private entity are college entrance exams, private scholarship exams, and college placement exams. Review courses given by private entities to prepare for all of these exams, as well as for exams sponsored by a government, would also fall within Section 309.

Section 309 ensures "that persons with disabilities are not foreclosed from educational, professional or trade opportunities because an examination or course is conducted in an inaccessible site or without an accommodation."[143]

A private entity offering an exam covered by this section must ensure that the exam is selected and administered so as to best ensure that, when the exam is administered to an individual with a disability that impairs sensory, manual, or speaking skills, the exam results accurately reflect the individual's aptitude or achievement level or whatever other factor the exam purports to measure—rather than reflecting the individual's impaired sensory, manual, or speaking skills (except where those skills are the factors that the examination purports to measure).[144]

Appropriate auxiliary aids must be provided to an individual taking an exam or course, which may include taped exams or texts, interpreters or other effective methods of making orally delivered materials available to individuals with hearing impairments, readers for individuals with visual impairments or learning disabilities, classroom equipment adapted for use by individuals with manual impairments, and other similar services and actions.[145] These aids do not need to be provided, however, if they would be an undue burden to furnish, or if they would fundamentally alter the particular exam or course.

---

[142] Id.

[143] Id. at 69.

[144] See Department of Justice regulation 28 CFR § 36.309(b)(1).

[145] See Department of Justice regulations 28 CFR §§ 36.309(b), 36.309(c).

If a private entity offered its programs at a location that was not accessible to the disabled, it would have to provide alternative accessible arrangements—arrangements that provided conditions comparable to those offered to others at the inaccessible location—to the disabled in order to meet its obligations under Section 309. For example, if a course or test is given in an inaccessible, comfortable classroom, the course or test must also be offered to the disabled at an accessible, comfortable location. Making the course or test available to the disabled in a cold, poorly lit basement would not be considered an alternative accessible arrangement.[146] A course could be offered through videotape, cassettes, or prepared notes, or the length of time permitted for its completion could be lengthened.[147] If an exam is given at an inaccessible location and no accessible equipment or facilities are available, the exam could be provided at the disabled person's home, with a proctor.[148]

[8] Warranty and Indemnification

A private entity, in purchasing or leasing a facility, in purchasing, leasing, remanufacturing, or altering a vehicle used to provide public transportation, and in constructing or altering a public accommodation covered by Title III, would be well advised to obtain a warranty from the vendor or contractor with whom the entity is dealing that the facility, vehicle, or work done complies with the accessibility standards of Title III of the ADA and all regulations and guidelines thereunder. Additionally, the private entity should ask such vendor or contractor to indemnify it against any loss stemming from a failure of the vehicle or work done to comply with Title III and the regulations and guidelines. Doing so will offer some protection to the private entity because if there is a violation of Title III, the private entity will bear the liability—even if it acted in good faith to comply with Title III and the error was by one of its vendors or contractors.

---

[146] H. Comm. on Jud. Rep. at 69.

[147] See Department of Justice regulation 28 CFR § 36.309(c).

[148] See Department of Justice regulation 28 CFR § 36.309(b)(4).

[9] Illegal Use of Drugs

Section 510(a) of the ADA provides that an individual with a disability does not include an individual who is currently engaging in the illegal use of drugs provided that the covered entity is acting on the basis of such use. Thus, for example, a public accommodation could properly refuse to serve a person whom it correctly perceived was a current drug user. However, it would be a violation of the ADA for a covered entity to discriminate against an individual who

1. Has successfully completed a supervised drug rehabilitation program and is no longer engaging in illegal use of drugs, or has otherwise been rehabilitated successfully and is no longer engaging in such use
2. Is participating in a supervised rehabilitation program and is no longer engaging in such use
3. Is erroneously regarded as engaging in such use, but is not engaging in such use[149]

It would not be a violation of the ADA for a covered entity to adopt or administer reasonable policies and procedures to ensure that a former drug user is no longer using illegal drugs, although Section 510 states that it is not meant to encourage, authorize, prohibit, or restrict the conducting of testing for illegal drug use.

As written, Section 510(a) would even allow a provider of health service to refuse to serve a current drug user. To avoid this result, Section 510(c) was added to prohibit the denial of health services, or services provided in connection with drug rehabilitation, on the basis of the current illegal use of drugs if the individual is otherwise entitled to such services. Accordingly, then, a current drug user cannot be refused service at a hospital for a broken leg if that individual is otherwise entitled to service.[150] Likewise, because Congress believed that vocational rehabilitation services are essential for the treatment and recovery of drug dependent persons, a vocational rehabil-

---

[149] See ADA § 510(b).

[150] H. Comm. on Jud. Rep. at 75.

itation program cannot deny its services to current drug users. [151]

¶ 5.05 NEW CONSTRUCTION AND ALTERATIONS

Section 303 sets forth additional areas in which failure to provide equal access to the disabled will be considered discrimination under the "full and equal enjoyment of the goods, services, facilities, privileges, advantages, or accommodations" standard of Section 302(a). Section 303 imposes an obligation in the construction of new facilities and substantial alteration of or addition to existing facilities to make such facilities accessible to the disabled. It does not force anyone to construct a new building or engage in alterations, but applies if new construction or alterations are voluntarily undertaken. The section covers both access by disabled members of the general public and by disabled employees.

Unlike Section 302, Section 303 does not apply just to public accommodations; it also covers commercial facilities. [152] An establishment that is a commercial facility but not a public accommodation is subject to Section 303 but not to other provisions of Title III, such as the ones setting forth the obligation to provide auxiliary aids or services. If a commercial facility is located within a private residence, Section 303 applies to that portion of the residence that is the commercial facility, as well as that portion of the residence used in connection with the commercial facility, i.e., indoor and outdoor walkways, restrooms. [153]

Currently, because of Section 504 of the Rehabilitation Act and the minimum guidelines developed thereunder by the ATBCB, recipients of federal financial assistance must ensure

---

[151] H. Comm. on Educ. and Lab. Rep. at 141. This provision is also consistent with Section 407 of the Drug Abuse Office and Treatment Act of 1972 (21 USC § 1174) and the regulations implementing the Rehabilitation Act (App. A-Analysis of Final Regulations, Subpart A-Definitions, 4; Drug addicts and alcoholics, paragraph 5, 42 Fed. Reg. 22686, reprinted in 45 CFR pt. 84 App. A (1986)).

[152] For a definition of commercial facility, see supra ¶ 5.02[2].

[153] See 28 CFR § 36.401(b).

that new construction and alterations to existing structures are done in such a manner as to make the facilities accessible to the disabled.[154] Section 303 is intended to extend this obligation to private, commercial establishments as well.[155]

The ATBCB was directed by the ADA to develop supplemental minimum guidelines partly to assist the Department of Justice in promulgating its regulations implementing Title III. These supplemental guidelines, entitled ADAAG, contain technical standards for construction, matters such as the dimensions and configuration of toilet stalls needed to accommodate persons in wheelchairs, the number of accessible telephones required on a building floor, and the number of accessible parking spaces needed in a parking lot.[156] The ADAAG are included in Appendix C.

The Department of Justice has incorporated the ADAAG into its regulations by mandating therein that new construction and alterations covered by Section 303 must comply with the technical standards contained in these guidelines in order to be considered as accessible to the disabled under the ADA.[157]

[1] New Construction

Section 303(a)(1) labels it as discrimination for a public accommodation or commercial facility to fail to design and construct a new facility so that it is readily accessible to and usable by the disabled, except where the public accommodation or commercial facility can demonstrate that it is structurally impracticable to do so in accordance with standards set forth or incorporated by reference in regulations issued under Title III. A grace period is provided, however, as this section only applies to facilities designed and constructed for first occupancy after January 26, 1993, thirty months after the enactment of the ADA.

---

[154] See UFAS ch. 4.

[155] H. Comm. on Educ. and Lab. Rep. at 116.

[156] The ATBCB's ADAAG can also be found at 56 Fed. Reg. 35,410 (July 26, 1991).

[157] See Department of Justice regulation 28 CFR § 36.406.

[a] Definitions

[i] First occupancy. The Department of Justice regulations interpret what is meant by first occupancy by stating that a facility is designed and constructed for first occupancy after January 26, 1993, only if the last application for a building permit or permit extension for the facility is received and certified to be complete by the appropriate governmental entity after January 26, 1992, and if the first certificate of occupancy is issued after January 26, 1993.[158]

[ii] Readily accessible to and usable by. The term "readily accessible to and usable by," though not defined in the ADA, does have its own history. In similar form, it has been used in the Architectural Barriers Act, the Fair Housing Act of 1968, as amended, the regulations implementing Section 504 of the Rehabilitation Act, and in some of the standards used by federal agencies and private industry (such as the UFAS).

In general, readily accessible to and usable by

is intended to enable people with disabilities (including mobility, sensory, and cognitive impairments) to get to, enter and use a facility. While the term does not necessarily require the accessibility of every part of every area of a facility, the term contemplates a high degree of convenient accessibility, entailing accessibility of parking areas, accessible routes to and from the facility, accessible entrances, usable bathrooms and water fountains, accessibility of public and common use areas, and access to the goods, services, programs, facilities, accommodations and work areas available at the facility.[159]

Importantly, though, not all parking spaces, bathrooms, and stalls within bathrooms must be disabled-accessible. Only a reasonable number must be accessible within a facility, depending on particular facts and circumstances, such as the use, location, and number of these items. Enough, however, should be accessi-

---

[158] See Department of Justice regulation 28 CFR § 36.401(a)(2).

[159] H. Comm. on Educ. and Lab. Rep. at 117, 118.

ble for each facility to provide both ready access to the facility and usability of its features and equipment and of the goods, services, and programs available therein—all on a basis equal to the access thereto for the nondisabled.

The ATBCB's ADAAG contain several definitions relating to accessibility. "Accessible" is defined simply as "a site, building, facility, or portion thereof that complies with these guidelines. An "accessible element" is "an element specified by these guidelines (for example, telephone, controls, and the like)." "Accessible space" is "space that complies with these guidelines," and an "accessible route" is defined as

> [a] continuous unobstructed path connecting all accessible elements and spaces in a building or facility. Interior accessible routes may include corridors, floors, ramps, elevators, lifts, and clear floor space at fixtures. Exterior accessible routes may include parking access aisles, curb ramps, crosswalks at vehicular ways, walks, ramps, and lifts.[160]

The more detailed technical requirements for making elements and spaces accessible are set forth in Chapter 4 of the ADAAG.

A facility referred to in this section is not just the building itself, or the exterior structure. It also includes the equipment and goods within the building. Each individual bathroom stall is a facility, for example.

As long as multiple facilities within a structure provide the same function, as indicated earlier, they do not all need to be accessible. But, where the facilities do not provide the same function, each facility must be accessible. For example, to provide equal service to the disabled and nondisabled, all check-out lanes in a supermarket should be built sufficiently wide to allow passage by individuals who use wheelchairs. Otherwise, if there are only one or two lanes wide enough to allow wheelchair passage, and these lanes are closed for portions of the day, persons in wheelchairs will essentially be denied access during those times. Similarly, different meeting rooms at a conference

---

[160] See ATBCB ADAAG at § 3.5.

center must all be made accessible since they may be used for different purposes at any given time.[161]

Section 303(a)(1) applies to the design as well as the construction of new buildings. A design company that fails to design a new building so that it is fully accessible to the disabled is guilty of discrimination. Likewise, corporate headquarters could not design a new store that is inaccessible; both headquarters and the actual operator of the store would be in violation of Section 303(a)(1).[162]

The two following examples are situations where the access requirements apply to areas that will be used by the general public as customers or patrons. The requirements apply as well to guaranteeing equal access to disabled employees. Facilities must be designed and constructed so that disabled employees have an accessible path of travel in and out of the work space, and around the work area. Unusual spaces where the disabled would not likely be, such as catwalks and fan rooms, do not have to be accessible, though.

1. *New medical and dental offices.* To be readily accessible to and usable by the disabled, a new office should include
   - A reasonable percentage of examining rooms that are fully accessible to the disabled
   - Waiting areas that are fully accessible
   - At least one bathroom that is fully accessible

2. *New hotels.* Readily accessible to and usable by includes, but is not limited to
   - Providing full access to the public use and common use portions of the hotel
   - Requiring that all doors and doorways designed to allow passage into and within all hotel rooms and bathrooms be sufficiently wide (exact width requirements will be included in the regulations) to allow passage by individuals who use wheelchairs

---

[161] H. Comm. on Educ. and Lab. Rep. at 118.

[162] 136 Cong. Rec. at H2624 (May 22, 1990) (Statement of Cong. Hamilton Fish, ranking minority member of the House Committee on the Judiciary).

- Making a percentage of each class of hotel rooms fully accessible by doing things such as including grab bars in bathroom and installing accessible counters
- Including audio loops in meeting areas
- Putting braille or raised letter words and numbers on elevators and areas containing public notices
- Installing flashing alarm lights to aid hearing-disabled persons
- Ramping stair areas and placing handrails on stairs and ramps

Hotels are not required to make every room fully disabled-accessible, just a reasonable number based on facts and circumstances. If a disabled person does not make an advance reservation and no fully accessible room is available at that time, the hotel is not guilty of discrimination as long as it is otherwise accessible and has a reasonable number of fully accessible rooms even though they are all occupied. If an advance reservation is made and the hotel is told then that a fully accessible room is needed, one must be provided if one is available at the time of the reservation (if all of the fully accessible rooms are already booked, the customer should be told so at the time he seeks to make the reservation).

If all the fully accessible rooms are not reserved, the hotel is not required to give up business to keep them open just in case a disabled person walks in the door. It may rent these rooms to nondisabled persons if it would lose the business otherwise, but if a disabled person subsequently comes in, the hotel should make an attempt to accommodate him if reasonable to do so — i.e., by moving the nondisabled person out of the fully accessible room if other rooms are available.

[b] Guidelines for New Facilities

An area within a new office, plant, factory, or warehouse that may be used by employees with disabilities must be designed and constructed so that individuals with disabilities can approach, enter, and exit the area. Each individual workstation, though, does not have to be built to be accessible or outfitted with fixtures, equipment, shelving, or the like that would make it disabled-accessible. The concept of modifying an individual workstation within a disabled-accessible area or facility to make it usable by a disabled employee would come into play only after a disabled person applies for a specific job; this would be governed by the standards in Title I as well as by the barrier removal and auxiliary aids requirements and limitations of Title III.

Though the ADA does not make it mandatory to do so, Congress has suggested that operators and designers of new facilities try to install equipment and the like that either is disabled-accessible or that can easily be made disabled-accessible (such as an adjustable-height light). If it is not a problem to do so, these installations should be made so that adjustments needed in the event of later-hired disabled employees can be easily made. [163]

Areas designed for either public use or common use by all employees, such as restrooms, employee lounges, employee cafeterias, gyms, and health facilities, must be accessible in accordance with the standards contained in the ATBCB's ADAAG.

There is no limit on size of the new facility to which Section 303 is applicable. Regardless of how small or large the facility or the facility operator and regardless of how many employees the operator has, Section 303 applies, and the new facility must be accessible to the disabled.

Departure from the technical standards and regulations regarding new construction issued by the ATBCB and the Department of Justice is permissible if the alternative methods used provide equivalent or greater access to and utilization of the facility by the disabled than would compliance with the guidelines or regulations, whether because of technical improvements or otherwise. [164]

---

[163] H. Comm. on Educ. and Lab. Rep. at 119.

[164] H. Comm. on Educ. and Lab. Rep. at 119; S. Comm. on Lab. and Hum. Resources Rep. at 70.

[c] Exception: Structural Impracticality

The only time an entity is not guilty of discrimination in failing to make a new facility accessible to the disabled under Section 303(a)(1) and the guidelines and regulations issued thereunder is if it is structurally impracticable to do so. This is meant to be "a narrow exception that will apply only in rare and unusual circumstances where unique characteristics of terrain make accessibility unusually difficult" or where making the facility accessible would destroy the physical integrity of the building.[165] One of few situations in which the exception would apply would be where a building must be built on stilts because of its location in marshlands or over water.[166]

The structurally impracticable exception in the ADA is meant to be analogous to a similar exception for peculiarities of terrain (the physical integrity exception) set out in the legislative history to the Fair Housing Amendments Act.[167] In both pieces of legislation, though accessibility was of extreme importance, Congress was simply being practical in wanting to make sure that the accessibility requirements did not destroy the facility.[168]

If it is structurally impracticable to construct a facility so as to make it fully accessible to the disabled, the owner should still try to do the next best thing—make it as accessible as is practical. If one part of a facility cannot be made accessible for structural reasons but another part can be, the owner must at least make this latter part accessible. If the structure cannot be made accessible to persons in wheelchairs but can be made accessible to the blind or deaf, they must be guaranteed access. Failure to

---

[165] H. Comm. on Educ. and Lab. Rep. at 120; S. Comm. on Lab. and Hum. Resources Rep. at 70.

[166] Id.

[167] H. Comm. on Educ. and Lab. Rep. at 120; S. Comm. on Lab. and Hum. Resources Rep. at 71.

[168] "Structural impracticability" is also a defined term in the FHA, though it is defined more broadly there than its use in the ADA. UFAS 3.5 defines it as "changes having little likelihood of being accomplished without removing or altering a load-bearing structural member and/or incurring an increased cost of 50 percent or more of the value of the element of the building or facility involved."

make a structure as accessible as is practicable under the circumstances would be discrimination. [169]

[2] Alterations to Existing Public Accommodations and Commercial Facilities

Section 303(a)(1) applies to the construction of new facilities. It does not require that any major, structural changes be made to any existing facilities. The only structural changes that existing facilities are *required* to make by Title III of the ADA are those types of barrier removals that are readily achievable—i.e., easy and inexpensive to make. This does not mean removal of walls or major structural redesign of premises, but instead encompasses such minor changes as putting up grab bars or ramping small sets of stairs.

If an existing facility chooses on its own to make a structural alteration that affects the usability of the facility, though, Section 303(a)(2) applies.

The mandate of Section 303(a)(2) takes effect on January 26, 1992, eighteen months after the enactment of the ADA. The Department of Justice regulations state that an alteration is deemed to be undertaken after January 26, 1992, if the physical alteration of the property begins after that date. [170]

In the bill reported by the House Committee on Education and Labor, the provision relating to alterations was contained in Section 302, which only applies to public accommodations, not to commercial facilities. Commercial facilities only had an obligation to make new construction and design accessible, under Section 303 of the education and labor bill. The House Judiciary Committee amended the legislation to move the provision dealing with alterations to Section 303, where the obligation to carry out building alterations in an accessible manner would extend to commercial facilities as well as to public accommodations. The sponsor of the amendment in the Judiciary Committee, Congressman Hamilton Fish, said that this amendment

---

[169] See Department of Justice regulation 28 CFR § 36.401(c).

[170] See Department of Justice regulation 28 CFR § 36.402(a)(2).

was intended to correct an oversight in previous bills where the alterations section only applied to public accommodations. The intent of the ADA is to assure that construction performed in the future results in accessibility and useability [sic] by people with disabilities. In order to accommodate the concerns of businesses, a line was drawn between existing buildings where only those accessibility changes which are readily achievable are required, and new construction which must be accessible. In keeping with this purpose, it made sense to require that alterations which affect usability also be accessible in all commercial facilities. The bill does not require that existing buildings be altered for accessibility purposes. It simply requires that if and when alterations are performed that they incorporate accessibility requirements. Without this amendment, the anomalous situation could arise that a new commercial facility which was required to be accessible under the ADA could be altered to make it inaccessible. [171]

Section 303(a)(2) requires that if structural alterations are being made, they be made so that the altered portions are, to the maximum extent possible, accessible to the disabled—including persons in wheelchairs. Additionally, if an entity chooses to make an alteration that affects or could affect the usability of or access to an area of the facility that contains a primary function of the facility, the alterations must be made in such a manner that, to the maximum extent feasible, the path of travel to the altered area and also to the bathrooms, telephones, and drinking fountains serving the altered area are made accessible to the disabled—unless the alterations to the path of travel or the bathrooms, telephones, and drinking fountains serving the altered area are disproportionate to the overall alterations in terms of cost and scope. The Attorney General is given the responsibility by the statute to develop criteria for determining when alterations are disproportionate. [172] Failure to meet the requirements set forth will be considered discrimination.

---

[171] 136 Cong. Rec. at H2624 (May 22, 1990) (Statement of Cong. Hamilton Fish).

[172] See infra ¶ 5.05[2][e].

[a] Definitions

[i] Areas of primary function. An area of the facility containing a primary function is one where significant goods, services, facilities, privileges, advantages, or accommodations are provided.[173] Examples of areas of primary function would include the customer service lobby of a bank, dining area of a cafeteria, examining room of a physician's office, meeting room of a conference center, viewing galleries of a museum, seating area of a theater, and the like—the places where business is conducted or the facility's purpose is carried out. Places that would not be areas of primary function include a mechanical room, boiler room, janitor's closet, storage closet, and catwalk.[174]

[ii] Path of travel. As used in Section 303(a)(2), path of travel is not defined in the statute. The legislative history explains it as follows, though:

> The "path of travel" to an altered area means a continuous, unobstructed way of pedestrian passage by means of which that area may be approached, entered, used, and exited; and which connects that area with an exterior approach (including sidewalks, streets, and parking areas), an entrance to the facility, and other parts of the facility. An accessible path of travel may consist of walks and sidewalks; curb ramps and other interior or exterior pedestrian ramps; clear floor paths through lobbies, corridors, rooms, and other improved areas; parking access aisles; elevators and lifts; or a combination of such elements.[175]

The Department of Justice's regulations adopt this definition.[176]

The concept of an accessible path of travel is similar to

---

[173] H. Comm. on Educ. and Lab. Rep. at 112.

[174] The concept of "area of primary function" is analogous to the concept in the UFAS of "functional spaces" or rooms of "major activities." See UFAS 3.5 (Apr. 1, 1988). See also 28 CFR § 36.403(b).

[175] H. Comm. on Educ. and Lab. Rep. at 113, 114.

[176] See Department of Justice regulation 28 CFR § 36.403(e).

"accessible route" and "circulation path," terms currently used in the UFAS. The UFAS defines accessible route as

> [a] continuous unobstructed path connecting all accessible elements and spaces in a building or facility. Interior accessible routes may include corridors, floors, ramps, elevators, lifts, and clear floor space at fixtures. Exterior accessible routes may include parking access aisles, curb ramps, walks, ramps, and lifts.[177]

A circulation path as used in the UFAS is "[a]n exterior or interior way of passage from one place to another for pedestrians, including, but not limited to, walks, hallways, courtyards, stairways, and stair landings."[178]

[iii] Maximum extent feasible. The legislation speaks in terms of providing access to a path of travel, restrooms, telephones, and drinking fountains both to the maximum extent feasible and where such alterations are not disproportionate to the overall scope and cost of the alterations. Maximum extent feasible in Section 303(a)(2) applies to the occasional case where the nature of an existing facility makes it impossible to comply fully with applicable accessibility standards through a planned alteration.[179] An example would be the rare case where the unique design pattern of an existing building—such as an ascending staircase design—would be totally destroyed by changes that would be needed to make the facility fully accessible. While it may not be feasible to make such a facility fully accessible to persons in wheelchairs as part of alterations, it would be feasible to make it accessible to the blind, or other disabled persons. Whatever level of accessibility can be provided, must be provided, subject to the disproportionality limitation.[180]

---

[177] UFAS 3.5 (Apr. 1, 1988).

[178] Id.

[179] See Department of Justice regulation 28 CFR § 36.402(c).

[180] Id.

[b] Alterations Affecting Usability

The regulations list several types of alterations that affect or could affect usability. These include, but are not limited to, remodeling, renovation, rehabilitation, reconstruction, historic restoration, changes or rearrangement in structural parts or elements, and extraordinary repairs.[181] Specific examples include relocating an electrical outlet, installing or replacing faucet controls, relocating a furnace or replacing a heating system in a manner that requires changes to other elements of the facility, and replacing door hardware such as door handles or hinges.[182] These alterations must meet the standards set forth in the ATBCB's ADAAG.[183]

General changes that normally will not affect usability include normal maintenance, reroofing, painting, wallpapering, asbestos removal, or changes to mechanical systems. Specific examples include replacing an electrical outlet without changing its location, replacing faucet washers, replacing a furnace with a similar furnace in the same location, and cosmetic changes such as repairing plaster, painting, or wallpapering.[184] Examples of alterations that would affect the usability of or access to an area containing a primary function are remodeling merchandise display areas or employee work areas in a department store, replacing an inaccessible floor surface in the customer service or employee work areas of a bank, redesigning the assembly line area of a factory, and installing a computer center in an accounting firm.[185]

The obligation to make an alteration "readily accessible to and usable by individuals with disabilities" has the same meaning in Section 303(a)(2) with respect to alterations as it does in Section 303(a)(1) in connection with new construction[186] —

---

[181] See Department of Justice regulation 28 CFR § 36.402(b)(1); see also ATBCB's ADAAG 3.5, defining "alteration."

[182] Id.

[183] Id.

[184] Id.

[185] See Department of Justice regulation 28 CFR § 36.403(c).

[186] See discussion of Section 303(a)(1) at supra ¶ 5.05.

namely, that the disabled must be able to get to, enter, and use a facility or an altered area. Access to all parts of the altered area is not required, but there must be a high degree of convenient accessibility, including (1) accessible routes to and from the altered area to usable bathrooms and water fountains nearby and to public and common use areas within the altered space and (2) access to the goods, services, programs, facilities, accommodations, and work areas in and around the altered area.

In order to trigger the requirement of accessibility in alterations, the alterations made must first be major ones, ones that affect the usability of the facility or a part thereof. Minor changes, such as painting or papering walls, replacing ceiling tiles, and similar alterations that do not affect usability, do not have to be made so that they are accessible to the disabled or so that paths of travel, bathrooms, telephones, and drinking fountains are accessible.[187]

A change to a facility's floor may or may not affect usability, depending upon the particular change involved. Routine maintenance, including repairing and sanding floors, generally would not affect access or usability. Normally, neither would laying new carpet, but if carpet was laid poorly or unevenly in some fashion, so that a wheelchair could not get across it, access and, consequently, usability would be affected. Failure to correct the diminished accessibility or to make alternative equal arrangements would be discrimination.[188]

A change such as totally pulling up and replacing a floor may be so substantial that it cannot help but affect access and usability. If so, the new floor must comply with the ADA and be accessible to all disabled persons. If the new floor is being put in an area of the facility that contains a primary function, the path of travel and bathrooms and water fountains nearby must also be made accessible (assuming the cost and scope is not disproportionate). As a good general rule, not all bathrooms, telephones, and water fountains need to be made accessible, but at

---

[187] H. Comm. on Educ. and Lab. Rep. at 111; H. Comm. on Jud. Rep. at 64.

[188] H. Comm. on Educ. and Lab. Rep. at 111, 112.

least one of each should be accessible in each area of primary function being altered. [189]

[c] Disproportionate Cost and Scope

As throughout the ADA, Congress did not want to place an absolute obligation upon public accommodations and facility owners to make the path of travel, bathrooms, telephones, and water fountains readily accessible to the disabled. Rather, this obligation is triggered only if the cost involved or scope of work that would need to be done to provide an accessible path of travel, accessible restrooms, drinking fountains, and telephones is not disproportionate to the other alterations being done. [190] Congress did not want the ADA to overwhelm, dominate, or inhibit an owner's ability to make needed alterations. "[W]here the tail (path of travel, accessible restrooms, etc.) would be wagging the dog (the overall alteration), the accessible path of travel and related accessibility features are not required." [191]

The key comparison to be made here is between the cost and scope of the alteration for accessibility and the cost and scope of the entire alterations. Congress rejected the approach used in some states of measuring the disproportionality by comparing the cost of ensuring accessibility to the entire value of the building in which the alterations are being made. [192]

The statute itself does not provide any guidelines for making the determination of when the cost and scope of accessibility is disproportionate, but directed that the specific parameters for doing this be included in regulations promulgated by the Attorney General.

Committee reports do shed some broad guidance on what these regulations could properly include. Both the House Judici-

---

[189] Id.

[190] HR Conf. Rep. No. 596, 101st Cong., 2d Sess. (1990), Conf. Rep. on S.933, Americans With Disabilities Act of 1990, Joint Explanatory Statement of the Committee of Conference at ¶ 51(b).

[191] H. Comm. on Educ. and Lab. Rep. at 112.

[192] H. Comm. on Jud. Rep. at 64; H. Comm. on Educ. and Lab. Rep. at 113.

ary Committee and Committee on Education and Labor felt it would be consistent with the ADA for a specific threshold, such as 30 percent of the alteration costs, to be established by the guidelines and regulations for determining whether the cost of making an alteration for accessibility is disproportionate.[193] The House Education and Labor Committee also stated that doubling the cost of a planned alteration to provide the necessary access is clearly disproportionate, and that in nearly all cases it would likewise be disproportionate if the accessibility costs were as high as 50 percent of the total alteration costs.[194] Importantly, though, these comments are just suggestions by the committees, and do not bind the Attorney General.

The Department of Justice's regulations define disproportionality by providing that alterations made to provide an accessible path of travel to the altered area will be presumed to be disproportionate to the overall alteration when the cost exceeds 20 percent of the cost of the alteration to the primary function area.[195]

Some examples of cost that may be counted as expenses required to provide an accessible path of travel are costs associated with:

1. Providing an accessible entrance and an accessible route to the altered area, for example, the cost of widening doorways or installing ramps
2. Making restrooms accessible, by doing things such as installing grab bars, enlarging toilet stalls, insulating pipes, or installing accessible faucet controls
3. Providing accessible telephones, by relocating the telephone to an accessible height, installing amplification devices, or installing a TDD
4. Relocating an inaccessible drinking fountain[196]

A public accommodation or commercial facility may con-

---

[193] Id.

[194] H. Comm. on Educ. and Lab. Rep. at 113.

[195] See Department of Justice regulation 28 CFR § 36.403(f)(1).

[196] See Department of Justice regulation 28 CFR § 36.403(f)(2).

ceivably attempt to evade the requirement of this section by dividing one major alteration project into many small projects to be carried out separately over a period. In this manner, the public accommodation or commercial facility could argue that the cost of ensuring accessibility is disproportionate to the cost of any one job. This argument would be unsuccessful, though. The appropriate cost and scope for comparison in this instance would not be the cost and scope of any one little job, but rather the aggregate cost of all the related alterations performed proximate in time.[197] Regulations state that this proximate time shall be three years, so that the total cost of alterations to the primary function areas on the path of travel during the preceding three-year period shall be considered in determining whether the cost of making that path of travel accessible is disproportionate.[198]

Under Section 302, if it is not readily achievable, that is, easy and inexpensive, for a public accommodation to provide total access to a disabled person, the public accommodation must still provide, through alternate methods, the best access that is readily achievable. If total equality of access is not possible, the ADA still requires that the disabled be given as much access as possible. Similarly, with the concept of disproportionality, if the cost of ensuring an accessible path of travel to the alterations, accessible restrooms, *and* accessible water fountains, is disproportionate, whichever of these individually can be made accessible must be. If a choice must be made as to which of these features to make accessible, the legislative history indicates that whichever one or ones provide the greatest use of the facility must be given highest priority and done first.[199] For example, making the entrance accessible would normally be more important than making a restroom or drinking fountain accessible—since one needs to be able to get inside a facility before the restroom matters.

By the same token, though, if a higher priority item such as an entrance cannot proportionately be made fully accessible,

---

[197] H. Comm. on Educ. and Lab. Rep. at 112; H. Comm. on Jud. Rep. at 64. See also 28 CFR § 36.403(h).

[198] See 28 CFR § 36.403(h)(2).

[199] H. Comm. on Educ. and Lab. Rep. at 113.

this does not automatically excuse the public accommodation or commercial facility from having to make other paths of travel, or a restroom, phone, or water fountain, accessible if these particular changes are not disproportionate. While some disabled persons will not be able to enter a building that does not have an accessible entrance, others will; these others will still need accessible water fountains, phones, and restrooms. Whatever is not disproportionate when an area of primary function is altered should be done. Providing the maximum amount of accessibility without incurring disproportionate cost or involving disproportionate scope is the goal.

Along this line, the Department of Justice's regulations provide a priority listing for elements that provide the greatest access; where full access cannot be provided because of disproportionality, the regulations say that at least partial access should be provided in the following order:

1. An accessible entrance
2. An accessible route to the altered area
3. At least one accessible restroom for each sex or a single unisex restroom
4. Accessible telephones
5. Accessible drinking fountains
6. Additional accessible elements such as parking, storage, and alarms when possible[200]

[3] Exception: Elevators

Section 303(a)(1) basically labels it as discrimination for a new public accommodation or commercial facility to be designed and constructed that is not accessible to the disabled. Section 303(a)(2) calls it discrimination when certain alterations, or paths of travel, water fountains and restrooms near these alterations are not disabled-accessible.

Section 303(a)(3) describes one specific type of accessibility feature that, despite the language of Sections 303(a)(1) and

---

[200] See Department of Justice regulation 28 CFR § 36.403(g)(2).

303(a)(2), need not be put into certain small buildings. It states that generally, if a facility has less than three stories, or if a facility has less than 3,000 square feet per story, it is not required to install an elevator to meet the requirements of accessibility in new construction under Section 303(a)(1) or accessibility in alterations to existing structures under Section 303(a)(2). The other accessibility requirements must still be met, where feasible or not disproportionate as set forth in Sections 303(a)(1) and 303(a)(2); it is just that the installation of an elevator is not required. Even if the only way of providing access is by putting in an elevator, the elevator does not have to be installed.

There are several instances, however, where this elevator exception does not apply to a new or altered facility. If the building is a shopping center, a shopping mall, or the professional office of a health care provider, an elevator must be installed if needed to ensure that any area housing a sales or rental establishment or a professional office of a health care provider is either on an accessible ground floor or on a floor served by an elevator.[201] If all sales or rental establishments and offices of health care providers are located on an accessible ground floor and the building otherwise qualifies for the elevator exception, no elevator is needed.

Although the statute lists a shopping center and a shopping mall separately, the Department of Justice's regulations combine them and define them identically. They are, with respect to new construction, "a building housing five or more sales or rental establishments" or "a series of buildings on a common site, either under common ownership or common control or developed either as one project or as a series of related projects, housing five or more sales or rental establishments."[202] A sales or rental establishment for this definition is one similar to a bakery, grocery store, clothing store, hardware store, or shopping center.[203] The definition only includes floor levels containing at least one sales or rental establishment, or any floor level designed or intended for use by at least one sales or rental

---

[201] 28 CFR §§ 36.401(d)(1), 36.404.

[202] 28 CFR § 36.401(d)(1)(ii).

[203] Id.

establishment.[204] The only difference with respect to alterations is that to qualify as a shopping center or mall, the buildings must be connected by a common pedestrian access route above or below the ground floor.[205]

A professional office of a health care provider is defined in the Attorney General's regulations as

> a location where a person or entity regulated by a State to provide professional services related to the physical or mental health of an individual makes such services available to the public. The facility housing the "professional offices of a health care provider" only includes floor levels containing at least one or more health care providers, or any floor level designed or intended for use by at least one health care provider.[206]

The statute also empowers the Attorney General to add additional categories of new or altered facilities to those that must have elevators regardless of square footage per story or number of stories, based on the nature of the usage of the facility. The Department of Justice's regulations add the following categories: a terminal, depot, or other station used for specified public transportation, or an airport passenger terminal.[207] All areas in these facilities that cater to passengers must be on an accessible route from an accessible entrance.

Though the ADA does not require the installation of an elevator in certain buildings, it still requires that in any new building, or in an altered building to an extent, each floor itself be made accessible to the disabled. For example, if the building qualifies for the elevator exception, the second floor of a small new accountants' office building will not be required to have an elevator leading up to it, but the second floor still must have disabled-accessible doorways, offices, water fountains, restrooms, and the like.

If a facility that is not required to have an elevator installs

---

[204] Id.

[205] 28 CFR § 36.404(a)(2).

[206] 28 CFR §§ 36.401(d)(1)(i), 36.404(a)(1).

[207] 28 CFR §§ 36.401(d)(2), 36.404(a).

one anyway, the elevator installed must be accessible to the disabled. It should be wide enough to permit easy entry by wheelchairs and should at least have braille tags next to the floor buttons.

[4] Obligations of Landlords and Tenants

Title III of the ADA generally prohibits an operator of a place of public accommodation from denying to any person the full and equal enjoyment of the goods, services, facilities, privileges, advantages, or accommodations of the place of public accommodation because of the person's disability. Where the operator of a place of public accommodation is a tenant or a subtenant, a question can arise as to whether a failure to make the place of public accommodation accessible to the disabled constitutes discrimination by the tenant or the landlord.

Whichever party is the one with legal control over the ability to make the needed changes, whether through barrier removal or other readily achievable change, is the one who would be guilty of discrimination for failing to do so. Often-times, the lease will set forth which party has the obligation to make structural changes or alterations. Other times, the responsibility will be placed upon one party, usually the landlord, by state law. From the tenant's standpoint, permission to make changes will more likely be stated as a right rather than an obligation in a lease; the tenant may be given the right to move an interior wall if it wishes, for example. If the tenant has the right to make a readily achievable change that would make the premises disabled-accessible and does not, the tenant, not the landlord, is guilty of discrimination. If all authority to make changes is reserved to the landlord, on the other hand, the landlord bears the responsibility under Title III.

The Department of Justice's regulations provide that allocation of responsibility between a landlord and tenant for complying with Title III can be determined by lease or other contract.[208] If a group rents space on a very short-term basis, so that alterations, barrier removal, or auxiliary aids are not feasi-

---

[208] See Department of Justice regulation 28 CFR § 36.201(b).

ble for it, the group would be well advised to include a provision in the lease specifying that responsibility for complying with the ADA rests with the landlord. The remaining time left on a tenant's lease can be a factor taken into account in determining whether a particular change is readily achievable.

If alterations are made by either a landlord or tenant that trigger the requirements of Section 303, only the party making the alterations is responsible for complying with the ADA.[209] Section 303(a)(2) deals in part with alterations that affect a primary function of a facility, triggering an obligation to guarantee an accessible path of travel, restroom, telephone, and water fountains during the alterations. If the landlord is doing the alterations, the landlord must comply with Section 303(a)(2). If the alterations are being done by the tenant, however, and the landlord is not doing alterations of its own, the landlord does not have an obligation to guarantee an accessible path of travel through common areas that might be affected by the tenant's alterations. Similarly, the tenant does not have an obligation to guarantee access on common areas, assuming it has no lease authority to make changes to common areas. The alterations done by the tenant on its own premises, however, cannot block access to existing accessible paths of travel, water fountains, telephones, and restrooms located in common areas.

Generally, unless altered by contract, the responsibility for providing auxiliary aids or making sure that displays are accessible rests with the lessee, not the landlord. Further, the landlord will not be held responsible for a particular tenant's policies (e.g., for a restaurant's refusing to admit a disabled person).

If a church, an entity exempt from the requirements of the ADA, leases space to a day-care center (a public accommodation), the church would not have to comply with Title III, but the day-care center would (as long as the day-care center is not owned or operated by the church). If a private club otherwise exempt from the ADA leases space to a day-care center, though, it becomes subject to the ADA, along with the day-care center, but only for the particular space leased. To the extent a private club not otherwise covered by the ADA makes its facilities

---

[209] H. Comm. on Educ. and Lab. Rep. at 115.

available to customers or patrons of a place of public accommodation, it is considered a place of public accommodation.

[5] Regulations Concerning Buildings and Facilities

Section 306(b) gave the Attorney General the responsibility to
issue regulations in an accessible format to carry out the provisions of Title III other than those covered by the Secretary of
Transportation's regulations. These regulations are to provide
standards and details for public accommodations to follow in
order to be considered as providing the disabled with full and
equal enjoyment of the goods, services, facilities, privileges,
advantages, or accommodations offered. Guidance is also to be
offered on the ADA's requirements concerning such items as
architectural and communication barrier removal, auxiliary
aids and services, necessary modification of private entities'
policies, and alternative methods required if barrier removal is
not possible. These regulations have been issued, and a copy is
included in Appendix C.[210]

As is the case with the regulations issued by the Secretary of
Transportation, the standards included in the Attorney General's regulations are required to be consistent with the ADAAG
issued by the ATBCB under Section 504(a) of the ADA, a copy
of which is included in Appendix C.[211] The purpose of the
ATBCB guidelines is to provide technical standards (i.e., number of accessible parking spaces required per parking lot, number of accessible public telephones required per floor of a
building, dimensions required for accessible toilet stalls) to
ensure that buildings, facilities, rail passenger cars, and vehicles
are accessible, in terms of architecture and design, transportation, and communication, to individuals with disabilities. The
new guidelines must not "reduce, weaken, narrow, or set less accessibility standards" than those contained in the ATBCB's minimum
guidelines that existed at the time of passage of the ADA.[212]

The Attorney General's regulations adopt and incorporate

---

[210] See 28 CFR pt. 36.

[211] See ADAAG issued by the ATBCB, 36 CFR pt. 1191, 56 Fed. Reg.
35,408 et seq. (July 26, 1991).

[212] H. Comm. on Educ. and Lab. Rep. at 139.

the ADAAG as the technical standards for accessible design for new construction and alterations. [213]

[a] Qualified Historic Properties

The ADAAG issued by the ATBCB under Section 504 of the ADA were required to include special procedures and requirements for alterations that will threaten or destroy the historic significance of qualified historic buildings and facilities. These procedures and requirements are set out in Rule 4.1.7 of the ADAAG. Generally, however, alterations to a qualified historic building or facility must comply with the ADAAG standards unless the historic significance of the building or facility would be impaired. At a minimum, a historic structure must have at least one accessible route to it.

The ADA incorporates the definition of "qualified historic buildings and facilities" from Section 4.1.7(1)(a) of the UFAS, which states:

> "Qualified" buildings or facilities are those buildings and facilities that are eligible for listing in the National Register of Historic Places, or such properties designated as historic under a statute of the appropriate state or local government body . . . . [214]

Section 504(c)(2) provides that whenever the ADA would otherwise require an alteration of a building or facility eligible for listing in the National Register of Historic Places, the following procedures from the UFAS shall apply:

> 1. Comments of the Advisory Council on Historic Preservation shall be obtained when required by section 106 of the National Historic Preservation Act of 1966, as amended, [215] before an alteration is made to a qualified historic building.
> 2. The Advisory Council shall determine, on a case-by-case basis, whether provisions for accessible exterior and interior routes, ramps, entrances, toilets, parking, and dis-

---

[213] 28 CFR § 36.406.

[214] UFAS 4.1.7(1)(a) (Apr. 1, 1988).

[215] 16 USC § 470; 36 CFR pt. 800.

plays and signage, would threaten or destroy the historic significance of the building or facility.

3. If the Advisory Council determines in writing that any of the accessibility requirements would threaten or destroy the historic significance of the building or facility, then the special minimum accessibility requirements for historic preservation set forth in UFAS 4.1.7(2) are to be followed.[216]

[b] Technical Assistance From the Attorney General

The Attorney General is also directed, by Section 506 of the ADA, in consultation with the Chair of the Equal Employment Opportunity Commission, the Secretary of Transportation, the Chair of the ATBCB, and the Chair of the Federal Communications Commission, to develop a plan to assist the public in understanding their obligations under all parts of the ADA. The agencies are to develop technical assistance manuals for public distribution; they may also make grants or enter into contracts with private individuals or entities to aid them in providing such technical assistance.

Some members of Congress were concerned about what might happen if the relevant agencies failed to satisfy the technical assistance requirements of Section 506. They did not want an entity covered under the ADA to be able to use such a failure as a defense to the entity's noncompliance with the ADA. Accordingly, Section 506(e) was included, which provides that

> [a]n employer, public accommodation, or other entity covered under the Act shall not be excused from compliance with the requirements of this Act because of any failure to receive technical assistance under this section, including any failure in the development or dissemination of any technical assistance manual authorized by this section.

¶ 5.06 TRANSPORTATION

By virtue of Sections 302(b)(2)(B), 302(b)(2)(C), 302(b)(2)(D), and 304, Title III applies to private entities that provide specified public transportation, whether or not the entities' primary

---

[216] UFAS 4.1.7(1), 4.1.7(2) (Apr. 1, 1988).

line of business is providing this transportation. Specified public transportation is defined in Section 301(10) as transportation by bus, rail, or any other conveyance (except by aircraft) that provides the general public with general or special service (including charter service) on a regular and continuing basis. Section 302 applies where the entity is not in the business of providing public transportation, and Section 304 applies where it is in this business. Thus, a private bus company and taxicab company, as well as a hotel that operates a shuttle service to and from an airport for its guests, are covered by Title III.

Public intercity rail and commuter rail operations are excepted from Title III, because Title II sets forth requirements for these types of transportation, but privately operated rail operations are included within Title III. Transportation by aircraft is also excluded from the scope of Title III—and from the ADA—because of the existence of the Air Carrier Access Act of 1986,[217] except for shuttle service operations operated by commercial airlines.[218]

Consistent with the exemption established in Title II for public school transportation,[219] Title III does not apply to the transportation of school children to and from a private elementary or secondary school and school-related activities. If the school is a recipient of federal assistance though, and therefore, subject to the provisions of Section 504 of the Rehabilitation Act, it must provide bus service to children with disabilities equivalent to that provided to children without disabilities.[220]

[1] Private Companies in the Business of Providing Transportation

Providers of transportation are not dealt with comprehensively by just one section of the ADA. The legislation divides the

---

[217] Pub. L. No. 99-435; see 49 USC App. 1301, 1374.

[218] Report of the House Comm. on Public Works and Transportation on the Americans With Disabilities Act of 1990, HR Rep. No. 485, 101st Cong., 2d Sess., pt. 1 (1990) (hereinafter cited as H. Comm. on Pub. Works and Transp. Rep.) at 38.

[219] See ADA § 221(2).

[220] H. Comm. on Pub. Works and Transp. Rep. at 36.

transportation world into different subsets, excludes some from coverage as duplicative, and treats others differently in different parts of the law. For example, public entities such as cities, counties, and municipalities that provide transportation ser- vices—like a city-operated public bus system or an intercity rail system—are generally prohibited from discriminating against the disabled by Title II of the ADA (though if these entities currently receive federal assistance, they are already prohibited from doing this by Section 504 of the Rehabilitation Act. Title II also reinforces the point that failure of public school bus systems to provide accessible transportation is a violation of the Reha- bilitation Act and the ADA.

Airline travel is excepted from the ADA because Congress felt the passage of the Air Carriers Access Act,[221] dealing with discrimination by air carriers, made additional coverage unnec- essary.[222] Public facilities associated with air travel, though, such as airports, fall within Title II of the ADA. Private provid- ers of transportation who do not offer transportation as their primary line of business, such as hotels that operate airport shuttle services, are treated by Section 303(b)(2)(B). Private ridesharing arrangements, where individuals form carpools or vanpools with volunteer drivers, are not covered at all by the ADA. If, however, a private company is formed that purchases vans, hires drivers, and then charges riders for carpool services, the company's operations are subject to the antidiscrimination provisions of Section 304.

Section 304 applies the general ADA prohibition against discrimination to private operators that provide "specified pub- lic transportation services" as their primary business, and whose operations affect interstate commerce. The disabled are guaran- teed full and equal access to and enjoyment of these transporta- tion systems. This general guaranty in Section 304 is similar to that provided to the disabled in their use of public accommoda- tions by Section 302.

Section 304(b) sets out specific types of conduct that would

---

[221] Pub. L. No. 99-435, amending 49 USC App. 1301, 1374.

[222] H. Comm. on Educ. and Lab. Rep. at 87, 121; S. Comm. on Lab. and Hum. Resources Rep. at 46, 72.

be considered discrimination if engaged in by a private entity that operates a specified public transportation service. In Sections 304(b)(1) and 304(b)(2), it makes the same general prohibitions applicable to these entities as Section 302(b)(2)(A)(i) through 302(b)(2)(A)(v) applies to owners and operators of public accommodations.[223] In addition, in Sections 304(b)(3) through 304(b)(7), certain specific conduct with respect to particular means of transportation are listed that constitute discrimination against the disabled. The regulations issued by the Secretary of Transportation pursuant to Section 306 will help carry out and provide additional guidance to the provisions of Section 304.

In any conflict between the more specific prohibitions of Sections 304(b)(3) through 304(b)(7) and the more generic prohibitions of Sections 304(b)(1) and 304(b)(2), the specific prohibitions govern.[224] For example, if an over-the-road bus is not required to have a wheelchair lift under Section 304(b)(4) and the regulations issued thereunder, a disabled person cannot successfully allege that for purposes of Section 304, the failure to provide such a lift constitutes discrimination under Section 304(b)(1) or Section 304(b)(2).[225]

[a] General Prohibitions

[i] Eligibility criteria. Discrimination by an entity covered by Section 304 includes the imposition or application by the entity of eligibility criteria that screen out or tend to screen out an individual with a disability or any class of individuals with disabilities from fully enjoying the specified public transportation services provided by the entity, unless such criteria can be shown to be necessary for the provision of the services being offered. It would be a violation of this section for a transit company to refuse to sell a monthly bus pass to someone just because the person is blind, for example, or to require that all persons walking with the aid of a cane sit in the back of the bus.

---

[223] See supra ¶ 5.04.

[224] H. Comm. on Pub. Works and Transp. Rep. at 39, 40.

[225] Id.

Eligibility criteria that tend to screen out equal enjoyment by the disabled—as opposed to criteria that actually screen out—would be policies that, while not creating a direct bar to enjoyment of the transportation services, diminish the chances of such individuals' enjoyment. Safety criteria that are neutral and necessary for the safe operation of the transportation service are not discriminatory just because certain disabled persons are screened out.

[ii] Failure to make reasonable modifications in policies. It is also discriminatory for an entity operating the transportation service to fail to make reasonable modifications in policies, practices, or procedures, when such modifications are necessary to afford full and equal enjoyment of specified transportation services to individuals with disabilities, unless the entity can demonstrate that making such modifications would fundamentally alter the nature of the specified transportation services provided. For example, the failure of a transportation operator to modify a policy banning all animals to accommodate seeing-eye and hearing-eye dogs would constitute discrimination.

[iii] Failure to provide auxiliary aids and services. An entity operating a transportation service must take steps to provide auxiliary aids and services to ensure that no individual with a disability is excluded, denied transportation, segregated, or otherwise treated differently than other individuals because of the disability. If the entity does not take such steps it constitutes discrimination, unless the entity can demonstrate that taking such steps would fundamentally alter the nature of the transportation service offered or would result in an undue burden.

This would make it discriminatory, for example, for a rail car operator subject to Section 304 generally to fail to provide an employee to take the order of and go to the food car for a person in a wheelchair who is unable to move the wheelchair from one rail car to another. Similarly, the failure of the operator to either provide a braille menu or have an employee read the dining car menu to a blind person would be discrimination.

The auxiliary aids and services contemplated are only those that are easily obtainable, not costly and difficult. The definition of this term in Section 3(1), while more relevant to public accommodations generally than to transportation operators specifically, shows this. As is the case in the public accommodations area, as technology develops new auxiliary aids and services, or makes existing aids easier to provide, the obligation of entities providing specified public transportation services will change to include these auxiliary aids and services.

The limiting concept of undue burden in the public transportation area is the same as in the public accommodation area and is analogous to undue hardship used in Title I. If an action requires significant difficulty or expense, it will be an undue burden.[226]

[iv] **Failure to remove barriers.** Section 304(b)(2)(C) makes it discriminatory for a provider of specified public transportation services to fail

1. To remove transportation barriers in existing vehicles and rail passenger cars, not including barriers that can only be removed through the retrofitting of vehicles or rail passenger cars, where such removal is readily achievable;

2. To take other reasonable steps to afford the disabled full and equal enjoyment of the transportation services if removal of transportation barriers is not readily achievable;

3. When making alterations to transportation vehicles that could affect the usability of the vehicles or part thereof, to make the alterations in a manner that, to the maximum extent feasible, the altered portions of the vehicle are readily accessible to and usable by individuals with disabilities, including individuals who use wheelchairs; and

4. When making alterations to transportation vehicles that affect or could affect usability of or access to an area of the vehicle containing a primary function (e.g., the seating area, or dining area if one exists), to make the alterations in such a manner that, to the maximum extent

---

[226] See supra ¶ 5.04 for further discussion of the term "undue burden."

feasible, the path of travel to the altered area and the bathrooms, telephones, and drinking fountains serving the altered area, are readily accessible to and usable by individuals with disabilities, where such latter alterations are not disproportionate in terms of cost and scope to the overall alterations (as determined under criteria established by regulations issued by the Secretary of Transportation).[227]

Section 304(b)(2)(C) incorporates these types of discrimination from Sections 302(b)(2)(A)(iv), 302(b)(2)(A)(v), and 303(a)(2).[228]

With respect to vehicles used for public transportation, "readily accessible to and usable" by is described by legislative history as meaning able to be entered into and exited from and safely and effectively used by individuals with disabilities, including individuals who use wheelchairs.[229] The proposed Department of Transportation regulations provide some assistance for interim interpretation, stating that to be considered accessible and usable by individuals with disabilities, a vehicle must meet three requirements:

1. It must meet the requirements of existing regulations 49 C.F.R. 609.15(d)–(i), which heretofore have applied in connection with the Urban Mass Transit Administration.

2. The vehicle shall be equipped with a lift or other level-change mechanism and shall have sufficient clearances to permit an individual using a wheelchair or other mobility device to reach a securement location.

3. There shall be at least one securement location on the vehicle. The securement device(s) at the securement location shall be sufficient to secure any wheelchair or other mobility device which the vehicle's lift and clearances per-

---

[227] Note that there is no requirement that the Secretary of Transportation's disproportionality criteria issued here be the same as the disproportionality criteria promulgated by the Attorney General in connection with Section 303(a)(2).

[228] Further discussion of these provisions is at supra ¶¶ 5.04 and 5.05[1].

[229] H. Comm. on Educ. and Lab. Rep. at 122; S. Comm. on Lab. and Hum. Resources Rep. at 73.

mit to enter the vehicle and proceed to the securement location.[230]

[b] Specific Prohibitions Applicable to Purchases or Leases

With several exceptions, Section 304(b)(3) requires a private entity that is primarily engaged in the business of transporting people that is going to purchase or lease a new vehicle to purchase or lease a new vehicle that is readily accessible to and usable by individuals with disabilities (including individuals who use wheelchairs). It applies in connection with any purchase or lease for which a solicitation is made thirty days after the July 26, 1990, enactment of the ADA.

The exceptions to this rule are as follows:

1. It does not apply to the purchase of an automobile.

2. It does not apply to the purchase of a van that has a seating capacity of less than eight passengers, counting the driver as one of the passengers (though Section 304(b)(5) restates the same rule and makes it applicable to the purchase or lease of a *new* van with less than eight passengers, but with a different effective date).

3. It does not apply to an over-the-road bus (see following discussion), which is defined in Section 301(5) as a bus characterized by an elevated passenger deck located over a baggage compartment—an intercity bus rather than a city transit bus.

4. A vehicle purchased to be used solely in a demand responsive system, that is, one in which the vehicles are not operated along a prescribed route according to a fixed schedule,[231] need not in and of itself be accessible if the system, when viewed in its entirety, provides a level of service to the disabled equivalent to the level of service provided to the general public. An entity that operates a demand responsive system may purchase a new vehicle that is not disabled-accessible as long as it has an accessible vehicle available (either that it owns or that it can borrow regu-

___

[230] See proposed Department of Transportation regulation 49 CFR § 37.31. Proposed (not final) Department of Transportation regulations can be found in the Federal Register dated October 4, 1990.

[231] See ADA § 301(3).

larly) in which to transport the disabled reasonably upon demand. "Equivalent service" to the disabled in this context is defined by the Department of Transportation in its proposed regulations as service provided in the most integrated setting feasible that is equivalent to service provided to the nondisabled with respect to response time, fares, geographic area of service, hours and days of service, restrictions based on trip purpose, availability of information and reservations capability, and any constraints on capacity or service availability. [232]

[c] Over-the-Road Buses

The failure of a private entity that is primarily engaged in the business of transporting people to comply with the regulations constitutes discrimination, under Section 304(b)(4). [233] Under the ADA, where over-the-road buses are concerned, both entities that are primarily in this business and operators that are not must follow the Secretary of Transportation's regulations and are guilty of discrimination if they do not. [234] There is, however, no requirement that the regulations be identical for each type of operator.

The requirements of Section 304(b)(4) with respect to over-the-road buses do not just apply to the purchase or lease of new buses. The section applies to the purchase or lease of used buses as well, to whatever extent they are included in the regulations.

The enacted version of the ADA differs from the House Education and Labor Committee reported version in that the final ADA has a much stronger emphasis on the issuance of regulations by the Secretary of Transportation governing accessibility in over-the-road buses. The determination under Section 304(b)(4) of whether discrimination has occurred is entirely tied

---

[232] See proposed Department of Transportation regulation 49 CFR § 37.29(b)(2).

[233] The regulations issued by the Secretary of Transportation cover over-the-road buses operated by entities that are not primarily engaged in the business of transporting people as well; failure of these operators to follow the regulations constitutes discrimination as well, but under Section 302(b)(2)(D)(ii).

[234] See ADA §§ 304(b)(4), 302(b)(2)(D)(ii).

to whether there has been compliance with the regulations. Given this, it is highly possible that the committee's original intent will not be met, and that standards for how many accessible spaces should be in a vehicle will not be left to the vehicle owner but will be included in the regulations.

[d] New Van With Fewer Than Eight Passengers

Section 304(b)(5) requires that a new van that has a seating capacity of less than eight passengers that is purchased or leased after thirty days following January 26, 1992, that is used to provide specified public transportation be accessible to the disabled, including persons in wheelchairs. The same standards for accessibility and usability previously described apply for such vans. The one exception is that a particular new van need not be accessible if the system for which the van was purchased or leased, when viewed in its entirety, provides equivalent service to the disabled and nondisabled. This is similar to one of the exceptions included in Section 304(b)(3) for demand responsive systems, except that here the exception applies to all new vans, whether used in a demand responsive system or a fixed route system.

To provide some frame of reference, equivalent service to the disabled for this purpose is defined by the proposed Department of Transportation regulations as service provided in the most integrated setting feasible that is equivalent to service provided to the nondisabled with respect to response time (if the system is demand responsive) or schedules/headways (if the system is a fixed route system), fares, geographic area of service, hours and days of service, restrictions based on trip purpose, availability of information and reservations capability, and any constraints on capacity or service availability.[235]

[e] Rail Passenger Cars

[i] New. Section 304(b)(6) requires that a new rail passenger car purchased or leased after thirty days following January

---

[235] See proposed Department of Transportation regulation 49 CFR § 37.29(c)(2).

26, 1992 (eighteen months after enactment), that is used to provide specified public transportation be accessible to the disabled, including individuals in wheelchairs. Like all of Section 304, this section only applies to purchases or leases by a private entity that is primarily engaged in the business of transporting people and whose operations affect commerce. The section does not apply to the National Railroad Passenger Corporation (Amtrak), to other rail operations operated by public entities, or to commuter railroads as defined in Sections 103(8) and 103(9) of the Rail Passenger Service Act.[236] These entities are covered by Part II of Title II of the ADA.[237]

Rail as used in Section 304 has the same meaning as railroad as used in Section 202(e) of the Federal Railroad Safety Act of 1970.[238] Under this act, railroad means

> all forms of non-highway ground transportation that run on rails or electromagnetic guideways, including (1) commuter and other short-haul rail passenger service in a metropolitan or suburban area, as well as any commuter rail service which was operated by the Consolidated Rail Corporation as of January 1, 1974, and (2) high speed ground transportation systems that connect metropolitan areas, without regard to whether they use new technologies not associated with traditional railroads. Such term does not include rapid

---

[236] 45 USC §§ 502(8), 502(9). Section 502(8) defines commuter authority as

> any State, local, or regional authority, corporation, or other entity established for purposes of providing commuter service, and includes the Metropolitan Transportation Authority, the Connecticut Department of Transportation, the Maryland Department of Transportation, the Southeastern Pennsylvania Transportation Authority, the New Jersey Transit Corporation, the Massachusetts Bay Transit Authority, the Port Authority Trans-Hudson Corporation, any successor agencies, and any entity created by one or more such agencies for the purpose of operating, or contracting for the operation of, commuter service.

Section 502(9) defines commuter service as "short-haul rail passenger service operated in metropolitan and suburban areas, whether within or across the geographical boundaries of a State, usually characterized by reduced fare, multiple ride, and commutation tickets and by morning and evening peak period operations."

[237] See ADA §§ 241–246.
[238] 45 USC § 431(e). See ADA § 301(8).

transit operations within an urban area that are not connected to the general railroad system of transportation.[239]

For purposes of this section, readily accessible to and usable by individuals with disabilities, including individuals who use wheelchairs, refers to the ability of the disabled, including persons in wheelchairs, to enter into, exit from, and safely and effectively use the rail passenger car.[240] The legislation emphasizes the particular need to make rail passenger cars accessible to persons in wheelchairs "because of past misinterpretations of the nature and extent of obligations under section 504 of the Rehabilitation Act of 1973."[241] However, the requirements of accessibility and usability naturally go beyond just applying to persons in wheelchairs and, as is the case throughout the ADA, apply to persons with all types of disabilities.

The legislative history suggested that the Department of Transportation's regulations implementing Section 304(b)(6) might require new railroad cars to

> include non-slip surfaces and contrast edges on steps, as well as handrails in boarding areas, to make the car accessible to and usable by individuals with mobility impairments who do not use wheelchairs. In addition, the design might be required to include adequate illumination in boarding areas, tactile markings for identifying basic amenities and circulation needs, contrasting characters on signage, a public address system for audible announcements, and automatic door closing alarms to make the car accessible . . . and usable.[242]

If the car is used as a light or rapid rail vehicle, it must meet the requirements set out in the existing regulation at 49 CFR Sections 609.19 and 609.17, respectively, at least until new standards are issued by the Department of Transportation. If the car

---

[239] 45 USC 431(e).

[240] Report of the House Comm. on Energy and Commerce on the Americans With Disabilities Act of 1990, HR Rep. No. 485, 101st Cong., 2d Sess., pt. 4 (1990) (hereinafter cited as H. Comm. on Energy and Com. Rep.) at 44.

[241] Id.

[242] Id.

is used as an intercity rail passenger car, it must meet the requirements set out in proposed regulation 49 CFR Section 37.87. If the car is used as a commuter rail car, it must meet the standards in proposed regulation 49 CFR Section 37.89, until new standards are developed.[243] It appears that in developing new standards, the Department of Transportation will apply the same accessibility and usability criteria in connection with rail cars owned by private entities as it will with rail cars owned by public entities under Title II of the ADA.

The obligation to provide lift service to assist the disabled in boarding rail passenger cars applies not just to persons in wheelchairs, but also to other persons who have difficulty in walking. People who use crutches, canes, or other similar mobility aids should be permitted to use a lift to board the car.

Importantly, the obligation to ensure that a new rail passenger car be accessible and usable to the disabled is not meant to require the provision of a lift, ramp, or other equipment in any particular circumstance.[244] This is because of the great variety to be found in design among train stations; presumably such equipment would not work at all stations. What is required is some way of affording the disabled access to the rail passenger car from the boarding platform that works. Providing an on-board lift is encouraged, but not required.

[ii] Remanufactured. Section 304(b)(7), which takes effect on January 26, 1992 (eighteen months after the effective date of the ADA), requires that if a private entity covered by the section remanufactures a rail passenger car so as to extend its usable life for ten years or more, or purchases or leases such a rail passenger car, the rail passenger car must be readily accessible to and usable by disabled persons, including persons in wheelchairs, to the maximum extent feasible. If the car is not so accessible and usable, it constitutes discrimination.

"Remanufacture" is not defined in this section, but some meaning can be ascertained from the legislative history dealing

---

[243] See proposed Department of Transportation regulation 49 CFR 37.29(d).

[244] H. Comm. on Energy and Com. Rep. at 61, 44.

with this same term in connection with Section 222(c) of the ADA. The House Committee on Public Works and Transportation stated in connection with Section 222(c) that the term "means that the vehicle is stripped to its frame and rebuilt."[245]

The same principles that apply to the purchase or lease of new rail passenger cars under Section 304(b)(6) are applicable here as well, with one primary difference. A qualifying new rail passenger car must be fully accessible and usable. A remanufactured rail passenger car must be accessible and usable only to the maximum extent feasible. This difference recognizes that in an existing car there may be rare instances in which the structural nature of the car is such as to make it virtually impossible to renovate it in a manner that renders it fully accessible and usable by persons with disabilities.[246]

It may be considered feasible to remanufacture a rail car to make it accessible to and usable by individuals with disabilities unless an engineering analysis demonstrates that doing so would have a significant adverse effect on the structural integrity of the car.[247]

[iii] Exception: historical or antique. Sections 304(b)(2)(C) and 304(b)(7) require barrier removal in rail passenger cars where it is readily achievable and accessibility when remanufacturing certain of these cars. Compliance with these requirements in historical or antiquated rail passenger cars used in public transportation, though, could well destroy the special, unique historical features and aspects of these cars. "Historical or antiquated rail passenger car" as used in this section is defined in Section 304(c)(2). Three tests must be met to fit the definition:

1. The rail passenger car must be thirty years old or older at the time of its use for transporting individuals.

---

[245] H. Comm. on Pub. Works and Transp. Rep. at 28.

[246] See, for purposes of analogy, discussion of "to the maximum extent feasible" in connection with Section 303(a)(2), at supra ¶ 5.05.

[247] See, i.e., proposed Department of Transportation regulation 49 CFR § 37.29(e).

2. Its manufacturer must no longer be in the business of manufacturing rail passenger cars; the manufacturer may still be in business, just not in the business of manufacturing rail passenger cars.

3. The car must have a consequential association with events or persons significant to the past *or* the car must embody, or be in the process of being restored to embody, either the distinctive characteristics of a type of car used in the past or to represent a period that has passed.

Part of the third portion of the definition is somewhat vague. Arguments may develop over whether events with which a particular rail passenger car may have been associated in the past are truly "significant" to the past. The first rail car to cross the country is clearly associated with a significant event. It is less clear, however, that a rail car that merely carried passengers from Washington to New York on a regular basis forty years ago was associated with anything "significant." This may be a concept difficult to clarify even in regulations. One way to avoid the problem, though, is to make sure the car meets the alternative prong of the third test—that it embodies a rail car used in the past or a past era. Thus, if the rail car that went from Washington to New York forty years ago still contains its essential features and characteristics, it will meet the third part of the definition regardless of whether it was associated with any significant event.

Generally, rail passenger cars that qualify as historical or antiquated cars will be used now for educational purposes, tourist attractions, excursions, or charters. As stated by the House Committee on Energy and Commerce, which added the exception for historical or antiquated cars to the ADA

Under the definition, a car does not suddenly become "historical or antiquated" merely because, for example, one furnishes it with a piece of antique furniture or hangs an antique fixture in an otherwise unremarkable setting. The passengers riding on these cars are generally attracted to such transportation, as opposed to other modes of transportation, for the ambience and experience provided by the historical or antiquated characteristics of the cars. These are the type of rail passenger cars that are intended to fall within the exception to the legislation.[248]

Making some changes to a historical or antiquated rail passenger car for the convenience of modern day passengers does not automatically cause a car to lose its status as a historical or antiquated car:

> Thus, for example, the installation of kitchens meeting [Federal Railroad Administration] and [Occupational Safety and Health Administration] safety standards, or the presence of air conditioning and modern plumbing, would not prevent a car from qualifying for the exception if these amenities do not detract from the overall historical or antiquated character of the car.[249]

However:

> Though an exception for historical or antiquated cars is provided, operators of these rail passenger cars should still make cars that fit within the exception accessible to disabled persons to whatever extent feasible. If accommodations can be made or barriers removed that would not significantly interfere with or change the historical or antiquated characteristics of the cars, they should be done.[250]

Structural modifications to historical or antique rail cars that might be necessary to comply with these requirements could result in changes to the rail passenger cars that would prevent them from meeting Federal Railroad Administration safety and mechanical standards.[251] In recognition of this, and because of the unique situation presented by these cars with respect to accessibility, an exception was created to balance the ADA's aim of ensuring access to transportation for the disabled against the need and congressional desire to preserve the heritage embodied

---

[248] H. Comm. on Energy and Com. Rep. at 62.

[249] Id.

[250] Id.

[251] Id.

in historical and antiquated rail passenger cars.[252]

Section 304(c) provides, therefore, that if complying with the barrier removal or remanufacture requirements of the section

> would significantly alter the historic or antiquated character of a historical or antiquated rail passenger, or a rail station served exclusively by such cars, or would result in violation of any rule, regulation, standard, or order issued by the Secretary of Transportation under the Federal Railroad Safety Act of 1970,[253] such compliance shall not be required.

[2] Entities Not Primarily in the Business of Providing Transportation

Sections 302(b)(2)(B), 302(b)(2)(C), and 302(b)(2)(D) deal with specific prohibitions against discriminatory conduct by three types of transportation systems—fixed route systems, demand responsive systems, and over-the-road buses. Application in these sections is limited to systems operated by private entities where the operating entity is not primarily engaged in the business of transporting people. In other words, the sections apply to transportation systems that are operated as an incidental portion of the operator's business—such as an airport shuttle service operated by a hotel, a limousine made available by a hotel, a shuttle bus service operated by a shopping center for its customers or by a private company for its employees, and the shuttle operations of recreational facilities, such as stadiums, zoos, amusement parks, and ski resorts.[254]

Sections 302(b)(2)(B), 302(b)(2)(C), and 302(b)(2)(D) do not cover private bus companies, taxicab companies, or other entities whose primary business is transporting people. Discrimination by these entities is prohibited instead by Section 304. Sections 302(b)(2)(B), 302(b)(2)(C), and 302(b)(2)(D) also do

---

[252] Id. at 61, 62.

[253] 45 USC 421 et seq.

[254] H. Comm. on Pub. Works and Transp. Rep. at 38.

not apply to transportation systems operated by public entities,[255] to public intercity rail service provided by Amtrak, or to commuter rail service.[256]

The sections apply to the purchase or lease of vehicles. Vehicle for purposes of Title III is defined only in the negative. It does not include a rail passenger car, railroad locomotive, railroad freight car, railroad caboose, intercity rail car, commuter rail car, or a railroad car covered elsewhere in Title III.[257]

Covered vehicles are subject to the Department of Justice regulations, and also to the more specifically directed Department of Transportation regulations.[258]

The section speaks in terms of requiring vehicles to be accessible to and usable by individuals with disabilities, including individuals who use wheelchairs. Until it issues permanent standards, the Department of Transportation's proposed regulations implementing these sections provide some guidance on what this entails, with three requirements:

1. The vehicle must meet the requirements set out in existing regulation 49 C.F.R. 609.15(d)(i), a provision originally issued in connection with the Urban Mass Transit Administration.

2. The vehicle shall be equipped with a lift or other level-change mechanism and shall have sufficient clearances to permit an individual using a wheelchair or other mobility device to reach a securement location.

3. There shall be at least one securement location on the vehicle. The securement device(s) at the securement location shall be sufficient to secure any wheelchair or other mobility device which the vehicle's lift and clearances permit to enter the vehicle and proceed to the securement location.[259]

---

[255] See ADA § 201(1).

[256] See Subtitle B, Part II, Title II of the ADA.

[257] See ADA § 301(11).

[258] See 28 CFR § 36.310.

[259] See proposed Department of Transportation regulation 49 CFR § 37.31. This interim regulation may conflict with limitations on what interim regulations can require—as set forth in Section 306(a)(2).

Further standards in this area may be issued by the Department of Transportation as part of its final regulations.

The sections contain varying standards based upon the seating capacity of a vehicle. Seating requirements will likely mean the capacity of the vehicle prior to any modifications made for accessibility reasons. In other words, if a van can be ordered from the manufacturer with over sixteen seats, it is considered as having a seating capacity in excess of sixteen persons even if after being modified to include a lift and wheelchair securement positions it can only carry less than sixteen passengers at one time.

[a] Fixed Route Systems

A "fixed route system" of transportation is defined in Section 301(4) as a system of providing transportation of individuals, other than by aircraft, on which a vehicle is operated along a prescribed route according to a fixed schedule. No advance reservation is necessary to guarantee service. As indicated above, the operator of this system must be a private entity for Title III to apply.

Under Section 302(b)(2)(B), it is considered discrimination for a private entity that operates a fixed route system to purchase or lease a vehicle with a seating capacity in excess of sixteen passengers (including the driver) for use on such system, for which a solicitation is made after the thirtieth day following the July 26, 1990, enactment of the ADA, if the vehicle is not readily accessible to and usable by individuals with disabilities, including individuals who use wheelchairs.

If the vehicle has more than sixteen seats, it must be built so as to afford equal access to the disabled. This could be accomplished by the inclusion of hydraulic lifts for wheelchairs, wide aisles and doors, and the like. It should be noted that this provision applies only to purchases for which the solicitation is made thirty days after the effective date. It does not apply to vehicles that are ordered before this time and delivered after the effective date, or to vehicles purchased after this date but for which the solicitation went out prior to the date.

If such a private entity purchases or leases a vehicle after July 26, 1990, that has a seating capacity of sixteen passengers or fewer (including the driver) that is not readily accessible to or usable by the disabled, the entity is guilty of discrimination only if its fixed route system, when viewed in its entirety, does not ensure a level of service to the disabled, including persons in wheelchairs, that is equivalent to the level of service provided to the nondisabled.

For vehicles with a seating capacity of less than sixteen passengers or fewer, the key date is the July 26, 1990, effective date of the ADA. There is no thirty-day grace period or solicitation period as is included for vehicles carrying over sixteen passengers. If such a smaller vehicle is purchased or leased the day after the effective date and is not accessible to the disabled, the "viewed-in-its-entirety" test applies.

According to the legislative history, in considering leases or purchases of vehicles with sixteen seats or less that are not accessible to the disabled, the standard of a "system viewed in its entirety providing an equivalent level of service" is met when an operator has, or has access to, a vehicle (including a vehicle operated in conjunction with a portable boarding assistance device) that is readily accessible to and usable by individuals with disabilities to meet the needs of such individuals on an "on-call" basis. Essentially, when all aspects of the system are analyzed, an individual with a disability must have an equivalent opportunity to use the system. [260]

For example, if a hotel that operates a fixed route airport shuttle does not need a vehicle with more than sixteen seats, it may still purchase one with sixteen seats or fewer that is not accessible to the disabled. The hotel, however, must make alternative equivalent arrangements for transporting the disabled who cannot board this vehicle. It may own another vehicle that is disabled-accessible that it can use to transport the disabled, it may make arrangements with another hotel or entity that has an accessible vehicle for that hotel to transport the disabled, it may borrow an accessible vehicle as needed, or it may use a portable

---

[260] H. Comm. on Pub. Works and Transp. Rep. at 38.

boarding assistance device to make an otherwise inaccessible vehicle accessible to the disabled. If the hotel makes these arrangements, its system, when viewed in its entirety, would afford equal service to the disabled.

The Department of Transportation's proposed regulations provide some interim guidance by stating that "equivalent service" in this context means that service that is available to the disabled, including persons in wheelchairs, must be provided in the most integrated setting feasible and must be equivalent to service provided other individuals with respect to schedules/headways, fares, geographic area of service, hours and days of service, availability of information, and any constraints on capacity or service availability.[261]

[b] Demand Responsive Systems

Section 302(b)(2)(C) applies to a demand responsive system operated by a private entity. A demand responsive system is any system, including one that provides transportation by request of the user, that provides transportation of individuals by a vehicle, and that is not a fixed route system. As with Section 302(b)(2)(B), Section 302(b)(2)(C) only applies to the operator of a demand responsive system that is not primarily in the business of providing transportation for people.

Generally, if a private system, such as a hotel's airport shuttle service, operates on a preset schedule, it will be considered a fixed route system. If it operates by request — that is, if the shuttle only runs when a guest needs to use it — then the system is a demand responsive one.

Like Section 302(b)(2)(B), Section 302(b)(2)(C) labels discriminatory a demand responsive system that purchases or leases a nonaccessible vehicle with seats for more than sixteen passengers for which solicitations are made after the thirtieth day following the ADA's July 26, 1990, enactment. There is, however, one key difference. A demand responsive system may properly purchase a nonaccessible vehicle with more than six-

---

[261] See proposed Department of Transportation regulation 49 CFR § 37.29(a)(2).

teen seats if it can demonstrate that the system, when viewed in its entirety, provides a level of service to the disabled equivalent to that provided persons without disabilities. The system may purchase and use large-seating vehicles that are not disabled-accessible as long as it has alternative means of transporting the disabled by accessible transportation or if it uses a boarding assistance device to enable persons with mobility impairments to access the otherwise inaccessible vehicle.

The Department of Transportation's proposed regulations provide some interim guidance by stating that equivalent service in this context means that service that is available to the disabled, including those in wheelchairs, must be provided in the most integrated setting feasible, and must be equivalent to service provided other individuals with respect to response time, fares, geographic area of service, hours and days of service, availability of information, and reservations capability, and any constraints on capacity or service availability.[262]

Even if a demand responsive system makes sure that vehicles it purchases or leases that have more than sixteen seats are accessible to the disabled, Section 302(b)(2)(C) still mandates (unlike Section 302(b)(2)(B) in a fixed route system) that the system when viewed in its entirety provide the disabled with a level of service equal to that offered to the nondisabled. A failure to do so would be discrimination.

This rule applies regardless of the number of seats in a particular vehicle purchased or leased by a demand responsive system. Because of this, a system may purchase an individual vehicle with less than sixteen seats that is not accessible, but only if the system overall still provides service to the disabled equivalent to service provided to the nondisabled.

[c] Exception: Over-the-Road Buses

Section 302(b)(2)(D) provides an exception for over-the-road buses operated by an entity not primarily in the business of providing transportation to people from the requirements of

---

[262] See proposed Department of Transportation regulation 49 CFR § 37.29(a)(3).

Sections 302(b)(2)(B) and 302(b)(2)(C). An over-the-road bus is a bus characterized by an elevated passenger deck located over a baggage compartment.[263] Most of the buses typically used in intercity, charter, or tour service would be considered over-the-road buses.

These over-the-road buses—as well as over-the-road buses operated by entities whose primary business is transporting people—will be subject to regulations promulgated by the Secretary of Transportation to ensure accessibility of the buses.[264] The permanent regulations will take into account the results of a detailed study of ways to promote accessibility in over-the-road buses to be conducted by the OTA.[265] Failure of an over-the-road bus to comply with the regulations issued will constitute discrimination.

[3] Regulations

[a] Over-the-Road Buses

Under the ADA, private entities that provide over-the-road bus service either as their primary business[266] or as something other than their primary business[267] must make the buses accessible to the disabled. This requirement goes into effect eighteen months after the July 26, 1990, enactment of the ADA. As defined in Section 301(5), an over-the-road bus is a bus "characterized by an elevated passenger deck located over a baggage compartment"—usually the type of bus associated with intercity transport.

Ways that were suggested to Congress by which over-the-road buses could be made accessible, particularly to individuals in wheelchairs, included wheelchair lifts and other boarding assistance devices. The cost and reliability of these devices was sufficiently disputed by some witnesses testifying at hearings on

---

[263] See ADA § 301(5).

[264] See ADA § 306(a).

[265] For discussion of the regulations and study, see infra § 5.06[3].

[266] See ADA § 304, particularly § 304(b)(4).

[267] See ADA § 302, particularly § 304(b)(2)(D)(ii).

the legislation, though, that Congress decided not to mandate the use of these or other specific devices in the ADA at the time of the ADA's passage.[268] Instead, it required that a comprehensive study be undertaken on the issue, with binding regulations to follow based on the results of the study.

[i] **The study.** Congressman Glenn Anderson, chairman of the House Public Works and Transportation Committee, the committee that added the study to the legislation, stated that "[b]ecause of the unique nature of their construction and the uncertain financial stability of the intercity bus industry, over-the-road buses will be subject to a special 3-year study to determine a method for making them accessible."[269] The OTA—an arm of Congress created to conduct research for Congress—was designated to conduct a study to determine the access needs of individuals with disabilities to over-the-road buses and over-the-road bus service and the most cost effective methods for providing access to the disabled, particularly those who use wheelchairs.

Different methods for providing access—such as wheelchair lifts—will be considered and evaluated for their effectiveness, cost, and practicality. Congressman John Paul Hammerschmidt, the ranking member of the House Public Works and Transportation Committee, stated as follows about the study:

[T]he OTA study is intended to be an objective analysis of the access needs of the disabled and cost-effective methods of providing accessibility to over-the-road buses. The study is needed in order to address questions which remain unanswered regarding accessibility to over-the-road buses. Very little experience exists currently with wheelchair lifts and other boarding assistance devices on over-the-road buses. Where lifts are in operation, use has been minimal. Most current lifts on over-the-road buses pose problems in terms of safety, compactness, reliability, and cost. Because of the

---

[268] H. Comm. on Pub. Works and Transp. Rep. at 41.

[269] 136 Cong. Rec. at H2436 (May 17, 1990) (Statement of Cong. Glenn Anderson).

high platform of an over-the-road bus, as opposed to a transit type bus, a lift must move to a greater height, posing both engineering and safety concerns. In addition, most lifts also take up substantial package express and passenger seating space, which impact revenues. The use of boarding chairs and ramps poses some problems in terms of portability and logistics. Some bus companies are meeting accessibility needs for their disabled passengers with a boarding chair and ramp system at the present time. I would expect that an analysis of the success of this method would be an important part of the study since it will be able to be reviewed in an actual service environment. In light of these facts, a thorough study of all methods of providing accessibility is necessary.[270]

The results of the study must be given to Congress and the president by July 26, 1993, three years after the enactment of the ADA. Recommendations for the best methods of promoting access to over-the-road buses and over-the-road bus service, as well as any policy options for legislative changes or additions, are to be included in the final product. The ATBCB will have an opportunity to comment on preliminary versions of the study, and any comments it has thereon must be included in the final version submitted to Congress and the president as long as the ATBCB's comments are given within 120 days of its receipt of the draft study from the OTA.

Section 305 lists several issues that the study must analyze, though this list is not meant to be all-inclusive.[271] These issues include the following:

1. The anticipated demand by the disabled for accessible over-the-road buses and over-the-road bus service.
2. The degree to which over-the-road buses and over-the-road bus service, including any service required under temporary regulations issued by the Secretary of Transportation, are readily accessible to and usable by the disabled.

---

[270] 136 Cong. Rec. at H2447 (May 17, 1990) (Statement of Cong. J.P. Hammerschmidt).

[271] H. Comm. on Pub. Works and Transp. Rep. at 41.

3. The effectiveness of various methods of providing accessibility to over-the-road buses and over-the-road bus service to the disabled. All types of methods—such as the use of boarding chairs, ramps, wheelchair lifts, and other boarding assistance devices—should be analyzed, including those that will and those that will not involve physical lifting.[272]

4. The cost of providing accessible over-the-road buses and bus service to the disabled, including consideration of recent technological and cost-saving developments in equipment and devices. Included in this should be an examination of alternative designs and technologies for both lifts and buses that may be developed to enable the disabled to board and exit buses without being carried.[273]

5. Possible design changes in over-the-road buses that could enhance accessibility, or better accommodate accessibility equipment, including the installation of accessible restrooms that do not result in a loss of seating capacity. Seating capacity as used here means a reduction in the number of seats on a bus in which passengers can ride comfortably; if a seat was reduced in size to accommodate a restroom, that seat would have to be capable of carrying a passenger as comfortably as an existing full-sized seat in order to avoid a finding of a loss in seating capacity.[274]

6. The impact of accessibility requirements on the continuation of over-the-road bus service, with particular consideration of the impact of such requirements on over-the-road bus service to rural communities.

This last item is a recognition that economic pressures on the bus industry have led to a reduction in service, particularly to the rural United States where many communities are not served by any other form of intercity public transportation. Congress does not want the ADA and the requirements of accessibility to cause over-the-road bus service to rural communities to deteriorate further. It does not want bus operators to be forced to

---

[272] Id.

[273] H. Comm. on Educ. and Lab. Rep. at 123.

[274] H. Comm. on Pub. Works and Transp. Rep. at 41.

eliminate service to some rural communities because of the cost or other difficulties of providing accessible transportation. The OTA study should analyze how the ADA can be complied with by bus operators without hurting service to rural communities and should make any appropriate policy recommendations.[275] The study should also go beyond this and look at how various methods of providing accessibility will impact on the intercity bus industry's ability to continue service to all communities given the economic history of the industry, passenger demographics, competition both in- and outside the industry, and future economic projections.[276]

The study could also examine current policies that make it difficult for private tour and charter operators that do not have accessible buses to borrow accessible buses from public entities that have them, as well as ways that intracity bus service providers of accessible bus service can link up with intercity providers to form "hub" arrangements where passengers are funneled from one provider of accessible services to another.[277]

The OTA is directed to establish an advisory committee to assist it with the study, though no specific duties of the advisory committee are set out in either the statute or the legislative history. The advisory committee will have members representing

1. Private operators and manufacturers of over-the-road buses
2. Disabled individuals (particularly ones in wheelchairs) who are potential users of the buses
3. Persons with technical knowledge and expertise in areas to be examined by the study (including manufacturers of boarding assistance equipment and devices)

The ADA does not set a size for this committee, but it does require that however many persons are appointed, the members

---

[275] H. Comm. on Educ. and Lab. Rep. at 123; S. Comm. on Lab. and Hum. Resources Rep. at 74.

[276] H. Comm. on Pub. Works and Transp. Rep. at 42.

[277] H. Comm. on Educ. and Lab. Rep. at 123; S. Comm. on Lab. and Hum. Resources Rep. at 74, 75.

representing the first two categories be equal to each other in number, and greater in aggregate number than the members appointed to represent the third category.

[ii] **Regulations.** By no later than July 26, 1991, the Secretary of Transportation is directed by Section 306(a)(2) to issue interim, temporary regulations to carry out the ADA's mandates that over-the-road bus service, by both operators whose primary business is transporting people and operators whose primary business is not transporting people, be accessible to the disabled.[278] These interim regulations will provide guidance for compliance with the ADA by over-the-road buses while affording time for the OTA study discussed earlier to be conducted, on which permanent regulations will be subsequently issued and based. There are two things that the statute prevents these interim regulations from requiring, however:

1. They cannot require that any structural changes be made to the buses in order to provide access to individuals in wheelchairs; and
2. They cannot require that boarding assistance devices, such as lifts, be purchased by bus operators to provide access.

While the interim regulations are in effect, therefore, it will not be considered discrimination for a private entity to purchase or lease an over-the-road bus that is not equipped with a wheelchair lift or that is not accompanied by a boarding chair and/or ramp. Naturally, however, the ADA does not prevent the entity from using or installing these devices anyway during the interim period.

The regulations can require additions to buses that do not involve structural changes or boarding assistance devices, though—additions such as the installation of nonskid strips on stairs, or special placement of grab bars. The failure of a private over-the-road bus operator to comply with the interim regulations during their applicability will constitute discrimination.

These interim regulations will remain in effect until perma-

---

[278] By August 9, 1991, however, these regulations had not been issued.

nent regulations to be issued subsequently by the Secretary of Transportation take effect, either six or seven years after the July 26, 1990, enactment of the ADA.[279]

The statute prevents the interim regulations from requiring that any structural changes be made to the buses in order to provide access to individuals who use wheelchairs, though, and may not require the operating entity to purchase a boarding assistance device to provide access to individuals in wheelchairs. Interim regulations could permissibly require the vehicle operator to provide employees to assist carrying an individual in a wheelchair onto an over-the-road bus. Additionally, they could require that drivers be trained to assist hearing- and sight-disabled persons in knowing when to disembark.

Once the results and recommendations from the OTA study have been received, the Secretary of Transportation is to develop permanent regulations to require better full access to over-the-road buses operated by private entities. Section 306(a)(2)(B)(ii) requires the secretary to issue these permanent regulations within one year after receiving the OTA study (and, as previously noted, this study must be completed by July 26, 1993). Taking into account the study's results and recommendations, the permanent regulations will require private entities that use an over-the-road bus to provide transportation that is accessible to the disabled, including individuals who use wheelchairs. The means by which the private entities must do this will in part come from the recommendations of the OTA study. A failure to comply with the permanent regulations will constitute discrimination.

When these permanent regulations take effect depends upon the size of the provider of transportation. For a smaller provider of transportation—and who qualifies as a small provider is to be determined by the Secretary of Transportation and

---

[279] The Senate-passed version of the ADA simply required that over-the-road buses be disabled-accessible by six or seven years after enactment. The House amendment included in the final legislation deleted this and required instead that purchases and leases of new over-the-road buses comply with specific regulations dealing with over-the-road buses to be issued by the Secretary of Transportation.

included in the regulations[280] — the regulations take effect seven years after enactment of the ADA, or on July 26, 1997. For other providers of transportation, July 26, 1996, six years after enactment, is the effective date. The additional year for small providers is in recognition of the increased burden that accessibility requirements could impose on operators with smaller fleets.[281]

Note that the effective dates for the regulations are not dependent on when the permanent regulations are completed by the Secretary of Transportation. Even if the OTA study is completed in twelve months instead of the thirty-six months allocated by the ADA, and even if the secretary then issues permanent regulations six months later instead of the allotted one year, the regulations will not take effect until either six or seven years after the ADA's enactment.

There could be one possible change to the effective dates for the permanent regulations. If the president determines that compliance with these regulations by the six- and seven-year deadlines included in the statute will result in a significant reduction in intercity over-the-road bus service, the president shall (not may) extend each deadline by one year.

The permanent regulations are not subject to the limitations of the temporary rules. The only statutory limitation on the permanent regulations is that these regulations cannot require the installation of accessible restrooms in over-the-road buses if the installation would result in a loss of seating capacity.[282] As used here, seating capacity refers to a reduction in the number of seats in which passengers can ride *comfortably*.[283]

As technology develops, however, that would allow installation of accessible restrooms without significant loss of seating, the Secretary of Transportation's regulations should require their installation.[284]

---

[280] The Secretary may permissibly define a small provider by using ICC class definitions in effect at the time of enactment of the ADA; see H. Comm. on Pub. Works and Transp. Rep. at 43.

[281] H. Comm. on Pub. Works and Transp. Rep. at 43.

[282] ADA § 306(a)(3).

[283] H. Comm. on Pub. Works and Transp. Rep. at 43.

[284] H. Comm. on Educ. and Lab. Rep. at 122.

Lifts or ramps, and fold-up seats or other wheelchair spaces with appropriate securement devices, are examples of currently available aids that can help make over-the-road buses accessible to the disabled.[285] In the House Committee on Education and Labor report, the committee stated that it does not intend for the regulations to spell out for each vehicle operator how many wheelchair or other mobility-aid spaces their vehicles must have, provided that at least some spaces on each vehicle purchased or leased after the effective date are accessible to individuals in wheelchairs or mobility-aids. The committee wanted this determination to be left up to the vehicle operator and be based upon a consideration of factors including the number of vehicles in the operator's fleet, seat vacancy rate, and usage by people with disabilities. The regulations issued by the Secretary of Transportation would help provide guidance on technical points, such as the size of a wheelchair space and specifications for lifts, ramps, securement devices, and the like.[286]

The regulations must include standards, or specifications, applicable to over-the-road buses. These standards must be consistent with the ADAAG issued by the ATBCB under Section 504 of the ADA.

[b] Other Transportation

Sections 302(b)(2)(B) and 302(b)(2)(C) deal with accessibility of vehicles operated by private entities that are not primarily in the business of providing transportation to people, in a fixed route system and a demand responsive system, respectively. Both sections took effect upon the July 26, 1990, enactment of the ADA.

Section 304 deals with accessibility of vehicles and rail passenger cars operated by private entities that are primarily in the business of providing transportation to people, without regard to the type of system in which the vehicles and rail passenger cars are used.

Congress intended for the regulations implementing these

---

[285] Id.

[286] Id.

sections to be issued by the Department of Transportation within one year of the ADA's enactment, by July 26, 1991. Just in case the regulations were not timely issued, though (and they were not), Congress wanted entities to have a point of reference to ensure that they were in compliance with the ADA until the regulations were issued.[287] This would also be of assistance in the interim period to entities covered by Sections 302(b)(2)(B), 302(b)(2)(C), and 304(b)(3), since these sections took effect on the July 26, 1990, enactment date.

Section 306(d) provides, therefore, that with respect to vehicles and rail passenger cars, a private entity will be considered to be in compliance with Title III's accessibility requirements if the design for the vehicle or rail car complies with the laws and regulations governing accessibility of such vehicles and cars—including the ATBCB's minimum guidelines and requirements in existence at the time of the ADA's enactment as well as its ADAAG issued pursuant to the ADA—to the extent that such laws and regulations are not inconsistent with Title III and are in effect at the time the vehicle or rail car design is substantially completed.

Reference is not made for compliance purposes here to the UFAS because the UFAS does not and is not contemplated to contain standards applicable to vehicle and rail passenger cars.[288]

¶ 5.07 ENFORCEMENT

[1] Private Rights of Action

The procedures for enforcing the ADA are set forth in Section 308. Section 308(a)(1) incorporates by reference the remedies and procedures available under Section 204(a) of Title II of the Civil Rights Act of 1964,[289] legislation that prohibits discrimina-

---

[287] H. Comm. on Educ. and Lab. Rep. at 125.

[288] H. Comm. on Energy and Com. Rep. at 63.

[289] 42 USC § 2000a-3(a).

tion in public accommodations on account of race, color, religion, or national origin. Section 204(a) reads as follows:

> Whenever any person has engaged or there are reasonable grounds to believe that any person is about to engage in any act or practice prohibited by section 203 [42 USC Section 2000a-2], a civil action for preventive relief, including an application for a permanent or temporary injunction, restraining order, or other order, may be instituted by the person aggrieved and, upon timely application, the court may, in its discretion, permit the Attorney General to intervene in such civil action if he certifies that the case is of general public importance. Upon application by the complainant and in such circumstances as the court may deem just, the court may appoint an attorney for such complainant and may authorize the commencement of the civil action without the payment of fees, costs or security.

Accordingly, a private civil action for *preventive relief* that can be brought under this provision of the Civil Rights Act, including an application for a permanent or temporary injunction, restraining order, or other order, is all that is permitted by Section 308(a)(1) of the ADA. Remedies in a private suit brought under Title III are limited to equitable relief.[290] Additionally, with court approval, the Attorney General may intervene in a case of general importance brought by a private plaintiff under the ADA because this is permitted under Section 204(a) of the Civil Rights Act.

Compensatory damages, including damages for emotional distress, and punitive damages are not permitted under Section 204(a) of the Civil Rights Act[291] and are not, therefore, recoverable by private plaintiffs under Title III of the ADA.

Likewise, no jury trial is permitted in an action under Section 204(a) of the Civil Rights Act because only injunctive relief

---

[290] 136 Cong. Rec. at H2439 (May 17, 1990) (Statement of Cong. Don Edwards, chairman of the House Judiciary Committee Subcommittee on Civil and Constitutional Rights).

[291] See, e.g., Newman v. Piggie Park Enters., Inc., 390 US 400 (1968); Lyle v. Village of Golden Valley, 310 F. Supp. 852 (D. Minn. 1970).

is available,[292] and no jury trial is consequently available in an action under Title III.

Attorney fees, including litigation expenses, and costs may be awarded to a prevailing party (other than the federal government), pursuant to Section 505 of the ADA. Consistent with the U.S. Supreme Court's holding in *Christianburg Garment Co. v. EEOC*,[293] courts and agencies shall not assess fees against a plaintiff or charging party unless it finds the claim to be frivolous.[294] Similarly, plaintiffs or charging parties should not be assessed the cost of experts, paralegals, or the like, unless the claim is groundless.[295]

Attorney fees are similarly permitted by Section 204(b) of the Civil Rights Act to encourage individuals injured by racial discrimination to seek judicial relief under the public accommodations provisions of Section 204(a). In cases brought to enforce Section 204(a), courts have said that in the absence of special circumstances that would render an award unjust, attorney fees should normally be awarded by the court to a successful plaintiff, payable by the losing defendant.[296]

It is intended that persons with disabilities have remedies and procedures available to them parallel to those available under comparable civil rights laws.[297] If Section 204(a) of the Civil Rights Act is amended to change the remedies or procedures available to persons discriminated against because of race, color, religion, or national origin, therefore, the change will affect the remedies or procedures available to the disabled under the ADA identically.[298]

---

[292] See, e.g., Adams v. Fazzio Real Estate Co., 268 F. Supp. 630 (ED La. 1967), aff'd, 396 F2d 146 (5th Cir. 1968).

[293] Christianburg Garment Co. v. EEOC, 434 US 412 (1978).

[294] H. Comm. on Educ. and Lab. Rep. at 140.

[295] Id.

[296] See, e.g., Newman v. Piggie Park Enters., Inc., 390 US 400 (1968); Wooten v. Moore, 400 F2d 239 (4th Cir. 1968), cert. denied, 393 US 1083 (1969); Evans v. Seaman, 452 F2d 749 (5th Cir. 1971), cert. denied, 408 US 924 (1972).

[297] H. Comm. on Jud. Rep. at 66.

[298] Id.

Section 308(a)(1) of the ADA makes the remedies and procedures of Section 204(a) of the Civil Rights Act available to two classes of people:

1. Any person who is subjected to discrimination on the basis of disability in violation of any part of Title III of the ADA

2. Any person who has reasonable grounds for believing that such person is about to be subjected to discrimination in violation of Section 303 of the ADA's provisions concerning new construction and alterations[299]

This could include a situation where a blueprint for new construction indicates that the new building will not be accessible to the disabled. Grounds would exist for a private action by the disabled alleging that they are "about to be" discriminated against because the building, when erected, will violate the ADA.[300]

Section 309(a)(1) of the ADA also states that nothing in Section 308 requires a person with a disability to engage in a futile gesture as a prerequisite to using the enforcement remedies and procedures available if that person has actual notice that a person or organization covered by Title III does not intend to comply with Title III's provisions. If an individual is about to be subjected to discrimination, the individual need not perform a useless action to confirm the discrimination before being able to file suit.[301]

Where a private person is discriminated against because of a disability, and the discrimination is a violation of either Section 302(b)(2)(A)(iv) (failure of a public accommodation to

---

[299] The original Senate-passed bill used the word "individual," not "person." The House-passed version, and the final legislation, used the word "person" because this word is what is used in Title II of the Civil Rights Act. See House Conf. Rep. No. 596, 101st Cong., 2d Sess. (1990), Conf. Rep. on S. 933, Americans With Disabilities Act of 1990, Joint Explanatory Statement of the Committee of Conference at ¶ 59(a).

[300] 136 Cong. Rec. at H2634 (May 22, 1990) (Statement of Cong. Patricia Schroeder).

[301] 136 Cong. Rec. at H2624 (May 22, 1990) (Statement of Cong. Hamilton Fish).

remove architectural and communication barriers) or Section 303(a) (failure of a public accommodation or commercial facility to make either new construction or alterations accessible), and where injunctive relief is granted by a court, the injunctive relief must include an order to alter the nonaccessible facility to make it readily accessible to and usable by individuals with disabilities to the extent required by Title III.[302]

Where appropriate, when injunctive relief is granted for a violation of Title III, it shall also require the provision of an auxiliary aid or service, modification of a policy, or provision of alternative methods to the extent required by Title III.

[2] Attorney General Right of Action

[a] Obligations

In addition to providing remedies to private persons, the ADA gives authority to enforce Title III to the Attorney General, in Section 308(b). In general, the Attorney General's primary obligations are threefold.

First, the Attorney General is to investigate alleged violations of Title III and to undertake periodic reviews of the compliance of entities covered by Title III, Section 308(b)(1)(A)(i). If there is reasonable cause to believe Title III is being violated, the Attorney General may file suit if necessary, as discussed later.

Second, the Attorney General may certify that a state law or local building code or similar ordinance that establishes accessibility requirements meets or exceeds the minimum requirements of the ADA for accessibility and usability of facilities covered by Title III. This certification of equivalency may be given after a state or local government files an application for it with the Assistant Attorney General for Civil Rights or his designee, following procedures set out in the Department of Justice's regulations.[303] Prior notice of a pending determination must be given in the Federal Register and a public hearing held at which

---

[302] See ADA § 308(a)(2).

[303] See Department of Justice regulations 28 CFR §§ 36.601–36.608.

persons, including the disabled, are provided an opportunity to testify against such certification. The hearing shall be held before an official of the Department of Justice, not before an administrative law judge,[304] and this certification is to be made by the Attorney General (the statute refers to the Attorney General, while the regulations empower the Assistant Attorney General for Civil Rights or his designee to issue the certification) in consultation with the ATBCB. The Department of Justice's regulations provide for the Assistant Attorney General for Civil Rights to make a preliminary determination of ADA-equivalency for a particular law or code, and then to hold a public hearing at least sixty days later.[305]

If certification is issued, it shall constitute rebuttable evidence that the state law or local ordinance in question does meet or exceed the minimum requirements of the ADA.[306] Under the statute, the Attorney General may establish priorities for considering requests for certification (though the proposed regulations do not do so), such as considering state laws before local laws, or considering laws first that incorporate model building codes that have already been approved for the ADA.[307] The certification provision is not intended in any way to permit any entities to avoid the purposes of the ADA; rather, it "is intended simply to allow builders and architects to use codes and laws with which they are familiar, if those laws, in fact, meet or exceed the requirements of this Act."[308]

A certification is only considered a certification of ADA-equivalency with respect to those features that are both covered by the code certified and addressed by the standards (Department of Justice regulations or ATBCB ADAAG) against which equivalency is measured. If a certified code is amended after

---

[304] H. Comm. on Jud. Rep. at 67.

[305] See Department of Justice regulation 28 CFR § 36.605(a).

[306] See Section 308(b)(1)(A)(i). Certification is not to be considered rulemaking for purposes of the Administrative Procedure Act, 5 USC § 551 et seq. If the minimum requirements are not met, certification will be denied.

[307] H. Comm. on Jud. Rep. at 67; H. Comm. on Educ. and Lab. Rep. at 127.

[308] H. Comm. on Educ. and Lab. Rep. at 126.

certification, the amendments are not considered part of the certification. [309]

Third, the Attorney General may institute court action against persons engaged in a pattern or practice of discrimination or resistance to the full enjoyment of rights granted by Title III, or when a person or group of persons has been discriminated against under Title III and such discrimination raises an issue of general public importance. [310] The Attorney General must have reasonable cause to believe that a violation of Title III has occurred before a suit can be brought. The obligation to initiate a court case, however, is discretionary rather than mandatory— the statute uses the words "may commence a civil action," not "shall commence." Because of this, nothing prevents the Attorney General from attempting to end discrimination informally, without filing suit.

[b] Authority of the Court

If an action is initiated by the Attorney General, jurisdiction lies in the appropriate U.S. district court. In such an action, the federal district court is given authority to grant three primary types of relief by Section 308(b)(2).

First, equitable relief, including: injunctive relief, providing an auxiliary aid or service, modification of policy, practice or procedure, or alternative method, and making facilities readily accessible to and usable by individuals with disabilities may be granted.

Second, other appropriate relief, including awarding monetary damages to the aggrieved persons when so requested by the Attorney General, may also be granted. The court, however, does not have the authority to award monetary damages if the Attorney General has not requested them. [311] If requested, the type of monetary damages that can be awarded include all forms of compensatory damages, including out-of-pocket expenses

---

[309] See Department of Justice regulation 28 CFR § 36.607.

[310] See ADA § 308(b)(1)(B).

[311] H. Comm. on Jud. Rep. at 68.

and damages for pain and suffering.[312] In addition to having the discretion to decide whether to seek monetary damages for private parties at all, the Attorney General has the discretion to decide exactly what type of damages to seek, and only those sought can be awarded.[313] Importantly, neither the monetary damages that can be awarded by the court in response to an Attorney General request, nor the "other relief" that the court can fashion, can include punitive damages, which are not permitted in a suit brought by the Attorney General.[314]

Third, a civil penalty may be awarded of up to $50,000 for a first violation and up to $100,000 for any subsequent violation. The penalty is assessed in order to vindicate the public interest against the entity that violated the ADA. These penalties are not meant to be imposed automatically in every case.[315] In considering whether to impose a penalty and in what amount, the court must give consideration to any good faith effort or attempt by the violating entity to comply with the ADA. As part of its evaluation of what constitutes good faith, the court must consider, among other factors it deems relevant, whether the violating entity could have reasonably anticipated the need for an appropriate type of auxiliary aid needed to accommodate the unique needs of a particular individual with a disability.

Substantial guidance to the courts on applying the good faith standard here is supplied by the House Committee on Education and Labor:

> The "good faith" standard referred to in this section is not intended to imply a willful or intentional standard—that is, an entity cannot demonstrate good faith simply by showing that it did not willfully, intentionally, or recklessly disregard the law. At the same time, the absence of such a course of conduct would be a factor a court should weigh in determining the existence of good faith.

---

[312] Id.; H. Comm. on Educ. and Lab. Rep. at 127. Compare to private rights of action, where monetary damages cannot be awarded.

[313] H. Comm. on Educ. and Lab. Rep. at 127; S. Comm. on Lab. and Hum. Resources Rep. at 77.

[314] See ADA § 308(b)(4).

[315] H. Comm. on Jud. Rep. at 68.

The "good faith" standard is a standard that should be seriously applied to protect from the assessment of civil penalties, as well as from the assessment of maximum civil penalties, those entities that have honestly and reasonably attempted to comply with the law. For example, a public accommodation is not required to anticipate all of the auxiliary aids that might be necessary to accommodate an individual with a unique disability. While, of course, a public accommodation is expected to anticipate such disabilities as visual, speech, hearing and mobility impairments, the Committee does not, as reflected in the statutory language, expect that civil penalties will be assessed against entities that reasonably and honestly could not have anticipated the unique needs of individuals with certain types of unusual disabilities and therefore may not have had some appropriate auxiliary aid at hand. Of course, once an individual has identified and requested a specific auxiliary aid, the public accommodation cannot subsequently claim that the aid could not have been reasonably anticipated. The public accommodation, of course, would still not have to provide the aid if it would impose an undue burden.

In sum, an honest effort to comply with the law should be a basic factor taken into account by the court in assessing whether any civil penalties, or the highest levels of those penalties, should apply against a public accommodation. As an additional example, assume that a public accommodation provided an auxiliary aid to a person with a disability, which the public accommodation reasonably believed would enable the person to effectively enjoy the goods and services provided by the accommodation. Assume further that a court ultimately determined that the auxiliary aid was not adequate for the person with a disability and therefore that the accommodation was in violation of the requirements of the Act. Assuming further that this action (or actions) somehow rose to the level of a case brought by the Attorney General, a court's assessment that the public accommodation had made a reasonable and honest effort to provide the auxiliary aid should obviously be taken into account by the court in determining good faith for the purposes of assessing any civil penalty.[316]

---

[316] H. Comm. on Educ. and Lab. Rep. at 128.

The House Judiciary Committee similarly offered guidance to the courts in this area, as follows:

> When making a determination regarding the amount of penalty, the court should consider the nature and circumstances of the violation, the degree of culpability, any history of price violations and financial circumstances of the violator, the goal of deterrence, and other matters as justice may require. [317]

Since the maximum amount of the penalty that can be awarded is dependent upon whether an entity's violation of the ADA is a first violation or not, a question can arise as to what constitutes a single violation. Section 308(b)(3) of the statute provides that determinations in the same action on liability that the entity has engaged in more than one discriminatory act— whether this determination is by judgment (including consent decree)[318] or settlement—are to be counted as just one violation. If the Attorney General brings an action and the court finds that the public accommodation has engaged in a series of acts that constitute a pattern or practice of discrimination, these acts together—even though actually multiple violations of the ADA —would be considered as just one violation for purposes of a civil penalty.[319] A second violation would not occur until a second suit was brought against the public accommodation and the public accommodation found to have committed another act or series of acts in violation of Title III.

---

[317] H. Comm. on Jud. Rep. at 68.

[318] H. Comm. on Educ. and Lab. Rep. at 127.

[319] H. Comm. on Jud. Rep. at 68; H. Comm. on Educ. and Lab. Rep. at 127.

CHAPTER **6**

ADA Title IV:
Telecommunications

¶ 6.01 PURPOSE OF TITLE IV

Title IV of the ADA contains provisions affording the disabled access to telephone and telecommunications services equal to that which the nondisabled enjoy. Title IV should not be viewed as establishing any new right for the disabled, but simply as an effort to ensure that the general mandate of the Communications Act of 1934, which is to provide efficient telephone service for all, is met for the disabled. The technology currently exists for doing so, but Congress felt that inadequate attention had been paid to the special needs of the disabled with respect to using the nation's telephone system.[1] Though the purpose of the Communications Act of 1934[2] is to provide "universal telephone service for all Americans," as much as possible,[3] the inability of hearing-impaired and speech-impaired persons to fully access the telephone system was seen by Congress as presenting a "serious threat" to the attainment of this goal.[4]

---

[1] Report of the House Comm. on Energy and Commerce on the Americans With Disabilities Act of 1990, HR Rep. No. 485, 101st Cong., 2d Sess., pt. 4 (1990) (hereinafter cited as H. Comm. on Energy and Com. Rep.) at 27; Report of the House Comm. on Education and Labor on the Americans With Disabilities Act of 1990, HR Rep. No. 485, 101st Cong., 2d Sess., pt. 2 (1990) (hereinafter cited as H. Comm. on Educ. and Lab. Rep.) at 129; Report of the Senate Comm. on Labor and Human Resources on the Americans With Disabilities Act of 1989, S. Rep. No. 116, 101st Cong., 1st Sess. (1989) (hereinafter cited as S. Comm. on Lab. and Hum. Resources Rep.) at 77.

[2] 47 USC 201 et seq.

[3] H. Comm. on Energy and Com. Rep. at 27.

[4] H. Comm. on Educ. and Lab. Rep. at 129; S. Comm. on Lab. and Hum. Resources Rep. at 77, 78.

The purpose of Title IV is in large measure "to establish a seamless interstate and intrastate relay system for the use of TDDs [telecommunications devices for the deaf] that will allow a communications-impaired caller to communicate with anyone who has a telephone, anywhere in the country."[5] Title IV is meant to ensure that the telephone service provided for the disabled is functionally equivalent to the service provided for persons without disabilities.[6] At the same time, Title IV is not meant in any way to discourage the development of new, advanced technologies that might make it easier for communications-impaired individuals to communicate by telephone.[7]

Title IV consists of just two sections. Section 401[8] adds a new section—Section 225—to the Communications Act of 1934, while Section 402 amends existing Section 711 of the Communications Act. Title IV permits state regulation and control over intrastate communications if a state wishes to so regulate, as long as such regulation and control meets the requirements set forth in new Section 225. The Federal Communications Commission (FCC) will regulate all interstate communications and all intrastate communications in states that do not choose to exercise independent regulation and control, and will ensure that states that do wish to exercise regulation and control do so in a manner that is consistent with Section 225.

Regulations implementing new Section 225 have been issued by the FCC.[9]

The statute itself does not specifically address whether a common carrier has an obligation to provide relay services in

---

[5] H. Comm. on Energy and Com. Rep. at 28.

[6] S. Comm. on Lab. and Hum. Resources Rep. at 78.

[7] H. Comm. on Educ. and Lab. Rep. at 130; S. Comm. on Lab. and Hum. Resources Rep. at 78.

[8] All of what is discussed in subsection (a) of Title IV, Section 401, is part of new Section 225 to the Communications Act of 1934. A subsection (b) is included in Title IV, Section 401, to make conforming amendments elsewhere in the Communications Act in order to acknowledge the FCC's new jurisdiction over intrastate carriers for the limited purpose of new Section 225.

[9] These regulations can be found at 47 CFR pt. 64.

languages other than English. The House Committee on Energy and Commerce, however, stated:

> [C]ommon carriers are encouraged to accommodate individuals who speak a language other than English. This is particularly important in areas in which there is a substantial population of individuals for whom English is not the primary language. However, carriers are not required to provide relay services in languages other than those which predominate among large sections of the population.[10]

¶ 6.02 NEW SECTION 225

Section 401 of Title IV adds a new Section 225 to the Communications Act of 1934 to carry out the title's mandate to provide telecommunications services for hearing- and speech-impaired persons. Unless otherwise noted, all references in the following discussion will be to subsections within the new Section 225.

[1] Definitions

Section 225(a) sets forth three definitions for purposes of the section, as outlined in the following discussion.

[a] Common Carrier or Carrier

A "common carrier or carrier" includes both interstate carriers as defined elsewhere in the Communications Act and intrastate carriers that are engaged in communication by wire or radio, without limitation. Section 3(h) of the Communications Act[11] (which applies to new Section 225 of the Communications Act) defines "common carrier" or "carrier" to mean

> any person engaged as a common carrier for hire, in interstate or foreign communication by wire or radio or interstate or foreign radio transmission of energy, except where reference is made to common carriers not subject to this

---

[10] H. Comm. on Energy and Com. Rep. at 66.

[11] 47 USC § 153(h).

chapter; but a person engaged in radio broadcasting shall not, insofar as such person is so engaged, be deemed a common carrier.

This would include cellular carriers, resale carriers, and all other carriers that provide voice-band telecommunications services.

[b] TDD

TDD is used in Title IV of the ADA to refer to a telecommunications device for the deaf, defined as any machine "that employs graphic communication in the transmission of coded signals through a wire or radio communication system." The TDD may be used by a variety of disabled individuals, though, not just deaf people. [12]

Individuals with hearing or speech disabilities can currently carry on telephone communications with each other by using these machines. TDDs use a typewriter-like machine with a screen or printer to send coded signals through the telephone network. A TDD on the other end of the call will decode the signal and print out or display the message for the receiving party. This works if both parties have TDDs, but does not allow a hearing- or speech-impaired person to communicate over the telephone with anyone who does not have a TDD. Since the bulk of the country consists of persons who do not have or use TDDs, the disabled are severely limited in who they can speak with by telephone.

Technology does currently exist to allow a disabled person using a TDD to communicate by telephone with a nondisabled person. TDDs can be connected to an operator relay system, where a person who is the relay operator also has a TDD and serves as an intermediary to the telephone conversation. The relay operator receives the TDD communication from the disabled person on the operator's TDD screen, and relays it by voice to the nondisabled person; the operator then takes the voice response from the nondisabled person and transmits it in coded form back to the disabled person's TDD, where the words are printed out on the disabled person's monitor or printer. The

---

[12] H. Comm. on Educ. and Lab. Rep. at 131.

operator relay system is being currently used in only a few states, and largely just for intrastate communications. As of July 1989, the FCC found that TDD operator relay systems were almost nonexistent for interstate communications. [13]

[c] Telecommunications Relay Services

The term "telecommunications relay services" is defined in Section 225(a) as

> telephone transmission services that provide the ability for an individual who has a hearing impairment or speech impairment to engage in communication by wire or radio with a hearing individual in a manner that is functionally equivalent to the ability of an individual who does not have a hearing impairment or speech impairment to communicate using voice communication services by wire or radio.

This definition includes services that enable two-way communication between individuals who use TDDs or similar devices and individuals who do not use these devices. To ensure inclusion of future technological advances that enable telephone communication between the disabled and the nondisabled, but that may be different from TDDs, the definition of "telecommunications relay services" is not limited in scope to just TDDs. This term supersedes the terms "dual party relay system," "message relay services," and "TDD relay." [14]

[2] Statutory Mandate: Equivalent Telephone Service

New Section 225(c) sets forth the basic mandate of Title IV: Not later than July 26, 1993, all common carriers providing telephone voice transmission services must provide relay services that permit access to telephone services to communications-impaired persons that are "functionally equivalent to voice telephone services provided to nonimpaired individuals." [15]

---

[13] H. Comm. on Energy and Com. Rep. at 27.

[14] See FCC regulation 47 CFR § 64.601(7).

[15] Id. at 65.

The statute gives the common carrier flexibility as to how the relay services can be provided. The common carrier may:

- Provide the relay services for its own system;
- Designate another company to do so for it;
- Select a vendor to provide the relay services through competitive bidding; or
- Band together with other common carriers to set up relay services that cover all of their telephone systems.

The FCC's regulations do not interfere with this flexibility and leave it largely to the carriers to decide exactly how to meet their responsibilities under the ADA. No matter how the common carrier goes about providing the relay services, though, the ultimate responsibility for statutory compliance remains with the carrier and cannot be transferred.[16]

[3] Which Regulations Govern?

Intrastate and interstate telecommunications relay services must be in compliance with regulations promulgated pursuant to Section 225. Because the statute offers states the opportunity to set up their own regulatory system for intrastate telecommunications relay services, the regulations that must be complied with differ, depending upon whether the common carrier is providing interstate or intrastate services and whether the particular state has chosen to regulate the area.

If a common carrier chooses to provide its relay services through another entity, then the common carrier would comply with the statute if the relay services provided by such entity meet the appropriate regulations.

[a] Interstate Carrier

For a common carrier providing interstate telephone service, the regulatory landscape is clear. It must provide telecommunications relay services in compliance with regulations issued by the FCC.

---

[16] H. Comm. on Energy and Com. Rep. at 66.

[b] Intrastate Carrier

A common carrier providing intrastate telephone service must first determine whether it is operating in a state that has established its own FCC-approved regulatory scheme. If it is, then the common carrier must only comply with the state regulations (though the state regulations must meet or exceed the FCC regulations). If the state within which the carrier is providing intrastate service has either not chosen to regulate, or has established a regulatory scheme that has not been approved by the FCC, then the carrier must comply with the FCC regulations. By contacting the FCC, a common carrier can ascertain whether a state has chosen to regulate the area and, if it has, whether the FCC has approved the scheme.

[4] Federal Communications Commission Regulations

The FCC has issued regulations to implement new Section 225, as required by the ADA.[17] Although the statute does not mandate everything that must be addressed in these regulations, new Section 225(d)(1) does list several specific points that must be covered.

[a] Requirements, Guidelines, and Procedures

The regulations must establish functional requirements, guidelines, and operations procedures for telecommunications relay services. This includes ensuring that a common carrier provide telecommunications relay services on a nondiscriminatory basis, twenty-four hours a day, to all users in the area served by a carrier.[18] As part of this, the FCC must include language to ensure that operators serving as relays are sufficiently trained to meet the needs of communications-disabled individuals.[19]

To carry out this intent, the FCC regulations provide, in part, as follows:

---

[17] Communications Act of 1934 § 225(d), 47 USC 201 et seq., which new section was added by the ADA (47 USC § 225).

[18] New Sections 225(d)(1)(A) and 225(d)(1)(C).

[19] H. Comm. on Educ. and Lab. Rep. at 133; S. Comm. on Lab. and Hum. Resources Rep. at 81.

- Telecommunications relay services (TRS) must have communications assistants (CA), or operators, who are properly trained to meet the specialized needs of individuals with speech and hearing disabilities. This includes ensuring the CAs have sufficient grammar and typing skills, as well as familiarity with U.S. sign language and speech disability cultures.
- TRS must include alternate staffing to provide callers with reasonably efficient access under projected calling volumes, so that the probability of a busy response due to CA unavailability is functionally equivalent to what a voice (nondisabled) caller would experience through the voice telephone network.
- TRS must, except during network failure, answer 85 percent of all calls within ten seconds, and no more than thirty seconds may elapse between receipt of dialing information and the dialing of the requested number.
- TRS must operate twenty-four hours a day.
- CAs must handle emergency calls in the same manner as other TRS calls.
- TRS users must have the same access to their chosen interchange carrier as other callers have, and they must be provided with the same operator services.[20]
- VCO and HCO technology must be standard features of TRS.

[b] Minimum Standards for Functional Equivalency

The ADA provides that regulations must establish minimum standards that must be met by a common carrier as part of its obligation to provide telecommunications relay services under Section 225(c). This will include technical and quality of service standards. In addition, standards must be established that will define what the functional equivalence is between telecommunications relay services and voice telephone transmission services. This latter point is very important because the broad purpose of the statute is to provide communications-disabled persons with telephone service that is functionally equivalent to that provided the nondisabled. Elaborating on

---

[20] See FCC regulation 47 CFR §§ 64.604(a), 64.604(b).

this, both the House Committee on Education and Labor and the Senate Committee on Labor and Human Resources stated that

> In determining factors necessary to establish functional equivalency, the FCC should include, for example, the requirement that telecommunications relay services transmit messages between the TDD and voice caller in real time, as well as the requirement that blockage rates for telecommunications relay services be no greater than standard industry blockage rates for voice telephone services. Other factors that should be included are the opportunity for telecommunications relay service users to choose an interstate carrier whenever possible. The FCC should enumerate other such measurable standards to ensure that hearing and non-hearing individuals have equivalent access to the Nation's telephone networks.[21]

The FCC's regulations contain these requirements.[22] They also specifically require that TDD relay systems be capable of communicating with either the American Standard Code for Information Interchange (ASCII) or Baudot signal format, at any speed generally in use.[23]

[c] Time and Availability of Relay Services

The statute says that regulations must require that telecommunications relay services operate every day for twenty-four hours a day. The regulations contain this requirement, and also provide that the relay systems have redundancy features functionally equivalent to the equipment in normal central offices, including uninterruptible power for emergency use.[24] Carriers are directed by the FCC to make the availability of relay service known to users, through inserts in bills and information in directories.[25]

---

[21] Id.

[22] See FCC regulation 47 CFR § 64.604(b)(4).

[23] See FCC regulation 47 CFR § 64.604(b)(1). This is also consistent with congressional intent. See H. Comm. on Energy and Com. Rep. at 67.

[24] See FCC regulation 47 CFR § 64.604(b)(4).

[25] See FCC regulation 47 CFR § 64.604(c)(2).

[d] Rates

The statute requires, and the FCC regulations mandate, that the rates for telephone service paid by communications-disabled persons be not greater than the rates paid by the nondisabled for a functionally equivalent communication of the same duration, made at the same time of day, and over the same distance. Special rate discounts that are not given to the nondisabled need not be afforded to disabled callers.[26] Transmitting a message by a telecommunications relay system will normally take longer than transmitting that same message by voice, so that some TDD relay calls will cost more than a voice call delivering the same message. A functionally equivalent communication would be a voice call of the same time duration at the same day and time and distance as the TDD call, not a voice call of the same message content.

[e] Relay Operators

The ADA requires the regulations to prohibit, and the regulations do so prohibit, relay operators from the following:

- Refusing to relay or accept certain calls (unless credit authorization is denied);
- Limiting in any way the length of calls from communications-disabled persons;
- Disclosing to anyone other than the recipient of the call the contents of any relayed conversation;
- Keeping records of the content of the call after the call is over (notes may be made by the operator during the call to aid in relaying the contents to the recipient, or to aid in summarizing the call if the TDD cannot transmit fast enough and the communications-disabled individual consents to receiving a summary, but they should be destroyed immediately afterwards); and
- Intentionally altering the content of a relayed call.[27]

---

[26] H. Comm. on Educ. and Lab. Rep. at 133; S. Comm. on Lab. and Hum. Resources Rep. at 82. See also proposed FCC regulation 47 CFR § 64.604(c)(3).

[27] See FCC regulation 47 CFR §§ 64.604(a)(2), 64.604(a)(3).

The operator may not allege tiredness or the end of a work shift as an excuse to terminate a call. A replacement operator should take over if necessary. Restrictions are necessary in order to protect the privacy rights of the callers. Relay operators are prohibited from violating callers' privacy rights. Records necessary to enable the carrier properly to bill the caller for the call may be kept—such as the time, duration, and distance of the call—but the actual content of the call is not considered such a record.

[f] New Technology

Section 225(d)(2) requires that the regulations issued by the FCC to implement Section 225 be consistent with Section 7(a) of the Communications Act, encourage the use of state-of-the-art technology, and not hamper in any way the development of new technology for communication by hearing- and speech-disabled persons. The regulations try to accomplish this objective simply by stating that the regulations are not intended to discourage or impair development of improved technology.[28]

[g] Allocation of Interstate and Intrastate Costs

Section 225(d)(3) requires that the regulations deal with the separation of costs for telecommunications relay services between interstate usage and intrastate usage in a manner consistent with Section 410 of the Communications Act.[29] The regulations do this by referencing the regulations adopted pursuant to Section 410 as providing the procedures and standards for such separation of costs.[30] No change is intended from the manner in which joint costs are currently allocated in the Communications Act between interstate and intrastate jurisdictions.[31]

The regulations are also required to provide, and do provide, that costs incurred by common carriers as a result of interstate telecommunications relay services be recovered by these

---

[28] See FCC regulation 47 CFR § 64.604(b)(5).

[29] 47 USC § 410.

[30] See FCC regulation 47 CFR § 64.604(c)(4).

[31] H. Comm. on Educ. and Lab. Rep. at 134; S. Comm. on Lab. and Hum. Resources Rep. at 82.

carriers from all interstate subscribers—not just TDD users. Costs incurred by intrastate carriers are to be recovered from the intrastate jurisdiction.[32] Additional details regarding cost recovery have not been included in the FCC's final regulations, because the FCC felt the record was not at that time adequate to develop a specific cost recovery mechanism. This will be addressed over time as the FCC builds a record, however.

The legislative history reveals a congressional intent requiring that the regulations ensure that all subscribers to every interstate service, including private line, public switched network services, and other common carrier services, contribute to the recovery of costs incurred in the provision of interstate relay services. However, the FCC is permitted to choose not to require "Lifeline" subscribers to pay for telecommunications relay services.[33] While the regulations do mandate cost recovery from all subscribers to interstate services, as indicated previously, they do not create the Lifeline exception.

Originally, Title IV contained a provision that prohibited the imposition of a fixed charge on all residential customers, disabled and nondisabled, to recover the costs of providing interstate telecommunications relay services, but this provision was deleted by the House Energy and Commerce Committee because it wanted to give the FCC broad discretion to determine the best way of ensuring cost recovery by the carriers.

In states choosing to regulate intrastate relay services, carriers must be permitted by the appropriate state regulatory commission to recover their costs in a manner consistent with Section 225 and the FCC regulations regarding cost recovery.[34]

[5] Enforcement of Section 225

Responsibility for ensuring that the general goals of Title IV of the ADA are met, and that the specific provisions of Section 225

---

[32] See new Section 225(d)(3); FCC regulation 47 CFR § 64.604(c)(4)(ii).

[33] H. Comm. on Energy and Com. Rep. at 67. Lifeline telephone service is generally service with some lower cost feature (i.e., half-price connection costs) offered to elderly persons on public assistance.

[34] See new Section 225(d)(3)(B); FCC regulation 47 CFR § 64.604(c)(4)(ii).

are carried out, rests with the FCC. The intent behind the regulatory scheme is for the FCC "to have sufficient enforcement authority to ensure that telecommunications relay services are provided nationwide and that certain minimum federal standards are met by all providers of the services."[35] This is true even though a certified state will have primary responsibility for enforcing the statute's goals pertaining to intrastate carriers. In addition, new Section 225(b) directs the FCC to ensure that intrastate and interstate telecommunications relay services are available, "to the extent possible and in the most efficient manner," to communications-disabled individuals.

[a] Interstate Communications — Basis of FCC Authority

The FCC clearly has the power and authority to enforce provisions of the Communications Act insofar as they affect interstate commerce. Once Congress decided to place Title IV within the Communications Act, no additional amendment of Title IV was required to give the FCC the same power and authority necessary to ensure the compliance of common carriers engaged in interstate communications already provided the FCC under other provisions of the Communications Act regarding interstate communications.

[b] Intrastate Communications — Basis of FCC Authority

There have been concerns about whether Congress can constitutionally give the FCC power over common carriers engaged in intrastate communications. These concerns, however, have been allayed, because intrastate communications become part of an interstate communications network. An impact and effect is therefore made upon interstate commerce, so Congress may properly regulate intrastate communications under the commerce clause of the U.S. Constitution.

---

[35] H. Comm. on Energy and Com. Rep. at 67; virtually identical quotation contained in H. Comm. on Educ. and Lab. Rep. at 134 and S. Comm. on Lab. and Hum. Resources Rep. at 82, 83.

[c] Basic Enforcement Scheme: Remedies and Complaints

In order to ensure compliance with Section 225 and punish violations thereof, the FCC is given sole authority to enforce the section against all interstate carriers, as well as against all intrastate carriers in states not having approved or certified regulatory schemes. The states that have such approved regulatory schemes are given enforcement authority against all intrastate carriers operating within them, and the FCC will refer complaints filed against such carriers to the states.[36]

Generally, the remedies available for violation of the Communications Act include the right by a private person to file either a suit in federal district court or a complaint with the FCC, and the power and authority of the FCC to undertake an investigation into a suspected violation and to order appropriate redress.[37] In any action brought to enforce Title IV, attorney fees, including litigation expenses and costs, may be awarded to a prevailing party (other than the federal government), pursuant to Section 505 of the ADA.

When a complaint alleging the violation of the statute is filed with the FCC, then the FCC must either:

1. Resolve the complaint within 180 days after the complaint is filed, if the complaint is about an interstate carrier or a carrier in a state with an unapproved or uncertified regulatory scheme; or
2. Immediately refer the complaint to an approved state enforcement agency, if the complaint is about an intrastate carrier in a state with an approved or certified scheme.

The FCC retains residual enforcement powers over intrastate carriers in an approved or certified state only if the state has not taken final action on a complaint within 180 days after the complaint has been filed with the state (or any shorter period prescribed for final action by the state's own regulations), or if

---

[36] See new Sections 225(e) and 225(g). See also FCC regulation 47 CFR § 64.604(c)(5)(i).

[37] 47 USC §§ 201–224.

the FCC determines that the state's regulatory program no longer meets FCC guidelines. [38]

[6] Federal Communications Commission Certification of State Regulatory Schemes

The key to a state's having any regulatory or enforcement powers over intrastate carriers rests with its obtaining certification — approval — of its regulatory scheme from the FCC. Any state wishing to seek certification must provide the FCC with documentation, by October 1, 1992, describing the state's program for implementing intrastate telecommunications relay services and the procedures and remedies the state will provide for enforcing the state's requirements. [39]

The FCC must grant certification if the state's program for making intrastate telecommunications relay services available to hearing- and speech-impaired individuals meets or exceeds the requirements of the FCC's own regulations, issued pursuant to new Section 225(d) [40] and if the program contains adequate procedures and remedies for its enforcement. The state program, similar to the FCC program, may make telecommunications relay services available through

- Designees;
- A competitively selected vendor;
- The regulation of intrastate carriers; or
- The state government itself. [41]

The FCC cannot refuse to certify a state's program based solely on the method the state chooses to fund the telecommunications relay services — i.e., the way costs of implementing the system will be recovered — unless the state's funding choice would cause users of the telecommunications relay services to

---

[38] See new Section 225(g). See 47 CFR § 64.604(c)(5) for the FCC's complaint procedures.

[39] See new Section 225(f); FCC regulation 47 CFR § 64.605.

[40] See 47 CFR § 64.604.

[41] H. Comm. on Energy and Com. Rep. at 68; H. Comm. on Educ. and Lab. Rep. at 134; S. Comm. on Lab. and Hum. Resources Rep. at 83.

pay a higher price for equivalent phone service than nonusers. The FCC's regulations, however, do prohibit funding mechanisms from being labeled in a manner that offends the public. [42]

Certification is good for five years, with renewals. The FCC may suspend or revoke its certification of a state's program if it determines that the certification is no longer warranted. [43] Suspension or revocation can only take place after the state is given both notice of the proposed action and the opportunity to present its position at a hearing before the FCC on the proposed action. If suspension or revocation of a state's certification occurs, the FCC is required to "provide a reasonable transition period to ensure both continuity of relay service for users and to provide a reasonable opportunity for common carriers to meet the requirements of the Commission's regulations after the suspension or revocation of the certified program." [44] Regulations simply state that upon suspension or revocation, the FCC will take such steps as may be necessary to ensure continuity of the relay services. [45]

¶ 6.03 CLOSED-CAPTIONING OF PUBLIC SERVICE ANNOUNCEMENTS

Section 402 of Title IV amends existing Section 711 of the Communications Act to require that any television public service announcement that is either partially or fully funded by the federal government, through any government agency or instrumentality, include closed-captioning of the verbal content of the announcement.

The aim of this amendment is to place the burden of compliance on the producer of the public service announcement and the producer's agents, and not on the television station/broadcaster. For example, if a public service announcement funded by the government is delivered to a television station without closed-captioning, the station is not required by

---

[42] See FCC regulation 47 CFR § 64.605(d).

[43] See new Section 225(f)(4); FCC regulation 47 CFR § 64.605(e).

[44] H. Comm. on Energy and Com. Rep. at 68.

[45] 47 CFR § 64.605(e).

the statute to supply the closed-captions. Additionally, a station will not be liable for broadcasting a government-funded public service announcement without the closed-captions unless closed-captions were included in the announcement as it was delivered to the station, and the station intentionally failed to show the closed-caption when it broadcast the public service announcement.

CHAPTER 7

Tax Considerations

This chapter discusses the tax implications of expenses incurred in complying with the ADA. Section 7.01 provides an overview of the general rules regarding deductibility and capitalization of expenditures. Section 7.02 discusses Section 190 of the Internal Revenue Code (IRC), a special provision allowing the deduction of accommodation expenses that otherwise would be deemed capital expenditures. Section 7.03 describes new IRC Section 44, which provides a tax credit for expenditures incurred in making businesses accessible to the disabled. Finally, Section 7.04 discusses a special job tax credit available to employers who hire certain qualified disabled individuals.

¶ 7.01 GENERAL TAX RULES

Compliance with the ADA will typically cause an employer/business to incur some expense. Whether the cost is small or large, the expenditure will allow, in most instances, for a reduction in taxes. Generally, the only issue will be whether the amounts incurred are deductible expenses (allowing for a reduction from gross income in the year expended) or capital expenditures (requiring depreciation over a number of tax years).

IRC Section 162 provides that individuals, corporations, and other taxpayers can deduct ordinary and necessary expenses paid or incurred during the tax year in carrying on any trade or business. An ordinary expense is one that is customary in the taxpayer's industry or is reasonably related to the taxpayer's business.[1] A necessary expense is one that is appropriate and beneficial in furthering the taxpayer's business.[2] Any expenditure reasonably related to complying with the ADA will meet the "ordinary and necessary" test of IRC Section 162.[3]

> EXAMPLE: Smith, who is disabled, seeks a position with Southern Company as a machine operator. In order for Smith to perform the essential functions of the job, he will require special training beyond that normally required for other machine operators. In order to accommodate Smith's disability, Southern Company agrees to pay for this extra training. Under such circumstances, Southern Company's training expenditures would be deductible.[4]

On the other hand, the deductibility of expenditures beyond those reasonably required by the ADA may be subject to challenge.[5] Deductions are a matter of legislative grace. Therefore, the burden of proof is always on the taxpayer to demonstrate that a deducted expense is both ordinary and necessary.

> EXAMPLE: Jones, who is blind, is the son of Northern Company's owner. Northern hires Jones as a product manager

---

[1] See, e.g., Welch v. Helvering, 290 US 111 (1933).

[2] Welch v. Helvering, 290 US 111 (1933).

[3] See, e.g., Rev. Rul. 71-59, 1971 CB 56 (mandatory contributions under state unemployment insurance laws held deductible); CB Smith, 44 TCM 1180, TC Memo. 1982-546 (cost of license required by local law held deductible).

[4] See Knoxville Iron Co., 18 TCM 251, TC Memo. 1959-54 (holding that training costs were deductible); Rev. Rul. 58-238, 1958-1 CB 90.

[5] See Cole v. Commissioner, 481 F2d 872 (2d Cir. 1973) (workers' compensation payments in excess of that required by state law held nondeductible).

and provides him with a driver to take him to and from work. The cost of such driver would likely be held nondeductible.[6] On the other hand, if Northern established a transportation system for all its disabled employees, the cost would likely be held deductible.

Adequate books and records of expenditures are generally required by the Internal Revenue Service (the Service) before a deduction will be allowed.[7] Although a taxpayer may attempt to estimate its actual costs when its records are inadequate, in reaching an approximation, the court may bear "heavily if it chooses upon the taxpayer whose inexactitude is of his own making."[8]

Not all ordinary and necessary expenses are currently deductible under IRC Section 162. Rather, under IRC Section 263, an ordinary and necessary expense that has an anticipated benefit beyond the tax year in which it is incurred is a capital expenditure and is not fully deductible in the year incurred. Except as allowed by IRC Section 190, which will be discussed in the next section, capital expenditures incurred in connection with the ADA may not be deducted from gross income except over the useful life of the item.[9]

As a general rule, capital expenditures are amounts paid for the acquisition of property or for a permanent improvement or betterment of property.[10] Capital expenditures may include any amounts paid or incurred to add to the value, or to substantially extend the useful life, of property owned by the taxpayer.[11] The costs of items qualifying as capital expenditures are added to the

---

[6] See ME Cole, 481 F2d 872 (2d Cir. 1973) (payments to cover traveling expenses of injured former employee and a companion held not to be required under applicable workers' compensation law and, therefore, not deductible).

[7] Treas. Reg. § 1.446-1(a)(4).

[8] Cohan v. Commissioner, 39 F2d 540 (2d Cir. 1930).

[9] A discussion of the rules relating to depreciation, accelerated cost recovery deductions, or amortization deductions of capital expenditures is beyond the scope of this book. A detailed analysis can be found in the Federal Tax Coordinator 2d Volume L-7400 (RIA 1991).

[10] IRC § 263; Treas. Reg. §§ 1.263(a)-1, 1.263(a)-2.

[11] IRC § 263; Treas. Reg. § 1.263(a)-(1).

basis of the property.[12] The essential distinction between a currently deductible expense and a capital expenditure is whether the anticipated benefit to be derived from the expenditure extends beyond a year. If the item has a useful life of less than a year, the cost is usually deductible as an expense from gross income. Otherwise, it will generally be deemed a capital expenditure. For example, the cost of printing sale items in braille would be a deductible expense, since such items have a minimal useful life. Similarly, the cost of retaining an expert in sign language to translate or assist in an interview would be currently deductible. On the other hand, the costs of building ramps, elevators, accessible workstations, and so on, would all be capital expenditures since these items have a useful life of more than one year (that is, their benefit extends beyond one tax year).[13] Likewise, the cost of equipment specially designed for the disabled will typically be deemed a capital expenditure.

The fact that such expenditures may be required by the ADA does not change them into currently deductible expenses.[14] For example, in *Blue Creek Coal, Inc.*,[15] the court held that costs incurred in putting cabs on bulldozers as required by safety regulations of the Mine Health and Safety Administration were capital expenditures. Another often cited decision is *RKO Theatres, Inc. v. United States*,[16] in which the court held that the cost of construction to comply with local fire regulations was not a deductible expense. According to the court in *RKO*, the fact that the construction was required by local law did not alter its character as a permanent improvement with a useful life of more than one year.

Although the U.S. Court of Claims has allowed small capital

---

[12] Treas. Reg. § 1.212-1(e).

[13] IRC § 263.

[14] See, e.g., Blue Creek Coal, Inc., TC Memo. 1984-579 (cost of including cabs on bulldozers as required by safety regulations of the Mine Health and Safety Administration were capital expenditures); Cerda v. United States, 53 AFTR2d 84-1460, 84-1 USTC ¶ 9490 (ND Ill. 1984) (plumbing, carpentry, and electrical work required by Chicago's building code were capital expenditures).

[15] Blue Creek Coal, Inc., TC Memo. 1984-579.

[16] RKO Theatres, Inc. v. United States, 163 F. Supp. 598 (Ct. Cl. 1958).

expenditures to be deducted currently, the Tax Court has held that expenses as small as $75 must be capitalized.[17]

¶ 7.02 SECTION 190 OF THE INTERNAL REVENUE CODE

The Tax Reform Act of 1976 enacted IRC Section 190, a special provision for the tax treatment of expenditures to remove architectural barriers to the disabled. IRC Section 190 allows qualified expenditures to be deducted rather than capitalized. The congressional Joint Committee Staff explained the purpose of this new rule as follows:

> In spite of previous Federal legislation to contend with the problem of architectural and transportation barriers to the handicapped and elderly, such barriers remain widespread in business and industry. The Congress believes that creating a tax incentive for a limited period could promote rapid modification of business facilities and vehicles. In addition, the removal of barriers to the handicapped and elderly would increase their involvement in economic, social and cultural activities.[18]

IRC Section 190 is available to individuals as well as to small businesses. It allows all persons a deduction of up to $15,000 (reduced from $35,000 by the 1990 Budget Agreement in return for a small business tax credit[19]) for "qualified" architectural and transportation barrier removal expenses. Individual taxpayers, partnerships, and affiliated groups of corporations filing a single return are subject to the $15,000 limitation. Amounts in excess of $15,000 are deemed capital expenses, and constitute adjustments to basis under IRC Section 1016(A).[20]

---

[17] Compare Cincinnati, New Orleans & Tex. Pac. Ry. Co. v. United States, 424 F2d 563 (Ct. Cl. 1970) with Klutz, TC Memo. 1979-169, 38 TCM 724.

[18] General Explanation of the Tax Reform Act of 1976 at 640 (RIA).

[19] See infra ¶ 7.03.

[20] Treas. Reg. § 1.190-1(b); IRC § 263.1016(a)(1).

For purposes of IRC Section 190, an "architectural and transportation barrier expense" is one whose purpose is to make any facility or public transportation vehicle more accessible to, or usable by, handicapped or elderly individuals. The vehicle or facility must be owned or leased by the taxpayer and used by it in connection with its trade or business.[21] Other key definitions under IRC Section 190 are as follows:

- A "facility" is all or any portion of a building, structure, equipment, road, walkway, parking lot, or other similar real or personal property.[22]
- "Public transportation" means a vehicle such as a bus or railroad car that provides transportation services to the public.[23]
- A "handicap" is a physical or mental impairment, including blindness and deafness, that constitutes or results in a functional limitation to employment or that substantially limits one or more major life activities, such as walking, speaking, or learning.[24]
- "Elderly" means sixty-five years of age or older.[25]

Expenditures are only deductible under IRC Section 190 if they are incurred in removing existing barriers. Comprehensive renovations or construction expenses typically are not covered.[26] Moreover, in order to qualify for the deduction, the removal of the barrier must not create a new barrier.[27]

In order to qualify for the deduction, the resulting removal must conform to specific requirements set forth in the regulations.[28]

---

[21] IRC § 190(b)(1).

[22] Treas. Reg. § 1.190-2(a)(1).

[23] Treas. Reg. § 1.190-2(a)(2).

[24] IRC § 190(b)(3).

[25] Treas. Reg. § 1.190-2(a)(4).

[26] Treas. Reg. § 1.190-2(b)(1).

[27] Treas. Reg. § 1.190-2(b)(22)(iii).

[28] Treas. Reg. § 1.190-2(b).

Walks

- A public walk must be at least 48 inches wide and must not slope more than 5 percent. A fairly long walk of maximum or near maximum steepness must have level areas at regular intervals. A walk or driveway must have a nonslip surface.
- The walk must have a continuous common surface and must not have steps or sudden changes in level.
- Where a walk crosses another walk, a driveway, or a parking lot, they must blend to a common level. However, this does not require the removal of curbs that are a safety feature for the handicapped, especially the blind.
- A sloping walk must have level platforms at the top and bottom. If a door swings out onto the platform at the top or bottom of the walk, the platform must be at least 5 feet deep and 5 feet wide. If a door does not swing onto the platform, the platform must be at least 3 feet deep and 5 feet wide. A platform must extend at least 1 foot past the opening side of any doorway.

Parking Lots

- At least one parking space near a facility must be set aside and marked for use by the handicapped.
- The parking space must be open on one side to allow room for people in wheelchairs or on braces or crutches to get in and out of a car onto a level surface.
- A parking space for the handicapped that is placed between two regular diagonal or head-on parking spaces must be at least 12 feet wide.
- The parking space must be located so that people in wheelchairs or on braces or crutches do not have to go behind parked cars.

Ramps

- A ramp must not slope more than 1 inch for each foot of length.
- The ramp must have at least one handrail that is 32 inches high, measured from the surface of the ramp. The hand-

rail must be smooth, and it must extend at least 1 foot past the top and bottom of the ramp. However, this does not require a handrail extension that is itself a hazard.

- The ramp must have a nonslip surface.
- The ramp must have level platforms at the top and bottom. If a door swings out onto a platform, the platform must be at least 5 feet deep and 5 feet wide. If a door does not swing onto a platform, the platform must be at least 3 feet deep and 5 feet wide. The platform must extend at least 1 foot past the opening side of any doorway.
- The ramp must have level platforms no farther than 30 feet apart and at any turn.
- A curb ramp must be provided at an intersection. The curb ramp must not be less than 4 feet wide and must not slope more than 1 inch for each foot of length. The two surfaces must blend smoothly. A curb ramp must have a nonslip surface.

Entrances

- A building must have at least one main entrance usable by people in wheelchairs. The entrance must be on a level accessible to an elevator.
- The international accessibility symbol must be displayed on routes to and at wheelchair-accessible entrances to facilities and public transportation vehicles.

Doors and doorways

- A door must have a clear opening at least 32 inches wide and must be operable by a single effort.
- The floor on the inside and outside of a doorway must be level for at least 5 feet from the door in the direction the door swings, and it must extend at least 1 foot past the opening side of the doorway.
- There must not be any sharp slopes or sudden changes in level at a doorway. The threshold must be flush with the floor. If the door has an automatic closer, it must be selected, placed, and set so as not to impair the use of the door by the handicapped.

Stairs

- Stairsteps must have round nosing of between 1 and 1½-inch radius.
- Stairs must have a handrail 32 inches high as measured from the front of the tread.
- Stairs must have at least one handrail that extends at least 18 inches past the top and bottom steps. However, this does not require a handrail extension that is itself a hazard.
- Each step must not be more than 7 inches high.

Floors

- Floors must have a nonslip surface.
- Floors on each story of a building must be on the same level or must be connected by a ramp.

Toilet rooms

- A toilet room must have enough space for people in wheelchairs.
- The toilet room must have at least one toilet stall that
  — Is at least 66 inches wide;
  — Is at least 60 inches deep;
  — Has a door that is at least 32 inches wide and swings out;
  — Has a handrail on one side that is 33 inches high and parallel to the floor, 1½ inches in outside diameter, 1½ inches away from the wall, and fastened securely at the ends and center; and
  — Has a toilet with a seat 19 to 20 inches from the floor with the centerline 18 inches from the side wall on which the handrail is located.
- The toilet room must have sinks with narrow aprons. Drain pipes and hot water pipes under a sink must be covered or insulated.
- A mirror and shelf above a sink must not be higher than 40 inches above the floor, measured from the top of the shelf and the bottom of the mirror.

- A toilet room for men must have wall-mounted urinals with the opening of the basin 15 to 19 inches from the floor or floor-mounted urinals that are level with the main floor.
- Towel racks, towel dispensers, and other dispensers and disposal units must not be mounted higher than 40 inches from the floor.

Water fountains

- A water fountain or cooler must have up-front spouts and controls.
- The water fountain or cooler must be hand-operated or hand-and-foot-operated.
- A water fountain mounted onto the side of a floor-mounted cooler must not be more than 30 inches above the floor.
- A wall-mounted, hand-operated water cooler must be mounted with the basin 36 inches from the floor.
- The water fountain must not be fully recessed and must not be set into an alcove unless the alcove is at least 36 inches wide.

Public telephones

- A public telephone must be placed so that the dial and the headset can be reached by people in wheelchairs.
- The public telephone must be equipped for those with hearing disabilities and be so identified with instructions for use.
- Coin slots of public telephones must not be more than 48 inches from the floor.

Elevators

- An elevator must be accessible to, and usable by, the handicapped and the elderly on the levels they use to enter the building and on all levels and areas normally used by them.
- Cab size must allow for turning a wheelchair. An elevator cab must measure at least 54 by 68 inches.

- Door clear opening width must be at least 32 inches.
- All controls needed must be within 48 to 54 inches from the cab floor. These controls must be usable by the blind and must be identifiable by touch.

Controls

- Switches and controls for light, heat, ventilation, windows, draperies, fire alarms, and all similar controls that are needed or used often must be placed within the reach of people in wheelchairs. These switches and controls must not be higher than 48 inches from the floor.

Hazards

- Hanging signs, ceiling lights, and similar objects and fixtures must be at least 7 feet from the floor.

Markings and signals

- Raised letters or numbers must be used to mark rooms and offices. These markings must be placed on the wall to the right or left of the door at a height of 54 to 66 inches from the floor.
- A door that might prove dangerous if a blind person were to use it, such as a door leading to a loading platform, boiler room, stage, or fire escape, must be identifiable by touch.
- An audible warning signal must be accompanied by a simultaneous visual signal for the benefit of those with hearing disabilities.
- A visual warning signal must be accompanied by a simultaneous audible signal for the benefit of the blind.

Rail facilities

- A rail facility must have at least one entrance with a clear opening at least 36 inches wide.
- A boarding platform edge bordering a drop-off or other dangerous condition must be marked with a strip of floor material that is different in color and texture from the rest

of the floor surface. The gap between boarding platform and vehicle doorway must be as small as possible.

Buses

- A bus must have a mechanism, such as a lift or ramp, to enable a wheelchair user to enter it and enough clearance to let a wheelchair user reach a secure location.
- The bus must have a wheelchair-securing device. However, this does not require a wheelchair-securing device that is itself a barrier or hazard.
- The vertical distance from the curb or from street level to the first front doorstep must not be more than 8 inches; each front doorstep after the first step up from the curb or street level must also not be more than 8 inches high; and the steps at the front and rear doors must be at least 12 inches deep.
- The bus must have clear signs indicating that seats in the front of the bus are priority seats for handicapped or elderly passengers and telling other passengers to make these seats available to handicapped and elderly passengers who want to use them.
- Handrails and stanchions must be provided in the entrance to the bus so that handicapped and elderly passengers can grasp them from outside the bus and use them while boarding and paying the fare. This system must include a rail across the front of the bus interior for passengers to lean against while paying fares. Overhead handrails must be continuous except for a gap at the rear doorway.
- Floors and steps must have nonslip surfaces. Each step edge must have a band of bright contrasting color running the full width of the step.
- A stepwell next to the driver must have, when the door is open, at least 2 footcandles of light measured on the step tread. Other stepwells must have, at all times, at least 2 footcandles of light measured at the step tread.
- The doorways of the bus must have outside lighting that provides at least 1 footcandle of light on the street surface for a distance of 3 feet from the bottom step edge. This

lighting must be below window level and must be shielded from the eyes of entering and exiting passengers.

- The fare box must be located as far forward as practical and must not block traffic in the vestibule.

Rapid and light rail vehicles

- Passenger doorways on the vehicle sides must have clear openings at least 32 inches wide.
- Audible or visual warning signals must be provided to alert passengers of closing doors.
- Handrails and stanchions must permit safe boarding, moving around, sitting, standing, and getting off by handicapped and elderly passengers. On a level-entry vehicle, handrails, stanchions, and seats must be located to allow a wheelchair user to enter the vehicle and position the wheelchair in a location that does not block the movement of other passengers. On a vehicle with steps, handrails and stanchions must be provided in the entrance so that handicapped and elderly persons can grasp them and use them from outside the vehicle while boarding.
- Floors must have nonslip surfaces. Each step edge on a light rail vehicle must have a band of bright contrasting color running the full width of the step.
- A stepwell next to the driver must have, when the door is open, at least 2 footcandles of light measured on the step tread. Other stepwells must have, at all times, at least 2 footcandles of light measured on the step tread.
- Doorways on a light rail vehicle must have outside lighting that provides at least 1 footcandle of light on the street surface for a distance of 3 feet from the bottom step edge. This lighting must be below window level and must be shielded from the eyes of entering and exiting passengers.

To be deductible, expenses of removing any barrier not covered by these standards must meet three tests: (1) The removed barrier must have been a substantial barrier to access or use of a facility or public transportation vehicle by handicapped or elderly people; (2) the removed barrier must have been a barrier for at least one major class of these persons (such as the blind, the deaf, or wheelchair users); and (3) the barrier must be removed without creating any new barrier that significantly impairs access to or use of the facility or vehicle by these persons. The burden of proof is on the taxpayer to establish that the requirements of the regulations have been satisfied. [29]

For partnerships, the $15,000 limit applies both to the partnership and to each partner. According to the regulations, [30] each partner must apply his $15,000 limit to the total of his (1) distributive share of the partnership's deductible expenses for the removal of barriers (after the $15,000 limit has been applied at the partnership level); (2) distributive share of any such IRC Section 190 expenses as are distributed to him from any other partnership; and (3) deductible expenses individually incurred for the removal of these barriers. In determining this limit, the partner may divide the $15,000 limit between any expenses that were individually incurred and any expenses that were received as a distributive share of a partnership's expenses. If this division results in all or part of a partner's distributive share not being deductible by him, the partnership may add the nondeductible part to the basis of the partnership property. In making the addition to the basis of a partnership's properties, the Service presumes that each partner's distributive share of qualified deductible expenses (after application of the $15,000 limit at the partnership level) was deductible in full by the partner. This presumption can be disproved only by showing that all or part of a partner's distributive share of such expenses was not deductible by him because it was more than his $15,000 limit as allocated by him. The Service gives the following example, using the pre-1989 $35,000 cap:

> In 1988 John Blue's distributive share of the Brown and Blue partnership's deductible expenses for the removal of architectural barriers to the handicapped and elderly was $25,000. John also had $20,000 of similar expenses in the operation of his sole proprietorship, which he chose to deduct in 1988. John allocated $20,000 of his $35,000 limit to his distributive share of the Brown and Blue partnership's expenses and $15,000 to his own expenses. John may

---

[29] IRC § 190(b)(2).

[30] Treas. Reg. § 1.190-1(b).

add to the basis of his own property his excess $5,000. Also, if Brown and Blue can show that John could not deduct $5,000 of his distributive share of the partnership's expenses, it may add that amount to the basis of the property.[31]

To qualify for the deduction, the modifications need only meet the requirements established by the Service. However, taxpayers should make sure that all building modifications meet local and state standards, which may be more stringent. Taxpayers should maintain careful records and documentation, including blueprints, contracts, and so on, in order to justify the deduction.[32]

¶ 7.03 SMALL BUSINESS TAX CREDITS

As part of the 1990 Budget Agreement, a tax credit was added to the IRC for certain expenditures incurred to make businesses accessible to the disabled. This provision will be codified as IRC Section 44 and entitled "Expenditures to Provide Access to Disabled Individuals."[33]

Under this new provision, an eligible small business that elects application of the credit will be allowed a nonrefundable income tax credit equal to 50 percent of the amount of eligible public accommodation access expenditures for any taxable year that exceed $250 but do not exceed $10,250.[34] An "eligible small business" is a business that had gross receipts for the preceding taxable year that did not exceed $1 million or that had no more than thirty full-time employees during such taxable year.[35] "Eligible access expenditures" are amounts paid or incurred by an

---

[31] IRS Publication 907.

[32] Treas. Reg. § 1.190-3(c).

[33] See Section 11611 of the Omnibus Budget Reconciliation Act of 1990, Pub. L. No. 101-508 (Oct. 27, 1990) (hereinafter cited as Budget Agreement).

[34] IRC § 44(a); Conference Report on the Omnibus Budget Reconciliation Act of 1990 (hereinafter cited as Budget Agreement Conference Report) at 159.

[35] IRC § 44(b).

eligible small business for the purpose of enabling an eligible small business to comply with the requirements of the ADA.[36]

New IRC Section 44 provides that eligible access expenditures include:

- Expenditures to remove architectural, communication, physical, or transportation barriers that prevent a business from being accessible to or usable by, individuals with disabilities;[37]
- Expenditures to provide qualified interpreters or otherwise to make aurally delivered materials available to individuals with hearing impairments;[38]
- Expenditures to provide qualified readers, taped texts, or otherwise to make visually delivered materials available to individuals with visual impairments;[39]
- Expenditures to acquire or modify equipment or devices for individuals with disabilities; and
- Expenditures to provide other similar services, modifications, materials, or equipment.[40]

To qualify as a deductible eligible access expenditure, an expenditure must be reasonable and necessary[41] and the resulting removal of any barrier (or the provision of any services, modifications, materials, or equipment) must meet the standards "promulgated by the Secretary with the concurrence of the Architectural and Transportation Compliance Board and set forth in regulations prescribed by the Secretary."[42] It is likely that such regulations will parallel the regulations issued under IRC Section 190 and discussed earlier. The Architectural and Transportation Compliance Board's proposed regulations on accessibility are set forth in Appendix C.

---

[36] IRC § 44(c); Budget Agreement Conference Report at 160.

[37] IRC § 44(c)(2)(A).

[38] IRC § 44(c)(2)(B).

[39] IRC § 44(c)(2)(C).

[40] IRC § 44(c)(2)(D); Budget Agreement Conference Report at 160.

[41] IRC § 44(c)(3); Budget Agreement Conference Report at 160.

[42] IRC § 44(c)(5).

To qualify for the credit, an expenditure must be incurred after the date of the Budget Agreement's enactment on November 5, 1990.[43] The portion of any unused business credit for any taxable year that is attributable to the disabled access credit cannot be carried back to taxable years ending before the date of enactment of the credit.[44] Because the disabled access credit is a general business credit, it is subject to the general limits on the amount of such credits that may be used for any taxable year.[45]

As under IRC Section 190, the limitation of the credit applies to both a partnership and its partners and an S corporation and its shareholders.[46]

In order to prevent a double benefit for taxpayers making eligible expenditures under both IRC Sections 190 and 44, IRC Section 44(d)(7) provides that "in the case of the amount of the credit determined under this section—(A) no deduction or credit shall be allowed for such amount under any other provision of this chapter and (B) no increase in the adjusted basis of any property shall result from such amount."

¶ 7.04 TARGETED JOBS CREDIT

IRC Section 51 provides a credit against taxes for employers who hire members of certain targeted groups. This provision was to expire at the end of September 1990, but the Budget Agreement extended the credit through December 31, 1991.[47] Among the targeted groups are those individuals who have a physical or mental impairment that constitutes a substantial handicap to employment and who were referred to the employer while receiving, or after completing, vocational rehabilitation services. The rehabilitation services must have been provided

---

[43] IRC § 44(c)(4).

[44] IRC § 39(d)(5) added by Budget Agreement; IRC § 44(c)(4); Budget Agreement Conference Report at 160.

[45] Section 11611(b) of the Budget Agreement; Budget Agreement Conference Report at 160.

[46] IRC § 44(d)(3).

[47] IRC § 51(c)(4); Section 11405(a) of the Budget Agreement.

under a state plan approved under the Rehabilitation Act or under a rehabilitation plan for veterans pursuant to Chapter 31 of Title 38 of the U.S. Code.[48] Under IRC Section 51, the employer may elect a credit against income tax of 40 percent of the first-year wages of the disabled individual, up to $6,000 of wages.

An employer will not be entitled to the credit unless the employer has received certification from the designated local agency that the individual is a member of a targeted group or has requested certification from the agency.[49] The employer must receive the certification before the employee begins his employment.[50] The employer's request for certification must be in writing, must state that the employer believes that the employee qualifies for certification under the requirements for the disabled, and must certify that the employer has made a good faith effort to determine whether the employee is in the targeted group.

---

[48] IRC § 51(d)(5).

[49] IRC § 51(d)(16)(A).

[50] Id.

Case Digests

A.01 IMPAIRMENT THAT IS A HANDICAP

[1] Specific Conditions Included

[a] Impairment Resulting From a Contagious Disease

A state department of education's bar on a teacher from his class-room duties, and his subsequent reassignment to an administra-tive position, after being diagnosed as having AIDS, violates Section 504 of the Rehabilitation Act of 1973. The plaintiff was a teacher of hearing-impaired students in the Orange County schools. In early 1987, he was hospitalized and diagnosed as having AIDS. Relying on the advice of a medical expert that there would be some risk to students if the plaintiff remained in his classroom, the department offered the plaintiff an administrative position preparing grant proposals at the same rate of pay and benefits as before, with the option to work out of his home. The plaintiff rejected this offer and brought an action in the district court, alleging discrimination due to his affliction, and moved for a preliminary injunction ordering the department to reinstate him to his classroom duties pending trial. The district court denied the motion. *Held*: The plaintiff is handicapped within the meaning of the Rehabilitation Act. The lower court used an erroneous standard of review in determining whether people with contagious diseases were within the Rehabilitation Act's coverage. Rather than requiring the plaintiff to disprove every theoretical possibility of harm to others, the department of education is required to prove that the transmission of the AIDS virus in the classroom setting is more than a mere theoretical possibility. Applying this standard, the Ninth Circuit determined that the plaintiff was entitled to preliminary injunctive relief.

[Chalk v. US District Court Cent. Dist. of Cal., 840 F2d 701 (9th Cir. 1988).]

Physical impairment resulting from a contagious disease may be considered a handicap. The plaintiff suffered from tuberculosis. For thirteen years, she had taught as an elementary school teacher in Nassau County, Florida. She was discharged in 1979 after suffering her third relapse of the disease. She sued, claiming that contagious diseases were included within the definition of a handicapped person under the Rehabilitation Act of 1973. *Held*: The definition of "handicapped person," under the Rehabilitation Act, and regulations issued under Section 504 by the Department of Health and Human Services, support a broad construction of the term "handicapped." The county's argument, that one could distinguish between the contagious effects of a disease and the disease's physical impact on a claimant, is rejected. It would be unfair to allow an employer to seize upon the distinction between the effects of a disease on others and the effects of a disease on a patient and use that distinction to justify discriminatory treatment.

[School Bd. of Nassau County v. Arline, 480 US 273 (1987).]

[b] Radical Mastectomy

An employee recovering from a radical mastectomy is disabled and entitled to reasonable accommodation of her condition. The plaintiff worked for the Department of the Army (DOA) in various positions over a fourteen-year period, all of which involved varying degrees of typing and filing. In 1977, she had a radical mastectomy operation as a treatment for cancer. The surgery involved not only the removal of one breast, but also significant portions of the muscles in her left arm, shoulder, and chest. When she returned to work following a recuperative period, she experienced difficulty in typing for prolonged periods, which was attributable to her operation. Although she requested lighter duty work, the DOA made only a limited effort to accommodate her. In response to an equal employment opportunity complaint, the DOA informed the plaintiff that they only had to offer her one position and that she could take it or leave it. She took it, despite the fact that the position required too much typing for her condition. Due to the stress of intensive typing duties, she was required to be taken by emergency ambulance to a hospital. *Held*: The plaintiff is indeed a handicapped person, because her physical condition substantially limited her ability to work. In addition, the DOA has an obligation to accommodate her impairment. It was totally inadequate and unacceptable for the DOA to place her in a position even more poorly suited to her impairment than her original one. Furthermore, given the overall size of the government's operation at that office, the budget, the number of employees, and the large number of positions of seemingly comparable skill requirements, the DOA clearly violated the reasonable accommodation requirement of the Rehabilitation Act of 1973.

[Harrison v. Marsh, 46 Fair Empl. Prac. Cas. (BNA) 971 (WD Mo. 1988).]

[c] Compulsive Gambling

Compulsive gambling is an impairment under the Rehabilitation Act of 1973. The plaintiff worked as a special agent for the Federal Bureau of Investigation (FBI) until he was dismissed for driving an FBI vehicle to Atlantic City where he gambled and lost $2,000 in government funds received by him as part of an undercover assignment. The plaintiff alleged that his actions were caused by a compulsive gambling disorder. After the Atlantic City incident, he entered a three-week treatment program, attended Gamblers Anonymous twice a week, and stopped gambling altogether. The plaintiff challenged his dismissal under the Rehabilitation Act. *Held*: Compulsive gambling is widely recognized as a mental disorder and is classified as a "psychological impairment" by the American Psychiatric Association.

[Rezza v. Department of Justice, 46 Fair Empl. Prac. Cas. (BNA) 1366 (ED Pa. 1988).]

[d] Impairment Resulting From Congenital Condition

An individual suffering from epilepsy is handicapped. The plaintiff was a clerk-typist. A few months after taking the job, she suffered the first of several epileptic seizures at work. Prior to her first seizure at work, she had not mentioned her epilepsy for fear of being denied the job. After her first seizure, she requested, among other things, that her supervisor provide additional training for her. This request was denied, and her work evaluation stated that she was less productive than average. Her supervisor informed her that if she could not process at least ten applications and issue at least five certificates per day, she would be dismissed. Despite the plaintiff's contention that this goal was unreasonable, she received notice that she was indeed going to be terminated as a clerk-typist. When she failed to meet the department's goals, she was discharged. *Held*: Epileptics are handicapped individuals. Epilepsy substantially limits one's ability to work, as federal and state regulations and policies restrict the types of jobs available to epileptics. As an epileptic, the plaintiff qualified as a handicapped individual. Because she could perform the essential duties of her position in spite of her epilepsy, she was also otherwise qualified.

[Reynolds v. Brock, 815 F2d 571 (9th Cir. 1987).]

[e] Back Injuries

An employee who sustained a back injury on the job, and whose injured condition affected her work and her ability to walk, sit,

stand, drive, and care for her home, is a handicapped person. The plaintiff was employed by the Philadelphia Housing Authority (PHA) as a receptionist-clerk. While at work, the plaintiff fell and sustained back and leg injuries that incapacitated her for more than two months. When the plaintiff returned to work after her accident, her requests for a wooden straight-back chair, use of the elevator, and coverage for regular breaks were ignored. Largely because the PHA did not provide the requested accommodations, Perez had to leave her job after a week and a half. The PHA thereafter terminated Perez. *Held*: The plaintiff is handicapped within the meaning of the Rehabilitation Act of 1973. The determination of who qualifies as a handicapped person under the act should be based on an inquiry of whether the particular impairment constitutes a significant barrier to employment for the particular person. The plaintiff's back problems caused her considerable pain, which not only affected her work, but also her ability to perform essential life functions.

[Perez v. Philadelphia Hous. Auth., 677 F. Supp. 357 (ED Pa. 1987).]

[f] Smoke Sensitivity

An employee who was hypersensitive to tobacco smoke qualifies as a handicapped person within the meaning of the Rehabilitation Act of 1973. The plaintiff worked for the Veterans Administration (VA). He was hypersensitive to tobacco smoke and had made this fact known to his superiors. In an effort to accommodate him, the VA physically separated the desks of the smokers and nonsmokers in the room where the plaintiff worked, secured a voluntary agreement from the smokers located in the same room as the plaintiff that they would not smoke in that room, secured the same agreement from the employees in another nearby room, and installed two ceiling vents in the plaintiff's office to withdraw smoke that might drift in from adjacent rooms. The plaintiff's supervisor even purchased an air purifier in an effort to alleviate the effects of smoking in his own office. Despite these efforts, the plaintiff filed an action against the VA alleging that their failure to accommodate his hypersensitivity to smoke by providing a smoke-free environment amounted to handicap discrimination. *Held*: The plaintiff was handicapped because of his hypersensitivity to smoke. The VA made reasonable efforts to accommodate his handicap while at the same time attempting to accommodate those who felt the need to smoke during working hours.

[Vickers v. Veterans Admin., 549 F. Supp. 85 (WD Wash. 1982).]

[2] Condition Regarded as a Handicap

An individual with a congenital spinal deformity is regarded as having an impairment and is, therefore, entitled to the protection of the Rehabilitation Act of 1973, even though he could meet the physical requirements of the job. The plaintiff was hired by the defendant as a utility man. The job required frequent lifting of up to 50 pounds of material and equipment and occasional lifting of up to 100 pounds. A doctor for the defendant concluded that, because of the plaintiff's back deformity, he could not lift more than 25 to 50 pounds. On that basis, the defendant discharged the plaintiff. Subsequently, a second physician examined the plaintiff and determined that the first doctor was wrong. Thereafter, the first physician reversed his initial opinion. Nevertheless, the defendant refused to rehire the plaintiff. *Held*: A person is handicapped not only if he has a substantially limiting impairment, but also if he is regarded as having such an impairment. The plaintiff's handicap was not his failure to meet the weight requirements of his position, but the congenital spine deformity, which the defendant perceived as imposing a disqualifying limitation event, though the plaintiff was able to perform the functions of his job. Thus, the plaintiff could be both handicapped and otherwise qualified for the job.

[Thornhill v. Marsh, 49 Fair Empl. Prac. Cas. (BNA) 6 (9th Cir. 1989).]

A.02 NO IMPAIRMENT OR HANDICAP

[1] Employment Opportunities Not Substantially Limited (Generally)

Whether the exclusion of an employee from a single job constitutes a substantial limitation on a major life activity, requires a

case-by-case analysis. The plaintiff was a member of a carpentry apprenticeship program. The program required 8,000 hours of field work to achieve journeyman status. During an employer medical examination, it was discovered that the applicant had a congenital back problem. This condition did not prevent the employee's performance of his apprentice duties, but did indicate a risk of future problems. Based on this risk, the government contractor/employer refused to hire the employee. The contractor contended that the Rehabilitation Act of 1973 only covered individuals who encounter difficulty with obtaining employment in general and not those persons who are merely denied a particular job or type of job because of associated risks. *Held*: The plaintiff's impairment did not substantially limit his employment opportunities. The following factors are to be applied on a case-by-case basis for determining whether a person's impairment substantially limits employment opportunities: (1) the number and types of jobs from which the impaired individual is disqualified; (2) the geographic area to which the applicant has reasonable access; (3) the applicant's own job expectations and training; (4) the criteria or qualifications in use generally; and (5) the types of jobs to which the rejection would apply. Under this test, it is assumed that all employers offering the same job or similar jobs would use the same requirement or screening process. Under this standard, the plaintiff was improperly denied employment. In addition, the risk of future injury was not a sufficient basis for discriminating against the plaintiff.

[EE Black, Ltd. v. Marshall, 497 F. Supp. 1088 (D. Haw. 1980).]

[2] Specific Conditions

[a] Transitory Illnesses

Maladaptive reactions to psychological stressors is a transitory illness not constituting a handicap. The plaintiff was employed with the U.S. General Services Administration (GSA) as a computer programmer analyst. He suffered from "maladaptive reaction to psychological stressors," an adjustment disorder often accompanied by violent emotion and conduct. The GSA terminated the plaintiff after he physically assaulted his supervisor and rampaged through the office damaging office equipment. *Held*: The plaintiff's condition was a transitory phenomenon, which could be expected to disappear when the "psychological stressor" (e.g., the plaintiff's supervisor) was removed.

[Adams v. US General Servs. Admin., 51 Fair Empl. Prac. Cas. (BNA) 647 (DDC 1989).]

An ill-defined transitory illness does not constitute a handicap. The plaintiff was employed by the Army and Air Force Exchange Service (AAFES) as a vehicle manager. After fourteen years of service with the AAFES, the plaintiff experienced health problems that required repeated absences from work and caused a decrease in performance. Ultimately, he was downgraded to a less demanding position. *Held*: The plaintiff was not handicapped, because his condition was ill-defined and, at worst, a transitory illness that had no permanent effect on the plaintiff's health. The downgrade in position, based on substantial evidence of poor job performance, was justified.

[Stevens v. Stubbs, 576 F. Supp. 1409 (ND Ga. 1983).]

[b] Sinus Condition, Hypertension

Sinus condition and hypertension do not constitute impairment. The plaintiff was a paraplegic who also suffered from hypertension and a sinus condition. Over the course of his employment, the plaintiff received numerous disciplinary actions for poor performance and lateness. He was also denied an opportunity for promotion. The plaintiff filed suit alleging, in part, that his treatment was a form of handicap discrimination. *Held*: The plaintiff's hypertension and sinus condition did not constitute a handicap. The plaintiff failed to prove that these conditions substantially limited a major life activity.

[Thomas v. General Servs. Admin., 49 Fair Empl. Prac. Cas. (BNA) 1602 (DDC 1989).]

[c] Left-Handedness

Being left-handed is not an impairment. The plaintiff was hired by the U.S. Postal Service as a part-time flexible letter carrier for a ninety-day probationary period in mid-1978. Because he took too long to complete his rounds during his training period, his supervisor recommended that he be given additional training. Despite the additional training and instruction in how to use his right hand to deliver mail, he continued to deliver mail with his left hand. The plaintiff received an unsatisfactory rating in four out of twelve categories on his thirty-day evaluation report, and was subsequently terminated. He alleged that his supervisors regarded his left-handedness as a handicap and that his discharge because of that handicap was discriminatory under the Rehabilitation Act of 1973. *Held*: Being left-handed is not an "impairment." Characteristics, such as average height or strength, that render an individual incapable of performing particular jobs are not covered by the statute because they are not impairments. Similarly, being left-handed is a physical characteristic, not a chronic illness, disorder or deformity, mental disability, or condition affecting health.

[de la Torres v. Bolger, 781 F2d 1134 (5th Cir. 1986).]

[d] Acrophobia

A utility systems repairer suffering from a fear of heights is not handicapped. The plaintiff was hired by the Department of Health and Human Services as a utility systems repairer and operator. The job description required that he be able to climb stairways and ladders both for emergencies and for routine maintenance. After he informed his supervisor that he could not climb past certain heights, he was terminated on the ground that he was medically unable to perform the full range of duties of his position. *Held*: The plaintiff was not handicapped because his life activities were not substantially limited by his fear of heights. An employee is neither disabled, nor regarded as disabled, merely because an employer finds him incapable of satisfying the singular demands of a particular job.

[Forrisi v. Bowen, 794 F2d 931 (4th Cir. 1986).]

[e] Service-Related Disabilities

An employee who is dismissed for excessive unscheduled absenteeism is not automatically "handicapped" because of his 30 per-

cent service-connected disability. The plaintiff suffered from diabetes and was established by the Veterans Administration (VA) to have a 30 percent service-related disability. The Postal Service terminated the plaintiff after he experienced a total of eleven unscheduled absences. He filed an action against the Postal Service following his termination, alleging, inter alia, that he had been discriminated against because of his handicap. *Held*: The plaintiff's 30 percent service-connected disability by the VA standards did not automatically render him a handicapped employee. The plaintiff's failure to comply with Executive Order 5396's requirement of advance notice of treatment and a certificate of treatment was especially important. Furthermore, the plaintiff's diabetes was not a substantial limitation on one or more of his major life activities.

[Wimbley v. Bolger, 642 F. Supp. 481 (WD Tenn. 1986).]

[f] Varicose Veins

Varicose veins do not constitute a handicap. The plaintiff began working for the Veterans Administration (VA) as a clerk-typist. The position required her to type and file, thus allowing her to sit and stand alternatively throughout the day. The VA later reduced its work force, and the plaintiff's position was eliminated. The plaintiff was reassigned to a mail clerk position, to which she objected on the ground that her varicose veins prevented her from standing or walking for long periods. She subsequently secured a position as a transcriptionist with the VA, but was removed from that position due to her low productivity and poor typing skills. The plaintiff alleged that the VA had violated the Rehabilitation Act of 1973's prohibition against handicap discrimination. *Held*: The plaintiff was not handicapped by virtue of her varicose veins within the meaning of the Rehabilitation Act. Four physicians who had examined the plaintiff found her condition of varicose veins to be only mild to moderate.

[Oesterling v. Walters, 760 F2d 859 (8th Cir. 1985).]

[g] Strabismus

A cross-eyed employee is not handicapped. The plaintiff was born with a mild case of strabismus, commonly known as crossed eyes. He was hired by the U.S. Postal Service after successfully passing the Letter Sorter Machine Vision Examination and other requirements for the position of distribution clerk machine trainee. When the plaintiff completed his probationary period, he was promoted to distribution clerk, part-time flexible (PTF), machine qualified. The duties of this new position required the plaintiff to operate a mail-sorting machine. After three months of work as a PTF machine operator, the plaintiff began to develop eye strain, headaches, and excessive tearing. The plaintiff's physician wrote a letter to the Postal Service indicating that the plaintiff's symptoms were the result of the detailed visual work required to operate the mail-sorting machine in combination with his strabismus. The plaintiff's condition, however, did not limit any other of his normal daily activities whatsoever. When the Postal Service discharged the plaintiff, he brought suit alleging handicap discrimination. *Held*: Although the plaintiff's impairment interfered with his ability to do a particular job, but did not significantly decrease his ability to obtain satisfactory employment otherwise, it was not substantially limiting within the meaning of the Rehabilitation Act of 1973. The plaintiff's strabismus never had any effect on any of his activities, including his past work history and ability to carry out other duties at the office apart from the operation of the mail-sorting machine.

[Jasany v. US Postal Serv., 755 F2d 1244 (6th Cir. 1985).]

[h] Voluntary Weight Gain

A body builder who applies for a position as a flight attendant, and who is rejected on the basis that his weight exceeds the weight restrictions for the job, is not handicapped if he gains weight voluntarily. The plaintiff was employed by United Airlines as a flight attendant. After seven years of service, he was terminated because his body-building activities brought his weight over the weight allowance for the job. United Airlines maintained its weight program in order to ensure the neat and pleasing appearance of its flight attendants. The program was not completely inflexible. It permitted a two-pound "buffer," as well as weight exceptions upon board approval. The plaintiff had in fact received a weight exception, but it was relinquished after United lost a sex discrimination case concerning the weight program. The plaintiff brought suit against United, claiming that his weight was a handicap that prevented him from obtaining a job for which he was otherwise qualified and, as such, that he had been the victim of handicap discrimination. *Held*: The plaintiff was not a handicapped individual. A person who exceeds the maximum weight for a flight attendant because he is an avid body builder is not limited in a major life activity—he is only prevented from having a single job. Furthermore, the plaintiff's weight problem was not the result of physiological disorders, cosmetic disfigurement, or anatomical loss. Rather, his weight and low-fat content were self-imposed and voluntary.

[Tudyman v. United Airlines, 608 F. Supp. 739 (CD Cal. 1984).]

[i] Minor Injuries

Minor injury to a knee from a fall does not constitute a handicap. The plaintiff, a probationary mail carrier, injured his knee while running from a dog. After the treating physician released him to return to work, the plaintiff sought a "second opinion" that also concluded that the plaintiff could indeed return to work without restrictions. Nevertheless, when the plaintiff notified his superior that he was capable of returning to work, he was informed that he had been terminated. The plaintiff brought suit alleging that he was being terminated because he was handicapped or perceived as being handicapped. *Held*: The plaintiff's condition did not constitute a handicap. His employer never considered the plaintiff to have been handicapped in any sense of the word.

[Alderson v. Postmaster Gen. of the US, 598 F. Supp. 49 (WD Okla. 1984).]

A.03 DUTY TO PROVIDE REASONABLE ACCOMMODATION

[1] Reassignment to Other Duties Is Possible

An employer discriminates against a handicapped employee if it waits three years to offer the employee limited duty work that was

available earlier. The plaintiff was employed with the Postal Service as a mail handler. During the course of his service, he suffered several injuries to his right knee, the most recent of which rendered him legally handicapped. Pursuant to a request from his treating physician, the Postal Service assigned the plaintiff to light-duty clerical work but this arrangement was terminated after complaints by a union at the worksite. As a result, there was a three-year period in which the plaintiff was out of work until he was reinstated performing limited duties as a mail handler. The plaintiff filed suit alleging that the Postal Service had violated the Rehabilitation Act of 1973 by neglecting to accommodate his physical limitations during the period he was out of work and collecting workers' compensation. *Held*: There is no difference between the "light" duties the plaintiff was originally assigned to, and the "limited" duties he was assigned to three years later. Both types of duties provided reasonable accommodation for the plaintiff while still performing the essential functions of a mail handler position. As such, the Postal Service had no excuse for failing to assign the plaintiff to these "limited" duties immediately after his "light"-duty status was terminated.

[Trimble v. Carlin, 633 F. Supp. 367 (ED Pa. 1986).]

[2] Alternative Accommodations Available

[a] Deafness

The Rehabilitation Act of 1973 protects a deaf plaintiff who is denied a position because she could not answer a telephone, even though she could perform the essential functions of the job. The plaintiff in this case was a thirty-two-year-old deaf woman. No mechanical device or medical treatment currently available would enable her to hear. She had worked at the Oak Brook, Illinois Post Office for thirteen years as a distribution clerk, a job requiring her to collect trays of mail and sort them by route. On two occasions, in 1986 and 1987, she sought the position of time and attendance clerk, and, in both instances, she was denied the job even though she had more seniority than the nondisabled persons selected. The plaintiff could perform all the duties of a time and attendance clerk except answering the telephone, a job function that had not been included in earlier job descriptions for this position. The time and attendance clerk position was also covered by the Postal Service's Qualification Standards for Bargaining Unit Positions that contain a requirement that all applicants have the "ability to hear the conversational voice, hearing aid permitted." While the job also required an ability to communicate with employees, the plaintiff could perform this role by reading lips, use of written notes, and expansion of the existing TTY keyboard telephone system. *Held*: The defendant had an affirmative obligation to enable the plaintiff to perform the essential functions of the time and attendance clerk position, and answering the telephone was not such a function. The qualification standard of an "ability to hear conversational voice" was not a necessary and legitimate physical requirement and, therefore, failed to satisfy the requirements of 29 CFR Section 1613.705, that qualifications be job-related and required by business necessity. A number of possible accommodations, ranging from laminating cards containing common phrases the plaintiff might need to use frequently, to preparing a list of phrases that individuals could point to when communicating with the plaintiff, would be reasonable, and would not require a substantial adjustment to the workplace. Finally, the defendant's contention, that not requiring the plaintiff to answer the telephone would lower morale and, therefore, be an "undue hardship," was rejected.

[Davis v. Frank, 50 Fair Empl. Prac. Cas. (BNA) 1188 (ND Ill. 1989).]

[b] Back Injuries

An employee who sustains a back injury on the job, and whose injured condition affects her work and her ability to walk, sit, stand, drive, and care for her home, is a handicapped person, and, therefore, her employer is obligated to accommodate her. The plaintiff was employed with the Philadelphia Housing Authority (PHA) as a receptionist-clerk. While at work, the plaintiff fell and sustained back and leg injuries that incapacitated her for more than two months. When the plaintiff returned to work after her accident, her requests for a wooden straight-back chair, use of the elevator, and coverage for regular breaks were ignored. Largely because the PHA did not provide the requested accommodations, Perez had to leave her job after a week and a half. The PHA thereafter terminated Perez. The plaintiff filed an action against the PHA alleging handicap discrimination. *Held*: The plaintiff was a handicapped person within the meaning of the Rehabilitation Act of 1973, which the PHA violated by refusing to grant the plaintiff the minimal accommodations she asked for and which she required to perform the physical requirements of her job.

[Perez v. Philadelphia Hous. Auth., 677 F. Supp. 357 (ED Pa. 1987).]

[c] Sarcoidosis

An employer's attempts to accommodate an employee's handicap of sarcoidosis are insufficient when the employee is not selected for positions for which he is qualified. The plaintiff was employed with the Department of the Army (DOA) for twenty-four years. While serving in the armed forces, the plaintiff was diagnosed as having sarcoidosis, a disease characterized by the formation of scar tissue and nodules in the organs and tissues affected. In addition, the plaintiff suffered from anorexia and was easily fatigued. Due to a restructuring of his employer's work force, the plaintiff was required to work a night shift. This new late night position had adverse effects upon the plaintiff's health. As a result, the plaintiff's personal physician wrote a letter to the plaintiff's supervisor explaining that his condition was exacerbated by the evening shift and that he recommended that the plaintiff continue his job on a day shift. As a result of this letter, the plaintiff was assigned to a temporary position on the day shift. The plaintiff remained there for approximately two years when the DOA eliminated the position and reassigned him back to the night shift. When the plaintiff suffered health problems, he once again requested reassignment. Although some effort was made to accommodate the plaintiff, the DOA refused to reassign him to a permanent position, and he was terminated. The plaintiff brought an action against the DOA, alleging violations of the Rehabilitation Act of 1973. *Held*: The DOA failed in its obligation to take further steps to accommodate the plaintiff's special needs so that he might remain in the federal service. Only a modified work schedule in the form of a day shift assignment would have been necessary to accommodate his handicap. The *Handbook on Reasonable Accommodation*, published by the Office of Personnel Management, sets forth options available for handicapped employees and applicants for federal service, and, of these options, reassignment as a means of accommodation was listed. While reassignment is not ordinarily mandated by the act, reassignment was indeed considered to be a reasonable accommodation by the Office of Personnel Management for handicapped federal agency employees. Therefore, there were positions for which the plaintiff was qualified, and they were available during the time that the DOA was attempting to accommodate him through reassignment.

[Rhone v. US Department of Army, 665 F. Supp. 734 (ED Mo. 1987).]

[d] Asthmatic Condition

An employer violates the California Fair Employment and Housing Act when it discharges an asthmatic employee who could perform the essential functions of her job and reasonable accommodations are available. Western Electric installs, modifies, and removes central office telecommunications equipment. The plaintiff was an installer for Western until she contracted a bronchial infection that aggravated a preexisting asthmatic condition. After an extended period, she was released to return to work subject to the restrictions that she stay away from dust and heavy exercise. Western determined that because of these restrictions the plaintiff could not perform the duties of an installer, and she was discharged. Thereafter, she brought suit alleging handicap discrimination under the California Fair Employment and Housing Act. *Held*: The plaintiff could perform the essential functions of an installer, and two accommodations were available: allowing the plaintiff to wear a paper mask when working with dust and reassigning strenuous tasks to her co-workers. The defendant's contention that there would be an imminent and substantial degree of risk to the employee if she continued to work were conclusory and speculative. Of particular importance is that Western had made no effort to experiment with the plaintiff's work restrictions prior to her discharge. Western's contention that reassigning part of the plaintiff's duties would constitute an undue hardship was rejected, because exposure to dust and heavy exercise were only a minimal aspect of an installer's job, and, therefore, such reassignment would not have been burdensome.

[Ackerman v. Western Elec. Co., 48 Fair Empl. Prac. Cas. (BNA) 1354 (ND Cal. 1986).]

[e] Multi-Handicapped

An education agency has an obligation to consider alternatives to eliminate a bus-driving requirement for a handicapped job applicant. The plaintiff is a multi-handicapped person. His handicaps include severe paralysis of his left side, as attributed to cerebral palsy, nocturnal epilepsy, and dyslexia. However, he has sufficient use of his left arm, hand, and leg, and is able to walk without assistance, lift children, and drive. In fact, the plaintiff has a chauffeur's license, and had driven cars, vans, and a U-haul without difficulty. The plaintiff's epilepsy is controlled by medication. The plaintiff sent the defendant a résumé and transcript in response to an advertisement placed by them seeking a preschool teacher of the handicapped and a special education instructor. After the defendant expressed interest in hiring the plaintiff, the plaintiff disclosed the extent of his impairments. The defendant responded that the preschool handicapped teacher had to be able to drive a school bus and that a state law required that a person have full and normal use of both hands, arms, feet, and legs in order to qualify for a bus driver's permit. The defendant then informed the plaintiff that it would be futile for him to come to the interview. The district court found that the plaintiff was better qualified, both in terms of education and experience, to teach preschool handicapped children than was the woman hired for the position he was seeking. The court also found that no teacher employed by the defendant had ever been required to drive a bus as part of his or her duties.

Further, the job description for a preschool handicapped teacher included no mention of bus driving. *Held*: Although state law imposed a physical requirement for school bus drivers, the defendant still had an obligation, under the Education of the Handicapped Act (20 USC Section 1400 et seq.) to try to accommodate the plaintiff by eliminating the need for him to drive a school bus. The defendant was wrong to give the plaintiff the impression that coming for the interview would be futile without considering whether accommodation was possible or suggesting to the plaintiff that it might be.

[Fitzgerald v. Green Valley Area Educ. Agency, 589 F. Supp. 1130 (SD Iowa 1984).]

[f] Blindness

Blind income maintenance workers (IMWs) who, with the assistance of readers, can meet all the requirements of their position, are otherwise qualified, and, therefore, their employer is required to provide reasonable accommodations, whether by readers or by other suitable means. The plaintiffs were all blind and employed by the Department of Public Welfare (DPW) as IMWs. The duties of an IMW consist of casework relating to a client's initial and continued eligibility for federal and state benefits. Many forms are used by an IMW, including a standardized five-page form that elicits information regarding a client's financial, vocational, and family situation that could conceivably bear upon the question of eligibility. Depending upon the client's situation, the IMW may also have to fill out other forms, such as a food stamp application worksheet or a child support form. In addition, while interviewing clients, an IMW will often have to review documents provided by the clients. Because the job of an IMW entails extensive paperwork, the plaintiffs were unable to perform their duties satisfactorily without the aid of a reader. Up until the time of the action brought against the DPW, the plaintiffs bore the expense of part-time hired readers, which permitted them to perform the requirements of their positions just as well as their sighted colleagues. The plaintiffs filed suit against the DPW under the Rehabilitation Act of 1973, claiming that the DPW had a duty to provide reasonable accommodation for their handicap or, more specifically, had a duty to assume the expense of the readers that enabled plaintiffs to perform their jobs. *Held*: Several modes of accommodation were available to enable the plaintiffs, who perform their jobs as well as sighted IMWs, to perform the essential functions of their job, aside from full-time readers. Of these alternatives, creating a braille version of the five-page client information form and printing copies of the *DPW Income Maintenance Manual*, the primary resource of the IMW, would prove to decrease the blind IMW's need for a reader by half. In view of the DPW's $300 million administrative budget, the modest cost of providing half-time readers, and the ease of adopting that accommodation without any disruption of the DPW's services, the accommodation would not be an undue burden of the DPW.

[Nelson v. Thornburgh, 567 F. Supp. 369 (ED Pa. 1983).]

A.04 NO DUTY TO PROVIDE REASONABLE ACCOMMODATION

[1] Reasonable Accommodation Already Provided

[a] Blindness

An employer reasonably accommodates a blind employee when it provides him with persons to act as readers, furnishes special equipment and office space, and decreases the employee's workload; there is no obligation to provide an employee with every accommodation he may request. The plaintiff, a blind employee, worked as a public affairs assistant for the Department of Education (DOE). His job duties included analyzing and responding to general inquiries directed to the Office of Civil Rights from members of Congress and the public. DOE provided the plaintiff with (1) part-time readers who spent a total of eighteen hours a week with him; (2) special equipment; and (3) a reduced workload of half that expected from a sighted employee in the same position. Dissatisfied with Carter's job performance and attitude, DOE sent the plaintiff a notice that he had thirty days to improve or face termination. Four months later, DOE terminated the plaintiff from his employment. The plaintiff brought suit against DOE alleging, in part, that it had not provided him with reasonable accommodation for his handicap as required under the Rehabilitation Act of 1973. Carter contended that he needed a voice-synthesized computer, a full-time reader of his choice, and easier access to office space as additional accommodations. *Held*: The employer is not obligated to provide the employee with every accommodation he may request, but only with reasonable accommodation as is necessary to enable him to perform his essential job responsibilities. Applying this standard, DOE carried its burden of persuasion on this issue by providing the plaintiff with reasonable accommodation.

[Carter v. Bennett, 840 F2d 63 (DC Cir. 1988).]

[b] Smoke Sensitivity

An employee who is hypersensitive to tobacco smoke qualifies as a handicapped person within the meaning of the Rehabilitation Act of 1973 but his employer is under no obligation to provide him with an environment entirely free of tobacco smoke. The plaintiff worked for the Veterans Administration (VA). He was hypersensitive to tobacco smoke and had made this known to his superiors. In an effort to accommodate him, the VA physically separated the desks of the smokers and nonsmokers in the room where the plaintiff worked, secured a voluntary agreement from the smokers located in the same room as the plaintiff that they would not smoke in that room, secured the same agreement from the employees in another nearby room, and installed two ceiling vents in the plaintiff's office to withdraw smoke that might drift in from adjacent rooms. The plaintiff's supervisor even purchased an air purifier in an effort to alleviate the effects of smoking in his own office. Despite these efforts, the plaintiff filed an action against the VA alleging that their failure to accommodate his hypersensitivity to smoke by providing a smoke-free environment amounted to handicap discrimination. *Held*: Although the plaintiff was handicapped because of his hypersensitivity to smoke, the VA made reasonable efforts to accommodate his handicap while, at the same time, attempting to accommodate those who felt the need to smoke during working hours.

[Vickers v. Veterans Admin., 549 F. Supp. 85 (WD Wash. 1982).]

[2] Employee Has Rejected Settlement

Once an employee rejects an employer's reasonable accommodation, she waives her right to seek any other form of accommodation. The plaintiff was terminated for reasons attributable to a disabling mental illness. While her skills were undisputably better than adequate, she had experienced emotional problems that led to excessive absenteeism and a pattern of disruptive behavior. Shortly before a scheduled hearing on her administrative appeal, the U.S. Postal Service (USPS) offered to alter the plaintiff's employment records to reflect a resignation, in lieu of a removal, and offered to rehire her at a grade 7 level if she were able to pass a fitness-for-duty exam. The plaintiff refused the settlement and went forward with her appeal, which resulted in a finding that the USPS had not discriminated against her. *Held*: A handicapped employee cannot dictate the measure of her employer's duty to accommodate, and, once she rejects a reasonable accommodation, she waives the right to demand some other form of accommodation.

[Matzo v. Postmaster Gen., 46 Fair Empl. Prac. Cas. (BNA) 869 (DDC 1987).]

[3] Interpreter for Hearing-Disabled Would Be Needed

A teaching hospital cannot be required, under Section 504 of the Rehabilitation Act of 1973, to hire an interpreter to accompany a prospective student with a hearing disability. The plaintiff, who suffered from a serious hearing disability, sought admission into Southeastern's nursing program. After Southeastern rejected the plaintiff's application, she sued under Section 504 of the Rehabilitation Act, alleging that she was an otherwise qualified handicapped individual and that her application was rejected "solely by reason of her handicap." *Held*: Section 504 was not violated; nothing in the Rehabilitation Act prohibits an educational institution from requiring reasonable physical qualifications for admission to a clinical training program. The school was not required to hire someone to follow the applicant around daily to interpret speech for the applicant whenever necessary. Section 504 does not compel educational institutions to disregard the disabilities of handicapped individuals or to make substantial modifications in their programs to allow the disabled to participate. A disabled individual is entitled to the protections of the Rehabilitation Act only if he demonstrates both that he is able to perform all the requirements of the job with or without accommodation, and that even though he is qualified, he was rejected for the position solely on the basis of his handicap.

[Southeastern Community College v. Davis, 442 US 397 (1979).]

[4] Violation of Collective-Bargaining Agreement Would Result

[a] Transfer of Employee Closer to Home

An employer is not required under the Rehabilitation Act of 1973 to transfer a handicapped employee to an office closer to his home if doing so would violate its collective-bargaining agreement. The plaintiff was a disabled Vietnam veteran suffering from an anxiety disorder. When his medical condition caused him to be absent quite often from his work with the Postal Service, the plaintiff's psychologist wrote letters explaining that the plaintiff's anxiety problem was exacerbated by driving to work in heavy traffic. To accommodate the plaintiff, he was reassigned to a position nearer his home, but was warned that the position was only temporary, and that if he desired a more permanent position near his home, he would have to bid for it using his seniority rights. However, when vacancies near his home became available, the plaintiff failed to apply. Ultimately, the Postal Service reassigned the plaintiff back to a position more than fifteen miles from his home. The plaintiff brought an action against the Postal Service alleging that under the Rehabilitation Act, the Postal Service was required to accommodate his medical needs by assigning him to a permanent daytime position close to his home. *Held*: The Postal Service could not be compelled to provide the plaintiff with an accommodation that would violate the seniority provisions of its collective-bargaining agreement. Under that agreement, assignments must be bid for and then awarded on the basis of seniority.

[Shea v. Tisch, 870 F2d 786 (1st Cir. 1989).]

[b] Reassignment of Employee to Less Onerous Duties

An employer is not required to assign a handicapped employee to a position of alternative light-duty employment if that employee cannot perform his job functions and if the employer's collective-bargaining agreement will be violated. The plaintiff was an asthmatic who was employed as a laborer-custodian with the U.S. Postal Service. Two years into his employment, however, the plaintiff suffered severe bouts of asthma. As a result, he was assigned to temporary light duty that relieved him of the obligation to perform tasks that required exertion or generated dust, factors likely to aggravate his asthma. The plaintiff later requested that his workload be further reduced, and filed a request for a permanent light-duty position. The Postal Service denied the plaintiff's request for two reasons. First, there were no permanent light-duty assignments available in the maintenance craft in which the plaintiff was employed. Second, the plaintiff was employed under a collective-bargaining agreement, which required an employee to have served five years before becoming eligible for a permanent light-duty assignment, and the plaintiff had only been with the Postal Service for three years at the time of his request. The Postal Service thereafter fired the plaintiff, reasoning that he was no longer capable of performing the functions of a laborer-custodian and no permanent light-duty position could be assigned to him. The plaintiff brought an action against the Postal Service, alleging discrimination and claiming that he was due reasonable accommodation for his handicapped condition under the Rehabilitation Act of 1973. *Held*: The Postal Service was not under an obligation to accommodate the plaintiff by assigning him to a permanent light-duty position. If a handicapped employee cannot do his job, he can be fired, and the employer is not required to assign him alternative employment. In addition, if the plaintiff were automatically reassigned to another department, then competition with other qualified employees would be eliminated, and their rights under the applicable collective-bargaining agreement would be violated.

[Carter v. Tisch, 822 F2d 465 (4th Cir. 1987).]

The rights afforded a qualified handicapped individual under the Rehabilitation Act of 1973 do not prevail over seniority rights

established by an applicable collective-bargaining agreement. The plaintiff was a Vietnam veteran with a 40 percent disability rating from the Veterans Administration (VA) as a result of shrapnel wounds to his knee and abdomen. The plaintiff performed his job as a carrier technician for seven years before he began to experience job-related physical difficulties, which rendered him unable to carry out all of his assigned duties. He therefore requested that he be reassigned to a vacancy on the Rural Carrier Craft, where the position would be less physically arduous. The Postal Service found him to be ineligible for the position under the applicable collective-bargaining agreement, which required the Postal Service to choose the most senior eligible employee for the position. *Held*: Rights created under bona fide seniority systems prevail over the rights created by the Rehabilitation Act.

[Hurst v. US Postal Serv., 653 F. Supp. 259 (ND Ga. 1986).]

An employer is not required to reassign a handicapped employee as a means of reasonable accommodation. The plaintiff was employed by the Postal Service as a laborer-custodian. While working in this capacity, he suffered from severe depression and was hospitalized. The plaintiff's treating physicians recommended that he not return to his custodial duties because the work exacerbated his depression. They suggested that the Postal Service assign the plaintiff to clerical work. The medical officer of the Postal Service office where the plaintiff worked concluded that the plaintiff was unable to perform his full duties as a laborer-custodian or any other position for which he may have been qualified. As a result, the Postal Service discharged the plaintiff from service. The plaintiff filed suit against the Postal Service, alleging that his condition was a job-related injury, and that he should have been reassigned because of his physical and/or mental handicap. *Held*: The severity and nature of the plaintiff's impairments rendered him handicapped and incapable of working as a laborer-custodian, and, while no authority indicates that reassignment is forbidden from possible forms of accommodation, no cases hold reassignment to be required. The duty to reasonably accommodate only contemplates accommodation of a qualified handicapped employee's present position and does not include a requirement to reassign or transfer an employee to another position. If the plaintiff had been automatically reassigned to another department, then his need to compete with other qualified employees would be eliminated, and their rights secured under the applicable collective-bargaining agreement might have been violated.

[Carty v. Carlin, 623 F. Supp. 1181 (D. Md. 1985).]

[5] Undue Hardship for Employer Would Result

[a] Employee's Inability to Work Around Dust or Fumes

A carpentry worker who became unable to work around hydrocarbon fumes or dust was rightly discharged because any further attempts to accommodate him would have placed an undue burden on the employer. The plaintiff was a carpentry worker with the U.S. Army for three years before he began to experience health problems related to an increased exposure to contact cement. After several episodes on the job of unruly, uncooperative, and unproductive behavior, the plaintiff was sent to the health clinic for examination. Because of dizziness and chest pains, the plaintiff was then taken to a hospital where he remained for five days. He did not return to work until three weeks after his release from the hospital. When the plaintiff returned to his job, he advised his supervisor that he could not be around dust or fumes. He was accordingly transferred to a warehouse, instructed to wear a respirator, and provided work that would not involve fumes or dust. The plaintiff's erratic conduct continued nonetheless, and, although attempts were made to reassign him to a position where he would not have to work around dust and fumes, he was ultimately discharged. The plaintiff filed an action alleging that his employer had failed to provide reasonable accommodation for his handicap. *Held*: Any further attempts by the department to accommodate the plaintiff would have placed an undue burden on the operations of the army depot where he worked. The department made affirmative attempts, although unsuccessful, to place the plaintiff in a position in which he could perform his duties in spite of his handicap. As a practical matter, the dustless and fumeless working environment that the plaintiff believed he required could not be provided because of the nature of the industrial processes performed at the depot.

[Rosiak v. US Department of Army, 46 Fair Empl. Prac. Cas. (BNA) 989 (MD Pa. 1987).]

[b] Employee's Nervousness and Heart Condition

A job applicant who suffers from nervousness and a heart condition is properly denied a position as a seasonal park technician, where any reasonable accommodation would place an undue burden on the employer. The plaintiff was rated by the Veteran's Administration (VA) as being 100 percent disabled based on a nervous condition and a heart impairment. Subsequent to this rating, the plaintiff underwent a quadruple bypass operation. Shortly thereafter, the plaintiff was denied a position as a seasonal park technician based upon his physical limitations. *Held*: Because the plaintiff could not safely perform the required job duties, such as operating a motorboat alone, walking over rough terrain, or handling disorderly park visitors, any attempt to reasonably accommodate him would have subjected the employer to an undue hardship. The essential nature of a particular job function is not determined solely by the amount of time devoted to it. Because a technician might be called upon to operate a motorboat alone only occasionally, does not make that job function any less essential or make it unrelated to the job. Only two to four other workers were available at any given time to patrol the 150,000 acres at the park, and, in light of the agency's limited resources, requiring these other park technicians to perform many of the plaintiff's duties (had he been hired), would impose an "undue hardship" on the Corps.

[Treadwell v. Alexander, 707 F2d 473 (11th Cir. 1983).]

[6] Employee Cannot Perform Essential Functions

[a] Inability to Perform Essential Functions of "Position in Question" (Generally)

The Rehabilitation Act of 1973's provision, requiring an employee to be able to perform the essential functions of the "position in question," does not refer to all positions to which a handicapped

employee may be assigned, but to the position from which the employee is actually terminated. The plaintiff was a federal protective officer (FPO) for many years. He performed his duties satisfactorily until he began to experience back problems associated with chronic low-back syndrome. As a result of this disability, the plaintiff could no longer perform the essential duties of his job. Consequently, he was placed on "light-duty" status, where he was responsible for filing, answering the telephone, mail delivery, and general clerical duties. Nearly three years later, he was discharged from his light-duty position. The plaintiff brought suit under the Rehabilitation Act, alleging that since he had been performing light duty for almost three years prior to his termination, his job was no longer an FPO but instead was the light-duty position that he was satisfactorily performing. The defendant contended, however, that the plaintiff was being discharged from the FPO job, a position for which he could not perform the essential functions. *Held*: The Rehabilitation Act's requirement, that an employee be able to perform the essential functions of the "position in question," refers to the job from which the plaintiff was dismissed. The "position in question" does not necessarily include all positions to which a handicapped person may have been reassigned. Thus, a trial was necessary to determine from which job the plaintiff was being terminated; that of FPO or the light-duty position.

[Dancy v. Kline, 639 F. Supp. 1076 (ND Ill. 1986).]

[b] Bilateral Carpal Tunnel Syndrome

The Rehabilitation Act of 1973 does not require an employer to provide light duty to an employee who suffers from bilateral carpal tunnel syndrome, since he cannot perform the essential functions of his given position. The plaintiff was employed with the U.S. Postal Service as a letter-sorting machine (LSM) distribution clerk. After contracting bilateral carpal tunnel syndrome, the plaintiff became incapable of working more than four hours per day. It was determined that this syndrome was caused and aggravated by keying on an LSM or by manually sorting mail. The Postal Service terminated the plaintiff upon finding that he was physically unable to perform the duties of his position any longer. The plaintiff brought an action against the Postal Service, alleging that they had an obligation to reassign him to a completely different position with duties he could perform. *Held*: Reassignment was not required under the Rehabilitation Act. An employee is properly fired if he cannot perform the essential functions of his given position.

[Black v. Frank, 52 Fair Empl. Prac. Cas. (BNA) 1059 (SD Ala. 1990).]

[c] Asthma

An employer is not required to assign a handicapped employee to a position of alternative light-duty employment if that employee cannot perform his job functions. The plaintiff was an asthmatic who was employed as a laborer-custodian with the U.S. Postal Service. Two years into his employment, however, the plaintiff suffered severe bouts of asthma. As a result, he was assigned to temporary light duty that relieved him of the obligation to perform tasks that required exertion or generated dust, factors likely to aggravate his asthma. The plaintiff later requested that his workload be further reduced, and filed a request for a permanent light-duty position. The Postal Service denied the plaintiff's request for two reasons. First, there were no permanent light-duty assignments available in the maintenance craft in which the plaintiff was employed. Second, the plaintiff was employed under a collective-bargaining agreement that required an employee to have served five years before becoming eligible for a permanent light-duty assignment, and the plaintiff had only been with the Postal Service for three years at the time of his request. The Postal Service thereafter fired the plaintiff, reasoning that he was no longer capable of performing the functions of a laborer-custodian and no permanent light-duty position could be assigned to him. The plaintiff brought an action against the Postal Service, alleging discrimination and claiming that he was due reasonable accommodation for his handicapped condition under the Rehabilitation Act of 1973. *Held*: The Postal Service was not under an obligation to accommodate the plaintiff by assigning him to a permanent light-duty position. If a handicapped employee cannot do his job, he can be fired, and the employer is not required to assign him alternative employment. In addition, if the plaintiff were automatically reassigned to another department, then competition with other qualified employees would be eliminated, and their rights under the applicable collective-bargaining agreement would have been violated.

[Carter v. Tisch, 822 F2d 465 (4th Cir. 1987).]

[d] Depression

An employer is not required to reassign a depressed employee as a means of reasonable accommodation if he is incapable of performing his job. The plaintiff was employed by the Postal Service as a laborer-custodian. While working in this capacity, he suffered from severe depression and was hospitalized. The plaintiff's treating physicians recommended that he not return to his custodial duties because the work exacerbated his depression. They suggested that the Postal Service assign the plaintiff to clerical work. The medical officer of the Postal Service office where the plaintiff worked concluded that the plaintiff was unable to perform his full duties as a laborer-custodian or any other position for which he may have been qualified. As a result, the Postal Service discharged the plaintiff from service. The plaintiff filed suit against the Postal Service, alleging that his condition was a job-related injury and that he should have been reassigned because of his physical and/or mental handicap. *Held*: The plaintiff was a handicapped individual under the Rehabilitation Act of 1973, but the severity and nature of the plaintiff's impairments rendered him incapable of working as a laborer-custodian. While no authority indicates that reassignment is forbidden from possible forms of accommodation, no cases hold reassignment to be required. The duty to reasonably accommodate only contemplates accommodation of a qualified handicapped employee's present position, and does not include a requirement to reassign or transfer an employee to another position.

[Carty v. Carlin, 623 F. Supp. 1181 (D. Md. 1985).]

[7] Employee Cannot Perform Job Safely

A job applicant who suffers from nervousness and a heart condition is properly denied a job as a seasonal park technician, where

the applicant could not safely perform his job alone. The plaintiff was rated by the Veteran's Administration (VA) as being 100 percent disabled based upon a nervous condition and a heart impairment. Subsequent to this rating, the plaintiff underwent a quadruple bypass operation. Shortly thereafter, the plaintiff was denied a position as a seasonal park technician based on his physical limitations. *Held*: The plaintiff could not safely perform the required job duties, such as operating a motorboat alone, walking over rough terrain, or handling disorderly park visitors. The plaintiff's argument that these functions were not "essential" because technicians did not regularly perform such duties was rejected. The essential nature of a particular job function is not determined solely by the amount of time devoted to it. That a technician might be called upon to operate a motorboat alone only occasionally, does not make that job function any less essential or make it unrelated to the job. As to the plaintiff's claim that the Corps had an obligation to make accommodation for his handicap, the court found that only two to four other workers were available at any given time to patrol the 150,000 acres at the park, and, in light of the agency's limited resources, requiring these other park technicians to perform many of the plaintiff's duties had he been hired would impose an "undue hardship" on the Corps.

[Treadwell v. Alexander, 707 F2d 473 (11th Cir. 1983).]

[8] Preferential Treatment Over Nondisabled and Disabled Would Result

[a] Reassignment to Other Duties

No reasonable accommodation is available for an employee with a borderline personality organization disorder with compulsive features (manifesting itself by shoplifting and anxiety over travel). The plaintiff was employed by the Department of Agriculture as a labor relations specialist. After it was discovered that he had been arrested on a number of occasions for shoplifting, he was fired. The plaintiff challenged his discharge contending that he suffered from a psychological condition causing him to have undue anxiety over traveling and a propensity to shoplift. *Held*:

The plaintiff's condition could not be accommodated by a transfer to another position. Reasonable accommodation does not require the government to reassign an employee, to create a new position for the employee, or to restructure a job in a way that would usurp the legitimate rights of other employees. Although many of these actions may be taken as a reasonable accommodation if no undue hardship would be imposed on the operation of an agency program, none were required in this case.

[Fields v. Lyng, 48 Fair Empl. Prac. Cas. (BNA) 1037 (D. Md. 1988).]

[b] Transfer to Office Closer to Home

An employer is not required to transfer a disabled employee to a job closer to her home, or otherwise give the plaintiff a preference over other disabled individuals. The plaintiff incurred debilitating injuries while working for the U.S. Postal Service. The injuries caused her to leave the service for a period of fourteen years, during which time she underwent rehabilitation. Subsequently, the Postal Service offered the plaintiff a permanent limited duty clerk's position. The plaintiff accepted the position, but almost immediately inquired into possible openings in an office closer to her home. The postmaster of the branch office near her home offered the plaintiff a part-time clerk assignment that would conform to her physical limitations. The plaintiff rejected this offer because of the part-time nature of the job and also because it required her to obtain an additional skill. She thereafter filed an action against the Postal Service, alleging handicap discrimination and failure to reasonably accommodate her condition. The plaintiff alleged that positions that suited her wants and needs actually existed in the branch office near her home, but were instead given to two other handicapped postal employees. *Held*: In favor of the Postal Service. The plaintiff sought a preference for one handicapped person over another for a given position. The purpose of the Rehabilitation Act of 1973 was to prevent treatment favorable to nonhandicapped individuals over the disabled. As this litigation involved no nonhandicapped employees, there could be no claim of handicap discrimination. The Postal Service had already accommodated Fowler by placing her in a limited duty clerk's position following her four-teen-year leave. This relieved the service from any further obligation to accommodate Fowler.

[Fowler v. Frank, 702 F. Supp. 143 (ED Mich. 1988).]

A.05 LEGITIMATE GROUNDS FOR REJECTING APPLICANT OR EMPLOYEE

[1] Nondisabled Applicant More Qualified

An employer does not violate the Rehabilitation Act of 1973 when it denies a blind job applicant the position of school librarian, in order to give the position to a more qualified applicant. The plaintiff had been legally blind since her childhood. While the vision in her right eye is correctable to 20/200, she could not read with her left eye even with accommodations. Despite her disability, the plaintiff received a bachelor's degree in library science and had obtained employment as an assistant librarian at a junior high school and as a teacher's aide. When she was rejected for a librarian position with the defendant, she sued, alleging handicap discrimination. The district court found in favor of the school district, focusing their decision on the issue of whether the nondisabled applicant was hired because she was more qualified or solely because the plaintiff was handicapped. *Held*: The school board did not violate the Rehabilitation Act when the board members regarded the plaintiff as qualified, but also regarded the selected person as simply the better candidate.

[Norcross v. Sneed, 755 F2d 113 (8th Cir. 1985).]

[2] Applicant or Employee Misconduct

[a] Poor Performance, Poor Attitude

An employee is not otherwise qualified because of his poor performance and poor attitude. The plaintiff was a paraplegic who also suffers from hypertension and a sinus condition. Over the course of his employment, the plaintiff received numerous disciplinary actions for poor performance and lateness. He was also denied an opportunity for promotion. The plaintiff filed suit, alleging, in part, that his treatment was a form of handicap discrimination. *Held*: The defendant was justified in taking adverse actions against the plaintiff for his failure to show up for work and training sessions on time. The plaintiff was not qualified, because he systematically abused leave privileges, performed poorly, was insubordinate, refused to be trained, was generally unavailable to work (which forced his supervisors to assign backup employees to all his assignments), and tended to make unsubstantiated accusations concerning his superiors whenever any attempt was made to discipline him.

[Thomas v. General Servs. Admin., 49 Fair Empl. Prac. Cas. (BNA) 1602 (DDC 1989).]

[b] Refusal to Take Medication to Control Condition

An employee's refusal to take medication to control her paranoid schizophrenia constitutes a waiver of her discrimination claim. The plaintiff suffered from paranoid schizophrenia. During the course of her employment with the U.S. Postal Service, she experienced four prolonged hospitalizations for psychiatric reasons. Prior to her dismissal, Franklin had on three separate occasions demonstrated a threatening and belligerent attitude toward public officials. Finally, when Franklin attempted to force her way into the White House, she was placed in a psychiatric hospital and discharged from her employment. *Held*: The plaintiff's failure to take prescribed medication was the cause of her violent incidents and that by failing to take it, she waived her claim of discrimination.

[Franklin v. Postal Serv., 46 Fair Empl. Prac. Cas. (BNA) 1734 (SD Ohio 1988).]

[c] Shoplifting

An employee with a borderline personality organization disorder with compulsive features (manifesting itself by shoplifting and anxiety over travel) is not an otherwise qualified individual for his position as a labor negotiator. The plaintiff was employed by the Department of Agriculture as a labor relations specialist. After it was discovered that he had been arrested on a number of occasions for shoplifting, he was fired. The plaintiff challenged his discharge, contending that he suffered from a psychological condition causing him to have undue anxiety over traveling and a propensity to shoplift. *Held*: The plaintiff was not otherwise qualified for the position of labor relations specialist because he could not travel safely or be trusted as a negotiator.

[Fields v. Lyng, 48 Fair Empl. Prac. Cas. (BNA) 1037 (D. Md. 1988).]

[d] False Representations on Job Application

An employer does not violate the Rehabilitation Act of 1973 when it terminates an epileptic criminal investigator who makes false representations on his pre-employment application as to his epilepsy. The plaintiff was a criminal investigator. The job description states that it is hazardous and that, therefore, criminal investigators must, if suffering from epilepsy, be seizure-free for two years without taking medication. During a pre-employment physical, the plaintiff falsely certified that he had never suffered seizures or convulsions, when, in fact, he had suffered at least three seizures in the past. One such seizure occurred while the plaintiff was with two other surveillance team members in a vehicle pursuing a hypothetical felon across state lines during an exercise. When this episode came to light, it was determined that the plaintiff was not medically qualified for the position of criminal investigator. When the plaintiff refused transfer to another position, he was terminated. *Held*: The plaintiff's intentional misrepresentation of his physical condition, which was his failure to disclose the three seizures he suffered prior to his pre-employment physical, justified the government's termination of the plaintiff's employment.

[Pineiro v. Lehman, 655 F. Supp. 483 (DPR 1987).]

A complaint of handicap discrimination brought by a discharged probationary mail carrier is dismissed, because of his failure to provide truthful answers on his employment application. The plaintiff applied for employment as a mail distributor with the Boston Post Office. In doing so, he submitted a form authorizing the release of his Veteran's Administration (VA) medical records. In response to a 60 percent disability rating from the

VA, the Postal Service requested that the plaintiff provide a report from an orthopedic surgeon as to his present physical condition. As requested, the plaintiff's surgeon wrote a letter to the Postal Service stating that the plaintiff could work without restrictions. The plaintiff was then hired as a probationary mail distributor, but, several days after he commenced work, the papers requested from the VA arrived. These records contradicted the orthopedic surgeon's finding that the plaintiff could work without restrictions. In fact, according to the VA, the plaintiff had told them that he was in constant pain and was under continuous treatment. In addition, the plaintiff had told the VA that he had not been able to work between 1981 and 1983. In his application to the Postal Service, however, he had stated that between the same years, he had worked from 60 to 120 hours a week. When confronted with the medical and employment discrepancies, the plaintiff admitted that he had lied to the VA. The plaintiff was subsequently terminated for falsification of records. *Held*: The Postal Service articulated a legitimate, nondiscriminatory reason for discharging the plaintiff, namely, the falsification made by the plaintiff during the application process.

[Lofgren v. Casey, 642 F. Supp. 1076 (D. Mass. 1986).]

[e] Child Abuse Conviction

An employee who is convicted of sexual child abuse is rightly stripped of his security clearance, which is necessary for his job, and is, therefore, no longer qualified for the position. The plaintiff worked for the Veterans Administration Medical Centers (VAMC) as a computer operator. Because of his access to confidential information, the plaintiff's job required a security clearance. During his employment, the plaintiff was convicted of sexual child abuse. Because of the conviction, the Inspector General's office determined that he was no longer able to hold a critical-sensitive position, revoked his security clearance, and demoted the plaintiff to the only job available at the time that did not require a security clearance. The plaintiff alleged, inter alia, that his mental disability, arising from a chronic condition of paranoid schizophrenia, was the cause of his demotion, and that this amounted to handicap discrimination. *Held*: The plaintiff's criminal misconduct rendered him not otherwise qualified for the position, due to the loss of his security clearance.

[Swann v. Walters, 620 F. Supp. 741 (DDC 1984).]

[3] Disabled Applicant or Employee Cannot Perform Essential Job Functions

[a] Personality-Disorder — Labor Negotiator

An employee with a borderline personality organization disorder with compulsive features (manifesting itself by shoplifting and anxiety over travel) is not an otherwise qualified individual for his position as a labor negotiator. The plaintiff was employed by the Department of Agriculture as a labor relations specialist. After it was discovered that he had been arrested on a number of occasions for shoplifting, he was fired. The plaintiff challenged his discharge, contending that he suffered from a psychological condition, causing him to have undue anxiety over traveling and a propensity to shoplift. *Held*: The plaintiff was not otherwise qualified for the position of labor relations specialist, because he could not travel safely or be trusted as a negotiator.

[Fields v. Lyng, 48 Fair Empl. Prac. Cas. (BNA) 1037 (D. Md. 1988).]

[b] Handicapped Writer/Editor (Cerebral Palsy)

An employer who refuses to promote an employee with cerebral palsy does not violate the Rehabilitation Act of 1973 because the employee cannot meet the accuracy standards required for the higher position. The plaintiff worked for the Office of the Federal Register. After having reached the GS-9 pay grade as a technical publication writer/editor, he was subsequently denied promotion on five occasions to GS-11. He brought suit under the Rehabilitation Act, alleging that the denials were based on his handicap. The primary distinction between the GS-9 and GS-11 jobs was that in the former, the employee's work was subject to review, while in the latter, he would be personally responsible for the final editing of publications with direct authority to release material to the printer. *Held*: Although the plaintiff was among the best qualified candidates in all instances, he lacked the accuracy required for the GS-11 position he sought, and, therefore, the Rehabilitation Act was not violated. Critically, there was absolutely no clear proof of any kind that the plaintiff's lack of accuracy was the result of, or related in any way to, his cerebral palsy. Even if the government had a duty to reasonably accommodate the plaintiff, so as to increase his likelihood of being promoted, it had already done so. The plaintiff had not been required to perform the same volume of work as his GS-9 colleagues. The Rehabilitation Act does not require the Office of the Federal Register to lower the GS-11's accuracy requirements.

[Bruegging v. Burke, 48 Fair Empl. Prac. Cas. (BNA) 140 (DDC 1987).]

[c] Cross-Eyed Postal Worker

Even where a cross-eyed employee is considered handicapped, if he cannot perform the essential functions of his job, he is not qualified under the Rehabilitation Act of 1973. The plaintiff was born with a mild case of strabismus, commonly known as crossed eyes. He was hired by the U.S. Postal Service after successfully passing the Letter Sorter Machine Vision Examination and other requirements for the position of distribution clerk machine trainee. When the plaintiff completed his probationary period, he was promoted to distribution clerk, part-time flexible (PTF), machine qualified. The duties of this new position required the plaintiff to operate a mail-sorting machine. After three months of work as a PTF machine operator, the plaintiff began to develop eye strain, headaches, and excessive tearing. The plaintiff's physician wrote a letter to the Postal Service indicating that the plaintiff's symptoms were the result of the detailed visual work required to operate the mail-sorting machine in combination with his strabismus. The plaintiff's condition, however, did not limit any other of his normal daily activities whatsoever. When the Postal Service discharged the plaintiff, he brought suit alleging handicap discrimination. *Held*: Even if the plaintiff were handicapped, he was not qualified to perform the duties for which he was hired, because he could not, with or without accommodation, continue to operate the mail-sorting machine. Accommodation for the plaintiff's condition would have required the Postal Service to eliminate the essential task of his job (the visual activity), which would have been unreasonable.

[Jasany v. US Postal Serv., 755 F2d 1244 (6th Cir. 1985).]

[d] Paraplegic Policeman

A paraplegic police officer who cannot perform forcible arrests and transfer requirements, which are necessary to the job, is not a "qualified handicapped individual" within the meaning of the Rehabilitation Act of 1973. The plaintiff was an officer in the St. Louis County Police Department. As a result of a gunshot wound sustained in the line of duty, he became a paraplegic. He was thereafter dismissed due to his inability to satisfy two police department requirements for commissioned officers—that they be able to effect a forceful arrest and that they be able to transfer among all positions within the department. The plaintiff brought suit under the Rehabilitation Act against the St. Louis County Police Department for reinstatement as a commissioned officer. *Held*: For the defendant, because both of the challenged physical requirements were nationwide standards for active commissioned police officers and were reasonable, legitimate, and necessary to guarantee effective police work, and the defendant's refusal to modify these requirements to accommodate the plaintiff was not unreasonable. An employer who denies an individual employment because of a handicap must show that the criteria used are job-related and that the applicant could not efficiently perform the essentials of the job. Applying this standard to the present case, the forceful arrest and transfer requirements were in fact necessary to the job and were uniformly applied.

[Simon v. St. Louis County, Mo., 735 F2d 1082 (8th Cir. 1984).]

[e] Back-Injured Postal Worker

An employee who can no longer perform the essential functions of the job for which she was hired, is not an otherwise qualified handicapped person under the Rehabilitation Act of 1973, and can be terminated from her employment. In 1977, the U.S. Postal Service advertised a vacancy for a position as a distribution clerk—machine operator trainee. The job entailed, among other things, operating a mail-sorting machine, moving large quantities of mail to and from the machine, and moving large quantities of mail in and out of the area of the machine. The plaintiff applied for, and was given, the position after successfully completing a written test and a pre-employment physical exam. The Postal Service assigned the plaintiff to a position that included transporting mail on dollies weighing up to 700 pounds when fully loaded. On the first day of this assignment, she attempted to move a dolly on her own and strained her back. She told her foreman that she could not perform the transporting work because of past back injuries. She was ultimately discharged due to her inability to perform the duties of her position and because a reassignment to a position of permanent light duty was prohibited by the national collective-bargaining agreement. The plaintiff filed suit against the Postal Service, alleging discrimination due to her handicap. *Held*: The plaintiff was not an otherwise qualified handicapped person because she could no longer perform the dolly-transporting work with or without reasonable accommodation.

[Daubert v. US Postal Serv., 733 F2d 1367 (10th Cir. 1984).]

[f] Schizophrenic Foreign Service Officer

A foreign service officer whose schizoid personality disorder requires support services available only in the United States, is not "otherwise qualified" to perform the essential functions of his job. The plaintiff worked as a foreign service officer in Uruguay for several years. He was dismissed from service after the Board of Foreign Service Appeals determined that he had compromised his ability to represent the United States abroad. The plaintiff attributed his conduct to acute alcohol addiction and a schizoid personality disorder. *Held*: Although either or both of the plaintiff's afflictions constituted a handicap, overseas service was an essential condition of the plaintiff's employment in the Foreign Service, and his need for continuing therapy in the United States precluded him from accepting an assignment abroad. Therefore, the plaintiff was not otherwise qualified.

[Guerriero v. Schultz, 557 F. Supp. 511 (DDC 1983).]

[g] Cardiac Condition—Engineer's Helper

An employer has no duty to inquire into the accuracy of medical reports indicating that a disabled employee cannot perform essential functions of his job. The plaintiff worked for the Federal Bureau of Investigation (FBI) as an operating engineer helper. He experienced such severe chest pains while at work one day that he was admitted to a hospital for examination. The treating cardiologist wrote to the plaintiff's supervisor that the plaintiff had a cardiac condition and that he should not be required to work at night, but that he could continue to perform strenuous labor if permitted to rest when tired. Although the plaintiff's supervisor made the suggested accommodations, the plaintiff nonetheless continued to experience chest pains. After reexamination by a second physician, it was determined that the plaintiff suffered from severe coronary artery disease and that he should be reassigned to a desk position without any stress. Although the plaintiff was then reassigned, he was soon discharged after failing tests for clerical positions. At the trial in the plaintiff's action under the Rehabilitation Act of 1973, it was brought to light that his condition was not nearly as severe as previously thought to be. *Held*: The plaintiff could not perform the duties of an operating engineer helper at the time he was terminated, and there are no cases, statutes, or regulations imposing a duty on the employer to inquire into the plaintiff's medical condition and to uncover the fact that his diagnosis was in error.

[Walker v. Attorney Gen. of the US, 572 F. Supp. 100 (DDC 1983).]

[4] Disabled Applicant or Employee a Threat to Self or to Others

[a] Physical Violence

An employee suffering from maladaptive reactions to psychological stressors is not otherwise qualified to perform his job where he is unable to refrain from using physical violence on his supervisor. The plaintiff was employed with the U.S. General Services Administration (GSA) as a computer programmer analyst. He suffered from a "maladaptive reaction to psychological stressor" condition, an adjustment disorder often accompanied by violent emotion and conduct. The GSA fired the plaintiff after he physically assaulted his supervisor and rampaged through the office damaging office equipment. *Held*: Even if the plaintiff's mental condition was considered a legitimate handicap, he was not "otherwise qualified" for his position, because he endangered the health and safety of himself and others.

[Adams v. US General Servs. Admin., 51 Fair Empl. Prac. Cas. (BNA) 647 (DDC 1989).]

[b] Insulin Dependency

A policy of the Federal Bureau of Investigation that precludes insulin-dependent persons from being employed in certain positions is found reasonable on the grounds of safety. The primary issue in this case was whether insulin-dependent persons could safely perform the essential functions of special agents and investigative specialists so as to invalidate an across-the-board rule prohibiting such persons from holding these positions. The plaintiff argued that the ability of a particular diabetic to perform the job should be decided on a case-by-case basis, rather than having all insulin-diabetics be excluded. *Held*: The preclusion of insulin-dependent diabetics from employment as special agents or investigative specialists does not violate the Rehabilitation Act of 1973, because there is no method of testing that could reliably determine whether certain individual insulin-dependent diabetics are at little or no risk of a severe hypoglycemic occurrence while on assignment. This blanket rule can be justified, because the requirements are directly connected with, and substantially promote, safety and job performance concerns.

[Davis v. Meese, 692 F. Supp. 505 (ED Pa. 1988).]

[5] Reasonable Accommodation Would Cause Undue Hardship for Employer

[a] Employee's Inability to Work Around Dust or Fumes

A carpentry worker who became unable to work around hydrocarbon fumes or dust was rightly discharged because any further

attempts to accommodate him would have placed an undue burden on the employer. The plaintiff was a carpentry worker with the U.S. Army for three years before he began to experience health problems related to an increased exposure to contact cement. After several episodes on the job of unruly, uncooperative, and unproductive behavior, the plaintiff was sent to the health clinic for examination. Because of dizziness and chest pains, the plaintiff was then taken to a hospital where he remained for five days. He did not return to work until three weeks after his release from the hospital. When the plaintiff returned to his job, he advised his supervisor that he could not be around dust or fumes. He was accordingly transferred to a warehouse, instructed to wear a respirator, and provided work that would not involve fumes or dust. The plaintiff's erratic conduct continued nonetheless, and, although attempts were made to reassign him to a position where he would not have to work around dust and fumes, he was ultimately discharged. The plaintiff filed an action alleging that his employer had failed to provide reasonable accommodation for his handicap. *Held*: Any further attempts by the department to accommodate the plaintiff would have placed an undue burden on the operations of the army depot where he worked. The department made affirmative attempts, although unsuccessful, to place the plaintiff in a position in which he could perform his duties in spite of his handicap. As a practical matter, the dustless and fumeless working environment that the plaintiff believed he required could not be provided, because of the nature of the industrial processes performed at the depot.

[Rosiak v. US Department of Army, 46 Fair Empl. Prac. Cas. (BNA) 989 (MD Pa. 1987).]

[b] Employee's Nervousness and Heart Condition

A job applicant who suffers from nervousness and a heart condition is properly denied a position as a seasonal park technician where any reasonable accommodation would place an undue burden on the employer. The plaintiff was rated by the Veteran's Administration (VA) as being 100 percent disabled based upon a nervous condition and a heart impairment. Subsequent to this rating, the plaintiff underwent a quadruple bypass operation.

Shortly thereafter, the plaintiff was denied a position as a seasonal park technician based upon his physical limitations. *Held*: Because the plaintiff could not safely perform the required job duties, such as operating a motorboat alone, walking over rough terrain, or handling disorderly park visitors, any attempt to reasonably accommodate him would have subjected the employer to an undue hardship. The essential nature of a particular job function is not determined solely by the amount of time devoted to it. Because a technician might be called upon to operate a motorboat alone only occasionally, does not make that job function any less essential or make it unrelated to the job. Only two to four other workers were available at any given time to patrol the 150,000 acres at the park, and, in light of the agency's limited resources, requiring these other park technicians to perform many of the plaintiff's duties (had he been hired) would impose an "undue hardship" on the Corps.

[Treadwell v. Alexander, 707 F2d 473 (11th Cir. 1983).]

A.06 ILLEGITIMATE GROUNDS FOR REJECTING APPLICANTS OR EMPLOYEES

[1] Disregarding Favorable Information on Applicant's or Employee's Condition

The Rehabilitation Act of 1973 is violated when an employer fails to accept the bona fide report of an employee's physician as to the limitations on her abilities to perform the essential functions of the job at issue. The plaintiff was employed full-time with a nursing home as the director of nursing up until the time she was diagnosed as having multiple sclerosis. The plaintiff's physician prepared a report that indicated that she was able to perform the duties of her job with the possible exception of walking or being on her feet for prolonged periods. The plaintiff's physician suggested that she return to work on a part-time basis, working herself up to full time before her three-month medical leave of absence would expire. Her employer refused to read the medical report. Although the employer ultimately offered her a part-time consulting position, it was not her original job. Thereafter, the plaintiff sued, alleging handicap discrimination. *Held*: The plaintiff was "otherwise qualified" to perform the director of nursing job. Standing or walking were not essential functions of the job, and the defendant should have accepted the bona fide conclusions of the plaintiff's doctor. The defendant was not permitted to require further assurances from the plaintiff that she could perform duties that were neither relevant to the director position nor to the health and safety of the defendant's patients or other employees. An employer, however, need not unquestionably accept the employee's doctor's view in all circumstances. Rather, an employer may, in an appropriate situation, require its own independent medical exam. The error made by the defendant was that it lacked adequate support for its assumptions concerning the plaintiff's ability. An employer's concerns about the abilities of a handicapped employee must be based on more than reflexive reactions about a handicapped individual's ability to do the job, no matter how well-intentioned.

[Carter v. Casa Cent., 849 F2d 1048 (7th Cir. 1988).]

The Rehabilitation Act of 1973 is violated when an applicant to a medical residency program qualifies for the program apart from his handicap, and the reasons articulated by the program's examining committee for rejecting the applicant are based on incorrect assumptions or inadequate factual grounds. The plaintiff was a medical doctor confined to a wheelchair and disabled in his abilities to walk and to write as a result of multiple sclerosis. He sought admission into the defendant's psychiatric residency program. He met all the requisite academic standards of the program. In addition, he submitted to the admissions committee a letter from his supervisor during one year of residency in psychiatry at another prestigious institution. The letter stated, among other things, that the plaintiff was hard-working, reliable, showed remarkable patience and understanding for his patients, and that his supervisors felt that his illness did not present any emotional impairment in his work. Moveover, the letter stated that the plaintiff was able to handle the most difficult case in a satisfactory manner. An examining board denied the plaintiff admittance to the residency program because his mean interview ratings were held to be too low. Each of the interviewers, in addition, made comments expressing their views about the plaintiff's capabilities. All of these comments reflected a doubt that he could handle either the emotional strain of caring for his patients or the physical load of the program due to his affliction. *Held*: The assumptions made by the admissions committee were sufficiently rebutted by the plaintiff's evidence to support the finding that the plaintiff was indeed qualified for the program and that his rejection was based on discriminatory reasoning.

[Pushkin v. Regents of Univ. of Colo., 658 F2d 1372 (10th Cir. 1981).]

[2] Disparate Treatment of Applicant or Employee Would Be Required

An employer violates the Rehabilitation Act of 1973 when the evidence establishes disparate treatment of the plaintiff. The plaintiff suffered from multiple physical disabilities, including an inability to speak clearly, a left hand with only three digits, a right hand that is severed above the wrist, and malformed feet. Despite her disabilities, she received a teaching degree and became licensed by the state of Nevada as a special education teacher. When four teaching positions became available with the defendant, offers were made to the plaintiff and three others. However, when the plaintiff began to exhibit unexplained symptoms of multiple sclerosis, increasingly causing her to miss work, the defendant refused to renew her contract. The plaintiff filed an action of handicap discrimination against the defendant. *Held*: The defendant had discriminated against the plaintiff, solely by reason of her handicap, based upon the following facts: (1) over a period of three years, she was not offered a standard teacher's contract in the district; (2) she was the only one of four teachers to receive a temporary one-year contract; (3) when one of the three failed to accept his permanent offer of employment, it was offered to a woman with no teaching experience and not to the plaintiff; (4) she was assigned the most difficult class of students; and (5) she was not provided adequate assistance after the first two assistants left.

[Recanzone v. Washoe County School Dist., 696 F. Supp. 1372 (D. Nev. 1988).]

[3] Invalid Condition of Employment

Dismissal of a hearing-impaired school bus driver is improper where the hearing requirement does not advance the essential purpose of the program. The plaintiff was hired and trained as a school bus driver by a private bus company that provided transportation for students in public school districts. After completing his training, the plaintiff took, and successfully passed, a school bus driver's license exam required by the Pennsylvania Department of Transportation (DOT). Shortly thereafter, DOT suspended the license on the ground that the plaintiff failed to satisfy a DOT regulation requiring all bus driver's license applicants to have no hearing loss greater than 25 decibels in the better ear, without a hearing aid. At the time of the plaintiff's suspension, however, he was in every respect, other than his hearing, qualified under DOT regulations to continue to be licensed to drive a school bus. In addition, with the use of his hearing aid, the plaintiff's hearing was corrected within the decibel requirements of the DOT safety regulations. The plaintiff filed a class action against the DOT in the district court, alleging, inter alia, that the suspension of his and members of the class's school bus driver's licenses violated the Rehabilitation Act of 1973. *Held*: The essential nature of the program is to prevent any appreciable risks, not just any risks, that a school bus driver will not be able to provide for the safety of his passengers. Since DOT permitted applicants who wore eyeglasses to earn their school bus driver's licenses, the distinction between the risks of eyeglasses becoming dislodged, and those of hearing aids becoming dislodged, was unfounded with respect to a bus driver's ability to provide for bus passengers' safety.

[Strathie v. Department of Transp., 716 F2d 227 (3d Cir. 1983).]

Despite state regulations, an employer is ordered to rehire a school bus driver whose leg had been amputated, because he is well qualified to drive and no expenditures by the employer are required to have the driver safely operate the bus. The plaintiff drove a school bus for several years prior to amputation of his left leg. After undergoing rehabilitative training to relearn driving skills, the plaintiff sought reemployment. His request was denied, based upon a state administrative regulation prohibiting the hiring of a school bus driver who did not possess both natural feet and legs. *Held*: Section 504 of the Rehabilitation Act of 1973 mandates that the plaintiff be rehired. The federal Rehabilitation Act takes precedence over any state law to the contrary. The plaintiff proved his ability to operate a school bus, despite the loss of his leg. He had undergone a substantial amount of rehabilitative driver training, and the Bureau of Rehabilitation Services had offered to provide the school system with the equipment necessary to accommodate the plaintiff's special needs, so that the school board would not have to expend any money to employ him.

[Coleman v. Casey County Bd. of Educ., 510 F. Supp. 301 (WD Ky. 1980).]

[4] Improper Testing

An employer who chooses a test that discriminates against the handicapped as its sole hiring criterion, and makes no meaningful accommodation for a handicapped applicant, violates the Rehabilitation Act of 1973. The plaintiff suffered from dyslexia. He applied for a position with the Tennessee Valley Authority (TVA) in an apprenticeship training program to become a heavy equipment operator. As its sole criterion for judging applicants, the TVA required the plaintiff to take the General Aptitude Test Battery (GATB), an examination used to predict the probability of success in the training program. The plaintiff received a low score on this examination due to his dyslexia. After receiving the results of his GATB test, the plaintiff had doctors evaluate him with nonwritten tests and was judged to have above-average intelligence, coordination, and aptitude for a position as a heavy equipment operator. The TVA attempted to persuade the testing service to administer an oral GATB to the plaintiff, but was unsuccessful, because scoring could not accurately be translated from an oral test. Despite the TVA's knowledge of the problems with the GATB, and, in spite of the unsuccessful efforts to obtain alternate forms of evaluation, the TVA rejected the plaintiff's application based solely on his low score on the written GATB. *Held*: The TVA had an obligation to do more in order to accommodate the plaintiff's handicap, such as developing alternative methods of testing. Moreover, both parties agreed that the main hiring criteria, the GATB test, could not accurately reflect the plaintiff's abilities.

[Stutts v. Freeman, 694 F2d 666 (11th Cir. 1983).]

[5] Inability to Perform Functions Not Listed in Job Description

An employer is responsible for the content of its standard position description, and, therefore, an employee is entitled to rely on it as a statement of the essential functions of her job. The plaintiff was a multiple position letter-sorting machine (MPLSM) operator. The job description of an MPLSM operator contained a list of duties and responsibilities expected of the operator, including manual distribution of mail, knowledge of distribution schemes, ability to operate the MPLSM with 98 percent accuracy, as well as minimum eyesight requirements. The plaintiff not only performed all of the tasks described above, but she also performed tasks not mentioned in the job description, including "culling" mail, a task that requires prolonged periods of standing. After being diagnosed in 1982 as having permanent osteoarthritis of the knee joints, and on the advice of her orthopedic surgeon, the plaintiff requested that the Postal Service assign her to "light" duty so as to avoid work requiring long periods of standing. She brought an action under the Rehabilitation Act of 1973, when employees performing light-duty work (but not MPLSM operators) were required to reduce their hours of work. The Postal Service defended on the ground that the plaintiff was not qualified to perform the essential functions of an MPLSM operator, because of her inability to stand for long periods. This was a job function not included in the position description, but nevertheless something that the plaintiff had done in the past. *Held*: The plaintiff was a qualified handicapped individual for the position of MPLSM operator, because she was able to perform any and every task described in the Postal Service's job description. This is true, even though she could not perform tasks not set forth in the description. Numerous courts entertaining Rehabilitation Act claims have looked to position descriptions in assessing the essential functions of a job. The plaintiff's willingness to stand for prolonged periods "culling" mail, a task not included in her job description, could not be turned against her to limit her rights to protection under the Rehabilitation Act. Moreover, because the Postal Service drafted the MPLSM operator job description, the plaintiff was entitled to rely on it as a statement of the essential functions of her job.

[Guinn v. Bolger, 598 F. Supp. 196 (DDC 1984).]

[6] Possibility of Future Injury

[a] Decision Should Not Be Based on Speculation and Conjecture

An employer violates the Rehabilitation Act of 1973 by rejecting an applicant for a cement-truck-driving position based upon the remote possibility that she may have a spasm (caused by a problem with her lower back) while driving. The Office of Federal Contract Compliance Programs (OFCCP) brought this action against Texas Industries, Inc. (TXI), on behalf of a disabled employee. TXI had refused to hire the employee as a cement truck driver because x-rays had revealed that she had a congenital deformity in her lower back. The x-rays also revealed that she had undergone a partial laminectomy for removal of a herniated disk. Based solely on the denial of the truck-driving position by TXI, the Department of Labor (DOL) determined that the employee was handicapped because she had been denied participation in a major life activity—employment. In addition, she was perceived as handicapped by TXI. The DOL next turned to the question of whether the employee was qualified for the position. TXI conceded that she had the experience for the job but argued that she was not qualified because she may endanger herself and others. This contention was based on TXI's medical experts who concluded that the employee could suffer sudden severe pain or a spasm while driving and that she might be unable to bring her truck to a safe stop. TXI relied upon a number of cases upholding a carrier's rejection of applicants for intercity bus driver positions because the applicants were older than the carrier's maximum hiring ages. These cases held that deference should be given to an employer's job qualification when that qualification is based on public safety. *Held*: The likelihood of injury, the seriousness of possible injury, or the imminence of the injury are factors that could be the basis for rejection of a qualified handicapped individual on the grounds of business necessity and safe performance of the job. Where an employer establishes the presence of such factors to a sufficient degree, it meets its burden of proving job-relatedness and consistency with business necessity and safe performance. In this case, TXI had failed to carry its burden of proof, for the evidence of an increased likelihood of the employee having a spasm while driving her cement truck was too speculative. In addition, even if she had such a spasm, the evidence that she could not safely bring her truck to a stop was based on conjecture. More than a remote possibility of future injury is needed to justify discrimination against the handicapped.

[Department of Labor, OFCCP v. Texas Indus., Inc., 47 Fair Empl. Prac. Cas. (BNA) 18 (DOL 1988).]

[b] Employer Has Duty to Evaluate All Relevant Medical Evidence

An employer must thoroughly evaluate all the relevant medical evidence when it intends to deny an employment opportunity to a disabled individual on the ground that there is an increased likelihood of injury to that person because of her condition. The plaintiff was an epileptic who applied for a position as a letter sorter machine operator for the U.S. Postal Service. At the time of her application, the plaintiff was employed at Motorola. She was described by her supervisor at Motorola as "very productive" and a person who could "work without difficulty." It was undisputed at trial that the machinery the plaintiff was exposed to at Motorola was more dangerous than that at the position she was seeking. After successfully passing the requisite written exam, the plaintiff was given a standard pre-employment physical exam. The examining doctor took her medical history, noted that she was taking medication, and that her epilepsy was adequately controlled. Nevertheless, the doctor recommended that the plaintiff not be placed in a position that would involve machinery with moving parts. The physician's recommendation was based upon a fear that the plaintiff's condition would increase the risk of injury to her while operating the machine.

Upon this recommendation, the defendant denied further consideration of the plaintiff's application. The plaintiff brought an action against the Postal Service, alleging that it had violated Section 501 of the Rehabilitation Act of 1973 when it denied her a position based on her physical handicap. *Held*: Since almost all handicapped persons are at a greater risk for work-related injuries, the standard for finding a disabled person not to be qualified must be more than a mere "elevated risk" of injury. A proper evaluation of a job applicant entails an analysis of all relevant information regarding the applicant's work and medical history. An employer has a duty to gather sufficient information from the applicant, and from qualified experts, to determine the applicant's abilities and the employer's methods of reasonable accommodation. Qualifications based on the risk of future injury must be examined with special care, so that the Rehabilitation Act will not easily be circumvented.

[Mantolete v. Bolger, 767 F2d 1416 (9th Cir. 1985).]

[c] No Sufficient Basis for Denial of Job

The possibility of future injury is not a sufficient reason for discriminating against the handicapped. The plaintiff was a member of a carpentry apprenticeship program. The program required 8,000 hours of field work to achieve journeyman status. During an employer medical examination, it was discovered that the applicant had a congenital back problem. This condition did not prevent the employee's performance of his apprentice duties but did indicate a risk of future problems. Based on this risk, the government contractor/employer refused to hire the employee. *Held*: The plaintiff's risk of future injury was not a sufficient basis for discriminating against the plaintiff.

[EE Black, Ltd. v. Marshall, 497 F. Supp. 1088 (D. Haw. 1980).]

A.07 NOTICE OF HANDICAP

[1] Employee Not Required to Give Employer Notice

A disabled individual cannot be required to put an employer on notice of handicap under the Rehabilitation Act of 1973. The plaintiff worked for the Department of the Treasury until he was removed from his position in early 1982 due to a reduction in work force. Later the same year, the plaintiff applied for rehire. At his interview, the plaintiff dressed as a woman, as he had during the previous eight years he was employed at the department. He was not rehired, but others with less seniority were. The plaintiff brought an action against the Treasury Department alleging that he had not been rehired because the personnel officer and director both regarded his transvestism as being a mental illness. The district court held that there was no violation of the act because the Treasury did not know that Blackwell was a transvestite, but believed him to be a homosexual, a condition not protected by the Rehabilitation Act. *Held*: The district court's opinion was vacated because a portion of the opinion could have been read to require the plaintiff to inform the Treasury of his handicap (i.e., his transvestism). Such a notice requirement was not supported by the case law, and was in conflict with the regulatory admonition against asking the prospective employee whether he or she is handicapped.

[Blackwell v. US Department of Treasury, 656 F. Supp. 713 (DDC 1986), opinion vacated, 830 F2d 1183 (DC Cir. 1987).]

[2] No Duty to Investigate Possibility of Handicap Without Clear Signs of Employee's Condition

Absent clear signs of the employee's alcoholism, an employer is not put on notice of the employee's alcoholism, and, therefore, an employer is not required to provide the employee with the protections required to be given to known alcoholics under the Rehabilitation Act of 1973. The plaintiff was employed as a securities transaction analyst with the Department of the Treasury. After missing a total of 443 hours of work in a period of six months, his supervisor placed him on leave restrictions. Subsequent to being placed on leave restrictions, the plaintiff was absent from work on numerous occasions. He attributed several of these unscheduled absences to "car trouble" and attributed a certain ten-day absence to a medical problem connected with low-back syndrome. As to this latter absence, he was advised that he needed to bring in medical documentation. While he did provide a letter signed by his doctor, the letter contained no substantive medical information and, at places, bordered on being incoherent. In response to the plaintiff's failure to obey his leave restrictions, the Department of the Treasury fired him. The plaintiff brought an action against his employer, alleging that he had been fired as a result of his handicaps, including his suffering from post-traumatic stress disorder and secondary alcoholism. In addition, he claimed that his supervisors should have been put on notice of his alcoholism, thus failing to provide him with the counseling he was due under terms of the Rehabilitation Act. *Held*: An employer is not required to investigate the possibility of alcoholism to the extent to which it must "ferret out" possible cases, but is required to investigate only those cases where there is a lot of evidence leading to suspicions of alcoholism. The plaintiff's alcoholism was not related to the reasons for his firing. These reasons were based on his failure to provide the required medical documentation for his other, non–alcohol-related illness. Moreover, because the plaintiff never informed his employer of his drinking problem, and also because the employer did not have enough "signs" to be put on notice of alcoholism, the employer did not violate its legal requirements, if such was the case. When presented with an employee whose work suffers because of his alcoholism, an employer must first offer counseling to the employee. If the employee rejects the offer, the employer must offer a firm choice between treatment and discipline. Then, the employer is obligated to evaluate whether keeping the employee would represent an undue hardship and to conduct a fitness-for-duty examination before taking disciplinary steps.

[Fong v. US Department of Treasury, 705 F. Supp. 41 (DDC 1989).]

[3] Employer Should Have Known of Employee's Condition

An employee's excessive absenteeism, frequent failure to return to work on the dates promised, and failure to obtain appropriate leave slips, occurring after twenty years of exemplary service, should have signaled the employee's underlying problem with alcoholism requiring further investigation, rather than the employee's dismissal. The plaintiff had been an employee of the National Marine Fisheries Service (NMFS) for approximately twenty years at the time of his dismissal in November 1983. Beginning in November 1980, the plaintiff was absent from work for 389 days. Although the plaintiff had a problem with alcohol, he never directly informed his supervisors of his illness until after his dismissal, despite its being the direct cause of his absenteeism and his violation of the employer's leave restrictions. The NMFS suspended the plaintiff for excessive absenteeism. The plaintiff phoned his supervisor and told her that he had something important to tell her about his problems, but was told to speak to another supervisor after his suspension was over. When the plaintiff returned to work following the suspension, he did not tell his superiors about his alcoholism. When the plaintiff's problems continued, he was discharged. The plaintiff brought suit, alleging that his employer should have known that he was an alcoholic, and thus failed to provide reasonable accommodation for his handicap. *Held*: Although generally, ignorance of a handicap relieves an agency from responsibility for reasonable accommodation, this duty attached in the present situation, because factors existed from which the NMFS could reasonably infer the plaintiff's alcoholism. Furthermore, by tolerating the plaintiff's erratic work performance for so long, the NMFS contributed to his disease by delaying entry into a rehabilitation program. Finally, a supervisor has a duty to conduct an interview with the employee, advising him of available programs, if he suspects an employee of having an alcohol problem.

[Ferguson v. US Department of Commerce, 46 Fair Empl. Prac. Cas. (BNA) 241 (MD Fla. 1988).]

A.08 DRUG AND ALCOHOL ABUSE

[1] No Impairment or Handicap

An alcoholic government employee is not qualified under the Rehabilitation Act of 1973 and is, therefore, not entitled to protection under the act. The plaintiff was employed with the District of Columbia government as a maintenance mechanic foreman. He was dismissed from his job for drunkenness on duty, discourteous treatment of other employees, and inexcusable absences without leave. Upon his dismissal, the plaintiff filed suit against the district, claiming that he had been discriminated against by virtue of his alcoholism, a disease that he contended constituted a "handicap." *Held*: Under Section 504 of the Rehabilitation Act, the term "handicapped" does not include any individual who is an alcoholic whose current use of alcohol prevents such individual from performing the duties of the job in question or whose employment, by reason of such current alcohol abuse, would constitute a direct threat to property or the safety of others. In addition, the plaintiff's alcoholism prevented him from performing his job. It also made him a threat to property and to others, and, thus, he was rightly dismissed.

[Garrison v. District of Columbia, 51 Fair Empl. Prac. Cas. (BNA) 94 (DDC 1989).]

[2] No Duty to Provide Further Reasonable Accommodation and Unjust Hardship on Employer

The termination of an alcoholic federal employee despite many attempts to accommodate her and despite her erratic conduct, does not violate the Rehabilitation Act of 1973. The plaintiff was employed as a contract specialist with the Federal Aviation Administration (FAA). Starting in early 1984, the effects of her alcoholism became apparent at her job. After observing the plaintiff at work intoxicated, an FAA psychiatrist took her for treatment at a hospital in-patient detoxification unit. The FAA advanced the plaintiff approximately five weeks of sick leave to enable her to complete this program. The plaintiff returned to work soon afterwards, but suffered a relapse in the autumn of 1984, resulting in unscheduled absences from the office and difficulties with co-workers. In August 1985, the FAA issued the plaintiff a letter of proposed termination. However, after the plaintiff's counsel informed the FAA that she had voluntarily entered a hospital's detoxification unit, the FAA rescinded the termination and granted the plaintiff a second leave of absence to facilitate treatment. When a third relapse occurred in late 1985, the FAA met with the plaintiff's counsel and agreed to stay her termination if she would (1) sign a statement of her agreement to get help and (2) would supply the FAA with a report from a prospective treating physician outlining a proposed treatment program. The plaintiff telephoned her supervisor to say that she thought it was ridiculous to pursue further treatment for her alcoholism and then failed to attend an appointment with the detoxification physician. The FAA thereafter terminated her. The plaintiff brought an action against the FAA, alleging that the FAA was required under the Rehabilitation Act to accommodate her handicap of alcoholism in lieu of terminating her employment. *Held*: The Rehabilitation Act did not require the FAA to make additional efforts to accommodate the plaintiff's condition. The previous attempts at accommodation were more than reasonable, and the plaintiff's erratic conduct had become an undue hardship to the agency's operations.

[LeMere v. Burnley, 683 F. Supp. 275 (DDC 1988).]

[3] Legitimate Grounds for Rejecting Applicant or Employee

[a] Applicant or Employee Misconduct

A compliance officer who is convicted of driving under the influence (DUI) three times is not qualified to carry out the responsibilities of his position, even though his alcoholism does not directly interfere with the performance of his duties or constitute a threat to property or the safety of others. The plaintiff was employed by the City of Macon as a compliance officer. Responsibilities of the position included carrying out the enforcement of federal, state, and local laws. While off duty, the plaintiff was charged and later convicted of DUI of alcohol and drugs on two separate occasions. He was later convicted of a third incident of DUI and was subsequently terminated. The plaintiff brought an action alleging that he had been fired because of his alcoholism. *Held*: The plaintiff's discharge was due to his three DUI convictions, as well as his failure to obtain adequate professional help for his drinking problem. The plaintiff could not function effectively as a compliance officer when he, himself, could not comply with the law, as evidenced by his three convictions for DUI.

[Huff v. Israel, 573 F. Supp. 107 (MD Ga. 1983).]

[b] Disabled Applicant or Employee Cannot Perform Essential Job Functions

A former undercover narcotics officer, hospitalized for drug dependence, stress, and depression, is not otherwise qualified to

perform the essential functions of his position. The plaintiff worked as an undercover narcotics officer with the Montgomery County Narcotics Enforcement Team (NET). As an undercover narcotics officer, the plaintiff had to assume different identities and, at times, had to take drugs so that his identity as a police officer would not be revealed to those who sold narcotics to him. During the four years that the plaintiff worked with NET, his use of drugs increased, and, eventually, he entered an in-patient drug rehabilitation program, remaining in the hospital for about a month. He later resigned his job. When his subsequent request for reinstatement was denied, he brought suit alleging handicap discrimination. The district court determined that the plaintiff's drug addiction qualified as a handicap. Furthermore, with respect to his claim that his stress and depression were handicaps, the court noted that because the defendants could not offer evidence to show that the plaintiff's hospitalization was solely for drug addiction, his mental illness would be considered a handicap within the meaning of the Rehabilitation Act of 1973. *Held*: Even though the plaintiff's drug addiction and mental illness were handicaps, requiring the police department to return the plaintiff to his undercover duties would be considered a substantial modification of an essential function, and, therefore, the plaintiff was not "otherwise qualified." While not every police officer who is impaired by stress and depression is not otherwise qualified, the plaintiff's stress and depression were so severe that they led him to the use of drugs and, thus, rendered him not qualified to perform the duties of his job.

[Desper v. Montgomery County, 52 Fair Empl. Prac. Cas. (BNA) 659 (ED Pa. 1990).]

[c] Disabled Applicant or Employee a Threat to Self and to Others

An alcoholic government employee is a direct threat to property and to others and, therefore, not entitled to protection under the Rehabilitation Act of 1973. The plaintiff was employed with the District of Columbia government as a maintenance mechanic foreman. He was dismissed from his job for drunkenness on duty, discourteous treatment of other employees, and inexcusable absences without leave. Upon his dismissal, the plaintiff

A-60

filed suit against the district, claiming that he had been discriminated against by virtue of his alcoholism, a disease that he contended constituted a "handicap." *Held*: Under Section 504 of the Rehabilitation Act, the term "handicapped" does not include any individual who is an alcoholic whose current use of alcohol prevents such individual from performing the duties of the job in question or whose employment, by reason of such current alcohol abuse, would constitute a direct threat to property or the safety of others. The plaintiff's alcoholism prevented him from performing his job, making him a threat to property and to others and, therefore, was rightly dismissed.

[Garrison v. District of Columbia, 51 Fair Empl. Prac. Cas. (BNA) 94 (DDC 1989).]

A compliance officer who is convicted of driving under the influence (DUI) three times is not qualified to carry out the responsibilities of his position, despite the fact that his alcoholism does not directly interfere with the performance of his duties or constitute a threat to property or safety of others. The plaintiff was employed by the City of Macon as a compliance officer. Responsibilities of the position included carrying out the enforcement of federal, state, and local laws. While off duty, the plaintiff was charged and later convicted of DUI of alcohol and drugs on two separate occasions. He was later convicted of a third incident of DUI and was subsequently terminated. The plaintiff brought an action alleging that he had been fired because of his alcoholism. *Held*: The plaintiff's discharge was due to his three DUI convictions, as well as his failure to obtain adequate professional help for his drinking problem. The plaintiff could not function effectively as a compliance officer when he, himself, could not comply with the law, as evidenced by his three convictions for DUI.

[Huff v. Israel, 573 F. Supp. 107 (MD Ga. 1983).]

[4] Notice of Handicap

[a] No Duty to Investigate Possibility of Handicap Without Clear Signs of Employee's Condition

Absent clear signs of the employee's alcoholism, an employer is not put on notice of the employee's alcoholism, and, therefore, an

employer is not required to provide the employee with the protections required to be given to known alcoholics under the Rehabilitation Act of 1973. The plaintiff was employed as a securities transaction analyst with the Department of the Treasury. After missing a total of 443 hours of work in a period of six months, his supervisor placed him on leave restrictions. Subsequent to being placed on leave restrictions, the plaintiff was absent from work on numerous occasions. He attributed several of these unscheduled absences to "car trouble" and attributed a certain ten-day absence to a medical problem connected with low-back syndrome. As to this latter absence, he was advised that he needed to bring in medical documentation. While he did provide a letter signed by his doctor, the letter contained no substantive medical information and, at places, bordered on being incoherent. In response to the plaintiff's failure to obey his leave restrictions, the Department of the Treasury fired him. The plaintiff brought an action against his employer, alleging that he had been fired as a result of his handicaps, including his suffering from post-traumatic stress disorder and secondary alcoholism. In addition, he claimed that his supervisors should have been put on notice of his alcoholism, thus failing to provide him with the counseling he was due under terms of the Rehabilitation Act. *Held*: An employer is not required to investigate the possibility of alcoholism to the extent to which it must "ferret out" possible cases, but is required to investigate only those cases where there is a lot of evidence leading to suspicions of alcoholism. The plaintiff's alcoholism was not related to the reasons for his firing. These reasons were based on his failure to provide the required medical documentation for his other, non–alcohol-related illness. Moreover, because the plaintiff never informed his employer of his drinking problem, and also because the employer did not have enough "signs" to be put on notice of alcoholism, the employer did not violate its legal requirements, if such was the case. When presented with an employee whose work suffers because of his alcoholism, an employer must first offer counseling to the employee. If the employee rejects the offer, the employer must offer a firm choice between treatment and discipline. Then, the employer is obligated to evaluate whether keeping the employee would represent an undue hardship and to conduct a fitness-for-duty examination before taking disciplinary steps.

[Fong v. US Department of Treasury, 705 F. Supp. 41 (DDC 1989).]

[b] Employer Should Have Known of Employee's Condition

An employee's excessive absenteeism, frequent failure to return to work on the dates promised, and failure to obtain appropriate leave slips, occurring after twenty years of exemplary service, should have signaled the employee's underlying problem with alcoholism requiring further investigation, rather than the employee's dismissal. The plaintiff had been an employee of the National Marine Fisheries Service (NMFS) for approximately twenty years at the time of his dismissal in November 1983. Beginning in November 1980, the plaintiff was absent from work for 389 days. Although the plaintiff had a problem with alcohol, he never directly informed his supervisors of his illness until after his dismissal, despite its being the direct cause of his absenteeism and his violation of the employer's leave restrictions. The NMFS suspended the plaintiff for excessive absenteeism. The plaintiff phoned his supervisor and told her that he had something important to tell her about his problems, but was told to speak to another supervisor after his suspension was over. When the plaintiff returned to work following the suspension, he did not tell his superiors about his alcoholism. When the plaintiff's problems continued, he was discharged. The plaintiff brought suit, alleging that his employer should have known that he was an alcoholic, and thus failed to provide reasonable accommodation for his handicap. *Held*: Although generally, ignorance of a handicap relieves an agency from responsibility for reasonable accommodation, this duty attached in the present situation, because factors existed from which the NMFS could reasonably infer the plaintiff's alcoholism. Furthermore, by tolerating the plaintiff's erratic work performance for so long, the NMFS contributed to his disease by delaying entry into a rehabilitation program. Finally, a supervisor has a duty to conduct an interview with the employee, advising him of available programs, if he suspects an employee of having an alcohol problem.

[Ferguson v. US Department of Commerce, 46 Fair Empl. Prac. Cas. (BNA) 241 (MD Fla. 1988).]

APPENDIX B

Americans With
Disabilities Act of 1990

PUBLIC LAW 101–336—JULY 26, 1990   104 STAT. 327

Public Law 101–336
101st Congress

An Act

To establish a clear and comprehensive prohibition of discrimination on the basis of disability.

July 26, 1990
[S. 933]

Be it enacted by the Senate and House of Representatives of the United States of America in Congress assembled,

SECTION 1. SHORT TITLE; TABLE OF CONTENTS.

(a) SHORT TITLE.—This Act may be cited as the "Americans with Disabilities Act of 1990".

(b) TABLE OF CONTENTS.—The table of contents is as follows:

Americans with Disabilities Act of 1990.

42 USC 12101 note.

42 USC 12101.   **SEC. 2. FINDINGS AND PURPOSES.**

(a) FINDINGS.—The Congress finds that—

(1) some 43,000,000 Americans have one or more physical or mental disabilities, and this number is increasing as the population as a whole is growing older;

(2) historically, society has tended to isolate and segregate individuals with disabilities, and, despite some improvements, such forms of discrimination against individuals with disabilities continue to be a serious and pervasive social problem;

(3) discrimination against individuals with disabilities persists in such critical areas as employment, housing, public accommodations, education, transportation, communication, recreation, institutionalization, health services, voting, and access to public services;

(4) unlike individuals who have experienced discrimination on the basis of race, color, sex, national origin, religion, or age, individuals who have experienced discrimination on the basis of disability have often had no legal recourse to redress such discrimination;

(5) individuals with disabilities continually encounter various forms of discrimination, including outright intentional exclusion, the discriminatory effects of architectural, transportation, and communication barriers, overprotective rules and policies,

failure to make modifications to existing facilities and practices, exclusionary qualification standards and criteria, segregation, and relegation to lesser services, programs, activities, benefits, jobs, or other opportunities;

(6) census data, national polls, and other studies have documented that people with disabilities, as a group, occupy an inferior status in our society, and are severely disadvantaged socially, vocationally, economically, and educationally;

(7) individuals with disabilities are a discrete and insular minority who have been faced with restrictions and limitations, subjected to a history of purposeful unequal treatment, and relegated to a position of political powerlessness in our society, based on characteristics that are beyond the control of such individuals and resulting from stereotypic assumptions not truly indicative of the individual ability of such individuals to participate in, and contribute to, society;

(8) the Nation's proper goals regarding individuals with disabilities are to assure equality of opportunity, full participation, independent living, and economic self-sufficiency for such individuals; and

(9) the continuing existence of unfair and unnecessary discrimination and prejudice denies people with disabilities the opportunity to compete on an equal basis and to pursue those opportunities for which our free society is justifiably famous, and costs the United States billions of dollars in unnecessary expenses resulting from dependency and nonproductivity.

(b) PURPOSE.—It is the purpose of this Act—

(1) to provide a clear and comprehensive national mandate for the elimination of discrimination against individuals with disabilities;

(2) to provide clear, strong, consistent, enforceable standards addressing discrimination against individuals with disabilities;

(3) to ensure that the Federal Government plays a central role in enforcing the standards established in this Act on behalf of individuals with disabilities; and

(4) to invoke the sweep of congressional authority, including the power to enforce the fourteenth amendment and to regulate commerce, in order to address the major areas of discrimination faced day-to-day by people with disabilities.

SEC. 3. DEFINITIONS.   42 USC 12102.

As used in this Act:

(1) AUXILIARY AIDS AND SERVICES.—The term "auxiliary aids and services" includes—

(A) qualified interpreters or other effective methods of making aurally delivered materials available to individuals with hearing impairments;

(B) qualified readers, taped texts, or other effective methods of making visually delivered materials available to individuals with visual impairments;

(C) acquisition or modification of equipment or devices; and

(D) other similar services and actions.

(2) DISABILITY.—The term "disability" means, with respect to an individual—

(A) a physical or mental impairment that substantially limits one or more of the major life activities of such individual;

(B) a record of such an impairment; or

(C) being regarded as having such an impairment.

(3) STATE.—The term "State" means each of the several States, the District of Columbia, the Commonwealth of Puerto Rico, Guam, American Samoa, the Virgin Islands, the Trust Territory of the Pacific Islands, and the Commonwealth of the Northern Mariana Islands.

TITLE I—EMPLOYMENT

42 USC 12111.

SEC. 101. DEFINITIONS.

As used in this title:

(1) COMMISSION.—The term "Commission" means the Equal Employment Opportunity Commission established by section 705 of the Civil Rights Act of 1964 (42 U.S.C. 2000e–4).

(2) COVERED ENTITY.—The term "covered entity" means an employer, employment agency, labor organization, or joint labor-management committee.

(3) DIRECT THREAT.—The term "direct threat" means a significant risk to the health or safety of others that cannot be eliminated by reasonable accommodation.

(4) EMPLOYEE.—The term "employee" means an individual employed by an employer.

(5) EMPLOYER.—

(A) IN GENERAL.—The term "employer" means a person engaged in an industry affecting commerce who has 15 or more employees for each working day in each of 20 or more calendar weeks in the current or preceding calendar year, and any agent of such person, except that, for two years following the effective date of this title, an employer means a person engaged in an industry affecting commerce who has 25 or more employees for each working day in each of 20 or more calendar weeks in the current or preceding year, and any agent of such person.

(B) EXCEPTIONS.—The term "employer" does not include—

(i) the United States, a corporation wholly owned by the government of the United States, or an Indian tribe; or

(ii) a bona fide private membership club (other than a labor organization) that is exempt from taxation under section 501(c) of the Internal Revenue Code of 1986.

(6) ILLEGAL USE OF DRUGS.—

(A) IN GENERAL.—The term "illegal use of drugs" means the use of drugs, the possession or distribution of which is unlawful under the Controlled Substances Act (21 U.S.C. 812). Such term does not include the use of a drug taken under supervision by a licensed health care professional, or other uses authorized by the Controlled Substances Act or other provisions of Federal law.

(B) DRUGS.—The term "drug" means a controlled substance, as defined in schedules I through V of section 202 of the Controlled Substances Act.

(7) PERSON, ETC.—The terms "person", "labor organization", "employment agency", "commerce", and "industry affecting commerce", shall have the same meaning given such terms in section 701 of the Civil Rights Act of 1964 (42 U.S.C. 2000e).

(8) QUALIFIED INDIVIDUAL WITH A DISABILITY.—The term "qualified individual with a disability" means an individual with a disability who, with or without reasonable accommodation, can perform the essential functions of the employment position that such individual holds or desires. For the purposes of this title, consideration shall be given to the employer's judgment as to what functions of a job are essential, and if an employer has prepared a written description before advertising or interviewing applicants for the job, this description shall be considered evidence of the essential functions of the job.

(9) REASONABLE ACCOMMODATION.—The term "reasonable accommodation" may include—

(A) making existing facilities used by employees readily accessible to and usable by individuals with disabilities; and

(B) job restructuring, part-time or modified work schedules, reassignment to a vacant position, acquisition or modification of equipment or devices, appropriate adjustment or modifications of examinations, training materials or policies, the provision of qualified readers or interpreters, and other similar accommodations for individuals with disabilities.

(10) UNDUE HARDSHIP.—

(A) IN GENERAL.—The term "undue hardship" means an action requiring significant difficulty or expense, when considered in light of the factors set forth in subparagraph (B).

(B) FACTORS TO BE CONSIDERED.—In determining whether an accommodation would impose an undue hardship on a covered entity, factors to be considered include—

(i) the nature and cost of the accommodation needed under this Act;

(ii) the overall financial resources of the facility or facilities involved in the provision of the reasonable accommodation; the number of persons employed at such facility; the effect on expenses and resources, or the impact otherwise of such accommodation upon the operation of the facility;

(iii) the overall financial resources of the covered entity; the overall size of the business of a covered entity with respect to the number of its employees; the number, type, and location of its facilities; and

(iv) the type of operation or operations of the covered entity, including the composition, structure, and functions of the workforce of such entity; the geographic separateness, administrative, or fiscal relationship of the facility or facilities in question to the covered entity.

SEC. 102. DISCRIMINATION.   42 USC 12112.

(a) GENERAL RULE.—No covered entity shall discriminate against a qualified individual with a disability because of the disability of such individual in regard to job application procedures, the hiring, advancement, or discharge of employees, employee compensation, job training, and other terms, conditions, and privileges of employment.

(b) CONSTRUCTION.—As used in subsection (a), the term "discriminate" includes—

(1) limiting, segregating, or classifying a job applicant or employee in a way that adversely affects the opportunities or status of such applicant or employee because of the disability of such applicant or employee;

(2) participating in a contractual or other arrangement or relationship that has the effect of subjecting a covered entity's qualified applicant or employee with a disability to the discrimination prohibited by this title (such relationship includes a relationship with an employment or referral agency, labor union, an organization providing fringe benefits to an employee of the covered entity, or an organization providing training and apprenticeship programs);

(3) utilizing standards, criteria, or methods of administration—

(A) that have the effect of discrimination on the basis of disability; or

(B) that perpetuate the discrimination of others who are subject to common administrative control;

(4) excluding or otherwise denying equal jobs or benefits to a qualified individual because of the known disability of an individual with whom the qualified individual is known to have a relationship or association;

(5)(A) not making reasonable accommodations to the known physical or mental limitations of an otherwise qualified individual with a disability who is an applicant or employee, unless such covered entity can demonstrate that the accommodation would impose an undue hardship on the operation of the business of such covered entity; or

(B) denying employment opportunities to a job applicant or employee who is an otherwise qualified individual with a disability, if such denial is based on the need of such covered entity to make reasonable accommodation to the physical or mental impairments of the employee or applicant;

(6) using qualification standards, employment tests or other selection criteria that screen out or tend to screen out an individual with a disability or a class of individuals with disabilities unless the standard, test or other selection criteria, as used by the covered entity, is shown to be job-related for the position in question and is consistent with business necessity; and

(7) failing to select and administer tests concerning employment in the most effective manner to ensure that, when such test is administered to a job applicant or employee who has a disability that impairs sensory, manual, or speaking skills, such test results accurately reflect the skills, aptitude, or whatever other factor of such applicant or employee that such test purports to measure, rather than reflecting the impaired sensory, manual, or speaking skills of such employee or applicant (except where such skills are the factors that the test purports to measure).

(c) MEDICAL EXAMINATIONS AND INQUIRIES.—

(1) IN GENERAL.—The prohibition against discrimination as referred to in subsection (a) shall include medical examinations and inquiries.

(2) PREEMPLOYMENT.—

(A) PROHIBITED EXAMINATION OR INQUIRY.—Except as provided in paragraph (3), a covered entity shall not conduct a medical examination or make inquiries of a job applicant as to whether such applicant is an individual with a disability or as to the nature or severity of such disability.

(B) ACCEPTABLE INQUIRY.—A covered entity may make preemployment inquiries into the ability of an applicant to perform job-related functions.

(3) EMPLOYMENT ENTRANCE EXAMINATION.—A covered entity may require a medical examination after an offer of employment has been made to a job applicant and prior to the commencement of the employment duties of such applicant, and may condition an offer of employment on the results of such examination, if—

(A) all entering employees are subjected to such an examination regardless of disability;

(B) information obtained regarding the medical condition or history of the applicant is collected and maintained on separate forms and in separate medical files and is treated as a confidential medical record, except that—

(i) supervisors and managers may be informed regarding necessary restrictions on the work or duties of the employee and necessary accommodations;

(ii) first aid and safety personnel may be informed, when appropriate, if the disability might require emergency treatment; and

(iii) government officials investigating compliance with this Act shall be provided relevant information on request; and

(C) the results of such examination are used only in accordance with this title.

(4) EXAMINATION AND INQUIRY.—

(A) PROHIBITED EXAMINATIONS AND INQUIRIES.—A covered entity shall not require a medical examination and shall not make inquiries of an employee as to whether such employee is an individual with a disability or as to the nature or severity of the disability, unless such examination or inquiry is shown to be job-related and consistent with business necessity.

(B) ACCEPTABLE EXAMINATIONS AND INQUIRIES.—A covered entity may conduct voluntary medical examinations, including voluntary medical histories, which are part of an employee health program available to employees at that work site. A covered entity may make inquiries into the ability of an employee to perform job-related functions.

(C) REQUIREMENT.—Information obtained under subparagraph (B) regarding the medical condition or history of any employee are subject to the requirements of subparagraphs (B) and (C) of paragraph (3).

SEC. 103. DEFENSES.   42 USC 12113.

(a) IN GENERAL.—It may be a defense to a charge of discrimination under this Act that an alleged application of qualification standards, tests, or selection criteria that screen out or tend to screen out or otherwise deny a job or benefit to an individual with a disability has been shown to be job-related and consistent with business necessity, and such performance cannot be accomplished by reasonable accommodation, as required under this title.

(b) QUALIFICATION STANDARDS.—The term "qualification standards" may include a requirement that an individual shall not pose a direct threat to the health or safety of other individuals in the workplace.

(c) RELIGIOUS ENTITIES.—

(1) IN GENERAL.—This title shall not prohibit a religious corporation, association, educational institution, or society from giving preference in employment to individuals of a particular religion to perform work connected with the carrying on by such corporation, association, educational institution, or society of its activities.

(2) RELIGIOUS TENETS REQUIREMENT.—Under this title, a religious organization may require that all applicants and employees conform to the religious tenets of such organization.

(d) LIST OF INFECTIOUS AND COMMUNICABLE DISEASES.—

(1) IN GENERAL.—The Secretary of Health and Human Services, not later than 6 months after the date of enactment of this Act, shall—

(A) review all infectious and communicable diseases which may be transmitted through handling the food supply;

(B) publish a list of infectious and communicable diseases which are transmitted through handling the food supply;

(C) publish the methods by which such diseases are transmitted; and

Public information.

(D) widely disseminate such information regarding the list of diseases and their modes of transmissability to the general public.

Such list shall be updated annually.

(2) APPLICATIONS.—In any case in which an individual has an infectious or communicable disease that is transmitted to others through the handling of food, that is included on the list developed by the Secretary of Health and Human Services under paragraph (1), and which cannot be eliminated by reasonable accommodation, a covered entity may refuse to assign or continue to assign such individual to a job involving food handling.

(3) CONSTRUCTION.—Nothing in this Act shall be construed to preempt, modify, or amend any State, county, or local law, ordinance, or regulation applicable to food handling which is designed to protect the public health from individuals who pose a significant risk to the health or safety of others, which cannot be eliminated by reasonable accommodation, pursuant to the list of infectious or communicable diseases and the modes of transmissability published by the Secretary of Health and Human Services.

42 USC 12114.

SEC. 104. ILLEGAL USE OF DRUGS AND ALCOHOL.

(a) QUALIFIED INDIVIDUAL WITH A DISABILITY.—For purposes of this title, the term "qualified individual with a disability" shall not include any employee or applicant who is currently engaging in the illegal use of drugs, when the covered entity acts on the basis of such use.

(b) RULES OF CONSTRUCTION.—Nothing in subsection (a) shall be construed to exclude as a qualified individual with a disability an individual who—

(1) has successfully completed a supervised drug rehabilitation program and is no longer engaging in the illegal use of drugs, or has otherwise been rehabilitated successfully and is no longer engaging in such use;

(2) is participating in a supervised rehabilitation program and is no longer engaging in such use; or

(3) is erroneously regarded as engaging in such use, but is not engaging in such use;

except that it shall not be a violation of this Act for a covered entity to adopt or administer reasonable policies or procedures, including but not limited to drug testing, designed to ensure that an individual described in paragraph (1) or (2) is no longer engaging in the illegal use of drugs.

(c) AUTHORITY OF COVERED ENTITY.—A covered entity—

(1) may prohibit the illegal use of drugs and the use of alcohol at the workplace by all employees;

(2) may require that employees shall not be under the influence of alcohol or be engaging in the illegal use of drugs at the workplace;

(3) may require that employees behave in conformance with the requirements established under the Drug-Free Workplace Act of 1988 (41 U.S.C. 701 et seq.);

(4) may hold an employee who engages in the illegal use of drugs or who is an alcoholic to the same qualification standards for employment or job performance and behavior that such entity holds other employees, even if any unsatisfactory performance or behavior is related to the drug use or alcoholism of such employee; and

(5) may, with respect to Federal regulations regarding alcohol and the illegal use of drugs, require that—

(A) employees comply with the standards established in such regulations of the Department of Defense, if the employees of the covered entity are employed in an industry subject to such regulations, including complying with regulations (if any) that apply to employment in sensitive positions in such an industry, in the case of employees of the covered entity who are employed in such positions (as defined in the regulations of the Department of Defense);

(B) employees comply with the standards established in such regulations of the Nuclear Regulatory Commission, if the employees of the covered entity are employed in an industry subject to such regulations, including complying with regulations (if any) that apply to employment in sensitive positions in such an industry, in the case of employees of the covered entity who are employed in such positions (as defined in the regulations of the Nuclear Regulatory Commission); and

(C) employees comply with the standards established in such regulations of the Department of Transportation, if the employees of the covered entity are employed in a transportation industry subject to such regulations, including complying with such regulations (if any) that apply to employment in sensitive positions in such an industry, in the case of employees of the covered entity who are employed in such positions (as defined in the regulations of the Department of Transportation).

(d) DRUG TESTING.—

(1) IN GENERAL.—For purposes of this title, a test to determine the illegal use of drugs shall not be considered a medical examination.

(2) CONSTRUCTION.—Nothing in this title shall be construed to encourage, prohibit, or authorize the conducting of drug testing for the illegal use of drugs by job applicants or employees or making employment decisions based on such test results.

(e) TRANSPORTATION EMPLOYEES.—Nothing in this title shall be construed to encourage, prohibit, restrict, or authorize the otherwise lawful exercise by entities subject to the jurisdiction of the Department of Transportation of authority to—

(1) test employees of such entities in, and applicants for, positions involving safety-sensitive duties for the illegal use of drugs and for on-duty impairment by alcohol; and

(2) remove such persons who test positive for illegal use of drugs and on-duty impairment by alcohol pursuant to paragraph (1) from safety-sensitive duties in implementing subsection (c).

42 USC 12115.   **SEC. 105. POSTING NOTICES.**

Every employer, employment agency, labor organization, or joint labor-management committee covered under this title shall post notices in an accessible format to applicants, employees, and members describing the applicable provisions of this Act, in the manner prescribed by section 711 of the Civil Rights Act of 1964 (42 U.S.C. 2000e-10).

42 USC 12116.   **SEC. 106. REGULATIONS.**

Not later than 1 year after the date of enactment of this Act, the Commission shall issue regulations in an accessible format to carry out this title in accordance with subchapter II of chapter 5 of title 5, United States Code.

42 USC 12117.   **SEC. 107. ENFORCEMENT.**

(a) POWERS, REMEDIES, AND PROCEDURES.—The powers, remedies, and procedures set forth in sections 705, 706, 707, 709, and 710 of the Civil Rights Act of 1964 (42 U.S.C. 2000e-4, 2000e-5, 2000e-6, 2000e-8, and 2000e-9) shall be the powers, remedies, and procedures this title provides to the Commission, to the Attorney General, or to any person alleging discrimination on the basis of disability in violation of any provision of this Act, or regulations promulgated under section 106, concerning employment.

(b) COORDINATION.—The agencies with enforcement authority for actions which allege employment discrimination under this title and under the Rehabilitation Act of 1973 shall develop procedures to ensure that administrative complaints filed under this title and under the Rehabilitation Act of 1973 are dealt with in a manner that avoids duplication of effort and prevents imposition of inconsistent or conflicting standards for the same requirements

Regulations.   under this title and the Rehabilitation Act of 1973. The Commission, the Attorney General, and the Office of Federal Contract Compliance Programs shall establish such coordinating mechanisms (similar to provisions contained in the joint regulations promulgated by the Commission and the Attorney General at part 42 of title 28 and part 1691 of title 29, Code of Federal Regulations, and the Memorandum of Understanding between the Commission and the Office of Federal Contract Compliance Programs dated January 16, 1981 (46 Fed. Reg. 7435, January 23, 1981)) in regulations implementing this title and Rehabilitation Act of 1973 not later than 18 months after the date of enactment of this Act.

SEC. 108. EFFECTIVE DATE.   42 USC 12111 note.

This title shall become effective 24 months after the date of enactment.

TITLE II—PUBLIC SERVICES

Subtitle A—Prohibition Against Discrimination and Other Generally Applicable Provisions

SEC. 201. DEFINITION.   42 USC 12131.

As used in this title:

(1) PUBLIC ENTITY.—The term "public entity" means—

(A) any State or local government;

(B) any department, agency, special purpose district, or other instrumentality of a State or States or local government; and

(C) the National Railroad Passenger Corporation, and any commuter authority (as defined in section 103(8) of the Rail Passenger Service Act).

(2) QUALIFIED INDIVIDUAL WITH A DISABILITY.—The term "qualified individual with a disability" means an individual with a disability who, with or without reasonable modifications to rules, policies, or practices, the removal of architectural, communication, or transportation barriers, or the provision of auxiliary aids and services, meets the essential eligibility requirements for the receipt of services or the participation in programs or activities provided by a public entity.

SEC. 202. DISCRIMINATION.   42 USC 12132.

Subject to the provisions of this title, no qualified individual with a disability shall, by reason of such disability, be excluded from participation in or be denied the benefits of the services, programs, or activities of a public entity, or be subjected to discrimination by any such entity.

SEC. 203. ENFORCEMENT.   42 USC 12133.

The remedies, procedures, and rights set forth in section 505 of the Rehabilitation Act of 1973 (29 U.S.C. 794a) shall be the remedies, procedures, and rights this title provides to any person alleging discrimination on the basis of disability in violation of section 202.

SEC. 204. REGULATIONS.   42 USC 12134.

(a) IN GENERAL.—Not later than 1 year after the date of enactment of this Act, the Attorney General shall promulgate regulations in an accessible format that implement this subtitle. Such regulations shall not include any matter within the scope of the authority of the Secretary of Transportation under section 223, 229, or 244.

(b) RELATIONSHIP TO OTHER REGULATIONS.—Except for "program accessibility, existing facilities", and "communications", regulations under subsection (a) shall be consistent with this Act and with the coordination regulations under part 41 of title 28, Code of Federal Regulations (as promulgated by the Department of Health, Education, and Welfare on January 13, 1978), applicable to recipients of Federal financial assistance under section 504 of the Rehabilitation Act of 1973 (29 U.S.C. 794). With respect to "program accessibility, existing facilities", and "communications", such regulations shall be consistent with regulations and analysis as in part 39 of title 28 of the Code of Federal Regulations, applicable to federally conducted activities under such section 504.

(c) STANDARDS.—Regulations under subsection (a) shall include standards applicable to facilities and vehicles covered by this subtitle, other than facilities, stations, rail passenger cars, and vehicles covered by subtitle B. Such standards shall be consistent with the minimum guidelines and requirements issued by the Architectural and Transportation Barriers Compliance Board in accordance with section 504(a) of this Act.

42 USC 12131 note.

SEC. 205. EFFECTIVE DATE.

(a) GENERAL RULE.—Except as provided in subsection (b), this subtitle shall become effective 18 months after the date of enactment of this Act.

(b) EXCEPTION.—Section 204 shall become effective on the date of enactment of this Act.

Subtitle B—Actions Applicable to Public Transportation Provided by Public Entities Considered Discriminatory

PART I—PUBLIC TRANSPORTATION OTHER THAN BY AIRCRAFT OR CERTAIN RAIL OPERATIONS

42 USC 12141.

SEC. 221. DEFINITIONS.

As used in this part:

(1) DEMAND RESPONSIVE SYSTEM.—The term "demand responsive system" means any system of providing designated public transportation which is not a fixed route system.

(2) DESIGNATED PUBLIC TRANSPORTATION.—The term "designated public transportation" means transportation (other than public school transportation) by bus, rail, or any other conveyance (other than transportation by aircraft or intercity or commuter rail transportation (as defined in section 241)) that provides the general public with general or special service (including charter service) on a regular and continuing basis.

(3) FIXED ROUTE SYSTEM.—The term "fixed route system" means a system of providing designated public transportation on which a vehicle is operated along a prescribed route according to a fixed schedule.

(4) OPERATES.—The term "operates", as used with respect to a fixed route system or demand responsive system, includes operation of such system by a person under a contractual or other arrangement or relationship with a public entity.

(5) PUBLIC SCHOOL TRANSPORTATION.—The term "public school transportation" means transportation by schoolbus vehicles of schoolchildren, personnel, and equipment to and from a public elementary or secondary school and school-related activities.

(6) SECRETARY.—The term "Secretary" means the Secretary of Transportation.

SEC. 222. PUBLIC ENTITIES OPERATING FIXED ROUTE SYSTEMS.   42 USC 12142.

(a) PURCHASE AND LEASE OF NEW VEHICLES.—It shall be considered discrimination for purposes of section 202 of this Act and section 504 of the Rehabilitation Act of 1973 (29 U.S.C. 794) for a public entity which operates a fixed route system to purchase or lease a new bus, a new rapid rail vehicle, a new light rail vehicle, or any other new vehicle to be used on such system, if the solicitation for such purchase or lease is made after the 30th day following the effective date of this subsection and if such bus, rail vehicle, or other vehicle is not readily accessible to and usable by individuals with disabilities, including individuals who use wheelchairs.

(b) PURCHASE AND LEASE OF USED VEHICLES.—Subject to subsection (c)(1), it shall be considered discrimination for purposes of section 202 of this Act and section 504 of the Rehabilitation Act of 1973 (29 U.S.C. 794) for a public entity which operates a fixed route system to purchase or lease, after the 30th day following the effective date of this subsection, a used vehicle for use on such system unless such entity makes demonstrated good faith efforts to purchase or lease a used vehicle for use on such system that is readily accessible to and usable by individuals with disabilities, including individuals who use wheelchairs.

(c) REMANUFACTURED VEHICLES.—

(1) GENERAL RULE.—Except as provided in paragraph (2), it shall be considered discrimination for purposes of section 202 of this Act and section 504 of the Rehabilitation Act of 1973 (29 U.S.C. 794) for a public entity which operates a fixed route system—

(A) to remanufacture a vehicle for use on such system so as to extend its usable life for 5 years or more, which remanufacture begins (or for which the solicitation is made) after the 30th day following the effective date of this subsection; or

(B) to purchase or lease for use on such system a remanufactured vehicle which has been remanufactured so as to extend its usable life for 5 years or more, which purchase or lease occurs after such 30th day and during the period in which the usable life is extended;

unless, after remanufacture, the vehicle is, to the maximum extent feasible, readily accessible to and usable by individuals with disabilities, including individuals who use wheelchairs.

(2) EXCEPTION FOR HISTORIC VEHICLES.—

(A) GENERAL RULE.—If a public entity operates a fixed route system any segment of which is included on the National Register of Historic Places and if making a vehicle of historic character to be used solely on such segment readily accessible to and usable by individuals with disabilities would significantly alter the historic character of such vehicle, the public entity only has to make (or to purchase or lease a remanufactured vehicle with) those modifications which are necessary to meet the requirements of paragraph

(1) and which do not significantly alter the historic character of such vehicle.

(B) VEHICLES OF HISTORIC CHARACTER DEFINED BY REGULATIONS.—For purposes of this paragraph and section 228(b), a vehicle of historic character shall be defined by the regulations issued by the Secretary to carry out this subsection.

42 USC 12143.   SEC. 223. PARATRANSIT AS A COMPLEMENT TO FIXED ROUTE SERVICE.

(a) GENERAL RULE.—It shall be considered discrimination for purposes of section 202 of this Act and section 504 of the Rehabilitation Act of 1973 (29 U.S.C. 794) for a public entity which operates a fixed route system (other than a system which provides solely commuter bus service) to fail to provide with respect to the operations of its fixed route system, in accordance with this section, paratransit and other special transportation services to individuals with disabilities, including individuals who use wheelchairs, that are sufficient to provide to such individuals a level of service (1) which is comparable to the level of designated public transportation services provided to individuals without disabilities using such system; or (2) in the case of response time, which is comparable, to the extent practicable, to the level of designated public transportation services provided to individuals without disabilities using such system.

(b) ISSUANCE OF REGULATIONS.—Not later than 1 year after the effective date of this subsection, the Secretary shall issue final regulations to carry out this section.

(c) REQUIRED CONTENTS OF REGULATIONS.—

(1) ELIGIBLE RECIPIENTS OF SERVICE.—The regulations issued under this section shall require each public entity which operates a fixed route system to provide the paratransit and other special transportation services required under this section—

(A)(i) to any individual with a disability who is unable, as a result of a physical or mental impairment (including a vision impairment) and without the assistance of another individual (except an operator of a wheelchair lift or other boarding assistance device), to board, ride, or disembark from any vehicle on the system which is readily accessible to and usable by individuals with disabilities;

(ii) to any individual with a disability who needs the assistance of a wheelchair lift or other boarding assistance device (and is able to board with such assistance) to board, ride, and disembark from any vehicle which is readily accessible to and usable by individuals with disabilities if the individual wants to travel on a route on the system during the hours of operation of the system at a time (or within a reasonable period of such time) when such a vehicle is not being used to provide designated public transportation on the route; and

(iii) to any individual with a disability who has a specific impairment-related condition which prevents such individual from traveling to a boarding location or from a disembarking location on such system;

(B) to one other individual accompanying the individual with the disability; and

(C) to other individuals, in addition to the one individual described in subparagraph (B), accompanying the individual with a disability provided that space for these additional individuals is available on the paratransit vehicle carrying the individual with a disability and that the transportation of such additional individuals will not result in a denial of service to individuals with disabilities.

For purposes of clauses (i) and (ii) of subparagraph (A), boarding or disembarking from a vehicle does not include travel to the boarding location or from the disembarking location.

(2) SERVICE AREA.—The regulations issued under this section shall require the provision of paratransit and special transportation services required under this section in the service area of each public entity which operates a fixed route system, other than any portion of the service area in which the public entity solely provides commuter bus service.

(3) SERVICE CRITERIA.—Subject to paragraphs (1) and (2), the regulations issued under this section shall establish minimum service criteria for determining the level of services to be required under this section.

(4) UNDUE FINANCIAL BURDEN LIMITATION.—The regulations issued under this section shall provide that, if the public entity is able to demonstrate to the satisfaction of the Secretary that the provision of paratransit and other special transportation services otherwise required under this section would impose an undue financial burden on the public entity, the public entity, notwithstanding any other provision of this section (other than paragraph (5)), shall only be required to provide such services to the extent that providing such services would not impose such a burden.

(5) ADDITIONAL SERVICES.—The regulations issued under this section shall establish circumstances under which the Secretary may require a public entity to provide, notwithstanding paragraph (4), paratransit and other special transportation services under this section beyond the level of paratransit and other special transportation services which would otherwise be required under paragraph (4).

(6) PUBLIC PARTICIPATION.—The regulations issued under this section shall require that each public entity which operates a fixed route system hold a public hearing, provide an opportunity for public comment, and consult with individuals with disabilities in preparing its plan under paragraph (7).

(7) PLANS.—The regulations issued under this section shall require that each public entity which operates a fixed route system—

(A) within 18 months after the effective date of this subsection, submit to the Secretary, and commence implementation of, a plan for providing paratransit and other special transportation services which meets the requirements of this section; and

(B) on an annual basis thereafter, submit to the Secretary, and commence implementation of, a plan for providing such services.

(8) PROVISION OF SERVICES BY OTHERS.—The regulations issued under this section shall—

(A) require that a public entity submitting a plan to the Secretary under this section identify in the plan any person or other public entity which is providing a paratransit or other special transportation service for individuals with disabilities in the service area to which the plan applies; and

(B) provide that the public entity submitting the plan does not have to provide under the plan such service for individuals with disabilities.

(9) OTHER PROVISIONS.—The regulations issued under this section shall include such other provisions and requirements as the Secretary determines are necessary to carry out the objectives of this section.

(d) REVIEW OF PLAN.—

(1) GENERAL RULE.—The Secretary shall review a plan submitted under this section for the purpose of determining whether or not such plan meets the requirements of this section, including the regulations issued under this section.

(2) DISAPPROVAL.—If the Secretary determines that a plan reviewed under this subsection fails to meet the requirements of this section, the Secretary shall disapprove the plan and notify the public entity which submitted the plan of such disapproval and the reasons therefor.

(3) MODIFICATION OF DISAPPROVED PLAN.—Not later than 90 days after the date of disapproval of a plan under this subsection, the public entity which submitted the plan shall modify the plan to meet the requirements of this section and shall submit to the Secretary, and commence implementation of, such modified plan.

(e) DISCRIMINATION DEFINED.—As used in subsection (a), the term "discrimination" includes—

(1) a failure of a public entity to which the regulations issued under this section apply to submit, or commence implementation of, a plan in accordance with subsections (c)(6) and (c)(7);

(2) a failure of such entity to submit, or commence implementation of, a modified plan in accordance with subsection (d)(3);

(3) submission to the Secretary of a modified plan under subsection (d)(3) which does not meet the requirements of this section; or

(4) a failure of such entity to provide paratransit or other special transportation services in accordance with the plan or modified plan the public entity submitted to the Secretary under this section.

(f) STATUTORY CONSTRUCTION.—Nothing in this section shall be construed as preventing a public entity—

(1) from providing paratransit or other special transportation services at a level which is greater than the level of such services which are required by this section,

(2) from providing paratransit or other special transportation services in addition to those paratransit and special transportation services required by this section, or

(3) from providing such services to individuals in addition to those individuals to whom such services are required to be provided by this section.

42 USC 12144.   **SEC. 224. PUBLIC ENTITY OPERATING A DEMAND RESPONSIVE SYSTEM.**

If a public entity operates a demand responsive system, it shall be considered discrimination, for purposes of section 202 of this Act and section 504 of the Rehabilitation Act of 1973 (29 U.S.C. 794), for such entity to purchase or lease a new vehicle for use on such system, for which a solicitation is made after the 30th day following the effective date of this section, that is not readily accessible to and usable by individuals with disabilities, including individuals who use wheelchairs, unless such system, when viewed in its entirety, provides a level of service to such individuals equivalent to the level of service such system provides to individuals without disabilities.

SEC. 225. TEMPORARY RELIEF WHERE LIFTS ARE UNAVAILABLE.   42 USC 12145.

(a) GRANTING.—With respect to the purchase of new buses, a public entity may apply for, and the Secretary may temporarily relieve such public entity from the obligation under section 222(a) or 224 to purchase new buses that are readily accessible to and usable by individuals with disabilities if such public entity demonstrates to the satisfaction of the Secretary—

(1) that the initial solicitation for new buses made by the public entity specified that all new buses were to be lift-equipped and were to be otherwise accessible to and usable by individuals with disabilities;

(2) the unavailability from any qualified manufacturer of hydraulic, electromechanical, or other lifts for such new buses;

(3) that the public entity seeking temporary relief has made good faith efforts to locate a qualified manufacturer to supply the lifts to the manufacturer of such buses in sufficient time to comply with such solicitation; and

(4) that any further delay in purchasing new buses necessary to obtain such lifts would significantly impair transportation services in the community served by the public entity.

(b) DURATION AND NOTICE TO CONGRESS.—Any relief granted under subsection (a) shall be limited in duration by a specified date, and the appropriate committees of Congress shall be notified of any such relief granted.

(c) FRAUDULENT APPLICATION.—If, at any time, the Secretary has reasonable cause to believe that any relief granted under subsection (a) was fraudulently applied for, the Secretary shall—

(1) cancel such relief if such relief is still in effect; and

(2) take such other action as the Secretary considers appropriate.

SEC. 226. NEW FACILITIES.   42 USC 12146.

For purposes of section 202 of this Act and section 504 of the Rehabilitation Act of 1973 (29 U.S.C. 794), it shall be considered discrimination for a public entity to construct a new facility to be used in the provision of designated public transportation services unless such facility is readily accessible to and usable by individuals with disabilities, including individuals who use wheelchairs.

SEC. 227. ALTERATIONS OF EXISTING FACILITIES.   42 USC 12147.

(a) GENERAL RULE.—With respect to alterations of an existing facility or part thereof used in the provision of designated public transportation services that affect or could affect the usability of the facility or part thereof, it shall be considered discrimination, for purposes of section 202 of this Act and section 504 of the Rehabilitation Act of 1973 (29 U.S.C. 794), for a public entity to fail to make such alterations (or to ensure that the alterations are made) in such a manner that, to the maximum extent feasible, the altered portions of the facility are readily accessible to and usable by individuals with disabilities, including individuals who use wheelchairs, upon the completion of such alterations. Where the public entity is undertaking an alteration that affects or could affect usability of or access to an area of the facility containing a primary function, the entity shall also make the alterations in such a manner that, to the maximum extent feasible, the path of travel to the altered area and the bathrooms, telephones, and drinking fountains serving the altered area, are readily accessible to and usable by individuals with disabilities, including individuals who use wheelchairs, upon completion of such alterations, where such alterations to the path of travel or the bathrooms, telephones, and drinking fountains serving the altered area are not disproportionate to the overall alterations in terms of cost and scope (as determined under criteria established by the Attorney General).

(b) SPECIAL RULE FOR STATIONS.—

(1) GENERAL RULE.—For purposes of section 202 of this Act and section 504 of the Rehabilitation Act of 1973 (29 U.S.C. 794), it shall be considered discrimination for a public entity that provides designated public transportation to fail, in accordance with the provisions of this subsection, to make key stations (as determined under criteria established by the Secretary by regulation) in rapid rail and light rail systems readily accessible to and usable by individuals with disabilities, including individuals who use wheelchairs.

(2) RAPID RAIL AND LIGHT RAIL KEY STATIONS.—

(A) ACCESSIBILITY.—Except as otherwise provided in this paragraph, all key stations (as determined under criteria established by the Secretary by regulation) in rapid rail and light rail systems shall be made readily accessible to and usable by individuals with disabilities, including individuals who use wheelchairs, as soon as practicable but in no event later than the last day of the 3-year period beginning on the effective date of this paragraph.

(B) EXTENSION FOR EXTRAORDINARILY EXPENSIVE STRUCTURAL CHANGES.—The Secretary may extend the 3-year period under subparagraph (A) up to a 30-year period for key stations in a rapid rail or light rail system which stations need extraordinarily expensive structural changes to, or replacement of, existing facilities; except that by the last day of the 20th year following the date of the enactment of this Act at least ⅔ of such key stations must be readily accessible to and usable by individuals with disabilities.

(3) PLANS AND MILESTONES.—The Secretary shall require the appropriate public entity to develop and submit to the Secretary a plan for compliance with this subsection—

(A) that reflects consultation with individuals with disabilities affected by such plan and the results of a public hearing and public comments on such plan, and

(B) that establishes milestones for achievement of the requirements of this subsection.

42 USC 12148.   SEC. 228. PUBLIC TRANSPORTATION PROGRAMS AND ACTIVITIES IN EXISTING FACILITIES AND ONE CAR PER TRAIN RULE.

(a) PUBLIC TRANSPORTATION PROGRAMS AND ACTIVITIES IN EXISTING FACILITIES.—

(1) IN GENERAL.—With respect to existing facilities used in the provision of designated public transportation services, it shall be considered discrimination, for purposes of section 202 of this Act and section 504 of the Rehabilitation Act of 1973 (29 U.S.C.

794), for a public entity to fail to operate a designated public transportation program or activity conducted in such facilities so that, when viewed in the entirety, the program or activity is readily accessible to and usable by individuals with disabilities.

(2) EXCEPTION.—Paragraph (1) shall not require a public entity to make structural changes to existing facilities in order to make such facilities accessible to individuals who use wheelchairs, unless and to the extent required by section 227(a) (relating to alterations) or section 227(b) (relating to key stations).

(3) UTILIZATION.—Paragraph (1) shall not require a public entity to which paragraph (2) applies, to provide to individuals who use wheelchairs services made available to the general public at such facilities when such individuals could not utilize or benefit from such services provided at such facilities.

(b) ONE CAR PER TRAIN RULE.—

(1) GENERAL RULE.—Subject to paragraph (2), with respect to 2 or more vehicles operated as a train by a light or rapid rail system, for purposes of section 202 of this Act and section 504 of the Rehabilitation Act of 1973 (29 U.S.C. 794), it shall be considered discrimination for a public entity to fail to have at least 1 vehicle per train that is accessible to individuals with disabilities, including individuals who use wheelchairs, as soon as practicable but in no event later than the last day of the 5-year period beginning on the effective date of this section.

(2) HISTORIC TRAINS.—In order to comply with paragraph (1) with respect to the remanufacture of a vehicle of historic character which is to be used on a segment of a light or rapid rail system which is included on the National Register of Historic Places, if making such vehicle readily accessible to and usable by individuals with disabilities would significantly alter the historic character of such vehicle, the public entity which operates such system only has to make (or to purchase or lease a remanufactured vehicle with) those modifications which are necessary to meet the requirements of section 222(c)(1) and which do not significantly alter the historic character of such vehicle.

SEC. 229. REGULATIONS.

42 USC 12149.

(a) IN GENERAL.—Not later than 1 year after the date of enactment of this Act, the Secretary of Transportation shall issue regulations, in an accessible format, necessary for carrying out this part (other than section 223).

(b) STANDARDS.—The regulations issued under this section and section 223 shall include standards applicable to facilities and vehicles covered by this subtitle. The standards shall be consistent with the minimum guidelines and requirements issued by the Architectural and Transportation Barriers Compliance Board in accordance with section 504 of this Act.

SEC. 230. INTERIM ACCESSIBILITY REQUIREMENTS.

42 USC 12150.

If final regulations have not been issued pursuant to section 229, for new construction or alterations for which a valid and appropriate State or local building permit is obtained prior to the issuance of final regulations under such section, and for which the construction or alteration authorized by such permit begins within one year of the receipt of such permit and is completed under the terms of such permit, compliance with the Uniform Federal Accessibility Standards in effect at the time the building permit is issued shall suffice to satisfy the requirement that facilities be readily accessible to and usable by persons with disabilities as required under sections 226 and 227, except that, if such final regulations have not been issued one year after the Architectural and Transportation Barriers Compliance Board has issued the supplemental minimum guidelines required under section 504(a) of this Act, compliance with such supplemental minimum guidelines shall be necessary to satisfy the requirement that facilities be readily accessible to and usable by persons with disabilities prior to issuance of the final regulations.

42 USC 12141 note.

SEC. 231. EFFECTIVE DATE.

(a) GENERAL RULE.—Except as provided in subsection (b), this part shall become effective 18 months after the date of enactment of this Act.

(b) EXCEPTION.—Sections 222, 223 (other than subsection (a)), 224, 225, 227(b), 228(b), and 229 shall become effective on the date of enactment of this Act.

PART II—PUBLIC TRANSPORTATION BY INTERCITY AND COMMUTER RAIL

42 USC 12161.

SEC. 241. DEFINITIONS.

As used in this part:

(1) COMMUTER AUTHORITY.—The term "commuter authority" has the meaning given such term in section 103(8) of the Rail Passenger Service Act (45 U.S.C. 502(8)).

(2) COMMUTER RAIL TRANSPORTATION.—The term "commuter rail transportation" has the meaning given the term "commuter service" in section 103(9) of the Rail Passenger Service Act (45 U.S.C. 502(9)).

(3) INTERCITY RAIL TRANSPORTATION.—The term "intercity rail transportation" means transportation provided by the National Railroad Passenger Corporation.

(4) RAIL PASSENGER CAR.—The term "rail passenger car" means, with respect to intercity rail transportation, single-level and bi-level coach cars, single-level and bi-level dining cars, single-level and bi-level sleeping cars, single-level and bi-level lounge cars, and food service cars.

(5) RESPONSIBLE PERSON.—The term "responsible person" means—

(A) in the case of a station more than 50 percent of which is owned by a public entity, such public entity;

(B) in the case of a station more than 50 percent of which is owned by a private party, the persons providing intercity or commuter rail transportation to such station, as allocated on an equitable basis by regulation by the Secretary of Transportation; and

(C) in a case where no party owns more than 50 percent of a station, the persons providing intercity or commuter rail transportation to such station and the owners of the station, other than private party owners, as allocated on an equitable basis by regulation by the Secretary of Transportation.

(6) Station.—The term "station" means the portion of a property located appurtenant to a right-of-way on which intercity or commuter rail transportation is operated, where such portion is used by the general public and is related to the provision of such transportation, including passenger platforms, designated waiting areas, ticketing areas, restrooms, and, where a public entity providing rail transportation owns the property, concession areas, to the extent that such public entity exercises control over the selection, design, construction, or alteration of the property, but such term does not include flag stops.

SEC. 242. INTERCITY AND COMMUTER RAIL ACTIONS CONSIDERED DISCRIMINATORY.   42 USC 12162.

(a) Intercity Rail Transportation.—

(1) One car per train rule.—It shall be considered discrimination for purposes of section 202 of this Act and section 504 of the Rehabilitation Act of 1973 (29 U.S.C. 794) for a person who provides intercity rail transportation to fail to have at least one passenger car per train that is readily accessible to and usable by individuals with disabilities, including individuals who use wheelchairs, in accordance with regulations issued under section 244, as soon as practicable, but in no event later than 5 years after the date of enactment of this Act.

(2) New intercity cars.—

(A) General rule.—Except as otherwise provided in this subsection with respect to individuals who use wheelchairs, it shall be considered discrimination for purposes of section 202 of this Act and section 504 of the Rehabilitation Act of 1973 (29 U.S.C. 794) for a person to purchase or lease any new rail passenger cars for use in intercity rail transportation, and for which a solicitation is made later than 30 days after the effective date of this section, unless all such rail cars are readily accessible to and usable by individuals with disabilities, including individuals who use wheelchairs, as prescribed by the Secretary of Transportation in regulations issued under section 244.

(B) Special rule for single-level passenger coaches for individuals who use wheelchairs.—Single-level passenger coaches shall be required to—

(i) be able to be entered by an individual who uses a wheelchair;

(ii) have space to park and secure a wheelchair;

(iii) have a seat to which a passenger in a wheelchair can transfer, and a space to fold and store such passenger's wheelchair; and

(iv) have a restroom usable by an individual who uses a wheelchair,

only to the extent provided in paragraph (3).

(C) Special rule for single-level dining cars for individuals who use wheelchairs.—Single-level dining cars shall not be required to—

(i) be able to be entered from the station platform by an individual who uses a wheelchair; or

(ii) have a restroom usable by an individual who uses a wheelchair if no restroom is provided in such car for any passenger.

(D) SPECIAL RULE FOR BI-LEVEL DINING CARS FOR INDIVIDUALS WHO USE WHEELCHAIRS.—Bi-level dining cars shall not be required to—

(i) be able to be entered by an individual who uses a wheelchair;

(ii) have space to park and secure a wheelchair;

(iii) have a seat to which a passenger in a wheelchair can transfer, or a space to fold and store such passenger's wheelchair; or

(iv) have a restroom usable by an individual who uses a wheelchair.

(3) ACCESSIBILITY OF SINGLE-LEVEL COACHES.—

(A) GENERAL RULE.—It shall be considered discrimination for purposes of section 202 of this Act and section 504 of the Rehabilitation Act of 1973 (29 U.S.C. 794) for a person who provides intercity rail transportation to fail to have on each train which includes one or more single-level rail passenger coaches—

(i) a number of spaces—

(I) to park and secure wheelchairs (to accommodate individuals who wish to remain in their wheelchairs) equal to not less than one-half of the number of single-level rail passenger coaches in such train; and

(II) to fold and store wheelchairs (to accommodate individuals who wish to transfer to coach seats) equal to not less than one-half of the number of single-level rail passenger coaches in such train, as soon as practicable, but in no event later than 5 years after the date of enactment of this Act; and

(ii) a number of spaces—

(I) to park and secure wheelchairs (to accommodate individuals who wish to remain in their wheelchairs) equal to not less than the total number of single-level rail passenger coaches in such train; and

(II) to fold and store wheelchairs (to accommodate individuals who wish to transfer to coach seats) equal to not less than the total number of single-level rail passenger coaches in such train, as soon as practicable, but in no event later than 10 years after the date of enactment of this Act.

(B) LOCATION.—Spaces required by subparagraph (A) shall be located in single-level rail passenger coaches or food service cars.

(C) LIMITATION.—Of the number of spaces required on a train by subparagraph (A), not more than two spaces to park and secure wheelchairs nor more than two spaces to fold and store wheelchairs shall be located in any one coach or food service car.

(D) OTHER ACCESSIBILITY FEATURES.—Single-level rail passenger coaches and food service cars on which the spaces required by subparagraph (A) are located shall have a restroom usable by an individual who uses a wheelchair and shall be able to be entered from the station platform by an individual who uses a wheelchair.

(4) FOOD SERVICE.—

(A) SINGLE-LEVEL DINING CARS.—On any train in which a single-level dining car is used to provide food service—

 (i) if such single-level dining car was purchased after the date of enactment of this Act, table service in such car shall be provided to a passenger who uses a wheelchair if—

  (I) the car adjacent to the end of the dining car through which a wheelchair may enter is itself accessible to a wheelchair;

  (II) such passenger can exit to the platform from the car such passenger occupies, move down the platform, and enter the adjacent accessible car described in subclause (I) without the necessity of the train being moved within the station; and

  (III) space to park and secure a wheelchair is available in the dining car at the time such passenger wishes to eat (if such passenger wishes to remain in a wheelchair), or space to store and fold a wheelchair is available in the dining car at the time such passenger wishes to eat (if such passenger wishes to transfer to a dining car seat); and

 (ii) appropriate auxiliary aids and services, including a hard surface on which to eat, shall be provided to ensure that other equivalent food service is available to individuals with disabilities, including individuals who use wheelchairs, and to passengers traveling with such individuals.

Unless not practicable, a person providing intercity rail transportation shall place an accessible car adjacent to the end of a dining car described in clause (i) through which an individual who uses a wheelchair may enter.

(B) BI-LEVEL DINING CARS.—On any train in which a bi-level dining car is used to provide food service—

 (i) if such train includes a bi-level lounge car purchased after the date of enactment of this Act, table service in such lounge car shall be provided to individuals who use wheelchairs and to other passengers; and

 (ii) appropriate auxiliary aids and services, including a hard surface on which to eat, shall be provided to ensure that other equivalent food service is available to individuals with disabilities, including individuals who use wheelchairs, and to passengers traveling with such individuals.

(b) COMMUTER RAIL TRANSPORTATION.—

 (1) ONE CAR PER TRAIN RULE.—It shall be considered discrimination for purposes of section 202 of this Act and section 504 of the Rehabilitation Act of 1973 (29 U.S.C. 794) for a person who provides commuter rail transportation to fail to have at least one passenger car per train that is readily accessible to and usable by individuals with disabilities, including individuals who use wheelchairs, in accordance with regulations issued under section 244, as soon as practicable, but in no event later than 5 years after the date of enactment of this Act.

 (2) NEW COMMUTER RAIL CARS.—

  (A) GENERAL RULE.—It shall be considered discrimination for purposes of section 202 of this Act and section 504 of the Rehabilitation Act of 1973 (29 U.S.C. 794) for a person to purchase or lease any new rail passenger cars for use in commuter rail transportation, and for which a solicitation is made later than 30 days after the effective date of this section, unless all such rail cars are readily accessible to and usable by individuals with disabilities, including individuals who use wheelchairs, as prescribed by the Secretary of Transportation in regulations issued under section 244.

(B) ACCESSIBILITY.—For purposes of section 202 of this Act and section 504 of the Rehabilitation Act of 1973 (29 U.S.C. 794), a requirement that a rail passenger car used in commuter rail transportation be accessible to or readily accessible to and usable by individuals with disabilities, including individuals who use wheelchairs, shall not be construed to require—

(i) a restroom usable by an individual who uses a wheelchair if no restroom is provided in such car for any passenger;

(ii) space to fold and store a wheelchair; or

(iii) a seat to which a passenger who uses a wheelchair can transfer.

(c) USED RAIL CARS.—It shall be considered discrimination for purposes of section 202 of this Act and section 504 of the Rehabilitation Act of 1973 (29 U.S.C. 794) for a person to purchase or lease a used rail passenger car for use in intercity or commuter rail transportation, unless such person makes demonstrated good faith efforts to purchase or lease a used rail car that is readily accessible to and usable by individuals with disabilities, including individuals who use wheelchairs, as prescribed by the Secretary of Transportation in regulations issued under section 244.

(d) REMANUFACTURED RAIL CARS.—

(1) REMANUFACTURING.—It shall be considered discrimination for purposes of section 202 of this Act and section 504 of the Rehabilitation Act of 1973 (29 U.S.C. 794) for a person to remanufacture a rail passenger car for use in intercity or commuter rail transportation so as to extend its usable life for 10 years or more, unless the rail car, to the maximum extent feasible, is made readily accessible to and usable by individuals with disabilities, including individuals who use wheelchairs, as prescribed by the Secretary of Transportation in regulations issued under section 244.

(2) PURCHASE OR LEASE.—It shall be considered discrimination for purposes of section 202 of this Act and section 504 of the Rehabilitation Act of 1973 (29 U.S.C. 794) for a person to purchase or lease a remanufactured rail passenger car for use in intercity or commuter rail transportation unless such car was remanufactured in accordance with paragraph (1).

(e) STATIONS.—

(1) NEW STATIONS.—It shall be considered discrimination for purposes of section 202 of this Act and section 504 of the Rehabilitation Act of 1973 (29 U.S.C. 794) for a person to build a new station for use in intercity or commuter rail transportation that is not readily accessible to and usable by individuals with disabilities, including individuals who use wheelchairs, as prescribed by the Secretary of Transportation in regulations issued under section 244.

(2) EXISTING STATIONS.—

(A) FAILURE TO MAKE READILY ACCESSIBLE.—

(i) GENERAL RULE.—It shall be considered discrimination for purposes of section 202 of this Act and section 504 of the Rehabilitation Act of 1973 (29 U.S.C. 794) for a responsible person to fail to make existing stations in the intercity rail transportation system, and existing key stations in commuter rail transportation systems, readily accessible to and usable by individuals with disabilities, including individuals who use wheelchairs, as prescribed by the Secretary of Transportation in regulations issued under section 244.

(ii) PERIOD FOR COMPLIANCE.—

(I) INTERCITY RAIL.—All stations in the intercity rail transportation system shall be made readily accessible to and usable by individuals with disabilities, including individuals who use wheelchairs, as soon as practicable, but in no event later than 20 years after the date of enactment of this Act.

(II) COMMUTER RAIL.—Key stations in commuter rail transportation systems shall be made readily accessible to and usable by individuals with disabilities, including individuals who use wheelchairs, as soon as practicable but in no event later than 3 years after the date of enactment of this Act, except that the time limit may be extended by the Secretary of Transportation up to 20 years after the date of enactment of this Act in a case where the raising of the entire passenger platform is the only means available of attaining accessibility or where other extraordinarily expensive structural changes are necessary to attain accessibility.

(iii) DESIGNATION OF KEY STATIONS.—Each commuter authority shall designate the key stations in its commuter rail transportation system, in consultation with individuals with disabilities and organizations representing such individuals, taking into consideration such factors as high ridership and whether such station serves as a transfer or feeder station. Before the final designation of key stations under this clause, a commuter authority shall hold a public hearing.

(iv) PLANS AND MILESTONES.—The Secretary of Transportation shall require the appropriate person to develop a plan for carrying out this subparagraph that reflects consultation with individuals with disabilities affected by such plan and that establishes milestones for achievement of the requirements of this subparagraph.

(B) REQUIREMENT WHEN MAKING ALTERATIONS.—

(i) GENERAL RULE.—It shall be considered discrimination, for purposes of section 202 of this Act and section 504 of the Rehabilitation Act of 1973 (29 U.S.C. 794), with respect to alterations of an existing station or part thereof in the intercity or commuter rail transportation systems that affect or could affect the usability of the station or part thereof, for the responsible person, owner, or person in control of the station to fail to make the alterations in such a manner that, to the maximum extent feasible, the altered portions of the station are readily accessible to and usable by individuals with disabilities, including individuals who use wheelchairs, upon completion of such alterations.

(ii) ALTERATIONS TO A PRIMARY FUNCTION AREA.—It shall be considered discrimination, for purposes of section 202 of this Act and section 504 of the Rehabilitation Act of 1973 (29 U.S.C. 794), with respect to alterations that affect or could affect the usability of or access to an area of the station containing a primary function, for the responsible person, owner, or person in control of the station to fail to make the alterations in such a manner that, to the maximum extent feasible, the path of travel to the altered area, and the bathrooms, telephones, and drinking fountains serving the altered area, are readily accessible to and usable by individuals with disabilities, including individuals who use wheelchairs, upon completion of such alterations, where such alterations to the path of travel or the bathrooms, telephones, and drinking fountains serving the altered area are not disproportionate to the overall alterations in terms of cost and scope (as determined under criteria established by the Attorney General).

(C) REQUIRED COOPERATION.—It shall be considered discrimination for purposes of section 202 of this Act and section 504 of the Rehabilitation Act of 1973 (29 U.S.C. 794) for an owner, or person in control, of a station governed by subparagraph (A) or (B) to fail to provide reasonable cooperation to a responsible person with respect to such station in that responsible person's efforts to comply with such subparagraph. An owner, or person in control, of a station shall be liable to a responsible person for any failure to provide reasonable cooperation as required by this subparagraph. Failure to receive reasonable cooperation required by this subparagraph shall not be a defense to a claim of discrimination under this Act.

42 USC 12163.   **SEC. 243. CONFORMANCE OF ACCESSIBILITY STANDARDS.**

Accessibility standards included in regulations issued under this part shall be consistent with the minimum guidelines issued by the Architectural and Transportation Barriers Compliance Board under section 504(a) of this Act.

42 USC 12164.   **SEC. 244. REGULATIONS.**

Not later than 1 year after the date of enactment of this Act, the Secretary of Transportation shall issue regulations, in an accessible format, necessary for carrying out this part.

42 USC 12165.   **SEC. 245. INTERIM ACCESSIBILITY REQUIREMENTS.**

(a) STATIONS.—If final regulations have not been issued pursuant to section 244, for new construction or alterations for which a valid and appropriate State or local building permit is obtained prior to the issuance of final regulations under such section, and for which the construction or alteration authorized by such permit begins within one year of the receipt of such permit and is completed under the terms of such permit, compliance with the Uniform Federal Accessibility Standards in effect at the time the building permit is issued shall suffice to satisfy the requirement that stations be readily accessible to and usable by persons with disabilities as required under section 242(e), except that, if such final regulations have not been issued one year after the Architectural and Transportation Barriers Compliance Board has issued the supplemental minimum guidelines required under section 504(a) of this Act, compliance with such supplemental minimum guidelines shall be necessary to satisfy the requirement that stations be readily accessible to and usable by persons with disabilities prior to issuance of the final regulations.

(b) RAIL PASSENGER CARS.—If final regulations have not been issued pursuant to section 244, a person shall be considered to have complied with the requirements of section 242 (a) through (d) that a rail passenger car be readily accessible to and usable by individuals with disabilities, if the design for such car complies with the laws and regulations (including the Minimum Guidelines and Requirements for Accessible Design and such supplemental minimum guidelines as are issued under section 504(a) of this Act) governing accessibility of such cars, to the extent that such laws and regulations are not inconsistent with this part and are in effect at the time such design is substantially completed.

SEC. 246. EFFECTIVE DATE.   42 USC 12161
                                                            note.
(a) GENERAL RULE.—Except as provided in subsection (b), this part shall become effective 18 months after the date of enactment of this Act.

(b) EXCEPTION.—Sections 242 and 244 shall become effective on the date of enactment of this Act.

TITLE III—PUBLIC ACCOMMODATIONS AND SERVICES OPERATED BY PRIVATE ENTITIES

SEC. 301. DEFINITIONS.   42 USC 12181.

As used in this title:

(1) COMMERCE.—The term "commerce" means travel, trade, traffic, commerce, transportation, or communication—

(A) among the several States;

(B) between any foreign country or any territory or possession and any State; or

(C) between points in the same State but through another State or foreign country.

(2) COMMERCIAL FACILITIES.—The term "commercial facilities" means facilities—

(A) that are intended for nonresidential use; and

(B) whose operations will affect commerce.

Such term shall not include railroad locomotives, railroad freight cars, railroad cabooses, railroad cars described in section 242 or covered under this title, railroad rights-of-way, or facilities that are covered or expressly exempted from coverage under the Fair Housing Act of 1968 (42 U.S.C. 3601 et seq.).

(3) DEMAND RESPONSIVE SYSTEM.—The term "demand responsive system" means any system of providing transportation of individuals by a vehicle, other than a system which is a fixed route system.

(4) FIXED ROUTE SYSTEM.—The term "fixed route system" means a system of providing transportation of individuals (other than by aircraft) on which a vehicle is operated along a prescribed route according to a fixed schedule.

(5) OVER-THE-ROAD BUS.—The term "over-the-road bus" means a bus characterized by an elevated passenger deck located over a baggage compartment.

(6) PRIVATE ENTITY.—The term "private entity" means any entity other than a public entity (as defined in section 201(1)).

(7) PUBLIC ACCOMMODATION.—The following private entities are considered public accommodations for purposes of this title, if the operations of such entities affect commerce—

(A) an inn, hotel, motel, or other place of lodging, except for an establishment located within a building that contains not more than five rooms for rent or hire and that is actually occupied by the proprietor of such establishment as the residence of such proprietor;

(B) a restaurant, bar, or other establishment serving food or drink;

(C) a motion picture house, theater, concert hall, stadium, or other place of exhibition or entertainment;

(D) an auditorium, convention center, lecture hall, or other place of public gathering;

(E) a bakery, grocery store, clothing store, hardware store, shopping center, or other sales or rental establishment;

(F) a laundromat, dry-cleaner, bank, barber shop, beauty shop, travel service, shoe repair service, funeral parlor, gas station, office of an accountant or lawyer, pharmacy, insurance office, professional office of a health care provider, hospital, or other service establishment;

(G) a terminal, depot, or other station used for specified public transportation;

(H) a museum, library, gallery, or other place of public display or collection;

(I) a park, zoo, amusement park, or other place of recreation;

(J) a nursery, elementary, secondary, undergraduate, or postgraduate private school, or other place of education;

(K) a day care center, senior citizen center, homeless shelter, food bank, adoption agency, or other social service center establishment; and

(L) a gymnasium, health spa, bowling alley, golf course, or other place of exercise or recreation.

(8) RAIL AND RAILROAD.—The terms "rail" and "railroad" have the meaning given the term "railroad" in section 202(e) of the Federal Railroad Safety Act of 1970 (45 U.S.C. 431(e)).

(9) READILY ACHIEVABLE.—The term "readily achievable" means easily accomplishable and able to be carried out without much difficulty or expense. In determining whether an action is readily achievable, factors to be considered include—

(A) the nature and cost of the action needed under this Act;

(B) the overall financial resources of the facility or facilities involved in the action; the number of persons employed at such facility; the effect on expenses and resources, or the impact otherwise of such action upon the operation of the facility;

(C) the overall financial resources of the covered entity; the overall size of the business of a covered entity with respect to the number of its employees; the number, type, and location of its facilities; and

(D) the type of operation or operations of the covered entity, including the composition, structure, and functions of the workforce of such entity; the geographic separateness, administrative or fiscal relationship of the facility or facilities in question to the covered entity.

(10) SPECIFIED PUBLIC TRANSPORTATION.—The term "specified public transportation" means transportation by bus, rail, or any other conveyance (other than by aircraft) that provides the general public with general or special service (including charter service) on a regular and continuing basis.

(11) VEHICLE.—The term "vehicle" does not include a rail passenger car, railroad locomotive, railroad freight car, railroad caboose, or a railroad car described in section 242 or covered under this title.

SEC. 302. PROHIBITION OF DISCRIMINATION BY PUBLIC ACCOMMODA-   42 USC 12182.
      TIONS.

(a) GENERAL RULE.—No individual shall be discriminated against on the basis of disability in the full and equal enjoyment of the goods, services, facilities, privileges, advantages, or accommodations of any place of public accommodation by any person who owns, leases (or leases to), or operates a place of public accommodation.

(b) CONSTRUCTION.—

(1) GENERAL PROHIBITION.—

(A) ACTIVITIES.—

(i) DENIAL OF PARTICIPATION.—It shall be discriminatory to subject an individual or class of individuals on the basis of a disability or disabilities of such individual or class, directly, or through contractual, licensing, or other arrangements, to a denial of the opportunity of the individual or class to participate in or benefit from the goods, services, facilities, privileges, advantages, or accommodations of an entity.

(ii) PARTICIPATION IN UNEQUAL BENEFIT.—It shall be discriminatory to afford an individual or class of individuals, on the basis of a disability or disabilities of such individual or class, directly, or through contractual, licensing, or other arrangements with the opportunity to participate in or benefit from a good, service, facility, privilege, advantage, or accommodation that is not equal to that afforded to other individuals.

(iii) SEPARATE BENEFIT.—It shall be discriminatory to provide an individual or class of individuals, on the basis of a disability or disabilities of such individual or class, directly, or through contractual, licensing, or other arrangements with a good, service, facility, privilege, advantage, or accommodation that is different or separate from that provided to other individuals, unless such action is necessary to provide the individual or class of individuals with a good, service, facility, privi-

PUBLIC LAW 101-336—JULY 26, 1990

lege, advantage, or accommodation, or other opportunity that is as effective as that provided to others.

(iv) INDIVIDUAL OR CLASS OF INDIVIDUALS.—For purposes of clauses (i) through (iii) of this subparagraph, the term "individual or class of individuals" refers to the clients or customers of the covered public accommodation that enters into the contractual, licensing or other arrangement.

(B) INTEGRATED SETTINGS.—Goods, services, facilities, privileges, advantages, and accommodations shall be afforded to an individual with a disability in the most integrated setting appropriate to the needs of the individual.

(C) OPPORTUNITY TO PARTICIPATE.—Notwithstanding the existence of separate or different programs or activities provided in accordance with this section, an individual with a disability shall not be denied the opportunity to participate in such programs or activities that are not separate or different.

(D) ADMINISTRATIVE METHODS.—An individual or entity shall not, directly or through contractual or other arrangements, utilize standards or criteria or methods of administration—

(i) that have the effect of discriminating on the basis of disability; or

(ii) that perpetuate the discrimination of others who are subject to common administrative control.

(E) ASSOCIATION.—It shall be discriminatory to exclude or otherwise deny equal goods, services, facilities, privileges, advantages, accommodations, or other opportunities to an individual or entity because of the known disability of an individual with whom the individual or entity is known to have a relationship or association.

(2) SPECIFIC PROHIBITIONS.—

(A) DISCRIMINATION.—For purposes of subsection (a), discrimination includes—

(i) the imposition or application of eligibility criteria that screen out or tend to screen out an individual with a disability or any class of individuals with disabilities from fully and equally enjoying any goods, services, facilities, privileges, advantages, or accommodations, unless such criteria can be shown to be necessary for the provision of the goods, services, facilities, privileges, advantages, or accommodations being offered;

(ii) a failure to make reasonable modifications in policies, practices, or procedures, when such modifications are necessary to afford such goods, services, facilities, privileges, advantages, or accommodations to individuals with disabilities, unless the entity can demonstrate that making such modifications would fundamentally alter the nature of such goods, services, facilities, privileges, advantages, or accommodations;

(iii) a failure to take such steps as may be necessary to ensure that no individual with a disability is excluded, denied services, segregated or otherwise treated differently than other individuals because of the absence of auxiliary aids and services, unless the entity can demonstrate that taking such steps would fundamentally alter the nature of the good, service, facility, privilege, advantage, or accommodation being offered or would result in an undue burden;

(iv) a failure to remove architectural barriers, and communication barriers that are structural in nature, in existing facilities, and transportation barriers in existing vehicles and rail passenger cars used by an establishment for transporting individuals (not including barriers that can only be removed through the retrofitting of vehicles or rail passenger cars by the installation of a hydraulic or other lift), where such removal is readily achievable; and

(v) where an entity can demonstrate that the removal of a barrier under clause (iv) is not readily achievable, a failure to make such goods, services, facilities, privileges, advantages, or accommodations available through alternative methods if such methods are readily achievable.

(B) FIXED ROUTE SYSTEM.—

(i) ACCESSIBILITY.—It shall be considered discrimination for a private entity which operates a fixed route system and which is not subject to section 304 to purchase or lease a vehicle with a seating capacity in excess of 16 passengers (including the driver) for use on such system, for which a solicitation is made after the 30th day following the effective date of this subparagraph, that is not readily accessible to and usable by individuals with disabilities, including individuals who use wheelchairs.

(ii) EQUIVALENT SERVICE.—If a private entity which operates a fixed route system and which is not subject to section 304 purchases or leases a vehicle with a seating capacity of 16 passengers or less (including the driver) for use on such system after the effective date of this subparagraph that is not readily accessible to or usable by individuals with disabilities, it shall be considered discrimination for such entity to fail to operate such system so that, when viewed in its entirety, such system ensures a level of service to individuals with disabilities, including individuals who use wheelchairs, equivalent to the level of service provided to individuals without disabilities.

(C) DEMAND RESPONSIVE SYSTEM.—For purposes of subsection (a), discrimination includes—

(i) a failure of a private entity which operates a demand responsive system and which is not subject to section 304 to operate such system so that, when viewed in its entirety, such system ensures a level of service to individuals with disabilities, including individuals who use wheelchairs, equivalent to the level of service provided to individuals without disabilities; and

(ii) the purchase or lease by such entity for use on such system of a vehicle with a seating capacity in excess of 16 passengers (including the driver), for which solicitations are made after the 30th day following the effective date of this subparagraph, that is not readily accessible to and usable by individuals with disabilities (including individuals who use wheelchairs) unless such entity can demonstrate that such system, when viewed in its entirety, provides a level of service to individuals with disabilities equivalent to that provided to individuals without disabilities.

(D) OVER-THE-ROAD BUSES.—

(i) LIMITATION ON APPLICABILITY.—Subparagraphs (B) and (C) do not apply to over-the-road buses.

(ii) ACCESSIBILITY REQUIREMENTS.—For purposes of subsection (a), discrimination includes (I) the purchase or lease of an over-the-road bus which does not comply with the regulations issued under section 306(a)(2) by a private entity which provides transportation of individuals and which is not primarily engaged in the business of transporting people, and (II) any other failure of such entity to comply with such regulations.

(3) SPECIFIC CONSTRUCTION.—Nothing in this title shall require an entity to permit an individual to participate in or benefit from the goods, services, facilities, privileges, advantages and accommodations of such entity where such individual poses a direct threat to the health or safety of others. The term "direct threat" means a significant risk to the health or safety of others that cannot be eliminated by a modification of policies, practices, or procedures or by the provision of auxiliary aids or services.

42 USC 12183.

SEC. 303. NEW CONSTRUCTION AND ALTERATIONS IN PUBLIC ACCOMMODATIONS AND COMMERCIAL FACILITIES.

(a) APPLICATION OF TERM.—Except as provided in subsection (b), as applied to public accommodations and commercial facilities, discrimination for purposes of section 302(a) includes—

(1) a failure to design and construct facilities for first occupancy later than 30 months after the date of enactment of this Act that are readily accessible to and usable by individuals with disabilities, except where an entity can demonstrate that it is structurally impracticable to meet the requirements of such subsection in accordance with standards set forth or incorporated by reference in regulations issued under this title; and

(2) with respect to a facility or part thereof that is altered by, on behalf of, or for the use of an establishment in a manner that affects or could affect the usability of the facility or part thereof, a failure to make alterations in such a manner that, to the maximum extent feasible, the altered portions of the facility are readily accessible to and usable by individuals with disabilities, including individuals who use wheelchairs. Where the entity is undertaking an alteration that affects or could affect usability of or access to an area of the facility containing a primary function, the entity shall also make the alterations in such a manner that, to the maximum extent feasible, the path of travel to the altered area and the bathrooms, telephones, and drinking fountains serving the altered area, are readily accessible to and usable by individuals with disabilities where such alterations to the path of travel or the bathrooms, telephones, and drinking fountains serving the altered area are not disproportionate to the overall alterations in terms of cost and

scope (as determined under criteria established by the Attorney General).

(b) ELEVATOR.—Subsection (a) shall not be construed to require the installation of an elevator for facilities that are less than three stories or have less than 3,000 square feet per story unless the building is a shopping center, a shopping mall, or the professional office of a health care provider or unless the Attorney General determines that a particular category of such facilities requires the installation of elevators based on the usage of such facilities.

SEC. 304. PROHIBITION OF DISCRIMINATION IN SPECIFIED PUBLIC TRANSPORTATION SERVICES PROVIDED BY PRIVATE ENTITIES.   42 USC 12184.

(a) GENERAL RULE.—No individual shall be discriminated against on the basis of disability in the full and equal enjoyment of specified public transportation services provided by a private entity that is primarily engaged in the business of transporting people and whose operations affect commerce.

(b) CONSTRUCTION.—For purposes of subsection (a), discrimination includes—

(1) the imposition or application by a entity described in subsection (a) of eligibility criteria that screen out or tend to screen out an individual with a disability or any class of individuals with disabilities from fully enjoying the specified public transportation services provided by the entity, unless such criteria can be shown to be necessary for the provision of the services being offered;

(2) the failure of such entity to—

(A) make reasonable modifications consistent with those required under section 302(b)(2)(A)(ii);

(B) provide auxiliary aids and services consistent with the requirements of section 302(b)(2)(A)(iii); and

(C) remove barriers consistent with the requirements of section 302(b)(2)(A) and with the requirements of section 303(a)(2);

(3) the purchase or lease by such entity of a new vehicle (other than an automobile, a van with a seating capacity of less than 8 passengers, including the driver, or an over-the-road bus) which is to be used to provide specified public transportation and for which a solicitation is made after the 30th day following the effective date of this section, that is not readily accessible to and usable by individuals with disabilities, including individuals who use wheelchairs; except that the new vehicle need not be readily accessible to and usable by such individuals if the new vehicle is to be used solely in a demand responsive system and if the entity can demonstrate that such system, when viewed in its entirety, provides a level of service to such individuals equivalent to the level of service provided to the general public;

(4)(A) the purchase or lease by such entity of an over-the-road bus which does not comply with the regulations issued under section 306(a)(2); and

(B) any other failure of such entity to comply with such regulations; and

(5) the purchase or lease by such entity of a new van with a seating capacity of less than 8 passengers, including the driver, which is to be used to provide specified public transportation and for which a solicitation is made after the 30th day following

PUBLIC LAW 101-336—JULY 26, 1990

the effective date of this section that is not readily accessible to or usable by individuals with disabilities, including individuals who use wheelchairs; except that the new van need not be readily accessible to and usable by such individuals if the entity can demonstrate that the system for which the van is being purchased or leased, when viewed in its entirety, provides a level of service to such individuals equivalent to the level of service provided to the general public;

(6) the purchase or lease by such entity of a new rail passenger car that is to be used to provide specified public transportation, and for which a solicitation is made later than 30 days after the effective date of this paragraph, that is not readily accessible to and usable by individuals with disabilities, including individuals who use wheelchairs; and

(7) the remanufacture by such entity of a rail passenger car that is to be used to provide specified public transportation so as to extend its usable life for 10 years or more, or the purchase or lease by such entity of such a rail car, unless the rail car, to the maximum extent feasible, is made readily accessible to and usable by individuals with disabilities, including individuals who use wheelchairs.

(c) HISTORICAL OR ANTIQUATED CARS.—

(1) EXCEPTION.—To the extent that compliance with subsection (b)(2)(C) or (b)(7) would significantly alter the historic or antiquated character of a historical or antiquated rail passenger car, or a rail station served exclusively by such cars, or would result in violation of any rule, regulation, standard, or order issued by the Secretary of Transportation under the Federal Railroad Safety Act of 1970, such compliance shall not be required.

(2) DEFINITION.—As used in this subsection, the term "historical or antiquated rail passenger car" means a rail passenger car—

(A) which is not less than 30 years old at the time of its use for transporting individuals;

(B) the manufacturer of which is no longer in the business of manufacturing rail passenger cars; and

(C) which—

(i) has a consequential association with events or persons significant to the past; or

(ii) embodies, or is being restored to embody, the distinctive characteristics of a type of rail passenger car used in the past, or to represent a time period which has passed.

42 USC 12185.   SEC. 305. STUDY.

(a) PURPOSES.—The Office of Technology Assessment shall undertake a study to determine—

(1) the access needs of individuals with disabilities to over-the-road buses and over-the-road bus service; and

(2) the most cost-effective methods for providing access to over-the-road buses and over-the-road bus service to individuals with disabilities, particularly individuals who use wheelchairs, through all forms of boarding options.

(b) CONTENTS.—The study shall include, at a minimum, an analysis of the following:

(1) The anticipated demand by individuals with disabilities for accessible over-the-road buses and over-the-road bus service.

(2) The degree to which such buses and service, including any service required under sections 304(b)(4) and 306(a)(2), are readily accessible to and usable by individuals with disabilities.

(3) The effectiveness of various methods of providing accessibility to such buses and service to individuals with disabilities.

(4) The cost of providing accessible over-the-road buses and bus service to individuals with disabilities, including consideration of recent technological and cost saving developments in equipment and devices.

(5) Possible design changes in over-the-road buses that could enhance accessibility, including the installation of accessible restrooms which do not result in a loss of seating capacity.

(6) The impact of accessibility requirements on the continuation of over-the-road bus service, with particular consideration of the impact of such requirements on such service to rural communities.

(c) ADVISORY COMMITTEE.—In conducting the study required by subsection (a), the Office of Technology Assessment shall establish an advisory committee, which shall consist of—

(1) members selected from among private operators and manufacturers of over-the-road buses;

(2) members selected from among individuals with disabilities, particularly individuals who use wheelchairs, who are potential riders of such buses; and

(3) members selected for their technical expertise on issues included in the study, including manufacturers of boarding assistance equipment and devices.

The number of members selected under each of paragraphs (1) and (2) shall be equal, and the total number of members selected under paragraphs (1) and (2) shall exceed the number of members selected under paragraph (3).

(d) DEADLINE.—The study required by subsection (a), along with recommendations by the Office of Technology Assessment, including any policy options for legislative action, shall be submitted to the President and Congress within 36 months after the date of the enactment of this Act. If the President determines that compliance with the regulations issued pursuant to section 306(a)(2)(B) on or before the applicable deadlines specified in section 306(a)(2)(B) will result in a significant reduction in intercity over-the-road bus service, the President shall extend each such deadline by 1 year.

President of U.S.

(e) REVIEW.—In developing the study required by subsection (a), the Office of Technology Assessment shall provide a preliminary draft of such study to the Architectural and Transportation Barriers Compliance Board established under section 502 of the Rehabilitation Act of 1973 (29 U.S.C. 792). The Board shall have an opportunity to comment on such draft study, and any such comments by the Board made in writing within 120 days after the Board's receipt of the draft study shall be incorporated as part of the final study required to be submitted under subsection (d).

SEC. 306. REGULATIONS.   42 USC 12186.

(a) TRANSPORTATION PROVISIONS.—

(1) GENERAL RULE.—Not later than 1 year after the date of the enactment of this Act, the Secretary of Transportation shall issue regulations in an accessible format to carry out sections

302(b)(2) (B) and (C) and to carry out section 304 (other than subsection (b)(4)).

(2) SPECIAL RULES FOR PROVIDING ACCESS TO OVER-THE-ROAD BUSES.—

(A) INTERIM REQUIREMENTS.—

(i) ISSUANCE.--Not later than 1 year after the date of the enactment of this Act, the Secretary of Transportation shall issue regulations in an accessible format to carry out sections 304(b)(4) and 302(b)(2)(D)(ii) that require each private entity which uses an over-the-road bus to provide transportation of individuals to provide accessibility to such bus; except that such regulations shall not require any structural changes in over-the-road buses in order to provide access to individuals who use wheelchairs during the effective period of such regulations and shall not require the purchase of boarding assistance devices to provide access to such individuals.

(ii) EFFECTIVE PERIOD.—The regulations issued pursuant to this subparagraph shall be effective until the effective date of the regulations issued under subparagraph (B).

(B) FINAL REQUIREMENT.—

(i) REVIEW OF STUDY AND INTERIM REQUIREMENTS.— The Secretary shall review the study submitted under section 305 and the regulations issued pursuant to subparagraph (A).

(ii) ISSUANCE.—Not later than 1 year after the date of the submission of the study under section 305, the Secretary shall issue in an accessible format new regulations to carry out sections 304(b)(4) and 302(b)(2)(D)(ii) that require, taking into account the purposes of the study under section 305 and any recommendations resulting from such study, each private entity which uses an over-the-road bus to provide transportation to individuals to provide accessibility to such bus to individuals with disabilities, including individuals who use wheelchairs.

(iii) EFFECTIVE PERIOD.—Subject to section 305(d), the regulations issued pursuant to this subparagraph shall take effect—

(I) with respect to small providers of transportation (as defined by the Secretary), 7 years after the date of the enactment of this Act; and

(II) with respect to other providers of transportation, 6 years after such date of enactment.

(C) LIMITATION ON REQUIRING INSTALLATION OF ACCESSIBLE RESTROOMS.—The regulations issued pursuant to this paragraph shall not require the installation of accessible restrooms in over-the-road buses if such installation would result in a loss of seating capacity.

(3) STANDARDS.—The regulations issued pursuant to this subsection shall include standards applicable to facilities and vehicles covered by sections 302(b)(2) and 304.

(b) OTHER PROVISIONS.—Not later than 1 year after the date of the enactment of this Act, the Attorney General shall issue regulations in an accessible format to carry out the provisions of this title not referred to in subsection (a) that include standards applicable to facilities and vehicles covered under section 302.

(c) CONSISTENCY WITH ATBCB GUIDELINES.—Standards included in regulations issued under subsections (a) and (b) shall be consistent with the minimum guidelines and requirements issued by the Architectural and Transportation Barriers Compliance Board in accordance with section 504 of this Act.

(d) INTERIM ACCESSIBILITY STANDARDS.—

(1) FACILITIES.—If final regulations have not been issued pursuant to this section, for new construction or alterations for which a valid and appropriate State or local building permit is obtained prior to the issuance of final regulations under this section, and for which the construction or alteration authorized by such permit begins within one year of the receipt of such permit and is completed under the terms of such permit, compliance with the Uniform Federal Accessibility Standards in effect at the time the building permit is issued shall suffice to satisfy the requirement that facilities be readily accessible to and usable by persons with disabilities as required under section 303, except that, if such final regulations have not been issued one year after the Architectural and Transportation Barriers Compliance Board has issued the supplemental minimum guidelines required under section 504(a) of this Act, compliance with such supplemental minimum guidelines shall be necessary to satisfy the requirement that facilities be readily accessible to and usable by persons with disabilities prior to issuance of the final regulations.

(2) VEHICLES AND RAIL PASSENGER CARS.—If final regulations have not been issued pursuant to this section, a private entity shall be considered to have complied with the requirements of this title, if any, that a vehicle or rail passenger car be readily accessible to and usable by individuals with disabilities, if the design for such vehicle or car complies with the laws and regulations (including the Minimum Guidelines and Requirements for Accessible Design and such supplemental minimum guidelines as are issued under section 504(a) of this Act) governing accessibility of such vehicles or cars, to the extent that such laws and regulations are not inconsistent with this title and are in effect at the time such design is substantially completed.

SEC. 307. EXEMPTIONS FOR PRIVATE CLUBS AND RELIGIOUS ORGANI-   42 USC 12187.
ZATIONS.

The provisions of this title shall not apply to private clubs or establishments exempted from coverage under title II of the Civil Rights Act of 1964 (42 U.S.C. 2000-a(e)) or to religious organizations or entities controlled by religious organizations, including places of worship.

SEC. 308. ENFORCEMENT.   42 USC 12188.

(a) IN GENERAL.—

(1) AVAILABILITY OF REMEDIES AND PROCEDURES.—The remedies and procedures set forth in section 204(a) of the Civil Rights Act of 1964 (42 U.S.C. 2000a-3(a)) are the remedies and procedures this title provides to any person who is being subjected to discrimination on the basis of disability in violation of this title or who has reasonable grounds for believing that such person is about to be subjected to discrimination in violation of

section 303. Nothing in this section shall require a person with a disability to engage in a futile gesture if such person has actual notice that a person or organization covered by this title does not intend to comply with its provisions.

(2) INJUNCTIVE RELIEF.—In the case of violations of sections 302(b)(2)(A)(iv) and section 303(a), injunctive relief shall include an order to alter facilities to make such facilities readily accessible to and usable by individuals with disabilities to the extent required by this title. Where appropriate, injunctive relief shall also include requiring the provision of an auxiliary aid or service, modification of a policy, or provision of alternative methods, to the extent required by this title.

(b) ENFORCEMENT BY THE ATTORNEY GENERAL.—

(1) DENIAL OF RIGHTS.—

(A) DUTY TO INVESTIGATE.—

(i) IN GENERAL.—The Attorney General shall investigate alleged violations of this title, and shall undertake periodic reviews of compliance of covered entities under this title.

(ii) ATTORNEY GENERAL CERTIFICATION.—On the application of a State or local government, the Attorney General may, in consultation with the Architectural and Transportation Barriers Compliance Board, and after prior notice and a public hearing at which persons, including individuals with disabilities, are provided an opportunity to testify against such certification, certify that a State law or local building code or similar ordinance that establishes accessibility requirements meets or exceeds the minimum requirements of this Act for the accessibility and usability of covered facilities under this title. At any enforcement proceeding under this section, such certification by the Attorney General shall be rebuttable evidence that such State law or local ordinance does meet or exceed the minimum requirements of this Act.

(B) POTENTIAL VIOLATION.—If the Attorney General has reasonable cause to believe that—

(i) any person or group of persons is engaged in a pattern or practice of discrimination under this title; or

(ii) any person or group of persons has been discriminated against under this title and such discrimination raises an issue of general public importance,

the Attorney General may commence a civil action in any appropriate United States district court.

(2) AUTHORITY OF COURT.—In a civil action under paragraph (1)(B), the court—

(A) may grant any equitable relief that such court considers to be appropriate, including, to the extent required by this title—

(i) granting temporary, preliminary, or permanent relief;

(ii) providing an auxiliary aid or service, modification of policy, practice, or procedure, or alternative method; and

(iii) making facilities readily accessible to and usable by individuals with disabilities;

(B) may award such other relief as the court considers to be appropriate, including monetary damages to persons aggrieved when requested by the Attorney General; and

(C) may, to vindicate the public interest, assess a civil penalty against the entity in an amount—

(i) not exceeding $50,000 for a first violation; and

(ii) not exceeding $100,000 for any subsequent violation.

(3) SINGLE VIOLATION.—For purposes of paragraph (2)(C), in determining whether a first or subsequent violation has occurred, a determination in a single action, by judgment or settlement, that the covered entity has engaged in more than one discriminatory act shall be counted as a single violation.

(4) PUNITIVE DAMAGES.—For purposes of subsection (b)(2)(B), the term "monetary damages" and "such other relief" does not include punitive damages.

(5) JUDICIAL CONSIDERATION.—In a civil action under paragraph (1)(B), the court, when considering what amount of civil penalty, if any, is appropriate, shall give consideration to any good faith effort or attempt to comply with this Act by the entity. In evaluating good faith, the court shall consider, among other factors it deems relevant, whether the entity could have reasonably anticipated the need for an appropriate type of auxiliary aid needed to accommodate the unique needs of a particular individual with a disability.

SEC. 309. EXAMINATIONS AND COURSES.

42 USC 12189.

Any person that offers examinations or courses related to applications, licensing, certification, or credentialing for secondary or post-secondary education, professional, or trade purposes shall offer such examinations or courses in a place and manner accessible to persons with disabilities or offer alternative accessible arrangements for such individuals.

SEC. 310. EFFECTIVE DATE.

42 USC 12181 note.

(a) GENERAL RULE.—Except as provided in subsections (b) and (c), this title shall become effective 18 months after the date of the enactment of this Act.

(b) CIVIL ACTIONS.—Except for any civil action brought for a violation of section 303, no civil action shall be brought for any act or omission described in section 302 which occurs—

(1) during the first 6 months after the effective date, against businesses that employ 25 or fewer employees and have gross receipts of $1,000,000 or less; and

(2) during the first year after the effective date, against businesses that employ 10 or fewer employees and have gross receipts of $500,000 or less.

(c) EXCEPTION.—Sections 302(a) for purposes of section 302(b)(2) (B) and (C) only, 304(a) for purposes of section 304(b)(3) only, 304(b)(3), 305, and 306 shall take effect on the date of the enactment of this Act.

TITLE IV—TELECOMMUNICATIONS

SEC. 401. TELECOMMUNICATIONS RELAY SERVICES FOR HEARING-IMPAIRED AND SPEECH-IMPAIRED INDIVIDUALS.

(a) TELECOMMUNICATIONS.—Title II of the Communications Act of 1934 (47 U.S.C. 201 et seq.) is amended by adding at the end thereof the following new section:

State and local governments.
47 USC 225.

"SEC. 225. TELECOMMUNICATIONS SERVICES FOR HEARING-IMPAIRED AND SPEECH-IMPAIRED INDIVIDUALS.

"(a) DEFINITIONS.—As used in this section—

"(1) COMMON CARRIER OR CARRIER.—The term 'common carrier' or 'carrier' includes any common carrier engaged in interstate communication by wire or radio as defined in section 3(h) and any common carrier engaged in intrastate communication by wire or radio, notwithstanding sections 2(b) and 221(b).

"(2) TDD.—The term 'TDD' means a Telecommunications Device for the Deaf, which is a machine that employs graphic communication in the transmission of coded signals through a wire or radio communication system.

"(3) TELECOMMUNICATIONS RELAY SERVICES.—The term 'telecommunications relay services' means telephone transmission services that provide the ability for an individual who has a hearing impairment or speech impairment to engage in communication by wire or radio with a hearing individual in a manner that is functionally equivalent to the ability of an individual who does not have a hearing impairment or speech impairment to communicate using voice communication services by wire or radio. Such term includes services that enable two-way communication between an individual who uses a TDD or other nonvoice terminal device and an individual who does not use such a device.

"(b) AVAILABILITY OF TELECOMMUNICATIONS RELAY SERVICES.—

"(1) IN GENERAL.—In order to carry out the purposes established under section 1, to make available to all individuals in the United States a rapid, efficient nationwide communication service, and to increase the utility of the telephone system of the Nation, the Commission shall ensure that interstate and intrastate telecommunications relay services are available, to the extent possible and in the most efficient manner, to hearing-impaired and speech-impaired individuals in the United States.

"(2) USE OF GENERAL AUTHORITY AND REMEDIES.—For the purposes of administering and enforcing the provisions of this section and the regulations prescribed thereunder, the Commission shall have the same authority, power, and functions with respect to common carriers engaged in intrastate communication as the Commission has in administering and enforcing the provisions of this title with respect to any common carrier engaged in interstate communication. Any violation of this section by any common carrier engaged in intrastate communication shall be subject to the same remedies, penalties, and procedures as are applicable to a violation of this Act by a common carrier engaged in interstate communication.

"(c) PROVISION OF SERVICES.—Each common carrier providing telephone voice transmission services shall, not later than 3 years after the date of enactment of this section, provide in compliance with the regulations prescribed under this section, throughout the area in which it offers service, telecommunications relay services, individually, through designees, through a competitively selected vendor, or in concert with other carriers. A common carrier shall be considered to be in compliance with such regulations—

"(1) with respect to intrastate telecommunications relay services in any State that does not have a certified program under subsection (f) and with respect to interstate telecommunications relay services, if such common carrier (or other entity through which the carrier is providing such relay services) is in compliance with the Commission's regulations under subsection (d); or

"(2) with respect to intrastate telecommunications relay services in any State that has a certified program under subsection (f) for such State, if such common carrier (or other entity through which the carrier is providing such relay services) is in compliance with the program certified under subsection (f) for such State.

"(d) REGULATIONS.—

"(1) IN GENERAL.—The Commission shall, not later than 1 year after the date of enactment of this section, prescribe regulations to implement this section, including regulations that—

"(A) establish functional requirements, guidelines, and operations procedures for telecommunications relay services;

"(B) establish minimum standards that shall be met in carrying out subsection (c);

"(C) require that telecommunications relay services operate every day for 24 hours per day;

"(D) require that users of telecommunications relay services pay rates no greater than the rates paid for functionally equivalent voice communication services with respect to such factors as the duration of the call, the time of day, and the distance from point of origination to point of termination;

"(E) prohibit relay operators from failing to fulfill the obligations of common carriers by refusing calls or limiting the length of calls that use telecommunications relay services;

"(F) prohibit relay operators from disclosing the content of any relayed conversation and from keeping records of the content of any such conversation beyond the duration of the call; and

"(G) prohibit relay operators from intentionally altering a relayed conversation.

"(2) TECHNOLOGY.—The Commission shall ensure that regulations prescribed to implement this section encourage, consistent with section 7(a) of this Act, the use of existing technology and do not discourage or impair the development of improved technology.

"(3) JURISDICTIONAL SEPARATION OF COSTS.—

"(A) IN GENERAL.—Consistent with the provisions of section 410 of this Act, the Commission shall prescribe regulations governing the jurisdictional separation of costs for the services provided pursuant to this section.

"(B) RECOVERING COSTS.—Such regulations shall generally provide that costs caused by interstate telecommunications relay services shall be recovered from all subscribers for every interstate service and costs caused by intrastate telecommunications relay services shall be recovered from the intrastate jurisdiction. In a State that has a certified program under subsection (f), a State commission shall permit a common carrier to recover the costs incurred in providing intrastate telecommunications relay services by a method consistent with the requirements of this section.

"(e) ENFORCEMENT.—

"(1) IN GENERAL.—Subject to subsections (f) and (g), the Commission shall enforce this section.

"(2) COMPLAINT.—The Commission shall resolve, by final order, a complaint alleging a violation of this section within 180 days after the date such complaint is filed.

"(f) CERTIFICATION.—

"(1) STATE DOCUMENTATION.—Any State desiring to establish a State program under this section shall submit documentation to the Commission that describes the program of such State for implementing intrastate telecommunications relay services and the procedures and remedies available for enforcing any requirements imposed by the State program.

"(2) REQUIREMENTS FOR CERTIFICATION.—After review of such documentation, the Commission shall certify the State program if the Commission determines that—

"(A) the program makes available to hearing-impaired and speech-impaired individuals, either directly, through designees, through a competitively selected vendor, or through regulation of intrastate common carriers, intrastate telecommunications relay services in such State in a manner that meets or exceeds the requirements of regulations prescribed by the Commission under subsection (d); and

"(B) the program makes available adequate procedures and remedies for enforcing the requirements of the State program.

"(3) METHOD OF FUNDING.—Except as provided in subsection (d), the Commission shall not refuse to certify a State program based solely on the method such State will implement for funding intrastate telecommunication relay services.

"(4) SUSPENSION OR REVOCATION OF CERTIFICATION.—The Commission may suspend or revoke such certification if, after notice and opportunity for hearing, the Commission determines that such certification is no longer warranted. In a State whose program has been suspended or revoked, the Commission shall take such steps as may be necessary, consistent with this section, to ensure continuity of telecommunications relay services.

"(g) COMPLAINT.—

"(1) REFERRAL OF COMPLAINT.—If a complaint to the Commission alleges a violation of this section with respect to intrastate telecommunications relay services within a State and certification of the program of such State under subsection (f) is in effect, the Commission shall refer such complaint to such State.

"(2) JURISDICTION OF COMMISSION.—After referring a complaint to a State under paragraph (1), the Commission shall exercise jurisdiction over such complaint only if—

"(A) final action under such State program has not been taken on such complaint by such State—

PUBLIC LAW 101–336—JULY 26, 1990   104 STAT. 369

"(i) within 180 days after the complaint is filed with such State; or
"(ii) within a shorter period as prescribed by the regulations of such State; or
"(B) the Commission determines that such State program is no longer qualified for certification under subsection (f).".
(b) CONFORMING AMENDMENTS.—The Communications Act of 1934 (47 U.S.C. 151 et seq.) is amended—
(1) in section 2(b) (47 U.S.C. 152(b)), by striking "section 224" and inserting "sections 224 and 225"; and
(2) in section 221(b) (47 U.S.C. 221(b)), by striking "section 301" and inserting "sections 225 and 301".

SEC. 402. CLOSED-CAPTIONING OF PUBLIC SERVICE ANNOUNCEMENTS.

Section 711 of the Communications Act of 1934 is amended to read as follows: 47 USC 611.

"SEC. 711. CLOSED-CAPTIONING OF PUBLIC SERVICE ANNOUNCEMENTS.

"Any television public service announcement that is produced or funded in whole or in part by any agency or instrumentality of Federal Government shall include closed captioning of the verbal content of such announcement. A television broadcast station licensee—
"(1) shall not be required to supply closed captioning for any such announcement that fails to include it; and
"(2) shall not be liable for broadcasting any such announcement without transmitting a closed caption unless the licensee intentionally fails to transmit the closed caption that was included with the announcement.".

TITLE V—MISCELLANEOUS PROVISIONS

SEC. 501. CONSTRUCTION.   42 USC 12201.

(a) IN GENERAL.—Except as otherwise provided in this Act, nothing in this Act shall be construed to apply a lesser standard than the standards applied under title V of the Rehabilitation Act of 1973 (29 U.S.C. 790 et seq.) or the regulations issued by Federal agencies pursuant to such title.
(b) RELATIONSHIP TO OTHER LAWS.—Nothing in this Act shall be construed to invalidate or limit the remedies, rights, and procedures of any Federal law or law of any State or political subdivision of any State or jurisdiction that provides greater or equal protection for the rights of individuals with disabilities than are afforded by this Act. Nothing in this Act shall be construed to preclude the prohibition of, or the imposition of restrictions on, smoking in places of employment covered by title I, in transportation covered by title II or III, or in places of public accommodation covered by title III.
(c) INSURANCE.—Titles I through IV of this Act shall not be construed to prohibit or restrict—
(1) an insurer, hospital or medical service company, health maintenance organization, or any agent, or entity that administers benefit plans, or similar organizations from underwriting risks, classifying risks, or administering such risks that are based on or not inconsistent with State law; or
(2) a person or organization covered by this Act from establishing, sponsoring, observing or administering the terms

of a bona fide benefit plan that are based on underwriting risks, classifying risks, or administering such risks that are based on or not inconsistent with State law; or

(3) a person or organization covered by this Act from establishing, sponsoring, observing or administering the terms of a bona fide benefit plan that is not subject to State laws that regulate insurance.

Paragraphs (1), (2), and (3) shall not be used as a subterfuge to evade the purposes of title I and III.

(d) ACCOMMODATIONS AND SERVICES.—Nothing in this Act shall be construed to require an individual with a disability to accept an accommodation, aid, service, opportunity, or benefit which such individual chooses not to accept.

42 USC 12202. SEC. 502. STATE IMMUNITY.

A State shall not be immune under the eleventh amendment to the Constitution of the United States from an action in Federal or State court of competent jurisdiction for a violation of this Act. In any action against a State for a violation of the requirements of this Act, remedies (including remedies both at law and in equity) are available for such a violation to the same extent as such remedies are available for such a violation in an action against any public or private entity other than a State.

42 USC 12203. SEC. 503. PROHIBITION AGAINST RETALIATION AND COERCION.

(a) RETALIATION.—No person shall discriminate against any individual because such individual has opposed any act or practice made unlawful by this Act or because such individual made a charge, testified, assisted, or participated in any manner in an investigation, proceeding, or hearing under this Act.

(b) INTERFERENCE, COERCION, OR INTIMIDATION.—It shall be unlawful to coerce, intimidate, threaten, or interfere with any individual in the exercise or enjoyment of, or on account of his or her having exercised or enjoyed, or on account of his or her having aided or encouraged any other individual in the exercise or enjoyment of, any right granted or protected by this Act.

(c) REMEDIES AND PROCEDURES.—The remedies and procedures available under sections 107, 203, and 308 of this Act shall be available to aggrieved persons for violations of subsections (a) and (b), with respect to title I, title II and title III, respectively.

42 USC 12204. SEC. 504. REGULATIONS BY THE ARCHITECTURAL AND TRANSPORTATION BARRIERS COMPLIANCE BOARD.

(a) ISSUANCE OF GUIDELINES.—Not later than 9 months after the date of enactment of this Act, the Architectural and Transportation Barriers Compliance Board shall issue minimum guidelines that shall supplement the existing Minimum Guidelines and Requirements for Accessible Design for purposes of titles II and III of this Act.

(b) CONTENTS OF GUIDELINES.—The supplemental guidelines issued under subsection (a) shall establish additional requirements, consistent with this Act, to ensure that buildings, facilities, rail passenger cars, and vehicles are accessible, in terms of architecture and design, transportation, and communication, to individuals with disabilities.

(c) QUALIFIED HISTORIC PROPERTIES.—

(1) IN GENERAL.—The supplemental guidelines issued under subsection (a) shall include procedures and requirements for

alterations that will threaten or destroy the historic significance of qualified historic buildings and facilities as defined in
4.1.7(1)(a) of the Uniform Federal Accessibility Standards.

(2) SITES ELIGIBLE FOR LISTING IN NATIONAL REGISTER.—With
respect to alterations of buildings or facilities that are eligible
for listing in the National Register of Historic Places under the
National Historic Preservation Act (16 U.S.C. 470 et seq.), the
guidelines described in paragraph (1) shall, at a minimum,
maintain the procedures and requirements established in 4.1.7
(1) and (2) of the Uniform Federal Accessibility Standards.

(3) OTHER SITES.—With respect to alterations of buildings or
facilities designated as historic under State or local law, the
guidelines described in paragraph (1) shall establish procedures
equivalent to those established by 4.1.7(1) (b) and (c) of the
Uniform Federal Accessibility Standards, and shall require, at a
minimum, compliance with the requirements established in
4.1.7(2) of such standards.

SEC. 505. ATTORNEY'S FEES.   42 USC 12205.

In any action or administrative proceeding commenced pursuant
to this Act, the court or agency, in its discretion, may allow the
prevailing party, other than the United States, a reasonable attorney's fee, including litigation expenses, and costs, and the United
States shall be liable for the foregoing the same as a private
individual.

SEC. 506. TECHNICAL ASSISTANCE.   42 USC 12206.

(a) PLAN FOR ASSISTANCE.—

(1) IN GENERAL.—Not later than 180 days after the date of
enactment of this Act, the Attorney General, in consultation
with the Chair of the Equal Employment Opportunity Commission, the Secretary of Transportation, the Chair of the Architectural and Transportation Barriers Compliance Board, and the
Chairman of the Federal Communications Commission, shall
develop a plan to assist entities covered under this Act, and
other Federal agencies, in understanding the responsibility of
such entities and agencies under this Act.

(2) PUBLICATION OF PLAN.—The Attorney General shall publish the plan referred to in paragraph (1) for public comment in
accordance with subchapter II of chapter 5 of title 5, United
States Code (commonly known as the Administrative Procedure
Act).

(b) AGENCY AND PUBLIC ASSISTANCE.—The Attorney General may
obtain the assistance of other Federal agencies in carrying out
subsection (a), including the National Council on Disability, the
President's Committee on Employment of People with Disabilities,
the Small Business Administration, and the Department of
Commerce.

(c) IMPLEMENTATION.—

(1) RENDERING ASSISTANCE.—Each Federal agency that has
responsibility under paragraph (2) for implementing this Act
may render technical assistance to individuals and institutions
that have rights or duties under the respective title or titles for
which such agency has responsibility.

(2) IMPLEMENTATION OF TITLES.—

(A) TITLE I.—The Equal Employment Opportunity
Commission and the Attorney General shall implement the

plan for assistance developed under subsection (a), for title I.

(B) TITLE II.—

(i) SUBTITLE A.—The Attorney General shall implement such plan for assistance for subtitle A of title II.

(ii) SUBTITLE B.—The Secretary of Transportation shall implement such plan for assistance for subtitle B of title II.

(C) TITLE III.—The Attorney General, in coordination with the Secretary of Transportation and the Chair of the Architectural Transportation Barriers Compliance Board, shall implement such plan for assistance for title III, except for section 304, the plan for assistance for which shall be implemented by the Secretary of Transportation.

(D) TITLE IV.—The Chairman of the Federal Communications Commission, in coordination with the Attorney General, shall implement such plan for assistance for title IV.

(3) TECHNICAL ASSISTANCE MANUALS.—Each Federal agency that has responsibility under paragraph (2) for implementing this Act shall, as part of its implementation responsibilities, ensure the availability and provision of appropriate technical assistance manuals to individuals or entities with rights or duties under this Act no later than six months after applicable final regulations are published under titles I, II, III, and IV.

(d) GRANTS AND CONTRACTS.—

(1) IN GENERAL.—Each Federal agency that has responsibility under subsection (c)(2) for implementing this Act may make grants or award contracts to effectuate the purposes of this section, subject to the availability of appropriations. Such grants and contracts may be awarded to individuals, institutions not organized for profit and no part of the net earnings of which inures to the benefit of any private shareholder or individual (including educational institutions), and associations representing individuals who have rights or duties under this Act. Contracts may be awarded to entities organized for profit, but such entities may not be the recipients or grants described in this paragraph.

(2) DISSEMINATION OF INFORMATION.—Such grants and contracts, among other uses, may be designed to ensure wide dissemination of information about the rights and duties established by this Act and to provide information and technical assistance about techniques for effective compliance with this Act.

(e) FAILURE TO RECEIVE ASSISTANCE.—An employer, public accommodation, or other entity covered under this Act shall not be excused from compliance with the requirements of this Act because of any failure to receive technical assistance under this section, including any failure in the development or dissemination of any technical assistance manual authorized by this section.

42 USC 12207.   **SEC. 507. FEDERAL WILDERNESS AREAS.**

(a) STUDY.—The National Council on Disability shall conduct a study and report on the effect that wilderness designations and wilderness land management practices have on the ability of individuals with disabilities to use and enjoy the National Wilderness Preservation System as established under the Wilderness Act (16 U.S.C. 1131 et seq.).

(b) SUBMISSION OF REPORT.—Not later than 1 year after the enactment of this Act, the National Council on Disability shall submit the report required under subsection (a) to Congress.

(c) SPECIFIC WILDERNESS ACCESS.—

(1) IN GENERAL.—Congress reaffirms that nothing in the Wilderness Act is to be construed as prohibiting the use of a wheelchair in a wilderness area by an individual whose disability requires use of a wheelchair, and consistent with the Wilderness Act no agency is required to provide any form of special treatment or accommodation, or to construct any facilities or modify any conditions of lands within a wilderness area in order to facilitate such use.

(2) DEFINITION.—For purposes of paragraph (1), the term "wheelchair" means a device designed solely for use by a mobility-impaired person for locomotion, that is suitable for use in an indoor pedestrian area.

SEC. 508. TRANSVESTITES.

42 USC 12208.

For the purposes of this Act, the term "disabled" or "disability" shall not apply to an individual solely because that individual is a transvestite.

SEC. 509. COVERAGE OF CONGRESS AND THE AGENCIES OF THE LEGISLATIVE BRANCH.

42 USC 12209.

(a) COVERAGE OF THE SENATE.—

(1) COMMITMENT TO RULE XLII.—The Senate reaffirms its commitment to Rule XLII of the Standing Rules of the Senate which provides as follows:

"No member, officer, or employee of the Senate shall, with respect to employment by the Senate or any office thereof—

"(a) fail or refuse to hire an individual;

"(b) discharge an individual; or

"(c) otherwise discriminate against an individual with respect to promotion, compensation, or terms, conditions, or privileges of employment

on the basis of such individual's race, color, religion, sex, national origin, age, or state of physical handicap.".

(2) APPLICATION TO SENATE EMPLOYMENT.—The rights and protections provided pursuant to this Act, the Civil Rights Act of 1990 (S. 2104, 101st Congress), the Civil Rights Act of 1964, the Age Discrimination in Employment Act of 1967, and the Rehabilitation Act of 1973 shall apply with respect to employment by the United States Senate.

(3) INVESTIGATION AND ADJUDICATION OF CLAIMS.—All claims raised by any individual with respect to Senate employment, pursuant to the Acts referred to in paragraph (2), shall be investigated and adjudicated by the Select Committee on Ethics, pursuant to S. Res. 338, 88th Congress, as amended, or such other entity as the Senate may designate.

(4) RIGHTS OF EMPLOYEES.—The Committee on Rules and Administration shall ensure that Senate employees are informed of their rights under the Acts referred to in paragraph (2).

(5) APPLICABLE REMEDIES.—When assigning remedies to individuals found to have a valid claim under the Acts referred to in paragraph (2), the Select Committee on Ethics, or such other entity as the Senate may designate, should to the extent

practicable apply the same remedies applicable to all other employees covered by the Acts referred to in paragraph (2). Such remedies shall apply exclusively.

(6) MATTERS OTHER THAN EMPLOYMENT.—

(A) IN GENERAL.—The rights and protections under this Act shall, subject to subparagraph (B), apply with respect to the conduct of the Senate regarding matters other than employment.

(B) REMEDIES.—The Architect of the Capitol shall establish remedies and procedures to be utilized with respect to the rights and protections provided pursuant to subparagraph (A). Such remedies and procedures shall apply exclusively, after approval in accordance with subparagraph (C).

(C) PROPOSED REMEDIES AND PROCEDURES.—For purposes of subparagraph (B), the Architect of the Capitol shall submit proposed remedies and procedures to the Senate Committee on Rules and Administration. The remedies and procedures shall be effective upon the approval of the Committee on Rules and Administration.

(7) EXERCISE OF RULEMAKING POWER.—Notwithstanding any other provision of law, enforcement and adjudication of the rights and protections referred to in paragraph (2) and (6)(A) shall be within the exclusive jurisdiction of the United States Senate. The provisions of paragraph (1), (3), (4), (5), (6)(B), and (6)(C) are enacted by the Senate as an exercise of the rulemaking power of the Senate, with full recognition of the right of the Senate to change its rules, in the same manner, and to the same extent, as in the case of any other rule of the Senate.

(b) COVERAGE OF THE HOUSE OF REPRESENTATIVES.—

(1) IN GENERAL.—Notwithstanding any other provision of this Act or of law, the purposes of this Act shall, subject to paragraphs (2) and (3), apply in their entirety to the House of Representatives.

(2) EMPLOYMENT IN THE HOUSE.—

(A) APPLICATION.—The rights and protections under this Act shall, subject to subparagraph (B), apply with respect to any employee in an employment position in the House of Representatives and any employing authority of the House of Representatives.

(B) ADMINISTRATION.—

(i) IN GENERAL.—In the administration of this paragraph, the remedies and procedures made applicable pursuant to the resolution described in clause (ii) shall apply exclusively.

(ii) RESOLUTION.—The resolution referred to in clause (i) is House Resolution 15 of the One Hundred First Congress, as agreed to January 3, 1989, or any other provision that continues in effect the provisions of, or is a successor to, the Fair Employment Practices Resolution (House Resolution 558 of the One Hundredth Congress, as agreed to October 4, 1988).

(C) EXERCISE OF RULEMAKING POWER.—The provisions of subparagraph (B) are enacted by the House of Representatives as an exercise of the rulemaking power of the House of Representatives, with full recognition of the right of the House to change its rules, in the same manner, and to the same extent as in the case of any other rule of the House.

(3) MATTERS OTHER THAN EMPLOYMENT.—

(A) IN GENERAL.—The rights and protections under this Act shall, subject to subparagraph (B), apply with respect to the conduct of the House of Representatives regarding matters other than employment.

(B) REMEDIES.—The Architect of the Capitol shall establish remedies and procedures to be utilized with respect to the rights and protections provided pursuant to subparagraph (A). Such remedies and procedures shall apply exclusively, after approval in accordance with subparagraph (C).

(C) APPROVAL.—For purposes of subparagraph (B), the Architect of the Capitol shall submit proposed remedies and procedures to the Speaker of the House of Representatives. The remedies and procedures shall be effective upon the approval of the Speaker, after consultation with the House Office Building Commission.

(c) INSTRUMENTALITIES OF CONGRESS.—

(1) IN GENERAL.—The rights and protections under this Act shall, subject to paragraph (2), apply with respect to the conduct of each instrumentality of the Congress.

(2) ESTABLISHMENT OF REMEDIES AND PROCEDURES BY INSTRUMENTALITIES.—The chief official of each instrumentality of the Congress shall establish remedies and procedures to be utilized with respect to the rights and protections provided pursuant to paragraph (1). Such remedies and procedures shall apply exclusively.

(3) REPORT TO CONGRESS.—The chief official of each instrumentality of the Congress shall, after establishing remedies and procedures for purposes of paragraph (2), submit to the Congress a report describing the remedies and procedures.

(4) DEFINITION OF INSTRUMENTALITIES.—For purposes of this section, instrumentalities of the Congress include the following: the Architect of the Capitol, the Congressional Budget Office, the General Accounting Office, the Government Printing Office, the Library of Congress, the Office of Technology Assessment, and the United States Botanic Garden.

(5) CONSTRUCTION.—Nothing in this section shall alter the enforcement procedures for individuals with disabilities provided in the General Accounting Office Personnel Act of 1980 and regulations promulgated pursuant to that Act.

SEC. 510. ILLEGAL USE OF DRUGS.   42 USC 12210.

(a) IN GENERAL.—For purposes of this Act, the term "individual with a disability" does not include an individual who is currently engaging in the illegal use of drugs, when the covered entity act. on the basis of such use.

(b) RULES OF CONSTRUCTION.—Nothing in subsection (a) shall be construed to exclude as an individual with a disability an individual who—

(1) has successfully completed a supervised drug rehabilitation program and is no longer engaging in the illegal use of drugs, or has otherwise been rehabilitated successfully and is no longer engaging in such use;

(2) is participating in a supervised rehabilitation program and is no longer engaging in such use; or

(3) is erroneously regarded as engaging in such use, but is not engaging in such use;

except that it shall not be a violation of this Act for a covered entity to adopt or administer reasonable policies or procedures, including but not limited to drug testing, designed to ensure that an individual described in paragraph (1) or (2) is no longer engaging in the illegal use of drugs; however, nothing in this section shall be construed to encourage, prohibit, restrict, or authorize the conducting of testing for the illegal use of drugs.

(c) HEALTH AND OTHER SERVICES.—Notwithstanding subsection (a) and section 511(b)(3), an individual shall not be denied health services, or services provided in connection with drug rehabilitation, on the basis of the current illegal use of drugs if the individual is otherwise entitled to such services.

(d) DEFINITION OF ILLEGAL USE OF DRUGS.—

(1) IN GENERAL.—The term "illegal use of drugs" means the use of drugs, the possession or distribution of which is unlawful under the Controlled Substances Act (21 U.S.C. 812). Such term does not include the use of a drug taken under supervision by a licensed health care professional, or other uses authorized by the Controlled Substances Act or other provisions of Federal law.

(2) DRUGS.—The term "drug" means a controlled substance, as defined in schedules I through V of section 202 of the Controlled Substances Act.

42 USC 12211.

SEC. 511. DEFINITIONS.

(a) HOMOSEXUALITY AND BISEXUALITY.—For purposes of the definition of "disability" in section 3(2), homosexuality and bisexuality are not impairments and as such are not disabilities under this Act.

(b) CERTAIN CONDITIONS.—Under this Act, the term "disability" shall not include—

(1) transvestism, transsexualism, pedophilia, exhibitionism, voyeurism, gender identity disorders not resulting from physical impairments, or other sexual behavior disorders;

(2) compulsive gambling, kleptomania, or pyromania; or

(3) psychoactive substance use disorders resulting from current illegal use of drugs.

SEC. 512. AMENDMENTS TO THE REHABILITATION ACT.

(a) DEFINITION OF HANDICAPPED INDIVIDUAL.—Section 7(8) of the Rehabilitation Act of 1973 (29 U.S.C. 706(8)) is amended by redesignating subparagraph (C) as subparagraph (D), and by inserting after subparagraph (B) the following subparagraph:

"(C)(i) For purposes of title V, the term 'individual with handicaps' does not include an individual who is currently engaging in the illegal use of drugs, when a covered entity acts on the basis of such use.

"(ii) Nothing in clause (i) shall be construed to exclude as an individual with handicaps an individual who—

"(I) has successfully completed a supervised drug rehabilitation program and is no longer engaging in the illegal use of drugs, or has otherwise been rehabilitated successfully and is no longer engaging in such use;

"(II) is participating in a supervised rehabilitation program and is no longer engaging in such use; or

"(III) is erroneously regarded as engaging in such use, but is not engaging in such use;

except that it shall not be a violation of this Act for a covered entity to adopt or administer reasonable policies or procedures, including but not limited to drug testing, designed to ensure that an individual described in subclause (I) or (II) is no longer engaging in the illegal use of drugs.

"(iii) Notwithstanding clause (i), for purposes of programs and activities providing health services and services provided under titles I, II and III, an individual shall not be excluded from the benefits of such programs or activities on the basis of his or her current illegal use of drugs if he or she is otherwise entitled to such services.

"(iv) For purposes of programs and activities providing educational services, local educational agencies may take disciplinary action pertaining to the use or possession of illegal drugs or alcohol against any handicapped student who currently is engaging in the illegal use of drugs or in the use of alcohol to the same extent that such disciplinary action is taken against nonhandicapped students. Furthermore, the due process procedures at 34 CFR 104.36 shall not apply to such disciplinary actions.

"(v) For purposes of sections 503 and 504 as such sections relate to employment, the term 'individual with handicaps' does not include any individual who is an alcoholic whose current use of alcohol prevents such individual from performing the duties of the job in question or whose employment, by reason of such current alcohol abuse, would constitute a direct threat to property or the safety of others.".

(b) DEFINITION OF ILLEGAL DRUGS.—Section 7 of the Rehabilitation Act of 1973 (29 U.S.C. 706) is amended by adding at the end the following new paragraph:

"(22)(A) The term 'drug' means a controlled substance, as defined in schedules I through V of section 202 of the Controlled Substances Act (21 U.S.C. 812).

"(B) The term 'illegal use of drugs' means the use of drugs, the possession or distribution of which is unlawful under the Controlled Substances Act. Such term does not include the use of a drug taken under supervision by a licensed health care professional, or other uses authorized by the Controlled Substances Act or other provisions of Federal law.".

(c) CONFORMING AMENDMENTS.—Section 7(8)(B) of the Rehabilitation Act of 1973 (29 U.S.C. 706(8)(B)) is amended—

(1) in the first sentence, by striking "Subject to the second sentence of this subparagraph," and inserting "Subject to subparagraphs (C) and (D),"; and

(2) by striking the second sentence.

SEC. 513. ALTERNATIVE MEANS OF DISPUTE RESOLUTION.   42 USC 12212.

Where appropriate and to the extent authorized by law, the use of alternative means of dispute resolution, including settlement negotiations, conciliation, facilitation, mediation, factfinding, minitrials,

104 STAT. 378   PUBLIC LAW 101-336—JULY 26, 1990

and arbitration, is encouraged to resolve disputes arising under this Act.

42 USC 12213.   SEC. 514. SEVERABILITY.

Should any provision in this Act be found to be unconstitutional by a court of law, such provision shall be severed from the remainder of the Act, and such action shall not affect the enforceability of the remaining provisions of the Act.

Approved July 26, 1990.

LEGISLATIVE HISTORY—S. 933 (H.R. 2273):

HOUSE REPORTS: No. 101-485, Pt. 1 (Comm. on Public Works and Transportation), Pt. 2 (Comm. on Education and Labor), Pt. 3 (Comm. on the Judiciary), and Pt. 4 (Comm. on Energy and Commerce) all accompanying H.R. 2273; and No. 101-558 and No. 101-569 both from (Comm. of Conference).
SENATE REPORTS: No. 101-116 (Comm. on Labor and Human Resources).
CONGRESSIONAL RECORD:
    Vol. 135 (1989): Sept. 7, considered and passed Senate.
    Vol. 136 (1990): May 17, 22, H.R. 2273 considered and passed House; S. 933 passed in lieu.
        July 11, Senate recommitted conference report.
        July 12, House agreed to conference report.
        July 13, Senate agreed to conference report.
WEEKLY COMPILATION OF PRESIDENTIAL DOCUMENTS, Vol. 26 (1990): July 26, Presidential remarks and statement.

APPENDIX **C**

Regulations Under the
ADA

Architectural and Transportation Barriers Compliance Board

36 CFR Part 1191
Americans With Disabilities Act (ADA)
Accessibility Guidelines for Buildings and
Facilities; Final Guidelines

**ARCHITECTURAL AND
TRANSPORTATION BARRIERS
COMPLIANCE BOARD**

36 CFR Part 1191

[Docket No. 90-2]

RIN 3014-AA09

**Americans With Disabilities Act (ADA)
Accessibility Guidelines for Buildings
and Facilities**

AGENCY: Architectural and
Transportation Barriers Compliance
Board.

ACTION: Final guidelines.

SUMMARY: The Architectural and
Transportation Barriers Compliance
Board is issuing final guidelines to assist
the Department of Justice to establish
accessibility standards for new
construction and alterations in places of
public accommodation and commercial
facilities, as required by title III the
Americans with Disabilities Act (ADA)
of 1990. The guidelines will ensure that
newly constructed and altered portions
of buildings and facilities covered by
title III of the ADA are readily
accessible to and usable by individuals
with disabilities in terms of architecture
and design, and communication. The
Department of Justice has proposed to
adopt the guidelines as the accessibility
standards for new construction and
alterations in places of public
accommodation and commercial
facilities for purposes of title III of the
ADA.

EFFECTIVE DATE: July 26, 1991.

FOR FURTHER INFORMATION CONTACT:
James Raggio, Office of the General
Counsel, Architectural and
Transportation Barriers Compliance
Board, 1111-18th Street, NW., Suite 501,
Washington, DC 20036. Telephone (202)
653-7834 (Voice/TDD). This is not a toll-
free number. This document is available
in accessible formats (cassette tape,
braille, large print, or computer disc)
upon request.

SUPPLEMENTARY INFORMATION:

Statutory Background

The Americans with Disabilities Act
(ADA) of 1990 extends to individuals
with disabilities comprehensive civil
rights protections similar to those
provided to persons on the basis of race,
sex, national origin, and religion under
the Civil Rights Act of 1964. Title III of
the ADA, which becomes effective on
January 26, 1992, prohibits
discrimination on the basis of disability
in places of public accommodation by
any person who owns, leases or leases
to, or operates a place of public

accommodation. As discussed below,
title III establishes accessibility
requirements for new construction and
alterations in places of public
accommodation and commercial
facilities.

"Public accommodation" is defined by
section 301(7) of the ADA as including
the following twelve categories of
private entities if their operations affect
commerce:

(1) An inn, hotel, motel, or other place of
lodging, except for an establishment located
within a building that contains not more than
five rooms for rent or hire and that is actually
occupied by the proprietor of such
establishment as the residence of such
proprietor;

(2) A restaurant, bar, or other
establishment serving food or drink;

(3) A motion picture house, theater, concert
hall, stadium, or other place of exhibition or
entertainment;

(4) An auditorium, convention center,
lecture hall, or other place of public
gathering;

(5) A bakery, grocery store, clothing store,
hardware store, shopping center, or other
sales or rental establishment;

(6) A laundromat, dry-cleaner, bank, barber
shop, beauty shop, travel service, shoe repair
service, funeral parlor, gas station, office of
an accountant or lawyer, pharmacy,
insurance office, professional office of a
health care provider, hospital, or other
service establishment;

(7) A terminal, depot, or other station used
for specified public transportation;

(8) A museum, library, gallery, or other
place of public display or collection;

(9) A park, zoo, amusement park, or other
place of recreation;

(10) A nursery, elementary, secondary,
undergraduate, or postgraduate private
school, or other place of education;

(11) A day care center, senior citizen
center, homeless shelter, food bank, adoption
agency, or other social service center
establishment; and

(12) A gymnasium health spa, bowling
alley, golf course, or other place of exercise
or recreation.

The legislative history states that
these twelve categories "should be
construed liberally consistent with the
intent of the legislation that people with
disabilities should have equal access to
the array of establishments that are
available to others who do not currently
have disabilities." H. Rept. 101-485, pt.
2, at 100.

"Commercial facilities" are defined by
section 301(1) of the ADA as facilities
that are intended for nonresidential use
and whose operations will affect
commerce. The legislative history states
that the term is to be interpreted broadly
to cover commercial establishments that
are not included within the specific
definition of "public accommodation"
such as office buildings, factories, and

other places in which employment will
occur. H. Rept. 101-485, pt. 2, at 116-17.

Section 303 of the ADA establishes
accessibility requirements for new
construction and alterations in places of
public accommodation and commercial
facilities. With respect to new
construction, section 303(a)1 requires
that places of public accommodation
and commercial facilities designed or
constructed for first occupancy after
January 26, 1993, must be readily
accessible to and usable by individuals
with disabilities, except where an entity
can demonstrate that it is structurally
impracticable. When alterations are
made that affect or could affect usability
of or access to a place of public
accommodation or commercial facility,
section 303(a)(2) requires that the
alterations be made in such a manner
that, to the maximum extent feasible,
the altered portions of the facility are
readily accessible to and usable by
individuals with disabilities. In addition,
where alterations affect or could affect
usability of or access to an area of the
facility containing a primary function,
section 303(a)(2) requires that the
alterations be made in such a manner
that, to the maximum extent feasible,
the path of travel to the altered area,
and the restrooms, telephones, and
drinking fountains serving the altered
area are readily accessible to and
usable by individuals with disabilities
unless it is disproportionate to the
overall alterations in terms of cost and
scope, as determined under criteria
established by the Attorney General.

Section 303(b) of the ADA contains an
exception which specifies that the
installation of an elevator is not
required for newly constructed or
altered facilities that are less than three
stories or have less than 3,000 square
feet per story unless the building is a
shopping center, shopping mall, the
professional office of a health care
provider, or another type of facility
determined by the Attorney General to
require the installation of an elevator
based on the usage of the facility.

According to the legislative history,
the term "readily accessible to and
usable by" is intended to provide "a
high degree of convenient accessibility"
and "enable people with disabilities
(including mobility, sensory, and
cognitive impairments) to get to, enter
and use a facility." H. Rept. 101-485, pt.
2, at 117-18. The term includes
"accessibility of parking areas,
accessible routes to and from the
facility, accessible entrances, usable
bathrooms and water fountains,
accessibility of public and common use
areas, and access to the goods, services,

programs, facilities, accommodations and work areas available at the facility.' Id. The legislative history further explains that when identical features will generally serve the same function, only a reasonable number must be accessible depending on such factors as their use, location, and number; however, when identical features will generally be used in different ways, each one must be accessible in most situations. H. Rept. 101-485, pt. 2, at 118; H. Rept. 101-485, pt. 3, at 61. For example, only a reasonable number of spaces in a parking lot or stalls within a restroom would have to be accessible, but all meeting rooms at a conference center would have to be accessible because each one may be used for different purposes at any given time. Id.

Under section 504 of the ADA, the Architectural and Transportation Barriers Compliance Board is required to issue guidelines to assist the Department of Justice to establish accessibility standards for new construction and alterations in places of public accommodation and commercial facilities covered by title III.[1] Section 504 requires that the guidelines supplement the existing Minimum Guidelines and Requirements for Accessible Design (MGRAD) and "establish additional requirements, consistent with this Act, to ensure that buildings (and) facilities * * * are accessible in terms of architecture and design * * * and communication, to individuals with disabilities.[2] Section

---

[1] The Board is an independent Federal agency established pursuant to section 502 of the Rehabilitation Act of 1973 to ensure that the requirements of the Architectural Barriers Act of 1968 are met and to propose alternative solutions to architectural, transportation, communication, and attitudinal barriers faced by individuals with disabilities. The Board consists of 12 members appointed by the President from among the general public, at least six of whom are required to be individuals with disabilities, and the heads of 11 Federal agencies or their designees whose positions are Executive Level IV or above. The Federal agencies are: The Departments of Health and Human Services, Education, Transportation, Housing and Urban Development, Labor, Interior, Defense, Justice, and Veterans Affairs; General Services Administration; and United States Postal Service

[2] The Board developed MGRAD to assist the General Services Administration, Department of Defense, Department of Housing and Urban Development, and United States Postal Service to establish accessibility standards for those federally owned, leased, or financed buildings covered by the Architectural Barriers Act of 1968. See 36 CFR part 1190. The standards established by those agencies are known as the Uniform Federal Accessibility Standards (UFAS) and are generally consistent with MGRAD.

504 also requires that the guidelines include provisions for alterations to qualified historic properties.

The Department of Justice is responsible for issuing final regulations to implement the provisions of title III of the ADA except for transportation vehicles. Section 306(c) of the ADA requires that the Department of Justice's final regulations include accessibility standards for new construction and alterations of buildings and facilities covered by title III of the ADA that are consistent with the Board's guidelines. On February 22, 1991, the Department of Justice proposed to adopt the Board's proposed guidelines with any changes made by the Board as the accessibility standards for purposes of title III of the ADA. See Department of Justice's proposed regulations, 28 CFR 34.406(a) and Appendix A to part 36—Standards for Accessible Design at 56 FR 7476, 7492, 7494 (February 22, 1991).

Proposed Guidelines

On January 22, 1991, the Board published a notice of proposed rulemaking (NPRM) in the **Federal Register** which contained the proposed Americans With Disabilities Act (ADA) Accessibility Guidelines For Buildings and Facilities (56 FR 2296). The proposed guidelines were modeled on the Uniform Federal Accessibility Standards (UFAS) which are generally consistent with MGRAD and use the same format and numbering system as the American National Standard Specifications for Making Buildings and Facilities Accessible to and Usable by Physically Handicapped People (ANSI A117.1-1980).[3] Where the ADA establishes requirements that differ from MGRAD or UFAS, the ADA requirements were followed.

The proposed guidelines contained:

• General provisions (sections 1 through 3) which include the purpose section, general information about the guidelines, miscellaneous instructions, and definitions.

• Scoping provisions (sections 4.1.1 through 4.1.7) which include the application section and scoping requirements for new construction of sites and exterior facilities, new construction of buildings and facilities, additions, alterations, and alterations to qualified historic properties.

---

[3] The ANSI A117.1 standard was revised in 1986 after UFAS was adopted. The 1980 and 1986 versions of the ANSI A117.1 standard are very similar and both are currently in use. As discussed under the general issues, the ANSI A117.1 standard is in the process of being revised again and the Board intends to coordinate its work with the ANSI A117 Committee.

• Technical specifications (sections 4.2 through 4.34) which reprint the text and illustrations of the ANSI A117.1–1980 standard with differences in the text noted by italics.

• Special application sections (sections 5 through 10) which include additional requirements for restaurants and cafeterias, medical care facilities, business and mercantile facilities, libraries, transient lodging, and transportation facilities.[4]

• An appendix which contains additional information to aid in understanding the guidelines, and designing buildings and facilities for greater accessibility.

The NPRM also asked questions and sought information on a number of specific issues related to the proposed guidelines.

Public Hearings and Comments

The Board held 14 public hearings around the country on the proposed guidelines between February 11, 1991 and March 7, 1991. A total of 450 people presented testimony on the proposed guidelines at the hearings. In addition, 1,585 written comments were submitted to the Board by the end of the comment period on March 25, 1991. Another 280 comments were received between March 26, 1991 and April 3, 1991. Although those comments were not timely, they were analyzed along with the comments received by March 25, 1991. The Board did not find it practical to consider comments received after April 3, 1991. In all, the Board received over 12,000 pages of comments and testimony on the proposed guidelines.

The Board received comments and testimony from a broad range of interested individuals and groups. Ten categories were identified and approximately the following numbers submitted timely comments or testimony for each category:

---

[4] The NPRM reserved section 10 for transportation facilities. The Board issued a supplemental notice of proposed rulemaking (SNPRM) in the **Federal Register** on March 20, 1990 which proposed additional requirements for transportation facilities that would make the guidelines also applicable to transportation facilities constructed or altered by public entities covered by title II of the ADA (56 FR 11874). The Department of Transportation has also proposed to adopt the Board's guidelines as the accessibility standards for transportation facilities for purposes of title II of the ADA. See Department of Transportation's proposed regulations, 49 CFR 37.13(b) and Appendix B to Part 37—Standards for Accessible Transportation Facilities at 56 FR 13861, 13881, and 13907 (April 4, 1991).

1270 Individuals who identified themselves as having a disability or who voiced a "consumer" perspective, and organizations representing these persons. For purposes of convenience, this category is referred to as "individuals with disabilities and their organizations" in the section-by-section analysis.

100 Government agencies involved with disability issues.

60 Building code officials and State agencies responsible for accessibility.

80 Architects, designers, engineers, and organizations representing these persons.

320 Businesses and organizations representing businesses.

60 Manufacturers.

20 Transit agencies.

50 Building owners and managers, and organizations representing these persons.

50 Other government agencies.

20 Other persons or organizations not in the above categories.

The comments and testimony were sorted by section and analyzed. For some sections, the comments were grouped around certain issues or questions identified in the NPRM. For other sections, the comments were scattered. A large number of commenters, especially individuals with disabilities and their organizations, expressed support for the guidelines, as proposed. Some commenters requested that sections be clarified or made recommendations for changes, including deletion of sections. Further, it was evident from some comments that a few of the proposed provisions in the NPRM were unclear and needed to be revised. With respect to those commenters who recommended changes, a few submitted data or studies in support of their recommendations; however, most recommendations were based on individual opinions or preferences. Where data or studies were not submitted in support of a recommended change, the Board was inclined to retain the provisions taken from the MGRAD, UFAS, and the ANSI A117.1 standard, especially with respect to the technical specifications in 4.2 through 4.34, unless more than a few commenters or an organization representing the interests of a large group believed that the provision was inadequate or otherwise in need of change. The Board considered each of those recommended changes on its merits. In some sections, commenters pointed out a need for new or additional requirements but further research or study is necessary for the Board to develop guidelines in the area. Some commenters asked questions regarding

application of the guidelines to specific situations.

Due to the large number of comments received and the deadline for issuing the final guidelines, it is not possible for the Board to respond to each comment in this preamble. The Board has made every effort within the time available to respond to significant comments in the section-by-section analysis. As discussed under specific sections, the Board has reserved action in some areas pending further study or research. The Board has an on-going research and technical assistance program and plans to periodically review and up-date the guidelines to ensure that they remain consistent with technological developments and changes in model codes and national standards, and meet the needs of individuals with disabilities.

General Issues

Coordination of Board and ANSI Processes

Many commenters generally supported using the ANSI A117.1—1980 standard as the basis for the technical specifications of the guidelines since that standard or its 1986 update is incorporated or reference in many State and local building codes and is generally accepted and understood by the building industry. The Council of American Building Officials (CABO), National Conference of States on Building Codes and Standards (NCSBCS), American Institute of Architects (AIA), and other commenters recommended that the Board coordinate any substantive changes to the ANSI A117.1 standard with the ANSI A117 Committee in order to maintain a consistent and uniform set of accessibility standards which can be efficiently and effectively implemented at the State and local level through established building regulatory processes.[5]

The Board is a member of the ANSI A117 Committee and is committed to working cooperatively with the Committee. The ANSI A117 Committee solicited proposals for changes to the

---

[5] The ANSI A117 Committee is responsible for periodically reviewing and up-dating the ANSI A117.1 standard. The Committee consists of 42 organizations representing individuals with disabilities, architects and designers, building owners and managers, building product manufacturers, model code groups, building code officials, and government agencies. The Committee operates under due process and consensus procedures established by the American National Standards Institute. See American National Standards Institute, Procedures for the Development and Coordination of American National Standards, approved by ANSI Board of Directors September 9, 1987.

ANSI A117.1 standard in July 1989, a full year before the ADA was enacted. When the ADA was enacted in July 1990, the Board was charged with the responsibility of issuing final guidelines in nine months. In order to meet this responsibility, the Board issued the NPRM on January 22, 1991. The ANSI A117 Committee published draft revisions to the ANSI A117.1 standard on February 22, 1991. The timing of these events did not permit the Board and the ANSI A117 Committee to fully coordinate their processes.[6]

Members of the ANSI A117 Committee have objected to various changes proposed in the February 1991 draft revisions to the ANSI A117.1 standard and the group is scheduled to meet in July 1991 to review the objections. In voting on the draft revisions to the ANSI A117.1 standard, the Board recommended that the ANSI A117 Committee consider the final ADA guidelines with the goal of establishing a single accessibility standard that meets the requirements of the ADA and that can be incorporated or referenced by the Federal government, model codes, and State and local building codes.

A single accessibility standard would greatly facilitate the certification of State and local codes by the Department of Justice.[7] Establishing a single accessibility standard that meets the requirements of the ADA and that can be incorporated or referenced by all levels of government will also ensure that the ADA requirements are routinely implemented at the design stage when building plans are reviewed and permits issued by state and local building officials and that non-compliance can be discovered and corrected through the building inspection process before buildings are occupied.

Several commenters also recommended that the Board adopt the draft scoping provisions developed by the CABO Board for the Coordination of the Model Codes (BCMC). The draft BCMC scoping provisions were developed before the ADA was enacted and do not meet all the requirements of the ADA. Further, the draft BCMC scoping provisions were not developed

---

[6] In an effort to make the guidelines generally consistent with the planned revisions to the ANSI A117.1 standard, the Board based some sections of the NPRM (e.g. alarms, detectable warnings, signage) on proposed changes considered by the ANSI A117 Committee.

[7] Section 308(b)(1)(A)(ii) of the ADA provides that, on the application of a state or local government, the Attorney General may, in consultation with the Board, and after prior notice and a public hearing, certify that a state or local code meets or exceeds the accessibility requirements of the ADA.

in accordance with the same due process and consensus procedures followed by the ANSI A117 Committee.[8] Nonetheless, as discussed under specific provisions, the Board has considered the draft BCMC scoping provisions where they are consistent with the requirements of the ADA.

Minimum Guidelines

Several commenters remarked that section 504 of the ADA provides that the guidelines issued by the Board are to be "minimum guidelines" and that the NPRM exceeded the Board's statutory authority. Specifically, some of the commenters noted that the provisions in the NPRM for areas of refuge [areas of rescue assistance in the final guidelines], visual alarms, detectable warnings, and signage go beyond existing codes and standards.

As discussed under the statutory background, section 504(a) of the ADA requires the Board to "issue minimum guidelines that shall supplement the existing Minimum Guidelines and Requirements for Accessible Design (MGRAD) * * *." The Board was authorized to develop MGRAD by the 1978 amendments to the Rehabilitation Act of 1973 which required the Board to "establish minimum guidelines and requirements for the standards issued pursuant to * * * the Architectural Barriers Act of 1968." 29 U.S.C. 502(b)(7).[9] As originally promulgated by the Board, MGRAD contained detailed technical specifications which described how to make entrances, telephones, drinking fountains, toilet rooms, and other elements and spaces of a building or facility accessible; and scoping provisions which specified the extent to which the technical specifications must be followed, including which and how many elements and spaces are to be made accessible within a building or facility. The scoping provisions and technical specifications in MGRAD are considered to be "minimum guidelines" in that the four standard setting agencies under the Architectural Barriers Act of 1968 may exceed

MGRAD's requirements and establish standard that provide a greater level of accessibility. The Department of Justice and other standard setting agencies under the ADA can also exceed the Board's "minimum guidelines" and establish standards that provide greater accessibility.

Congress specifically required in section 504 of the ADA that the Board "supplement the existing [MGRAD]" for purposes of title III of the ADA and further required that the "supplemental guidelines * * * establish additional requirements, consistent with this Act, to ensure that buildings (and) facilities * * * are accessible in terms of architecture and design, * * * and communication, to individuals with disabilities." The legislative history further explains the Board's responsibilities as follows:

In issuing the supplemental minimum guidelines and requirements called for under this legislation, the Board should consider whether other revisions or improvements of the existing MGRAD (including scoping provisions) are called for to achieve consistency with the intent and the requirements of this legislation. Particular attention should be paid to providing greater guidance regarding communication accessibility.

In no event shall the minimum guidelines issued under this legislation reduce, weaken, narrow, or set less accessibility standards than those included in existing MGRAD. H. Rept. 101–485, pt. 2, at 139.

Further, Congress was clear that it intended "a high degree of convenient accessibility" and that minimum guidelines do not mean "minimal accessibility." H. Rept. 101–485, pt. 2, at 118. Thus, Congress authorized the Board to revise MGRAD and to establish new requirements where appropriate to ensure that newly constructed and altered buildings and facilities covered by title III of the ADA provide a high degree of convenient accessibility to individuals with disabilities.

In carrying out its responsibilities, the Board considered research and studies which have been conducted since MGRAD was last revised; the work of the ANSI A117 Committee in updating the ANSI A117.1 standard; and developments in the model codes. As directed by Congress, the Board paid particular attention to those areas relating to communication accessibility, including public telephones equipped with volume controls, public text telephones, assistive listening systems for assembly areas, visual alarms, detectable warnings, and signage. Where possible and consistent with the ADA, the Board attempted to make

provisions in the NPRM consistent with the planned revisions to the ANSI A117.1 standard. This was done for visual alarms, detectable warnings, and signage. In developing provisions for areas of rescue assistance, as further explained in the NPRM the Board looked to the proposed BCMC scoping provisions for the ANSI A117.1 standard and the 1991 Uniform Building Code. See 56 FR 2296, at 2304 and 2309 (January 22, 1991).

The Board received many comments on the new provisions proposed in the NPRM. As futher discussed under the section-by-section analysis, the Board has carefully considered all the comments and many of the new provisions have been revised or clarified based on the comments. The Board believes that it has acted consistent with the statute in supplementing MGRAD and establishing new requirements where appropriate to ensure that buildings and facilities covered by title III of the ADA provide a high degree of convenient accessibility to individuals with disabilities.

"User Friendly" Guidelines

Several commenters recommended editorial changes to the guidelines. Some of these commenters noted that editorial changes have been proposed to the ANSI A117.1 standard and requested that the Board incorporate the proposed changes in the guidelines.

The Board has attempted to make the guidelines as "user friendly" as possible, including using the ANSI format and numbering system and providing additional explanatory information in the appendix to the guidelines. The Board also intends to make available manuals explaining the guidelines and to provide training and technical assistance. With respect to the proposed editorial changes to the ANSI A117.1 standard, the Board will consider all editorial changes to that standard after they have been approved by the ANSI A117 Committee.

Relationship to Other Regulations and Laws

A number of commenters requested clarification of the relationship between the Board's guidelines and section 302(b)(2)(A)(iv) of the ADA which requires the removal of architectural barriers, and communication barriers that are structural in nature, in existing facilities, where such removal is readily achievable.

The Board's guidelines are to be applied to the design, construction, and alteration of buildings and facilities to the extent required by regulations issued

---

[8] The February 22, 1991 draft revisions to the ANSI A117.1 standard reprinted the draft BCMC scoping provisions with modifications as an appendix to the standard. However, the draft BCMC scoping provisions are not part of the ANSI A117.1 standard and are not approved by the American National Standards Institute.

[9] The Architectural Barriers Act of 1968 requires that certain federally owned, leased, or financed buildings be accessible to individuals with disabilities. The General Services Administration, Department of Defense, Department of Housing and Urban Development, and United States Postal Service are responsible for establishing accessibility standards for those buildings covered by the Architectural Barriers Act of 1968.

by other Federal agencies, including the Department of Justice, under the ADA. The Department of Justice's final regulations will address whether the Board's guidelines are applicable to removal of barriers in existing facilities where measures are taken solely to comply with section 302(b)(2)(A)(iv) of the ADA.

Several commenters also requested the Board to clarify the relationship between its guidelines and areas used only by employees as work areas. As futher discussed under the section-by-section analysis, the provision in 4.1.1(3) has been revised to clarify that such areas must be designed and constructed so that individuals with disabilities can approach, enter and exit the areas. Modifications to particular work areas to meet the needs of an individual employee or applicant with a disability would be addressed by title I of the ADA which prohibits discrimination in employment on the basis of disability and which requires reasonable accommodation. This issue is within the jurisdiction of the Equal Employment Opportunity Commission.

Some commenters requested clarification regarding what requirements apply if an entity is covered by both the ADA and other Federal laws or regulations which require accessibility in new construction and alterations such as the Architectural Barriers Act of 1968 or section 504 of the Rehabilitation Act of 1973. UFAS is the applicable standard for purposes of the Architectural Barriers Act of 1968 and is also referenced as the accessibility standard in many regulations issued by other Federal agencies under section 504 of the Rehabilitation Act of 1973. In some areas, the ADA guidelines provide for greater accessibility than UFAS (e.g., provisions relating to communication access); and in other areas, UFAS provides for greater accessibility than the ADA guidelines (e.g., no elevator exception for facilities that are less than three stories or that have less than 3,000 square feet per story). An entity that is covered by both the ADA and another Federal law or regulation which requires compliance with accessibility standards must comply with the specific provisions that provide for greater accessibility.

State and Local Government Buildings

The Board is also required by section 504 of the ADA to issue accessibility guidelines for newly constructed and altered State and local government buildings which are covered by title II of the ADA. The requirements in title II of the ADA for State and local government buildings differ in some aspects from those in title III for places of public

accommodation and commercial facilities. For example, the title III structural impracticability exception in new construction and the elevator exception for newly constructed or altered facilities that are less than three stories or have less than 3,000 square feet per story do not apply to State and local government buildings. The NPRM requested information on several issues relating to State and local government buildings for purposes of developing accessibility guidelines for those facilities, including providing access to various areas in courthouses (e.g., jury boxes, witness standards, and judge's benches); experience of detention and correctional facilities in complying with the UFAS scoping provisions under current regulations issued under section 504 of the Rehabilitation Act of 1973; and whether the requirements for alterations to State and local government buildings should be the same as for places of public accommodation and commercial facilities. The Board received many comments on these issues. The Board intends to further analyze those comments and to issue proposed guidelines for State and local government buildings for public comment after these final guidelines and the final guidelines for transportation vehicles and facilities are published.

The Department of Justice's final regulations will include requirements for new construction and alterations of State and local government buildings and further address the applicable accessibility standards.

Children's Environments and Recreational Facilities

The NPRM also requested information relevant to establishing accessibility guidelines for children's environments and recreational facilities. The Board received comments in each of these areas. The Board has undertaken several activities in preparation for developing accessibility guidelines in these areas. The Board is sponsoring a research project on "Accessibility Standards for Children's Environments". The Board is also working with the U.S. Forest Service, National Park Service, and other Federal agencies with recreation responsibilities in the development of comprehensive accessibility guidelines for outdoor recreational facilities, including boating access, water access at beaches, fishing piers, and horse back riding. It is anticipated that these projects will be completed in the Fall of 1991 and the Board intends to initiate rulemaking activity in the areas of children's

environments and recreational facilities at that time.

Although the final guidelines do not include accessibility guidelines for children's environments and recreational facilities at this time, newly constructed or altered children's facilities and recreational facilities subject to title III of the ADA must comply with these guidelines where applicable. For example, an accessible route must be provided to a swimming pool deck area even though the guidelines do not presently include specific requirements for providing access to the pool itself. Technical assistance is available from the Board in this area.

Chemical and Environmental Sensitivities

The Board received over 400 comments from individuals who identified themselves as chemically sensitive. Many of the comments were sent in on preprinted postcards distributed by the National Center for Environmental Health Strategies (NCEHS). The commenters described the health problems that they have experienced due to exposure to chemical substances and indoor contaminants in buildings, including certain building materials, furnishings, cleaning products and fragrances, and tobacco smoke. They requested that the Board address their need for access to place of public accommodation and commercial facilities. Action on Smoking and Health (ASH) also requested the Board to address tobacco smoke in buildings. NCEHS and the Environmental Health Network provided additional background materials on chemical sensitivities. Among the suggestions made to lessen exposure to chemical substances and indoor contaminants in buildings were providing windows that open; improving the design and requirements for heating, cooling, and ventilation systems; and selecting building materials and furnishings that do not contain certain chemical substances.

Chemical and environmental sensitivities present some complex issues which require coordination and cooperation with other Federal agencies and private standard setting agencies. Pending further study of these issues, the Board does not believe it is appropriate to address them at this time.

Section-by-Section Analysis

This section of the preamble contains a concise summary of the significant comments received on the NPRM, the

Board's response to those comments, and any changes made to the guidelines.

1. Purpose

The purpose section has been clarified to state that the guidelines are to be applied during the design, construction, and alteration of places of public accommodation and commercial facilities to the extent required by regulations issued by Federal agencies, including the Department of Justice, under the ADA. The Department of Justice's final regulations will address the extent to which the guidelines are applicable to places of public accommodation and commercial facilities under new construction and alteration sections, including alterations to an area containing a primary function and cost disproportionality. The Department of Justice's final regulations will also address whether the guidelines are applicable to the removal of architectural barriers, and communications barriers that are structural in nature, in existing buildings and facilities where such removal is readily achievable. The Equal Employment Opportunity Commission's final regulations will address whether the guidelines are applicable for purposes of reasonable accommodation under title I of the ADA.

2. General

2.1   Provisions for Adults

There were no comments on this section. As discussed under the general issues, the Board will develop guidelines for children's environments.

2.2   Equivalent Facilitation

Comment. Commenters generally supported the equivalent facilitation provision which permits departures from the guidelines where substantially equivalent or greater access to or usability of a building or facility is provided. Some commenters requested that the guidelines include examples of alternatives that would provide equivalent facilitation. Other commenters expressed concerns about enforcement and a few recommended that a process be established for reviewing whether equivalent facilitation is provided.

Response. The equivalent facilitation provision has been clarified by substituting the words "designs and technologies" for "methods." The purpose of the provision is to allow for flexibility to design for unique and special circumstances and to facilitate the application of new technologies. The accessibility and usability of design solutions developed for unique and

special circumstances must be evaluated on a case by case basis. In the case of new technologies which provide equivalent facilitation, as those technologies become more common, the Board will consider incorporating them in the guidelines.

The final guidelines in corporate specific provisions for equivalent facilitation in five sections. In 4.1.6(3)(c), in the case of alterations to an existing facility the guidelines permit an elevator car to have different dimensions when usability can be demonstrated and all other elements required to be accessible comply with the applicable provisions of 4.10 (e.g., a 49 inch by 60 inch elevator car with a door opening on the narrow dimension could accommodate the standard wheelchair clearances shown in figure 4). In 4.31.9, the guidelines permit the use of a portable text telephone if it is readily available for use with a nearby public pay telephone that is equipped with a shelf; an electrical outlet within, or adjacent to, the telephone enclosure; and a long enough telephone handset cord to allow connection of the text telephone and the telephone receiver if an acoustic coupler is used. In 7.2, the guidelines provide for equivalent facilitation at counters that may not have a cash register but at which goods or services are distributed (e.g., teller stations in banks, registration counters in hotels and motels) by permitting use of a folding shelf attached to the main counter on which an individual with a disability can write, and use of the space on the side of the counter or at the concierge desk for handling materials back and forth. In 9.1.4, the guidelines deem it equivalent facilitation if the operator of a hotel or similar place of transient lodging elects to limit construction of accessible rooms to those intended for multiple occupancy provided that such rooms are made available to an individual with a disability who requests a single-occupancy room. In 9.2.2(b)(d), hotels and other similar places of transient lodging are permitted to utilize a higher door threshold or a change in level at patios, terraces and balconies where necessary to protect the integrity of the unit from wind and water damage but equivalent facilitation is required where it results in patios, terraces, or balconies that are not on an accessible level (e.g., raised decking or a ramp must be provided to permit access to the patio, terrace or balcony).

Equivalent facilitation is appropriate and applies to the entire guidelines and not only those sections mentioned above. For example, other areas where equivalent facilitation may be appropriate include the use of automatic

door openers for double leaf doors, and provision of audible signage for individuals with vision impairments. The use of a portable ramp, however, is not considered equivalent facilitation.

The ADA does not require any process to be established for reviewing whether equivalent facilitation is provided.

3. Miscellaneous Instructions and Definitions

3.1   Graphic Conventions

3.2   Dimensional Tolerances

3.3   Notes

3.4   General Terminology

Few comments were receive on these sections and they did not warrant any changes.

3.5   Definitions

Comment. Several commenters recommended that the term "individual with a disability" should be defined the same as in the ADA.

Response. The definition of the term "individual with a disability" has been deleted from the guidelines as unnecessary since the guidelines will be incorporated in the Department of Justice's regulations implementing title III of the ADA which will include a definition of the term. The NPRM defined "accessible" in terms of being used "by individuals with disabilities, including those affecting mobility, sensory, or cognitive functions." The definition of the term "accessible" has been revised in the final guidelines to mean a site, building, facility, or portion thereof that complies with the guidelines. In other words, buildings and facilities that meet the requirements of the guidelines are by definiton accessbile to individuals with disabilities.

Comment. Commenters made several recommendations for changes in the definition of the term "technically infeasible."

Response. The Definition of the term "technically infeasible" has been revised and moved to the scoping provisions for alterations at 4.1.6(1)(j). Changes to that definition are discussed under that section. A new term "structural frame" has been added to 3.5 in connection with the revised definition of "technically infeasible" which is also discussed under the scoping provision for alterations.

Comment. A commenter requested that the term "text telephone" be used in place of "telecommunication display device or telecommunication device for the deaf (TDD)."

Response. The term "text telephone" is used in the final guidelines. The term "TDD" is often understood to include devices which use only the Baudot code. Many newer models are also capable of transmitting in the ASCII code and this appears to be the trend. Other systems of communication based on computer hardware and software are also being used for communication by individuals with disabilities and their rapid proliferation suggests that they may become the dominant modes of communication in the future. The Board is concerned that the term "TDD" will become outmoded, and that entities will assume that they have satisfied their responsibilities by providing access only in an obsolete format that may be incompatible with many devices. By using the more inclusive term "text telephone," the Board intends that, as technology develops in this rapidly changing area, entities will be able to choose from a broader range of appropriate devices and formats.

Further, although the term TDD refers to a "telecommunication device for the deaf," TDDs are not used only by individuals who are deaf. Nor do all individuals who are deaf use TDDs to communicate over the telephone. The legislative history recognizes that many individuals who are deaf, hard of hearing, and speech impaired use other kinds of non-voice terminal devices. The term "text telephone" would encompass the various types of telecommunication devices. This term is currently used in Europe to describe telephones with keyboards and visual screens, and is generally understood to mean TDDs, computer hardware and software, and other non-voice terminal devices. "Text telephones" do not include facsimile (fax) equipment.

4. Accessible Elements and Spaces: Scope and Technical Requirements

4.1 Minimum Requirements

The scoping provisions are contained in 4.1.1 through 4.1.7 and are discussed below.

4.1.1 Application

This section describes the application of the guidelines.

General (4.1.1 (1))

Comment. Several commenters requested that the application of the guidelines be clarified with respect to existing buildings.

Response. The general provision in 4.1.1(1) has been revised to clarify that all areas of newly designed or constructed buildings and facilities, and altered portions of existing buildings

and facilities required to be accessible by 4.1.6, must comply with the guidelines unless otherwise provided in 4.1.1 or a special application section. The specific requirements for alterations to existing buildings are discussed under 4.1.6.

Application Based on Building Use (4.1.1(2))

Comment. Several commenters requested that application of the guidelines be clarifed with respect to transportation facilities.

Response. The special application sections 5 through 10 provide additional requirements for restaurants and cafeterias, medical care facilities, business and mercantile facilities, libraries, transient lodging, and transportation facilities. Section 10 on transportation facilities was reserved in the NPRM. The Board issued a supplemental notice of proposed rulemaking (SNPRM) on March 20, 1991 in connection with its proposed guidelines on transportation vehicles containing proposed additional requirements for transportation facilities (56 FR 11874).[10] A final section 10 on transportation facilities will be issued at the same time as the final guidelines for transportation vehicles. Although the final guidelines do not contain any additional requirements for transportation facilities at this time, newly constructed or altered transportation facilities subject to title III of the ADA must comply with these guidelines where applicable. For example, the restrooms in a newly constructed transportation facility such as a bus depot must comply with the requirements for accessible toilet facilities.

Areas Used Only By Employees As Work Areas (4.1.1(3))

Comment. A number of commenters requested that the application of the guidelines to areas used only by employees as work areas be clarified. Some commenters wanted employee work areas to be adaptable with adjustable elements and to comply with requirements for clear floor space, reach ranges and visual alarms.

Response. The legislative history explains that areas used only by employees as work areas are covered by the guidelines but individual work

---

[10] The SNPRM also proposed to amend the guidelines to make them applicable to transportation facilities constructed or altered by public entities covered by title II of the ADA. Until final notice of the amended guidelines is published in the Federal Register, the guidelines do not apply to transportation facilities constructed or altered by public entities coverd by title II of the ADA.

stations are not required to be constructed in a fully accessible manner. H. Rept. 101–485, pt. 3, at 63. Modifications to an individual workstation would be covered by reasonable accommodation under title I of the ADA which prohibits discrimination in employment on the basis of disability. The Equal Employment Opportunity Commission is responsible for issuing regulations to implement title I of the ADA.

The provision in 4.1.1(3) has been revised to clarify that areas that are used only by employees as work areas shall be designed and constructed so that individuals with disabilities can approach, enter, and exit the areas. For instance, individual office rooms in a typical office building must be on an accessible route and the doors to the rooms must comply with the technical specifications in 4.13.

The guidelines do not require that any work areas be constructed to permit maneuvering within the work area (e.g., maneuvering spaces around a desk) or that fixed or built-in equipment be accessible (e.g., counters or shelves). However, modifications may be required to a particular work area for an individual employee or applicant with a disability as a reasonable accommodation under title I of the ADA.

The appendix includes advisory guidance on individual work stations at A4.1.1(3). Where there are a series of built-in or fixed individual work stations of the same type (e.g., laboratories, service counters, ticket booths), in order to facilitate reasonable accommodation at a future date, it is recommended that 5% or at least one of each type of work station should be constructed so that an individual with disabilities can maneuver within the work station. Consideration should also be given to placing shelves in an employee work area at a convenient height for accessibility or installing commercially available shelving that is adjustable so that reasonable accommodations can be made in the future.

Comment. The NPRM requested information on fixed or built-in equipment in physician's offices that is used by patients and should be addressed by the guidelines. Commenters recommended that examining tables, diagnostic machinery, and dental chairs should be accessible or adaptable. However, anecdotal information suggests that most of the equipment is not fixed or built-in the structure of the building. No information was submitted on technical specifications for such equipment.

Response. These guidelines are intended to address only that equipment that is fixed or built into the structure of the building. The Board believes that this issue requires further study before it can be addressed in the guidelines. The Board may provide technical assistance in this area.

Temporary Structures (4.1.1(4))

Comment. The NPRM asked whether trailers at construction sites should be included in the list of temporary structures in 4.1.1(4) covered by the guidelines. Most of the commenters from each category who responded to the question stated that such structures should not be required to comply with the guidelines. The Associated General Contractors of America pointed out that the legislative history specifically states that construction sites are not to be considered a public accommodation. See H. Rept. 101–485, pt. 1, at 36.

Response. Based on legislative history, the list of temporary structures in 4.1.1(4) has been revised to state that construction trailers are not included.

General Exceptions (4.1.1(5))

Comment. With respect to the exception in 4.1.1(5)(a) for structural impracticability in new construction, some commenters questioned whether such an exception is necessary in new construction. Other commenters requested that the term be further defined. A few commenters suggested that the exception implied that the entire building or facility was exempt from the guidelines.

Response. The exception in 4.1.1(5)(a) is based on section 303(a)(1) of the ADA. The legislative history explains that the exception is a narrow one and applies only in rare circumstances where unique characteristics of terrain prevent the incorporation of accessibility features. H. Rept. 101–485, pt. 2, at 120. The legislative history further explains that the exception is not to be viewed as totally exempting the entire building or facility for the guidelines. id. The exception has been revised to clarify that if full compliance with the guidelines is structurally impracticable in new construction, the entity must comply with the guidelines to the extent that it is not structurally impracticable. Any portion of the building or facility which can be made accessible and is required by the guidelines to be accessible must comply with the guidelines.

Comment. The NPRM asked whether other spaces should be included in the list in 4.1.1(5)(b) of spaces exempt from complying with the guidelines and whether functional criteria should be developed for identifying such spaces. Most of the commenters who responded to the question favored the functional criteria approach. Commenters also recommended specific spaces to be included in the exception.

Response. The exception in 4.1.1(5)(b) has been revised to include functional criteria and exempts non-occupiable spaces that are: (a) Accessed only by ladders, catwalks, crawl spaces, very narrow passageways, or freight or non-passenger elevators; and (b) frequented only by service personnel for repair purposes. Such spaces include but are not limited to elevator pits, elevator penthouses, and piping or equipment catwalks. Some of the spaces recommended by commenters such as cooling towers and utility tunnels would be covered by the functional criteria. Other spaces suggested by commenters such as mechanical rooms or closets that are not accessed by ladders or very narrow passageways are considered employee work areas and are covered under 4.1.1(3) which only requires that individuals with disabilities be able to approach, enter, and exit the area but does not require maneuvering space to be provided in the area.

Observation galleries that are raised to look out over an area below and are used primarily for security purposes have also been included in the spaces exempt from the guidelines. This exemption prevails over the requirement in 4.1.1(3) that employee work areas be designed and constructed so that individuals with disabilities can approach, enter, and exit the area. Under the exemption, a vertical means of accessibility is not required to such galleries. However, modifications to such galleries to provide a vertical means of access to an employee with a disability may be required as a reasonable accommodation under title I of the ADA.

4.1.2 Accessible Sites and Exterior Facilities

This section contains scoping provisions for accessible sites and exterior facilities.

Accessible Route (4.1.2(1) and (2))

Protruding Objects (4.1.2(3))

Ground Surfaces (4.1.2(4))

Few comments were received on these scoping provisions and they did not warrant any changes.

Parking (4.1.2(5))

Comment. A number of commenters from each category stated that the number of accessible parking spaces specified in the table in 4.1.2.(5)(a) is adequate. Some commenters stated that the number should be increased, and other commenters stated that the number should be reduced. One commenter submitted a report prepared for the institute of Traffic Engineers (ITE) which was based on a survey of 198 sites taken between 1986 and 1987. The ITE report recommended that the number of accessible spaces be based on occupancy type and gross floor area of the building or facility. The National Parking Association (NPA) and some members of its Parking Consultants Council (PCC) submitted recommended standards based on the ITE report. The NPA/PCC standards recommend that three categories be established for accessible parking spaces: High use, moderate use, and low use. The high use category would provide a number of accessible parking spaces similar to that contained in the table in 4.1.2(5)(a) and apply to occupancy types where an above average number of individuals with disabilities might reasonably be anticipated. The NPA/PCC suggested that high use occupancy types would include hospitals, nursing homes, medical office buildings, and social service agencies. The low use category would provide for approximately one-half the number of accessible spaces as the high use category and apply to occupancy types which generate primarily regular, long-term parking (3 hours or more in duration) such as airports, schools, universities, office buildings (except medical), warehousing, manufacturing, and industries. The medium use category would provide for a number of accessible parking spaces between the high use and low use categories and apply to any occupancy type that does not clearly qualify as either high or low use. The NPA submitted a revised set of recommendations after the close of the comment period based on a recent survey by its members. In place of the high, medium, and low use categories, the NPA recommended three classes of occupancy types. Class I would consist of medical facilities and have a slightly higher number of accessible parking spaces then contained in the table in 4.1.2(5)(a). Class II would consist of public accommodations except those specifically included in Classes I or III and provide for a number of accessible parking spaces similar to that contained in the table in 4.1.2(5)(a). According to the NPA, the recent survey data showed the number of parking spaces specified in the table in 4.1.2(5)(a) "appears to reasonably fit the Class II uses [public accommodations] and the requirements of smaller facilities are not unreasonable." Class III would consist of commercial uses, mixed uses in which the majority of parkers are generated by a commercial use, public parking facilities in central business districts, and universities and provide for about one-half the number of accessible parking spaces specified in the table in 4.1.2(5)(a).

Response. The number of parking spaces required for specific occupancy uses is usually established by State and local zoning and land use codes. The guidelines require that a percentage of the parking spaces required under State and local codes be accessible. As noted above, the recent NPA survey supports the adequacy of the table contained in 4.1.2(5)(a) for most public accommodations. A recent study conducted for the Board on accessible parking spaces and loading zones concluded that the table in 4.1.2(5)(a) was adequate and recommended that surveys be taken every two to three years to evaluate its continuing adequacy. No changes have been made in the table contained in 4.1.2(5)(a) because the comments and two surveys support the table.

A sentence has been added to 4.1.2(5)(a) to clarify that spaces required by the table need not be provided in the particular lot. They may be provided in a different location if equivalent or greater accessibility in terms of distance from an accessible entrance, cost, and convenience is ensured.

The NPRM proposed to add a provision to 4.1.5(a) requiring accessible parking spaces to be located as close as practical to an accessible entrance. In the final guidelines, requirements regarding the location of accessible parking spaces have been consolidated in the technical specifications for parking at 4.6.2 and are further discussed there.

Facilities that provide medical care and other services for persons with mobility impairments are discussed under a separate comment below. As for so called "low use" of "Class III" occupancy types, the ITE and NPA surveys apparently did not consider the level of accessibility provided at the buildings and facilities which would affect usage by individuals with disabilities. The Board finds no basis for concluding that individuals with disabilities have less need for using buildings and facilities included in the so called "low use" or "Class III" occupancy types, including airports, schools, universities, office buildings, and public parking facilities in central business districts. The passage and implementation of the ADA will enable and encourage many more individuals

with disabilities to use these buildings and facilities and, therefore, the Board rejects establishing a separate table with a lower number of accessible parking spaces for so called "low use" or "Class III" occupancy types.

Comment. The NPRM asked whether accessible parking spaces should be required for vans and, if so, whether such spaces should be in addition to the number of accessible parking spaces specified in the table in 4.1.2(5)(a) or a percentage of those spaces. Most of the persons in each category who responded to the question were in favor of requiring accessible parking spaces for vans and recommended that those spaces should be a percentage of the spaces specified in the table in 4.1.2(5)(a). Specific recommendations ranged from 0.5% to 75%. Commenters also submitted various recommendations for the minimum width of accessible parking spaces needed to accommodate vans which ranged from 13 feet to 18 feet, including an adjacent access aisle. Recommendations for vertical clearance needed for vans ranged from 96 inches to 144 inches. Several commenters recommended that all accessible parking spaces should be the same size and be capable of accommodating vans. Some commenters recommended adoption of the universal parking design guidelines developed by the City of Phoenix Fire Department which provides for all accessible parking spaces to be at least 11 feet wide and to have an adjacent access aisle at least 5 feet wide.

Response. The technical specification in 4.6.3 for accessible parking spaces require such spaces to be 8 feet (96 inches) wide minimum and to have an adjacent access aisle 5 feet (60 inches) wide minimum. Two accessible parking spaces may share a common access aisle. An access aisle that is 60 inches wide does not provide sufficient space to permit a lift to be deployed from the side of a van and still leave room for a person using a wheelchair or other mobility aid to exit from the lift platform. A recent Board sponsored study on accessible parking and loading zones conducted tests with various van, lift, and wheelchair combinations and found that a parking space and access aisle almost 17 feet wide is needed to deploy a lift and exit conveniently.

Requirements have been added to the scoping provisions in 4.1.2(5)(b) requiring that one in every eight accessible parking spaces, but not less than one, be served by an access aisle 96 inches (8 feet) wide minimum and be designated "van accessible." For instance, if there are 16 accessible

parking spaces, at least two wider access aisles must be provided. If a wider access aisle is placed between two accessible parking spaces, both parking spaces can accommodate vans.

Requirements have also been added to the technical specifications in 4.6.5 regarding the vertical clearance to be provided at van accessible parking spaces. The NPRM proposed that the minimum vertical clearances should be 114 inches. This figure was taken from MGRAD and UFAS which was based on a survey of paratransit vehicles for purposes of establishing the vertical clearance needed at passenger loading zones. The survey found that the highest paratransit vehicle had a height of 120 inches but that a vertical clearance of 114 inches would accommodate most paratransit vehicles. MGRAD and UFAS used the same figure for accessible parking spaces for vans; however, such spaces were not mandatory. Personal vans are usually not as tall as paratransit vehicles. This is especially true with growing use of accessible mini-vans. California requires a minimum vertical clearance of 98 inches which accommodates most vans without seriously affecting multi-level parking structures. Based on the experience with the California standard, the technical specifications in 4.6.5 adopt a minimum vertical clearance of 98 inches for van accessible parking spaces. The vertical clearance must be provided along at least one vehicle access route from the site entrance(s) and exit(s) to the van accessible parking space. The technical specifications in 4.6.5 permit the van accessible parking spaces to be grouped on one level of a parking structure.

An exception has also been added to 4.1.2(5)(a) permitting all required accessible parking spaces to conform to the universal parking design guidelines developed by the City of Phoenix Fire Department. As discussed above, those guidelines provide for accessible parking spaces to be at least 11 feet wide and to have an adjacent access aisle at least 5 feet wide. Additional information on the universal parking design guidelines is provided in the appendix at A4.6.3.

Comment. A number of commenters recommended that the scoping provision for accessible parking spaces at transient lodging (4.1.2(5)(d) in the NPRM) be revised. The provision would require that where parking is provided for all occupants, one accessible parking space be provided for each accessible unit or sleeping room; and where parking is provided for visitors, 2% of the spaces or a least one be accessible.

C-10

Some commenters pointed out that the provision was not workable because many places of transient lodging, such as hotels, do not provide parking spaces for each room.

Response. The provision was based on similar requirement in MGRAD and UFAS which was intended for accessible housing. The provision may not be applicable to all places of transient lodging and has been deleted from the final guidelines. Instead, places of transient lodging must provide the number of accessible parking spaces specified in the table in 4.1.2(5)(a).

Comment. The NPRM asked whether the scoping provision in 4.1.2(5)(d) (4.1.2(5)(e) in the NPRM) should require nonmedical facilities that specialize in providing services for persons with mobility impairments such as vocational rehabilitation facilities to provide a higher number of accessible parking spaces. Most of the commenters who responded to the question favored requiring such facilities to provide a higher number of accessible parking spaces. Some commenters recommended that the percentage be greater than that proposed in the NPRM.

Response. The scoping provision in 4.1.2(5)(d) (4.1.2(5)(e) in the NPRM) has been revised and clarified. The provision has been clarified as applying to facilities that provide medical care and other services for persons with mobility impairments and units of such facilities. Generally, facilities that provide medical care and other services for persons with mobility impairments are required to provide the number of accessible parking spaces specified in the table in 4.1.2(5)(a) except in two cases. The first case applies to outpatient units and facilities where 10% of the total number of parking spaces serving each such unit or facility must be accessible. The second case applies to units and facilities that specialize in treatment or services for persons with mobility impairments where 20% of the total number of parking spaces serving each such unit or facility must be accessible. The latter case would include vocational rehabilitation facilities.

Comment. The National Parking Association (NPA) requested that valet parking facilities not be required to comply with the guidelines.

Response. Valet parking facilities are different from self-parking facilities. In valet parking facilities, the driver and passenger usually leave the vehicle at the entrance of the facility and another person parks the vehicle. The final guidelines require in 4.1.2(5)(e) that valet parking facilities provide an accessible passenger loading zone located on an accessible route to the entrance of the facility. Additional advisory material on valet parking is included in the appendix at A4.1.2(5)(e).

Portable Toilet and Bathing Units (4.1.2(6))

Comment. The NPRM asked whether the scoping provision of accessible portable toilets and bathing units should be advisory or mandatory. Most persons who responded to the question favored making the provision mandatory. As for how many accessible units should be required when single user units are clustered at a single location, the recommendations ranged from at least one unit to 100%.

Response. The provision has been revised to require that where single user portable toilet or bathing units are clustered at a single location, at least 5% but no less than one of the units at each cluster must be accessible.

Comment. Several commenters recommended that portable toilet units at construction sites should not be required to be accessible.

Response. An exception has been added for portable toilet units at construction sites used exclusively by construction personnel.

Exterior Signage (4.1.2(7))

Comment. Based on the comments received from graphic designers and sign manufacturers, the Board concluded that the scoping provisions and technical specifications for signage were unclear and needed to be revised. Many interpreted the NPRM as requiring all signs to have raised and brailled characters and all upper case letters.

Response. The scoping provisions for exterior and interior signage and the accompanying technical specifications have been clarified and revised in response to the comments. See 4.1.3(16) for scoping provisions for interior signage; and 4.30 for technical specifications for signage. Exterior signs which designate permanent rooms and spaces must comply with the technical specifications in 4.30.1 and 4.30.4 through 4.30.6 for raised and brailled characters, finish and contrast, and mounting location and height. For instance, signs on toilet facilities at a zoo must have raised and brailled characters designating the men's and women's toilet facilities, and also meet the finish and contrast, and mounting location and height requirements. Exterior signs which provide directions to or information about functional spaces of a building or facility must comply with the technical specifications in 4.30.1, 4.30.2 and 4.30.5 for character proportion, and finish and contrast. The technical specifications in 4.30.3 for character height must also be complied with if the signage is suspended or projected overhead in compliance with the technical specifications in 4.4.2 for head room for protruding objects. For instance, a sign adjacent to a pedestrian walkway directing the public to an accessible entrance to a building or facility must meet the character proportion and finish and contrast requirements, as well as the character height requirements if suspended or projected above the walkway in compliance with 4.4.2.

4.1.3 Accessible Buildings: New Construction

This section contains scoping provisions for new construction of accessible buildings and facilities.

Accessible Route (4.1.3(1))

Protruding Objects (4.1.3(2))

Ground and Floor Surfaces (4.1.3(3))

Few comments were received on these scoping provisions and they did not warrant any changes.

Stairs (4.1.3(4))

Comment. Several commenters requested clarification regarding whether 4.1.3(4) applies to exterior stairs, as well as interior stairs.

Response. The provision has been clarified that interior and exterior stairs must comply with the technical specifications in 4.9 for stairs when they connect levels that are not connected by an elevator or other accessible means of vertical access (e.g., ramp or lift). In other words, for example, if an elevator serves as a means of going from one floor to another, the stairs connecting the two floors are not required to comply with 4.9.

Comment. The NPRM asked whether in new construction stairs connecting levels that are also served by an elevator should be required to comply with the technical specifications in 4.9 for stairs especially since stairs must be used in emergency evacuations. Most persons who responded to the question favored such a requirement. Several commenters recommended that the provision should apply only to stairs required by State and local building codes for egress. Other commenters noted that the model codes are incorporating more safety features for stairs and that it is unnecessary to address the same features in accessibility standards.

Response. The technical specifications in 4.9 regarding stair treads and risers, nosings, and handrails are safety features which affect all members of the public. As the model codes are updated, more general safety features which also provide greater accessibility are being incorporated in those codes. The problem identified in the NPRM may be addressed through the model codes. The Board plans to monitor the development of the model codes and has not made any changes to the scoping provision for stairs other than to clarify that the provisions applies to exterior stairs, as well as interior stairs.

Elevators (4.1.3(5))

Elevator Exemption (4.1.3(5) Exception1).

Comment. A number of commenters objected to exempting buildings and facilities that are less than three stories or have less than 3,000 square feet per story from the elevator requirement unless the building or facility is a shopping center, a shopping mall, the professional office of a health care provider, or another type of facility that has been determined by the Attorney General to require an elevator.

Response. The elevator exemption is based on section 303(b) of the ADA. The Department of Justice is responsible for implementing this section of the ADA and that agency's final regulations will address definitions and application of the section.

A statement has been added to the appendix at 4.1.3(8) explaining that if a building or facility is exempt from the elevator requirement, it is not necessary to provide another accessible means of vertical access (e.g., ramps, platform lifts or wheelchair lifts) between each level of the building or facility.

Comment. Some commenters requested that basements, attics, and mezzanines be counted for purposes of determining whether a building or facility is less than three stories. Other commenters requested that basements, attics, and mezzanines not be counted.

Response. A "story" is defined in 3.5 as including "occupiable" space which in turn is defined as space that is: (a) Designed for human occupancy in which individuals congregate for amusement, educational or similar purposes, or in which occupants are engaged at labor; and (b) equipped with means of egress, light, and ventilation. If a basement or attic is designed or intended to be used as occupiable space or is later altered to be occupiable, it is counted for purposes of determining whether a building or facility is less than three stories.

As for mezzanines, the model codes do not consider mezzanines to be a story. Where possible, the Board defines

terms in the guidelines to be consistent with the model codes when they are also consistent with the ADA and, therefore, mezzanines are not counted for purposes of determining whether a building or facility is less than three stories. However, as further discussed below, if a building or facility is exempt from the elevator requirement, but nonetheless has a full passenger elevator, that elevator must serve each level, including the mezzanine.

Comment. Several commenters questioned why buildings and facilities that are exempt from the elevator requirement must comply with other requirements in 4.1.3 on floors above or below the accessible ground floor.

Response. This provision is based on the legislative history which states that "the exception regarding elevators does not obviate or limit in any way the obligation to comply with the other accessibility requirements established by this legislation, including requirements applicable to floors which, pursuant to the exception, are not served by an elevator." H. Rept. 101–485, pt 2, at 114. There are several reasons for this provision. Some individuals who are mobility impaired may work on a building's second floor, which they can reach by stairs and the use of crutches; however, the same individuals, once they reach the second floor, may then use a wheelchair that is kept in the office. Further, an elevator may be installed at a future date, or an addition to the building or a second building which is later connected may include an elevator. The second floor must also be accessible to individuals with visual or hearing impairments.

Comment. With respect to a new building or facility that is exempt from the elevator requirement but an elevator is nonetheless planned, the NPRM asked whether it was appropriate to require the elevator in such a building or facility to meet the technical specifications in 4.10 for elevators and to serve each level in the building or facility. Most persons who responded to the question favored the requirement. Some commenters recommended that the provision be limited to full passenger elevators and not freight elevators.

Response. This provision is also based on the legislative history. See H. Rept. 101–485, pt. 2, at 114. The Board agrees that the provision should apply only to full passenger elevators and has added appropriate language to the elevator exemption. A sentence has also been added to the provision that if a full passenger elevator provides service from a garage to only one level of a building or facility, it is not required to

serve the other levels of the building or facility.

Platform Lifts/Wheelchair Lifts (4.1.3(5) Exception 4)

Comment. The NPRM noted that some building codes and the proposed BCMC scoping provisions prohibit the installation of platform lifts or wheelchair lifts as part of a required accessible route in new construction and asked a series of questions regarding their use. Individuals with disabilities and their organizations who responded to the questions viewed platform lifts or wheelchair lifts as inferior to ramps, not independently operated, poorly maintained, dangerous, and undignified. However, some of these commenters acknowledged that in some alteration projects, and in limited areas in new construction, a platform lift or wheelchair lift may be the only viable option for accessibility. Lift manufacturers and vendors acknowledged that there have been significant problems in the past but believed that improvements have been made, and gave examples where a platform lift or wheelchair lift provided a better design solution than a ramp. Several architects and other commenters recommended that the Board specify conditions for the use of platform lifts or wheelchair lifts.

Response. Rather than prohibit platform lifts or wheelchair lifts in new construction, the Board believes that the better approach is to specify the conditions where their use is allowed. The applicable exception under 4.1.3(5) has been revised to permit the use of platform lifts or wheelchair lifts complying with 4.11 and applicable State or local codes in new construction under the following conditions:

(a) To provide an accessible route to performing area in an assembly occupancy;

(b) To comply with the wheelchair viewing position line-of-sight and dispersion requirements of 4.33.3 (e.g., to provide access to seating areas located above a cross aisle or to box seats);

(c) To provide access to incidental occupant spaces and rooms which are not open to the general public and which house no more than five persons (e.g., equipment control rooms, projection booths, radio and news booths, raised pharmacy platforms, manager's stations in food stores); and

(d) To provide access when existing site constraints or other constraints make use of a ramp or an elevator infeasible.

The last condition allows the use of platform lifts or wheelchair lifts only in very limited circumstances where use of a ramp or an elevator is infeasible due to existing site constraints or other constraints. For example, if a new infill building is being constructed incorporating a historic facade which must be maintained, thereby effectively predetermining the entry floor level, and space for a ramp to the entry floor level was not available, a platform lift or wheelchair lift would be permitted.

Windows (4.1.3(6))

The NPRM proposed to require that operable windows comply with the technical specifications in 4.12 for windows. For reasons explained under 4.12, the Board has decided to reserve the technical specifications for windows in the final guidelines and, therefore, the scoping provision is also reserved.

Doors (4.1.3(7))

Comment. Several commenters requested that a requirement be added for at least one automated door at a principal entrance, or at each entrance, or at certain rooms (e.g., restrooms, meeting rooms).

Response. The force required to open a door can affect usability of a building or facility by individuals with disabilities. This is especially true for exterior doors where a variety of factors can affect closing force (e.g., wind pressure, weight of door, heating and ventilation systems, positive or negative pressure within a building). Neither UFAS nor these guidelines specify an opening force for exterior doors because of these variable factors. Requiring an automated door in certain occupancies or large buildings could provide a solution to the problem. The Board plans to study this issue to determine where and in what types of buildings and facilities automated doors may be practical or necessary and cost feasible for future revision of the guidelines.

Entrances (4.1.3(8))

Comment. The NPRM asked two questions regarding entrances in new construction. First, in the case of buildings that have more than one ground floor level (e.g., buildings with a split level entrance leading only to stairs or escalators which connect with upper and lower levels less than one story above or below grade, and buildings built on hillsides with more than one floor having direct access to grade), should each ground floor level have an accessible entrance? [11] Second, should

[11] This question was suggested by the legislative history which stated that: "[a]ccessibility requirements shall not be evaded by constructing facilities in such a way that no story constitutes a

all entrances to every building be accessible. Businesses generally favored providing an accessible entrance at only one ground floor level in response to the first question and making some but not all entrances accessible in response to the second question. Individuals with disabilities and their organizations, and commenters from other categories, generally favored providing an accessible entrance at each ground floor level in response to the first question and making all entrances accessible in response to the second question.

Response. The NPRM proposed to follow UFAS which establishes two requirements for entrances. First, at least one principal entrance at each ground floor would be required to be accessible.[12] Second, when a building or facility has entrances which normally serve transportation facilities, passenger loading zones, accessible parking facilities, public streets and sidewalks, or accessible interior vertical access, at least one of the entrances serving each function would have to be accessible.

Depending on the interpretation of what it means for an entrance to "normally serve" a function, the NPRM could result in all the entrances to a building being accessible as illustrated by the following example. A building has four entrances: One on each side. Two of the entrances lead directly to parking lots of equal size on opposite sides of the building. People who use the building usually arrive by car and enter through the two parking lot entrances making them principal entrances. Each parking lot has accessible parking spaces and the two parking lot entrances are accessible and connected by an accessible route to the accessible parking spaces. The third entrance leads directly to a driveway with a bus stop and the fourth entrance leads directly to a public sidewalk. Even if the bus stop and the public sidewalk are connected by an accessible route to the two parking lot entrances, the third and fourth entrances could nonetheless be required to be accessible under the NPRM if an entrance which "normally serves" a function means the nearest entrance which directly leads to the function.

'ground floor,' for example, by constructing a building whose main entrance leads only to stairways or escalators that connect with upper or lower floors; at least one accessible ground story must be provided." H. Rept. 101–596, at 77.
[12] UFAS defines a "principal entrance" as "the main door through which most people enter." The NPRM defined a "principal entrance" as "one through which a significant number of people enter" in recognition of the fact that buildings, especially larger ones, typically have several principal entrances.

The legislative history makes clear that not every feature of every building needs to be accessible but rather a high level of convenient access is contemplated. The legislative history further states that "(a)ccessibility requirements shall not be evaded by constructing facilities in such a way that no story constitutes a 'ground floor,' for example, by constructing a building whose main entrance leads to stairways or escalators that connect with upper and lower floors; at least one accessible ground story must be provided." H. Rept. 101–596, at 77. Thus, each newly constructed building or facility must have at least one ground story entrance and at least one accessible entrance. The legislative history does not state that all or even most entrances must be accessible.

The Board wants to ensure a high level of access to all new buildings consistent with the statute. The Board has sought to require accessible entrances in a number that is easily definable and reasonable. The Board also wants to ensure that the requirements can be and will be met in all instances, except in those rare cases where the structural impracticability exception applies. In some urban and suburban areas, much new construction is "infill" between existing facilities and is constricted by slope and other site considerations, such as existing sidewalks and nearby property lines. In some areas there are land use plans and other restrictions that, in effect, limit development to sites where slopes are between 10% and 25%. For example, Maryland is considering imposing a land use plan on its localities which would preserve "agricultural" land (generally less than 10% slope) and steeply sloped land (more than 25% slope) and thus focus new development in areas with slopes between 10% and 25%. The Board understands that other States are considering similar proposals. Structural impracticability is a very narrow exception and, as explained in the legislative history, does not apply to situations where a building is constructed on "hilly" terrain or on a plot of land with steep slopes. H. Rept. 101–485, pt. 2, at 120. The Board believes it would be unreasonable to require all entrances to be accessible in such cases.

There is very little data available concerning the impact of site considerations on entrance accessibility. The Department of Housing and Urban Development's analysis of its Fair Housing Accessibility (FHA) Guidelines estimated the cost of providing 27 accessible entrances in new constructions at three different apartment complexes at sites having slopes of less than 10%, as ranging from an additional $240 to $1636 per entrance. The average cost was $836 per entrance. This data is not easily transferable to commercial construction because of the differences between residential and commercial construction and the differences in the FHA guidelines and the ADA guidelines. The Board's draft final regulatory impact analysis estimates the cost of an accessible building entrance ramp with a 1:12 slope for a 5-feet rise and railings extensions to be $8460 for offices and hotels. This cost does not take grading or retaining walls into account.

Thus, the Board is not at this time mandating 100% accessible entrances in new construction. At the same time, the Board recognizes that providing only one accessible entrance to a building with multiple public entrances will not always achieve the high level of convenient access contemplated by the ADA. In light of all these concerns, the Board has established two independent requirements for entrances in 4.1.3(8) (a) and (b). First, 4.1.3(8)(a)(i) requires that at least 50% of all public entrances be accessible. One of these must be a ground floor entrance. In addition, 4.1.3(8)(a)(ii) requires that accessible entrances must be provided in a number at least equivalent to the number of exits required by the applicable State or local building or life safety code. This provision acknowledges the importance of life safety issues in access to, use of, and egress from a building. Model building and life safety codes are generally consistent in their method of determining the number of exits required, the exit width necessary, and the separation of exits needed to ensure safe egress during an emergency. Since not all exits are required to serve as entrances, if only one building entrance is planned, and a building or life safety code requires two fire exits, 4.1.3(8)(ii) would not require the provision of more than the one planned entrance. Furthermore, 4.1.8(a)(iii) requires accessible entrances be provided to each tenancy in a facility. One entrance may be considered as meeting more than one of the requirements in 4.1.3(8)(a) (i) through (iii). Where feasible, the accessible entrances must be the entrances used by the majority of people visiting or working in the building.

Second, 4.1.3(8)(b) (i) and (ii) require that accessible entrances be provided from any indoor garages, pedestrian tunnels, or elevated walkways that have entrances to the facility. One entrance

may be considered as meeting more than one of the requirements in 4.1.3(8)(b) (i) and (ii).

The Board believes that these provisions, combined with the other requirements described above, will ensure access at least equivalent to that required by MGRAD and UFAS and intended by Congress.

The NPRM included a requirement in the technical specifications for signage at 4.30.1 that entrances which are not accessible to have directional signage complying with 4.30 indicating the location of the nearest accessible entrance. This requirement has been placed in the scoping provisions for entrances in the final guidelines.

Comment. Several commenters recommended including sections from the proposed BCMC scoping provisions in the guidelines requiring an accessible entrance to be provided to each tenancy within a building (e.g., retail stores in a strip shopping center), and all entrances having walkways with a change in elevation of 6 inches or less at the entrance to be accessible.

Response. Multi-tenant facilities such as a strip shopping center are generally viewed as one building. To ensure that each retail store and other places of public accommodation within such facilities are accessible, a requirement has been added to 4.1.3(8)(a)(iii) for an accessible entrance to be provided to each tenancy within a building. As for entrances having walkways with a change in elevation of 6 inches or less at the entrance, the provision is not necessary in light of 4.1.3(8) in its entirety. Further, the proposed BCMC scoping provision does not address the fact that site preparation can usually be made to ensure an elevation change of more than 6 inches, thereby circumventing the intent of the requirement.

Egress and Areas of Rescue Assistance (4.1.3(9))

Comment. The NPRM proposed to require "areas of refuge" in newly constructed buildings and facilities which were defined as areas, which have direct access to an exit stairway, where people who are unable to use stairs may remain safely to await further instructions or assistance during emergency evacuation. Building owners and managers and businesses objected to the concept of "area of refuge." Many of these commenters, including the Building Owners and Managers Association (BOMA), expressed concern that such areas would result in restricting evacuation of individuals with disabilities during an emergency. Evacuation plans were recommended

instead. Individuals with disabilities and their organizations who commented on the provision supported it.

Response. The Board wishes to emphasize that the purpose of areas of refuge is to facilitate and not restrict the evacuation of wheelchair users and other individuals with mobility impairments during an emergency. MGRAD, UFAS, and the ANSI A117.1 standard, all require that accessible routes connect to an accessible place of refuge in the event of an emergency. Since elevators are generally not available for egress during a fire, a safe area is needed where wheelchair users and other individuals with mobility impairments who cannot exit by stairways can temporarily await further instructions or evacuation assistance. To clarify this point, the area has been renamed "areas of rescue assistance" in the final guidelines. The appendix to the guidelines recognizes in A4.3.10 that an emergency management plan for the evacuation of people with disabilities is essential in providing for fire safety in buildings and facilities. However, an evacuation plan alone is not sufficient to ensure the safety of individuals with mobility impairments during an emergency since individuals may not be able to transfer to an evacuation device or may require assistance from trained personnel.

The final guidelines incorporate modified scoping provisions and technical specifications from chapter 31, section 3104 of the 1991 Uniform Building Code. In buildings and facilities, or portions of buildings and facilities, required to be accessible under the ADA, accessible means of egress must be provided in the same number as required for exits by State or local buidling and life safety codes. Where a required exit from an occupiable level above or below a level of accessible exit discharge is not accessible, areas of rescue assistance must be provided on each level in a number equal to that of inaccessible required exits. A horizontal exit which meets the requirements of state or local building or life safety codes may also be used for an area of rescue assistance.

The scoping provisions in 4.1.3(9) for areas of rescue assistance do not apply to exterior facilities covered by 4.1.2. For example, parking lots and open parking garages are covered only by 4.1.2 and are not required to comply with the scoping provisions in 4.1.3(9) for areas of rescue assistance.

The technical specifications for areas of rescue assistance are discussed under 4.3.11 and provide several alternatives for design of such areas. The draft final regulatory impact estimates the additional direct costs for creation of an area of rescue assistance in a portion of a stairway landing in a new building to be $824. Although there are less expensive alternatives, this option was analyzed in the draft final regulatory impact analysis because it is commonly used at the current time in buildings that provide area of rescue assistance and because it represents the highest range of cost that will be incurred. Based on this estimate, the additional direct costs for providing areas of rescue assistance in stairway landings in a new low-rise office building 6 stories and 40,000 square feet per story would be $6,240 or $.03 per square foot of building area; and in a high-rise office building with 25 stories 30,000 square feet per story would be $29,952 or $.04 per square foot of building area. In many cases the cost of providing areas of rescue assistance will be much lower because such areas can be provided in elevator lobbies, office rooms, and similar space used for other purposes. No costs will be incurred in alterations or in new buildings with supervised automatic sprinkler systems because of exceptions which are included in the final guidelines as explained below. The Board believes these costs to be reasonable in light of this important life safety issue.

Comment. Several commenters requested that buildings and facilities equipped with a supervised automatic sprinkler system be exempted from the requirements for areas of rescue assistance.

Response. An exception has been added exempting buildings and facilities having a supervised automatic sprinkler from the requirements for areas of rescue assistance. Supervised automatic sprinkler systems have built in signals for monitoring features of the system such as the opening and closing of water control valves, the power supplies for needed pumps, and water tank levels, and for indicating conditions that will impair the satisfactory operation of the sprinkler system. Because of these monitoring features, supervised automatic sprinkler systems have a high level of satisfactory performance and response to fire conditions and the Board does not believe that additional measures are needed in buildings and facilities with such systems.

Comment. The American Hotel and Motel Association requested that in the case of hotels and motels on floors used exclusively for guest rooms, such rooms be permitted to serve as areas of rescue assistance because State and local

building and life safety codes require them to be fire-resistive.

Response. The organization responsible for development of the Uniform Building Code rejected this proposal on the grounds that it is inappropriate to designate a room or space that is not available to the public as an area of rescue assistance. The Board declines to accept the proposal for the same reason. In addition, there are some inconsistencies among State and local building and life safety codes regarding requirements for fire-resistive construction.

Comment. Several commenters raised questions regarding the application of the requirements for areas of rescue of assistance to alterations of existing facilities.

Response. The guidelines require areas of rescue assistance only in new construction. For the reasons discussed under 4.1.6(1)(g), a paragraph has been added to the scoping provisions for alterations to clarify that the requirements for areas of rescue assistance do not apply to alterations of existing facilities.

Drinking Fountains (4.1.3(10))

Comment. The NPRM asked whether a specific percentage of accessible drinking fountains would be required and, if so, whether at least 50% would be an appropriate number. Most persons who commented on the question stated that at least 50% was an appropriate number. Several commenters requested that the provisions address the distance between accessible drinking fountains.

Response. The Board wants to ensure that drinking fountains are accessible to wheelchair users and individuals who have difficulty bending or stooping. The final guidelines provide that where there is only one drinking fountain on a floor, there must be a drinking fountain that is accessible to wheelchair users in accordance with 4.15 and individuals who have difficulty bending or stooping. This can be accomplished by use of a "hi-lo" drinking fountain; by providing one drinking fountain accessible to wheelchair users and one drinking fountain at a standard height convenient for those who have difficulty bending or stooping; by providing a drinking fountain accessible under 4.15 and a water cooler; or by such other means as would achieve the required accessibility for each group on each floor. Where more than one drinking fountain or water cooler is provided on a floor, 50% of those provided must comply with 4.15 and be on an accessible route. In the event an odd number of drinking fountains are provided on a floor, the requirement can be met by rounding

down the odd number to an even number and calculating 50% of the even number. Additional advisory material on drinking fountains is included in the appendix at A4.1.3(10).

Toilet Rooms (4.1.3(11))

Comment. Some commenters were opposed to the scoping provision in 4.1.3(11) requiring that each public and common use toilet room be accessible.

Response. Although each common and public use toilet room must be accessible, if more than one toilet stall, lavatory, or other feature is provided in such a toilet room, generally only one of each feature is required to be accessible. See 4.22.4 through 4.22.7. Toilet rooms serving specific sleeping accommodations in dormitories, hotels, and other similar places of transient lodging are not public or common use toilet rooms.

Comment. A few commenters objected to requiring other toilet rooms to be adaptable.

Response. The scoping provision in 4.1.3(11) has been clarified that the adaptability requirement applies to toilet rooms that are designed or intended for the use of the occupant of a specific space such as a private toilet room which is part of an executive's office. Exempting such toilet rooms in new construction from the adaptability requirement would make reasonable accommodation in the future impossible in many cases.

Comment. Several commenters requested clarification whether every toilet room provided as part of a sleeping accommodation in medical care facilities and transient lodging must be accessible or adaptable.

Response. As stated in 4.1.1(1), in new construction all areas of buildings and facilities must comply with 4.1 through 4.35, unless otherwise provided in the general application section or a special application section. Medical care facilities and transient lodging are covered by special application sections 6 and 9 respectively which require that a specific percentage of sleeping accommodations, including toilet rooms, be accessible. The guidelines do not require toilet rooms in other sleeping accommodations to be accessible except that, in the case of hotels, motels and other similar places of transient lodging, doors and doorways must be designed to allow passage into the toilet room.

Comment. A few commenters recommended that an accessible unisex toilet room should be required either in addition to or in place of separate toilet rooms for men and women.

Response. Unisex toilet rooms are discussed in the technical specifications for toilet rooms in 4.22.

Storage, Shelving and Display Units (4.1.3(12))

Comment. Several commenters requested clarification regarding whether all storage, shelving and display units must be within the forward and side reach ranges for wheelchair users.

Response. The scoping provision in 4.1.3(12)(a) applies only to fixed cabinets, shelves, closets, and drawers and expressly states that additional storage space may be provided outside the forward and side reach ranges for wheelchair users. The technical specifications for reach ranges for storage spaces have also been clarified. See 4.25.3; and figures 38a and 38b.

The scoping provision in 4.1.3(12)(b) applies to fixed shelves or display units allowing self-service by customers and requires such shelves and display units be located on an accessible route. A sentence has been added to the provision to clarify that compliance with the forward and side reach ranges for wheelchair users is not required.

Comment. Businesses requested that shelves in employee work areas (e.g., stockrooms, baggage rooms, maids closets) be exempt from the scoping provision 4.1.3(12)(a).

Response. As stated in 4.1.1(1), in new construction all areas of buildings and facilities must comply with 4.1 through 4.35, unless otherwise provided in the general application section or a special application section. Areas used only by employees as work areas are covered by 4.1.1(3) which requires that such areas be designed and constructed so that individuals with disabilities can approach, enter, and exit the areas. This provision expressly states that employee work areas are not required to be equipped with accessible shelves. The appendix includes advisory guidance at A4.1.1(3) that consideration should be given to placing shelves in employee work areas at a convenient height for accessibility or installing commercially available shelving that is adjustable so that reasonable accommodation can be made in the future.

Controls and Operating Maintenance (4.1.3(13))

Comment. Several commenters requested clarification whether controls not intended for public use must be within the forward or side reach ranges for wheelchair users.

Response. An exception has been added to the technical specifications in 4.27.3 stating that the forward and side reach range requirements do not apply where the use of special equipment dictates otherwise or where electrical and communications systems receptacles are not normally intended for use by building occupants.

Audible and Visual Alarms (4.1.3(14))

Comment. Commenters generally supported the inclusion of visual alarms in the guidelines. Some businesses considered requiring visual alarms in new buildings and facilities to be excessive and recommended that such alarms should be provided only in areas where an individual with a hearing impairment was an occupant or that portable or personal alarm devices should be permitted. A few commenters requested that buildings with automatic sprinkler systems be exempt from the requirement for visual alarms.

Response. Builders and designers cannot know in advance whether a space will be occupied by a person with a hearing impairment. If visual alarms are not included in the design of new buildings and facilities but instead are required only where an individual with a hearing impairment was an occupant, buildings and facilities would have to be retrofitted at potentially greater cost. Further, visual alarms are intended to alert visitors, and not just regular tenants, to emergencies. Portable or personal alarm devices are carried by an individual and are triggered by a signal from the building emergency alarm system. Provision of these devices is not an acceptable alternative, especially in places of public accommodation such as retail stores, assembly areas, and transportation facilities where the number of visitors and temporary users greatly exceeds the number of tenants. They have been demonstrably ineffective in both drill and emergency situations in such places and have resulted in visitors being left unaware of the need for evacuation. The only situation where portable or personal alarm devices are permitted under the guidelines is in sleeping accommodations in hotels and other similar places of transient lodging where guests are assigned temporarily to a specific room and can be provided appropriate devices when registering for the room. See 9.3.2. Even then, hallways, lobbies and other common areas in hotels and other similar places of transient lodging must have permanently installed visual alarms.

As for buildings with automatic sprinkler systems, visual alarms are generally required only where audible alarms are required or provided. Since buildings with automatic sprinkler systems are required to provide audible alarms, the Board believes that persons with hearing impairments are entitled to access the same emergency warning system.

The draft final regulatory impact analysis estimates the direct additional cost per visual alarm device in new construction, including installation, to be $169. A high-rise office building with 25 stores and 30,000 square feet per story is estimated to require 160 devices for a total cost of $27,040 or $.04 per square foot of building area. The Board believes that this cost is reasonable in light of the importance of this life safety issue.

Detectable Warnings (4.1.3(15))

A large number of comments was received in support of and in opposition to detectable warnings in general and at specific locations. As further discussed under 4.29, the requirements for detectable warnings have been revised and some sections have been reserved pending further study and research for future revisions to the guidelines. An editorial change has been made to 4.1.3(15) stating that detectable warnings shall be provided at locations specified in 4.29.

Interior Signage (4.1.3(16))

Comment. As discussed under 4.1.2(7), the Board has concluded based on review of the comments that the scoping provisions and technical specifications for signage were unclear and needed to be revised.

Response. The scoping provisions for interior and exterior signage and the accompanying technical specifications have been clarified and revised in response to the comments. See 4.1.2(7) for scoping provisions for exterior signage; and 4.30 for technical specifications for signage. Interior signs which designate permanent rooms and spaces must comply with the technical specifications in 4.30.1 and 4.30.4 through 4.30.6 for raised and brailled characters, finish and contrast, and mounting locations and height. For instance, numbers on hotel guest rooms, patient rooms in hospitals, office suites, and signs designating men's and women's toilet facilities must have raised and brailled characters, and also must meet the finish and contrast, and mounting height requirements. Interior signs which provide direction to or information about functional spaces of a building or facility must comply with the technical specifications in 4.30.1, 4.30.2 and 4.30.5 for character proportion and finish and contrast. The technical specifications in 4.30.3 for character height must also be complied with if the signage is suspended or projected overhead in compliance with the technical specifications in 4.4.2 for head room for protruding objects.

An exception has also been added to 4.1.3(16) to clarify that building directories, menus, and other signs which provide temporary information about rooms and spaces such as the current occupant's name do not have to comply with the requirements for signage.

Comment. The NPRM asked whether additional types of signage such as informational and directional signage about functional spaces, rules of conduct, or hazards should be tactile (i.e., comply with technical specifications in 4.30.4 and 4.30.6 for raised and braille characters and mounting location and height). The NPRM also requested information on available technologies such as audible signs for overhead and remote signage. Comments from individuals with disabilities and their organizations regarding additional types of signage that should be tactile were scattered with no clear consensus of opinion that would be useful for purposes of establishing guidelines. Technical information was submitted by Love Electronics regarding infrared signage.

Response. Although technology is available for making overhead and remote signage accessible, the Board plans to further study this issue to determine where and in what types of buildings and facilities such technology may be necessary for future revision of the guidelines.

Accessible Public Telephones (4.1.17(a))

Comment. Individuals with disabilities and their organizations requested that more accessible telephones be required. One commenter recommended that a maximum distance of 300 feet be established between accessible public telephones in large buildings and facilities. A telephone company objected to requiring at least one public telephone per floor to meet the technical specifications in 4.31.2 for forward reach by wheelchair users when two or more banks of telephones are provided on each floor. One commenter recommended that the exception under 4.1.3(17)(a) for exterior public telephones should permit a side reach telephone instead of a forward reach telephone if dial tone first service is available.

Response. The exception under 4.1.3(17)(a) has been revised as recommended. It has also been clarified that accessible public telephones required by 4.1.3(17)(a) do not include

text telephones which are covered by 4.1.3(17)(c).

Public Telephones Equipped With Volume Controls (4.1.3(17)(b))

Comment. Most individuals with disabilities and their organizations supported the NPRM proposal to require 25% of public telephones in newly constructed buildings and facilities to be equipped with a volume control in addition to the requirement in 4.1.3(17)(a) for accessible public telephones. A few requested that the number be increased. Some recommended that scoping be based on occupancy. Telephone companies responded that they have adopted voluntary programs to install public telephones equipped with volume controls and recommended that the Board defer to a Federal Communication Commission (FCC) proceeding which declined to require 25% of all public telephones to be equipped with volume controls. See Order Completing Inquiry and Providing Further Notice of Proposed Rulemaking, CC Docket No. 87–124 (July 27, 1989).

Response. The FCC declined to require 25% of all public telephones to be equipped with volume controls based on cost estimates provided by telephone companies for retrofitting all existing public telephones with a volume control. The NPRM proposal was more modest and only required 25% of public telephones installed in newly constructed buildings and facilities to be accessible. The American Telephone and Telegraph Company reported that its newly designed public telephones incorporate volume controls as a standard feature. Southwestern Bell Telephone Company also reported that it installs volume controls in its public telephones free upon the request of its customers. Cost data provided by other telephone companies for equipping public telephones with volume controls ranged from $10 to $80. Since the additional direct cost of requiring 25% of public telephones in newly constructed buildings and facilities is nothing to minimal depending on the telephone manufacturer or company, the requirement has been retained in the final guidelines.

Comment. The American Public Communication Council requested that the requirement be postponed for one year to permit suppliers to test and evaluate equipment.

Response. The American Telephone and Telegraph Company and other telephone companies currently offer public telephones equipped with volume controls as a standard feature or upon request. In addition, many telephone

companies incorporate the volume control feature into the base of the telephone rather than the handset which has virtually eliminated concerns about vandalism. The Board does not believe that any delay is warranted beyond the January 26, 1992 effective date for title III of the ADA.

Public Text Telephones (4.1.3(17)(c)–(d))

Comment. The NPRM asked whether the scoping provision for public text telephones should be based on the total number of public pay telephones in a building or facility and whether six public pay telephones should be the trigger point. As an alternative, the NPRM asked whether the scoping provision should be based on occupancy type as is done in Michigan. The NPRM also asked for information about the need for public text telephones in general and at specific types of facilities. Most individuals with disabilities and their organizations and other commenters who responded to the questions recommended basing the scoping provision on occupancy type in addition to the total number of public pay telephones in a building or facility and generally supported the need for public text telephones in the same occupancy types as required in Michigan (e.g., transportation facilities, hospitals, shopping malls, convention centers, hotels with a convention center). Many of these commenters expressed concern that smaller or rural communities may have buildings and facilities where there is a need for public text telephones regardless of the number of public pay telephones. As for the trigger point for a scoping provision based on total number of public pay telephones, many individuals with disabilities and their organizations and other commenters recommended that the trigger point be less than six public pay telephones and offered a variety of percentage, bank, and cluster options. Businesses and telephone companies were generally opposed to public text telephones and expressed concerns about cost, utilization, and maintenance. One telephone company stated that the presence of six public telephones would indicate a high volume of traffic and suggests a potential for cost recovery. Other telephone companies referred to a Federal Communications Commission proceeding to gather information concerning the telecommunication needs of individuals with hearing impairments which concluded that "requiring that pay telephones be designed to accommodate portable TDDs, however, should be less costly, and may well provide benefits that outweigh the costs." Order Completing Inquiry and Providing Further Notice of Proposed Rulemaking, CC Docket No. 87–124 (July 27, 1989) at paragraph 110.

Response. A number of changes have been made to the scoping provision for public text telephones in response to the comments. The final guidelines include requirements based on (1) the total number of interior and exterior public pay telephones provided at a site and (2) certain occupancy types, regardless of the number or public pay telephones provided at the site. The trigger point has been set at four or more interior and exterior public pay telephones at a site where at least one is in an interior location. For instance, if a building or facility has two exterior and two interior public pay telephones on the site, the scoping provisions for a public text telephone is triggered. On the other hand, if all public pay telephones are located outdoors, a public text telephone is not required because text telephones do not currently work well outdoors and the use of portable text telephones at such locations is impractical.

The final guidelines further provide that if an interior public pay telephone is provided in a stadium or arena, a convention center, a hotel with a convention center, or a covered mall, at least one interior public text telephone must be provided in the facility. In the case of hospitals, if a public pay telephone is located in or adjacent to an emergency room, recovery room, or waiting room, one public text telephone must be provided at each such location.

The scoping provision for public text telephones in transportation facilities will be included in section 10 of the final guidelines. The Board will also incorporate a scoping provision for public text telephones in State and local government buildings when the guidelines are supplemented for purposes of title II of the ADA.

The final guidelines also include new technical specifications for public text telephones at 4.31.9 and additional explanatory information in the appendix at A4.31.9. The technical specifications permit the use of either an integrated text telephone and pay telephone unit, or a conventional text telephone that is permanently affixed within, or adjacent to, the telephone enclosure. In addition, the technical specifications permit the use of portable text telephones as equivalent facilitation under certain conditions. At the present time, pocket-type text telephones do not accommodate a wide range of individuals with disabilities and are not considered appropriate for purposes of equivalent facilitation. As technology develops, this may change. To be

considered equivalent facilitation, the portable text telephone must be readily available for use with nearby public pay telephones. For example, if a hotel has portable text telephones available at the registration desk on a 24 hour basis for use with nearby public pay telephones, substantially equivalent access to and usability of the public pay telephone would be provided. On the other hand, if the portable text telephone is kept at a remote location from the public pay telephones or is stored in a space near the public pay telephones but the user must search for personnel not regularly stationed near the public pay telephones, substantially equivalent access to and use of the public pay telephone would not be provided. If a portable text telephone is provided as equivalent facilitation, at least one nearby public pay telephone must be equipped with a shelf and an electrical outlet to accommodate the portable text telephone. The technical specifications for the shelf are in 4.31.9(2). If an acoustic coupler is used, the telephone handset cord must be long enough to connect the public pay phone with the text telephone. Regardless of whether the public text telephone is portable or permanently affixed, the technical specifications for signage in 4.30.7(3) require that directional signage indicating the location of the nearest public text telephone must be provided near all banks of telephones which do not contain a text telephone. If a building or facility has no banks of telephones, the directional signage must be provided at the entrance (e.g., in a building directory).

Comment. Several commenters recommended that, in addition to requiring at least one public text telephone in certain buildings and facilities, public pay telephones should be designed to accommodate portable text telephones so that individuals who carry their own devices can use public pay telephones, especially in larger facilities where one may have to walk a considerable distance to find a public text telephone.

Response. A new scoping provision has been added at 4.1.3(17)(d) requiring at least one public pay telephone in each bank of three or more interior public pay telephones to be designed to accommodate a portable text telephone. The public pay telephone must comply with the technical specifications in 4.31.9(2), and be equipped with a shelf on which to place a portable text telephone, an electrical outlet, and a telephone handset cord long enough to reach the shelf for acoustical coupling. Some telephone enclosure companies currently have several models on the

market which comply with these requirements.

Fixed Seating and Tables (4.1.3(18))

Comment. The NPRM asked whether the five percent scoping provision for fixed seating and tables was adequate. Many commenters interpreted the provision as applying to seating in assembly areas or restaurants and stated that the number was too low. Some commenters stated that similar scoping provisions in their states were adequate.

Response. Wheelchair seating spaces in assembly areas and restaurants are addressed in separate provisions. See 4.1.3(19)(a) for assembly areas; and 5.1 for restaurants. The five percent figure has not been changed. Several editorial changes have been made to the provision to be consistent with 4.1.1(3) regarding areas used only by employees as work areas. The term "accessible public or common use areas" has been substituted for "accessible spaces" and the reference to "work surfaces" has been deleted. As clarified, the provision applies to fixed seating and tables in accessible public and common use areas such as study carrels or laboratory stations in a classroom.

Wheelchair Seating Spaces in Assembly Areas (4.1.3(19)(a))

Comment. Individuals with disabilities and their organizations and other commenters recommended that the scoping provisions for wheelchair seating spaces in assembly areas include such spaces for areas with less than 50 seats and generally favored an increase in the number of wheelchair seating spaces. Several commenters, including theater owners, believed that the requirements for wheelchair seating spaces in assembly areas were excessive.

Response. The table in 4.1.3(19)(a) specifying the number of wheelchair seating spaces in assembly areas has been revised in response to the comments. The new scoping provision is generally taken from the California building code. In smaller assembly areas, one wheelchair seating space is required in areas having a seating capacity of 4 to 25, and two wheelchair seating spaces are required in areas having a seating capacity of 26 to 50. The NPRM required no accessible seating in assembly areas with fewer than 50 seats. Unlike the NPRM, the new scoping provision also requires that one percent, but not less than one, of all fixed seats be aisle seats that have either no armrests, or removable or folding armrests on the aisle side of the seat to increase accessibility for wheelchair users who wish to transfer to a fixed seat and individuals with other mobility impairments for whom armrests present an obstacle. These seats must be identified by a sign or marker and a sign must be posted in the ticket office notifying patrons of their availability.

The total number of seating spaces for individuals with mobility impairments is generally the same under the NPRM and the final guidelines. For instance, in an assembly area with a seating capacity of 200, the NPRM required 6 wheelchair seating spaces; and the final guidelines require 4 wheelchair seating spaces and 2 accessible aisle seats. In an assembly area with a seating capacity of 1,000, the NPRM required 20 wheelchair seating spaces; and the final guidelines require 11 wheelchair seating spaces and 10 accessible aisle seats. To address the concerns regarding the number of wheelchair seating spaces required in larger facilities, a paragraph has been added to the appendix explaining that readily removable or folding seating units may be installed in wheelchair seating spaces which may be used by other persons when not needed for wheelchair users or individuals with other mobility impairments. Folding seating units usually consists of two fixed seats that can be easily folded into a fixed center bar to allow for open spaces for wheelchair users when needed.

Assistive Listening Systems (4.1.3(19)(b))

Comment. The NPRM asked whether certain assembly areas with fixed seating should be required to have permanently installed assistive listening systems, and whether other areas should be permitted to have an adequate number of electrical outlets or other supplementary wiring to accommodate portable assistive listening systems. Most commenters who responded to the question favored requiring permanently installed assistive listening systems in assembly areas with fixed seating and permitting the use of portable systems in other areas. For instance, hotels pointed out that larger meeting rooms are frequently subdivided into smaller meeting rooms and a permanently installed assistive listening system may not be usable in such areas. Some commenters recommended that all assistive listening systems should be portable.

Response. The scoping provision for assistive listening systems has been revised. The provision applies to concert and lecture halls, playhouses and movie theaters, meeting rooms, and other assembly areas where audible

communication is integral to use of the space. If such an assembly area (a) accommodates at least 50 persons or has an audioamplification system and (b) has fixed seating, a permanently installed assistive listening system is required. Other assembly areas are permitted to have an adequate number of electrical outlets or other supplementary wiring to accommodate portable assistive listening systems. The requirement assures that individuals with hearing impairments can attend functions in assembly areas with fixed seating without having to give advance notice or disrupt the event to have a portable assistive listening system set up. The requirement also provides for flexibility for smaller assembly areas and rooms and spaces with changeable seating arrangements.

The provision in the NPRM which would have required assistive listening systems to be installed in rooms if they are used regularly as meeting or conference rooms was deleted because it would have covered individual offices which are used for meetings which was not intended.

Comment. Several commenters requested that the scoping provision not be limited to indoor assembly areas and include such facilities as baseball stadiums.

Response. The baseball stadium in Boston has a permanently installed assistive listening system. Since the technology currently exists for providing communication access to such facilities, the scoping provision is not limited to indoor assembly areas.

Comment. Most commenters supported requiring that the minimum number of receivers be equal to four percent of the total number of seats but not less than two. Some commenters believed that the number was excessive and other commenters wanted the number to be increased.

Response. The four percent figure is based on a Bureau of the Census estimate of the number of persons aged 15 and over who have difficulty hearing what is said in a normal conversation with another person, excluding those who cannot hear at all. See Bureau of Census, Disability Functional Limitation and Insurance Coverage, 1984–85. There are other studies which indicate that the numbers may be as high as eight to ten percent. As assistive listening systems become more readily available, it is expected that their usage will increase. The Board intends to monitor this issue and if a need for an increase in the number of receivers is demonstrated, the scoping provision will be revised.

Comment. The NPRM requested information regarding which types of assistive listening systems (induction loop, FM, and infra red) work best in particular environments. Each of the three types of systems received some support for all applications. Many commenters described their personal experiences with particular types of systems. Those who provided extensive information on the advantages and disadvantages of the various systems recommended that a specific type should be selected only after consultation with experts in the field.

Response. The appendix in A4.33.6 has been expanded to provide additional information on the various types of assistive listening systems. The appendix includes a table reprinted from a National Institute of Disability and Rehabilitation Research "Rehab Brief" which shows some of the advantages and disadvantages of each system and typical applications. New York has also adopted technical specifications which may be useful. A pamphlet is available from the Board which lists demonstration centers across the country where technical assistance can be obtained in selecting and installing appropriate systems.

Comment. The NPRM also requested information regarding the need for an assistive listening device at sales and service counters, teller windows, box offices, and information kiosks where a physical barrier separates service personnel and customers. Most commenters favored the provision of an assistive listening device at these places. Those who were opposed to this provision recommended alternative means to address the problem such as training personnel how to communicate effectively with individuals who have hearing impairments.

Response. A provision has been added to the appendix at A7.2(3) recommending that at least one permanently installed assistive listening system be installed at sales and service counters, teller windows, box offices, and information kiosks where a physical barrier separates service personnel and customers.

Automated Teller Machines (4.1.3 (20))

The legislative history of the ADA specifically mentions automatic teller machines (ATMs) as covered by the accessibility requirements. The NPRM included proposed scoping provisions and technical specifications for ATMs. The scoping provisions in the final guidelines have been revised and require that where ATMs are provided, each machine shall comply with 4.34

except where two or more machines are provided at one location, then only one machine shall comply with 4.34. For example, if a large shopping mall has an ATM located at each end of the mall, then each ATM must be accessible. On the other hand, if the ATMs are located adjacent to each other, then only one ATM must be accessible. Comments regarding ATMs and the requirements of the final guidelines are discussed under the technical specifications at 4.34.

Dressing and Fitting Rooms (4.1.3(21))

Comment. The NPRM asked whether the guidelines should include requirements for accessible dressing and fitting rooms. Individuals with disabilities and their organizations supported such requirements. Businesses expressed concern about having sufficient space for accessible dressing and fitting rooms, especially in existing buildings and facilities.

Response. A new scoping provision has been added at 4.1.3(21) for new construction requiring that where dressing and fitting rooms are provided for use by the public or employees, 5 percent, but not less than one, of such rooms for each type of use in each cluster of dressing rooms must be accessible. For instance, in a hospital where dressing rooms are provided for specific treatment or examination rooms, 5 percent, but not less than one, of the dressing rooms provided for each type of treatment or examination rooms must be accessible.

The Board recognizes that in some cases it may be technically infeasible to comply with the scoping provisions for new construction when altering dressing rooms in existing facilities due to space limitations and has included a provision in 4.1.6(3)(h) that requires only one dressing room for each sex on each level to be accessible in alterations where technical infeasibility can be demonstrated. Accessible unisex dressing rooms may be used to meet the requirement in 4.1.6(3)(h) where only unisex dressing rooms are provided.

Technical specifications for accessible dressing rooms are provided in 4.35.

4.1.5   Accessible Buildings: Additions

This section contains the scoping provisions for additions to existing buildings and facilities.

Comment. Several commenters raised questions regarding whether an addition to an existing building is to be treated as new construction or an alteration.

Response. Additions to existing buildings have attributes of both new construction and an alteration. To the extent that a space or element in the addition is newly constructed, each new

space or element must comply with the applicable scoping provisions of 4.1.1 to 4.1.3 for new construction, the applicable technical specifications of 4.2 through 4.35, and the applicable special application sections 5 through 10. For instance, if a restroom is provided in the addition, it must comply with the requirements for new construction. Construction of an addition does not, however, create an obligation to retrofit the entire existing building or facility to meet requirements for new construction. Rather, the addition is to be regarded as an alteration and to the extent that it affects or could affect the usability of or access to an area containing a primary function, the requirements in 4.1.6(2) are triggered with respect to providing an accessible path of travel to the altered area and making the restrooms, telephones, and drinking fountains serving the altered area accessible. For example, if a museum adds a new wing that does not have a separate entrance as part of the addition, an accessible path of travel would have to be provided through the existing building or facility unless it is disproportionate to the overall cost and scope of the addition as determined under criteria established by the Attorney General. The scoping provision in 4.1.5 has been clarified to reflect these requirements.

4.1.6   Accessible Buildings: Alterations

This section contains scoping provisions for alterations.

General (4.1.6(1))

Comment. Some commenters pointed out that the provision in 4.1.6(1)(a) prohibiting any decrease in accessibility when an alteration is undertaken was inconsistent with the provision in 4.1.6(1)(d) [4.1.6(1)(e) in the NPRM] which does not impose any greater requirements in alterations than in new construction.

Response. The provision has been revised to state that no alteration shall be undertaken which decreases or has the affect of decreasing accessibility or usability of a building or facility below the requirements for new construction at the time of the alteration.

Comment. Several businesses expressed concern about minor alterations triggering extensive retrofitting of existing buildings and facilities to meet the requirements for new construction.

Response. The Board wishes to make it clear that minor alterations do not trigger extensive retrofitting of existing buildings. There are three general principles for alterations. First, if any existing element, space, or common area is altered, the altered element, space, or

common area must meet new construction requirements. 4.1.6(1)(b). Second, if alterations to the elements in a space when considered together amount to an alteration of the space, the entire space must meet new construction requirements. 4.1.6(1)(c). Third, if the alteration affects or could affect the usability of or access to an area containing a primary function, the path of travel to the altered area and the restrooms, drinking fountains, and telephones serving the altered area must be made accessible unless it is disproportionate to the overall alterations in terms of cost and scope as determined under criteria established by the Attorney General. 4.1.6(2). This last requirement will be addressed in greater detail in the Department of Justice's final regulations.

There are two general exceptions that apply to alterations. First, compliance with a specific scoping provision or technical specification is not required if it is technically infeasible. 4.1.6(1)(j). As further discussed below, the definition of the term "technically infeasible" has been revised and does not require compliance with new construction requirements where existing structural conditions would require removing or altering a load-bearing member which is an essential part of the structural frame or where existing physical or site constraints prohibit full and strict compliance. Second, the installation of an elevator is not required in an altered building or facility that is less than three stories or has less than 3,000 square feet per story unless the building is a shopping center, a shopping mall, the professional office of a health care provider, or another type of facility determined by the Attorney General. 4.1.6(1)(k). The elevator exception is established by section 303(b) of the ADA and is the same as that contained in the scoping provisions for new construction. As discussed above, if a building or facility is not exempt from the elevator requirement and the requirement for an accessible path of travel is triggered under 4.1.6(2), the installation of an elevator is subject to the disproportionality limitation. However, if an escalator or stair is planned or installed where none existed previously and major structural modifications are necessary for such installation, then an elevator or other vertical means of access must be provided. 4.1.6(1)(f).

The following examples illustrate the application of these principles and exceptions:

1. If a door handle is replaced, the new door handle must comply with

4.13.9 which states that door hardware shall have a shape that is easy to grasp and does not require tight grasping, tight pinching, or turning of the wrist (e.g., lever handles, U-shaped handles). Replacing the door handle does not trigger any other accessibility requirements for the door.

2. A common practice when replacing doors is to install a complete door assembly consisting of the frame and a pre-hung door. In interior light-frame construction (e.g., wood or metal studs), a wider door assembly can be installed without altering a load-bearing structural member which is an essential part of the structural frame. If a complete door assembly is installed in interior light-frame construction and space is available to comply with the clear width and maneuvering clearances specified in 4.13.5 and 4.13.6, those requirements must be met. However, if space is restricted, as in the case of some hotel guest rooms where narrow doorways are defined by bathroom and closet walls, it may be technically infeasible to comply with the clear width or maneuvering clearances specified in 4.13.5 and 4.13.6 due to existing physical constraints.

3. If a parking lot is resurfaced and does not have the number of accessible parking spaces required by 4.1.2(5) or the parking spaces do not comply with 4.6.3, those requirements must be met with unless it is technically infeasible. If the resurfacing does not include regrading, it may be technically infeasible to comply with the requirement in 4.6.3 that accessible parking spaces and access aisles be level with surface slopes not exceeding 1:50 (2%) in all directions due to existing site constraints. If a local zoning or land use code requires the parking lot to have a certain number of parking spaces and providing the number of accessible parking spaces in 4.1.2(5) would result in reducing the total number of parking spaces below that required by the local code, it would be technically infeasible to fully comply with the scoping provision due to site constraints resulting from legitimate requirements of the local code. For instance, if 4.1.2(5) requires five accessible parking spaces to be provided, but the parking lot can only accommodate four accessible parking spaces and still meet the local code requirement for total number of parking spaces, then four accessible parking spaces must be provided.

4. If the water closets, toilet stalls, lavatories and mirrors in a toilet room are all replaced, the new fixtures must comply with the technical specifications in 4.16, 4.17, and 4.19 for those elements.

Since replacing the water closets, toilet stalls, lavatories and mirrors also amounts to an alteration of the toilet room, the entire toilet room must comply with the technical specifications in 4.22 for toilet rooms which include a requirement for the doors to the toilet room to comply with 4.13.

The Board has added provisions to the final guidelines to clarify when accessible routes and accessible entrances are required in alterations to existing buildings and facilities. A provision has been added at 4.1.6(1)(b) that, if the requirements for new construction provide for an element, space, or common area to be on an accessible route, alteration of the element, space, or common area does not trigger the requirement for an accessible route unless the alteration affects the usability of or access to an area containing a primary function in which case an accessible path of travel is required by 4.1.6(2) subject to the disproportionality limitation. For instance, in new construction the scoping provision in 4.1.3(10) requires that drinking fountains be on an accessible route. If a drinking fountain is replaced on the third story of a building that does not have an elevator, installation of a new accessible drinking fountain does not trigger the installation of an elevator.

A provision has also been added to the final guidelines at 4.1.6(1)(h) that, if a planned alteration entails alterations to an entrance, and the building has an accessible entrance, the entrance being altered is not required to comply with the new construction requirements unless the alteration affects the usability of or access to an area containing a primary function in which case an accessible path of travel is required by 4.1.6(2) subject to the disproportionality limitation. If an entrance is altered and is not made accessible, appropriate signage must be provided indicating the location of the nearest accessible entrance. Additional advisory material on alterations to entrances is included in the appendix at A4.1.6(2)(h).

Comment. A few commenters requested that a waiver process be established.

Response. The ADA does not provide for a waiver process. The technical infeasibility and elevator exceptions in 4.1.6(1) (i) and (j) are similar to a waiver in that compliance with specific scoping provisions and technical specifications is not required if certain conditions are met. Special scoping provisions and technical specifications are provided for in the case of some elements and spaces where technical infeasibility exists. See

4.1.6(3). However, the exceptions differ from a waiver in that to obtain a waiver an entity must usually submit documentation to a reviewing authority showing that conditions exist to warrant not complying with a specific scoping provision or technical specification and the reviewing authority must decide whether to grant or deny the waiver. The ADA only provides for review after the fact if a complaint is filed with the Department of Justice or a court. Entities should maintain documentation of conditions warranting an exemption in the event of such review.

Comment. Several commenters questioned why altered elements and spaces must be made accessible if the rest of the building or facility is inaccessible.

Response. Congress recognized that it would be costly to retrofit entire buildings and facilities to be accessible and that it would be more cost effective to incorporate accessibility gradually as elements and spaces are altered. See H. Rept. 101–485, pt. 3, at 60. The scoping provisions are based on the statute and ensure that individuals with disabilities will have access to the goods, services, and employment available in the altered parts of buildings and facilities.

Comment. Several commenters requested that the guidelines specifically address when public text telephones are required in existing buildings and facilities.

If alterations to existing buildings or facilities with less than four interior or exterior public pay telephones would increase the number to four or more public pay telephones with at least one in an interior location, then at least one interior public text telephone must be provided. For instance, if an existing building or facility has one interior and one exterior public pay telephone and two more are added, then at least one interior public text telephone would be required. If one or more interior or exterior public pay telephones in an existing facility with four or more public pay telephones with at least one in an interior location is altered, then at least one interior public text telephone must be provided. For instance, if an existing building or facility has two interior and two exterior public pay telephones and one or more of them is replaced, then at least one interior public text telephone would be required.

Comment. Several commenters requested that areas of rescue assistance not be required in existing buildings and facilities because it would require costly and extensive renovations.

Response. The Board recognizes that providing areas of rescue assistance in existing buildings may require costly and extensive renovations. Pending further study, a provision has been added in 4.1.6(1)(g) stating that the requirements in 4.1.6(9), 4.3.10, and 4.3.11 regarding areas of rescue assistance do not apply to alterations of existing buildings.

Comment. Several commenters requested that hazardous materials abatement and automatic sprinkling retrofitting be added to the list of alterations in 4.1.6(1)(i) (4.1.6(1)(f) in the NPRM) exempt from guidelines.

Response. Alterations which are limited solely to hazardous materials abatement and automatic sprinkling retrofitting and which do not involve changes to any elements or spaces required to be accessible by the guidelines have been added to the list of alterations in 4.1.6(1)(i) exempt from the guidelines.

Comment. A number of commenters requested changes in the definition of the term "technically infeasible." Some commenters requested that in the case of alterations that would require removing or altering a load-bearing member, a distinction should be made between: (a) wood and metal studs or joists used in light-frame construction of interior walls and floors; and (b) concrete, masonry, heavy timber or steel columns, beams, girders and structural slabs. Other commenters requested that a cost factor be included in the definition of "technically infeasible."

Response. The definition of "technically infeasible" has been moved from the definitions in 3.5 to 4.1.6(1)(i). With respect to alterations that would require removing or altering a load-bearing member, the definition has been revised to apply to a load-bearing member which is an essential part of the structural frame. The structural frame is defined in 3.5 as consisting of the columns and the girders, beams, trusses and spandrels having direct connections to the columns, and all other members which are essential to the stability of the building as a whole. This definition would not include wood or metal studs or joists used in light-frame construction of interior walls and floors. With respect to existing physical or site constraints prohibiting full and strict compliance, such constraints can result from legitimate legal requirements (e.g., a right of way agreement preventing construction of a ramp in front of a building).

As for costs, that factor has been taken into account in several places in the scoping provisions for alterations. First, as further discussed above where

requirements for an accessible path of travel, including vertical access by means of an elevator, ramp, or platform lift or wheelchair lift, are triggered by an alteration that affects access to or usability of an area containing a primary function, there is a disproportionality limitation which will be addressed in the Department of Justice's final regulations. See 4.1.6(2). Second, the technical infeasibility exception is designed to limit costs by not requiring the removal or alteration of a load-bearing member which is an essential part of the structural frame and not requiring compliance with new construction requirements where there are existing physical or site constraints. Third, where commenters have pointed out specific new construction requirements which would require costly and extensive renovations to existing buildings and facilities such as those for areas of rescue assistance, the Board has not required them. See 4.1.6(1)(g). Fourth, the installation of elevators is not required in alterations of existing buildings and facilities which are less than three stories or have less than 3,000 square feet per story except for certain types of facilities. See 4.1.6(1)(k).

4.1.6(2)   Alterations To An Area Containing A Primary Function

Comment. A number of commenters requested that the terms "an area containing a primary function;" "path of travel;" and "disproportionate" be defined.

Response. The Department of Justice's final regulations will define and apply these terms.

4.1.6(3)   Special Technical Provisions For Alterations

Comment. A few commenters requested that the application of the special provisions in 4.1.6(3) be clarified. Some commenters objected to allowing a short ramp to be steeper and elevators to have a 48 inch by 48 inch inside car dimension. Other commenters made recommendations for elevator car sizes and alternative provisions that require further study or will be discussed in the technical assistance manual.

Response. The special provisions in 4.1.6(3) contain requirements for ramps, stairs, elevators, doors, toilet facilities, assembly areas, and dressing and fitting rooms that may be used in alterations to existing buildings and facilities when it is technically infeasible to comply with new construction requirements or other specified conditions exist. The Board recognizes that the special provisions for ramps and elevators do not accommodate as many individuals with

disabilities as do the technical specifications in 4.7.2, 4.8.2, and 4.10.9. However, faced with the choice between providing no access or a lesser degree of access to existing buildings and facilities that are altered, the Board has opted for the latter. As noted above, other recommendations have been made for elevator car sizes and alternative provisions that will be studied for future revision of the guidelines or will be discussed in the technical assistance manual.

A new provision has been added at 4.1.6(3)(g) that platform lifts or wheelchair lifts complying with 4.11 and applicable State and local codes are allowed as part of an accessible route in alterations and that the use of lifts is not limited to the conditions specified in the scoping provisions for new construction.

4.1.7   Accessible Buildings: Historic Preservation

This section contains scoping provisions and alternative requirements for alterations to qualified historic buildings and facilities.

Comment. A number of commenters requested that the Board clarify the application of 4.1.7(1) and the procedures under section 106 of the National Historic Preservation Act.

Response: The provision has been revised to clarify that alterations to a qualified historic building or facility shall comply with the scoping provisions for alterations (4.1.6), the applicable technical specifications (4.2 through 4.35), and the applicable special application sections (5 through 10) unless it is determined in accordance with the procedures discussed below that compliance with the requirements for accessible routes (exterior and interior), ramps, entrances, or toilets would threaten or destroy the historic significance of the building or facility in which case the alternative requirements in 4.1.7(3) (4.1.7(2) in the NPRM) may be used. The alternative requirements allow for flexibility to accommodate the national interest in historic preservation.

The definition of a "qualified historic building or facility" has been moved to 4.1.7(1)(b) and retains the UFAS definition as required by section 504(c)(1) of the ADA.

New paragraphs have been added at 4.1.7(2)(a)(i) and (ii) to clarify the procedures under section 106 of the National Historic Preservation Act (16 U.S.C. 470f) and their application to alterations covered by the ADA. Section 106 requires that a Federal agency with jurisdiction over a Federal, federally assisted, or federally licensed undertaking consider the effects of the agency's undertaking on buildings and facilities listed in or eligible for listing in the National Register of Historic Places and give the Advisory Council on Historic Preservation a reasonable opportunity to comment on the undertaking prior to approval of the undertaking. The Advisory Council on Historic Preservation has established a process to implement section 106. See 36 CFR part 800. The section 106 process provides for the Federal agency to consult with the State Historic Preservation Officer established under section 101(b) of the National Historic Preservation Act (16 U.S.C. 470a(b)) whose responsibilities include cooperating with Federal and State agencies, local governments, and organizations and individuals to ensure that historic properties are taken into consideration at all levels of planning and development. The section 106 process encourages the Federal agency and State Historic Preservation Officer to agree on alternatives to avoid or minimize adverse effects on buildings and facilities listed in or eligible for listing in the National Register of Historic Places. The section 106 process does not apply to buildings and facilities that are designated as historic under an appropriate State or local law but are not listed in or eligible for listing in the National Register of Historic Places. For example, the section 106 process applies if the National Park Service leases a federally owned building listed in the National Register of Historic Places to a private entity with permission to renovate the building for use as a bed and breakfast inn or if the Small Business Administration loans funds to a private entity to renovate a building eligible for listing in the National Register of Historic Places for use as a restaurant. Where alterations are undertaken to a qualified historic building or facility that is subject to section 106 of the National Historic Preservation Act, the Federal agency with jurisdiction over the undertaking is responsible for following the section 106 process. If the State Historic Preservation Officer or Advisory Council on Historic Preservation agrees that compliance with the requirements for accessible routes (exterior and interior), ramps, entrances, or toilets would threaten or destroy the historic significance of the building or facility, the alternative requirements may be used.

Comment: Section 504(c)(3) of the ADA requires the Board to establish procedures for determining whether the alternative requirements may be used for qualified historic buildings and

facilities that are not subject to section 106 of the National Historic Preservation Act. The NPRM requested information on what procedures should be followed. The National Park Service, Advisory Council on Historic Preservation, National Conference of State Historic Preservation Officers, and other commenters responsible for historic preservation programs recommended that an entity undertaking alterations to a qualified historic building or facility should consult with the State Historic Preservation Officer whenever the entity believes that compliance with the accessibility requirements would threaten or destroy the historical significance of the building or facility and that the alternative requirements should be used. Individuals with disabilities and their organizations requested that criteria be established for determining whether compliance with the accessibility requirements would threaten or destroy the historical significance of a building or facility and that State and local accessibility officials and organizations representing individuals with disabilities should be involved in the consultation process.

Response: The State Historic Preservation Officer is a key public official in the Federal-State partnership envisioned under the National Historic Preservation Act. Every State currently has a State Historic Preservation Officer approved by the Secretary of the Interior whose responsibilities include advising and assisting Federal and State agencies and local governments in carrying out their historic preservation responsibilities; cooperating with organizations and individuals to ensure that historic properties are taken into consideration at all levels of planning and development; and providing technical assistance relating to Federal and State historic preservation programs. See 16 U.S.C. 470a(b)(3)(E) through (F). The State Historic Preservation Officer is required to have a full-time professional staff in each of the following disciplines: history, archeology, and architectural history. See 36 CFR 61.4(d).

The Board believes that it is consistent with the State Historic Preservation Officer's existing responsibilities under the National Historic Preservation Act to provide for that official to be consulted with whenever an entity undertakes alterations to a qualified historic building or facility that is not subject to the section 106 process and the entity believes that compliance with the accessibility requirements would threaten or destroy the historical

significance of the building or facility and that the alternative requirements should be used. An entity may not unilaterally decide to use the alternative requirements. Rather, if an entity wants to use the alternative requirements, the entity must consult with the State Historic Preservation Officer and if that official agrees that compliance with the accessibility requirements would threaten or destroy the historic significance of the building or facility, then the alternative requirements may be used. A new paragraph has been added at 4.1.7(2)(b) for this purpose.

The Board wishes to emphasize that when applying this provision, the inquiry should focus on whether compliance with the accessibility requirements would threaten or destroy the characteristics of a building or facility that make it eligible for listing in the National Register of Historic Places or designation as historic under an appropriate State or local law. The National Park Service and Advisory Council on Historic Preservation have had considerable experience with making accessible alterations to qualified historic buildings and facilities and have expressed interest in working with the Board to develop technical guidance and procedures to assist State Historic Preservation Officers in carrying out their consultation responsibilities and to ensure consistent and uniform application of the provision at the State and local level.

The National Conference of State Historic Preservation Officers reported that some State historic preservation programs have established good working relationships with their State and local accessibility officials and that the guidelines should encourage these relationships. The section 106 process also provides for involving other interested parties in the consultation process. See 36 CFR 800.5(e)(1). A new paragraph has been added at 4.1.7(2)(c) recommending that State and local accessibility officials, and individuals with disabilities and their organizations be involved in the consultation process.

Section 101(c)(1) of the National Historic Preservation Act (16 U.S.C. 407a(c)(1)) allows for responsibilities to be delegated to a local government historic preservation program certified by the State Historic Preservation Officer and the Secretary of the Interior. To be certified, a local government must meet certain minimum requirements, including professional expertise in architectural history. See 36 CFR 61.5. There are about 600 certified local governments. A new paragraph has been added at 4.1.7(2)(d) to allow the

State Historic Preservation Officer to delegate consultation responsibilities for purposes of this section to a certified local government.

Comment: Commenters generally expressed support for using the alternative requirements in 4.1.7(3) (4.1.7(2) in the NPRM) in those cases were accessibility cannot be achieved without threatening or destroying the historical significance of a building or facility. The National Park Service noted that based on its experience accessibility can be achieved in most cases with some alteration of non-significant features. The National Park Service, Advisory Council on Historic Preservation, National Trust for Historic Preservation, and other commenters with historic preservation responsibilites expressed a need for greater flexibility in providing accessibility to qualified historic buildings and facilities. These commenters expressed concern that it may be technically infeasible to comply with specific accessibility requirements in the case of some buildings and facilities. These commenters also recommended that an exception be established for a small group of buildings and facilities such as a historic house museum that has only one entrance and where modifying the doorway or cutting out a window to create an accessible entrance would destroy the characteristics that make the building eligible for listing on the National Register of Historic Places.

Response: As stated in 4.1.7(1)(a), the provisions of 4.1.6 relating to alterations apply to qualified historic buildings and facilities. If it is technically infeasible to comply with a specific accessibility requirement, the other elements and features of the building or facility that are being altered and can be made accessible must be made accessible within the scope of the alteration. See 4.1.6(1)(g). Flexibility is also allowed under 2.2 which permits alternative designs and technologies to be used on a case-by-case basis where they will provide substantially equivalent or greater access to and usability of a building or facility. As for those buildings and facilities where it may not be possible to achieve compliance with the alternative requirements without destroying the historic significance of the building, the Board plans to consult with the National Park Service and Advisory Council on Historic Preservation about this issue and propose an exception in the next phase of rulemaking. An exception is reserved under 4.1.7(1)(a) for this purpose.

Comment: With respect to the exception in 4.1.7(3)(b) (4.1.7(2)(b) in the NPRM) which permits access by means of an entrance not generally used by the public if a public entrance cannot be made accessible provided that the alternative entrance is unlocked and directional signage is provided, the NPRM asked how security concerns can be addressed and convenient and independent access facilitated at the same time. Most persons who responded to the question favored retaining the requirement that the alternative entrance be unlocked and independently operable, and recommended that a notification system also be provided.

Response: The requirement for the alternative entrance to be unlocked has been retained and a new requirement has been added for a notification system to be provided. A provision has also been added permitting use of a remote monitoring system where security is a concern. If a remote monitoring system is used, the alternative entrance must remain unlocked.

4.2 through 4.35 Technical Specifications

Sections 4.2 through 4.35 contain the technical specifications for elements and spaces required to be accessible by the scoping provisions (4.1 through 4.1.7) and special application sections (5 through 10). The technical specifications are the same as the 1980 version of ANSI A117.1 standard, except as noted in the text of italics.[13]

4.2 Space Allowances and Reach Ranges

Comment. Several commenters recommended that the technical specifications for clear floor turning, and maneuvering spaces should be increased for individuals who use power wheelchairs and three wheeled scooters. A few commenters also recommended changes to the side reach ranges.

Response. Additional research is needed regarding space allowances and reach ranges for individuals who use power wheelchairs and three wheeled scooters. No change has been made in the guidelines.

4.3 Accessible Route

Comment. A number of commenters recommended that skywalks and tunnels be specifically included as part of accessible routes.

[13] The ANSI A117.1 standard is reprinted with permission from the American National Standards Institute. Copies of the ANSI A117.1 standard may be purchased from the American National Standards Institute at 1430 Broadway, New York, NY 10016.

Response. Since skywalks and tunnels can be part of an accessible route, they have been specifically included in 4.3.1.

Comment. The NPRM requested comments on various options for language to include in 4.3.2 regarding travel distances between points on an accessible route. Most commenters from each category who responded to the question favored stating that the accessible route shall, to the maximum extent feasible, coincide with the route for the general public.

Response. A requirement has been added to 4.3.2 that the accessible route shall, to the maximum extent feasible, coincide with the route for the general public. Since the route provided for the general public is usually the shortest and most direct route, the requirement will result in that route being made accessible in most cases.

Comment. Several commenters stated that the minimum widths for accessible routes and passing space requirements were not adequate and should be increased. No research or supportive data was provided.

Response. No changes have been made.

4.3.11 Areas of Rescue Assistance

Comment. Many commenters favored including technical specifications for areas of rescue assistance in the guidelines. Commenters, including the National Fire Protection Association (NFPA), submitted various recommendations for changes to the technical specifications, including permitting the use of exit stairway landings with a standpipe and areas having direct access to elevators specifically designed for emergency evacuation purposes. Several commenters recommended that the 1991 Uniform Building Code provisions for areas of rescue assistance be adopted.

Response. The 1991 Uniform Building Code provisions for areas of rescue assistance have been modified and incorporated in 4.3.11 since they represent the most current and comprehensive provisions on the subject. See 1991 Uniform Building Code, chapter 31, section 3104(b). The final guidelines permit seven different areas meeting certain conditions to be used as areas of rescue assistance. The final guidelines do not restrict the use of exit stairway landings with standpipes because the first duty of firefighters is to assist in the evacuation of individuals from the building or facility before undertaking the protection of property. The final guidelines also permit use of elevator lobbies with direct access to an emergency evacuation elevator when elevator shafts and adjacent lobbies are pressurized as required for smokeproof enclosures by local regulations and when complying with certain other requirements. The Uniform Building Code provisions for size, stairway width, two-way communication and signage have also been adopted with a clarification that the communication system must include both visual and audible signals.

4.4 Protruding Objects

Comment. The NPRM asked questions regarding the adequacy of the technical specifications for protruding objects. About one-fourth of the commenters believed that they were adequate. The other commenters made over 30 different suggestions for changes.

Response. No changes have been made. The comments suggest that additional research is needed in this area.

4.5 Ground and Floor Surfaces

Comment. The NPRM asked whether a quantitative value should be assigned for slip resistance of ground and floor surfaces. Although there was general support for the concept, commenters presented information on a variety of issues, including the variability of measurement techniques and the likelihood of obtaining different values; lack of consensus regarding appropriate testing methods; and manufacturers certification of products.

Response. Recommended values for slip resistant surfaces on accessible routes and ramps have been included in the appendix at A 4.5.1. Many common building materials suitable for flooring are now labelled with information on the static coefficient of friction. Although it may not be possible to compare one product directly with another, or to guarantee a constant measure, builders and designers are encouraged to specify materials with appropriate values. As more products include information on slip resistance, improved uniformity in measurement and specification is likely.

Comment. The greenhouse industry raised questions about the coverage of gravel pathways in greenhouses.

Response. If a greenhouse is used only as an employee work area, the guidelines only require that the work area be designed and constructed so that individuals with disabilities can approach, enter, and exit the area. See 4.1.1(3) Thus, ground and floor surfaces within the greenhouse are not required to comply with 4.5 where the facility is used only as an employee work area. On the other hand, if the greenhouse is also used for retail sales purposes, the

facility must be designed and constructed to be accessible, including having an accessible route which has a ground or floor surface that complies with 4.5. Gravel is generally used for drainage under plant beds and walkways can be made of asphalt or concrete. Even where walkway drainage is needed, there are a variety of methods for providing firm, stable, and slip resistant surfaces.

Comment. A number of comments were received on the technical specifications for carpets in 4.5.3. Some commenters expressed concern about the 1/2 inch maximum pile height and recommended that it should not apply to carpeting off an accessible route. Other commenters recommended that performance requirements should be developed for carpets with pile height higher than 1/2 inch.

Response. The technical specifications for carpets in 4.5.3 are taken directly from the ANSI A117.1 standard. The requirements only apply to ground and floor surfaces along accessible routes and in accessible rooms and spaces, including public use and common use areas. If an area is used only as an employee work area, the ground and floor surfaces within the work area are not required to comply with 4.5, consistent with the provision in 4.1.1(3) that requires the work area to be designed and constructed so that individuals with disabilities can approach, enter, and exit the area. Additional advisory material on carpets is included in the appendix at A4.5.3.

4.6 Parking and Passenger Loading Zones [14]

Comment. Several commenters requested that the requirements regarding the location of accessible parking spaces be clarified. Some commenters recommended that a maximum distance such as 200 feet be specified between accessible parking spaces and accessible entrances.

Response. The technical specifications in 4.6.2 have been revised based on the proposed BCMC scoping provisions and provide that accessible parking spaces serving a particular building must be located on the shortest accessible route of travel from adjacent parking to an accessible entrance. In parking facilities that do not serve a particular building, the accessible parking spaces must be located on the shortest accessible route of travel to an

[14] As discussed under the scoping provisions for parking in 4.1.2(5), the final guidelines include requirements for van accessible parking spaces and the technical specifications in 4.6.4 and 4.6.5 relating to vans have been modified.

accessible pedestrian entrance of the parking facility. In buildings with multiple accessible entrances with adjacent parking, accessible parking spaces must be dispersed and located closest to the accessible entrances. For instance, at a shopping mall with several accessible entrances or a strip shopping center where each separate tenancy is required to have an accessible entrance, the accessible parking spaces would be dispersed and located closest to the accessible entrances.

A maximum distance has not been included in the guidelines because the requirement that accessible parking spaces be located on the shortest accessible route of travel to an accessible entrance will in most cases result in the spaces being located as close as practical to the nearest accessible entrance. Specifying a maximum distance such as 200 feet could result in the provision being misinterpreted as requiring that the spaces be within 200 feet but not necessarily located closest to an accessible entrance.

Comment. Several commenters from the parking industry questioned the requirement in 4.6.3 that accessible parking spaces and adjacent access aisles must be level with surface slopes not exceeding 1:50 (2%) in all directions. For instance, the National Parking Association (NPA) noted that paved surfaces must have a designed slope of at least 1:100 (1%) to provide drainage and that structural systems frequently used in parking structures have cambered elements where the member must be sloped more than 2% to get a 1% actual slope at the high end of element.

Response. The requirement in 4.6.3 for a level surface with slopes not exceeding 1:50 (2%) applies only to accessible parking spaces and adjacent access aisles and not to the entire floor area of the parking facility. A level surface is necessary at accessible parking spaces and adjacent access aisles to enable individuals who use wheelchairs to safely transfer to and from a vehicle and to permit the deployment of lifts from vans. As the NPA's comment recognizes, it is possible to achieve an actual 1% slope at parts of the floor area of the parking facility. When planned for in the early design phase, it is possible to achieve a level surface with a slope not exceeding 1:50 (2%) at the accessible spaces and adjacent access aisles.

Comment. Several commenters recommended additional requirements for access aisles, including location of curb ramps and striping or otherwise designating access aisles.

Response. Figure 9 shows that the access aisle must be demarcated (a wide parking space alone is not in compliance) and that the connection to the accessible route is at the front of the aisle. Additional information has been included in the appendix on access aisles. The access aisle must be connected to an accessible route to the appropriate accessible entrance of a building a facility. The access aisle must either blend with the accessible route or have a curb ramp complying with 4.7. The curb ramp opening must be located within the boundaries of the access aisle, and not the parking space, and the curb ramp cannot project into the aisle. The required dimensions of the access aisle cannot be restricted by planters, curbs, or wheel stops.

4.7 Curb Ramps

Few comments were received on the technical specifications for curb ramps in 4.7 and they did not warrant any changes. Some comments concerned wayfinding for persons with visual impairments and detectable warnings at curb ramps which are addressed under 4.29.

4.8 Ramps

Comment. The NPRM asked whether the technical specification in 4.8.2 requiring a maximum 1:12 slope for ramps in new construction should be changed. Most persons in each category who responded to the question favored retaining the maximum 1:12 ramp slope. Those commenters who recommended a change preferred ramp slopes between 1:16 and 1:20.

Response. The technical specification in 4.8.2 has not been changed. However, information has been added in the appendix at A4.8.2 explaining that the ability to manage an incline is related to both its slope and its length. Wheelchair users with disabilities affecting their arms or with low stamina have serious difficulty managing inclines. Many wheelchair users, for instance, cannot manage a slope of 1:12 for 30 feet. Most wheelchair users and people with mobility impairments who are ambulatory can manage a slope of 1:16. For these reasons, ramp slopes between 1:16 and 1:20 are preferred. The technical specifications in 4.8.4 have also been revised to clarify that a level landing is required at the top of each ramp and each ramp run. A statement has been added to the appendix at A4.8.4 explaining that level landings are essential toward maintaining an aggregate slope that complies with the guidelines. A ramp landing that is not

level can cause individuals using wheelchairs to tip backward or bottom out when the ramp is approached.

Comment. Several commenters recommended changes to the technical specifications for handrails in 4.8.5, including making the height ranges consistent with the model codes and not requiring handrails on ramps adjacent to seating in assembly areas.

Response. The height ranges for handrails in 4.8.5(5) has been changed from "between 30 inches and 34 inches" to "between 34 inches and 38 inches" to be consistent with the model codes. A similar change has been made to the technical specifications for handrails on stairs in 4.9.4. A provision has also been added to 4.8.5 clarifying that handrails are not required on ramps adjacent to seating in assembly areas.

Comment. A number of commenters recommended that additional railings or higher edge protection be provided for persons with visual impairments.

Response. These recommendations will be studied for future revisions of the guidelines.

4.9 Stairs

Comment. Several commenters recommended that open risers should be permitted on stairs under certain conditions such as where ventilation is critical or on monumental and decorative stairs.

Response. The prohibition against open risers in 4.9.2 applies only to stairs covered by the scoping provision in 4.1.3(4). That provision requires that interior and exterior stairs connecting levels that are not connected by an elevator must comply with 4.9. Thus, open risers may be used on stairs which connect levels also served by an elevator or other accessible means of vertical access.

Comment. Several commenters recommended that steps should have contrasting nosings or tread markings. Some commenters also recommend that the nosing projection should be reduced from 1½ inches to ½ inch maximum.

Response. The Board is not aware of any research that supports these recommendations. There is some controversy over whether each step should have the contrast nosing or only the top and bottom step of each stair. The Board is aware that the February 1991 draft revisions to the ANSI A117.1 standard proposed to add a technical specification for tread markings on stairs. Pending further research or action by the ANSI A117 Committee, the Board is not inclined to include this provision in the guidelines.

Comment. Commenters made several recommendations for changes to the

technical specifications for handrails in 4.9.4, including making the height ranges consistent with the model codes; permitting the 1½ inch clearance between handrails and the wall to be a minimum; and adopting a provision from the California code on handrail extensions. Some commenters also presented detailed comments regarding wayfinding problems when persons who are visually impaired encounter diagonal or circular stairs.

Response. The height range for handrails in 4.9.4(5) has been changed from "between 30 inches and 34 inches" to "between 34 inches and 38 inches" to be consistent with the model codes. A similar change has been made to the technical specifications for handrails on ramps in 4.8.5. The Board has retained the 1½ inch clearance between the handrails and the wall as an absolute. As explained in the appendix at A4.26.1, many people brace their forearms between supports and walls to give them more leverage and stability in maintaining balance. The 1½ inch clearance is a safety clearance to prevent injuries from arms slipping through the openings. It also provides adequate gripping room. The other recommendations require further study.

Comment. A number of comments were received raising safety concerns about the use of the raised truncated domes as detectable warnings at stairs. These comments are further discussed under 4.29.

Response. For the reasons explained under 4.29, the requirement in 4.9.5 for detectable warnings at stairs has been reserved until further research is conducted regarding the use of raised truncated domes as a detectable warning at stairs.

4.10 Elevators

Comment. Several commenters recommended that the February 1991 draft revisions to the ANSI A117.1 standard be adopted. Some commenters also recommended that references to the elevator safety code be updated.

Response. The February 1991 draft revisions to the ANSI A117.1 standard proposed to establish separate technical specifications for new and existing elevators. The Board believes that it is best to await futher action by the ANSI A117 Committee in this area. In the meantime, the references to the elevator safety code in 4.10.1, 4.10.6, and 4.10.14 have been updated to the current code, ASME A17.1–1990. The reference to platform lifts or wheelchair lifts has also been deleted from 4.10.1 in light of the revised scoping provisions for those devices in 4.1.3(5) and 4.1.6(3)(g).

Comment. Commenters generally supported the requirement for braille characters on hoistway entrances, control panels, and emergency communication systems. Several commenters requested that the technical specifications in 4.10.5, 4.10.12, and 4.10.14 be clarified to specify that raised characters must be accompanied by braille. Some commenters requested that the reference to the use of recessed letters or symbols in 4.10.14 for identifying emergency communication systems be deleted. A number of commenters recommended that automatic verbal announcements of floor stops be required in place of audible signals.

Response. The NPRM provided in 4.10.5, 4.10.12, and 4.10.14 that hoistway entrances, control panels, and emergency communication systems have raised characters complying with 4.30.4. That provision provided for raised characters to be accompanied by braille. The final guidelines have been clarified by including the requirement for brailled characters in 4.10.5, 4.10.12, and 4.10.14. The technical specifications in 4.30.4 do not permit the use of recessed letters. To be consistent with that provision, the reference to recessed letters or symbols in 4.10.14 for identifying emergency communication systems has been deleted.

The Board recognizes that automatic verbal announcements of floor stops is preferred by individuals with visual impairments. The technical specifications in 4.10.13 permit their use in place of audible signals.

Comment. A number of commenters recommended that the ANSI A117.1—1986 standard for control panel height should be adopted in place of the NPRM.

Response. The NPRM provided in 4.10.12(3) that all floor buttons on elevator control panels be no higher than 48 inches, unless there is a substantial increase in cost, in which case the maximum mounting height may be increased to 54 inches. Commenters questioned what constitutes a "substantial increase in cost" and pointed out that the ANSI A117.1–1986 standard provides for greater flexibility by requiring all floor buttons to be no higher than 54 inches above the floor for side approach and 48 inches for front approach. The final guidelines adopt the ANSI A117.1–1986 standard for control panel height in 4.10.12(3).

Comment. A number of commenters requested additional guidance on the technical specification in 4.10.14 for an emergency two-way communication system.

Response. Additional information has been included in the appendix at A4.10.14 on emergency two-way communication systems. Such systems should ideally provide both voice and visual display intercommunication so that persons with visual impairments and persons with speech and hearing impairments can receive information regarding the status of a rescue. A voice intercommunication system cannot be the only means of communication because it is not accessible to persons with speech and hearing impairments. While a voice intercommunication system is not required, at a minimum, the system must provide both an audio and visual indication, such as a recorded message and flashing light, to announce that a rescue is on the way.

4.11   Platform Lifts/Wheelchair Lifts

Comment. Most of the comments received on platform lifts or wheelchair lifts were in response to questions in the NPRM regarding scoping provisions which are discussed under 4.1.3(5). Commenters from the lift industry recommended that the technical specifications should reference current safety standards. Individuals with disabilities and their organizations recommended that the technical specifications should specifically provide for independent operation.

Response. The technical specifications in 4.11.2 have been revised to reference the current safety standard, ASME A17.1–1990, part XX. The scoping provisions in 4.1.3(5) Exception 4 also require that platform lifts or wheelchair lifts comply with applicable state or local codes. The technical specification in 4.11.3 has also been revised in response to comments regarding independent operation to specifically require the platform lifts or wheelchair lifts provide for unassisted operation. This requirement does not preclude the use of a key to operate a lift as long as the key is readily available and allows for unassisted operation. The appendix in A4.11 has also been revised to provide more up-to-date information on platform lifts or wheelchair lifts.

Comment. Commenters from the lift industry requested that an exception be established to permit the use of inclined lifts with a 30 inch by 48 inch platform size in stairwells with space limitations.

Response. Inclined lifts are required to comply with the technical specifications in 4.2.4 for clear floor space which provides for a minimum clear space of 30 inches by 48 inches to accommodate a wheelchair user. The Board is aware that this space will not accommodate some powered wheelchairs or three

wheeled scooters which are increasing in popularity, especially among older people. The Board does not believe that any exceptions should be established permitting the use of shorter platform lifts or wheelchair lifts.

4.12   Windows

Comment. The NPRM proposed to adopt the ANSI A117.1 standard for windows which provides for a maximum 5 pounds of force (lbf.) to open operable windows and for locks, cranks, and other hardware to comply with the technical specifications for controls and operating mechanisms, including reach ranges for forward or side approaches. A number of commenters expressed concern that the 5 lbf. maximum force requirement is not currently achievable.

Response. The technical specifications for windows have been reserved in the final guidelines and information from the ANSI A117.1 standard has been placed in the appendix at A4.12.1 and A4.12.2. When the Board issued MGRAD in 1982, it reserved the technical specifications for windows pending further study or experience with the ANSI A117.1 standard. See 47 FR 33862. (August 4, 1982). The Board subsequently sponsored a research project on hand anthropometrics which studied the capabilities of selected individuals with disabilities to operate mechanisms and building components. The findings from the research project suggested design criteria for window opening hardware and indicated appropriate operable forces based on specific types of hardware that were compatible with the ANSI A117.1 standard. Based on the results of the research project, Board adopted the ANSI A117.1 standard when it revised MGRAD in 1989. See 36 CFR 1190.31(j), 54 FR 5434 (February 3, 1989). Information obtained during the current rulemaking revealed that the existing industry standards for operable windows are 25 lbf. for sliding windows and 45 lbf. for double hung windows and that windows meeting the ANSI A117.1 standard are not commonly available for use in heavy construction. The Board needs additional information about existing products and technologies before it can adopt final technical specifications for windows.

4.13   Doors

Comment. Commenters made individual recommendations for changes or clarifications to the technical specifications for doors in 4.13 and the accompanying figures. For instance, clarification was requested regarding whether all or part of the clear space on the latch side of the door in figure 25(a) can be provided by other accessible space such as an open space for hanging clothes in a hotel guestroom.

Response. Two minor changes have been included in the technical specifications for door hardware in 4.13.9. First, the sentence in the NPRM referring to doors in dwelling units has been deleted since it was not consistent with the requirements for doors in accessible units in transient lodging in 9.2.2(3) which requires all doors designed to allow passage into and within all accessible sleeping rooms and units to comply with 4.13. Second, the sentence in the NPRM referring to doors to hazardous areas has been deleted because the technical specifications in 4.29.3 for detectable warnings on doors to hazardous areas have been reserved. An additional change has been made to 4.13.6 to label the exemption in the last sentence of that technical specification as an "exception."

With regard to figure 25(a), the guidelines do not preclude other accessible space from being used to provide the required clearance on the latch side of the door as long as the specified dimensions are met and other uses of the space do not interfere with or intrude upon the clearance required by a wheelchair user or crutch user to reach and open the door or present other barriers not allowed in the guidelines. For example, an open rack mounted on the wall in such a way so as to provide clearance for a wheelchair user or crutch user could be a protruding object. An enclosed closet area would not likely permit adequate maneuvering space.

4.14   Entrances

All the comments on entrances concerned the scoping provision and are discussed under 4.1.3(8). No changes have been made to the technical specifications.

4.15   Drinking Fountains and Water Coolers

Comment. Commenters made individual recommendations for changes or clarifications to the technical specifications for drinking fountains and water coolers in 4.15. For instance, clarification was requested regarding the spout location on a drinking fountain with a round or oval bowl.

Response. A sentence has been added to the technical specification for spout location in 4.15.3 to clairfy that on a drinking fountain with a round or oval bowl, the spout must be positioned so the flow of water is within 3 inches of the front edge of the fountain. The sentence in appendix at A4.15.2 has also been clairified that two drinking

fountains, mounted side by side or on a single post, are usable by individuals with disabilities and people who find it difficult to bend over.

4.16   Water Closets

Comment. Commenters made individual recommendations for changes or clarifications to the technical specifications for water closets in 4.16 and accompanying figures. For instance, clarification was requested regarding the dimensions of the grab bar behind the water closet in figure 29(a) and the location of the lavatory in figure 28.

Response. A sentence has been added to the technical specifications in 4.16.4 to clarify that the grab bar behind the water closet must be 36 inches minimum. The grab bar dimensions have also been clarified in figure 29(a). Additional information has been provided in the appendix at A4.22 regarding figure 28 and the placement of the lavatory. The dotted lines in figure 28 designate the minimum clear floor space, depending on the direction of approach, required for wheelchair users to transfer onto the water closet. The dimensions of 48 inches and 60 inches, respectively, correspond to the space required for wheelchair users to perform a diagonal approach transfer and side approach transfer. See Fig. A6 (a) and (b). Placement of the lavatory to the immediate side of the water closet will preclude use of the side approach transfer. To accommodate the side approach transfer, the space adjacent to the water closet must remain clear of obstruction for 42 inches from the center line of the toilet and the lavatory must not be located within this space. A turning circle or T-turn, the clear floor space of the lavatory, and maneuvering space at the door must be considered when determining the possible wall location. See Fig. 3, 25 and 32.

4.17   Toilet Stalls

Comment. The NPRM presented two approaches for accommodating the needs of persons with mobility impairments who are ambulatory with respect to use of toilet stalls: (a) provide for moveable grab bar in the 60 inch wide standard stall; or (b) provide for a 36 inch wide alternate stall or a conventional, non-accessible stall equipped with dual parallel grab bars in addition to the 60 inch standard stall. Most persons in each category who commented on the two approaches opposed the use of moveable grab bars and supported the provisions of a 36 inch wide alternate stall with dual grab bars in addition to the 60 inch wide standard stall. Some commenters questioned why the 36 inch or 48 inch

alternate stalls are only permitted in alterations where the provision of a 60 inch wide standard stall is technically infeasible.

Response. The guidelines require use of the 60 inch wide standard stall unless it is technically infeasible in alterations because that stall provides clear floor space and grab bars to enable wheelchair users to perform a side approach transfer or diagonal approach transfer from a wheelchair to the toilet. See Fig. A6 (a) and (b). Although many wheelchair users are unable to use either alternate stall, persons with mobility impairments who are ambulatory can use them. Many of those persons find it more convenient to use the two parallel grab bars in the 36 inch wide alternate stall. Based on the comments, a provision has been added to the technical specifications for toilet rooms in 4.22.4 requiring that a 36 inch wide alternate stall with parallel grab bars be provided in addition to the 60 inch wide standard stall where six or more toilet stalls are provided. Since the stall is primarily intended for use by persons with mobility impairments who are ambulatory rather than wheelchair users, the length of the stall could be conventional. The door, however, must swing outward to ensure a usable space by persons with mobility impairments who are ambulatory.

Comment. Several commenters recommended that the width dimensions in figure 30 (a) and (b) should be labeled as minimum. A number of commenters requested that the requirements for hardware on toilet stall doors be clarified.

Response. The width dimensions in figure 30 (a) and (b) have been labeled as minimum. The technical specification in 4.19.5 has been clarified that toilet stall doors including hardware, must comply with 4.13. That provision requires in relevant part at 4.13.9 that handles, pulls, latches, locks, and other operating devices on accessible doors must have a shape that is easy to grasp with one hand and does not require tight grasping, tight pinching, or twisting of the wrist to operate.

4.18   Urinals

Few comments were received on the technical specifications for urinals in 4.18 and they did not warrant any changes.

4.19   Lavatories and Mirrors

Comment. Commenters made individual recommendations for changes or clarifications to the technical specification for lavatories and mirrors in 4.19. For instance, it was pointed out that hot water and drain pipes under lavatories can be configured near the back wall so as to prevent contact but the technical specifications only allowed insulation for protection.

Response. The technical specifications for exposed pipes and surfaces in 4.19.4 have been revised to require that hot water and drain pipes under lavatories be insulated or otherwise configured to protect against contact.

4.20 Bathtubs

Comment. Commenters made individual recommendations for changes or clarifications to the technical specifications for bathtubs in 4.20. For instance, clarification was requested that the lavatory in figure 33 must provide clear space under it to reach the bathtub control area and that the shower spray unit required by 4.20.6 can be used both as a fixed shower head and as a hand-held shower.

Response. The technical specifications for lavatories in 4.19.2 and 4.19.3 require that a clearance of at least 29 inches be provided from the floor to the bottom of the apron of the lavatory and that a clear floor space of 30 inches by 48 inches be provided in front of the lavatory. The technical specifications in 4.20.6 has been clarified to provide that the shower spray unit can be used both as a fixed shower head and as a hand-held shower.

Comment. The NPRM asked whether a vertical grab bar should be provided in addition to the dual horizontal grab bars required by 4.20.4. Most persons in each category who responded to the question favored the provision of a vertical grab bar. However, the commenters made differing recommendations regarding the location and size of the vertical grab bar.

Response. The location and size of the vertical grab bar requires further study before it can be specified.

4.21 Shower Stalls

Comment. As further discussed under 9.1.2, the final guidelines require that hotels with 50 or more sleeping rooms or suites must provide a certain number of sleeping rooms or suites that include a 30 inch by 60 inch or 36 inch by 60 inch roll-in shower as illustrated in figure 57 (a) and (b). The NPRM asked several questions regarding the design of the roll-in shower. Most persons from each category who responded to the question favored: (a) including a fold-up seat in the shower; (b) requiring the seat to be slip-resistant; (c) allowing the shower head and controls to be located in the center of the long wall of the shower;

and (d) providing two mounting hooks for the shower spray unit.

Response. The technical specifications for seats in 4.21.3 have been revised to add a provision for a fold-up seat in the 30 inch by 60 inch roll-in shower required for hotels. The seat must be mounted on the wall adjacent to the controls or shower as shown in figure 57. A requirement has not been included for the seat to be slip-resistant pending further study. A note has been added to figure 37(b) allowing the shower head to be located on the long wall or on either side wall. A requirement has not been included for two mounting hooks pending further study of mounting heights. However, the technical specification in 4.20.6 has been clarified to provide that the shower spray unit must be useable both as a fixed shower head and as a hand-held shower.

Comment. One commenter pointed out that the American Society of Testing and Materials (ASTM) and the Consumer Product Safety Commission have developed slip resistant standards for shower stalls. Another commenter submitted data showing that shower stall drains should be located in a corner to avoid the potential hazards of slipping on a sloping surface and to provide an even surface for portable shower seats.

Response. These matters will be further studied for future revisions of the guidelines.

4.22 Toilet Rooms

Comment. As further discussed under 4.17, most persons who responded to questions in the NPRM regarding accommodating the needs of persons with mobility impairments who are ambulatory with respect to use of toilet stalls favored the provision of a 36 inch wide alternate stall with dual grab bars in addition to the 60 inch wide standard stall.

Response. A provision has been added to the technical specifications for toilet rooms in 4.22.4 requiring that a 36 inch wide alternate stall with parallel grab bars be provided in addition to the 60 inch wide standard stall where six or more toilet stalls are provided. Additional information on the design of this stall is provided in the appendix at A4.17.3 and is discussed under 4.17.

Comment. Some commenters recommended that accessible "unisex" toilet rooms are preferred by some wheelchair users, especially those who may be assisted by another person. Information on the design of accessible "unisex" toilet rooms has been included in the

appendix at A4.22.3. The appendix recommends that consideration be given to providing accessible "unisex" toilet rooms in new construction, in addition to providing the required accessible toilet stalls in other rest rooms. The appendix also points out that accessible "unisex" toilet rooms are permitted in alterations where it is technically infeasible to make existing toilet rooms accessible.

4.23 Bathrooms, Bathing Facilities, and Shower Rooms

Comment. Commenters made individual recommendations for changes to the technical specifications for bathrooms, bathing facilities, and shower rooms. For instance, it was recommended that group showers in locker rooms be addressed.

Response. Group showers will be more fully addressed in future revisions of the guidelines. The technical specifications for the placement of controls and the shower head in roll-in showers can be used in a corner of a group shower to provide access.

4.24 Sinks

Few comments were received on the technical specifications for sinks in 4.24 and they did not warrant any changes. To be consistent with the change made to technical specifications for lavatories in 4.19, 4.24.6 has been revised to require that hot water and drain pipes under sinks be insulated or otherwise configured to protect against contact.

4.25 Storage

Comment. Commenters made individual recommendations for changes or clarifications to the technical specifications for storage in 4.25. For instance, it was requested that the height and depth for closet rods and shelves be clarified.

Response. The technical specifications in 4.25.3 for the height and depth of closet rods and shelves have been clarified. Accessible storage must be within the reach ranges in 4.2.5 or 4.2.6 for a forward approach (Fig. 5) or a side approach (Fig. 6). For a side approach where the distance from the wheelchair to the clothes rod or shelves does not exceed 10 inches, the height of the clothes rod canot exceed 54 inches and shelves must be provided between 9 inches and 54 inches. In reach-in closets without accessible doors where the distance from the wheelchair to the clothes rod or shelves exceeds 10 inches, but is less than 21 inches, the height of the clothes rod cannot exceed 48 inches and shelves must be provided between 9 inches and 48 inches. These dimensions are shown in figures 38 (a) and (b). An additional closet rod or shelves may be provided outside the specified dimensions.

4.26 Handrails, Grab Bars, and Tub and Shower Seats

Few comments were received on the technical specifications for handrails and grab bars in 4.26 and they did not warrant any changes.

4.27 Controls and Operating Mechanisms

Comment. Several commenters asked whether controls and operating mechanisms that are not normally intended for public use must comply with the technical specifications in 4.27.

Response. An exception has been added to the technical specifications at 4.27.3 which provides that the requirements do not apply where the use of special equipment dictates otherwise or where electrical and communications systems receptacles are not normally intended for use by building occupants. For instance, electrical receptacles installed specifically for wall-mounted clocks and refrigerators or microwave ovens in transient lodging or lunch rooms in an office building are not required to be placed within the specified reach ranges if the receptacles are not intended for regular or frequent use by building occupants.

Comment. The American Hotel and Motel Association (AHMA) stated, without any explanation, that thermostats must be mounted at 60 inches and cannot be placed at an accessible height. A few commenters also expressed concern that State and local codes require electrical outlets be placed lower than 15 inches above the floor.

Response. The technical specifications in 4.27.3 require that the highest operable part of controls, dispensers, receptacles, and other operable equipment be placed within the forward reach range in 4.2.5 (maximum high forward reach is 48 inches and minimum low forward reach is 15 inches, where there is no obstruction) or the side reach range in 4.2.6 (maximum high side reach is 54 inches and minimum low side reach is 9 inches, where there is no obstruction). Thermostats and electrical outlets that are intended for use by building occupants are controls subject to 4.27. The technical specifications in 4.27.3 regarding the location of such controls are taken directly from the ANSI A117.1 standard. AHMA did not cite to any State or local code provision that requires thermostats to be mounted at 60 inches and the Board is not aware of

any. State and local building codes allow the lower placement of electrical outlets but do not preclude what is required in 4.27.3. The Fair Housing Accessibility Guidelines also provide for thermostats and electrical outlets to be placed within similar heights. Therefore, there is no basis for establishing different requirements for thermostats or electrical outlets.

4.28 Alarms

Comment. The NPRM asked whether requirements should be established for the standardization of audible alarms to distinguish them from other sounds. The commenters were divided on the issue. The National Fire Protection Association (NFPA) and several other commenters recommended that the technical specifications for audible alarms in 4.28.2 should be consistent with the NFPA 72A Standard for Protective Signalling Systems. NFPA 72A recommends that the duration of a sound which an alarm should exceed by 5 decibels should be 60 seconds rather than 30 seconds. NFPA 72A also recommends a 130 decibel maximum sound level. NFPA further recommended that the requirements should be stated in terms of the "A" weighted scale.

Response. The technical specifications for audible alarms in 4.28.2 have been revised to conform to NFPA 72A, except that the maximum sound level of 120 decibels has not been changed. The Board understands that the 120 decibel level is commonly known as the "threshold of pain." The 130 decibel level recommended in NFPA 72A was primarily intended for industrial application where noise is a problem and may be appropriate only for industrial occupancies. The 120 decibel level limit has been retained pending further information. The comments did not otherwise present any information beyond that obtained through the Board's research project which concluded that there was not enough known about the problem to develop specific requirements for the standardization of audible alarms. Instead, additional information developed by the Board's research project has been included in the appendix to assist builders and designers in selecting appropriate systems.

Comment. NFPA and several other commenters recommended that the technical specifications for visual alarms in 4.28.3 should be consistent with NFPA 72G Guide for Installation, Maintenance, and Use of Notification Appliances for Protective Signalling Systems. A few commenters recommended that the Board reserve

establishing any requirements for visual alarms until it evaluated a recent study by the Underwriters Laboratory (UL) on such alarms. Some building owners and managers requested that the requirements should be more performance oriented. For example, a system was suggested in which some or all of the building lights would flash in some fashion. Several commenters stated that the requirements should address ambient light levels due to concern that the intensity of the visual signal might temporarily blind people in areas with low light. A few commenters were also concerned about the effect of strobe lights in inducing seizures in certain individuals.

Response. The technical specifications for visual alarms in 4.28.3 have been revised as follows to be consistent with NFPA 72G:

(a) A new paragraph has been added at 4.28.3(3) to provide for a maximum pulse duration of 0.2 sec. with a maximum duty cycle of 40%.

(b) The maximum 120 candela intensity has been deleted from 4.28.3(4) (4.28.3(3) in the NPRM). NFPA 72G permits intensities up to 1000 candela and the UL study found no evidence that such bright devices caused any eye damage in view of the shortness of the flash pulse.

(c) The height requirement for placement of visual signal devices in 4.28.3(6) (4.28.3(5) in the NPRM) has been amended to specify that the devices be at least 6 inches below the ceiling to reduce the potential concealment by smoke.

The requirements in 4.28.3 (7) and (8) (4.28.3 (6) and (7) in the NPRM) have been revised to clarify that the spacing distance applies only in rooms or spaces which are required to have visual signal appliances. The requirement that no place be more than 50 feet from the signal means that the signaling devices would be spaced 100 feet apart as recommended in NFPA 72G. A sentence has also been added to address the spacing of signaling devices in large rooms and spaces such as auditoriums that are more than 100 feet across and are not divided by walls or partitions above 6 feet. In such rooms and spaces, the signaling devices may be placed 100 feet apart around the perimeter of the room or space instead of suspending the devices from the ceiling.

The Board has reviewed the UL study and it generally supports the technical specifications in 4.28.3. The Board notes that NFPA 72G is scheduled to be revised in 1993 and that the UL is planning to develop standards for visual signal devices. The Board intends to monitor these standards and update the guidelines, as appropriate.

The Board has not opted for more performance oriented requirements because the lack of specificity in the current UFAS and ANSI A117.1 standards have resulted in the provision of some ineffective visual alarm systems. As new systems and technologies are developed and tested, the equivalent facilitation provision in 2.2 provides sufficient flexibility for builders and designers to use them. The Board will also consider new systems and technologies when it periodically updates the guidelines.

NFPA 72G and the UL study indicate that the 75 candela minimum signal intensity specified in 4.28.3(4) is not harmful at different lighting levels. The ambient lighting level of typical offices, classrooms, and hotel rooms as tested by UL ranges from 20 to 75 lumens per square foot. NFPA 72G recommends a signal intensity of 100 to 1000 candela for that lighting level. The UL study tested strobe lights with intensity levels equivalent to those required by 4.28.3(4), including tests conducted in a totally dark room where the strobe flash provided the only light. Not only were the subjects not blinded, but they were able to move about the room and find specific objects on a table. As for the possible effect of strobe lights on inducing seizures in certain individuals, the Board's research project and other available information indicate that the problem does not occur if the flash rate is less than 5 HZ. The Board has set the maximum rate at 3 HZ for additional safety.

Comment. Several commenters pointed out that if portable visual alarms are permitted in dwelling units and sleeping rooms, they should be triggered by the emergency alarm system for the building. A few commenters recommended that portable vibrating alarms should also be required to awaken sleepers. Some commenters noted that the requirement that the signal be visible in all areas of the dwelling unit or sleeping room would be difficult in some unusually shaped rooms and spaces.

Response. The intent of the technical specifications for auxiliary alarms in 4.28.4 is that the portable devices will be equivalent to a permanently installed visual alarm that is connected to the building emergency alarm system. The requirement has been clarified by specifying that a means must be provided by which a signal from the building emergency alarm system can trigger the auxiliary alarm. This can be accomplished by providing a separate circuit or transmitting a signal through

the normal wiring system to trigger the portable device.

The UL study found that it required a signal of 110 candela to wake a sleeping person compared to a 15 candela signal to alert people in normal work situations. The UL study also found that vibrating alarms were more effective than visual signals for waking sleeping persons. This information has been included in the appendix at A4.28.4.

The requirement that the signal be visible in all areas of the dwelling unit or sleeping room is reasonable since the purpose of the alarm is to alert persons to emergencies. NFPA 72G states that the signal should be visible "regardless of the orientation" of the individual. The signal can reflect off the walls and be visible in various areas of the room. Some unusually shaped rooms and spaces may require more than one visual alarm device. Builders and designers should take this into consideration when designing and building new facilities.

4.29 Detectable Warnings

Comment. The NPRM proposed to include new provisions for detectable warnings based on research and planned revisions to the ANSI A117.1 standard. A detectable warning is a standardized surface feature built in or applied to walking surfaces or other elements to warn individuals with visual impairments of hazards on a circulation path. The detectable warning should consist of raised truncated domes. Comments were received in support of and in opposition to including detectable warnings in the guidelines. Commenters who opposed detectable warnings gave a variety of reasons. Some individuals with visual impairments stated that with proper training and use of mobility aids they can avoid dangers in the physical environment. These commenters believed that detectable warnings are unnecessary and the people with visual impairments may tend to rely on detectable warnings rather than learn adequate mobility skills. They also expressed concern that detectable warnings might cause hazards for people with visual impairments because the warnings are distracting and can cause people to lose their balance. They noted that detectable warnings may also be hazardous for people with mobility impairments who are ambulatory especially in outdoor conditions where ice and snow removal may be adversely affected by the raised truncated domes. Other commenters stated that detectable warnings create and perpetuate misconceptions and attitudinal barriers about people who

have visual impairments. They expressed concern that detectable warnings would negatively affect the employment of people with visual impairments because employers might mistakenly perceive that such individuals cannot function in an environment that is not specially equipped. In their view, detectable warnings could result in "unintended discriminatory effects." A few commenters questioned the adequacy of the research; the long term durability of raised truncated domes; the ability of the construction industry to comply with the requirement; and the aesthetics of detectable warnings.

Commenters who supported detectable warnings also gave a variety of reasons. They pointed out that there is a significant number of people with visual impairments who are not able to fully master mobility skills due to a range of factors, including age of onset, type of disability, and innate abilities. They further pointed out that necessary cues such as traffic sounds are not always distinguishable due to various circumstances which are beyond the control of the individual. These commenters were concerned about the safety of persons who cannot depend on using mobility skills to detect hazardous conditions. They believed that detectable warnings can prevent unnecessary accidents and deaths and do not stigmatize people who have visual impairments because the warnings are helpful to all people. They noted that detectable warnings are frequently used in industrial settings to warn workers whose vision may be temporarily obscured of hazards in the workplace and have been proven effective in preventing accidents and injuries.

Some commenters generally supported the concept of detectable warnings but suggested that the guidelines should allow for a variety of surface treatments in order to accommodate variations in walking surfaces and design techniques.

Response. Accessibility includes ensuring that individuals with disabilities can safely use the built environment. Some of the requirements in the guidelines such as those for areas of rescue assistance and visual alarms are based primarily on concern for the safety of individuals with disabilities. The purpose of detectable warnings is to alert individuals with visual impairments of hazards on a circulation path that might otherwise go unnoticed and result in serious injury. Although mobility training is essential, as some of the commenters pointed out, a significant number of people with visual impairments are not able to fully master mobility skills. Further, mobility training is not always readily available.

The Board's goal is to provide appropriate cues in the built environment to facilitate the use of mobility skills. The Board does not believe that detectable warnings are any more stigmatizing than ramps. Like other accessibility features, detectable warnings benefit all people.

As discussed in the NPRM, studies have demonstrated the raised truncated dome pattern to be an effective detectable warning. See Tactile Warnings to Promote Safety in the Vicinity of Transit Platform Edges, Urban Mass Transportation Administration (1987); Pathfinder Tactile Tile Demonstration Test Project, Metro-Dade Transit Agency (1988). The domes can be constructed using a variety of methods including concrete stamping or the application of a prefabricated surface treatment. Although there are other common surface treatments that are detectable, the concept of a detectable warning is to provide consistent and uniform surface treatment that is distinctive from other materials and consistently recognized as a warning in order to alert pedestrians that they are approaching a potentially dangerous area.

The final guidelines retain the requirements in 4.29.2 for detectable warnings to consist of raised truncated domes. The requirement for detectable warnings used on interior surfaces to differ from adjoining walking surfaces in resiliency or sound on cane contract has also been retained. However, for the reasons discussed under the comments below, the Board has limited the application of detectable warnings to hazardous vehicular ways, reflecting pools that are not otherwise protected, and curb ramps. The provisions for detectable warnings at stairs and on doors to hazardous areas have been reserved pending further study.

Comment. The NPRM provided in 4.29.2 for detectable warnings to contrast visually with adjoining surfaces and proposed to specify a 70% contrast ratio. The NPRM asked several questions regarding the proposed contrast ratio, including whether it was too difficult to achieve and whether a one inch black band between the detectable warning and adjoining surfaces would provide sufficient contrast for persons with low vision. Most of the persons who responded to the question objected to the contrast ratio. Several commenters stated that it could not be measured or enforced under field conditions. Some

commenters noted that materials with demonstrated low maintenance and durability characteristics often have low reflective values and would not meet the criteria. Many commenters also opposed the use of a black band. Several commenters recommended that detectable warnings should be a yellow color.

Response. The final guidelines provide in 4.29.2 that detectable warnings must contrast visually with adjoining surfaces, either light-on-dark or dark-on-light. The 70% contrast ratio has been placed in the appendix at A4.29.2 and is advisory only.

Comment. A number of commenters opposed the requirements in 4.9.5 and 4.29.4 for detectable warnings at stairs primarily based on concern that the raised truncated domes will create a tripping hazard. Several commenters, including industries which use detectable warnings to alert workers of hazards such as loading docks, requested that the depth of the warning be decreased from 36 inches to 24 inches.

Response. Although detectable warnings have been successfully used at such locations as transit platform edges and loading dock edges, there is no data available regarding this application at stairs. People may use a different gait when they approach stairs compared to other walking surfaces. The requirement in 4.9.5 and 4.29.4 for detectable warnings at stairs have been reserved pending further study regarding possible tripping hazards. The requirements in 4.29.3 and 4.29.7 for detectable warnings on doors to hazardous areas and for standardization of such warnings within a building, facility or site have also been reserved pending further study.

Comment. A number of commenters requested that detectable warnings also be required at uncurbed and unprotected drop off areas where a fall may be extremely hazardous or life threatening such as transit platforms and loading docks. Some commenters were opposed to detectable warnings at those locations. Several commenters recommended that detectable warnings should be required where the drop-off separating the pedestrian and vehicular way is more than curb height.

Response. The requirement in 4.29.5 has been clarified that a detectable warning is required when a walk crosses or adjoins a vehicular way, and the walking surfaces are not separated-by curbs, railings, or other elements between the pedestrian areas and vehicular areas. For instance, some hotels have driveways that adjoin walkways at entrances. If there is no curb separating the pedestrian and

vehicular area, a detectable warning would have to be provided. Detectable warnings for transportation facilities will be addressed in section 10 of the final guidelines which will be published separately in the **Federal Register**. Detectable warnings have not been required at loading docks and loading ramps because those areas are generally not open to the public. If an individual employee with a visual impairment works in an area with hazardous drop-offs, detectable warnings would be covered by reasonable accommodation under title I of the ADA.

Comment. Some commenters questioned the requirement in 4.7.7 for detectable warnings at curb ramps. A few commenters expressed concerns about maintenance, including snow and ice removal. Other commenters suggested changes to the requirement that the detectable warnings extend the full width and depth of the curb ramp.

Response. Properly designed curb ramps have gentle slopes which may not be easily detectable by some persons with visual impairments. Furthermore, changes in slope along pedestrian ways are commonplace and persons with visual impairments cannot predictably know when a change in slope indicates the presence of a curb ramp. The Board is concerned about the safety of persons with visual impairments who may unknowingly enter a vehicular way due to the lack of any cue or warnings at curb ramps to prevent serious injuries and deaths. The requirement in 4.7.7 for detectable warnings at curb ramps has therefore been retained.

4.30 Signage

Comment. A number of commenters, including graphic designers and sign manufacturers, objected to the technical specifications for character height and letter spacing in 4.30.3. Their primary concern was the impact of the requirements on the size of the sign. For instance, the NPRM proposed that letters on building directories by ⅝-inch minimum. One commenter pointed out that the current industry standard for film negative directories is ³⁄₁₆ inch which is roughly ¼ the size proposed in the NPRM. Building directories would need to be 16 times their current size (4 times as high and 4 times as wide) to meet the ⅝-inch minimum. The commenter noted that larger office buildings have difficulty just accommodating a directory large enough to list their occupants in ³⁄₁₆-inch type. Several individuals with disabilities and other commenters objected to wide letter spacing because they believed it would make it more difficult to read by word shape or "footprint."

Response. The minimum height requirements for building directories and wall mounted signs and the provision for wide letter spacing have been deleted from the technical specifications in 4.30.3. Signs that are suspended or projected overhead in compliance with the technical specifications for protruding objects in 4.4.2 (i.e., more than 80 inches above the floor or ground) are required to have a character height of 3 inches minimum. A sentence has also been added to 4.30.3 to clarify that lower case letters are permitted.

Comment. Individuals with disabilities and government agencies involved with disability issues supported the technical specifications for raised and brailled characters in 4.30.4. Many of the commenters who opposed the technical specifications, including graphic designers and sign manufacturers, interpreted the NPRM as requiring all signs to have raised and brailled characters and all upper case letters and apparently objected to the scoping provisions and technical specifications on that basis. A few commenters also expressed concern that raised and braille characters may be more prone to vandalism.

Response. As discussed earlier, the scoping provisions for exterior and interior signage have been clarified in response to the comments. See 4.1.2(7) and 4.1.3(16). Only those signs which designate permanent rooms and spaces must comply with the technical specifications in 4.30.4 through 4.30.6 for raised and brailled characters, finish and contrast, and mounting location and height. No changes have been made to the technical specifications for raised and brailled characters in 4.30.4. Raised and brailled characters can be designed to be as vandal resistant as other signage.

Comment. Several graphic designers and sign manufacturers objected to eggshell finish being specified in the technical specifications for finish and contrast in 4.30.5. They felt that it unnecessarily restricts the industry. A number of commenters also objected to the 70% contrast ratio proposed in the NPRM because they believed that it could not be measured or enforced in the field.

Response. The Board sponsored research project on which the technical specifications for finish and contrast in 4.30.5 are based found that eggshell and matte finishes are equally readable by persons with low vision. The NPRM proposed to require only eggshell because of its relative resistance to

soiling compared to matte. The final guidelines provide for eggshell, matte, or other non-glare finish. The 70% contrast formula has been placed in the appendix at A4.30.5 and is advisory only. The appendix also recommends an eggshell finish and light characters on a dark background.

Comment. The NPRM proposed in 4.30.6 that signs providing permanent identification of rooms and spaces be mounted on the wall adjacent to the latch side of the door at a height between 54 and 66 inches. These signs are required to include raised and brailled characters. A number of commenters recommended different mounting heights. Some pointed out that the 66 inch height was not within the reach range for wheelchair users. Other commenters pointed out that a more uniform and consistent mounting height would make it easier for persons with visual impairments to locate the signage.

Response. The technical specifications in 4.30.6 have been revised to require that signs providing permanent identification of rooms and spaces be mounted 60 inches above the finish floor to the center of the sign. The 60 inch mounting height was recommended in the original research for the ANSI A117.1—1980 standard. See *Accessible Buildings for People with Severe Visual Impairments*, Steinfeld (1978). Lowering the maximum height also reduces the viewing distance for persons with low vision and places the sign at a more comfortable reading height for users of braille and raised characters. A sentence has also been added to 4.30.6 clarifying that where there is no wall space to the latch side of the door, including at double leaf doors, signs are to be placed on the nearest adjacent wall.

Comment. A number of commenters recommended that the international symbol of access for hearing loss be used to identify the availability of permanently installed assistive listening systems in assembly areas required to have such systems by 4.1.3(19)(b).

Response. A requirement has been added to the technical specifications for symbols of accessibility in 4.30.7 that assistive listening systems be identified by signage that includes the international symbol of access for hearing loss. See Fig. 43(d). Additional information is provided in the appendix at A4.30.7 regarding appropriate messages to include with the symbol (e.g., infrared Assistive Listening System Available—Please Ask).

Comment. The NPRM proposed in 4.30.8 that illumination levels on the sign surface be in the 200 to 300 lux range (10 to 30 footcandles) and that the

illumination level on the surface of the sign not be significantly exceeded by the ambient light or visible bright lighting source behind or in front of the sign. A number of commenters objected to this provision as unenforceable. Other commenters noted that the proposed levels were generally met or exceeded in indoor lighted areas.

Response. The technical specifications for illumination levels in 4.30.8 has been reserved pending further study. The NPRM provision has been included in the appendix at A4.30.8 and is advisory only.

4.31 Telephones

Comment. The NPRM asked what decibel range should be specified for volume control telephones. Persons who responded to the question generally favored a range of 12 decibels to 18 decibels. Some commenters requested higher levels, stating that those with lower levels were not helpful. Although most telephone companies who responded to the question indicated that their equipment would fall within this range, they were opposed to specifying any decibel level.

Response. The final guidelines provide in 4.31.5(2) that public telephones required to be equipped with volume controls by 4.1.3(17)(b) must be capable of a minimum of 12 decibels and a maximum of 18 decibels above normal because higher levels can damage the ear. If an automatic reset button is provided, the 18 decibel level may be exceeded.

Comment. A number of commenters recommended that the requirement in 4.31.5 for a magnetic field in the area of the receiver cup should be changed to require hearing aid compatible telephones.

Response. The technical specifications in 4.31.5(1) have been revised to require that public telephones required to be equipped with volume controls by 4.1.3(17)(b) must be hearing aid compatible. The Hearing Aid Compatibility Act of 1988 requires that nearly all telephones be hearing aid compatible.

4.32 Fixed or Built-In Seating and Tables

Comment. Commenters made individual recommendations for changes and clarifications to the technical specifications for fixed or built-in seating and tables in 4.32. For instance, it was recommended that the depth requirement under tables be increased to accommodate guide dogs.

Response. The reference to "work surfaces" have been deleted from the technical specifications in 4.32 since those features are not required to be accessible by 4.1.1(3). The appendix recommends at A4.1.1(3) that if individual work stations are made accessible, they should comply with the applicable technical specifications. As for change to the depth requirements under tables, further study is needed.

4.33 Assembly Areas

Comment. Individuals with disabilities and their organizations supported the requirements in 4.33.3 for wheelchair seating spaces to be dispersed throughout the seating area. Several commenters requested that companion seating also be provided next to wheelchair seating spaces. Commenters from the theater industry expressed concern about the loss of seats if wheelchair seating spaces are placed mid-row. Motion picture theater owners pointed out that new movie theaters are typically a multiplex of small auditoriums each of which seats between 150 and 300 people and that each seat is situated to provide a clear line of sight to the screen. They requested that such small auditoriums be exempt from the dispersal requirement. A few commenters recommended that ramped aisles which are part of an accessible route to wheelchair seating spaces should be permitted to have steeper slopes if necessary to provide adequate sightlines.

Response. The requirements in 4.33.3 for dispersal of wheelchair seating spaces have been modified. Wheelchair seating spaces must be an integral part of any fixed seating plan and be situated so as to provide wheelchair users a choice of admission prices and lines of sight comparable to those available to the rest of the public. A provision has been added for at least one companion fixed seat to be provided next to each wheelchair seating space. The final guidelines require that when the seating capacity exceeds 300, wheelchair seating spaces must be provided in more than one location. This provision is based on the California code and balances considerations of cost and lost of other seating spaces with the need for access. It should be noted, however, that the guidelines do not require wheelchair seating spaces to be placed mid-row. No significant loss of seats is anticipated. As discussed under the scoping provisions in 4.1.3(19)(a), to address concerns regarding the number of wheelchair seating spaces required in large facilities, a provision has also been added to 4.33.3 permitting readily removable seats to be installed in wheelchair seating spaces which may be

used by other persons when these spaces are not needed by wheelchair users or other individuals with mobility impairments. As explained in the appendix at 4.33.3, folding seating units usually consist of two fixed seats that can be easily folded into a fixed center bar to allow for open spaces for wheelchair users when needed.

As for ramped aisles which are part of an accessible route to wheelchair seating spaces, the Board is not convinced that slopes steeper than the maximum 1:12 permitted in 4.8.2 are necessary to provide adequate sightlines. Sightlines and visibility are affected by several factors, including the slope of the floor; the height of the screen; the distance between rows; and the staggering of seats. The Board understands that there are theaters designed with ramp aisles that comply with the maximum 1:12 slope and provide adequate sightlines.

Comment. The NPRM asked questions regarding row spacing and lines of sight over standing spectators in sports arenas and other similar assembly areas. Many of the persons who responded to the question stated that they have difficulty accessing mid-row seats in an assembly area. Many commenters also recommended that lines of sight should be provided over standing spectators.

Response. Building and life safety codes set minimum distances between rows of fixed seats with consideration of the number of seats in a row, the exit aisle width and arrangement, and the location of exit doors. Because row spacing is related to these other factors, the Board does not believe that it is appropriate for the guidelines to set requirements in this area. However, information has been included in the appendix at A4.33.3 on "continental" seating which allows a greater number of seats per row with a commensurate increase in row spacing and exit doors. This alternative increases ease of access to mid-row seats for people who walk with difficulty and facilitates emergency egress for all people. Builders and designers are encouraged to consider "continental" seating along with other factors when planning seating in assembly areas.

The issue of lines of sight over standing spectators will be addressed in guidelines for recreational facilities.

Comment. As discussed under the scoping provision in 4.1.3(19)(b) for assistive listening systems in assembly areas, the NPRM requested information regarding which types of assistive listening systems (magnetic induction loops, FM, and infra-red) work best in

particular environments. Many comments described their personal experiences with particular types of systems. Those who provide extensive information on the various systems recommended that a specific type should be selected only after consultation with experts in the field.

Response. Additional information on assistive listening systems is provided in the technical specifications in 4.33.6 and in the appendix at A4.33.6. The type of assistive listening system appropriate for a particular application depends on the characteristics of the setting, the nature of the program, and the intended audience. The appendix includes a table reprinted from a National Institute of Disability and Rehabilitation Research "Rehab Brief" which shows some of the advantages and disadvantages of each system and typical applications. New York has also adopted technical specifications which may be useful. A pamphlet is available from the Board which lists demonstration centers across the country where technical assistance can be obtained in selecting and installing appropriate systems.

4.34 Automated Teller Machines

Comment. The NPRM contained an exception in 4.1.3(20) for drive-up-only ATMs, which provided that drive-up ATMs are not required to comply with the requirements in 4.34.2 and 4.34.3 for controls and clearances and reach ranges because they are designed to be used from motor vehicles. The NPRM requested information on reach range requirements from standard size motor vehicles. The American Bankers Association (ABA) stated:

A number of uncontrollable variables are inherent in designing drive-up ATMs, e.g., the size of the driver; car dimensions; the skill of the driver in stopping the car close to the ATM. * * * However, given the number of uncontrollable variables, it is inevitable that certain drivers will be unable to use comfortably the drive-up ATM or will have to exit the car in order to complete a transaction.

Response. Because of the uncontrollable variables involved in utilizing drive-up ATMs, the Board, in the NPRM, provided an exception in the scoping provisions in 4.1.3(20) for drive-up ATMs. The drive-up ATMs do not have to comply with 4.34.2 (Controls) (which refers to 4.27) and 4.34.3 (Clearances and Reach Range) because they are designed to be used from motor vehicles. The Board maintained that exception with a minor change in referencing the provisions. The current provision states that the drive-up ATMs are not required to comply with 4.27.2, 4.27.3 and 4.34.3.

Comment. The ABA took the position that drive-up ATMs should be exempt from requirements that they be accessible to persons with visual impairments. The basis for their position was that drive-up ATMs are supposed to be used by the driver of the car who must have sufficient vision to drive legally. Should a passenger wish to use the ATM, stated the ABA, the driver could assist. Another commenter supported this position stating that a person who is visually impaired cannot use the drive-up ATM from the rear seat because most newer cars do not have fully openable windows.

Response. While the Board understands that the driver must have sufficient vision to operate the automobile, a passenger riding in either the front or back seat of the automobile may be visually impaired. Although the ABA cites the availability of the driver for assistance, this method would not allow the individual to use the ATM independently. In responding to the issue of drive-up ATMs in general, the ABA stated that given the number of uncontrollable variables, it is inevitable that some drivers will have to exit the car in order to complete a transaction. Thus it is entirely conceivable and not unexpected that a passenger may exit the automobile to use the drive-up ATM and this passenger may be an individual who is visually impaired. Furthermore, while some cars do not have fully operable rear windows, many cars do and, as with the front seat passenger, the individual in the rear seat may exit the car to utilize the ATM.

Consistent with the scoping provisions in 4.1.3(20) where a drive-up ATM is located adjacent to a walk-up ATM, only one ATM would have to be accessible to persons with visual impairments. Operational issues regarding the availability of accessible ATM services (e.g., accessible ATM being open same hours as non-accessible ATM) would be covered by the Department of Justice's regulations.

Comment. Section 4.34.4 provides that instructions and all information for use of ATMs shall be made accessible to and independently usable by persons with vision impairments. In the NPRM, the Board sought additional information on equipment presently in use or available technologies for making instructions and other information relating to the use of ATMs accessible to persons with vision impairments. There were over 50 different suggestions for making ATMs accessible to persons with vision impairments including (1) The installation of a handset voice

output telephone device; (2) using large print and braille; (3) a "talking machine"; (4) using phone type receivers behind locked doors; (5) cassette instructions; (6) braille instructions; and (7) using a consumer electronics bus or universal interface bus for output accessibility.

The ABA took the position that while some technology does exist to assist many visually impaired persons, there does not appear to be technology to ensure in every case ATM accessibility to all visually impaired persons. The ABA stated that current technology supplied to assist visually impaired persons includes raised key identification overlay; high quality contrast screens; character font design selections to ensure easiest reading; and character enlargement. The ABA suggested that educational audio tapes and braille manuals offer at least one source of immediate accommodation for persons with vision impairments.

The ABA further recommended that the regulations concerning ATMs be "flexible and fluid." The ABA stated that "(i)t would be unfortunate if the initial or later regulations locked in specifications and standards in a manner which discourages future innovations and improvements" and that "(a)s technology develops and improves and as disabled persons determine and convey their suggestions, the facilities should evolve to provide better accessibility to disabled persons." The ABA was of the opinion that flexibility is particularly crucial with regard to providing ATM access to persons with vision impairments.

Response. While not stated specifically in the rule, braille and large print instructions (as proposed in the planned revisions to the ANSI A117.1 standard), when used in conjunction with tactually marked keys or other means of identification, do serve as one source of accommodation for persons with vision impairments. In an article recently published in the ABA Banking Journal, it was noted that at least one manufacturer provides ATMs with brailled keys as a standard feature. The manufacturer also provides training kits for bank customers with vision impairments that include a braille workbook on how to use the machine. Access Comes to ATMs, ABA Banking Journal (November 1990).

In light of the evolving technology in this area and to allow flexibility in design, the Board has stated the requirement for accessibility for persons with vision impairments in general performance terms. No changes were made to this section from the proposed rule which provides that instructions

and all information for use of ATMs shall be made accessible to and independently usable by persons with vision impairments. While the planned revisions to the ANSI A117.1 standard may contain more specific provisions with respect to equipping ATMs for use by persons with vision impairments, the Board has chosen to maintain its position of flexibility in this area.

Comment. The Board sought comment on whether or not visual displays should be required to maintain accessibility for persons with hearing impairments where telephone handsets are used to convey printed and displayed information to persons with vision impairments. The Board queried whether there was a possibility that handsets would entirely replace video display screens. The overwhelming majority of comments from individuals with disabilities and their organizations indicated that where telephone handsets are used, visual displays should also be provided. The ABA took the position that it is inconceivable at this time that telephone handsets would ever replace a visual display. The American Council of the Blind was in agreement with this position stating that whatever accommodations that are made for persons with visual impairments should not preclude use by persons with other disabilities. One commenter indicated that visual displays must be maintained for people with limited use of arms or hands and another commenter stated that many persons with hearing loss are not able to use instructions via telephones or intercoms.

Response. The Board is also of the opinion that if telephone handsets or similar devices are provided, these will be in addition to and not preclude video display screens. Although it is unlikely that this should ever occur, the Board may address this issue in the future.

Comment. The Board also sought information concerning vandalism and the use of telephone handsets. The ABA took the position that telephone handsets furnished with ATMs are more susceptible to vandalism than telephone handsets currently used for public telephones, citing the reason that ATM telephone handsets are often vandalized for reasons which do not apply to telephone handsets. As an example, the ABA cited the instance where people who try to access someone else's account using a debit card which does not belong to them could become angry enough to vandalize an ATM when they are denied access to the ATM. The Wells Fargo Bank, the Service Centers Corporation and other commenters also expressed concern that telephone handsets are subject to vandalism.

Response. The Board is not requiring telephone handsets. Telephone handsets were suggested because they are one way that some banks have chosen to address the need for accommodation for persons with visual impairments. As cited in the ABA article, other means are available for providing information for use of ATMs by persons with vision impairments. These other means are not precluded should the banks prefer to use them. (The handset alternative was chosen to cost out in the regulatory impact analysis because of its high initial cost.)

Comment. The Board sought comment on whether information provided on video display screens (such as "deposit or withdrawal" and "checking or savings") can also be provided in braille when the user presses various keys. Additionally, the Board inquired whether receipts can be made accessible by braille or voice synthesis if a telephone handset or other listening device is used. Since many ATMs are located in an outdoor environment, the Board requested comment on how screen illumination and contrast can be provided in an outdoor environment where glare may be a problem.

The ABA stated that they are not aware of the availability of video display screens which are capable of displaying information in braille. Braille printers for receipts are available; however, the ABA took the position that such printers cannot be integrated with ATMs as a practical matter.

Further, according to the ABA, ATM manufacturers have researched in depth how to minimize glare through screen illumination and contrast. The ABA further stated that as new materials and techniques are developed, the effects of glare will be reduced and readability improved. They took the position that the Board should not enumerate specific contrast and color requirements as competition alone will ensure that the most readable combinations are marketed and used.

Response. Given the lack of technology which allows for the practical integration of braille printers in ATMs, the Board has not required braille printers at this time. The Board believes that technology in the industry must improve before specific contrast and color requirements can be included in the guidelines. The Board believes that this area needs further research.

Comment. The Board invited comments on how privacy needs can be met in the context of accessible ATMs. Comments received in response to this section were primarily based on individual concerns and no research or supportive documentation was included. The ABA took the position that given the unavailability of voice synthesis, the use of a speaker is a viable option at this point which will not threaten the privacy of the user. Another commenter suggested using a system of beeps to confirm the transaction, while other commenters noted that audio output could result in a loss of privacy and security. Other suggestions for increased privacy included (1) installation of a "next in line" area behind which the visual display is unreadable; (2) making the display of information optional; (3) having a screen with a narrow viewing range or one which is not readable from all directions and angles; (4) enclosing ATMs in a booth; and (5) modifying the video display or viewing slot so it can be angled down farther or turned to the left or right, both manually and automatically, for individuals who use wheelchairs and others.

An issue which is interrelated with privacy matters is the concern for security. The Board sought comments concerning what security issues, if any, should be considered relative to an individual with a disability and whether or not there were considerations with respect to the environment around ATMs that may cause difficulty complying with the provisions of this section. The majority of the comments received addressed the need for security at ATMs based on use by the general public and not just by those individuals with disabilities. A limited number of commenters took the position that individuals with disabilities are "easier prey" and that use by visually impaired persons may increase the opportunity for criminal activity. One commenter stated that complex or costly security measures may be unreasonable in relation to the actual use by disabled people. Many commenters stressed the need for proper lighting at ATMs. Several other commenters took the position that security must not be compromised for access, and another comment asked that flexibility be allowed because the location and security considerations at ATMs vary widely. Suggestions to improve security included (1) using a telephone handset (audio output through speakers is undesirable since it can be overheard by others) or shaded screen and keeping the handset in a closed compartment accessible by card users only to prevent vandalism; (2) providing both ¼ and ¼ inch jacks so personal headphones can be plugged into an ATM (the jacks can be protected from tampering or vandalism by a sliding cover until the ATM is activated by logging in a correct user identification); and (3) video monitoring around ATMs, as is done in convenience stores.

Response. Based on the response that the Board received concerning these areas, it is apparent that security and privacy are issues of general concern which apply to all ATM users and not just to individuals with disabilities and are issues which the industry must address. Until such time as additional research can be conducted into the issues of security and privacy at ATMs, the Board does not propose to include requirements for such measures.

Comment. The Board sought comment on whether other point of sale machines, such as machines selling insurance at airports or machines used for overnight delivery of letters and packages, should be covered by these guidelines and, if so, what requirements would be appropriate. Many persons who responded to the question favored providing access to the machines. A few commenters questioned whether the machines were fixed or built-in parts of a building or facility. Some commenters recommended that the machines should be addressed on a case-by-case basis as the services develop because blanket coverage in the early development stage could significantly lessen their distribution and the variety and quality of services provided.

Response. The Board believes this issue needs further study. However, the Board tends to agree with comments saying that a majority of the machines are equipment and therefore not within the Board's purview.

4.35 Dressing and Fitting Rooms

As discussed in the scoping provisions at 4.1.3(21), requirements have been added to the final guidelines for accessible dressing and fitting rooms. Technical specifications are provided for clear floor space, doors, a bench, and mirrors where provided.

5. Restaurants and Cafeterias

5.1 General

Section 5 contains specific requirements for restaurants and cafeterias, in addition to those contained in 4.1 through 4.35 and provides that where fixed tables are provided (or dining counters where food is consumed but there is no service) at least 5 percent, but not less than one, of the fixed tables (or a portion of the dining counter) shall be accessible and comply with 4.32 as required in 4.1.3(18).

Comment. The NPRM did not contain a specific reference to "counters" and a number of the commenters questioned whether restaurants that provide only high counters along the wall are covered.

Response. Such counters are covered by the guidelines and the Board has clarified this coverage by specifically referencing "counters" in this section. The board further clarified the language to reflect that the 5% requirement of fixed or built-in seating or tables is not in addition to section 4.1.3(18). To avoid confusion with section 5.2 (Counters and Bars), the Board inserted language to clarify that this section refers to dining counters where food is consumed but is not served at the counter as opposed to section 5.2 which addresses counters where food or drink is served at the counter for consumption. Where counters are provided solely for the sale of food and drink and not consumption then those counters must comply with 7.2 Sales and Service Counters.

Comment. The Board invited comment on whether requiring that at least 5%, but not less than one, of the fixed tables be accessible and comply with 4.32 (Seating Tables, and Work Surfaces) was adequate or whether a higher or lower percent should be specified. The Board sought comment on the impact of the different percentages on space layouts and revenues.

Response. While a slight majority of the commenters favored a higher percentage, little supporting information was provided to assess the impact of the higher (or lower) percentage on space layouts and revenues. The requirement of 5% accessibility of fixed tables is based on current building codes. The Board retained the 5% provision with no further changes to this paragraph.

5.2   Counters and Bars

This section requires that where food or drink is served at counters exceeding 34 inches in height to customers seated on stools or standing at the counter, a portion of the main counter which is 60 inches in length minimum shall be provided in compliance with 4.32 (Fixed or Built-in Seating and Tables) or service shall be available at accessible tables within the same area.

Comment. The NPRM did not explain the term "portion" and at least half of those responding to this section urged the Board to clarify the reference to a "portion".

Response. The Board provided language to reflect that a "portion of the counter" refers to a portion of the main counter which is 60 inches in length minimum. The 60 inches space provides for two wheelchairs or one wheelchair and one seat or chair.

5.3   Access Aisles

This section contains technical specifications for access aisles to accessible fixed tables. No changes were made to this paragraph.

5.4   Dining Areas

Section 5.4 requires that, in newly constructed restaurants and cafeterias, raised or sunken dining areas, loggias, and outdoor seating areas must be accessible. In alterations, accessibility to raised or sunken dining areas, or to all parts of outdoors seating areas is not required provided that the same services and decor are provided in an accessible space usable by the general public and not restricted to use by people with disabilities.

In non-elevator buildings, an accessible means of vertical access to the mezzanine is not required provided the area of mezzanine seating measures no more than 33 percent of the area of the accessible seating area and the same services and decor are provided in an accessible space usable by the general public and are not restricted to use by persons with disabilities. This exception does not apply to buildings required to have an elevator.

Comment. Several commenters indicated that clarification was needed regarding the requirement that dining rooms be accessible. Based on the language of the NPRM, it was unclear whether all dining rooms or just those which are raised or sunken are required to be accessible.

Response. The Board clarified its intent that all dining areas are to be accessible in new construction.

5.5   Food Service Lines

Section 5.5 is taken from UFAS and provides technical specification for accessible food service lines. Instead of requiring a "reasonable portion" of self-service shelves to be within forward and side reach ranges (4.2.5 and 4.2.6), the guidelines require at least 50% of each type of self-service shelves to be within the required reach ranges. No changes were made to this paragraph.

5.6   Tableware and Condiment Areas

This section requires that self-service shelves and dispensing devices for tableware, dishware, condiments, food and beverages be installed to comply with 4.2 (Space Allowance and Reach Ranges). No changes were made to this section.

5.7   Raised Platforms

Section 5.7 requires that a raised platform used for the head table or speaker's lectern in banquet rooms or spaces shall be accessible by means of a ramp or platform lift complying with 4.8 or 4.11, respectively. Open edges of a raised platform must be protected by the placement of tables or by a curb. No changes were made to this section.

5.8   Vending Machines and Other Equipment

This section requires that spaces for vending machines and other equipment shall comply with 4.2 and shall be located on an accessible route. The NPRM also provided that the equipment comply with 4.27 (Controls and Operating Mechanisms). This latter provision was deleted as it relates to equipment not under the jurisdiction of these guidelines.

5.9   Quiet Areas (Reserved)

Comment. A significant number of responses raised the issue of the need for "Quiet Areas" in restaurants. According to these commenters, extraneous noise and dim lights make it difficult for persons with hearing impairments to communicate when dining out.

Response. The Board has reserved this section until such time as research can be conducted on appropriate requirements which address the need for a quiet area in restaurants.

6. *Medical Care Facilities*

These sections establish specific requirements for medical care facilities, in addition to those contained in 4.1 through 4.35. The sections apply to medical care facilities such as hospitals where persons may need assistance in responding to an emergency and where the period of stay may exceed twenty-four hours. Doctors' and dentists' offices are not included in this section but are subject to the requirements of section 4.

6.1   General

Comment. Regarding the scoping provision for hospitals specifically approximately half of the commenters proposed increasing the percentage while the other half suggested that it be reduced. In addition to those comments, there were other commenters who favored increasing the percentage for medical facilities in general. Those arguing for a reduced figure in hospitals, did so based on the impact on cost and space. Humana Inc. expressed concern that the requirements of the guidelines for accessible bed and toilet rooms could result in a loss of 10% of beds in alterations. They further expressed concern about the requirement that all employee work areas be accessible. The American Hospital Association estimated cost increases of 20% for new construction and 40% to 60% for alterations.

Response. The scoping requirement of 10% is based on the current MGRAD. The draft final regulatory impact analysis shows that the cost per square foot increase is $1.00 per square foot for an overall percentage increase in new construction costs of 1.02%. The draft final regulatory analysis further shows that the cost increase per bed in a 100 bed hospital is $879.50. Over the 40 year useful life of the facility this cost amounts to $21.99 per bed per year. These figures support the requirement for 10% accessibility.

A portion of the commenters' anticipated cost was attributable to the health care industry's concern over the perceived 100% accessibility required in employee areas. To avoid any misunderstanding that the Board is requiring 100% accessibility for all rooms as a result of the reference to "employee use areas," the Board has deleted that reference. Provisions concerning areas used only by employees as work areas and individual work stations are covered under section 4.1.1(3). That section requires access to employee work areas to the extent that individuals with disabilities can approach, enter, and exit the areas.

Furthermore, retrofitting existing facilities solely for accessibility reasons is not required by the guidelines. Additionally, the distribution of accessible beds in a hospital can vary based on the anticipated need in different specialized units. For example, more than 10% may be needed in a general surgical unit and less than 10% in obstetrics and pediatrics.

The loss of beds referenced in the comments could result only from alteration of existing units and would be unlikely in most situations. A new section 6.1(4) has been added to address concerns about the impact of the alterations requirements. Section 6.1(4)(a) provides that when patient bedrooms (and toilet/bath rooms that are part of the patient bedroom) are being added or altered as part of a planned renovation to a discrete department of an existing medical facility, accessible patient bedrooms shall be provided in a percentage consistent with the percentage of rooms required to be accessible by the applicable requirements of 6.1(1), 6.1(2), or 6.1(3), until the number of accessible patient bedrooms in the facility equals the overall number of accessible patient bedrooms that would be required if the facility were newly constructed. For example, if 20 patient bedrooms are being altered in the obstetrics department of a hospital, 2 of the altered

rooms must be made accessible. If 20 patient bedrooms are being altered in a unit within the same hospital that specializes in treating mobility impairments, all of the altered rooms must be made accessible.

Section 6.1(4)(b) addresses alterations within departments that are not undergoing a complete renovation. Under section 6.1(4)(b), when patient bedrooms are being added or altered individually, and not as part of an alteration of the entire area, the altered patent bedrooms shall comply with 6.3, unless either (1) the number of accessible rooms provided in the department or area containing the altered patient bedroom equals the number of accessible patient bedrooms that would be required if the percentage requirements of 6.1(1), 6.1(2), or 6.1(3) were applied to that department or area or (2) the number of accessible patient bedrooms in the facility equals the overall number that would be required if the facility were newly constructed. For example, if a patient bedroom in a rehabilitation unit in a general hospital is altered, it must be made accessible because 6.1(2) requires all rehabilitation unit beds to be accessible. A patient bedroom in the obstetrics ward of a general hospital which is altered must be made accessible unless 10% of the beds in that ward are currently accessible or unless the facility as a whole already meets the new construction accessibility requirements. Where toilet or bath rooms are part of patient bedrooms which are added or altered and are required to be accessible, each such patient toilet or bathroom shall comply with 6.4. These provisions will enable a medical care facility to ensure that accessible rooms are distributed appropriately among the various units within the facility.

Comment. Many of the comments received on this section addressed the issue of scoping requirements for nursing homes. The majority of the comments received from nursing homes felt that the requirement for 50% of the patient bedrooms and toilets, all public use, common use and employee use areas was too excessive and suggested a figure of 5%. The justification given for the reduction was the substantial impact this requirement would have on cost and space. Many of those comments estimated that the cost increase per bed would be $8,000.

Response. The scoping requirement of 50% is based on the current MGRAD. The draft final regulatory impact analysis shows that the cost per square foot increase is $1.70 per square foot for an overall percentage increase in new construction costs of 1.74%. The draft

final regulatory impact analysis further shows that the cost increase per bed in a 76 bed nursing home is $1553. Over the 40 year useful life of the facility this cost amounts to $38.83 per year. These figures support the requirement for 50% accessibility.

Comment. The majority of the comments received from the nursing homes took the position that, "residential care facilities" should be exempt from the guidelines. The basis for their position was that, by definition, those facilities are not medical care facilities since they are primarily residential in nature and are not providing medical care.

Response. The Board considered the issue of residential care facilities. It is the understanding of the Board that clarification of the applicability of these guidelines to "residential care facilities" will be addressed in the rules to be issued by the Department of Justice. To avoid any misunderstanding, the term "period of residence" used in this section was revised to read "period of stay".

Comment. The responses from the nursing homes took exception to requiring that "employee work areas" be accessible. Those commenters reasoned that since nursing facility residents are dependent upon staff to assist them in the event of a fire or life-threatening emergency, staff must be physically capable of providing assistance as a requirement of employment. The provision for employee access to all patient rooms was characterized as a needless expense.

Response. The Board is of the opinion that not all nursing home staff are expected to be physically capable of providing assistance in emergency situations (e.g. clinicians, administrative personnel). As indicated above, to avoid any misunderstanding that the Board is requiring 100% accessibility for all rooms as a result of the reference to "employee use areas," the Board has deleted that reference.

Comment. The Board sought comment on whether other types of facilities should be listed in the scoping table. A majority of the responses supported the provision as proposed in the NPRM. Approximately 25% of the responses recommended adding clinics. Other facilities which were recommended for inclusion were outpatient/ambulatory care facilities, medical professional buildings, and dentist offices. Also suggested were hospices, assisted living and congregate care facilities and rehabilitation facilities.

Response. Clinics can vary considerably in the type of services provided, and many do not provide patient bedrooms or provide overnight accommodation. If the clinics do provide patient bedrooms or overnight accommodation, they are covered under the provisions of this section of the guidelines, otherwise, they would be subject only to the requirements of section 4. The medical care facilities listed are meant to be illustrative. If a specific medical care facility is not mentioned, it is required to meet the requirements for the type of facility that it most closely resembles. For instance, an orthopedic hospital would be considered a rehabilitation facility. The Board considered outpatient care facilities, medical professional buildings and dentists offices, but did not consider these to be medical care facilities under this section as the period of stay does not exceed 24 hours.

The Board considered and included rehabilitation facilities in the guidelines based on the reason that those facilities would also specialize in treating conditions that affect mobility.

Additionally, the Board revised the language to reflect that if a hospital or a rehabilitation facility has a "unit" within the facility that specializes in treating conditions that affect mobility, then that unit, not the entire facility must meet the higher level of requirements for accessibility.

6.2 Entrances

This section contains technical specifications for entrances. No changes were made to this paragraph.

6.3 Patient Bedrooms

Section 6.3 provides that accessible patient bedrooms shall be provided in compliance with 4.1 through 4.35. Each accessible bedroom shall have a door that complies with 4.13, except that entry doors to acute care hospital bedrooms for in-patients shall be exempted from the requirement in 4.13.6 for maneuvering space at the latch side of the door if the door is at least 44 inches wide. Each accessible bedroom shall also have adequate space to provide a maneuvering space that complies with 4.2.3. In rooms with 2 beds, it is preferable that this space be located between beds. Furthermore, each accessible bedroom shall have adequate space to provide a minimum clear floor space of 36 inches along each side of the bed and to provide an accessible route complying with 4.3.3 to each side of each bed.

Comment. The NPRM provided that each bedroom would have a turning space preferably located near the entrance and a minimum clear floor space of 36 inches along each side of the

bed. Approximately one-third of the comments received which addressed this section considered the space requirements at entrances to patient bedrooms and along side beds to be too restrictive or excessive and would have a substantial impact on costs and availability of space. The American Association of Homes for the Aging (AAHA) recommended that the guidelines only require a minimum amount of square footage per room and leave the configuration of the room to the discretion of facility operators. The AAHA argued that existing requirements such as those issued by the Health Care Finance Administration (HCFA) on environmental quality already address the needs of patients including those who are disabled.

Response. The HCFA requirements cannot be regarded as an effective alternative to these guidelines as they address environmental quality and are not designed to address accessibility.

The NPRM recommended that a turning space in compliance with 4.2.3 be located near the entrance. As the provisions in 4.13 for doors addresses the issue of maneuvering space at doors, this was deleted.

In the NPRM, the Board distinguished between requirements for two-bed rooms and four-bed rooms. With the exception of stating that in rooms with two beds, it is preferable that the maneuvering space be located between the beds, the Board has revised the language to provide that each bedroom shall have adequate space to provide a minimum clear floor space of 36 inches along each side of the bed and to provide an accessible route complying with 4.3.3 to each side of the bed. The Board determined that the additional requirements for space between the foot of the bed and the wall or the foot of the opposing bed of 42 and 48 inches was excessive and not consistent with other accessibility requirements in the guidelines. Accordingly, the Board revised the guidelines to provide that only a provision of 36 inches along all sides of the bed is required.

For purposes of clarity, the Board restated the exception to 4.13 that entry doors to acute care hospital bedrooms for in-patients shall be exempted from the requirement in 4.13.6 for maneuvering space at the latch side of the door if the door is at least 44 inches wide.

6.4 Patient Toilet Rooms

This section was revised to clarify that where private toilet/bath rooms are provided as part of an accessible patient bedroom, the toilet/bath room must

comply with 4.22 or 4.23 and be on an accessible route.

7. Business and Mercantile

7.1   General

These sections contain specific requirements for all areas used for business transactions with the public, and are in addition to those in 4.1 through 4.35.

The comments received on this section generally involved operational issues which, pursuant to the ADA, are under the jurisdiction of the Department of Justice and not these guidelines. With the exception of providing that the provisions of this section are in addition to those in 4.1 through 4.35 (as opposed to 4.34 in the NPRM), no changes were made to this paragraph.

7.2   Sales and Service Counters, Teller Windows, Information Counters

Section 7.2 requires that where counters with cash registers are provided in department stores and miscellaneous retail stores for sales or distribution of goods or services to the public, at least one of each type shall have a portion of the counter which is at least 36 inches in length with a maximum height of 36 inches above the finish floor. It shall be on an accessible route complying with 4.3. The accessible counters must be dispersed throughout the building or facility. In alterations where it is technically infeasible to provide an accessible counter, an auxiliary counter meeting these requirements may be provided. Where counters without cash registers are provided and at which goods or services are sold or distributed, this section provides for three options: (1) A portion of the main counter which is a minimum of 36 inches in length shall be provided with a maximum height of 36 inches in; (or) (2) an auxiliary counter with a maximum height of 36 inches in close proximity to the main counter shall be provided; or (3) equivalent facilitation shall be provided. All accessible sales and service counters shall be on an accessible route complying with 4.3.

Comment. The NPRM did not explain the term "portion" and the Board was urged to clarify the reference to "portion".

Response. The Board provided language to reflect that a "portion of the counter" refers to a portion of the counter which is at least 36 inches in length with a maximum height of 36 inches above the finish floor.

Comment. The Board sought comments on whether a portion of each teller station or ticketing area should be accessible or whether a percentage of the stations should be accessible where services are available at several points. Approximately 25% of the commenters to this section supported the requirement that a percentage should comply. Only a third of those responses recommended a specific percentage which ranged from 5% to 100%, but not less than one. Almost 50% of the responses preferred that a portion of each counter/station comply. The latter group of commenters argued that a portion of each is better because (1) it is difficult to ensure that the accessible counter will be staffed at all times; (2) it eliminates the stigma of a "handicap counter"; (3) counter functions may change throughout the day; (4) often there is only one queuing line rather than a separate line for each station which lessens the chance of getting the "accessible station"; and (5) equipment may break down rendering the accessible counter unusable.

Comments from banking institutions raised the concern that lower counters are a security risk for their tellers, banks, employees and customers. The hotel/motel industry was equally concerned over the security risks for their employees and also raised the issue that a higher counter is more ergonomically efficient for standing work areas. Supermarkets were concerned with how to make the refrigerated display cases in the meat, deli, and seafood accessible. They proposed serving disabled customers at the end of the counter. Retailers were concerned over the showcase islands which they use, as well as security and the loss of storage and display areas if they have to have a lower counter at every island.

Response. The Board amended the language of this section to take into consideration the different types of businesses and the varying uses of counters.

Counters with cash registers: In a department store or other retail store where counters with cash registers are provided, there must be at least one of each type which shall have a portion of the counter which is at least 36 inches with a maximum height of 36 inches above the finish floor. It shall be on an accessible route complying with 4.3. Accordingly, if the retailer chooses to have an express cash lane and one which takes only charges, one of each must be accessible.

Counters without cash registers, but where goods or services are sold or distributed: Where there are no cash registers at the counter, the Board provided for three options: (1) A portion of the main counter that is 36 inches in width minimum shall be provided with a maximum height of 36 inches; or (2) an auxiliary counter with a height of 36 inches in close proximity to the main counter shall be provided; or (3) equivalent facilitation shall be provided.

The NPRM provided that where counters exceeding 36 inches in height are provided, a portion of the main counter shall be provided with a maximum height of between 28 inches to 34 inches above the floor. To address the concerns of safety raised by the commenters in response to the Board's question, the Board changed the scoping from "a portion of the main counter" to "at least one of each type" and raised the height requirement to a maximum of 36 inches above the finish floor. Additionally, where there is a cash register, only a portion of the counter need comply and that portion would not have to contain the cash register. Furthermore, for counters where there is no cash register, equivalent facilitation such as providing an auxiliary counter in close proximity to the main counter can be provided and may accommodate security concerns.

The Board has also added a provision in the appendix which recommends that an assistive listening device which complies with 4.33 be permanently installed at each location or series.

7.3 Check-out Aisles

Section 7.2 refers to counters without aisles whereas this section concerns counters with aisles which are identified here as check out aisles. A counter without an aisle can be approached in more than one direction such as in a convenience store, whereas a counter with an aisle has a circulation route having one approach and one exit and is therefore only approachable in one direction.

Comment. Of the comments received on this section, there was strong support from individuals with disabilities and their organizations for requiring that all check-out aisles be accessible. The response from the business community was strong in its opposition to requiring 100% accessibility. In support of their position, the business industry cited security risks, expense and difficult employee working conditions. The businesses provided statistics to support their concern for the costs involved. In connection with the cost impact of lost space, the International Mass Retail Association advised that sales per square foot equalled $185 in the last year and on the average it was $224.

Response. In the NPRM, the Board pointed out options which are available that can be designed and constructed to be accessible with only minor variations from what is considered the "typical" design and little or no increase in overall square footage. The Board cited examples such as cashiers' stations that can be staggered front-to-back, or two narrow check-out aisles can be combined into a double-wide aisle served by cashiers on both the right and left sides of the aisle. The Board sought comments relating to the experience of stores which have utilized these designs to provide wider check-out aisles and whether the designs presented security considerations or required additional space. The comments received from the business industry reflected a concern over the loss of store space that would result with each accessible aisle and security problems. The Board has addressed these concerns by changing the requirement for 100% accessibility to a requirement that the number of accessible aisles be provided in accordance with a sliding scale which is based on the number of each type of check-out aisles. Check-out aisles of different design include those which are specifically designed to serve different functions and includes the following features: length of belt or no belt; or permanent signage designating the aisle as an express lane. Signage identifying accessible check-out aisles shall comply with 4.30.7 and shall be mounted above the check-out aisle in the same location where the check-out number or type of check-out is displayed. For small businesses, where the selling space is under 5000 square feet, only one check-out aisle is required to be accessible.

In alterations, at least one check-out aisle shall be accessible in facilities under 5000 square feet of selling space. In facilities over 5000 square feet of selling space, at least one of each design of check-out aisle shall be made accessible when altered until the number of accessible check-out aisles of each design equals the number required in new construction.

7.4 Security Bollards

No changes were made to this paragraph.

8. Libraries

These sections are taken from UFAS without change and provide specific requirements for the design of all public areas of libraries, including reading and study areas, stacks, reference rooms, reserve areas, and special facilities and collections. They are in addition to the requirements contained in 4.1 through 4.35.

Comment. The majority of the comments received regarding this section were from individuals with disabilities and their organizations and included changes related primarily to individual concerns or preferences. Except for one commenter who stated that the North Carolina Building Code requires all fixed tables, stacks and carrels to be accessible, no research or supporting data was cited in the recommended changes.

Several commenters did raise concerns over the lack of requirements for braille/voice input/output terminals for book catalogs and existing electronic catalogs.

Response. The issue of braille/voice input/output terminals is an operational matter and is under the purview of the Department of Justice and is not addressed in the guidelines.

The Board retained the language of this section with only two minor changes. In section 8.3, the reference for the check out area was changed to reference 7.2(1) to be consistent with the requirements under sales and service counters. In section 8.4 (Card Catalogs and Magazine Displays), the term "reference stacks" was deleted to avoid confusion with section 8.5 which places no limit on the height of "stacks".

9. Accessible Transient Lodging

Section 9 contains specific requirements for transient lodging which are in addition to those contained in section 4.1 through 4.35.

Comment. Many of the comments on this particular section came from the hotel industry, the majority of which recommended that the cross-reference to sections 5 and 7 should be deleted as it is redundant.

Response. Since 4.1.1(2) identifies the requirements for buildings with multiple functions, the cross-reference to sections 5 and 7 has been deleted.

Comment. The response from individuals with disabilities and their organizations generally recommended additional provisions for signage for persons who are visually impaired, such as requirements for tactile characters on doors, braille instructions on the use of phones, television, appliances, environmental controls, and other necessities and amenities which are provided by the hotel, as well as directional signage.

Response. No changes were made to this section regarding signage since section 4.30 addresses this issue and is applicable to transient lodging. In particular, sections 4.30.4 through 4.30.6 provide for permanent identification of rooms and spaces. Requiring brailled instructions for the use of phones, televisions and other portable items as suggested by commenters, is an operational issue which falls under the

jurisdiction of the Department of Justice and is not addressed in these guidelines.

Comment. One commenter noted that requiring all rooms to be on an accessible route would require the installation of elevators in two story hotels previously excluded in 4.1.3(5).

Response. In lieu of installing an elevator, the accessible rooms may be located on a ground floor which is accessible and thus elevators are not mandatory in two story hotels.

Section 9.1 Hotels, Motels, Inns, Boarding Houses, Dormitories, Resorts and other Similar Places of Transient Lodging

The proposed guidelines provided that all public use and common use areas and five percent, but never fewer than one, of each class of sleeping rooms or suites are required to be designed and constructed to comply with section 4 and sections 9.2 through 9.3. The proposed guidelines further provided that in addition to the 5% accessible room requirement, another 5% must comply with 9.3 (sleeping accommodations for persons with hearing impairments) for a total of 10% of each class.

These requirements were enumerated in paragraph 9.1 of the proposed guidelines. The final guidelines address these areas in individually numbered sub-paragraphs in 9.1. They are discussed below in the order they appear under the new numbering system.

9.1.2 Accessible Units, Sleeping Rooms, and Suites

Comment—Number of accessible rooms. The majority of the comments from individuals with disabilities and their organizations supported the provision of a minimum of 5% accessible rooms. A small number of commenters suggested that the percentage of accessible rooms should equal the percentage of persons with disabilities; that at least 8% of the rooms should be accessible; that the 5% figure should increase to 10% in new construction; the exemption for facilities with fewer than 5 units should be deleted or that long term lodging (i.e. dormitories) should have additional rooms if the demand exceeds the supply.

Comments received from the business and industry groups strongly argued against the 5% figure stating that there was no foundation to support that requirement. Several commenters suggested a 2 to 4% figure. The American Hotel and Motel Association (AHMA) argued for a lower figure citing (1) the Department of Justice Preliminary Regulatory Impact Analysis which

states that according to a 1984 study by Mathematica Policy Research, 645,000 persons use wheelchairs; and (2) the US Travel Data Center statistics which found that 65% of all US residents take one or more trips for business or pleasure at least 100 miles away from home each year. Using these statistics, the AHMA found that a goal of achieving an equivalent amount of travel for disabled people would result in 419,000 travelers who use wheelchairs in the United States which equates to less than 0.3% of all travelers. Using the Board's statistics, of 1,341,000 people who use a wheelchair and/or a walker (National Health Institute Services, Home Care Supplement: 1980) and assuming 65% traveling, the AHMA found this to result in slightly more than 0.5%. The AHMA also cited the 1990 California Hotel and Motel Association survey of its members which indicated that the "incidence of demand as demonstrated by reservations for wheelchair accessible rooms was less than 0.1%." Based on that survey, the AHMA proposed that only 1% of the rooms should be required to be accessible.

Comment. Roll-in showers. The Board invited comments relative to a requirement for the larger roll-in showers in transient lodging. The majority of the responses received were strongly in favor of the larger stalls but varied on the number which should be required. Some of the issues raised in the responses included (1) requiring roll-in showers for people with disabilities who are unable to transfer into a bathtub or onto a shower seat; (2) requiring 5 feet by 5 feet showers; (3) providing fold down bench seats in all shower stalls; (4) placing shower controls along the side wall adjacent to the bathroom; (5) requiring both bath tubs and showers in accessible units; and (6) providing accessible shower chairs.

Response. The Board based the requirement for 5% accessible rooms on Board sponsored research which provided that 1,341,000 are reported to use a wheelchair and/or walker (National Health Institute Services, Home Care Supplement: 1980); and 5,191,000 individuals have other mobility impairments (Bureau of Census, Disability Functional Limitation and Insurance coverage: 1984–85). While the statistics provided by AHMA and others in the lodging industry would suggest a much lower percentage of 1%, the comments received from individuals with disabilities and their organizations were overwhelmingly in favor of a higher percentage citing instances where no rooms or an insufficient number of rooms were available, thus making travel difficult or impossible for individuals with disabilities. The Board took note of a voluntary standard approved by the AHMA Executive Engineers Committee and published by both AHMA and the Paralyzed Veterans of America. The standard proposed a 2% to 4% criteria for the number of accessible guest rooms in newly constructed hotels and motels (An Interpretation of ANSI A117.1 (1986) The American National Standard for Buildings and Facilities—Providing Accessibility and Usability for Physically Handicapped People as applicable to New Hotels and Motels).

Taking into consideration the additional statistics provided by AHMA regarding the percentage of people who travel as well the response from individuals with disabilities and their organizations regarding the difficulty experienced in traveling and the overwhelmingly favorable response to requiring a roll-in shower, the Board revised this section to provide that accessible sleeping rooms and roll-in showers in compliance with 9.2, 4.21 and Figure 57 shall be provided on a sliding scale in accordance with the table in 9.1.2. The table provides for 4% of the first 100 rooms to be accessible, decreasing to 20 accessible rooms in a facility with 1000 rooms, plus 1% for each 100 over that 1000. The table also provides that in facilities with over 50 rooms, 1% of the rooms shall have roll-in showers.

9.1.3 Sleeping Accommodations for Persons with Hearing Impairments

Comment. A number of commenters misunderstood the provisions relating to the number of rooms which must comply with section 9.3 (Visual Alarms, Notification Devices, and Telephones). Many did not understand that the requirement that a number of rooms must comply with 9.3 was in addition to those required to comply with 9.2.

Response. The Board has revised the language to clearly reflect that the provision for sleeping accommodations for persons with hearing impairments is in addition to the accessible room requirements for section 9.2.

Comment. As with 9.1.2, there was strong support from individuals with disabilities and their organizations in support of accessible rooms for people with hearing impairments, and strong objections from the business community over the basis for requiring 5%. The lodging industry based its objections on statistics cited by the Board in its preamble which provide that 1,741,000 individuals are deaf in both ears

(National Institute on Disability and Rehabilitation Research, Data on Disability from the National Health Interview Survey: 1983) and the US Travel Data Center statistics which found that 65% of all US residents take one or more trips for business or pleasure at least 100 miles away from home each year. Using these statistics, the result would be .7% travelers. The lodging industry suggested that 1% would be a more appropriate requirement.

Response. In the preamble to the proposed guidelines, the Board also cited the Bureau of Census statistics which stated that 7,694,000 individuals have difficulty hearing what is said in a normal conversation with another person, including those who cannot hear at all (Bureau of Census, Disability Functional Limitation and Insurance Coverage: 1984–85). The Board further pointed out that an analysis of demographic date reveals there are at least as many persons with hearing impairments as there are persons with mobility impairments. Other studies indicate that a greater percentage of individuals have a hearing impairment (i.e., the National Center for Health Statistics found a 7.9 percent rate, National Health Interview Survey, 1979–80). Based on that data and the ADA's mandate that the Board provide greater guidance with respect to communication accessibility, the proposed guidelines required compliance with section 9.3 for an additional number of rooms equal to that requried to comply with section 9.2. Taking into consideration the statistical data provided by the AHMA regarding the percentage of travelers as discussed in 9.1.2 above, the Board has revised this section to provide that in addition to those accessible sleeping rooms and suites required by 9.1.2, sleeping rooms which comply with 9.3 shall be provided in conformance with the table in 9.1.3. That table provides for 4% of the first 100 rooms to comply with 9.3, decreasing to 20 accessible rooms in a facility with 1000 rooms, plus 1% for each 100 over that 1000.

9.1.4 Classes of Sleeping Accommodations

Comment. The majority of the comments received from individuals with disabilities and their organizations suggested that "class" should take into consideration price, the size of the room (i.e. number of beds) and the various amenities and features provided. Two commenters from the building code group/state access agency category suggested that in lieu of using the term "class" it would be preferable to require that the rooms be dispersed throughout

the facility to ensure that a person with a disability the fullest range of room reservations available to the general public.

The lodging industry urged the use of the "standard industry classification" to define "class": (a) Standard rooms; (b) premium rooms (where a distinctly different level of service is provided); (c) suites (all types). Use of this classification would take into consideration the size of the room, amenities and features and, indirectly, price.

Response. In order to provide persons with disabilities with a range of options which are available to others, the Board has revised this section to provide that the rooms will be dispersed among the various classes of sleeping accommodations available. Factors to be considered in determining the various classes include room size, cost, amenities provided, and the number of beds provided.

The Board added a provision for equivalent facilitation to this section which allows the operator of a facility to limit construction of accessible rooms to those intended for multiple occupancy, provided that such rooms are made available to those who request a single occupancy room at the cost of a single occupancy room. This provision allows for more flexibility in the distribution of accessible rooms for the operator of a facility and provides accessible rooms for those who request a single occupancy room and rate.

9.1.5 Alterations to Accessible Units, Sleeping Rooms, and Suites

The Board took the pcsition that a section on alterations specifically for transient lodging was appropriate for the reason that there are a number of problems peculiar to hotels, which regularly implement a seven or eight year cycle of alterations. For instance, if a percentage of rooms is required to be accessible and the hotel later alters a non-accessible room, a question is raised as to whether to make that room an accessible room or that element an accessible element, and as to how this would apply to wings of hotels. Accordingly, the Board has added a paragraph to section 9 which provides requirements for accessibility when sleeping rooms or a portion of the rooms are altered in an existing facility. The guidelines provide that where alterations occur, at least one sleeping room or suite that complies with the requirement of 9.2 (Requirements for Accessible Units, Sleeping Rooms, and Suites) shall be provided for each 25 sleeping rooms, or fraction thereof, of rooms being altered until the number of such rooms provided equals the number required to be accessible by 9.1.2. For each 25 sleeping rooms, or fraction, of rooms being altered, at least one sleeping room or suite that complies with the requirement of 9.3 (Visual Alarms, Notification Devices, and telephones) shall be provided until the number of such rooms equals the number required to be accessible by 9.1.3. For further discussion regarding alteration requirements which directly affect transient lodging, see 4.1.6 (Accessible Buildings: Alterations).

9.2 Requirements for Accessible Units, Sleeping Rooms and Suites

9.2.1 General

This section provides that units, sleeping rooms and suites required to be accessible by 9.1 shall comply with 9.2.

No comments were received for this section and the Board has not made any changes.

9.2.2 Minimum Requirements

This section provides the minimum requirements for accessible units, sleeping rooms and suites.

Maneuvering Space (9.2.2(1))

This section requires a maneuvering space of 36 inches clear width located along both sides of a bed, except that where two beds are provided, this requirement can be met by providing a 36 inches wide maneuvering space located between the two beds.

Comment. The Board sought comments on whether maneuvering space should be required along both sides of a bed to accommodate individuals who use wheelchairs and can transfer from a wheelchair to a bed from only one side. The results were divided among individuals with disabilities and their organizations and the business organizations. Individuals with disabilities and their organizations, government agencies involved with disability issues and other government agencies overwhelmingly supported the provision of maneuvering space on both sides of a bed. The lodging industry however, overwhelmingly took the opposite position based on the reasoning that the maneuvering clearances required by section 9.2.2(1) allow forward or reverse approach, thus permitting side access from either the right or the left.

Response. Because an individual can transfer from the left or the right as a result of the ability to go forward or reverse, does not mean that the individual can also turn themselves around 180 degrees to be at one end of

the bed or the other. Thus, such an individual would not be able to utilize amenities provided such as television or necessities such as telephones. For this reason, the forward and reverse argument of the lodging industry was not acceptable.

The Board took the position that a maneuvering space should be required on both sides of a bed and that a 36 inches clear width maneuvering space was appropriate. Where two beds are provided, the requirement is met by providing the maneuvering space between the two beds.

Accessible Route (9.2.2.(2))

This section requires that an accessible route complying with 4.3 connect all accessible spaces and elements including telephones within the unit. This does not require an elevator in multi-story units as long as the spaces identified in 9.2.2 (6) and (7) are on accessible levels and the accessible sleeping area is suitable for dual occupancy.

Comment. One commenter suggested that the route should be required into and through the unit. This latter was reference to HUD's guidelines which provides in 24 CFR 100.205(c)(3)(ii) that there shall be an accessible route into and through the covered dwelling.

The lodging industry noted that there are a number of transient lodging facilities that have types of sleeping accomodations or dwelling units that are multi-story or split level. They took the position that vertical access should not be required to each story or level as long as all primary functions are available on accessible levels.

Response. To require an accessible route into and through each multi-story unit would be cost prohibitive unless the occupant exited their living space into a common area, used public use elevator, and reentered the unit from a different level at great inconvenience to the occupant.

The final guidelines address the concerns of the lodging industry and clarify that it is not the Board's intent to require vertical access to each story or level. However, this is provided that the spaces identified in 9.2.2 (6) and (7) are on accessible levels and are suitable for dual occupancy.

Doors (9.2.2(3))

This section requires that doors and doorways designed to allow passage into and within all sleeping rooms, suites or other covered units shall comply with 4.13.

Comment. The AHMA and other members of the lodging industry took the position that the Board should not

require doors to non-usable space to be accessible.

Response. The response from individuals with disabilities and their organizations was overwhelmingly in favor of this requirement. Many individuals with disabilities stated that rooms not required to be fully accessible would still be usable by some if they were able to enter the doorways. For instance, if the doorways are accessible, individuals with varying mobility impairments may be able to use a room that does not have grab bars or a room that does not have maneuvering space.

The legislative history of the ADA states that, with respect to hotels, accessibility includes "requiring all doors and doorways designed to allow passage into and within all hotel rooms and bathrooms to be sufficiently wide to allow passage by individuals who use wheelchairs." H. Rept. 101–485, pt. 2, at 118. The Board retained this provision with no changes.

Storage (9.2.2(4))

This section requires that if fixed or built-in storage facilities such as cabinets, shelves, closets, and drawers are provided in accessible spaces, at least one of each type provided shall contain storage space complying with 4.25. Additional storage may be provided outside those dimensions.

Comment. The majority of the comments on this section were from the lodging industry, who suggested that the accessible rooms should also be usable by other than disabled guests. This could be accomplished they suggested, by such practices as installing two door viewers, two clothes closet rods—one at an "accessible" height and one at a standard height.

Response. The Board has addressed the concerns of the lodging industry by clarifying that as long as the minimum requirements are met, additional storage may be provided outside the dimensions required in 4.25.

Controls (9.2.2(5))

This section provides that all controls shall comply with 4.27. No changes were made to this section.

Accessible Areas (9.2.2(6))

This section requires that where provided the following shall be accessible and on an accessible route:

(a) The living area; (b) the dining area; (c) at least one sleeping area; (d) patios, terraces or balconies; (e) at least one full bathroom; (f) if only half baths are provided, at least one half bath, and (g) carports, garages or parking spaces.

Of the comments received on transient lodging, the majority concerned this section. The comments mainly focused on two areas—(d) patios and terraces; and (e) the bathroom area. Those areas are addressed below.

Patios, Terraces and Balconies (9.2.2(6)(d))

Comment. One commenter objected to this provision as it placed an unreasonable restraint on exterior architecture and window/door systems. The AHMA and others in the lodging industry however, were almost unanimous in their opposition to this requirement due to weather protection needs at ocean side resort property and other areas subject to high wind and water damage from hurricanes and storms which result in door sills higher than ½ inch.

Response. The Board understands the need to protect the integrity of the unit from water and weather damage and that many local building codes require higher door thresholds or a change in the level of the balcony to prevent structural damage from water. The Board also recognizes that to provide for higher thresholds or a change in level would, in all probability, eliminate the use of a balcony or deck area by individuals with disabilities. The final guidelines therefore provide that the requirements of 4.13.8 (Thresholds at Doorways) and 4.3.8 (Changes in Level) do no apply where it is necessary to utilize a higher door threshold or a change in level to protect the integrity of the unit from wind and water damage. The final guidelines also provide that where the exception to 4.13.8 and 4.3.8 would result in an inaccessible route to patios, terraces or balconies, that equivalent facilitation shall be provided. Equivalent facilitation at a hotel patio or balcony might consist of providing raised decking or a ramp to achieve accessibility.

Bathrooms (9.2.2(6)(e))

Comment. The responses to this paragraph were primarily from the disability community and focused on the need for accessible showers.

Response. The Board has responded to the issue of a roll-in shower under section 9.1.2 (Accessible Units, Sleeping Rooms, and Suites) and has included a requirement for a roll-in shower based on a sliding scale.

Kitchens, Kitchenettes, or Wet Bars (9.2.2(7))

This section provides for minimum requirements when kitchens, kitchenettes or wet bars are provided as accessory to a sleeping room or suite.

Comment. The AHMA and other commenters from the lodging industry urged the Board to reduce the requirement that 50% of the shelf space shall be accessible to 20% due to conventional design and cabinet fabrication practices.

Response. The Board considered the position of the lodging industry, however no further data was submitted in support of this position. The Board is of the opinion that current conventional design and fabrication practices are available which allow for the provision of 50% accessibility.

Comment. The AHMA and others in the lodging industry also expressed concern that many appliances are not manufactured with controls which are accessible according to 4.27 (such as coffee makers, toasters, microwave ovens, and other appliances).

Response. Under the ADA, the Board has jurisdiction to provide guidelines for built in applicances—not items such as toasters and coffee makers. Those items are therefore not addressed in the guidelines. Although portable devices are allowed under equivalent facilitation, the guidelines do not prescribe the features or controls of such devices. The Board does propose to address the issue of such appliances in the ADA manual.

9.3 Sleeping Room Accommodations for Persons with Hearing Impairments

9.3.1 General.

These requirements were enumerated in paragraph 9.3 of the proposed guidelines. The final guidelines address this area in 9.3.1. This section specifies the features which must be provided in units, sleeping rooms, or suites required to accommodate persons with hearing impairments. Visual alarms which comply with 4.28.4 must be provided. Visual notification devices which alert room occupants of incoming telephone calls and a door knock or bell must also be provided. The visual notification device may not be connected to visual alarm signal applicances. If a permanently installed telephone is provided, it shall have a volume control. An accessible electrical outlet within 4 feet of a telephone connection shall be provided to facilitate the use of a text telephone.

Comment. The disability groups generally supported the requirements of this provision. The comments suggested additional considerations which primarily involved the provision of portable devices. Members of the lodging industry took the position that guests could provide their own

notification devices and that only electrical outlets should be required.

In the PRM, the Board noted the availability of both portable and built-in visual alarms and visual notification devices. The Board sought information on the effectiveness and usability of portable devices as compared to built-in devices.

Generally, individuals with disabilities and their organizations were divided on which was preferable. In all, 25% of the comments (the majority of which were from the disability community) preferred built-in devices while 23% of the comments (the majority of which were from the disability community) preferred portable devices; 12% of the comments stated that portable devices were acceptable; 2% of the comments supported the use of portable devices when built-in devices are not available; 5% of the comments opposed the use of portable devices; and 18% of the comments supported the use of both.

The lodging industry took the position that if it was the intent of the guidelines to use portable devices only when they can be activated by a building alarm system then permanent devices will be required due to the lack of availability of such a portable system. The lodging industry stated that permanent devices will result in excessive costs and less flexibility in room selections.

Response. The guidelines require that auxiliary visual alarms shall be provided and comply with 4.28.4. Visual notification devices shall also be provided to alert room occupants of incoming telephone calls and a door knock or bell. The guidelines do allow for equivalent facilitation which requires the installation of electrical outlets and telephone wiring in order to enable the use of portable visual alarms and communications devices provided by the operator of the facility.

9.4 Other Sleeping Rooms and Suites

This section provides that doors and doorways designed to allow passage into and within all sleeping units or other covered units shall comply with 4.13.5.

Comment. The responses from individuals with disabilities and their organizations were overwhelmingly in favor of the accessibility of all doors and doorways. Responses from the lodging industry however, were overwhelmingly against this provision arguing that accessible doors should not be required to non-usable units as it is an undue burden without proven demand. Comments from the lodging industry cite the incurring of extraordinary costs by necessitating greater square footage in guest rooms and bathrooms to accommodate door swings and clearance. As for existing buildings which are altered, the industry commenters argued that it would be prohibitively expensive and architecturally or structurally impractical. The industry further took the position that the 32-inch minimum clearance should apply only to the guestroom entrance doors and only in new construction.

Response. Comments from individuals with disabilities however, frequently identified situations where a standard room could be used if it has an accessible entrance and bathroom doors.

The legislative history of the ADA states that, with respect to hotels, accessibility includes "requiring all doors and doorways designed to allow passage into and within all hotel rooms and bathrooms to be sufficiently wide to allow passage by individuals who use wheelchairs." H. Rept. 101–485, pt. 2, at 118.

The Board retained this provision with no changes.

9.5 Transient Lodging in Homeless Shelters, Halfway Houses, Transient Group Homes, and other Social Services Establishments

The Board received few comments specifically from organizations who were advocates for the homeless, however overall the comments received on this section from individuals with disabilities, disability groups and the business community generally expressed a sensitivity to the issues of cost and availability and the needs of those who are homeless.

9.5.1 New Construction

This section provides that in new construction all public use and common use areas are required to comply with section 4. At least one of each type of amenity in each common area shall be accessible and shall be located on an accessible route to any accessible unit or sleeping accommodation.

Comment. The Board sought comment on whether it is necessary or appropriate to require at least one of every amenity to be accessible in each of the common areas. The majority of the responses were from individuals with disabilities and their organizations. The responses were split on whether or not the Board should amend the proposed language to provide that at least one of each type of amenity be available in an accessible common area.

Response. The Board has retained the language of this provision without

change but has added a provision to acknowledge the elevator exception provided in section 4.1.3(5). Where elevators are not provided, as allowed in 4.1.3(5), accessible amenities are not required on inaccessible floors as long as one of each type is provided in common areas on accessible floors.

9.5.2 Alterations

This section was previously reserved in the NPRM. The Board recognized that unique problems may arise when homeless shelters and similar establishments are placed in existing facilities originally designed for different purposes. The Board sought comments on what scoping provisions should apply to homeless shelters. Factors to be considered are the needs of the population to be served, service availability, and the significant demand for these important and scarce facilities.

Comment. Approximately 25% of the commenters took the position that the scoping should be the same as in other transient lodging. Just over 10% suggested that the scoping should be less than that in transient lodging. Some commenters responded by urging the Board to consider the cost vs. usage issue and to be sensitive to the realization that the number of shelters may be limited by the standards. A few commenters suggested a proportion (5% to 10%) of the shelter space should be accessible.

Response. The Board is mindful of the considerations in assessing the appropriate scoping requirements for alterations in homeless shelters and sought comments concerning this issue. The responses, however did not provide sufficient information regarding the need and the impact of applying the guidelines developed for other transient lodging, such as hotel and motels, to homeless shelters.

The Board is concerned that without homeless shelters, the most vulnerable members of society, including those homeless people who are disabled, will be without shelter. The Board wishes to avoid guidelines which result in a shelter not opening or expanding or result in the closing of shelters which are out of compliance.

The Board intends to conduct further study of this issue. Until such research is completed and guidelines are adopted, the Board has provided interim minimum guidelines.

The guidelines provide the provisions of 9.5.3 (Accessible Sleeping Accommodations in New Construction) and 9.1.5 (Alterations to Accessible Units, Sleeping Rooms, and Suites) shall apply to sleeping rooms and beds in social service establishments which are

not homeless shelters and the alterations of other areas in such establishments shall be consistent with the new construction provisions of 9.5.1 (New Construction).

In homeless shelters, where the following elements are altered, the following requirements apply: (a) at least one public entrance shall allow a person with mobility impairments to approach, enter and exit including a minimum clear door width of 32 inches; (b) sleeping space for homeless persons as provided in the scoping provision of 9.1.2 (Accessible Units, Sleeping Rooms, and Suites in Transient Lodging) shall include doors to the sleeping area with a minimum clear width of 32 inches and maneuvering space around the beds for persons with mobility impairments complying with 9.2.2(1); (c) at least one toilet room for each gender or one unisex toilet room shall have a minimum clear door width of 32 inches, minimum turning space complying with 4.2.3 (Wheelchair Turning Space), one water closet complying with 4.16 (Water Closets), one lavatory complying with 4.19 (Lavatories and Mirrors), and the door shall have a privacy latch and, if provided, at least one tub or shower shall comply with 4.20 (Bathtubs) or 4.21 (Shower Stalls) respectively; (d) at least one common area which a person with mobility impairments can approach, enter and exit including a minimum clear door width of 32 inches; (e) at least one route connecting elements (a), (b), (c) and (d) which a person with mobility impairments can use including minimum clear width of 36 inches, passing space complying with 4.3.4 (Passing Space) turning space complying with 4.2.3 (Wheelchair Turning Space) and changes in levels complying with 4.3.8 (Changes in Levels); and (f) homeless shelters can comply with the provisions of (a)-(e) by providing the above elements on one floor.

9.5.3 Accessible Sleeping Accommodations in New Construction

The Board previously reserved this section in the NPRM and sought comments on whether the Board should require 5% of sleeping accommodations to be fully accessible, with an additional 2% for people with hearing impairments.

Comment. With respect to accessible sleeping rooms, approximately 50% of the responses supported requiring 5% of the sleeping rooms to be fully accessible.

Response. The Board is mindful of the desire to balance the need for accessibility in homeless shelters versus the impact of additional construction requirements. In the section on transient lodging for establishments such as hotels and motels, the Board adopted a sliding scale and it is the position of the Board that homeless shelters should not be held to more stringent scoping provisions. Accordingly, the scoping provisions for homeless shelters in new construction provide for accessible sleeping rooms in accordance with the table in 9.1.2 (Accessible Units, Sleeping Rooms, and Suites) and shall comply with 9.2 (Accessible Units, Sleeping Rooms and Suites) where such items are provided.

The Board recognizes that in some homeless shelters, the room or rooms contain a number of beds. In those instances, a percentage of the beds equal to the table provided in 9.1.2 shall comply with 9.2.2(1).

Comment. With respect to sleeping accommodations for persons with hearing impairments, approximately 25% of the responses favored requiring an additional 2% of the rooms to accommodate persons with hearing impairments. Approximately 50% of the commenters took the position that the 2% was too low. A number of commenters suggested that 9.5.3 should be consistent with the requirements for hotels, motels and other similar establishments.

Response. As in the requirements for accessible sleeping rooms in homeless shelters, the Board took the position that scoping provisions equal to those applicable to hotels, motels and similar establishments were appropriate. The guidelines provide that in addition to the rooms required to comply with the table in 9.1.2 (Accessible Units, Sleeping Rooms, and Suites), sleeping rooms that comply with 9.3 (Visual Alarms, Notification Devices and Telephones) shall be provided in accordance with the table in 9.1.3 (Sleeping Accommodations for Persons with Hearing Impairments).

10. Transportation Facilities [Reserved]

Regulatory Process Matters

The guidelines are issued to assist the Department of Justice to establish accessibility standards for new construction and alterations in places of public accommodation and commercial facilities as required by title III of the ADA. The Department of Justice has proposed to incorporate the guidelines in its final regulations as the accessibility standards for purposes of title III of the ADA. The guidelines thus meet the criteria for a major rule under Executive Order 12291 and have been reviewed by the Office of Management and Budget.

The Board has prepared a draft final regulatory impact analysis (RIA) of the guidelines. The draft final RIA is available for public comment. The Board will provide copies of the document to the public upon request. The public is encouraged to provide additional information as to the costs and benefits associated with the guidelines. Comments on costs and benefits that are received within 60 days of publication of these guidelines will be analyzed in the final RIA which will be completed by Janaury 1, 1992.

Accessibility does not generally add features to a building or facility but rather simply requires that features commonly provided have certain characteristics. Several studies discussed in the draft final RIA have shown that designing buildings and facilities to be accessible, from the conceptual phase onward, adds less than 1% to the total construction costs. The draft final RIA analyzes the cost impact of accessibility elements which have the potential of adding to the cost of a building or facility. Included in the analysis are: Areas of rescue assistance; parking (signage); curb ramps (detectable warnings); ramps (handrail extensions and edge protection); stairs (handrail extensions); elevators (raised characters on hoistway entrances, reopening devices, tactile and braille control indicators, and audible signage for car position); entrances (ramps); water closets and toilet stalls (grab bars); lavatories and sinks (insulation of hot water and drain pipes); bath tubs and shower stalls (seat, grab bars, and hand-held showers); alarms (visual systems); signage (tactile and braille characters); telephones (volume controls, text telephones, and signage); assembly areas (assistive listening systems); automated teller machines (equipment for persons with visual impairments); dressing and fitting rooms (curtained opening and swinging door); and roll-in showers and visual notification devices for accessible sleeping accommodations.

The draft final RIA also assesses the cost of space increases in certain building and facility types which are caused when accessible elements are repeated (e.g., accessible parking spaces in a parking lot and a parking garage; accessible patient bedrooms in a hospital and a nursing home). The element related costs are aggregated to estimate the costs for certain building types, including high-rise and low-rise office buildings, high-rise and low-rise hotels, auditoriums and movie theaters, parking lots and parking garages, and hospitals and nursing homes. For parking lots and parking garages, and hospitals and nursing homes, the aggregate costs also include the cost of space increases. The draft final RIA also discusses the indirect costs of the accessibility elements such as maintenance, operation and opportunity costs. Space allocation and re-allocation issues are analyzed with respect to maneuvering space in corridors; the standard toilet stall versus the alternate toilet stall; check-out aisles; and areas of rescue assistance.

As for regulatory alternatives, section 504 of the ADA specifically requires that the guidelines "supplement the existing (MGRAD)" on which the current UFAS is based and "establish additional requirements, consistent with this Act, to ensure that buildings (and) facilities * * * are accessible, in terms of architecture and design, * * * and communication, to individuals with disabilities." The legislative history states that the guidelines may not "reduce, weaken, narrow, or set less accessibility standards than those included in existing MGRAD" and should provide greater guidance in the area of communication accessibility for individuals with hearing and visual impairments. As mandated by the statute, the final guidelines use MGRAD and UFAS as their base or floor. The draft final RIA discusses regulatory alternatives considered for major provisions which go beyond MGRAD and UFAS. These include provisions for accessible parking; areas of rescue assistance; volume controls for public telephones; text telephones; detectable warnings; assistive listening systems; signage; and automated teller machines.

The draft final RIA also contains information that would be included in a final regulatory flexibility analysis under the Regulatory Flexibility Act and the final RIA will serve as the final regulatory flexibility analysis. The extensive notice and public comment procedure followed by the Board in the promulgation of these guidelines, which included public hearings, dissemination of materials, and provision of speakers to affected groups, clearly provided any interested small entities with the notice and opportunity for comment provided under the Regulatory Flexibility Act procedures.

The Board wishes to point out that Congress amended the Internal Revenue Code in 1990 to facilitate compliance by small entities with the ADA. Under section 44 of the Internal Revenue Code, as amended, eligible small businesses can receive a tax credit for certain costs of compliance with the ADA. An eligible small business is one whose gross receipts do not exceed $1,000,000 or whose workforce does not consist of more than 30 full-time workers.

Qualifying businesses may claim a credit of up to 50 percent of eligible access expenditures that exceed $250 but do not exceed $10,250. Examples of eligible access expenditures include the necessary and reasonable costs of removing barriers, providing auxiliary aids, and acquiring or modifying equipment or devices. Section 190 of the Internal Revenue Code, as amended, also provides for a deduction of up to $15,000 per year for expenses associated with the removal of qualified architectural and transportation barriers for any entity, regardless of size.

The guidelines do not preempt State and local regulation of the construction and alteration of places of public accommodation and commercial facilities. Section 308(b)(1)(A)(ii) of the ADA permits State and local governments to apply to the Attorney General for certification that a State or local code meets or exceeds the accessibility requirements of the ADA. Therefore, a Federalism assessment has not been prepared under Executive Order 12612.

The guidelines are effective immediately so that they can be incorporated in the Department of Justice's final regulations. The Department of Justice's final regulations will establish the effective date for the accessibility standards.

List of Subjects in 36 CFR Part 1191

Buildings, Civil rights, Handicapped, Individuals with disabilities.

Authorized by vote of the Board on July 1 and 12, 1991.

William H. McCabe,

Chairman, Architectural and Transportation Barriers Compliance Board.

For the reasons set forth in the preamble, the Board adds part 1191 to title 36 of the Code of Federal Regulations to read as follows:

PART 1191—AMERICANS WITH DISABILITIES ACT (ADA) ACCESSIBILITY GUIDELINES FOR BUILDINGS AND FACILITIES

Sec.
1191.1   Accessibility guidelines.
Appendix to part 1191—Americans With Disabilities Act (ADA) Accessibility Guidelines for Buildings and Facilities.

Authority: Americans With Disabilities Act of 1990, Pub. L. 101–336, 42 U.S.C. 12204.

§ 1191.11   Accessibility guidelines.

The accessibility guidelines for buildings and facilities for purposes of the Americans With Disabilities Act are found in the appendix to this part. The guidelines are issued to assist the Department of Justice to establish accessibility standards to implement the legislation.

BILLING CODE 8150-01-M

Americans with Disabilities Act (ADA)

Accessibility Guidelines for Buildings and Facilities

U.S. Architectural & Transportation Barriers
Compliance Board
1111 18th Street, N.W., Suite 501
Washington, D.C. 20036-3894
(202) 653-7834 v/TDD
(202) 653-7863 FAX

ADA ACCESSIBILITY GUIDELINES
FOR BUILDINGS AND FACILITIES
TABLE OF CONTENTS

i

1. PURPOSE.

This document sets guidelines for accessibility to places of public accommodation and commercial facilities by individuals with disabilities. These guidelines are to be applied during the design, construction, and alteration of such buildings and facilities to the extent required by regulations issued by Federal agencies, including the Department of Justice, under the Americans with Disabilities Act of 1990.

The technical specifications 4.2 through 4.35, of these guidelines are the same as those of the American National Standard Institute's document A117.1-1980, except as noted in this text by italics. However, sections 4.1.1 through 4.1.7 and sections 5 through 10 are different from ANSI A117.1 in their entirety and are printed in standard type.

The illustrations and text of ANSI A117.1 are reproduced with permission from the American National Standards Institute. Copies of the standard may be purchased from the American National Standards Institute at 1430 Broadway, New York, New York 10018.

2. GENERAL.

2.1 Provisions for Adults. *The specifications in these guidelines are based upon adult dimensions and anthropometrics.*

2.2* Equivalent Facilitation. *Departures from particular technical and scoping requirements of this guideline by the use of other designs and technologies are permitted where the alternative designs and technologies used will provide substantially equivalent or greater access to and usability of the facility.*

3. MISCELLANEOUS INSTRUCTIONS AND DEFINITIONS.

3.1 Graphic Conventions. Graphic conventions are shown in Table 1. Dimensions that are not marked minimum or maximum are absolute, unless otherwise indicated in the text or captions.

Table 1
Graphic Conventions

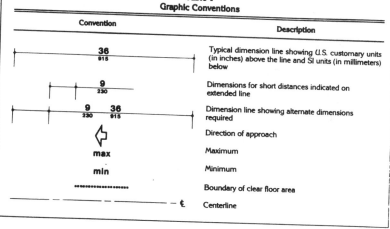

Convention	Description
36 / 915	Typical dimension line showing U.S. customary units (in inches) above the line and SI units (in millimeters) below
9 / 230	Dimensions for short distances indicated on extended line
9 / 230 36 / 915	Dimension line showing alternate dimensions required
⇦	Direction of approach
max	Maximum
min	Minimum
••••••••••••••••••••	Boundary of clear floor area
——————— ₵	Centerline

1

3.2 Dimensional Tolerances. All dimensions are subject to conventional building industry tolerances for field conditions.

3.3 Notes. The text of *these guidelines* does not contain notes or footnotes. Additional information, explanations, and advisory materials are located in the Appendix. Paragraphs marked with an asterisk have related, non-mandatory material in the Appendix. In the Appendix, the corresponding paragraph numbers are preceded by an A.

3.4 General Terminology.

comply with. Meet one or more specifications of *these guidelines.*

if, if ... then. Denotes a specification that applies only when the conditions described are present.

may. Denotes an option or alternative.

shall. Denotes a mandatory specification or requirement.

should. Denotes an advisory specification or recommendation.

3.5 Definitions.

Access Aisle. An accessible pedestrian space between elements, such as parking spaces, seating, and desks, that provides clearances appropriate for use of the elements.

Accessible. Describes a site, building, facility, or portion thereof that complies with *these guidelines.*

Accessible Element. An *element* specified by *these guidelines* (for example, telephone, controls, and the like).

Accessible Route. A continuous unobstructed path connecting all accessible elements and spaces of a building or facility. Interior accessible routes may include corridors, floors, ramps, elevators, lifts, and clear floor space at fixtures. Exterior accessible routes may include parking access aisles, curb ramps, *crosswalks at vehicular ways,* walks, ramps, and lifts.

Accessible Space. Space that complies with these guidelines.

Adaptability. The ability of certain building spaces and elements, such as kitchen counters, sinks, and grab bars, to be added or altered so as to accommodate the needs of *individuals with or without disabilities* or to accommodate the needs of persons with different types or degrees of disability.

Addition. An expansion, extension, or increase in the gross floor area of a building or facility.

Administrative Authority. A governmental agency that adopts or enforces regulations and *guidelines* for the design, construction, or alteration of buildings and facilities.

Alteration. An alteration is a change to a building or facility made by, on behalf of, or for the use of a public accommodation or commercial facility, that affects or could affect the usability of the building or facility or part thereof. Alterations include, but are not limited to, remodeling, renovation, rehabilitation, reconstruction, historic restoration, changes or rearrangement of the structural parts or elements, and changes or rearrangement in the plan configuration of walls and full-height partitions. Normal maintenance, reroofing, painting or wallpapering, or changes to mechanical and electrical systems are not alterations unless they affect the usability of the building or facility.

Area of Rescue Assistance. An area, which has direct access to an exit, where people who are unable to use stairs may remain temporarily in safety to await further instructions or assistance during emergency evacuation.

Assembly Area. A room or space accommodating a group of individuals for recreational, educational, political, social, or amusement purposes, or for the consumption of food and drink.

Automatic Door. A door equipped with a power-operated mechanism and controls that open and close the door automatically upon receipt of a momentary actuating signal. The switch that begins the automatic cycle may be a photoelectric device, floor mat, or manual switch (see power-assisted door).

2

C-52

Building. Any structure used and intended for supporting or sheltering any use or occupancy.

Circulation Path. An exterior or interior way of passage from one place to another for pedestrians, including, but not limited to, walks, hallways, courtyards, stairways, and stair landings.

Clear. Unobstructed.

Clear Floor Space. *The minimum unobstructed floor or ground space required to accommodate a single, stationary wheelchair and occupant.*

Closed Circuit Telephone. *A telephone with dedicated line(s) such as a house phone, courtesy phone or phone that must be used to gain entrance to a facility.*

Common Use. Refers to those interior and exterior rooms, spaces, or elements that are made available for the use of a restricted group of people (for example, *occupants of a homeless shelter*, the occupants of an office building, or the guests of such occupants).

Cross Slope. The slope that is perpendicular to the direction of travel (see running slope).

Curb Ramp. A short ramp cutting through a curb or built up to it.

Detectable Warning. *A standardized surface feature built in or applied to walking surfaces or other elements to warn visually impaired people of hazards on a circulation path.*

Dwelling Unit. A single unit which provides a kitchen or food preparation area, in addition to rooms and spaces for living, bathing, sleeping, and the like. *Dwelling units include a single family home or a townhouse used as a transient group home; an apartment building used as a shelter; guestrooms in a hotel that provide sleeping accommodations and food preparation areas; and other similar facilities used on a transient basis. For purposes of these guidelines, use of the term "Dwelling Unit" does not imply the unit is used as a residence.*

Egress, Means of. *A continuous and unobstructed way of exit travel from any point in a building or facility to a public way. A means of egress comprises vertical and horizontal travel* and may include intervening room spaces, doorways, hallways, corridors, passageways, balconies, ramps, stairs, enclosures, lobbies, horizontal exits, courts and yards. An accessible means of egress is one that complies with these guidelines and does not include stairs, steps, or escalators. Areas of rescue assistance or evacuation elevators may be included as part of accessible means of egress.

Element. *An architectural or mechanical component of a building, facility, space, or site, e.g., telephone, curb ramp, door, drinking fountain, seating, or water closet.*

Entrance. *Any access point to a building or portion of a building or facility used for the purpose of entering. An entrance includes the approach walk, the vertical access leading to the entrance platform, the entrance platform itself, vestibules if provided, the entry door(s) or gate(s), and the hardware of the entry door(s) or gate(s).*

Facility. *All or any portion of buildings, structures, site improvements, complexes, equipment, roads, walks, passageways, parking lots, or other real or personal property located on a site.*

Ground Floor. *Any occupiable floor less than one story above or below grade with direct access to grade. A building or facility always has at least one ground floor and may have more than one ground floor as where a split level entrance has been provided or where a building is built into a hillside.*

Mezzanine or Mezzanine Floor. *That portion of a story which is an intermediate floor level placed within the story and having occupiable space above and below its floor.*

Marked Crossing. A crosswalk or other identified path intended for pedestrian use in crossing a vehicular way.

Multifamily Dwelling. Any building containing more than two dwelling units.

Occupiable. *A room or enclosed space designed for human occupancy in which individuals congregate for amusement, educational or similar purposes, or in which occupants are engaged at labor, and which is equipped with means of egress, light, and ventilation.*

3

C-53

3.5 Definitions

Operable Part. A part of a piece of equipment or appliance used to insert or withdraw objects, or to activate, deactivate, or adjust the equipment or appliance (for example, coin slot, pushbutton, handle).

Path of Travel. (Reserved).

Power-assisted Door. A door used *for human passage* with a mechanism that helps to open the door, or relieves the opening resistance of a door, upon the activation of a switch or a continued force applied to the door itself.

Public Use. Describes interior or exterior rooms or spaces that are made available to the general public. Public use may be provided at a building or facility that is privately or publicly owned.

Ramp. A walking surface which has a running slope greater than 1:20.

Running Slope. The slope that is parallel to the direction of travel (see cross slope).

Service Entrance. An entrance intended primarily for delivery of goods or services.

Signage. *Displayed* verbal, symbolic, *tactile*, and pictorial information.

Site. A parcel of land bounded by a property line or a designated portion of a public right-of-way.

Site Improvement. Landscaping, paving for pedestrian and vehicular ways, outdoor lighting, recreational facilities, and the like, added to a site.

Sleeping Accommodations. Rooms in which people sleep; for example, dormitory and hotel or motel guest rooms or suites.

Space. A definable area, e.g., room, toilet room, hall, assembly area, entrance, storage room, alcove, courtyard, or lobby.

Story. That portion of a building included between the upper surface of a floor and upper surface of the floor or roof next above. If such

portion of a building does not include occupiable space, it is not considered a story for purposes of these guidelines. There may be more than one floor level within a story as in the case of a mezzanine or mezzanines.

Structural Frame. The structural frame shall be considered to be the columns and the girders, beams, trusses and spandrels having direct connections to the columns and all other members which are essential to the stability of the building as a whole.

Tactile. Describes an object that can be perceived using the sense of touch.

Text Telephone. Machinery or equipment that employs interactive graphic (i.e., typed) communications through the transmission of coded signals across the standard telephone network. Text telephones can include, for example, devices known as TDD's (telecommunication display devices or telecommunication devices for deaf persons) or computers.

Transient Lodging. A building, facility, or portion thereof, excluding inpatient medical care facilities, that contains one or more dwelling units or sleeping accommodations. Transient lodging may include, but is not limited to, resorts, group homes, hotels, motels, and dormitories.

Vehicular Way. A route intended for vehicular traffic, such as a street, driveway, or parking lot.

Walk. An exterior pathway with a prepared surface intended for pedestrian use, including general pedestrian areas such as plazas and courts.

NOTE: Sections 4.1.1 through 4.1.7 are different from ANSI A117.1 in their entirety and are printed in standard type (ANSI A117.1 does not include scoping provisions).

4

4. ACCESSIBLE ELEMENTS AND SPACES: SCOPE AND TECHNICAL REQUIREMENTS.

4.1 Minimum Requirements

4.1.1* Application.

(1) General. All areas of newly designed or newly constructed buildings and facilities required to be accessible by 4.1.2 and 4.1.3 and altered portions of existing buildings and facilities required to be accessible by 4.1.6 shall comply with these guidelines, 4.1 through 4.35, unless otherwise provided in this section or as modified in a special application section.

(2) Application Based on Building Use. Special application sections 5 through 10 provide additional requirements for restaurants and cafeterias, medical care facilities, business and mercantile, libraries, accessible transient lodging, and transportation facilities. When a building or facility contains more than one use covered by a special application section, each portion shall comply with the requirements for that use.

(3)* Areas Used Only by Employees as Work Areas. Areas that are used only as work areas shall be designed and constructed so that individuals with disabilities can approach, enter, and exit the areas. These guidelines do not require that any areas used only as work areas be constructed to permit maneuvering within the work area or be constructed or equipped (i.e., with racks or shelves) to be accessible.

(4) Temporary Structures. These guidelines cover temporary buildings or facilities as well as permanent facilities. Temporary buildings and facilities are not of permanent construction but are extensively used or are essential for public use for a period of time. Examples of temporary buildings or facilities covered by these guidelines include, but are not limited to: reviewing stands, temporary classrooms, bleacher areas, exhibit areas, temporary banking facilities, temporary health screening services, or temporary safe pedestrian passageways around a construction site. Structures, sites and equipment directly associated with the actual processes of construction, such as scaffolding, bridging, materials hoists, or construction trailers are not included.

(5) General Exceptions.

(a) In new construction, a person or entity is not required to meet fully the requirements of these guidelines where that person or entity can demonstrate that it is structurally impracticable to do so. Full compliance will be considered structurally impracticable only in those rare circumstances when the unique characteristics of terrain prevent the incorporation of accessibility features. If full compliance with the requirements of these guidelines is structurally impracticable, a person or entity shall comply with the requirements to the extent it is not structurally impracticable. Any portion of the building or facility which can be made accessible shall comply to the extent that it is not structurally impracticable.

(b) Accessibility is not required to (i) observation galleries used primarily for security purposes; or (ii) in non-occupiable spaces accessed only by ladders, catwalks, crawl spaces, very narrow passageways, or freight (non-passenger) elevators, and frequented only by service personnel for repair purposes; such spaces include, but are not limited to, elevator pits, elevator penthouses, piping or equipment catwalks.

4.1.2 Accessible Sites and Exterior Facilities: New Construction. An accessible site shall meet the following minimum requirements:

(1) At least one accessible route complying with 4.3 shall be provided within the boundary of the site from public transportation stops, accessible parking spaces, passenger loading zones if provided, and public streets or sidewalks, to an accessible building entrance.

(2) At least one accessible route complying with 4.3 shall connect accessible buildings, accessible facilities, accessible elements, and accessible spaces that are on the same site.

(3) All objects that protrude from surfaces or posts into circulation paths shall comply with 4.4.

5

4.1.2 Accessible Sites and Exterior Facilities: New Construction

(4) Ground surfaces along accessible routes and in accessible spaces shall comply with 4.5.

(5) (a) If parking spaces are provided for self-parking by employees or visitors, or both, then accessible spaces complying with 4.6 shall be provided in each such parking area in conformance with the table below. Spaces required by the table need not be provided in the particular lot. They may be provided in a different location if equivalent or greater accessibility, in terms of distance from an accessible entrance, cost and convenience is ensured.

Total Parking in Lot	Required Minimum Number of Accessible Spaces
1 to 25	1
26 to 50	2
51 to 75	3
76 to 100	4
101 to 150	5
151 to 200	6
201 to 300	7
301 to 400	8
401 to 500	9
501 to 1000	2 percent of total
1001 and over	20 plus 1 for each 100 over 1000

Except as provided in (b), access aisles adjacent to accessible spaces shall be 60 in (1525 mm) wide minimum.

(b) One in every eight accessible spaces, but not less than one, shall be served by an access aisle 96 in (2440 mm) wide minimum and shall be designated "van accessible" as required by 4.6.4. The vertical clearance at such spaces shall comply with 4.6.5. All such spaces may be grouped on one level of a parking structure.

EXCEPTION: Provision of all required parking spaces in conformance with "Universal Parking Design" (see appendix A4.6.3) is permitted.

(c) If passenger loading zones are provided, then at least one passenger loading zone shall comply with 4.6.6.

(d) At facilities providing medical care and other services for persons with mobility impairments, parking spaces complying with 4.6 shall

be provided in accordance with 4.1.2(5)(a) except as follows:

(i) Outpatient units and facilities: 10 percent of the total number of parking spaces provided serving each such outpatient unit or facility;

(ii) Units and facilities that specialize in treatment or services for persons with mobility impairments: 20 percent of the total number of parking spaces provided serving each such unit or facility.

(e)*Valet parking: Valet parking facilities shall provide a passenger loading zone complying with 4.6.6 located on an accessible route to the entrance of the facility. Paragraphs 5(a), 5(b), and 5(d) of this section do not apply to valet parking facilities.

(6) If toilet facilities are provided on a site, then each such public or common use toilet facility shall comply with 4.22. If bathing facilities are provided on a site, then each such public or common use bathing facility shall comply with 4.23.

For single user portable toilet or bathing units clustered at a single location, at least 5% but no less than one toilet unit or bathing unit complying with 4.22 or 4.23 shall be installed at each cluster whenever typical inaccessible units are provided. Accessible units shall be identified by the International Symbol of Accessibility.

EXCEPTION: Portable toilet units at construction sites used exclusively by construction personnel are not required to comply with 4.1.2(6).

(7) Building Signage. Signs which designate permanent rooms and spaces shall comply with 4.30.1, 4.30.4, 4.30.5 and 4.30.6. Other signs which provide direction to, or information about, functional spaces of the building shall comply with 4.30.1, 4.30.2, 4.30.3, and 4.30.5. Elements and spaces of accessible facilities which shall be identified by the International Symbol of Accessibility and which shall comply with 4.30.7 are:

(a) Parking spaces designated as reserved for individuals with disabilities;

6

(b) Accessible passenger loading zones;

(c) Accessible entrances when not all are accessible (inaccessible entrances shall have directional signage to indicate the route to the nearest accessible entrance);

(d) Accessible toilet and bathing facilities when not all are accessible.

4.1.3 Accessible Buildings: New Construction. Accessible buildings and facilities shall meet the following minimum requirements:

(1) At least one accessible route complying with 4.3 shall connect accessible building or facility entrances with all accessible spaces and elements within the building or facility.

(2) All objects that overhang or protrude into circulation paths shall comply with 4.4.

(3) Ground and floor surfaces along accessible routes and in accessible rooms and spaces shall comply with 4.5.

(4) Interior and exterior stairs connecting levels that are not connected by an elevator, ramp, or other accessible means of vertical access shall comply with 4.9.

(5)* One passenger elevator complying with 4.10 shall serve each level, including mezzanines, in all multi-story buildings and facilities unless exempted below. If more than one elevator is provided, each full passenger elevator shall comply with 4.10.

EXCEPTION 1: Elevators are not required in facilities that are less than three stories or that have less than 3000 square feet per story unless the building is a shopping center, a shopping mall, or the professional office of a health care provider, or another type of facility as determined by the Attorney General. The elevator exemption set forth in this paragraph does not obviate or limit in any way the obligation to comply with the other accessibility requirements established in section 4.1.3. For example, floors above or below the accessible ground floor must meet the requirements of this section except for elevator service. If toilet or bathing facilities are provided on a level not served by an elevator, then toilet or bathing facilities must be provided on the accessible ground floor. In new construction if a building or facility is eligible for this exemption but a full passenger elevator is nonetheless planned, that elevator shall meet the requirements of 4.10 and shall serve each level in the building. A full passenger elevator that provides service from a garage to only one level of a building or facility is not required to serve other levels.

EXCEPTION 2: Elevator pits, elevator penthouses, mechanical rooms, piping or equipment catwalks are exempted from this requirement.

EXCEPTION 3: Accessible ramps complying with 4.8 may be used in lieu of an elevator.

EXCEPTION 4: Platform lifts (wheelchair lifts) complying with 4.11 of this guideline and applicable state or local codes may be used in lieu of an elevator only under the following conditions:

(a) To provide an accessible route to a performing area in an assembly occupancy.

(b) To comply with the wheelchair viewing position line-of-sight and dispersion requirements of 4.33.3.

(c) To provide access to incidental occupiable spaces and rooms which are not open to the general public and which house no more than five persons, including but not limited to equipment control rooms and projection booths.

(d) To provide access where existing site constraints or other constraints make use of a ramp or an elevator infeasible.

(6) Windows: (Reserved).

(7) Doors:

(a) At each accessible entrance to a building or facility, at least one door shall comply with 4.13.

(b) Within a building or facility, at least one door at each accessible space shall comply with 4.13.

(c) Each door that is an element of an accessible route shall comply with 4.13.

7

4.1.3 Accessible Buildings: New Construction

(d) Each door required by 4.3.10, Egress, shall comply with 4.13.

(8) In new construction, at a minimum, the requirements in (a) and (b) below shall be satisfied independently:

(a)(i) At least 50% of all public entrances (excluding those in (b) below) must be accessible. At least one must be a ground floor entrance. Public entrances are any entrances that are not loading or service entrances.

(ii) Accessible entrances must be provided in a number at least equivalent to the number of exits required by the applicable building/fire codes. (This paragraph does not require an increase in the total number of entrances planned for a facility.)

(iii) An accessible entrance must be provided to each tenancy in a facility (for example, individual stores in a strip shopping center).

One entrance may be considered as meeting more than one of the requirements in (a). Where feasible, accessible entrances shall be the entrances used by the majority of people visiting or working in the building.

(b)(i) In addition, if direct access is provided for pedestrians from an enclosed parking garage to the building, at least one direct entrance from the garage to the building must be accessible.

(ii) If access is provided for pedestrians from a pedestrian tunnel or elevated walkway, one entrance to the building from each tunnel or walkway must be accessible.

One entrance may be considered as meeting more than one of the requirements in (b).

Because entrances also serve as emergency exits whose proximity to all parts of buildings and facilities is essential, it is preferable that all entrances be accessible.

(c) If the only entrance to a building, or tenancy in a facility, is a service entrance, that entrance shall be accessible.

(d) Entrances which are not accessible shall have directional signage complying with 4.30.1,

4.30.2, 4.30.3, and 4.30.5, which indicates the location of the nearest accessible entrance.

(9)* In buildings or facilities, or portions of buildings or facilities, required to be accessible, accessible means of egress shall be provided in the same number as required for exits by local building/life safety regulations. Where a required exit from an occupiable level above or below a level of accessible exit discharge is not accessible, an area of rescue assistance shall be provided on each such level (in a number equal to that of inaccessible required exits). Areas of rescue assistance shall comply with 4.3.11. A horizontal exit, meeting the requirements of local building/life safety regulations, shall satisfy the requirement for an area of rescue assistance.

EXCEPTION: Areas of rescue assistance are not required in buildings or facilities having a supervised automatic sprinkler system.

(10)* Drinking Fountains:

(a) Where only one drinking fountain is provided on a floor there shall be a drinking fountain which is accessible to individuals who use wheelchairs in accordance with 4.15 and one accessible to those who have difficulty bending or stooping. (This can be accommodated by the use of a "hi-lo" fountain; by providing one fountain accessible to those who use wheelchairs and one fountain at a standard height convenient for those who have difficulty bending; by providing a fountain accessible under 4.15 and a water cooler; or by such other means as would achieve the required accessibility for each group on each floor.)

(b) Where more than one drinking fountain or water cooler is provided on a floor, 50% of those provided shall comply with 4.15 and shall be on an accessible route.

(11) Toilet Facilities: If toilet rooms are provided, then each public and common use toilet room shall comply with 4.22. Other toilet rooms provided for the use of occupants of specific spaces (i.e., a private toilet room for the occupant of a private office) shall be adaptable. If bathing rooms are provided, then each public and common use bathroom shall comply with 4.23. Accessible toilet rooms and bathing facilities shall be on an accessible route.

8

4.1.3 Accessible Buildings: New Construction

(12) Storage, Shelving and Display Units:

(a) If fixed or built-in storage facilities such as cabinets, shelves, closets, and drawers are provided in accessible spaces, at least one of each type provided shall contain storage space complying with 4.25. Additional storage may be provided outside of the dimensions required by 4.25.

(b) Shelves or display units allowing self-service by customers in mercantile occupancies shall be located on an accessible route complying with 4.3. Requirements for accessible reach range do not apply.

(13) Controls and operating mechanisms in accessible spaces, along accessible routes, or as parts of accessible elements (for example, light switches and dispenser controls) shall comply with 4.27.

(14) If emergency warning systems are provided, then they shall include both audible alarms and visual alarms complying with 4.28. Sleeping accommodations required to comply with 9.3 shall have an alarm system complying with 4.28. Emergency warning systems in medical care facilities may be modified to suit standard health care alarm design practice.

(15) Detectable warnings shall be provided at locations as specified in 4.29.

(16) Building Signage:

(a) Signs which designate permanent rooms and spaces shall comply with 4.30.1, 4.30.4, 4.30.5 and 4.30.6.

(b) Other signs which provide direction to or information about functional spaces of the building shall comply with 4.30.1, 4.30.2, 4.30.3, and 4.30.5.

EXCEPTION: Building directories, menus, and all other signs which are temporary are not required to comply.

(17) Public Telephones:

(a) If public pay telephones, public closed circuit telephones, or other public telephones are provided, then they shall comply with 4.31.2 through 4.31.8 to the extent required by the following table:

Number of each type of telephone provided on each floor	Number of telephones required to comply with 4.31.2 through 4.31.8[1]
1 or more single unit	1 per floor
1 bank[2]	1 per floor
2 or more banks[2]	1 per bank. Accessible unit may be installed as a single unit in proximity (either visible or with signage) to the bank. At least one public telephone per floor shall meet the requirements for a forward reach telephone[3].

[1] Additional public telephones may be installed at any height. Unless otherwise specified, accessible telephones may be either forward or side reach telephones.

[2] A bank consists of two or more adjacent public telephones, often installed as a unit.

[3] EXCEPTION: For exterior installations only, if dial tone first service is available, then a side reach telephone may be installed instead of the required forward reach telephone (i.e., one telephone in proximity to each bank shall comply with 4.31).

(b)* All telephones required to be accessible and complying with 4.31.2 through 4.31.8 shall be equipped with a volume control. In addition, 25 percent, but never less than one, of all other public telephones provided shall be equipped with a volume control and shall be dispersed among all types of public telephones, including closed circuit telephones, throughout the building or facility. Signage complying with applicable provisions of 4.30.7 shall be provided.

(c) The following shall be provided in accordance with 4.31.9:

(i) If a total number of four or more public pay telephones (including both interior and exterior phones) is provided at a site, and at least one is in an interior location, then at least one interior public text telephone shall be provided.

(ii) If an interior public pay telephone is provided in a stadium or arena, in a convention center, in a hotel with a convention center, or

9

C-59

4.1.3 Accessible Buildings: New Construction

in a covered mall, at least one interior public text telephone shall be provided in the facility.

(iii) if a public pay telephone is located in or adjacent to a hospital emergency room, hospital recovery room, or hospital waiting room, one public text telephone shall be provided at each such location.

(d) Where a bank of telephones in the interior of a building consists of three or more public pay telephones, at least one public pay telephone in each such bank shall be equipped with a shelf and outlet in compliance with 4.31.9(2).

(18) If fixed or built-in seating or tables (including, but not limited to, study carrels and student laboratory stations), are provided in accessible public or common use areas, at least five percent (5%), but not less than one, of the fixed or built-in seating areas or tables shall comply with 4.32. An accessible route shall lead to and through such fixed or built-in seating areas, or tables.

(19)* Assembly areas:

(a) In places of assembly with fixed seating accessible wheelchair locations shall comply with 4.33.2, 4.33.3, and 4.33.4 and shall be provided consistent with the following table:

Capacity of Seating in Assembly Areas	Number of Required Wheelchair Locations
4 to 25	1
26 to 50	2
51 to 300	4
301 to 500	6
over 500	6, plus 1 additional space for each total seating capacity increase of 100

In addition, one percent, but not less than one, of all fixed seats shall be aisle seats with no armrests on the aisle side, or removable or folding armrests on the aisle side. Each such seat shall be identified by a sign or marker. Signage notifying patrons of the availability of such seats shall be posted at the ticket office. Aisle seats are not required to comply with 4.33.4.

(b) This paragraph applies to assembly areas where audible communications are integral to the use of the space (e.g., concert and lecture halls, playhouses and movie theaters, meeting rooms, etc.). Such assembly areas, if (1) they accommodate at least 50 persons, or if they have audio-amplification systems, and (2) they have fixed seating, shall have a permanently installed assistive listening system complying with 4.33. For other assembly areas, a permanently installed assistive listening system, or an adequate number of electrical outlets or other supplementary wiring necessary to support a portable assistive listening system shall be provided. The minimum number of receivers to be provided shall be equal to 4 percent of the total number of seats, but in no case less than two. Signage complying with applicable provisions of 4.30 shall be installed to notify patrons of the availability of a listening system.

(20) Where automated teller machines (ATMs) are provided, each ATM shall comply with the requirements of 4.34 except where two or more are provided at a location, then only one must comply.

EXCEPTION: Drive-up-only automated teller machines are not required to comply with 4.27.2, 4.27.3 and 4.34.3.

(21) Where dressing and fitting rooms are provided for use by the general public, patients, customers or employees, 5 percent, but never less than one, of dressing rooms for each type of use in each cluster of dressing rooms shall be accessible and shall comply with 4.35.

Examples of types of dressing rooms are those serving different genders or distinct and different functions as in different treatment or examination facilities.

4.1.4 (Reserved).

4.1.5 Accessible Buildings: Additions.
Each addition to an existing building or facility shall be regarded as an alteration. Each space or element added to the existing building or facility shall comply with the applicable provisions of 4.1.1 to 4.1.3, Minimum Requirements (for New Construction) and the applicable technical specifications of 4.2 through 4.35 and sections 5 through 10. Each addition that

10

affects or could affect the usability of an area containing a primary function shall comply with 4.1.6(2).

4.1.6 Accessible Buildings: Alterations.

(1) General. Alterations to existing buildings and facilities shall comply with the following:

(a) No alteration shall be undertaken which decreases or has the effect of decreasing accessibility or usability of a building or facility below the requirements for new construction at the time of alteration.

(b) If existing elements, spaces, or common areas are altered, then each such altered element, space, feature, or area shall comply with the applicable provisions of 4.1.1 to 4.1.3 Minimum Requirements (for New Construction). If the applicable provision for new construction requires that an element, space, or common area be on an accessible route, the altered element, space, or common area is not required to be on an accessible route except as provided in 4.1.6(2) (Alterations to an Area Containing a Primary Function.)

(c) If alterations of single elements, when considered together, amount to an alteration of a room or space in a building or facility, the entire space shall be made accessible.

(d) No alteration of an existing element, space, or area of a building or facility shall impose a requirement for greater accessibility than that which would be required for new construction. For example, if the elevators and stairs in a building are being altered and the elevators are, in turn, being made accessible, then no accessibility modifications are required to the stairs connecting levels connected by the elevator. If stair modifications to correct unsafe conditions are required by other codes, the modifications shall be done in compliance with these guidelines unless technically infeasible.

(e) At least one interior public text telephone complying with 4.31.9 shall be provided if:

(i) alterations to existing buildings or facilities with less than four exterior or interior public pay telephones would increase the total number to four or more telephones with at least one in an interior location; or

(ii) alterations to one or more exterior or interior public pay telephones occur in an existing building or facility with four or more public telephones with at least one in an interior location.

(f) If an escalator or stair is planned or installed where none existed previously and major structural modifications are necessary for such installation, then a means of accessible vertical access shall be provided that complies with the applicable provisions of 4.7, 4.8, 4.10, or 4.11.

(g) In alterations, the requirements of 4.1.3(9), 4.3.10 and 4.3.11 do not apply.

(h) *Entrances: If a planned alteration entails alterations to an entrance, and the building has an accessible entrance, the entrance being altered is not required to comply with 4.1.3(8), except to the extent required by 4.1.6(2). If a particular entrance is not made accessible, appropriate accessible signage indicating the location of the nearest accessible entrance(s) shall be installed at or near the inaccessible entrance, such that a person with disabilities will not be required to retrace the approach route from the inaccessible entrance.

(i) If the alteration work is limited solely to the electrical, mechanical, or plumbing system, or to hazardous material abatement, or automatic sprinkler retrofitting, and does not involve the alteration of any elements or spaces required to be accessible under these guidelines, then 4.1.6(2) does not apply.

(j) EXCEPTION: In alteration work, if compliance with 4.1.6 is technically infeasible, the alteration shall provide accessibility to the maximum extent feasible. Any elements or features of the building or facility that are being altered and can be made accessible shall be made accessible within the scope of the alteration.

Technically Infeasible. Means, with respect to an alteration of a building or a facility, that it has little likelihood of being accomplished because existing structural conditions would require removing or altering a load-bearing member which is an essential part of the structural frame; or because other existing physical or site constraints prohibit modification or

4.1.6 Accessible Buildings: Alterations

addition of elements, spaces, or features which are in full and strict compliance with the minimum requirements for new construction and which are necessary to provide accessibility.

(k) EXCEPTION:

(i) These guidelines do not require the installation of an elevator in an altered facility that is less than three stories or has less than 3,000 square feet per story unless the building is a shopping center, a shopping mall, the professional office of a health care provider, or another type of facility as determined by the Attorney General.

(ii) The exemption provided in paragraph (i) does not obviate or limit in any way the obligation to comply with the other accessibility requirements established in these guidelines. For example, alterations to floors above or below the ground floor must be accessible regardless of whether the altered facility has an elevator. If a facility subject to the elevator exemption set forth in paragraph (i) nonetheless has a full passenger elevator, that elevator shall meet, to the maximum extent feasible, the accessibility requirements of these guidelines.

(2) Alterations to an Area Containing a Primary Function: In addition to the requirements of 4.1.6(1), an alteration that affects or could affect the usability of or access to an area containing a primary function shall be made so as to ensure that, to the maximum extent feasible, the path of travel to the altered area and the restrooms, telephones, and drinking fountains serving the altered area, are readily accessible to and usable by individuals with disabilities, unless such alterations are disproportionate to the overall alterations in terms of cost and scope (as determined under criteria established by the Attorney General).

(3) Special Technical Provisions for Alterations to Existing Buildings and Facilities:

(a) Ramps: Curb ramps and interior or exterior ramps to be constructed on sites or in existing buildings or facilities where space limitations prohibit the use of a 1:12 slope or less may have slopes and rises as follows:

(i) A slope between 1:10 and 1:12 is allowed for a maximum rise of 6 inches.

(ii) A slope between 1:8 and 1:10 is allowed for a maximum rise of 3 inches. A slope steeper than 1:8 is not allowed.

(b) Stairs: Full extension of handrails at stairs shall not be required in alterations where such extensions would be hazardous or impossible due to plan configuration.

(c) Elevators:

(i) If safety door edges are provided in existing automatic elevators, automatic door reopening devices may be omitted (see 4.10.6).

(ii) Where existing shaft configuration or technical infeasibility prohibits strict compliance with 4.10.9, the minimum car plan dimensions may be reduced by the minimum amount necessary, but in no case shall the inside car area be smaller than 48 in by 48 in.

(iii) Equivalent facilitation may be provided with an elevator car of different dimensions when usability can be demonstrated and when all other elements required to be accessible comply with the applicable provisions of 4.10. For example, an elevator of 47 in by 69 in (1195 mm by 1755 mm) with a door opening on the narrow dimension, could accommodate the standard wheelchair clearances shown in Figure 4.

(d) Doors:

(i) Where it is technically infeasible to comply with clear opening width requirements of 4.13.5, a projection of 5/8 in maximum will be permitted for the latch side stop.

(ii) If existing thresholds are 3/4 in high or less, and have (or are modified to have) a beveled edge on each side, they may remain.

(e) Toilet Rooms:

(i) Where it is technically infeasible to comply with 4.22 or 4.23, the installation of at least one unisex toilet/bathroom per floor, located in the same area as existing toilet facilities, will be permitted in lieu of modifying existing toilet facilities to be accessible. Each unisex toilet room shall contain one water closet complying with 4.16 and one lavatory complying with 4.19, and the door shall have a privacy latch.

12

4.1.7 Accessible Buildings: Historic Preservation

(ii) Where it is technically infeasible to install a required standard stall (Fig. 30(a)), or where other codes prohibit reduction of the fixture count (i.e., removal of a water closet in order to create a double-wide stall), either alternate stall (Fig.30(b)) may be provided in lieu of the standard stall.

(iii) When existing toilet or bathing facilities are being altered and are not made accessible, signage complying with 4.30.1, 4.30.2, 4.30.3, 4.30.5, and 4.30.7 shall be provided indicating the location of the nearest accessible toilet or bathing facility within the facility.

(f) Assembly Areas:

(i) Where it is technically infeasible to disperse accessible seating throughout an altered assembly area, accessible seating areas may be clustered. Each accessible seating area shall have provisions for companion seating and shall be located on an accessible route that also serves as a means of emergency egress.

(ii) Where it is technically infeasible to alter all performing areas to be on an accessible route, at least one of each type of performing area shall be made accessible.

(g) Platform Lifts (Wheelchair Lifts): In alterations, platform lifts (wheelchair lifts) complying with 4.11 and applicable state or local codes may be used as part of an accessible route. The use of lifts is not limited to the four conditions in exception 4 of 4.1.3(5).

(h) Dressing Rooms: In alterations where technical infeasibility can be demonstrated, one dressing room for each sex on each level shall be made accessible. Where only unisex dressing rooms are provided, accessible unisex dressing rooms may be used to fulfill this requirement.

4.1.7 Accessible Buildings: Historic Preservation.

(1) Applicability:

(a) General Rule. Alterations to a qualified historic building or facility shall comply with 4.1.6 Accessible Buildings: Alterations, the applicable technical specifications of 4.2

through 4.35 and the applicable special application sections 5 through 10 unless it is determined in accordance with the procedures in 4.1.7(2) that compliance with the requirements for accessible routes (exterior and interior), ramps, entrances, or toilets would threaten or destroy the historic significance of the building or facility in which case the alternative requirements in 4.1.7(3) may be used for the feature.

EXCEPTION: (Reserved).

(b) Definition. A qualified historic building or facility is a building or facility that is:

(i) Listed in or eligible for listing in the National Register of Historic Places; or

(ii) Designated as historic under an appropriate State or local law.

(2) Procedures:

(a) Alterations to Qualified Historic Buildings and Facilities Subject to Section 106 of the National Historic Preservation Act:

(i) Section 106 Process. Section 106 of the National Historic Preservation Act (16 U.S.C. 470 f) requires that a Federal agency with jurisdiction over a Federal, federally assisted, or federally licensed undertaking consider the effects of the agency's undertaking on buildings and facilities listed in or eligible for listing in the National Register of Historic Places and give the Advisory Council on Historic Preservation a reasonable opportunity to comment on the undertaking prior to approval of the undertaking.

(ii) ADA Application. Where alterations are undertaken to a qualified historic building or facility that is subject to section 106 of the National Historic Preservation Act, the Federal agency with jurisdiction over the undertaking shall follow the section 106 process. If the State Historic Preservation Officer or Advisory Council on Historic Preservation agrees that compliance with the requirements for accessible routes (exterior and interior), ramps, entrances, or toilets would threaten or destroy the historic significance of the building or facility, the alternative requirements in 4.1.7(3) may be used for the feature.

13

(b) Alterations to Qualified Historic Buildings and Facilities Not Subject to Section 106 of the National Historic Preservation Act. Where alterations are undertaken to a qualified historic building or facility that is not subject to section 106 of the National Historic Preservation Act, if the entity undertaking the alterations believes that compliance with the requirements for accessible routes (exterior and interior), ramps, entrances, or toilets would threaten or destroy the historic significance of the building or facility and that the alternative requirements in 4.1.7(3) should be used for the feature, the entity should consult with the State Historic Preservation Officer. If the State Historic Preservation Officer agrees that compliance with the accessibility requirements for accessible routes (exterior and interior), ramps, entrances or toilets would threaten or destroy the historical significance of the building or facility, the alternative requirements in 4.1.7(3) may be used.

(c) Consultation With Interested Persons. Interested persons should be invited to participate in the consultation process, including State or local accessibility officials, individuals with disabilities, and organizations representing individuals with disabilities.

(d) Certified Local Government Historic Preservation Programs. Where the State Historic Preservation Officer has delegated the consultation responsibility for purposes of this section to a local government historic preservation program that has been certified in accordance with section 101(c) of the National Historic Preservation Act of 1966 (16 U.S.C. 470a (c)) and implementing regulations (36 CFR 61.5), the responsibility may be carried out by the appropriate local government body or official.

(3) Historic Preservation: Minimum Requirements:

(a) At least one accessible route complying with 4.3 from a site access point to an accessible entrance shall be provided.

EXCEPTION: A ramp with a slope no greater than 1:6 for a run not to exceed 2 ft (610 mm) may be used as part of an accessible route to an entrance.

(b) At least one accessible entrance complying with 4.14 which is used by the public shall be provided.

EXCEPTION: If it is determined that no entrance used by the public can comply with 4.14, then access at any entrance not used by the general public but open (unlocked) with directional signage at the primary entrance may be used. The accessible entrance shall also have a notification system. Where security is a problem, remote monitoring may be used.

(c) If toilets are provided, then at least one toilet facility complying with 4.22 and 4.1.6 shall be provided along an accessible route that complies with 4.3. Such toilet facility may be unisex in design.

(d) Accessible routes from an accessible entrance to all publicly used spaces on at least the level of the accessible entrance shall be provided. Access shall be provided to all levels of a building or facility in compliance with 4.1 whenever practical.

(e) Displays and written information, documents, etc., should be located where they can be seen by a seated person. Exhibits and signage displayed horizontally (e.g., open books), should be no higher than 44 in (1120 mm) above the floor surface.

NOTE: The technical provisions of sections 4.2 through 4.35 are the same as those of the American National Standard Institute's document A117.1-1980, except as noted in the text.

4.2 Space Allowance and Reach Ranges.

4.2.1* Wheelchair Passage Width. The minimum clear width for single wheelchair passage shall be 32 in (815 mm) at a point and 36 in (915 mm) continuously (see Fig. 1 and 24(e)).

4.2.2 Width for Wheelchair Passing. The minimum width for two wheelchairs to pass is 60 in (1525 mm) (see Fig. 2).

4.2.3* Wheelchair Turning Space. The space required for a wheelchair to make a 180-degree turn is a clear space of 60 in (1525 mm)

14

4.2.4° Clear Floor or Ground Space for Wheelchairs

diameter (see Fig. 3(a)) or a T-shaped space (see Fig. 3(b)).

4.2.4° Clear Floor or Ground Space for Wheelchairs.

4.2.4.1 Size and Approach. The minimum clear floor or ground space required to accommodate a single, stationary wheelchair and occupant is 30 in by 48 in (760 mm by 1220 mm) (see Fig. 4(a)). The minimum clear floor or ground space for wheelchairs may be positioned for forward or parallel approach to an object (see Fig. 4(b) and (c)). Clear floor or ground space for wheelchairs may be part of the knee space required under some objects.

4.2.4.2 Relationship of Maneuvering Clearance to Wheelchair Spaces. One full unobstructed side of the clear floor or ground space for a wheelchair shall adjoin or overlap an accessible route or adjoin another wheelchair clear floor space. If a clear floor space is located in an alcove or otherwise confined on all or part of three sides, additional maneuvering clearances shall be provided as shown in Fig. 4(d) and (e).

4.2.4.3 Surfaces for Wheelchair Spaces. Clear floor or ground spaces for wheelchairs shall comply with 4.5.

4.2.5° Forward Reach. If the clear floor space only allows forward approach to an object, the maximum high forward reach allowed shall be 48 in (1220 mm) (see Fig. 5(a)). *The minimum low forward reach is 15 in (380 mm).* If the high forward reach is over an obstruction, reach and clearances shall be as shown in Fig. 5(b).

4.2.6° Side Reach. If the clear floor space allows parallel approach by a person in a wheelchair, the maximum high side reach allowed shall be 54 in (1370 mm) and the low side reach shall be no less than 9 in (230 mm) above the floor (Fig. 6(a) and (b)). If the side reach is over an obstruction, the reach and clearances shall be as shown in Fig 6(c).

4.3 Accessible Route.

4.3.1° General. All walks, halls, corridors, aisles, *skywalks, tunnels,* and other spaces

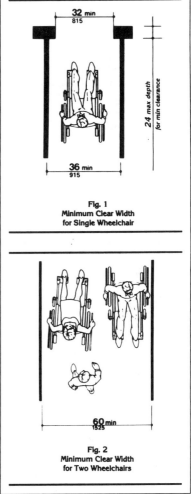

Fig. 1
Minimum Clear Width
for Single Wheelchair

Fig. 2
Minimum Clear Width
for Two Wheelchairs

15

C-65

4.3 Accessible Route

that are part of an accessible route shall comply with 4.3.

4.3.2 Location.

(1) At least one accessible route *within the boundary of the site* shall be provided from public transportation stops, accessible parking, and accessible passenger loading zones, and public streets or sidewalks to the accessible building entrance they serve. *The accessible route shall, to the maximum extent feasible, coincide with the route for the general public.*

(2) At least one accessible route shall connect accessible buildings, facilities, elements, and spaces that are on the same site.

(3) At least one accessible route shall connect accessible building or facility entrances with all accessible spaces and elements and with all accessible dwelling units within the building or facility.

(4) An accessible route shall connect at least one accessible entrance of each accessible

dwelling unit with those exterior and interior spaces and facilities that serve the accessible dwelling unit.

4.3.3 Width. The minimum clear width of an accessible route shall be 36 in (915 mm) except at doors (see 4.13.5 and 4.13.6). If a person in a wheelchair must make a turn around an obstruction, the minimum clear width of the accessible route shall be as shown in Fig. 7(a) and (b).

4.3.4 Passing Space. If an accessible route has less than 60 in (1525 mm) clear width, then passing spaces at least 60 in by 60 in (1525 mm by 1525 mm) shall be located at reasonable intervals not to exceed 200 ft (61 m). A T-intersection of two corridors or walks is an acceptable passing place.

4.3.5 Head Room. Accessible routes shall comply with 4.4.2.

4.3.6 Surface Textures. The surface of an accessible route shall comply with 4.5.

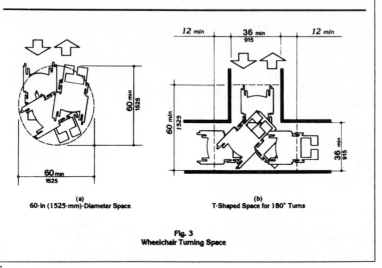

(a)
60-in (1525-mm)-Diameter Space

(b)
T-Shaped Space for 180° Turns

Fig. 3
Wheelchair Turning Space

16

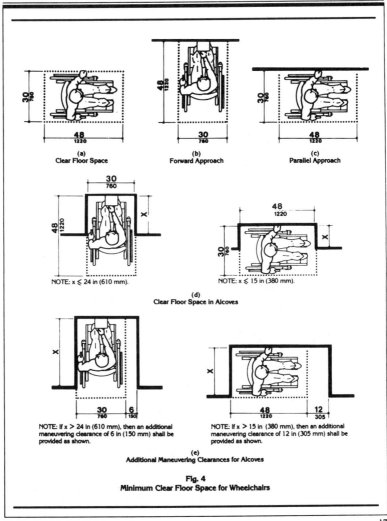

(a)
Clear Floor Space

(b)
Forward Approach

(c)
Parallel Approach

NOTE: x ≤ 24 in (610 mm).

NOTE: x ≤ 15 in (380 mm).

(d)
Clear Floor Space in Alcoves

NOTE: If x > 24 in (610 mm), then an additional maneuvering clearance of 6 in (150 mm) shall be provided as shown.

NOTE: If x > 15 in (380 mm), then an additional maneuvering clearance of 12 in (305 mm) shall be provided as shown.

(e)
Additional Maneuvering Clearances for Alcoves

Fig. 4
Minimum Clear Floor Space for Wheelchairs

17

4.3 Accessible Route

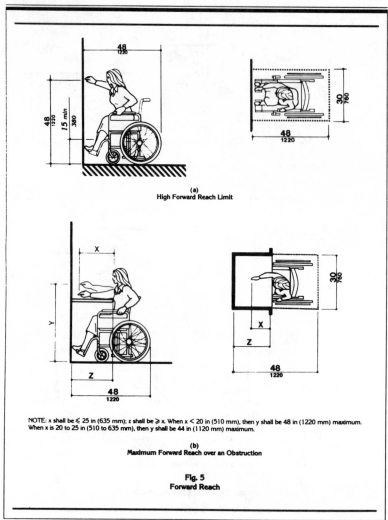

(a)
High Forward Reach Limit

NOTE: x shall be ⩽ 25 in (635 mm); z shall be ⩾ x. When x < 20 in (510 mm), then y shall be 48 in (1220 mm) maximum. When x is 20 to 25 in (510 to 635 mm), then y shall be 44 in (1120 mm) maximum.

(b)
Maximum Forward Reach over an Obstruction

Fig. 5
Forward Reach

18

C-68

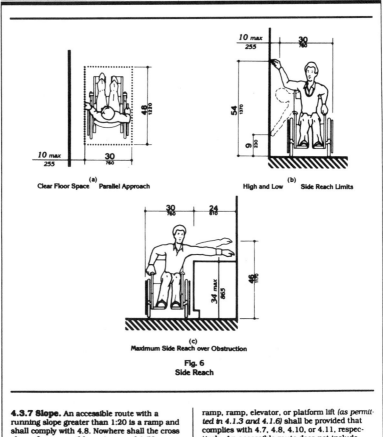

(a)
Clear Floor Space   Parallel Approach

(b)
High and Low   Side Reach Limits

(c)
Maximum Side Reach over Obstruction

Fig. 6
Side Reach

4.3.7 Slope. An accessible route with a running slope greater than 1:20 is a ramp and shall comply with 4.8. Nowhere shall the cross slope of an accessible route exceed 1:50.

4.3.8 Changes in Levels. Changes in levels along an accessible route shall comply with 4.5.2. If an accessible route has changes in level greater than 1/2 in (13 mm), then a curb ramp, ramp, elevator, or platform lift (as permitted in 4.1.3 and 4.1.6) shall be provided that complies with 4.7, 4.8, 4.10, or 4.11, respectively. An accessible route does not include stairs, steps, or escalators. See definition of "egress, means of" in 3.5.

4.3.9 Doors. Doors along an accessible route shall comply with 4.13.

19

4.3.10* Egress

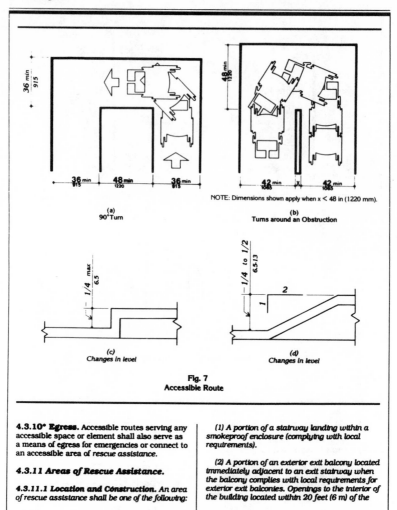

NOTE: Dimensions shown apply when x < 48 in (1220 mm).

(a)
90°Turn

(b)
Turns around an Obstruction

(c)
Changes in level

(d)
Changes in level

Fig. 7
Accessible Route

4.3.10* Egress. Accessible routes serving any accessible space or element shall also serve as a means of egress for emergencies or connect to an accessible area of *rescue assistance.*

4.3.11 *Areas of Rescue Assistance.*

4.3.11.1 Location and Construction. *An area of rescue assistance shall be one of the following:*

(1) A portion of a stairway landing within a smokeproof enclosure (complying with local requirements).

(2) A portion of an exterior exit balcony located immediately adjacent to an exit stairway when the balcony complies with local requirements for exterior exit balconies. Openings to the interior of the building located within 20 feet (6 m) of the

20

area of rescue assistance shall be protected with fire assemblies having a three-fourths hour fire protection rating.

(3) A portion of a one-hour fire-resistive corridor (complying with local requirements for fire-resistive construction and for openings) located immediately adjacent to an exit enclosure.

(4) A vestibule located immediately adjacent to an exit enclosure and constructed to the same fire-resistive standards as required for corridors and openings.

(5) A portion of a stairway landing within an exit enclosure which is vented to the exterior and is separated from the interior of the building with not less than one-hour fire-resistive doors.

(6) When approved by the appropriate local authority, an area or a room which is separated from other portions of the building by a smoke barrier. Smoke barriers shall have a fire-resistive rating of not less than one hour and shall completely enclose the area or room. Doors in the smoke barrier shall be tight-fitting smoke- and draft-control assemblies having a fire-protection rating of not less than 20 minutes and shall be self-closing or automatic closing. The area or room shall be provided with an exit directly to an exit enclosure. Where the room or area exits into an exit enclosure which is required to be of more than one-hour fire-resistive construction, the room or area shall have the same fire-resistive construction, including the same opening protection, as required for the adjacent exit enclosure.

(7) An elevator lobby when elevator shafts and adjacent lobbies are pressurized as required for smokeproof enclosures by local regulations and when complying with requirements herein for size, communication, and signage. Such pressurization system shall be activated by smoke detectors on each floor located in a manner approved by the appropriate local authority. Pressurization equipment and its duct work within the building shall be separated from other portions of the building by a minimum two-hour fire-resistive construction.

4.3.11.2 Size. Each area of rescue assistance shall provide at least two accessible areas each being not less than 30 inches by 48 inches (760 mm by 1220 mm). The area of rescue

assistance shall not encroach on any required exit width. The total number of such 30-inch by 48-inch (760 mm by 1220 mm) areas per story shall be not less than one for every 200 persons of calculated occupant load served by the area of rescue assistance.

EXCEPTION: The appropriate local authority may reduce the minimum number of 30-inch by 48-inch (760 mm by 1220 mm) areas to one for each area of rescue assistance on floors where the occupant load is less than 200.

4.3.11.3* Stairway Width. Each stairway adjacent to an area of rescue assistance shall have a minimum clear width of 48 inches between handrails.

4.3.11.4* Two-way Communication. A method of two-way communication, with both visible and audible signals, shall be provided between each area of rescue assistance and the primary entry. The fire department or appropriate local authority may approve a location other than the primary entry.

4.3.11.5 Identification. Each area of rescue assistance shall be identified by a sign which states "AREA OF RESCUE ASSISTANCE" and displays the international symbol of accessibility. The sign shall be illuminated when exit sign illumination is required. Signage shall also be installed at all inaccessible exits and where otherwise necessary to clearly indicate the direction to areas of rescue assistance. In each area of rescue assistance, instructions on the use of the area under emergency conditions shall be posted adjoining the two-way communication system.

4.4 Protruding Objects.

4.4.1* General. Objects projecting from walls (for example, telephones) with their leading edges between 27 in and 80 in (685 mm and 2030 mm) above the finished floor shall protrude no more than 4 in (100 mm) into walks, halls, corridors, passageways, or aisles (see Fig. 8(a)). Objects mounted with their leading edges at or below 27 in (685 mm) above the finished floor may protrude any amount (see Fig. 8(a) and (b)). Free-standing objects mounted on posts or pylons may overhang 12 in (305 mm) maximum from 27 in to 80 in (685 mm to 2030 mm) above the ground or

4.4 Protruding Objects

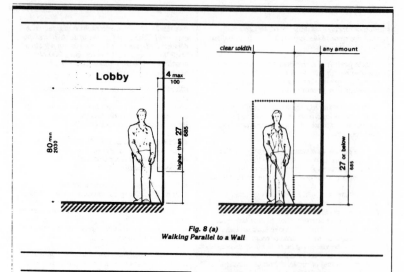

Fig. 8 (a)
Walking Parallel to a Wall

Fig. 8 (b)
Walking Perpendicular to a Wall

Fig. 8
Protruding Objects

finished floor (see Fig. 8(c) and (d)). Protruding objects shall not reduce the clear width of an accessible route or maneuvering space (see Fig. 8(e)).

4.4.2 Head Room. Walks, halls, corridors, passageways, aisles, or other circulation spaces shall have 80 in (2030 mm) minimum clear head room (see Fig. 8(a)). *If vertical clearance of an area adjoining an accessible route is reduced to less than 80 in (nominal dimension), a barrier to warn blind or visually-impaired persons shall be provided (see Fig. 8(c-1)).*

4.5 Ground and Floor Surfaces.

4.5.1* General. Ground and floor surfaces along accessible routes and in accessible rooms and spaces including floors, walks, ramps, stairs, and curb ramps, shall be stable, firm, slip-resistant, and shall comply with 4.5.

4.5.2 Changes in Level. Changes in level up to 1/4 in (6 mm) may be vertical and without edge treatment (see Fig. 7(c)). Changes in level between 1/4 in and 1/2 in (6 mm and 13 mm)

4.4 Protruding Objects

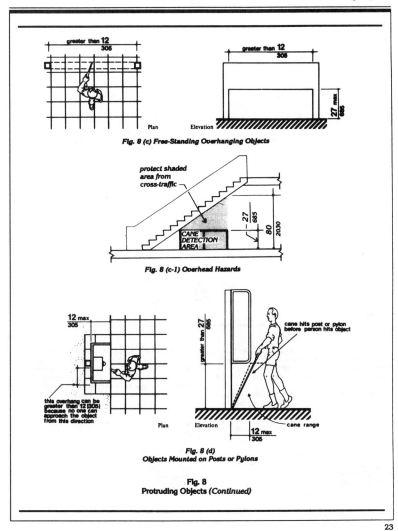

Fig. 8 (c) Free-Standing Overhanging Objects

Fig. 8 (c-1) Overhead Hazards

Fig. 8 (d)
Objects Mounted on Posts or Pylons

Fig. 8
Protruding Objects (Continued)

23

4.5 Ground and Floor Surfaces

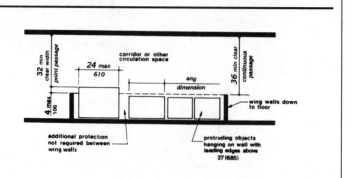

Fig. 8 (e)
Example of Protection around Wall-Mounted Objects and Measurements of Clear Widths

Fig. 8
Protruding Objects *(Continued)*

shall be beveled with a slope no greater than 1:2 *(see Fig. 7(d))*. Changes in level greater than 1/2 in (13 mm) shall be accomplished by means of a ramp that complies with 4.7 or 4.8.

4.5.3* Carpet. If carpet or carpet tile is used on a ground or floor surface, then it shall be securely attached; have a firm cushion, pad, or backing, or no cushion or pad; and have a level loop, textured loop, level cut pile, or level cut/uncut pile texture. The maximum pile *thickness* shall be 1/2 in (13 mm) (see Fig. 8(f)). Exposed edges of carpet shall be fastened to floor surfaces and have trim along the entire length of the exposed edge. Carpet edge trim shall comply with 4.5.2.

4.5.4 Gratings. If gratings are located in walking surfaces, then they shall have spaces no greater than 1/2 in (13 mm) wide in one direction *(see Fig. 8(g))*. If gratings have elongated openings, then they shall be placed so that the long dimension is perpendicular to the dominant direction of travel *(see Fig. 8(h))*.

4.6 Parking and Passenger Loading Zones.

4.6.1 Minimum Number. *Parking spaces required to be accessible by 4.1 shall comply with 4.6.2 through 4.6.5. Passenger loading zones required to be accessible by 4.1 shall comply with 4.6.5 and 4.6.6.*

24

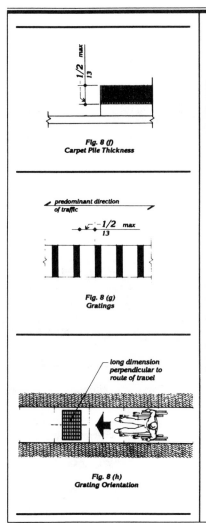

Fig. 8 (f)
Carpet Pile Thickness

Fig. 8 (g)
Gratings

Fig. 8 (h)
Grating Orientation

4.6.2 Location. *Accessible parking spaces serving* a particular building shall be located on the shortest accessible route of travel *from adjacent parking* to an accessible entrance. *In parking facilities* that do not serve a particular building, *accessible parking* shall be located on the shortest accessible route *of travel* to an accessible pedestrian entrance of the parking facility. *In buildings with multiple accessible entrances with adjacent parking, accessible parking spaces shall be dispersed and located closest to the accessible entrances.*

4.6.3* Parking Spaces. *Accessible* parking spaces shall be at least 96 in (2440 mm) wide. Parking access aisles shall be part of an accessible route to the building or facility entrance and shall comply with 4.3. Two accessible parking spaces may share a common access aisle (see Fig. 9). Parked vehicle overhangs shall not reduce the clear width of an accessible route. *Parking spaces and access aisles shall be level with surface slopes not exceeding 1:50 (2%) in all directions.*

4.6.4* Signage. Accessible parking spaces shall be designated as reserved by a sign showing the symbol of accessibility (see 4.30.7). *Spaces complying with 4.1.2(5)(b) shall have an additional sign "Van-Accessible" mounted below the symbol of accessibility. Such signs shall be located so they cannot be obscured by a vehicle parked in the space.*

4.6.5* Vertical Clearance. *Provide minimum vertical clearance of 114 in (2895 mm) at accessible passenger loading zones and along at least one vehicle access route to such areas from site entrance(s) and exit(s). At parking spaces complying with 4.1.2(5)(b), provide minimum vertical clearance of 98 in (2490 mm) at the parking space and along at least one vehicle access route to such spaces from site entrance(s) and exit(s).*

4.6.6 Passenger Loading Zones. Passenger loading zones shall provide an access aisle at least 60 in (1525 mm) wide and 20 ft (240 in) (6100 mm) long adjacent and parallel to the vehicle pull-up space (see Fig. 10). If there are curbs between the access aisle and the vehicle pull-up space, then a curb ramp complying with 4.7 shall be provided. *Vehicle standing spaces and access aisles shall be level with*

25

C-75

4.7 Curb Ramps

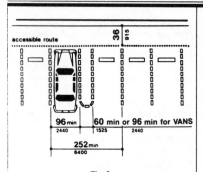

96 min
2440

60 min or 96 min for VANS
1525   2440

252 min
6400

Fig. 9
Dimensions of Parking Spaces

surface slopes not exceeding 1:50 (2%) in all directions.

4.7 Curb Ramps.

4.7.1 Location. Curb ramps complying with 4.7 shall be provided wherever an accessible route crosses a curb.

4.7.2 Slope. Slopes of curb ramps shall comply with 4.8.2. The slope shall be measured as shown in Fig. 11. *Transitions from ramps to walks, gutters, or streets shall be flush and free of abrupt changes. Maximum slopes of adjoining gutters, road surface immediately adjacent to the curb ramp, or accessible route shall not exceed 1:20.*

4.7.3 Width. The minimum width of a curb ramp shall be 36 in (915 mm), exclusive of flared sides.

4.7.4 Surface. Surfaces of curb ramps shall comply with 4.5.

4.7.5 Sides of Curb Ramps. If a curb ramp is located where pedestrians must walk across the ramp, *or where it is not protected by hand-rails or guardrails,* it shall have flared sides; the maximum slope of the flare shall be 1:10 (see Fig. 12(a)). Curb ramps with returned curbs

may be used where pedestrians would not normally walk across the ramp (see Fig. 12(b)).

4.7.6 Built-up Curb Ramps. Built-up curb ramps shall be located so that they do not project into vehicular traffic lanes (see Fig. 13).

4.7.7 *Detectable Warnings.* A curb ramp shall have a *detectable* warning complying with 4.29.2. *The detectable warning shall extend* the full width and depth of the curb ramp.

4.7.8 Obstructions. Curb ramps shall be located or protected to prevent their obstruction by parked vehicles.

4.7.9 Location at Marked Crossings. Curb ramps at marked crossings shall be wholly contained within the markings, excluding any flared sides (see Fig. 15).

4.7.10 Diagonal Curb Ramps. If diagonal (or corner type) curb ramps have returned curbs or other well-defined edges, such edges shall be parallel to the direction of pedestrian flow. The bottom of diagonal curb ramps shall have 48 in (1220 mm) minimum clear space as shown in Fig. 15(c) and (d). If diagonal curb ramps are provided at marked crossings, the 48 in (1220 mm) clear space shall be within the markings (see Fig. 15(c) and (d)). If diagonal curb ramps have flared sides, they shall also have at least a 24 in (610 mm) long segment of straight curb located on each side of the curb ramp and within the marked crossing (see Fig. 15(c)).

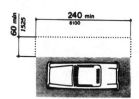

240 min
6100

60 min
1525

Fig. 10
Access Aisle at Passenger Loading Zones

26

4.8 Ramps

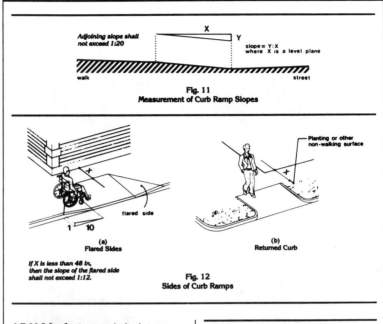

Fig. 11
Measurement of Curb Ramp Slopes

(a)
Flared Sides

(b)
Returned Curb

*If X is less than 48 in,
then the slope of the flared side
shall not exceed 1:12.*

Fig. 12
Sides of Curb Ramps

4.7.11 Islands. Any raised islands in crossings shall be cut through level with the street or have curb ramps at both sides and a level area at least 48 in (1220 mm) long between the curb ramps in the part of the island intersected by the crossings (see Fig. 15(a) and (b)).

4.8 Ramps.

4.8.1° General. Any part of an accessible route with a slope greater than 1:20 shall be considered a ramp and shall comply with 4.8.

4.8.2° Slope and Rise. The least possible slope shall be used for any ramp. The maximum slope of a ramp in new construction shall be 1:12. The maximum rise for any run shall be 30 in (760 mm) (see Fig. 16). Curb ramps

Fig. 13
Built-Up Curb Ramp

and ramps to be constructed on existing sites or in existing buildings or facilities may have slopes and rises as *allowed in 4.1.6(3)(a)* if space limitations prohibit the use of a 1:12 slope or less.

27

4.8 Ramps

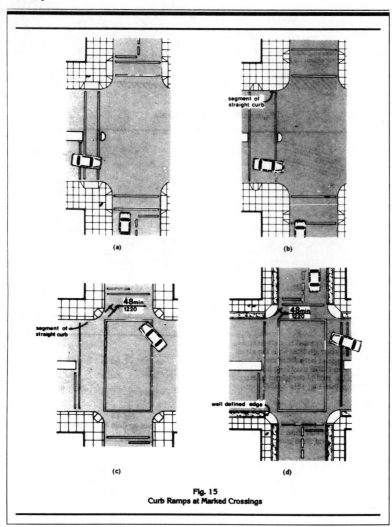

Fig. 15
Curb Ramps at Marked Crossings

4.8 Ramps

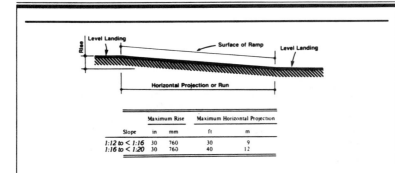

Fig. 16
Components of a Single Ramp Run and Sample Ramp Dimensions

	Maximum Rise		Maximum Horizontal Projection	
Slope	in	mm	ft	m
1:12 to < 1:16	30	760	30	9
1:16 to < 1:20	30	760	40	12

4.8.3 Clear Width. The minimum clear width of a ramp shall be 36 in (915 mm).

4.8.4* Landings. Ramps shall have level landings at bottom and top of *each ramp and each ramp run.* Landings shall have the following features:

(1) The landing shall be at least as wide as the ramp run leading to it.

(2) The landing length shall be a minimum of 60 in (1525 mm) clear.

(3) If ramps change direction at landings, the minimum landing size shall be 60 in by 60 in (1525 mm by 1525 mm).

(4) If a doorway is located at a landing, then the area in front of the doorway shall comply with 4.13.6.

4.8.5* Handrails. If a ramp run has a rise greater than 6 in (150 mm) or a horizontal projection greater than 72 in (1830 mm), then it shall have handrails on both sides. Handrails are not required on curb ramps *or adjacent to seating in assembly areas.* Handrails shall comply with 4.26 and shall have the following features:

(1) Handrails shall be provided along both sides of ramp segments. The inside handrail on switchback or dogleg ramps shall always be continuous.

(2) If handrails are not continuous, they shall extend at least 12 in (305 mm) beyond the top and bottom of the ramp segment and shall be parallel with the floor or ground surface (see Fig. 17).

(3) The clear space between the handrail and the wall shall be 1 - 1/2 in (38 mm).

(4) Gripping surfaces shall be continuous.

(5) *Top of handrail gripping surfaces shall be mounted between 34 in and 38 in (865 mm and 965 mm) above ramp surfaces.*

(6) *Ends of handrails shall be either rounded or returned smoothly to floor, wall, or post.*

(7) *Handrails shall not rotate within their fittings.*

4.8.6 Cross Slope and Surfaces. The cross slope of ramp surfaces shall be no greater than 1:50. Ramp surfaces shall comply with 4.5.

29

4.8.7 Edge Protection. Ramps and landings with drop-offs shall have curbs, walls, railings, or projecting surfaces that prevent people from slipping off the ramp. Curbs shall be a minimum of 2 in (50 mm) high (see Fig. 17).

4.8.8 Outdoor Conditions. Outdoor ramps and their approaches shall be designed so that water will not accumulate on walking surfaces.

4.9 Stairs.

4.9.1* Minimum Number. *Stairs required to be accessible by 4.1 shall comply with 4.9.*

4.9.2 Treads and Risers. On any given flight of stairs, all steps shall have uniform riser heights and uniform tread widths. Stair treads shall be no less than 11 in (280 mm) wide, measured from riser to riser (see Fig. 18(a)). *Open risers are not permitted.*

4.9.3 Nosings. The undersides of nosings shall not be abrupt. The radius of curvature at the leading edge of the tread shall be no greater than 1/2 in (13 mm). Risers shall be sloped or the underside of the nosing shall have an angle not less than 60 degrees from the horizontal. Nosings shall project no more than 1-1/2 in (38 mm) (see Fig. 18).

4.9.4 Handrails. Stairways shall have handrails at both sides of all stairs. Handrails shall comply with 4.26 and shall have the following features:

(1) Handrails shall be continuous along both sides of stairs. The inside handrail on switchback or dogleg stairs shall always be continuous (see Fig. 19(a) and (b)).

(2) If handrails are not continuous, they shall extend at least 12 in (305 mm) beyond the top riser and at least 12 in (305 mm) plus the width of one tread beyond the bottom riser. At the top, the extension shall be parallel with the floor or ground surface. At the bottom, the handrail shall continue to slope for a distance of the width of one tread from the bottom riser; the remainder of the extension shall be horizontal (see Fig. 19(c) and (d)). Handrail extensions shall comply with 4.4.

(3) The clear space between handrails and wall shall be 1-1/2 in (38 mm).

(4) Gripping surfaces shall be uninterrupted by newel posts, other construction elements, or obstructions.

(5) Top of handrail gripping surface shall be mounted between 34 in and 38 in (865 mm and 965 mm) above stair nosings.

(6) Ends of handrails shall be either rounded or returned smoothly to floor, wall or post.

(7) Handrails shall not rotate within their fittings.

4.9.5 *Detectable Warnings* at Stairs. *(Reserved).*

4.9.6 Outdoor Conditions. Outdoor stairs and their approaches shall be designed so that water will not accumulate on walking surfaces.

4.10 Elevators.

4.10.1 General. *Accessible* elevators shall be on an accessible route and shall comply with 4.10 and with the *ASME A17.1-1990, Safety Code for Elevators and Escalators. Freight elevators shall not be considered as meeting the requirements of this section unless the only elevators provided are used as combination passenger and freight elevators for the public and employees.*

4.10.2 Automatic Operation. Elevator operation shall be automatic. Each car shall be equipped with a self-leveling feature that will automatically bring the car to floor landings within a tolerance of 1/2 in (13 mm) under rated loading to zero loading conditions. This self-leveling feature shall be automatic and independent of the operating device and shall correct the overtravel or undertravel.

4.10.3 Hall Call Buttons. Call buttons in elevator lobbies and halls shall be centered at 42 in (1065 mm) above the floor. Such call buttons shall have visual signals to indicate when each call is registered and when each call is answered. Call buttons shall be a minimum of 3/4 in (19 mm) in the smallest dimension. The button designating the up direction shall be on top. (See Fig. 20.) *Buttons shall be raised or flush. Objects mounted beneath hall call buttons shall not project into the elevator lobby more than 4 in (100 mm).*

30

C-80

4.10 Elevators

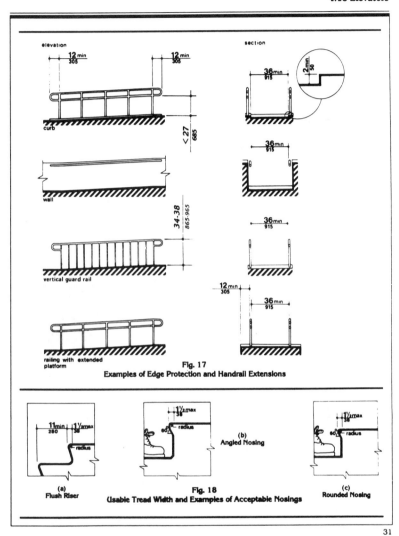

Fig. 17
Examples of Edge Protection and Handrail Extensions

(a)
Flush Riser

(b)
Angled Nosing

(c)
Rounded Nosing

Fig. 18
Usable Tread Width and Examples of Acceptable Nosings

31

C-81

4.10 Elevators

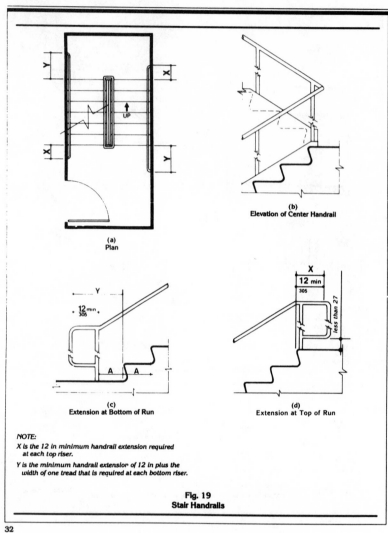

(a)
Plan

(b)
Elevation of Center Handrail

(c)
Extension at Bottom of Run

(d)
Extension at Top of Run

NOTE:

X is the 12 in minimum handrail extension required
at each top riser.

Y is the minimum handrail extension of 12 in plus the
width of one tread that is required at each bottom riser.

Fig. 19
Stair Handrails

32

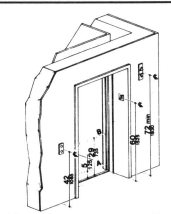

NOTE: The automatic door reopening device is activated if an object passes through either line A or line B. Line A and line B represent the vertical locations of the door reopening device not requiring contact.

Fig. 20
Holstway and Elevator Entrances

4.10.4 Hall Lanterns. A visible and audible signal shall be provided at each hoistway entrance to indicate which car is answering a call. Audible signals shall sound once for the up direction and twice for the down direction or shall have verbal annunciators that say "up" or "down." Visible signals shall have the following features:

(1) Hall lantern fixtures shall be mounted so that their centerline is at least 72 in (1830 mm) above the lobby floor. (See Fig. 20.)

(2) Visual elements shall be at least 2-1/2 in (64 mm) in the smallest dimension.

(3) Signals shall be visible from the vicinity of the hall call button (see Fig. 20). In-car lanterns located in cars, visible from the vicinity of hall call buttons, and conforming to the above requirements, shall be acceptable.

4.10.5 Raised and Braille Characters on Hoistway Entrances. All elevator hoistway entrances shall have *raised and Braille* floor designations provided on both jambs. The centerline of the characters shall be 60 in (1525 mm) *above finish* floor. Such characters shall be 2 in (50 mm) high and shall comply with 4.30.4. Permanently applied plates are acceptable if they are permanently fixed to the jambs. (See Fig. 20).

4.10.6* Door Protective and Reopening Device. Elevator doors shall open and close automatically. They shall be provided with a reopening device that will stop and reopen a car door and hoistway door automatically if the door becomes obstructed by an object or person. The device shall be capable of completing these operations without requiring contact for an obstruction passing through the opening at heights of 5 in and 29 in (125 mm and 735 mm) above finish floor (see Fig. 20). Door reopening devices shall remain effective for at least 20 seconds. After such an interval, doors may close in accordance with the requirements of *ASME A17.1-1990.*

4.10.7* Door and Signal Timing for Hall Calls. The minimum acceptable time from notification that a car is answering a call until the doors of that car start to close shall be calculated from the following equation:

$$T = D/(1.5 \text{ ft/s}) \text{ or } T = D/(445 \text{ mm/s})$$

where T total time in seconds and D distance (in feet or millimeters) from a point in the lobby or corridor 60 in (1525 mm) directly in front of the farthest call button controlling that car to the centerline of its hoistway door (see Fig. 21). For cars with in-car lanterns, T begins when the lantern is visible from the vicinity of hall call buttons and an audible signal is sounded. *The minimum acceptable notification time shall be 5 seconds.*

4.10.8 Door Delay for Car Calls. The minimum time for elevator doors to remain fully open in response to a car call shall be 3 seconds.

4.10.9 Floor Plan of Elevator Cars. The floor area of elevator cars shall provide space for wheelchair users to enter the car, maneuver

33

4.10.12 Car Controls

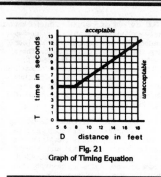

Fig. 21
Graph of Timing Equation

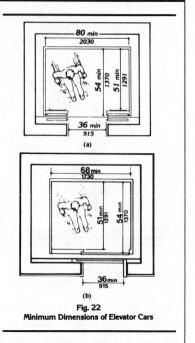

(a)

(b)

Fig. 22
Minimum Dimensions of Elevator Cars

within reach of controls, and exit from the car. Acceptable door opening and inside dimensions shall be as shown in Fig. 22. The clearance between the car platform sill and the edge of any hoistway landing shall be no greater than 1-1/4 in (32 mm).

4.10.10 Floor Surfaces. Floor surfaces shall comply with 4.5.

4.10.11 Illumination Levels. The level of illumination at the car controls, platform, and car threshold and landing sill shall be at least 5 footcandles (53.8 lux).

4.10.12* Car Controls. Elevator control panels shall have the following features:

(1) Buttons. All control buttons shall be at least 3/4 in (19 mm) in their smallest dimension. They *shall* be *raised* or flush.

(2) Tactile, *Braille,* and Visual Control Indicators. All control buttons shall be designated by *Braille and by raised* standard alphabet characters for letters, arabic characters for numerals, or standard symbols as shown in Fig. 23(a), and as required in *ASME A17.1-1990. Raised and Braille* characters and symbols shall comply with 4.30. The call button for the main entry floor shall be designated by a *raised* star at the left of the floor designation (see Fig. 23(a)). All raised designations for control buttons shall be placed immediately to the left of the button to which they apply. Applied plates,

permanently attached, are an acceptable means to provide raised control designations. Floor buttons shall be provided with visual indicators to show when each call is registered. The visual indicators shall be extinguished when each call is answered.

(3) Height. All floor buttons shall be no higher than 54 in (1370 mm) above the *finish* floor *for side approach and 48 in (1220 mm) for front approach.* Emergency controls, including the emergency alarm and emergency stop, shall be grouped at the bottom of the panel and shall have their centerlines no less than 35 in (890 mm) above the finish floor (see Fig. 23(a) and (b)).

34

4.10.13° Car Position Indicators

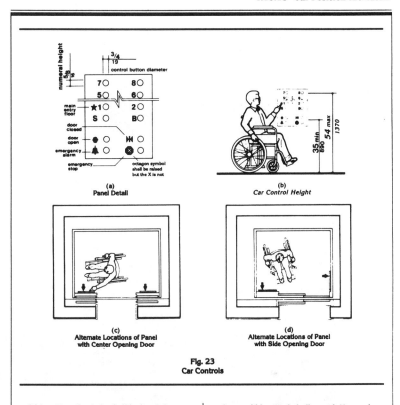

(a)
Panel Detail

(b)
Car Control Height

(c)
Alternate Locations of Panel
with Center Opening Door

(d)
Alternate Locations of Panel
with Side Opening Door

Fig. 23
Car Controls

(4) Location. Controls shall be located on a front wall if cars have center opening doors, and at the side wall or at the front wall next to the door if cars have side opening doors (see Fig. 23(c) and (d)).

4.10.13° Car Position Indicators. In elevator cars, a visual car position indicator shall be provided above the car control panel or over the door to show the position of the elevator in the hoistway. As the car passes or stops at a floor served by the elevators, the corresponding numerals shall illuminate, and an audible signal shall sound. Numerals shall be a minimum of 1/2 in (13 mm) high. The audible signal shall be no less than 20 decibels with a frequency no higher than 1500 Hz. An automatic verbal announcement of the floor number at which a car stops or which a car passes may be substituted for the audible signal.

4.10.14° Emergency Communications. If provided, emergency two-way communication systems between the elevator and a point outside the hoistway shall comply with *ASME*

35

4.11 Platform Lifts (Wheelchair Lifts)

A17.1-1990. The highest operable part of a two-way communication system shall be a maximum of *48 in (1220 mm)* from the floor of the car. It shall be identified by a raised symbol and lettering complying with 4.30 and located adjacent to the device. If the system uses a handset then the length of the cord from the panel to the handset shall be at least 29 in (735 mm). *If the system is located in a closed compartment the compartment door hardware shall conform to 4.27. Controls and Operating Mechanisms. The emergency inter-communication system shall not require voice communication.*

4.11 Platform Lifts (Wheelchair Lifts).

4.11.1 Location. *Platform lifts (wheelchair lifts) permitted by 4.1 shall comply with the requirements of 4.11.*

4.11.2* Other Requirements. If platform lifts (wheelchair lifts) are used, they shall comply with 4.2.4, 4.5, 4.27, and *ASME A17.1 Safety Code for Elevators and Escalators, Section XX, 1990.*

4.11.3 Entrance. *If platform lifts are used then they shall facilitate unassisted entry, operation, and exit from the lift in compliance with 4.11.2.*

4.12 Windows.

4.12.1* General. *(Reserved).*

4.12.2* Window Hardware. *(Reserved).*

4.13 Doors.

4.13.1 General. *Doors required to be acces-sible by 4.1 shall comply with the requirements of 4.13.*

4.13.2 Revolving Doors and Turnstiles. Revolving doors or turnstiles shall not be the only means of passage at an accessible entrance or along an accessible route. *An accessible gate or door shall be provided adja-cent to the turnstile or revolving door and shall be so designed as to facilitate the same use pattern.*

4.13.3 Gates. Gates, including ticket gates, shall meet all applicable specifications of 4.13.

4.13.4 Double-Leaf Doorways. If doorways have two *independently operated* door leaves, then at least one leaf shall meet the specifica-tions in 4.13.5 and 4.13.6. That leaf shall be an active leaf.

4.13.5 Clear Width. Doorways shall have a minimum clear opening of 32 in (815 mm) with the door open 90 degrees, measured between the face of the door and the *opposite stop* (see Fig. 24(a), (b), (c), and (d)). Openings more than 24 in (610 mm) in depth shall comply with 4.2.1 and 4.3.3 (see Fig. 24(e)).

EXCEPTION: Doors not requiring full user passage, such as shallow closets, may have the clear opening reduced to 20 in (510 mm) minimum.

4.13.6 Maneuvering Clearances at Doors. Minimum maneuvering clearances at doors that are not automatic or power-assisted shall be as shown in Fig. 25. The floor or ground area within the required clearances shall be level and clear.

EXCEPTION: Entry doors to acute care hospital bedrooms for in-patients shall be exempted from the requirement for space at the latch side of the door (see dimension "x" in Fig. 25) if the door is at least 44 in (1120 mm) wide.

4.13.7 Two Doors in Series. The minimum space between two hinged or pivoted doors in series shall be 48 in (1220 mm) plus the width of any door swinging into the space. Doors in series shall swing either in the same direction or away from the space between the doors (see Fig. 26).

4.13.8* Thresholds at Doorways. Thresholds at doorways shall not exceed 3/4 in (19 mm) in height for exterior sliding doors or 1/2 in (13 mm) for other types of doors. Raised thresholds and floor level changes at accessible doorways shall be beveled with a slope no greater than 1:2 (see 4.5.2).

4.13.9* Door Hardware. Handles, pulls, latches, locks, and other operating devices on accessible doors shall have a shape that is easy

36

4.13 Doors

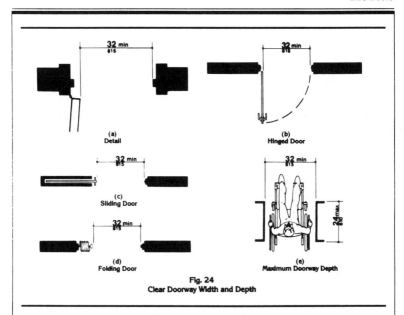

(a)
Detail

(b)
Hinged Door

(c)
Sliding Door

(d)
Folding Door

(e)
Maximum Doorway Depth

Fig. 24
Clear Doorway Width and Depth

to grasp with one hand and does not require tight grasping, tight pinching, or twisting of the wrist to operate. Lever-operated mechanisms, push-type mechanisms, and U-shaped handles are acceptable designs. When sliding doors are fully open, operating hardware shall be exposed and usable from both sides. *Hardware required for accessible door passage shall be mounted no higher than 48 in (1220 mm) above finished floor.*

4.13.10° Door Closers. If a door has a closer, then the sweep period of the closer shall be adjusted so that from an open position of 70 degrees, the door will take at least 3 seconds to move to a point 3 in (75 mm) from the latch, measured to the leading edge of the door.

4.13.11° Door Opening Force. The maximum force for pushing or pulling open a door shall be as follows:

(1) Fire doors shall have the minimum opening force allowable by the appropriate administrative authority.

(2) Other doors.

(a) exterior hinged doors: *(Reserved).*

(b) interior hinged doors: 5 lbf (22.2N)

(c) sliding or folding doors: 5 lbf (22.2N)

These forces do not apply to the force required to retract latch bolts or disengage other devices that may hold the door in a closed position.

37

C-87

4.13 Doors

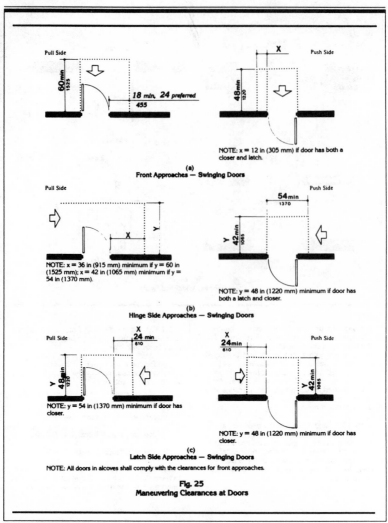

NOTE: x = 12 in (305 mm) if door has both a closer and latch.

(a)
Front Approaches — Swinging Doors

NOTE: x = 36 in (915 mm) minimum if y = 60 in (1525 mm); x = 42 in (1065 mm) minimum if y = 54 in (1370 mm).

NOTE: y = 48 in (1220 mm) minimum if door has both a latch and closer.

(b)
Hinge Side Approaches — Swinging Doors

NOTE: y = 54 in (1370 mm) minimum if door has closer.

NOTE: y = 48 in (1220 mm) minimum if door has closer.

(c)
Latch Side Approaches — Swinging Doors

NOTE: All doors in alcoves shall comply with the clearances for front approaches.

Fig. 25
Maneuvering Clearances at Doors

38

C-88

4.13 Doors

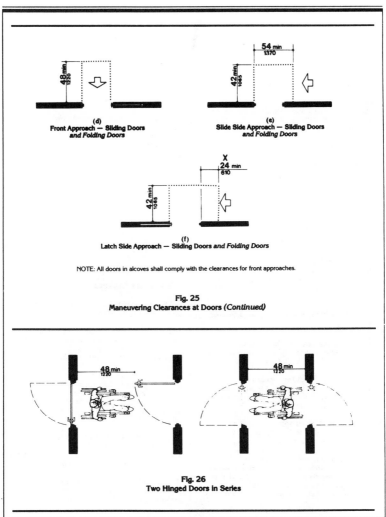

**(d)
Front Approach — Sliding Doors
and Folding Doors**

**(e)
Slide Side Approach — Sliding Doors
and Folding Doors**

**(f)
Latch Side Approach — Sliding Doors and Folding Doors**

NOTE: All doors in alcoves shall comply with the clearances for front approaches.

**Fig. 25
Maneuvering Clearances at Doors (Continued)**

**Fig. 26
Two Hinged Doors in Series**

39

C-89

4.13.12* Automatic Doors and Power-Assisted Doors. If an automatic door is used, then it shall comply with *ANSI/BHMA A156.10-1985*. Slowly opening, low-powered, automatic doors shall *comply with ANSI A156.19-1984*. Such doors shall not open to back check faster than 3 seconds and shall require no more than 15 lbf (66.6N) to stop door movement. If a power-assisted door is used, its door-opening force shall comply with 4.13.11 and its closing shall conform to the requirements in *ANSI A156.19-1984*.

4.14 Entrances.

4.14.1 Minimum Number. *Entrances required to be accessible by 4.1* shall be part of an accessible route complying with 4.3. Such entrances shall be connected by an accessible route to public transportation stops, to accessible parking and passenger loading zones, and to public streets or sidewalks if available (see 4.3.2(1)). They shall also be connected by an accessible route to all accessible spaces or elements within the building or facility.

4.14.2 Service Entrances. A service entrance shall not be the sole accessible entrance unless it is the only entrance to a building or facility (for example, in a factory or garage).

4.15 Drinking Fountains and Water Coolers.

4.15.1 Minimum Number. *Drinking fountains or water coolers required to be accessible by 4.1* shall comply with 4.15.

4.15.2* Spout Height. Spouts shall be no higher than 36 in (915 mm), measured from the floor or ground surfaces to the spout outlet (see Fig. 27(a)).

4.15.3 Spout Location. The spouts of drinking fountains and water coolers shall be at the front of the unit and shall direct the water flow in a trajectory that is parallel or nearly parallel to the front of the unit. The spout shall provide a flow of water at least 4 in (100 mm) high so as to allow the insertion of a cup or glass under the flow of water. *On an accessible drinking fountain with a round or oval bowl, the spout must be positioned so the flow of water is within 3 in (75 mm) of the front edge of the fountain.*

4.15.4 Controls. Controls shall comply with 4.27.4. *Unit controls shall be front mounted or side mounted near the front edge.*

4.15.5 Clearances.

(1) Wall- and post-mounted cantilevered units shall have a clear knee space between the bottom of the apron and the floor or ground at least 27 in (685 mm) high, 30 in (760 mm) wide, and 17 in to 19 in (430 mm to 485 mm) deep (see Fig. 27(a) and (b)). Such units shall also have a minimum clear floor space 30 in by 48 in (760 mm by 1220 mm) to allow a person in a wheelchair to approach the unit facing forward.

(2) Free-standing or built-in units not having a clear space under them shall have a clear floor space at least 30 in by 48 in (760 mm by 1220 mm) that allows a person in a wheelchair to make a parallel approach to the unit (see Fig. 27(c) and (d)). This clear floor space shall comply with 4.2.4.

4.16 Water Closets.

4.16.1 General. Accessible water closets shall comply with 4.16.

4.16.2 Clear Floor Space. Clear floor space for water closets not in stalls shall comply with Fig. 28. Clear floor space may be arranged to allow either a left-handed or right-handed approach.

4.16.3* Height. The height of water closets shall be 17 in to 19 in (430 mm to 485 mm), measured to the top of the toilet seat (see Fig. 29(b)). *Seats shall not be sprung to return to a lifted position.*

4.16.4* Grab Bars. Grab bars for water closets not located in stalls shall comply with 4.26 and Fig. 29. *The grab bar behind the water closet shall be 36 in (915 mm) minimum.*

4.16.5* Flush Controls. Flush controls shall be hand operated *or automatic* and shall comply with 4.27.4. Controls for flush valves shall be mounted on the wide side of toilet areas no more than 44 in (1120 mm) above the floor.

4.16.6 Dispensers. Toilet paper dispensers shall be installed within reach, as shown in Fig. 29(b). *Dispensers that control delivery, or that do not permit continuous paper flow, shall not be used.*

4.17 Toilet Stalls.

4.17.1 Location. Accessible toilet stalls shall be on an accessible route and shall meet the requirements of 4.17.

4.17.2 Water Closets. Water closets in accessible stalls shall comply with 4.16.

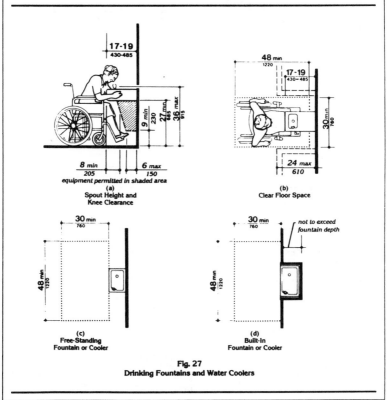

Fig. 27
Drinking Fountains and Water Coolers

41

4.17 Toilet Stalls

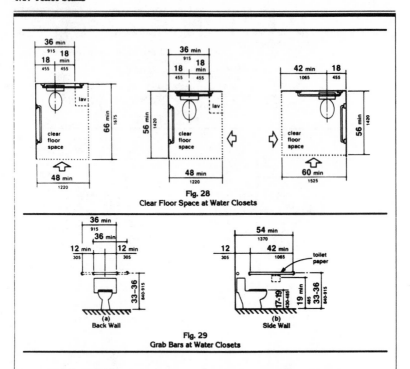

Fig. 28
Clear Floor Space at Water Closets

Fig. 29
Grab Bars at Water Closets

4.17.3° Size and Arrangement. The size and arrangement of the standard toilet stall shall comply with Fig. 30(a), *Standard Stall.* Standard toilet stalls with a minimum depth of 56 in (1420 mm) (see Fig. 30(a)) shall have wall-mounted water closets. If the depth of a standard toilet stall is increased at least 3 in (75 mm), then a floor-mounted water closet may be used. Arrangements shown for standard toilet stalls may be reversed to allow either a left- or right-hand approach. Additional stalls shall be provided in conformance with 4.22.4.

EXCEPTION: In instances of alteration work where provision of a standard stall (Fig. 30(a))

is technically infeasible or where plumbing code requirements prevent combining existing stalls to provide space, either alternate stall (Fig. 30(b)) may be provided in lieu of the standard stall.

4.17.4 Toe Clearances. In standard stalls, the front partition and at least one side partition shall provide a toe clearance of at least 9 in (230 mm) above the floor. If the depth of the stall is greater than 60 in (1525 mm), then the toe clearance is not required.

4.17.5° Doors. Toilet stall doors, *including door hardware,* shall comply with 4.13. *If toilet stall approach is from the latch side of the stall door, clearance between the door side of the*

42

C-92

4.17 Toilet Stalls

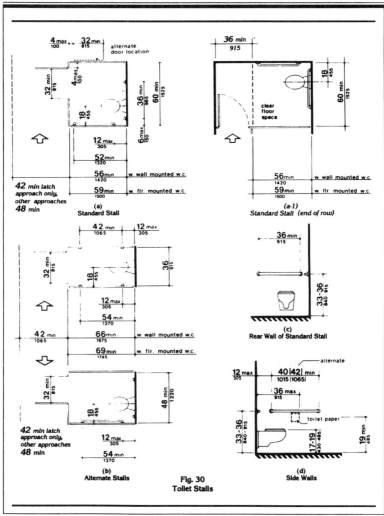

Fig. 30
Toilet Stalls

43

C-93

4.19 Lavatories and Mirrors

stall and any obstruction may be reduced to a minimum of 42 in (1065 mm) (Fig. 30).

4.17.6 Grab Bars. Grab bars complying with the length and positioning shown in Fig. 30(a), (b), (c), and (d) shall be provided. Grab bars may be mounted with any desired method as long as they have a gripping surface at the locations shown and do not obstruct the required clear floor area. Grab bars shall comply with 4.26.

4.18 Urinals.

4.18.1 General. Accessible urinals shall comply with 4.18.

4.18.2 Height. Urinals shall be stall-type or wall-hung with an elongated rim at a maximum of 17 in (430 mm) above the finish floor.

4.18.3 Clear Floor Space. A clear floor space 30 in by 48 in (760 mm by 1220 mm) shall be provided in front of urinals to allow forward approach. This clear floor space shall adjoin or overlap an accessible route and shall comply with 4.2.4. *Urinal shields that do not extend beyond the front edge of the urinal rim may be provided with 29 in (735 mm) clearance between them.*

4.18.4 Flush Controls. Flush controls shall be hand operated or automatic, and shall comply with 4.27.4, and shall be mounted no more than 44 in (1120 mm) above the finish floor.

4.19 Lavatories and Mirrors.

4.19.1 General. The requirements of 4.19 shall apply to lavatory fixtures, vanities, and built-in lavatories.

4.19.2 Height and Clearances. Lavatories shall be mounted with *the rim or counter surface no higher than 34 in (865 mm) above the finish floor.* Provide a clearance of at least 29 in (735 mm) above the finish floor to the bottom of the apron. Knee and toe clearance shall comply with Fig. 31.

4.19.3 Clear Floor Space. A clear floor space 30 in by 48 in (760 mm by 1220 mm) complying with 4.2.4 shall be provided in front of a lavatory to allow forward approach. Such

clear floor space shall adjoin or overlap an accessible route and shall extend a maximum of 19 in (485 mm) underneath the lavatory (see Fig. 32).

4.19.4 Exposed Pipes and Surfaces. Hot water and drain pipes under lavatories shall be insulated or otherwise *configured to protect against contact.* There shall be no sharp or abrasive surfaces under lavatories.

4.19.5 Faucets. Faucets shall comply with 4.27.4. Lever-operated, push-type, and electronically controlled mechanisms are examples of acceptable designs. *If self-closing valves are*

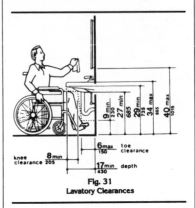

Fig. 31
Lavatory Clearances

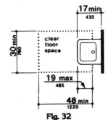

Fig. 32
Clear Floor Space at Lavatories

44

used the faucet *shall remain* open for at least 10 seconds.

4.19.6° Mirrors. Mirrors shall be mounted with the bottom edge *of the reflecting surface* no higher than 40 in (1015 mm) *above the finish* floor (see Fig. 31).

4.20 Bathtubs.

4.20.1 General. Accessible bathtubs shall comply with 4.20.

4.20.2 Floor Space. Clear floor space in front of bathtubs shall be as shown in Fig. 33.

4.20.3 Seat. An in-tub seat or a seat at the head end of the tub shall be provided as shown in Fig. 33 and 34. The structural strength of seats and their attachments shall comply with 4.26.3. Seats shall be mounted securely and shall not slip during use.

4.20.4 Grab Bars. Grab bars complying with 4.26 shall be provided as shown in Fig. 33 and 34.

4.20.5 Controls. Faucets and other controls complying with 4.27.4 shall be located as shown in Fig. 34.

4.20.6 Shower Unit. A shower spray unit with a hose at least 60 in (1525 mm) long that can be used *both* as a fixed shower head *and* as a hand-held shower shall be provided.

4.20.7 Bathtub Enclosures. If provided, enclosures for bathtubs shall not obstruct controls or transfer from wheelchairs onto bathtub seats or into tubs. Enclosures on bathtubs shall not have tracks mounted on their rims.

4.21 Shower Stalls.

4.21.1° General. Accessible shower stalls shall comply with 4.21.

4.21.2 Size and Clearances. Except as specified in 9.1.2, shower stall size and clear floor space shall comply with Fig. 35(a) or (b). The shower stall in Fig. 35(a) shall be 36 in by 36 in (915 mm by 915 mm). Shower stalls required by 9.1.2 shall comply with Fig. 57(a)

or (b). The shower stall in Fig. 35(b) will fit into the space required for a bathtub.

4.21.3 Seat. A seat shall be provided in shower stalls 36 in by 36 in (915 mm by 915 mm) and shall be as shown in Fig. 36. The seat shall be mounted 17 in to 19 in (430 mm to 485 mm) from the bathroom floor and shall extend the full depth of the stall. In a 36 in by 36 in (915 mm by 915 mm) shower stall, the seat shall be on the wall opposite the controls. *Where a fixed seat is provided in a 30 in by 60 in minimum (760 mm by 1525 mm) shower stall, it shall be a folding type and shall be mounted on the wall adjacent to the controls as shown in Fig. 57.* The structural strength of seats and their attachments shall comply with 4.26.3.

4.21.4 Grab Bars. Grab bars complying with 4.26 shall be provided as shown in Fig. 37.

4.21.5 Controls. Faucets and other controls complying with 4.27.4 shall be located as shown in Fig. 37. In shower stalls 36 in by 36 in (915 mm by 915 mm), all controls, faucets, and the shower unit shall be mounted on the side wall opposite the seat.

4.21.6 Shower Unit. A shower spray unit with a hose at least 60 in (1525 mm) long that can be used *both* as a fixed shower head *and* as a hand-held shower shall be provided.

EXCEPTION: In unmonitored facilities where vandalism is a consideration, a fixed shower head mounted at 48 in (1220 mm) above the shower floor may be used in lieu of a hand-held shower head.

4.21.7 Curbs. If provided, curbs in shower stalls 36 in by 36 in (915 mm by 915 mm) shall be no higher than 1/2 in (13 mm). Shower stalls that are 30 in by 60 in (760 mm by 1525 mm) minimum shall not have curbs.

4.21.8 Shower Enclosures. If provided, enclosures for shower stalls shall not obstruct controls or obstruct transfer from wheelchairs onto shower seats.

4.22 Toilet Rooms.

4.22.1 Minimum Number. *Toilet facilities required to be accessible by 4.1 shall comply*

4.21 Shower Stalls

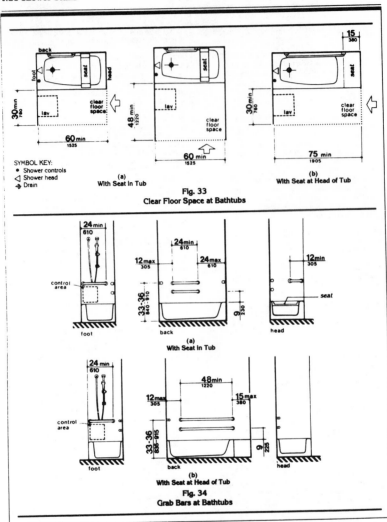

SYMBOL KEY:
- Shower controls
- Shower head
- Drain

(a)
With Seat in Tub

(b)
With Seat at Head of Tub

Fig. 33
Clear Floor Space at Bathtubs

(a)
With Seat in Tub

(b)
With Seat at Head of Tub

Fig. 34
Grab Bars at Bathtubs

46

C-96

with 4.22. Accessible toilet rooms shall be on an accessible route.

4.22.2 Doors. All doors to accessible toilet rooms shall comply with 4.13. Doors shall not swing into the clear floor space required for any fixture.

4.22.3° Clear Floor Space. The accessible fixtures and controls required in 4.22.4, 4.22.5, 4.22.6, and 4.22.7 shall be on an accessible route. An unobstructed turning space complying with 4.2.3 shall be provided within an accessible toilet room. The clear floor space at fixtures and controls, the accessible route, and the turning space may overlap.

4.22.4 Water Closets. If toilet stalls are provided, then at least one shall be a standard

toilet stall complying with 4.17; *where 6 or more stalls are provided, in addition to the stall complying with 4.17.3, at least one stall 36 in (915 mm) wide with an outward swinging, self-closing door and parallel grab bars complying with Fig. 30(d) and 4.26 shall be provided.* Water closets in such stalls shall comply with 4.16. If water closets are not in stalls, then at least one shall comply with 4.16.

4.22.5 Urinals. If urinals are provided, *then* at least one shall comply with 4.18.

4.22.6 Lavatories and Mirrors. If lavatories and mirrors are provided, *then* at least one of each shall comply with 4.19.

4.22.7 Controls and Dispensers. If controls, dispensers, receptacles, or other

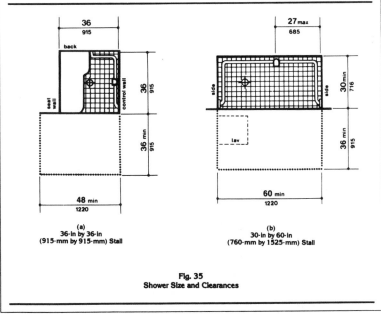

Fig. 35
Shower Size and Clearances

4.23 Bathrooms, Bathing Facilities, and Shower Rooms

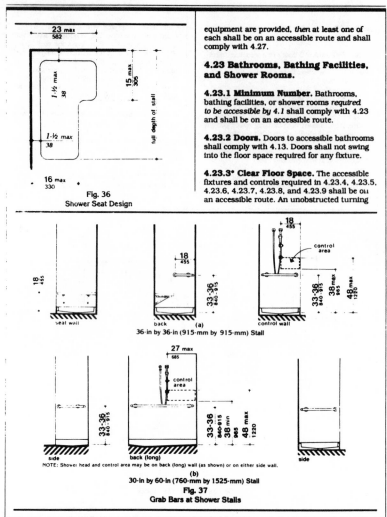

Fig. 36
Shower Seat Design

equipment are provided, *then* at least one of each shall be on an accessible route and shall comply with 4.27.

4.23 Bathrooms, Bathing Facilities, and Shower Rooms.

4.23.1 Minimum Number. Bathrooms, bathing facilities, or shower rooms *required to be accessible by 4.1* shall comply with 4.23 and shall be on an accessible route.

4.23.2 Doors. Doors to accessible bathrooms shall comply with 4.13. Doors shall not swing into the floor space required for any fixture.

4.23.3* Clear Floor Space. The accessible fixtures and controls required in 4.23.4, 4.23.5, 4.23.6, 4.23.7, 4.23.8, and 4.23.9 shall be on an accessible route. An unobstructed turning

36-in by 36-in (915-mm by 915-mm) Stall

NOTE: Shower head and control area may be on back (long) wall (as shown) or on either side wall.

(b)
30-in by 60-in (760-mm by 1525-mm) Stall

Fig. 37
Grab Bars at Shower Stalls

48

space complying with 4.2.3 shall be provided within an accessible bathroom. The clear floor spaces at fixtures and controls, the accessible route, and the turning space may overlap.

4.23.4 Water Closets. If toilet stalls are provided, then at least one shall be a standard toilet stall complying with 4.17; *where 6 or more stalls are provided, in addition to the stall complying with 4.17.3, at least one stall 36 in (915 mm) wide with an outward swinging, self-closing door and parallel grab bars complying with Fig. 30(d) and 4.26 shall be provided. Water closets in such stalls* shall comply with 4.16. If water closets are not in stalls, then at least one shall comply with 4.16.

4.23.5 Urinals. If urinals are provided, then at least one shall comply with 4.18.

4.23.6 Lavatories and Mirrors. If lavatories and mirrors are provided, then at least one of each shall comply with 4.19.

4.23.7 Controls and Dispensers. If controls, dispensers, receptacles, or other equipment *are* provided, *then* at least one of each shall be on an accessible route and shall comply with 4.27.

4.23.8 Bathing and Shower Facilities. If tubs or showers are provided, then at least one accessible tub that complies with 4.20 or at least one accessible shower that complies with 4.21 shall be provided.

4.23.9* Medicine Cabinets. If medicine cabinets are provided, at least one shall be located with a usable shelf no higher than 44 in (1120 mm) above the floor space. The floor space shall comply with 4.2.4.

4.24 Sinks.

4.24.1 General. Sinks *required to be accessible by 4.1* shall comply with 4.24.

4.24.2 Height. Sinks shall be mounted with the counter or rim no higher than 34 in (865 mm) *above the finish* floor.

4.24.3 Knee Clearance. Knee clearance that is at least 27 in (685 mm) high, 30 in (760 mm) wide, and 19 in (485 mm) deep shall be pro-

vided underneath sinks.

4.24.4 Depth. Each sink shall be a maximum of 6-1/2 in (165 mm) deep.

4.24.5 Clear Floor Space. A clear floor space at least 30 in by 48 in (760 mm by 1220 mm) complying with 4.2.4 shall be provided in front of a sink to allow forward approach. The clear floor space shall be on an accessible route and shall extend a maximum of 19 in (485 mm) underneath the sink (see Fig. 32).

4.24.6 Exposed Pipes and Surfaces. Hot water and drain pipes exposed under sinks shall be insulated or otherwise *configured so as to protect against contact.* There shall be no sharp or abrasive surfaces under sinks.

4.24.7 Faucets. Faucets shall comply with 4.27.4. Lever-operated, push-type, touch-type, or electronically controlled mechanisms are acceptable designs.

4.25 Storage.

4.25.1 General. *Fixed* storage facilities such as cabinets, shelves, closets, and drawers *required to be accessible by 4.1* shall comply with 4.25.

4.25.2 Clear Floor Space. A clear floor space at least 30 in by 48 in (760 mm by 1220 mm) complying with 4.2.4 that allows either a forward or parallel approach by a person using a wheelchair shall be provided at accessible storage facilities.

4.25.3 Height. Accessible storage spaces shall be within at least one of the reach ranges specified in 4.2.5 and 4.2.6 *(see Fig. 5 and Fig. 6).* Clothes rods or shelves shall be a maximum of 54 in (1370 mm) *above the finish floor for a side approach. Where the distance from the wheelchair to the clothes rod or shelf exceeds 10 in (255 mm) (as in closets without accessible doors) the height and depth to the rod or shelf shall comply with Fig. 38(a) and Fig. 38(b).*

4.25.4 Hardware. Hardware for accessible storage facilities shall comply with 4.27.4. Touch latches and U-shaped pulls are acceptable.

49

4.26 Handrails, Grab Bars, and Tub and Shower Seats

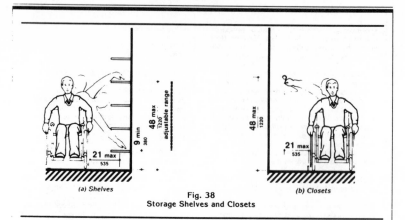

(a) Shelves

(b) Closets

Fig. 38
Storage Shelves and Closets

4.26 Handrails, Grab Bars, and Tub and Shower Seats.

4.26.1* General. All handrails, grab bars, and tub and shower seats *required to be accessible by 4.1, 4.8, 4.9, 4.16, 4.17, 4.20 or 4.21* shall comply with 4.26.

4.26.2* Size and Spacing of Grab Bars and Handrails. The diameter or width of the gripping surfaces of a handrail or grab bar shall be 1-1/4 in to 1-1/2 in (32 mm to 38 mm), or the shape shall provide an equivalent gripping surface. If handrails or grab bars are mounted adjacent to a wall, the space between the wall and the grab bar shall be 1-1/2 in (38 mm) (see Fig. 39(a), (b), (c), and (e)). Handrails may be located in a recess if the recess is a maximum of 3 in (75 mm) deep and extends at least 18 in (455 mm) above the top of the rail (see Fig. 39(d)).

4.26.3 Structural Strength. The structural strength of grab bars, tub and shower seats, fasteners, and mounting devices shall meet the following specification:

(1) Bending stress in a grab bar or seat induced by the maximum bending moment from the application of 250 lbf (1112N) shall be less than the allowable stress for the material of the grab bar or seat.

(2) Shear stress induced in a grab bar or seat by the application of 250 lbf (1112N) shall be less than the allowable shear stress for the material of the grab bar or seat. If the connection between the grab bar or seat and its mounting bracket or other support is considered to be fully restrained, then direct and torsional shear stresses shall be totaled for the combined shear stress, which shall not exceed the allowable shear stress.

(3) Shear force induced in a fastener or mounting device from the application of 250 lbf (1112N) shall be less than the allowable lateral load of either the fastener or mounting device or the supporting structure, whichever is the smaller allowable load.

(4) Tensile force induced in a fastener by a direct tension force of 250 lbf (1112N) plus the maximum moment from the application of 250 lbf (1112N) shall be less than the allowable withdrawal load between the fastener and the supporting structure.

(5) Grab bars shall not rotate within their fittings.

4.26 Handrails, Grab Bars, and Tub and Shower Seats

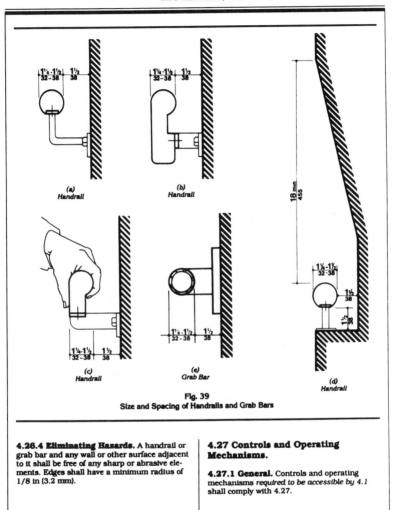

(a)
Handrail

(b)
Handrail

(c)
Handrail

(e)
Grab Bar

(d)
Handrail

Fig. 39
Size and Spacing of Handrails and Grab Bars

4.26.4 Eliminating Hazards. A handrail or grab bar and any wall or other surface adjacent to it shall be free of any sharp or abrasive elements. Edges shall have a minimum radius of 1/8 in (3.2 mm).

4.27 Controls and Operating Mechanisms.

4.27.1 General. Controls and operating mechanisms *required to be accessible by 4.1* shall comply with 4.27.

51

C-101

4.27.2 Clear Floor Space. Clear floor space complying with 4.2.4 that allows a forward or a parallel approach by a person using a wheelchair shall be provided at controls, dispensers, receptacles, and other operable equipment.

4.27.3° Height. The highest operable part of controls, dispensers, receptacles, and other operable equipment shall be placed within at least one of the reach ranges specified in 4.2.5 and 4.2.6. Electrical and communications system receptacles on walls shall be mounted no less than 15 in (380 mm) above the floor.

EXCEPTION: These requirements do not apply where the use of special equipment dictates otherwise or where electrical and communications systems receptacles are not normally intended for use by building occupants.

4.27.4 Operation. Controls and operating mechanisms shall be operable with one hand and shall not require tight grasping, pinching, or twisting of the wrist. The force required to activate controls shall be no greater than 5 lbf (22.2 N).

4.28 Alarms.

4.28.1 General. Alarm systems required to be accessible by 4.1 shall comply with 4.28. At a minimum, visual signal appliances shall be provided in buildings and facilities in each of the following areas: restrooms and any other general usage areas (e.g., meeting rooms), hallways, lobbies, and any other area for common use.

4.28.2° Audible Alarms. If provided, audible emergency alarms shall produce a sound that exceeds the prevailing equivalent sound level in the room or space by at least 15 dbA or exceeds any maximum sound level with a duration of 60 seconds by 5 dbA, whichever is louder. Sound levels for alarm signals shall not exceed 120 dbA.

4.28.3° Visual Alarms. Visual alarm signal appliances shall be integrated into the building or facility alarm system. If single station audible alarms are provided then single station visual alarm signals shall be provided. Visual alarm signals shall have the following minimum photometric and location features:

(1) The lamp shall be a xenon strobe type or equivalent.

(2) The color shall be clear or nominal white (i.e., unfiltered or clear filtered white light).

(3) The maximum pulse duration shall be two-tenths of one second (0.2 sec) with a maximum duty cycle of 40 percent. The pulse duration is defined as the time interval between initial and final points of 10 percent of maximum signal.

(4) The intensity shall be a minimum of 75 candela.

(5) The flash rate shall be a minimum of 1 Hz and a maximum of 3 Hz.

(6) The appliance shall be placed 80 in (2030 mm) above the highest floor level within the space or 6 in (152 mm) below the ceiling, whichever is lower.

(7) In general, no place in any room or space required to have a visual signal appliance shall be more than 50 ft (15 m) from the signal (in the horizontal plane). In large rooms and spaces exceeding 100 ft (30 m) across, without obstructions 6 ft (2 m) above the finish floor, such as auditoriums, devices may be placed around the perimeter, spaced a maximum 100 ft (30 m) apart, in lieu of suspending appliances from the ceiling.

(8) No place in common corridors or hallways in which visual alarm signalling appliances are required shall be more than 50 ft (15 m) from the signal.

4.28.4° Auxiliary Alarms. Units and sleeping accommodations shall have a visual alarm connected to the building emergency alarm system or shall have a standard 110-volt electrical receptacle into which such an alarm can be connected and a means by which a signal from the building emergency alarm system can trigger such an auxiliary alarm. When visual alarms are in place the signal shall be visible in all areas of the unit or room. Instructions for use of the auxiliary alarm or receptacle shall be provided.

4.29 Detectable Warnings.

4.29.1 General. Detectable warnings required by 4.1 and 4.7 shall comply with 4.29.

4.29.2* Detectable Warnings on Walking Surfaces. Detectable warnings shall consist of raised truncated domes with a diameter of nominal 0.9 in (23 mm), a height of nominal 0.2 in (5 mm) and a center-to-center spacing of nominal 2.35 in (60 mm) and shall contrast visually with adjoining surfaces, either light-on-dark, or dark-on-light.

The material used to provide contrast shall be an integral part of the walking surface. Detectable warnings used on interior surfaces shall differ from adjoining walking surfaces in resiliency or sound-on-cane contact.

4.29.3 Detectable Warnings on Doors To Hazardous Areas. (Reserved).

4.29.4 Detectable Warnings at Stairs. (Reserved).

4.29.5 Detectable Warnings at Hazardous Vehicular Areas. If a walk crosses or adjoins a vehicular way, and the walking surfaces are not separated by curbs, railings, or other elements between the pedestrian areas and vehicular areas, the boundary between the areas shall be defined by a continuous detectable warning which is 36 in (915 mm) wide, complying with 4.29.2.

4.29.6 Detectable Warnings at Reflecting Pools. The edges of reflecting pools shall be protected by railings, walls, curbs, or detectable warnings complying with 4.29.2.

4.29.7 Standardization. (Reserved).

4.30 Signage.

4.30.1* General. Signage required to be accessible by 4.1 shall comply with the applicable provisions of 4.30.

4.30.2* Character Proportion. Letters and numbers on signs shall have a width-to-height ratio between 3:5 and 1:1 and a stroke-width-to-height ratio between 1:5 and 1:10.

4.30.3 Character Height. Characters and numbers on signs shall be sized according to the viewing distance from which they are to be read. The minimum height is measured using an upper case X. Lower case characters are permitted.

Height Above Finished Floor	Minimum Character Height
Suspended or Projected Overhead in compliance with 4.4.2	3 in. (75 mm) minimum

4.30.4* Raised and Brailled Characters and Pictorial Symbol Signs (Pictograms). Letters and numerals shall be raised 1/32 in, upper case, sans serif or simple serif type and shall be accompanied with Grade 2 Braille. Raised characters shall be at least 5/8 in (16 mm) high, but no higher than 2 in (50 mm). Pictograms shall be accompanied by the equivalent verbal inscription placed directly below the pictogram. The border dimension of the pictogram shall be 6 in (152 mm) minimum in height.

4.30.5* Finish and Contrast. The characters and background of signs shall be eggshell, matte, or other non-glare finish. Characters and symbols shall contrast with their background — either light characters on a dark background or dark characters on a light background.

4.30.6 Mounting Location and Height. Where permanent identification is provided for rooms and spaces, signs shall be installed on the wall adjacent to the latch side of the door. Where there is no wall space to the latch side of the door, including at double leaf doors, signs shall be placed on the nearest adjacent wall. Mounting height shall be 60 in (1525 mm) above the finish floor to the centerline of the sign. Mounting location for such signage shall be so that a person may approach within 3 in (76 mm) of signage without encountering protruding objects or standing within the swing of a door.

4.30.7* Symbols of Accessibility.

(1) Facilities and elements required to be identified as accessible by 4.1 shall use the international symbol of accessibility. The

53

C-103

4.30 Signage

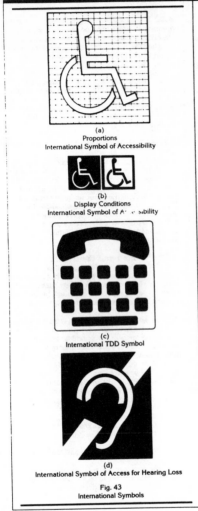

(a)
Proportions
International Symbol of Accessibility

(b)
Display Conditions
International Symbol of A··· ·sibility

(c)
International TDD Symbol

(d)
International Symbol of Access for Hearing Loss

Fig. 43
International Symbols

symbol shall be displayed as shown in Fig. 43(a) and (b).

(2) Volume Control Telephones. Telephones required to have a volume control by 4.1.3(17)(b) shall be identified by a sign containing a depiction of a telephone handset with radiating sound waves.

(3) Text Telephones. Text telephones required by 4.1.3 (17)(c) shall be identified by the international TDD symbol (Fig 43(c)). In addition, if a facility has a public text telephone, directional signage indicating the location of the nearest text telephone shall be placed adjacent to all banks of telephones which do not contain a text telephone. Such directional signage shall include the international TDD symbol. If a facility has no banks of telephones, the directional signage shall be provided at the entrance (e.g., in a building directory).

(4) Assistive Listening Systems. In assembly areas where permanently installed assistive listening systems are required by 4.1.3(19)(b) the availability of such systems shall be identified with signage that includes the international symbol of access for hearing loss (Fig 43(d)).

4.30.8° Illumination Levels. *(Reserved).*

4.31 Telephones.

4.31.1 General. Public telephones required to be accessible by 4.1 shall comply with 4.31.

4.31.2 Clear Floor or Ground Space. A clear floor or ground space at least 30 in by 48 in (760 mm by 1220 mm) that allows either a forward or parallel approach by a person using a wheelchair shall be provided at telephones (see Fig. 44). The clear floor or ground space shall comply with 4.2.4. Bases, enclosures, and fixed seats shall not impede approaches to telephones by people who use wheelchairs.

4.31.3° Mounting Height. The highest operable part of the telephone shall be within the reach ranges specified in 4.2.5 or 4.2.6.

4.31.4 *Protruding Objects.* *Telephones shall comply with 4.4.*

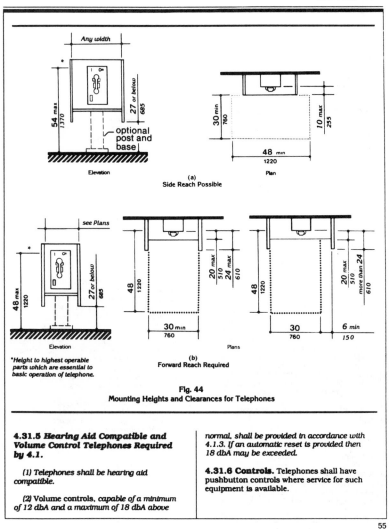

Fig. 44
Mounting Heights and Clearances for Telephones

4.31.5 Hearing Aid Compatible and Volume Control Telephones Required by 4.1.

(1) Telephones shall be hearing aid compatible.

(2) Volume controls, capable of a minimum of 12 dbA and a maximum of 18 dbA above normal, shall be provided in accordance with 4.1.3. If an automatic reset is provided then 18 dbA may be exceeded.

4.31.6 Controls. Telephones shall have pushbutton controls where service for such equipment is available.

55

4.32 *Fixed or Built-in Seating and Tables*

4.31.7 Telephone Books. Telephone books, if provided, shall be located *in a position that complies with the reach ranges specified in 4.2.5 and 4.2.6.*

4.31.8 Cord Length. The cord from the telephone to the handset shall be at least 29 in (735 mm) long.

4.31.9* Text Telephones Required by 4.1.

(1) Text telephones used with a pay telephone shall be permanently affixed within, or adjacent to, the telephone enclosure. If an acoustic coupler is used, the telephone cord shall be sufficiently long to allow connection of the text telephone and the telephone receiver.

(2) Pay telephones designed to accommodate a portable text telephone shall be equipped with a shelf and an electrical outlet within or adjacent to the telephone enclosure. The telephone handset shall be capable of being placed flush on the surface of the shelf. The shelf shall be capable of accommodating a text telephone and shall have 6 in (152 mm) minimum vertical clearance in the area where the text telephone is to be placed.

(3) Equivalent facilitation may be provided. For example, a portable text telephone may be made available in a hotel at the registration desk if it is available on a 24-hour basis for use with nearby public pay telephones. In this instance, at least one pay telephone shall comply with paragraph 2 of this section. In addition, if an acoustic coupler is used, the telephone handset cord shall be sufficiently long so as to allow connection of the text telephone and the telephone receiver. Directional signage shall be provided and shall comply with 4.30.7.

4.32 Fixed or Built-in Seating and Tables.

4.32.1 Minimum Number. Fixed or built-in seating or tables *required to be accessible by* 4.1 shall comply with 4.32.

4.32.2 Seating. If seating spaces for people in wheelchairs are provided at *fixed* tables or counters, clear floor space complying with 4.2.4 shall be provided. Such clear floor space

shall not overlap knee space by more than 19 in (485 mm) (see Fig. 45).

4.32.3 Knee Clearances. If seating for people in wheelchairs is provided at tables *or* counters, knee spaces at least 27 in (685 mm) high, 30 in (760 mm) wide, and 19 in (485 mm) deep shall be provided (see Fig. 45).

4.32.4* Height of Tables or Counters. The tops of *accessible* tables and *counters* shall be from 28 in to 34 in (710 mm to 865 mm) *above the finish* floor or ground.

4.33 Assembly Areas.

4.33.1 Minimum Number. Assembly *and associated areas required to be accessible by* 4.1 shall comply with 4.33.

4.33.2* Size of Wheelchair Locations. Each wheelchair location shall provide minimum clear ground or floor spaces as shown in Fig. 46.

4.33.3* Placement of Wheelchair Locations. Wheelchair areas shall be an integral part of any fixed seating plan and shall be provided so as to provide people with physical disabilities a choice of admission prices and lines of sight comparable to those for members of the general public. They shall adjoin an accessible route that also serves as a means of egress in case of emergency. At least one companion fixed seat shall be provided next to each wheelchair seating area. When the seating capacity exceeds 300, wheelchair spaces shall be provided in more than one location. Readily removable seats may be installed in wheelchair spaces when the spaces are not required to accommodate wheelchair users.

EXCEPTION: Accessible viewing positions may be clustered for bleachers, balconies, and other areas having sight lines that require slopes of greater than 5 percent. Equivalent accessible viewing positions may be located on levels having accessible egress.

4.33.4 Surfaces. The ground or floor at wheelchair locations shall be level and shall comply with 4.5.

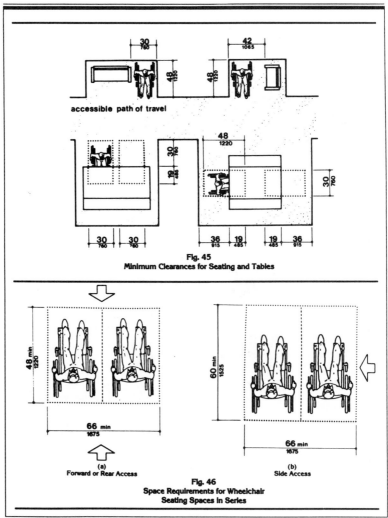

Fig. 45
Minimum Clearances for Seating and Tables

(a)
Forward or Rear Access

(b)
Side Access

Fig. 46
Space Requirements for Wheelchair
Seating Spaces in Series

57

4.33.5 Access to Performing Areas.
An accessible route shall connect wheelchair seating locations with performing areas, including stages, arena floors, dressing rooms, locker rooms, and other spaces used by performers.

4.33.6* Placement of Listening Systems.
If the listening system provided serves individual fixed seats, then such seats shall be located within a 50 ft (15 m) viewing distance of the stage or playing area and shall have a complete view of the stage or playing area.

4.33.7* Types of Listening Systems.
Assistive listening systems (ALS) are intended to augment standard public address and audio systems by providing signals which can be received directly by persons with special receivers or their own hearing aids and which eliminate or filter background noise. The type of assistive listening system appropriate for a particular application depends on the characteristics of the setting, the nature of the program, and the intended audience. Magnetic induction loops, infra-red and radio frequency systems are types of listening systems which are appropriate for various applications.

4.34 Automated Teller Machines.

4.34.1 General. *Each machine required to be accessible by 4.1.3 shall be on an accessible route and shall comply with 4.34.*

4.34.2 Controls. *Controls for user activation shall comply with the requirements of 4.27.*

4.34.3 Clearances and Reach Range.
Free standing or built-in units not having a clear space under them shall comply with 4.27.2 and 4.27.3 and provide for a parallel approach and both a forward and side reach to the unit allowing a person in a wheelchair to access the controls and dispensers.

4.34.4 Equipment for Persons with Vision Impairments. *Instructions and all information for use shall be made accessible to and independently usable by persons with vision impairments.*

4.35 Dressing and Fitting Rooms.

4.35.1 General. *Dressing and fitting rooms required to be accessible by 4.1 shall comply with 4.35 and shall be on an accessible route.*

4.35.2 Clear Floor Space. *A clear floor space allowing a person using a wheelchair to make a 180-degree turn shall be provided in every accessible dressing room entered through a swinging or sliding door. No door shall swing into any part of the turning space. Turning space shall not be required in a private dressing room entered through a curtained opening at least 32 in (815 mm) wide if clear floor space complying with section 4.2 renders the dressing room usable by a person using a wheelchair.*

4.35.3 Doors. *All doors to accessible dressing rooms shall be in compliance with section 4.13.*

4.35.4 Bench. *Every accessible dressing room shall have a 24 in by 48 in (610 mm by 1220 mm) bench fixed to the wall along the longer dimension. The bench shall be mounted 17 in to 19 in (430 mm to 485 mm) above the finish floor. Clear floor space shall be provided alongside the bench to allow a person using a wheelchair to make a parallel transfer onto the bench. The structural strength of the bench and attachments shall comply with 4.26.3. Where installed in conjunction with showers, swimming pools, or other wet locations, water shall not accumulate upon the surface of the bench and the bench shall have a slip-resistant surface.*

4.35.5 Mirror. *Where mirrors are provided in dressing rooms of the same use, then in an accessible dressing room, a full-length mirror, measuring at least 18 in wide by 54 in high (460 mm by 1370 mm), shall be mounted in a position affording a view to a person on the bench as well as to a person in a standing position.*

NOTE: Sections 4.1.1 through 4.1.7 and sections 5 through 10 are different from ANSI A117.1 in their entirety and are printed in standard type.

5. RESTAURANTS AND CAFETERIAS.

5.1° General. Except as specified or modified in this section, restaurants and cafeterias shall comply with the requirements of 4.1 to 4.35. Where fixed tables (or dining counters where food is consumed but there is no service) are provided, at least 5 percent, but not less than one, of the fixed tables (or a portion of the dining counter) shall be accessible and shall comply with 4.32 as required in 4.1.3(18). In establishments where separate areas are designated for smoking and non-smoking patrons, the required number of accessible fixed tables (or counters) shall be proportionally distributed between the smoking and non-smoking areas. In new construction, and where practicable in alterations, accessible fixed tables (or counters) shall be distributed throughout the space or facility.

5.2 Counters and Bars. Where food or drink is served at counters exceeding 34 in (865 mm) in height for consumption by customers seated on stools or standing at the counter, a portion of the main counter which is 60 in (1525 mm) in length minimum shall be provided in compliance with 4.32 or service shall be available at accessible tables within the same area.

5.3 Access Aisles. All accessible fixed tables shall be accessible by means of an access aisle at least 36 in (915 mm) clear between parallel edges of tables or between a wall and the table edges.

5.4 Dining Areas. In new construction, all dining areas, including raised or sunken dining areas, loggias, and outdoor seating areas, shall be accessible. In non-elevator buildings, an accessible means of vertical access to the mezzanine is not required under the following conditions: 1) the area of mezzanine seating measures no more than 33 percent of the area of the total accessible seating area; 2) the same services and decor are provided in an accessible space usable by the general public; and, 3) the accessible areas are not restricted to use by people with disabilities. In alterations, accessibility to raised or sunken dining areas, or to all parts of outdoor seating areas is not required provided that the same services and decor are provided in an accessible space usable by the general public and are not restricted to use by people with disabilities.

5.5 Food Service Lines. Food service lines shall have a minimum clear width of 36 in (915 mm), with a preferred clear width of 42 in (1065 mm) to allow passage around a person using a wheelchair. Tray slides shall be mounted no higher than 34 in (865 mm) above the floor (see Fig. 53). If self-service shelves

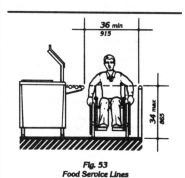

Fig. 53
Food Service Lines

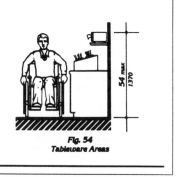

Fig. 54
Tableware Areas

59

are provided, at least 50 percent of each type must be within reach ranges specified in 4.2.5 and 4.2.6.

5.6 Tableware and Condiment Areas. Self-service shelves and dispensing devices for tableware, dishware, condiments, food and beverages shall be installed to comply with 4.2 (see Fig. 54).

5.7 Raised Platforms. In banquet rooms or spaces where a head table or speaker's lectern is located on a raised platform, the platform shall be accessible in compliance with 4.8 or 4.11. Open edges of a raised platform shall be protected by placement of tables or by a curb.

5.8 Vending Machines and Other Equipment. Spaces for vending machines and other equipment shall comply with 4.2 and shall be located on an accessible route.

5.9 Quiet Areas. (Reserved).

6. MEDICAL CARE FACILITIES.

6.1 General. Medical care facilities included in this section are those in which people receive physical or medical treatment or care and where persons may need assistance in responding to an emergency and where the period of stay may exceed twenty-four hours. In addition to the requirements of 4.1 through 4.35, medical care facilities and buildings shall comply with 6.

(1) Hospitals - general purpose hospitals, psychiatric facilities, detoxification facilities — At least 10 percent of patient bedrooms and toilets, and all public use and common use areas are required to be designed and constructed to be accessible.

(2) Hospitals and rehabilitation facilities that specialize in treating conditions that affect mobility, or units within either that specialize in treating conditions that affect mobility — All patient bedrooms and toilets, and all public use and common use areas are required to be designed and constructed to be accessible.

(3) Long term care facilities, nursing homes — At least 50 percent of patient bedrooms and toilets, and all public use and common use areas are required to be designed and constructed to be accessible.

(4) Alterations to patient bedrooms.

(a) When patient bedrooms are being added or altered as part of a planned renovation of an entire wing, a department, or other discrete area of an existing medical facility, a percentage of the patient bedrooms that are being added or altered shall comply with 6.3. The percentage of accessible rooms provided shall be consistent with the percentage of rooms required to be accessible by the applicable requirements of 6.1(1), 6.1(2), or 6.1(3), until the number of accessible patient bedrooms in the facility equals the overall number that would be required if the facility were newly constructed. (For example, if 20 patient bedrooms are being altered in the obstetrics department of a hospital, 2 of the altered rooms must be made accessible. If, within the same hospital, 20 patient bedrooms are being altered in a unit that specializes in treating mobility impairments, all of the altered rooms must be made accessible.) Where toilet/bath rooms are part of patient bedrooms which are added or altered and required to be accessible, each such patient toilet/bathroom shall comply with 6.4.

(b) When patient bedrooms are being added or altered individually, and not as part of an alteration of the entire area, the altered patient bedrooms shall comply with 6.3, unless either: a) the number of accessible rooms provided in the department or area containing the altered patient bedroom equals the number of accessible patient bedrooms that would be required if the percentage requirements of 6.1(1), 6.1(2), or 6.1(3) were applied to that department or area; or b) the number of accessible patient bedrooms in the facility equals the overall number that would be required if the facility were newly constructed. Where toilet/bathrooms are part of patient bedrooms which are added or altered and required to be accessible, each such toilet/bathroom shall comply with 6.4.

6.2 Entrances. At least one accessible entrance that complies with 4.14 shall be protected from the weather by canopy or roof overhang. Such entrances shall incorporate a passenger loading zone that complies with 4.6.6.

6.3 Patient Bedrooms. Provide accessible patient bedrooms in compliance with 4.1 through 4.35. Accessible patient bedrooms shall comply with the following:

(1) Each bedroom shall have a door that complies with 4.13.

EXCEPTION: Entry doors to acute care hospital bedrooms for in-patients shall be exempted from the requirement in 4.13.6 for maneuvering space at the latch side of the door if the door is at least 44 in (1120 mm) wide.

(2) Each bedroom shall have adequate space to provide a maneuvering space that complies with 4.2.3. In rooms with 2 beds, it is preferable that this space be located between beds.

(3) Each bedroom shall have adequate space to provide a minimum clear floor space of 36 in (915 mm) along each side of the bed and to provide an accessible route complying with 4.3.3 to each side of each bed.

6.4 Patient Toilet Rooms. Where toilet/bath rooms are provided as a part of a patient bedroom, each patient bedroom that is required to be accessible shall have an accessible toilet/bath room that complies with 4.22 or 4.23 and shall be on an accessible route.

7. BUSINESS AND MERCANTILE.

7.1 General. In addition to the requirements of 4.1 to 4.35, the design of all areas used for business transactions with the public shall comply with 7.

7.2 Sales and Service Counters, Teller Windows, Information Counters.

(1) In department stores and miscellaneous retail stores where counters have cash registers and are provided for sales or distribution of goods or services to the public, at least one of each type shall have a portion of the counter which is at least 36 in (915 mm) in length with a maximum height of 36 in (915 mm) above the finish floor. It shall be on an accessible route complying with 4.3. The accessible counters must be dispersed throughout the building or facility. In alterations where it is technically infeasible to provide an accessible counter, an auxiliary counter meeting these requirements may be provided.

(2) At ticketing counters, teller stations in a bank, registration counters in hotels and motels, box office ticket counters, and other counters that may not have a cash register but at which goods or services are sold or distributed, either:

(i) a portion of the main counter which is a minimum of 36 in (915 mm) in length shall be provided with a maximum height of 36 in (915 mm); or

(ii) an auxiliary counter with a maximum height of 36 in (915 mm) in close proximity to the main counter shall be provided; or

(iii) equivalent facilitation shall be provided (e.g., at a hotel registration counter, equivalent facilitation might consist of: (1) provision of a folding shelf attached to the main counter on which an individual with disabilities can write, and (2) use of the space on the side of the counter or at the concierge desk, for handing materials back and forth).

All accessible sales and service counters shall be on an accessible route complying with 4.3.

(3)* Assistive Listening Devices. (Reserved)

61

C-111

7.3* Check-out Aisles.

(1) In new construction, accessible check-out aisles shall be provided in conformance with the table below:

Total Check-out Aisles of Each Design	Minimum Number of Accessible Check-out Aisles (of each design)
1 – 4	1
5 – 8	2
8 – 15	3
over 15	3, plus 20% of additional aisles

EXCEPTION: In new construction, where the selling space is under 5000 square feet, only one check-out aisle is required to be accessible.

EXCEPTION: In alterations, at least one check-out aisle shall be accessible in facilities under 5000 square feet of selling space. In facilities of 5000 or more square feet of selling space, at least one of each design of check-out aisle shall be made accessible when altered until the number of accessible check-out aisles of each design equals the number required in new construction.

Examples of check-out aisles of different "design" include those which are specifically designed to serve different functions. Different "design" includes but is not limited to the following features - length of belt or no belt; or permanent signage designating the aisle as an express lane.

(2) Clear aisle width for accessible check-out aisles shall comply with 4.2.1 and maximum adjoining counter height shall not exceed 38 in (965 mm) above the finish floor. The top of the lip shall not exceed 40 in (1015 mm) above the finish floor.

(3) Signage identifying accessible check-out aisles shall comply with 4.30.7 and shall be mounted above the check-out aisle in the same location where the check-out number or type of check-out is displayed.

7.4 Security Bollards.
Any device used to prevent the removal of shopping carts from store premises shall not prevent access or egress to people in wheelchairs. An alternate entry that is equally convenient to that provided for the ambulatory population is acceptable.

8. | LIBRARIES.

8.1 General. In addition to the requirements of 4.1 to 4.35, the design of all public areas of a library shall comply with 8, including reading and study areas, stacks, reference rooms, reserve areas, and special facilities or collections.

8.2 Reading and Study Areas. At least 5 percent or a minimum of one of each element of fixed seating, tables, or study carrels shall comply with 4.2 and 4.32. Clearances between fixed accessible tables and between study carrels shall comply with 4.3.

8.3 Check-Out Areas. At least one lane at each check-out area shall comply with 7.2(1). Any traffic control or book security gates or turnstiles shall comply with 4.13.

8.4 Card Catalogs and Magazine Displays. Minimum clear aisle space at card catalogs and magazine displays shall comply with Fig. 55. Maximum reach height shall comply with 4.2, with a height of 48 in (1220 mm) preferred irrespective of approach allowed.

8.5 Stacks. Minimum clear aisle width between stacks shall comply with 4.3, with a minimum clear aisle width of 42 in (1065 mm) preferred where possible. Shelf height in stack areas is unrestricted (see Fig. 56).

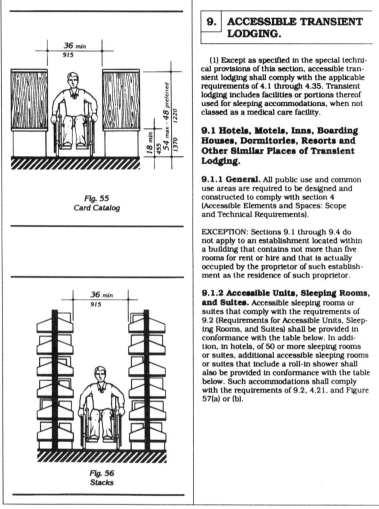

Fig. 55
Card Catalog

Fig. 56
Stacks

9. ACCESSIBLE TRANSIENT LODGING.

(1) Except as specified in the special technical provisions of this section, accessible transient lodging shall comply with the applicable requirements of 4.1 through 4.35. Transient lodging includes facilities or portions thereof used for sleeping accommodations, when not classed as a medical care facility.

9.1 Hotels, Motels, Inns, Boarding Houses, Dormitories, Resorts and Other Similar Places of Transient Lodging.

9.1.1 General. All public use and common use areas are required to be designed and constructed to comply with section 4 (Accessible Elements and Spaces: Scope and Technical Requirements).

EXCEPTION: Sections 9.1 through 9.4 do not apply to an establishment located within a building that contains not more than five rooms for rent or hire and that is actually occupied by the proprietor of such establishment as the residence of such proprietor.

9.1.2 Accessible Units, Sleeping Rooms, and Suites. Accessible sleeping rooms or suites that comply with the requirements of 9.2 (Requirements for Accessible Units, Sleeping Rooms, and Suites) shall be provided in conformance with the table below. In addition, in hotels, of 50 or more sleeping rooms or suites, additional accessible sleeping rooms or suites that include a roll-in shower shall also be provided in conformance with the table below. Such accommodations shall comply with the requirements of 9.2, 4.21, and Figure 57(a) or (b).

63

C-113

9.1.3 Sleeping Accommodations for Persons with Hearing Impairments

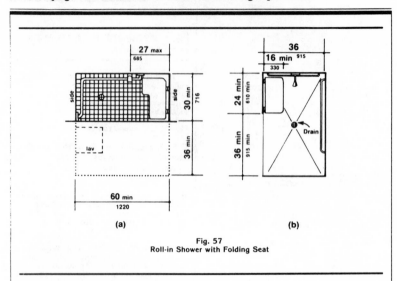

Fig. 57
Roll-in Shower with Folding Seat

Number of Rooms	Accessible Rooms	Rooms with Roll-in Showers
1 to 25	1	
26 to 50	2	
51 to 75	3	1
76 to 100	4	1
101 to 150	5	2
151 to 200	6	2
201 to 300	7	3
301 to 400	8	4
401 to 500	9	4 plus one for each additional 100 over 400
501 to 1000	2% of total	
1001 and over	20 plus 1 for each 100 over 1000	

9.1.3 Sleeping Accommodations for Persons with Hearing Impairments.
In addition to those accessible sleeping rooms and suites required by 9.1.2, sleeping rooms and suites that comply with 9.3 (Visual Alarms, Notification Devices, and Telephones) shall be provided in conformance with the following table:

Number of Elements	Accessible Elements
1 to 25	1
26 to 50	2
51 to 75	3
76 to 100	4
101 to 150	5
151 to 200	6
201 to 300	7
301 to 400	8
401 to 500	9
501 to 1000	2% of total
1001 and over	20 plus 1 for each 100 over 1000

64

9.1.4 Classes of Sleeping Accommodations.

(1) In order to provide persons with disabilities a range of options equivalent to those available to other persons served by the facility, sleeping rooms and suites required to be accessible by 9.1.2 shall be dispersed among the various classes of sleeping accommodations available to patrons of the place of transient lodging. Factors to be considered include room size, cost, amenities provided, and the number of beds provided.

(2) Equivalent Facilitation. For purposes of this section, it shall be deemed equivalent facilitation if the operator of a facility elects to limit construction of accessible rooms to those intended for multiple occupancy, provided that such rooms are made available at the cost of a single-occupancy room to an individual with disabilities who requests a single-occupancy room.

9.1.5. Alterations to Accessible Units, Sleeping Rooms, and Suites.

When sleeping rooms are being altered in an existing facility, or portion thereof, subject to the requirements of this section, at least one sleeping room or suite that complies with the requirements of 9.2 (Requirements for Accessible Units, Sleeping Rooms, and Suites) shall be provided for each 25 sleeping rooms, or fraction thereof, of rooms being altered until the number of such rooms provided equals the number required to be accessible with 9.1.2. In addition, at least one sleeping room or suite that complies with the requirements of 9.3 (Visual Alarms, Notification Devices, and Telephones) shall be provided for each 25 sleeping rooms, or fraction thereof, of rooms being altered until the number of such rooms equals the number required to be accessible by 9.1.3.

9.2 Requirements for Accessible Units, Sleeping Rooms and Suites.

9.2.1 General. Units, sleeping rooms, and suites required to be accessible by 9.1 shall comply with 9.2.

9.2.2 Minimum Requirements. An accessible unit, sleeping room or suite shall be on an accessible route complying with 4.3 and have the following accessible elements and spaces.

(1) Accessible sleeping rooms shall have a 36 in (915 mm) clear width maneuvering space located along both sides of a bed, except that where two beds are provided, this requirement can be met by providing a 36 in (915 mm) wide maneuvering space located between the two beds.

(2) An accessible route complying with 4.3 shall connect all accessible spaces and elements, including telephones, within the unit, sleeping room, or suite. This is not intended to require an elevator in multi-story units as long as the spaces identified in 9.2.2(6) and (7) are on accessible levels and the accessible sleeping area is suitable for dual occupancy.

(3) Doors and doorways designed to allow passage into and within all sleeping rooms, suites or other covered units shall comply with 4.13.

(4) If fixed or built-in storage facilities such as cabinets, shelves, closets, and drawers are provided in accessible spaces, at least one of each type provided shall contain storage space complying with 4.25. Additional storage may be provided outside of the dimensions required by 4.25.

(5) All controls in accessible units, sleeping rooms, and suites shall comply with 4.27.

(6) Where provided as part of an accessible unit, sleeping room, or suite, the following spaces shall be accessible and shall be on an accessible route:

    (a) the living area.

    (b) the dining area.

    (c) at least one sleeping area.

    (d) patios, terraces, or balconies.

EXCEPTION: The requirements of 4.13.8 and 4.3.8 do not apply where it is necessary to utilize a higher door threshold or a change in level to protect the integrity of the unit from wind/water damage. Where this exception results in patios, terraces or balconies that are not at an accessible level, equivalent facilitation shall be provided. (E.g., equivalent facilitation at a hotel patio or balcony might consist of providing raised decking or a ramp to provide accessibility.)

(e) at least one full bathroom (i.e., one with a water closet, a lavatory, and a bathtub or shower).

(f) if only half baths are provided, at least one half bath.

(g) carports, garages or parking spaces.

(7) Kitchens, Kitchenettes, or Wet Bars. When provided as accessory to a sleeping room or suite, kitchens, kitchenettes, wet bars, or similar amenities shall be accessible. Clear floor space for a front or parallel approach to cabinets, counters, sinks, and appliances shall be provided to comply with 4.2.4. Countertops and sinks shall be mounted at a maximum height of 34 in (865 mm) above the floor. At least fifty percent of shelf space in cabinets or refrigerator/freezers shall be within the reach ranges of 4.2.5 or 4.2.6 and space shall be designed to allow for the operation of cabinet and/or appliance doors so that all cabinets and appliances are accessible and usable. Controls and operating mechanisms shall comply with 4.27.

(8) Sleeping room accommodations for persons with hearing impairments required by 9.1 and complying with 9.3 shall be provided in the accessible sleeping room or suite.

9.3 Visual Alarms, Notification Devices and Telephones.

9.3.1 General. In sleeping rooms required to comply with this section, auxiliary visual alarms shall be provided and shall comply with 4.28.4. Visual notification devices shall also be provided in units, sleeping rooms and suites to alert room occupants of incoming telephone calls and a door knock or bell. Notification devices shall not be connected to auxiliary visual alarm signal appliances. Permanently installed telephones shall have volume controls complying with 4.31.5; an accessible electrical outlet within 4 ft (1220 mm) of a telephone connection shall be provided to facilitate the use of a text telephone.

9.3.2 Equivalent Facilitation. For purposes of this section, equivalent facilitation shall include the installation of electrical outlets (including outlets connected to a facility's central alarm system) and telephone wiring in sleeping rooms and suites to enable persons with hearing impairments to utilize portable visual alarms and communication devices provided by the operator of the facility.

9.4 Other Sleeping Rooms and Suites.
Doors and doorways designed to allow passage into and within all sleeping units or other covered units shall comply with 4.13.5.

9.5 Transient Lodging in Homeless Shelters, Halfway Houses, Transient Group Homes, and Other Social Service Establishments.

9.5.1 New Construction. In new construction all public use and common use areas are required to be designed and constructed to comply with section 4. At least one of each type of amenity (such as washers, dryers and similar equipment installed for the use of occupants) in each common area shall be accessible and shall be located on an accessible route to any accessible unit or sleeping accommodation.

EXCEPTION: Where elevators are not provided as allowed in 4.1.3(5), accessible amenities are not required on inaccessible floors as long as one of each type is provided in common areas on accessible floors.

9.5.2 Alterations.

(1) Social service establishments which are not homeless shelters:

(a) The provisions of 9.5.3 and 9.1.5 shall apply to sleeping rooms and beds.

(b) Alteration of other areas shall be consistent with the new construction provisions of 9.5.1.

(2) Homeless shelters. If the following elements are altered, the following requirements apply:

(a) at least one public entrance shall allow a person with mobility impairments to approach, enter and exit including a minimum clear door width of 32 in (815 mm).

(b) sleeping space for homeless persons as provided in the scoping provisions of 9.1.2 shall include doors to the sleeping area with a minimum clear width of 32 in (815 mm) and maneuvering space around the beds for persons with mobility impairments complying with 9.2.2(1).

(c) at least one toilet room for each gender or one unisex toilet room shall have a minimum clear door width of 32 in (815 mm), minimum turning space complying with 4.2.3, one water closet complying with 4.16, one lavatory complying with 4.19 and the door shall have a privacy latch; and, if provided, at least one tub or shower shall comply with 4.20 or 4.21, respectively.

(d) at least one common area which a person with mobility impairments can approach, enter and exit including a minimum clear door width of 32 in (815 mm).

(e) at least one route connecting elements (a), (b), (c) and (d) which a person with mobility impairments can use including minimum clear width of 36 in (915 mm), passing space complying with 4.3.4, turning space complying with 4.2.3 and changes in levels complying with 4.3.8.

(f) homeless shelters can comply with the provisions of (a)-(e) by providing the above elements on one accessible floor.

9.5.3. Accessible Sleeping Accommodations in New Construction.
Accessible sleeping rooms shall be provided in conformance with the table in 9.1.2 and shall comply with 9.2 Accessible Units, Sleeping Rooms and Suites (where the items are provided). Additional sleeping rooms that comply with 9.3 Sleeping Accommodations for Persons with Hearing Impairments shall be provided in conformance with the table provided in 9.1.3.

In facilities with multi-bed rooms or spaces, a percentage of the beds equal to the table provided in 9.1.2 shall comply with 9.2.2(1).

10.	TRANSPORTATION FACILITIES. (Reserved).

APPENDIX

This appendix contains *materials of an advisory nature* and provides additional information that should help the reader to understand the minimum requirements of the *guidelines* or to design buildings or facilities for greater accessibility. The paragraph numbers correspond to the sections or paragraphs of the *guideline* to which the material relates and are therefore not consecutive (for example, A4.2.1 contains additional information relevant to 4.2.1). Sections *of the guidelines* for which additional material appears in this appendix have been indicated by an asterisk. *Nothing in this appendix shall in any way obviate any obligation to comply with the requirements of the guidelines itself.*

A2.2 Equivalent Facilitation. *Specific examples of equivalent facilitation are found in the following sections:*

4.1.6(3)(c)	*Elevators in Alterations*
4.31.9	*Text Telephones*
7.2	*Sales and Service Counters, Teller Windows, Information Counters*
9.1.4	*Classes of Sleeping Accommodations*
9.2.2(6)(d)	*Requirements for Accessible Units, Sleeping Rooms, and Suites*

A4.1.1 Application.

A4.1.1(3) Areas Used Only by Employees as Work Areas. *Where there are a series of individual work stations of the same type (e.g., laboratories, service counters, ticket booths), 5%, but not less than one, of each type of work station should be constructed so that an individual with disabilities can maneuver within the work stations. Rooms housing individual offices in a typical office building must meet the requirements of the guidelines concerning doors, accessible routes, etc. but do not need to allow for maneuvering space around individual desks. Modifications required to permit maneuvering within the work area may be accomplished as a reasonable accommodation to individual employees with disabilities under Title I of the ADA. Consideration should also be given to placing shelves in employee work areas at a convenient height for accessibility or installing commercially available shelving that is adjustable so that reasonable accommodations can be made in the future.*

If work stations are made accessible they should comply with the applicable provisions of 4.2 through 4.35.

A4.1.2 Accessible Sites and Exterior Facilities: New Construction.

A4.1.2(5)(e) Valet Parking. *Valet parking is not always usable by individuals with disabilities. For instance, an individual may use a type of vehicle controls that render the regular controls inoperable or the driver's seat in a van may be removed. In these situations, another person cannot park the vehicle. It is recommended that some self-parking spaces be provided at valet parking facilities for individuals whose vehicles cannot be parked by another person and that such spaces be located on an accessible route to the entrance of the facility.*

A4.1.3 Accessible Buildings: New Construction.

A4.1.3(5) *Only full passenger elevators are covered by the accessibility provisions of 4.10. Materials and equipment hoists, freight elevators not intended for passenger use, dumbwaiters, and construction elevators are not covered by these guidelines. If a building is exempt from the elevator requirement, it is not necessary to provide a platform lift or other means of vertical access in lieu of an elevator.*

Under Exception 4, platform lifts are allowed where existing conditions make it impractical to install a ramp or elevator. Such conditions generally occur where it is essential to provide access to small raised or lowered areas where space may not be available for a ramp. Examples include, but are not limited to, raised pharmacy platforms, commercial offices raised above a sales floor, or radio and news booths.

A4.1.3(9) *Supervised automatic sprinkler systems have built in signals for monitoring features of the system such as the opening and closing of water control valves, the power supplies for needed pumps, water tank levels, and for indicating conditions that will impair the satisfactory operation of the sprinkler system.*

A1

A4.2 Space Allowances and Reach Ranges

Because of these monitoring features, super-vised automatic sprinkler systems have a high level of satisfactory performance and response to fire conditions.

A4.1.3(10) *If an odd number of drinking fountains is provided on a floor, the requirement in 4.1.3(10)(b) may be met by rounding down the odd number to an even number and calculating 50% of the even number. When more than one drinking fountain on a floor is required to comply with 4.15, those fountains should be dispersed to allow wheelchair users convenient access. For example, in a large facility such as a convention center that has water fountains at several locations on a floor, the accessible water fountains should be located so that wheelchair users do not have to travel a greater distance than other people to use a drinking fountain.*

A4.1.3(17)(b) *In addition to the requirements of section 4.1.3(17)(b), the installation of additional volume controls is encouraged. Volume controls may be installed on any telephone.*

A4.1.3(19)(a) *Readily removable or folding seating units may be installed in lieu of providing an open space for wheelchair users. Folding seating units are usually two fixed seats that can be easily folded into a fixed center bar to allow for one or two open spaces for wheelchair users when necessary. These units are more easily adapted than removable seats which generally require the seat to be removed in advance by the facility management.*

Either a sign or a marker placed on seating with removable or folding arm rests is required by this section. Consideration should be given for ensuring identification of such seats in a darkened theater. For example, a marker which contrasts (light on dark or dark on light) and which also reflects light could be placed on the side of such seating so as to be visible in a lighted auditorium and also to reflect light from a flashlight.

A4.1.6 Accessible Buildings: Alterations.

A4.1.6(1)(h) *When an entrance is being altered, it is preferable that those entrances being altered be made accessible to the extent feasible.*

A4.2 Space Allowances and Reach Ranges.

A4.2.1 Wheelchair Passage Width.

(1) Space Requirements for Wheelchairs. Many persons who use wheelchairs need a 30 in (760 mm) clear opening width for doorways, gates, and the like, when the latter are entered head-on. If the *person* is unfamiliar with a building, if competing traffic is heavy, if sudden or frequent movements are needed, or if the wheelchair must be turned at an opening, then greater clear widths are needed. For most situations, the addition of an inch of leeway on either side is sufficient. Thus, a minimum clear width of 32 in (815 mm) will provide adequate clearance. However, when an opening or a restriction in a passageway is more than 24 in (610 mm) long, it is essentially a passageway and must be at least 36 in (915 mm) wide.

(2) Space Requirements for Use of Walking Aids. Although people who use walking aids can maneuver through clear width openings of 32 in (815 mm), they need 36 in (915 mm) wide passageways and walks for comfortable gaits. Crutch tips, often extending down at a wide angle, are a hazard in narrow passageways where they might not be seen by other pedestrians. Thus, the 36 in (915 mm) width provides a safety allowance both for the person *with a disability* and for others.

(3) Space Requirements for Passing. Ablebodied *persons* in winter clothing, walking

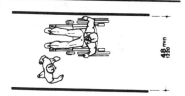

Fig. A1
Minimum Passage Width for One Wheelchair and One Ambulatory Person

A2

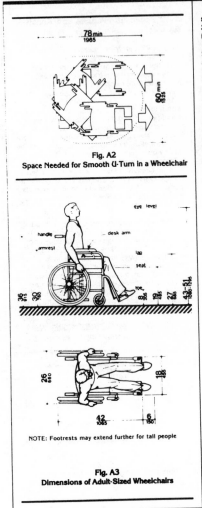

Fig. A2
Space Needed for Smooth U-Turn in a Wheelchair

straight ahead with arms swinging, need 32 in (815 mm) of width, which includes 2 in (50 mm) on either side for sway, and another 1 in (25 mm) tolerance on either side for clearing nearby objects or other pedestrians. Almost all wheelchair users and those who use walking aids can also manage within this 32 in (815 mm) width for short distances. Thus, two streams of traffic can pass in 64 in (1625 mm) in a comfortable flow. Sixty inches (1525 mm) provides a minimum width for a somewhat more restricted flow. If the clear width is less than 60 in (1525 mm), two wheelchair users will not be able to pass but will have to seek a wider place for passing. Forty-eight inches (1220 mm) is the minimum width needed for an ambulatory person to pass a nonambulatory or semi-ambulatory person. Within this 48 in (1220 mm) width, the ambulatory person will have to twist to pass a wheelchair user, a person with a *service animal*, or a

NOTE: Footrests may extend further for tall people

Fig. A3
Dimensions of Adult-Sized Wheelchairs

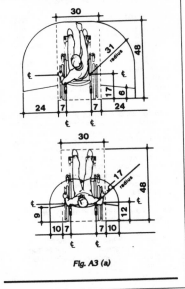

Fig. A3 (a)

A3

C-120

A4.3 Accessible Route

semi-ambulatory person. There will be little leeway for swaying or missteps (see Fig. A1).

A4.2.3 Wheelchair Turning Space.
These guidelines specify a minimum space of 60 in (1525 mm) diameter or a 60 in by 60 in (1525 mm by 1525 mm) T-shaped space for a pivoting 180-degree turn of a wheelchair. This space is usually satisfactory for turning around, but many people will not be able to turn without repeated tries and bumping into surrounding objects. The space shown in Fig. A2 will allow most wheelchair users to complete U-turns without difficulty.

A4.2.4 Clear Floor or Ground Space for Wheelchairs. The wheelchair and user shown in Fig. A3 represent typical dimensions for a large adult male. The space requirements in this *guideline* are based upon maneuvering clearances that will accommodate most wheelchairs. Fig. A3 provides a uniform reference for design not covered by this *guideline*.

A4.2.5 & A4.2.6 Reach. *Reach ranges for persons seated in wheelchairs may be further clarified by Fig. A3(a). These drawings approximate in the plan view the information shown in Fig. 4, 5, and 6.*

A4.3 Accessible Route.

A4.3.1 General.

(1) Travel Distances. Many people with mobility impairments can move at only very slow speeds; for many, traveling 200 ft (61 m) could take about 2 minutes. This assumes a rate of about 1.5 ft/s (455 mm/s) on level ground. It also assumes that the traveler would move continuously. However, on trips over 100 ft (30 m), disabled people are apt to rest frequently, which substantially increases their trip times. Resting periods of 2 minutes for every 100 ft (30 m) can be used to estimate travel times for people with severely limited stamina. In inclement weather, slow progress and resting can greatly increase a disabled person's exposure to the elements.

(2) Sites. Level, indirect routes or those with running slopes lower than 1:20 can sometimes provide more convenience than direct routes with maximum allowable slopes or with ramps.

A4

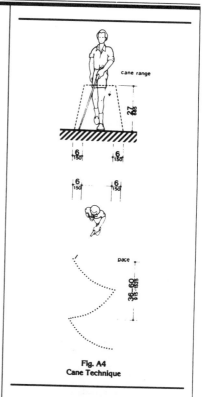

**Fig. A4
Cane Technique**

A4.3.10 Egress. Because people with disabilities may visit, be employed or be a resident in any building, emergency management plans with specific provisions to ensure their safe evacuation also play an essential role in fire safety and life safety.

A4.3.11.3 Stairway Width. *A 48 inch (1220 mm) wide exit stairway is needed to allow assisted evacuation (e.g., carrying a person in a wheelchair) without encroaching on the exit path for ambulatory persons.*

A4.3.11.4 Two-way Communication. *It is essential that emergency communication not be dependent on voice communications alone because the safety of people with hearing or speech impairments could be jeopardized. The visible signal requirement could be satisfied with something as simple as a button in the area of rescue assistance that lights, indicating that help is on the way, when the message is answered at the point of entry.*

A4.4 Protruding Objects.

A4.4.1 General. Service animals are trained to recognize and avoid hazards. However, most people with severe impairments of vision use the long cane as an aid to mobility. The two principal cane techniques are the touch technique, where the cane arcs from side to side and touches points outside both shoulders; and the diagonal technique, where the cane is held in a stationary position diagonally across the body with the cane tip touching or just above the ground at a point outside one shoulder and the handle or grip extending to a point outside the other shoulder. The touch technique is used primarily in uncontrolled areas, while the diagonal technique is used primarily in certain limited, controlled, and familiar environments. Cane users are often trained to use both techniques.

Potential hazardous objects are noticed only if they fall within the detection range of canes (see Fig. A4). Visually impaired people walking toward an object can detect an overhang if its lowest surface is not higher than 27 in (685 mm). When walking alongside *protruding* objects, they cannot detect overhangs. Since proper cane and *service animal* techniques keep people away from the edge of a path or from walls, a slight overhang of no more than 4 in (100 mm) is not hazardous.

A4.5 Ground and Floor Surfaces.

A4.5.1 General. People who have difficulty walking or maintaining balance or who use crutches, canes, or walkers, and those with restricted gaits are particularly sensitive to slipping and tripping hazards. For such people, a stable and regular surface is necessary for safe walking, particularly on stairs. Wheelchairs can be propelled most easily on surfaces that are hard, stable, and regular. Soft loose surfaces such as shag carpet, loose sand or gravel, wet clay, and irregular surfaces such as cobblestones can significantly impede wheelchair movement.

Slip resistance is based on the frictional force necessary to keep a shoe heel or crutch tip from slipping on a walking surface under conditions likely to be found on the surface. While the *dynamic* coefficient of friction during walking varies in a complex and non-uniform way, the *static* coefficient of friction, which can be measured in several ways, provides a close approximation of the slip resistance of a surface. Contrary to popular belief, some slippage is *necessary* to walking, especially for persons with restricted gaits; a truly "non-slip" surface could not be negotiated.

The Occupational Safety and Health Administration recommends that walking surfaces have a static coefficient of friction of 0.5. A research project sponsored by the Architectural and Transportation Barriers Compliance Board (Access Board) conducted tests with persons with disabilities and concluded that a higher coefficient of friction was needed by such persons. A static coefficient of friction of 0.6 is recommended for accessible routes and 0.8 for ramps.

It is recognized that the coefficient of friction varies considerably due to the presence of contaminants, water, floor finishes, and other factors not under the control of the designer or builder and not subject to design and construction guidelines and that compliance would be difficult to measure on the building site. Nevertheless, many common building materials suitable for flooring are now labeled with information on the static coefficient of friction. While it may not be possible to compare one product directly with another, or to guarantee a constant measure, builders and designers are encouraged to specify materials with appropriate values. As more products include information on slip resistance, improved uniformity in measurement and specification is likely. The Access Board's advisory guidelines on Slip Resistant Surfaces provides additional information on this subject.

Cross slopes on walks and ground or floor surfaces can cause considerable difficulty in propelling a wheelchair in a straight line.

A5

A4.6 Parking and Passenger Loading Zones

A4.5.3 Carpet. Much more needs to be done in developing both quantitative and qualitative criteria for carpeting (i.e., problems associated with texture and weave need to be studied). However, certain functional characteristics are well established. When both carpet and padding are used, it is desirable to have minimum movement (preferably none) between the floor and the pad and the pad and the carpet which would allow the carpet to hump or warp. In heavily trafficked areas, a thick, soft (plush) pad or cushion, particularly in combination with long carpet pile, makes it difficult for individuals in wheelchairs and those with other ambulatory disabilities to get about. Firm carpeting can be achieved through proper selection and combination of pad and carpet, sometimes with the elimination of the pad or cushion, and with proper installation. Carpeting designed with a weave that causes a zig-zag effect when wheeled across is strongly discouraged.

A4.6 Parking and Passenger Loading Zones.

A4.6.3 Parking Spaces. The increasing use of vans with side-mounted lifts or ramps by persons with disabilities has necessitated some revisions in specifications for parking spaces and adjacent access aisles. The typical accessible parking space is 96 in (2440 mm) wide with an adjacent 60 in (1525 mm) access aisle. However, this aisle does not permit lifts or ramps to be deployed and still leave room for a person using a wheelchair or other mobility aid to exit the lift platform or ramp. In tests conducted with actual lift/van/wheelchair combinations, (under a Board-sponsored Accessible Parking and Loading Zones Project) researchers found that a space and aisle totaling almost 204 in (5180 mm) wide was needed to deploy a lift and exit conveniently. The "van accessible" parking space required by these guidelines provides a 96 in (2440 mm) wide space with a 96 in (2440 mm) adjacent access aisle which is just wide enough to maneuver and exit from a side mounted lift. If a 96 in (2440 mm) access aisle is placed between two spaces, two "van accessible" spaces are created. Alternatively, if the wide access aisle is provided at the end of a row (an area often unused), it may be possible to provide the wide access aisle without additional space (see Fig. A5(a)).

A sign is needed to alert van users to the presence of the wider aisle, but the space is not intended to be restricted only to vans.

"Universal" Parking Space Design. An alternative to the provision of a percentage of spaces with a wide aisle, and the associated need to include additional signage, is the use of what has been called the "universal" parking space design. Under this design, all accessible spaces are 132 in (3350 mm) wide with a 60 in (1525 mm) access aisle (see Fig. A5(b)). One

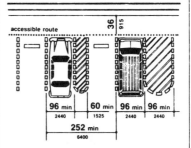

(a)
Van Accessible Space at End Row

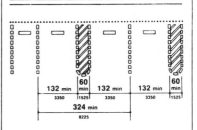

(b)
Universal Parking Space Design

Fig. A5
Parking Space Alternatives

A6

advantage to this design is that no additional signage is needed because all spaces can accommodate a van with a side-mounted lift or ramp. Also, there is no competition between cars and vans for spaces since all spaces can accommodate either. Furthermore, the wider space permits vehicles to park to one side or the other within the 132 in (3350 mm) space to allow persons to exit and enter the vehicle on either the driver or passenger side, although, in some cases, this would require exiting or entering without a marked access aisle.

An essential consideration for any design is having the access aisle level with the parking space. Since a person with a disability, using a lift or ramp, must maneuver within the access aisle, the aisle cannot include a ramp or sloped area. The access aisle must be connected to an accessible route to the appropriate accessible entrance of a building or facility. The parking access aisle must either blend with the accessible route or have a curb ramp complying with 4.7. Such a curb ramp opening must be located within the access aisle boundaries, not within the parking space boundaries. Unfortunately, many facilities are designed with a ramp that is blocked when any vehicle parks in the accessible space. Also, the required dimensions of the access aisle cannot be restricted by planters, curbs or wheel stops.

A4.6.4 Signage. Signs designating parking places for disabled people can be seen from a driver's seat if the signs are mounted high enough above the ground and located at the front of a parking space.

A4.6.5 *Vertical Clearance.* High-top vans, which disabled people or transportation services often use, require higher clearances in parking garages than automobiles.

A4.8 Ramps.

A4.8.1 General. Ramps are essential for wheelchair users if elevators or lifts are not available to connect different levels. However, some people who use walking aids have difficulty with ramps and prefer stairs.

A4.8.2 *Slope and Rise.* Ramp slopes between 1:16 and 1:20 are preferred. The ability to manage an incline is related to both its slope and its length. Wheelchair users with

disabilities affecting their arms or with low stamina have serious difficulty using inclines. Most ambulatory people and most people who use wheelchairs can manage a slope of 1:16. Many people cannot manage a slope of 1:12 for 30 ft (9 m).

A4.8.4 *Landings.* *Level landings are essential toward maintaining an aggregate slope that complies with these guidelines. A ramp landing that is not level causes individuals using wheelchairs to tip backward or bottom out when the ramp is approached.*

A4.8.5 Handrails. The requirements for stair and ramp handrails in this guideline are for adults. When children are principal users in a building or facility, a second set of handrails at an appropriate height can assist them and aid in preventing accidents.

A4.9 Stairs.

A4.9.1 *Minimum Number.* *Only interior and exterior stairs connecting levels that are not connected by an elevator, ramp, or other accessible means of vertical access have to comply with 4.9.*

A4.10 Elevators.

A4.10.6 Door Protective and Reopening Device. The required door reopening device would hold the door open for 20 seconds if the doorway remains obstructed. After 20 seconds, the door may begin to close. However, if designed in accordance with *ASME A17.1-1990,* the door closing movement could still be stopped if a person or object exerts sufficient force at any point on the door edge.

A4.10.7 Door and Signal Timing for Hall Calls. This paragraph allows variation in the location of call buttons, advance time for warning signals, and the door-holding period used to meet the time requirement.

A4.10.12 Car Controls. Industry-wide standardization of elevator control panel design would make all elevators significantly more convenient for use by people with severe visual impairments. In many cases, it will be possible to locate the highest control on elevator panels within 48 in (1220 mm) from the floor.

A7

A4.11 Platform Lifts (Wheelchair Lifts)

A4.10.13 Car Position Indicators. A special button may be provided that would activate the audible signal within the given elevator only for the desired trip, rather than maintaining the audible signal in constant operation.

A4.10.14 Emergency Communications. A device that requires no handset is easier to use by people who have difficulty reaching. Also, small handles on handset compartment doors are not usable by people who have difficulty grasping.

Ideally, emergency two-way communication systems should provide both voice and visual display intercommunication so that persons with hearing impairments and persons with vision impairments can receive information regarding the status of a rescue. A voice intercommunication system cannot be the only means of communication because it is not accessible to people with speech and hearing impairments. While a voice intercommunication system is not required, at a minimum, the system should provide both an audio and visual indication that a rescue is on the way.

A4.11 Platform Lifts (Wheelchair Lifts).

A4.11.2 Other Requirements. *Inclined stairway chairlifts, and inclined and vertical platform lifts (wheelchair lifts) are available for short-distance, vertical transportation of people with disabilities. Care should be taken in selecting lifts as some lifts are not equally suitable for use by both wheelchair users and semi-ambulatory individuals.*

A4.12 Windows.

A4.12.1 General. *Windows intended to be operated by occupants in accessible spaces should comply with 4.12.*

A4.12.2 Window Hardware. *Windows requiring pushing, pulling, or lifting to open (for example, double-hung, sliding, or casement and awning units without cranks) should require no more than 5 lbf (22.2 N) to open or close. Locks, cranks, and other window hardware should comply with 4.27.*

A4.13 Doors.

A4.13.8 Thresholds at Doorways. Thresholds and surface height changes in doorways are particularly inconvenient for wheelchair users who also have low stamina or restrictions in arm movement because complex maneuvering is required to get over the level change while operating the door.

A4.13.9 Door Hardware. Some disabled persons must push against a door with their chair or walker to open it. Applied kickplates on doors with closers can reduce required maintenance by withstanding abuse from wheelchairs and canes. To be effective, they should cover the door width, less approximately 2 in (51 mm), up to a height of 16 in (405 mm) from its bottom edge and be centered across the *width of the door.*

A4.13.10 Door Closers. Closers with delayed action features give a person more time to maneuver through doorways. They are particularly useful on frequently used interior doors such as entrances to toilet rooms.

A4.13.11 Door Opening Force. Although most people with disabilities can exert at least 5 lbf (22.2N), both pushing and pulling from a stationary position, a few people with severe disabilities cannot exert 3 lbf (13.13N). Although some people cannot manage the allowable forces in this guideline and many others have difficulty, door closers must have certain minimum closing forces to close doors satisfactorily. Forces for pushing or pulling doors open are measured with a push-pull scale under the following conditions:

(1) Hinged doors: Force applied perpendicular to the door at the door opener or 30 in (760 mm) from the hinged side, whichever is farther from the hinge.

(2) Sliding or folding doors: Force applied parallel to the door at the door pull or latch.

(3) Application of force: Apply force gradually so that the applied force does not exceed the resistance of the door. In high-rise buildings, air-pressure differentials may require a modification of this specification in order to meet the functional intent.

A8

A4.13.12 Automatic Doors and Power-Assisted Doors. Sliding automatic doors do not need guard rails and are more convenient for wheelchair users and visually impaired people to use. If slowly opening automatic doors can be reactivated before their closing cycle is completed, they will be more convenient in busy doorways.

A4.15 Drinking Fountains and Water Coolers.

A4.15.2 Spout Height. *Two drinking fountains, mounted side by side or on a single post, are usable by people with disabilities and people who find it difficult to bend over.*

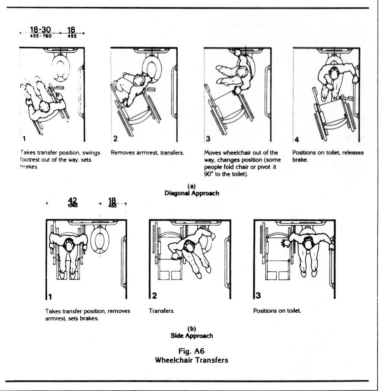

1 Takes transfer position, swings footrest out of the way, sets brakes.

2 Removes armrest, transfers.

3 Moves wheelchair out of the way, changes position (some people fold chair or pivot it 90° to the toilet).

4 Positions on toilet, releases brake.

(a)
Diagonal Approach

1 Takes transfer position, removes armrest, sets brakes.

2 Transfers.

3 Positions on toilet.

(b)
Side Approach

Fig. A6
Wheelchair Transfers

A9

A4.16 Water Closets

A4.16 Water Closets.

A4.16.3 Height. Height preferences for toilet seats vary considerably among disabled people. Higher seat heights may be an advantage to some ambulatory disabled people, but are often a disadvantage for wheelchair users and others. Toilet seats 18 in (455 mm) high seem to be a reasonable compromise. Thick seats and filler rings are available to adapt standard fixtures to these requirements.

A4.16.4 Grab Bars. Fig. A6(a) and (b) show the diagonal and side approaches most commonly used to transfer from a wheelchair to a water closet. Some wheelchair users can transfer from the front of the toilet while others use a 90-degree approach. Most people who use the two additional approaches can also use either the diagonal approach or the side approach.

A4.16.5 Flush Controls. Flush valves and related plumbing can be located behind walls or to the side of the toilet, or a toilet seat lid can be provided if plumbing fittings are directly behind the toilet seat. Such designs reduce the chance of injury and imbalance caused by leaning back against the fittings. Flush controls for tank-type toilets have a standardized mounting location on the left side of the tank (facing the tank). Tanks can be obtained by special order with controls mounted on the right side. If administrative authorities require flush controls for flush valves to be located in a position that conflicts with the location of the rear grab bar, then that bar may be split or shifted toward the wide side of the toilet area.

A4.17 Toilet Stalls.

A4.17.3 Size and Arrangement. *This section requires use of the 60 in (1525 mm) standard stall (Figure 30(a)) and permits the 36 in (915 mm) or 48 in (1220 mm) wide alternate stall (Figure 30(b)) only in alterations where provision of the standard stall is technically infeasible or where local plumbing codes prohibit reduction in the number of fixtures. A standard stall provides a clear space on one side of the water closet to enable persons who use wheelchairs to perform a side or diagonal transfer from the wheelchair to the water closet. However, some persons with disabilities who use mobility aids such as walkers, canes or crutches*

are better able to use the two parallel grab bars in the 36 in (915 mm) wide alternate stall to achieve a standing position.

In large toilet rooms, where six or more toilet stalls are provided, it is therefore required that a 36 in (915 mm) wide stall with parallel grab bars be provided in addition *to the standard stall required in new construction. The 36 in (915 mm) width is necessary to achieve proper use of the grab bars; wider stalls would position the grab bars too far apart to be easily used and narrower stalls would position the grab bars too close to the water closet. Since the stall is primarily intended for use by persons using canes, crutches and walkers, rather than wheelchairs, the length of the stall could be conventional. The door, however, must swing outward to ensure a usable space for people who use crutches or walkers.*

A4.17.5 Doors. To make it easier for wheelchair users to close toilet stall doors, doors can be provided with closers, spring hinges, or a pull bar mounted on the inside surface of the door near the hinge side.

A4.19 Lavatories and Mirrors.

A4.19.6 Mirrors. If mirrors are to be used by both ambulatory people and wheelchair users, then they must be at least 74 in (1880 mm) high at their topmost edge. A single full length mirror can accommodate all people, including children.

A4.21 Shower Stalls.

A4.21.1 General. Shower stalls that are 36 in by 36 in (915 mm by 915 mm) wide provide additional safety to people who have difficulty maintaining balance because all grab bars and walls are within easy reach. Seated people use the walls of 36 in by 36 in (915 mm by 915 mm) showers for back support. Shower stalls that are 60 in (1525 mm) wide and have no curb may increase usability of a bathroom by wheelchair users because the shower area provides additional maneuvering space.

A4.22 Toilet Rooms.

A4.22.3 Clear Floor Space. *In many small facilities, single-user restrooms may be the only* *facilities provided for all building users. In addition, the guidelines allow the use of "unisex" or "family" accessible toilet rooms in alterations when technical infeasibility can be demonstrated. Experience has shown that the provision of accessible "unisex" or single-user restrooms is a reasonable way to provide access for wheelchair users and any attendants, especially when attendants are of the opposite sex. Since these facilities have proven so useful, it is often considered advantageous to install a "unisex" toilet room in new facilities in addition to making the multi-stall restrooms accessible, especially in shopping malls, large auditoriums, and convention centers.*

Figure 28 (section 4.16) provides minimum clear floor space dimensions for toilets in accessible "unisex" toilet rooms. The dotted lines designate the minimum clear floor space, depending on the direction of approach, required for wheelchair users to transfer onto the water closet. The dimensions of 48 in (1220 mm) and 60 in (1525 mm), respectively, correspond to the space required for the two common transfer approaches utilized by wheelchair users (see Fig. A6). It is important to keep in mind that the placement of the lavatory to the immediate side of the water closet will preclude the side approach transfer illustrated in Figure A6(b).

To accommodate the side transfer, the space adjacent to the water closet must remain clear of obstruction for 42 in (1065 mm) from the centerline of the toilet (Figure 28) and the lavatory must not be located within this clear space. A turning circle or T-turn, the clear floor space at the lavatory, and maneuvering space at the door must be considered when determining the possible wall locations. A privacy latch or other accessible means of ensuring privacy during use should be provided at the door.

RECOMMENDATIONS:

1. In new construction, accessible single-user restrooms may be desirable in some situations because they can accommodate a wide variety of building users. However, they cannot be used in lieu of making the multi-stall toilet rooms accessible as required.

2. Where strict compliance to the guidelines for accessible toilet facilities is technically infeasible in the alteration of existing facilities, accessible "unisex" toilets are a reasonable alternative.

3. In designing accessible single-user restrooms, the provisions of adequate space to allow a side transfer will provide accommodation to the largest number of wheelchair users.

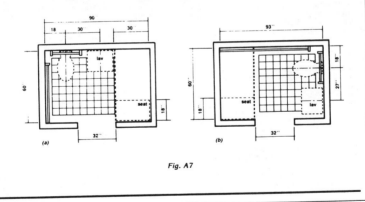

Fig. A7

A4.23 Bathrooms, Bathing Facilities, and Shower Rooms

A4.23 Bathrooms, Bathing Facilities, and Shower Rooms.

A4.23.3 Clear Floor Space. *Figure A7 shows two possible configurations of a toilet room with a roll-in shower. The specific shower shown is designed to fit exactly within the dimensions of a standard bathtub. Since the shower does not have a lip, the floor space can be used for required maneuvering space. This would permit a toilet room to be smaller than would be permitted with a bathtub and still provide enough floor space to be considered accessible. This design can provide accessibility in facilities where space is at a premium (i.e., hotels and medical care facilities). The alternate roll-in shower (Fig. 57b) also provides sufficient room for the "T-turn" and does not require plumbing to be on more than one wall.*

A4.23.9 Medicine Cabinets. Other alternatives for storing medical and personal care items are very useful to disabled people. Shelves, drawers, and floor-mounted cabinets can be provided within the reach ranges of disabled people.

A4.26 Handrails, Grab Bars, and Tub and Shower Seats.

A4.26.1 General. Many disabled people rely heavily upon grab bars and handrails to maintain balance and prevent serious falls. Many people brace their forearms between supports and walls to give them more leverage and stability in maintaining balance or for lifting. The grab bar clearance of 1-1/2 in (38 mm) required in this guideline is a safety clearance to prevent injuries resulting from arms slipping through the openings. It also provides adequate gripping room.

A4.26.2 Size and Spacing of Grab Bars and Handrails. This specification allows for alternate shapes of handrails as long as they allow an opposing grip similar to that provided by a circular section of 1-1/4 in to 1-1/2 in (32 mm to 38 mm).

A4.27 Controls and Operating Mechanisms.

A4.27.3 Height. *Fig. A8 further illustrates*

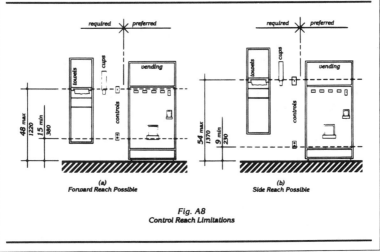

(a)
Forward Reach Possible

(b)
Side Reach Possible

Fig. A8
Control Reach Limitations

A12

mandatory and advisory control mounting height provisions for typical equipment.

Electrical receptacles installed to serve individual appliances and not intended for regular or frequent use by building occupants are not required to be mounted within the specified reach ranges. Examples would be receptacles installed specifically for wall-mounted clocks, refrigerators, and microwave ovens.

A4.28 Alarms.

A4.28.2 Audible Alarms. Audible emergency signals must have an intensity and frequency that can attract the attention of individuals who have partial hearing loss. People over 60 years of age generally have difficulty perceiving frequencies higher than 10,000 Hz. An alarm signal which has a periodic element to its signal, such as single stroke bells (clang-pause-clang-pause), hi-low (up-down-up-down) and fast whoop (on-off-on-off) are best. Avoid continuous or reverberating tones. Select a signal which has a sound characterized by three or four clear tones without a great deal of "noise" in between.

A4.28.3 Visual Alarms. The specifications in this section do not preclude the use of zoned or coded alarm systems.

A4.28.4 Auxiliary Alarms. Locating visual emergency alarms in rooms where persons who are deaf may work or reside alone can ensure that they will always be warned when an emergency alarm is activated. To be effective, such devices must be located and oriented so that they will spread signals and reflections throughout a space or raise the overall light level sharply. However, visual alarms alone are not necessarily the best means to alert sleepers. A study conducted by Underwriters Laboratory (UL) concluded that a flashing light more than seven times brighter was required (110 candela v. 15 candela, at the same distance) to awaken sleepers as was needed to alert awake subjects in a normal daytime illuminated room.

For hotel and other rooms where people are likely to be asleep, a signal-activated vibrator placed between mattress and box spring or under a pillow was found by UL to be much more effective in alerting sleepers. Many readily available devices are sound-activated so that they could respond to an alarm clock, clock

radio, wake-up telephone call or room smoke detector. Activation by a building alarm system can either be accomplished by a separate circuit activating an auditory alarm which would, in turn, trigger the vibrator or by a signal transmitted through the ordinary 110-volt outlet. Transmission of signals through the power line is relatively simple and is the basis of common, inexpensive remote light control systems sold in many department and electronic stores for home use. So-called "wireless" intercoms operate on the same principal.

A4.29 Detectable Warnings.

A4.29.2 Detectable Warnings on Walking Surfaces. The material used to provide contrast should contrast by at least 70%. Contrast in percent is determined by:

$$Contrast = [(B_1 - B_2)/B_1] \times 100$$

where B_1 = light reflectance value (LRV) of the lighter area
and B_2 = light reflectance value (LRV) of the darker area.

Note that in any application both white and black are never absolute; thus, B_1 never equals 100 and B_2 is always greater than 0.

A4.30 Signage.

A4.30.1 General. In building complexes where finding locations independently on a routine basis may be a necessity (for example, college campuses), tactile maps or prerecorded instructions can be very helpful to visually impaired people. Several maps and auditory instructions have been developed and tested for specific applications. The type of map or instructions used must be based on the information to be communicated, which depends highly on the type of buildings or users.

Landmarks that can easily be distinguished by visually impaired individuals are useful as orientation cues. Such cues include changes in illumination level, bright colors, unique patterns, wall murals, location of special equipment or other architectural features.

Many people with disabilities have limitations in movement of their heads and reduced peripheral vision. Thus, signage positioned

A4.30 Signage

perpendicular to the path of travel is easiest for them to notice. People can generally distinguish signage within an angle of 30 degrees to either side of the centerlines of their faces without moving their heads.

A4.30.2 Character Proportion. The legibility of printed characters is a function of the viewing height, character height, the ratio of the stroke width to the height of the character, the contrast of color between character and background, and print font. The size of characters must be based upon the intended viewing distance. A severely nearsighted person may have to be much closer to recognize a character of a given size than a person with normal visual acuity.

A4.30.4 Raised and Brailled Characters and Pictorial Symbol Signs (Pictograms). *The standard dimensions for literary Braille are as follows:*

Dot diameter	.059 in.
Inter-dot spacing	.090 in.
Horizontal separation between cells	.241 in.
Vertical separation between cells	.395 in.

Raised borders around *signs containing* raised characters may make them confusing to read unless the border is set far away from the characters. *Accessible signage with descriptive materials about public buildings, monuments, and objects of cultural interest may not provide sufficiently detailed and meaningful information. Interpretive guides, audio tape devices, or other methods may be more effective in presenting such information.*

A4.30.5 Finish and Contrast. *An eggshell finish (11 to 19 degree gloss on 60 degree glossimeter) is recommended. Research indicates that signs are more legible for persons with low vision when characters contrast with their background by at least 70 percent. Contrast in percent shall be determined by:*

$$Contrast = [(B_1 - B_2)/B_1] \times 100$$

where B_1 = *light reflectance value (LRV) of the lighter area and* B_2 = *light reflectance value (LRV) of the darker area.*

Note that in any application both white and black are never absolute; thus, B_1 *never equals 100 and* B_2 *is always greater than 0.*

The greatest readability is usually achieved through the use of light-colored characters or symbols on a dark background.

A4.30.7 Symbols of Accessibility for Different Types of Listening Systems. *Paragraph 4 of this section requires signage indicating the availability of an assistive listening system. An appropriate message should be displayed with the international symbol of access for hearing loss since this symbol conveys general accessibility for people with hearing loss. Some suggestions are:*

INFRARED
ASSISTIVE LISTENING SYSTEM
AVAILABLE
——PLEASE ASK——

AUDIO LOOP IN USE
TURN T-SWITCH FOR
BETTER HEARING
——OR ASK FOR HELP——

FM
ASSISTIVE LISTENING
SYSTEM AVAILABLE
——PLEASE ASK——

The symbol may be used to notify persons of the availability of other auxiliary aids and services such as: real time captioning, captioned note taking, sign language interpreters, and oral interpreters.

A4.30.8 Illumination Levels. *Illumination levels on the sign surface shall be in the 100 to 300 lux range (10 to 30 footcandles) and shall be uniform over the sign surface. Signs shall be located such that the illumination level on the surface of the sign is not significantly exceeded by the ambient light or visible bright lighting source behind or in front of the sign.*

A14

A4.31 Telephones.

A4.31.3 Mounting Height. In localities where the dial-tone first system is in operation, calls can be placed at a coin telephone through the operator without inserting coins. The operator button is located at a height of 46 in (1170 mm) if the coin slot of the telephone is at 54 in (1370 mm). A generally available public telephone with a coin slot mounted lower on the equipment would allow universal installation of telephones at a height of 48 in (1220 mm) or less to all operable parts.

A4.31.9 Text Telephones. *A public text telephone may be an integrated text telephone pay phone unit or a conventional portable text telephone that is permanently affixed within, or adjacent to, the telephone enclosure. In order to be usable with a pay phone, a text telephone which is not a single integrated text telephone pay phone unit will require a shelf large enough (10 in (255mm) wide by 10 in (255 mm) deep with a 6 in (150 mm) vertical clearance minimum) to accommodate the device, an electrical outlet, and a power cord. Movable or portable text telephones may be used to provide equivalent facilitation. A text telephone should be readily available so.that a person using it may access the text telephone easily and conveniently. As currently designed pocket-type text telephones for personal use do not accommodate a wide range of users. Such devices would not be considered substantially equivalent to conventional text telephones. However, in the future as technology develops this could change.*

A4.32 Fixed or Built-in Seating and Tables.

A4.32.4 Height of Tables or Counters. Different types of work require different *table or counter* heights for comfort and optimal performance. Light detailed work such as writing requires a *table or counter* close to elbow height for a standing person. Heavy manual work such as rolling dough requires *a counter or table* height about 10 in (255 mm) below elbow height for a standing person. This principle of *high/low table or counter heights* also applies for seated persons; however, the limiting condition for seated manual work is clearance under the *table or counter*.

Table A1 shows convenient *counter heights* for seated persons. The great variety of heights for comfort and optimal performance indicates a need for alternatives or a compromise in height if people who stand and people who sit will be using the same counter area.

Table A1
Convenient Heights of Tables and Counters for Seated People[1]

Conditions of Use	Short Women in mm		Tall Men in mm	
Seated in a wheelchair:				
Manual work–				
Desk or removeable armrests	26	660	30	760
Fixed, full-size armrests[2]	32[3]	815	32[3]	815
Light detailed work:				
Desk or removable armrests	29	735	34	865
Fixed, full-size armrests[2]	32[3]	815	34	865
Seated in a 16-in. (405-mm)				
High chair:				
Manual work	26	660	27	685
Light detailed work	28	710	31	785

[1] All dimensions are based on a work-surface thickness of 1 1/2 in (38 mm) and a clearance of 1 1/2 in (38 mm) between legs and the underside of a work surface.

[2] This type of wheelchair arm does not interfere with the positioning of a wheelchair under a work surface.

[3] This dimension is limited by the height of the armrests: a lower height would be preferable. Some people in this group prefer lower work surfaces, which require positioning the wheelchair back from the edge of the counter.

A4.33 Assembly Areas.

A4.33.2 Size of Wheelchair Locations. Spaces large enough for two wheelchairs allow people who are coming to a performance together to sit together.

A4.33.3 Placement of Wheelchair Locations. The location of wheelchair areas can be planned so that a variety of positions

A15

Table A2. Summary of Assistive Listening Devices

within the seating area are provided. This will allow choice in viewing and price categories.

Building/life safety codes set minimum distances between rows of fixed seats with consideration of the number of seats in a row, the exit aisle width and arrangement, and the location of exit doors. "Continental" seating, with a greater number of seats per row and a *commensurate increase in row spacing and exit doors, facilitates emergency egress for all people and increases ease of access to mid-row seats especially for people who walk with difficulty. Consideration of this positive attribute of "continental" seating should be included along with all other factors in the design of fixed seating areas.*

Table A2. Summary of Assistive Listening Devices

System	Advantages	Disadvantages	Typical Applications
Induction Loop Transmitter: Transducer wired to induction loop around listening area. Receiver: Self-contained induction receiver or personal hearing aid with telecoil.	Cost-Effective Low Maintenance Easy to use Unobtrusive May be possible to integrate into existing public address system. Some hearing aids can function as receivers.	Signal spills over to adjacent rooms. Susceptible to electrical interference. Limited portability Inconsistent signal strength. Head position affects signal strength. Lack of standards for induction coil performance.	Meeting areas Theaters Churches and Temples Conference rooms Classrooms TV viewing
FM Transmitter: Flashlight-sized worn by speaker. Receiver: With personal hearing aid via DAI or induction neck-loop and telecoil; or self-contained with earphone(s).	Highly portable Different channels allow use by different groups within the same room. High user mobility Variable for large range of hearing losses.	High cost of receivers Equipment fragile Equipment obtrusive High maintenance Expensive to maintain Custom fitting to individual user may be required.	Classrooms Tour groups Meeting areas Outdoor events One-on-one
Infrared Transmitter: Emitter in line-of-sight with receiver. Receiver: Self-contained. Or with personal hearing aid via DAI or induction neckloop and telecoil.	Easy to use Insures privacy or confidentiality Moderate cost Can often be integrated into existing public address system.	Line-of-sight required between emitter and receiver. Ineffective outdoors Limited portability Requires installation	Theaters Churches and Temples Auditoriums Meetings requiring confidentiality TV viewing

Source: Rehab Brief, National Institute on Disability and Rehabilitation Research, Washington, DC, Vol. XII, No. 10, (1990).

A16

A4.33.6 Placement of Listening Systems.
A distance of 50 ft (15 m) allows a person to distinguish performers' facial expressions.

A4.33.7 Types of Listening Systems.
An assistive listening system appropriate for an assembly area for a group of persons or where the specific individuals are not known in advance, such as a playhouse, lecture hall or movie theater, may be different from the system appropriate for a particular individual provided as an auxiliary aid or as part of a reasonable accommodation. The appropriate device for an individual is the type that individual can use, whereas the appropriate system for an assembly area will necessarily be geared toward the "average" or aggregate needs of various individuals. A listening system that can be used from any seat in a seating area is the most flexible way to meet this specification. Earphone jacks with variable volume controls can benefit only people who have slight hearing loss and do not help people who use hearing aids. At the present time, *magnetic induction* loops are the most feasible type of listening system for people who use hearing aids *equipped with* "T-coils," but people without hearing aids or those with hearing aids not equipped with inductive pick-ups cannot use them *without special receivers*. Radio frequency systems can be extremely effective and inexpensive. People without hearing aids can use them, but people with hearing aids need a special receiver to use them as they are presently designed. If hearing aids had a jack to allow a by-pass of microphones, then radio frequency systems would be suitable for people with and without hearing aids. Some listening systems may be subject to interference from other equipment and feedback from hearing aids of people who are using the systems. Such interference can be controlled by careful engineering design that anticipates feedback sources in the surrounding area.

Table A2, reprinted from a National Institute of Disability and Rehabilitation Research "Rehab Brief," shows some of the advantages and disadvantages of different types of assistive listening systems. In addition, the Architectural and Transportation Barriers Compliance Board (Access Board) has published a pamphlet on Assistive Listening Systems which lists demonstration centers across the country where technical assistance can be obtained in selecting and installing appropriate systems. The state of New York has also adopted a detailed technical specification which may be useful.

A5.0 Restaurants and Cafeterias.

A5.1 General.
Dining counters (where there is no service) are typically found in small carry-out restaurants, bakeries, or coffee shops and may only be a narrow eating surface attached to a wall. This section requires that where such a dining counter is provided, a portion of the counter shall be at the required accessible height.

A7.0 Business and Mercantile.

A7.2(3) Assistive Listening Devices.
At all sales and service counters, teller windows, box offices, and information kiosks where a physical barrier separates service personnel and customers, it is recommended that at least one permanently installed assistive listening device complying with 4.33 be provided at each location or series. Where assistive listening devices are installed, signage should be provided identifying those stations which are so equipped.

A7.3 Check-out Aisles.
Section 7.2 refers to counters without aisles; section 7.3 concerns check-out aisles. A counter without an aisle (7.2) can be approached from more than one direction such as in a convenience store. In order to use a check-out aisle (7.3), customers must enter a defined area (an aisle) at a particular point, pay for goods, and exit at a particular point.

[FR Doc. 91–17481 Filed 7–25–91; 8:45 am]

BILLING CODE 8150–01–C

A17

Department of Justice

Office of the Attorney General

28 CFR Part 36
Nondiscrimination on the Basis of
Disability by Public Accommodations and
in Commercial Facilities; Final Rule

DEPARTMENT OF JUSTICE

Office of the Attorney General

28 CFR Part 36

[Order No. 1513–91]

Nondiscrimination on the Basis of Disability by Public Accommodations and in Commercial Facilities

AGENCY: Department of Justice.

ACTION: Final rule.

SUMMARY: This rule implements title III of the Americans with Disabilities Act, Public Law 101–336, which prohibits discrimination on the basis of disability by private entities in places of public accommodation, requires that all new places of public accommodation and commercial facilities be designed and constructed so as to be readily accessible to and usable by persons with disabilities, and requires that examinations or courses related to licensing or certification for professional and trade purposes be accessible to persons with disabilities.

EFFECTIVE DATE: January 26, 1992.

FOR FURTHER INFORMATION CONTACT: Barbara S. Drake, Deputy Assistant Attorney General, Civil Rights Division; Stewart B. Oneglia, Chief, Coordination and Review Section, Civil Rights Division; and John Wodatch, Director, Office on the Americans with Disabilities Act, Civil Rights Division; all of the U.S Department of Justice, Washington, DC 20530. They may be contacted through the Division's ADA Information Line at (202) 514–0301 (Voice), (202) 514–0381 (TDD), or (202) 514–0383 (TDD). These telephone numbers are not toll-free numbers.

Copies of this rule are available in the following alternate formats: large print, Braille, electronic file on computer disk, and audio-tape. Copies may be obtained from the Office on the Americans with Disabilities Act at (202) 514–0301 (Voice) or (202) 514–0381 (TDD). The rule is also available on electronic bulletin board at (202) 514–6193. These telephone numbers are not toll-free numbers.

SUPPLEMENTARY INFORMATION:

Background

The landmark Americans with Disabilities Act ("ADA" or "the Act"), enacted on July 26, 1990, provides comprehensive civil rights protections to individuals with disabilities in the areas of employment, public accommodations, State and local government services, and telecommunications.

The legislation was originally developed by the National Council on Disability, an independent Federal agency that reviews and makes recommendations concerning Federal laws, programs, and policies affecting individuals with disabilities. In its 1986 study, "Toward Independence," the National Council on Disability recognized the inadequacy of the existing, limited patchwork of protections for individuals with disabilities, and recommended the enactment of a comprehensive civil rights law requiring equal opportunity for individuals with disabilities throughout American life. Although the 100th Congress did not act on the legislation, which was first introduced in 1988, then-Vice-President George Bush endorsed the concept of comprehensive disability rights legislation during his presidential campaign and became a dedicated advocate of the ADA.

The ADA was reintroduced in modified form in May 1989 for consideration by the 101st Congress. In June 1989, Attorney General Dick Thornburg, in testimony before the Senate Committee on Labor and Human Resources, reiterated the Bush Administration's support for the ADA and suggested changes in the proposed legislation. After extensive negotiations between Senate sponsors and the Administration, the Senate passed an amended version of the ADA on September 7, 1989, by a vote of 76–8.

In the House, jurisdiction over the ADA was divided among four committees, each of which conducted extensive hearings and issued detailed committee reports: the Committee on Education and Labor, the Committee on the Judiciary, the Committee on Public Works and Transportation, and the Committee on Energy and Commerce. On October 12, 1989, the Attorney General testified in favor of the legislation before the Committee on the Judiciary. The Civil Rights Division, on February 22, 1990, provided testimony to the Committee on Small Business, which although technically without jurisdiction over the bill, conducted hearings on the legislation's impact on small business.

After extensive committee consideration and floor debate, the House of Representatives passed an amended version of the Senate bill on May 22, 1990, by a vote of 403–20. After resolving their differences in conference, the Senate and House took final action on the bill—the House passing it by a vote of 377–28 on July 12, 1990, and the Senate, a day later, by a vote of 91–6. The ADA was enacted into law with the President's signature at a White House ceremony on July 26, 1990.

Rulemaking History

On February 22, 1991, the Department of Justice published a notice of proposed rulemaking (NPRM) implementing title III of the ADA in the **Federal Register** (56 FR 7452). On February 28, 1991, the Department published a notice of proposed rulemaking implementing subtitle A of title II of the ADA in the **Federal Register** (56 FR 8538). Each NPRM solicited comments on the definitions, standards, and procedures of the proposed rules. By the April 29, 1991, close of the comment period of the NPRM for title II, the Department had received 2,718 comments on the two proposed rules. Following the close of the comment period, the Department received an additional 222 comments.

In order to encourage public participation in the development of the Department's rules under the ADA, the Department held four public hearings. Hearings were held in Dallas, Texas on March 4–5, 1991; in Washington, DC on March 13–14–15, 1991; in San Francisco, California on March 18–19, 1991; and in Chicago, Illinois on March 27–28, 1991. At these hearings, 329 persons testified and 1,567 pages of testimony were compiled. Transcripts of the hearings were included in the Department's rulemaking docket.

The comments that the Department received occupy almost six feet of shelf space and contain over 10,000 pages. The Department received comments from individuals from all fifty States and the District of Columbia. Nearly 75% of the comments came from individuals and from organizations representing the interests of persons with disabilities. The Department received 292 comments from entities covered by the ADA and trade associations representing businesses in the private sector, and 67 from government units, such as mayors' offices, public school districts, and various State agencies working vith individuals with disabilities.

The Department received one comment from a consortium of 511 organizations representing a broad spectrum of persons with disabilities. In addition, at least another 25 commenters endorsed the position expressed by this consortium or submitted identical comments on one or both proposed regulations.

An organization representing persons with hearing impairments submitted a large number of comments. This organization presented the Department with 479 individual comments, each providing in chart form a detailed representation of what type of auxiliary aid or service would be useful in the various categories of places of public accommodation.

The Department received a number of comments based on almost ten different form letters. For example, individuals who have a heightened sensitivity to a variety of chemical substances submitted 266 postcards detailing how exposure to various environmental conditions restricts their access to places of public accommodation and to commercial facilities. Another large group of form letters came from groups affiliated with independent living centers.

The vast majority of the comments addressed the Department's proposal implementing title III. Just over 100 comments addressed only issues presented in the proposed title II regulation.

The Department read and analyzed each comment that was submitted in a timely fashion. Transcripts of the four hearings were analyzed along with the written comments. The decisions that the Department has made in response to these comments, however, were not made on the basis of the number of commenters addressing any one point but on a thorough consideration of the merits of the points of view expressed in the comments. Copies of the written comments, including transcripts of the four hearings, will remain available for public inspection in room 854 of the HOLC Building, 320 First Street, NW., Washington, DC from 10 a.m. to 5 p.m., Monday through Friday, except for legal holidays, until August 30, 1991.

The Americans with Disabilities Act gives to individuals with disabilities civil rights protections with respect to discrimination that are parallel to those provided to individuals on the basis of race, color, national origin, sex, and religion. It combines in its own unique formula elements drawn principally from two key civil rights statutes—the Civil Rights Act of 1964 and title V of the Rehabilitation Act of 1973. The ADA generally employs the framework of titles II (42 U.S.C. 2000a to 2000a–6) and VII (42 U.S.C. 2000e to 2000e–16) of the Civil Rights Act of 1964 for coverage and enforcement and the terms and concepts of section 504 of the Rehabilitation Act of 1973 (29 U.S.C. 794) for what constitutes discrimination.

Other recently enacted legislation will facilitate compliance with the ADA. As amended in 1990, the Internal Revenue Code allows a deduction of up to $15,000 per year for expenses associated with the removal of qualified architectural and transportation barriers. The 1990 amendment also permits eligible small businesses to receive a tax credit for certain costs of compliance with the

ADA. An eligible small business is one whose gross receipts do not exceed $1,000,000 or whose workforce does not consist of more than 30 full-time workers. Qualifying businesses may claim a credit of up to 50 percent of eligible access expenditures that exceed $250 but do not exceed $10,250. Examples of eligible access expenditures include the necessary and reasonable costs of removing barriers, providing auxiliary aids, and acquiring or modifying equipment or devices.

In addition, the Communications Act of 1934 has been amended by the Television Decoder Circuitry Act of 1990, Public Law 101–431, to require as of July 1, 1993, that all televisions with screens of 13 inches or wider have built-in decoder circuitry for displaying closed captions. This new law will eventually lessen dependence on the use of portable decoders in achieving compliance with the auxiliary aids and services requirements of the rule.

Overview of the Rule

The final rule establishes standards and procedures for the implementation of title III of the Act, which addresses discrimination by private entities in places of public accommodation, commercial facilities, and certain examinations and courses. The careful consideration Congress gave title III is reflected in the detailed statutory provisions and the expansive reports of the Senate Committee on Labor and Human Resources and the House Committees on the Judiciary, and Education and Labor. The final rule follows closely the language of the Act and supplements it, where appropriate, with interpretive material found in the committee reports.

The rule is organized into six subparts. Subpart A, "General," includes the purpose and application sections, describes the relationship of the Act to other laws, and defines key terms used in the regulation.

Subpart B, "General Requirements," contains material derived from what the statute calls the "General Rule," and the "General Prohibition," in sections 302(a) and 302(b)(1), respectively, of the Act. Topics addressed by this subpart include discriminatory denials of access or participation, the provision of unequal benefits, indirect discrimination through contracting, the participation of individuals with disabilities in the most integrated setting appropriate to their needs, and discrimination based on association with individuals with disabilities. Subpart B also contains a number of "miscellaneous" provisions derived from title V of the Act that

involve issues such as retaliation and coercion for asserting ADA rights, illegal drug use, insurance, and restrictions on smoking in places of public accommodation. Finally, subpart B contains additional general provisions regarding direct threats to health or safety, maintenance of accessible features of facilities and equipment, and the coverage of places of public accommodation located in private residences.

Subpart C, "Specific Requirements," addresses the "Specific Prohibitions" in section 302(b)(2) of the Act. Included in this subpart are topics such as discriminatory eligibility criteria; reasonable modifications in policies, practices or procedures; auxiliary aids and services; the readily achievable removal of barriers and alternatives to barrier removal; the extent to which inventories of accessible or special goods are required; seating in assembly areas; personal devices and services; and transportation provided by public accommodations. Subpart C also incorporates the requirements of section 309 of title III relating to examinations and courses.

Subpart D, "New Construction and Alterations," sets forth the requirements for new construction and alterations based on section 303 of the Act. It addresses such issues as what facilities are covered by the new construction requirements, what an alteration is, the application of the elevator exception, the path of travel obligations resulting from an alteration to a primary function area, requirements for commercial facilities located in private residences, and the application of alterations requirements to historic buildings and facilities.

Subpart E, "Enforcement," describes the Act's title III enforcement procedures, including private actions, as well as investigations and litigation conducted by the Attorney General. These provisions are based on sections 308 and 310(b) of the Act.

Subpart F, "Certification of State Laws or Local Building Codes," establishes procedures for the certification of State or local building accessibility ordinances that meet or exceed the new construction and alterations requirements of the ADA. These provisions are based on section 308(b)(1)(A)(ii) of the Act.

The section-by-section analysis of the rule explains in detail the provisions of each of these subparts.

The Department is also today publishing a final rule for the implementation and enforcement of subtitle A of title II of the Act. This rule prohibits discrimination on the basis of disability against qualified individuals with disabilities in all services, programs, or activities of State and local government.

Regulatory Process Matters

This final rule has been reviewed by the Office of Management and Budget (OMB) under Executive Order 12291. The Department is preparing a regulatory impact analysis (RIA) of this rule, and the Architectural and Transportation Barriers Compliance Board is preparing an RIA for its Americans with Disabilities Act Accessibility Guidelines for Buildings and Facilities (ADAAG) that are incorporated in Appendix A of the Department's final rule. Draft copies of both preliminary RIAs are available for comment; the Department will provide copies of these documents to the public upon request. Commenters are urged to provide additional information as to the costs and benefits associated with this rule. This will facilitate the development of a final RIA by January 1, 1992.

The Department's RIA will evaluate the economic impact of the final rule. Included among those title III provisions that are likely to result in significant economic impact are the requirements for auxiliary aids, barrier removal in existing facilities, and readily accessible new construction and alterations. An analysis of the costs of these provisions will be included in the RIA.

The preliminary RIA prepared for the notice of proposed rulemaking contained all of the available information that would have been included in a preliminary regulatory flexibility analysis, had one been prepared under the Regulatory Flexibility Act, concerning the rule's impact on small entities. The final RIA will contain all of the information that is required in a final regulatory flexibility analysis, and will serve as such an analysis. Moreover, the extensive notice and comment procedure followed by the Department in the promulgation of this rule, which included public hearings, dissemination of materials, and provision of speakers to affected groups, clearly provided any interested small entities with the notice and opportunity for comment provided for under the Regulatory Flexibility Act procedures.

This final rule will preempt State laws affecting entities subject to the ADA only to the extent that those laws directly conflict with the statutory requirements of the ADA. Therefore, this rule is not subject to Executive Order 12612, and a Federalism Assessment is not required.

The reporting and recordkeeping requirements described in subpart F of the rule are considered to be information collection requirements as that term is defined by the Office of Management and Budget in 5 CFR part 1320. Accordingly, those information collection requirements have been submitted to OMB for review pursuant to the Paperwork Reduction Act.

Section-By-Section Analysis and Response to Comments

Subpart A—General

Section 36.101 Purpose

Section 36.101 states the purpose of the rule. which is to effectuate title III of the Americans with Disabilities Act of 1990. This title prohibits discrimination on the basis of disability by public accommodations, requires places of public accommodation and commercial facilities to be designed, constructed, and altered in compliance with the accessibility standards established by this part, and requires that examinations or courses related to licensing or certification for professional or trade purposes be accessible to persons with disabilities.

Section 36.102 Application

Section 36.102 specifies the range of entities and facilities that have obligations under the final rule. The rule applies to any public accommodation or commercial facility as those terms are defined in § 36.104. It also applies, in accordance with section 309 of the ADA, to private entities that offer examinations or courses related to applications, licensing, certification, or credentialing for secondary or postsecondary education, professional, or trade purposes. Except as provided in § 36.206, "Retaliation or coercion," this part does not apply to individuals other than public accommodations or to public entities. Coverage of private individuals and public entities is discussed in the preamble to § 36.206.

As defined in § 36.104, a public accommodation is a private entity that owns, leases or leases to, or operates a place of public accommodation. Section 36.102(b)(2) emphasizes that the general and specific public accommodations requirements of subparts B and C obligate a public accommodation only with respect to the operations of a place of public accommodation. This distinction is drawn in recognition of the fact that a private entity that meets the regulatory definition of public accommodation could also own, lease or lease to, or operate facilities that are not places of public accommodation. The rule would exceed the reach of the ADA

if it were to apply the public accommodations requirements of subparts B and C to the operations of a private entity that do not involve a place of public accommodation. Similarly, § 36.102(b)(3) provides that the new construction and alterations requirements of subpart D obligate a public accommodation only with respect to facilities used as, or designed or constructed for use as, places of public accommodation or commercial facilities.

On the other hand, as mandated by the ADA and reflected in § 36.102(c), the new construction and alterations requirements of subpart D apply to a commercial facility whether or not the facility is a place of public accommodation, or is owned, leased, leased to, or operated by a public accommodation.

Section 36.102(e) states that the rule does not apply to any private club, religious entity, or public entity. Each of these terms is defined in § 36.104. The exclusion of private clubs and religious entities is derived from section 307 of the ADA; and the exclusion of public entities is based on the statutory definition of public accommodation in section 301(7) of the ADA, which excludes entities other than private entities from coverage under title III of the ADA.

Section 36.103 Relationship to Other Laws

Section 36.103 is derived from sections 501 (a) and (b) of the ADA. Paragraph (a) provides that, except as otherwise specifically provided by this part, the ADA is not intended to apply lesser standards than are required under title V of the Rehabilitation Act of 1973, as amended (29 U.S.C. 790–794), or the regulations implementing that title. The standards of title V of the Rehabilitation Act apply for purposes of the ADA to the extent that the ADA has not explicitly adopted a different standard from title V. Where the ADA explicitly provides a different standard from section 504, the ADA standard applies to the ADA, but not to section 504. For example, section 504 requires that all federally assisted programs and activities be readily accessible to and usable by individuals with handicaps, even if major structural alterations are necessary to make a program accessible. Title III of the ADA, in contrast, only requires alterations to existing facilities if the modifications are "readily achievable," that is, able to be accomplished easily and without much difficulty or expense. A public accommodation that is covered under both section 504 and the ADA is still required to meet the "program accessibility" standard in order to comply with section 504, but would not be in violation of the ADA unless it failed to make "readily achievable" modifications. On the other hand, an entity covered by the ADA is required to make "readily achievable" modifications, even if the program can be made accessible without any architectural modifications. Thus, an entity covered by both section 504 and title III of the ADA must meet both the "program accessibility" requirement and the "readily achievable" requirement.

Paragraph (b) makes explicit that the rule does not affect the obligation of recipients of Federal financial assistance to comply with the requirements imposed under section 504 of the Rehabilitation Act of 1973.

Paragraph (c) makes clear that Congress did not intend to displace any of the rights or remedies provided by other Federal laws or other State or local laws (including State common law) that provide greater or equal protection to individuals with disabilities. A plaintiff may choose to pursue claims under a State law that does not confer greater substantive rights, or even confers fewer substantive rights, if the alleged violation is protected under the alternative law and the remedies are greater. For example, assume that a person with a physical disability seeks damages under a State law that allows compensatory and punitive damages for discrimination on the basis of physical disability, but does not allow them on the basis of mental disability. In that situation, the State law would provide narrower coverage, by excluding mental disabilities, but broader remedies, and an individual covered by both laws could choose to bring an action under both laws. Moreover, State tort claims confer greater remedies and are not preempted by the ADA. A plaintiff may join a State tort claim to a case brought under the ADA. In such a case, the plaintiff must, of course, prove all the elements of the State tort claim in order to prevail under that cause of action.

A commenter had concerns about privacy requirements for banking transactions using telephone relay services. Title IV of the Act provides adequate protections for ensuring the confidentiality of communications using the relay services. This issue is more appropriately addressed by the Federal Communications Commission in its regulation implementing title IV of the Act.

Section 36.104 Definitions

"Act." The word "Act" is used in the regulation to refer to the Americans with Disabilities Act of 1990, Pub. L. 101–336, which is also referred to as the "ADA."

"Commerce." The definition of "commerce" is identical to the statutory definition provided in section 301(l) of the ADA. It means travel, trade, traffic, commerce, transportation, or communication among the several States, between any foreign country or any territory or possession and any State, or between points in the same State but through another State or foreign country. Commerce is defined in the same manner as in title II of the Civil Rights Act of 1964, which prohibits racial discrimination in public accommodations.

The term "commerce" is used in the definition of "place of public accommodation." According to that definition, one of the criteria that an entity must meet before it can be considered a place of public accommodation is that its operations affect commerce. The term "commerce" is similarly used in the definition of "commercial facility."

The use of the phrase "operations affect commerce" applies the full scope of coverage of the Commerce Clause of the Constitution in enforcing the ADA. The Constitution gives Congress broad authority to regulate interstate commerce, including the activities of local business enterprises (e.g., a physician's office, a neighborhood restaurant, a laundromat, or a bakery) that affect interstate commerce through the purchase or sale of products manufactured in other States, or by providing services to individuals from other States. Because of the integrated nature of the national economy, the ADA and this final rule will have extremely broad application.

"Commercial facilities" are those facilities that are intended for nonresidential use by a private entity and whose operations affect commerce. As explained under § 36.401, "New construction," the new construction and alteration requirements of subpart D of the rule apply to all commercial facilities, whether or not they are places of public accommodation. Those commercial facilities that are not places of public accommodation are not subject to the requirements of subparts B and C (e.g., those requirements concerning auxiliary aids and general nondiscrimination provisions).

Congress recognized that the employees within commercial facilities would generally be protected under title I (employment) of the Act. However, as the House Committee on Education and Labor pointed out, "[t]o the extent that new facilities are built in a manner that make[s] them accessible to all

individuals, including potential employees, there will be less of a need for individual employers to engage in reasonable accommodations for particular employees." H.R. Rep. No. 485, 101st Cong., 2d Sess., pt. 2, at 117 (1990) [hereinafter "Education and Labor report"]. While employers of fewer than 15 employees are not covered by title I's employment discrimination provisions, there is no such limitation with respect to new construction covered under title III. Congress chose not to so limit the new construction provisions because of its desire for a uniform requirement of accessibility in new construction, because accessibility can be accomplished easily in the design and construction stage, and because future expansion of a business or sale or lease of the property to a larger employer or to a business that is a place of public accommodation is always a possibility.

The term "commercial facilities" is not intended to be defined by dictionary or common industry definitions. Included in this category are factories, warehouses, office buildings, and other buildings in which employment may occur. The phrase, "whose operations affect commerce," is to be read broadly, to include all types of activities reached under the commerce clause of the Constitution.

Privately operated airports are also included in the category of commercial facilities. They are not, however, places of public accommodation because they are not terminals used for "specified public transportation." (Transportation by aircraft is specifically excluded from the statutory definition of "specified public transportation.") Thus, privately operated airports are subject to the new construction and alteration requirements of this rule (subpart D) but not to subparts B and C. (Airports operated by public entities are covered by title II of the Act.) Places of public accommodation located within airports, such as restaurants, shops, lounges, or conference centers, however, are covered by subparts B and C of this part.

The statute's definition of "commercial facilities" specifically includes only facilities "that are intended for nonresidential use" and specifically exempts those facilities that are covered or expressly exempted from coverage under the Fair Housing Act of 1968, as amended (42 U.S.C. 3601–3631). The interplay between the Fair Housing Act and the ADA with respect to those facilities that are "places of public accommodation" was the subject of many comments and is addressed in the preamble discussion of the definition of "place of public accommodation."

"Current illegal use of drugs." The phrase "current illegal use of drugs" is used in § 36.209. Its meaning is discussed in the preamble for that section.

"Disability." The definition of the term "disability" is comparable to the definition of the term "individual with handicaps" in section 7(8)(B) of the Rehabilitation Act and section 802(h) of the Fair Housing Act. The Education and Labor Committee report makes clear that the analysis of the term "individual with handicaps" by the Department of Health, Education, and Welfare in its regulations implementing section 504 (42 FR 22685 (May 4, 1977)) and the analysis by the Department of Housing and Urban Development in its regulation implementing the Fair Housing Amendments Act of 1988 (54 FR 3232 (Jan. 23, 1989)) should also apply fully to the term "disability" (Education and Labor report at 50).

The use of the term "disability" instead of "handicap" and the term "individual with a disability" instead of "individual with handicaps" represents an effort by the Congress to make use of up-to-date, currently accepted terminology. The terminology applied to individuals with disabilities is a very significant and sensitive issue. As with racial and ethnic terms, the choice of words to describe a person with a disability is overlaid with stereotypes, patronizing attitudes, and other emotional connotations. Many individuals with disabilities, and organizations representing such individuals, object to the use of such terms as "handicapped person" or "the handicapped." In other recent legislation, Congress also recognized this shift in terminology, e.g., by changing the name of the National Council on the Handicapped to the National Council on Disability (Pub. L. 100–630).

In enacting the Americans with Disabilities Act, Congress concluded that it was important for the current legislation to use terminology most in line with the sensibilities of most Americans with disabilities. No change in definition or substance is intended nor should be attributed to this change in phraseology.

The term "disability" means, with respect to an individual—

(A) A physical or mental impairment that substantially limits one or more of the major life activities of such individual;

(B) A record of such an impairment; or

(C) Being regarded as having such an impairment.

If an individual meets any one of these three tests, he or she is considered to be an individual with a disability for purposes of coverage under the Americans with Disabilities Act.

Congress adopted this same basic definition of "disability," first used in the Rehabilitation Act of 1973 and in the Fair Housing Amendments Act of 1988, for a number of reasons. It has worked well since it was adopted in 1974. There is a substantial body of administrative interpretation and judicial precedent on this definition. Finally, it would not be possible to guarantee comprehensiveness by providing a list of specific disabilities, especially because new disorders may be recognized in the future, as they have since the definition was first established in 1974.

Test A—A Physical or Mental Impairment That Substantially Limits One or More of the Major Life Activities of Such Individual

Physical or mental impairment. Under the first test, an individual must have a physical or mental impairment. As explained in paragraph (1) (i) of the definition, "impairment" means any physiological disorder or condition, cosmetic disfigurement, or anatomical loss affecting one or more of the following body systems: Neurological; musculoskeletal; special sense organs (including speech organs that are not respiratory, such as vocal cords, soft palate, and tongue); respiratory, including speech organs; cardiovascular; reproductive; digestive; genitourinary; hemic and lymphatic; skin; and endocrine. It also means any mental or psychological disorder, such as mental retardation, organic brain syndrome, emotional or mental illness, and specific learning disabilities. This list closely tracks the one used in the regulations for section 504 of the Rehabilitation Act of 1973 (see, e.g., 45 CFR 84.3(j)(2)(i)).

Many commenters asked that "traumatic brain injury" be added to the list in paragraph (1)(i). Traumatic brain injury is already included because it is a physiological condition affecting one of the listed body systems, i.e., "neurological." Therefore, it was unnecessary for the Department to add the term to the regulation.

It is not possible to include a list of all the specific conditions, contagious and noncontagious diseases, or infections that would constitute physical or mental impairments because of the difficulty of ensuring the comprehensiveness of such a list, particularly in light of the fact that other conditions or disorders may be identified in the future. However, the list of examples in paragraph (1)(iii) of the

definition includes: Orthopedic, visual, speech and hearing impairments; cerebral palsy; epilepsy, muscular dystrophy, multiple sclerosis, cancer, heart disease, diabetes, mental retardation, emotional illness, specific learning disabilities, HIV disease (symptomatic or asymptomatic), tuberculosis, drug addiction, and alcoholism.

The examples of "physical or mental impairments" in paragraph (1)(iii) are the same as those contained in many section 504 regulations, except for the addition of the phrase "contagious and noncontagious" to describe the types of diseases and conditions included, and the addition of "HIV disease (symptomatic or asymptomatic)" and "tuberculosis" to the list of examples. These additions are based on the ADA committee reports, caselaw, and official legal opinions interpreting section 504. In *School Board of Nassau County* v. *Arline*, 480 U.S. 273 (1987), a case involving an individual with tuberculosis, the Supreme Court held that people with contagious diseases are entitled to the protections afforded by section 504. Following the *Arline* decision, this Department's Office of Legal Counsel issued a legal opinion that concluded that symptomatic HIV disease is an impairment that substantially limits a major life activity; therefore it has been included in the definition of disability under this part. The opinion also concluded that asymptomatic HIV disease is an impairment that substantially limits a major life activity, either because of its actual effect on the individual with HIV disease or because the reactions of other people to individuals with HIV disease cause such individuals to be treated as though they are disabled. See Memorandum from Douglas W. Kmiec, Acting Assistant Attorney General, Office of Legal Counsel, Department of Justice, to Arthur B. Culvahouse, Jr., Counsel to the President (Sept. 27, 1988), *reprinted in* Hearings on S. 933, the Americans with Disabilities Act, Before the Subcomm. on the Handicapped of the Senate Comm. on Labor and Human Resources, 101st Cong., 1st Sess. 346 (1989). The phrase "symptomatic or asymptomatic" was inserted in the final rule after "HIV disease" in response to commenters who suggested that the clarification was necessary to give full meaning to the Department's opinion.

Paragraph (1)(iv) of the definition states that the phrase "physical or mental impairment" does not include homosexuality or bisexuality. These conditions were never considered impairments under other Federal disability laws. Section 511(a) of the statute makes clear that they are likewise not to be considered impairments under the Americans with Disabilities Act.

Physical or mental impairment does not include simple physical characteristics, such as blue eyes or black hair. Nor does it include environmental, cultural, economic, or other disadvantages, such as having a prison record, or being poor. Nor is age a disability. Similarly, the definition does not include common personality traits such as poor judgment or a quick temper where these are not symptoms of a mental or psychological disorder. However, a person who has these characteristics and also has a physical or mental impairment may be considered as having a disability for purposes of the Americans with Disabilities Act based on the impairment.

Substantial limitation of a major life activity. Under Test A, the impairment must be one that "substantially limits a major life activity." Major life activities include such things as caring for one's self, performing manual tasks, walking, seeing, hearing, speaking, breathing, learning, and working. For example, a person who is paraplegic is substantially limited in the major life activity of walking, a person who is blind is substantially limited in the major life activity of seeing, and a person who is mentally retarded is substantially limited in the major life activity of learning. A person with traumatic brain injury is substantially limited in the major life activities of caring for one's self, learning, and working because of memory deficit, confusion, contextual difficulties, and inability to reason appropriately.

A person is considered an individual with a disability for purposes of Test A, the first prong of the definition, when the individual's important life activities are restricted as to the conditions, manner, or duration under which they can be performed in comparison to most people. A person with a minor, trivial impairment, such as a simple infected finger, is not impaired in a major life activity. A person who can walk for 10 miles continuously is not substantially limited in walking merely because, on the eleventh mile, he or she begins to experience pain, because most people would not be able to walk eleven miles without experiencing some discomfort.

The Department received many comments on the proposed rule's inclusion of the word "temporary" in the definition of "disability." The preamble indicated that impairments are not necessarily excluded from the definition

of "disability" simply because they are temporary, but that the duration, or expected duration, of an impairment is one factor that may properly be considered in determining whether the impairment substantially limits a major life activity. The preamble recognized, however, that temporary impairments, such as a broken leg, are not commonly regarded as disabilities, and only in rare circumstances would the degree of the limitation and its expected duration be substantial: Nevertheless, many commenters objected to inclusion of the word "temporary" both because it is not in the statute and because it is not contained in the definition of "disability" set forth in the title I regulations of the Equal Employment Opportunity Commission (EEOC). The word "temporary" has been deleted from the final rule to conform with the statutory language. The question of whether a temporary impairment is a disability must be resolved on a case-by-case basis, taking into consideration both the duration (or expected duration) of the impairment and the extent to which it actually limits a major life activity of the affected individual.

The question of whether a person has a disability should be assessed without regard to the availability of mitigating measures, such as reasonable modifications or auxiliary aids and services. For example, a person with hearing loss is substantially limited in the major life activity of hearing, even though the loss may be improved through the use of a hearing aid. Likewise, persons with impairments, such as epilepsy or diabetes, that substantially limit a major life activity, are covered under the first prong of the definition of disability, even if the effects of the impairment are controlled by medication.

Many commenters asked that environmental illness (also known as multiple chemical sensitivity) as well as allergy to cigarette smoke be recognized as disabilities. The Department, however, declines to state categorically that these types of allergies or sensitivities are disabilities, because the determination as to whether an impairment is a disability depends on whether, given the particular circumstances at issue, the impairment substantially limits one or more major life activities (or has a history of, or is regarded as having such an effect).

Sometimes respiratory or neurological functioning is so severely affected that an individual will satisfy the requirements to be considered disabled under the regulation. Such an individual would be entitled to all of the protections afforded by the Act and this

part. In other cases, individuals may be sensitive to environmental elements or to smoke but their sensitivity will not rise to the level needed to constitute a disability. For example, their major life activity of breathing may be somewhat, but not substantially, impaired. In such circumstances, the individuals are not disabled and are not entitled to the protections of the statute despite their sensitivity to environmental agents.

In sum, the determination as to whether allergies to cigarette smoke, or allergies or sensitivities characterized by the commenters as environmental illness are disabilities covered by the regulation must be made using the same case-by-case analysis that is applied to all other physical or mental impairments. Moreover, the addition of specific regulatory provisions relating to environmental illness in the final rule would be inappropriate at this time pending future consideration of the issue by the Architectural and Transportation Barriers Compliance Board, the Environmental Protection Agency, and the Occupational Safety and Health Administration of the Department of Labor.

Test B—A Record of Such an Impairment

This test is intended to cover those who have a record of an impairment. As explained in paragraph (3) of the rule's definition of disability, this includes a person who has a history of an impairment that substantially limited a major life activity, such as someone who has recovered from an impairment. It also includes persons who have been misclassified as having an impairment.

This provision is included in the definition in part to protect individuals who have recovered from a physical or mental impairment that previously substantially limited them in a major life activity. Discrimination on the basis of such a past impairment is prohibited. Frequently occurring examples of the first group (those who have a history of an impairment) are persons with histories of mental or emotional illness, heart disease, or cancer; examples of the second group (those who have been misclassified as having an impairment) are persons who have been misclassified as having mental retardation or mental illness.

Test C—Being Regarded as Having Such an Impairment

This test, as contained in paragraph (4) of the definition, is intended to cover persons who are treated by a private entity or public accommodation as having a physical or mental impairment that substantially limits a major life activity. It applies when a person is treated as if he or she has an impairment that substantially limits a major life activity, regardless of whether that person has an impairment.

The Americans with Disabilities Act uses the same "regarded as" test set forth in the regulations implementing section 504 of the Rehabilitation Act. *See, e.g.,* 28 CFR 42.540(k)(2)(iv), which provides:

(iv) "Is regarded as having an impairment" means (A) Has a physical or mental impairment that does not substantially limit major life activities but that is treated by a recipient as constituting such a limitation; (B) Has a physical or mental impairment that substantially limits major life activities only as a result of the attitudes of others toward such impairment; or (C) Has none of the impairments defined in paragraph (k)(2)(i) of this section but is treated by a recipient as having such an impairment.

The perception of the private entity or public accommodation is a key element of this test. A person who perceives himself or herself to have an impairment, but does not have an impairment, and is not treated as if he or she has an impairment, is not protected under this test. A person would be covered under this test if a restaurant refused to serve that person because of a fear of "negative reactions" of others to that person. A person would also be covered if a public accommodation refused to serve a patron because it perceived that the patron had an impairment that limited his or her enjoyment of the goods or services being offered.

For example, persons with severe burns often encounter discrimination in community activities, resulting in substantial limitation of major life activities. These persons would be covered under this test based on the attitudes of others towards the impairment, even if they did not view themselves as "impaired."

The rationale for this third test, as used in the Rehabilitation Act of 1973, was articulated by the Supreme Court in *Arline,* 480 U.S. 273 (1987). The Court noted that, although an individual may have an impairment that does not in fact substantially limit a major life activity, the reaction of others may prove just as disabling. "Such an impairment might not diminish a person's physical or mental capabilities, but could nevertheless substantially limit that person's ability to work as a result of the negative reactions of others to the impairment." *Id.* at 283. The Court concluded that, by including this test in the Rehabilitation Act's definition, "Congress acknowledged that society's

accumulated myths and fears about disability and disease are as handicapping as are the physical limitations that flow from actual impairment." *Id.* at 284.

Thus, a person who is not allowed into a public accommodation because of the myths, fears, and stereotypes associated with disabilities would be covered under this third test whether or not the person's physical or mental condition would be considered a disability under the first or second test in the definition.

If a person is refused admittance on the basis of an actual or perceived physical or mental condition, and the public accommodation can articulate no legitimate reason for the refusal (such as failure to meet eligibility criteria), a perceived concern about admitting persons with disabilities could be inferred and the individual would qualify for coverage under the "regarded as" test. A person who is covered because of being regarded as having an impairment is not required to show that the public accommodation's perception is inaccurate (e.g., that he will be accepted by others, or that insurance rates will not increase) in order to be admitted to the public accommodation.

Paragraph (5) of the definition lists certain conditions that are not included within the definition of "disability." The excluded conditions are: transvestism, transsexualism, pedophilia, exhibitionism, voyeurism, gender identity disorders not resulting from physical impairments, other sexual behavior disorders, compulsive gambling, kleptomania, pyromania, and psychoactive substance use disorders resulting from current illegal use of drugs. Unlike homosexuality and bisexuality, which are not considered impairments under either the Americans with Disabilities Act (see the definition of "disability," paragraph (1)(iv)) or section 504, the conditions listed in paragraph (5), except for transvestism, are not necessarily excluded as impairments under section 504. (Transvestism was excluded from the definition of disability for section 504 by the Fair Housing Amendments Act of 1988, Pub. L. 100–430, § 6(b).) The phrase "current illegal use of drugs" used in this definition is explained in the preamble to § 36.209.

"Drug." The definition of the term "drug" is taken from section 510(d)(2) of the ADA.

"Facility." "Facility" means all or any portion of buildings, structures, sites, complexes, equipment, rolling stock or other conveyances, roads, walks, passageways, parking lots, or other real or personal property, including the site

where the building, property, structure, or equipment is located. Committee reports made clear that the definition of facility was drawn from the definition of facility in current Federal regulations (*see, e.g.,* Education and Labor report at 114). It includes both indoor and outdoor areas where human-constructed improvements, structures, equipment, or property have been added to the natural environment.

The term "rolling stock or other conveyances" was not included in the definition of facility in the proposed rule. However, commenters raised questions about the applicability of this part to places of public accommodation operated in mobile facilities (such as cruise ships, floating restaurants, or mobile health units). Those places of public accommodation are covered under this part, and would be included in the definition of "facility." Thus the requirements of subparts B and C would apply to those places of public accommodation. For example, a covered entity could not discriminate on the basis of disability in the full and equal enjoyment of the facilities (§ 36.201). Similarly, a cruise line could not apply eligibility criteria to potential passengers in a manner that would screen out individuals with disabilities, unless the criteria are "necessary," as provided in § 36.301.

However, standards for new construction and alterations of such facilities are not yet included in the Americans with Disabilities Act Accessibility Guidelines for Buildings and Facilities (ADAAG) adopted by § 36.406 and incorporated in Appendix A. The Department therefore will not interpret the new construction and alterations provisions of subpart D to apply to the types of facilities discussed here, pending further development of specific requirements.

Requirements pertaining to accessible transportation services provided by public accommodations are included in § 36.310 of this part; standards pertaining to accessible vehicles will be issued by the Secretary of Transportation pursuant to section 306 of the Act, and will be codified at 49 CFR part 37.

A public accommodation has obligations under this rule with respect to a cruise ship to the extent that its operations are subject to the laws of the United States.

The definition of "facility" only includes the site over which the private entity may exercise control or on which a place of public accommodation or a commercial facility is located. It does not include, for example, adjacent roads or walks controlled by a public entity that is not subject to this part. Public entities are subject to the requirements of title II of the Act. The Department's regulation implementing title II, which will be codified at 28 CFR part 35, addresses the obligations of public entities to ensure accessibility by providing curb ramps at pedestrian walkways.

"Illegal use of drugs." The definition of "illegal use of drugs" is taken from section 510(d)(1) of the Act and clarifies that the term includes the illegal use of one or more drugs.

"Individual with a disability" means a person who has a disability but does not include an individual who is currently illegally using drugs, when the public accommodation acts on the basis of such use. The phrase "current illegal use of drugs" is explained in the preamble to § 36.209.

"Place of public accommodation." The term "place of public accommodation" is an adaptation of the statutory definition of "public accommodation" in section 301(7) of the ADA and appears as an element of the regulatory definition of public accommodation. The final rule defines "place of public accommodation" as a facility, operated by a private entity, whose operations affect commerce and fall within at least one of 12 specified categories. The term "public accommodation," on the other hand, is reserved by the final rule for the private entity that owns, leases (or leases to), or operates a place of public accommodation. It is the public accommodation, and not the place of public accommodation, that is subject to the regulation's nondiscrimination requirements. Placing the obligation not to discriminate on the public accommodation, as defined in the rule, is consistent with section 302(a) of the ADA, which places the obligation not to discriminate on any person who owns, leases (or leases to), or operates a place of public accommodation.

Facilities operated by government agencies or other public entities as defined in this section do not qualify as places of public accommodation. The actions of public entities are governed by title II of the ADA and will be subject to regulations issued by the Department of Justice under that title. The receipt of government assistance by a private entity does not by itself preclude a facility from being considered as a place of public accommodation.

The definition of place of public accommodation incorporates the 12 categories of facilities represented in the statutory definition of public accommodation in section 301(7) of the ADA:

1. Places of lodging.
2. Establishments serving food or drink.
3. Places of exhibition or entertainment.
4. Places of public gathering.
5. Sales or rental establishments.
6. Service establishments.
7. Stations used for specified public transportation.
8. Places of public display or collection.
9. Places of recreation.
10. Places of education.
11. Social service center establishments.
12. Places of exercise or recreation.

In order to be a place of public accommodation, a facility must be operated by a private entity, its operations must affect commerce, and it must fall within one of these 12 categories. While the list of categories is exhaustive, the representative examples of facilities within each category are not. Within each category only a few examples are given. The category of social service center establishments would include not only the types of establishments listed, day care centers, senior citizen centers, homeless shelters, food banks, adoption agencies, but also establishments such as substance abuse treatment centers, rape crisis centers, and halfway houses. As another example, the category of sales or rental establishments would include an innumerable array of facilities that would sweep far beyond the few examples given in the regulation. For example, other retail or wholesale establishments selling or renting items, such as bookstores, videotape rental stores, car rental establishment, pet stores, and jewelry stores would also be covered under this category, even though they are not specifically listed.

Several commenters requested clarification as to the coverage of wholesale establishments under the category of "sales or rental establishments." The Department intends for wholesale establishments to be covered under this category as places of public accommodation except in cases where they sell exclusively to other businesses and not to individuals. For example, a company that grows food produce and supplies its crops exclusively to food processing corporations on a wholesale basis does not become a public accommodation because of these transactions. If this company operates a road side stand where its crops are sold to the public, the road side stand would be a sales establishment covered by the ADA. Conversely, a sales establishment that markets its goods as "wholesale to the

public" and sells to individuals would not be exempt from ADA coverage despite its use of the word "wholesale" as a marketing technique.

Of course, a company that operates a place of public accommodation is subject to this part only in the operation of that place of public accommodation. In the example given above, the wholesale produce company that operates a road side stand would be a public accommodation only for the purposes of the operation of that stand. The company would be prohibited from discriminating on the basis of disability in the operation of the road side stand, and it would be required to remove barriers to physical access to the extent that it is readily achievable to do so (see § 36.304); however, in the event that it is not readily achievable to remove barriers, for example, by replacing a gravel surface or regrading the area around the stand to permit access by persons with mobility impairments, the company could meet its obligations through alternative methods of making its goods available, such as delivering produce to a customer in his or her car (see § 36.305). The concepts of readily achievable barrier removal and alternatives to barrier removal are discussed further in the preamble discussion of §§ 36.304 and 36.305.

Even if a facility does not fall within one of the 12 categories, and therefore does not qualify as a place of public accommodation, it still may be a commercial facility as defined in § 36.104 and be subject to the new construction and alterations requirements of subpart D.

A number of commenters questioned the treatment of residential hotels and other residential facilities in the Department's proposed rule. These commenters were essentially seeking resolution of the relationship between the Fair Housing Act and the ADA concerning facilities that are both residential in nature and engage in activities that would cause them to be classified as "places of public accommodation" under the ADA. The ADA's express exemption relating to the Fair Housing Act applies only to "commercial facilities" and not to "places of public accommodation."

A facility whose operations affect interstate commerce is a place of public accommodation for purposes of the ADA to the extent that its operations include those types of activities engaged in or services provided by the facilities contained on the list of 12 categories in section 301(7) of the ADA. Thus, a facility that provides social services would be considered a "social service center establishment." Similarly, the category "places of lodging" would exclude solely residential facilities because the nature of a place of lodging contemplates the use of the facility for short-term stays.

Many facilities, however, are mixed use facilities. For example, in a large hotel that has a separate residential apartment wing, the residential wing would not be covered by the ADA because of the nature of the occupancy of that part of the facility. This residential wing would, however, be covered by the Fair Housing Act. The separate nonresidential accommodations in the rest of the hotel would be a place of lodging, and thus a public accommodation subject to the requirements of this final rule. If a hotel allows both residential and short-term stays, but does not allocate space for these different uses in separate, discrete units, both the ADA and the Fair Housing Act may apply to the facility. Such determinations will need to be made on a case-by-case basis. Any place of lodging of the type described in paragraph (1) of the definition of place of public accommodation and that is an establishment located within a building that contains not more than five rooms for rent or hire and is actually occupied by the proprietor of the establishment as his or her residence is not covered by the ADA. (This exclusion from coverage does not apply to other categories of public accommodations, for example, professional offices or homeless shelters, that are located in a building that is also occupied as a private residence.)

A number of commenters noted that the term "residential hotel" may also apply to a type of hotel commonly known as a "single room occupancy hotel." Although such hotels or portions of such hotels may fall under the Fair Housing Act when operated or used as long-term residences, they are also considered "places of lodging" under the ADA when guests of such hotels are free to use them on a short-term basis. In addition, "single room occupancy hotels" may provide social services to their guests, often through the operation of Federal or State grant programs. In such a situation, the facility would be considered a "social service center establishment" and thus covered by the ADA as a place of public accommodation, regardless of the length of stay of the occupants.

A similar analysis would also be applied to other residential facilities that provide social services, including homeless shelters, shelters for people seeking refuge from domestic violence,

nursing homes, residential care facilities, and other facilities where persons may reside for varying lengths of time. Such facilities should be analyzed under the Fair Housing Act to determine the application of that statute. The ADA, however, requires a separate and independent analysis. For example, if the facility, or a portion of the facility, is intended for or permits short-term stays, or if it can appropriately be categorized as a service establishment or as a social service establishment, then the facility or that portion of the facility used for the covered purpose is a place of public accommodation under the ADA. For example, a homeless shelter that is intended and used only for long-term residential stays and that does not provide social services to its residents would not be covered as a place of public accommodation. However, if this facility permitted short-term stays or provided social services to its residents, it would be covered under the ADA either as a "place of lodging" or as a "social service center establishment," or as both.

A private home, by itself, does not fall within any of the 12 categories. However, it can be covered as a place of public accommodation to the extent that it is used as a facility that would fall within one of the 12 categories. For example, if a professional office of a dentist, doctor, or psychologist is located in a private home, the portion of the home dedicated to office use (including areas used both for the residence and the office, e.g., the entrance to the home that is also used as the entrance to the professional office) would be considered a place of public accommodation. Places of public accommodation located in residential facilities are specifically addressed in § 36.207.

If a tour of a commercial facility that is not otherwise a place of public accommodation, such as, for example, a factory or a movie studio production set, is open to the general public, the route followed by the tour is a place of public accommodation and the tour must be operated in accordance with the rule's requirements for public accommodations. The place of public accommodation defined by the tour does not include those portions of the commercial facility that are merely viewed from the tour route. Hence, the barrier removal requirements of § 36.304 only apply to the physical route followed by the tour participants and not to work stations or other areas that are merely adjacent to, or within view of, the tour route. If the tour is not open to the general public, but rather is

conducted, for example, for selected business colleagues, partners, customers, or consultants, the tour route is not a place of public accommodation and the tour is not subject to the requirements for public accommodations.

Public accommodations that receive Federal financial assistance are subject to the requirements of section 504 of the Rehabilitation Act as well as the requirements of the ADA.

Private schools, including elementary and secondary schools, are covered by the rule as places of public accommodation. The rule itself, however, does not require a private school to provide a free appropriate education or develop an individualized education program in accordance with regulations of the Department of Education implementing section 504 of the Rehabilitation Act of 1973, as amended (34 CFR part 104), and regulations implementing the Individuals with Disabilities Education Act (34 CFR part 300). The receipt of Federal assistance by a private school, however, would trigger application of the Department of Education's regulations to the extent mandated by the particular type of assistance received.

"Private club." The term "private club" is defined in accordance with section 307 of the ADA as a private club or establishment exempted from coverage under title II of the Civil Rights Act of 1964. Title II of the 1964 Act exempts any "private club or other establishment not in fact open to the public, except to the extent that the facilities of such establishment are made available to the customers or patrons of [a place of public accommodation as defined in title II]." The rule, therefore, as reflected in § 36.102(e) of the application section, limits the coverage of private clubs accordingly. The obligations of a private club that rents space to any other private entity for the operation of a place of public accommodation are discussed further in connection with § 36.201.

In determining whether a private entity qualifies as a private club under title II, courts have considered such factors as the degree of member control of club operations, the selectivity of the membership selection process, whether substantial membership fees are charged, whether the entity is operated on a nonprofit basis, the extent to which the facilities are open to the public, the degree of public funding, and whether the club was created specifically to avoid compliance with the Civil Rights

Act. See *e.g., Tillman* v. *Wheaton-Haven Recreation Ass'n*, 410 U.S. 431 (1973); *Daniel* v. *Paul*, 395 U.S. 298 (1969); *Olzman* v. *Lake Hills Swim Club, Inc.*, 495 F.2d 1333 (2d Cir. 1974); *Anderson* v. *Pass Christian Isles Golf Club, Inc.*, 488 F.2d 855 (5th Cir. 1974); *Smith* v. *YMCA*, 462 F.2d 634 (5th Cir. 1972); *Stout* v. *YMCA*, 404 F.2d 687 (5th Cir. 1968); *United States* v. *Richberg*, 398 F.2d 523 (5th Cir. 1968); *Nesmith* v. *YMCA*, 397 F.2d 96 (4th Cir. 1968); *United States* v. *Lansdowne Swim Club*, 713 F. Supp. 785 (E.D. Pa. 1989); *Durham* v. *Red Lake Fishing and Hunting Club, Inc.*, 666 F. Supp. 954 (W.D. Tex. 1987); *New York* v. *Ocean Club, Inc.*, 602 F. Supp. 489 (E.D.N.Y. 1984); *Brown* v. *Loudoun Golf and Country Club, Inc.*, 573 F. Supp. 399 (E.D. Va. 1983); *United States* v. *Trustees of Fraternal Order of Eagles*, 472 F. Supp. 1174 (E.D. Wis. 1979); *Cornelius* v. *Benevolent Protective Order of Elks*, 382 F. Supp. 1182 (D. Conn. 1974).

"Private entity." The term "private entity" is defined as any individual or entity other than a public entity. It is used as part of the definition of "public accommodation" in this section.

The definition adds "individual" to the statutory definition of private entity (see section 301(6) of the ADA). This addition clarifies that an individual may be a private entity and, therefore, may be considered a public accommodation if he or she owns, leases (or leases to), or operates a place of public accommodation. The explicit inclusion of individuals under the definition of private entity is consistent with section 302(a) of the ADA, which broadly prohibits discrimination on the basis of disability by any person who owns, leases (or leases to), or operates a place of public accommodation.

"Public accommodation." The term "public accommodation" means a private entity that owns, leases (or leases to), or operates a place of public accommodation. The regulatory term, "public accommodation," corresponds to the statutory term, "person," in section 302(a) of the ADA. The ADA prohibits discrimination "by any person who owns, leases (or leases to), or operates a place of public accommodation." The text of the regulation consequently places the ADA's nondiscrimination obligations on "public accommodations" rather than on "persons" or on "places of public accommodation."

As stated in § 36.102(b)(2), the requirements of subparts B and C obligate a public accommodation only with respect to the operations of a place of public accommodation. A public accommodation must also meet the requirements of subpart D with respect to facilities used as, or designed or constructed for use as, places of public accommodation or commercial facilities.

"Public entity." The term "public entity" is defined in accordance with section 201(1) of the ADA as any State or local government; any department, agency, special purpose district, or other instrumentality of a State or States or local government; and the National Railroad Passenger Corporation, and any commuter authority (as defined in section 103(8) of the Rail Passenger Service Act). It is used in the definition of "private entity" in § 36.104. Public entities are excluded from the definition of private entity and therefore cannot qualify as public accommodations under this regulation. However, the actions of public entities are covered by title II of the ADA and by the Department's title II regulations codified at 28 CFR part 35.

"Qualified interpreter." The Department received substantial comment regarding the lack of a definition of "qualified interpreter." The proposed rule defined auxiliary aids and services to include the statutory term, "qualified interpreters" (§ 36.303(b)), but did not define that term. Section 36.303 requires the use of a qualified interpreter where necessary to achieve effective communication, unless an undue burden or fundamental alteration would result. Commenters stated that a lack of guidance on what the term means would create confusion among those trying to secure interpreting services and often result in less than effective communication.

Many commenters were concerned that, without clear guidance on the issue of "qualified" interpreter, the rule would be interpreted to mean "available, rather than qualified" interpreters. Some claimed that few public accommodations would understand the difference between a qualified interpreter and a person who simply knows a few signs or how to fingerspell.

In order to clarify what is meant by "qualified interpreter" the Department has added a definition of the term to the final rule. A qualified interpreter means an interpreter who is able to interpret effectively, accurately, and impartially both receptively and expressively, using any necessary specialized vocabulary. This definition focuses on the actual ability of the interpreter in a particular interpreting context to facilitate effective communication between the public accommodation and the individual with disabilities.

Public comment also revealed that public accommodations have at times asked persons who are deaf to provide family members or friends to interpret.

In certain circumstances, notwithstanding that the family member or friend is able to interpret or is a certified interpreter, the family member or friend may not be qualified to render the necessary interpretation because of factors such as emotional or personal involvement or considerations of confidentiality that may adversely affect the ability to interpret "effectively, accurately, and impartially."

"Readily achievable." The definition of "readily achievable" follows the statutory definition of that term in section 301(9) of the ADA. Readily achievable means easily accomplishable and able to be carried out without much difficulty or expense. The term is used as a limitation on the obligation to remove barriers under §§ 36.304(a), 36.305(a), 36.308(a), and 36.310(b). Further discussion of the meaning and application of the term "readily achievable" may be found in the preamble section for § 36.304.

The definition lists factors to be considered in determining whether barrier removal is readily achievable in any particular circumstance. A significant number of commenters objected to § 36.306 of the proposed rule, which listed identical factors to be considered for determining "readily achievable" and "undue burden" together in one section. They asserted that providing a consolidated section blurred the distinction between the level of effort required by a public accommodation under the two standards. The readily achievable standard is a "lower" standard than the "undue burden" standard in terms of the level of effort required, but the factors used in determining whether an action is readily achievable or would result in an undue burden are identical (See Education and Labor report at 109). Although the preamble to the proposed rule clearly delineated the relationship between the two standards, to eliminate any confusion the Department has deleted § 36.306 of the proposed rule. That section, in any event, as other commenters noted, had merely repeated the lists of factors contained in the definitions of readily achievable and undue burden.

The list of factors included in the definition is derived from section 301(9) of the ADA. It reflects the congressional intention that a wide range of factors be considered in determining whether an action is readily achievable. It also takes into account that many local facilities are owned or operated by parent corporations or entities that conduct operations at many different sites. This section makes clear that, in some instances, resources beyond those of the local facility where the barrier must be removed may be relevant in determining whether an action is readily achievable. One must also evaluate the degree to which any parent entity has resources that may be allocated to the local facility.

The statutory list of factors in section 301(9) of the Act uses the term "covered entity" to refer to the larger entity of which a particular facility may be a part. "Covered entity" is not a defined term in the ADA and is not used consistently throughout the Act. The definition, therefore, substitutes the term "parent entity" in place of "covered entity" in paragraphs (3), (4), and (5) when referring to the larger private entity whose overall resources may be taken into account. This usage is consistent with the House Judiciary Committee's use of the term "parent company" to describe the larger entity of which the local facility is a part (H.R. Rep. No. 485, 101st Cong., 2d Sess., pt. 3, at 40–41, 54–55 [1990] [hereinafter "Judiciary report"]).

A number of commenters asked for more specific guidance as to when and how the resources of a parent corporation or entity are to be taken into account in determining what is readily achievable. The Department believes that this complex issue is most appropriately resolved on a case-by-case basis. As the comments reflect, there is a wide variety of possible relationships between the site in question and any parent corporation or other entity. It would be unwise to posit legal ramifications under the ADA of even generic relationships (e.g., banks involved in foreclosures or insurance companies operating as trustees or in other similar fiduciary relationships), because any analysis will depend so completely on the detailed fact situations and the exact nature of the legal relationships involved. The final rule does, however, reorder the factors to be considered. This shift and the addition of the phrase "if applicable" make clear that the line of inquiry concerning resources will start at the site involved in the action itself. This change emphasizes that the overall resources, size, and operations of the parent corporation or entity should be considered to the extent appropriate in light of "the geographic separateness, and the administrative or fiscal relationship of the site or sites in question to any parent corporation or entity."

Although some commenters sought more specific numerical guidance on the definition of readily achievable, the Department has declined to establish in the final rule any kind of numerical formula for determining whether an action is readily achievable. It would be difficult to devise a specific ceiling on compliance costs that would take into account the vast diversity of enterprises covered by the ADA's public accommodations requirements and the economic situation that any particular entity would find itself in at any moment. The final rule, therefore, implements the flexible case-by-case approach chosen by Congress.

A number of commenters requested that security considerations be explicitly recognized as a factor in determining whether a barrier removal action is readily achievable. The Department believes that legitimate safety requirements, including crime prevention measures, may be taken into account so long as they are based on actual risks and are necessary for safe operation of the public accommodation. This point has been included in the definition.

Some commenters urged the Department not to consider acts of barrier removal in complete isolation from each other in determining whether they are readily achievable. The Department believes that it is appropriate to consider the cost of other barrier removal actions as one factor in determining whether a measure is readily achievable.

"Religious entity." The term "religious entity" is defined in accordance with section 307 of the ADA as a religious organization or entity controlled by a religious organization, including a place of worship. Section 36.102(e) of the rule states that the rule does not apply to any religious entity.

The ADA's exemption of religious organizations and religious entities controlled by religious organizations is very broad, encompassing a wide variety of situations. Religious organizations and entities controlled by religious organizations have no obligations under the ADA. Even when a religious organization carries out activities that would otherwise make it a public accommodation, the religious organization is exempt from ADA coverage. Thus, if a church itself operates a day care center, a nursing home, a private school, or a diocesan school system, the operations of the center, home, school, or schools would not be subject to the requirements of the ADA or this part. The religious entity would not lose its exemption merely because the services provided were open to the general public. The test is whether the church or other religious organization operates the public accommodation, not which individuals receive the public accommodation's services.

Religious entities that are controlled by religious organizations are also exempt from the ADA's requirements. Many religious organizations in the United States use lay boards and other secular or corporate mechanisms to operate schools and an array of social services. The use of a lay board or other mechanism does not itself remove the ADA's religious exemption. Thus, a parochial school, having religious doctrine in its curriculum and sponsored by a religious order, could be exempt either as a religious organization or as an entity controlled by a religious organization, even if it has a lay board. The test remains a factual one—whether the church or other religious organization controls the operations of the school or of the service or whether the school or service is itself a religious organization.

Although a religious organization or a religious entity that is controlled by a religious organization has no obligations under the rule, a public accommodation that is not itself a religious organization, but that operates a place of public accommodation in leased space on the property of a religious entity, which is not a place of worship, is subject to the rule's requirements if it is not under control of a religious organization. When a church rents meeting space, which is not a place of worship, to a local community group or to a private, independent day care center, the ADA applies to the activities of the local community group and day care center if a lease exists and consideration is paid.

"Service animal." The term "service animal" encompasses any guide dog, signal dog, or other animal individually trained to provide assistance to an individual with a disability. The term is used in § 36.302(c), which requires public accommodations generally to modify policies, practices, and procedures to accommodate the use of service animals in places of public accommodation.

"Specified public transportation." The definition of "specified public transportation" is identical to the statutory definition in section 301(10) of the ADA. The term means transportation by bus, rail, or any other conveyance (other than by aircraft) that provides the general public with general or special service (including charter service) on a regular and continuing basis. It is used in category (7) of the definition of "place of public accommodation," which includes stations used for specified public transportation.

The effect of this definition, which excludes transportation by aircraft, is that it excludes privately operated airports from coverage as places of public accommodation. However, places of public accommodation located within airports would be covered by this part. Airports that are operated by public entities are covered by title II of the ADA and, if they are operated as part of a program receiving Federal financial assistance, by section 504 of the Rehabilitation Act. Privately operated airports are similarly covered by section 504 if they are operated as part of a program receiving Federal financial assistance. The operations of any portion of any airport that are under the control of an air carrier are covered by the Air Carrier Access Act. In addition, airports are covered as commercial facilities under this rule.

"State." The definition of "State" is identical to the statutory definition in section 3(3) of the ADA. The term is used in the definitions of "commerce" and "public entity" in § 36.104.

"Undue burden." The definition of "undue burden" is analogous to the statutory definition of "undue hardship" in employment under section 101(10) of the ADA. The term undue burden means "significant difficulty or expense" and serves as a limitation on the obligation to provide auxiliary aids and services under § 36.303 and §§ 36.309 (b)(3) and (c)(3). Further discussion of the meaning and application of the term undue burden may be found in the preamble discussion of § 36.303.

The definition lists factors considered in determining whether provision of an auxiliary aid or service in any particular circumstance would result in an undue burden. The factors to be considered in determining whether an action would result in an undue burden are identical to those to be considered in determining whether an action is readily achievable. However, "readily achievable" is a lower standard than "undue burden" in that it requires a lower level of effort on the part of the public accommodation (see Education and Labor report at 109). Further analysis of the factors to be considered in determining undue burden may be found in the preamble discussion of the definition of the term "readily achievable."

Subpart B—General Requirements

Subpart B includes general prohibitions restricting a public accommodation from discriminating against people with disabilities by denying them the opportunity to benefit from goods or services, by giving them

unequal goods or services, or by giving them different or separate goods or services. These general prohibitions are patterned after the basic, general prohibitions that exist in other civil rights laws that prohibit discrimination on the basis of race, sex, color, religion, or national origin.

Section 36.201 General

Section 36.201(a) contains the general rule that prohibits discrimination on the basis of disability in the full and equal enjoyment of goods, services, facilities, privileges, advantages, and accommodations of any place of public accommodation.

Full and equal enjoyment means the right to participate and to have an equal opportunity to obtain the same results as others to the extent possible with such accommodations as may be required by the Act and these regulations. It does not mean that an individual with a disability must achieve an identical result or level of achievement as persons without a disability. For example, an exercise class cannot exclude a person who uses a wheelchair because he or she cannot do all of the exercises and derive the same result from the class as persons without a disability.

Section 302(a) of the ADA states that the prohibition against discrimination applies to "any person who owns, leases (or leases to), or operates a place of public accommodation," and this language is reflected in § 36.201(a). The coverage is quite extensive and would include sublessees, management companies, and any other entity that owns, leases, leases to, or operates a place of public accommodation, even if the operation is only for a short time.

The first sentence of paragraph (b) of § 36.201 reiterates the general principle that both the landlord that owns the building that houses the place of public accommodation, as well as the tenant that owns or operates the place of public accommodation, are public accommodations subject to the requirements of this part. Although the statutory language could be interpreted as placing equal responsibility on all private entities, whether lessor, lessee, or operator of a public accommodation, the committee reports suggest that liability may be allocated. Section 36.201(b) of that section of the proposed rule attempted to allocate liability in the regulation itself. Paragraph (b)(2) of that section made a specific allocation of liability for the obligation to take readily achievable measures to remove barriers, and paragraph (b)(3) made a specific allocation for the obligation to provide auxiliary aids.

Numerous commenters pointed out that these allocations would not apply in all situations. Some asserted that paragraph (b)(2) of the proposed rule only addressed the situation when a lease gave the tenant the right to make alterations with permission of the landlord, but failed to address other types of leases, e.g., those that are silent on the right to make alterations, or those in which the landlord is not permitted to enter a tenant's premises to make alterations. Several commenters noted that many leases contain other clauses more relevant to the ADA than the alterations clause. For example, many leases contain a "compliance clause," a clause which allocates responsibility to a particular party for compliance with all relevant Federal, State, and local laws. Many commenters pointed out various types of relationships that were left unaddressed by the regulation, e.g., sale and leaseback arrangements where the landlord is a financial institution with no control or responsibility for the building; franchises; subleases; and management companies which, at least in the hotel industry, often have control over operations but are unable to make modifications to the premises.

Some commenters raised specific questions as to how the barrier removal allocation would work as a practical matter. Paragraph (b)(2) of the proposed rule provided that the burden of making readily achievable modifications within the tenant's place of public accommodation would shift to the landlord when the modifications were not readily achievable for the tenant or when the landlord denied a tenant's request for permission to make such modifications. Commenters noted that the rule did not specify exactly when the burden would actually shift from tenant to landlord and whether the landlord would have to accept a tenant's word that a particular action is not readily achievable. Others questioned if the tenant should be obligated to use alternative methods of barrier removal before the burden shifts. In light of the fact that readily achievable removal of barriers can include such actions as moving of racks and displays, some commenters doubted the appropriateness of requiring a landlord to become involved in day-to-day operations of its tenants' businesses.

The Department received widely differing comments in response to the preamble question asking whether landlord and tenant obligations should vary depending on the length of time remaining on an existing lease. Many suggested that tenants should have no responsibilities in "shorter leases."

which commenters defined as ranging anywhere from 90 days to three years. Other commenters pointed out that the time remaining on the lease should not be a factor in the rule's allocation of responsibilities, but is relevant in determining what is readily achievable for the tenant. The Department agrees with this latter approach and will interpret the rule in that manner.

In recognition of the somewhat limited applicability of the allocation scheme contained in the proposed rule, paragraphs (b)(2) and (b)(3) have been deleted from the final rule. The Department has substituted instead a statement that allocation of responsibility as between the parties for taking readily achievable measures to remove barriers and to provide auxiliary aids and services both in common areas and within places of public accommodation may be determined by the lease or other contractual relationships between the parties. The ADA was not intended to change existing landlord/tenant responsibilities as set forth in the lease. By deleting specific provisions from the rule, the Department gives full recognition to this principle. As between the landlord and tenant, the extent of responsibility for particular obligations may be, and in many cases probably will be, determined by contract.

The suggested allocation of responsibilities contained in the proposed rule may be used if appropriate in a particular situation. Thus, the landlord would generally be held responsible for making readily achievable changes and providing auxiliary aids and services in common areas and for modifying policies, practices, or procedures applicable to all tenants, and the tenant would generally be responsible for readily achievable changes, provision of auxiliary aids, and modification of policies within its own place of public accommodation.

Many commenters objected to the proposed rule's allocation of responsibility for providing auxiliary aids and services solely to the tenant, pointing out that this exclusive allocation may not be appropriate in the case of larger public accommodations that operate their businesses by renting space out to smaller public accommodations. For example, large theaters often rent to smaller traveling companies and hospitals often rely on independent contractors to provide childbirth classes. Groups representing persons with disabilities objected to the proposed rule because, in their view, it permitted the large theater or hospital to evade ADA responsibilities by leasing

to independent smaller entities. They suggested that these types of public accommodations are not really landlords because they are in the business of providing a service, rather than renting space, as in the case of a shopping center or office building landlord. These commenters believed that responsibility for providing auxiliary aids should shift to the landlord, if the landlord relies on a smaller public accommodation or independent contractor to provide services closely related to those of the larger public accommodation, and if the needed auxiliary aids prove to be an undue burden for the smaller public accommodation. The final rule no longer lists specific allocations to specific parties but, rather, leaves allocation of responsibilities to the lease negotiations. Parties are, therefore, free to allocate the responsibility for auxiliary aids.

Section 36.201(b)(4) of the proposed rule, which provided that alterations by a tenant on its own premises do not trigger a path of travel obligation on the landlord, has been moved to § 36.403(d) of the final rule.

An entity that is not in and of itself a public accommodation, such as a trade association or performing artist, may become a public accommodation when it leases space for a conference or performance at a hotel, convention center, or stadium. For an entity to become a public accommodation when it is the lessee of space, however, the Department believes that consideration in some form must be given. Thus, a Boy Scout troop that accepts donated space does not become a public accommodation because the troop has not "leased" space, as required by the ADA.

As a public accommodation, the trade association or performing artist will be responsible for compliance with this part. Specific responsibilities should be allocated by contract, but, generally, the lessee should be responsible for providing auxiliary aids and services (which could include interpreters, Braille programs, etc.) for the participants in its conference or performance as well as for assuring that displays are accessible to individuals with disabilities.

Some commenters suggested that the rule should allocate responsibilities for areas other than removal of barriers and auxiliary aids. The final rule leaves allocation of all areas to the lease negotiations. However, in general landlords should not be given responsibility for policies a tenant applies in operating its business, if such policies are solely those of the tenant. Thus, if a restaurant tenant

discriminates by refusing to seat a patron, it would be the tenant, and not the landlord, who would be responsible, because the discriminatory policy is imposed solely by the tenant and not by the landlord. If, however, a tenant refuses to modify a "no pets" rule to allow service animals in its restaurant because the landlord mandates such a rule, then both the landlord and the tenant would be liable for violation of the ADA when a person with a service dog is refused entrance. The Department wishes to emphasize, however, that the parties are free to allocate responsibilities in any way they choose.

Private clubs are also exempt from the ADA. However, consistent with title II of the Civil Rights Act (42 U.S.C. 2000a(e), a private club is considered a public accommodation to the extent that "the facilities of such establishment are made available to the customers or patrons" of a place of public accommodation. Thus, if a private club runs a day care center that is open exclusively to its own members, the club, like the church in the example above, would have no responsibility for compliance with the ADA. Nor would the day care center have any responsibilities because it is part of the private club exempt from the ADA.

On the other hand, if the private club rents to a day care center that is open to the public, then the private club would have the same obligations as any other public accommodation that functions as a landlord with respect to compliance with title III within the day care center. In such a situation, both the private club that "leases to" a public accommodation and the public accommodation lessee (the day care center) would be subject to the ADA. This same principle would apply if the private club were to rent to, for example, a bar association, which is not generally a public accommodation but which, as explained above, becomes a public accommodation when it leases space for a conference.

Section 36.202   Activities

Section 36.202 sets out the general forms of discrimination prohibited by title III of the ADA. These general prohibitions are further refined by the specific prohibitions in subpart C. Section 36.213 makes clear that the limitations on the ADA's requirements contained in subpart C, such as "necessity" (§ 36.301(a)) and "safety" (§ 36.301(b)), are applicable to the prohibitions in § 36.202. Thus, it is unnecessary to add these limitations to § 36.202 as has been requested by some commenters. In addition, the language of § 36.202 very closely tracks the language of section 302(b)(1)(A) of the Act, and that statutory provision does not expressly contain these limitations.

Deny participation—Section 36.202(a) provides that it is discriminatory to deny a person with a disability the right to participate in or benefit from the goods, services, facilities, privileges, advantages, or accommodations of a place of public accommodation.

A public accommodation may not exclude persons with disabilities on the basis of disability for reasons other than those specifically set forth in this part. For example, a public accommodation cannot refuse to serve a person with a disability because its insurance company conditions coverage or rates on the absence of persons with disabilities. This is a frequent basis of exclusion from a variety of community activities and is prohibited by this part.

Unequal benefit—Section 36.202(b) prohibits services or accommodations that are not equal to those provided others. For example, persons with disabilities must not be limited to certain performances at a theater.

Separate benefit—Section 36.202(c) permits different or separate benefits or services only when necessary to provide persons with disabilities opportunities as effective as those provided others. This paragraph permitting separate benefits "when necessary" should be read together with § 36.203(a), which requires integration in "the most integrated setting appropriate to the needs of the individual." The preamble to that section provides further guidance on separate programs. Thus, this section would not prohibit the designation of parking spaces for persons with disabilities.

Each of the three paragraphs (a)–(c) prohibits discrimination against an individual or class of individuals "either directly or through contractual, licensing, or other arrangements." The intent of the contractual prohibitions of these paragraphs is to prohibit a public accommodation from doing indirectly, what it may not do directly. Thus, the "individual or class of individuals" referenced in the three paragraphs is intended to refer to the clients and customers of the public accommodation that entered into a contractual arrangement. It is not intended to encompass the clients or customers of other entities. A public accommodation, therefore, is not liable under this provision for discrimination that may be practiced by those with whom it has a contractual relationship, when that discrimination is not directed against its own clients or customers. For example, if an amusement park contracts with a

food service company to operate its restaurants at the park, the amusement park is not responsible for other operations of the food service company that do not involve clients or customers of the amusement park. Section 36.202(d) makes this clear by providing that the term "individual or class of individuals" refers to the clients or customers of the public accommodation that enters into the contractual, licensing, or other arrangement.

Section 36.203   Integrated Settings

Section 36.203 addresses the integration of persons with disabilities. The ADA recognizes that the provision of goods and services in an integrated manner is a fundamental tenet of nondiscrimination on the basis of disability. Providing segregated accommodations and services relegates persons with disabilities to the status of second-class citizens. For example, it would be a violation of this provision to require persons with mental disabilities to eat in the back room of a restaurant or to refuse to allow a person with a disability the full use of a health spa because of stereotypes about the person's ability to participate. Section 36.203(a) states that a public accommodation shall afford goods, services, facilities, privileges, advantages, and accommodations to an individual with a disability in the most integrated setting appropriate to the needs of the individual. Section 36.203(b) specifies that, notwithstanding the existence of separate or different programs or activities provided in accordance with this section, an individual with a disability shall not be denied the opportunity to participate in such programs or activities that are not separate or different. Section 306.203(c), which is derived from section 501(d) of the Americans with Disabilities Act, states that nothing in this part shall be construed to require an individual with a disability to accept an accommodation, aid, service, opportunity, or benefit that he or she chooses not to accept.

Taken together, these provisions are intended to prohibit exclusion and segregation of individuals with disabilities and the denial of equal opportunities enjoyed by others, based on, among other things, presumptions, patronizing attitudes, fears, and stereotypes about individuals with disabilities. Consistent with these standards, public accommodations are required to make decisions based on facts applicable to individuals and not on the basis of presumptions as to what a class of individuals with disabilities can or cannot do.

Sections 36.203 (b) and (c) make clear that individuals with disabilities cannot be denied the opportunity to participate in programs that are not separate or different. This is an important and overarching principle of the Americans with Disabilities Act. Separate, special, or different programs that are designed to provide a benefit to persons with disabilities cannot be used to restrict the participation of persons with disabilities in general, integrated activities.

For example, a person who is blind may wish to decline participating in a special museum tour that allows persons to touch sculptures in an exhibit and instead tour the exhibit at his or her own pace with the museum's recorded tour. It is not the intent of this section to require the person who is blind to avail himself or herself of the special tour. Modified participation for persons with disabilities must be a choice, not a requirement.

Further, it would not be a violation of this section for an establishment to offer recreational programs specially designed for children with mobility impairments in those limited circumstances. However, it would be a violation of this section if the entity then excluded these children from other recreational services made available to nondisabled children, or required children with disabilities to attend only designated programs.

Many commenters asked that the Department clarify a public accommodation's obligations within the integrated program when it offers a separate program, but an individual with a disability chooses not to participate in the separate program. It is impossible to make a blanket statement as to what level of auxiliary aids or modifications are required in the integrated program. Rather, each situation must be assessed individually. Assuming the integrated program would be appropriate for a particular individual, the extent to which that individual must be provided with modifications will depend not only on what the individual needs but also on the limitations set forth in subpart C. For example, it may constitute an undue burden for a particular public accommodation, which provides a full-time interpreter in its special guided tour for individuals with hearing impairments, to hire an additional interpreter for those individuals who choose to attend the integrated program. The Department cannot identify categorically the level of assistance or aid required in the integrated program.

The preamble to the proposed rule contained a statement that some interpreted as encouraging the continuation of separate schools, sheltered workshops, special recreational programs, and other similar programs. It is important to emphasize that § 36.202(c) only calls for separate programs when such programs are "necessary" to provide as effective an opportunity to individuals with disabilities as to other individuals. Likewise, § 36.203(a) only permits separate programs when a more integrated setting would not be "appropriate." Separate programs are permitted, then, in only limited circumstances. The sentence at issue has been deleted from the preamble because it was too broadly stated and had been erroneously interpreted as Departmental encouragement of separate programs without qualification.

The proposed rule's reference in § 36.203(b) to separate programs or activities provided in accordance with "this section" has been changed to "this subpart" in recognition of the fact that separate programs or activities may, in some limited circumstances, be permitted not only by § 36.203(a) but also by § 36.202(c).

In addition, some commenters suggested that the individual with the disability is the only one who can decide whether a setting is "appropriate" and what the "needs" are. Others suggested that only the public accommodation can make these determinations. The regulation does not give exclusive responsibility to either party. Rather, the determinations are to be made based on an objective view, presumably one which would take into account views of both parties.

Some commenters expressed concern that § 36.203(c), which states that nothing in the rule requires an individual with a disability to accept special accommodations and services provided under the ADA, could be interpreted to allow guardians of infants or older people with disabilities to refuse medical treatment for their wards. Section 36.203(c) has been revised to make it clear that paragraph (c) is inapplicable to the concern of the commenters. A new paragraph (c)(2) has been added stating that nothing in the regulation authorizes the representative or guardian of an individual with a disability to decline food, water, medical treatment, or medical services for that individual. New paragraph (c) clarifies that neither the ADA nor the regulation alters current Federal law ensuring the rights of incompetent individuals with disabilities to receive food, water, and medical treatment. See, e.g., Child Abuse Amendments of 1984

(42 U.S.C. 5106a(b)(10), 5106g(10)); Rehabilitation Act of 1973, as amended (29 U.S.C 794); Developmentally Disabled Assistance and Bill of Rights Act (42 U.S.C. 6042).

Sections 36.203(c) (1) and (2) are based on section 501(d) of the ADA. Section § 501(d) was designed to clarify that nothing in the ADA requires individuals with disabilities to accept special accommodations and services for individuals with disabilities that may segregate them:

The Committee added this section (501(d)) to clarify that nothing in the ADA is intended to permit discriminatory treatment on the basis of disability, even when such treatment is rendered under the guise of providing an accommodation, service, aid or benefit to the individual with disability. For example, a blind individual may choose not to avail himself or herself of the right to go to the front of a line, even if a particular public accommodation has chosen to offer such a modification of a policy for blind individuals. Or, a blind individual may choose to decline to participate in a special museum tour that allows persons to touch sculptures in an exhibit and instead tour the exhibits at his or her own pace with the museum's recorded tour.

(Judiciary report at 71–72.) The Act is not to be construed to mean that an individual with disabilities must accept special accommodations and services for individuals with disabilities when that individual chooses to participate in the regular services already offered. Because medical treatment, including treatment for particular conditions, is not a special accommodation or service for individuals with disabilities under section 501(d), neither the Act nor this part provides affirmative authority to suspend such treatment. Section 501(d) is intended to clarify that the Act is not designed to foster discrimination through mandatory acceptance of special services when other alternatives are provided; this concern does not reach to the provision of medical treatment for the disabling condition itself.

Section 36.213 makes clear that the limitations contained in subpart C are to be read into subpart B. Thus, the integration requirement is subject to the various defenses contained in subpart C, such as safety, if eligibility criteria are at issue (§ 36.301(b)), or fundamental alteration and undue burden, if the concern is provision of auxiliary aids (§ 36.303(a)).

Section 36.204 Administrative Methods

Section 36.204 specifies that an individual or entity shall not, directly, or through contractual or other arrangements, utilize standards or criteria or methods of administration

that have the effect of discriminating on the basis of disability or that perpetuate the discrimination of others who are subject to common administrative control. The preamble discussion of § 36.301 addresses eligibility criteria in detail.

Section 36.204 is derived from section 302(b)(1)(D) of the Americans with Disabilities Act, and it uses the same language used in the employment section of the ADA (section 102(b)(3)). Both sections incorporate a disparate impact standard to ensure the effectiveness of the legislative mandate to end discrimination. This standard is consistent with the interpretation of section 504 by the U.S. Supreme Court in *Alexander* v. *Choate*, 469 U.S. 287 (1985). The Court in *Choate* explained that members of Congress made numerous statements during passage of section 504 regarding eliminating architectural barriers, providing access to transportation, and eliminating discriminatory effects of job qualification procedures. The Court then noted: "These statements would ring hollow if the resulting legislation could not rectify the harms resulting from action that discriminated by effect as well as by design." *Id* at 297 (footnote omitted).

Of course, § 36.204 is subject to the various limitations contained in subpart C including, for example, necessity (§ 36.301(a)), safety (§ 36.301(b)), fundamental alteration (§ 36.302(a)), readily achievable (§ 36.304(a)), and undue burden (§ 36.303(a)).

Section 36.205 Association

Section 36.205 implements section 302(b)(1)(E) of the Act, which provides that a public accommodation shall not exclude or otherwise deny equal goods, services, facilities, privileges, advantages, accommodations, or other opportunities to an individual or entity because of the known disability of an individual with whom the individual or entity is known to have a relationship or association. This section is unchanged from the proposed rule.

The individuals covered under this section include any individuals who are discriminated against because of their known association with an individual with a disability. For example, it would be a violation of this part for a day care center to refuse admission to a child because his or her brother has HIV disease.

This protection is not limited to those who have a familial relationship with the individual who has a disability. If a place of public accommodation refuses admission to a person with cerebral palsy and his or her companions, the companions have an independent right of action under the ADA and this section.

During the legislative process, the term "entity" was added to section 302(b)(1)(E) to clarify that the scope of the provision is intended to encompass not only persons who have a known association with a person with a disability, but also entities that provide services to or are otherwise associated with such individuals. This provision was intended to ensure that entities such as health care providers, employees of social service agencies, and others who provide professional services to persons with disabilities are not subjected to discrimination because of their professional association with persons with disabilities. For example, it would be a violation of this section to terminate the lease of a entity operating an independent living center for persons with disabilities, or to seek to evict a health care provider because that individual or entity provides services to persons with mental impairments.

Section 36.206 Retaliation or Coercion

Section 36.206 implements section 503 of the ADA, which prohibits retaliation against any individual who exercises his or her rights under the Act. This section is unchanged from the proposed rule. Paragraph (a) of § 36.206 provides that no private entity or public entity shall discriminate against any individual because that individual has exercised his or her right to oppose any act or practice made unlawful by this part, or because that individual made a charge, testified, assisted, or participated in any manner in an investigation, proceeding, or hearing under the Act or this part.

Paragraph (b) provides that no private entity or public entity shall coerce, intimidate, threaten, or interfere with any individual in the exercise of his or her rights under this part or because that individual aided or encouraged any other individual in the exercise or enjoyment of any right granted or protected by the Act or this part.

Illustrations of practices prohibited by this section are contained in paragraph (c), which is modeled on a similar provision in the regulations issued by the Department of Housing and Urban Development to implement the Fair Housing Act (see 24 CFR 100.400(c)(l)). Prohibited actions may include:

(1) Coercing an individual to deny or limit the benefits, services, or advantages to which he or she is entitled under the Act or this part;

(2) Threatening, intimidating, or interfering with an individual who is seeking to obtain or use the goods, services, facilities, privileges, advantages, or accommodations of a public accommodation;

(3) Intimidating or threatening any person because that person is assisting or encouraging an individual or group entitled to claim the rights granted or protected by the Act or this part to exercise those rights; or

(4) Retaliating against any person because that person has participated in any investigation or action to enforce the Act or this part.

This section protects not only individuals who allege a violation of the Act or this part, but also any individuals who support or assist them. This section applies to all investigations or proceedings initiated under the Act or this part without regard to the ultimate resolution of the underlying allegations. Because this section prohibits any act of retaliation or coercion in response to an individual's effort to exercise rights established by the Act and this part (or to support the efforts of another individual), the section applies not only to public accommodations that are otherwise subject to this part, but also to individuals other than public accommodations or to public entities. For example, it would be a violation of the Act and this part for a private individual, e.g., a restaurant customer, to harass or intimidate an individual with a disability in an effort to prevent that individual from patronizing the restaurant. It would, likewise, be a violation of the Act and this part for a public entity to take adverse action against an employee who appeared as a witness on behalf of an individual who sought to enforce the Act.

Section 36.207 Places of Public Accommodation Located in Private Residences

A private home used exclusively as a residence is not covered by title III because it is neither a "commercial facility" nor a "place of public accommodation." In some situations, however, a private home is not used exclusively as a residence, but houses a place of public accommodation in all or part of a home (e.g., an accountant who meets with his or her clients at his or her residence). Section 36.207(a) provides that those portions of the private residence used in the operation of the place of public accommodation are covered by this part.

For instance, a home or a portion of a home may be used as a day care center during the day and a residence at night. If all parts of the house are used for the day care center, then the entire residence is a place of public accommodation because no part of the house is used exclusively as a residence. If an accountant uses one room in the house solely as his or her professional office, then a portion of the house is used exclusively as a place of public accommodation and a portion is used exclusively as a residence. Section 36.207 provides that when a portion of a residence is used exclusively as a residence, that portion is not covered by this part. Thus, the portions of the accountant's house, other than the professional office and areas and spaces leading to it, are not covered by this part. All of the requirements of this rule apply to the covered portions, including requirements to make reasonable modifications in policies, eliminate discriminatory eligibility criteria, take readily achievable measures to remove barriers or provide readily achievable alternatives (e.g., making house calls), provide auxiliary aids and services and undertake only accessible new construction and alterations.

Paragraph (b) was added in response to comments that sought clarification on the extent of coverage of the private residence used as the place of public accommodation. The final rule makes clear that the place of accommodation extends to all areas of the home used by clients and customers of the place of public accommodation. Thus, the ADA would apply to any door or entry way, hallways, a restroom, if used by customers and clients; and any other portion of the residence, interior or exterior, used by customers or clients of the public accommodation. This interpretation is simply an application of the general rule for all public accommodations, which extends statutory requirements to all portions of the facility used by customers and clients, including, if applicable, restrooms, hallways, and approaches to the public accommodation. As with other public accommodations, barriers at the entrance and on the sidewalk leading up to the public accommodation, if the sidewalk is under the control of the public accommodation, must be removed if doing so is readily achievable.

The Department recognizes that many businesses that operate out of personal residences are quite small, often employing only the homeowner and having limited total revenues. In these circumstances the effect of ADA coverage would likely be quite minimal. For example, because the obligation to remove existing architectural barriers is limited to those that are easily accomplishable without much difficulty or expense (see § 36.304), the range of required actions would be quite modest.

It might not be readily achievable for such a place of public accommodation to remove any existing barriers. If it is not readily achievable to remove existing architectural barriers, a public accommodation located in a private residence may meet its obligations under the Act and this part by providing its goods or services to clients or customers with disabilities through the use of alternative measures, including delivery of goods or services in the home of the customer or client, to the extent that such alternative measures are readily achievable (See § 36.305).

Some commenters asked for clarification as to how the new construction and alteration standards of subpart D will apply to residences. The new construction standards only apply to the extent that the residence or portion of the residence was designed or intended for use as a public accommodation. Thus, for example, if a portion of a home is designed or constructed for use exclusively as a lawyer's office or for use both as a lawyer's office and for residential purposes, then it must be designed in accordance with the new construction standards in the appendix. Likewise, if a homeowner is undertaking alterations to convert all or part of his residence to a place of public accommodation, that work must be done in compliance with the alterations standards in the appendix.

The preamble to the proposed rule addressed the applicable requirements when a commercial facility is located in a private residence. That situation is now addressed in § 36.401(b) of subpart D.

Section 36.208   Direct Threat

Section 36.208(a) implements section 302(b)(3) of the Act by providing that this part does not require a public accommodation to permit an individual to participate in or benefit from the goods, services, facilities, privileges, advantages and accommodations of the public accommodation, if that individual poses a direct threat to the health or safety of others. This section is unchanged from the proposed rule.

The Department received a significant number of comments on this section. Commenters representing individuals with disabilities generally supported this provision, but suggested revisions to further limit its application. Commenters representing public accommodations generally endorsed modifications that would permit a public accommodation to exercise its own judgment in determining whether an individual poses a direct threat.

The inclusion of this provision is not intended to imply that persons with disabilities pose risks to others. It is intended to address concerns that may arise in this area. It establishes a strict standard that must be met before denying service to an individual with a disability or excluding that individual from participation.

Paragraph (b) of this section explains that a "direct threat" is a significant risk to the health or safety of others that cannot be eliminated by a modification of policies, practices, or procedures, or by the provision of auxiliary aids and services. This paragraph codifies the standard first applied by the Supreme Court in *School Board of Nassau County* v. *Arline*, 480 U.S. 273 (1987), in which the Court held that an individual with a contagious disease may be an "individual with handicaps" under section 504 of the Rehabilitation Act. In *Arline*, the Supreme Court recognized that there is a need to balance the interests of people with disabilities against legitimate concerns for public safety. Although persons with disabilities are generally entitled to the protection of this part, a person who poses a significant risk to others may be excluded if reasonable modifications to the public accommodation's policies, practices, or procedures will not eliminate that risk. The determination that a person poses a direct threat to the health or safety of others may not be based on generalizations or stereotypes about the effects of a particular disability; it must be based on an individual assessment that conforms to the requirements of paragraph (c) of this section.

Paragraph (c) establishes the test to use in determining whether an individual poses a direct threat to the health or safety of others. A public accommodation is required to make an individualized assessment, based on reasonable judgment that relies on current medical evidence or on the best available objective evidence, to determine: The nature, duration, and severity of the risk; the probability that the potential injury will actually occur; and whether reasonable modifications of policies, practices, or procedures will mitigate the risk. This is the test established by the Supreme Court in *Arline*. Such an inquiry is essential if the law is to achieve its goal of protecting disabled individuals from discrimination based on prejudice, stereotypes, or unfounded fear, while giving appropriate weight to legitimate concerns, such as the need to avoid exposing others to significant health and safety risks. Making this assessment will not usually require the services of a physician. Sources for medical knowledge include guidance from public health authorities, such as the U.S. Public Health Service, the Centers for Disease Control, and the National Institutes of Health, including the National Institute of Mental Health.

Many of the commenters sought clarification of the inquiry requirement. Some suggested that public accommodations should be prohibited from making any inquiries to determine if an individual with a disability would pose a direct threat to other persons. The Department believes that to preclude all such inquiries would be inappropriate. Under § 36.301 of this part, a public accommodation is permitted to establish eligibility criteria necessary for the safe operation of the place of public accommodation. Implicit in that right is the right to ask if an individual meets the criteria. However, any eligibility or safety standard established by a public accommodation must be based on actual risk, not on speculation or stereotypes; it must be applied to all clients or customers of the place of public accommodation; and inquiries must be limited to matters necessary to the application of the standard.

Some commenters suggested that the test established in the *Arline* decision, which was developed in the context of an employment case, is too stringent to apply in a public accommodations context where interaction between the public accommodation and its client or customer is often very brief. One suggested alternative was to permit public accommodations to exercise "good faith" judgment in determining whether an individual poses a direct threat, particularly when a public accommodation is dealing with a client or customer engaged in disorderly or disruptive behavior.

The Department believes that the ADA clearly requires that any determination to exclude an individual from participation must be based on an objective standard. A public accommodation may establish neutral eligibility criteria as a condition of receiving its goods or services. As long as these criteria are necessary for the safe provision of the public accommodation's goods and services and applied neutrally to all clients or customers, regardless of whether they are individuals with disabilities, a person who is unable to meet the criteria may be excluded from participation without inquiry into the underlying reason for the inability to comply. In places of public accommodation such as restaurants, theaters, or hotels, where the contact between the public accommodation and its clients is transitory, the uniform application of an eligibility standard precluding violent or disruptive behavior by any client or customer should be sufficient to enable a public accommodation to conduct its business in an orderly manner.

Some other commenters asked for clarification of the application of this provision to persons, particularly children, who have short-term, contagious illnesses, such as fevers, influenza, or the common cold. It is common practice in schools and day care settings to exclude persons with such illnesses until the symptoms subside. The Department believes that these commenters misunderstand the scope of this rule. The ADA only prohibits discrimination against an individual with a disability. Under the ADA and this part, a "disability" is defined as a physical or mental impairment that substantially limits one or more major life activities. Common, short-term illnesses that predictably resolve themselves within a matter of days do not "substantially limit" a major life activity; therefore, it is not a violation of this part to exclude an individual from receiving the services of a public accommodation because of such transitory illness. However, this part does apply to persons who have long-term illnesses. Any determination with respect to a person who has a chronic or long-term illness must be made in compliance with the requirements of this section.

Section 36.209 Illegal Use of Drugs

Section 36.209 effectuates section 510 of the ADA, which clarifies the Act's application to people who use drugs illegally. Paragraph (a) provides that this part does not prohibit discrimination based on an individual's current illegal use of drugs.

The Act and the regulation distinguish between illegal use of drugs and the legal use of substances, whether or not those substances are "controlled substances," as defined in the Controlled Substances Act (21 U.S.C. 812). Some controlled substances are prescription drugs that have legitimate medical uses. Section 36.209 does not affect use of controlled substances pursuant to a valid prescription, under supervision by a licensed health care professional, or other use that is authorized by the Controlled Substances Act or any other provision of Federal law. It does apply to illegal use of those substances, as well as to illegal use of controlled substances that are not prescription drugs. The key question is

whether the individual's use of the substance is illegal, not whether the substance has recognized legal uses. Alcohol is not a controlled substance, so use of alcohol is not addressed by § 36.209. Alcoholics are individuals with disabilities, subject to the protections of the statute.

A distinction is also made between the use of a substance and the status of being addicted to that substance. Addiction is a disability, and addicts are individuals with disabilities protected by the Act. The protection, however, does not extend to actions based on the illegal use of the substance. In other words, an addict cannot use the fact of his or her addiction as a defense to an action based on illegal use of drugs. This distinction is not artificial. Congress intended to deny protection to people who engage in the illegal use of drugs, whether or not they are addicted, but to provide protection to addicts so long as they are not currently using drugs.

A third distinction is the difficult one between current use and former use. The definition of "current illegal use of drugs" in § 36.104, which is based on a report of the Conference Committee, H.R. Conf. Rep. No. 596, 101st Cong., 2d Sess. 64 (1990), is "illegal use of drugs that occurred recently enough to justify a reasonable belief that a person's drug use is current or that continuing use is a real and ongoing problem."

Paragraph (a)(2)(i) specifies that an individual who has successfully completed a supervised drug rehabilitation program or has otherwise been rehabilitated successfully and who is not engaging in current illegal use of drugs is protected. Paragraph (a)(2)(ii) clarifies that an individual who is currently participating in a supervised rehabilitation program and is not engaging in current illegal use of drugs is protected. Paragraph (a)(2)(iii) provides that a person who is erroneously regarded as engaging in current illegal use of drugs, but who is not engaging in such use, is protected.

Paragraph (b) provides a limited exception to the exclusion of current illegal users of drugs from the protections of the Act. It prohibits denial of health services, or services provided in connection with drug rehabilitation, to an individual on the basis of current illegal use of drugs, if the individual is otherwise entitled to such services. As explained further in the discussion of § 36.302, a health care facility that specializes in a particular type of treatment, such as care of burn victims, is not required to provide drug rehabilitation services, but it cannot refuse to treat an individual's burns on

the grounds that the individual is illegally using drugs.

A commenter argued that health care providers should be permitted to use their medical judgment to postpone discretionary medical treatment of individuals under the influence of alcohol or drugs. The regulation permits a medical practitioner to take into account an individual's use of drugs in determining appropriate medical treatment. Section 36.209 provides that the prohibitions on discrimination in this part do not apply when the public accommodation acts on the basis of current illegal use of drugs. Although those prohibitions do apply under paragraph (b), the limitations established under this part also apply. Thus, under § 36.208, a health care provider or other public accommodation covered under § 36.209(b) may exclude an individual whose current illegal use of drugs poses a direct threat to the health or safety of others, and, under § 36.301, a public accommodation may impose or apply eligibility criteria that are necessary for the provision of the services being offered, and may impose legitimate safety requirements that are necessary for safe operation. These same limitations also apply to individuals with disabilities who use alcohol or prescription drugs. The Department believes that these provisions address this commenter's concerns.

Other commenters pointed out that abstention from the use of drugs is an essential condition for participation in some drug rehabilitation programs, and may be a necessary requirement in inpatient or residential settings. The Department believes that this comment is well-founded. Congress clearly did not intend to exclude from drug treatment programs the very individuals who need such programs because of their use of drugs. In such a situation, however, once an individual has been admitted to a program, abstention may be a necessary and appropriate condition to continued participation. The final rule therefore provides that a drug rehabilitation or treatment program may deny participation to individuals who use drugs while they are in the program.

Paragraph (c) expresses Congress' intention that the Act be neutral with respect to testing for illegal use of drugs. This paragraph implements the provision in section 510(b) of the Act that allows entities "to adopt or administer reasonable policies or procedures, including but not limited to drug testing," that ensure an individual who is participating in a supervised rehabilitation program, or who has completed such a program or otherwise been rehabilitated successfully, is no longer engaging in the illegal use of drugs. Paragraph (c) is not to be construed to encourage, prohibit, restrict, or authorize the conducting of testing for the illegal use of drugs.

Paragraph (c) of § 36.209 clarifies that it is not a violation of this part to adopt or administer reasonable policies or procedures to ensure that an individual who formerly engaged in the illegal use of drugs is not currently engaging in illegal use of drugs. Any such policies or procedures must, of course, be reasonable, and must be designed to identify accurately the illegal use of drugs. This paragraph does not authorize inquiries, tests, or other procedures that would disclose use of substances that are not controlled substances or are taken under supervision by a licensed health care professional, or other uses authorized by the Controlled Substances Act or other provisions of Federal law, because such uses are not included in the definition of "illegal use of drugs."

One commenter argued that the rule should permit testing for lawful use of prescription drugs, but most favored the explanation that tests must be limited to *unlawful* use in order to avoid revealing the use of prescription medicine used to treat disabilities. Tests revealing legal use of prescription drugs might violate the prohibition in § 36.301 of attempts to unnecessarily identify the existence of a disability.

Section 36.210   Smoking

Section 36.210 restates the clarification in section 501(b) of the Act that the Act does not preclude the prohibition of, or imposition of restrictions on, smoking. Some commenters argued that § 36.210 does not go far enough, and that the regulation should prohibit smoking in all places of public accommodation. The reference to smoking in section 501 merely clarifies that the Act does not require public accommodations to accommodate smokers by permitting them to smoke in places of public accommodations.

Section 36.211   Maintenance of Accessible Features

Section 36.211 provides that a public accommodation shall maintain in operable working condition those features of facilities and equipment that are required to be readily accessible to and usable by persons with disabilities by the Act or this part. The Act requires that, to the maximum extent feasible, facilities must be accessible to, *and*

usable by, individuals with disabilities. This section recognizes that it is not sufficient to provide features such as accessible routes, elevators, or ramps, if those features are not maintained in a manner that enables individuals with disabilities to use them. Inoperable elevators, locked accessible doors, or "accessible" routes that are obstructed by furniture, filing cabinets, or potted plants are neither "accessible to" nor "usable by" individuals with disabilities.

Some commenters objected that this section appeared to establish an absolute requirement and suggested that language from the preamble be included in the text of the regulation. It is, of course, impossible to guarantee that mechanical devices will never fail to operate. Paragraph (b) of the final regulation provides that this section does not prohibit isolated or temporary interruptions in service or access due to maintenance or repairs. This paragraph is intended to clarify that temporary obstructions or isolated instances of mechanical failure would not be considered violations of the Act or this part. However, allowing obstructions or "out of service" equipment to persist beyond a reasonable period of time would violate this part, as would repeated mechanical failures due to improper or inadequate maintenance. Failure of the public accommodation to ensure that accessible routes are properly maintained and free of obstructions, or failure to arrange prompt repair of inoperable elevators or other equipment intended to provide access, would also violate this part.

Other commenters requested that this section be expanded to include specific requirements for inspection and maintenance of equipment, for training staff in the proper operation of equipment, and for maintenance of specific items. The Department believes that this section properly establishes the general requirement for maintaining access and that further, more detailed requirements are not necessary.

Section 36.212   Insurance

The Department received numerous comments on proposed § 36.212. Most supported the proposed regulation but felt that it did not go far enough in protecting individuals with disabilities and persons associated with them from discrimination. Many commenters argued that language from the preamble to the proposed regulation should be included in the text of the final regulation. Other commenters argued that even that language was not strong enough, and that more stringent standards should be established. Only a

few commenters argued that the Act does not apply to insurance underwriting practices or the terms of insurance contracts. These commenters cited language from the Senate committee report (S. Rep. No. 116, 101st Cong., 1st Sess., at 84–86 (1989) (hereinafter "Senate report")), indicating that Congress did not intend to affect existing insurance practices.

The Department has decided to adopt the language of the proposed rule without change. Sections 36.212 (a) and (b) restate section 501(c) of the Act, which provides that the Act shall not be construed to restrict certain insurance practices on the part of insurance companies and employers, as long as such practices are not used to evade the purposes of the Act. Section 36.212(c) is a specific application of § 36.202(a), which prohibits denial of participation on the basis of disability. It provides that a public accommodation may not refuse to serve an individual with a disability because of limitations on coverage or rates in its insurance policies (see Judiciary report at 56).

Many commenters supported the requirements of § 36.212(c) in the proposed rule because it addressed an important reason for denial of services by public accommodations. One commenter argued that services could be denied if the insurance coverage required exclusion of people whose disabilities were reasonably related to the risks involved in that particular place of public accommodation. Sections 36.208 and 36.301 establish criteria for denial of participation on the basis of legitimate safety concerns. This paragraph does not prohibit consideration of such concerns in insurance policies, but provides that any exclusion on the basis of disability must be based on the permissible criteria, rather than on the terms of the insurance contract.

Language in the committee reports indicates that Congress intended to reach insurance practices by prohibiting differential treatment of individuals with disabilities in insurance offered by public accommodations unless the differences are justified. "Under the ADA, a person with a disability cannot be denied insurance or be subject to different terms or conditions of insurance based on disability alone, if the disability does not pose increased risks" (Senate report at 84; Education and Labor report at 136). Section 501(c) (1) of the Act was intended to emphasize that "insurers may continue to sell to and underwrite individuals applying for life, health, or other insurance on an individually underwritten basis, or to service such insurance products, *so long as the standards used are based on sound actuarial data and not on speculation*" (Judiciary report at 70 (emphasis added); see also Senate report at 85; Education and Labor report at 137).

The committee reports indicate that underwriting and classification of risks must be "based on sound actuarial principles or be related to actual or reasonably anticipated experience" (see, *e.g.,* Judiciary report at 71). Moreover, "while a plan which limits certain kinds of coverage based on classification of risk would be allowed * * *, the plan may not refuse to insure, or refuse to continue to insure, or limit the amount, extent, or kind of coverage available to an individual, or charge a different rate for the same coverage solely because of a physical or mental impairment, except where the refusal, limitation, or rate differential is based on sound actuarial principles or is related to actual or reasonably anticipated experience" (Senate report at 85; Education and Labor report at 136–37; Judiciary report at 71). The ADA, therefore, does not prohibit use of legitimate actuarial considerations to justify differential treatment of individuals with disabilities in insurance.

The committee reports provide some guidance on how nondiscrimination principles in the disability rights area relate to insurance practices. For example, a person who is blind may not be denied coverage based on blindness independent of actuarial risk classification. With respect to group health insurance coverage, an individual with a pre-existing condition may be denied coverage for that condition for the period specified in the policy, but cannot be denied coverage for illness or injuries unrelated to the pre-existing condition. Also, a public accommodation may offer insurance policies that limit coverage for certain procedures or treatments, but may not entirely deny coverage to a person with a disability.

The Department requested comment on the extent to which data that would establish statistically sound correlations are available. Numerous commenters cited pervasive problems in the availability and cost of insurance for individuals with disabilities and parents of children with disabilities. No commenters cited specific data, or sources of data, to support specific exclusionary practices. Several commenters reported that, even when statistics are available, they are often outdated and do not reflect current medical technology and treatment methods. Concern was expressed that adequate efforts are not made to distinguish those individuals who are high users of health care from individuals in the same diagnostic groups who may be low users of health care. One insurer reported that "hard data and actuarial statistics are not available to provide precise numerical justifications for every underwriting determination," but argued that decisions may be based on "logical principles generally accepted by actuarial science and fully consistent with state insurance laws." The commenter urged that the Department recognize the validity of information other than statistical data as a basis for insurance determinations.

The most frequent comment was a recommendation that the final regulation should require the insurance company to provide a copy of the actuarial data on which its actions are based when requested by the applicant. Such a requirement would be beyond anything contemplated by the Act or by Congress and has therefore not been included in the Department's final rule. Because the legislative history of the ADA clarifies that different treatment of individuals with disabilities in insurance may be justified by sound actuarial data, such actuarial data will be critical to any potential litigation on this issue. This information would presumably be obtainable in a court proceeding where the insurer's actuarial data was the basis for different treatment of persons with disabilities. In addition, under some State regulatory schemes, insurers may have to file such actuarial information with the State regulatory agency and this information may be obtainable at the State level.

A few commenters representing the insurance industry conceded that underwriting practices in life and health insurance are clearly covered, but argued that property and casualty insurance are not covered. The Department sees no reason for this distinction. Although life and health insurance are the areas where the regulation will have its greatest application, the Act applies equally to unjustified discrimination in all types of insurance provided by public accommodations. A number of commenters, for example, reported difficulties in obtaining automobile insurance because of their disabilities, despite their having good driving records.

Section 36.213   Relationship of Subpart B to Subparts C and D

This section explains that subpart B sets forth the general principles of nondiscrimination applicable to all entities subject to this regulation, while subparts C and D provide guidance on the application of this part to specific situations. The specific provisions in subparts C and D, including the limitations on those provisions, control over the general provisions in circumstances where both specific and general provisions apply. Resort to the general provisions of subpart B is only appropriate where there are no applicable specific rules of guidance in subparts C or D. This interaction between the specific requirements and the general requirements operates with regard to contractual obligations as well.

One illustration of this principle is its application to the obligation of a public accommodation to provide access to services by removal of architectural barriers or by alternatives to barrier removal. The general requirement, established in subpart B by § 36.203, is that a public accommodation must provide its services to individuals with disabilities in the most integrated setting appropriate. This general requirement would appear to categorically prohibit "segregated" seating for persons in wheelchairs. Section 36.304, however, only requires removal of architectural barriers to the extent that removal is "readily achievable." If providing access to all areas of a restaurant, for example, would not be "readily achievable," a public accommodation may provide access to selected areas only. Also, § 36.305 provides that, where barrier removal is not readily achievable, a public accommodation may use alternative, readily achievable methods of making services available, such as curbside service or home delivery. Thus, in this manner, the specific requirements of §§ 36.304 and 36.305 control over the general requirement of § 36.203.

Subpart C—Specific Requirements

In general, subpart C implements the "specific prohibitions" that comprise section 302(b)(2) of the ADA. It also addresses the requirements of section 309 of the ADA regarding examinations and courses.

Section 36.301   Eligibility Criteria

Section 36.301 of the rule prohibits the imposition or application of eligibility criteria that screen out or tend to screen out an individual with a disability or any class of individuals with disabilities from fully and equally enjoying any goods, services, facilities, privileges, advantages, and accommodations, unless such criteria can be shown to be necessary for the provision of the goods, services, facilities, privileges, advantages, or accommodations being offered. This prohibition is based on section 302(b)(2)(A)(i) of the ADA.

It would violate this section to establish exclusive or segregative eligibility criteria that would bar, for example, all persons who are deaf from playing on a golf course or all individuals with cerebral palsy from attending a movie theater, or limit the seating of individuals with Down's syndrome to only particular areas of a restaurant. The wishes, tastes, or preferences of other customers may not be asserted to justify criteria that would exclude or segregate individuals with disabilities.

Section 36.301 also prohibits attempts by a public accommodation to unnecessarily identify the existence of a disability; for example, it would be a violation of this section for a retail store to require an individual to state on a credit application whether the applicant has epilepsy, mental illness, or any other disability, or to inquire unnecessarily whether an individual has HIV disease.

Section 36.301 also prohibits policies that unnecessarily impose requirements or burdens on individuals with disabilities that are not placed on others. For example, public accommodations may not require that an individual with a disability be accompanied by an attendant. As provided by § 36.306, however, a public accommodation is not required to provide services of a personal nature including assistance in toileting, eating, or dressing.

Paragraph (c) of § 36.301 provides that public accommodations may not place a surcharge on a particular individual with a disability or any group of individuals with disabilities to cover the costs of measures, such as the provision of auxiliary aids and services, barrier removal, alternatives to barrier removal, and reasonable modifications in policies, practices, and procedures, that are required to provide that individual or group with the nondiscriminatory treatment required by the Act or this part.

A number of commenters inquired as to whether deposits required for the use of auxiliary aids, such as assistive listening devices, are prohibited surcharges. It is the Department's view that reasonable, completely refundable, deposits are not to be considered surcharges prohibited by this section. Requiring deposits is an important means of ensuring the availability of

equipment necessary to ensure compliance with the ADA.

Other commenters sought clarification as to whether § 36.301(c) prohibits professionals from charging for the additional time that it may take in certain cases to provide services to an individual with disabilities. The Department does not intend § 36.301(c) to prohibit professionals who bill on the basis of time from charging individuals with disabilities on that basis. However, fees may not be charged for the provision of auxiliary aids and services, barrier removal, alternatives to barrier removal, reasonable modifications in policies, practices, and procedures, or any other measures necessary to ensure compliance with the ADA.

Other commenters inquired as to whether day care centers may charge for extra services provided to individuals with disabilities. As stated above, § 36.302(c) is intended only to prohibit charges for measures necessary to achieve compliance with the ADA.

Another commenter asserted that charges may be assessed for home delivery provided as an alternative to barrier removal under § 36.305, when home delivery is provided to all customers for a fee. Charges for home delivery are permissible if home delivery is not considered an alternative to barrier removal. If the public accommodation offers an alternative, such as curb, carry-out, or sidewalk service for which no surcharge is assessed, then it may charge for home delivery in accordance with its standard pricing for home delivery.

In addition, § 36.301 prohibits the imposition of criteria that "tend to" screen out an individual with a disability. This concept, which is derived from current regulations under section 504 (see, e.g., 45 CFR 84.13), makes it discriminatory to impose policies or criteria that, while not creating a direct bar to individuals with disabilities, indirectly prevent or limit their ability to participate. For example, requiring presentation of a driver's license as the sole means of identification for purposes of paying by check would violate this section in situations where, for example, individuals with severe vision impairments or developmental disabilities or epilepsy are ineligible to receive a driver's license and the use of an alternative means of identification, such as another photo I.D. or credit card, is feasible.

A public accommodation may, however, impose neutral rules and criteria that screen out, or tend to screen out, individuals with disabilities, if the criteria are necessary for the safe

operation of the public accommodation. Examples of safety qualifications that would be justifiable in appropriate circumstances would include height requirements for certain amusement park rides or a requirement that all participants in a recreational rafting expedition be able to meet a necessary level of swimming proficiency. Safety requirements must be based on actual risks and not on speculation, stereotypes, or generalizations about individuals with disabilities.

Section 36.302   Modifications in Policies, Practices, or Procedures

Section 36.302 of the rule prohibits the failure to make reasonable modifications in policies, practices, and procedures when such modifications may be necessary to afford any goods, services, facilities, advantages, or accommodations, unless the entity can demonstrate that making such modifications would fundamentally alter the nature of such goods, services, facilities, privileges, advantages, or accommodations. This prohibition is based on section 302(b)(2)(A)(ii) of the ADA.

For example, a parking facility would be required to modify a rule barring all vans or all vans with raised roofs, if an individual who uses a wheelchair-accessible van wishes to park in that facility, and if overhead structures are high enough to accommodate the height of the van. A department store may need to modify a policy of only permitting one person at a time in a dressing room, if an individual with mental retardation needs and requests assistance in dressing from a companion. Public accommodations may need to revise operational policies to ensure that services are available to individuals with disabilities. For instance, a hotel may need to adopt a policy of keeping an accessible room unoccupied until an individual with a disability arrives at the hotel, assuming the individual has properly reserved the room.

One example of application of this principle is specifically included in a new § 36.302(d) on check-out aisles. That paragraph provides that a store with check-out aisles must ensure that an adequate number of accessible check-out aisles is kept open during store hours, or must otherwise modify its policies and practices, in order to ensure that an equivalent level of convenient service is provided to individuals with disabilities as is provided to others. For example, if only one check-out aisle is accessible, and it is generally used for express service, one way of providing equivalent service is to allow persons with mobility impairments to make all of their purchases at that aisle. This principle also applies with respect to other accessible elements and services. For example, a particular bank may be in compliance with the accessibility guidelines for new construction incorporated in appendix A with respect to automated teller machines (ATM) at a new branch office by providing one accessible walk-up machine at that location, even though an adjacent walk-up ATM is not accessible and the drive-up ATM is not accessible. However, the bank would be in violation of this section if the accessible ATM was located in a lobby that was locked during evening hours while the drive-up ATM was available to customers without disabilities during those same hours. The bank would need to ensure that the accessible ATM was available to customers during the hours that any of the other ATM's was available.

A number of commenters inquired as to the relationship between this section and § 36.307, "Accessible or special goods." Under § 36.307, a public accommodation is not required to alter its inventory to include accessible or special goods that are designed for, or facilitate use by, individuals with disabilities. The rule enunciated in § 36.307 is consistent with the "fundamental alteration" defense to the reasonable modifications requirement of § 36.302. Therefore, § 36.302 would not require the inventory of goods provided by a public accommodation to be altered to include goods with accessibility features. For example, § 36.302 would not require a bookstore to stock Brailled books or order Brailled books, if it does not do so in the normal course of its business.

The rule does not require modifications to the legitimate areas of specialization of service providers. Section 36.302(b) provides that a public accommodation may refer an individual with a disability to another public accommodation, if that individual is seeking or requires, treatment or services outside of the referring public accommodation's area of specialization, and if, in the normal course of its operations, the referring public accommodation would make a similar referral for an individual without a disability who seeks or requires the same treatment or services.

For example, it would not be discriminatory for a physician who specializes only in burn treatment to refer an individual who is deaf to another physician for treatment of an injury other than a burn injury. To require a physician to accept patients outside of his or her specialty would fundamentally alter the nature of the medical practice and, therefore, not be required by this section.

A clinic specializing exclusively in drug rehabilitation could similarly refuse to treat a person who is not a drug addict, but could not refuse to treat a person who is a drug addict simply because the patient tests positive for HIV. Conversely, a clinic that specializes in the treatment of individuals with HIV could refuse to treat an individual that does not have HIV, but could not refuse to treat a person for HIV infection simply because that person is also a drug addict.

Some commenters requested clarification as to how this provision would apply to situations where manifestations of the disability in question, itself, would raise complications requiring the expertise of a different practitioner. It is not the Department's intention in § 36.302(b) to prohibit a physician from referring an individual with a disability to another physician, if the disability itself creates specialized complications for the patient's health that the physician lacks the experience or knowledge to address (see Education and Labor report at 106).

Section 36.302(c)(1) requires that a public accommodation modify its policies, practices, or procedures to permit the use of a service animal by an individual with a disability in any area open to the general public. The term "service animal" is defined in § 36.104 to include guide dogs, signal dogs, or any other animal individually trained to provide assistance to an individual with a disability.

A number of commenters pointed to the difficulty of making the distinction required by the proposed rule between areas open to the general public and those that are not. The ambiguity and uncertainty surrounding these provisions has led the Department to adopt a single standard for all public accommodations.

Section 36.302(c)(1) of the final rule now provides that "[g]enerally, a public accommodation shall modify policies, practices, and procedures to permit the use of a service animal by an individual with a disability." This formulation reflects the general intent of Congress that public accommodations take the necessary steps to accommodate service animals and to ensure that individuals with disabilities are not separated from their service animals. It is intended that the broadest feasible access be provided to service animals in all places of public accommodation, including movie theaters, restaurants, hotels, retail stores, hospitals, and nursing homes (see Education and Labor report at 106; Judiciary report at 59). The section also acknowledges, however, that, in rare circumstances, accommodation of service animals may not be required because a fundamental alteration would result in the nature of the goods, services, facilities, privileges, or accommodations offered or provided, or the safe operation of the public accommodation would be jeopardized.

As specified in § 36.302(c)(2), the rule does not require a public accommodation to supervise or care for any service animal. If a service animal must be separated from an individual with a disability in order to avoid a fundamental alteration or a threat to safety, it is the responsibility of the individual with the disability to arrange for the care and supervision of the animal during the period of separation.

A museum would not be required by § 36.302 to modify a policy barring the touching of delicate works of art in order to enhance the participation of individuals who are blind, if the touching threatened the integrity of the work. Damage to a museum piece would clearly be a fundamental alteration that is not required by this section.

Section 36.303 Auxiliary Aids and Services.

Section 36.303 of the final rule requires a public accommodation to take such steps as may be necessary to ensure that no individual with a disability is excluded, denied services, segregated or otherwise treated differently than other individuals because of the absence of auxiliary aids and services, unless the public accommodation can demonstrate that taking such steps would fundamentally alter the nature of the goods, services, facilities, advantages, or accommodations being offered or would result in an undue burden. This requirement is based on section 302(b)(2)(A)(iii) of the ADA.

Implicit in this duty to provide auxiliary aids and services is the underlying obligation of a public accommodation to communicate effectively with its customers, clients, patients, or participants who have disabilities affecting hearing, vision, or speech. To give emphasis to this underlying obligation, § 36.303(c) of the rule incorporates language derived from section 504 regulations for federally conducted programs (see *e.g.*, 28 CFR 39.160(a)) that requires that appropriate auxiliary aids and services be furnished to ensure that communication with persons with disabilities is as effective as communication with others.

Auxiliary aids and services include a wide range of services and devices for ensuring effective communication. Use of the most advanced technology is not required so long as effective communication is ensured. The Department's proposed § 36.303(b) provided a list of examples of auxiliary aids and services that was taken from the definition of auxiliary aids and services in section 3(1) of the ADA and was supplemented by examples from regulations implementing section 504 in federally conducted programs (see *e.g.*, 28 CFR 39.103). A substantial number of commenters suggested that additional examples be added to this list. The Department has added several items to this list but wishes to clarify that the list is not an all-inclusive or exhaustive catalogue of possible or available auxiliary aids or services. It is not possible to provide an exhaustive list, and such an attempt would omit new devices that will become available with emerging tech..iology.

The Department has added videotext displays, computer-aided transcription services, and open and closed captioning to the list of examples. Videotext displays have become an important means of accessing auditory communications through a public address system. Transcription services are used to relay aurally delivered material almost simultaneously in written form to persons who are deaf or hard of hearing. This technology is often used at conferences, conventions, and hearings. While the proposed rule expressly included television decoder equipment as an auxiliary aid or service, it did not mention captioning itself. The final rule rectifies this omission by mentioning both closed and open captioning.

In this section, the Department has changed the proposed rule's phrase, "orally delivered materials," to the phrase, "aurally delivered materials." This new phrase tracks the language in the definition of "auxiliary aids and services" in section 3 of the ADA and is meant to include nonverbal sounds and alarms and computer-generated speech.

Several persons and organizations requested that the Department replace the term "telecommunications devices for deaf persons" or "TDD's" with the term "text telephone." The Department has declined to do so. The Department is aware that the Architectural and Transportation Barriers Compliance Board has used the phrase "text telephone" in lieu of the statutory term "TDD" in its final accessibility

guidelines. Title IV of the ADA, however, uses the term "Telecommunications Device for the Deaf," and the Department believes it would be inappropriate to abandon this statutory term at this time.

Paragraph (b)(2) lists examples of aids and services for making visually delivered materials accessible to persons with visual impairments. Many commenters proposed additional examples such as signage or mapping, audio description services, secondary auditory programs (SAP), telebraillers, and reading machines. While the Department declines to add these items to the list in the regulation, they may be considered appropriate auxiliary aids and services.

Paragraph (b)(3) refers to the acquisition or modification of equipment or devices. For example, tape players used for an audio-guided tour of a museum exhibit may require the addition of Brailled adhesive labels to the buttons on a reasonable number of the tape players to facilitate their use by individuals who are blind. Similarly, permanent or portable assistive listening systems for persons with hearing impairments may be required at a hotel conference center.

Several commenters suggested the addition of current technological innovations in microelectronics and computerized control systems (e.g., voice recognition systems, automatic dialing telephones, and infrared elevator and light control systems) to the list of auxiliary aids and services. The Department interprets auxiliary aids and services as those aids and services designed to provide effective communications, i. e., making aurally and visually delivered information available to persons with hearing, speech, and vision impairments. Methods of making services, programs, or activities accessible to, or usable by, individuals with mobility or manual dexterity impairments are addressed by other sections of this part, including the requirements for modifications in policies, practices, or procedures (§ 36.302), the elimination of existing architectural barriers (§ 36.304), and the provision of alternatives to barriers removal (§ 36.305).

Paragraph (b)(4) refers to other similar services and actions. Several commenters asked for clarification that "similar services and actions" include retrieving items from shelves, assistance in reaching a marginally accessible seat, pushing a barrier aside in order to provide an accessible route, or assistance in removing a sweater or coat. While retrieving an item from a shelf might be an "auxiliary aid or

service" for a blind person who could not locate the item without assistance, it might be a readily achievable alternative to barrier removal for a person using a wheelchair who could not reach the shelf, or a reasonable modification to a self-service policy for an individual who lacked the ability to grasp the item. (Of course, a store would not be required to provide a personal shopper.) As explained above, auxiliary aids and services are those aids and services required to provide effective communications. Other forms of assistance are more appropriately addressed by other provisions of the final rule.

The auxiliary aid requirement is a flexible one. A public accommodation can choose among various alternatives as long as the result is effective communication. For example, a restaurant would not be required to provide menus in Braille for patrons who are blind, if the waiters in the restaurant are made available to read the menu. Similarly, a clothing boutique would not be required to have Brailled price tags if sales personnel could provide price information orally upon request; and a bookstore would not be required to make available a sign language interpreter, because effective communication can be conducted by notepad.

A critical determination is what constitutes an effective auxiliary aid or service. The Department's proposed rule recommended that, in determining what auxiliary aid to use, the public accommodation consult with an individual before providing him or her with a particular auxiliary aid or service. This suggestion sparked a significant volume of public comment. Many persons with disabilities, particularly persons who are deaf or hard of hearing, recommended that the rule should require that public accommodations give "primary consideration" to the "expressed choice" of an individual with a disability. These commenters asserted that the proposed rule was inconsistent with congressional intent of the ADA, with the Department's proposed rule implementing title II of the ADA, and with longstanding interpretations of section 504 of the Rehabilitation Act.

Based upon a careful review of the ADA legislative history, the Department believes that Congress did not intend under title III to impose upon a public accommodation the requirement that it give primary consideration to the request of the individual with a disability. To the contrary, the legislative history demonstrates congressional intent to strongly encourage consulting with persons with disabilities. In its analysis of the ADA's auxiliary aids requirement for public accommodations, the House Education and Labor Committee stated that it "expects" that "public accommodation(s) will consult with the individual with a disability before providing a particular auxiliary aid or service" (Education and Labor report at 107). Some commenters also cited a different committee statement that used mandatory language as evidence of legislative intent to require primary consideration. However, this statement was made in the context of reasonable accommodations required by title I with respect to employment (Education and Labor report at 67). Thus, the Department finds that strongly encouraging consultation with persons with disabilities, in lieu of mandating primary consideration of their expressed choice, is consistent with congressional intent.

The Department wishes to emphasize that public accommodations must take steps necessary to ensure that an individual with a disability will not be excluded, denied services, segregated or otherwise treated differently from other individuals because of the use of inappropriate or ineffective auxiliary aids. In those situations requiring an interpreter, the public accommodations must secure the services of a qualified interpreter, unless an undue burden would result.

In the analysis of § 36.303(c) in the proposed rule, the Department gave as an example the situation where a note pad and written materials were insufficient to permit effective communication in a doctor's office when the matter to be decided was whether major surgery was necessary. Many commenters objected to this statement, asserting that it gave the impression that only decisions about major surgery would merit the provision of a sign language interpreter. The statement would, as the commenters also claimed, convey the impression to other public accommodations that written communications would meet the regulatory requirements in all but the most extreme situations. The Department, when using the example of major surgery, did not intend to limit the provision of interpreter services to the most extreme situations.

Other situations may also require the use of interpreters to ensure effective communication depending on the facts of the particular case. It is not difficult to imagine a wide range of communications involving areas such as

health, legal matters, and finances that would be sufficiently lengthy or complex to require an interpreter for effective communication. In some situations, an effective alternative to use of a notepad or an interpreter may be the use of a computer terminal upon which the representative of the public accommodation and the customer or client can exchange typewritten messages.

Section 36.303(d) specifically addresses requirements for TDD's. Partly because of the availability of telecommunications relay services to be established under title IV of the ADA, § 36.303(d)(2) provides that a public accommodation is not required to use a telecommunication device for the deaf (TDD) in receiving or making telephone calls incident to its operations. Several commenters were concerned that relay services would not be sufficient to provide effective access in a number of situations. Commenters argued that relay systems (1) do not provide effective access to the automated systems that require the caller to respond by pushing a button on a touch tone phone, (2) cannot operate fast enough to convey messages on answering machines, or to permit a TDD user to leave a recorded message, and (3) are not appropriate for calling crisis lines relating to such matters as rape, domestic violence, child abuse, and drugs where confidentiality is a concern. The Department believes that it is more appropriate for the Federal Communications Commission to address these issues in its rulemaking under title IV.

A public accommodation is, however, required to make a TDD available to an individual with impaired hearing or speech, if it customarily offers telephone service to its customers, clients, patients, or participants on more than an incidental convenience basis. Where entry to a place of public accommodation requires use of a security entrance telephone, a TDD or other effective means of communication must be provided for use by an individual with impaired hearing or speech.

In other words, individual retail stores, doctors' offices, restaurants, or similar establishments are not required by this section to have TDD's, because TDD users will be able to make inquiries, appointments, or reservations with such establishments through the relay system established under title IV of the ADA. The public accommodation will likewise be able to contact TDD users through the relay system. On the other hand, hotels, hospitals, and other

similar establishments that offer nondisabled individuals the opportunity to make outgoing telephone calls on more than an incidental convenience basis must provide a TDD on request.

Section 36.303(e) requires places of lodging that provide televisions in five or more guest rooms and hospitals to provide, upon request, a means for decoding closed captions for use by an individual with impaired hearing. Hotels should also provide a TDD or similar device at the front desk in order to take calls from guests who use TDD's in their rooms. In this way guests with hearing impairments can avail themselves of such hotel services as making inquiries of the front desk and ordering room service. The term "hospital" is used in its general sense and should be interpreted broadly.

Movie theaters are not required by § 36.303 to present open-captioned films. However, other public accommodations that impart verbal information through soundtracks on films, video tapes, or slide shows are required to make such information accessible to persons with hearing impairments. Captioning is one means to make the information accessible to individuals with disabilities.

The rule specifies that auxiliary aids and services include the acquisition or modification of equipment or devices. For example, tape players used for an audio-guided tour of a museum exhibit may require the addition of Brailled adhesive labels to the buttons on a reasonable number of the tape players to facilitate their use by individuals who are blind. Similarly, a hotel conference center may need to provide permanent or portable assistive listening systems for persons with hearing impairments.

As provided in § 36.303(f), a public accommodation is not required to provide any particular aid or service that would result either in a fundamental alteration in the nature of the goods, services, facilities, privileges, advantages, or accommodations offered or in an undue burden. Both of these statutory limitations are derived from existing regulations and caselaw under section 504 and are to be applied on a case-by-case basis (see, e.g., 28 CFR 39.160(d) and *Southeastern Community College* v. *Davis*, 442 U.S. 397 (1979)). Congress intended that "undue burden" under § 36.303 and "undue hardship," which is used in the employment provisions of title I of the ADA, should be determined on a case-by-case basis under the same standards and in light of the same factors (Judiciary report at 59). The rule, therefore, in accordance with the definition of undue hardship in section 101(10) of the ADA, defines undue burden as "significant difficulty or expense" (see §§ 36.104 and 36.303(a)) and requires that undue burden be determined in light of the factors listed in the definition in 36.104.

Consistent with regulations implementing section 504 in federally conducted programs (see, e.g., 28 CFR 39.160(d)), § 36.303(f) provides that the fact that the provision of a particular auxiliary aid or service would result in an undue burden does not relieve a public accommodation from the duty to furnish an alternative auxiliary aid or service, if available, that would not result in such a burden.

Section 36.303(g) of the proposed rule has been deleted from this section and included in a new § 36.306. That new section continues to make clear that the auxiliary aids requirement does not mandate the provision of individually prescribed devices, such as prescription eyeglasses or hearing aids.

The costs of compliance with the requirements of this section may not be financed by surcharges limited to particular individuals with disabilities or any group of individuals with disabilities (§ 36.301(c)).

Section 36.304   Removal of Barriers

Section 36.304 requires the removal of architectural barriers and communication barriers that are structural in nature in existing facilities, where such removal is readily achievable, i.e., easily accomplishable and able to be carried out without much difficulty or expense. This requirement is based on section 302(b)(2)(A)(iv) of the ADA.

A number of commenters interpreted the phrase "communication barriers that are structural in nature" broadly to encompass the provision of communications devices such as TDD's, telephone handset amplifiers, assistive listening devices, and digital check-out displays. The statute, however, as read by the Department, limits the application of the phrase "communications barriers that are structural in nature" to those barriers that are an integral part of the physical structure of a facility. In addition to the communications barriers posed by permanent signage and alarm systems noted by Congress (see Education and Labor report at 110), the Department would also include among the communications barriers covered by § 36.304 the failure to provide adequate sound buffers, and the presence of physical partitions that hamper the passage of sound waves between employees and customers. Given that § 36.304's proper focus is on the removal

of physical barriers, the Department believes that the obligation to provide communications equipment and devices such as TDD's, telephone handset amplifiers, assistive listening devices, and digital check-out displays is more appropriately determined by the requirements for auxiliary aids and services under § 36.303 (see Education and Labor report at 107–108). The obligation to remove communications barriers that are structural in nature under § 36.304, of course, is independent of any obligation to provide auxiliary aids and services under § 36.303.

The statutory provision also requires the readily achievable removal of certain barriers in existing vehicles and rail passenger cars. This transportation requirement is not included in § 36.304, but rather in § 36.310(b) of the rule.

In striking a balance between guaranteeing access to individuals with disabilities and recognizing the legitimate cost concerns of businesses and other private entities, the ADA establishes different standards for existing facilities and new construction. In existing facilities, where retrofitting may prove costly, a less rigorous degree of accessibility is required than in the case of new construction and alterations (see §§ 36.401–36.406) where accessibility can be more conveniently and economically incorporated in the initial stages of design and construction.

For example, a bank with existing automatic teller machines (ATM's) would have to remove barriers to the use of the ATM's, if it is readily achievable to do so. Whether or not it is necessary to take actions such as ramping a few steps or raising or lowering an ATM would be determined by whether the actions can be accomplished easily and without much difficulty or expense.

On the other hand, a newly constructed bank with ATM's would be required by § 36.401 to have an ATM that is "readily accessible to and usable by" persons with disabilities in accordance with accessibility guidelines incorporated under § 36.406.

The requirement to remove architectural barriers includes the removal of physical barriers of any kind. For example, § 36.304 requires the removal, when readily achievable, of barriers caused by the location of temporary or movable structures, such as furniture, equipment, and display racks. In order to provide access to individuals who use wheelchairs, for example, restaurants may need to rearrange tables and chairs, and department stores may need to reconfigure display racks and shelves.

As stated in § 36.304(f), such actions are not readily achievable to the extent that they would result in a significant loss of selling or serving space. If the widening of all aisles in selling or serving areas is not readily achievable, then selected widening should be undertaken to maximize the amount of merchandise or the number of tables accessible to individuals who use wheelchairs. Access to goods and services provided in any remaining inaccessible areas must be made available through alternative methods to barrier removal, as required by § 36.305.

Because the purpose of title III of the ADA is to ensure that public accommodations are accessible to their customers, clients, or patrons (as opposed to their employees, who are the focus of title I), the obligation to remove barriers under § 36.304 does not extend to areas of a facility that are used exclusively as employee work areas.

Section 36.304(b) provides a wide-ranging list of the types of modest measures that may be taken to remove barriers and that are likely to be readily achievable. The list includes examples of measures, such as adding raised letter markings on elevator control buttons and installing flashing alarm lights, that would be used to remove communications barriers that are structural in nature. It is not an exhaustive list, but merely an illustrative one. Moreover, the inclusion of a measure on this list does not mean that it is readily achievable in all cases. Whether or not any of these measures is readily achievable is to be determined on a case-by-case basis in light of the particular circumstances presented and the factors listed in the definition of readily achievable (§ 36.104).

A public accommodation generally would not be required to remove a barrier to physical access posed by a flight of steps, if removal would require extensive ramping or an elevator. Ramping a single step, however, will likely be readily achievable, and ramping several steps will in many circumstances also be readily achievable. The readily achievable standard does not require barrier removal that requires extensive restructuring or burdensome expense. Thus, where it is not readily achievable to do, the ADA would not require a restaurant to provide access to a restroom reachable only by a flight of stairs.

Like § 36.405, this section permits deference to the national interest in preserving significant historic structures. Barrier removal would not be considered "readily achievable" if it would threaten or destroy the historic significance of a building or facility that is eligible for listing in the National Register of Historic Places under the National Historic Preservation Act (16 U.S.C. 470, *et seq.*), or is designated as historic under State or local law.

The readily achievable defense requires a less demanding level of exertion by a public accommodation than does the undue burden defense to the auxiliary aids requirements of § 36.303. In that sense, it can be characterized as a "lower" standard than the undue burden standard. The readily achievable defense is also less demanding than the undue hardship defense in section 102(b)(5) of the ADA, which limits the obligation to make reasonable accommodation in employment. Barrier removal measures that are not easily accomplishable and are not able to be carried out without much difficulty or expense are not required under the readily achievable standard, even if they do not impose an undue burden or an undue hardship.

Section 36.304(f)(1) of the proposed rule, which stated that "barrier removal is not readily achievable if it would result in significant loss of profit or significant loss of efficiency of operation," has been deleted from the final rule. Many commenters objected to this provision because it impermissibly introduced the notion of profit into a statutory standard that did not include it. Concern was expressed that, in order for an action not to be considered readily achievable, a public accommodation would inappropriately have to show, for example, not only that the action could not be done without "much difficulty or expense", but that a significant loss of profit would result as well. In addition, some commenters asserted use of the word "significant," which is used in the definition of undue hardship under title I (the standard for interpreting the meaning of undue burden as a defense to title III's auxiliary aids requirements) (see §§ 36.104, 36.303(f)), blurs the fact that the readily achievable standard requires a lower level of effort on the part of a public accommodation than does the undue burden standard.

The obligation to engage in readily achievable barrier removal is a continuing one. Over time, barrier removal that initially was not readily achievable may later be required because of changed circumstances. Many commenters expressed support for the Department's position that the obligation to comply with § 36.304 is continuing in nature. Some urged that the rule require public accommodations

to assess their compliance on at least an annual basis in light of changes in resources and other factors that would be relevant to determining what barrier removal measures would be readily achievable.

Although the obligation to engage in readily achievable barrier removal is clearly a continuing duty, the Department has declined to establish any independent requirement for an annual assessment or self-evaluation. It is best left to the public accommodations subject to § 36.304 to establish policies to assess compliance that are appropriate to the particular circumstances faced by the wide range of public accommodations covered by the ADA. However, even in the absence of an explicit regulatory requirement for periodic self-evaluations, the Department still urges public accommodations to establish procedures for an ongoing assessment of their compliance with the ADA's barrier removal requirements. The Department recommends that this process include appropriate consultation with individuals with disabilities or organizations representing them. A serious effort at self-assessment and consultation can diminish the threat of litigation and save resources by identifying the most efficient means of providing required access.

The Department has been asked for guidance on the best means for public accommodations to comply voluntarily with this section. Such information is more appropriately part of the Department's technical assistance effort and will be forthcoming over the next several months. The Department recommends, however, the development of an implementation plan designed to achieve compliance with the ADA's barrier removal requirements before they become effective on January 26, 1992. Such a plan, if appropriately designed and diligently executed, could serve as evidence of a good faith effort to comply with the requirements of § 36.104. In developing an implementation plan for readily achievable barrier removal, a public accommodation should consult with local organizations representing persons with disabilities and solicit their suggestions for cost-effective means of making individual places of public accommodation accessible. Such organizations may also be helpful in allocating scarce resources and establishing priorities. Local associations of businesses may want to encourage this process and serve as the forum for discussions on the local level

between disability rights organizations and local businesses.

Section 36.304(c) recommends priorities for public accommodations in removing barriers in existing facilities. Because the resources available for barrier removal may not be adequate to remove all existing barriers at any given time, § 36.304(c) suggests priorities for determining which types of barriers should be mitigated or eliminated first. The purpose of these priorities is to facilitate long-term business planning and to maximize, in light of limited resources, the degree of effective access that will result from any given level of expenditure.

Although many commenters expressed support for the concept of establishing priorities, a significant number objected to their mandatory nature in the proposed rule. The Department shares the concern of these commenters that mandatory priorities would increase the likelihood of litigation and inappropriately reduce the discretion of public accommodations to determine the most effective mix of barrier removal measures to undertake in particular circumstances. Therefore, in the final rule the priorities are no longer mandatory.

In response to comments that the priorities failed to address communications issues, the Department wishes to emphasize that the priorities encompass the removal of communications barriers that are structural in nature. It would be counter to the ADA's carefully wrought statutory scheme to include in this provision the wide range of communication devices that are required by the ADA's provisions on auxiliary aids and services. The final rule explicitly includes Brailled and raised letter signage and visual alarms among the examples of steps to remove barriers provided in § 36.304(c)(2).

Section 36.304(c)(1) places the highest priority on measures that will enable individuals with disabilities to physically enter a place of public accommodation. This priority on "getting through the door" recognizes that providing actual physical access to a facility from public sidewalks, public transportation, or parking is generally preferable to any alternative arrangements in terms of both business efficiency and the dignity of individuals with disabilities.

The next priority, which is established in § 36.304(c)(2), is for measures that provide access to those areas of a place of public accommodation where goods and services are made available to the public. For example, in a hardware store, to the extent that it is readily achievable to do so, individuals with disabilities should be given access not only to assistance at the front desk, but also access, like that available to other customers, to the retail display areas of the store.

The Department agrees with those commenters who argued that access to the areas where goods and services are provided is generally more important than the provision of restrooms. Therefore, the final rule reverses priorities two and three of the proposed rule in order to give lower priority to accessible restrooms. Consequently, the third priority in the final rule (§ 36.304(c)(3)) is for measures to provide access to restroom facilities and the last priority is placed on any remaining measures required to remove barriers.

Section 36.304(d) requires that measures taken to remove barriers under § 36.304 be subject to subpart D's requirements for alterations (except for the path of travel requirements in § 36.403). It only permits deviations from the subpart D requirements when compliance with those requirements is not readily achievable. In such cases, § 36.304(d) permits measures to be taken that do not fully comply with the subpart D requirements, so long as the measures do not pose a significant risk to the health or safety of individuals with disabilities or others.

This approach represents a change from the proposed rule which stated that "readily achievable" measures taken solely to remove barriers under § 36.304 are exempt from the alterations requirements of subpart D. The intent of the proposed rule was to maximize the flexibility of public accommodations in undertaking barrier removal by allowing deviations from the technical standards of subpart D. It was thought that allowing slight deviations would provide access and release additional resources for expanding the amount of barrier removal that could be obtained under the readily achievable standard.

Many commenters, however, representing both businesses and individuals with disabilities, questioned this approach because of the likelihood that unsafe or ineffective measures would be taken in the absence of the subpart D standards for alterations as a reference point. Some advocated a rule requiring strict compliance with the subpart D standard.

The Department in the final rule has adopted the view of many commenters that (1) public accommodations should in the first instance be required to comply with the subpart D standards for alterations where it is readily achievable to do so and (2) safe, readily achievable measures must be taken when compliance with the subpart D standards is not readily achievable. Reference to the subpart D standards in this manner will promote certainty and good design at the same time that permitting slight deviations will expand the amount of barrier removal that may be achieved under § 36.304.

Because of the inconvenience to individuals with disabilities and the safety problems involved in the use of portable ramps, § 36.304(e) permits the use of a portable ramp to comply with § 36.304(a) only when installation of a permanent ramp is not readily achievable. In order to promote safety, § 36.304(e) requires that due consideration be given to the incorporation of features such as nonslip surfaces, railings, anchoring, and strength of materials in any portable ramp that is used.

Temporary facilities brought in for use at the site of a natural disaster are subject to the barrier removal requirements of § 36.304.

A number of commenters requested clarification regarding how to determine when a public accommodation has discharged its obligation to remove barriers in existing facilities. For example, is a hotel required by § 36.304 to remove barriers in all of its guest rooms? Or is some lesser percentage adequate? A new paragraph (g) has been added to § 36.304 to address this issue. The Department believes that the degree of barrier removal required under § 36.304 may be less, but certainly would not be required to exceed, the standards for alterations under the ADA Accessibility Guidelines incorporated by subpart D of this part (ADAAG). The ADA's requirements for readily achievable barrier removal in existing facilities are intended to be substantially less rigorous than those for new construction and alterations. It, therefore, would be obviously inappropriate to require actions under § 36.304 that would exceed the ADAAG requirements. Hotels, then, in order to satisfy the requirements of § 36.304, would not be required to remove barriers in a higher percentage of rooms than required by ADAAG. If relevant standards for alterations are not provided in ADAAG, then reference should be made to the standards for new construction.

Section 36.305   Alternatives to Barrier Removal

Section 36.305 specifies that where a public accommodation can demonstrate that removal of a barrier is not readily achievable, the public accommodation must make its goods, services, facilities, privileges, advantages, or accommodations available through alternative methods, if such methods are readily achievable. This requirement is based on section 302(b)(2)(A)(v) of the ADA.

For example, if it is not readily achievable for a retail store to raise, lower, or remove shelves or to rearrange display racks to provide accessible aisles, the store must, if readily achievable, provide a clerk or take other alternative measures to retrieve inaccessible merchandise. Similarly, if it is not readily achievable to ramp a long flight of stairs leading to the front door of a restaurant or a pharmacy, the restaurant or the pharmacy must take alternative measures, if readily achievable, such as providing curb service or home delivery. If, within a restaurant, it is not readily achievable to remove physical barriers to a certain section of a restaurant, the restaurant must, where it is readily achievable to do so, offer the same menu in an accessible area of the restaurant.

Where alternative methods are used to provide access, a public accommodation may not charge an individual with a disability for the costs associated with the alternative method (see § 36.301(c)). Further analysis of the issue of charging for alternative measures may be found in the preamble discussion of § 36.301(c).

In some circumstances, because of security considerations, some alternative methods may not be readily achievable. The rule does not require a cashier to leave his or her post to retrieve items for individuals with disabilities, if there are no other employees on duty.

Section 36.305(c) of the proposed rule has been deleted and the requirements have been included in a new § 36.306. That section makes clear that the alternative methods requirement does not mandate the provision of personal devices, such as wheelchairs, or services of a personal nature.

In the final rule, § 36.305(c) provides specific requirements regarding alternatives to barrier removal in multiscreen cinemas. In some situations, it may not be readily achievable to remove enough barriers to provide access to all of the theaters of a multiscreen cinema. If that is the case, § 36.305(c) requires the cinema to establish a film rotation schedule that provides reasonable access for individuals who use wheelchairs to films being presented by the cinema. It further requires that reasonable notice be provided to the public as to the location and time of accessible showings. Methods for providing notice include appropriate use of the international accessibility symbol in a cinema's print advertising and the addition of accessibility information to a cinema's recorded telephone information line.

Section 36.306 Personal Devices and Services

The final rule includes a new § 36.306, entitled "Personal devices and services." Section 36.306 of the proposed rule, "Readily achievable and undue burden: Factors to be considered," was deleted for the reasons described in the preamble discussion of the definition of the term "readily achievable" in § 36.104. In place of §§ 36.303(g) and 36.305(c) of the proposed rule, which addressed the issue of personal devices and services in the contexts of auxiliary aids and alternatives to barrier removal, § 36.306 provides a general statement that the regulation does not require the provision of personal devices and services. This section states that a public accommodation is not required to provide its customers, clients, or participants with personal devices, such as wheelchairs; individually prescribed devices, such as prescription eyeglasses or hearing aids; or services of a personal nature including assistance in eating, toileting, or dressing.

This statement serves as a limitation on all the requirements of the regulation. The personal devices and services limitation was intended to have general application in the proposed rule in all contexts where it was relevant. The final rule, therefore, clarifies this point by including a general provision that will explicitly apply not just to auxiliary aids and services and alternatives to barrier removal, but across-the-board to include such relevant areas as modifications in policies, practices, and procedures (§ 36.302) and examinations and courses (§ 36.309), as well.

The Department wishes to clarify that measures taken as alternatives to barrier removal, such as retrieving items from shelves or providing curb service or home delivery, are not to be considered personal services. Similarly, minimal actions that may be required as modifications in policies, practices, or procedures under § 36.302, such as a waiter's removing the cover from a customer's straw, a kitchen's cutting up food into smaller pieces, or a bank's filling out a deposit slip, are not services of a personal nature within the meaning of § 36.306. (Of course, such modifications may be required under § 36.302 only if they are "reasonable.") Similarly, this section does not preclude

the short-term loan of personal receivers that are part of an assistive listening system.

Of course, if personal services are customarily provided to the customers or clients of a public accommodation, e.g., in a hospital or senior citizen center, then these personal services should also be provided to persons with disabilities using the public accommodation.

Section 36.307 Accessible or Special Goods.

Section 36.307 establishes that the rule does not require a public accommodation to alter its inventory to include accessible or special goods with accessibility features that are designed for, or facilitate use by, individuals with disabilities. As specified in § 36.307(c), accessible or special goods include such items as Brailled versions of books, books on audio-cassettes, closed captioned video tapes, special sizes or lines of clothing, and special foods to meet particular dietary needs.

The purpose of the ADA's public accommodations requirements is to ensure accessibility to the goods offered by a public accommodation, not to alter the nature or mix of goods that the public accommodation has typically provided. In other words, a bookstore, for example, must make its facilities and sales operations accessible to individuals with disabilities, but is not required to stock Brailled or large print books. Similarly, a video store must make its facilities and rental operations accessible, but is not required to stock closed-captioned video tapes. The Department has been made aware, however, that the most recent titles in video-tape rental establishments are, in fact, closed captioned.

Although a public accommodation is not required by § 36.307(a) to modify its inventory, it is required by § 36.307(b), at the request of an individual with disabilities, to order accessible or special goods that it does not customarily maintain in stock if, in the normal course of its operation, it makes special orders for unstocked goods, and if the accessible or special goods can be obtained from a supplier with whom the public accommodation customarily does business. For example, a clothing store would be required to order specially-sized clothing at the request of an individual with a disability, if it customarily makes special orders for clothing that it does not keep in stock, and if the clothing can be obtained from one of the store's customary suppliers.

One commenter asserted that the proposed rule could be interpreted to require a store to special order

accessible or special goods of all types, even if only one type is specially ordered in the normal course of its business. The Department, however, intends for § 36.307(b) to require special orders only of those particular types of goods for which a public accommodation normally makes special orders. For example, a book and recording store would not have to specially order Brailled books if, in the normal course of its business, it only specially orders recordings and not books.

Section 36.308 Seating in Assembly Areas.

Section 36.308 establishes specific requirements for removing barriers to physical access in assembly areas, which include such facilities as theaters, concert halls, auditoriums, lecture halls, and conference rooms. This section does not address the provision of auxiliary aids or the removal of communications barriers that are structural in nature. These communications requirements are the focus of other provisions of the regulation (see §§ 36.303–36.304).

Individuals who use wheelchairs historically have been relegated to inferior seating in the back of assembly areas separate from accompanying family members and friends. The provisions of § 36.308 are intended to promote integration and equality in seating.

In some instances it may not be readily achievable for auditoriums or theaters to remove seats to allow individuals with wheelchairs to sit next to accompanying family members or friends. In these situations, the final rule retains the requirement that the public accommodation provide portable chairs or other means to allow the accompanying individuals to sit with the persons in wheelchairs. Persons in wheelchairs should have the same opportunity to enjoy movies, plays, and similar events with their families and friends, just as other patrons do. The final rule specifies that portable chairs or other means to permit family members or companions to sit with individuals who use wheelchairs must be provided only when it is readily achievable to do so.

In order to facilitate seating of wheelchair users who wish to transfer to existing seating, paragraph (a)(1) of the final rule adds a requirement that, to the extent readily achievable, a reasonable number of seats with removable aisle-side armrests must be provided. Many persons in wheelchairs are able to transfer to existing seating with this relatively minor modification. This solution avoids the potential safety hazard created by the use of portable chairs and fosters integration. The final ADA Accessibility Guidelines incorporated by subpart D (ADAAG) also add a requirement regarding aisle seating that was not in the proposed guidelines. In situations when a person in a wheelchair transfers to existing seating, the public accommodation shall provide assistance in handling the wheelchair of the patron with the disability.

Likewise, consistent with ADAAG, the final rule adds in § 36.308(a)(1)(ii)(B) a requirement that, to the extent readily achievable, wheelchair seating provide lines of sight and choice of admission prices comparable to those for members of the general public.

Finally, because Congress intended that the requirements for barrier removal in existing facilities be substantially less rigorous than those required for new construction and alterations, the final rule clarifies in § 36.308(a)(3) that in no event can the requirements for existing facilities be interpreted to exceed the standards for alterations under ADAAG. For example, § 4.33 of ADAAG only requires wheelchair spaces to be provided in more than one location when the seating capacity of the assembly area exceeds 300. Therefore, paragraph (a) of § 36.308 may not be interpreted to require readily achievable dispersal of wheelchair seating in assembly areas with 300 or fewer seats. Similarly, § 4.1.3(19) of ADAAG requires six accessible wheelchair locations in an assembly area with 301 to 500 seats. The reasonable number of wheelchair locations required by paragraph (a), therefore, may be less than six, but may not be interpreted to exceed six.

Proposed Section 36.309 Purchase of Furniture and Equipment

Section 36.309 of the proposed rule would have required that newly purchased furniture or equipment made available for use at a place of public accommodation be accessible, to the extent such furniture or equipment is available, unless this requirement would fundamentally alter the goods, services, facilities, privileges, advantages, or accommodations offered, or would not be readily achievable. Proposed § 36.309 has been omitted from the final rule because the Department has determined that its requirements are more properly addressed under other sections, and because there are currently no appropriate accessibility standards addressing many types of furniture and equipment.

Some types of equipment will be required to meet the accessibility requirements of subpart D. For example, ADAAG establishes technical and scoping requirements in new construction and alterations for automated teller machines and telephones. Purchase or modification of equipment is required in certain instances by the provisions in §§ 36.201 and 36.202. For example, an arcade may need to provide accessible video machines in order to ensure full and equal enjoyment of the facilities and to provide an opportunity to participate in the services and facilities it provides. The barrier removal requirements of § 36.304 will apply as well to furniture and equipment (lowering shelves, rearranging furniture, adding Braille labels to a vending machine).

Section 36.309 Examinations and Courses

Section 36.309(a) sets forth the general rule that any private entity that offers examinations or courses related to applications, licensing, certification, or credentialing for secondary or postsecondary education, professional, or trade purposes shall offer such examinations or courses in a place and manner accessible to persons with disabilities or offer alternative accessible arrangements for such individuals.

Paragraph (a) restates section 309 of the Americans with Disabilities Act. Section 309 is intended to fill the gap that is created when licensing, certification, and other testing authorities are not covered by section 504 of the Rehabilitation Act or title II of the ADA. Any such authority that is covered by section 504, because of the receipt of Federal money, or by title II, because it is a function of a State or local government, must make all of its programs accessible to persons with disabilities, which includes physical access as well as modifications in the way the test is administered, e.g., extended time, written instructions, or assistance of a reader.

Many licensing, certification, and testing authorities are not covered by section 504, because no Federal money is received; nor are they covered by title II of the ADA because they are not State or local agencies. However, States often require the licenses provided by such authorities in order for an individual to practice a particular profession or trade. Thus, the provision was included in the ADA in order to assure that persons with disabilities are not foreclosed from educational, professional, or trade opportunities because an examination or course is conducted in an

inaccessible site or without needed modifications.

As indicated in the "Application" section of this part (§ 36.102), § 36.309 applies to any private entity that offers the specified types of examinations or courses. This is consistent with section 309 of the Americans with Disabilities Act, which states that the requirements apply to "any person" offering examinations or courses.

The Department received a large number of comments on this section, reflecting the importance of ensuring that the key gateways to education and employment are open to individuals with disabilities. The most frequent comments were objections to the fundamental alteration and undue burden provisions in §§ 36.309 (b)(3) and (c)(3) and to allowing courses and examinations to be provided through alternative accessible arrangements, rather than in an integrated setting.

Although section 309 of the Act does not refer to a fundamental alteration or undue burden limitation, those limitations do appear in section 302(b)(2)(A)(iii) of the Act, which establishes the obligation of public accommodations to provide auxiliary aids and services. The Department, therefore, included it in the paragraphs of § 36.309 requiring the provision of auxiliary aids. One commenter argued that similar limitations should apply to all of the requirements of § 36.309, but the Department did not consider this extension appropriate.

Commenters who objected to permitting "alternative accessible arrangements" argued that such arrangements allow segregation and should not be permitted, unless they are the least restrictive available alternative, for example, for someone who cannot leave home. Some commenters made a distinction between courses, where interaction is an important part of the educational experience, and examinations, where it may be less important. Because the statute specifically authorizes alternative accessible arrangements as a method of meeting the requirements of section 309, the Department has not adopted this suggestion. The Department notes, however, that, while examinations of the type covered by § 36.309 may not be covered elsewhere in the regulation, courses will generally be offered in a "place of education," which is included in the definition of "place of public accommodation" in § 36.104, and, therefore, will be subject to the integrated setting requirement of § 36.203.

Section 36.309(b) sets forth specific requirements for examinations. Examinations covered by this section would include a bar exam or the Scholastic Aptitude Test prepared by the Educational Testing Service. Paragraph (b)(1) is adopted from the Department of Education's section 504 regulation on admission tests to postsecondary educational programs (34 CFR 104.42(b)(3)). Paragraph (b)(1)(i) requires that a private entity offering an examination covered by the section must assure that the examination is selected and administered so as to best ensure that the examination accurately reflects an individual's aptitude or achievement level or other factor the examination purports to measure, rather than reflecting the individual's impaired sensory, manual, or speaking skills (except where those skills are the factors that the examination purports to measure).

Paragraph (b)(1)(ii) requires that any examination specially designed for individuals with disabilities be offered as often and in as timely a manner as other examinations. Some commenters noted that persons with disabilities may be required to travel long distances when the locations for examinations for individuals with disabilities are limited, for example, to only one city in a State instead of a variety of cities. The Department has therefore revised this paragraph to add a requirement that such examinations be offered at locations that are as convenient as the location of other examinations.

Commenters representing organizations that administer tests wanted to be able to require individuals with disabilities to provide advance notice and appropriate documentation, at the applicants' expense, of their disabilities and of any modifications or aids that would be required. The Department agrees that such requirements are permissible, provided that they are not unreasonable and that the deadline for such notice is no earlier than the deadline for others applying to take the examination. Requiring individuals with disabilities to file earlier applications would violate the requirement that examinations designed for individuals with disabilities be offered in as timely a manner as other examinations.

Examiners may require evidence that an applicant is entitled to modifications or aids as required by this section, but requests for documentation must be reasonable and must be limited to the need for the modification or aid requested. Appropriate documentation might include a letter from a physician

or other professional, or evidence of a prior diagnosis or accommodation, such as eligibility for a special education program. The applicant may be required to bear the cost of providing such documentation, but the entity administering the examination cannot charge the applicant for the cost of any modifications or auxiliary aids, such as interpreters, provided for the examination.

Paragraph (b)(1)(iii) requires that examinations be administered in facilities that are accessible to individuals with disabilities or alternative accessible arrangements are made.

Paragraph (b)(2) gives examples of modifications to examinations that may be necessary in order to comply with this section. These may include providing more time for completion of the examination or a change in the manner of giving the examination, e.g., reading the examination to the individual.

Paragraph (b)(3) requires the provision of auxiliary aids and services, unless the private entity offering the examination can demonstrate that offering a particular auxiliary aid would fundamentally alter the examination or result in an undue burden. Examples of auxiliary aids include taped examinations, interpreters or other effective methods of making aurally delivered materials available to individuals with hearing impairments, readers for individuals with visual impairments or learning disabilities, and other similar services and actions. The suggestion that individuals with learning disabilities may need readers is included, although it does not appear in the Department of Education regulation, because, in fact, some individuals with learning disabilities have visual perception problems and would benefit from a reader.

Many commenters pointed out the importance of ensuring that modifications provide the individual with a disability an equal opportunity to demonstrate his or her knowledge or ability. For example, a reader who is unskilled or lacks knowledge of specific terminology used in the examination may be unable to convey the information in the questions or to follow the applicant's instructions effectively. Commenters pointed out that, for persons with visual impairments who read Braille, Braille provides the closest functional equivalent to a printed test. The Department has, therefore, added Brailled examinations to the examples of auxiliary aids and services that may be required. For similar reasons, the

Department also added to the list of examples of auxiliary aids and services large print examinations and answer sheets; "qualified" readers; and transcribers to write answers

A commenter suggested that the phrase "fundamentally alter the examination" in this paragraph of the proposed rule be revised to more accurately reflect the function affected. In the final rule the Department has substituted the phrase "fundamentally alter the measurement of the skills or knowledge the examination is intended to test."

Paragraph (b)(4) gives examples of alternative accessible arrangements. For instance, the private entity might be required to provide the examination at an individual's home with a proctor. Alternative arrangements must provide conditions for individuals with disabilities that are comparable to the conditions under which other individuals take the examinations. In other words, an examination cannot be offered to an individual with a disability in a cold, poorly lit basement, if other individuals are given the examination in a warm, well lit classroom.

Some commenters who provide examinations for licensing or certification for particular occupations or professions urged that they be permitted to refuse to provide modifications or aids for persons seeking to take the examinations if those individuals, because of their disabilities, would be unable to perform the essential functions of the profession or occupation for which the examination is given, or unless the disability is reasonably determined in advance as not being an obstacle to certification. The Department has not changed its rule based on this comment. An examination is one stage of a licensing or certification process. An individual should not be barred from attempting to pass that stage of the process merely because he or she might be unable to meet other requirements of the process. If the examination is not the first stage of the qualification process, an applicant may be required to complete the earlier stages prior to being admitted to the examination. On the other hand, the applicant may not be denied admission to the examination on the basis of doubts about his or her abilities to meet requirements that the examination is not designed to test.

Paragraph (c) sets forth specific requirements for courses. Paragraph (c)(1) contains the general rule that any course covered by this section must be modified to ensure that the place and manner in which the course is given is accessible. Paragraph (c)(2) gives examples of possible modifications that might be required, including extending the time permitted for completion of the course, permitting oral rather than written delivery of an assignment by a person with a visual impairment, or adapting the manner in which the course is conducted (i.e., providing cassettes of class handouts to an individual with a visual impairment). In response to comments, the Department has added to the examples in paragraph (c)(2) specific reference to distribution of course materials. If course materials are published and available from other sources, the entity offering the course may give advance notice of what materials will be used so as to allow an individual to obtain them in Braille or on tape but materials provided by the course offerer must be made available in alternative formats for individuals with disabilities.

In language similar to that of paragraph (b), paragraph (c)(3) requires auxiliary aids and services, unless a fundamental alteration or undue burden would result, and paragraph (c)(4) requires that courses be administered in accessible facilities. Paragraph (c)(5) gives examples of alternative accessible arrangements. These may include provision of the course through videotape, cassettes, or prepared notes. Alternative arrangements must provide comparable conditions to those provided to others, including similar lighting, room temperature, and the like. An entity offering a variety of courses, to fulfill continuing education requirements for a profession, for example, may not limit the selection or choice of courses available to individuals with disabilities.

Section 36.310   Transportation Provided by Public Accommodations

Section 36.310 contains specific provisions relating to public accommodations that provide transportation to their clients or customers. This section has been substantially revised in order to coordinate the requirements of this section with the requirements applicable to these transportation systems that will be contained in the regulations issued by the Secretary of Transportation pursuant to section 306 of the ADA, to be codified at 49 CFR part 37. The Department notes that, although the responsibility for issuing regulations applicable to transportation systems operated by public accommodations is divided between this Department and the Department of -Transportation, enforcement authority is assigned only to the Department of Justice.

The Department received relatively few comments on this section of the proposed rule. Most of the comments addressed issues that are not specifically addressed in this part, such as the standards for accessible vehicles and the procedure for determining whether equivalent service is provided. Those standards will be contained in the regulation issued by the Department of Transportation. Other commenters raised questions about the types of transportation that will be subject to this section. In response to these inquiries, the Department has revised the list of examples contained in the regulation.

Paragraph (a)(1) states the general rule that covered public accommodations are subject to all of the specific provisions of subparts B, C, and D, except as provided in § 36.310. Examples of operations covered by the requirements are listed in paragraph (a)(2). The stated examples include hotel and motel airport shuttle services, customer shuttle bus services operated by private companies and shopping centers, student transportation, and shuttle operations of recreational facilities such as stadiums, zoos, amusement parks, and ski resorts. This brief list is not exhaustive. The section applies to any fixed route or demand responsive transportation system operated by a public accommodation for the benefit of its clients or customers. The section does not apply to transportation services provided only to employees. Employee transportation will be subject to the regulations issued by the Equal Employment Opportunity Commission to implement title I of the Act. However, if employees and customers or clients are served by the same transportation system, the provisions of this section will apply.

Paragraph (b) specifically provides that a public accommodation shall remove transportation barriers in existing vehicles to the extent that it is readily achievable to do so, but that the installation of hydraulic or other lifts is not required.

Paragraph (c) provides that public accommodations subject to this section shall comply with the requirements for transportation vehicles and systems contained in the regulations issued by the Secretary of Transportation.

Subpart D—New Construction and Alterations

Subpart D implements section 303 of the Act, which requires that newly constructed or altered places of public accommodation or commercial facilities be readily accessible to and usable by individuals with disabilities. This

requirement contemplates a high degree of convenient access. It is intended to ensure that patrons and employees of places of public accommodation and employees of commercial facilities are able to get to, enter, and use the facility.

Potential patrons of places of public accommodation, such as retail establishments, should be able to get to a store, get into the store, and get to the areas where goods are being provided. Employees should have the same types of access, although those individuals require access to and around the employment area as well as to the area in which goods and services are provided.

The ADA is geared to the future—its goal being that, over time, access will be the rule, rather than the exception. Thus, the Act only requires modest expenditures, of the type addressed in § 36.304 of this part, to provide access to existing facilities not otherwise being altered, but requires all new construction and alterations to be accessible.

The Act does not require new construction or alterations; it simply requires that, when a public accommodation or other private entity undertakes the construction or alteration of a facility subject to the Act, the newly constructed or altered facility must be made accessible. This subpart establishes the requirements for new construction and alterations.

As explained under the discussion of the definition of "facility," § 36.104, pending development of specific requirements, the Department will not apply this subpart to places of public accommodation located in mobile units, boats, or other conveyances.

Section 36.401   New Construction

General

Section 36.401 implements the new construction requirements of the ADA. Section 303 (a)(1) of the Act provides that discrimination for purposes of section 302(a) of the Act includes a failure to design and construct facilities for first occupancy later than 30 months after the date of enactment (i.e., after January 26, 1993) that are readily accessible to and usable by individuals with disabilities.

Paragraph 36.401(a)(1) restates the general requirement for accessible new construction. The proposed rule stated that "any public accommodation or other private entity responsible for design and construction" must ensure that facilities conform to this requirement. Various commenters suggested that the proposed language was not consistent with the statute because it substituted "private entity responsible for design and construction" for the statutory language; because it did not address liability on the part of architects, contractors, developers, tenants, owners, and other entities; and because it limited the liability of entities responsible for commercial facilities. In response, the Department has revised this paragraph to repeat the language of section 303(a) of the ADA. The Department will interpret this section in a manner consistent with the intent of the statute and with the nature of the responsibilities of the various entities for design, for construction, or for both.

Designed and Constructed for First Occupancy

According to paragraph (a)(2), a facility is subject to the new construction requirements only if a completed application for a building permit or permit extension is filed after January 26, 1992, and the facility is occupied after January 26, 1993.

The proposed rule set forth for comment two alternative ways by which to determine what facilities are subject to the Act and what standards apply. Paragraph (a)(2) of the final rule is a slight variation on Option One in the proposed rule. The reasons for the Department's choice of Option One are discussed later in this section.

Paragraph (a)(2) acknowledges that Congress did not contemplate having actual occupancy be the sole trigger for the accessibility requirements, because the statute prohibits a failure to "design and construct for first occupancy," rather than requiring accessibility in facilities actually occupied after a particular date.

The commenters overwhelmingly agreed with the Department's proposal to use a date certain; many cited the reasons given in the preamble to the proposed rule. First, it is helpful for designers and builders to have a fixed date for accessible design, so that they can determine accessibility requirements early in the planning and design stage. It is difficult to determine accessibility requirements in anticipation of the actual date of first occupancy because of unpredictable and uncontrollable events (e.g., strikes affecting suppliers or labor, or natural disasters) that may delay occupancy. To redesign or reconstruct portions of a facility if it begins to appear that occupancy will be later than anticipated would be quite costly. A fixed date also assists those responsible for enforcing, or monitoring compliance with, the statute, and those protected by it.

The Department considered using as a trigger date for application of the accessibility standards the date on which a permit is granted. The Department chose instead the date on which a complete permit application is certified as received by the appropriate government entity. Almost all commenters agreed with this choice of a trigger date. This decision is based partly on information that several months or even years can pass between application for a permit and receipt of a permit. Design is virtually complete at the time an application is complete (i.e., certified to contain all the information required by the State, county, or local government). After an application is filed, delays may occur before the permit is granted due to numerous factors (not necessarily relating to accessibility): for example, hazardous waste discovered on the property, flood plain requirements, zoning disputes, or opposition to the project from various groups. These factors should not require redesign for accessibility if the application was completed before January 26, 1992. However, if the facility must be redesigned for other reasons, such as a change in density or environmental preservation, and the final permit is based on a new application, the rule would require accessibility if that application was certified complete after January 26, 1992.

The certification of receipt of a complete application for a building permit is an appropriate point in the process because certifications are issued in writing by governmental authorities. In addition, this approach presents a clear and objective standard. However, a few commenters pointed out that in some jurisdictions it is not possible to receive a "certification" that an application is complete, and suggested that in those cases the fixed date should be the date on which an application for a permit is received by the government agency. The Department has included such a provision in § 36.401(a)(2)(i).

The date of January 26, 1992, is relevant only with respect to the last application for a permit or permit extension for a facility. Thus, if an entity has applied for only a "foundation" permit, the date of that permit application has no effect, because the entity must also apply for and receive a permit at a later date for the actual superstructure. In this case, it is the date of the later application that would control, unless construction is not completed within the time allowed by the permit, in which case a third permit would be issued and the date of the

application for that permit would be determinative for purposes of the rule.

Choice of Option One for Defining "Designed and Constructed for First Occupancy"

Under the option the Department has chosen for determining applicability of the new construction standards, a building would be considered to be "for first occupancy" after January 26, 1993, only (1) if the last application for a building permit or permit extension for the facility is certified to be complete (or, in some jurisdictions, received) by a State, county, or local government after January 26, 1992, and (2) if the first certificate of occupancy is issued after January 26, 1993. The Department also asked for comment on an Option Two, which would have imposed new construction requirements if a completed application for a building permit or permit extension was filed after the enactment of the ADA (July 26, 1990), and the facility was occupied after January 26, 1993.

The request for comment on this issue ‎ ew a large number of comments expressing a wide range of views. Most business groups and some disability rights groups favored Option One, and some business groups and most disability rights groups favored Option Two. Individuals and government entities were equally divided; several commenters proposed other options.

Those favoring Option One pointed out that it is more reasonable in that it allows time for those subject to the new construction requirements to anticipate those requirements and to receive technical assistance pursuant to the Act. Numerous commenters said that time frames for designing and constructing some types of facilities (for example, health care facilities) can range from two to four years or more. They expressed concerns that Option Two, which would apply to some facilities already under design or construction as of the date the Act was signed, and to some on which construction began shortly after enactment, could result in costly redesign or reconstruction of those facilities. Option One supporters found Option Two objectionable on due process grounds. In their view, Option Two would mean that in July 1991 (upon issuance of the final DOJ rule) the responsible entities would learn that ADA standards had been in effect since July 26, 1990, and this would amount to retroactive application of standards. Numerous commenters characterized Option Two as having no support in the statute and Option One as being more consistent with congressional intent.

Those who favored Option Two pointed out that it would include more facilities within the coverage of the new construction standards. They argued that because similar accessibility requirements are in effect under State laws, no hardship would be imposed by this option. Numerous commenters said that hardship would also be eliminated in light of their view that the ADA requires compliance with the Uniform Federal Accessibility Standards (UFAS) until issuance of DOJ standards. Those supporting Option Two claimed that it was more consistent with the statute and its legislative history.

The Department has chosen Option One rather than Option Two, primarily on the basis of the language of three relevant sections of the statute. First, section 303(a) requires compliance with accessibility standards set forth, or incorporated by reference in, regulations to be issued by the Department of Justice. Standing alone, this section cannot be read to require compliance with the Department's standards before those standards are issued (through th' rulemaking). Second, according to section 310 of the statute, section 303 becomes effective on January 26, 1992. Thus, section 303 cannot impose requirements on the design of buildings before that date. Third, while section 306(d) of the Act requires compliance with UFAS if final regulations have not been issued, that provision cannot reasonably be read to take effect until July 26, 1991, the date by which the Department must issue final regulations under title III.

Option Two was based on the premise that the interim standards in section 306(d) take effect as of the ADA's enactment (July 26, 1990), rather than on the date by which the Department of Justice regulations are due to be issued (July 26, 1991). The initial clause of section 306(d)(1) itself is silent on this question:

If final regulations have not been issued pursuant to this section, for new construction for which a * * * building permit is obtained prior to the issuance of final regulations * * * (interim standards apply).

The approach in Option Two relies partly on the language of section 310 of the Act, which provides that section 306, the interim standards provision, takes effect on the date of enactment. Under this interpretation the interim standards provision would prevail over the operative provision, section 303, which requires that new construction be accessible and which becomes effective January 26, 1992. This approach would also require construing the language of section 306(d)(1) to take effect before the Department's standards are due to be issued. The preferred reading of section 306 is that it would require that, if the Department's final standards had not been issued by July 26, 1991, UFAS would apply to certain buildings until such time as the Department's standards were issued.

General Substantive Requirements of the New Construction Provisions

The rule requires, as does the statute, that covered newly constructed facilities be readily accessible to and usable by individuals with disabilities. The phrase "readily accessible to and usable by individuals with disabilities" is a term that, in slightly varied formulations, has been used in the Architectural Barriers Act of 1968, the Fair Housing Act, the regulations implementing section 504 of the Rehabilitation Act of 1973, and current accessibility standards. It means, with respect to a facility or a portion of a facility, that it can be approached, entered, and used by individuals with disabilities (including mobility, sensory, and cognitive impairments) easily and conveniently. A facility that is constructed to meet the requirements of the rule's accessibility standards will be considered readily accessible and usable with respect to construction. To the extent that a particular type or element of a facility is not specifically addressed by the standards, the language of this section is the safest guide.

A private entity that renders an "accessible" building inaccessible in its operation, through policies or practices, may be in violation of section 302 of the Act. For example, a private entity can render an entrance to a facility inaccessible by keeping an accessible entrance open only during certain hours (whereas the facility is available to others for a greater length of time). A facility could similarly be rendered inaccessible if a person with disabilities is significantly limited in her or his choice of a range of accommodations.

Ensuring access to a newly constructed facility will include providing access to the facility from the street or parking lot, to the extent the responsible entity has control over the route from those locations. In some cases, the private entity will have no control over access at the point where streets, curbs, or sidewalks already exist, and in those instances the entity is encouraged to request modifications to a sidewalk, including installation of curb cuts, from a public entity responsible for them. However, as some commenters pointed out, there is no obligation for a private entity subject to title III of the ADA to seek or ensure compliance by a public entity with title II. Thus, although a locality may have an obligation under title II of the Act to install curb cuts at a particular location, that responsibility is separate from the private entity's title III obligation, and any involvement by a private entity in seeking cooperation from a public entity is purely voluntary in this context.

Work Areas

Proposed paragraph 36.401(b) addressed access to employment areas, rather than to the areas where goods or services are being provided. The preamble noted that the proposed paragraph provided guidance for new construction and alterations until more specific guidance was issued by the ATBCB and reflected in this Department's regulation. The entire paragraph has been deleted from this section in the final rule. The concepts of paragraphs (b) (1), (2), and (5) of the proposed rule are included, with modifications and expansion, in ADAAG. Paragraphs (3) and (4) of the proposed rule, concerning fixtures and equipment, are not included in the rule or in ADAAG.

Some commenters asserted that questions relating to new construction and alterations of work areas should be addressed by the EEOC under title I, as employment concerns. However, the legislative history of the statute clearly indicates that the new construction and alterations requirements of title III were intended to ensure accessibility of new facilities to all individuals, including employees. The language of section 303 sweeps broadly in its application to all public accommodations and commercial facilities. EEOC's title I regulations will address accessibility requirements that come into play when "reasonable accommodation" to individual employees or applicants with disabilities is mandated under title I.

The issues dealt with in proposed § 36.401(b) (1) and (2) are now addressed in ADAAG section 4.1.1(3). The Department's proposed paragraphs would have required that areas that will be used only by employees as work stations be constructed so that individuals with disabilities could approach, enter, and exit the areas. They would not have required that all individual work stations be constructed or equipped (for example, with shelves that are accessible or adaptable) to be accessible. This approach was based on the theory that, as long as an employee with disabilities could enter the building and get to and around the employment area, modifications in a particular work station could be instituted as a "reasonable accommodation" to that employee if the modifications were necessary and they did not constitute an undue hardship.

Almost all of the commenters agreed with the proposal to require access to a work area but not to require accessibility of each individual work station. This principle is included in ADAAG 4.1.1(3). Several of the comments related to the requirements of the proposed ADAAG and have been addressed in the accessibility standards.

Proposed paragraphs (b) (3) and (4) would have required that consideration be given to placing fixtures and equipment at accessible heights in the first instance, and to purchasing new equipment and fixtures that are adjustable. These paragraphs have not been included in the final rule because the rule in most instances does not establish accessibility standards for purchased equipment. (See discussion elsewhere in the preamble of proposed § 36.309.) While the Department encourages entities to consider providing accessible or adjustable fixtures and equipment for employees, this rule does not require them to do so.

Paragraph (b)(5) of proposed § 36.401 clarified that proposed paragraph (b) did not limit the requirement that employee areas other than individual work stations must be accessible. For example, areas that are employee "common use" areas and are not solely used as work stations (e.g., employee lounges, cafeterias, health units, exercise facilities) are treated no differently under this regulation than other parts of a building; they must be constructed or altered in compliance with the accessibility standards. This principle is not stated in § 36.401 but is implicit in the requirements of this section and ADAAG.

Commercial Facilities in Private Residences

Section 36.401(b) of the final rule is a new provision relating to commercial facilities located in private residences. The proposed rule addressed these requirements in the preamble to § 36.207, "Places of public accommodation located in private residences." The preamble stated that the approach for commercial facilities would be the same as that for places of public accommodation, i.e., those portions used exclusively as a commercial facility or used as both a commercial facility and for residential purposes would be covered. Because commercial facilities are only subject to new construction and alterations

requirements, however, the covered portions would only be subject to subpart D. This approach is reflected in § 36.401(b)(1).

The Department is aware that the statutory definition of "commercial facility" excludes private residences because they are "expressly exempted from coverage under the Fair Housing Act of 1968, as amended." However, the Department interprets that exemption as applying only to facilities that are exclusively residential. When a facility is used as both a residence and a commercial facility, the exemption does not apply.

Paragraph (b)(2) is similar to the new paragraph (b) under § 36.207, "Places of public accommodation located in private residences." The paragraph clarifies that the covered portion includes not only the space used as a commercial facility, but also the elements used to enter the commercial facility, e.g., the homeowner's front sidewalk, if any; the doorway; the hallways; the restroom, if used by employees or visitors of the commercial facility; and any other portion of the residence, interior or exterior, used by employees or visitors of the commercial facility.

As in the case of public accommodations located in private residences, the new construction standards only apply to the extent that a portion of the residence is designed or intended for use as a commercial facility. Likewise, if a homeowner alters a portion of his home to convert it to a commercial facility, that work must be done in compliance with the alterations standards in appendix A.

Structural Impracticability

Proposed § 36.401(c) is included in the final rule with minor changes. It details a statutory exception to the new construction requirement: the requirement that new construction be accessible does not apply where an entity can demonstrate that it is structurally impracticable to meet the requirements of the regulation. This provision is also included in ADAAG, at section 4.1.1(5)(a).

Consistent with the legislative history of the ADA, this narrow exception will apply only in rare and unusual circumstances where unique characteristics of terrain make accessibility unusually difficult. Such limitations for topographical problems are analogous to an acknowledged limitation in the application of the accessibility requirements of the Fair Housing Amendments Act (FHAA) of 1988.

Almost all commenters supported this interpretation. Two commenters argued that the DOJ requirement is too limiting and would not exempt some buildings that should be exempted because of soil conditions, terrain, and other unusual site conditions. These commenters suggested consistency with HUD's Fair Housing Accessibility Guidelines (5u FR 9472 (1991)), which generally would allow exceptions from accessibility requirements, or allow compliance with less stringent requirements, on sites with slopes exceeding 10%.

The Department is aware of the provisions in HUD's guidelines, which were issued on March 6, 1991, after passage of the ADA and publication of the Department's proposed rule. The approach taken in these guidelines, which apply to different types of construction and implement different statutory requirements for new construction, does not bind this Department in regulating under the ADA. The Department has included in the final rule the substance of the proposed provision, which is faithful to the intent of the statute, as expressed in the legislative history. (See Senate report at 70–71; Education and Labor report at 120.)

The limited structural impracticability exception means that it is acceptable to deviate from accessibility requirements only where unique characteristics of terrain prevent the incorporation of accessibility features and where providing accessibility would destroy the physical integrity of a facility. A situation in which a building must be built on stilts because of its location in marshlands or over water is an example of one of the few situations in which the exception for structural impracticability would apply.

This exception to accessibility requirements should not be applied to situations in which a facility is located in "hilly" terrain or on a plot of land upon which there are steep grades. In such circumstances, accessibility can be achieved without destroying the physical integrity of a structure, and is required in the construction of new facilities.

Some commenters asked for clarification concerning when and how to apply the ADA rules or the Fair Housing Accessibility Guidelines, especially when a facility may be subject to both because of mixed use. Guidance on this question is provided in the discussion of the definitions of place of public accommodation and commercial facility. With respect to the structural impracticability exception, a mixed-use facility could not take advantage of the Fair Housing exemption, to the extent that it is less stringent than the ADA exemption, except for those portions of the facility that are subject only to the Fair Housing Act.

As explained in the preamble to the proposed rule, in those rare circumstances in which it is structurally impracticable to achieve full compliance with accessibility retirements under the ADA, places of public accommodation and commercial facilities should still be designed and constructed to incorporate accessibility features to the extent that the features are structurally practicable. The accessibility requirements should not be viewed as an all-or-nothing proposition in such circumstances.

If it is structurally impracticable for a facility in its entirety to be readily accessible to and usable by people with disabilities, then those portions that can be made accessible should be made accessible. If a building cannot be constructed in compliance with the full range of accessibility requirements because of structural impracticability, then it should still incorporate those features that are structurally practicable. If it is structurally impracticable to make a particular facility accessible to persons who have particular types of disabilities, it is still appropriate to require it to be made accessible to persons with other types of disabilities. For example, a facility that is of necessity built on stilts and cannot be made accessible to persons who use wheelchairs because it is structurally impracticable to do so, must be made accessible for individuals with vision or hearing impairments or other kinds of disabilities.

Elevator Exemption

Section 36.401(d) implements the "elevator exemption" for new construction in section 303(b) of the ADA. The elevator exemption is an exception to the general requirement that new facilities be readily accessible to and usable by individuals with disabilities. Generally, an elevator is the most common way to provide individuals who use wheelchairs "ready access" to floor levels above or below the ground floor of a multi-story building. Congress, however, chose not to require elevators in new small buildings, that is, those with less than three stories or less than 3,000 square feet per story. In buildings eligible for the exemption, therefore, "ready access" from the building entrance to a floor above or below the ground floor is not required, because the statute does not require that an elevator be installed in such buildings. The elevator exemption

does not apply, however, to a facility housing a shopping center, a shopping mall, or the professional office of a health care provider, or other categories of facilities as determined by the Attorney General. For example, a new office building that will have only two stories, with no elevator planned, will not be required to have an elevator, even if each story has 20,000 square feet. In other words, having either less than 3000 square feet per story or less than three stories qualifies a facility for the exemption; it need not qualify for the exemption on both counts. Similarly, a facility that has five stories of 2800 square feet each qualifies for the exemption. If a facility has three or more stories at any point, it is not eligible for the elevator exemption unless all the stories are less than 3000 square feet.

The terms "shopping center or shopping mall" and "professional office of a health care provider" are defined in this section. They are substantially identical to the definitions included in the proposed rule in § 36.104, "Definitions." They have been moved to this section because, as commenters pointed out, they are relevant only for the purposes of the elevator exemption, and inclusion in the general definitions section could give the incorrect impression that an office of a health care provider is not covered as a place of public accommodation under other sections of the rule, unless the office falls within the definition.

For purposes of § 36.401, a "shopping center or shopping mall" is (1) a building housing five or more sales or rental establishments, or (2) a series of buildings on a common site, either under common ownership or common control or developed either as one project or as a series of related projects, housing five or more sales or rental establishments. The term "shopping center or shopping mall" only includes floor levels containing at least one sales or rental establishment, or any floor level that was designed or intended for use by at least one sales or rental establishment.

Any sales or rental establishment of the type that is included in paragraph (5) of the definition of "place of public accommodation" (for example, a bakery, grocery store, clothing store, or hardware store) is considered a sales or rental establishment for purposes of this definition; the other types of public accommodations (e.g., restaurants, laundromats, banks, travel services, health spas) are not.

In the preamble to the proposed rule, the Department sought comment on whether the definition of "shopping center or mall" should be expanded to

include any of these other types of public accommodations. The Department also sought comment on whether a series of buildings should fall within the definition only if they are physically connected.

Most of those responding to the first question (overwhelmingly groups representing people with disabilities, or individual commenters) urged that the definition encompass more places of public accommodation, such as restaurants, motion picture houses, laundromats, dry cleaners, and banks. They pointed out that often it is not known what types of establishments will be tenants in a new facility. In addition, they noted that malls are advertised as entities, that their appeal is in the "package" of services offered to the public, and that this package often includes the additional types of establishments mentioned.

Commenters representing business groups sought to exempt banks, travel services, grocery stores, drug stores, and freestanding retail stores from the elevator requirement. They based this request on the desire to continue the practice in some locations of incorporating mezzanines housing administrative offices, raised pharmacist areas, and raised areas in the front of supermarkets that house safes and are used by managers to oversee operations of check-out aisles and other functions. Many of these concerns are adequately addressed by ADAAG. Apart from those addressed by ADAAG, the Department sees no reason to treat a particular type of sales or rental establishment differently from any other. Although banks and travel services are not included as "sales or rental establishments," because they do not fall under paragraph (5) of the definition of place of public accommodation, grocery stores and drug stores are included.

The Department has declined to include places of public accommodation other than sales or rental establishments in the definition. The statutory definition of "public accommodation" (section 301(7)) lists 12 types of establishments that are considered public accommodations. Category (E) includes "a bakery, grocery store, clothing store, hardware store, shopping center, or other sales or rental establishment." This arrangement suggests that it is only these types of establishments that would make up a shopping center for purposes of the statute. To include all types of places of public accommodation, or those from 6 or 7 of the categories, as commenters suggest, would overly limit the elevator exemption; the universe of facilities covered by the definition of "shopping center" could well exceed the number of multitenant facilities *not* covered, which would render the exemption almost meaningless.

For similar reasons, the Department is retaining the requirement that a building or series of buildings must house five or more sales or rental establishments before it falls within the definition of "shopping center." Numerous commenters objected to the number and requested that the number be lowered from five to three or four. Lowering the number in this manner would include an inordinately large number of two-story multitenant buildings within the category of those required to have elevators.

The responses to the question concerning whether a series of buildings should be connected in order to be covered were varied. Generally, disability rights groups and some government agencies said a series of buildings should not have to be connected, and pointed to a trend in some areas to build shopping centers in a garden or village setting. The Department agrees that this design choice should not negate the elevator requirement for new construction. Some business groups answered the question in the affirmative, and some suggested a different definition of shopping center. For example, one commenter recommended the addition of a requirement that the five or more establishments be physically connected on the non-ground floors by a common pedestrian walkway or pathway, because otherwise a series of stand-alone facilities would have to comply with the elevator requirement, which would be unduly burdensome and perhaps infeasible. Another suggested use of what it characterized as the standard industry definition: "A group of retail stores and related business facilities, the whole planned, developed, operated and managed as a unit." While the rule's definition would reach a series of related projects that are under common control but were not developed as a single project, the Department considers such a facility to be a shopping center within the meaning of the statute. However, in light of the hardship that could confront a series of existing small stand-alone buildings if elevators were required in alterations, the Department has included a common access route in the definition of shopping center or shopping mall for purposes of § 36.404.

Some commenters suggested that access to restrooms and other shared facilities open to the public should be required even if those facilities were not on a shopping floor. Such a provision with respect to toilet or bathing facilities is included in the elevator exception in final ADAAG 4.1.3(5).

For purposes of this subpart, the rule does not distinguish between a "shopping mall" (usually a building with a roofed-over common pedestrian area serving more than one tenant in which a majority of the tenants have a main entrance from the common pedestrian area) and a "shopping center" (e.g., a "shopping strip"). Any facility housing five or more of the types of sales or rental establishments described, regardless of the number of other types of places of public accommodation housed there (e.g., offices, movie theatres, restaurants), is a shopping center or shopping mall.

For example, a two-story facility built for mixed-use occupancy on both floors (e.g., by sales and rental establishments, a movie theater, restaurants, and general office space) is a shopping center or shopping mall if it houses five or more sales or rental establishments. If none of these establishments is located on the second floor, then only the ground floor, which contains the sales or rental establishments, would be a "shopping center or shopping mall," unless the second floor was designed or intended for use by at least one sales or rental establishment. In determining whether a floor was intended for such use, factors to be considered include the types of establishments that first occupied the floor, the nature of the developer's marketing strategy, i.e., what types of establishments were sought, and inclusion of any design features particular to rental and sales establishments.

A "professional office of a health care provider" is defined as a location where a person or entity regulated by a State to provide professional services related to the physical or mental health of an individual makes such services available to the public. In a two-story development that houses health care providers only on the ground floor, the "professional office of a health care provider" is limited to the ground floor unless the second floor was designed or intended for use by a health care provider. In determining if a floor was intended for such use, factors to be considered include whether the facility was constructed with special plumbing, electrical, or other features needed by health care providers, whether the developer marketed the facility as a medical office center, and whether any of the establishments that first occupied

the floor was, in fact, a health care provider.

In addition to requiring that a building that is a shopping center, shopping mall, or the professional office of a health care provider have an elevator regardless of square footage or number of floors, the ADA (section 303(b)) provides that the Attorney General may determine that a particular category of facilities requires the installation of elevators based on the usage of the facilities. The Department, as it proposed to do, has added to the nonexempt categories terminals, depots, or other stations used for specified public transportation, and airport passenger terminals. Numerous commenters in all categories endorsed this proposal; none opposed it. It is not uncommon for an airport passenger terminal or train station, for example, to have only two floors, with gates on both floors. Because of the significance of transportation, because a person with disabilities could be arriving or departing at any gate, and because inaccessible facilities could result in a total denial of transportation services, it is reasonable to require that newly constructed transit facilities be accessible, regardless of square footage or number of floors. One comment suggested an amendment that would treat terminals and stations similarly to shopping centers, by requiring an accessible route only to those areas used for passenger loading and unloading and for other passenger services. Paragraph (d)(2)(ii) has been modified accordingly.

Some commenters suggested that other types of facilities (e.g., educational facilities, libraries, museums, commercial facilities, and social service facilities) should be included in the category of nonexempt facilities. The Department has not found adequate justification for including any other types of facilities in the nonexempt category at this time.

Section 36.401(d)(2) establishes the operative requirements concerning the elevator exemption and its application to shopping centers and malls, professional offices of health care providers, transit stations, and airport passenger terminals. Under the rule's framework, it is necessary first to determine if a new facility (including one or more buildings) houses places of public accommodation or commercial facilities that are in the categories for which elevators are required. If so, and the facility is a shopping center or shopping mall, or a professional office of a health care provider, then any area housing such an office or a sales or rental establishment or the professional office of a health care provider is not entitled to the elevator exemption.

The following examples illustrate the application of these principles:

1. A shopping mall has an upper and a lower level. There are two "anchor stores" (in this case, major department stores) at either end of the mall, both with exterior entrances and an entrance on each level from the common area). In addition, there are 30 stores (sales or rental establishments) on the upper level, all of which have entrances from a common central area. There are 30 stores on the lower level, all of which have entrances from a common central area. According to the rule, elevator access must be provided to each store and to each level of the anchor stores. This requirement could be satisfied with respect to the 60 stores through elevators connecting the two pedestrian levels, provided that an individual could travel from the elevator to any other point on that level (i.e., into any store through a common pedestrian area) on an accessible path.

2. A commercial (nonresidential) "townhouse" development is composed of 20 two-story attached buildings. The facility is developed as one project, with common ownership, and the space will be leased to retailers. Each building has one accessible entrance from a pedestrian walk to the first floor. From that point, one can enter a store on the first floor, or walk up a flight of stairs to a store on the second floor. All 40 stores must be accessible at ground floor level or by accessible vertical access from that level. This does not mean, however, that 20 elevators must be installed. Access could be provided to the second floor by an elevator from the pedestrian area on the lower level to an upper walkway connecting all the areas on the second floor.

3. In the same type of development, it is planned that retail stores will be housed exclusively on the ground floor, with only office space (not professional offices of health care providers) on the second. Elevator access need not be provided to the second floor because all the sales or rental establishments (the entities that make the facility a shopping center) are located on an accessible ground floor.

4. In the same type of development, the space is designed and marketed as medical or office suites, or as a medical office facility. Accessible vertical access must be provided to all areas, as described in example 2.

Some commenters suggested that building owners who knowingly lease or rent space to nonexempt places of public accommodation would violate § 36.401. However, the Department does not consider leasing or renting inaccessible space in itself to constitute a violation of this part. Nor does a change in use of a facility, with no accompanying alterations (e.g., if a psychiatrist replaces an attorney as a tenant in a second-floor office, but no alterations are made to the office) trigger accessibility requirements.

Entities cannot evade the requirements of this section by constructing facilities in such a way that no story is intended to constitute a "ground floor." For example, if a private entity constructs a building whose main entrance leads only to stairways or escalators that connect with upper or lower floors, the Department would consider at least one level of the facility a ground story.

The rule requires in § 36.401(d)(3), consistent with the proposed rule, that, even if a building falls within the elevator exemption, the floor or floors other than the ground floor must nonetheless be accessible, except for elevator access, to individuals with disabilities, including people who use wheelchairs. This requirement applies to buildings that do not house sales or rental establishments or the professional offices of a health care provider as well as to those in which such establishments or offices are all located on the ground floor. In such a situation, little added cost is entailed in making the second floor accessible, because it is similar in structure and floor plan to the ground floor.

There are several reasons for this provision. First, some individuals who are mobility impaired may work on a building's second floor, which they can reach by stairs and the use of crutches; however, the same individuals, once they reach the second floor, may then use a wheelchair that is kept in the office. Secondly, because the first floor will be accessible, there will be little additional cost entailed in making the second floor, with the same structure and generally the same floor plan, accessible. In addition, the second floor must be accessible to those persons with disabilities who do not need elevators for level changes (for example, persons with sight or hearing impairments and those with certain mobility impairments). Finally, if an elevator is installed in the future for any reason, full access to the floor will be facilitated.

One commenter asserted that this provision goes beyond the Department's authority under the Act, and disagreed with the Department's claim that little additional cost would be entailed in compliance. However, the provision is taken directly from the legislative history (see Education and Labor report at 114).

One commenter said that where an elevator is not required, platform lifts should be required. Two commenters pointed out that the elevator exemption is really an exemption from the requirement for providing an accessible route to a second floor not served by an elevator. The Department agrees with the latter comment. Lifts to provide access between floors are not required in buildings that are not required to have elevators. This point is specifically addressed in the appendix to ADAAG (§ 4.1.3(5)). ADAAG also addresses in detail the situations in which lifts are permitted or required.

Section 36.402   Alterations

Sections 36.402–36.405 implement section 303(a)(2) of the Act, which requires that alterations to existing facilities be made in a way that ensures that the altered portion is readily accessible to and usable by individuals with disabilities. This part does not require alterations; it simply provides that when alterations are undertaken, they must be made in a manner that provides access.

Section 36.402(a)(1) provides that any alteration to a place of public accommodation or a commercial facility, after January 26, 1992, shall be made so as to ensure that, to the maximum extent feasible, the altered portions of the facility are readily accessible to and usable by individuals with disabilities, including individuals who use wheelchairs.

The proposed rule provided that an alteration would be deemed to be undertaken after January 26, 1992, if the physical alteration of the property is in progress after that date. Commenters pointed out that this provision would, in some cases, produce an unjust result by requiring the redesign or retrofitting of projects initiated before this part established the ADA accessibility standards. The Department agrees that the proposed rule would, in some instances, unfairly penalize projects that were substantially completed before the effective date. Therefore, paragraph (a)(2) has been revised to specify that an alteration will be deemed to be undertaken after January 26, 1992, if the physical alteration of the property begins after that date. As a matter of interpretation, the Department will construe this provision to apply to alterations that require a permit from a State, County or local government, if physical alterations pursuant to the terms of the permit begin after January 26, 1992. The Department recognizes that this application of the effective date may require redesign of some facilities that were planned prior to the publication of this part, but no retrofitting will be required of facilities on which the physical alterations were initiated prior to the effective date of the Act. Of course, nothing in this section in any way alters the obligation of any facility to remove architectural barriers in existing facilities to the extent that such barrier removal is readily achievable.

Paragraph (b) provides that, for the purposes of this part, an "alteration" is a change to a place of public accommodation or a commercial facility that affects or could affect the usability of the building or facility or any part thereof. One commenter suggested that the concept of usability should apply only to those changes that affect access by persons with disabilities. The Department remains convinced that the Act requires the concept of "usability" to be read broadly to include any change that affects the usability of the facility, not simply changes that relate directly to access by individuals with disabilities.

The Department received a significant number of comments on the examples provided in paragraphs (b)(1) and (b)(2) of the proposed rule. Some commenters urged the Department to limit the application of this provision to major structural modifications, while others asserted that it should be expanded to include cosmetic changes such as painting and wallpapering. The Department believes that neither approach is consistent with the legislative history, which requires this Department's regulation to be consistent with the accessibility guidelines (ADAAG) developed by the Architectural and Transportation Barriers Compliance Board (ATBCB). Although the legislative history contemplates that, in some instances, the ADA accessibility standards will exceed the current MGRAD requirements, it also clearly indicates the view of the drafters that "minor changes such as painting or papering walls * * * do not affect usability" (Education and Labor report at 111, Judiciary report at 64), and, therefore, are not alterations. The proposed rule was based on the existing MGRAD definition of "alteration." The language of the final rule has been revised to be consistent with ADAAG, incorporated as appendix A to this part.

Some commenters sought clarification of the intended scope of this section. The proposed rule contained illustrations of changes that affect

usability and those that do not. The intent of the illustrations was to explain the scope of the alterations requirement; the effect was to obscure it. As a result of the illustrations, some commenters concluded that any alteration to a facility, even a minor alteration such as relocating an electrical outlet, would trigger an extensive obligation to provide access throughout an entire facility. That result was never contemplated.

Therefore, in this final rule paragraph (b)(1) has been revised to include the major provisions of paragraphs (b)(1) and (b)(2) of the proposed rule. The examples in the proposed rule have been deleted. Paragraph (b)(1) now provides that alterations include, but are not limited to, remodeling, renovation, rehabilitation, reconstruction, historic restoration, changes or rearrangement in structural parts or elements, and changes or rearrangement in the plan configuration of walls and full-height partitions. Normal maintenance, reroofing, painting or wallpapering, asbestos removal, or changes to mechanical and electrical systems are not alterations unless they affect the usability of building or facility.

Paragraph (b)(2) of this final rule was added to clarify the scope of the alterations requirement. Paragraph (b)(2) provides that if existing elements, spaces, or common areas are altered, then each such altered element, space, or area shall comply with the applicable provisions of appendix A (ADAAG). As provided in § 36.403, if an altered space or area is an area of the facility that contains a primary function, then the requirements of that section apply.

Therefore, when an entity undertakes a minor alteration to a place of public accommodation or commercial facility, such as moving an electrical outlet, the new outlet must be installed in compliance with ADAAG. (Alteration of the elements listed in § 36.403(c)(2) cannot trigger a path of travel obligation.) If the alteration is to an area, such as an employee lounge or locker room, that is not an area of the facility that contains a primary function, that area must comply with ADAAG. It is only when an alteration affects access to or usability of an area containing a primary function, as opposed to other areas or the elements listed in § 36.403(c)(2), that the path of travel to the altered area must be made accessible.

The Department received relatively few comments on paragraph (c), which explains the statutory phrase "to the maximum extent feasible." Some commenters suggested that the

regulation should specify that cost is a factor in determining whether it is feasible to make an altered area accessible. The legislative history of the ADA indicates that the concept of feasibility only reaches the question of whether it is possible to make the alteration accessible in compliance with this part. Costs are to be considered only when an alteration to an area containing a primary function triggers an additional requirement to make the path of travel to the altered area accessible.

Section 36.402(c) is, therefore, essentially unchanged from the proposed rule. At the recommendation of a commenter, the Department has inserted the word "virtually" to modify "impossible" to conform to the language of the legislative history. It explains that the phrase "to the maximum extent feasible" as used in this section applies to the occasional case where the nature of an existing facility makes it virtually impossible to comply fully with applicable accessibility standards through a planned alteration. In the occasional cases in which full compliance is impossible, alterations shall provide the maximum physical accessibility feasible. Any features of the facility that are being altered shall be made accessible unless it is technically infeasible to do so. If providing accessibility in conformance with this section to individuals with certain disabilities (e.g., those who use wheelchairs) would not be feasible, the facility shall be made accessible to persons with other types of disabilities (e.g., those who use crutches or who have impaired vision or hearing, or those who have other types of impairments).

Section 36.403 Alterations: Path of Travel

Section 36.403 implements the statutory requirement that any alteration that affects or could affect the usability of or access to an area of a facility that contains a primary function shall be made so as to ensure that, to the maximum extent feasible, the path of travel to the altered area, and the restrooms, telephones, and drinking fountains serving the altered area, are readily accessible to and usable by individuals with disabilities, including individuals who use wheelchairs, unless the cost and scope of such alterations is disproportionate to the cost of the overall alteration. Paragraph (a) restates this statutory requirement.

Paragraph (b) defines a "primary function" as a major activity for which the facility is intended. This paragraph is unchanged from the proposed rule.

Areas that contain a primary function include, but are not limited to, the customer services lobby of a bank, the dining area of a cafeteria, the meeting rooms in a conference center, as well as offices and all other work areas in which the activities of the public accommodation or other private entities using the facility are carried out. The concept of "areas containing a primary function" is analogous to the concept of "functional spaces" in § 3.5 of the existing Uniform Federal Accessibility Standards, which defines "functional spaces" as "[t]he rooms and spaces in a building that house the major activities for which the building or facility is intended."

Paragraph (b) provides that areas such as mechanical rooms, boiler rooms, supply storage rooms, employee lounges and locker rooms, janitorial closets, entrances, corridors, and restrooms are not areas containing a primary function. There may be exceptions to this general rule. For example, the availability of public restrooms at a place of public accommodation at a roadside rest stop may be a major factor affecting customers' decisions to patronize the public accommodation. In that case, a restroom would be considered to be an "area containing a primary function" of the facility.

Most of the commenters who addressed this issue supported the approach taken by the Department; but a few commenters suggested that areas not open to the general public or those used exclusively by employees should be excluded from the definition of primary function. The preamble to the proposed rule noted that the Department considered an alternative approach to the definition of "primary function," under which a primary function of a commercial facility would be defined as a major activity for which the facility was intended, while a primary function of a place of public accommodation would be defined as an activity which involves providing significant goods, services, facilities, privileges, advantages, or accommodations. However, the Department concluded that, although portions of the legislative history of the ADA support this alternative, the better view is that the language now contained in § 36.403(b) most accurately reflects congressional intent. No commenter made a persuasive argument that the Department's interpretation of the legislative history is incorrect.

When the ADA was introduced, the requirement to make alterations accessible was included in section 302 of the Act, which identifies the practices that constitute discrimination by a public accommodation. Because section 302 applies only to the operation of a place of public accommodation, the alterations requirement was intended only to provide access to clients and customers of a public accommodation. It was anticipated that access would be provided to employees with disabilities under the "reasonable accommodation" requirements of title I. However, during its consideration of the ADA, the House Judiciary Committee amended the bill to move the alterations provision from section 302 to section 303, which applies to commercial facilities as well as public accommodations. The Committee report accompanying the bill explains that:

New construction and alterations of both public accommodations and commercial facilities must be made readily accessible to and usable by individuals with disabilities * * *. Essentially, [this requirement] is designed to ensure that patrons *and employees* of public accommodations and commercial facilities are able to get to, enter and use the facility * * *. The rationale for making new construction accessible applies with equal force to alterations.

Judiciary report at 62–63 (emphasis added).

The ADA, as enacted, contains the language of section 303 as it was reported out of the Judiciary Committee. Therefore, the Department has concluded that the concept of "primary function" should be applied in the same manner to places of public accommodation and to commercial facilities, thereby including employee work areas in places of public accommodation within the scope of this section.

Paragraph (c) provides examples of alterations that affect the usability of or access to an area containing a primary function. The examples include: Remodeling a merchandise display area or employee work areas in a department store; installing a new floor surface to replace an inaccessible surface in the customer service area or employee work areas of a bank; redesigning the assembly line area of a factory; and installing a computer center in an accounting firm. This list is illustrative, not exhaustive. Any change that affects the usability of or access to an area containing a primary function triggers the statutory obligation to make the path of travel to the altered area accessible.

When the proposed rule was drafted, the Department believed that the rule made it clear that the ADA would require alterations to the path of travel only when such alterations are not disproportionate to the alteration to the primary function area. However, the comments that the Department received

indicated that many commenters believe that even minor alterations to individual elements would require additional alterations to the path of travel. To address the concern of these commenters, a new paragraph (c)(2) has been added to the final rule to provide that alterations to such elements as windows, hardware, controls (e.g. light switches or thermostats), electrical outlets, or signage will not be deemed to be alterations that affect the usability of or access to an area containing a primary function. Of course, each element that is altered must comply with ADAAG (appendix A). The cost of alterations to individual elements would be included in the overall cost of an alteration for purposes of determining disproportionality and would be counted when determining the aggregate cost of a series of small alterations in accordance with § 36.401(h) if the area is altered in a manner that affects access to or usability of an area containing a primary function.

Paragraph (d) concerns the respective obligations of landlords and tenants in the cases of alterations that trigger the path of travel requirement under § 36.403. This paragraph was contained in the landlord/tenant section of the proposed rule, § 36.201(b). If a tenant is making alterations upon its premises pursuant to terms of a lease that grant it the authority to do so (even if they constitute alterations that trigger the path of travel requirement), and the landlord is not making alterations to other parts of the facility, then the alterations by the tenant on its own premises do not trigger a path of travel obligation upon the landlord in areas of the facility under the landlord's authority that are not otherwise being altered. The legislative history makes clear that the path of travel requirement applies only to the entity that is already making the alteration, and thus the Department has not changed the final rule despite numerous comments suggesting that the tenant be required to provide a path of travel.

Paragraph (e) defines a "path of travel" as a continuous, unobstructed way of pedestrian passage by means of which an altered area may be approached, entered, and exited; and which connects the altered area with an exterior approach (including sidewalks, streets, and parking areas), an entrance to the facility, and other parts of the facility. This concept of an accessible path of travel is analogous to the concepts of "accessible route" and "circulation path" contained in section 3.5 of the current UFAS. Some commenters suggested that this paragraph should address emergency egress. The Department disagrees. "Path of travel" as it is used in this section is a term of art under the ADA that relates only to the obligation of the public accommodation or commercial facility to provide additional accessible elements when an area containing a primary function is altered. The Department recognizes that emergency egress is an important issue, but believes that it is appropriately addressed in ADAAG (appendix A), not in this paragraph. Furthermore, ADAAG does not require changes to emergency egress areas in alterations.

Paragraph (e)(2) is drawn from section 3.5 of UFAS. It provides that an accessible path of travel may consist of walks and sidewalks, curb ramps and other interior or exterior pedestrian ramps; clear floor paths through lobbies, corridors, rooms, and other improved areas; parking access aisles; elevators and lifts; or a combination of such elements. Paragraph (e)(3) provides that, for the purposes of this part, the term "path of travel" also includes the restrooms, telephones, and drinking fountains serving an altered area.

Although the Act establishes an expectation that an accessible path of travel should generally be included when alterations are made to an area containing a primary function, Congress recognized that, in some circumstances, providing an accessible path of travel to an altered area may be sufficiently burdensome in comparison to the alteration being undertaken to the area containing a primary function as to render this requirement unreasonable. Therefore, Congress provided, in section 303(a)(2) of the Act, that alterations to the path of travel that are disproportionate in cost and scope to the overall alteration are not required.

The Act requires the Attorney General to determine at what point the cost of providing an accessible path of travel becomes disproportionate. The proposed rule provided three options for making this determination.

Two committees of Congress specifically addressed this issue: the House Committee on Education and Labor and the House Committee on the Judiciary. The reports issued by each committee suggested that accessibility alterations to a path of travel might be "disproportionate" if they exceed 30% of the alteration costs (Education and Labor report at 113; Judiciary report at 64). Because the Department believed that smaller percentage rates might be appropriate, the proposed rule sought comments on three options: 10%, 20%, or 30%.

The Department received a significant number of comments on this section. Commenters representing individuals with disabilities generally supported the use of 30% (or more); commenters representing covered entities supported a figure of 10% (or less). The Department believes that alterations made to provide an accessible path of travel to the altered area should be deemed disproportionate to the overall alteration when the cost exceeds 20% of the cost of the alteration to the primary function area. This approach appropriately reflects the intent of Congress to provide access for individuals with disabilities without causing economic hardship for the covered public accommodations and commercial facilities.

The Department has determined that the basis for this cost calculation shall be the cost of the alterations to the area containing the primary function. This approach will enable the public accommodation or other private entity that is making the alteration to calculate its obligation as a percentage of a clearly ascertainable base cost, rather than as a percentage of the "total" cost, an amount that will change as accessibility alterations to the path of travel are made.

Paragraph (f)(2) (paragraph (e)(2) in the proposed rule) is unchanged. It provides examples of costs that may be counted as expenditures required to provide an accessible path of travel. They include:

• Costs associated with providing an accessible entrance and an accessible route to the altered area, for example, the cost of widening doorways or installing ramps;

• Costs associated with making restrooms accessible, such as installing grab bars, enlarging toilet stalls, insulating pipes, or installing accessible faucet controls;

• Costs associated with providing accessible telephones, such as relocating telephones to an accessible height, installing amplification devices, or installing telecommunications devices for deaf persons (TDD's);

• Costs associated with relocating an inaccessible drinking fountain.

Paragraph (f)(1) of the proposed rule provided that when the cost of alterations necessary to make the path of travel serving an altered area fully accessible is disproportionate to the cost of the overall alteration, the path of travel shall be made accessible to the maximum extent feasible. In response to the suggestion of a commenter, the Department has made an editorial change in the final rule (paragraph (g)(1)) to clarify that if the cost of

providing a fully accessible path of travel is disproportionate, the path of travel shall be made accessible "to the extent that it can be made accessible without incurring disproportionate costs."

Paragraph (g)(2) (paragraph (f)(2) in the NPRM) establishes that priority should be given to those elements that will provide the greatest access, in the following order: An accessible entrance; an accessible route to the altered area; at least one accessible restroom for each sex or a single unisex restroom; accessible telephones; accessible drinking fountains; and, whenever possible, additional accessible elements such as parking, storage, and alarms. This paragraph is unchanged from the proposed rule.

Paragraph (h) (paragraph (g) in the proposed rule) provides that the obligation to provide an accessible path of travel may not be evaded by performing a series of small alterations to the area served by a single path of travel if those alterations could have been performed as a single undertaking. If an area containing a primary function has been altered without providing an accessible path of travel to serve that area, and subsequent alterations of that area, or a different area on the same path of travel, are undertaken within three years of the original alteration, the total cost of alterations to primary function areas on that path of travel during the preceding three year period shall be considered in determining whether the cost of making the path of travel serving that area accessible is disproportionate. Only alterations undertaken after January 26, 1992, shall be considered in determining if the cost of providing accessible features is disproportionate to the overall cost of the alterations.

Section 36.404 Alterations: Elevator Exemption

Section 36.404 implements the elevator exemption in section 303(b) of the Act as it applies to altered facilities. The provisions of section 303(b) are discussed in the preamble to § 36.401(d) above. The statute applies the same exemption to both new construction and alterations. The principal difference between the requirements of § 36.401(d) and § 36.404 is that, in altering an existing facility that is not eligible for the statutory exemption, the public accommodation or other private entity responsible for the alteration is not required to install an elevator if the installation of an elevator would be disproportionate in cost and scope to the cost of the overall alteration as provided in § 36.403(f)(1). In addition, the standards referenced in § 36.406 (ADAAG) provide that installation of an elevator in an altered facility is not required if it is "technically infeasible."

This section has been revised to define the terms "professional office of a health care provider" and "shopping center or shopping mall" for the purposes of this section. The definition of "professional office of a health care provider" is identical to the definition included in § 36.401(d).

It has been brought to the attention of the Department that there is some misunderstanding about the scope of the elevator exemption as it applies to the professional office of a health care provider. A public accommodation, such as the professional office of a health care provider, is required to remove architectural barriers to its facility to the extent that such barrier removal is readily achievable (see § 36.304), but it is not otherwise required by this part to undertake new construction or alterations. This part does not require that an existing two story building that houses the professional office of a health care provider be altered for the purpose of providing elevator access. If, however, alterations to the area housing the office of the health care provider are undertaken for other purposes, the installation of an elevator might be ~~d, but only if the cost of the ᵤᵢₑ ᵥtor is not disproportionate to the ₛt of the overall alteration. Neither the ᵢct nᵤᵣ this part prohibits a health care ᵣ ᵣovider from locating his or her professional office in an existing facility that does not have an elevator.

Because of the unique challenges presented in altering existing facilities, ᵢhe Department has adopted a definition of "shopping center or shopping mall" for the purposes of this section that is ᵢghtly different from the definition ᵢⁱopted under § 36.401(d). For the ᵢposes of this section, a "shopping center or shopping mall" is (1) a building housing five or more sales or rental establishments, or (2) a series of buildings on a common site, connected by a common pedestrian access route above or below the ground floor, either under common ownership or common control or developed either as one project or as a series of related projects, housing five or more sales or rental establishments. As is the case with new construction, the term "shopping center or shopping mall" only includes floor levels housing at least one sales or rental establishment, or any floor level that was designed or intended for use by at least one sales or rental establishment.

The Department believes that it is appropriate to use a different definition of "shopping center or shopping mall" for this section than for § 36.401, in order to make it clear that a series of existing buildings on a common site that is altered for the use of sales or rental establishments does not become a "shopping center or shopping mall" required to install an elevator, unless there is a common means of pedestrian access above or below the ground floor. Without this exemption, separate, but adjacent, buildings that were initially designed and constructed independently of each other could be required to be retrofitted with elevators, if they were later renovated for a purpose not contemplated at the time of construction.

Like § 36.401(d), § 36.404 provides that the exemptions in this paragraph do not obviate or limit in any way the obligation to comply with the other accessibility requirements established in this subpart. For example, alterations to floors above or below the ground floor must be accessible regardless of whether the altered facility has an elevator. If a facility that is not required to install an elevator nonetheless has an elevator, that elevator shall meet, to the maximum extent feasible, the accessibility requirements of this section.

Section 36.405 Alterations: Historic Preservation

Section 36.405 gives effect to the intent of Congress, expressed in section 504(c) of the Act, that this part recognize the national interest in preserving significant historic structures. Commenters criticized the Department's use of descriptive terms in the proposed rule that are different from those used in the ADA to describe eligible historic properties. In addition, some commenters criticized the Department's decision to use the concept of "substantially impairing" the historic features of a property, which is a concept employed in regulations implementing section 504 of the Rehabilitation Act of 1973. Those commenters recommended that the Department adopt the criteria of "adverse effect" published by the Advisory Council on Historic Preservation under the National Historic Preservation Act (36 CFR 800.9) as the standard for determining whether an historic property may be altered.

The Department agrees with these comments to the extent that they suggest that the language of the rule should conform to the language employed by Congress in the ADA. Therefore, the language of this section has been

revised to make it clear that this provision applies to buildings or facilities that are eligible for listing in the National Register of Historic Places under the National Historic Preservation Act (16 U.S.C. 470 *et seq.*) and to buildings or facilities that are designated as historic under State or local law. The Department believes, however, that the criteria of adverse effect employed under the National Historic Preservation Act are inappropriate for this rule because section 504(c) of the ADA specifies that special alterations provisions shall apply only when an alteration would "threaten or destroy the historic significance of qualified historic buildings and facilities."

The Department intends that the exception created by this section be applied only in those very rare situations in which it is not possible to provide access to an historic property using the special access provisions in ADAAG. Therefore, paragraph (a) of § 36.405 has been revised to provide that alterations to historic properties shall comply, to the maximum extent feasible, with section 4.1.7 of ADAAG. Paragraph (b) of this section has been revised to provide that if it has been determined, under the procedures established in ADAAG, that it is not feasible to provide physical access to an historic property that is a place of public accommodation in a manner that will not threaten or destroy the historic significance of the property, alternative methods of access shall be provided pursuant to the requirements of Subpart C.

Section 36.406 Standards for New Construction and Alterations

Section 36.406 implements the requirements of sections 306(b) and 306(c) of the Act, which require the Attorney General to promulgate standards for accessible design for buildings and facilities subject to the Act and this part that are consistent with the supplemental minimum guidelines and requirements for accessible design published by the Architectural and Transportation Barriers Compliance Board (ATBCB or Board) pursuant to section 504 of the Act. This section of the rule provides that new construction and alterations subject to this part shall comply with the standards for accessible design published as appendix A to this part.

Appendix A contains the Americans with Disabilities Act Accessibility Guidelines for Buildings and Facilities (ADAAG) which is being published by the ATBCB as a final rule elsewhere in this issue of the Federal Register. As proposed in this Department's proposed rule, § 36.406(a) adopts ADAAG as the accessibility standard applicable under this rule.

Paragraph (b) was not included in the proposed rule. It provides, in chart form, guidance for using ADAAG together with subparts A through D of this part when determining requirements for a particular facility. This chart is intended solely as guidance for the user; it has no effect for purposes of compliance or enforcement. It does not necessarily provide complete or mandatory information.

Proposed § 36.406(b) is not included in the final rule. That provision, which would have taken effect only if the final rule had followed the proposed Option Two for § 36.401(a), is unnecessary because the Department has chosen Option One, as explained in the preamble for that section.

Section 504(a) of the ADA requires the ATBCB to issue minimum guidelines to supplement the existing Minimum Guidelines and Requirements for Accessible Design (MGRAD) (36 CFR part 1190) for purposes of title III. According to section 504(b) of the Act, the guidelines are to establish additional requirements, consistent with the Act, "to ensure that buildings and facilities are accessible, in terms of architecture and design, . . . and communication, to individuals with disabilities." Section 306(c) of the Act requires that the accessibility standards included in the Department's regulations be consistent with the minimum guidelines, in this case ADAAG.

As explained in the ATBCB's preamble to ADAAG, the substance and form of the guidelines are drawn from several sources. They use as their model the 1984 Uniform Federal Accessibility Standards (UFAS) (41 CFR part 101, subpart 101–19.6, appendix), which are the standards implementing the Architectural Barriers Act. UFAS is based on the Board's 1982 MGRAD. ADAAG follows the numbering system and format of the private sector American National Standard Institute's ANSI A117.1 standards. (American National Specifications for Making Buildings and Facilities Accessible to and Usable by Physically Handicapped People (ANSI A117–1980) and American National Standard for Buildings and Facilities—Providing Accessibility and Usability for Physically Handicapped People (ANSI A117.1–1986).) ADAAG supplements MGRAD. In developing ADAAG, the Board made every effort to be consistent with MGRAD and the current and proposed ANSI Standards, to the extent consistent with the ADA.

ADAAG consists of nine main sections and a separate appendix. Sections 1 through 3 contain general provisions and definitions. Section 4 contains scoping provisions and technical specifications applicable to all covered buildings and facilities. The scoping provisions are listed separately for new construction of sites and exterior facilities; new construction of buildings; additions; alterations; and alterations to historic properties. The technical specifications generally reprint the text and illustrations of the ANSI A117.1 standard, except where differences are noted by italics. Sections 5 through 9 of the guidelines are special application sections and contain additional requirements for restaurants and cafeterias, medical care facilities, business and mercantile facilities, libraries, and transient lodging. The appendix to the guidelines contains additional information to aid in understanding the technical specifications. The section numbers in the appendix correspond to the sections of the guidelines to which they relate. An asterisk after a section number indicates that additional information appears in the appendix.

ADAAG's provisions are further explained under Summary of ADAAG below.

General Comments

One commenter urged the Department to move all or portions of subpart D, New Construction and Alterations, to the appendix (ADAAG) or to duplicate portions of subpart D in the appendix. The commenter correctly pointed out that subpart D is inherently linked to ADAAG, and that a self-contained set of rules would be helpful to users. The Department has attempted to simplify use of the two documents by deleting some paragraphs from subpart D (e.g., those relating to work areas), because they are included in ADAAG. However, the Department has retained in subpart D those sections that are taken directly from the statute or that give meaning to specific statutory concepts (e.g., structural impracticability, path of travel). While some of the subpart D provisions are duplicated in ADAAG, others are not. For example, issues relating to path of travel and disproportionality in alterations are not addressed in detail in ADAAG. (The structure and contents of the two documents are addressed below under Summary of ADAAG.) While the Department agrees that it would be useful to have one self-contained document, the different focuses of this rule and ADAAG do not permit this result at this time. However, the chart

included in § 36.406(b) should assist users in applying the provisions of subparts A through D, and ADAAG together.

Numerous business groups have urged the Department not to adopt the proposed ADAAG as the accessibility standards, because the requirements established are too high, reflect the "state of the art," and are inflexible, rigid, and impractical. Many of these objections have been lodged on the basis that ADAAG exceeds the statutory mandate to establish "minimum" guidelines. In the view of the Department, these commenters have misconstrued the meaning of the term "minimum guidelines." The statute clearly contemplates that the guidelines establish a level of access—a minimum—that the standards must meet or exceed. The guidelines are not to be "minimal" in the sense that they would provide for a low level of access. To the contrary, Congress emphasized that the ADA requires a "high degree of convenient access." Education and Labor report at 117–18. The legislative history explains that the guidelines may not "reduce, weaken, narrow or set less accessibility standards than those included in existing MGRAD" and should provide greater guidance in communication accessibility for individuals with hearing and vision impairments. Id. at 139. Nor did Congress contemplate a set of guidelines less detailed than ADAAG; the statute requires that the ADA guidelines supplement the existing MGRAD. When it established the statutory scheme, Congress was aware of the content and purpose of the 1982 MGRAD; as ADAAG does with respect to ADA, MGRAD establishes a minimum level of access that the Architectural Barriers Act standards (i.e., UFAS) must meet or exceed, and includes a high level of detail.

Many of the same commenters urged the Department to incorporate as its accessibility standards the ANSI standard's technical provisions and to adopt the proposed scoping provisions under development by the Council of American Building Officials' Board for the Coordination of Model Codes (BCMC). They contended that the ANSI standard is familiar to and accepted by professionals, and that both documents are developed through consensus. They suggested that ADAAG will not stay current, because it does not follow an established cyclical review process, and that it is not likely to be adopted by nonfederal jurisdictions in State and local codes. They urged the Department and the Board to coordinate the

ADAAG provisions and any substantive changes to them with the ANSI A117 committee in order to maintain a consistent and uniform set of accessibility standards that can be efficiently and effectively implemented at the State and local level through the existing building regulatory processes.

The Department shares the commenters' goal of coordination between the private sector and Federal standards, to the extent that coordination can lead to substantive requirements consistent with the ADA. A single accessibility standard, or consistent accessibility standards, that can be used for ADA purposes and that can be incorporated or referenced by State and local governments, would help to ensure that the ADA requirements are routinely implemented at the design stage. The Department plans to work toward this goal.

The Department, however, must comply with the requirements of the ADA, the Federal Advisory Committee Act (5 U.S.C app. 1 *et seq.*) and the Administrative Procedure Act (5 U.S.C 551 *et seq.*). Neither the Department nor the Board can adopt private requirements wholesale. Furthermore, neither the 1991 ANSI A117 Standard revision nor the BCMC process is complete. Although the ANSI and BCMC provisions are not final, the Board has carefully considered both the draft BCMC scoping provisions and draft ANSI technical standards and included their language in ADAAG wherever consistent with the ADA.

Some commenters requested that, if the Department did not adopt ANSI by reference, the Department declare compliance with ANSI/BCMC to constitute equivalency with the ADA standards. The Department has not adopted this recommendation but has instead worked as a member of the ATBCB to ensure that its accessibility standards are practical and usable. In addition, as explained under subpart F, Certification of State Laws or Local Building Codes, the proper forum for further evaluation of this suggested approach would be in conjunction with the certification process.

Some commenters urged the Department to allow an additional comment period after the Board published its guidelines in final form, for purposes of affording the public a further opportunity to evaluate the appropriateness of including them as the Departments accessibility standards. Such an additional comment period is unnecessary and would unduly delay the issuance of final regulations. The Department put the public on notice, through the proposed rule, of its intention to adopt the proposed ADAAG, with any changes made by the Board, as the accessibility standards. As a member of the Board and of its ADA Task Force, the Department participated actively in the public hearings held on the proposed guidelines and in preparation of both the proposed and final versions of ADAAG. Many individuals and groups commented directly to the Department's docket, or at its public hearings, about ADAAG. The comments received on ADAAG, whether by the Board or by this Department, were thoroughly analyzed and considered by the Department in the context of whether the proposed ADAAG was consistent with the ADA and suitable for adoption as both guidelines and standards. The Department is convinced that ADAAG as adopted in its final form is appropriate for these purposes. The final guidelines, adopted here as standards, will ensure the high level of access contemplated by Congress, consistent with the ADA's balance between the interests of people with disabilities and the business community.

A few commenters, citing the Senate report (at 70) and the Education and Labor report (at 119), asked the Department to include in the regulations a provision stating that departures from particular technical and scoping requirements of the accessibility standards will be permitted so long as the alternative methods used will provide substantially equivalent or greater access to and utilization of the facility. Such a provision is found in ADAAG 2.2 and by virtue of that fact is included in these regulations.

Comments on specific provisions of proposed ADAAG

During the course of accepting comments on its proposed rule, the Department received numerous comments on ADAAG. Those areas that elicited the heaviest response included assistive listening systems, automated teller machines, work areas, parking, areas of refuge, telephones (scoping for TDD's and volume controls) and visual alarms. Strenuous objections were raised by some business commenters to the proposed provisions of the guidelines concerning check-out aisles, counters, and scoping for hotels and nursing facilities. All these comments were considered in the same manner as other comments on the Department's proposed rule and, in the Department's view, have been addressed adequately in the final ADAAG.

Largely in response to comments, the Board made numerous changes from its proposal, including the following:

• Generally, at least 50% of public entrances to new buildings must be accessible, rather than all entrances, as would often have resulted from the proposed approach.

• Not all check-out aisles are required to be accessible.

• The final guidelines provide greater flexibility in providing access to sales counters, and no longer require a portion of every counter to be accessible.

• Scoping for TDD's or text telephones was increased. One TDD or text telephone, for speech and hearing impaired persons, must be provided at locations with 4, rather than 6, pay phones, and in hospitals and shopping malls. Use of portable (less expensive) TDD's is allowed.

• Dispersal of wheelchair seating areas in theaters will be required only where there are more than 300 seats, rather than in all cases. Seats with removable armrests (i.e., seats into which persons with mobility impairments can transfer) will also be required.

• Areas of refuge (areas with direct access to a stairway, and where people who cannot use stairs may await assistance during a emergency evacuation) will be required, as proposed, but the final provisions are based on the Uniform Building Code. Such areas are not required in alterations.

• Rather than requiring 5% of new hotel rooms to be accessible to people with mobility impairments, between 2 and 4% accessibility (depending on total number of rooms) is required. In addition, 1% of the rooms must have roll-in showers.

• The proposed rule reserved the provisions on alterations to homeless shelters. The final guidelines apply alterations requirements to homeless shelters, but the requirements are less stringent than those applied to other types of facilities.

• Parking spaces that can be used by people in vans (with lifts) will be required.

• As mandated by the ADA, the Board has established a procedure to be followed with respect to alterations to historic facilities.

Summary of ADAAG

This section of the preamble summarizes the structure of ADAAG, and highlights the more important portions.

• *Sections 1 Through 3*

Sections 1 through 3 contain general requirements, including definitions.

• *Section 4.1.1, Application*

Section 4 contains scoping requirements. Section 4.1.1, Application, provides that all areas of newly designed or newly constructed buildings and facilities and altered portions of existing buildings and facilities required to be accessible by § 4.1.6 must comply with the guidelines unless otherwise provided in § 4.1.1 or a special application section. It addresses areas used only by employees as work areas, temporary structures, and general exceptions.

Section 4.1.1(3) preserves the basic principle of the proposed rule: Areas that may be used by employees with disabilities shall be designed and constructed so that an individual with a disability can approach, enter, and exit the area. The language has been clarified to provide that it applies to any area used only as a work area (not just to areas "that may be used by employees with disabilities"), and that the guidelines do not require that any area used as an individual work station be designed with maneuvering space or equipped to be accessible. The appendix to ADAAG explains that work areas must meet the guidelines' requirements for doors and accessible routes, and recommends, but does not require, that 5% of individual work stations be designed to permit a person using a wheelchair to maneuver within the space.

Further discussion of work areas is found in the preamble concerning proposed § 36.401(b).

Section 4.1.1(5)(a) includes an exception for structural impracticability that corresponds to the one found in § 36.401(c) and discussed in that portion of the preamble.

• *Section 4.1.2, Accessible Sites and Exterior Facilities: New Construction*

This section addresses exterior features, elements, or spaces such as parking, portable toilets, and exterior signage, in new construction. Interior elements and spaces are covered by § 4.1.3.

The final rule retains the UFAS scoping for parking but also requires that at least one of every eight accessible parking spaces be designed with adequate adjacent space to deploy a lift used with a van. These spaces must have a sign indicating that they are van-accessible, but they are not to be reserved exclusively for van users.

• *Section 4.1.3, Accessible Buildings: New Construction*

This section establishes scoping requirements for new construction of buildings and facilities.

Sections 4.1.3 (1) through (4) cover accessible routes, protruding objects, ground and floor surfaces, and stairs.

Section 4.1.3(5) generally requires elevators to serve each level in a newly constructed building, with four exceptions included in the subsection. Exception 1 is the "elevator exception" established in § 36.401(d), which must be read with this section. Exception 4 allows the use of platform lifts under certain conditions.

Section 4.1.3(6), Windows, is reserved. Section 4.1.3(7) applies to doors.

Under § 4.1.3(8), at least 50% of all public entrances must be accessible. In addition, if a building is designed to provide access to enclosed parking, pedestrian tunnels, or elevated walkways, at least one entrance that serves each such function must be accessible. Each tenancy in a building must be served by an accessible entrance. Where local regulations (e.g., fire codes) require that a minimum number of exits be provided, an equivalent number of accessible entrances must be provided. (The latter provision does not require a greater number of entrances than otherwise planned.)

ADAAG Section 4.1.3(9), with accompanying technical requirements in Section 4.3, requires an area of rescue assistance (*i.e.*, an area with direct access to an exit stairway and where people who are unable to use stairs may await assistance during an emergency evacuation) to be established on each floor of a multi-story building. This was one of the most controversial provisions in the guidelines. The final ADAAG is based on current Uniform Building Code requirements and retains the requirement that areas of refuge (renamed "areas of rescue assistance") be provided, but specifies that this requirement does not apply to buildings that have a supervised automatic sprinkler system. Areas of refuge are not required in alterations.

The next seven subsections deal with drinking fountains (§ 4.1.3(10)); toilet facilities (§ 4.1.3(11)); storage, shelving, and display units (§ 4.1.3(12)); controls and operating mechanisms (§ 4.1.3(13)), emergency warning systems (§ 4.1.3(14)), detectable warnings (§ 4.1.3(15)), and building signage (§ 4.1.3(16)). Paragraph 11 requires that toilet facilities comply with § 4.22, which requires one accessible toilet stall (60″ × 60″) in each newly constructed restroom. In response

to public comments, the final rule requires that a second accessible stall (36″ × 60″) be provided in restrooms that have six or more stalls.

ADAAG Section 4.1.3(17) establishes requirements for accessibility of pay phones to persons with mobility impairments, hearing impairments (requiring some phones with volume controls), and those who cannot use voice telephones. It requires one interior "text telephone" to be provided at any facility that has a total of four or more public pay phones. (The term "text telephone" has been adopted to reflect current terminology and changes in technology.) In addition, text telephones will be required in specific locations, such as covered shopping malls, hospitals (in emergency rooms, waiting rooms, and recovery areas), and convention centers.

Paragraph 18 of Section 4.1.3 generally requires that at least five percent of fixed or built-in seating or tables be accessible.

Paragraph 19, covering assembly areas, specifies the number of wheelchair seating spaces and types and numbers of assistive listening systems required. It requires dispersal of wheelchair seating locations in facilities where there are more than 300 seats. The guidelines also require that at least one percent of all fixed seats be aisle seats without armrests (or with moveable armrests) on the aisle side to increase accessibility for persons with mobility impairments who prefer to transfer from their wheelchairs to fixed seating. In addition, the final ADAAG requires that fixed seating for a companion be located adjacent to each wheelchair location.

Paragraph 20 requires that where automated teller machines are provided, at least one must comply with section 4.34, which, among other things, requires accessible controls, and instructions and other information that are accessible to persons with sight impairments.

Under paragraph 21, where dressing rooms are provided, five percent or at least one must comply with section 4.35.

• *Section 4.1.5, Additions*

Each addition to an existing building or facility is regarded as an alteration subject to §§ 36.402 through 36.406 of subpart D, including the date established in § 36.402(a). But additions also have attributes of new construction, and to the extent that a space or element in the addition is newly constructed, each new space or element must comply with the applicable scoping provisions of sections 4.1.1 to 4.1.3 for new construction, the applicable technical specifications of sections 4.2 through 4.34, and any applicable special provisions in sections 5 through 10. For instance, if a restroom is provided in the addition, it must comply with the requirements for new construction. Construction of an addition does not, however, create an obligation to retrofit the entire existing building or facility to meet requirements for new construction. Rather, the addition is to be regarded as an alteration and to the extent that it affects or could affect the usability of or access to an area containing a primary function, the requirements in section 4.1.6(2) are triggered with respect to providing an accessible path of travel to the altered area and making the restrooms, telephones, and drinking fountains serving the altered area accessible. For example, if a museum adds a new wing that does not have a separate entrance as part of the addition, an accessible path of travel would have to be provided through the existing building or facility unless it is disproportionate to the overall cost and scope of the addition as established in § 36.403(f).

• *Section 4.1.6, Alterations*

An alteration is a change to a building or facility that affects or could affect the usability of or access to the building or facility or any part thereof. There are three general principles for alterations. First, if any existing element or space is altered, the altered element or space must meet new construction requirements (section 4.1.6(1)(b)). Second, if alterations to the elements in a space when considered together amount to an alteration of the space, the entire space must meet new construction requirements (section 4.1.6(1)(c)). Third, if the alteration affects or could affect the usability of or access to an area containing a primary function, the path of travel to the altered area and the restrooms, drinking fountains, and telephones serving the altered area must be made accessible unless it is disproportionate to the overall alterations in terms of cost and scope as determined under criteria established by the Attorney General (§ 4.1.6(2)).

Section 4.1.6 should be read with §§ 36.402 through 36.405. Requirements concerning alterations to an area serving a primary function are addressed with greater detail in the latter sections than in section 4.1.6(2). Section 4.1.6(1)(j) deals with technical infeasibility. Section 4.1.6(3) contains special technical provisions for alterations to existing buildings and facilities.

• *Section 4.1.7, Historic Preservation*

This section contains scoping provisions and alternative requirements for alterations to qualified historic buildings and facilities. It clarifies the procedures under the National Historic Preservation Act and their application to alterations covered by the ADA. An individual seeking to alter a facility that is subject to the ADA guidelines and to State or local historic preservation statutes shall consult with the State Historic Preservation Officer to determine if the planned alteration would threaten or destroy the historic significance of the facility.

• *Sections 4.2 Through 4.35*

Sections 4.2 through 4.35 contain the technical specifications for elements and spaces required to be accessible by the scoping provisions (sections 4.1 through 4.1.7) and special application sections (sections 5 through 10). The technical specifications are the same as the 1980 version of ANSI A117.1 standard, except as noted in the text by italics.

• *Sections 5 Through 9*

These are special application sections and contain additional requirements for restaurants and cafeterias, medical care facilities, business and mercantile facilities, libraries, and transient lodging. For example, at least 5 percent, but not less than one, of the fixed tables in a restaurant must be accessible.

In section 7, Business and Mercantile, paragraph 7.2 (Sales and Service Counters, Teller Windows, Information Counters) has been revised to provide greater flexibility in new construction than did the proposed rule. At least one of each type of sales or service counter where a cash register is located shall be made accessible. Accessible counters shall be dispersed throughout the facility. At counters such as bank teller windows or ticketing counters, alternative methods of compliance are permitted. A public accommodation may lower a portion of the counter, provide an auxiliary counter, or provide equivalent facilitation through such means as installing a folding shelf on the front of the counter at an accessible height to provide a work surface for a person using a wheelchair.

Section 7.3., Check-out Aisles, provides that, in new construction, a certain number of each design of check-out aisle, as listed in a chart based on the total number of check-out aisles of each design, shall be accessible. The percentage of check-outs required to be accessible generally ranges from 20% to 40%. In a newly constructed or altered

facility with less than 5,000 square feet of selling space, at least one of each type of check-out aisle must be accessible. In altered facilities with 5,000 or more square feet of selling space, at least one of each design of check-out aisle must be made accessible when altered, until the number of accessible aisles equals the number that would be required for new construction.

• *Section 9, Accessible Transient Lodging*

Section 9 addresses two types of transient lodging: hotels, motels, inns, boarding houses, dormitories, resorts, and other similar places (sections 9.1 through 9.4); and homeless shelters, halfway houses, transient group homes, and other social service establishments (section 9.5). The interplay of the ADA and Fair Housing Act with respect to such facilities is addressed in the preamble discussion of the definition of "place of public accommodation" in § 36.104.

The final rule establishes scoping requirements for accessibility of newly constructed hotels. Four percent of the first hundred rooms, and roughly two percent of rooms in excess of 100, must meet certain requirements for accessibility to persons with mobility or hearing impairments, and an additional identical percentage must be accessible to persons with hearing impairments. An additional 1% of the available rooms must be equipped with roll-in showers, raising the actual scoping for rooms accessible to persons with mobility impairments to 5% of the first hundred rooms and 3% thereafter. The final ADAAG also provides that when a hotel is being altered, one fully accessible room and one room equipped with visual alarms, notification devices, and amplified telephones shall be provided for each 25 rooms being altered until the number of accessible rooms equals that required under the new construction standard. Accessible rooms must be dispersed in a manner that will provide persons with disabilities with a choice of single or multiple-bed accommodations.

In new construction, homeless shelters and other social service entities must comply with ADAAG; at least one type of amenity in each common area must be accessible. In a facility that is not required to have an elevator, it is not necessary to provide accessible amenities on the inaccessible floors if at least one of each type of amenity is provided in accessible common areas. The percentage of accessible sleeping accommodations required is the same as that required for other places of transient lodging. Requirements for facilities altered for use as a homeless shelter parallel the current MGRAD accessibility requirements for leased buildings. A shelter located in an altered facility must have at least one accessible entrance, accessible sleeping accommodations in a number equivalent to that established for new construction, at least one accessible toilet and bath, at least one accessible common area, and an accessible route connecting all accessible areas. All accessible areas in a homeless shelter in an altered facility may be located on one level.

Section 10, Transportation Facilities

Section 10 of ADAAG is reserved. On March 20, 1991, the ATBCB published a supplemental notice of proposed rulemaking (56 FR 11874) to establish special access requirements for transportation facilities. The Department anticipates that when the ATBCB issues final guidelines for transportation facilities, this part will be amended to include those provisions.

Subpart E—Enforcement

Because the Department of Justice does not have authority to establish procedures for judicial review and enforcement, subpart E generally restates the statutory procedures for enforcement.

Section 36.501 describes the procedures for private suits by individuals and the judicial remedies available. In addition to the language in section 308(a)(1) of the Act, § 36.501(a) of this part includes the language from section 204(a) of the Civil Rights Act of 1964 (42 U.S.C. 2000a–3(a)) which is incorporated by reference in the ADA. A commenter noted that the proposed rule did not include the provision in section 204(a) allowing the court to appoint an attorney for the complainant and authorize the commencement of the civil action without the payment of fees, costs, or security. That provision has been included in the final rule.

Section 308(a)(1) of the ADA permits a private suit by an individual who has reasonable grounds for believing that he or she is "about to be" subjected to discrimination in violation of section 303 of the Act (subpart D of this part), which requires that new construction and alterations be readily accessible to and usable by individuals with disabilities. Authorizing suits to prevent construction of facilities with architectural barriers will avoid the necessity of costly retrofitting that might be required if suits were not permitted until after the facilities were completed. To avoid unnecessary suits, this section

requires that the individual bringing the suit have 'reasonable grounds" for believing that a violation is about to occur, but does not require the individual to engage in a futile gesture if he or she has notice that a person or organization covered by title III of the Act does not intend to comply with its provisions.

Section 36.501(b) restates the provisions of section 308(a)(2) of the Act, which states that injunctive relief for the failure to remove architectural barriers in existing facilities or the failure to make new construction and alterations accessible "shall include" an order to alter these facilities to make them readily accessible to and usable by persons with disabilities to the extent required by title III. The Report of the Energy and Commerce Committee notes that "an order to make a facility readily accessible to and usable by individuals with disabilities is mandatory" under this standard. H.R. Rep. No. 485, 101st Cong., 2d Sess, pt 4, at 64 (1990). Also, injunctive relief shall include, where appropriate, requiring the provision of an auxiliary aid or service, modification of a policy, or provision of alternative methods, to the extent required by title III of the Act and this part.

Section 36.502 is based on section 308(b)(1)(A)(i) of the Act, which provides that the Attorney General shall investigate alleged violations of title III and undertake periodic reviews of compliance of covered entities. Although the Act does not establish a comprehensive administrative enforcement mechanism for investigation and resolution of all complaints received, the legislative history notes that investigation of alleged violations and periodic compliance reviews are essential to effective enforcement of title III, and that the Attorney General is expected to engage in active enforcement and to allocate sufficient resources to carry out this responsibility. Judiciary Report at 67.

Many commenters argued for inclusion of more specific provisions for administrative resolution of disputes arising under the Act and this part in order to promote voluntary compliance and avoid the need for litigation. Administrative resolution is far more efficient and economical than litigation, particularly in the early stages of implementation of complex legislation when the specific requirements of the statute are not widely understood. The Department has added a new paragraph (c) to this section authorizing the Attorney General to initiate a compliance review where he or she has

reason to believe there may be a violation of this rule.

Section 36.503 describes the procedures for suits by the Attorney General set out in section 308(b)(1)(B) of the Act. If the Department has reasonable cause to believe that any person or group of persons is engaged in a pattern or practice of resistance to the full enjoyment of any of the rights granted by title III or that any person or group of persons has been denied any of the rights granted by title III and such denial raises an issue of general public importance, the Attorney General may commence a civil action in any appropriate United States district court. The proposed rule provided for suit by the Attorney General "or his or her designee." The reference to a "designee" has been omitted in the final rule because it is unnecessary. The Attorney General has delegated enforcement authority under the ADA to the Assistant Attorney General for Civil Rights. 55 FR 40653 (October 4, 1990) (to be codified at 28 CFR 0.50(l).)

Section 36.504 describes the relief that may be granted in a suit by the Attorney General under section 308(b)(2) of the Act. In such an action, the court may grant any equitable relief it considers to be appropriate, including granting temporary, preliminary, or permanent relief, providing an auxiliary aid or service, modification of policy or alternative method, or making facilities readily accessible to and usable by individuals with disabilities, to the extent required by title III. In addition, a court may award such other relief as the court considers to be appropriate, including monetary damages to persons aggrieved, when requested by the Attorney General.

Furthermore, the court may vindicate the public interest by assessing a civil penalty against the covered entity in an amount not exceeding $50,000 for a first violation and not exceeding $100,000 for any subsequent violation. Section 36.504(b) of the rule adopts the standard of section 308(b)(3) of the Act. This section makes it clear that, in counting the number of previous determinations of violations for determining whether a "first" or "subsequent" violation has occurred, determinations in the same action that the entity has engaged in more than one discriminatory act are to be counted as a single violation. A "second violation" would not accrue to that entity until the Attorney General brought another suit against the entity and the entity was again held in violation. Again, all of the violations found in the second suit would be cumulatively considered as a "subsequent violation."

Section 36.504(c) clarifies that the terms "monetary damages" and "other relief" do not include punitive damages. They do include, however, all forms of compensatory damages, including out-of-pocket expenses and damages for pain and suffering.

Section 36.504(a)(3) is based on section 308(b)(2)(C) of the Act, which provides that, "to vindicate the public interest," a court may assess a civil penalty against the entity that has been found to be in violation of the Act in suits brought by the Attorney General. In addition, § 36.504(d), which is taken from section 308(b)(5) of the Act, further provides that, in considering what amount of civil penalty, if any, is appropriate, the court shall give consideration to "any good faith effort or attempt to comply with this part." In evaluating such good faith, the court shall consider "among other factors it deems relevant, whether the entity could have reasonably anticipated the need for an appropriate type of auxiliary aid needed to accommodate the unique needs of a particular individual with a disability."

The "good faith" standard referred to in this section is not intended to imply a willful or intentional standard—that is, an entity cannot demonstrate good faith simply by showing that it did not willfully, intentionally, or recklessly disregard the law. At the same time, the absence of such a course of conduct would be a factor a court should weigh in determining the existence of good faith.

Section 36.505 states that courts are authorized to award attorneys fees, including litigation expenses and costs, as provided in section 505 of the Act. Litigation expenses include items such as expert witness fees, travel expenses, etc. The Judiciary Committee Report specifies that such items are included under the rubric of "attorneys fees" and not "costs" so that such expenses will be assessed against a plaintiff only under the standard set forth in *Christiansburg Garment Co.* v. *Equal Employment Opportunity Commission,* 434 U.S. 412 (1978). (Judiciary report at 73.)

Section 36.506 restates section 513 of the Act, which encourages use of alternative means of dispute resolution. Section 36.507 explains that, as provided in section 506(e) of the Act, a public accommodation or other private entity is not excused from compliance with the requirements of this part because of any failure to receive technical assistance.

Section 36.305   Effective Date

In general, title III is effective 18 months after enactment of the Americans with Disabilities Act, i.e., January 26, 1992. However, there are several exceptions to this general rule contained throughout title III. Section 36.508 sets forth all of these exceptions in one place.

Paragraph (b) contains the rule on civil actions. It states that, except with respect to new construction and alterations, no civil action shall be brought for a violation of this part that occurs before July 26, 1992, against businesses with 25 or fewer employees and gross receipts of $1,000,000 or less; and before January 26, 1993, against businesses with 10 or fewer employees and gross receipts of $500,000 or less. In determining what constitutes gross receipts, it is appropriate to exclude amounts collected for sales taxes.

Paragraph (c) concerns transportation services provided by public accommodations not primarily engaged in the business of transporting people. The 18-month effective date applies to all of the transportation provisions except those requiring newly purchased or leased vehicles to be accessible. Vehicles subject to that requirement must be accessible to and usable by individuals with disabilities if the solicitation for the vehicle is made on or after August 26, 1990.

Subpart F—Certification of State Labs or Local Building Codes

Subpart F establishes procedures to implement section 308(b)(1)(A)(ii) of the Act, which provides that, on the application of a State or local government, the Attorney General may certify that a State law or local building code or similar ordinance meets or exceeds the minimum accessibility requirements of the Act. In enforcement proceedings, this certification will constitute rebuttable evidence that the law or code meets or exceeds the ADA's requirements.

Three significant changes, further explained below, were made from the proposed subpart, in response to comments. First, the State or local jurisdiction is required to hold a public hearing on its proposed request for certification and to submit to the Department, as part of the information and materials in support of a request for certification, a transcript of the hearing. Second, the time allowed for interested persons and organizations to comment on the request filed with the Department (§ 36.605(a)(1)) has been changed from 30 to 60 days. Finally, a new § 36.606,

Guidance concerning model codes, has been added.

Section 36.601 establishes the definitions to be used for purposes of this subpart. Two of the definitions have been modified, and a definition of "model code" has been added. First, in response to a comment, a reference to a code "or part thereof" has been added to the definition of "code." The purpose of this addition is to clarify that an entire code need not be submitted if only part of it is relevant to accessibility, or if the jurisdiction seeks certification of only some of the portions that concern accessibility. The Department does not intend to encourage "piecemeal" requests for certification by a single jurisdiction. In fact, the Department expects that in some cases, rather than certifying portions of a particular code and refusing to certify others, it may notify a submitting jurisdiction of deficiencies and encourage a reapplication that cures those deficiencies, so that the entire code can be certified eventually. Second, the definition of "submitting official" has been modified. The proposed rule defined the submitting official to be the State or local official who has principal responsibility for administration of a code. Commenters pointed out that in some cases more than one code within the same jurisdiction is relevant for purposes of certification. It was also suggested that the Department allow a State to submit a single application on behalf of the State, as well as on behalf of any local jurisdictions required to follow the State accessibility requirements. Consistent with these comments, the Department has added to the definition language clarifying that the official can be one authorized to submit a code on behalf of a jurisdiction.

A definition of "model code" has been added in light of new § 36.606.

Most commenters generally approved of the proposed certification process. Some approved of what they saw as the Department's attempt to bring State and local codes into alignment with the ADA. A State agency said that this section will be the backbone of the intergovernmental cooperation essential if the accessibility provisions of the ADA are to be effective.

Some comments disapproved of the proposed process as timeconsuming and laborious for the Department, although some of these comments pointed out that, if the Attorney General certified model codes on which State and local codes are based, many perceived problems would be alleviated. (This point is further addressed by new § 36.608.)

Many of the comments received from business organizations, as well as those from some individuals and disability rights groups, addressed the relationship of the ADA requirements and their enforcement, to existing State and local codes and code enforcement systems. These commenters urged the Department to use existing code-making bodies for interpretations of the ADA, and to actively participate in the integration of the ADA into the text of the national model codes that are adopted by State and local enforcement agencies. These issues are discussed in preamble section 36.406 under General comments.

Many commenters urged the Department to evaluate or certify the entire code enforcement system (including any process for hearing appeals from builders of denials by the building code official of requests for variances, waivers, or modifications). Some urged that certification not be allowed in jurisdictions where waivers can be granted, unless there is a clearly identified decision-making process, with written rulings and notice to affected parties of any waiver or modification request. One commenter urged establishment of a dispute resolution mechanism, providing for interpretation (usually through a building official) and an administrative appeals mechanism (generally called Boards of Appeal, Boards of Construction Appeals, or Boards of Review), before certification could be granted.

The Department thoroughly considered these proposals but has declined to provide for certification of processes of enforcement or administration of State and local codes. The statute clearly authorizes the Department to certify the codes themselves for equivalency with the statute; it would be ill-advised for the Department at this point to inquire beyond the face of the code and written interpretations of it. It would be inappropriate to require those jurisdictions that grant waivers or modifications to establish certain procedures before they can apply for certification, or to insist that no deviations can be permitted. In fact, the Department expects that many jurisdictions will allow slight variations from a particular code, consistent with ADAAG itself. ADAAG includes in § 2.2 a statement allowing departures from particular requirements where substantially equivalent or greater access and usability is provided. Several sections specifically allow for

alternative methods providing equivalent facilitation and, in some cases, provide examples. (See, e.g., section 4.31.9, Text Telephones; section 7.2(2) (iii), Sales and Service Counters.) Section 4.1.6 includes less stringent requirements that are permitted in alterations, in certain circumstances.

However, in an attempt to ensure that it does not certify a code that in practice has been or will be applied in a manner that defeats its equivalency with the ADA, the Department will require that the submitting official include, with the application for certification, any relevant manuals, guides, or any other interpretive information issued that pertain to the code. (§ 36.603(c)(1).) The requirement that this information be provided is in addition to the NPRM's requirement that the official provide any pertinent formal opinions of the State Attorney General or the chief legal officer of the jurisdiction.

The first step in the certification process is a request for certification, filed by a "submitting official" (§ 36.603). The Department will not accept requests for certification until after January 26, 1992, the effective date of this part. The Department received numerous comments from individuals and organizations representing a variety of interests, urging that the hearing required to be held by the Assistant Attorney General in Washington, DC, after a preliminary determination of equivalency (§ 36.605(a)(2)), be held within the State or locality requesting certification, in order to facilitate greater participation by all interested parties. While the Department has not modified the requirement that it hold a hearing in Washington, it has added a new subparagraph 36.603(b)(3) requiring a hearing within the State or locality before a request for certification is filed. The hearing must be held after adequate notice to the public and must be on the record; a transcript must be provided with the request for certification. This procedure will insure input from the public at the State or local level and will also insure a Washington, DC, hearing as mentioned in the legislative history.

The request for certification, along with supporting documents (§ 36.603(c)), must be filed in duplicate with the office of the Assistant Attorney General for Civil Rights. The Assistant Attorney General may request further information. The request and supporting materials will be available for public examination at the office of the Assistant Attorney General and at the office of the State or local agency charged with administration and enforcement of the code. The submitting

official must publish public notice of the request for certification.

Next, under § 36.604, the Assistant Attorney General's office will consult with the ATBCB and make a preliminary determination to either (1) find that the code is equivalent (make a "preliminary determination of equivalency") or (2) deny certification. The next step depends on which of these preliminary determinations is made.

If the preliminary determination is to find equivalency, the Assistant Attorney General, under § 36.605, will inform the submitting official in writing of the preliminary determination and publish a notice in the **Federal Register** informing the public of the preliminary determination and inviting comment for 60 days. (This time period has been increased from 30 days in light of public comment pointing out the need for more time within which to evaluate the code.) After considering the information received in response to the comments, the Department will hold a hearing in Washington. This hearing will not be subject to the formal requirements of the Administrative Procedure Act. In fact, this requirement could be satisfied by a meeting with interested parties. After the hearing, the Assistant Attorney General's office will consult again with the ATBCB and make a final determination of equivalency or a final determination to deny the request for certification, with a notice of the determination published in the **Federal Register.**

If the preliminary determination is to deny certification, there will be no hearing (§ 36.606). The Department will notify the submitting official of the preliminary determination, and may specify how the code could be modified in order to receive a preliminary determination of equivalency. The Department will allow at least 15 days for the submitting official to submit relevant material in opposition to the preliminary denial. If none is received, no further action will be taken. If more information is received, the Department will consider it and make either a final decision to deny certification or a preliminary determination of equivalency. If at that stage the Assistant Attorney General makes a preliminary determination of equivalency, the hearing procedures set out in § 36.605 will be followed.

Section 36.607 addresses the effect of certification. First, certification will only be effective concerning those features or elements that are both (1) covered by the certified code and (2) addressed by the regulations against which they are being certified. For example, if children's facilities are not addressed by the Department's standards, and the building in question is a private elementary school, certification will not be effective for those features of the building to be used by children. And if the Department's regulations addressed equipment but the local code did not, a building's equipment would not be covered by the certification.

In addition, certification will be effective only for the particular edition of the code that is certified. Amendments will not automatically be considered certified, and a submitting official will need to reapply for certification of the changed or additional provisions.

Certification will not be effective in those situations where a State or local building code official allows a facility to be constructed or altered in a manner that does not follow the technical or scoping provisions of the certified code. Thus, if an official either waives an accessible element or feature or allows a change that does not provide equivalent facilitation, the fact that the Department has certified the code itself will not stand as evidence that the facility has been constructed or altered in accordance with the minimum accessibility requirements of the ADA. The Department's certification of a code is effective only with respect to the standards in the code; it is not to be interpreted to apply to a State or local government's application of the code. The fact that the Department has certified a code with provisions concerning waivers, variances, or equivalent facilitation shall not be interpreted as an endorsement of actions taken pursuant to those provisions.

The final rule includes a new § 36.608 concerning model codes. It was drafted in response to concerns raised by numerous commenters, many of which have been discussed under General comments (§ 36.406). It is intended to assist in alleviating the difficulties posed by attempting to certify possibly tens of thousands of codes. It is included in recognition of the fact that many codes are based on, or incorporate, model or consensus standards developed by nationally recognized organizations (e.g., the American National Standards Institute (ANSI); Building Officials and Code Administrators (BOCA) International; Council of American Building Officials (CABO) and its Board for the Coordination of Model Codes (BCMC); Southern Building Code Congress International (SBCCI)). While the Department will not certify or

"precertify" model codes, as urged by some commenters, it does wish to encourage the continued viability of the consensus and model code process consistent with the purposes of the ADA.

The new section therefore allows an authorized representative of a private entity responsible for developing a model code to apply to the Assistant Attorney General for review of the code. The review process will be informal and will not be subject to the procedures of §§ 36.602 through 36.607. The result of the review will take the form of guidance from the Assistant Attorney General as to whether and in what respects the model code is consistent with the ADA's requirements. The guidance will not be binding on any entity or on the Department; it will assist in evaluations of individual State or local codes and may serve as a basis for establishing priorities for consideration of individual codes. The Department anticipates that this approach will foster further cooperation among various government levels, the private entities developing standards, and individuals with disabilities.

List of Subjects in 28 CFR Part 36

Administrative practice and procedure, Alcoholism, Americans with disabilities, Buildings, Business and industry, Civil rights, Consumer protection, Drug abuse, Handicapped, Historic preservation, Reporting and recordkeeping requirements.

By the authority vested in me as Attorney General by 28 U.S.C. 509, 510, 5 U.S.C. 301, and section 306(b) of the Americans with Disabilities Act, Public Law 101-336, and for the reasons set forth in the preamble, Chapter I of title 28 of the Code of Federal Regulations is amended by adding a new part 36 to read as follows:

PART 36—NONDISCRIMINATION ON THE BASIS OF DISABILITY BY PUBLIC ACCOMMODATIONS AND IN COMMERCIAL FACILITIES

Subpart A—General

Sec.
36.101   Purpose.
36.102   Application.
36.103   Relationship to other laws.
36.104   Definitions.
36.105—36.200   [Reserved]

Subpart B—General Requirements

36.201   General.
36.202   Activities.
36.203   Integrated settings.
36.204   Administrative methods.
36.205   Association.
36.206   Retaliation or coercion.

36.207   Places of public accommodations located in private residences.
36.208   Direct threat.
36.209   Illegal use of drugs.
36.210   Smoking.
36.211   Maintenance of accessible features.
36.212   Insurance.
36.213   Relationship of subpart B to subparts C and D of this part.
36.214—36.300   [Reserved]

Subpart C—Specific Requirements

36.301   Eligibility criteria.
36.302   Modifications in policies, practices, or procedures.
36.303   Auxiliary aids and services.
36.304   Removal of barriers.
36.305   Alternatives to barrier removal.
36.306   Personal devices and services.
36.307   Accessible or special goods.
36.308   Seating in assembly areas.
36.309   Examinations and courses.
36.310   Transportation provided by public accommodations.
36.311—36.400   [Reserved]

Subpart D—New Construction and Alterations

36.401   New construction.
36.402   Alterations.
36.403   Alterations: Path of travel.
36.404   Alterations: Elevator exemption.
36.405   Alterations: Historic preservation.
36.406   Standards for new construction and alterations.
36.407—36.500   [Reserved]

Subpart E—Enforcement

36.501   Private suits.
36.502   Investigations and compliance reviews.
36.503   Suit by the Attorney General.
36.504   Relief.
36.505   Attorneys fees.
36.506   Alternative means of dispute resolution.
36.507   Effect of unavailability of technical assistance.
36.508   Effective date.
36.509—36.600   [Reserved]

Subpart F—Certification of State Laws or Local Building Codes

36.601   Definitions.
36.602   General rule.
36.603   Filing a request for certification.
36.604   Preliminary determination.
36.605   Procedure following preliminary determination of equivalency.
36.606   Procedure following preliminary denial of certification.
36.607   Effect of certification.
36.608   Guidance concerning model codes.
36.609—36.999   [Reserved]

Appendix A to Part 36—Standards for Accessible Design

Appendix B to Part 36—Preamble to Regulation on Nondiscrimination on the Basis of Disability by Public Accommodations and in Commercial Facilities (Published July 26, 1991)

Authority: 5 U.S.C. 301; 28 U.S.C. 509, 510; Pub. L. 101-336, 42 U.S.C. 12186.

Subpart A—General

§ 36.101   Purpose.

The purpose of this part is to implement title III of the Americans with Disabilities Act of 1990 (42 U.S.C. 12181), which prohibits discrimination on the basis of disability by public accommodations and requires places of public accommodation and commercial facilities to be designed, constructed, and altered in compliance with the accessibility standards established by this part.

§ 36.102   Application.

(a) *General.* This part applies to any—
(1) Public accommodation;
(2) Commercial facility; or
(3) Private entity that offers examinations or courses related to applications, licensing, certification, or credentialing for secondary or postsecondary education, professional, or trade purposes.

(b) *Public accommodations.* (1) The requirements of this part applicable to public accommodations are set forth in subparts B, C, and D of this part.

(2) The requirements of subparts B and C of this part obligate a public accommodation only with respect to the operations of a place of public accommodation.

(3) The requirements of subpart D of this part obligate a public accommodation only with respect to—

(i) A facility used as, or designed or constructed for use as, a place of public accommodation; or

(ii) A facility used as, or designed and constructed for use as, a commercial facility.

(c) *Commercial facilities.* The requirements of this part applicable to commercial facilities are set forth in subpart D of this part.

(d) *Examinations and courses.* The requirements of this part applicable to private entities that offer examinations or courses as specified in paragraph (a) of this section are set forth in § 36.309.

(e) *Exemptions and exclusions.* This part does not apply to any private club (except to the extent that the facilities of the private club are made available to customers or patrons of a place of public accommodation), or to any religious entity or public entity.

§ 36.103   Relationship to other laws.

(a) *Rule of interpretation.* Except as otherwise provided in this part, this part shall not be construed to apply a lesser standard than the standards applied under title V of the Rehabilitation Act of 1973 (29 U.S.C. 791) or the regulations issued by Federal agencies pursuant to that title.

(b) *Section 504.* This part does not affect the obligations of a recipient of Federal financial assistance to comply with the requirements of section 504 of the Rehabilitation Act of 1973 (29 U.S.C. 794) and regulations issued by Federal agencies implementing section 504.

(c) *Other laws.* This part does not invalidate or limit the remedies, rights, and procedures of any other Federal laws, or State or local laws (including State common law) that provide greater or equal protection for the rights of individuals with disabilities and individuals associated with them.

§ 36.104   Definitions.

For purposes of this part, the term—

Act means the Americans with Disabilities Act of 1990 (Pub. L. 101–336, 104 Stat. 327, 42 U.S.C. 12101–12213 and 47 U.S.C. 225 and 611).

Commerce means travel, trade, traffic, commerce, transportation, or communication—

(1) Among the several States;
(2) Between any foreign country or any territory or possession and any State; or
(3) Between points in the same State but through another State or foreign country.

Commercial facilities means facilities—

(1) Whose operations will affect commerce;
(2) That are intended for nonresidential use by a private entity; and
(3) That are not—

(i) Facilities that are covered or expressly exempted from coverage under the Fair Housing Act of 1968, as amended (42 U.S.C. 3601–3631);
(ii) Aircraft; or
(iii) Railroad locomotives, railroad freight cars, railroad cabooses, commuter or intercity passenger rail cars (including coaches, dining cars, sleeping cars, lounge cars, and food service cars), any other railroad cars described in section 242 of the Act or covered under title II of the Act, or railroad rights-of-way. For purposes of this definition, "rail" and "railroad" have the meaning given the term "railroad" in section 202(e) of the Federal Railroad Safety Act of 1970 (45 U.S.C. 431(e)).

Current illegal use of drugs means illegal use of drugs that occurred recently enough to justify a reasonable belief that a person's drug use is current or that continuing use is a real and ongoing problem.

Disability means, with respect to an individual, a physical or mental impairment that substantially limits one or more of the major life activities of such individual; a record of such an impairment; or being regarded as having such an impairment.

(1) The phrase *physical or mental impairment* means—

(i) Any physiological disorder or condition, cosmetic disfigurement, or anatomical loss affecting one or more of the following body systems: neurological; musculoskeletal; special sense organs; respiratory, including speech organs; cardiovascular; reproductive; digestive; genitourinary; hemic and lymphatic; skin; and endocrine;

(ii) Any mental or psychological disorder such as mental retardation, organic brain syndrome, emotional or mental illness, and specific learning disabilities;

(iii) The phrase physical or mental impairment includes, but is not limited to, such contagious and noncontagious diseases and conditions as orthopedic, visual, speech, and hearing impairments, cerebral palsy, epilepsy, muscular dystrophy, multiple sclerosis, cancer, heart disease, diabetes, mental retardation, emotional illness, specific learning disabilities, HIV disease (whether symptomatic or asymptomatic), tuberculosis, drug addiction, and alcoholism;

(iv) The phrase *physical or mental impairment* does not include homosexuality or bisexuality.

(2) The phrase *major life activities* means functions such as caring for one's self, performing manual tasks, walking, seeing, hearing, speaking, breathing, learning, and working.

(3) The phrase *has a record of such an impairment* means has a history of, or has been misclassified as having, a mental or physical impairment that substantially limits one or more major life activities.

(4) The phrase *is regarded as having an impairment* means—

(i) Has a physical or mental impairment that does not substantially limit major life activities but that is treated by a private entity as constituting such a limitation;

(ii) Has a physical or mental impairment that substantially limits major life activities only as a result of the attitudes of others toward such impairment; or

, (iii) Has none of the impairments defined in paragraph (1) of this definition but is treated by a private entity as having such an impairment.

(5) The term *disability* does not include—

(i) Transvestism, transsexualism, pedophilia, exhibitionism, voyeurism, gender identity disorders not resulting from physical impairments, or other sexual behavior disorders;

(ii) Compulsive gambling, kleptomania, or pyromania; or

(iii) Psychoactive substance use disorders resulting from current illegal use of drugs.

Drug means a controlled substance, as defined in schedules I through V of section 202 of the Controlled Substances Act (21 U.S.C. 812).

Facility means all or any portion of buildings, structures, sites, complexes, equipment, rolling stock or other conveyances, roads, walks, passageways, parking lots, or other real or personal property, including the site where the building, property, structure, or equipment is located.

Illegal use of drugs means the use of one or more drugs, the possession or distribution of which is unlawful under the Controlled Substances Act (21 U.S.C. 812). The term "illegal use of drugs" does not include the use of a drug taken under supervision by a licensed health care professional, or other uses authorized by the Controlled Substances Act or other provisions of Federal law.

Individual with a disability means a person who has a disability. The term "individual with a disability" does not include an individual who is currently engaging in the illegal use of drugs, when the private entity acts on the basis of such use.

Place of public accommodation means a facility, operated by a private entity, whose operations affect commerce and fall within at least one of the following categories—

(1) An inn, hotel, motel, or other place of lodging, except for an establishment located within a building that contains not more than five rooms for rent or hire and that is actually occupied by the proprietor of the establishment as the residence of the proprietor;

(2) A restaurant, bar, or other establishment serving food or drink;

(3) A motion picture house, theater, concert hall, stadium, or other place of exhibition or entertainment;

(4) An auditorium, convention center, lecture hall, or other place of public gathering;

(5) A bakery, grocery store, clothing store, hardware store, shopping center, or other sales or rental establishment;

(6) A laundromat, dry-cleaner, bank, barber shop, beauty shop, travel service, shoe repair service, funeral parlor, gas station, office of an accountant or lawyer, pharmacy, insurance office, professional office of a health care provider, hospital, or other service establishment;

(7) A terminal, depot, or other station used for specified public transportation;

(8) A museum, library, gallery, or other place of public display or collection;

(9) A park, zoo, amusement park, or other place of recreation;

(10) A nursery, elementary, secondary, undergraduate, or postgraduate private school, or other place of education;

(11) A day care center, senior citizen center, homeless shelter, food bank, adoption agency, or other social service center establishment; and

(12) A gymnasium, health spa, bowling alley, golf course, or other place of exercise or recreation.

Private club means a private club or establishment exempted from coverage under title II of the Civil Rights Act of 1964 (42 U.S.C. 2000a(e)).

Private entity means a person or entity other than a public entity.

Public accommodation means a private entity that owns (or leases (or leases to), or operates a place of public accommodation.

Public entity means—

(1) Any State or local government;

(2) Any department, agency, special purpose district, or other instrumentality of a State or States or local government; and

(3) The National Railroad Passenger Corporation, and any commuter authority (as defined in section 103(8) of the Rail Passenger Service Act). (45 U.S.C. 541)

Qualified interpreter means an interpreter who is able to interpret effectively, accurately and impartially both receptively and expressively, using any necessary specialized vocabulary.

Readily achievable means easily accomplishable and able to be carried out without much difficulty or expense. In determining whether an action is readily achievable factors to be considered include—

(1) The nature and cost of the action needed under this part;

(2) The overall financial resources of the site or sites involved in the action; the number of persons employed at the site; the effect on expenses and resources; legitimate safety requirements that are necessary for safe operation, including crime prevention measures; or the impact otherwise of the action upon the operation of the site;

(3) The geographic separateness, and the administrative or fiscal relationship of the site or sites in question to any parent corporation or entity;

(4) If applicable, the overall financial resources of any parent corporation or entity; the overall size of the parent corporation or entity with respect to the number of its employees; the number, type, and location of its facilities; and

(5) If applicable, the type of operation or operations of any parent corporation or entity, including the composition, structure, and functions of the workforce of the parent corporation or entity.

Religious entity means a religious organization, including a place of worship.

Service animal means any guide dog, signal dog, or other animal individually trained to do work or perform tasks for the benefit of an individual with a disability, including, but not limited to, guiding individuals with impaired vision, alerting individuals with impaired hearing to intruders or sounds, providing minimal protection or rescue work, pulling a wheelchair, or fetching dropped items.

Specified public transportation means transportation by bus, rail, or any other conveyance (other than by aircraft) that provides the general public with general or special service (including charter service) on a regular and continuing basis.

State means each of the several States, the District of Columbia, the Commonwealth of Puerto Rico, Guam, American Samoa, the Virgin Islands, the Trust Territory of the Pacific Islands, and the Commonwealth of the Northern Mariana Islands.

Undue burden means significant difficulty or expense. In determining whether an action would result in an undue burden, factors to be considered include—

(1) The nature and cost of the action needed under this part;

(2) The overall financial resources of the site or sites involved in the action; the number of persons employed at the site; the effect on expenses and resources; legitimate safety requirements that are necessary for safe operation, including crime prevention measures; or the impact otherwise of the action upon the operation of the site;

(3) The geographic separateness, and the administrative or fiscal relationship of the site or sites in question to any parent corporation or entity;

(4) If applicable, the overall financial resources of any parent corporation or entity; the overall size of the parent corporation or entity with respect to the number of its employees; the number, type, and location of its facilities; and

(5) If applicable, the type of operation or operations of any parent corporation or entity, including the composition, structure, and functions of the workforce of the parent corporation or entity.

C-186

§§ 36.105–36.200 [Reserved]

Subpart B—General Requirements

§ 36.201 General.

(a) *Prohibition of discrimination*. No individual shall be discriminated against on the basis of disability in the full and equal enjoyment of the goods, services, facilities, privileges, advantages, or accommodations of any place of public accommodation by any private entity who owns, leases (or leases to), or operates a place of public accommodation.

(b) *Landlord and tenant responsibilities*. Both the landlord who owns the building that houses a place of public accommodation and the tenant who owns or operates the place of public accommodation are public accommodations subject to the requirements of this part. As between the parties, allocation of responsibility for complying with the obligations of this part may be determined by lease or other contract.

§ 36.202 Activities.

(a) *Denial of participation*. A public accommodation shall not subject an individual or class of individuals on the basis of a disability or disabilities of such individual or class, directly, or through contractual, licensing, or other arrangements, to a denial of the opportunity of the individual or class to participate in or benefit from the goods, services, facilities, privileges, advantages, or accommodations of a place of public accommodation.

(b) *Participation in unequal benefit*. A public accommodation shall not afford an individual or class of individuals, on the basis of a disability or disabilities of such individual or class, directly, or through contractual, licensing, or other arrangements, with the opportunity to participate in or benefit from a good, service, facility, privilege, advantage, or accommodation that is not equal to that afforded to other individuals.

(c) *Separate benefit*. A public accommodation shall not provide an individual or class of individuals, on the basis of a disability or disabilities of such individual or class, directly, or through contractual, licensing, or other arrangements with a good, service, facility, privilege, advantage, or accommodation that is different or separate from that provided to other individuals, unless such action is necessary to provide the individual or class of individuals with a good, service, facility, privilege, advantage, or accommodation, or other opportunity that is as effective as that provided to others.

(d) *Individual or class of individuals*. For purposes of paragraphs (a) through (c) of this section, the term "individual or class of individuals" refers to the clients or customers of the public accommodation that enters into the contractual, licensing, or other arrangement.

§ 36.203 Integrated settings.

(a) *General*. A public accommodation shall afford goods, services, facilities, privileges, advantages, and accommodations to an individual with a disability in the most integrated setting appropriate to the needs of the individual.

(b) *Opportunity to participate*. Notwithstanding the existence of separate or different programs or activities provided in accordance with this subpart, a public accommodation shall not deny an individual with a disability an opportunity to participate in such programs or activities that are not separate or different.

(c) *Accommodations and services*. (1) Nothing in this part shall be construed to require an individual with a disability to accept an accommodation, aid, service, opportunity, or benefit available under this part that such individual chooses not to accept.

(2) Nothing in the Act or this part authorizes the representative or guardian of an individual with a disability to decline food, water, medical treatment, or medical services for that individual.

§ 36.204 Administrative methods.

A public accommodation shall not, directly or through contractual or other arrangements, utilize standards or criteria or methods of administration that have the effect of discriminating on the basis of disability, or that perpetuate the discrimination of others who are subject to common administrative control.

§ 36.205 Association.

A public accommodation shall not exclude or otherwise deny equal goods, services, facilities, privileges, advantages, accommodations, or other opportunities to an individual or entity because of the known disability of an individual with whom the individual or entity is known to have a relationship or association.

§ 36.206 Retaliation or coercion.

(a) No private or public entity shall discriminate against any individual because that individual has opposed any act or practice made unlawful by this part, or because that individual made a charge, testified, assisted, or participated in any manner in an investigation, proceeding, or hearing under the Act or this part.

(b) No private or public entity shall coerce, intimidate, threaten, or interfere with any individual in the exercise or enjoyment of, or on account of his or her having exercised or enjoyed, or on account of his or her having aided or encouraged any other individual in the exercise or enjoyment of, any right granted or protected by the Act or this part.

(c) Illustrations of conduct prohibited by this section include, but are not limited to:

(1) Coercing an individual to deny or limit the benefits, services, or advantages to which he or she is entitled under the Act or this part;

(2) Threatening, intimidating, or interfering with an individual with a disability who is seeking to obtain or use the goods, services, facilities, privileges, advantages, or accommodations of a public accommodation;

(3) Intimidating or threatening any person because that person is assisting or encouraging an individual or group entitled to claim the rights granted or protected by the Act or this part to exercise those rights; or

(4) Retaliating against any person because that person has participated in any investigation or action to enforce the Act or this part.

§ 36.207 Places of public accommodation located in private residences.

(a) When a place of public accommodation is located in a private residence, the portion of the residence used exclusively as a residence is not covered by this part, but that portion used exclusively in the operation of the place of public accommodation or that portion used both for the place of public accommodation and for residential purposes is covered by this part.

(b) The portion of the residence covered under paragraph (a) of this section extends to those elements used to enter the place of public accommodation, including the homeowner's front sidewalk, if any, the door or entryway, and hallways; and those portions of the residence, interior or exterior, available to or used by customers or clients, including restrooms.

§ 36.208 Direct threat.

(a) This part does not require a public accommodation to permit an individual to participate in or benefit from the goods, services, facilities, privileges, advantages and accommodations of that public accommodation when that individual poses a direct threat to the health or safety of others.

(b) *Direct threat* means a significant risk to the health or safety of others that cannot be eliminated by a modification of policies, practices, or procedures, or by the provision of auxiliary aids or services.

(c) In determining whether an individual poses a direct threat to the health or safety of others, a public accommodation must make an individualized assessment, based on reasonable judgment that relies on current medical knowledge or on the best available objective evidence, to ascertain: the nature, duration, and severity of the risk; the probability that the potential injury will actually occur; and whether reasonable modifications of policies, practices, or procedures will mitigate the risk.

§ 36.209 Illegal use of drugs.

(a) *General.* (1) Except as provided in paragraph (b) of this section, this part does not prohibit discrimination against an individual based on that individual's current illegal use of drugs.

(2) A public accommodation shall not discriminate on the basis of illegal use of drugs against an individual who is not engaging in current illegal use of drugs and who—

(i) Has successfully completed a supervised drug rehabilitation program or has otherwise been rehabilitated successfully;

(ii) Is participating in a supervised rehabilitation program; or

(iii) Is erroneously regarded as engaging in such use.

(b) *Health and drug rehabilitation services.* (1) A public accommodation shall not deny health services, or services provided in connection with drug rehabilitation, to an individual on the basis of that individual's current illegal use of drugs, if the individual is otherwise entitled to such services.

(2) A drug rehabilitation or treatment program may deny participation to individuals who engage in illegal use of drugs while they are in the program.

(c) *Drug testing.* (1) This part does not prohibit a public accommodation from adopting or administering reasonable policies or procedures, including but not limited to drug testing, designed to ensure that an individual who formerly engaged in the illegal use of drugs is not now engaging in current illegal use of drugs.

(2) Nothing in this paragraph (c) shall be construed to encourage, prohibit, restrict, or authorize the conducting of testing for the illegal use of drugs.

§ 36.210 Smoking.

This part does not preclude the prohibition of, or the imposition of restrictions on, smoking in places of public accommodation.

§ 36.211 Maintenance of accessible features.

(a) A public accommodation shall maintain in operable working condition those features of facilities and equipment that are required to be readily accessible to and usable by persons with disabilities by the Act or this part.

(b) This section does not prohibit isolated or temporary interruptions in service or access due to maintenance or repairs.

§ 36.212 Insurance.

(a) This part shall not be construed to prohibit or restrict—

(1) An insurer, hospital or medical service company, health maintenance organization, or any agent, or entity that administers benefit plans, or similar organizations from underwriting risks, classifying risks, or administering such risks that are based on or not inconsistent with State law; or

(2) A person or organization covered by this part from establishing, sponsoring, observing or administering the terms of a bona fide benefit plan that are based on underwriting risks, classifying risks, or administering such risks that are based on or not inconsistent with State law; or

(3) A person or organization covered by this part from establishing, sponsoring, observing or administering the terms of a bona fide benefit plan that is not subject to State laws that regulate insurance.

(b) Paragraphs (a) (1), (2), and (3) of this section shall not be used as a subterfuge to evade the purposes of the Act or this part.

(c) A public accommodation shall not refuse to serve an individual with a disability because its insurance company conditions coverage or rates on the absence of individuals with disabilities.

§ 36.213 Relationship of subpart B to subparts C and D of this part.

Subpart B of this part sets forth the general principles of nondiscrimination applicable to all entities subject to this part. Subparts C and D of this part provide guidance on the application of the statute to specific situations. The specific provisions, including the limitations on those provisions, control over the general provisions in circumstances where both specific and general provisions apply.

§§ 36.214–36.300 [Reserved]

Subpart C—Specific Requirements

§ 36.301 Eligibility criteria.

(a) *General.* A public accommodation shall not impose or apply eligibility criteria that screen out or tend to screen out an individual with a disability or any class of individuals with disabilities from fully and equally enjoying any goods, services, facilities, privileges, advantages, or accommodations, unless such criteria can be shown to be necessary for the provision of the goods, services, facilities, privileges, advantages, or accommodations being offered.

(b) *Safety.* A public accommodation may impose legitimate safety requirements that are necessary for safe operation. Safety requirements must be based on actual risks and not on mere speculation, stereotypes, or generalizations about individuals with disabilities.

(c) *Charges.* A public accommodation may not impose a surcharge on a particular individual with a disability or any group of individuals with disabilities to cover the costs of measures, such as the provision of auxiliary aids, barrier removal, alternatives to barrier removal, and reasonable modifications in policies, practices, or procedures, that are required to provide that individual or group with the nondiscriminatory treatment required by the Act or this part.

§ 36.302 Modifications in policies, practices, or procedures.

(a) *General.* A public accommodation shall make reasonable modifications in policies, practices, or procedures, when the modifications are necessary to afford goods, services, facilities, privileges, advantages, or accommodations to individuals with disabilities, unless the public accommodation can demonstrate that making the modifications would fundamentally alter the nature of the goods, services, facilities, privileges, advantages, or accommodations.

(b) *Specialties*—(1) *General.* A public accommodation may refer an individual with a disability to another public accommodation, if that individual is seeking, or requires, treatment or services outside of the referring public accommodation's area of specialization, and if, in the normal course of its operations, the referring public accommodation would make a similar referral for an individual without a disability who seeks or requires the same treatment or services.

(2) *Illustration—medical specialties.* A health care provider may refer an individual with a disability to another provider, if that individual is seeking, or requires, treatment or services outside of the referring provider's area of specialization, and if the referring provider would make a similar referral for an individual without a disability who seeks or requires the same treatment or services. A physician who specializes in treating only a particular condition cannot refuse to treat an individual with a disability for that condition, but is not required to treat the individual for a different condition.

(c) *Service animals—*(1) *General.* Generally, a public accommodation shall modify policies, practices, or procedures to permit the use of a service animal by an individual with a disability.

(2) *Care or supervision of service animals.* Nothing in this part requires a public accommodation to supervise or care for a service animal.

(d) *Check-out aisles.* A store with check-out aisles shall ensure that an adequate number of accessible check-out aisles are kept open during store hours, or shall otherwise modify its policies and practices, in order to ensure that an equivalent level of convenient service is provided to individuals with disabilities as is provided to others. If only one check-out aisle is accessible, and it is generally used for express service, one way of providing equivalent service is to allow persons with mobility impairments to make all their purchases at that aisle.

§ 36.303   Auxiliary aids and services.

(a) *General.* A public accommodation shall take those steps that may be necessary to ensure that no individual with a disability is excluded, denied services, segregated or otherwise treated differently than other individuals because of the absence of auxiliary aids and services, unless the public accommodation can demonstrate that taking those steps would fundamentally alter the nature of the goods, services, facilities, privileges, advantages, or accommodations being offered or would result in an undue burden, i.e., significant difficulty or expense.

(b) *Examples.* The term "auxiliary aids and services" includes—

(1) Qualified interpreters, notetakers, computer-aided transcription services, written materials, telephone handset amplifiers, assistive listening devices, assistive listening systems, telephones compatible with hearing aids, closed caption decoders, open and closed captioning, telecommunications devices for deaf persons (TDD's), videotext displays, or other effective methods of making aurally delivered materials available to individuals with hearing impairments;

(2) Qualified readers, taped texts, audio recordings, Brailled materials, large print materials, or other effective methods of making visually delivered materials available to individuals with visual impairments;

(3) Acquisition or modification of equipment or devices; and

(4) Other similar services and actions.

(c) *Effective communication.* A public accommodation shall furnish appropriate auxiliary aids and services where necessary to ensure effective communication with individuals with disabilities.

(d) *Telecommunication devices for the deaf (TDD's).* (1) A public accommodation that offers a customer, client, patient, or participant the opportunity to make outgoing telephone calls on more than an incidental convenience basis shall make available, upon request, a TDD for the use of an individual who has impaired hearing or a communication disorder.

(2) This part does not require a public accommodation to use a TDD for receiving or making telephone calls incident to its operations.

(e) *Closed caption decoders.* Places of lodging that provide televisions in five or more guest rooms and hospitals that provide televisions for patient use shall provide, upon request, a means for decoding captions for use by an individual with impaired hearing.

(f) *Alternatives.* If provision of a particular auxiliary aid or service by a public accommodation would result in a fundamental alteration in the nature of the goods, services, facilities, privileges, advantages, or accommodations being offered or in an undue burden, i.e., significant difficulty or expense, the public accommodation shall provide an alternative auxiliary aid or service, if one exists, that would not result in an alteration or such burden but would nevertheless ensure that, to the maximum extent possible, individuals with disabilities receive the goods, services, facilities, privileges, advantages, or accommodations offered by the public accommodation.

§ 36.304   Removal of barriers.

(a) *General.* A public accommodation shall remove architectural barriers in existing facilities, including communication barriers that are structural in nature, where such removal is readily achievable, i.e., easily accomplishable and able to be carried out without much difficulty or expense.

(b) *Examples.* Examples of steps to remove barriers include, but are not limited to, the following actions—

(1) Installing ramps;

(2) Making curb cuts in sidewalks and entrances;

(3) Repositioning shelves;

(4) Rearranging tables, chairs, vending machines, display racks, and other furniture;

(5) Repositioning telephones;

(6) Adding raised markings on elevator control buttons;

(7) Installing flashing alarm lights;

(8) Widening doors;

(9) Installing offset hinges to widen doorways;

(10) Eliminating a turnstile or providing an alternative accessible path;

(11) Installing accessible door hardware;

(12) Installing grab bars in toilet stalls;

(13) Rearranging toilet partitions to increase maneuvering space;

(14) Insulating lavatory pipes under sinks to prevent burns;

(15) Installing a raised toilet seat;

(16) Installing a full-length bathroom mirror;

(17) Repositioning the paper towel dispenser in a bathroom;

(18) Creating designated accessible parking spaces;

(19) Installing an accessible paper cup dispenser at an existing inaccessible water fountain;

(20) Removing high pile, low density carpeting; or

(21) Installing vehicle hand controls.

(c) *Priorities.* A public accommodation is urged to take measures to comply with the barrier removal requirements of this section in accordance with the following order of priorities.

(1) First, a public accommodation should take measures to provide access to a place of public accommodation from public sidewalks, parking, or public transportation. These measures include for example, installing an entrance ramp, widening entrances, and providing accessible parking spaces.

(2) Second, a public accommodation should take measures to provide access to those areas of a place of public accommodation where goods and services are made available to the public. These measures include, for example, adjusting the layout of display racks, rearranging tables, providing Brailled and raised character signage, widening doors, providing visual alarms, and installing ramps.

(3) Third, a public accommodation should take measures to provide access to restroom facilities. These measures include, for example, removal of

obstructing furniture or vending machines, widening of doors, installation of ramps, providing accessible signage, widening of toilet stalls, and installation of grab bars.

(4) Fourth, a public accommodation should take any other measures necessary to provide access to the goods, services, facilities, privileges, advantages, or accommodations of a place of public accommodation.

(d) *Relationship to alterations requirements of subpart D of this part.* (1) Except as provided in paragraph (d)(2) of this section, measures taken to comply with the barrier removal requirements of this section shall comply with the applicable requirements for alterations in § 36.402 and §§ 36.404–36.406 of this part for the element being altered. The path of travel requirements of § 36.403 shall not apply to measures taken solely to comply with the barrier removal requirements of this section.

(2) If, as a result of compliance with the alterations requirements specified in paragraph (d)(1) of this section, the measures required to remove a barrier would not be readily achievable, a public accommodation may take other readily achievable measures to remove the barrier that do not fully comply with the specified requirements. Such measures include, for example, providing a ramp with a steeper slope or widening a doorway to a narrower width than that mandated by the alterations requirements. No measure shall be taken, however, that poses a significant risk to the health or safety of individuals with disabilities or others.

(e) *Portable ramps.* Portable ramps should be used to comply with this section only when installation of a permanent ramp is not readily achievable. In order to avoid any significant risk to the health or safety of individuals with disabilities or others in using portable ramps, due consideration shall be given to safety features such as nonslip surfaces, railings, anchoring, and strength of materials.

(f) *Selling or serving space.* The rearrangement of temporary or movable structures, such as furniture, equipment, and display racks is not readily achievable to the extent that it results in a significant loss of selling or serving space.

(g) *Limitation on barrier removal obligations.* (1) The requirements for barrier removal under § 36.304 shall not be interpreted to exceed the standards for alterations in subpart D of this part.

(2) To the extent that relevant standards for alterations are not provided in subpart D of this part, then the requirements of § 36.304 shall not be

interpreted to exceed the standards for new construction in subpart D of this part.

(3) This section does not apply to rolling stock and other conveyances to the extent that § 36.310 applies to rolling stock and other conveyances.

§ 36.305 **Alternatives to barrier removal.**

(a) *General.* Where a public accommodation can demonstrate that barrier removal is not readily achievable, the public accommodation shall not fail to make its goods, services, facilities, privileges, advantages, or accommodations available through alternative methods, if those methods are readily achievable.

(b) *Examples.* Examples of alternatives to barrier removal include, but are not limited to, the following actions—

(1) Providing curb service or home delivery;

(2) Retrieving merchandise from inaccessible shelves or racks;

(3) Relocating activities to accessible locations;

(c) *Multiscreen cinemas.* If it is not readily achievable to remove barriers to provide access by persons with mobility impairments to all of the theaters of a multiscreen cinema, the cinema shall establish a film rotation schedule that provides reasonable access for individuals who use wheelchairs to all films. Reasonable notice shall be provided to the public as to the location and time of accessible showings.

§ 36.306 **Personal devices and services.**

This part does not require a public accommodation to provide its customers, clients, or participants with personal devices, such as wheelchairs; individually prescribed devices, such as prescription eyeglasses or hearing aids; or services of a personal nature including assistance in eating, toileting, or dressing.

§ 36.307 **Accessible or special goods.**

(a) This part does not require a public accommodation to alter its inventory to include accessible or special goods that are designed for, or facilitate use by, individuals with disabilities.

(b) A public accommodation shall order accessible or special goods at the request of an individual with disabilities, if, in the normal course of its operation, it makes special orders on request for unstocked goods, and if the accessible or special goods can be obtained from a supplier with whom the public accommodation customarily does business.

(c) Examples of accessible or special goods include items such as Brailled

versions of books, books on audio cassettes, closed-captioned video tapes, special sizes or lines of clothing, and special foods to meet particular dietary needs.

§ 36.308 **Seating in assembly areas.**

(a) *Existing facilities.* (1) To the extent that it is readily achievable, a public accommodation in assembly areas shall—

(i) Provide a reasonable number of wheelchair seating spaces and seats with removable aisle-side arm rests; and

(ii) Locate the wheelchair seating spaces so that they—

(A) Are dispersed throughout the seating area;

(B) Provide lines of sight and choice of admission prices comparable to those for members of the general public;

(C) Adjoin an accessible route that also serves as a means of egress in case of emergency; and

(D) Permit individuals who use wheelchairs to sit with family members or other companions.

(2) If removal of seats is not readily achievable, a public accommodation shall provide, to the extent that it is readily achievable to do so, a portable chair or other means to permit a family member or other companion to sit with an individual who uses a wheelchair.

(3) The requirements of paragraph (a) of this section shall not be interpreted to exceed the standards for alterations in subpart D of this part.

(b) *New construction and alterations.* The provision and location of wheelchair seating spaces in newly constructed or altered assembly areas shall be governed by the standards for new construction and alterations in subpart D of this part.

§ 36.309 **Examinations and courses.**

(a) *General.* Any private entity that offers examinations or courses related to applications, licensing, certification, or credentialing for secondary or postsecondary education, professional, or trade purposes shall offer such examinations or courses in a place and manner accessible to persons with disabilities or offer alternative accessible arrangements for such individuals.

(b) *Examinations.* (1) Any private entity offering an examination covered by this section must assure that—

(i) The examination is selected and administered so as to best ensure that, when the examination is administered to an individual with a disability that impairs sensory, manual, or speaking skills, the examination results accurately reflect the individual's aptitude or achievement level or whatever other factor the examination purports to measure, rather than reflecting the individual's impaired sensory, manual, or speaking skills (except where those skills are the factors that the examination purports to measure);

(ii) An examination that is designed for individuals with impaired sensory, manual, or speaking skills is offered at equally convenient locations, as often, and in as timely a manner as are other examinations; and

(iii) The examination is administered in facilities that are accessible to individuals with disabilities or alternative accessible arrangements are made.

(2) Required modifications to an examination may include changes in the length of time permitted for completion of the examination and adaptation of the manner in which the examination is given.

(3) A private entity offering an examination covered by this section shall provide appropriate auxiliary aids for persons with impaired sensory, manual, or speaking skills, unless that private entity can demonstrate that offering a particular auxiliary aid would fundamentally alter the measurement of the skills or knowledge the examination is intended to test or would result in an undue burden. Auxiliary aids and services required by this section may include taped examinations, interpreters or other effective methods of making orally delivered materials available to individuals with hearing impairments, Brailled or large print examinations and answer sheets or qualified readers for individuals with visual impairments or learning disabilities, transcribers for individuals with manual impairments, and other similar services and actions.

(4) Alternative accessible arrangements may include, for example, provision of an examination at an individual's home with a proctor if accessible facilities or equipment are unavailable. Alternative arrangements must provide comparable conditions to those provided for nondisabled individuals.

(c) *Courses.* (1) Any private entity that offers a course covered by this section must make such modifications to that course as are necessary to ensure that the place and manner in which the course is given are accessible to individuals with disabilities.

(2) Required modifications may include changes in the length of time permitted for the completion of the course, substitution of specific requirements, or adaptation of the manner in which the course is

conducted or course materials are distributed.

(3) A private entity that offers a course covered by this section shall provide appropriate auxiliary aids and services for persons with impaired sensory, manual, or speaking skills, unless the private entity can demonstrate that offering a particular auxiliary aid or service would fundamentally alter the course or would result in an undue burden. Auxiliary aids and services required by this section may include taped texts, interpreters or other effective methods of making orally delivered materials available to individuals with hearing impairments, Brailled or large print texts or qualified readers for individuals with visual impairments and learning disabilities, classroom equipment adapted for use by individuals with manual impairments, and other similar services and actions.

(4) Courses must be administered in facilities that are accessible to individuals with disabilities or alternative accessible arrangements must be made.

(5) Alternative accessible arrangements may include, for example, provision of the course through videotape, cassettes, or prepared notes. Alternative arrangements must provide comparable conditions to those provided for nondisabled individuals.

§ 36.310 **Transportation provided by public accommodations.**

(a) *General.* (1) A public accommodation that provides transportation services, but that is not primarily engaged in the business of transporting people, is subject to the general and specific provisions in subparts B, C, and D of this part for its transportation operations, except as provided in this section.

(2) *Examples.* Transportation services subject to this section include, but are not limited to, shuttle services operated between transportation terminals and places of public accommodation, customer shuttle bus services operated by private companies and shopping centers, student transportation systems, and transportation provided within recreational facilities such as stadiums, zoos, amusement parks, and ski resorts.

(b) *Barrier removal.* A public accommodation subject to this section shall remove transportation barriers in existing vehicles and rail passenger cars used for transporting individuals (not including barriers that can only be removed through the retrofitting of vehicles or rail passenger cars by the installation of a hydraulic or other lift)

where such removal is readily achievable.

(c) *Requirements for vehicles and systems.* A public accommodation subject to this section shall comply with the requirements pertaining to vehicles and transportation systems in the regulations issued by the Secretary of Transportation pursuant to section 306 of the Act.

§§ 36.311–36.400 **[Reserved]**

Subpart D—New Construction and Alterations

§ 36.401 **New construction.**

(a) *General.* (1) Except as provided in paragraphs (b) and (c) of this section, discrimination for purposes of this part includes a failure to design and construct facilities for first occupancy after January 26, 1993, that are readily accessible to and usable by individuals with disabilities.

(2) For purposes of this section, a facility is designed and constructed for first occupancy after January 26, 1993, only—

(i) If the last application for a building permit or permit extension for the facility is certified to be complete, by a State, County, or local government after January 26, 1992 (or, in those jurisdictions where the government does not certify completion of applications, if the last application for a building permit or permit extension for the facility is received by the State, County, or local government after January 26, 1992); and

(ii) If the first certificate of occupancy for the facility is issued after January 26, 1993.

(b) *Commercial facilities located in private residences.* (1) When a commercial facility is located in a private residence, the portion of the residence used exclusively as a residence is not covered by this subpart, but that portion used exclusively in the operation of the commercial facility or that portion used both for the commercial facility and for residential purposes is covered by the new construction and alterations requirements of this subpart.

(2) The portion of the residence covered under paragraph (b)(1) of this section extends to those elements used to enter the commercial facility, including the homeowner's front sidewalk, if any, the door or entryway, and hallways; and those portions of the residence, interior or exterior, available to or used by employees or visitors of the commercial facility, including restrooms.

(c) *Exception for structural impracticability.* (1) Full compliance with the requirements of this section is not required where an entity can demonstrate that it is structurally impracticable to meet the requirements. Full compliance will be considered structurally impracticable only in those rare circumstances when the unique characteristics of terrain prevent the incorporation of accessibility features.

(2) If full compliance with this section would be structurally impracticable, compliance with this section is required to the extent that it is not structurally impracticable. In that case, any portion of the facility that can be made accessible shall be made accessible to the extent that it is not structurally impracticable.

(3) If providing accessibility in conformance with this section to individuals with certain disabilities (e.g., those who use wheelchairs) would be structurally impracticable, accessibility shall nonetheless be ensured to persons with other types of disabilities (e.g., those who use crutches or who have sight, hearing, or mental impairments) in accordance with this section.

(d) *Elevator exemption.* (1) For purposes of this paragraph (d)—

(i) *Professional office of a health care provider* means a location where a person or entity regulated by a State to provide professional services related to the physical or mental health of an individual make such services available to the public. The facility housing the "professional office of a health care provider" only includes floor levels housing at least one health care provider, or any floor level designed or intended for use by at least one health care provider.

(ii) *Shopping center or shopping mall means*—

(A) A building housing five or more sales or rental establishments; or

(B) A series of buildings on a common site, either under common ownership or common control or developed either as one project or as a series of related projects, housing five or more sales or rental establishments. For purposes of this section, places of public accommodation of the types listed in paragraph (5) of the definition of "place of public accommodation" in section § 36.104 are considered sales or rental establishments. The facility housing a "shopping center or shopping mall" only includes floor levels housing at least one sales or rental establishment, or any floor level designed or intended for use by at least one sales or rental establishment.

(2) This section does not require the installation of an elevator in a facility that is less than three stories or has less than 3000 square feet per story, except

with respect to any facility that houses one or more of the following:

(i) A shopping center or shopping mall, or a professional office of a health care provider.

(ii) A terminal, depot, or other station used for specified public transportation, or an airport passenger terminal. In such a facility, any area housing passenger services, including boarding and debarking, loading and unloading, baggage claim, dining facilities, and other common areas open to the public, must be on an accessible route from an accessible entrance.

(3) The elevator exemption set forth in this paragraph (d) does not obviate or limit, in any way the obligation to comply with the other accessibility requirements established in paragraph (a) of this section. For example, in a facility that houses a shopping center or shopping mall, or a professional office of a health care provider, the floors that are above or below an accessible ground floor and that do not house sales or rental establishments or a professional office of a health care provider, must meet the requirements of this section but for the elevator.

§ 36.402 Alterations.

(a) *General.* (1) Any alteration to a place of public accommodation or a commercial facility, after January 26, 1992, shall be made so as to ensure that, to the maximum extent feasible, the altered portions of the facility are readily accessible to and usable by individuals with disabilities, including individuals who use wheelchairs.

(2) An alteration is deemed to be undertaken after January 26, 1992, if the physical alteration of the property begins after that date.

(b) *Alteration.* For the purposes of this part, an alteration is a change to a place of public accommodation or a commercial facility that affects or could affect the usability of the building or facility or any part thereof.

(1) Alterations include, but are not limited to, remodeling, renovation, rehabilitation, reconstruction, historic restoration, changes or rearrangement in structural parts or elements, and changes or rearrangement in the plan configuration of walls and full-height partitions. Normal maintenance, reroofing, painting or wallpapering, asbestos removal, or changes to mechanical and electrical systems are not alterations unless they affect the usability of the building or facility.

(2) If existing elements, spaces, or common areas are altered, then each such altered element, space, or area shall comply with the applicable provisions of appendix A to this part.

(c) *To the maximum extent feasible.* The phrase "to the maximum extent feasible," as used in this section, applies to the occasional case where the nature of an existing facility makes it virtually impossible to comply fully with applicable accessibility standards through a planned alteration. In these circumstances, the alteration shall provide the maximum physical accessibility feasible. Any altered features of the facility that can be made accessible shall be made accessible. If providing accessibility in conformance with this section to individuals with certain disabilities (e.g., those who use wheelchairs) would not be feasible, the facility shall be made accessible to persons with other types of disabilities (e.g., those who use crutches, those who have impaired vision or hearing, or those who have other impairments).

§ 36.403 Alterations: Path of travel.

(a) *General.* An alteration that affects or could affect the usability of or access to an area of a facility that contains a primary function shall be made so as to ensure that, to the maximum extent feasible, the path of travel to the altered area and the restrooms, telephones, and drinking fountains serving the altered area, are readily accessible to and usable by individuals with disabilities, including individuals who use wheelchairs, unless the cost and scope of such alterations is disproportionate to the cost of the overall alteration.

(b) *Primary function.* A "primary function" is a major activity for which the facility is intended. Areas that contain a primary function include, but are not limited to, the customer services lobby of a bank, the dining area of a cafeteria, the meeting rooms in a conference center, as well as offices and other work areas in which the activities of the public accommodation or other private entity using the facility are carried out. Mechanical rooms, boiler rooms, supply storage rooms, employee lounges or locker rooms, janitorial closets, entrances, corridors, and restrooms are not areas containing a primary function.

(c) *Alterations to an area containing a primary function.* (1) Alterations that affect the usability of or access to an area containing a primary function include, but are not limited to—

(i) Remodeling merchandise display areas or employee work areas in a department store;

(ii) Replacing an inaccessible floor surface in the customer service or employee work areas of a bank;

(iii) Redesigning the assembly line area of a factory; or

(iv) Installing a computer center in an accounting firm.

(2) For the purposes of this section, alterations to windows, hardware, controls, electrical outlets, and signage shall not be deemed to be alterations that affect the usability of or access to an area containing a primary function.

(d) *Landlord/tenant:* If a tenant is making alterations as defined in § 36.402 that would trigger the requirements of this section, those alterations by the tenant in areas that only the tenant occupies do not trigger a path of travel obligation upon the landlord with respect to areas of the facility under the landlord's authority, if those areas are not otherwise being altered.

(e) *Path of travel.* (1) A "path of travel" includes a continuous, unobstructed way of pedestrian passage by means of which the altered area may be approached, entered, and exited, and which connects the altered area with an exterior approach (including sidewalks, streets, and parking areas), an entrance to the facility, and other parts of the facility.

(2) An accessible path of travel may consist of walks and sidewalks, curb ramps and other interior or exterior pedestrian ramps; clear floor paths through lobbies, corridors, rooms, and other improved areas; parking access aisles; elevators and lifts; or a combination of these elements.

(3) For the purposes of this part, the term "path of travel" also includes the restrooms, telephones, and drinking fountains serving the altered area.

(f) *Disproportionality.* (1) Alterations made to provide an accessible path of travel to the altered area will be deemed disproportionate to the overall alteration when the cost exceeds 20% of the cost of the alteration to the primary function area.

(2) Costs that may be counted as expenditures required to provide an accessible path of travel may include:

(i) Costs associated with providing an accessible entrance and an accessible route to the altered area, for example, the cost of widening doorways or installing ramps;

(ii) Costs associated with making restrooms accessible, such as installing grab bars, enlarging toilet stalls, insulating pipes, or installing accessible faucet controls;

(iii) Costs associated with providing accessible telephones, such as relocating the telephone to an accessible height, installing amplification devices, or installing a telecommunications device for deaf persons (TDD);

(iv) Costs associated with relocating an inaccessible drinking fountain.

(g) *Duty to provide accessible features in the event of disproportionality.* (1) When the cost of alterations necessary to make the path of travel to the altered area fully accessible is disproportionate to the cost of the overall alteration, the path of travel shall be made accessible to the extent that it can be made accessible without incurring disproportionate costs.

(2) In choosing which accessible elements to provide, priority should be given to those elements that will provide the greatest access, in the following order:

(i) An accessible entrance;

(ii) An accessible route to the altered area;

(iii) At least one accessible restroom for each sex or a single unisex restroom;

(iv) Accessible telephones;

(v) Accessible drinking fountains; and

(vi) When possible, additional accessible elements such as parking, storage, and alarms.

(h) *Series of smaller alterations.* (1) The obligation to provide an accessible path of travel may not be evaded by performing a series of small alterations to the area served by a single path of travel if those alterations could have been performed as a single undertaking.

(2) (i) If an area containing a primary function has been altered without providing an accessible path of travel to that area, and subsequent alterations of that area, or a different area on the same path of travel, are undertaken within three years of the original alteration, the total cost of alterations to the primary function areas on that path of travel during the preceding three year period shall be considered in determining whether the cost of making that path of travel accessible is disproportionate.

(ii) Only alterations undertaken after January 26, 1992, shall be considered in determining if the cost of providing an accessible path of travel is disproportionate to the overall cost of the alterations.

§ 36.404 Alterations: Elevator exemption.

(a) This section does not require the installation of an elevator in an altered facility that is less than three stories or has less than 3,000 square feet per story, except with respect to any facility that houses a shopping center, a shopping mall, the professional office of a health care provider, a terminal, depot, or other station used for specified public transportation, or an airport passenger terminal.

(1) For the purposes of this section, "professional office of a health care provider" means a location where a person or entity regulated by a State to

provide professional services related to the physical or mental health of an individual makes such services available to the public. The facility that houses a "professional office of a health care provider" only includes floor levels housing by at least one health care provider, or any floor level designed or intended for use by at least one health care provider.

(2) For the purposes of this section, shopping center or shopping mall means—

(i) A building housing five or more sales or rental establishments; or

(ii) A series of buildings on a common site, connected by a common pedestrian access route above or below the ground floor, that is either under common ownership or common control or developed either as one project or as a series of related projects, housing five or more sales or rental establishments. For purposes of this section, places of public accommodation of the types listed in paragraph (5) of the definition of "place of public accommodation" in § 36.104 are considered sales or rental establishments. The facility housing a "shopping center or shopping mall" only includes floor levels housing at least one sales or rental establishment, or any floor level designed or intended for use by at least one sales or rental establishment.

(b) The exemption provided in paragraph (a) of this section does not obviate or limit in any way the obligation to comply with the other accessibility requirements established in this subpart. For example, alterations to floors above or below the accessible ground floor must be accessible regardless of whether the altered facility has an elevator.

§ 36.405 Alterations: Historic preservation.

(a) Alterations to buildings or facilities that are eligible for listing in the National Register of Historic Places under the National Historic Preservation Act (16 U.S.C. 470 *et seq.*), or are designated as historic under State or local law, shall comply to the maximum extent feasible with section 4.1.7 of appendix A to this part.

(b) If it is determined under the procedures set out in section 4.1.7 of appendix A that it is not feasible to provide physical access to an historic property that is a place of public accommodation in a manner that will not threaten or destroy the historic significance of the building or facility, alternative methods of access shall be provided pursuant to the requirements of subpart C of this part.

§ 36.406 Standards for new construction and alterations.

(a) New construction and alterations subject to this part shall comply with the standards for accessible design published as appendix A to this part (ADAAG).

(b) The chart in the appendix to this section provides guidance to the user in reading appendix A to this part (ADAAG) together with subparts A through D of this part, when determining requirements for a particular facility.

Appendix to § 36.406

This chart has no effect for purposes of compliance or enforcement. It does not necessarily provide complete or mandatory information.

	Subparts A–D	ADAAG
Application, General.	36.102(b)(3): public accommodations. 36.102(c): commercial facilities. 36.102(e): public entities. 36.103 (other laws). 36.401 ("for first occupancy"). 36.402(a) (alterations).	1, 2, 3, 4.1.1.
Definitions......	36.104: commercial facilities, facility, place of public accommodation, private club, public accommodation, public entity, religious entity. 36.401(d)(1)(ii), 36.404(a)(2): shopping center or shopping mall. 36.401(d)(1)(i), 36.404(a)(1): professional office of a health care provider. 36.402: alteration; usability. 36.402(c): to the maximum extent feasible.	3.5 Definitions, including: addition, alteration, building, element, facility, space, story. 4.1.6(j), technical infeasibility.
New Construc-tion:.	36.401(a) General.	4.1.2.

	Subparts A–D	ADAAG
General..........	36.401(b) Commercial facilities in private residences. 36.207 Places of public accommodation in private residences.	4.1.3.
Work Areas......		4.1.1(3).
Structural Impracticability.	36.401(c)............	4.1.1(5)(a).
Elevator Exemption.	36.401(d)............ 36.404.............	4.1.3(5). 4.1.1(5), 4.1.3(5) and throughout.
Other Exceptions.		
Alterations: General.	36.401(b): commercial facilities in private residences. 36.402............ 36.403............	4.1.6(1). 4.1.6(2).
Alterations Affecting an Area Containing A Primary Function; Path of Travel; Disproportionality.		
Alterations: Special Technical Provisions.		4.1.6(3).
Additions........	36.401–36.405..... 36.405.............	4.1.5. 4.1.7.
Historic Preservation.		
Technical Provisions.		4.2 through 4.35.
Restaurants and Cafeterias.		5.
Medical Care Facilities.		6.
Business and Mercantile.		7.
Libraries........		8.
Transient Lodging (Hotels, Homeless Shelters, Etc.).		9.
Transportation Facilities.		[10, Reserved].

§§ 36.407–36.500 [Reserved]

Subpart E—Enforcement

§ 36.501 Private suits.

(a) *General.* Any person who is being subjected to discrimination on the basis of disability in violation of the Act or this part or who has reasonable grounds for believing that such person is about to be subjected to discrimination in violation of section 303 of the Act or subpart D of this part may institute a civil action for preventive relief, including an application for a permanent or temporary injunction, restraining order, or other order. Upon timely application, the court may, in its discretion, permit the Attorney General to intervene in the civil action if the Attorney General or his or her designee certifies that the case is of general public importance. Upon application by the complainant and in such circumstances as the court may deem just, the court may appoint an attorney for such complainant and may authorize the commencement of the civil action without the payment of fees, costs, or security. Nothing in this section shall require a person with a disability to engage in a futile gesture if the person has actual notice that a person or organization covered by title III of the Act or this part does not intend to comply with its provisions.

(b) *Injunctive relief.* In the case of violations of § 36.304, § 36.308, § 36.310(b), § 36.401, § 36.402, § 36.403, and § 36.405 of this part, injunctive relief shall include an order to alter facilities to make such facilities readily accessible to and usable by individuals with disabilities to the extent required by the Act or this part. Where appropriate, injunctive relief shall also include requiring the provision of an auxiliary aid or service, modification of a policy, or provision of alternative methods, to the extent required by the Act or this part.

§ 36.502 Investigations and compliance reviews.

(a) The Attorney General shall investigate alleged violations of the Act or this part.

(b) Any individual who believes that he or she or a specific class of persons has been subjected to discrimination prohibited by the Act or this part may request the Department to institute an investigation.

(c) Where the Attorney General has reason to believe that there may be a violation of this part, he or she may initiate a compliance review.

§ 36.503 Suit by the Attorney General.

Following a compliance review or investigation under § 36.502, or at any other time in his or her discretion, the Attorney General may commence a civil action in any appropriate United States district court if the Attorney General has reasonable cause to believe that—

(a) Any person or group of persons is engaged in a pattern or practice of discrimination in violation of the Act or this part; or

(b) Any person or group of persons has been discriminated against in violation of the Act or this part and the discrimination raises an issue of general public importance.

§ 36.504 Relief.

(a) *Authority of court.* In a civil action under § 36.503, the court—

(1) May grant any equitable relief that such court considers to be appropriate, including, to the extent required by the Act or this part—

(i) Granting temporary, preliminary, or permanent relief;

(ii) Providing an auxiliary aid or service, modification of policy, practice, or procedure, or alternative method; and

(iii) Making facilities readily accessible to and usable by individuals with disabilities;

(2) May award other relief as the court considers to be appropriate, including monetary damages to persons aggrieved when requested by the Attorney General; and

(3) May, to vindicate the public interest, assess a civil penalty against the entity in an amount

(i) Not exceeding $50,000 for a first violation; and

(ii) Not exceeding $100,000 for any subsequent violation.

(b) *Single violation.* For purposes of paragraph (a) (3) of this section, in determining whether a first or subsequent violation has occurred, a determination in a single action, by judgment or settlement, that the covered entity has engaged in more than one discriminatory act shall be counted as a single violation.

(c) *Punitive damages.* For purposes of paragraph (a)(2) of this section, the terms "monetary damages" and "such other relief" do not include punitive damages.

(d) *Judicial consideration.* In a civil action under § 36.503, the court, when considering what amount of civil penalty, if any, is appropriate, shall give consideration to any good faith effort or attempt to comply with this part by the entity. In evaluating good faith, the court shall consider, among other factors it deems relevant, whether the entity could have reasonably anticipated the need for an appropriate type of auxiliary aid needed to accommodate the unique needs of a particular individual with a disability.

§ 36.505 Attorneys fees.

In any action or administrative proceeding commenced pursuant to the Act or this part, the court or agency, in its discretion, may allow the prevailing party, other than the United States, a reasonable attorney's fee, including litigation expenses, and costs, and the United States shall be liable for the foregoing the same as a private individual.

§ 36.506 Alternative means of dispute resolution.

Where appropriate and to the extent authorized by law, the use of alternative means of dispute resolution, including settlement negotiations, conciliation, facilitation, mediation, factfinding, minitrials, and arbitration, is encouraged to resolve disputes arising under the Act and this part.

§ 36.507 Effect of unavailability of technical assistance.

A public accommodation or other private entity shall not be excused from compliance with the requirements of this part because of any failure to receive technical assistance, including any failure in the development or dissemination of any technical assistance manual authorized by the Act.

§ 36.508 Effective date.

(a) *General.* Except as otherwise provided in this section and in this part, this part shall become effective on January 26, 1992.

(b) *Civil actions.* Except for any civil action brought for a violation of section 303 of the Act, no civil action shall be brought for any act or omission described in section 302 of the Act that occurs—

(1) Before July 26, 1992, against businesses with 25 or fewer employees and gross receipts of $1,000,000 or less.

(2) Before January 26, 1993, against businesses with 10 or fewer employees and gross receipts of $500,000 or less.

(c) *Transportation services provided by public accommodations.* Newly purchased or leased vehicles required to be accessible by § 36.310 must be readily accessible to and usable by individuals with disabilities, including individuals who use wheelchairs, if the solicitation for the vehicle is made after August 25, 1990.

§§ 36.509–36.600 [Reserved]

Subpart F—Certification of State Laws or Local Building Codes

§ 36.601 Definitions.

Assistant Attorney General means the Assistant Attorney General for Civil Rights or his or her designee.

Certification of equivalency means a final certification that a code meets or exceeds the minimum requirements of title III of the Act for accessibility and usability of facilities covered by that title.

Code means a State law or local building code or similar ordinance, or part thereof, that establishes accessibility requirements.

Model code means a nationally recognized document developed by a private entity for use by State or local jurisdictions in developing codes as defined in this section. A model code is intended for incorporation by reference or adoption in whole or in part, with or without amendment, by State or local jurisdictions.

Preliminary determination of equivalency means a preliminary determination that a code appears to meet or exceed the minimum requirements of title III of the Act for accessibility and usability of facilities covered by that title.

Submitting official means the State or local official who—

(1) Has principal responsibility for administration of a code, or is authorized to submit a code on behalf of a jurisdiction; and

(2) Files a request for certification under this subpart.

§ 36.602 General rule.

On the application of a State or local government, the Assistant Attorney General may certify that a code meets or exceeds the minimum requirements of the Act for the accessibility and usability of places of public accommodation and commercial facilities under this part by issuing a certification of equivalency. At any enforcement proceeding under title III of the Act, such certification shall be rebuttable evidence that such State law or local ordinance does meet or exceed the minimum requirements of title III.

§ 36.603 Filing request for certification.

(a) A submitting official may file a request for certification of a code under this subpart.

(b) Before filing a request for certification of a code, the submitting official shall ensure that—

(1) Adequate public notice of intention to file a request for certification, notice of a hearing, and notice of the location at which the request and materials can be inspected is published within the relevant jurisdiction;

(2) Copies of the proposed request and supporting materials are made available for public examination and copying at the office of the State or local agency charged with administration and enforcement of the code; and

(3) The local or State jurisdiction holds a public hearing on the record, in the State or locality, at which the public is invited to comment on the proposed request for certification.

(c) The submitting official shall include the following materials and information in support of the request:

(1) The text of the jurisdiction's code; any standard, regulation, code, or other relevant document incorporated by reference or otherwise referenced in the code; the law creating and empowering the agency; any relevant manuals, guides, or any other interpretive information issued that pertain to the code; and any formal opinions of the State Attorney General or the chief legal officer of the jurisdiction that pertain to the code;

(2) Any model code or statute on which the pertinent code is based, and an explanation of any differences between the model and the pertinent code;

(3) A transcript of the public hearing required by paragraph (b)(3) of this section; and

(4) Any additional information that the submitting official may wish to be considered.

(d) The submitting official shall file the original and one copy of the request and of supporting materials with the Assistant Attorney General. The submitting official shall clearly label the request as a "request for certification" of a code. A copy of the request and supporting materials will be available for public examination and copying at the offices of the Assistant Attorney General in Washington, DC. The submitting official shall ensure that copies of the request and supporting materials are available for public examination and copying at the office of the State or local agency charged with administration and enforcement of the code. The submitting official shall ensure that adequate public notice of the request for certification and of the location at which the request and materials can be inspected is published within the relevant jurisdiction.

(e) Upon receipt of a request for certification, the Assistant Attorney General may request further information that he or she considers relevant to the determinations required to be made under this subpart.

§ 36.604 Preliminary determination.

After consultation with the Architectural and Transportation Barriers Compliance Board, the Assistant Attorney General shall make a preliminary determination of equivalency or a preliminary determination to deny certification.

§ 36.605 Procedure following preliminary determination of equivalency.

(a) If the Assistant Attorney General makes a preliminary determination of equivalency under § 36.604, he or she shall inform the submitting official, in writing, of that preliminary determination. The Assistant Attorney General shall also—

(1) Publish a notice in the Federal Register that advises the public of the preliminary determination of equivalency with respect to the particular code, and invite interested persons and organizations, including individuals with disabilities, during a period of at least 60 days following publication of the notice, to file written comments relevant to whether a final certification of equivalency should be issued;

(2) After considering the information received in response to the notice described in paragraph (a) of this section, and after publishing a separate notice in the Federal Register, hold an informal hearing in Washington, DC at which interested persons, including individuals with disabilities, are provided an opportunity to express their views with respect to the preliminary determination of equivalency; and

(b) The Assistant Attorney General, after consultation with the Architectural and Transportation Barriers Compliance Board, and consideration of the materials and information submitted pursuant to this section and § 36.603, shall issue either a certification of equivalency or a final determination to deny the request for certification. He or she shall publish notice of the certification of equivalency or denial of certification in the Federal Register.

§ 36.606 Procedure following preliminary denial of certification.

(a) If the Assistant Attorney General makes a Preliminary determination to deny certification of a code under § 36.604, he or she shall notify the submitting official of the determination. The notification may include specification of the manner in which the code could be amended in order to qualify for certification.

(b) The Assistant Attorney General shall allow the submitting official not less than 15 days to submit data, views, and arguments in opposition to the preliminary determination to deny certification. If the submitting official does not submit materials, the Assistant Attorney General shall not be required to take any further action. If the submitting official submits materials, the Assistant Attorney General shall evaluate those materials and any other relevant information. After evaluation of any newly submitted materials, the Assistant Attorney General shall make either a final denial of certification or a preliminary determination of equivalency.

§ 36.607 Effect of certification.

(a)(1) A certification shall be considered a certification of equivalency only with respect to those features or elements that are both covered by the certified code and addressed by the standards against which equivalency is measured.

(2) For example, if certain equipment is not covered by the code, the determination of equivalency cannot be used as evidence with respect to the question of whether equipment in a building built according to the code satisfies the Act's requirements with respect to such equipment. By the same token, certification would not be relevant to construction of a facility for children, if the regulations against which equivalency is measured do not address children's facilities.

(b) A certification of equivalency is effective only with respect to the particular edition of the code for which certification is granted. Any amendments or other changes to the code after the date of the certified edition are not considered part of the certification.

(c) A submitting official may reapply for certification of amendments or other changes to a code that has already received certification.

§ 36.608 Guidance concerning model codes.

Upon application by an authorized representative of a private entity responsible for developing a model code, the Assistant Attorney General may review the relevant model code and issue guidance concerning whether and in what respects the model code is consistent with the minimum requirements of the Act for the accessibility and usability of places of public accommodation and commercial facilities under this part.

§§ 36.609–36.999 [Reserved]
BILLING CODE 4410-01-M

Appendix A to Part 36—Standards for Accessible Design

ADA ACCESSIBILITY GUIDELINES
FOR BUILDINGS AND FACILITIES
TABLE OF CONTENTS

i

1. PURPOSE.

This document sets guidelines for accessibility to places of public accommodation and commercial facilities by individuals with disabilities. These guidelines are to be applied during the design, construction, and alteration of such buildings and facilities to the extent required by regulations issued by Federal agencies, including the Department of Justice, under the Americans with Disabilities Act of 1990.

The technical specifications 4.2 through 4.35, of these guidelines are the same as those of the American National Standard Institute's document A117.1-1980, except as noted in this text by italics. However, sections 4.1.1 through 4.1.7 and sections 5 through 10 are different from ANSI A117.1 in their entirety and are printed in standard type.

The illustrations and text of ANSI A117.1 are reproduced with permission from the American National Standards Institute. Copies of the standard may be purchased from the American National Standards Institute at 1430 Broadway, New York, New York 10018.

2. GENERAL.

2.1 Provisions for Adults. *The specifica-tions in these guidelines are based upon adult dimensions and anthropometrics.*

2.2* Equivalent Facilitation. *Departures from particular technical and scoping require-ments of this guideline by the use of other designs and technologies are permitted where the alternative designs and technologies used will provide substantially equivalent or greater access to and usability of the facility.*

3. MISCELLANEOUS INSTRUCTIONS AND DEFINITIONS.

3.1 Graphic Conventions. Graphic conventions are shown in Table 1. Dimensions that are not marked minimum or maximum are absolute, unless otherwise indicated in the text or captions.

Table 1
Graphic Conventions

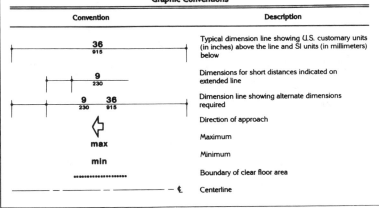

Convention	Description
36 / 915	Typical dimension line showing U.S. customary units (in inches) above the line and SI units (in millimeters) below
9 / 230	Dimensions for short distances indicated on extended line
9 / 230 36 / 915	Dimension line showing alternate dimensions required
	Direction of approach
max	Maximum
min	Minimum
	Boundary of clear floor area
℄	Centerline

3.2 Dimensional Tolerances. All dimensions are subject to conventional building industry tolerances for field conditions.

3.3 Notes. The text of *these guidelines* does not contain notes or footnotes. Additional information, explanations, and advisory materials are located in the Appendix. Paragraphs marked with an asterisk have related, nonmandatory material in the Appendix. In the Appendix, the corresponding paragraph numbers are preceded by an A.

3.4 General Terminology.

comply with. Meet one or more specifications of *these guidelines*.

if, if ... then. Denotes a specification that applies only when the conditions described are present.

may. Denotes an option or alternative.

shall. Denotes a mandatory specification or requirement.

should. Denotes an advisory specification or recommendation.

3.5 Definitions.

Access Aisle. An accessible pedestrian space between elements, such as parking spaces, seating, and desks, that provides clearances appropriate for use of the elements.

Accessible. Describes a site, building, facility, or portion thereof that complies with *these guidelines*.

Accessible Element. An *element* specified by *these guidelines* (for example, telephone, controls, and the like).

Accessible Route. A continuous unobstructed path connecting all accessible elements and spaces of a building or facility. Interior accessible routes may include corridors, floors, ramps, elevators, lifts, and clear floor space at fixtures. Exterior accessible routes may include parking access aisles, curb ramps, *crosswalks at vehicular ways*, walks, ramps, and lifts.

Accessible Space. Space that complies with these guidelines.

Adaptability. The ability of certain building spaces and elements, such as kitchen counters, sinks, and grab bars, to be added or altered so as to accommodate the needs of *individuals with or without disabilities* or to accommodate the needs of persons with different types or degrees of disability.

Addition. An expansion, extension, or increase in the gross floor area of a building or facility.

Administrative Authority. A governmental agency that adopts or enforces regulations and guidelines for the design, construction, or alteration of buildings and facilities.

Alteration. An alteration is a change to a building or facility made by, on behalf of, or for the use of a public accommodation or commercial facility, that affects or could affect the usability of the building or facility or part thereof. Alterations include, but are not limited to, remodeling, renovation, rehabilitation, reconstruction, historic restoration, changes or rearrangement of the structural parts or elements, and changes or rearrangement in the plan configuration of walls and full-height partitions. Normal maintenance, reroofing, painting or wallpapering, or changes to mechanical and electrical systems are not alterations unless they affect the usability of the building or facility.

Area of Rescue Assistance. An area, which has direct access to an exit, where people who are unable to use stairs may remain temporarily in safety to await further instructions or assistance during emergency evacuation.

Assembly Area. A room or space accommodating a group of individuals for recreational, educational, political, social, or amusement purposes, or for the consumption of food and drink.

Automatic Door. A door equipped with a power-operated mechanism and controls that open and close the door automatically upon receipt of a momentary actuating signal. The switch that begins the automatic cycle may be a photoelectric device, floor mat, or manual switch (see power-assisted door).

2

Building. Any structure used and intended for supporting or sheltering any use or occupancy.

Circulation Path. An exterior or interior way of passage from one place to another for pedestrians, including, but not limited to, walks, hallways, courtyards, stairways, and stair landings.

Clear. Unobstructed.

Clear Floor Space. The minimum unobstructed floor or ground space required to accommodate a single, stationary wheelchair and occupant.

Closed Circuit Telephone. A telephone with dedicated line(s) such as a house phone, courtesy phone or phone that must be used to gain entrance to a facility.

Common Use. Refers to those interior and exterior rooms, spaces, or elements that are made available for the use of a restricted group of people (for example, occupants of a homeless shelter, the occupants of an office building, or the guests of such occupants).

Cross Slope. The slope that is perpendicular to the direction of travel (see running slope).

Curb Ramp. A short ramp cutting through a curb or built up to it.

Detectable Warning. A standardized surface feature built in or applied to walking surfaces or other elements to warn visually impaired people of hazards on a circulation path.

Dwelling Unit. A single unit which provides a kitchen or food preparation area, in addition to rooms and spaces for living, bathing, sleeping, and the like. Dwelling units include a single family home or a townhouse used as a transient group home; an apartment building used as a shelter; guestrooms in a hotel that provide sleeping accommodations and food preparation areas; and other similar facilities used on a transient basis. For purposes of these guidelines, use of the term "Dwelling Unit" does not imply the unit is used as a residence.

Egress, Means of. A continuous and unobstructed way of exit travel from any point in a building or facility to a public way. A means of egress comprises vertical and horizontal travel and may include intervening room spaces, doorways, hallways, corridors, passageways, balconies, ramps, stairs, enclosures, lobbies, horizontal exits, courts and yards. An accessible means of egress is one that complies with these guidelines and does not include stairs, steps, or escalators. Areas of rescue assistance or evacuation elevators may be included as part of accessible means of egress.

Element. An architectural or mechanical component of a building, facility, space, or site, e.g., telephone, curb ramp, door, drinking fountain, seating, or water closet.

Entrance. Any access point to a building or portion of a building or facility used for the purpose of entering. An entrance includes the approach walk, the vertical access leading to the entrance platform, the entrance platform itself, vestibules if provided, the entry door(s) or gate(s), and the hardware of the entry door(s) or gate(s).

Facility. All or any portion of buildings, structures, site improvements, complexes, equipment, roads, walks, passageways, parking lots, or other real or personal property located on a site.

Ground Floor. Any occupiable floor less than one story above or below grade with direct access to grade. A building or facility always has at least one ground floor and may have more than one ground floor as where a split level entrance has been provided or where a building is built into a hillside.

Mezzanine or Mezzanine Floor. That portion of a story which is an intermediate floor level placed within the story and having occupiable space above and below its floor.

Marked Crossing. A crosswalk or other identified path intended for pedestrian use in crossing a vehicular way.

Multifamily Dwelling. Any building containing more than two dwelling units.

Occupiable. A room or enclosed space designed for human occupancy in which individuals congregate for amusement, educational or similar purposes, or in which occupants are engaged at labor, and which is equipped with means of egress, light, and ventilation.

3

3.5 Definitions

Operable Part. A part of a piece of equipment or appliance used to insert or withdraw objects, or to activate, deactivate, or adjust the equipment or appliance (for example, coin slot, pushbutton, handle).

Path of Travel. *(Reserved).*

Power-assisted Door. A door used *for human passage* with a mechanism that helps to open the door, or relieves the opening resistance of a door, upon the activation of a switch or a continued force applied to the door itself.

Public Use. Describes interior or exterior rooms or spaces that are made available to the general public. Public use may be provided at a building or facility that is privately or publicly owned.

Ramp. A walking surface which has a running slope greater than 1:20.

Running Slope. The slope that is parallel to the direction of travel (see cross slope).

Service Entrance. An entrance intended primarily for delivery of goods or services.

Signage. Displayed verbal, symbolic, *tactile*, and pictorial information.

Site. A parcel of land bounded by a property line or a designated portion of a public right-of-way.

Site Improvement. Landscaping, paving for pedestrian and vehicular ways, outdoor lighting, recreational facilities, and the like, added to a site.

Sleeping Accommodations. Rooms in which people sleep; for example, dormitory and hotel or motel guest rooms or suites.

Space. *A definable area, e.g., room, toilet room, hall, assembly area, entrance, storage room, alcove, courtyard, or lobby.*

Story. *That portion of a building included between the upper surface of a floor and upper surface of the floor or roof next above. If such*

portion of a building does not include occupiable space, it is not considered a story for purposes of these guidelines. There may be more than one floor level within a story as in the case of a mezzanine or mezzanines.

Structural Frame. The structural frame shall be considered to be the columns and the girders, beams, trusses and spandrels having direct connections to the columns and all other members which are essential to the stability of the building as a whole.

Tactile. Describes an object that can be perceived using the sense of touch.

Text Telephone. *Machinery or equipment that employs interactive graphic (i.e., typed) communications through the transmission of coded signals across the standard telephone network. Text telephones can include, for example, devices known as TDD's (telecommunication display devices or telecommunication devices for deaf persons) or computers.*

Transient Lodging. *A building, facility, or portion thereof, excluding inpatient medical care facilities, that contains one or more dwelling units or sleeping accommodations. Transient lodging may include, but is not limited to, resorts, group homes, hotels, motels, and dormitories.*

Vehicular Way. A route intended for vehicular traffic, such as a street, driveway, or parking lot.

Walk. An exterior pathway with a prepared surface intended for pedestrian use, including general pedestrian areas such as plazas and courts.

NOTE: Sections 4.1.1 through 4.1.7 are different from ANSI A117.1 in their entirety and are printed in standard type (ANSI A117.1 does not include scoping provisions).

4

4.	ACCESSIBLE ELEMENTS AND SPACES: SCOPE AND TECHNICAL REQUIREMENTS.

4.1 Minimum Requirements

4.1.1* Application.

(1) General. All areas of newly designed or newly constructed buildings and facilities required to be accessible by 4.1.2 and 4.1.3 and altered portions of existing buildings and facilities required to be accessible by 4.1.6 shall comply with these guidelines, 4.1 through 4.35, unless otherwise provided in this section or as modified in a special application section.

(2) Application Based on Building Use. Special application sections 5 through 10 provide additional requirements for restaurants and cafeterias, medical care facilities, business and mercantile, libraries, accessible transient lodging, and transportation facilities. When a building or facility contains more than one use covered by a special application section, each portion shall comply with the requirements for that use.

(3)* Areas Used Only by Employees as Work Areas. Areas that are used only as work areas shall be designed and constructed so that individuals with disabilities can approach, enter, and exit the areas. These guidelines do not require that any areas used only as work areas be constructed to permit maneuvering within the work area or be constructed or equipped (i.e., with racks or shelves) to be accessible.

(4) Temporary Structures. These guidelines cover temporary buildings or facilities as well as permanent facilities. Temporary buildings and facilities are not of permanent construction but are extensively used or are essential for public use for a period of time. Examples of temporary buildings or facilities covered by these guidelines include, but are not limited to: reviewing stands, temporary classrooms, bleacher areas, exhibit areas, temporary banking facilities, temporary health screening services, or temporary safe pedestrian passageways around a construction site. Structures, sites and equipment directly associated with the actual processes of construction, such as scaffolding, bridging, materials hoists, or construction trailers are not included.

(5) General Exceptions.

(a) In new construction, a person or entity is not required to meet fully the requirements of these guidelines where that person or entity can demonstrate that it is structurally impracticable to do so. Full compliance will be considered structurally impracticable only in those rare circumstances when the unique characteristics of terrain prevent the incorporation of accessibility features. If full compliance with the requirements of these guidelines is structurally impracticable, a person or entity shall comply with the requirements to the extent it is not structurally impracticable. Any portion of the building or facility which can be made accessible shall comply to the extent that it is not structurally impracticable.

(b) Accessibility is not required to (i) observation galleries used primarily for security purposes; or (ii) in non-occupiable spaces accessed only by ladders, catwalks, crawl spaces, very narrow passageways, or freight (non-passenger) elevators, and frequented only by service personnel for repair purposes; such spaces include, but are not limited to, elevator pits, elevator penthouses, piping or equipment catwalks.

4.1.2 Accessible Sites and Exterior Facilities: New Construction. An accessible site shall meet the following minimum requirements:

(1) At least one accessible route complying with 4.3 shall be provided within the boundary of the site from public transportation stops, accessible parking spaces, passenger loading zones if provided, and public streets or sidewalks, to an accessible building entrance.

(2) At least one accessible route complying with 4.3 shall connect accessible buildings, accessible facilities, accessible elements, and accessible spaces that are on the same site.

(3) All objects that protrude from surfaces or posts into circulation paths shall comply with 4.4.

5

C-203

4.1.2 Accessible Sites and Exterior Facilities: New Construction

(4) Ground surfaces along accessible routes and in accessible spaces shall comply with 4.5.

(5) (a) If parking spaces are provided for self-parking by employees or visitors, or both, then accessible spaces complying with 4.6 shall be provided in each such parking area in conformance with the table below. Spaces required by the table need not be provided in the particular lot. They may be provided in a different location if equivalent or greater accessibility, in terms of distance from an accessible entrance, cost and convenience is ensured.

Total Parking in Lot	Required Minimum Number of Accessible Spaces
1 to 25	1
26 to 50	2
51 to 75	3
76 to 100	4
101 to 150	5
151 to 200	6
201 to 300	7
301 to 400	8
401 to 500	9
501 to 1000	2 percent of total
1001 and over	20 plus 1 for each 100 over 1000

Except as provided in (b), access aisles adjacent to accessible spaces shall be 60 in (1525 mm) wide minimum.

(b) One in every eight accessible spaces, but not less than one, shall be served by an access aisle 96 in (2440 mm) wide minimum and shall be designated "van accessible" as required by 4.6.4. The vertical clearance at such spaces shall comply with 4.6.5. All such spaces may be grouped on one level of a parking structure.

EXCEPTION: Provision of all required parking spaces in conformance with "Universal Parking Design" (see appendix A4.6.3) is permitted.

(c) If passenger loading zones are provided, then at least one passenger loading zone shall comply with 4.6.6.

(d) At facilities providing medical care and other services for persons with mobility impairments, parking spaces complying with 4.6 shall be provided in accordance with 4.1.2(5)(a) except as follows:

(i) Outpatient units and facilities: 10 percent of the total number of parking spaces provided serving each such outpatient unit or facility;

(ii) Units and facilities that specialize in treatment or services for persons with mobility impairments: 20 percent of the total number of parking spaces provided serving each such unit or facility.

(e)*Valet parking: Valet parking facilities shall provide a passenger loading zone complying with 4.6.6 located on an accessible route to the entrance of the facility. Paragraphs 5(a), 5(b), and 5(d) of this section do not apply to valet parking facilities.

(6) If toilet facilities are provided on a site, then each such public or common use toilet facility shall comply with 4.22. If bathing facilities are provided on a site, then each such public or common use bathing facility shall comply with 4.23.

For single user portable toilet or bathing units clustered at a single location, at least 5% but no less than one toilet unit or bathing unit complying with 4.22 or 4.23 shall be installed at each cluster whenever typical inaccessible units are provided. Accessible units shall be identified by the International Symbol of Accessibility.

EXCEPTION: Portable toilet units at construction sites used exclusively by construction personnel are not required to comply with 4.1.2(6).

(7) Building Signage. Signs which designate permanent rooms and spaces shall comply with 4.30.1, 4.30.4, 4.30.5 and 4.30.6. Other signs which provide direction to, or information about, functional spaces of the building shall comply with 4.30.1, 4.30.2, 4.30.3, and 4.30.5. Elements and spaces of accessible facilities which shall be identified by the International Symbol of Accessibility and which shall comply with 4.30.7 are:

(a) Parking spaces designated as reserved for individuals with disabilities;

6

(b) Accessible passenger loading zones;

(c) Accessible entrances when not all are accessible (inaccessible entrances shall have directional signage to indicate the route to the nearest accessible entrance);

(d) Accessible toilet and bathing facilities when not all are accessible.

4.1.3 Accessible Buildings: New Construction. Accessible buildings and facilities shall meet the following minimum requirements:

(1) At least one accessible route complying with 4.3 shall connect accessible building or facility entrances with all accessible spaces and elements within the building or facility.

(2) All objects that overhang or protrude into circulation paths shall comply with 4.4.

(3) Ground and floor surfaces along accessible routes and in accessible rooms and spaces shall comply with 4.5.

(4) Interior and exterior stairs connecting levels that are not connected by an elevator, ramp, or other accessible means of vertical access shall comply with 4.9.

(5)* One passenger elevator complying with 4.10 shall serve each level, including mezzanines, in all multi-story buildings and facilities unless exempted below. If more than one elevator is provided, each full passenger elevator shall comply with 4.10.

EXCEPTION 1: Elevators are not required in facilities that are less than three stories or that have less than 3000 square feet per story unless the building is a shopping center, a shopping mall, or the professional office of a health care provider, or another type of facility as determined by the Attorney General. The elevator exemption set forth in this paragraph does not obviate or limit in any way the obligation to comply with the other accessibility requirements established in section 4.1.3. For example, floors above or below the accessible ground floor must meet the requirements of this section except for elevator service. If toilet or bathing facilities are provided on a level not served by an elevator, then toilet or bathing facilities must be provided on the accessible ground floor. In new construction if a building or facility is eligible for this exemption but a full passenger elevator is nonetheless planned, that elevator shall meet the requirements of 4.10 and shall serve each level in the building. A full passenger elevator that provides service from a garage to only one level of a building or facility is not required to serve other levels.

EXCEPTION 2: Elevator pits, elevator penthouses, mechanical rooms, piping or equipment catwalks are exempted from this requirement.

EXCEPTION 3: Accessible ramps complying with 4.8 may be used in lieu of an elevator.

EXCEPTION 4: Platform lifts (wheelchair lifts) complying with 4.11 of this guideline and applicable state or local codes may be used in lieu of an elevator only under the following conditions:

(a) To provide an accessible route to a performing area in an assembly occupancy.

(b) To comply with the wheelchair viewing position line-of-sight and dispersion requirements of 4.33.3.

(c) To provide access to incidental occupiable spaces and rooms which are not open to the general public and which house no more than five persons, including but not limited to equipment control rooms and projection booths.

(d) To provide access where existing site constraints or other constraints make use of a ramp or an elevator infeasible.

(6) Windows: (Reserved).

(7) Doors:

(a) At each accessible entrance to a building or facility, at least one door shall comply with 4.13.

(b) Within a building or facility, at least one door at each accessible space shall comply with 4.13.

(c) Each door that is an element of an accessible route shall comply with 4.13.

7

4.1.3 Accessible Buildings: New Construction

(d) Each door required by 4.3.10, Egress, shall comply with 4.13.

(8) In new construction, at a minimum, the requirements in (a) and (b) below shall be satisfied independently:

(a)(i) At least 50% of all public entrances (excluding those in (b) below) must be accessible. At least one must be a ground floor entrance. Public entrances are any entrances that are not loading or service entrances.

(ii) Accessible entrances must be provided in a number at least equivalent to the number of exits required by the applicable building/fire codes. (This paragraph does not require an increase in the total number of entrances planned for a facility.)

(iii) An accessible entrance must be provided to each tenancy in a facility (for example, individual stores in a strip shopping center).

One entrance may be considered as meeting more than one of the requirements in (a). Where feasible, accessible entrances shall be the entrances used by the majority of people visiting or working in the building.

(b)(i) In addition, if direct access is provided for pedestrians from an enclosed parking garage to the building, at least one direct entrance from the garage to the building must be accessible.

(ii) If access is provided for pedestrians from a pedestrian tunnel or elevated walkway, one entrance to the building from each tunnel or walkway must be accessible.

One entrance may be considered as meeting more than one of the requirements in (b).

Because entrances also serve as emergency exits whose proximity to all parts of buildings and facilities is essential, it is preferable that all entrances be accessible.

(c) If the only entrance to a building, or tenancy in a facility, is a service entrance, that entrance shall be accessible.

(d) Entrances which are not accessible shall have directional signage complying with 4.30.1, 4.30.2, 4.30.3, and 4.30.5, which indicates the location of the nearest accessible entrance.

(9)* In buildings or facilities, or portions of buildings or facilities, required to be accessible, accessible means of egress shall be provided in the same number as required for exits by local building/life safety regulations. Where a required exit from an occupiable level above or below a level of accessible exit discharge is not accessible, an area of rescue assistance shall be provided on each such level (in a number equal to that of inaccessible required exits). Areas of rescue assistance shall comply with 4.3.11. A horizontal exit, meeting the requirements of local building/life safety regulations, shall satisfy the requirement for an area of rescue assistance.

EXCEPTION: Areas of rescue assistance are not required in buildings or facilities having a supervised automatic sprinkler system.

(10)* Drinking Fountains:

(a) Where only one drinking fountain is provided on a floor there shall be a drinking fountain which is accessible to individuals who use wheelchairs in accordance with 4.15 and one accessible to those who have difficulty bending or stooping. (This can be accommodated by the use of a "hi-lo" fountain; by providing one fountain accessible to those who use wheelchairs and one fountain at a standard height convenient for those who have difficulty bending; by providing a fountain accessible under 4.15 and a water cooler; or by such other means as would achieve the required accessibility for each group on each floor.)

(b) Where more than one drinking fountain or water cooler is provided on a floor, 50% of those provided shall comply with 4.15 and shall be on an accessible route.

(11) Toilet Facilities: If toilet rooms are provided, then each public and common use toilet room shall comply with 4.22. Other toilet rooms provided for the use of occupants of specific spaces (i.e., a private toilet room for the occupant of a private office) shall be adaptable. If bathing rooms are provided, then each public and common use bathroom shall comply with 4.23. Accessible toilet rooms and bathing facilities shall be on an accessible route.

8

(12) Storage, Shelving and Display Units:

(a) If fixed or built-in storage facilities such as cabinets, shelves, closets, and drawers are provided in accessible spaces, at least one of each type provided shall contain storage space complying with 4.25. Additional storage may be provided outside of the dimensions required by 4.25.

(b) Shelves or display units allowing self-service by customers in mercantile occupancies shall be located on an accessible route complying with 4.3. Requirements for accessible reach range do not apply.

(13) Controls and operating mechanisms in accessible spaces, along accessible routes, or as parts of accessible elements (for example, light switches and dispenser controls) shall comply with 4.27.

(14) If emergency warning systems are provided, then they shall include both audible alarms and visual alarms complying with 4.28. Sleeping accommodations required to comply with 9.3 shall have an alarm system complying with 4.28. Emergency warning systems in medical care facilities may be modified to suit standard health care alarm design practice.

(15) Detectable warnings shall be provided at locations as specified in 4.29.

(16) Building Signage:

(a) Signs which designate permanent rooms and spaces shall comply with 4.30.1, 4.30.4, 4.30.5 and 4.30.6.

(b) Other signs which provide direction to or information about functional spaces of the building shall comply with 4.30.1, 4.30.2, 4.30.3, and 4.30.5.

EXCEPTION: Building directories, menus, and all other signs which are temporary are not required to comply.

(17) Public Telephones:

(a) If public pay telephones, public closed circuit telephones, or other public telephones are provided, then they shall comply with 4.31.2 through 4.31.8 to the extent required by the following table:

Number of each type of telephone provided on each floor	Number of telephones required to comply with 4.31.2 through 4.31.8[1]
1 or more single unit	1 per floor
1 bank[2]	1 per floor
2 or more banks[2]	1 per bank. Accessible unit may be installed as a single unit in proximity (either visible or with signage) to the bank. At least one public telephone per floor shall meet the requirements for a forward reach telephone[3].

[1] Additional public telephones may be installed at any height. Unless otherwise specified, accessible telephones may be either forward or side reach telephones.

[2] A bank consists of two or more adjacent public telephones, often installed as a unit.

[3] EXCEPTION: For exterior installations only, if dial tone first service is available, then a side reach telephone may be installed instead of the required forward reach telephone (i.e., one telephone in proximity to each bank shall comply with 4.31).

(b)* All telephones required to be accessible and complying with 4.31.2 through 4.31.8 shall be equipped with a volume control. In addition, 25 percent, but never less than one, of all other public telephones provided shall be equipped with a volume control and shall be dispersed among all types of public telephones, including closed circuit telephones, throughout the building or facility. Signage complying with applicable provisions of 4.30.7 shall be provided.

(c) The following shall be provided in accordance with 4.31.9:

(i) If a total number of four or more public pay telephones (including both interior and exterior phones) is provided at a site, and at least one is in an interior location, then at least one interior public text telephone shall be provided.

(ii) If an interior public pay telephone is provided in a stadium or arena, in a convention center, in a hotel with a convention center, or

9

4.1.3 Accessible Buildings: New Construction

in a covered mall, at least one interior public text telephone shall be provided in the facility.

(iii) If a public pay telephone is located in or adjacent to a hospital emergency room, hospital recovery room, or hospital waiting room, one public text telephone shall be provided at each such location.

(d) Where a bank of telephones in the interior of a building consists of three or more public pay telephones, at least one public pay telephone in each such bank shall be equipped with a shelf and outlet in compliance with 4.31.9(2).

(18) If fixed or built-in seating or tables (including, but not limited to, study carrels and student laboratory stations), are provided in accessible public or common use areas, at least five percent (5%), but not less than one, of the fixed or built-in seating areas or tables shall comply with 4.32. An accessible route shall lead to and through such fixed or built-in seating areas, or tables.

(19)* Assembly areas:

(a) In places of assembly with fixed seating accessible wheelchair locations shall comply with 4.33.2, 4.33.3, and 4.33.4 and shall be provided consistent with the following table:

Capacity of Seating in Assembly Areas	Number of Required Wheelchair Locations
4 to 25	1
26 to 50	2
51 to 300	4
301 to 500	6
over 500	6, plus 1 additional space for each total seating capacity increase of 100

In addition, one percent, but not less than one, of all fixed seats shall be aisle seats with no armrests on the aisle side, or removable or folding armrests on the aisle side. Each such seat shall be identified by a sign or marker. Signage notifying patrons of the availability of such seats shall be posted at the ticket office. Aisle seats are not required to comply with 4.33.4.

(b) This paragraph applies to assembly areas where audible communications are integral to the use of the space (e.g., concert and lecture halls, playhouses and movie theaters, meeting rooms, etc.). Such assembly areas, if (1) they accommodate at least 50 persons, or if they have audio-amplification systems, and (2) they have fixed seating, shall have a permanently installed assistive listening system complying with 4.33. For other assembly areas, a permanently installed assistive listening system, or an adequate number of electrical outlets or other supplementary wiring necessary to support a portable assistive listening system shall be provided. The minimum number of receivers to be provided shall be equal to 4 percent of the total number of seats, but in no case less than two. Signage complying with applicable provisions of 4.30 shall be installed to notify patrons of the availability of a listening system.

(20) Where automated teller machines (ATMs) are provided, each ATM shall comply with the requirements of 4.34 except where two or more are provided at a location, then only one must comply.

EXCEPTION: Drive-up-only automated teller machines are not required to comply with 4.27.2, 4.27.3 and 4.34.3.

(21) Where dressing and fitting rooms are provided for use by the general public, patients, customers or employees, 5 percent, but never less than one, of dressing rooms for each type of use in each cluster of dressing rooms shall be accessible and shall comply with 4.35.

Examples of types of dressing rooms are those serving different genders or distinct and different functions as in different treatment or examination facilities.

4.1.4 (Reserved).

4.1.5 Accessible Buildings: Additions.
Each addition to an existing building or facility shall be regarded as an alteration. Each space or element added to the existing building or facility shall comply with the applicable provisions of 4.1.1 to 4.1.3, Minimum Requirements (for New Construction) and the applicable technical specifications of 4.2 through 4.35 and sections 5 through 10. Each addition that

10

affects or could affect the usability of an area containing a primary function shall comply with 4.1.6(2).

4.1.6 Accessible Buildings: Alterations.

(1) General. Alterations to existing buildings and facilities shall comply with the following:

(a) No alteration shall be undertaken which decreases or has the effect of decreasing accessibility or usability of a building or facility below the requirements for new construction at the time of alteration.

(b) If existing elements, spaces, or common areas are altered, then each such altered element, space, feature, or area shall comply with the applicable provisions of 4.1.1 to 4.1.3 Minimum Requirements (for New Construction). If the applicable provision for new construction requires that an element, space, or common area be on an accessible route, the altered element, space, or common area is not required to be on an accessible route except as provided in 4.1.6(2) (Alterations to an Area Containing a Primary Function.)

(c) If alterations of single elements, when considered together, amount to an alteration of a room or space in a building or facility, the entire space shall be made accessible.

(d) No alteration of an existing element, space, or area of a building or facility shall impose a requirement for greater accessibility than that which would be required for new construction. For example, if the elevators and stairs in a building are being altered and the elevators are, in turn, being made accessible, then no accessibility modifications are required to the stairs connecting levels connected by the elevator. If stair modifications to correct unsafe conditions are required by other codes, the modifications shall be done in compliance with these guidelines unless technically infeasible.

(e) At least one interior public text telephone complying with 4.31.9 shall be provided if:

(i) alterations to existing buildings or facilities with less than four exterior or interior public pay telephones would increase the total number to four or more telephones with at least one in an interior location; or

(ii) alterations to one or more exterior or interior public pay telephones occur in an existing building or facility with four or more public telephones with at least one in an interior location.

(f) If an escalator or stair is planned or installed where none existed previously and major structural modifications are necessary for such installation, then a means of accessible vertical access shall be provided that complies with the applicable provisions of 4.7, 4.8, 4.10, or 4.11.

(g) In alterations, the requirements of 4.1.3(9), 4.3.10 and 4.3.11 do not apply.

(h)*Entrances: If a planned alteration entails alterations to an entrance, and the building has an accessible entrance, the entrance being altered is not required to comply with 4.1.3(8), except to the extent required by 4.1.6(2). If a particular entrance is not made accessible, appropriate accessible signage indicating the location of the nearest accessible entrance(s) shall be installed at or near the inaccessible entrance, such that a person with disabilities will not be required to retrace the approach route from the inaccessible entrance.

(i) If the alteration work is limited solely to the electrical, mechanical, or plumbing system, or to hazardous material abatement, or automatic sprinkler retrofitting, and does not involve the alteration of any elements or spaces required to be accessible under these guidelines, then 4.1.6(2) does not apply.

(j) EXCEPTION: In alteration work, if compliance with 4.1.6 is technically infeasible, the alteration shall provide accessibility to the maximum extent feasible. Any elements or features of the building or facility that are being altered and can be made accessible shall be made accessible within the scope of the alteration.

Technically Infeasible. Means, with respect to an alteration of a building or a facility, that it has little likelihood of being accomplished because existing structural conditions would require removing or altering a load-bearing member which is an essential part of the structural frame; or because other existing physical or site constraints prohibit modification or

4.1.6 Accessible Buildings: Alterations

addition of elements, spaces, or features which are in full and strict compliance with the minimum requirements for new construction and which are necessary to provide accessibility.

(k) EXCEPTION:

(i) These guidelines do not require the installation of an elevator in an altered facility that is less than three stories or has less than 3,000 square feet per story unless the building is a shopping center, a shopping mall, the professional office of a health care provider, or another type of facility as determined by the Attorney General.

(ii) The exemption provided in paragraph (i) does not obviate or limit in any way the obligation to comply with the other accessibility requirements established in these guidelines. For example, alterations to floors above or below the ground floor must be accessible regardless of whether the altered facility has an elevator. If a facility subject to the elevator exemption set forth in paragraph (i) nonetheless has a full passenger elevator, that elevator shall meet, to the maximum extent feasible, the accessibility requirements of these guidelines.

(2) Alterations to an Area Containing a Primary Function: In addition to the requirements of 4.1.6(1), an alteration that affects or could affect the usability of or access to an area containing a primary function shall be made so as to ensure that, to the maximum extent feasible, the path of travel to the altered area and the restrooms, telephones, and drinking fountains serving the altered area, are readily accessible to and usable by individuals with disabilities, unless such alterations are disproportionate to the overall alterations in terms of cost and scope (as determined under criteria established by the Attorney General).

(3) Special Technical Provisions for Alterations to Existing Buildings and Facilities:

(a) Ramps: Curb ramps and interior or exterior ramps to be constructed on sites or in existing buildings or facilities where space limitations prohibit the use of a 1:12 slope or less may have slopes and rises as follows:

(i) A slope between 1:10 and 1:12 is allowed for a maximum rise of 6 inches.

(ii) A slope between 1:8 and 1:10 is allowed for a maximum rise of 3 inches. A slope steeper than 1:8 is not allowed.

(b) Stairs: Full extension of handrails at stairs shall not be required in alterations where such extensions would be hazardous or impossible due to plan configuration.

(c) Elevators:

(i) If safety door edges are provided in existing automatic elevators, automatic door reopening devices may be omitted (see 4.10.6).

(ii) Where existing shaft configuration or technical infeasibility prohibits strict compliance with 4.10.9, the minimum car plan dimensions may be reduced by the minimum amount necessary, but in no case shall the inside car area be smaller than 48 in by 48 in.

(iii) Equivalent facilitation may be provided with an elevator car of different dimensions when usability can be demonstrated and when all other elements required to be accessible comply with the applicable provisions of 4.10. For example, an elevator of 47 in by 69 in (1195 mm by 1755 mm) with a door opening on the narrow dimension, could accommodate the standard wheelchair clearances shown in Figure 4.

(d) Doors:

(i) Where it is technically infeasible to comply with clear opening width requirements of 4.13.5, a projection of 5/8 in maximum will be permitted for the latch side stop.

(ii) If existing thresholds are 3/4 in high or less, and have (or are modified to have) a beveled edge on each side, they may remain.

(e) Toilet Rooms:

(i) Where it is technically infeasible to comply with 4.22 or 4.23, the installation of at least one unisex toilet/bathroom per floor, located in the same area as existing toilet facilities, will be permitted in lieu of modifying existing toilet facilities to be accessible. Each unisex toilet room shall contain one water closet complying with 4.16 and one lavatory complying with 4.19, and the door shall have a privacy latch.

12

(ii) Where it is technically infeasible to install a required standard stall (Fig. 30(a)), or where other codes prohibit reduction of the fixture count (i.e., removal of a water closet in order to create a double-wide stall), either alternate stall (Fig.30(b)) may be provided in lieu of the standard stall.

(iii) When existing toilet or bathing facilities are being altered and are not made accessible, signage complying with 4.30.1, 4.30.2, 4.30.3, 4.30.5, and 4.30.7 shall be provided indicating the location of the nearest accessible toilet or bathing facility within the facility.

(f) Assembly Areas:

(i) Where it is technically infeasible to disperse accessible seating throughout an altered assembly area, accessible seating areas may be clustered. Each accessible seating area shall have provisions for companion seating and shall be located on an accessible route that also serves as a means of emergency egress.

(ii) Where it is technically infeasible to alter all performing areas to be on an accessible route, at least one of each type of performing area shall be made accessible.

(g) Platform Lifts (Wheelchair Lifts): In alterations, platform lifts (wheelchair lifts) complying with 4.11 and applicable state or local codes may be used as part of an accessible route. The use of lifts is not limited to the four conditions in exception 4 of 4.1.3(5).

(h) Dressing Rooms: In alterations where technical infeasibility can be demonstrated, one dressing room for each sex on each level shall be made accessible. Where only unisex dressing rooms are provided, accessible unisex dressing rooms may be used to fulfill this requirement.

4.1.7 Accessible Buildings: Historic Preservation.

(1) Applicability:

(a) General Rule. Alterations to a qualified historic building or facility shall comply with 4.1.6 Accessible Buildings: Alterations, the applicable technical specifications of 4.2

through 4.35 and the applicable special application sections 5 through 10 unless it is determined in accordance with the procedures in 4.1.7(2) that compliance with the requirements for accessible routes (exterior and interior), ramps, entrances, or toilets would threaten or destroy the historic significance of the building or facility in which case the alternative requirements in 4.1.7(3) may be used for the feature.

EXCEPTION: (Reserved).

(b) Definition. A qualified historic building or facility is a building or facility that is:

(i) Listed in or eligible for listing in the National Register of Historic Places; or

(ii) Designated as historic under an appropriate State or local law.

(2) Procedures:

(a) Alterations to Qualified Historic Buildings and Facilities Subject to Section 106 of the National Historic Preservation Act:

(i) Section 106 Process. Section 106 of the National Historic Preservation Act (16 U.S.C. 470 f) requires that a Federal agency with jurisdiction over a Federal, federally assisted, or federally licensed undertaking consider the effects of the agency's undertaking on buildings and facilities listed in or eligible for listing in the National Register of Historic Places and give the Advisory Council on Historic Preservation a reasonable opportunity to comment on the undertaking prior to approval of the undertaking.

(ii) ADA Application. Where alterations are undertaken to a qualified historic building or facility that is subject to section 106 of the National Historic Preservation Act, the Federal agency with jurisdiction over the undertaking shall follow the section 106 process. If the State Historic Preservation Officer or Advisory Council on Historic Preservation agrees that compliance with the requirements for accessible routes (exterior and interior), ramps, entrances, or toilets would threaten or destroy the historic significance of the building or facility, the alternative requirements in 4.1.7(3) may be used for the feature.

13

4.2 Space Allowance and Reach Ranges

(b) Alterations to Qualified Historic Buildings and Facilities Not Subject to Section 106 of the National Historic Preservation Act. Where alterations are undertaken to a qualified historic building or facility that is not subject to section 106 of the National Historic Preservation Act, if the entity undertaking the alterations believes that compliance with the requirements for accessible routes (exterior and interior), ramps, entrances, or toilets would threaten or destroy the historic significance of the building or facility and that the alternative requirements in 4.1.7(3) should be used for the feature, the entity should consult with the State Historic Preservation Officer. If the State Historic Preservation Officer agrees that compliance with the accessibility requirements for accessible routes (exterior and interior), ramps, entrances or toilets would threaten or destroy the historical significance of the building or facility, the alternative requirements in 4.1.7(3) may be used.

(c) Consultation With Interested Persons. Interested persons should be invited to participate in the consultation process, including State or local accessibility officials, individuals with disabilities, and organizations representing individuals with disabilities.

(d) Certified Local Government Historic Preservation Programs. Where the State Historic Preservation Officer has delegated the consultation responsibility for purposes of this section to a local government historic preservation program that has been certified in accordance with section 101(c) of the National Historic Preservation Act of 1966 (16 U.S.C. 470a (c)) and implementing regulations (36 CFR 61.5), the responsibility may be carried out by the appropriate local government body or official.

(3) Historic Preservation: Minimum Requirements:

(a) At least one accessible route complying with 4.3 from a site access point to an accessible entrance shall be provided.

EXCEPTION: A ramp with a slope no greater than 1:6 for a run not to exceed 2 ft (610 mm) may be used as part of an accessible route to an entrance.

(b) At least one accessible entrance complying with 4.14 which is used by the public shall be provided.

EXCEPTION: If it is determined that no entrance used by the public can comply with 4.14, then access at any entrance not used by the general public but open (unlocked) with directional signage at the primary entrance may be used. The accessible entrance shall also have a notification system. Where security is a problem, remote monitoring may be used.

(c) If toilets are provided, then at least one toilet facility complying with 4.22 and 4.1.6 shall be provided along an accessible route that complies with 4.3. Such toilet facility may be unisex in design.

(d) Accessible routes from an accessible entrance to all publicly used spaces on at least the level of the accessible entrance shall be provided. Access shall be provided to all levels of a building or facility in compliance with 4.1 whenever practical.

(e) Displays and written information, documents, etc., should be located where they can be seen by a seated person. Exhibits and signage displayed horizontally (e.g., open books), should be no higher than 44 in (1120 mm) above the floor surface.

NOTE: The technical provisions of sections 4.2 through 4.35 are the same as those of the American National Standard Institute's document A117.1-1980, except as noted in the text.

4.2 Space Allowance and Reach Ranges.

4.2.1* Wheelchair Passage Width. The minimum clear width for single wheelchair passage shall be 32 in (815 mm) at a point and 36 in (915 mm) continuously (see Fig. 1 and 24(e)).

4.2.2 Width for Wheelchair Passing. The minimum width for two wheelchairs to pass is 60 in (1525 mm) (see Fig. 2).

4.2.3* Wheelchair Turning Space. The space required for a wheelchair to make a 180-degree turn is a clear space of 60 in (1525 mm)

14

4.2.4* Clear Floor or Ground Space for Wheelchairs

diameter (see Fig. 3(a)) or a T-shaped space (see Fig. 3(b)).

4.2.4* Clear Floor or Ground Space for Wheelchairs.

4.2.4.1 Size and Approach. The minimum clear floor or ground space required to accommodate a single, stationary wheelchair and occupant is 30 in by 48 in (760 mm by 1220 mm) (see Fig. 4(a)). The minimum clear floor or ground space for wheelchairs may be positioned for forward or parallel approach to an object (see Fig. 4(b) and (c)). Clear floor or ground space for wheelchairs may be part of the knee space required under some objects.

4.2.4.2 Relationship of Maneuvering Clearance to Wheelchair Spaces. One full unobstructed side of the clear floor or ground space for a wheelchair shall adjoin or overlap an accessible route or adjoin another wheelchair clear floor space. If a clear floor space is located in an alcove or otherwise confined on all or part of three sides, additional maneuvering clearances shall be provided as shown in Fig. 4(d) and (e).

4.2.4.3 Surfaces for Wheelchair Spaces. Clear floor or ground spaces for wheelchairs shall comply with 4.5.

4.2.5* Forward Reach. If the clear floor space only allows forward approach to an object, the maximum high forward reach allowed shall be 48 in (1220 mm) (see Fig. 5(a)). *The minimum low forward reach is 15 in (380 mm).* If the high forward reach is over an obstruction, reach and clearances shall be as shown in Fig. 5(b).

4.2.6* Side Reach. If the clear floor space allows parallel approach by a person in a wheelchair, the maximum high side reach allowed shall be 54 in (1370 mm) and the low side reach shall be no less than 9 in (230 mm) above the floor (Fig. 6(a) and (b)). If the side reach is over an obstruction, the reach and clearances shall be as shown in Fig 6(c).

4.3 Accessible Route.

4.3.1* General. All walks, halls, corridors, aisles, *skywalks*, *tunnels*, and other spaces

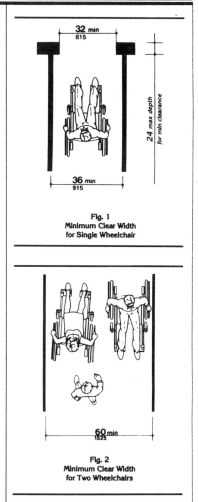

Fig. 1
Minimum Clear Width
for Single Wheelchair

Fig. 2
Minimum Clear Width
for Two Wheelchairs

15

C-213

4.3 Accessible Route

that are part of an accessible route shall comply with 4.3.

4.3.2 Location.

(1) At least one accessible route *within the boundary of the site* shall be provided from public transportation stops, accessible parking, and accessible passenger loading zones, and public streets or sidewalks to the accessible building entrance they serve. *The accessible route shall, to the maximum extent feasible, coincide with the route for the general public.*

(2) At least one accessible route shall connect accessible buildings, facilities, elements, and spaces that are on the same site.

(3) At least one accessible route shall connect accessible building or facility entrances with all accessible spaces and elements and with all accessible dwelling units within the building or facility.

(4) An accessible route shall connect at least one accessible entrance of each accessible dwelling unit with those exterior and interior spaces and facilities that serve the accessible dwelling unit.

4.3.3 Width. The minimum clear width of an accessible route shall be 36 in (915 mm) except at doors (see 4.13.5 and 4.13.6). If a person in a wheelchair must make a turn around an obstruction, the minimum clear width of the accessible route shall be as shown in Fig. 7(a) and (b).

4.3.4 Passing Space. If an accessible route has less than 60 in (1525 mm) clear width, then passing spaces at least 60 in by 60 in (1525 mm by 1525 mm) shall be located at reasonable intervals not to exceed 200 ft (61 m). A T-intersection of two corridors or walks is an acceptable passing place.

4.3.5 Head Room. Accessible routes shall comply with 4.4.2.

4.3.6 Surface Textures. The surface of an accessible route shall comply with 4.5.

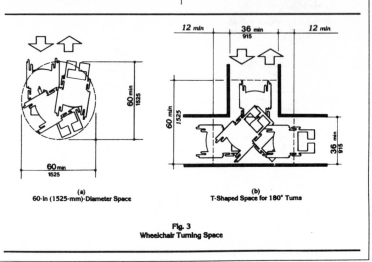

(a)
60-in (1525-mm)-Diameter Space

(b)
T-Shaped Space for 180° Turns

Fig. 3
Wheelchair Turning Space

16

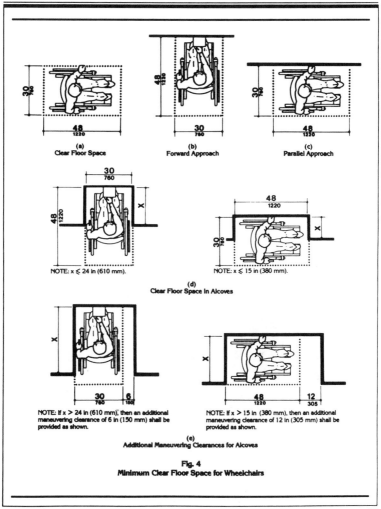

Fig. 4
Minimum Clear Floor Space for Wheelchairs

4.3 Accessible Route

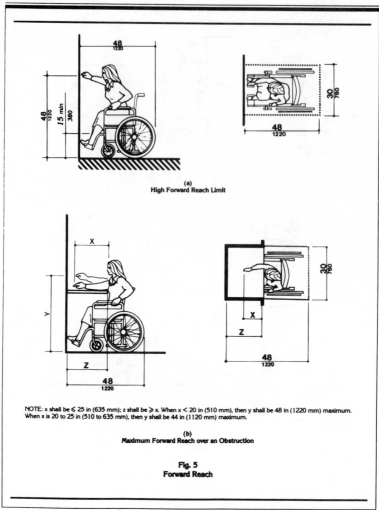

NOTE: x shall be ≤ 25 in (635 mm); z shall be ≥ x. When x < 20 in (510 mm), then y shall be 48 in (1220 mm) maximum. When x is 20 to 25 in (510 to 635 mm), then y shall be 44 in (1120 mm) maximum.

(b)
Maximum Forward Reach over an Obstruction

Fig. 5
Forward Reach

18

C-216

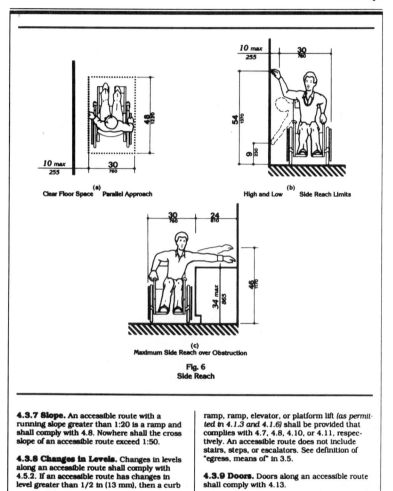

(a)
Clear Floor Space   Parallel Approach

(b)
High and Low   Side Reach Limits

(c)
Maximum Side Reach over Obstruction

Fig. 6
Side Reach

4.3.7 Slope. An accessible route with a running slope greater than 1:20 is a ramp and shall comply with 4.8. Nowhere shall the cross slope of an accessible route exceed 1:50.

4.3.8 Changes in Levels. Changes in levels along an accessible route shall comply with 4.5.2. If an accessible route has changes in level greater than 1/2 in (13 mm), then a curb

ramp, ramp, elevator, or platform lift (as permitted in 4.1.3 and 4.1.6) shall be provided that complies with 4.7, 4.8, 4.10, or 4.11, respectively. An accessible route does not include stairs, steps, or escalators. See definition of "egress, means of" in 3.5.

4.3.9 Doors. Doors along an accessible route shall comply with 4.13.

19

4.3.10* Egress

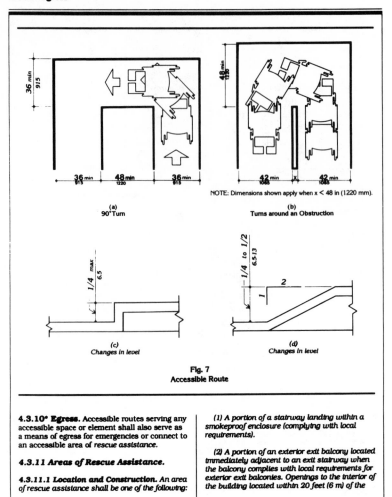

NOTE: Dimensions shown apply when x < 48 in (1220 mm).

(a)
90° Turn

(b)
Turns around an Obstruction

(c)
Changes in level

(d)
Changes in level

**Fig. 7
Accessible Route**

4.3.10* Egress. Accessible routes serving any accessible space or element shall also serve as a means of egress for emergencies or connect to an accessible area of *rescue assistance*.

4.3.11 Areas of Rescue Assistance.

4.3.11.1 Location and Construction. An area of *rescue assistance* shall be one of the following:

(1) A portion of a stairway landing within a smokeproof enclosure (complying with local requirements).

(2) A portion of an exterior exit balcony located immediately adjacent to an exit stairway when the balcony complies with local requirements for exterior exit balconies. Openings to the interior of the building located within 20 feet (6 m) of the

20

area of rescue assistance shall be protected with fire assemblies having a three-fourths hour fire protection rating.

(3) A portion of a one-hour fire-resistive corridor (complying with local requirements for fire-resistive construction and for openings) located immediately adjacent to an exit enclosure.

(4) A vestibule located immediately adjacent to an exit enclosure and constructed to the same fire-resistive standards as required for corridors and openings.

(5) A portion of a stairway landing within an exit enclosure which is vented to the exterior and is separated from the interior of the building with not less than one-hour fire-resistive doors.

(6) When approved by the appropriate local authority, an area or a room which is separated from other portions of the building by a smoke barrier. Smoke barriers shall have a fire-resistive rating of not less than one hour and shall completely enclose the area or room. Doors in the smoke barrier shall be tight-fitting smoke-and draft-control assemblies having a fire-protection rating of not less than 20 minutes and shall be self-closing or automatic closing. The area or room shall be provided with an exit directly to an exit enclosure. Where the room or area exits into an exit enclosure which is required to be of more than one-hour fire-resistive construction, the room or area shall have the same fire-resistive construction, including the same opening protection, as required for the adjacent exit enclosure.

(7) An elevator lobby when elevator shafts and adjacent lobbies are pressurized as required for smokeproof enclosures by local regulations and when complying with requirements herein for size, communication, and signage. Such pressurization system shall be activated by smoke detectors on each floor located in a manner approved by the appropriate local authority. Pressurization equipment and its duct work within the building shall be separated from other portions of the building by a minimum two-hour fire-resistive construction.

4.3.11.2 Size. Each area of rescue assistance shall provide at least two accessible areas each being not less than 30 inches by 48 inches (760 mm by 1220 mm). The area of rescue assistance shall not encroach on any required exit width. The total number of such 30-inch by 48-inch (760 mm by 1220 mm) areas per story shall be not less than one for every 200 persons of calculated occupant load served by the area of rescue assistance.

EXCEPTION: The appropriate local authority may reduce the minimum number of 30-inch by 48-inch (760 mm by 1220 mm) areas to one for each area of rescue assistance on floors where the occupant load is less than 200.

4.3.11.3° Stairway Width. Each stairway adjacent to an area of rescue assistance shall have a minimum clear width of 48 inches between handrails.

4.3.11.4° Two-way Communication. A method of two-way communication, with both visible and audible signals, shall be provided between each area of rescue assistance and the primary entry. The fire department or appropriate local authority may approve a location other than the primary entry.

4.3.11.5 Identification. Each area of rescue assistance shall be identified by a sign which states "AREA OF RESCUE ASSISTANCE" and displays the international symbol of accessibility. The sign shall be illuminated when exit sign illumination is required. Signage shall also be installed at all inaccessible exits and where otherwise necessary to clearly indicate the direction to areas of rescue assistance. In each area of rescue assistance, instructions on the use of the area under emergency conditions shall be posted adjoining the two-way communication system.

4.4 Protruding Objects.

4.4.1° General. Objects projecting from walls (for example, telephones) with their leading edges between 27 in and 80 in (685 mm and 2030 mm) above the finished floor shall protrude no more than 4 in (100 mm) into walks, halls, corridors, passageways, or aisles (see Fig. 8(a)). Objects mounted with their leading edges at or below 27 in (685 mm) above the finished floor may protrude any amount (see Fig. 8(a) and (b)). Free-standing objects mounted on posts or pylons may overhang 12 in (305 mm) maximum from 27 in to 80 in (685 mm to 2030 mm) above the ground or

4.4 Protruding Objects

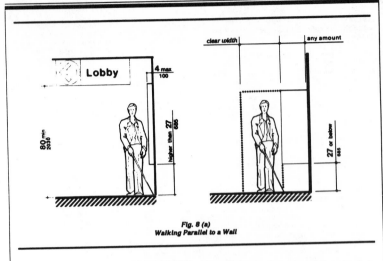

Fig. 8 (a)
Walking Parallel to a Wall

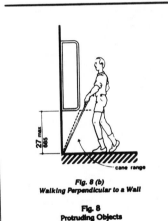

Fig. 8 (b)
Walking Perpendicular to a Wall

Fig. 8
Protruding Objects

finished floor (see Fig. 8(c) and (d)). Protruding objects shall not reduce the clear width of an accessible route or maneuvering space (see Fig. 8(e)).

4.4.2 Head Room. Walks, halls, corridors, passageways, aisles, or other circulation spaces shall have 80 in (2030 mm) minimum clear head room (see Fig. 8(a)). *If vertical clearance of an area adjoining an accessible route is reduced to less than 80 in (nominal dimension), a barrier to warn blind or visually-impaired persons shall be provided (see Fig. 8(c-1)).*

4.5 Ground and Floor Surfaces.

4.5.1° General. Ground and floor surfaces along accessible routes and in accessible rooms and spaces including floors, walks, ramps, stairs, and curb ramps, shall be stable, firm, slip-resistant, and shall comply with 4.5.

4.5.2 Changes in Level. Changes in level up to 1/4 in (6 mm) may be vertical and without edge treatment *(see Fig. 7(c))*. Changes in level between 1/4 in and 1/2 in (6 mm and 13 mm)

22

4.4 Protruding Objects

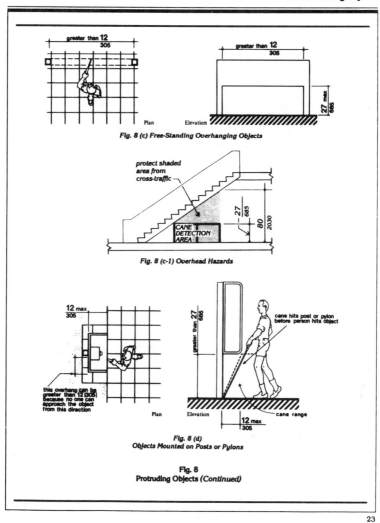

Fig. 8 (c) Free-Standing Overhanging Objects

Fig. 8 (c-1) Overhead Hazards

Fig. 8 (d)
Objects Mounted on Posts or Pylons

Fig. 8
Protruding Objects (Continued)

23

C-221

4.5 Ground and Floor Surfaces

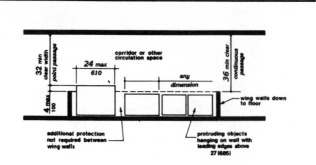

Fig. 8 (e)
Example of Protection around Wall-Mounted Objects and Measurements of Clear Widths

Fig. 8
Protruding Objects *(Continued)*

shall be beveled with a slope no greater than 1:2 *(see Fig. 7(d))*. Changes in level greater than 1/2 in (13 mm) shall be accomplished by means of a ramp that complies with 4.7 or 4.8.

4.5.3* Carpet. If carpet or carpet tile is used on a ground or floor surface, then it shall be securely attached; have a firm cushion, pad, or backing, or no cushion or pad; and have a level loop, textured loop, level cut pile, or level cut/uncut pile texture. The maximum pile *thickness* shall be 1/2 in (13 mm) (see Fig. 8(f)). Exposed edges of carpet shall be fastened to floor surfaces and have trim along the entire length of the exposed edge. Carpet edge trim shall comply with 4.5.2.

4.5.4 Gratings. If gratings are located in walking surfaces, then they shall have spaces no greater than 1/2 in (13 mm) wide in one direction *(see Fig. 8(g))*. If gratings have elongated openings, then they shall be placed so that the long dimension is perpendicular to the dominant direction of travel *(see Fig. 8(h))*.

4.6 Parking and Passenger Loading Zones.

4.6.1 Minimum Number. *Parking spaces required to be accessible by 4.1 shall comply with 4.6.2 through 4.6.5. Passenger loading zones required to be accessible by 4.1 shall comply with 4.6.5 and 4.6.6.*

24

4.6 Parking and Passenger Loading Zones

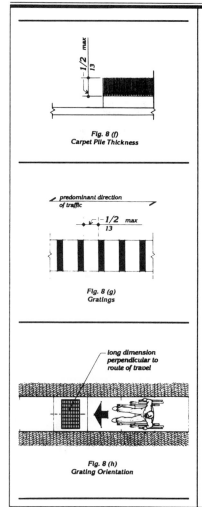

Fig. 8 (f)
Carpet Pile Thickness

Fig. 8 (g)
Gratings

Fig. 8 (h)
Grating Orientation

4.6.2 Location. *Accessible parking spaces serving* a particular building shall be located on the shortest accessible route of travel *from adjacent parking* to an accessible entrance. *In parking facilities* that do not serve a particular building, *accessible parking* shall be located on the shortest accessible route *of travel* to an accessible pedestrian entrance of the parking facility. *In buildings with multiple accessible entrances with adjacent parking, accessible parking spaces shall be dispersed and located closest to the accessible entrances.*

4.6.3° Parking Spaces. *Accessible* parking spaces shall be at least 96 in (2440 mm) wide. Parking access aisles shall be part of an accessible route to the building or facility entrance and shall comply with 4.3. Two accessible parking spaces may share a common access aisle (see Fig. 9). Parked vehicle overhangs shall not reduce the clear width of an accessible route. *Parking spaces and access aisles shall be level with surface slopes not exceeding 1:50 (2%) in all directions.*

4.6.4° Signage. Accessible parking spaces shall be designated as reserved by a sign showing the symbol of accessibility (see 4.30.7). *Spaces complying with 4.1.2(5)(b) shall have an additional sign "Van-Accessible" mounted below the symbol of accessibility. Such signs shall be located so they cannot be obscured by a vehicle* parked in the space.

4.6.5° Vertical Clearance. *Provide minimum vertical clearance of 114 in (2895 mm) at accessible passenger loading zones and along at least one vehicle access route to such areas from site entrance(s) and exit(s). At parking spaces complying with 4.1.2(5)(b), provide minimum vertical clearance of 98 in (2490 mm) at the parking space and along at least one vehicle access route to such spaces from site entrance(s) and exit(s).*

4.6.6 Passenger Loading Zones. Passenger loading zones shall provide an access aisle at least 60 in (1525 mm) wide and 20 ft (240 in) (6100 mm) long adjacent and parallel to the vehicle pull-up space (see Fig. 10). If there are curbs between the access aisle and the vehicle pull-up space, then a curb ramp complying with 4.7 shall be provided. *Vehicle standing spaces and access aisles shall be level with*

25

4.7 Curb Ramps

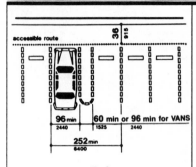

Fig. 9
Dimensions of Parking Spaces

---

surface slopes not exceeding 1:50 (2%) in all directions.

4.7 Curb Ramps.

4.7.1 Location. Curb ramps complying with 4.7 shall be provided wherever an accessible route crosses a curb.

4.7.2 Slope. Slopes of curb ramps shall comply with 4.8.2. The slope shall be measured as shown in Fig. 11. *Transitions from ramps to walks, gutters, or streets shall be flush and free of abrupt changes. Maximum slopes of adjoining gutters, road surface immediately adjacent to the curb ramp, or accessible route shall not exceed 1:20.*

4.7.3 Width. The minimum width of a curb ramp shall be 36 in (915 mm), exclusive of flared sides.

4.7.4 Surface. Surfaces of curb ramps shall comply with 4.5.

4.7.5 Sides of Curb Ramps. If a curb ramp is located where pedestrians must walk across the ramp, *or where it is not protected by handrails or guardrails,* it shall have flared sides; the maximum slope of the flare shall be 1:10 (see Fig. 12(a)). Curb ramps with returned curbs

may be used where pedestrians would not normally walk across the ramp (see Fig. 12(b)).

4.7.6 Built-up Curb Ramps. Built-up curb ramps shall be located so that they do not project into vehicular traffic lanes (see Fig. 13).

4.7.7 Detectable Warnings. A curb ramp shall have a *detectable* warning complying with 4.29.2. *The detectable warning shall extend the* full width and depth of the curb ramp.

4.7.8 Obstructions. Curb ramps shall be located or protected to prevent their obstruction by parked vehicles.

4.7.9 Location at Marked Crossings. Curb ramps at marked crossings shall be wholly contained within the markings, excluding any flared sides (see Fig. 15).

4.7.10 Diagonal Curb Ramps. If diagonal (or corner type) curb ramps have returned curbs or other well-defined edges, such edges shall be parallel to the direction of pedestrian flow. The bottom of diagonal curb ramps shall have 48 in (1220 mm) minimum clear space as shown in Fig. 15(c) and (d). If diagonal curb ramps are provided at marked crossings, the 48 in (1220 mm) clear space shall be within the markings (see Fig. 15(c) and (d)). If diagonal curb ramps have flared sides, they shall also have at least a 24 in (610 mm) long segment of straight curb located on each side of the curb ramp and within the marked crossing (see Fig. 15(c)).

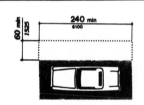

Fig. 10
Access Aisle at Passenger Loading Zones

26

4.8 Ramps

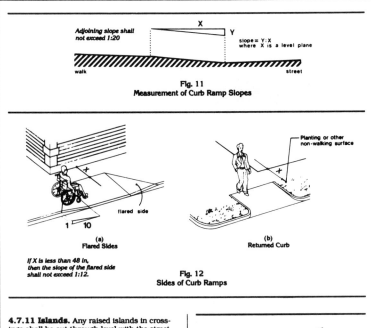

Fig. 11
Measurement of Curb Ramp Slopes

(a)
Flared Sides

(b)
Returned Curb

If X is less than 48 in,
then the slope of the flared side
shall not exceed 1:12.

Fig. 12
Sides of Curb Ramps

4.7.11 Islands. Any raised islands in crossings shall be cut through level with the street or have curb ramps at both sides and a level area at least 48 in (1220 mm) long between the curb ramps in the part of the island intersected by the crossings (see Fig. 15(a) and (b)).

4.8 Ramps.

4.8.1° General. Any part of an accessible route with a slope greater than 1:20 shall be considered a ramp and shall comply with 4.8.

4.8.2° Slope and Rise. The least possible slope shall be used for any ramp. The maximum slope of a ramp in new construction shall be 1:12. The maximum rise for any run shall be 30 in (760 mm) (see Fig. 16). Curb ramps

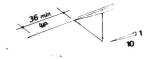

Fig. 13
Built-Up Curb Ramp

and ramps to be constructed on existing sites or in existing buildings or facilities may have slopes and rises as *allowed in 4.1.6(3)(a)* if space limitations prohibit the use of a 1:12 slope or less.

27

4.8 Ramps

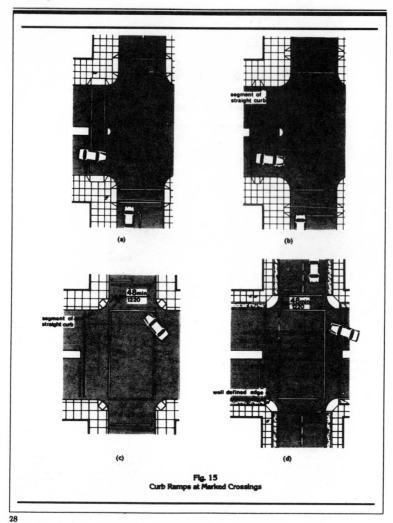

**Fig. 15
Curb Ramps at Marked Crossings**

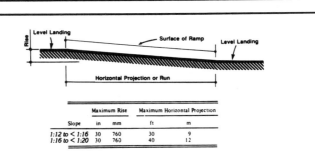

	Maximum Rise		Maximum Horizontal Projection	
Slope	in	mm	ft	m
1:12 to < 1:16	30	760	30	9
1:16 to < 1:20	30	760	40	12

Fig. 16
Components of a Single Ramp Run and Sample Ramp Dimensions

4.8.3 Clear Width. The minimum clear width of a ramp shall be 36 in (915 mm).

4.8.4° Landings. Ramps shall have level landings at bottom and top of *each ramp and each ramp* run. Landings shall have the following features:

(1) The landing shall be at least as wide as the ramp run leading to it.

(2) The landing length shall be a minimum of 60 in (1525 mm) clear.

(3) If ramps change direction at landings, the minimum landing size shall be 60 in by 60 in (1525 mm by 1525 mm).

(4) If a doorway is located at a landing, then the area in front of the doorway shall comply with 4.13.6.

4.8.5° Handrails. If a ramp run has a rise greater than 6 in (150 mm) or a horizontal projection greater than 72 in (1830 mm), then it shall have handrails on both sides. Handrails are not required on curb ramps *or adjacent to seating in assembly areas.* Handrails shall comply with 4.26 and shall have the following features:

(1) Handrails shall be provided along both sides of ramp segments. The inside handrail on switchback or dogleg ramps shall always be continuous.

(2) If handrails are not continuous, they shall extend at least 12 in (305 mm) beyond the top and bottom of the ramp segment and shall be parallel with the floor or ground surface (see Fig. 17).

(3) The clear space between the handrail and the wall shall be 1 - 1/2 in (38 mm).

(4) Gripping surfaces shall be continuous.

(5) *Top of handrail gripping surfaces shall be mounted between 34 in and 38 in (865 mm and 965 mm) above ramp surfaces.*

(6) *Ends of handrails shall be either rounded or returned smoothly to floor, wall, or post.*

(7) *Handrails shall not rotate within their fittings.*

4.8.6 Cross Slope and Surfaces. The cross slope of ramp surfaces shall be no greater than 1:50. Ramp surfaces shall comply with 4.5.

29

4.8.7 Edge Protection. Ramps and landings with drop-offs shall have curbs, walls, railings, or projecting surfaces that prevent people from slipping off the ramp. Curbs shall be a minimum of 2 in (50 mm) high (see Fig. 17).

4.8.8 Outdoor Conditions. Outdoor ramps and their approaches shall be designed so that water will not accumulate on walking surfaces.

4.9 Stairs.

4.9.1* Minimum Number. *Stairs required to be accessible by 4.1 shall comply with 4.9.*

4.9.2 Treads and Risers. On any given flight of stairs, all steps shall have uniform riser heights and uniform tread widths. Stair treads shall be no less than 11 in (280 mm) wide, measured from riser to riser (see Fig. 18(a)). *Open risers are not permitted.*

4.9.3 Nosings. The undersides of nosings shall not be abrupt. The radius of curvature at the leading edge of the tread shall be no greater than 1/2 in (13 mm). Risers shall be sloped or the underside of the nosing shall have an angle not less than 60 degrees from the horizontal. Nosings shall project no more than 1-1/2 in (38 mm) (see Fig. 18).

4.9.4 Handrails. Stairways shall have handrails at both sides of all stairs. Handrails shall comply with 4.26 and shall have the following features:

(1) Handrails shall be continuous along both sides of stairs. The inside handrail on switchback or dogleg stairs shall always be continuous (see Fig. 19(a) and (b)).

(2) If handrails are not continuous, they shall extend at least 12 in (305 mm) beyond the top riser and at least 12 in (305 mm) plus the width of one tread beyond the bottom riser. At the top, the extension shall be parallel with the floor or ground surface. At the bottom, the handrail shall continue to slope for a distance of the width of one tread from the bottom riser; the remainder of the extension shall be horizontal (see Fig. 19(c) and (d)). Handrail extensions shall comply with 4.4.

(3) The clear space between handrails and wall shall be 1-1/2 in (38 mm).

(4) Gripping surfaces shall be uninterrupted by newel posts, other construction elements, or obstructions.

(5) *Top of handrail gripping surface shall be mounted between 34 in and 38 in (865 mm and 965 mm) above stair nosings.*

(6) *Ends of handrails shall be either rounded or returned smoothly to floor, wall or post.*

(7) *Handrails shall not rotate within their fittings.*

4.9.5 Detectable Warnings at Stairs. (Reserved).

4.9.6 Outdoor Conditions. Outdoor stairs and their approaches shall be designed so that water will not accumulate on walking surfaces.

4.10 Elevators.

4.10.1 General. *Accessible* elevators shall be on an accessible route and shall comply with 4.10 and with the *ASME A17.1-1990*, Safety Code for Elevators and Escalators. *Freight elevators shall not be considered as meeting the requirements of this section unless the only elevators provided are used as combination passenger and freight elevators for the public and employees.*

4.10.2 Automatic Operation. Elevator operation shall be automatic. Each car shall be equipped with a self-leveling feature that will automatically bring the car to floor landings within a tolerance of 1/2 in (13 mm) under rated loading to zero loading conditions. This self-leveling feature shall be automatic and independent of the operating device and shall correct the overtravel or undertravel.

4.10.3 Hall Call Buttons. Call buttons in elevator lobbies and halls shall be centered at 42 in (1065 mm) above the floor. Such call buttons shall have visual signals to indicate when each call is registered and when each call is answered. Call buttons shall be a minimum of 3/4 in (19 mm) in the smallest dimension. The button designating the up direction shall be on top. (See Fig. 20.) Buttons shall be raised or flush. Objects mounted beneath hall call buttons shall not project into the elevator lobby more than 4 in (100 mm).

30

4.10 Elevators

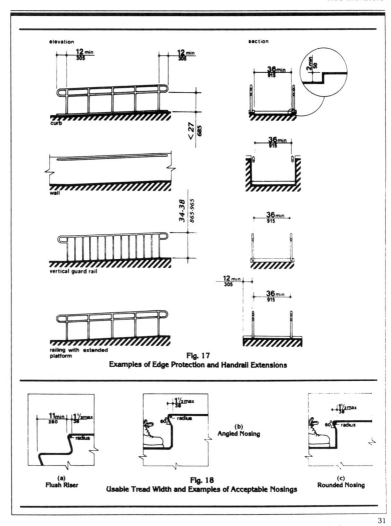

Fig. 17
Examples of Edge Protection and Handrail Extensions

Fig. 18
Usable Tread Width and Examples of Acceptable Nosings

(a) Flush Riser

(b) Angled Nosing

(c) Rounded Nosing

31

4.10 Elevators

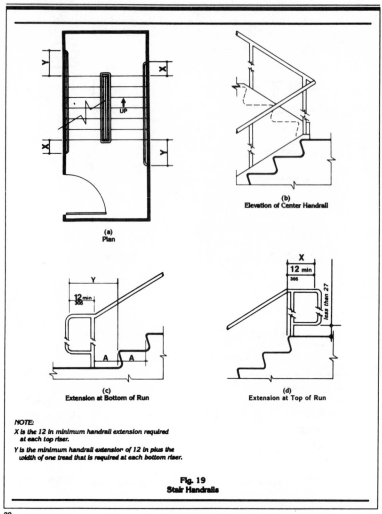

(a)
Plan

(b)
Elevation of Center Handrail

(c)
Extension at Bottom of Run

(d)
Extension at Top of Run

NOTE:

*X is the 12 in minimum handrail extension required
at each top riser.*

*Y is the minimum handrail extension of 12 in plus the
width of one tread that is required at each bottom riser.*

**Fig. 19
Stair Handrails**

32

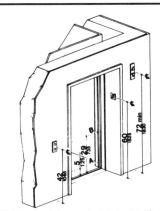

NOTE: The automatic door reopening device is activated if an object passes through either line A or line B. Line A and line B represent the vertical locations of the door reopening device not requiring contact.

Fig. 20
Hoistway and Elevator Entrances

4.10.4 Hall Lanterns. A visible and audible signal shall be provided at each hoistway entrance to indicate which car is answering a call. Audible signals shall sound once for the up direction and twice for the down direction or shall have verbal annunciators that say "up" or "down." Visible signals shall have the following features:

(1) Hall lantern fixtures shall be mounted so that their centerline is at least 72 in (1830 mm) above the lobby floor. (See Fig. 20.)

(2) Visual elements shall be at least 2-1/2 in (64 mm) in the smallest dimension.

(3) Signals shall be visible from the vicinity of the hall call button (see Fig. 20). In-car lanterns located in cars, visible from the vicinity of hall call buttons, and conforming to the above requirements, shall be acceptable.

4.10.5 Raised and Braille Characters on Hoistway Entrances. All elevator hoistway entrances shall have raised and Braille floor designations provided on both jambs. The centerline of the characters shall be 60 in (1525 mm) above finish floor. Such characters shall be 2 in (50 mm) high and shall comply with 4.30.4. Permanently applied plates are acceptable if they are permanently fixed to the jambs. (See Fig. 20).

4.10.6° Door Protective and Reopening Device. Elevator doors shall open and close automatically. They shall be provided with a reopening device that will stop and reopen a car door and hoistway door automatically if the door becomes obstructed by an object or person. The device shall be capable of completing these operations without requiring contact for an obstruction passing through the opening at heights of 5 in and 29 in (125 mm and 735 mm) above finish floor (see Fig. 20). Door reopening devices shall remain effective for at least 20 seconds. After such an interval, doors may close in accordance with the requirements of ASME A17.1-1990.

4.10.7° Door and Signal Timing for Hall Calls. The minimum acceptable time from notification that a car is answering a call until the doors of that car start to close shall be calculated from the following equation:

$$T = D/(1.5 \text{ ft/s}) \text{ or } T = D/(445 \text{ mm/s})$$

where T total time in seconds and D distance (in feet or millimeters) from a point in the lobby or corridor 60 in (1525 mm) directly in front of the farthest call button controlling that car to the centerline of its hoistway door (see Fig. 21). For cars with in-car lanterns, T begins when the lantern is visible from the vicinity of hall call buttons and an audible signal is sounded. *The minimum acceptable notification time shall be 5 seconds.*

4.10.8 Door Delay for Car Calls. The minimum time for elevator doors to remain fully open in response to a car call shall be 3 seconds.

4.10.9 Floor Plan of Elevator Cars. The floor area of elevator cars shall provide space for wheelchair users to enter the car, maneuver

33

C-231

4.10.12 Car Controls

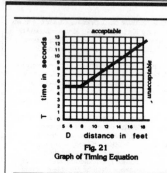

Fig. 21
Graph of Timing Equation

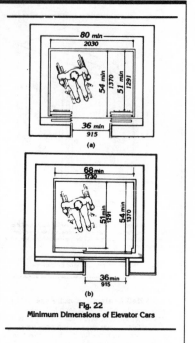

(a)

(b)

Fig. 22
Minimum Dimensions of Elevator Cars

within reach of controls, and exit from the car. Acceptable door opening and inside dimensions shall be as shown in Fig. 22. The clearance between the car platform sill and the edge of any hoistway landing shall be no greater than 1-1/4 in (32 mm).

4.10.10 Floor Surfaces. Floor surfaces shall comply with 4.5.

4.10.11 Illumination Levels. The level of illumination at the car controls, platform, and car threshold and landing sill shall be at least 5 footcandles (53.8 lux).

4.10.12* Car Controls. Elevator control panels shall have the following features:

(1) Buttons. All control buttons shall be at least 3/4 in (19 mm) in their smallest dimension. They *shall* be *raised* or flush.

(2) Tactile, *Braille*, and Visual Control Indicators. All control buttons shall be designated by *Braille and by raised* standard alphabet characters for letters, arabic characters for numerals, or standard symbols as shown in Fig. 23(a), and as required in *ASME A17.1-1990*. *Raised and Braille* characters and symbols shall comply with 4.30. The call button for the main entry floor shall be designated by a *raised* star at the left of the floor designation (see Fig. 23(a)). All raised designations for control buttons shall be placed immediately to the left of the button to which they apply. Applied plates,

permanently attached, are an acceptable means to provide raised control designations. Floor buttons shall be provided with visual indicators to show when each call is registered. The visual indicators shall be extinguished when each call is answered.

(3) Height. All floor buttons shall be no higher than 54 in (1370 mm) above the *finish floor for side approach and* 48 in (1220 mm) *for front approach.* Emergency controls, including the emergency alarm and emergency stop, shall be grouped at the bottom of the panel and shall have their centerlines no less than 35 in (890 mm) above the finish floor (see Fig. 23(a) and (b)).

34

C-232

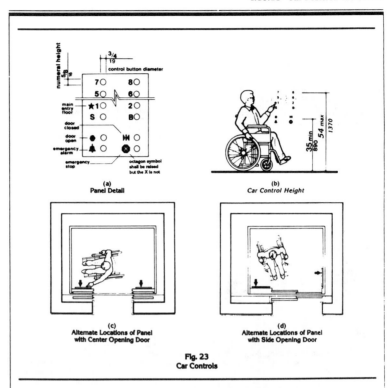

(a)
Panel Detail

(b)
Car Control Height

(c)
**Alternate Locations of Panel
with Center Opening Door**

(d)
**Alternate Locations of Panel
with Side Opening Door**

**Fig. 23
Car Controls**

(4) Location. Controls shall be located on a front wall if cars have center opening doors, and at the side wall or at the front wall next to the door if cars have side opening doors (see Fig. 23(c) and (d)).

4.10.13* Car Position Indicators. In elevator cars, a visual car position indicator shall be provided above the car control panel or over the door to show the position of the elevator in the hoistway. As the car passes or stops at a floor served by the elevators, the corresponding numerals shall illuminate,

and an audible signal shall sound. Numerals shall be a minimum of 1/2 in (13 mm) high. The audible signal shall be no less than 20 decibels with a frequency no higher than 1500 Hz. An automatic verbal announcement of the floor number at which a car stops or which a car passes may be substituted for the audible signal.

4.10.14* Emergency Communications. If provided, emergency two-way communication systems between the elevator and a point outside the hoistway shall comply with *ASME*

35

C-233

4.11 Platform Lifts (Wheelchair Lifts)

A17.1-1990. The highest operable part of a two-way communication system shall be a maximum of 48 in (1220 mm) from the floor of the car. It shall be identified by a raised symbol and lettering complying with 4.30 and located adjacent to the device. If the system uses a handset then the length of the cord from the panel to the handset shall be at least 29 in (735 mm). *If the system is located in a closed compartment the compartment door hardware shall conform to 4.27, Controls and Operating Mechanisms. The emergency intercommunication system shall not require voice communication.*

4.11 Platform Lifts (Wheelchair Lifts).

4.11.1 Location. *Platform lifts (wheelchair lifts) permitted by 4.1 shall comply with the requirements of 4.11.*

4.11.2* Other Requirements. If platform lifts (wheelchair lifts) are used, they shall comply with 4.2.4, 4.5, 4.27, and *ASME A17.1 Safety Code for Elevators and Escalators, Section XX, 1990.*

4.11.3 Entrance. *If platform lifts are used then they shall facilitate unassisted entry, operation, and exit from the lift in compliance with 4.11.2.*

4.12 Windows.

4.12.1* General. *(Reserved).*

4.12.2* Window Hardware. *(Reserved).*

4.13 Doors.

4.13.1 General. *Doors required to be accessible by 4.1 shall comply with the requirements of 4.13.*

4.13.2 Revolving Doors and Turnstiles. Revolving doors or turnstiles shall not be the only means of passage at an accessible entrance or along an accessible route. *An accessible gate or door shall be provided adjacent to the turnstile or revolving door and shall be so designed as to facilitate the same use pattern.*

4.13.3 Gates. Gates, including ticket gates, shall meet all applicable specifications of 4.13.

4.13.4 Double-Leaf Doorways. If doorways have two *independently operated* door leaves, then at least one leaf shall meet the specifications in 4.13.5 and 4.13.6. That leaf shall be an active leaf.

4.13.5 Clear Width. Doorways shall have a minimum clear opening of 32 in (815 mm) with the door open 90 degrees, measured between the face of the door and the *opposite* stop (see Fig. 24(a), (b), (c), and (d)). Openings more than 24 in (610 mm) in depth shall comply with 4.2.1 and 4.3.3 (see Fig. 24(e)).

EXCEPTION: Doors not requiring full user passage, such as shallow closets, may have the clear opening reduced to 20 in (510 mm) minimum.

4.13.6 Maneuvering Clearances at Doors. Minimum maneuvering clearances at doors that are not automatic or power-assisted shall be as shown in Fig. 25. The floor or ground area within the required clearances shall be level and clear.

EXCEPTION: Entry doors to acute care hospital bedrooms for in-patients shall be exempted from the requirement for space at the latch side of the door (see dimension "x" in Fig. 25) if the door is at least 44 in (1120 mm) wide.

4.13.7 Two Doors in Series. The minimum space between two hinged or pivoted doors in series shall be 48 in (1220 mm) plus the width of any door swinging into the space. Doors in series shall swing either in the same direction or away from the space between the doors (see Fig. 26).

4.13.8* Thresholds at Doorways. Thresholds at doorways shall not exceed 3/4 in (19 mm) in height for exterior sliding doors or 1/2 in (13 mm) for other types of doors. Raised thresholds and floor level changes at accessible doorways shall be beveled with a slope no greater than 1:2 (see 4.5.2).

4.13.9* Door Hardware. Handles, pulls, latches, locks, and other operating devices on accessible doors shall have a shape that is easy

4.13 Doors

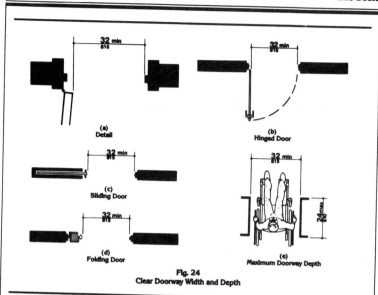

(a)
Detail

(b)
Hinged Door

(c)
Sliding Door

(d)
Folding Door

(e)
Maximum Doorway Depth

Fig. 24
Clear Doorway Width and Depth

to grasp with one hand and does not require tight grasping, tight pinching, or twisting of the wrist to operate. Lever-operated mechanisms, push-type mechanisms, and U-shaped handles are acceptable designs. When sliding doors are fully open, operating hardware shall be exposed and usable from both sides. *Hardware required for accessible door passage shall be mounted no higher than 48 in (1220 mm) above finished floor.*

4.13.10° Door Closers. If a door has a closer, then the sweep period of the closer shall be adjusted so that from an open position of 70 degrees, the door will take at least 3 seconds to move to a point 3 in (75 mm) from the latch, measured to the leading edge of the door.

4.13.11° Door Opening Force. The maximum force for pushing or pulling open a door shall be as follows:

(1) Fire doors shall have the minimum opening force allowable by the appropriate administrative authority.

(2) Other doors.

  (a) exterior hinged doors: *(Reserved).*

  (b) interior hinged doors: 5 lbf (22.2N)

  (c) sliding or folding doors:.5 lbf (22.2N)

These forces do not apply to the force required to retract latch bolts or disengage other devices that may hold the door in a closed position.

37

C-235

4.13 Doors

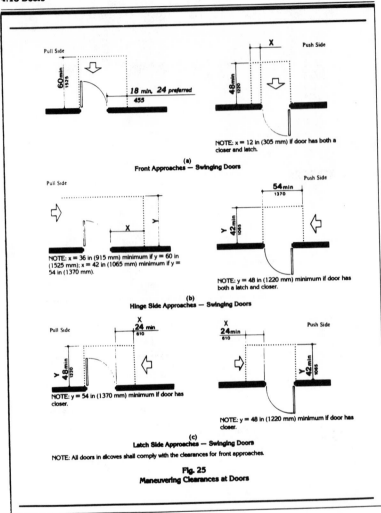

NOTE: x = 12 in (305 mm) if door has both a closer and latch.

(a)
Front Approaches — Swinging Doors

NOTE: x = 36 in (915 mm) minimum if y = 60 in (1525 mm); x = 42 in (1065 mm) minimum if y = 54 in (1370 mm).

NOTE: y = 48 in (1220 mm) minimum if door has both a latch and closer.

(b)
Hinge Side Approaches — Swinging Doors

NOTE: y = 54 in (1370 mm) minimum if door has closer.

NOTE: y = 48 in (1220 mm) minimum if door has closer.

(c)
Latch Side Approaches — Swinging Doors

NOTE: All doors in alcoves shall comply with the clearances for front approaches.

Fig. 25
Maneuvering Clearances at Doors

38

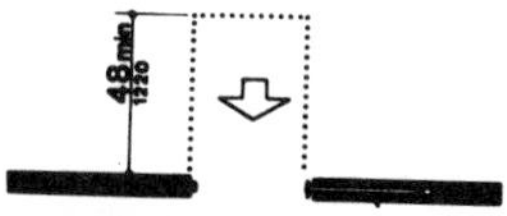

(d)
Front Approach — Sliding Doors
and Folding Doors

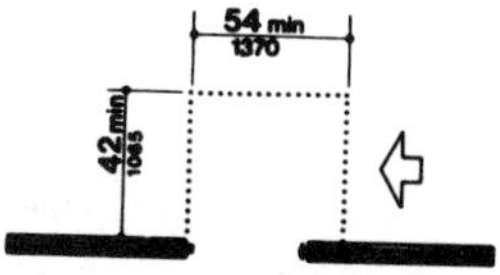

(e)
Slide Side Approach — Sliding Doors
and Folding Doors

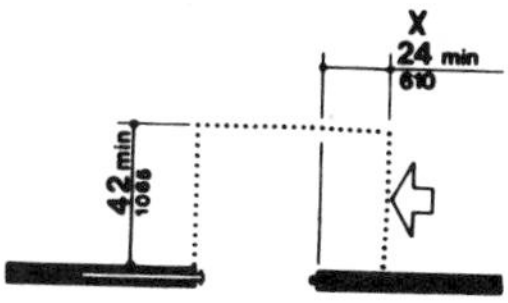

(f)
Latch Side Approach — Sliding Doors and Folding Doors

NOTE: All doors in alcoves shall comply with the clearances for front approaches.

Fig. 25
Maneuvering Clearances at Doors *(Continued)*

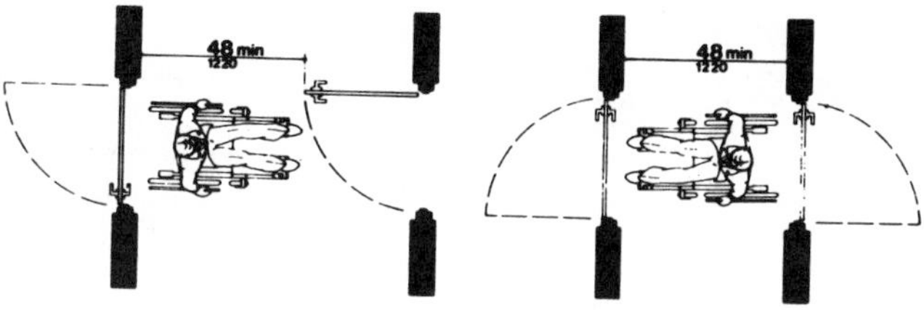

Fig. 26
Two Hinged Doors in Series

4.13.12° Automatic Doors and Power-Assisted Doors. If an automatic door is used, then it shall comply with *ANSI/BHMA A156.10-1985.* Slowly opening, low-powered, automatic doors shall *comply with ANSI A156.19-1984.* Such doors shall not open to back check faster than 3 seconds and shall require no more than 15 lbf (66.6N) to stop door movement. If a power-assisted door is used, its door-opening force shall comply with 4.13.11 and its closing shall conform to the requirements in *ANSI A156.19-1984.*

4.14 Entrances.

4.14.1 Minimum Number. *Entrances required to be accessible by 4.1* shall be part of an accessible route complying with 4.3. Such entrances shall be connected by an accessible route to public transportation stops, to accessible parking and passenger loading zones, and to public streets or sidewalks if available (see 4.3.2(1)). They shall also be connected by an accessible route to all accessible spaces or elements within the building or facility.

4.14.2 Service Entrances. A service entrance shall not be the sole accessible entrance unless it is the only entrance to a building or facility (for example, in a factory or garage).

4.15 Drinking Fountains and Water Coolers.

4.15.1 Minimum Number. *Drinking fountains or water coolers required to be accessible by 4.1* shall comply with 4.15.

4.15.2° Spout Height. Spouts shall be no higher than 36 in (915 mm), measured from the floor or ground surfaces to the spout outlet (see Fig. 27(a)).

4.15.3 Spout Location. The spouts of drinking fountains and water coolers shall be at the front of the unit and shall direct the water flow in a trajectory that is parallel or nearly parallel to the front of the unit. The spout shall provide a flow of water at least 4 in (100 mm) high so as to allow the insertion of a cup or glass under the flow of water. *On an accessible drinking fountain with a round or oval bowl, the spout must be positioned so the flow of water is within 3 in (75 mm) of the front edge of the fountain.*

4.15.4 Controls. Controls shall comply with 4.27.4. *Unit controls shall be front mounted or side mounted near the front edge.*

4.15.5 Clearances.

(1) Wall- and post-mounted cantilevered units shall have a clear knee space between the bottom of the apron and the floor or ground at least 27 in (685 mm) high, 30 in (760 mm) wide, and 17 in to 19 in (430 mm to 485 mm) deep (see Fig. 27(a) and (b)). Such units shall also have a minimum clear floor space 30 in by 48 in (760 mm by 1220 mm) to allow a person in a wheelchair to approach the unit facing forward.

(2) Free-standing or built-in units not having a clear space under them shall have a clear floor space at least 30 in by 48 in (760 mm by 1220 mm) that allows a person in a wheelchair to make a parallel approach to the unit (see Fig. 27(c) and (d)). This clear floor space shall comply with 4.2.4.

4.16 Water Closets.

4.16.1 General. Accessible water closets shall comply with 4.16.

4.16.2 Clear Floor Space. Clear floor space for water closets not in stalls shall comply with Fig. 28. Clear floor space may be arranged to allow either a left-handed or right-handed approach.

4.16.3° Height. The height of water closets shall be 17 in to 19 in (430 mm to 485 mm), measured to the top of the toilet seat (see Fig. 29(b)). *Seats shall not be sprung to return to a lifted position.*

4.16.4° Grab Bars. Grab bars for water closets not located in stalls shall comply with 4.26 and Fig. 29. *The grab bar behind the water closet shall be 36 in (915 mm) minimum.*

4.16.5° Flush Controls. Flush controls shall be hand operated *or automatic* and shall comply with 4.27.4. Controls for flush valves shall be mounted on the wide side of toilet areas no more than 44 in (1120 mm) above the floor.

4.16.6 Dispensers. Toilet paper dispensers shall be installed within reach, as shown in Fig. 29(b). *Dispensers that control delivery, or that do not permit continuous paper flow, shall not be used.*

4.17 Toilet Stalls.

4.17.1 Location. Accessible toilet stalls shall be on an accessible route and shall meet the requirements of 4.17.

4.17.2 Water Closets. Water closets in accessible stalls shall comply with 4.16.

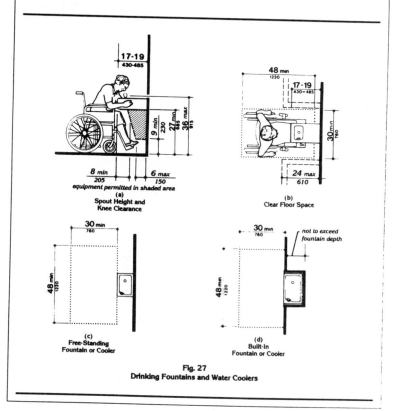

(a)
Spout Height and
Knee Clearance

(b)
Clear Floor Space

(c)
Free-Standing
Fountain or Cooler

(d)
Built-In
Fountain or Cooler

Fig. 27
Drinking Fountains and Water Coolers

41

4.17 Toilet Stalls

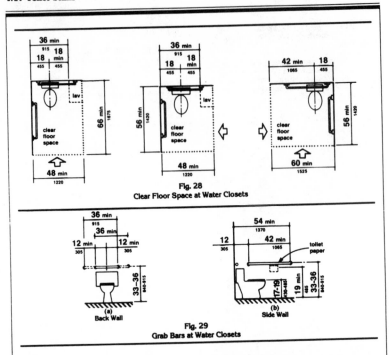

Fig. 28
Clear Floor Space at Water Closets

Fig. 29
Grab Bars at Water Closets

4.17.3° Size and Arrangement. The size and arrangement of the standard toilet stall shall comply with Fig. 30(a), *Standard Stall*. Standard toilet stalls with a minimum depth of 56 in (1420 mm) (see Fig. 30(a)) shall have wall-mounted water closets. If the depth of a standard toilet stall is increased at least 3 in (75 mm), then a floor-mounted water closet may be used. Arrangements shown for standard toilet stalls may be reversed to allow either a left- or right-hand approach. Additional stalls shall be provided in conformance with 4.22.4.

EXCEPTION: In instances of alteration work where provision of a standard stall (Fig. 30(a))

is technically infeasible or where plumbing code requirements prevent combining existing stalls to provide space, either alternate stall (Fig. 30(b)) may be provided in lieu of the standard stall.

4.17.4 Toe Clearances. In standard stalls, the front partition and at least one side partition shall provide a toe clearance of at least 9 in (230 mm) above the floor. If the depth of the stall is greater than 60 in (1525 mm), then the toe clearance is not required.

4.17.5° Doors. Toilet stall doors, *including door hardware*, shall comply with 4.13. *If toilet stall approach is from the latch side of the stall door, clearance between the door side of the*

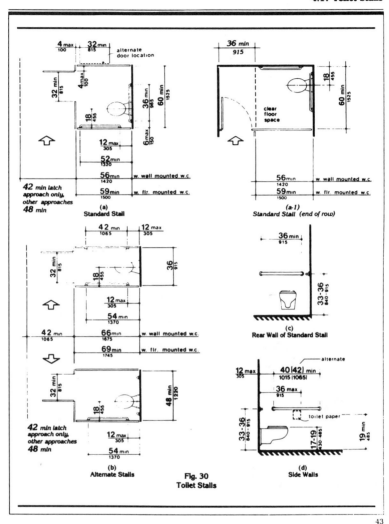

Fig. 30
Toilet Stalls

43

4.19 Lavatories and Mirrors

stall and any obstruction may be reduced to a minimum of 42 in (1065 mm) (Fig. 30).

4.17.6 Grab Bars. Grab bars complying with the length and positioning shown in Fig. 30(a), (b), (c), and (d) shall be provided. Grab bars may be mounted with any desired method as long as they have a gripping surface at the locations shown and do not obstruct the required clear floor area. Grab bars shall comply with 4.26.

4.18 Urinals.

4.18.1 General. Accessible urinals shall comply with 4.18.

4.18.2 Height. Urinals shall be stall-type or wall-hung with an elongated rim at a maximum of 17 in (430 mm) above the finish floor.

4.18.3 Clear Floor Space. A clear floor space 30 in by 48 in (760 mm by 1220 mm) shall be provided in front of urinals to allow forward approach. This clear space shall adjoin or overlap an accessible route and shall comply with 4.2.4. *Urinal shields that do not extend beyond the front edge of the urinal rim may be provided with 29 in (735 mm) clearance between them.*

4.18.4 Flush Controls. Flush controls shall be hand operated or automatic, and shall comply with 4.27.4, and shall be mounted no more than 44 in (1120 mm) above the finish floor.

4.19 Lavatories and Mirrors.

4.19.1 General. The requirements of 4.19 shall apply to lavatory fixtures, vanities, and built-in lavatories.

4.19.2 Height and Clearances. Lavatories shall be mounted with *the rim or counter surface no higher than 34 in (865 mm) above the finish floor.* Provide a clearance of at least 29 in (735 mm) above the finish floor to the bottom of the apron. Knee and toe clearance shall comply with Fig. 31.

4.19.3 Clear Floor Space. A clear floor space 30 in by 48 in (760 mm by 1220 mm) complying with 4.2.4 shall be provided in front of a lavatory to allow forward approach. Such

clear floor space shall adjoin or overlap an accessible route and shall extend a maximum of 19 in (485 mm) underneath the lavatory (see Fig. 32).

4.19.4 Exposed Pipes and Surfaces. Hot water and drain pipes under lavatories shall be insulated or otherwise *configured to protect against contact.* There shall be no sharp or abrasive surfaces under lavatories.

4.19.5 Faucets. Faucets shall comply with 4.27.4. Lever-operated, push-type, and electronically controlled mechanisms are examples of acceptable designs. *If self-closing valves are*

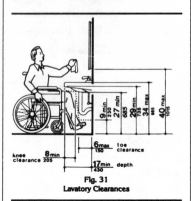

Fig. 31
Lavatory Clearances

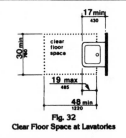

Fig. 32
Clear Floor Space at Lavatories

44

used the faucet *shall remain* open for at least 10 seconds.

4.19.6° Mirrors. Mirrors shall be mounted with the bottom edge *of the reflecting surface* no higher than 40 in (1015 mm) *above the finish* floor (see Fig. 31).

4.20 Bathtubs.

4.20.1 General. Accessible bathtubs shall comply with 4.20.

4.20.2 Floor Space. Clear floor space in front of bathtubs shall be as shown in Fig. 33.

4.20.3 Seat. An in-tub seat or a seat at the head end of the tub shall be provided as shown in Fig. 33 and 34. The structural strength of seats and their attachments shall comply with 4.26.3. Seats shall be mounted securely and shall not slip during use.

4.20.4 Grab Bars. Grab bars complying with 4.26 shall be provided as shown in Fig. 33 and 34.

4.20.5 Controls. Faucets and other controls complying with 4.27.4 shall be located as shown in Fig. 34.

4.20.6 Shower Unit. A shower spray unit with a hose at least 60 in (1525 mm) long that can be used *both* as a fixed shower head *and* as a hand-held shower shall be provided.

4.20.7 Bathtub Enclosures. If provided, enclosures for bathtubs shall not obstruct controls or transfer from wheelchairs onto bathtub seats or into tubs. Enclosures on bathtubs shall not have tracks mounted on their rims.

4.21 Shower Stalls.

4.21.1° General. Accessible shower stalls shall comply with 4.21.

4.21.2 Size and Clearances. Except as specified in 9.1.2, shower stall size and clear floor space shall comply with Fig. 35(a) or (b). The shower stall in Fig. 35(a) shall be 36 in by 36 in (915 mm by 915 mm). Shower stalls required by 9.1.2 shall comply with Fig. 57(a)

or (b). The shower stall in Fig. 35(b) will fit into the space required for a bathtub.

4.21.3 Seat. A seat shall be provided in shower stalls 36 in by 36 in (915 mm by 915 mm) and shall be as shown in Fig. 36. The seat shall be mounted 17 in to 19 in (430 mm to 485 mm) from the bathroom floor and shall extend the full depth of the stall. In a 36 in by 36 in (915 mm by 915 mm) shower stall, the seat shall be on the wall opposite the controls. *Where a fixed seat is provided in a 30 in by 60 in minimum (760 mm by 1525 mm) shower stall, it shall be a folding type and shall be mounted on the wall adjacent to the controls as shown in Fig. 57.* The structural strength of seats and their attachments shall comply with 4.26.3.

4.21.4 Grab Bars. Grab bars complying with 4.26 shall be provided as shown in Fig. 37.

4.21.5 Controls. Faucets and other controls complying with 4.27.4 shall be located as shown in Fig. 37. In shower stalls 36 in by 36 in (915 mm by 915 mm), all controls, faucets, and the shower unit shall be mounted on the side wall opposite the seat.

4.21.6 Shower Unit. A shower spray unit with a hose at least 60 in (1525 mm) long that can be used *both* as a fixed shower head *and* as a hand-held shower shall be provided.

EXCEPTION: In unmonitored facilities where vandalism is a consideration, a fixed shower head mounted at 48 in (1220 mm) above the shower floor may be used in lieu of a hand-held shower head.

4.21.7 Curbs. If provided, curbs in shower stalls 36 in by 36 in (915 mm by 915 mm) shall be no higher than 1/2 in (13 mm). Shower stalls that are 30 in by 60 in (760 mm by 1525 mm) minimum shall not have curbs.

4.21.8 Shower Enclosures. If provided, enclosures for shower stalls shall not obstruct controls or obstruct transfer from wheelchairs onto shower seats.

4.22 Toilet Rooms.

4.22.1 Minimum Number. *Toilet facilities required to be accessible by 4.1 shall comply*

4.21 Shower Stalls

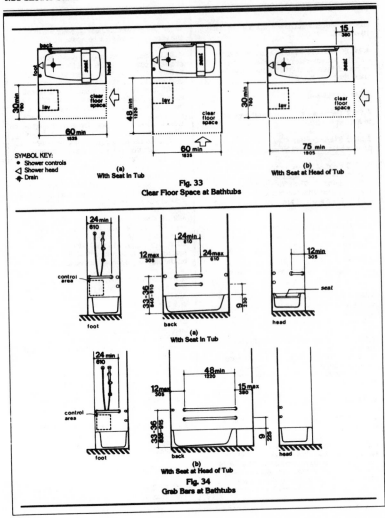

SYMBOL KEY:
- Shower controls
◁ Shower head
✦ Drain

(a)
With Seat in Tub

(b)
With Seat at Head of Tub

Fig. 33
Clear Floor Space at Bathtubs

(a)
With Seat in Tub

(b)
With Seat at Head of Tub

Fig. 34
Grab Bars at Bathtubs

46

with 4.22. Accessible toilet rooms shall be on an accessible route.

4.22.2 Doors. All doors to accessible toilet rooms shall comply with 4.13. Doors shall not swing into the clear floor space required for any fixture.

4.22.3* Clear Floor Space. The accessible fixtures and controls required in 4.22.4, 4.22.5, 4.22.6, and 4.22.7 shall be on an accessible route. An unobstructed turning space complying with 4.2.3 shall be provided within an accessible toilet room. The clear floor space at fixtures and controls, the accessible route, and the turning space may overlap.

4.22.4 Water Closets. If toilet stalls are provided, then at least one shall be a standard

toilet stall complying with 4.17; *where 6 or more stalls are provided, in addition to the stall complying with 4.17.3, at least one stall 36 in (915 mm) wide with an outward swinging, self-closing door and parallel grab bars complying with Fig. 30(d) and 4.26 shall be provided. Water closets in such stalls shall comply with 4.16.* If water closets are not in stalls, then at least one shall comply with 4.16.

4.22.5 Urinals. If urinals are provided, *then* at least one shall comply with 4.18.

4.22.6 Lavatories and Mirrors. If lavatories and mirrors are provided, *then* at least one of each shall comply with 4.19.

4.22.7 Controls and Dispensers. If controls, dispensers, receptacles, or other

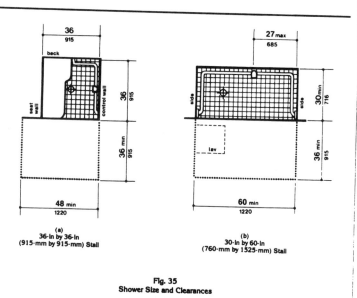

(a)
36-in by 36-in
(915-mm by 915-mm) Stall

(b)
30-in by 60-in
(760-mm by 1525-mm) Stall

**Fig. 35
Shower Size and Clearances**

4.23 Bathrooms, Bathing Facilities, and Shower Rooms

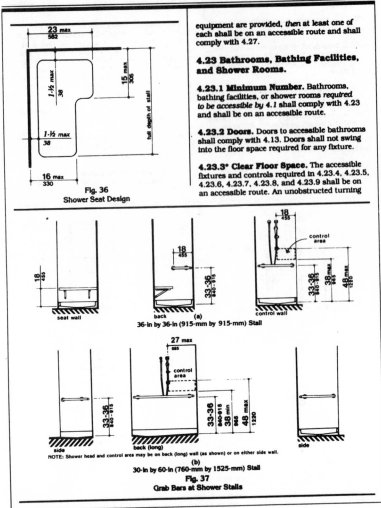

equipment are provided, *then* at least one of each shall be on an accessible route and shall comply with 4.27.

4.23 Bathrooms, Bathing Facilities, and Shower Rooms.

4.23.1 Minimum Number. Bathrooms, bathing facilities, or shower rooms *required to be accessible by 4.1* shall comply with 4.23 and shall be on an accessible route.

4.23.2 Doors. Doors to accessible bathrooms shall comply with 4.13. Doors shall not swing into the floor space required for any fixture.

4.23.3° Clear Floor Space. The accessible fixtures and controls required in 4.23.4, 4.23.5, 4.23.6, 4.23.7, 4.23.8, and 4.23.9 shall be on an accessible route. An unobstructed turning

Fig. 36
Shower Seat Design

NOTE: Shower head and control area may be on back (long) wall (as shown) or on either side wall.

Fig. 37
Grab Bars at Shower Stalls

48

space complying with 4.2.3 shall be provided within an accessible bathroom. The clear floor spaces at fixtures and controls, the accessible route, and the turning space may overlap.

4.23.4 Water Closets. If toilet stalls are provided, then at least one shall be a standard toilet stall complying with 4.17; *where 6 or more stalls are provided, in addition to the stall complying with 4.17.3, at least one stall 36 in (915 mm) wide with an outward swinging, self-closing door and parallel grab bars complying with Fig. 30(d) and 4.26 shall be provided.* Water closets in such stalls shall comply with 4.16. If water closets are not in stalls, then at least one shall comply with 4.16.

4.23.5 Urinals. If urinals are provided, then at least one shall comply with 4.18.

4.23.6 Lavatories and Mirrors. If lavatories and mirrors are provided, then at least one of each shall comply with 4.19.

4.23.7 Controls and Dispensers. If controls, dispensers, receptacles, or other equipment *are* provided, *then* at least one of each shall be on an accessible route and shall comply with 4.27.

4.23.8 Bathing and Shower Facilities. If tubs or showers are provided, then at least one accessible tub that complies with 4.20 or at least one accessible shower that complies with 4.21 shall be provided.

4.23.9* Medicine Cabinets. If medicine cabinets are provided, at least one shall be located with a usable shelf no higher than 44 in (1120 mm) above the floor space. The floor space shall comply with 4.2.4.

4.24 Sinks.

4.24.1 General. Sinks *required to be accessible by 4.1* shall comply with 4.24.

4.24.2 Height. Sinks shall be mounted with the counter or rim no higher than 34 in (865 mm) *above the finish floor.*

4.24.3 Knee Clearance. Knee clearance that is at least 27 in (685 mm) high, 30 in (760 mm) wide, and 19 in (485 mm) deep shall be pro-

vided underneath sinks.

4.24.4 Depth. Each sink shall be a maximum of 6-1/2 in (165 mm) deep.

4.24.5 Clear Floor Space. A clear floor space at least 30 in by 48 in (760 mm by 1220 mm) complying with 4.2.4 shall be provided in front of a sink to allow forward approach. The clear floor space shall be on an accessible route and shall extend a maximum of 19 in (485 mm) underneath the sink (see Fig. 32).

4.24.6 Exposed Pipes and Surfaces. Hot water and drain pipes exposed under sinks shall be insulated or otherwise *configured so as to protect against contact.* There shall be no sharp or abrasive surfaces under sinks.

4.24.7 Faucets. Faucets shall comply with 4.27.4. Lever-operated, push-type, touch-type, or electronically controlled mechanisms are acceptable designs.

4.25 Storage.

4.25.1 General. *Fixed* storage facilities such as cabinets, shelves, closets, and drawers *required to be accessible by 4.1* shall comply with 4.25.

4.25.2 Clear Floor Space. A clear floor space at least 30 in by 48 in (760 mm by 1220 mm) complying with 4.2.4 that allows either a forward or parallel approach by a person using a wheelchair shall be provided at accessible storage facilities.

4.25.3 Height. Accessible storage spaces shall be within at least one of the reach ranges specified in 4.2.5 and 4.2.6 *(see Fig. 5 and Fig. 6).* Clothes rods or shelves shall be a maximum of 54 in (1370 mm) *above the finish floor for a side approach. Where the distance from the wheelchair to the clothes rod or shelf exceeds 10 in (255 mm) (as in closets without accessible doors) the height and depth to the rod or shelf shall comply with Fig. 38(a) and Fig. 38(b).*

4.25.4 Hardware. Hardware for accessible storage facilities shall comply with 4.27.4. Touch latches and U-shaped pulls are acceptable.

49

C-247

4.26 Handrails, Grab Bars, and Tub and Shower Seats

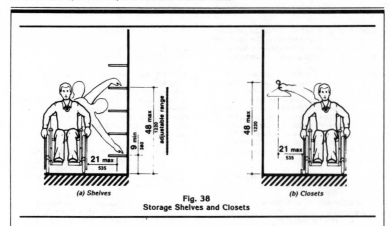

(a) Shelves

Fig. 38
Storage Shelves and Closets

(b) Closets

4.26 Handrails, Grab Bars, and Tub and Shower Seats.

4.26.1* General. All handrails, grab bars, and tub and shower seats *required to be accessible by 4.1, 4.8, 4.9, 4.16, 4.17, 4.20 or 4.21* shall comply with 4.26.

4.26.2* Size and Spacing of Grab Bars and Handrails. The diameter or width of the gripping surfaces of a handrail or grab bar shall be 1-1/4 in to 1-1/2 in (32 mm to 38 mm), or the shape shall provide an equivalent gripping surface. If handrails or grab bars are mounted adjacent to a wall, the space between the wall and the grab bar shall be 1-1/2 in (38 mm) (see Fig. 39(a), (b), (c), and (e)). Handrails may be located in a recess if the recess is a maximum of 3 in (75 mm) deep and extends at least 18 in (455 mm) above the top of the rail (see Fig. 39(d)).

4.26.3 Structural Strength. The structural strength of grab bars, tub and shower seats, fasteners, and mounting devices shall meet the following specification:

(1) Bending stress in a grab bar or seat induced by the maximum bending moment from the application of 250 lbf (1112N) shall be less than the allowable stress for the material of the grab bar or seat.

(2) Shear stress induced in a grab bar or seat by the application of 250 lbf (1112N) shall be less than the allowable shear stress for the material of the grab bar or seat. If the connection between the grab bar or seat and its mounting bracket or other support is considered to be fully restrained, then direct and torsional shear stresses shall be totaled for the combined shear stress, which shall not exceed the allowable shear stress.

(3) Shear force induced in a fastener or mounting device from the application of 250 lbf (1112N) shall be less than the allowable lateral load of either the fastener or mounting device or the supporting structure, whichever is the smaller allowable load.

(4) Tensile force induced in a fastener by a direct tension force of 250 lbf (1112N) plus the maximum moment from the application of 250 lbf (1112N) shall be less than the allowable withdrawal load between the fastener and the supporting structure.

(5) Grab bars shall not rotate within their fittings.

50

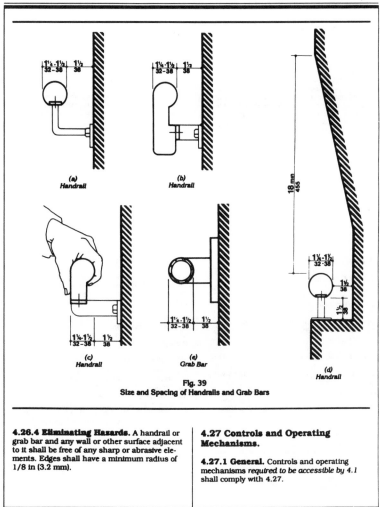

Fig. 39
Size and Spacing of Handrails and Grab Bars

4.26.4 Eliminating Hazards. A handrail or grab bar and any wall or other surface adjacent to it shall be free of any sharp or abrasive elements. Edges shall have a minimum radius of 1/8 in (3.2 mm).

4.27 Controls and Operating Mechanisms.

4.27.1 General. Controls and operating mechanisms *required to be accessible by 4.1* shall comply with 4.27.

51

C-249

4.27.2 Clear Floor Space. Clear floor space complying with 4.2.4 that allows a forward or a parallel approach by a person using a wheelchair shall be provided at controls, dispensers, receptacles, and other operable equipment.

4.27.3° Height. The highest operable part of controls, dispensers, receptacles, and other operable equipment shall be placed within at least one of the reach ranges specified in 4.2.5 and 4.2.6. Electrical and communications system receptacles on walls shall be mounted no less than 15 in (380 mm) above the floor.

EXCEPTION: These requirements do not apply where the use of special equipment dictates otherwise or where electrical and communications systems receptacles are not normally intended for use by building occupants.

4.27.4 Operation. Controls and operating mechanisms shall be operable with one hand and shall not require tight grasping, pinching, or twisting of the wrist. The force required to activate controls shall be no greater than 5 lbf (22.2 N).

4.28 Alarms.

4.28.1 General. Alarm systems required to be accessible by 4.1 shall comply with 4.28. At a minimum, visual signal appliances shall be provided in buildings and facilities in each of the following areas: restrooms and any other general usage areas (e.g., meeting rooms), hallways, lobbies, and any other area for common use.

4.28.2° Audible Alarms. If provided, audible emergency alarms shall produce a sound that exceeds the prevailing equivalent sound level in the room or space by at least 15 dbA or exceeds any maximum sound level with a duration of 60 seconds by 5 dbA, whichever is louder. Sound levels for alarm signals shall not exceed 120 dbA.

4.28.3° Visual Alarms. Visual alarm signal appliances shall be integrated into the building or facility alarm system. If single station audible alarms are provided then single station visual alarm signals shall be provided. Visual alarm signals shall have the following minimum photometric and location features:

(1) The lamp shall be a xenon strobe type or equivalent.

(2) The color shall be clear or nominal white (i.e., unfiltered or clear filtered white light).

(3) The maximum pulse duration shall be two-tenths of one second (0.2 sec) with a maximum duty cycle of 40 percent. The pulse duration is defined as the time interval between initial and final points of 10 percent of maximum signal.

(4) The intensity shall be a minimum of 75 candela.

(5) The flash rate shall be a minimum of 1 Hz and a maximum of 3 Hz.

(6) The appliance shall be placed 80 in (2030 mm) above the highest floor level within the space or 6 in (152 mm) below the ceiling, whichever is lower.

(7) In general, no place in any room or space required to have a visual signal appliance shall be more than 50 ft (15 m) from the signal (in the horizontal plane). In large rooms and spaces exceeding 100 ft (30 m) across, without obstructions 6 ft (2 m) above the finish floor, such as auditoriums, devices may be placed around the perimeter, spaced a maximum 100 ft (30 m) apart, in lieu of suspending appliances from the ceiling.

(8) No place in common corridors or hallways in which visual alarm signalling appliances are required shall be more than 50 ft (15 m) from the signal.

4.28.4° Auxiliary Alarms. Units and sleeping accommodations shall have a visual alarm connected to the building emergency alarm system or shall have a standard 110-volt electrical receptacle into which such an alarm can be connected and a means by which a signal from the building emergency alarm system can trigger such an auxiliary alarm. When visual alarms are in place the signal shall be visible in all areas of the unit or room. Instructions for use of the auxiliary alarm or receptacle shall be provided.

4.29 Detectable Warnings.

4.29.1 General. *Detectable* warnings required by 4.1 and 4.7 shall comply with 4.29.

4.29.2* Detectable Warnings on Walking Surfaces. *Detectable warnings shall consist of raised truncated domes with a diameter of nominal 0.9 in (23 mm), a height of nominal 0.2 in (5 mm) and a center-to-center spacing of nominal 2.35 in (60 mm) and shall contrast visually with adjoining surfaces, either light-on-dark, or dark-on-light.*

The material used to provide contrast shall be an integral part of the walking surface. Detectable warnings used on interior surfaces shall differ from adjoining walking surfaces in resiliency or sound-on-cane contact.

4.29.3 Detectable Warnings on Doors To Hazardous Areas. *(Reserved).*

4.29.4 Detectable Warnings at Stairs. *(Reserved).*

4.29.5 Detectable Warnings at Hazardous Vehicular Areas. If a walk crosses or adjoins a vehicular way, *and the walking surfaces are not separated by* curbs, railings, or other elements *between the pedestrian areas and vehicular areas,* the boundary between the areas shall be defined by a continuous *detectable* warning *which is* 36 in (915 mm) wide, complying with 4.29.2.

4.29.6 Detectable Warnings at Reflecting Pools. The edges of reflecting pools shall be protected by railings, walls, curbs, or *detectable* warnings complying with 4.29.2.

4.29.7 Standardization. *(Reserved).*

4.30 Signage.

4.30.1* General. Signage *required to be accessible by 4.1 shall comply with the applicable provisions of 4.30.*

4.30.2* Character Proportion. Letters and numbers on signs shall have a width-to-height ratio between 3:5 and 1:1 and a stroke-width-to-height ratio between 1:5 and 1:10.

4.30.3 *Character Height.* *Characters and numbers on signs shall be sized according to the viewing distance from which they are to be read. The minimum height is measured using an upper case X. Lower case characters are permitted.*

Height Above Finished Floor	Minimum Character Height
Suspended or Projected Overhead in compliance with 4.4.2	3 in. (75 mm) minimum

4.30.4* Raised and Brailled Characters and Pictorial Symbol Signs (Pictograms). Letters and numerals shall be raised 1/32 in, upper case, sans serif or simple serif type and shall be accompanied with Grade 2 Braille. Raised characters shall be at least 5/8 in (16 mm) high, but no higher than 2 in (50 mm). Pictograms shall be accompanied by the equivalent verbal description placed directly below the pictogram. The border dimension of the pictogram shall be 6 in (152 mm) minimum in height.

4.30.5* Finish and Contrast. The characters and background of signs shall be eggshell, matte, or other non-glare finish. Characters and symbols shall contrast with their background — either light characters on a dark background or dark characters on a light background.

4.30.6 *Mounting Location and Height.* *Where permanent identification is provided for rooms and spaces, signs shall be installed on the wall adjacent to the latch side of the door. Where there is no wall space to the latch side of the door, including at double leaf doors, signs shall be placed on the nearest adjacent wall. Mounting height shall be 60 in (1525 mm) above the finish floor to the centerline of the sign. Mounting location for such signage shall be so that a person may approach within 3 in (76 mm) of signage without encountering protruding objects or standing within the swing of a door.*

4.30.7* Symbols of Accessibility.

(1) Facilities and elements required to be identified as accessible by 4.1 shall use the international symbol of accessibility. The

53

C-251

4.30 Signage

(a)
Proportions
International Symbol of Accessibility

(b)
Display Conditions
International Symbol of Accessibility

(c)
International TDD Symbol

(d)
International Symbol of Access for Hearing Loss

Fig. 43
International Symbols

symbol shall be displayed as shown in Fig. 43(a) and (b).

(2) Volume Control Telephones. Telephones required to have a volume control by 4.1.3(17)(b) shall be identified by a sign containing a depiction of a telephone handset with radiating sound waves.

(3) Text Telephones. Text telephones required by 4.1.3 (17)(c) shall be identified by the international TDD symbol (Fig 43(c)). In addition, if a facility has a public text telephone, directional signage indicating the location of the nearest text telephone shall be placed adjacent to all banks of telephones which do not contain a text telephone. Such directional signage shall include the international TDD symbol. If a facility has no banks of telephones, the directional signage shall be provided at the entrance (e.g., in a building directory).

(4) Assistive Listening Systems. In assembly areas where permanently installed assistive listening systems are required by 4.1.3(19)(b) the availability of such systems shall be identified with signage that includes the international symbol of access for hearing loss (Fig 43(d)).

4.30.8* Illumination Levels. *(Reserved).*

4.31 Telephones.

4.31.1 General. Public telephones *required to be accessible by 4.1* shall comply with 4.31.

4.31.2 Clear Floor or Ground Space. A clear floor or ground space at least 30 in by 48 in (760 mm by 1220 mm) that allows either a forward or parallel approach by a person using a wheelchair shall be provided at telephones (see Fig. 44). The clear floor or ground space shall comply with 4.2.4. Bases, enclosures, and fixed seats shall not impede approaches to telephones by people who use wheelchairs.

4.31.3* Mounting Height. The highest operable part of the telephone shall be within the reach ranges specified in 4.2.5 or 4.2.6.

4.31.4 Protruding Objects. *Telephones shall comply with 4.4.*

54

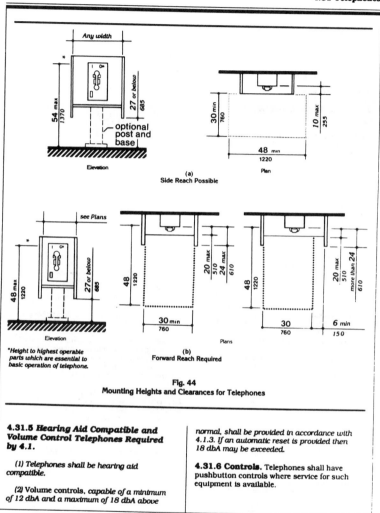

Fig. 44
Mounting Heights and Clearances for Telephones

4.31.5 Hearing Aid Compatible and Volume Control Telephones Required by 4.1.

(1) Telephones shall be hearing aid compatible.

(2) Volume controls, *capable of a minimum of 12 dbA and a maximum of 18 dbA above* normal, shall be provided in accordance with 4.1.3. If an automatic reset is provided then 18 dbA may be exceeded.

4.31.6 Controls. Telephones shall have pushbutton controls where service for such equipment is available.

55

4.31.7 Telephone Books. Telephone books, if provided, shall be located *in a position that complies with the reach ranges specified in 4.2.5 and 4.2.6.*

4.31.8 Cord Length. The cord from the telephone to the handset shall be at least 29 in (735 mm) long.

4.31.9° Text Telephones Required by 4.1.

(1) Text telephones used with a pay telephone shall be permanently affixed within, or adjacent to, the telephone enclosure. If an acoustic coupler is used, the telephone cord shall be sufficiently long to allow connection of the text telephone and the telephone receiver.

(2) Pay telephones designed to accommodate a portable text telephone shall be equipped with a shelf and an electrical outlet within or adjacent to the telephone enclosure. The telephone handset shall be capable of being placed flush on the surface of the shelf. The shelf shall be capable of accommodating a text telephone and shall have 6 in (152 mm) minimum vertical clearance in the area where the text telephone is to be placed.

(3) Equivalent facilitation may be provided. For example, a portable text telephone may be made available in a hotel at the registration desk if it is available on a 24-hour basis for use with nearby public pay telephones. In this instance, at least one pay telephone shall comply with paragraph 2 of this section. In addition, if an acoustic coupler is used, the telephone handset cord shall be sufficiently long so as to allow connection of the text telephone and the telephone receiver. Directional signage shall be provided and shall comply with 4.30.7.

4.32 Fixed or Built-in Seating and Tables.

4.32.1 Minimum Number. Fixed or built-in seating or tables required to be *accessible by 4.1* shall comply with 4.32.

4.32.2 Seating. If seating spaces for people in wheelchairs are provided at *fixed* tables or counters, clear floor space complying with 4.2.4 shall be provided. Such clear floor space

shall not overlap knee space by more than 19 in (485 mm) (see Fig. 45).

4.32.3 Knee Clearances. If seating for people in wheelchairs is provided at tables or counters, knee spaces at least 27 in (685 mm) high, 30 in (760 mm) wide, and 19 in (485 mm) deep shall be provided (see Fig. 45).

4.32.4° Height of Tables or Counters. The tops of *accessible* tables and *counters* shall be from 28 in to 34 in (710 mm to 865 mm) *above the finish floor or ground.*

4.33 Assembly Areas.

4.33.1 Minimum Number. Assembly *and associated* areas *required to be accessible by 4.1* shall comply with 4.33.

4.33.2° Size of Wheelchair Locations. Each wheelchair location shall provide minimum clear ground or floor spaces as shown in Fig. 46.

4.33.3° Placement of Wheelchair Locations. Wheelchair areas shall be an integral part of any fixed seating plan and shall be provided so as to provide people with physical disabilities a choice of admission prices and lines of sight comparable to those for members of the general public. They shall adjoin an accessible route that also serves as a means of egress in case of emergency. At least one companion fixed seat shall be provided next to each wheelchair seating area. When the seating capacity exceeds 300, wheelchair spaces shall be provided in more than one location. Readily removable seats may be installed in wheelchair spaces when the spaces are not required to accommodate wheelchair users.

EXCEPTION: Accessible viewing positions may be clustered for bleachers, balconies, and other areas having sight lines that require slopes of greater than 5 percent. Equivalent accessible viewing positions may be located on levels having accessible egress.

4.33.4 Surfaces. The ground or floor at wheelchair locations shall be level and shall comply with 4.5.

56

4.33 Assembly Areas

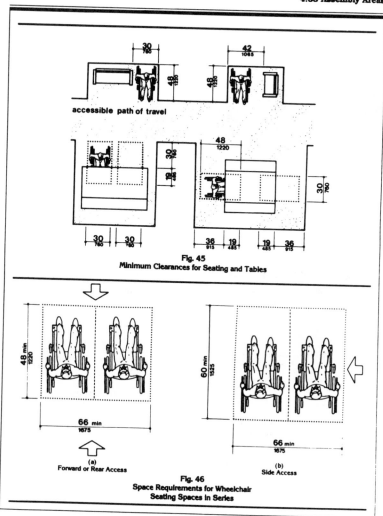

Fig. 45
Minimum Clearances for Seating and Tables

accessible path of travel

(a)
Forward or Rear Access

(b)
Side Access

Fig. 46
Space Requirements for Wheelchair
Seating Spaces in Series

57

C-255

4.33.5 Access to Performing Areas.
An accessible route shall connect wheelchair seating locations with performing areas, including stages, arena floors, dressing rooms, locker rooms, and other spaces used by performers.

4.33.6* Placement of Listening Systems.
If the listening system provided serves individual fixed seats, then such seats shall be located within a 50 ft (15 m) viewing distance of the stage or playing area and shall have a complete view of the stage or playing area.

4.33.7* Types of Listening Systems.
Assistive listening systems (ALS) are intended to augment standard public address and audio systems by providing signals which can be received directly by persons with special receivers or their own hearing aids and which eliminate or filter background noise. The type of assistive listening system appropriate for a particular application depends on the characteristics of the setting, the nature of the program, and the intended audience. Magnetic induction loops, infra-red and radio frequency systems are types of listening systems which are appropriate for various applications.

4.34 Automated Teller Machines.

4.34.1 General. *Each machine required to be accessible by 4.1.3 shall be on an accessible route and shall comply with 4.34.*

4.34.2 Controls. *Controls for user activation shall comply with the requirements of 4.27.*

4.34.3 Clearances and Reach Range.
Free standing or built-in units not having a clear space under them shall comply with 4.27.2 and 4.27.3 and provide for a parallel approach and both a forward and side reach to the unit allowing a person in a wheelchair to access the controls and dispensers.

4.34.4 Equipment for Persons with Vision Impairments. *Instructions and all information for use shall be made accessible to and independently usable by persons with vision impairments.*

4.35 Dressing and Fitting Rooms.

4.35.1 General. *Dressing and fitting rooms required to be accessible by 4.1 shall comply with 4.35 and shall be on an accessible route.*

4.35.2 Clear Floor Space. *A clear floor space allowing a person using a wheelchair to make a 180-degree turn shall be provided in every accessible dressing room entered through a swinging or sliding door. No door shall swing into any part of the turning space. Turning space shall not be required in a private dressing room entered through a curtained opening at least 32 in (815 mm) wide if clear floor space complying with section 4.2 renders the dressing room usable by a person using a wheelchair.*

4.35.3 Doors. *All doors to accessible dressing rooms shall be in compliance with section 4.13.*

4.35.4 Bench. *Every accessible dressing room shall have a 24 in by 48 in (610 mm by 1220 mm) bench fixed to the wall along the longer dimension. The bench shall be mounted 17 in to 19 in (430 mm to 485 mm) above the finish floor. Clear floor space shall be provided alongside the bench to allow a person using a wheelchair to make a parallel transfer onto the bench. The structural strength of the bench and attachments shall comply with 4.26.3. Where installed in conjunction with showers, swimming pools, or other wet locations, water shall not accumulate upon the surface of the bench and the bench shall have a slip-resistant surface.*

4.35.5 Mirror. *Where mirrors are provided in dressing rooms of the same use, then in an accessible dressing room, a full-length mirror, measuring at least 18 in wide by 54 in high (460 mm by 1370 mm), shall be mounted in a position affording a view to a person on the bench as well as to a person in a standing position.*

NOTE: Sections 4.1.1 through 4.1.7 and sections 5 through 10 are different from ANSI A117.1 in their entirety and are printed in standard type.

5. | RESTAURANTS AND CAFETERIAS.

5.1* General. Except as specified or modified in this section, restaurants and cafeterias shall comply with the requirements of 4.1 to 4.35. Where fixed tables (or dining counters where food is consumed but there is no service) are provided, at least 5 percent, but not less than one, of the fixed tables (or a portion of the dining counter) shall be accessible and shall comply with 4.32 as required in 4.1.3(18). In establishments where separate areas are designated for smoking and non-smoking patrons, the required number of accessible fixed tables (or counters) shall be proportionally distributed between the smoking and non-smoking areas. In new construction, and where practicable in alterations, accessible fixed tables (or counters) shall be distributed throughout the space or facility.

5.2 Counters and Bars. Where food or drink is served at counters exceeding 34 in (865 mm) in height for consumption by customers seated on stools or standing at the counter, a portion of the main counter which is 60 in (1525 mm) in length minimum shall be provided in compliance with 4.32 or service shall be available at accessible tables within the same area.

5.3 Access Aisles. All accessible fixed tables shall be accessible by means of an access aisle at least 36 in (915 mm) clear between parallel edges of tables or between a wall and the table edges.

5.4 Dining Areas. In new construction, all dining areas, including raised or sunken dining areas, loggias, and outdoor seating areas, shall be accessible. In non-elevator buildings, an accessible means of vertical access to the mezzanine is not required under the following conditions: 1) the area of mezzanine seating measures no more than 33 percent of the area of the total accessible seating area; 2) the same services and decor are provided in an accessible space usable by the general public; and, 3) the accessible areas are not restricted to use by people with disabilities. In alterations, accessibility to raised or sunken dining areas, or to all parts of outdoor seating areas is not required provided that the same services and decor are provided in an accessible space usable by the general public and are not restricted to use by people with disabilities.

5.5 Food Service Lines. Food service lines shall have a minimum clear width of 36 in (915 mm), with a preferred clear width of 42 in (1065 mm) to allow passage around a person using a wheelchair. Tray slides shall be mounted no higher than 34 in (865 mm) above the floor (see Fig. 53). If self-service shelves

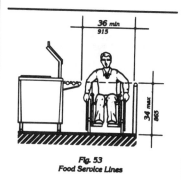

Fig. 53
Food Service Lines

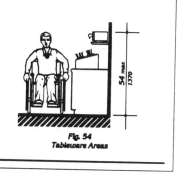

Fig. 54
Tableware Areas

are provided, at least 50 percent of each type must be within reach ranges specified in 4.2.5 and 4.2.6.

5.6 Tableware and Condiment Areas.
Self-service shelves and dispensing devices for tableware, dishware, condiments, food and beverages shall be installed to comply with 4.2 (see Fig. 54).

5.7 Raised Platforms.
In banquet rooms or spaces where a head table or speaker's lectern is located on a raised platform, the platform shall be accessible in compliance with 4.8 or 4.11. Open edges of a raised platform shall be protected by placement of tables or by a curb.

5.8 Vending Machines and Other Equipment.
Spaces for vending machines and other equipment shall comply with 4.2 and shall be located on an accessible route.

5.9 Quiet Areas. (Reserved).

6. MEDICAL CARE FACILITIES.

6.1 General.
Medical care facilities included in this section are those in which people receive physical or medical treatment or care and where persons may need assistance in responding to an emergency and where the period of stay may exceed twenty-four hours. In addition to the requirements of 4.1 through 4.35, medical care facilities and buildings shall comply with 6.

(1) Hospitals - general purpose hospitals, psychiatric facilities, detoxification facilities — At least 10 percent of patient bedrooms and toilets, and all public use and common use areas are required to be designed and constructed to be accessible.

(2) Hospitals and rehabilitation facilities that specialize in treating conditions that affect mobility, or units within either that specialize in treating conditions that affect mobility — All patient bedrooms and toilets, and all public use and common use areas are required to be designed and constructed to be accessible.

(3) Long term care facilities, nursing homes — At least 50 percent of patient bedrooms and toilets, and all public use and common use areas are required to be designed and constructed to be accessible.

(4) Alterations to patient bedrooms.

(a) When patient bedrooms are being added or altered as part of a planned renovation of an entire wing, a department, or other discrete area of an existing medical facility, a percentage of the patient bedrooms that are being added or altered shall comply with 6.3. The percentage of accessible rooms provided shall be consistent with the percentage of rooms required to be accessible by the applicable requirements of 6.1(1), 6.1(2), or 6.1(3), until the number of accessible patient bedrooms in the facility equals the overall number that would be required if the facility were newly constructed. (For example, if 20 patient bedrooms are being altered in the obstetrics department of a hospital, 2 of the altered rooms must be made accessible. If, within the same hospital, 20 patient bedrooms are being altered in a unit that specializes in treating mobility impairments, all of the altered rooms must be made accessible.) Where toilet/bath rooms are part of patient bedrooms which are added or altered and required to be accessible, each such toilet/bathroom shall comply with 6.4.

(b) When patient bedrooms are being added or altered individually, and not as part of an alteration of the entire area, the altered patient bedrooms shall comply with 6.3, unless either: a) the number of accessible rooms provided in the department or area containing the altered patient bedroom equals the number of accessible patient bedrooms that would be required if the percentage requirements of 6.1(1), 6.1(2), or 6.1(3) were applied to that department or area; or b) the number of accessible patient bedrooms in the facility equals the overall number that would be required if the facility were newly constructed. Where toilet/bath rooms are part of patient bedrooms which are added or altered and required to be accessible, each such toilet/bathroom shall comply with 6.4.

6.2 Entrances. At least one accessible entrance that complies with 4.14 shall be protected from the weather by canopy or roof overhang. Such entrances shall incorporate a passenger loading zone that complies with 4.6.6.

6.3 Patient Bedrooms. Provide accessible patient bedrooms in compliance with 4.1 through 4.35. Accessible patient bedrooms shall comply with the following:

(1) Each bedroom shall have a door that complies with 4.13.

EXCEPTION: Entry doors to acute care hospital bedrooms for in-patients shall be exempted from the requirement in 4.13.6 for maneuvering space at the latch side of the door if the door is at least 44 in (1120 mm) wide.

(2) Each bedroom shall have adequate space to provide a maneuvering space that complies with 4.2.3. In rooms with 2 beds, it is preferable that this space be located between beds.

(3) Each bedroom shall have adequate space to provide a minimum clear floor space of 36 in (915 mm) along each side of the bed and to provide an accessible route complying with 4.3.3 to each side of each bed.

6.4 Patient Toilet Rooms. Where toilet/bath rooms are provided as a part of a patient bedroom, each patient bedroom that is required to be accessible shall have an accessible toilet/bath room that complies with 4.22 or 4.23 and shall be on an accessible route.

7. BUSINESS AND MERCANTILE.

7.1 General. In addition to the requirements of 4.1 to 4.35, the design of all areas used for business transactions with the public shall comply with 7.

7.2 Sales and Service Counters, Teller Windows, Information Counters.

(1) In department stores and miscellaneous retail stores where counters have cash registers and are provided for sales or distribution of goods or services to the public, at least one of each type shall have a portion of the counter which is at least 36 in (915 mm) in length with a maximum height of 36 in (915 mm) above the finish floor. It shall be on an accessible route complying with 4.3. The accessible counters must be dispersed throughout the building or facility. In alterations where it is technically infeasible to provide an accessible counter, an auxiliary counter meeting these requirements may be provided.

(2) At ticketing counters, teller stations in a bank, registration counters in hotels and motels, box office ticket counters, and other counters that may not have a cash register but at which goods or services are sold or distributed, either:

(i) a portion of the main counter which is a minimum of 36 in (915 mm) in length shall be provided with a maximum height of 36 in (915 mm); or

(ii) an auxiliary counter with a maximum height of 36 in (915 mm) in close proximity to the main counter shall be provided; or

(iii) equivalent facilitation shall be provided (e.g., at a hotel registration counter, equivalent facilitation might consist of: (1) provision of a folding shelf attached to the main counter on which an individual with disabilities can write, and (2) use of the space on the side of the counter or at the concierge desk, for handing materials back and forth).

All accessible sales and service counters shall be on an accessible route complying with 4.3.

(3)* Assistive Listening Devices. (Reserved)

61

C-259

7.3* Check-out Aisles.

(1) In new construction, accessible check-out aisles shall be provided in conformance with the table below:

Total Check-out Aisles of Each Design	Minimum Number of Accessible Check-out Aisles (of each design)
1 – 4	1
5 – 8	2
8 – 15	3
over 15	3, plus 20% of additional aisles

EXCEPTION: In new construction, where the selling space is under 5000 square feet, only one check-out aisle is required to be accessible.

EXCEPTION: In alterations, at least one check-out aisle shall be accessible in facilities under 5000 square feet of selling space. In facilities of 5000 or more square feet of selling space, at least one of each design of check-out aisle shall be made accessible when altered until the number of accessible check-out aisles of each design equals the number required in new construction.

Examples of check-out aisles of different "design" include those which are specifically designed to serve different functions. Different "design" includes but is not limited to the following features - length of belt or no belt; or permanent signage designating the aisle as an express lane.

(2) Clear aisle width for accessible check-out aisles shall comply with 4.2.1 and maximum adjoining counter height shall not exceed 38 in (965 mm) above the finish floor. The top of the lip shall not exceed 40 in (1015 mm) above the finish floor.

(3) Signage identifying accessible check-out aisles shall comply with 4.30.7 and shall be mounted above the check-out aisle in the same location where the check-out number or type of check-out is displayed.

7.4 Security Bollards.
Any device used to prevent the removal of shopping carts from store premises shall not prevent access or egress to people in wheelchairs. An alternate entry that is equally convenient to that provided for the ambulatory population is acceptable.

8. | LIBRARIES.

8.1 General. In addition to the requirements of 4.1 to 4.35, the design of all public areas of a library shall comply with 8, including reading and study areas, stacks, reference rooms, reserve areas, and special facilities or collections.

8.2 Reading and Study Areas. At least 5 percent or a minimum of one of each element of fixed seating, tables, or study carrels shall comply with 4.2 and 4.32. Clearances between fixed accessible tables and between study carrels shall comply with 4.3.

8.3 Check-Out Areas. At least one lane at each check-out area shall comply with 7.2(1). Any traffic control or book security gates or turnstiles shall comply with 4.13.

8.4 Card Catalogs and Magazine Displays. Minimum clear aisle space at card catalogs and magazine displays shall comply with Fig. 55. Maximum reach height shall comply with 4.2, with a height of 48 in (1220 mm) preferred irrespective of approach allowed.

8.5 Stacks. Minimum clear aisle width between stacks shall comply with 4.3, with a minimum clear aisle width of 42 in (1065 mm) preferred where possible. Shelf height in stack areas is unrestricted (see Fig. 56).

62

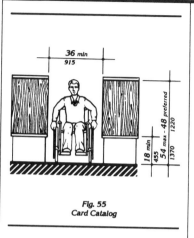

Fig. 55
Card Catalog

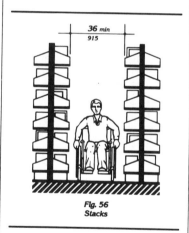

Fig. 56
Stacks

9. ACCESSIBLE TRANSIENT LODGING.

(1) Except as specified in the special technical provisions of this section, accessible transient lodging shall comply with the applicable requirements of 4.1 through 4.35. Transient lodging includes facilities or portions thereof used for sleeping accommodations, when not classed as a medical care facility.

9.1 Hotels, Motels, Inns, Boarding Houses, Dormitories, Resorts and Other Similar Places of Transient Lodging.

9.1.1 General. All public use and common use areas are required to be designed and constructed to comply with section 4 (Accessible Elements and Spaces: Scope and Technical Requirements).

EXCEPTION: Sections 9.1 through 9.4 do not apply to an establishment located within a building that contains not more than five rooms for rent or hire and that is actually occupied by the proprietor of such establishment as the residence of such proprietor.

9.1.2 Accessible Units, Sleeping Rooms, and Suites. Accessible sleeping rooms or suites that comply with the requirements of 9.2 (Requirements for Accessible Units, Sleeping Rooms, and Suites) shall be provided in conformance with the table below. In addition, in hotels, of 50 or more sleeping rooms or suites, additional accessible sleeping rooms or suites that include a roll-in shower shall also be provided in conformance with the table below. Such accommodations shall comply with the requirements of 9.2, 4.21, and Figure 57(a) or (b).

63

C-261

9.1.3 Sleeping Accommodations for Persons with Hearing Impairments

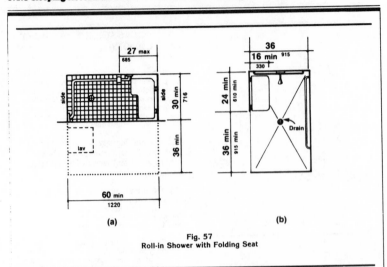

Fig. 57
Roll-in Shower with Folding Seat

Number of Rooms	Accessible Rooms	Rooms with Roll-in Showers
1 to 25	1	
26 to 50	2	
51 to 75	3	1
76 to 100	4	1
101 to 150	5	2
151 to 200	6	2
201 to 300	7	3
301 to 400	8	4
401 to 500	9	4 plus one for each additional 100 over 400
501 to 1000	2% of total	
1001 and over	20 plus 1 for each 100 over 1000	

9.1.3 Sleeping Accommodations for Persons with Hearing Impairments.
In addition to those accessible sleeping rooms and suites required by 9.1.2, sleeping rooms

and suites that comply with 9.3 (Visual Alarms, Notification Devices, and Telephones) shall be provided in conformance with the following table:

Number of Elements	Accessible Elements
1 to 25	1
26 to 50	2
51 to 75	3
76 to 100	4
101 to 150	5
151 to 200	6
201 to 300	7
301 to 400	8
401 to 500	9
501 to 1000	2% of total
1001 and over	20 plus 1 for each 100 over 1000

9.1.4 Classes of Sleeping Accommodations.

(1) In order to provide persons with disabilities a range of options equivalent to those available to other persons served by the facility, sleeping rooms and suites required to be accessible by 9.1.2 shall be dispersed among the various classes of sleeping accommodations available to patrons of the place of transient lodging. Factors to be considered include room size, cost, amenities provided, and the number of beds provided.

(2) Equivalent Facilitation. For purposes of this section, it shall be deemed equivalent facilitation if the operator of a facility elects to limit construction of accessible rooms to those intended for multiple occupancy, provided that such rooms are made available at the cost of a single-occupancy room to an individual with disabilities who requests a single-occupancy room.

9.1.5. Alterations to Accessible Units, Sleeping Rooms, and Suites.
When sleeping rooms are being altered in an existing facility, or portion thereof, subject to the requirements of this section, at least one sleeping room or suite that complies with the requirements of 9.2 (Requirements for Accessible Units, Sleeping Rooms, and Suites) shall be provided for each 25 sleeping rooms, or fraction thereof, of rooms being altered until the number of such rooms provided equals the number required to be accessible with 9.1.2. In addition, at least one sleeping room or suite that complies with the requirements of 9.3 (Visual Alarms, Notification Devices, and Telephones) shall be provided for each 25 sleeping rooms, or fraction thereof, of rooms being altered until the number of such rooms equals the number required to be accessible by 9.1.3.

9.2 Requirements for Accessible Units, Sleeping Rooms and Suites.

9.2.1 General.
Units, sleeping rooms, and suites required to be accessible by 9.1 shall comply with 9.2.

9.2.2 Minimum Requirements.
An accessible unit, sleeping room or suite shall be on an accessible route complying with 4.3 and have the following accessible elements and spaces.

(1) Accessible sleeping rooms shall have a 36 in (915 mm) clear width maneuvering space located along both sides of a bed, except that where two beds are provided, this requirement can be met by providing a 36 in (915 mm) wide maneuvering space located between the two beds.

(2) An accessible route complying with 4.3 shall connect all accessible spaces and elements, including telephones, within the unit, sleeping room, or suite. This is not intended to require an elevator in multi-story units as long as the spaces identified in 9.2.2(6) and (7) are on accessible levels and the accessible sleeping area is suitable for dual occupancy.

(3) Doors and doorways designed to allow passage into and within all sleeping rooms, suites or other covered units shall comply with 4.13.

(4) If fixed or built-in storage facilities such as cabinets, shelves, closets, and drawers are provided in accessible spaces, at least one of each type provided shall contain storage space complying with 4.25. Additional storage may be provided outside of the dimensions required by 4.25.

(5) All controls in accessible units, sleeping rooms, and suites shall comply with 4.27.

(6) Where provided as part of an accessible unit, sleeping room, or suite, the following spaces shall be accessible and shall be on an accessible route:

(a) the living area.

(b) the dining area.

(c) at least one sleeping area.

(d) patios, terraces, or balconies.

EXCEPTION: The requirements of 4.13.8 and 4.3.8 do not apply where it is necessary to utilize a higher door threshold or a change in level to protect the integrity of the unit from wind/water damage. Where this exception results in patios, terraces or balconies that are not at an accessible level, equivalent facilitation

65

shall be provided. (E.g., equivalent facilitation at a hotel patio or balcony might consist of providing raised decking or a ramp to provide accessibility.)

(e) at least one full bathroom (i.e., one with a water closet, a lavatory, and a bathtub or shower).

(f) if only half baths are provided, at least one half bath.

(g) carports, garages or parking spaces.

(7) Kitchens, Kitchenettes, or Wet Bars. When provided as accessory to a sleeping room or suite, kitchens, kitchenettes, wet bars, or similar amenities shall be accessible. Clear floor space for a front or parallel approach to cabinets, counters, sinks, and appliances shall be provided to comply with 4.2.4. Countertops and sinks shall be mounted at a maximum height of 34 in (865 mm) above the floor. At least fifty percent of shelf space in cabinets or refrigerator/freezers shall be within the reach ranges of 4.2.5 or 4.2.6 and space shall be designed to allow for the operation of cabinet and/or appliance doors so that all cabinets and appliances are accessible and usable. Controls and operating mechanisms shall comply with 4.27.

(8) Sleeping room accommodations for persons with hearing impairments required by 9.1 and complying with 9.3 shall be provided in the accessible sleeping room or suite.

9.3 Visual Alarms, Notification Devices and Telephones.

9.3.1 General. In sleeping rooms required to comply with this section, auxiliary visual alarms shall be provided and shall comply with 4.28.4. Visual notification devices shall also be provided in units, sleeping rooms and suites to alert room occupants of incoming telephone calls and a door knock or bell. Notification devices shall not be connected to auxiliary visual alarm signal appliances. Permanently installed telephones shall have volume controls complying with 4.31.5; an accessible electrical outlet within 4 ft (1220 mm) of a telephone connection shall be provided to facilitate the use of a text telephone.

9.3.2 Equivalent Facilitation. For purposes of this section, equivalent facilitation shall include the installation of electrical outlets (including outlets connected to a facility's central alarm system) and telephone wiring in sleeping rooms and suites to enable persons with hearing impairments to utilize portable visual alarms and communication devices provided by the operator of the facility.

9.4 Other Sleeping Rooms and Suites.
Doors and doorways designed to allow passage into and within all sleeping units or other covered units shall comply with 4.13.5.

9.5 Transient Lodging in Homeless Shelters, Halfway Houses, Transient Group Homes, and Other Social Service Establishments.

9.5.1 New Construction. In new construction all public use and common use areas are required to be designed and constructed to comply with section 4. At least one of each type of amenity (such as washers, dryers and similar equipment installed for the use of occupants) in each common area shall be accessible and shall be located on an accessible route to any accessible unit or sleeping accommodation.

EXCEPTION: Where elevators are not provided as allowed in 4.1.3(5), accessible amenities are not required on inaccessible floors as long as one of each type is provided in common areas on accessible floors.

9.5.2 Alterations.

(1) Social service establishments which are not homeless shelters:

(a) The provisions of 9.5.3 and 9.1.5 shall apply to sleeping rooms and beds.

(b) Alteration of other areas shall be consistent with the new construction provisions of 9.5.1.

(2) Homeless shelters. If the following elements are altered, the following requirements apply:

(a) at least one public entrance shall allow a person with mobility impairments to approach, enter and exit including a minimum clear door width of 32 in (815 mm).

(b) sleeping space for homeless persons as provided in the scoping provisions of 9.1.2 shall include doors to the sleeping area with a minimum clear width of 32 in (815 mm) and maneuvering space around the beds for persons with mobility impairments complying with 9.2.2(1).

(c) at least one toilet room for each gender or one unisex toilet room shall have a minimum clear door width of 32 in (815 mm), minimum turning space complying with 4.2.3, one water closet complying with 4.16, one lavatory complying with 4.19 and the door shall have a privacy latch; and, if provided, at least one tub or shower shall comply with 4.20 or 4.21, respectively.

(d) at least one common area which a person with mobility impairments can approach, enter and exit including a minimum clear door width of 32 in (815 mm).

(e) at least one route connecting elements (a), (b), (c) and (d) which a person with mobility impairments can use including minimum clear width of 36 in (915 mm), passing space complying with 4.3.4, turning space complying with 4.2.3 and changes in levels complying with 4.3.8.

(f) homeless shelters can comply with the provisions of (a)-(e) by providing the above elements on one accessible floor.

9.5.3. Accessible Sleeping Accommodations in New Construction. Accessible sleeping rooms shall be provided in conformance with the table in 9.1.2 and shall comply with 9.2 Accessible Units, Sleeping Rooms and Suites (where the items are provided). Additional sleeping rooms that comply with 9.3 Sleeping Accommodations for Persons with Hearing Impairments shall be provided in conformance with the table provided in 9.1.3.

In facilities with multi-bed rooms or spaces, a percentage of the beds equal to the table provided in 9.1.2 shall comply with 9.2.2(1).

10. TRANSPORTATION FACILITIES. (Reserved).

67

C-265

APPENDIX

This appendix contains *materials of an advisory nature* and provides additional information that should help the reader to understand the minimum requirements of the *guidelines* or to design buildings or facilities for greater accessibility. The paragraph numbers correspond to the sections or paragraphs of the *guideline* to which the material relates and are therefore not consecutive (for example, A4.2.1 contains additional information relevant to 4.2.1). Sections *of the guidelines* for which additional material appears in this appendix have been indicated by an asterisk. *Nothing in this appendix shall in any way obviate any obligation to comply with the requirements of the guidelines itself.*

A2.2 Equivalent Facilitation. *Specific examples of equivalent facilitation are found in the following sections:*

4.1.6(3)(c)	*Elevators in Alterations*
4.31.9	*Text Telephones*
7.2	*Sales and Service Counters, Teller Windows, Information Counters*
9.1.4	*Classes of Sleeping Accommodations*
9.2.2(6)(d)	*Requirements for Accessible Units, Sleeping Rooms, and Suites*

A4.1.1 Application.

A4.1.1(3) Areas Used Only by Employees as Work Areas. *Where there are a series of individual work stations of the same type (e.g., laboratories, service counters, ticket booths), 5%, but not less than one, of each type of work station should be constructed so that an individual with disabilities can maneuver within the work stations. Rooms housing individual offices in a typical office building must meet the requirements of the guidelines concerning doors, accessible routes, etc. but do not need to allow for maneuvering space around individual desks. Modifications required to permit maneuvering within the work area may be accomplished as a reasonable accommodation to individual employees with disabilities under Title I of the ADA. Consideration should also be given to placing shelves in employee work areas at a* convenient height for accessibility or installing commercially available shelving that is adjustable so that reasonable accommodations can be made in the future.

If work stations are made accessible they should comply with the applicable provisions of 4.2 through 4.35.

A4.1.2 Accessible Sites and Exterior Facilities: New Construction.

A4.1.2(5)(e) Valet Parking. *Valet parking is not always usable by individuals with disabilities. For instance, an individual may use a type of vehicle controls that render the regular controls inoperable or the driver's seat in a van may be removed. In these situations, another person cannot park the vehicle. It is recommended that some self-parking spaces be provided at valet parking facilities for individuals whose vehicles cannot be parked by another person and that such spaces be located on an accessible route to the entrance of the facility.*

A4.1.3 Accessible Buildings: New Construction.

A4.1.3(5) *Only full passenger elevators are covered by the accessibility provisions of 4.10. Materials and equipment hoists, freight elevators not intended for passenger use, dumbwaiters, and construction elevators are not covered by these guidelines. If a building is exempt from the elevator requirement, it is not necessary to provide a platform lift or other means of vertical access in lieu of an elevator.*

Under Exception 4, platform lifts are allowed where existing conditions make it impractical to install a ramp or elevator. Such conditions generally occur where it is essential to provide access to small raised or lowered areas where space may not be available for a ramp. Examples include, but are not limited to, raised pharmacy platforms, commercial offices raised above a sales floor, or radio and news booths.

A4.1.3(9) *Supervised automatic sprinkler systems have built in signals for monitoring features of the system such as the opening and closing of water control valves, the power supplies for needed pumps, water tank levels, and for indicating conditions that will impair the satisfactory operation of the sprinkler system.*

A1

A4.2 Space Allowances and Reach Ranges

Because of these monitoring features, supervised automatic sprinkler systems have a high level of satisfactory performance and response to fire conditions.

A4.1.3(10) *If an odd number of drinking fountains is provided on a floor, the requirement in 4.1.3(10)(b) may be met by rounding down the odd number to an even number and calculating 50% of the even number. When more than one drinking fountain on a floor is required to comply with 4.15, those fountains should be dispersed to allow wheelchair users convenient access. For example, in a large facility such as a convention center that has water fountains at several locations on a floor, the accessible water fountains should be located so that wheelchair users do not have to travel a greater distance than other people to use a drinking fountain.*

A4.1.3(17)(b) *In addition to the requirements of section 4.1.3(17)(b), the installation of additional volume controls is encouraged. Volume controls may be installed on any telephone.*

A4.1.3(19)(a) *Readily removable or folding seating units may be installed in lieu of providing an open space for wheelchair users. Folding seating units are usually two fixed seats that can be easily folded into a fixed center bar to allow for one or two open spaces for wheelchair users when necessary. These units are more easily adapted than removable seats which generally require the seat to be removed in advance by the facility management.*

Either a sign or a marker placed on seating with removable or folding arm rests is required by this section. Consideration should be given for ensuring identification of such seats in a darkened theater. For example, a marker which contrasts (light on dark or dark on light) and which also reflects light could be placed on the side of such seating so as to be visible in a lighted auditorium and also to reflect light from a flashlight.

A4.1.6 Accessible Buildings: Alterations.

A4.1.6(1)(h) *When an entrance is being altered, it is preferable that those entrances being altered be made accessible to the extent feasible.*

A2

A4.2 Space Allowances and Reach Ranges.

A4.2.1 Wheelchair Passage Width.

(1) Space Requirements for Wheelchairs. Many persons who use wheelchairs need a 30 in (760 mm) clear opening width for doorways, gates, and the like, when the latter are entered head-on. If the *person* is unfamiliar with a building, if competing traffic is heavy, if sudden or frequent movements are needed, or if the wheelchair must be turned at an opening, then greater clear widths are needed. For most situations, the addition of an inch of leeway on either side is sufficient. Thus, a minimum clear width of 32 in (815 mm) will provide adequate clearance. However, when an opening or a restriction in a passageway is more than 24 in (610 mm) long, it is essentially a passageway and must be at least 36 in (915 mm) wide.

(2) Space Requirements for Use of Walking Aids. Although people who use walking aids can maneuver through clear width openings of 32 in (815 mm), they need 36 in (915 mm) wide passageways and walks for comfortable gaits. Crutch tips, often extending down at a wide angle, are a hazard in narrow passageways where they might not be seen by other pedestrians. Thus, the 36 in (915 mm) width provides a safety allowance both for the person *with a disability* and for others.

(3) Space Requirements for Passing. Able-bodied *persons* in winter clothing, walking

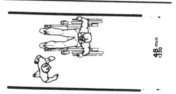

Fig. A1
Minimum Passage Width for One Wheelchair and One Ambulatory Person

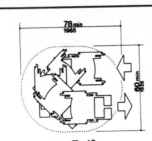

Fig. A2
Space Needed for Smooth U-Turn in a Wheelchair

straight ahead with arms swinging, need 32 in (815 mm) of width, which includes 2 in (50 mm) on either side for sway, and another 1 in (25 mm) tolerance on either side for clearing nearby objects or other pedestrians. Almost all wheelchair users and those who use walking aids can also manage within this 32 in (815 mm) width for short distances. Thus, two streams of traffic can pass in 64 in (1625 mm) in a comfortable flow. Sixty inches (1525 mm) provides a minimum width for a somewhat more restricted flow. If the clear width is less than 60 in (1525 mm), two wheelchair users will not be able to pass but will have to seek a wider place for passing. Forty-eight inches (1220 mm) is the minimum width needed for an ambulatory person to pass a nonambulatory or semi-ambulatory person. Within this 48 in (1220 mm) width, the ambulatory person will have to twist to pass a wheelchair user, a person with a *service animal*, or a

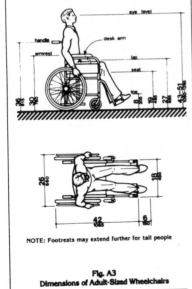

NOTE: Footrests may extend further for tall people

Fig. A3
Dimensions of Adult-Sized Wheelchairs

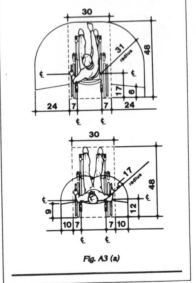

Fig. A3 (a)

A3

A4.3 Accessible Route

semi-ambulatory person. There will be little leeway for swaying or missteps (see Fig. A1).

A4.2.3 Wheelchair Turning Space.
These guidelines specify a minimum space of 60 in (1525 mm) diameter or a 60 in by 60 in (1525 mm by 1525 mm) T-shaped space for a pivoting 180-degree turn of a wheelchair. This space is usually satisfactory for turning around, but many people will not be able to turn without repeated tries and bumping into surrounding objects. The space shown in Fig. A2 will allow most wheelchair users to complete U-turns without difficulty.

A4.2.4 Clear Floor or Ground Space for Wheelchairs.
The wheelchair and user shown in Fig. A3 represent typical dimensions for a large adult male. The space requirements in this *guideline* are based upon maneuvering clearances that will accommodate most wheelchairs. Fig. A3 provides a uniform reference for design not covered by this *guideline*.

A4.2.5 & A4.2.6 Reach.
Reach ranges for persons seated in wheelchairs may be further clarified by Fig. A3(a). These drawings approximate in the plan view the information shown in Fig. 4, 5, and 6.

A4.3 Accessible Route.

A4.3.1 General.

(1) Travel Distances. Many people with mobility impairments can move at only very slow speeds; for many, traveling 200 ft (61 m) could take about 2 minutes. This assumes a rate of about 1.5 ft/s (455 mm/s) on level ground. It also assumes that the traveler would move continuously. However, on trips over 100 ft (30 m), disabled people are apt to rest frequently, which substantially increases their trip times. Resting periods of 2 minutes for every 100 ft (30 m) can be used to estimate travel times for people with severely limited stamina. In inclement weather, slow progress and resting can greatly increase a disabled person's exposure to the elements.

(2) Sites. Level, indirect routes or those with running slopes lower than 1:20 can sometimes provide more convenience than direct routes with maximum allowable slopes or with ramps.

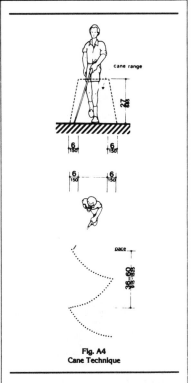

Fig. A4
Cane Technique

A4.3.10 Egress.
Because people with disabilities may visit, be employed or be a resident in any building, emergency management plans with specific provisions to ensure their safe evacuation also play an essential role in fire safety and life safety.

A4.3.11.3 Stairway Width.
A 48 inch (1220 mm) wide exit stairway is needed to allow assisted evacuation (e.g., carrying a person in a wheelchair) without encroaching on the exit path for ambulatory persons.

A4

A4.3.11.4 Two-way Communication. *It is essential that emergency communication not be dependent on voice communications alone because the safety of people with hearing or speech impairments could be jeopardized. The visible signal requirement could be satisfied with something as simple as a button in the area of rescue assistance that lights, indicating that help is on the way, when the message is answered at the point of entry.*

A4.4 Protruding Objects.

A4.4.1 General. Service animals are trained to recognize and avoid hazards. However, most people with severe impairments of vision use the long cane as an aid to mobility. The two principal cane techniques are the touch technique, where the cane arcs from side to side and touches points outside both shoulders; and the diagonal technique, where the cane is held in a stationary position diagonally across the body with the cane tip touching or just above the ground at a point outside one shoulder and the handle or grip extending to a point outside the other shoulder. The touch technique is used primarily in uncontrolled areas, while the diagonal technique is used primarily in certain limited, controlled, and familiar environments. Cane users are often trained to use both techniques.

Potential hazardous objects are noticed only if they fall within the detection range of canes (see Fig. A4). Visually impaired people walking toward an object can detect an overhang if its lowest surface is not higher than 27 in (685 mm). When walking alongside *protruding* objects, they cannot detect overhangs. Since proper cane and *service animal* techniques keep people away from the edge of a path or from walls, a slight overhang of no more than 4 in (100 mm) is not hazardous.

A4.5 Ground and Floor Surfaces.

A4.5.1 General. *People who have difficulty walking or maintaining balance or who use crutches, canes, or walkers, and those with restricted gaits are particularly sensitive to slipping and tripping hazards. For such people, a stable and regular surface is necessary for safe walking, particularly on stairs. Wheelchairs can be propelled most easily on surfaces that are hard, stable, and regular. Soft loose* surfaces such as shag carpet, loose sand or gravel, wet clay, and irregular surfaces such as cobblestones can significantly impede wheelchair movement.

Slip resistance is based on the frictional force necessary to keep a shoe heel or crutch tip from slipping on a walking surface under conditions likely to be found on the surface. *While the dynamic coefficient of friction during walking varies in a complex and non-uniform way, the static coefficient of friction, which can be measured in several ways, provides a close approximation of the slip resistance of a surface. Contrary to popular belief, some slippage is necessary to walking, especially for persons with restricted gaits; a truly "non-slip" surface could not be negotiated.*

The Occupational Safety and Health Administration recommends that walking surfaces have a static coefficient of friction of 0.5. A research project sponsored by the Architectural and Transportation Barriers Compliance Board (Access Board) conducted tests with persons with disabilities and concluded that a higher coefficient of friction was needed by such persons. A static coefficient of friction of 0.6 is recommended for accessible routes and 0.8 for ramps.

It is recognized that the coefficient of friction varies considerably due to the presence of contaminants, water, floor finishes, and other factors not under the control of the designer or builder and not subject to design and construction guidelines and that compliance would be difficult to measure on the building site. Nevertheless, many common building materials suitable for flooring are now labeled with information on the static coefficient of friction. While it may not be possible to compare one product directly with another, or to guarantee a constant measure, builders and designers are encouraged to specify materials with appropriate values. As more products include information on slip resistance, improved uniformity in measurement and specification is likely. The Access Board's advisory guidelines on Slip Resistant Surfaces provides additional information on this subject.

Cross slopes on walks and ground or floor surfaces can cause considerable difficulty in propelling a wheelchair in a straight line.

A5

A4.6 Parking and Passenger Loading Zones

A4.5.3 Carpet. Much more needs to be done in developing both quantitative and qualitative criteria for carpeting (*i.e., problems associated with texture and weave need to be studied*). However, certain functional characteristics are well established. When both carpet and padding are used, it is desirable to have minimum movement (preferably none) between the floor and the pad and the pad and the carpet which would allow the carpet to hump or warp. In heavily trafficked areas, a thick, soft (plush) pad or cushion, particularly in combination with long carpet pile, makes it difficult for individuals in wheelchairs and those with other ambulatory disabilities to get about. Firm carpeting can be achieved through proper selection and combination of pad and carpet, sometimes with the elimination of the pad or cushion, and with proper installation. *Carpeting designed with a weave that causes a zig-zag effect when wheeled across is strongly discouraged.*

A4.6 Parking and Passenger Loading Zones.

A4.6.3 Parking Spaces. *The increasing use of vans with side-mounted lifts or ramps by persons with disabilities has necessitated some revisions in specifications for parking spaces and adjacent access aisles. The typical accessible parking space is 96 in (2440 mm) wide with an adjacent 60 in (1525 mm) access aisle. However, this aisle does not permit lifts or ramps to be deployed and still leave room for a person using a wheelchair or other mobility aid to exit the lift platform or ramp. In tests conducted with actual lift/van/wheelchair combinations, (under a Board-sponsored Accessible Parking and Loading Zones Project) researchers found that a space and aisle totaling almost 204 in (5180 mm) wide was needed to deploy a lift and exit conveniently. The "van accessible" parking space required by these guidelines provides a 96 in (2440 mm) wide space with a 96 in (2440 mm) adjacent access aisle which is just wide enough to maneuver and exit from a side mounted lift. If a 96 in (2440 mm) access aisle is placed between two spaces, two "van accessible" spaces are created. Alternatively, if the wide access aisle is provided at the end of a row (an area often unused), it may be possible to provide the wide access aisle without additional space (see Fig. A5(a)).*

A sign is needed to alert van users to the presence of the wider aisle, but the space is not intended to be restricted only to vans.

"Universal" Parking Space Design. An alternative to the provision of a percentage of spaces with a wide aisle, and the associated need to include additional signage, is the use of what has been called the "universal" parking space design. Under this design, all accessible spaces are 132 in (3350 mm) wide with a 60 in (1525 mm) access aisle (see Fig. A5(b)). One

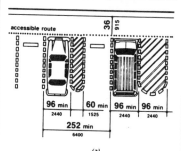

(a)
Van Accessible Space at End Row

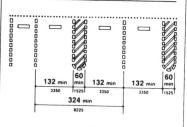

(b)
Universal Parking Space Design

Fig. A5
Parking Space Alternatives

A6

advantage to this design is that no additional signage is needed because all spaces can accommodate a van with a side-mounted lift or ramp. Also, there is no competition between cars and vans for spaces since all spaces can accommodate either. Furthermore, the wider space permits vehicles to park to one side or the other within the 132 in (3350 mm) space to allow persons to exit and enter the vehicle on either the driver or passenger side, although, in some cases, this would require exiting or entering without a marked access aisle.

An essential consideration for any design is having the access aisle level with the parking space. Since a person with a disability, using a lift or ramp, must maneuver within the access aisle, the aisle cannot include a ramp or sloped area. The access aisle must be connected to an accessible route to the appropriate accessible entrance of a building or facility. The parking access aisle must either blend with the accessible route or have a curb ramp complying with 4.7. Such a curb ramp opening must be located within the access aisle boundaries, not within the parking space boundaries. Unfortunately, many facilities are designed with a ramp that is blocked when any vehicle parks in the accessible space. Also, the required dimensions of the access aisle cannot be restricted by planters, curbs or wheel stops.

A4.6.4 Signage. Signs designating parking places for disabled people can be seen from a driver's seat if the signs are mounted high enough above the ground and located at the front of a parking space.

A4.6.5 Vertical Clearance. High-top vans, which disabled people or transportation services often use, require higher clearances in parking garages than automobiles.

A4.8 Ramps.

A4.8.1 General. Ramps are essential for wheelchair users if elevators or lifts are not available to connect different levels. However, some people who use walking aids have difficulty with ramps and prefer stairs.

A4.8.2 Slope and Rise. *Ramp slopes between 1:16 and 1:20 are preferred.* The ability to manage an incline is related to both its slope and its length. Wheelchair users with

disabilities affecting their arms or with low stamina have serious difficulty using inclines. Most ambulatory people and most people who use wheelchairs can manage a slope of 1:16. Many people cannot manage a slope of 1:12 for 30 ft (9 m).

A4.8.4 Landings. *Level landings are essential toward maintaining an aggregate slope that complies with these guidelines. A ramp landing that is not level causes individuals using wheelchairs to tip backward or bottom out when the ramp is approached.*

A4.8.5 Handrails. The requirements for stair and ramp handrails in this *guideline* are for adults. When children are principal users in a building or facility, a second set of handrails at an appropriate height can assist them and aid in preventing accidents.

A4.9 Stairs.

A4.9.1 Minimum Number. *Only interior and exterior stairs connecting levels that are not connected by an elevator, ramp, or other accessible means of vertical access have to comply with 4.9.*

A4.10 Elevators.

A4.10.6 Door Protective and Reopening Device. The required door reopening device would hold the door open for 20 seconds if the doorway remains obstructed. After 20 seconds, the door may begin to close. However, if designed in accordance with *ASME A17.1-1990*, the door closing movement could still be stopped if a person or object exerts sufficient force at any point on the door edge.

A4.10.7 Door and Signal Timing for Hall Calls. This paragraph allows variation in the location of call buttons, advance time for warning signals, and the door-holding period used to meet the time requirement.

A4.10.12 Car Controls. Industry-wide standardization of elevator control panel design would make all elevators significantly more convenient for use by people with severe visual impairments. In many cases, it will be possible to locate the highest control on elevator panels within 48 in (1220 mm) from the floor.

A7

A4.11 Platform Lifts (Wheelchair Lifts)

A4.10.13 Car Position Indicators. A special button may be provided that would activate the audible signal within the given elevator only for the desired trip, rather than maintaining the audible signal in constant operation.

A4.10.14 Emergency Communications. A device that requires no handset is easier to use by people who have difficulty reaching. *Also, small handles on handset compartment doors are not usable by people who have difficulty grasping.*

Ideally, emergency two-way communication systems should provide both voice and visual display intercommunication so that persons with hearing impairments and persons with vision impairments can receive information regarding the status of a rescue. A voice intercommunication system cannot be the only means of communication because it is not accessible to people with speech and hearing impairments. While a voice intercommunication system is not required, at a minimum, the system should provide both an audio and visual indication that a rescue is on the way.

A4.11 Platform Lifts (Wheelchair Lifts).

A4.11.2 Other Requirements. *Inclined stairway chairlifts, and inclined and vertical platform lifts (wheelchair lifts) are available for short-distance, vertical transportation of people with disabilities. Care should be taken in selecting lifts as some lifts are not equally suitable for use by both wheelchair users and semi-ambulatory individuals.*

A4.12 Windows.

A4.12.1 General. *Windows intended to be operated by occupants in accessible spaces should comply with 4.12.*

A4.12.2 Window Hardware. *Windows requiring pushing, pulling, or lifting to open (for example, double-hung, sliding, or casement and awning units without cranks) should require no more than 5 lbf (22.2 N) to open or close. Locks, cranks, and other window hardware should comply with 4.27.*

A4.13 Doors.

A4.13.8 Thresholds at Doorways. Thresholds and surface height changes in doorways are particularly inconvenient for wheelchair users who also have low stamina or restrictions in arm movement because complex maneuvering is required to get over the level change while operating the door.

A4.13.9 Door Hardware. Some disabled persons must push against a door with their chair or walker to open it. Applied kickplates on doors with closers can reduce required maintenance by withstanding abuse from wheelchairs and canes. To be effective, they should cover the door width, less approximately 2 in (51 mm), up to a height of 16 in (405 mm) from its bottom edge and be centered across the *width of the door.*

A4.13.10 Door Closers. Closers with delayed action features give a person more time to maneuver through doorways. They are particularly useful on frequently used interior doors such as entrances to toilet rooms.

A4.13.11 Door Opening Force. Although most people with disabilities can exert at least 5 lbf (22.2N), both pushing and pulling from a stationary position, a few people with severe disabilities cannot exert 3 lbf (13.13N). Although some people cannot manage the allowable forces in this guideline and many others have difficulty, door closers must have certain minimum closing forces to close doors satisfactorily. Forces for pushing or pulling doors open are measured with a push-pull scale under the following conditions:

(1) Hinged doors: Force applied perpendicular to the door at the door opener or 30 in (760 mm) from the hinged side, whichever is farther from the hinge.

(2) Sliding or folding doors: Force applied parallel to the door at the door pull or latch.

(3) Application of force: Apply force gradually so that the applied force does not exceed the resistance of the door. In high-rise buildings, air-pressure differentials may require a modification of this specification in order to meet the functional intent.

A8

A4.15 Drinking Fountains and Water Coolers

A4.13.12 Automatic Doors and Power-Assisted Doors. Sliding automatic doors do not need guard rails and are more convenient for wheelchair users and visually impaired people to use. If slowly opening automatic doors can be reactivated before their closing cycle is completed, they will be more convenient in busy doorways.

A4.15 Drinking Fountains and Water Coolers.

A4.15.2 Spout Height. Two drinking fountains, mounted side by side or on a single post, are usable by people with disabilities and people who find it difficult to bend over.

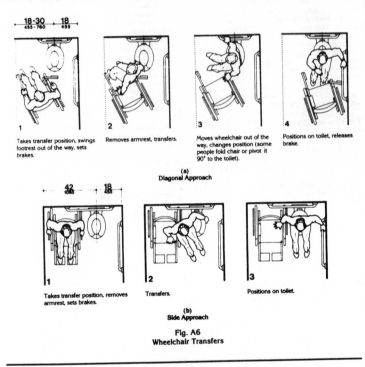

1 — Takes transfer position, swings footrest out of the way, sets brakes.

2 — Removes armrest, transfers.

3 — Moves wheelchair out of the way, changes position (some people fold chair or pivot it 90° to the toilet).

4 — Positions on toilet, releases brake.

(a)
Diagonal Approach

1 — Takes transfer position, removes armrest, sets brakes.

2 — Transfers.

3 — Positions on toilet.

(b)
Side Approach

Fig. A6
Wheelchair Transfers

A9

A4.16 Water Closets

A4.16 Water Closets.

A4.16.3 Height. Height preferences for toilet seats vary considerably among disabled people. Higher seat heights may be an advantage to some ambulatory disabled people, but are often a disadvantage for wheelchair users and others. Toilet seats 18 in (455 mm) high seem to be a reasonable compromise. Thick seats and filler rings are available to adapt standard fixtures to these requirements.

A4.16.4 Grab Bars. Fig. A6(a) and (b) show the diagonal and side approaches most commonly used to transfer from a wheelchair to a water closet. Some wheelchair users can transfer from the front of the toilet while others use a 90-degree approach. Most people who use the two additional approaches can also use either the diagonal approach or the side approach.

A4.16.5 Flush Controls. Flush valves and related plumbing can be located behind walls or to the side of the toilet, or a toilet seat lid can be provided if plumbing fittings are directly behind the toilet seat. Such designs reduce the chance of injury and imbalance caused by leaning back against the fittings. Flush controls for tank-type toilets have a standardized mounting location on the left side of the tank (facing the tank). Tanks can be obtained by special order with controls mounted on the right side. If administrative authorities require flush controls for flush valves to be located in a position that conflicts with the location of the rear grab bar, then that bar may be split or shifted toward the wide side of the toilet area.

A4.17 Toilet Stalls.

A4.17.3 Size and Arrangement. This section requires use of the 60 in (1525 mm) standard stall (Figure 30(a)) and permits the 36 in (915 mm) or 48 in (1220 mm) wide alternate stall (Figure 30(b)) only in alterations where provision of the standard stall is technically infeasible or where local plumbing codes prohibit reduction in the number of fixtures. A standard stall provides a clear space on one side of the water closet to enable persons who use wheelchairs to perform a side or diagonal transfer from the wheelchair to the water closet. However, some persons with disabilities who use mobility aids such as walkers, canes or crutches

are better able to use the two parallel grab bars in the 36 in (915 mm) wide alternate stall to achieve a standing position.

In large toilet rooms, where six or more toilet stalls are provided, it is therefore required that a 36 in (915 mm) wide stall with parallel grab bars be provided in addition to the standard stall required in new construction. The 36 in (915 mm) width is necessary to achieve proper use of the grab bars; wider stalls would position the grab bars too far apart to be easily used and narrower stalls would position the grab bars too close to the water closet. Since the stall is primarily intended for use by persons using canes, crutches and walkers, rather than wheelchairs, the length of the stall could be conventional. The door, however, must swing outward to ensure a usable space for people who use crutches or walkers.

A4.17.5 Doors. To make it easier for wheelchair users to close toilet stall doors, doors can be provided with closers, spring hinges, or a pull bar mounted on the inside surface of the door near the hinge side.

A4.19 Lavatories and Mirrors.

A4.19.6 Mirrors. If mirrors are to be used by both ambulatory people and wheelchair users, then they must be at least 74 in (1880 mm) high at their topmost edge. A single full length mirror can accommodate all people, including children.

A4.21 Shower Stalls.

A4.21.1 General. Shower stalls that are 36 in by 36 in (915 mm by 915 mm) wide provide additional safety to people who have difficulty maintaining balance because all grab bars and walls are within easy reach. Seated people use the walls of 36 in by 36 in (915 mm by 915 mm) showers for back support. Shower stalls that are 60 in (1525 mm) wide and have no curb may increase usability of a bathroom by wheelchair users because the shower area provides additional maneuvering space.

A4.22 Toilet Rooms.

A4.22.3 Clear Floor Space. In many small facilities, single-user restrooms may be the only facilities provided for all building users. In addition, the guidelines allow the use of "unisex" or "family" accessible toilet rooms in alterations when technical infeasibility can be demonstrated. Experience has shown that the provision of accessible "unisex" or single-user restrooms is a reasonable way to provide access for wheelchair users and any attendants, especially when attendants are of the opposite sex. Since these facilities have proven so useful, it is often considered advantageous to install a "unisex" toilet room in new facilities in addition to making the multi-stall restrooms accessible, especially in shopping malls, large auditoriums, and convention centers.

Figure 28 (section 4.16) provides minimum clear floor space dimensions for toilets in accessible "unisex" toilet rooms. The dotted lines designate the minimum clear floor space, depending on the direction of approach, required for wheelchair users to transfer onto the water closet. The dimensions of 48 in (1220 mm) and 60 in (1525 mm), respectively, correspond to the space required for the two common transfer approaches utilized by wheelchair users (see Fig. A6). It is important to keep in mind that the placement of the lavatory to the immediate side of the water closet will preclude the side approach transfer illustrated in Figure A6(b).

To accommodate the side transfer, the space adjacent to the water closet must remain clear of obstruction for 42 in (1065 mm) from the centerline of the toilet (Figure 28) and the lavatory must not be located within this clear space. A turning circle or T-turn, the clear floor space at the lavatory, and maneuvering space at the door must be considered when determining the possible wall locations. A privacy latch or other accessible means of ensuring privacy during use should be provided at the door.

RECOMMENDATIONS:

1. In new construction, accessible single-user restrooms may be desirable in some situations because they can accommodate a wide variety of building users. However, they cannot be used in lieu of making the multi-stall toilet rooms accessible as required.

2. Where strict compliance to the guidelines for accessible toilet facilities is technically infeasible in the alteration of existing facilities, accessible "unisex" toilets are a reasonable alternative.

3. In designing accessible single-user restrooms, the provisions of adequate space to allow a side transfer will provide accommodation to the largest number of wheelchair users.

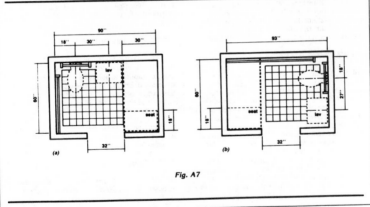

Fig. A7

A4.23 Bathrooms, Bathing Facilities, and Shower Rooms

A4.23 Bathrooms, Bathing Facilities, and Shower Rooms.

A4.23.3 Clear Floor Space. Figure A7 shows two possible configurations of a toilet room with a roll-in shower. The specific shower shown is designed to fit exactly within the dimensions of a standard bathtub. Since the shower does not have a lip, the floor space can be used for required maneuvering space. This would permit a toilet room to be smaller than would be permitted with a bathtub and still provide enough floor space to be considered accessible. This design can provide accessibility in facilities where space is at a premium (i.e., hotels and medical care facilities). The alternate roll-in shower (Fig. 57b) also provides sufficient room for the "T-turn" and does not require plumbing to be on more than one wall.

A4.23.9 Medicine Cabinets. Other alternatives for storing medical and personal care items are very useful to disabled people. Shelves, drawers, and floor-mounted cabinets can be provided within the reach ranges of disabled people.

A4.26 Handrails, Grab Bars, and Tub and Shower Seats.

A4.26.1 General. Many disabled people rely heavily upon grab bars and handrails to maintain balance and prevent serious falls. Many people brace their forearms between supports and walls to give them more leverage and stability in maintaining balance or for lifting. The grab bar clearance of 1-1/2 in (38 mm) required in this guideline is a safety clearance to prevent injuries resulting from arms slipping through the openings. It also provides adequate gripping room.

A4.26.2 Size and Spacing of Grab Bars and Handrails. This specification allows for alternate shapes of handrails as long as they allow an opposing grip similar to that provided by a circular section of 1-1/4 in to 1-1/2 in (32 mm to 38 mm).

A4.27 Controls and Operating Mechanisms.

A4.27.3 Height. Fig. A8 further illustrates

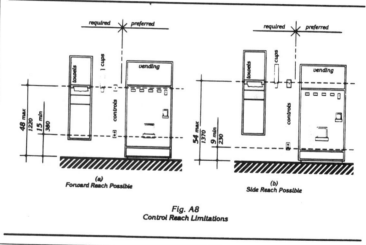

Fig. A8
Control Reach Limitations

A12

mandatory and advisory control mounting height provisions for typical equipment.

Electrical receptacles installed to serve individual appliances and not intended for regular or frequent use by building occupants are not required to be mounted within the specified reach ranges. Examples would be receptacles installed specifically for wall-mounted clocks, refrigerators, and microwave ovens.

A4.28 Alarms.

A4.28.2 Audible Alarms. Audible emergency signals must have an intensity and frequency that can attract the attention of individuals who have partial hearing loss. People over 60 years of age generally have difficulty perceiving frequencies higher than 10,000 Hz. An alarm signal which has a periodic element to its signal, such as single stroke bells (clang-pause-clang-pause), hi-low (up-down-up-down) and fast whoop (on-off-on-off) are best. Avoid continuous or reverberating tones. Select a signal which has a sound characterized by three or four clear tones without a great deal of "noise" in between.

A4.28.3 Visual Alarms. The specifications in this section do not preclude the use of zoned or coded alarm systems.

A4.28.4 Auxiliary Alarms. Locating visual emergency alarms in rooms where persons who are deaf may work or reside alone can ensure that they will always be warned when an emergency alarm is activated. To be effective, such devices must be located and oriented so that they will spread signals and reflections throughout a space or raise the overall light level sharply. However, visual alarms alone are not necessarily the best means to alert sleepers. A study conducted by Underwriters Laboratory (UL) concluded that a flashing light more than seven times brighter was required (110 candela v. 15 candela, at the same distance) to awaken sleepers as was needed to alert awake subjects in a normal daytime illuminated room.

For hotel and other rooms where people are likely to be asleep, a signal-activated vibrator placed between mattress and box spring or under a pillow was found by UL to be much more effective in alerting sleepers. Many readily available devices are sound-activated so that they could respond to an alarm clock, clock

radio, wake-up telephone call or room smoke detector. Activation by a building alarm system can either be accomplished by a separate circuit activating an auditory alarm which would, in turn, trigger the vibrator or by a signal transmitted through the ordinary 110-volt outlet. Transmission of signals through the power line is relatively simple and is the basis of common, inexpensive remote light control systems sold in many department and electronic stores for home use. So-called "wireless" intercoms operate on the same principal.

A4.29 Detectable Warnings.

A4.29.2 Detectable Warnings on Walking Surfaces. The material used to provide contrast should contrast by at least 70%. Contrast in percent is determined by:

$$\text{Contrast} = [(B_1 - B_2)/B_1] \times 100$$

where B_1 = light reflectance value (LRV) of the lighter area
and B_2 = light reflectance value (LRV) of the darker area.

Note that in any application both white and black are never absolute; thus, B_1 never equals 100 and B_2 is always greater than 0.

A4.30 Signage.

A4.30.1 General. In building complexes where finding locations independently on a routine basis may be a necessity (for example, college campuses), tactile maps or prerecorded instructions can be very helpful to visually impaired people. Several maps and auditory instructions have been developed and tested for specific applications. The type of map or instructions used must be based on the information to be communicated, which depends highly on the type of buildings or users.

Landmarks that can easily be distinguished by visually impaired individuals are useful as orientation cues. Such cues include changes in illumination level, bright colors, unique patterns, wall murals, location of special equipment or other architectural features.

Many people with disabilities have limitations in movement of their heads and reduced peripheral vision. Thus, signage positioned

A13

A4.30 Signage

perpendicular to the path of travel is easiest for them to notice. People can generally distinguish signage within an angle of 30 degrees to either side of the centerlines of their faces without moving their heads.

A4.30.2 Character Proportion. The legibility of printed characters is a function of the viewing distance, character height, the ratio of the stroke width to the height of the character, the contrast of color between character and background, and print font. The size of characters must be based upon the intended viewing distance. A severely nearsighted person may have to be much closer to recognize a character of a given size than a person with normal visual acuity.

A4.30.4 Raised and Brailled Characters and Pictorial Symbol Signs
(Pictograms). *The standard dimensions for literary Braille are as follows:*

Dot diameter	.059 in.
Inter-dot spacing	.090 in.
Horizontal separation between cells	.241 in.
Vertical separation between cells	.395 in.

Raised borders around signs containing raised characters may make them confusing to read unless the border is set far away from the characters. *Accessible signage with descriptive materials about public buildings, monuments, and objects of cultural interest may not provide sufficiently detailed and meaningful information. Interpretive guides, audio tape devices, or other methods may be more effective in presenting such information.*

A4.30.5 Finish and Contrast. *An eggshell finish (11 to 19 degree gloss on 60 degree glossimeter) is recommended. Research indicates that signs are more legible for persons with low vision when characters contrast with their background by at least 70 percent. Contrast in percent shall be determined by:*

$$Contrast = [(B_1 - B_2)/B_1] \times 100$$

*where B_1 = light reflectance value (LRV) of the lighter area
and B_2 = light reflectance value (LRV) of the darker area.*

Note that in any application both white and black are never absolute; thus, B_1 never equals 100 and B_2 is always greater than 0.

The greatest readability is usually achieved through the use of light-colored characters or symbols on a dark background.

A4.30.7 Symbols of Accessibility for Different Types of Listening Systems. *Paragraph 4 of this section requires signage indicating the availability of an assistive listening system. An appropriate message should be displayed with the international symbol of access for hearing loss since this symbol conveys general accessibility for people with hearing loss. Some suggestions are:*

INFRARED
ASSISTIVE LISTENING SYSTEM
AVAILABLE
——PLEASE ASK——

AUDIO LOOP IN USE
TURN T-SWITCH FOR
BETTER HEARING
——OR ASK FOR HELP——

FM
ASSISTIVE LISTENING
SYSTEM AVAILABLE
——PLEASE ASK——

The symbol may be used to notify persons of the availability of other auxiliary aids and services such as: real time captioning, captioned note taking, sign language interpreters, and oral interpreters.

A4.30.8 Illumination Levels. *Illumination levels on the sign surface shall be in the 100 to 300 lux range (10 to 30 footcandles) and shall be uniform over the sign surface. Signs shall be located such that the illumination level on the surface of the sign is not significantly exceeded by the ambient light or visible bright lighting source behind or in front of the sign.*

A14

A4.31 Telephones.

A4.31.3 Mounting Height. In localities where the dial-tone first system is in operation, calls can be placed at a coin telephone through the operator without inserting coins. The operator button is located at a height of 46 in (1170 mm) if the coin slot of the telephone is at 54 in (1370 mm). A generally available public telephone with a coin slot mounted lower on the equipment would allow universal installation of telephones at a height of 48 in (1220 mm) or less to all operable parts.

A4.31.9 Text Telephones. A public text telephone may be an integrated text telephone pay phone unit or a conventional portable text telephone that is permanently affixed within, or adjacent to, the telephone enclosure. In order to be usable with a pay phone, a text telephone which is not a single integrated text telephone pay phone unit will require a shelf large enough (10 in (255mm) wide by 10 in (255 mm) deep with a 6 in (150 mm) vertical clearance minimum) to accommodate the device, an electrical outlet, and a power cord. Movable or portable text telephones may be used to provide equivalent facilitation. A text telephone should be readily available so that a person using it may access the text telephone easily and conveniently. As currently designed pocket-type text telephones for personal use do not accommodate a wide range of users. Such devices would not be considered substantially equivalent to conventional text telephones. However, in the future as technology develops this could change.

A4.32 Fixed or Built-in Seating and Tables.

A4.32.4 Height of Tables or Counters. Different types of work require different *table or counter* heights for comfort and optimal performance. Light detailed work such as writing requires a *table or counter* close to elbow height for a standing person. Heavy manual work such as rolling dough requires *a counter or table* height about 10 in (255 mm) below elbow height for a standing person. This principle of *high/low table or counter heights* also applies for seated persons; however, the limiting condition for seated manual work is clearance under the *table or counter.*

Table A1 shows convenient *counter heights* for seated persons. The great variety of heights for comfort and optimal performance indicates a need for alternatives or a compromise in height if people who stand and people who sit will be using the same counter area.

Table A1
Convenient Heights of Tables and Counters for Seated People[1]

Conditions of Use	Short Women in mm		Tall Men in mm	
Seated in a wheelchair:				
Manual work–				
Desk or removeable armrests	26	660	30	760
Fixed, full-size armrests[2]	32[3]	815	32[3]	815
Light detailed work:				
Desk or removeable armrests	29	735	34	865
Fixed, full-size armrests[3]	32[3]	815	34	865
Seated in a 16-in. (405-mm)				
High chair:				
Manual work	26	660	27	685
Light detailed work	28	710	31	785

[1] All dimensions are based on a work-surface thickness of 1 1/2 in (38 mm) and a clearance of 1 1/2 in (38 mm) between legs and the underside of a work surface.

[2] This type of wheelchair arm does not interfere with the positioning of a wheelchair under a work surface.

[3] This dimension is limited by the height of the armrests: a lower height would be preferable. Some people in this group prefer lower work surfaces, which require positioning the wheelchair back from the edge of the counter.

A4.33 Assembly Areas.

A4.33.2 Size of Wheelchair Locations. Spaces large enough for two wheelchairs allow people who are coming to a performance together to sit together.

A4.33.3 Placement of Wheelchair Locations. The location of wheelchair areas can be planned so that a variety of positions

Table A2. Summary of Assistive Listening Devices

within the seating area are provided. This will allow choice in viewing and price categories.

Building/life safety codes set minimum distances between rows of fixed seats with consideration of the number of seats in a row, the exit aisle width and arrangement, and the location of exit doors. "Continental" seating, with a greater number of seats per row and a

commensurate increase in row spacing and exit doors, facilitates emergency egress for all people and increases ease of access to mid-row seats especially for people who walk with difficulty. Consideration of this positive attribute of "continental" seating should be included along with all other factors in the design of fixed seating areas.

Table A2. *Summary of Assistive Listening Devices*

System	Advantages	Disadvantages	Typical Applications
Induction Loop Transmitter: Transducer wired to induction loop around listening area. Receiver: Self-contained induction receiver or personal hearing aid with telecoil.	Cost-Effective Low Maintenance Easy to use Unobtrusive May be possible to integrate into existing public address system. Some hearing aids can function as receivers.	Signal spills over to adjacent rooms. Susceptible to electrical interference. Limited portability Inconsistent signal strength. Head position affects signal strength. Lack of standards for induction coil performance.	Meeting areas Theaters Churches and Temples Conference rooms Classrooms TV viewing
FM Transmitter: Flashlight-sized worn by speaker. Receiver: With personal hearing aid via DAI or induction neck-loop and telecoil; or self-contained with earphone(s).	Highly portable Different channels allow use by different groups within the same room. High user mobility Variable for large range of hearing losses.	High cost of receivers Equipment fragile Equipment obtrusive High maintenance Expensive to maintain Custom fitting to individual user may be required.	Classrooms Tour groups Meeting areas Outdoor events One-on-one
Infrared Transmitter: Emitter in line-of-sight with receiver. Receiver: Self-contained. Or with personal hearing aid via DAI or induction neckloop and telecoil.	Easy to use Insures privacy or confidentiality Moderate cost Can often be integrated into existing public address system.	Line-of-sight required between emitter and receiver. Ineffective outdoors Limited portability Requires installation	Theaters Churches and Temples Auditoriums Meetings requiring confidentiality TV viewing

Source: Rehab Brief, National Institute on Disability and Rehabilitation Research, Washington, DC, Vol. XII, No. 10, (1990).

A16

A4.33.6 Placement of Listening Systems. A distance of 50 ft (15 m) allows a person to distinguish performers' facial expressions.

A4.33.7 Types of Listening Systems. An assistive listening system appropriate for an assembly area for a group of persons or where the specific individuals are not known in advance, such as a playhouse, lecture hall or movie theater, may be different from the system appropriate for a particular individual provided as an auxiliary aid or as part of a reasonable accommodation. The appropriate device for an individual is the type that individual can use, whereas the appropriate system for an assembly area will necessarily be geared toward the "average" or aggregate needs of various individuals. A listening system that can be used from any seat in a seating area is the most flexible way to meet this specification. Earphone jacks with variable volume controls can benefit only people who have slight hearing loss and do not help people who use hearing aids. At the present time, *magnetic induction* loops are the most feasible type of listening system for people who use hearing aids *equipped with* "T-coils," but people without hearing aids or those with hearing aids not equipped with inductive pick-ups cannot use them *without special receivers.* Radio frequency systems can be extremely effective and inexpensive. People without hearing aids can use them, but people with hearing aids need a special receiver to use them as they are presently designed. If hearing aids had a jack to allow a by-pass of microphones, then radio frequency systems would be suitable for people with and without hearing aids. Some listening systems may be subject to interference from other equipment and feedback from hearing aids of people who are using the systems. Such interference can be controlled by careful engineering design that anticipates feedback sources in the surrounding area.

Table A2, reprinted from a National Institute of Disability and Rehabilitation Research "Rehab Brief," shows some of the advantages and disadvantages of different types of assistive listening systems. In addition, the Architectural and Transportation Barriers Compliance Board (Access Board) has published a pamphlet on Assistive Listening Systems which lists demonstration centers across the country where technical assistance can be obtained in selecting and installing appropriate systems. The state of New York has also adopted a detailed technical specification which may be useful.

A5.0 Restaurants and Cafeterias.

A5.1 General. Dining counters (where there is no service) are typically found in small carry-out restaurants, bakeries, or coffee shops and may only be a narrow eating surface attached to a wall. This section requires that where such a dining counter is provided, a portion of the counter shall be at the required accessible height.

A7.0 Business and Mercantile.

A7.2(3) Assistive Listening Devices. At all sales and service counters, teller windows, box offices, and information kiosks where a physical barrier separates service personnel and customers, it is recommended that at least one permanently installed assistive listening device complying with 4.33 be provided at each location or series. Where assistive listening devices are installed, signage should be provided identifying those stations which are so equipped.

A7.3 Check-out Aisles. Section 7.2 refers to counters without aisles; section 7.3 concerns check-out aisles. A counter without an aisle (7.2) can be approached from more than one direction such as in a convenience store. In order to use a check-out aisle (7.3), customers must enter a defined area (an aisle) at a particular point, pay for goods, and exit at a particular point.

C-282

Appendix B to Part 36—Preamble to Regulation on Nondiscrimination on the Basis of Disability by Public Accommodations and in Commercial Facilities (Published July 26, 1991)

Note: For the convenience of the reader, this appendix contains the text of the preamble to the final regulation on nondiscrimination on the basis of disability by public accommodations and in commercial facilities beginning at the heading "Section-by-Section Analysis and Response to Comments" and ending before "List of Subjects in 28 CFR part 36" (56 FR July 26, 1991).

Dated: July 17, 1991.

Dick Thornburgh,
Attorney General.

[FR Doc. 91–17482 Filed 7–25–91; 8:45 am]

BILLING CODE 4410-01-M

Department of Justice

Office of the Attorney General

28 CFR Part 35
Nondiscrimination on the Basis of
Disability in State and Local Government
Services; Final Rule

DEPARTMENT OF JUSTICE

28 CFR Part 35

[Order No. 1512-91]

Nondiscrimination on the Basis of Disability in State and Local Government Services

AGENCY: Department of Justice.

ACTION: Final rule.

SUMMARY: This rule implements subtitle A of title II of the Americans with Disabilities Act, Public Law 101–336, which prohibits discrimination on the basis of disability by public entities. Subtitle A protects qualified individuals with disabilities from discrimination on the basis of disability in the services, programs, or activities of all State and local governments. It extends the prohibition of discrimination in federally assisted programs established by section 504 of the Rehabilitation Act of 1973 to all activities of State and local governments, including those that do not receive Federal financial assistance, and incorporates specific prohibitions of discrimination on the basis of disability from titles I, III, and V of the Americans with Disabilities Act. This rule, therefore, adopts the general prohibitions of discrimination established under section 504, as well as the requirements for making programs accessible to individuals with disabilities and for providing equally effective communications. It also sets forth standards for what constitutes discrimination on the basis of mental or physical disability, provides a definition of disability and qualified individual with a disability, and establishes a complaint mechanism for resolving allegations of discrimination.

EFFECIVE DATE: January 26, 1992.

FOR FURTHER INFORMATION CONTACT: Barbara S. Drake, Deputy Assistant Attorney General, Civil Rights Division; Stewart B. Oneglia, Chief, Coordination and Review Section, Civil Rights Division; John L. Wodatch, Director, Office on the Americans with Disabilities Act, Civil Rights Division; all of the U.S. Department of Justice, Washington, DC 20530. These individuals may be contacted through the Division's ADA Information Line at (202) 514–0301 (Voice), (202) 514–0381 (TDD), or (202) 514–0383 (TDD). These telephone numbers are not toll-free numbers.

SUPPLEMENTARY INFORMATION:

Background

The landmark Americans with Disabilities Act ("ADA" or "the Act"), enacted on July 26, 1990, provides comprehensive civil rights protections to individuals with disabilities in the areas of employment, public accommodations, State and local government services, and telecommunications.

This regulation implements subtitle A of title II of the ADA, which applies to State and local governments. Most programs and activities of State and local governments are recipients of Federal financial assistance from one or more Federal funding agencies and, therefore, are already covered by section 504 of the Rehabilitation Act of 1973, as amended (29 U.S.C. 794) ("section 504"), which prohibits discrimination on the basis of handicap in federally assisted programs and activities. Because title II of the ADA essentially extends the nondiscrimination mandate of section 504 to those State and local governments that do not receive Federal financial assistance, this rule hews closely to the provisions of existing section 504 regulations. This approach is also based on section 204 of the ADA, which provides that the regulations issued by the Attorney General to implement title II shall be consistent with the ADA and with the Department of Health, Education, and Welfare's coordination regulation, now codified at 28 CFR part 41, and, with respect to "program accessibility, existing facilities," and "communications," with the Department of Justice's regulation for its federally conducted programs and activities, codified at 28 CFR part 39.

The first regulation implementing section 504 was issued in 1977 by the Department of Health, Education, and Welfare (HEW) for the programs and activities to which it provided Federal financial assistance. The following year, HEW issued its coordination regulation for federally assisted programs, which served as the model for regulations issued by the other Federal agencies that administer grant programs. HEW's coordination authority, and the coordination regulation issued under that authority, were transferred to the Department of Justice by Executive Order 12250 in 1980.

In 1978, Congress extended application of section 504 to programs and activities conducted by Federal Executive agencies and the United States Postal Service. Pursuant to Executive Order 12250, the Department of Justice developed a prototype regulation to implement the 1978 amendment for federally conducted programs and activities. More than 80 Federal agencies have now issued final regulations based on that prototype,

prohibiting discrimination based on handicap in the programs and activities they conduct.

Despite the large number of regulations implementing section 504 for federally assisted and federally conducted programs and activities, there is very little variation in their substantive requirements, or even in their language. Major portions of this regulation, therefore, are taken directly from the existing regulations.

In addition, section 204(b) of the ADA requires that the Department's regulation implementing subtitle A of title II be consistent with the ADA. Thus, the Department's final regulation includes provisions and concepts from titles I and III of the ADA.

Rulemaking History

On February 22, 1991, the Department of Justice published a notice of proposed rulemaking (NPRM) implementing title III of the ADA in the **Federal Register**. 56 FR 7452. On February 28, 1991, the Department published a notice of proposed rulemaking implementing subtitle A of title II of the ADA in the **Federal Register**. 56 FR 8538. Each NPRM solicited comments on the definitions, standards, and procedures of the proposed rules. By the April 29, 1991, close of the comment period of the NPRM for title II, the Department had received 2,718 comments. Following the close of the comment period, the Department received an additional 222 comments.

In order to encourage public participation in the development of the Department's rules under the ADA, the Department held four public hearings. Hearings were held in Dallas, Texas on March 4–5, 1991, in Washington, DC on March 13–15, 1991, in San Francisco, California on March 18–19, 1991, and in Chicago, Illinois on March 27–28, 1991. At these hearings, 329 persons testified and 1,567 pages of testimony were compiled. Transcripts of the hearings were included in the Department's rulemaking docket.

The comments that the Department received occupy almost six feet of shelf space and contain over 10,000 pages. The Department received comments from individuals from all fifty States and the District of Columbia. Nearly 75% of the comments that the Department received came from individuals and from organizations representing the interests of persons with disabilities. The Department received 292 comments from entities covered by the ADA and trade associations representing businesses in the private sector, and 67 from government units, such as mayors' offices, public school districts, and various State agencies working with individuals with disabilities.

The Department received one comment from a consortium of 540 organizations representing a broad spectrum of persons with disabilities. In addition, at least another 25 commenters endorsed the position expressed by this consortium, or submitted identical comments on one or both proposed regulations.

An organization representing persons with hearing impairments submitted a large number of comments. This organization presented the Department with 479 individual comments, each providing in chart form a detailed representation of what type of auxiliary aid or service would be useful in the various categories of places of public accommodation.

The Department received a number of comments based on almost ten different form letters. For example, individuals who have a heightened sensitivity to a variety of chemical substances submitted 266 post cards detailing how exposure to various environmental conditions restricts their access to public and commercial buildings. Another large group of form letters came from groups affiliated with independent living centers.

The vast majority of the comments addressed the Department's proposal implementing title III. Slightly more than 100 comments addressed only issues presented in the proposed title II regulation.

The Department read and analyzed each comment that was submitted in a timely fashion. Transcripts of the four hearings were analyzed along with the written comments. The decisions that the Department has made in response to these comments, however, were not made on the basis of the number of commenters addressing any one point but on a thorough consideration of the merits of the points of view expressed in the comments. Copies of the written comments, including transcripts of the four hearings, will remain available for public inspection in room 854 of the HOLC Building, 320 First Street, NW., Washington, DC from 10 a.m. to 5 p.m., Monday through Friday, except for legal holidays, until August 30, 1991.

Overview of the Rule

The rule is organized into seven subparts. Subpart A, "General," includes the purpose and application sections, describes the relationship of the Act to other laws, and defines key terms used in the regulation. It also includes administrative requirements adapted from section 504 regulations for self-evaluations, notices, designation of responsible employees, and adoption of grievance procedures by public entities.

Subpart B, "General Requirements," contains the general prohibitions of discrimination based on the Act and the section 504 regulations. It also contains certain "miscellaneous" provisions derived from title V of the Act that involve issues such as retaliation and coercion against those asserting ADA rights, illegal use of drugs, and restrictions on smoking. These provisions are also included in the Department's proposed title III regulation, as is the general provision on maintenance of accessible features.

Subpart C addresses employment by public entities, which is also covered by title I of the Act. Subpart D, which is also based on the section 504 regulations, sets out the requirements for program accessibility in existing facilities and for new construction and alterations. Subpart E contains specific requirements relating to communications.

Subpart F establishes administrative procedures for enforcement of title II. As provided by section 203 of the Act, these are based on the procedures for enforcement of section 504, which, in turn, are based on the enforcement procedures for title VI of the Civil Rights Act of 1964 (42 U.S.C. 2000d to 2000d-4a). Subpart F also restates the provisions of title V of the ADA on attorneys fees, alternative means of dispute resolution, the effect of unavailability of technical assistance, and State immunity.

Subpart G designates the Federal agencies responsible for investigation of complaints under this part. It assigns enforcement responsibility for particular public entities, on the basis of their major functions, to eight Federal agencies that currently have substantial responsibilities for enforcing section 504. It provides that the Department of Justice would have enforcement responsibility for all State and local government entities not specifically assigned to other designated agencies, but that the Department may further assign specific functions to other agencies. The part would not, however, displace the existing enforcement authorities of the Federal funding agencies under section 504.

Regulatory Process Matters

This final rule has been reviewed by the Office of Management and Budget under Executive Order 12291. The Department is preparing a final regulatory impact analysis (RIA) of this rule and the Architectural and Transportation Barriers Compliance Board is preparing an RIA for its Americans with Disabilities Act Accessibility Guidelines for Buildings and Facilities (ADAAG) that are incorporated in appendix A of the Department's final rule implementing title III of the ADA. Draft copies of both preliminary RIAs are available for comment; the Department will provide copies of these documents to the public upon request. Commenters are urged to provide additional information as to the costs and benefits associated with this rule. This will facilitate the development of a final RIA by January 1, 1992.

The Department's RIA will evaluate the economic impact of the final rule. Included among those title II provisions that are likely to result in significant economic impact are the requirements for auxiliary aids, barrier removal in existing facilities, and readily accessible new construction and alterations. An analysis of these costs will be included in the RIA.

The Preliminary RIA prepared for the notice of proposed rulemaking contained all of the available information that would have been included in a preliminary regulatory flexibility analysis, had one been prepared under the Regulatory Flexibility Act, concerning the rule's impact on small entities. The final RIA will contain all of the information that is required in a final regulatory flexibility analysis and will serve as such an analysis. Moreover, the extensive notice and comment procedure followed by the Department in the promulgation of this rule, which included public hearings, dissemination of materials, and provision of speakers to affected groups, clearly provided any interested small entities with the notice and opportunity for comment provided for under the Regulatory Flexibility Act procedures.

The Department is preparing a statement of the federalism impact of the rule under Executive Order 12612 and will provide copies of this statement on request.

The reporting and recordkeeping requirements described in the rule are considered to be information collection requirements as that term is defined by the Office of Management and Budget in 5 CFR part 1320. Accordingly, those information collection requirements have been submitted to OMB for review pursuant to the Paperwork Reduction Act.

Section-by-Section Analysis

Subpart A—General

Section 35.101   Purpose

Section 35.101 states the purpose of the rule, which is to effectuate subtitle A of title II of the Americans with Disabilities Act of 1990 (the Act), which prohibits discrimination on the basis of disability by public entities. This part does not, however, apply to matters within the scope of the authority of the Secretary of Transportation under subtitle B of title II of the Act.

Section 35.102   Application

This provision specifies that, except as provided in paragraph (b), the regulation applies to all services, programs, and activities provided or made available by public entities, as that term is defined in § 35.104. Section 504 of the Rehabilitation Act of 1973 (29 U.S.C. 794), which prohibits discrimination on the basis of handicap in federally assisted programs and activities, already covers those programs and activities of public entities that receive Federal financial assistance. Title II of the ADA extends this prohibition of discrimination to include all services, programs, and activities provided or made available by State and local governments or any of their instrumentalities or agencies, regardless of the receipt of Federal financial assistance. Except as provided in § 35.134, this part does not apply to private entities.

The scope of title II's coverage of public entities is comparable to the coverage of Federal Executive agencies under the 1978 amendment to section 504, which extended section 504's application to all programs and activities "conducted by" Federal Executive agencies, in that title II applies to anything a public entity does. Title II coverage, however, is not limited to "Executive" agencies, but includes activities of the legislative and judicial branches of State and local governments. All governmental activities of public entities are covered, even if they are carried out by contractors. For example, a State is obligated by title II to ensure that the services, programs, and activities of a State park inn operated under contract by a private entity are in compliance with title II's requirements. The private entity operating the inn would also be subject to the obligations of public accommodations under title III of the Act and the Department's title III regulations at 28 CFR part 36.

Aside from employment, which is also covered by title I of the Act, there are two major categories of programs or activities covered by this regulation: those involving general public contact as part of ongoing operations of the entity and those directly administered by the entities for program beneficiaries and participants. Activities in the first category include communication with the public (telephone contacts, office walk-ins, or interviews) and the public's use of the entity's facilities. Activities in the second category include programs that provide State or local government services or benefits.

Paragraph (b) of § 35.102 explains to the extent that the public transportation services, programs, and activities of public entities are covered by subtitle B of title II of the Act, they are subject to the regulation of the Department of Transportation (DOT) at 49 CFR part 37, and are not covered by this part. The Department of Transportation's ADA regulation establishes specific requirements for construction of transportation facilities and acquisition of vehicles. Matters not covered by subtitle B, such as the provision of auxiliary aids, are covered by this rule. For example, activities that are covered by the Department of Transportation's regulation implementing subtitle B are not required to be included in the self-evaluation required by § 35.105. In addition, activities not specifically addressed by DOT's ADA regulation may be covered by DOT's regulation implementing section 504 for its federally assisted programs and activities at 49 CFR part 27. Like other programs of public entities that are also recipients of Federal financial assistance, those programs would be covered by both the section 504 regulation and this part. Although airports operated by public entities are not subject to DOT's ADA regulation, they are subject to subpart A of title II and to this rule.

Some commenters asked for clarification about the responsibilities of public school systems under section 504 and the ADA with respect to programs, services, and activities that are not covered by the Individuals with Disabilities Education Act (IDEA), including, for example, programs open to parents or to the public, graduation ceremonies, parent-teacher organization meetings, plays and other events open to the public, and adult education classes. Public school systems must comply with the ADA in all of their services, programs, or activities, including those that are open to parents or to the public. For instance, public school systems must provide program accessibility to parents and guardians with disabilities to these programs, activities, or services, and appropriate auxiliary aids and services whenever necessary to ensure effective communication, as long as the provision of the auxiliary aids results neither in an undue burden or in a fundamental alteration of the program.

Section 35.103   Relationship to Other Laws

Section 35.103 is derived from sections 501 (a) and (b) of the ADA. Paragraph (a) of this section provides that, except as otherwise specifically provided by this part, title II of the ADA is not intended to apply lesser standards than are required under title V of the Rehabilitation Act of 1973, as amended (29 U.S.C. 790–94), or the regulations implementing that title. The standards of title V of the Rehabilitation Act apply for purposes of the ADA to the extent that the ADA has not explicitly adopted a different standard than title V. Because title II of the ADA essentially extends the antidiscrimination prohibition embodied in section 504 to all actions of State and local governments, the standards adopted in this part are generally the same as those required under section 504 for federally assisted programs. Title II, however, also incorporates those provisions of titles I and III of the ADA that are not inconsistent with the regulations implementing section 504. Judiciary Committee report, H.R. Rep. No. 485, 101st Cong., 2d Sess., pt. 3, at 51 (1990) (hereinafter "Judiciary report") ; Education and Labor Committee report, H.R. Rep. No. 485, 101st Cong., 2d Sess., pt. 2, at 84 (1990) (hereinafter "Education and Labor report"). Therefore, this part also includes appropriate provisions derived from the regulations implementing those titles. The inclusion of specific language in this part, however, should not be interpreted as an indication that a requirement is not included under a regulation implementing section 504.

Paragraph (b) makes clear that Congress did not intend to displace any of the rights or remedies provided by other Federal laws (including section 504) or other State laws (including State common law) that provide greater or equal protection to individuals with disabilities. As discussed above, the standards adopted by title II of the ADA for State and local government services are generally the same as those required under section 504 for federally assisted programs and activities. Subpart F of the regulation establishes compliance procedures for processing complaints covered by both this part and section 504.

With respect to State law, a plaintiff may choose to pursue claims under a State law that does not confer greater substantive rights, or even confers fewer substantive rights, if the alleged violation is protected under the alternative law and the remedies are greater. For example, a person with a physical disability could seek damages under a State law that allows compensatory and punitive damages for discrimination on the basis of physical disability, but not on the basis of mental disability. In that situation, the State law would provide narrower coverage, by excluding mental disabilities, but broader remedies, and an individual covered by both laws could choose to bring an action under both laws. Moreover, State tort claims confer greater remedies and are not preempted by the ADA. A plaintiff may join a State tort claim to a case brought under the ADA. In such a case, the plaintiff must, of course, prove all the elements of the State tort claim in order to prevail under that cause of action.

Section 35.104   Definitions

"Act." The word "Act" is used in this part to refer to the Americans with Disabilities Act of 1990, Public Law 101–336, which is also referred to as the "ADA."

"Assistant Attorney General." The term "Assistant Attorney General" refers to the Assistant Attorney General of the Civil Rights Division of the Department of Justice.

"Auxiliary aids and services." Auxiliary aids and services include a wide range of services and devices for ensuring effective communication. The proposed definition in § 35.104 provided a list of examples of auxiliary aids and services that were taken from the definition of auxiliary aids and services in section 3(1) of the ADA and were supplemented by examples from regulations implementing section 504 in federally conducted programs (see 28 CFR 39.103).

A substantial number of commenters suggested that additional examples be added to this list. The Department has added several items to this list but wishes to clarify that the list is not an all-inclusive or exhaustive catalogue of possible or available auxiliary aids or services. It is not possible to provide an exhaustive list, and an attempt to do so would omit the new devices that will become available with emerging technology.

Subparagraph (1) lists several examples, which would be considered auxiliary aids and services to make aurally delivered materials available to individuals with hearing impairments.

The Department has changed the phrase used in the proposed rules, "orally delivered materials," to the statutory phrase, "aurally delivered materials," to track section 3 of the ADA and to include non-verbal sounds and alarms, and computer generated speech.

The Department has added videotext displays, transcription services, and closed and open captioning to the list of examples. Videotext displays have become an important means of accessing auditory communications through a public address system. Transcription services are used to relay aurally delivered material almost simultaneously in written form to persons who are deaf or hearing-impaired. This technology is often used at conferences, conventions, and hearings. While the proposed rule expressly included television decoder equipment as an auxiliary aid or service, it did not mention captioning itself. The final rule rectifies this omission by mentioning both closed and open captioning.

Several persons and organizations requested that the Department replace the term "telecommunications devices for deaf persons" or "TDD's" with the term "text telephone." The Department has declined to do so. The Department is aware that the Architectural and Transportation Barriers Compliance Board (ATBCB) has used the phrase "text telephone" in lieu of the statutory term "TDD" in its final accessibility guidelines. Title IV of the ADA, however, uses the term "Telecommunications Device for the Deaf" and the Department believes it would be inappropriate to abandon this statutory term at this time.

Several commenters urged the Department to include in the definition of "auxiliary aids and services" devices that are now available or that may become available with emerging technology. The Department declines to do so in the rule. The Department, however, emphasizes that, although the definition would include "state of the art" devices, public entities are not required to use the newest or most advanced technologies as long as the auxiliary aid or service that is selected affords effective communication.

Subparagraph (2) lists examples of aids and services for making visually delivered materials accessible to persons with visual impairments. Many commenters proposed additional examples, such as signage or mapping, audio description services, secondary auditory programs, telebraillers, and reading machines. While the Department declines to add these items to the list, they are auxiliary aids and

services and may be appropriate depending on the circumstances.

Subparagraph (3) refers to acquisition or modification of equipment or devices. Several commenters suggested the addition of current technological innovations in microelectronics and computerized control systems (e.g., voice recognition systems, automatic dialing telephones, and infrared elevator and light control systems) to the list of auxiliary aids. The Department interprets auxiliary aids and services as those aids and services designed to provide effective communications, i.e., making aurally and visually delivered information available to persons with hearing, speech, and vision impairments. Methods of making services, programs, or activities accessible to, or usable by, individuals with mobility or manual dexterity impairments are addressed by other sections of this part, including the provision for modifications in policies, practices, or procedures (§ 35.130 (b)(7)).

Paragraph (b)(4) deals with other similar services and actions. Several commenters asked for clarification that "similar services and actions" include retrieving items from shelves, assistance in reaching a marginally accessible seat, pushing a barrier aside in order to provide an accessible route, or assistance in removing a sweater or coat. While retrieving an item from a shelf might be an "auxiliary aid or service" for a blind person who could not locate the item without assistance, it might be a method of providing program access for a person using a wheelchair who could not reach the shelf, or a reasonable modification to a self-service policy for an individual who lacked the ability to grasp the item. As explained above, auxiliary aids and services are those aids and services required to provide effective communications. Other forms of assistance are more appropriately addressed by other provisions of the final rule.

"Complete complaint." "Complete complaint" is defined to include all the information necessary to enable the Federal agency designated under subpart G as responsible for investigation of a complaint to initiate its investigation.

"Current illegal use of drugs." The phrase "current illegal use of drugs" is used in § 35.131. Its meaning is discussed in the preamble for that section.

"Designated agency." The term "designated agency" is used to refer to the Federal agency designated under subpart G of this rule as responsible for carrying out the administrative enforcement responsibilities established by subpart F of the rule.

"Disability." The definition of the term "disability" is the same as the definition in the title III regulation codified at 28 CFR part 36. It is comparable to the definition of the term "individual with handicaps" in section 7(8) of the Rehabilitation Act and section 802(h) of the Fair Housing Act. The Education and Labor Committee report makes clear that the analysis of the term "individual with handicaps" by the Department of Health, Education, and Welfare (HEW) in its regulations implementing section 504 (42 FR 22685 (May 4, 1977)) and the analysis by the Department of Housing and Urban Development in its regulation implementing the Fair Housing Amendments Act of 1988 (54 FR 3232 (Jan. 23, 1989)) should also apply fully to the term "disability" (Education and Labor report at 50).

The use of the term "disability" instead of "handicap" and the term "individual with a disability" instead of "individual with handicaps" represents an effort by Congress to make use of up-to-date, currently accepted terminology. As with racial and ethnic epithets, the choice of terms to apply to a person with a disability is overlaid with stereotypes, patronizing attitudes, and other emotional connotations. Many individuals with disabilities, and organizations representing such individuals, object to the use of such terms as "handicapped person" or "the handicapped." In other recent legislation, Congress also recognized this shift in terminology, e.g., by changing the name of the National Council on the Handicapped to the National Council on Disability (Pub. L. 100-630).

In enacting the Americans with Disabilities Act, Congress concluded that it was important for the current legislation to use terminology most in line with the sensibilities of most Americans with disabilities. No change in definition or substance is intended nor should one be attributed to this change in phraseology.

The term "disability" means, with respect to an individual—

(A) A physical or mental impairment that substantially limits one or more of the major life activities of such individual;

(B) A record of such an impairment; or

(C) Being regarded as having such an impairment. If an individual meets any one of these three tests, he or she is considered to be an individual with a disability for purposes of coverage under the Americans with Disabilities Act.

Congress adopted this same basic definition of "disability," first used in the Rehabilitation Act of 1973 and in the Fair Housing Amendments Act of 1988, for a number of reasons. First, it has worked well since it was adopted in 1974. Second, it would not be possible to guarantee comprehensiveness by providing a list of specific disabilities, especially because new disorders may be recognized in the future, as they have since the definition was first established in 1974.

Test A—A physical or mental impairment that substantially limits one or more of the major life activities of such individual

Physical or mental impairment. Under the first test, an individual must have a physical or mental impairment. As explained in paragraph (1)(i) of the definition, "impairment" means any physiological disorder or condition, cosmetic disfigurement, or anatomical loss affecting one or more of the following body systems: neurological; musculoskeletal; special sense organs (which would include speech organs that are not respiratory such as vocal cords, soft palate, tongue, etc.); respiratory, including speech organs; cardiovascular; reproductive; digestive; genitourinary; hemic and lymphatic; skin; and endocrine. It also means any mental or psychological disorder, such as mental retardation, organic brain syndrome, emotional or mental illness, and specific learning disabilities. This list closely tracks the one used in the regulations for section 504 of the Rehabilitation Act of 1973 (see, *e.g.*, 45 CFR 84.3(j)(2)(i)).

Many commenters asked that "traumatic brain injury" be added to the list in paragraph (1)(i). Traumatic brain injury is already included because it is a physiological condition affecting one of the listed body systems, i.e., "neurological." Therefore, it was unnecessary to add the term to the regulation, which only provides representative examples of physiological disorders.

It is not possible to include a list of all the specific conditions, contagious and noncontagious diseases, or infections that would constitute a list of physical impairments because of the difficulty of ensuring the comprehensiveness of such a list, particularly in light of the fact that other conditions or disorders may be identified in the future. However, the list of examples in paragraph (1)(ii) of the definition includes: orthopedic, visual, speech and hearing impairments, cerebral palsy, epilepsy, muscular dystrophy, multiple sclerosis, cancer, heart disease, diabetes, mental

retardation, emotional illness, specific learning disabilities, HIV disease (symptomatic or asymptomatic), tuberculosis, drug addiction, and alcoholism. The phrase "symptomatic or asymptomatic" was inserted in the final rule after "HIV disease" in response to commenters who suggested the clarification was necessary.

The examples of "physical or mental impairments" in paragraph (1)(ii) are the same as those contained in many section 504 regulations, except for the addition of the phrase "contagious and noncontagious" to describe the types of diseases and conditions included, and the addition of "HIV disease (symptomatic or asymptomatic)" and "tuberculosis" to the list of examples. These additions are based on the committee reports, caselaw, and official legal opinions interpreting section 504. In *School Board of Nassau County* v. *Arline*, 480 U.S. 273 (1987), a case involving an individual with tuberculosis, the Supreme Court held that people with contagious diseases are entitled to the protections afforded by section 504. Following the *Arline* decision, this Department's Office of Legal Counsel issued a legal opinion that concluded that symptomatic HIV disease is an impairment that substantially limits a major life activity; therefore it has been included in the definition of disability under this part. The opinion also concluded that asymptomatic HIV disease is an impairment that substantially limits a major life activity, either because of its actual effect on the individual with HIV disease or because the reactions of other people to individuals with HIV disease cause such individuals to be treated as though they are disabled. See Memorandum from Douglas W. Kmiec, Acting Assistant Attorney General, Office of Legal Counsel, Department of Justice, to Arthur B. Culvahouse, Jr., Counsel to the President (Sept. 27, 1988), reprinted in Hearings on S. 933, the Americans with Disabilities Act, Before the Subcomm. on the Handicapped of the Senate Comm. on Labor and Human Resources, 101st. Cong., 1st Sess. 346 (1989).

Paragraph (1)(iii) states that the phrase "physical or mental impairment" does not include homosexuality or bisexuality. These conditions were never considered impairments under other Federal disability laws. Section 511(a) of the statute makes clear that they are likewise not to be considered impairments under the Americans with Disabilities Act.

Physical or mental impairment does not include simple physical characteristics, such as blue eyes or black hair. Nor does it include environmental, cultural, economic, or other disadvantages, such as having a prison record, or being poor. Nor is age a disability. Similarly, the definition does not include common personality traits such as poor judgment or a quick temper where these are not symptoms of a mental or psychological disorder. However, a person who has these characteristics and also has a physical or mental impairment may be considered as having a disability for purposes of the Americans with Disabilities Act based on the impairment.

Substantial Limitation of a Major Life Activity. Under Test A, the impairment must be one that "substantially limits a major life activity." Major life activities include such things as caring for one's self, performing manual tasks, walking, seeing, hearing, speaking, breathing, learning, and working.

For example, a person who is paraplegic is substantially limited in the major life activity of walking, a person who is blind is substantially limited in the major life activity of seeing, and a person who is mentally retarded is substantially limited in the major life activity of learning. A person with traumatic brain injury is substantially limited in the major life activities of caring for one's self, learning, and working because of memory deficit, confusion, contextual difficulties, and inability to reason appropriately.

A person is considered an individual with a disability for purposes of Test A, the first prong of the definition, when the individual's important life activities are restricted as to the conditions, manner, or duration under which they can be performed in comparison to most people. A person with a minor, trivial impairment, such as a simple infected finger, is not impaired in a major life activity. A person who can walk for 10 miles continuously is not substantially limited in walking merely because, on the eleventh mile, he or she begins to experience pain, because most people would not be able to walk eleven miles without experiencing some discomfort.

The Department received many comments on the proposed rule's inclusion of the word "temporary" in the definition of "disability." The preamble indicated that impairments are not necessarily excluded from the definition of "disability" simply because they are temporary, but that the duration, or expected duration, of an impairment is one factor that may properly be considered in determining whether the impairment substantially limits a major life activity. The preamble recognized,

however, that temporary impairments, such as a broken leg, are not commonly regarded as disabilities, and only in rare circumstances would the degree of the limitation and its expected duration be substantial. Nevertheless, many commenters objected to inclusion of the word "temporary" both because it is not in the statute and because it is not contained in the definition of "disability" set forth in the title I regulations of the Equal Employment Opportunity Commission (EEOC). The word "temporary" has been deleted from the final rule to conform with the statutory language.

The question of whether a temporary impairment is a disability must be resolved on a case-by-case basis, taking into consideration both the duration (or expected duration) of the impairment and the extent to which it actually limits a major life activity of the affected individual.

The question of whether a person has a disability should be assessed without regard to the availability of mitigating measures, such as reasonable modification or auxiliary aids and services. For example, a person with hearing loss is substantially limited in the major life activity of hearing, even though the loss may be improved through the use of a hearing aid. Likewise, persons with impairments, such as epilepsy or diabetes, that substantially limit a major life activity, are covered under the first prong of the definition of disability, even if the effects of the impairment are controlled by medication.

Many commenters asked that environmental illness (also known as multiple chemical sensitivity) as well as allergy to cigarette smoke be recognized as disabilities. The Department, however, declines to state categorically that these types of allergies or sensitivities are disabilities, because the determination as to whether an impairment is a disability depends on whether, given the particular circumstances at issue, the impairment substantially limits one or more major life activities (or has a history of, or is regarded as having such an effect).

Sometimes respiratory or neurological functioning is so severely affected that an individual will satisfy the requirements to be considered disabled under the regulation. Such an individual would be entitled to all of the protections afforded by the Act and this part. In other cases, individuals may be sensitive to environmental elements or to smoke but their sensitivity will not rise to the level needed to constitute a disability. For example, their major life activity of breathing may be somewhat,

but not substantially, impaired. In such circumstances, the individuals are not disabled and are not entitled to the protections of the statute despite their sensitivity to environmental agents.

In sum, the determination as to whether allergies to cigarette smoke, or allergies or sensitivities characterized by the commenters as environmental illness are disabilities covered by the regulation must be made using the same case-by-case analysis that is applied to all other physical or mental impairments. Moreover, the addition of specific regulatory provisions relating to environmental illness in the final rule would be inappropriate at this time pending future consideration of the issue by the Architectural and Transportation Barriers Compliance Board, the Environmental Protection Agency, and the Occupational Safety and Health Administration of the Department of Labor.

Test B—A record of such an impairment

This test is intended to cover those who have a record of an impairment. As explained in paragraph (3) of the rule's definition of disability, this includes a person who has a history of an impairment that substantially limited a major life activity, such as someone who has recovered from an impairment. It also includes persons who have been misclassified as having an impairment.

This provision is included in the definition in part to protect individuals who have recovered from a physical or mental impairment that previously substantially limited them in a major life activity. Discrimination on the basis of such a past impairment is prohibited. Frequently occurring examples of the first group (those who have a history of an impairment) are persons with histories of mental or emotional illness, heart disease, or cancer; examples of the second group (those who have been misclassified as having an impairment) are persons who have been misclassified as having mental retardation or mental illness.

Test C—Being regarded as having such an impairment

This test, as contained in paragraph (4) of the definition, is intended to cover persons who are treated by a public entity as having a physical or mental impairment that substantially limits a major life activity. It applies when a person is treated as if he or she has an impairment that substantially limits a major life activity, regardless of whether that person has an impairment.

The Americans with Disabilities Act uses the same "regarded as" test set forth in the regulations implementing section 504 of the Rehabilitation Act. See, e.g., 28 CFR 42.540(k)(2)(iv), which provides:

(iv) "Is regarded as having an impairment" means (A) Has a physical or mental impairment that does not substantially limit major life activities but that is treated by a recipient as constituting such a limitation; (B) Has a physical or mental impairment that substantially limits major life activities only as a result of the attitudes of others toward such impairment; or (C) Has none of the impairments defined in paragraph (k)(2)(i) of this section but is treated by a recipient as having such an impairment.

The perception of the covered entity is a key element of this test. A person who perceives himself or herself to have an impairment, but does not have an impairment, and is not treated as if he or she has an impairment, is not protected under this test.

A person would be covered under this test if a public entity refused to serve the person because it perceived that the person had an impairment that limited his or her enjoyment of the goods or services being offered.

For example, persons with severe burns often encounter discrimination in community activities, resulting in substantial limitation of major life activities. These persons would be covered under this test based on the attitudes of others towards the impairment, even if they did not view themselves as "impaired."

The rationale for this third test, as used in the Rehabilitation Act of 1973, was articulated by the Supreme Court in *Arline*, 480 U.S. 273 (1987). The Court noted that although an individual may have an impairment that does not in fact substantially limit a major life activity, the reaction of others may prove just as disabling. "Such an impairment might not diminish a person's physical or mental capabilities, but could nevertheless substantially limit that person's ability to work as a result of the negative reactions of others to the impairment." *Id.* at 283. The Court concluded that, by including this test in the Rehabilitation Act's definition, "Congress acknowledged that society's accumulated myths and fears about disability and diseases are as handicapping as are the physical limitations that flow from actual impairment." *Id.* at 284.

Thus, a person who is denied services or benefits by a public entity because of myths, fears, and stereotypes associated with disabilities would be covered under this third test whether or not the person's physical or mental condition would be considered a disability under the first or second test in the definition.

If a person is refused admittance on the basis of an actual or perceived physical or mental condition, and the public entity can articulate no legitimate reason for the refusal (such as failure to meet eligibility criteria), a perceived concern about admitting persons with disabilities could be inferred and the individual would qualify for coverage under the "regarded as" test. A person who is covered because of being regarded as having an impairment is not required to show that the public entity's perception is inaccurate (e.g., that he will be accepted by others) in order to receive benefits from the public entity.

Paragraph (5) of the definition lists certain conditions that are not included within the definition of "disability." The excluded conditions are: Transvestism, transsexualism, pedophilia, exhibitionism, voyeurism, gender identity disorders not resulting from physical impairments, other sexual behavior disorders, compulsive gambling, kleptomania, pyromania, and psychoactive substance use disorders resulting from current illegal use of drugs. Unlike homosexuality and bisexuality, which are not considered impairments under either section 504 or the Americans with Disabilities Act (see the definition of "disability," paragraph (1)(iv)), the conditions listed in paragraph (5), except for transvestism, are not necessarily excluded as impairments under section 504. (Transvestism was excluded from the definition of disability for section 504 by the Fair Housing Amendments Act of 1988, Pub. L. 100–430, section 6(b)).

"Drug." The definition of the term "drug" is taken from section 510(d)(2) of the ADA.

"Facility." "Facility" means all or any portion of buildings, structures, sites, complexes, equipment, rolling stock or other conveyances, roads, walks, passageways, parking lots, or other real or personal property, including the site where the building, property, structure, or equipment is located. It includes both indoor and outdoor areas where human-constructed improvements, structures, equipment, or property have been added to the natural environment.

Commenters raised questions about the applicability of this part to activities operated in mobile facilities, such as bookmobiles or mobile health screening units. Such activities would be covered by the requirement for program accessibility in § 35.150, and would be included in the definition of "facility" as "other real or personal property," although standards for new construction and alterations of such facilities are not yet included in the accessibility standards adopted by § 35.151. Sections

35.150 and 35.151 specifically address the obligations of public entities to ensure accessibility by providing curb ramps at pedestrian walkways.

"Historic preservation programs" and "Historic properties" are defined in order to aid in the interpretation of §§ 35.150 (a)(2) and (b)(2), which relate to accessibility of historic preservation programs, and § 35.151(d), which relates to the alteration of historic properties.

"Illegal use of drugs." The definition of "illegal use of drugs" is taken from section 510(d)(1) of the Act and clarifies that the term includes the illegal use of one or more drugs.

"Individual with a disability" means a person who has a disability but does not include an individual who is currently illegally using drugs, when the public entity acts on the basis of such use. The phrase "current illegal use of drugs" is explained in § 35.131.

"Public entity." The term "public entity" is defined in accordance with section 201(1) of the ADA as any State or local government; any department, agency, special purpose district, or other instrumentality of a State or States or local government; or the National Railroad Passenger Corporation, and any commuter authority (as defined in section 103(8) of the Rail Passenger Service Act).

"Qualified individual with a disability." The definition of "qualified individual with a disability" is taken from section 201(2) of the Act, which is derived from the definition of "qualified handicapped person" in the Department of Health and Human Services' regulation implementing section 504 (45 CFR § 84.3(k)). It combines the definition at 45 CFR 84.3(k)(1) for employment ("a handicapped person who, with reasonable accommodation, can perform the essential functions of the job in question") with the definition for other services at 45 CFR 84.3(k)(4) ("a handicapped person who meets the essential eligibility requirements for the receipt of such services").

Some commenters requested clarification of the term "essential eligibility requirements." Because of the variety of situations in which an individual's qualifications will be at issue, it is not possible to include more specific criteria in the definition. The "essential eligibility requirements" for participation in some activities covered under this part may be minimal. For example, most public entities provide information about their operations as a public service to anyone who requests it. In such situations, the only "eligibility requirement" for receipt of such information would be the request for it.

Where such information is provided by telephone, even the ability to use a voice telephone is not an "essential eligibility requirement," because § 35.161 requires a public entity to provide equally effective telecommunication systems for individuals with impaired hearing or speech.

For other activities, identification of the "essential eligibility requirements" may be more complex. Where questions of safety are involved, the principles established in § 36.208 of the Department's regulation implementing title III of the ADA, to be codified at 28 CFR, part 36, will be applicable. That section implements section 302(b)(3) of the Act, which provides that a public accommodation is not required to permit an individual to participate in or benefit from the goods, services, facilities, privileges, advantages and accommodations of the public accommodation, if that individual poses a direct threat to the health or safety of others.

A "direct threat" is a significant risk to the health or safety of others that cannot be eliminated by a modification of policies, practices, or procedures, or by the provision of auxiliary aids or services. In *School Board of Nassau County* v. *Arline*, 480 U.S. 273 (1987), the Supreme Court recognized that there is a need to balance the interests of people with disabilities against legitimate concerns for public safety. Although persons with disabilities are generally entitled to the protection of this part, a person who poses a significant risk to others will not be "qualified," if reasonable modifications to the public entity's policies, practices, or procedures will not eliminate that risk.

The determination that a person poses a direct threat to the health or safety of others may not be based on generalizations or stereotypes about the effects of a particular disability. It must be based on an individualized assessment, based on reasonable judgment that relies on current medical evidence or on the best available objective evidence, to determine: the nature, duration, and severity of the risk; the probability that the potential injury will actually occur; and whether reasonable modifications of policies, practices, or procedures will mitigate the risk. This is the test established by the Supreme Court in *Arline*. Such an inquiry is essential if the law is to achieve its goal of protecting disabled individuals from discrimination based on prejudice, stereotypes, or unfounded fear, while giving appropriate weight to legitimate concerns, such as the need to avoid exposing others to significant

health and safety risks. Making this assessment will not usually require the services of a physician. Sources for medical knowledge include guidance from public health authorities, such as the U.S. Public Health Service, the Centers for Disease Control, and the National Institutes of Health, including the National Institute of Mental Health.

"Qualified interpreter." The Department received substantial comment regarding the lack of a definition of "qualified interpreter." The proposed rule defined auxiliary aids and services to include the statutory term, "qualified interpreters" (§ 35.104), but did not define it. Section 35.160 requires the use of auxiliary aids including qualified interpreters and commenters stated that a lack of guidance on what the term means would create confusion among those trying to secure interpreting services and often result in less than effective communication.

Many commenters were concerned that, without clear guidance on the issue of "qualified" interpreter, the rule would be interpreted to mean "available, rather than qualified" interpreters. Some claimed that few public entities would understand the difference between a qualified interpreter and a person who simply knows a few signs or how to fingerspell.

In order to clarify what is meant by "qualified interpreter" the Department has added a definition of the term to the final rule. A qualified interpreter means an interpreter who is able to interpret effectively, accurately, and impartially both receptively and expressively, using any necessary specialized vocabulary. This definition focuses on the actual ability of the interpreter in a particular interpreting context to facilitate effective communication between the public entity and the individual with disabilities.

Public comment also revealed that public entities have at times asked persons who are deaf to provide family members or friends to interpret. In certain circumstances, notwithstanding that the family member of friend is able to interpret or is a certified interpreter, the family member or friend may not be qualified to render the necessary interpretation because of factors such as emotional or personal involvement or considerations of confidentiality that may adversely affect the ability to interpret effectively, accurately, and impartially."

The definition of "qualified interpreter" in this rule does not invalidate or limit standards for interpreting services of any State or local law that are equal to or more

stringent than those imposed by this definition. For instance, the definition would not supersede any requirement of State law for use of a certified interpreter in court proceedings.

"Section 504." The Department added a definition of "section 504" because the term is used extensively in subpart F of this part.

"State." The definition of "State" is identical to the statutory definition in section 3(3) of the ADA.

Section 35.105   Self-evaluation

Section 35.105 establishes a requirement, based on the section 504 regulations for federally assisted and federally conducted programs, that a public entity evaluate its current policies and practices to identify and correct any that are not consistent with the requirements of this part. As noted in the discussion of § 35.102, activities covered by the Department of Transportation's regulation implementing subtitle B of title II are not required to be included in the self-evaluation required by this section.

Experience has demonstrated the self-evaluation process to be a valuable means of establishing a working relationship with individuals with disabilities, which has promoted both effective and efficient implementation of section 504. The Department expects that it will likewise be useful to public entities newly covered by the ADA.

All public entities are required to do a self-evaluation. However, only those that employ 50 or more persons are required to maintain the self-evaluation on file and make it available for public inspection for three years. The number 50 was derived from the Department of Justice's section 504 regulations for federally assisted programs, 28 CFR 42.505(c). The Department received comments critical of this limitation, some suggesting the requirement apply to all public entities and others suggesting that the number be changed from 50 to 15. The final rule has not been changed. Although many regulations implementing section 504 for federally assisted programs do use 15 employees as the cut-off for this record-keeping requirement, the Department believes that it would be inappropriate to extend it to those smaller public entities covered by this regulation that do not receive Federal financial assistance. This approach has the benefit of minimizing paperwork burdens on small entities.

Paragraph (d) provides that the self-evaluation required by this section shall apply only to programs not subject to section 504 or those policies and practices, such as those involving communications access, that have not already been included in a self-evaluation required under an existing regulation implementing section 504. Because most self-evaluations were done from five to twelve years ago, however, the Department expects that a great many public entities will be reexamining all of their policies and programs. Programs and functions may have changed, and actions that were supposed to have been taken to comply with section 504 may not have been fully implemented or may no longer be effective. In addition, there have been statutory amendments to section 504 which have changed the coverage of section 504, particularly the Civil Rights Restoration Act of 1987, Public Law No. 100-259, 102 Stat. 28 (1988), which broadened the definition of a covered program or activity."

Several commenters suggested that the Department clarify public entities' liability during the one-year period for compliance with the self-evaluation requirement. The self-evaluation requirement does not stay the effective date of the statute nor of this part. Public entities are, therefore, not shielded from discrimination claims during that time.

Other commenters suggested that the rule require that every self-evaluation include an examination of training efforts to assure that individuals with disabilities are not subjected to discrimination because of insensitivity, particularly in the law enforcement area. Although the Department has not added such a specific requirement to the rule, it would be appropriate for public entities to evaluate training efforts because, in many cases, lack of training leads to discriminatory practices, even when the policies in place are nondiscriminatory.

Section 35.106 Notice

Section 35.106 requires a public entity to disseminate sufficient information to applicants, participants, beneficiaries; and other interested persons to inform them of the rights and protections afforded by the ADA and this regulation. Methods of providing this information include, for example, the publication of information in handbooks, manuals, and pamphlets that are distributed to the public to describe a public entity's programs and activities; the display of informative posters in service centers and other public places; or the broadcast of information by television or radio. In providing the notice, a public entity must comply with the requirements for effective communication in § 35.160. The

preamble to that section gives guidance on how to effectively communicate with individuals with disabilities.

Section 35.107 Designation of Responsible Employee and Adoption of Grievance Procedures

Consistent with § 35.105, self-evaluation, the final rule requires that public entities with 50 or more employees designate a responsible employee and adopt grievance procedures. Most of the commenters who suggested that the requirement that self-evaluation be maintained on file for three years not be limited to those employing 50 or more persons made a similar suggestion concerning § 35.107. Commenters recommended either that all public entities be subject to § 35.107, or that "50 or more persons" be changed to "15 or more persons." As explained in the discussion of § 35.105, the Department has not adopted this suggestion.

The requirement for designation of an employee responsible for coordination of efforts to carry out responsibilities under this part is derived from the HEW regulation implementing section 504 in federally assisted programs. The requirement for designation of a particular employee and dissemination of information about how to locate that employee helps to ensure that individuals dealing with large agencies are able to easily find a responsible person who is familiar with the requirements of the Act and this part and can communicate those requirements to other individuals in the agency who may be unaware of their responsibilities. This paragraph in no way limits a public entity's obligation to ensure that all of its employees comply with the requirements of this part, but it ensures that any failure by individual employees can be promptly corrected by the designated employee.

Section 35.107(b) requires public entities with 50 or more employees to establish grievance procedures for resolving complaints of violations of this part. Similar requirements are found in the section 504 regulations for federally assisted programs (see, e.g., 45 CFR 84.7(b)). The rule, like the regulations for federally assisted programs, provides for investigation and resolution of complaints by a Federal enforcement agency. It is the view of the Department that public entities subject to this part should be required to establish a mechanism for resolution of complaints at the local level without requiring the complainant to resort to the Federal complaint procedures established under subpart F. Complainants would not, however, be required to exhaust the

public entity's grievance procedures before filing a complaint under subpart F. Delay in filing the complaint at the Federal level caused by pursuit of the remedies available under the grievance procedure would generally be considered good cause for extending the time allowed for filing under § 35.170(b).

Subpart B—General Requirements

Section 35.130 General Prohibitions Against Discrimination

The general prohibitions against discrimination in the rule are generally based on the prohibitions in existing regulations implementing section 504 and, therefore, are already familiar to State and local entities covered by section 504. In addition, § 35.130 includes a number of provisions derived from title III of the Act that are implicit to a certain degree in the requirements of regulations implementing section 504.

Several commenters suggested that this part should include the section of the proposed title III regulation that implemented section 309 of the Act, which requires that courses and examinations related to applications, licensing, certification, or credentialing be provided in an accessible place and manner or that alternative accessible arrangements be made. The Department has not adopted this suggestion. The requirements of this part, including the general prohibitions of discrimination in this section, the program access requirements of subpart D, and the communications requirements of subpart E, apply to courses and examinations provided by public entities. The Department considers these requirements to be sufficient to ensure that courses and examinations administered by public entities meet the requirements of section 309. For example, a public entity offering an examination must ensure that modifications of policies, practices, or procedures or the provision of auxiliary aids and services furnish the individual with a disability an equal opportunity to demonstrate his or her knowledge or ability. Also, any examination specially designed for individuals with disabilities must be offered as often and in as timely a manner as are other examinations. Further, under this part, courses and examinations must be offered in the most integrated setting appropriate. The analysis of § 35.130(d) is relevant to this determination.

A number of commenters asked that the regulation be amended to require training of law enforcement personnel to recognize the difference between criminal activity and the effects of seizures or other disabilities such as mental retardation, cerebral palsy, traumatic brain injury, mental illness, or deafness. Several disabled commenters gave personal statements about the abuse they had received at the hands of law enforcement personnel. Two organizations that commented cited the Judiciary report at 50 as authority to require law enforcement training.

The Department has not added such a training requirement to the regulation. Discriminatory arrests and brutal treatment are already unlawful police activities. The general regulatory obligation to modify policies, practices, or procedures requires law enforcement to make changes in policies that result in discriminatory arrests or abuse of individuals with disabilities. Under this section law enforcement personnel would be required to make appropriate efforts to determine whether perceived strange or disruptive behavior or unconsciousness is the result of a disability. The Department notes that a number of States have attempted to address the problem of arresting disabled persons for noncriminal conduct resulting from their disability through adoption of the Uniform Duties to Disabled Persons Act, and encourages other jurisdictions to consider that approach.

Paragraph (a) restates the nondiscrimination mandate of section 202 of the ADA. The remaining paragraphs in § 35.130 establish the general principles for analyzing whether any particular action of the public entity violates this mandate.

Paragraph (b) prohibits overt denials of equal treatment of individuals with disabilities. A public entity may not refuse to provide an individual with a disability with an equal opportunity to participate in or benefit from its program simply because the person has a disability.

Paragraph (b)(1)(i) provides that it is discriminatory to deny a person with a disability the right to participate in or benefit from the aid, benefit, or service provided by a public entity. Paragraph (b)(1)(ii) provides that the aids, benefits, and services provided to persons with disabilities must be equal to those provided to others, and paragraph (b)(1)(iii) requires that the aids, benefits, or services provided to individuals with disabilities must be as effective in affording equal opportunity to obtain the same result, to gain the same benefit, or to reach the same level of achievement as those provided to others. These paragraphs are taken from the regulations implementing section 504 and simply restate principles long established under section 504.

Paragraph (b)(1)(iv) permits the public entity to develop separate or different aids, benefits, or services when necessary to provide individuals with disabilities with an equal opportunity to participate in or benefit from the public entity's programs or activities, but only when necessary to ensure that the aids, benefits, or services are as effective as those provided to others. Paragraph (b)(1)(iv) must be read in conjunction with paragraphs (b)(2), (d), and (e). Even when separate or different aids, benefits, or services would be more effective, paragraph (b)(2) provides that a qualified individual with a disability still has the right to choose to participate in the program that is not designed to accommodate individuals with disabilities. Paragraph (d) requires that a public entity administer services, programs, and activities in the most integrated setting appropriate to the needs of qualified individuals with disabilities.

Paragraph (b)(2) specifies that, notwithstanding the existence of separate or different programs or activities provided in accordance with this section, an individual with a disability shall not be denied the opportunity to participate in such programs or activities that are not separate or different. Paragraph (e), which is derived from section 501(d) of the Americans with Disabilities Act, states that nothing in this part shall be construed to require an individual with a disability to accept an accommodation, aid, service, opportunity, or benefit that he or she chooses not to accept.

Taken together, these provisions are intended to prohibit exclusion and segregation of individuals with disabilities and the denial of equal opportunities enjoyed by others, based on, among other things, presumptions, patronizing attitudes, fears, and stereotypes about individuals with disabilities. Consistent with these standards, public entities are required to ensure that their actions are based on facts applicable to individuals and not on presumptions as to what a class of individuals with disabilities can or cannot do.

Integration is fundamental to the purposes of the Americans with Disabilities Act. Provision of segregated accommodations and services relegates persons with disabilities to second-class status. For example, it would be a violation of this provision to require persons with disabilities to eat in the back room of a government cafeteria or to refuse to allow a person with a disability the full use of recreation or exercise facilities because of

stereotypes about the person's ability to participate.

Many commenters objected to proposed paragraphs (b)(1)(iv) and (d) as allowing continued segregation of individuals with disabilities. The Department recognizes that promoting integration of individuals with disabilities into the mainstream of society is an important objective of the ADA and agrees that, in most instances, separate programs for individuals with disabilities will not be permitted. Nevertheless, section 504 does permit separate programs in limited circumstances, and Congress clearly intended the regulations issued under title II to adopt the standards of section 504. Furthermore, Congress included authority for separate programs in the specific requirements of title III of the Act. Section 302(b)(1)(A)(iii) of the Act provides for separate benefits in language similar to that in § 35.130(b)(1)(iv), and section 302(b)(1)(B) includes the same requirement for "the most integrated setting appropriate" as in § 35.130(d).

Even when separate programs are permitted, individuals with disabilities cannot be denied the opportunity to participate in programs that are not separate or different. This is an important and overarching principle of the Americans with Disabilities Act. Separate, special, or different programs that are designed to provide a benefit to persons with disabilities cannot be used to restrict the participation of persons with disabilities in general, integrated activities.

For example, a person who is blind may wish to decline participating in a special museum tour that allows persons to touch sculptures in an exhibit and instead tour the exhibit at his or her own pace with the museum's recorded tour. It is not the intent of this section to require the person who is blind to avail himself or herself of the special tour. Modified participation for persons with disabilities must be a choice, not a requirement.

In addition, it would not be a violation of this section for a public entity to offer recreational programs specially designed for children with mobility impairments. However, it would be a violation of this section if the entity then excluded these children from other recreational services for which they are qualified to participate when these services are made available to nondisabled children, or if the entity required children with disabilities to attend only designated programs.

Many commenters asked that the Department clarify a public entity's obligations within the integrated program when it offers a separate program but an individual with a disability chooses not to participate in the separate program. It is impossible to make a blanket statement as to what level of auxiliary aids or modifications would be required in the integrated program. Rather, each situation must be assessed individually. The starting point is to question whether the separate program is in fact necessary or appropriate for the individual. Assuming the separate program would be appropriate for a particular individual, the extent to which that individual must be provided with modifications in the integrated program will depend not only on what the individual needs but also on the limitations and defenses of this part. For example, it may constitute an undue burden for a public accommodation, which provides a full-time interpreter in its special guided tour for individuals with hearing impairments, to hire an additional interpreter for those individuals who choose to attend the integrated program. The Department cannot identify categorically the level of assistance or aid required in the integrated program.

Paragraph (b)(1)(v) provides that a public entity may not aid or perpetuate discrimination against a qualified individual with a disability by providing significant assistance to an agency, organization, or person that discriminates on the basis of disability in providing any aid, benefit, or service to beneficiaries of the public entity's program. This paragraph is taken from the regulations implementing section 504 for federally assisted programs.

Paragraph (b)(1)(vi) prohibits the public entity from denying a qualified individual with a disability the opportunity to participate as a member of a planning or advisory board.

Paragraph (b)(1)(vii) prohibits the public entity from limiting a qualified individual with a disability in the enjoyment of any right, privilege, advantage, or opportunity enjoyed by others receiving any aid, benefit, or service.

Paragraph (b)(3) prohibits the public entity from utilizing criteria or methods of administration that deny individuals with disabilities access to the public entity's services, programs, and activities or that perpetuate the discrimination of another public entity, if both public entities are subject to common administrative control or are agencies of the same State. The phrase "criteria or methods of administration" refers to official written policies of the public entity and to the actual practices of the public entity. This paragraph

prohibits both blatantly exclusionary policies or practices and nonessential policies and practices that are neutral on their face, but deny individuals with disabilities an effective opportunity to participate. This standard is consistent with the interpretation of section 504 by the U.S. Supreme Court in *Alexander* v. *Choate*, 469 U.S. 287 (1985). The Court in *Choate* explained that members of Congress made numerous statements during passage of section 504 regarding eliminating architectural barriers, providing access to transportation, and eliminating discriminatory effects of job qualification procedures. The Court then noted: "These statements would ring hollow if the resulting legislation could not rectify the harms resulting from action that discriminated by effect as well as by design." *Id.* at 297 (footnote omitted).

Paragraph (b)(4) specifically applies the prohibition enunciated in § 35.130(b)(3) to the process of selecting sites for construction of new facilities or selecting existing facilities to be used by the public entity. Paragraph (b)(4) does not apply to construction of additional buildings at an existing site.

Paragraph (b)(5) prohibits the public entity, in the selection of procurement contractors, from using criteria that subject qualified individuals with disabilities to discrimination on the basis of disability.

Paragraph (b)(6) prohibits the public entity from discriminating against qualified individuals with disabilities on the basis of disability in the granting of licenses or certification. A person is a "qualified individual with a disability" with respect to licensing or certification if he or she can meet the essential eligibility requirements for receiving the license or certification (see § 35.104).

A number of commenters were troubled by the phrase "essential eligibility requirements" as applied to State licensing requirements, especially those for health care professions. Because of the variety of types of programs to which the definition of "qualified individual with a disability" applies, it is not possible to use more specific language in the definition. The phrase "essential eligibility requirements," however, is taken from the definitions in the regulations implementing section 504, so caselaw under section 504 will be applicable to its interpretation. In *Southeastern Community College* v. *Davis*, 442 U.S. 397, for example, the Supreme Court held that section 504 does not require an institution to "lower or effect substantial modifications of standards to accommodate a handicapped person," 442 U.S. at 413, and that the school had

established that the plaintiff was not "qualified" because she was not able to "serve the nursing profession in all customary ways," *id.* Whether a particular requirement is "essential" will, of course, depend on the facts of the particular case.

In addition, the public entity may not establish requirements for the programs or activities of licensees or certified entities that subject qualified individuals with disabilities to discrimination on the basis of disability. For example, the public entity must comply with this requirement when establishing safety standards for the operations of licensees. In that case the public entity must ensure that standards that it promulgates do not discriminate against the employment of qualified individuals with disabilities in an impermissible manner.

Paragraph (b)(6) does not extend the requirements of the Act or this part directly to the programs or activities of licensees or certified entities themselves. The programs or activities of licensees or certified entities are not themselves programs or activities of the public entity merely by virtue of the license or certificate.

Paragraph (b)(7) is a specific application of the requirement under the general prohibitions of discrimination that public entities make reasonable modifications in policies, practices, or procedures where necessary to avoid discrimination on the basis of disability. Section 302(b)(2)(A)(ii) of the ADA sets out this requirement specifically for public accommodations covered by title III of the Act, and the House Judiciary Committee Report directs the Attorney General to include those specific requirements in the title II regulation to the extent that they do not conflict with the regulations implementing section 504. Judiciary report at 52.

Paragraph (b)(8), a new paragraph not contained in the proposed rule, prohibits the imposition or application of eligibility criteria that screen out or tend to screen out an individual with a disability or any class of individuals with disabilities from fully and equally enjoying any service, program, or activity, unless such criteria can be shown to be necessary for the provision of the service, program, or activity being offered. This prohibition is also a specific application of the general prohibitions of discrimination and is based on section 302(b)(2)(A)(i) of the ADA. It prohibits overt denials of equal treatment of individuals with disabilities, or establishment of exclusive or segregative criteria that would bar individuals with disabilities from participation in services, benefits, or activities.

Paragraph (b)(8) also prohibits policies that unnecessarily impose requirements or burdens on individuals with disabilities that are not placed on others. For example, public entities may not require that a qualified individual with a disability be accompanied by an attendant. A public entity is not, however, required to provide attendant care, or assistance in toileting, eating, or dressing to individuals with disabilities, except in special circumstances, such as where the individual is an inmate of a custodial or correctional institution.

In addition, paragraph (b)(8) prohibits the imposition of criteria that "tend to" screen out an individual with a disability. This concept, which is derived from current regulations under section 504 (see, e.g., 45 CFR 84.13), makes it discriminatory to impose policies or criteria that, while not creating a direct bar to individuals with disabilities, indirectly prevent or limit their ability to participate. For example, requiring presentation of a driver's license as the sole means of identification for purposes of paying by check would violate this section in situations where, for example, individuals with severe vision impairments or developmental disabilities are ineligible to receive a driver's license and the use of an alternative means of identification, such as another photo I.D. or credit card, is feasible.

A public entity may, however, impose neutral rules and criteria that screen out, or tend to screen out, individuals with disabilities if the criteria are necessary for the safe operation of the program in question. Examples of safety qualifications that would be justifiable in appropriate circumstances would include eligibility requirements for drivers' licenses, or a requirement that all participants in a recreational rafting expedition be able to meet a necessary level of swimming proficiency. Safety requirements must be based on actual risks and not on speculation, stereotypes, or generalizations about individuals with disabilities.

Paragraph (c) provides that nothing in this part prohibits a public entity from providing benefits, services, or advantages to individuals with disabilities, or to a particular class of individuals with disabilities, beyond those required by this part. It is derived from a provision in the section 504 regulations that permits programs conducted pursuant to Federal statute or Executive order that are designed to benefit only individuals with disabilities or a given class of individuals with

disabilities to be limited to those individuals with disabilities. Section 504 ensures that federally assisted programs are made available to all individuals, without regard to disabilities, unless the Federal program under which the assistance is provided is specifically limited to individuals with disabilities or a particular class of individuals with disabilities. Because coverage under this part is not limited to federally assisted programs, paragraph (c) has been revised to clarify that State and local governments may provide special benefits, beyond those required by the nondiscrimination requirements of this part, that are limited to individuals with disabilities or a particular class of individuals with disabilities, without thereby incurring additional obligations to persons without disabilities or to other classes of individuals with disabilities.

Paragraphs (d) and (e), previously referred to in the discussion of paragraph (b)(1)(iv), provide that the public entity must administer services, programs, and activities in the most integrated setting appropriate to the needs of qualified individuals with disabilities, i.e., in a setting that enables individuals with disabilities to interact with nondisabled persons to the fullest extent possible, and that persons with disabilities must be provided the option of declining to accept a particular accommodation.

Some commenters expressed concern that § 35.130(e), which states that nothing in the rule requires an individual with a disability to accept special accommodations and services provided under the ADA, could be interpreted to allow guardians of infants or older people with disabilities to refuse medical treatment for their wards. Section 35.130(e) has been revised to make it clear that paragraph (e) is inapplicable to the concern of the commenters. A new paragraph (e)(2) has been added stating that nothing in the regulation authorizes the representative or guardian of an individual with a disability to decline food, water, medical treatment, or medical services for that individual. New paragraph (e) clarifies that neither the ADA nor the regulation alters current Federal law ensuring the rights of incompetent individuals with disabilities to receive food, water, and medical treatment. See, e.g., Child Abuse Amendments of 1984 (42 U.S.C. 5106a(b)(10), 5106g(10)); Rehabilitation Act of 1973, as amended (29 U.S.C. 794); the Developmentally Disabled Assistance and Bill of Rights Act (42 U.S.C. 6042).

Sections 35.130(e).(1) and (2) are based on section 501(d) of the ADA.

Section 501(d) was designed to clarify that nothing in the ADA requires individuals with disabilities to accept special accommodations and services for individuals with disabilities that may segregate them:

The Committee added this section [501(d)] to clarify that nothing in the ADA is intended to permit discriminatory treatment on the basis of disability, even when such treatment is rendered under the guise of providing an accommodation, service, aid or benefit to the individual with disability. For example, a blind individual may choose not to avail himself or herself of the right to go to the front of a line, even if a particular public accommodation has chosen to offer such a modification of a policy for blind individuals. Or, a blind individual may choose to decline to participate in a special museum tour that allows persons to touch sculptures in an exhibit and instead tour the exhibits at his or her own pace with the museum's recorded tour.

Judiciary report at 71–72. The Act is not to be construed to mean that an individual with disabilities must accept special accommodations and services for individuals with disabilities when that individual can participate in the regular services already offered. Because medical treatment, including treatment for particular conditions, is not a special accommodation or service for individuals with disabilities under section 501(d), neither the Act nor this part provides affirmative authority to suspend such treatment. Section 501(d) is intended to clarify that the Act is not designed to foster discrimination through mandatory acceptance of special services when other alternatives are provided; this concern does not reach to the provision of medical treatment for the disabling condition itself.

Paragraph (f) provides that a public entity may not place a surcharge on a particular individual with a disability, or any group of individuals with disabilities, to cover any costs of measures required to provide that individual or group with the nondiscriminatory treatment required by the Act or this part. Such measures may include the provision of auxiliary aids or of modifications required to provide program accessibility.

Several commenters asked for clarification that the costs of interpreter services may not be assessed as an element of "court costs." The Department has already recognized that imposition of the cost of courtroom interpreter services is impermissible under section 504. The preamble to the Department's section 504 regulation for its federally assisted programs states that where a court system has an obligation to provide qualified interpreters, "it has the corresponding responsibility to pay for the services of the interpreters." (45 FR 37630 (June 3, 1980)). Accordingly, recouping the costs of interpreter services by assessing them as part of court costs would also be prohibited.

Paragraph (g), which prohibits discrimination on the basis of an individual's or entity's known relationship or association with an individual with a disability, is based on sections 102(b)(4) and 302(b)(1)(E) of the ADA. This paragraph was not contained in the proposed rule. The individuals covered under this paragraph are any individuals who are discriminated against because of their known association with an individual with a disability. For example, it would be a violation of this paragraph for a local government to refuse to allow a theater company to use a school auditorium on the grounds that the company had recently performed for an audience of individuals with HIV disease.

This protection is not limited to those who have a familial relationship with the individual who has a disability. Congress considered, and rejected, amendments that would have limited the scope of this provision to specific associations and relationships. Therefore, if a public entity refuses admission to a person with cerebral palsy and his or her companions, the companions have an independent right of action under the ADA and this section.

During the legislative process, the term "entity" was added to section 302(b)(1)(E) to clarify that the scope of the provision is intended to encompass not only persons who have a known association with a person with a disability, but also entities that provide services to or are otherwise associated with such individuals. This provision was intended to ensure that entities such as health care providers, employees of social service agencies, and others who provide professional services to persons with disabilities are not subjected to discrimination because of their professional association with persons with disabilities.

Section 35.131 Illegal Use of Drugs

Section 35.131 effectuates section 510 of the ADA, which clarifies the Act's application to people who use drugs illegally. Paragraph (a) provides that this part does not prohibit discrimination based on an individual's current illegal use of drugs.

The Act and the regulation distinguish between illegal use of drugs and the legal use of substances, whether or not

those substances are "controlled substances," as defined in the Controlled Substances Act (21 U.S.C. 812). Some controlled substances are prescription drugs that have legitimate medical uses. Section 35.131 does not affect use of controlled substances pursuant to a valid prescription under supervision by a licensed health care professional, or other use that is authorized by the Controlled Substances Act or any other provision of Federal law. It does apply to illegal use of those substances, as well as to illegal use of controlled substances that are not prescription drugs. The key question is whether the individual's use of the substance is illegal, not whether the substance has recognized legal uses. Alcohol is not a controlled substance, so use of alcohol is not addressed by § 35.131 (although alcoholics are individuals with disabilities, subject to the protections of the statute).

A distinction is also made between the use of a substance and the status of being addicted to that substance. Addiction is a disability, and addicts are individuals with disabilities protected by the Act. The protection, however, does not extend to actions based on the illegal use of the substance. In other words, an addict cannot use the fact of his or her addiction as a defense to an action based on illegal use of drugs. This distinction is not artificial. Congress intended to deny protection to people who engage in the illegal use of drugs, whether or not they are addicted, but to provide protection to addicts so long as they are not currently using drugs.

A third distinction is the difficult one between current use and former use. The definition of "current illegal use of drugs" in § 35.104, which is based on the report of the Conference Committee, H.R. Conf. Rep. No. 596, 101st Cong., 2d Sess. 64 (1990) (hereinafter "Conference report"), is "illegal use of drugs that occurred recently enough to justify a reasonable belief that a person's drug use is current or that continuing use is a real and ongoing problem."

Paragraph (a)(2)(i) specifies that an individual who has successfully completed a supervised drug rehabilitation program or has otherwise been rehabilitated successfully and who is not engaging in current illegal use of drugs is protected. Paragraph (a)(2)(ii) clarifies that an individual who is currently participating in a supervised rehabilitation program and is not engaging in current illegal use of drugs is protected. Paragraph (a)(2)(iii) provides that a person who is erroneously regarded as engaging in current illegal use of drugs, but who is not engaging in such use, is protected.

Paragraph (b) provides a limited exception to the exclusion of current illegal users of drugs from the protections of the Act. It prohibits denial of health services, or services provided in connection with drug rehabilitation to an individual on the basis of current illegal use of drugs, if the individual is otherwise entitled to such services. A health care facility, such as a hospital or clinic, may not refuse treatment to an individual in need of the services it provides on the grounds that the individual is illegally using drugs, but it is not required by this section to provide services that it does not ordinarily provide. For example, a health care facility that specializes in a particular type of treatment, such as care of burn victims, is not required to provide drug rehabilitation services, but it cannot refuse to treat a individual's burns on the grounds that the individual is illegally using drugs.

Some commenters pointed out that abstention from the use of drugs is an essential condition of participation in some drug rehabilitation programs, and may be a necessary requirement in inpatient or residential settings. The Department believes that this comment is well-founded. Congress clearly intended to prohibit exclusion from drug treatment programs of the very individuals who need such programs because of their use of drugs, but, once an individual has been admitted to a program, abstention may be a necessary and appropriate condition to continued participation. The final rule therefore provides that a drug rehabilitation or treatment program may prohibit illegal use of drugs by individuals while they are participating in the program.

Paragraph (c) expresses Congress' intention that the Act be neutral with respect to testing for illegal use of drugs. This paragraph implements the provision in section 510(b) of the Act that allows entities "to adopt or administer reasonable policies or procedures, including but not limited to drug testing," that ensure that an individual who is participating in a supervised rehabilitation program, or who has completed such a program or otherwise been rehabilitated successfully is no longer engaging in the illegal use of drugs. The section is not to be "construed to encourage, prohibit, restrict, or authorize the conducting of testing for the illegal use of drugs."

Paragraph 35.131(c) clarifies that it is not a violation of this part to adopt or administer reasonable policies or procedures to ensure that an individual who formerly engaged in the illegal use of drugs is not currently engaging in illegal use of drugs. Any such policies or procedures must, of course, be reasonable, and must be designed to identify accurately the illegal use of drugs. This paragraph does not authorize inquiries, tests, or other procedures that would disclose use of substances that are not controlled substances or are taken under supervision by a licensed health care professional, or other uses authorized by the Controlled Substances Act or other provisions of Federal law, because such uses are not included in the definition of "illegal use of drugs." A commenter argued that the rule should permit testing for lawful use of prescription drugs, but most commenters preferred that tests must be limited to unlawful use in order to avoid revealing the lawful use of prescription medicine used to treat disabilities.

Section 35.132   Smoking

Section 35.132 restates the clarification in section 501(b) of the Act that the Act does not preclude the prohibition of, or imposition of restrictions on, smoking in transportation covered by title II. Some commenters argued that this section is too limited in scope, and that the regulation should prohibit smoking in all facilities used by public entities. The reference to smoking in section 501, however, merely clarifies that the Act does not require public entities to accommodate smokers by permitting them to smoke in transportation facilities.

Section 35.133   Maintenance of Accessible Features

Section 35.133 provides that a public entity shall maintain in operable working condition those features of facilities and equipment that are required to be readily accessible to and usable by persons with disabilities by the Act or this part. The Act requires that, to the maximum extent feasible, facilities must be accessible to, and usable by, individuals with disabilities. This section recognizes that it is not sufficient to provide features such as accessible routes, elevators, or ramps, if those features are not maintained in a manner that enables individuals with disabilities to use them. Inoperable elevators, locked accessible doors, or "accessible" routes that are obstructed by furniture, filing cabinets, or potted plants are neither "accessible to" nor "usable by" individuals with disabilities.

Some commenters objected that this section appeared to establish an absolute requirement and suggested that language from the preamble be included

in the text of the regulation. It is, of course, impossible to guarantee that mechanical devices will never fail to operate. Paragraph (b) of the final regulation provides that this section does not prohibit isolated or temporary interruptions in service or access due to maintenance or repairs. This paragraph is intended to clarify that temporary obstructions or isolated instances of mechanical failure would not be considered violations of the Act or this part. However, allowing obstructions or "out of service" equipment to persist beyond a reasonable period of time would violate this part, as would repeated mechanical failures due to improper or inadequate maintenance. Failure of the public entity to ensure that accessible routes are properly maintained and free of obstructions, or failure to arrange prompt repair of inoperable elevators or other equipment intended to provide access would also violate this part.

Other commenters requested that this section be expanded to include specific requirements for inspection and maintenance of equipment, for training staff in the proper operation of equipment, and for maintenance of specific items. The Department believes that this section properly establishes the general requirement for maintaining access and that further details are not necessary.

Section 35.134   Retaliation or Coercion

Section 35.134 implements section 503 of the ADA, which prohibits retaliation against any individual who exercises his or her rights under the Act. This section is unchanged from the proposed rule. Paragraph (a) of § 35.134 provides that no private or public entity shall discriminate against any individual because that individual has exercised his or her right to oppose any act or practice made unlawful by this part, or because that individual made a charge, testified, assisted, or participated in any manner in an investigation, proceeding, or hearing under the Act or this part.

Paragraph (b) provides that no private or public entity shall coerce, intimidate, threaten, or interfere with any individual in the exercise of his or her rights under this part or because that individual aided or encouraged any other individual in the exercise or enjoyment of any right granted or protected by the Act or this part.

This section protects not only individuals who allege a violation of the Act or this part, but also any individuals who support or assist them. This section applies to all investigations or proceedings initiated under the Act or this part without regard to the ultimate

resolution of the underlying allegations. Because this section prohibits any act of retaliation or coercion in response to an individual's effort to exercise rights established by the Act and this part (or to support the efforts of another individual), the section applies not only to public entities subject to this part, but also to persons acting in an individual capacity or to private entities. For example, it would be a violation of the Act and this part for a private individual to harass or intimidate an individual with a disability in an effort to prevent that individual from attending a concert in a State-owned park. It would, likewise, be a violation of the Act and this part for a private entity to take adverse action against an employee who appeared as a witness on behalf of an individual who sought to enforce the Act.

Section 35.135   Personal Devices and Services

The final rule includes a new § 35.135, entitled "Personal devices and services," which states that the provision of personal devices and services is not required by title II. This new section, which serves as a limitation on all of the requirements of the regulation, replaces § 35.160(b)(2) of the proposed rule, which addressed the issue of personal devices and services explicitly only in the context of communications. The personal devices and services limitation was intended to have general application in the proposed rule in all contexts where it was relevant. The final rule, therefore, clarifies this point by including a general provision that will explicitly apply not only to auxiliary aids and services but across-the-board to include other relevant areas such as, for example, modifications in policies, practices, and procedures (§ 35.130(b)(7)). The language of § 35.135 parallels an analogous provision in the Department's title III regulations (28 CFR 36.306) but preserves the explicit reference to "readers for personal use or study" in § 35.160(b)(2) of the proposed rule. This section does not preclude the short-term loan of personal receivers that are part of an assistive listening system.

Subpart C—Employment

Section 35.140   Employment Discrimination Prohibited

Title II of the ADA applies to all activities of public entities, including their employment practices. The proposed rule cross-referenced the definitions, requirements, and procedures of title I of the ADA, as established by the Equal Employment

Opportunity Commission in 29 CFR part 1630. This proposal would have resulted in use, under § 35.140, of the title I definition of "employer," so that a public entity with 25 or more employees would have become subject to the requirements of § 35.140 on July 26, 1992, one with 15 to 24 employees on July 26, 1994, and one with fewer than 15 employees would have been excluded completely.

The Department received comments objecting to this approach. The commenters asserted that Congress intended to establish nondiscrimination requirements for employment by all public entities, including those that employ fewer than 15 employees; and that Congress intended the employment requirements of title II to become effective at the same time that the other requirements of this regulation become effective, January 26, 1992. The Department has reexamined the statutory language and legislative history of the ADA on this issue and has concluded that Congress intended to cover the employment practices of all public entities and that the applicable effective date is that of title II.

The statutory language of section 204(b) of the ADA requires the Department to issue a regulation that is consistent with the ADA and the Department's coordination regulation under section 504, 28 CFR part 41. The coordination regulation specifically requires nondiscrimination in employment, 28 CFR 41.52–41.55, and does not limit coverage based on size of employer. Moreover, under all section 504 implementing regulations issued in accordance with the Department's coordination regulation, employment coverage under section 504 extends to all employers with federally assisted programs or activities, regardless of size, and the effective date for those employment requirements has always been the same as the effective date for nonemployment requirements established in the same regulations. The Department therefore concludes that § 35.140 must apply to all public entities upon the effective date of this regulation.

In the proposed regulation the Department cross-referenced the regulations implementing title I of the ADA, issued by the Equal Employment Opportunity Commission at 29 CFR part 1630, as a compliance standard for § 35.140 because, as proposed, the scope of coverage and effective date of coverage under title II would have been coextensive with title I. In the final regulation this language is modified slightly Subparagraph (1) of new

paragraph (b) makes it clear that the standards established by the Equal Employment Opportunity Commission in 29 CFR part 1630 will be the applicable compliance standards if the public entity is subject to title I. If the public entity is not covered by title I, or until it is covered by title I, subparagraph (b)(2) cross-references section 504 standards for what constitutes employment discrimination, as established by the Department of Justice in 28 CFR part 41. Standards for title I of the ADA and section 504 of the Rehabilitation Act are for the most part identical because title I of the ADA was based on requirements set forth in regulations implementing section 504.

The Department, together with the other Federal agencies responsible for the enforcement of Federal laws prohibiting employment discrimination on the basis of disability, recognizes the potential for jurisdictional overlap that exists with respect to coverage of public entities and the need to avoid problems related to overlapping coverage. The other Federal agencies include the Equal Employment Opportunity Commission, which is the agency primarily responsible for enforcement of title I of the ADA, the Department of Labor, which is the agency responsible for enforcement of section 503 of the Rehabilitation Act of 1973, and 26 Federal agencies with programs of Federal financial assistance, which are responsible for enforcing section 504 in those programs. Section 107 of the ADA requires that coordination mechanisms be developed in connection with the administrative enforcement of complaints alleging discrimination under title I and complaints alleging discrimination in employment in violation of the Rehabilitation Act. Although the ADA does not specifically require inclusion of employment complaints under title II in the coordinating mechanisms required by title I, Federal investigations of title II employment complaints will be coordinated on a government-wide basis also. The Department is currently working with the EEOC and other affected Federal agencies to develop effective coordinating mechanisms, and final regulations on this issue will be issued on or before January 26, 1992.

Subpart D—Program Accessibility

Section 35.149 Discrimination Prohibited

Section 35.149 states the general nondiscrimination principle underlying the program accessibility requirements of §§ 35.150 and 35.151.

Section 35.150 Existing Facilities

Consistent with section 204(b) of the Act, this regulation adopts the program accessibility concept found in the section 504 regulations for federally conducted programs or activities (e.g., 28 CFR part 39). The concept of "program accessibility" was first used in the section 504 regulation adopted by the Department of Health, Education, and Welfare for its federally assisted programs and activities in 1977. It allowed recipients to make their federally assisted programs and activities available to individuals with disabilities without extensive retrofitting of their existing buildings and facilities, by offering those programs through alternative methods. Program accessibility has proven to be a useful approach and was adopted in the regulations issued for programs and activities conducted by Federal Executive agencies. The Act provides that the concept of program access will continue to apply with respect to facilities now in existence, because the cost of retrofitting existing facilities is often prohibitive.

Section 35.150 requires that each service, program, or activity conducted by a public entity, when viewed in its entirety, be readily accessible to and usable by individuals with disabilities. The regulation makes clear, however, that a public entity is not required to make each of its existing facilities accessible (§ 35.150(a)(1)). Unlike title III of the Act, which requires public accommodations to remove architectural barriers where such removal is "readily achievable," or to provide goods and services through alternative methods, where those methods are "readily achievable," title II requires a public entity to make its programs accessible in all cases, except where to do so would result in a fundamental alteration in the nature of the program or in undue financial and administrative burdens. Congress intended the "undue burden" standard in title II to be significantly higher than the "readily achievable" standard in title III. Thus, although title II may not require removal of barriers in some cases where removal would be required under title III, the program access requirement of title II should enable individuals with disabilities to participate in and benefit from the services, programs, or activities of public entities in all but the most unusual cases.

Paragraph (a)(2), which establishes a special limitation on the obligation to ensure program accessibility in historic preservation programs, is discussed below in connection with paragraph (b).

Paragraph (a)(3), which is taken from the section 504 regulations for federally conducted programs, generally codifies case law that defines the scope of the public entity's obligation to ensure program accessibility. This paragraph provides that, in meeting the program accessibility requirement, a public entity is not required to take any action that would result in a fundamental alteration in the nature of its service, program, or activity or in undue financial and administrative burdens. A similar limitation is provided in § 35.164.

This paragraph does not establish an absolute defense; it does not relieve a public entity of all obligations to individuals with disabilities. Although a public entity is not required to take actions that would result in a fundamental alteration in the nature of a service, program, or activity or in undue financial and administrative burdens, it nevertheless must take any other steps necessary to ensure that individuals with disabilities receive the benefits or services provided by the public entity.

It is the Department's view that compliance with § 35.150(a), like compliance with the corresponding provisions of the section 504 regulations for federally conducted programs, would in most cases not result in undue financial and administrative burdens on a public entity. In determining whether financial and administrative burdens are undue, all public entity resources available for use in the funding and operation of the service, program, or activity should be considered. The burden of proving that compliance with paragraph (a) of § 35.150 would fundamentally alter the nature of a service, program, or activity or would result in undue financial and administrative burdens rests with the public entity.

The decision that compliance would result in such alteration or burdens must be made by the head of the public entity or his or her designee and must be accompanied by a written statement of the reasons for reaching that conclusion. The Department recognizes the difficulty of identifying the official responsible for this determination, given the variety of organizational forms that may be taken by public entities and their components. The intention of this paragraph is that the determination must be made by a high level official, no lower than a Department head, having budgetary authority and responsibility for making spending decisions.

Any person who believes that he or she or any specific class of persons has been injured by the public entity head's

decision or failure to make a decision may file a complaint under the compliance procedures established in subpart F.

Paragraph (b)(1) sets forth a number of means by which program accessibility may be achieved, including redesign of equipment, reassignment of services to accessible buildings, and provision of aides.

The Department wishes to clarify that, consistent with longstanding interpretation of section 504, carrying an individual with a disability is considered an ineffective and therefore an unacceptable method for achieving program accessibility. Department of Health, Education, and Welfare, Office of Civil Rights, Policy Interpretation No. 4, 43 FR 36035 (August 14, 1978). Carrying will be permitted only in manifestly exceptional cases, and only if all personnel who are permitted to participate in carrying an individual with a disability are formally instructed on the safest and least humiliating means of carrying. "Manifestly exceptional" cases in which carrying would be permitted might include, for example, programs conducted in unique facilities, such as an oceanographic vessel, for which structural changes and devices necessary to adapt the facility for use by individuals with mobility impairments are unavailable or prohibitively expensive. Carrying is not permitted as an alternative to structural modifications such as installation of a ramp or a chairlift.

In choosing among methods, the public entity shall give priority consideration to those that will be consistent with provision of services in the most integrated setting appropriate to the needs of individuals with disabilities. Structural changes in existing facilities are required only when there is no other feasible way to make the public entity's program accessible. (It should be noted that "structural changes" include all physical changes to a facility; the term does not refer only to changes to structural features, such as removal of or alteration to a load-bearing structural member.) The requirements of § 35.151 for alterations apply to structural changes undertaken to comply with this section. The public entity may comply with the program accessibility requirement by delivering services at alternate accessible sites or making home visits as appropriate.

Historic Preservation Programs

In order to avoid possible conflict between the congressional mandates to preserve historic properties, on the one

hand, and to eliminate discrimination against individuals with disabilities on the other, paragraph (a)(2) provides that a public entity is not required to take any action that would threaten or destroy the historic significance of an historic property. The special limitation on program accessibility set forth in paragraph (a)(2) is applicable only to historic preservation programs, as defined in § 35.104, that is, programs that have preservation of historic properties as a primary purpose. Narrow application of the special limitation is justified because of the inherent flexibility of the program accessibility requirement. Where historic preservation is not a primary purpose of the program, the public entity is not required to use a particular facility. It can relocate all or part of its program to an accessible facility, make home visits, or use other standard methods of achieving program accessibility without making structural alterations that might threaten or destroy significant historic features of the historic property. Thus, government programs located in historic properties, such as an historic State capitol, are not excused from the requirement for program access.

Paragraph (a)(2), therefore, will apply only to those programs that uniquely concern the preservation and experience of the historic property itself. Because the primary benefit of an historic preservation program is the experience of the historic property, paragraph (b)(2) requires the public entity to give priority to methods of providing program accessibility that permit individuals with disabilities to have physical access to the historic property. This priority on physical access may also be viewed as a specific application of the general requirement that the public entity administer programs in the most integrated setting appropriate to the needs of qualified individuals with disabilities (§ 35.130(d)). Only when providing physical access would threaten or destroy the historic significance of an historic property, or would result in a fundamental alteration in the nature of the program or in undue financial and administrative burdens, may the public entity adopt alternative methods for providing program accessibility that do not ensure physical access. Examples of some alternative methods for providing program access are provided in paragraph (b)(2).

Time Periods

Paragraphs (c) and (d) establish time periods for complying with the program accessibility requirement. Like the regulations for federally assisted programs (e.g., 28 CFR 41.57(b)), paragraph (c) requires the public entity to make any necessary structural changes in facilities as soon as practicable, but in no event later than three years after the effective date of this regulation.

The proposed rule provided that, aside from structural changes, all other necessary steps to achieve compliance with this part must be taken within sixty days. The sixty day period was taken from regulations implementing section 504, which generally were effective no more than thirty days after publication. Because this regulation will not be effective until January 26, 1992, the Department has concluded that no additional transition period for non-structural changes is necessary, so the sixty day period has been omitted in the final rule. Of course, this section does not reduce or eliminate any obligations that are already applicable to a public entity under section 504.

Where structural modifications are required, paragraph (d) requires that a transition plan be developed by an entity that employs 50 or more persons, within six months of the effective date of this regulation. The legislative history of title II of the ADA makes it clear that, under title II, "local and state governments are required to provide curb cuts on public streets." Education and Labor report at 84. As the rationale for the provision of curb cuts, the House report explains, "The employment, transportation, and public accommodation sections of * * * (the ADA) would be meaningless if people who use wheelchairs were not afforded the opportunity to travel on and between the streets." Id. Section 35.151(e), which establishes accessibility requirements for new construction and alterations, requires that all newly constructed or altered streets, roads, or highways must contain curb ramps or other sloped areas at any intersection having curbs or other barriers to entry from a street level pedestrian walkway, and all newly constructed or altered street level pedestrian walkways must have curb ramps or other sloped areas at intersections to streets, roads, or highways. A new paragraph (d)(2) has been added to the final rule to clarify the application of the general requirement for program accessibility to the provision of curb cuts at existing crosswalks. This paragraph requires that the transition plan include a schedule for providing curb ramps or other sloped areas at existing pedestrian walkways, giving priority to walkways serving entities covered by the Act, including State and local government offices and

facilities, transportation, public accommodations, and employers, followed by walkways serving other areas. Pedestrian "walkways" include locations where access is required for use of public transportation, such as bus stops that are not located at intersections or crosswalks.

Similarly, a public entity should provide an adequate number of accessible parking spaces in existing parking lots or garages over which it has jurisdiction.

Paragraph (d)(3) provides that, if a public entity has already completed a transition plan required by a regulation implementing section 504, the transition plan required by this part will apply only to those policies and practices that were not covered by the previous transition plan. Some commenters suggested that the transition plan should include all aspects of the public entity's operations, including those that may have been covered by a previous transition plan under section 504. The Department believes that such a duplicative requirement would be inappropriate. Many public entities may find, however, that it will be simpler to include all of their operations in the transition plan than to attempt to identify and exclude specifically those that were addressed in a previous plan. Of course, entities covered under section 504 are not shielded from their obligations under that statute merely because they are included under the transition plan developed under this section.

Section 35.151   New Construction and Alterations

Section 35.151 provides that those buildings that are constructed or altered by, on behalf of, or for the use of a public entity shall be designed, constructed, or altered to be readily accessible to and usable by individuals with disabilities if the construction was commenced after the effective date of this part. Facilities under design on that date will be governed by this section if the date that bids were invited falls after the effective date. This interpretation is consistent with Federal practice under section 504.

Section 35.151(c) establishes two standards for accessible new construction and alteration. Under paragraph (c), design, construction, or alteration of facilities in conformance with the Uniform Federal Accessibility Standards (UFAS) or with the Americans with Disabilities Act Accessibility Guidelines for Buildings and Facilities (hereinafter ADAAG) shall be deemed to comply with the requirements of this section with respect

to those facilities except that, if ADAAG is chosen, the elevator exemption contained in §§ 36.401(d) and 36.404 does not apply. ADAAG is the standard for private buildings and was issued as guidelines by the Architectural and Transportation Barriers Compliance Board (ATBCB) under title III of the ADA. It has been adopted by the Department of Justice and is published as appendix A to the Department's title III rule in today's Federal Register. Departures from particular requirements of these standards by the use of other methods shall be permitted when it is clearly evident that equivalent access to the facility or part of the facility is thereby provided. Use of two standards is a departure from the proposed rule.

The proposed rule adopted UFAS as the only interim accessibility standard because that standard was referenced by the regulations implementing section 504 of the Rehabilitation Act promulgated by most Federal funding agencies. It is, therefore, familiar to many State and local government entities subject to this rule. The Department, however, received many comments objecting to the adoption of UFAS. Commenters pointed out that, except for the elevator exemption, UFAS is not as stringent as ADAAG. Others suggested that the standard should be the same to lessen confusion.

Section 204(b) of the Act states that title II regulations must be consistent not only with section 504 regulations but also with "this act." Based on this provision, the Department has determined that a public entity should be entitled to choose to comply either with ADAAG or UFAS.

Public entities who choose to follow ADAAG, however, are not entitled to the elevator exemption contained in title III of the Act and implemented in the title III regulation at § 36.401(d) for new construction and § 36.404 for alterations. Section 303(b) of title III states that, with some exceptions, elevators are not required in facilities that are less than three stories or have less than 3000 square feet per story. The section 504 standard, UFAS, contains no such exemption. Section 501 of the ADA makes clear that nothing in the Act may be construed to apply a lesser standard to public entities than the standards applied under section 504. Because permitting the elevator exemption would clearly result in application of a lesser standard than that applied under section 504, paragraph (c) states that the elevator exemption does not apply when public entities choose to follow ADAAG. Thus, a two-story courthouse, whether built according to UFAS or

ADAAG, must be constructed with an elevator. It should be noted that Congress did not include an elevator exemption for public transit facilities covered by subtitle B of title II, which covers public transportation provided by public entities, providing further evidence that Congress intended that public buildings have elevators.

Section 504 of the ADA requires the ATBCB to issue supplemental Minimum Guidelines and Requirements for Accessible Design of buildings and facilities subject to the Act, including title II. Section 204(c) of the ADA provides that the Attorney General shall promulgate regulations implementing title II that are consistent with the ATBCB's ADA guidelines. The ATBCB has announced its intention to issue title II guidelines in the future. The Department anticipates that, after the ATBCB's title II guidelines have been published, this rule will be amended to adopt new accessibility standards consistent with the ATBCB's rulemaking. Until that time, however, public entities will have a choice of following UFAS or ADAAG, without the elevator exemption.

Existing buildings leased by the public entity after the effective date of this part are not required by the regulation to meet accessibility standards simply by virtue of being leased. They are subject, however, to the program accessibility standard for existing facilities in § 35.150. To the extent the buildings are newly constructed or altered, they must also meet the new construction and alteration requirements of § 35.151.

The Department received many comments urging that the Department require that public entities lease only accessible buildings. Federal practice under section 504 has always treated newly leased buildings as subject to the existing facility program accessibility standard. Section 204(b) of the Act states that, in the area of "program accessibility, existing facilities," the title II regulations must be consistent with section 504 regulations. Thus, the Department has adopted the section 504 principles for these types of leased buildings. Unlike the construction of new buildings where architectural barriers can be avoided at little or no cost, the application of new construction standards to an existing building being leased raises the same prospect of retrofitting buildings as the use of an existing Federal facility, and the same program accessibility standard should apply to both owned and leased existing buildings. Similarly, requiring that public entities only lease accessible space would significantly restrict the

options of State and local governments in seeking leased space, which would be particularly burdensome in rural or sparsely populated areas.

On the other hand, the more accessible the leased space is, the fewer structural modifications will be required in the future for particular employees whose disabilities may necessitate barrier removal as a reasonable accommodation. Pursuant to the requirements for leased buildings contained in the Minimum Guidelines and Requirements for Accessible Design published under the Architectural Barriers Act by the ATBCB, 36 CFR 1190.34, the Federal Government may not lease a building unless it contains (1) One accessible route from an accessible entrance to those areas in which the principal activities for which the building is leased are conducted, (2) accessible toilet facilities, and (3) accessible parking facilities, if a parking area is included within the lease (36 CFR 1190.34). Although these requirements are not applicable to buildings leased by public entities covered by this regulation, such entities are encouraged to look for the most accessible space available to lease and to attempt to find space complying at least with these minimum Federal requirements.

Section 35.151(d) gives effect to the intent of Congress, expressed in section 504(c) of the Act, that this part recognize the national interest in preserving significant historic structures. Commenters criticized the Department's use of descriptive terms in the proposed rule that are different from those used in the ADA to describe eligible historic properties. In addition, some commenters criticized the Department's decision to use the concept of "substantially impairing" the historic features of a property, which is a concept employed in regulations implementing section 504 of the Rehabilitation Act of 1973. Those commenters recommended that the Department adopt the criteria of "adverse effect" published by the Advisory Council on Historic Preservation under the National Historic Preservation Act, 36 CFR 800.9, as the standard for determining whether an historic property may be altered.

The Department agrees with these comments to the extent that they suggest that the language of the rule should conform to the language employed by Congress in the ADA. A definition of "historic property," drawn from section 504 of the ADA, has been added to § 35.104 to clarify that the term applies to those properties listed or eligible for

listing in the National Register of Historic Places, or properties designated as historic under State or local law.

The Department intends that the exception created by this section be applied only in those very rare situations in which it is not possible to provide access to an historic property using the special access provisions established by UFAS and ADAAG. Therefore, paragraph (d)(1) of § 35.151 has been revised to clearly state that alterations to historic properties shall comply, to the maximum extent feasible, with section 4.1.7 of UFAS or section 4.1.7 of ADAAG. Paragraph (d)(2) has been revised to provide that, if it has been determined under the procedures established in UFAS and ADAAG that it is not feasible to provide physical access to an historic property in a manner that will not threaten or destroy the historic significance of the property, alternative methods of access shall be provided pursuant to the requirements of § 35.150.

In response to comments, the Department has added to the final rule a new paragraph (e) setting out the requirements of § 36.151 as applied to curb ramps. Paragraph (e) is taken from the statement contained in the preamble to the proposed rule that all newly constructed or altered streets, roads, and highways must contain curb ramps at any intersection having curbs or other barriers to entry from a street level pedestrian walkway, and that all newly constructed or altered street level pedestrian walkways must have curb ramps at intersections to streets, roads, or highways.

Subpart E—Communications

Section 35.160   General

Section 35.160 requires the public entity to take such steps as may be necessary to ensure that communications with applicants, participants, and members of the public with disabilities are as effective as communications with others.

Paragraph (b)(1) requires the public entity to furnish appropriate auxiliary aids and services when necessary to afford an individual with a disability an equal opportunity to participate in, and enjoy the benefits of, the public entity's service, program, or activity. The public entity must provide an opportunity for individuals with disabilities to request the auxiliary aids and services of their choice. This expressed choice shall be given primary consideration by the public entity (§ 35.160(b)(2)). The public entity shall honor the choice unless it can demonstrate that another effective means of communication exists or that use of the means chosen would not be required under § 35.164.

Deference to the request of the individual with a disability is desirable because of the range of disabilities, the variety of auxiliary aids and services, and different circumstances requiring effective communication. For instance, some courtrooms are now equipped for "computer-assisted transcripts," which allow virtually instantaneous transcripts of courtroom argument and testimony to appear on displays. Such a system might be an effective auxiliary aid or service for a person who is deaf or has a hearing loss who uses speech to communicate, but may be useless for someone who uses sign language.

Although in some circumstances a notepad and written materials may be sufficient to permit effective communication, in other circumstances they may not be sufficient. For example, a qualified interpreter may be necessary when the information being communicated is complex, or is exchanged for a lengthy period of time. Generally, factors to be considered in determining whether an interpreter is required include the context in which the communication is taking place, the number of people involved, and the importance of the communication.

Several commenters asked that the rule clarify that the provision of readers is sometimes necessary to ensure access to a public entity's services, programs or activities. Reading devices or readers should be provided when necessary for equal participation and opportunity to benefit from any governmental service, program, or activity, such as reviewing public documents, examining demonstrative evidence, and filling out voter registration forms or forms needed to receive public benefits. The importance of providing qualified readers for examinations administered by public entities is discussed under § 35.130. Reading devices and readers are appropriate auxiliary aids and services where necessary to permit an individual with a disability to participate in or benefit from a service, program, or activity.

Section 35.160(b)(2) of the proposed rule, which provided that a public entity need not furnish individually prescribed devices, readers for personal use or study, or other devices of a personal nature, has been deleted in favor of a new section in the final rule on personal devices and services (see § 35.135).

In response to comments, the term "auxiliary aids and services" is used in place of "auxiliary aids" in the final rule. This phrase better reflects the

range of aids and services that may be required under this section.

A number of comments raised questions about the extent of a public entity's obligation to provide access to television programming for persons with hearing impairments. Television and videotape programming produced by public entities are covered by this section. Access to audio portions of such programming may be provided by closed captioning.

Section 35.161   Telecommunication Devices for the Deaf (TDD's)

Section 35.161 requires that, where a public entity communicates with applicants and beneficiaries by telephone, TDD's or equally effective telecommunication systems be used to communicate with individuals with impaired speech or hearing.

Problems arise when a public entity which does not have a TDD needs to communicate with an individual who uses a TDD or vice versa. Title IV of the ADA addresses this problem by requiring establishment of telephone relay services to permit communications between individuals who communicate by TDD and individuals who communicate by the telephone alone. The relay services required by title IV would involve a relay operator using both a standard telephone and a TDD to type the voice messages to the TDD user and read the TDD messages to the standard telephone user.

Section 204(b) of the ADA requires that the regulation implementing title II with respect to communications be consistent with the Department's regulation implementing section 504 for its federally conducted programs and activities at 28 CFR part 39. Section 35.161, which is taken from § 39.160(a)(2) of that regulation, requires the use of TDD's or equally effective telecommunication systems for communication with people who use TDD's. Of course, where relay services, such as those required by title IV of the ADA are available, a public entity may use those services to meet the requirements of this section.

Many commenters were concerned that public entities should not rely heavily on the establishment of relay services. The commenters explained that while relay services would be of vast benefit to both public entities and individuals who use TDD's, the services are not sufficient to provide access to all telephone services. First, relay systems do not provide effective access to the increasingly popular automated systems that require the caller to respond by pushing a button on a touch tone phone. Second, relay systems cannot operate

fast enough to convey messages on answering machines, or to permit a TDD user to leave a recorded message. Third, communication through relay systems may not be appropriate in cases of crisis lines pertaining to rape, domestic violence, child abuse, and drugs. The Department believes that it is more appropriate for the Federal Communications Commission to address these issues in its rulemaking under title IV.

Some commenters requested that those entities with frequent contacts with clients who use TDD's have on-site TDD's to provide for direct communication between the entity and the individual. The Department encourages those entities that have extensive telephone contact with the public such as city halls, public libraries, and public aid offices, to have TDD's to insure more immediate access. Where the provision of telephone service is a major function of the entity, TDD's should be available.

Section 35.162   Telephone Emergency Services

Many public entities provide telephone emergency services by which individuals can seek immediate assistance from police, fire, ambulance, and other emergency services. These telephone emergency services— including "911" services—are clearly an important public service whose reliability can be a matter of life or death. The legislative history of title II specifically reflects congressional intent that public entities must ensure that telephone emergency services, including 911 services, be accessible to persons with impaired hearing and speech through telecommunication technology (Conference report at 67; Education and Labor report at 84–85).

Proposed § 35.162 mandated that public entities provide emergency telephone services to persons with disabilities that are "functionally equivalent" to voice services provided to others. Many commenters urged the Department to revise the section to make clear that direct access to telephone emergency services is required by title II of the ADA as indicated by the legislative history (Conference report at 67–68; Education and Labor report at 85). In response, the final rule mandates "direct access," instead of "access that is functionally equivalent" to that provided to all other telephone users. Telephone emergency access through a third party or through a relay service would not satisfy the requirement for direct access.

Several commenters asked about a separate seven-digit emergency call number for the 911 services. The requirement for direct access disallows the use of a separate seven-digit number where 911 service is available. Separate seven-digit emergency call numbers would be unfamiliar to many individuals and also more burdensome to use. A standard emergency 911 number is easier to remember and would save valuable time spent in searching in telephone books for a local seven-digit emergency number.

Many commenters requested the establishment of minimum standards of service (e.g., the quantity and location of TDD's and computer modems needed in a given emergency center). Instead of establishing these scoping requirements, the Department has established a performance standard through the mandate for direct access.

Section 35.162 requires public entities to take appropriate steps, including equipping their emergency systems with modern technology, as may be necessary to promptly receive and respond to a call from users of TDD's and computer modems. Entities are allowed the flexibility to determine what is the appropriate technology for their particular needs. In order to avoid mandating use of particular technologies that may become outdated, the Department has eliminated the references to the Baudot and ASCII formats in the proposed rule.

Some commenters requested that the section require the installation of a voice amplification device on the handset of the dispatcher's telephone to amplify the dispatcher's voice. In an emergency, a person who has a hearing loss may be using a telephone that does not have an amplification device. Installation of speech amplification devices on the handsets of the dispatchers' telephones would respond to that situation. The Department encourages their use.

Several commenters emphasized the need for proper maintenance of TDD's used in telephone emergency services. Section 35.133, which mandates maintenance of accessible features, requires public entities to maintain in operable working condition TDD's and other devices that provide direct access to the emergency system.

Section 35.163 Information and Signage

Section 35.163(a) requires the public entity to provide information to individuals with disabilities concerning accessible services, activities, and facilities. Paragraph (b) requires the public entity to provide signage at all inaccessible entrances to each of its facilities that directs users to an accessible entrance or to a location with information about accessible facilities.

Several commenters requested that, where TDD-equipped pay phones or portable TDD's exist, clear signage should be posted indicating the location of the TDD. The Department believes that this is required by paragraph (a). In addition, the Department recommends that, in large buildings that house TDD's, directional signage indicating the location of available TDD's should be placed adjacent to banks of telephones that do not contain a TDD.

Section 35.164 Duties

Section 35.164, like paragraph (a)(3) of § 35.150, is taken from the section 504 regulations for federally conducted programs. Like paragraph (a)(3), it limits the obligation of the public entity to ensure effective communication in accordance with *Davis* and the circuit court opinions interpreting it. It also includes specific requirements for determining the existence of undue financial and administrative burdens. The preamble discussion of § 35.150(a) regarding that determination is applicable to this section and further explains the public entity's obligation to comply with §§ 35.160–35.164. Because of the essential nature of the services provided by telephone emergency systems, the Department assumes that § 35.164 will rarely be applied to § 35.162.

Subpart F—Compliance Procedures

Subpart F sets out the procedures for administrative enforcement of this part. Section 203 of the Act provides that the remedies, procedures, and rights set forth in section 505 of the Rehabilitation Act of 1973 (29 U.S.C. 794a) for enforcement of section 504 of the Rehabilitation Act, which prohibits discrimination on the basis of handicap in programs and activities that receive Federal financial assistance, shall be the remedies, procedures, and rights for enforcement of title II. Section 505, in turn, incorporates by reference the remedies, procedures, and rights set forth in title VI of the Civil Rights Act of 1964 (42 U.S.C. 2000d to 2000d–4a). Title VI, which prohibits discrimination on the basis of race, color, or national origin in federally assisted programs, is enforced by the Federal agencies that provide the Federal financial assistance to the covered programs and activities in question. If voluntary compliance cannot be achieved, Federal agencies enforce title VI either by the termination of Federal funds to a program that is found to discriminate, following an administrative hearing, or by a referral to this Department for judicial enforcement.

Title II of the ADA extended the requirements of section 504 to all services, programs, and activities of State and local governments, not only those that receive Federal financial assistance. The House Committee on Education and Labor explained the enforcement provisions as follows:

It is the Committee's intent that administrative enforcement of section 202 of the legislation should closely parallel the Federal government's experience with section 504 of the Rehabilitation Act of 1973. The Attorney General should use section 504 enforcement procedures and the Department's coordination role under Executive Order 12250 as models for regulation in this area.

The Committee envisions that the Department of Justice will identify appropriate Federal agencies to oversee compliance activities for State and local governments. As with section 504, these Federal agencies, including the Department of Justice, will receive, investigate, and where possible, resolve complaints of discrimination. If a Federal agency is unable to resolve a complaint by voluntary means, * * * the major enforcement sanction for the Federal government will be referral of cases by these Federal agencies to the Department of Justice.

The Department of Justice may then proceed to file suits in Federal district court. As with section 504, there is also a private right of action for persons with disabilities, which includes the full panoply of remedies. Again, consistent with section 504, it is not the Committee's intent that persons with disabilities need to exhaust Federal administrative remedies before exercising their private right of action.

Education & Labor report at 98. See also S. Rep. No. 116, 101st Cong., 1st Sess., at 57–58 (1989).

Subpart F effectuates the congressional intent by deferring to section 504 procedures where those procedures are applicable, that is, where a Federal agency has jurisdiction under section 504 by virtue of its provision of Federal financial assistance to the program or activity in which the discrimination is alleged to have occurred. Deferral to the 504 procedures also makes the sanction of fund termination available where necessary to achieve compliance. Because the Civil Rights Restoration Act (Pub. L. 100–259) extended the application of section 504 to all of the operations of the public entity receiving the Federal financial assistance, many activities of State and local governments are already covered by section 504. The procedures in subpart F apply to complaints concerning services, programs, and activities of public entities that are covered by the ADA.

Subpart G designates the Federal agencies responsible for enforcing the ADA with respect to specific components of State and local government. It does not, however, displace existing jurisdiction under section 504 of the various funding agencies. Individuals may still file discrimination complaints against recipients of Federal financial assistance with the agencies that provide that assistance, and the funding agencies will continue to process those complaints under their existing procedures for enforcing section 504. The substantive standards adopted in this part for title II of the ADA are generally the same as those required under section 504 for federally assisted programs, and public entities covered by the ADA are also covered by the requirements of section 504 to the extent that they receive Federal financial assistance. To the extent that title II provides greater protection to the rights of individuals with disabilities, however, the funding agencies will also apply the substantive requirements established under title II and this part in processing complaints covered by both this part and section 504, except that fund termination procedures may be used only for violations of section 504.

Subpart F establishes the procedures to be followed by the agencies designated in subpart G for processing complaints against State and local government entities when the designated agency does not have jurisdiction under section 504.

Section 35.170   Complaints

Section 35.170 provides that any individual who believes that he or she or a specific class of individuals has been subjected to discrimination on the basis of disability by a public entity may, by himself or herself or by an authorized representative, file a complaint under this part within 180 days of the date of the alleged discrimination, unless the time for filing is extended by the agency for good cause. Although § 35.107 requires public entities that employ 50 or more persons to establish grievance procedures for resolution of complaints, exhaustion of those procedures is not a prerequisite to filing a complaint under this section. If a complainant chooses to follow the public entity's grievance procedures, however, any resulting delay may be considered good cause for extending the time allowed for filing a complaint under this part.

Filing the complaint with any Federal agency will satisfy the requirement for timely filing. As explained below, a complaint filed with an agency that has jurisdiction under section 504 will be processed under the agency's procedures for enforcing section 504.

Some commenters objected to the complexity of allowing complaints to be filed with different agencies. The multiplicity of enforcement jurisdiction is the result of following the statutorily mandated enforcement scheme. The Department has, however, attempted to simplify procedures for complainants by making the Federal agency that receives the complaint responsible for referring it to an appropriate agency.

The Department has also added a new paragraph (c) to this section providing that a complaint may be filed with any agency designated under subpart G of this part, or with any agency that provides funding to the public entity that is the subject of the complaint, or with the Department of Justice. Under § 35.171(a)(2), the Department of Justice will refer complaints for which it does not have jurisdiction under section 504 to an agency that does have jurisdiction under section 504, or to the agency designated under subpart G as responsible for complaints filed against the public entity that is the subject of the complaint or in the case of an employment complaint that is also subject to title I of the Act, to the Equal Employment Opportunity Commission. Complaints filed with the Department of Justice may be sent to the Coordination and Review Section, P.O. Box 66118, Civil Rights Division, U.S. Department of Justice, Washington, DC 20035–6118.

Section 35.171   Acceptance of Complaints

Section 35.171 establishes procedures for determining jurisdiction and responsibility for processing complaints against public entities. The final rule provides complainants an opportunity to file with the Federal funding agency of their choice. If that agency does not have jurisdiction under section 504, however, and is not the agency designated under subpart G responsible for that public entity, the agency must refer the complaint to the Department of Justice, which will be responsible for referring it either to an agency that does have jurisdiction under section 504 or to the appropriate designated agency, or in the case of an employment complaint that is also subject to title I of the Act, to the Equal Employment Opportunity Commission.

Whenever an agency receives a complaint over which it has jurisdiction under section 504, it will process the complaint under its section 504 procedures. When the agency designated under subpart G receives a complaint for which it does not have jurisdiction under section 504, it will treat the complaint as an ADA complaint under the procedures established in this subpart.

Section 35.171 also describes agency responsibilities for the processing of employment complaints. As described in connection with § 35.140, additional procedures regarding the coordination of employment complaints will be established in a coordination regulation issued by DOJ and EEOC. Agencies with jurisdiction under section 504 for complaints alleging employment discrimination also covered by title I will follow the procedures established by the coordination regulation for those complaints. Complaints covered by title I but not section 504 will be referred to the EEOC, and complaints covered by this part but not title I will be processed under the procedures in this part.

Section 35.172   Resolution of Complaints

Section 35.172 requires the designated agency to either resolve the complaint or issue to the complainant and the public entity a Letter of Findings containing findings of fact and conclusions of law and a description of a remedy for each violation found.

The Act requires the Department of Justice to establish administrative procedures for resolution of complaints, but does not require complainants to exhaust these administrative remedies. The Committee Reports make clear that Congress intended to provide a private right of action with the full panoply of remedies for individual victims of discrimination. Because the Act does not require exhaustion of administrative remedies, the complainant may elect to proceed with a private suit at any time.

Section 35.173   Voluntary Compliance Agreements

Section 35.173 requires the agency to attempt to resolve all complaints in which it finds noncompliance through voluntary compliance agreements enforceable by the Attorney General.

Section 35.174   Referral

Section 35.174 provides for referral of the matter to the Department of Justice if the agency is unable to obtain voluntary compliance.

Section 35.175   Attorney's Fees

Section 35.175 states that courts are authorized to award attorneys fees, including litigation expenses and costs, as provided in section 505 of the Act. Litigation expenses include items such as expert witness fees, travel expenses, etc. The Judiciary Committee Report specifies that such items are included under the rubric of "attorneys fees" and not "costs" so that such expenses will be assessed against a plaintiff only under the standard set forth in *Christiansburg Garment Co.* v. *Equal Employment Opportunity Commission,* 434 U.S. 412 (1978). (Judiciary report at 73.)

Section 35.176   Alternative Means of Dispute Resolution

Section 35.176 restates section 513 of the Act, which encourages use of alternative means of dispute resolution.

Section 35.177   Effect of Unavailability of Technical Assistance

Section 35.177 explains that, as provided in section 506(e) of the Act, a public entity is not excused from compliance with the requirements of this part because of any failure to receive technical assistance.

Section 35.178   State Immunity

Section 35.178 restates the provision of section 502 of the Act that a State is not immune under the eleventh amendment to the Constitution of the United States from an action in Federal or State court for violations of the Act, and that the same remedies are available for any such violations as are available in an action against an entity other than a State.

Subpart G—Designated Agencies

Section 35.190   Designated Agencies

Subpart G designates the Federal agencies responsible for investigating complaints under this part. At least 26 agencies currently administer programs of Federal financial assistance that are subject to the nondiscrimination requirements of section 504 as well as other civil rights statutes. A majority of these agencies administer modest programs of Federal financial assistance and/or devote minimal resources exclusively to "external" civil rights enforcement activities. Under Executive Order 12250, the Department of Justice has encouraged the use of delegation agreements under which certain civil rights compliance responsibilities for a class of recipients funded by more than one agency are delegated by an agency or agencies to a "lead" agency. For example, many agencies that fund institutions of higher education have signed agreements that designate the Department of Education as the "lead" agency for this class of recipients.

The use of delegation agreements reduces overlap and duplication of effort, and thereby strengthens overall civil rights enforcement. However, the use of these agreements to date generally has been limited to education and health care recipients. These classes of recipients are funded by numerous agencies and the logical connection to a lead agency is clear (e.g., the Department of Education for colleges and universities, and the Department of Health and Human Services for hospitals).

The ADA's expanded coverage of State and local government operations further complicates the process of establishing Federal agency jurisdiction for the purpose of investigating complaints of discrimination on the basis of disability. Because all operations of public entities now are covered irrespective of the presence or absence of Federal financial assistance, many additional State and local government functions and organizations now are subject to Federal jurisdiction. In some cases, there is no historical or single clear-cut subject matter relationship with a Federal agency as was the case in the education example described above. Further, the 33,000 governmental jurisdictions subject to the ADA differ greatly in their organization, making a detailed and workable division of Federal agency jurisdiction by individual State, county, or municipal entity unrealistic.

This regulation applies the delegation concept to the investigation of complaints of discrimination on the basis of disability by public entities under the ADA. It designates eight agencies, rather than all agencies currently administering programs of Federal financial assistance, as responsible for investigating complaints under this part. These "designated agencies" generally have the largest civil rights compliance staffs, the most experience in complaint investigations and disability issues, and broad yet clear subject area responsibilities. This division of responsibilities is made functionally rather than by public entity type or name designation. For example, all entities (regardless of their title) that exercise responsibilities, regulate, or administer services or programs relating to lands and natural resources fall within the jurisdiction of the Department of Interior.

Complaints under this part will be investigated by the designated agency most closely related to the functions exercised by the governmental component against which the complaint is lodged. For example, a complaint against a State medical board, where such a board is a recognizable entity, will be investigated by the Department of Health and Human Services (the designated agency for regulatory activities relating to the provision of health care), even if the board is part of a general umbrella department of planning and regulation (for which the Department of Justice is the designated agency). If two or more agencies have apparent responsibility over a complaint, § 35.190(c) provides that the Assistant Attorney General shall determine which one of the agencies shall be the designated agency for purposes of that complaint.

Thirteen commenters, including four proposed designated agencies, addressed the Department of Justice's identification in the proposed regulation of nine "designated agencies" to investigate complaints under this part. Most comments addressed the proposed specific delegations to the various individual agencies. The Department of Justice agrees with several commenters who pointed out that responsibility for "historic and cultural preservation" functions appropriately belongs with the Department of Interior rather than the Department of Education. The Department of Justice also agrees with the Department of Education that "museums" more appropriately should be delegated to the Department of Interior, and that "preschool and daycare programs" more appropriately should be assigned to the Department of Health and Human Services, rather than to the Department of Education. The final rule reflects these decisions.

The Department of Commerce opposed its listing as the designated agency for "commerce and industry, including general economic development, banking and finance, consumer protection, insurance, and small business". The Department of Commerce cited its lack of a substantial existing section 504 enforcement program and experience with many of the specific functions to be delegated. The Department of Justice accedes to the Department of Commerce's position, and has assigned itself as the designated agency for these functions.

In response to a comment from the Department of Health and Human Services, the regulation's category of "medical and nursing schools" has been clarified to read "schools of medicine, dentistry, nursing, and other health-related fields". Also in response to a comment from the Department of Health and Human Services, "correctional institutions" have been specifically added to the public safety and administration of justice functions assigned to the Department of Justice.

The regulation also assigns the Department of Justice as the designated agency responsible for all State and local government functions not assigned to other designated agencies. The Department of Justice, under an agreement with the Department of the Treasury, continues to receive and coordinate the investigation of complaints filed under the Revenue Sharing Act. This entitlement program, which was terminated in 1986, provided civil rights compliance jurisdiction for a wide variety of complaints regarding the use of Federal funds to support various general activities of local governments. In the absence of any similar program of Federal financial assistance administered by another Federal agency, placement of designated agency responsibilities for miscellaneous and otherwise undesignated functions with the Department of Justice is an appropriate continuation of current practice.

The Department of Education objected to the proposed rule's inclusion of the functional area of "arts and humanities" within its responsibilities, and the Department of Housing and Urban Development objected to its proposed designation as responsible for activities relating to rent control, the real estate industry, and housing code enforcement. The Department has deleted these areas from the lists assigned to the Departments of Education and Housing and Urban Development, respectively, and has added a new paragraph (c) to § 35.190, which provides that the Department of Justice may assign responsibility for components of State or local governments that exercise responsibilities, regulate, or administer services, programs, or activities relating to functions not assigned to specific designated agencies by paragraph (b) of this section to other appropriate agencies. The Department believes that this approach will provide more flexibility in determining the appropriate agency for investigation of complaints involving those components of State and local governments not specifically addressed by the listings in paragraph (b). As provided in §§ 35.170 and 35.171, complaints filed with the Department of Justice will be referred to the appropriate agency.

Several commenters proposed a stronger role for the Department of Justice, especially with respect to the receipt and assignment of complaints, and the overall monitoring of the effectiveness of the enforcement activities of Federal agencies. As discussed above, §§ 35.170 and 35.171 have been revised to provide for referral of complaints by the Department of Justice to appropriate enforcement

agencies. Also, language has been added to § 35.190(a) of the final regulation stating that the Assistant Attorney General shall provide policy guidance and interpretations to designated agencies to ensure the consistent and effective implementation of this part.

List of Subjects in 28 CFR Part 35

Administrative practice and procedure, Alcoholism, Americans with disabilities, Buildings, Civil rights, Drug abuse, Handicapped, Historic preservation, Intergovernmental relations, Reporting and recordkeeping requirements.

By the authority vested in me as Attorney General by 28 U.S.C. 509, 510, 5 U.S.C. 301, and section 204 of the Americans with Disabilities Act, and for the reasons set forth in the preamble, chapter I of title 28 of the Code of Federal Regulations is amended by adding a new part 35 to read as follows:

PART 35—NONDISCRIMINATION ON THE BASIS OF DISABILITY IN STATE AND LOCAL GOVERNMENT SERVICES

Subpart A—General

Sec.
35.101   Purpose.
35.102   Application.
35.103   Relationship to other laws.
35.104   Definitions.
35.105   Self-evaluation.
35.106   Notice.
35.107   Designation of responsible employee and adoption of grievance procedures.
35.108—35.129   [Reserved]

Subpart B—General Requirements

35.130   General prohibitions against discrimination.
35.131   Illegal use of drugs.
35.132   Smoking.
35.133   Maintenance of accessible features.
35.134   Retaliation or coercion.
35.135   Personal devices and services.
35.136—35.139   [Reserved]

Subpart C—Employment

35.140   Employment discrimination prohibited.
35.141—35.148   [Reserved]

Subpart D—Program Accessibility

35.149   Discrimination prohibited.
35.150   Existing facilities.
35.151   New construction and alterations.
35.152—35.159   [Reserved]

Subpart E—Communications

35.160   General.
35.161   Telecommunication devices for the deaf (TDD's).
35.162   Telephone emergency services.
35.163   Information and signage.
35.164   Duties.
35.165—35.169   [Reserved]

Subpart F—Compliance Procedures

35.170   Complaints.
35.171   Acceptance of complaints.
35.172   Resolution of complaints.
35.173   Voluntary compliance agreements.
35.174   Referral.
35.175   Attorney's fees.
35.176   Alternative means of dispute resolution.
35.177   Effect of unavailability of technical assistance.
35.178   State immunity.
35.179—35.189   [Reserved]

Subpart G—Designated Agencies

35.190   Designated agencies.
35.191—35.999   [Reserved]

Appendix A to Part 35—Preamble to Regulation on Nondiscrimination on the Basis of Disability in State and Local Government Services (Published July 26, 1991)

Authority: 5 U.S.C. 301; 28 U.S.C. 509, 510; Title II, Pub. L. 101–336 (42 U.S.C. 12134).

Subpart A—General

§ 35.101   Purpose.

The purpose of this part is to effectuate subtitle A of title II of the Americans with Disabilities Act of 1990, (42 U.S.C. 12131), which prohibits discrimination on the basis of disability by public entities.

§ 35.102   Application.

(a) Except as provided in paragraph (b) of this section, this part applies to all services, programs, and activities provided or made available by public entities.

(b) To the extent that public transportation services, programs, and activities of public entities are covered by subtitle B of title II of the ADA (42 U.S.C. 12141), they are not subject to the requirements of this part.

§ 35.103   Relationship to other laws.

(a) *Rule of interpretation.* Except as otherwise provided in this part, this part shall not be construed to apply a lesser standard than the standards applied under title V of the Rehabilitation Act of 1973 (29 U.S.C. 791) or the regulations issued by Federal agencies pursuant to that title.

(b) *Other laws.* This part does not invalidate or limit the remedies, rights, and procedures of any other Federal laws, or State or local laws (including State common law) that provide greater or equal protection for the rights of individuals with disabilities or individuals associated with them.

§ 35.104   Definitions.

For purposes of this part, the term—
Act means the Americans with Disabilities Act (Pub. L. 101–336, 104

Stat. 327, 42 U.S.C. 12101–12213 and 47 U.S.C. 225 and 611).

Assistant Attorney General means the Assistant Attorney General, Civil Rights Division, United States Department of Justice.

Auxiliary aids and services includes—

(1) Qualified interpreters, notetakers, transcription services, written materials, telephone handset amplifiers, assistive listening devices, assistive listening systems, telephones compatible with hearing aids, closed caption decoders, open and closed captioning, telecommunications devices for deaf persons (TDD's), videotext displays, or other effective methods of making aurally delivered materials available to individuals with hearing impairments;

(2) Qualified readers, taped texts, audio recordings, Brailled materials, large print materials, or other effective methods of making visually delivered materials available to individuals with visual impairments;

(3) Acquisition or modification of equipment or devices; and

(4) Other similar services and actions.

Complete complaint means a written statement that contains the complainant's name and address and describes the public entity's alleged discriminatory action in sufficient detail to inform the agency of the nature and date of the alleged violation of this part. It shall be signed by the complainant or by someone authorized to do so on his or her behalf. Complaints filed on behalf of classes or third parties shall describe or identify (by name, if possible) the alleged victims of discrimination.

Current illegal use of drugs means illegal use of drugs that occurred recently enough to justify a reasonable belief that a person's drug use is current or that continuing use is a real and ongoing problem.

Designated agency means the Federal agency designated under subpart G of this part to oversee compliance activities under this part for particular components of State and local governments.

Disability means, with respect to an individual, a physical or mental impairment that substantially limits one or more of the major life activities of such individual; a record of such an impairment; or being regarded as having such an impairment.

(1)(i) The phrase *physical or mental impairment* means—

(A) Any physiological disorder or condition, cosmetic disfigurement, or anatomical loss affecting one or more of the following body systems: Neurological, musculoskeletal, special sense organs, respiratory (including

speech organs), cardiovascular, reproductive, digestive, genitourinary, hemic and lymphatic, skin, and endocrine;

(B) Any mental or psychological disorder such as mental retardation, organic brain syndrome, emotional or mental illness, and specific learning disabilities.

(ii) The phrase *physical or mental impairment* includes, but is not limited to, such contagious and noncontagious diseases and conditions as orthopedic, visual, speech and hearing impairments, cerebral palsy, epilepsy, muscular dystrophy, multiple sclerosis, cancer, heart disease, diabetes, mental retardation, emotional illness, specific learning disabilities, HIV disease (whether symptomatic or asymptomatic), tuberculosis, drug addiction, and alcoholism.

(iii) The phrase *physical or mental impairment* does not include homosexuality or bisexuality.

(2) The phrase *major life activities* means functions such as caring for one's self, performing manual tasks, walking, seeing, hearing, speaking, breathing, learning, and working.

(3) The phrase *has a record of such an impairment* means has a history of, or has been misclassified as having, a mental or physical impairment that substantially limits one or more major life activities.

(4) The phrase *is regarded as having an impairment* means—

(i) Has a physical or mental impairment that does not substantially limit major life activities but that is treated by a public entity as constituting such a limitation;

(ii) Has a physical or mental impairment that substantially limits major life activities only as a result of the attitudes of others toward such impairment; or

(iii) Has none of the impairments defined in paragraph (1) of this definition but is treated by a public entity as having such an impairment.

(5) The term *disability* does not include—

(i) Transvestism, transsexualism, pedophilia, exhibitionism, voyeurism, gender identity disorders not resulting from physical impairments, or other sexual behavior disorders;

(ii) Compulsive gambling, kleptomania, or pyromania; or

(iii) Psychoactive substance use disorders resulting from current illegal use of drugs.

Drug means a controlled substance, as defined in schedules I through V of section 202 of the Controlled Substances Act (21 U.S.C. 812).

Facility means all or any portion of buildings, structures, sites, complexes, equipment, rolling stock or other conveyances, roads, walks, passageways, parking lots, or other real or personal property, including the site where the building, property, structure, or equipment is located.

Historic preservation programs means programs conducted by a public entity that have preservation of historic properties as a primary purpose.

Historic Properties means those properties that are listed or eligible for listing in the National Register of Historic Places or properties designated as historic under State or local law.

Illegal use of drugs means the use of one or more drugs, the possession or distribution of which is unlawful under the Controlled Substances Act (21 U.S.C. 812). The term *illegal use of drugs* does not include the use of a drug taken under supervision by a licensed health care professional, or other uses authorized by the Controlled Substances Act or other provisions of Federal law.

Individual with a disability means a person who has a disability. The term *individual with a disability* does not include an individual who is currently engaging in the illegal use of drugs, when the public entity acts on the basis of such use.

Public entity means—

(1) Any State or local government;

(2) Any department, agency, special purpose district, or other instrumentality of a State or States or local government; and

(3) The National Railroad Passenger Corporation, and any commuter authority (as defined in section 103(8) of the Rail Passenger Service Act).

Qualified individual with a disability means an individual with a disability who, with or without reasonable modifications to rules, policies, or practices, the removal of architectural, communication, or transportation barriers, or the provision of auxiliary aids and services, meets the essential eligibility requirements for the receipt of services or the participation in programs or activities provided by a public entity.

Qualified interpreter means an interpreter who is able to interpret effectively, accurately, and impartially both receptively and expressively, using any necessary specialized vocabulary.

Section 504 means section 504 of the Rehabilitation Act of 1973 (Pub. L. 93–112, 87 Stat. 394 (29 U.S.C. 794)), as amended.

State means each of the several States, the District of Columbia, the Commonwealth of Puerto Rico, Guam, American Samoa, the Virgin Islands, the

Trust Territory of the Pacific Islands, and the Commonwealth of the Northern Mariana Islands.

§ 35.105 Self-evaluation.

(a) A public entity shall, within one year of the effective date of this part, evaluate its current services, policies, and practices, and the effects thereof, that do not or may not meet the requirements of this part and, to the extent modification of any such services, policies, and practices is required, the public entity shall proceed to make the necessary modifications.

(b) A public entity shall provide an opportunity to interested persons, including individuals with disabilities or organizations representing individuals with disabilities, to participate in the self-evaluation process by submitting comments.

(c) A public entity that employs 50 or more persons shall, for at least three years following completion of the self-evaluation, maintain on file and make available for public inspection:

(1) A list of the interested persons consulted;

(2) A description of areas examined and any problems identified; and

(3) A description of any modifications made.

(d) If a public entity has already complied with the self-evaluation requirement of a regulation implementing section 504 of the Rehabilitation Act of 1973, then the requirements of this section shall apply only to those policies and practices that were not included in the previous self-evaluation.

§ 35.106 Notice.

A public entity shall make available to applicants, participants, beneficiaries, and other interested persons information regarding the provisions of this part and its applicability to the services, programs, or activities of the public entity, and make such information available to them in such manner as the head of the entity finds necessary to apprise such persons of the protections against discrimination assured them by the Act and this part.

§ 35.107 Designation of responsible employee and adoption of grievance procedures.

(a) Designation of responsible employee. A public entity that employs 50 or more persons shall designate at least one employee to coordinate its efforts to comply with and carry out its responsibilities under this part, including any investigation of any complaint communicated to it alleging its noncompliance with this part or

alleging any actions that would be prohibited by this part. The public entity shall make available to all interested individuals the name, office address, and telephone number of the employee or employees designated pursuant to this paragraph.

(b) Complaint procedure. A public entity that employs 50 or more persons shall adopt and publish grievance procedures providing for prompt and equitable resolution of complaints alleging any action that would be prohibited by this part.

§§ 35.108–35.129 [Reserved]

Subpart B—General Requirements

§ 35.130 General prohibitions against discrimination.

(a) No qualified individual with a disability shall, on the basis of disability, be excluded from participation in or be denied the benefits of the services, programs, or activities of a public entity, or be subjected to discrimination by any public entity.

(b) (1) A public entity, in providing any aid, benefit, or service, may not, directly or through contractual, licensing, or other arrangements, on the basis of disability—

(i) Deny a qualified individual with a disability the opportunity to participate in or benefit from the aid, benefit, or service;

(ii) Afford a qualified individual with a disability an opportunity to participate in or benefit from the aid, benefit, or service that is not equal to that afforded others;

(iii) Provide a qualified individual with a disability with an aid, benefit, or service that is not as effective in affording equal opportunity to obtain the same result, to gain the same benefit, or to reach the same level of achievement as that provided to others;

(iv) Provide different or separate aids, benefits, or services to individuals with disabilities or to any class of individuals with disabilities than is provided to others unless such action is necessary to provide qualified individuals with disabilities with aids, benefits, or services that are as effective as those provided to others;

(v) Aid or perpetuate discrimination against a qualified individual with a disability by providing significant assistance to an agency, organization, or person that discriminates on the basis of disability in providing any aid, benefit, or service to beneficiaries of the public entity's program;

(vi) Deny a qualified individual with a disability the opportunity to participate as a member of planning or advisory boards;

(vii) Otherwise limit a qualified individual with a disability in the enjoyment of any right, privilege, advantage, or opportunity enjoyed by others receiving the aid, benefit, or service.

(2) A public entity may not deny a qualified individual with a disability the opportunity to participate in services, programs, or activities that are not separate or different, despite the existence of permissibly separate or different programs or activities.

(3) A public entity may not, directly or through contractual or other arrangements, utilize criteria or methods of administration:

(i) That have the effect of subjecting qualified individuals with disabilities to discrimination on the basis of disability;

(ii) That have the purpose or effect of defeating or substantially impairing accomplishment of the objectives of the public entity's program with respect to individuals with disabilities; or

(iii) That perpetuate the discrimination of another public entity if both public entities are subject to common administrative control or are agencies of the same State.

(4) A public entity may not, in determining the site or location of a facility, make selections—

(i) That have the effect of excluding individuals with disabilities from, denying them the benefits of, or otherwise subjecting them to discrimination; or

(ii) That have the purpose or effect of defeating or substantially impairing the accomplishment of the objectives of the service, program, or activity with respect to individuals with disabilities.

(5) A public entity, in the selection of procurement contractors, may not use criteria that subject qualified individuals with disabilities to discrimination on the basis of disability.

(6) A public entity may not administer a licensing or certification program in a manner that subjects qualified individuals with disabilities to discrimination on the basis of disability, nor may a public entity establish requirements for the programs or activities of licensees or certified entities that subject qualified individuals with disabilities to discrimination on the basis of disability. The programs or activities of entities that are licensed or certified by a public entity are not, themselves, covered by this part.

(7) A public entity shall make reasonable modifications in policies, practices, or procedures when the modifications are necessary to avoid discrimination on the basis of disability,

unless the public entity can demonstrate that making the modifications would fundamentally alter the nature of the service, program, or activity.

(8) A public entity shall not impose or apply eligibility criteria that screen out or tend to screen out an individual with a disability or any class of individuals with disabilities from fully and equally enjoying any service, program, or activity, unless such criteria can be shown to be necessary for the provision of the service, program, or activity being offered.

(c) Nothing in this part prohibits a public entity from providing benefits, services, or advantages to individuals with disabilities, or to a particular class of individuals with disabilities beyond those required by this part.

(d) A public entity shall administer services, programs, and activities in the most integrated setting appropriate to the needs of qualified individuals with disabilities.

(e)(1) Nothing in this part shall be construed to require an individual with a disability to accept an accommodation, aid, service, opportunity, or benefit provided under the ADA or this part which such individual chooses not to accept.

(2) Nothing in the Act or this part authorizes the representative or guardian of an individual with a disability to decline food, water, medical treatment, or medical services for that individual.

(f) A public entity may not place a surcharge on a particular individual with a disability or any group of individuals with disabilities to cover the costs of measures, such as the provision of auxiliary aids or program accessibility, that are required to provide that individual or group with the nondiscriminatory treatment required by the Act or this part.

(g) A public entity shall not exclude or otherwise deny equal services, programs, or activities to an individual or entity because of the known disability of an individual with whom the individual or entity is known to have a relationship or association.

§ 35.131 Illegal use of drugs.

(a) *General.* (1) Except as provided in paragraph (b) of this section, this part does not prohibit discrimination against an individual based on that individual's current illegal use of drugs.

(2) A public entity shall not discriminate on the basis of illegal use of drugs against an individual who is not engaging in current illegal use of drugs and who—

(i) Has successfully completed a supervised drug rehabilitation program or has otherwise been rehabilitated successfully;

(ii) Is participating in a supervised rehabilitation program; or

(iii) Is erroneously regarded as engaging in such use.

(b) *Health and drug rehabilitation services.* (1) A public entity shall not deny health services, or services provided in connection with drug rehabilitation, to an individual on the basis of that individual's current illegal use of drugs, if the individual is otherwise entitled to such services.

(2) A drug rehabilitation or treatment program may deny participation to individuals who engage in illegal use of drugs while they are in the program.

(c) *Drug testing.* (1) This part does not prohibit a public entity from adopting or administering reasonable policies or procedures, including but not limited to drug testing, designed to ensure that an individual who formerly engaged in the illegal use of drugs is not now engaging in current illegal use of drugs.

(2) Nothing in paragraph (c) of this section shall be construed to encourage, prohibit, restrict, or authorize the conduct of testing for the illegal use of drugs.

§ 35.132 Smoking.

This part does not preclude the prohibition of, or the imposition of restrictions on, smoking in transportation covered by this part.

§ 35.133 Maintenance of accessible features.

(a) A public accommodation shall maintain in operable working condition those features of facilities and equipment that are required to be readily accessible to and usable by persons with disabilities by the Act or this part.

(b) This section does not prohibit isolated or temporary interruptions in service or access due to maintenance or repairs.

§ 35.134 Retaliation or coercion.

(a) No private or public entity shall discriminate against any individual because that individual has opposed any act or practice made unlawful by this part, or because that individual made a charge, testified, assisted, or participated in any manner in an investigation, proceeding, or hearing under the Act or this part.

(b) No private or public entity shall coerce, intimidate, threaten, or interfere with any individual in the exercise or enjoyment of, or on account of his or her having exercised or enjoyed, or on account of his or her having aided or encouraged any other individual in the exercise or enjoyment of, any right granted or protected by the Act or this part.

§ 35.135 Personal devices and services.

This part does not require a public entity to provide to individuals with disabilities personal devices, such as wheelchairs; individually prescribed devices, such as prescription eyeglasses or hearing aids; readers for personal use or study; or services of a personal nature including assistance in eating, toileting, or dressing.

§§ 35.136–35.139 [Reserved]

Subpart C—Employment

§ 35.140 Employment discrimination prohibited.

(a) No qualified individual with a disability shall, on the basis of disability, be subjected to discrimination in employment under any service, program, or activity conducted by a public entity.

(b)(1) For purposes of this part, the requirements of title I of the Act, as established by the regulations of the Equal Employment Opportunity Commission in 29 CFR part 1630, apply to employment in any service, program, or activity conducted by a public entity if that public entity is also subject to the jurisdiction of title I.

(2) For the purposes of this part, the requirements of section 504 of the Rehabilitation Act of 1973, as established by the regulations of the Department of Justice in 28 CFR part 41, as those requirements pertain to employment, apply to employment in any service, program, or activity conducted by a public entity if that public entity is not also subject to the jurisdiction of title I.

§§ 35.141–35.148 [Reserved]

Subpart D—Program Accessibility

§ 35.149 Discrimination prohibited.

Except as otherwise provided in § 35.150, no qualified individual with a disability shall, because a public entity's facilities are inaccessible to or unusable by individuals with disabilities, be excluded from participation in, or be denied the benefits of the services, programs, or activities of a public entity, or be subjected to discrimination by any public entity.

§ 35.150 Existing facilities.

(a) *General.* A public entity shall operate each service, program, or activity so that the service, program, or activity, when viewed in its entirety, is readily accessible to and usable by individuals with disabilities. This paragraph does not—

(1) Necessarily require a public entity to make each of its existing facilities accessible to and usable by individuals with disabilities;

(2) Require a public entity to take any action that would threaten or destroy the historic significance of an historic property; or

(3) Require a public entity to take any action that it can demonstrate would result in a fundamental alteration in the nature of a service, program, or activity or in undue financial and administrative burdens. In those circumstances where personnel of the public entity believe that the proposed action would fundamentally alter the service, program, or activity or would result in undue financial and administrative burdens, a public entity has the burden of proving that compliance with § 35.150(a) of this part would result in such alteration or burdens. The decision that compliance would result in such alteration or burdens must be made by the head of a public entity or his or her designee after considering all resources available for use in the funding and operation of the service, program, or activity, and must be accompanied by a written statement of the reasons for reaching that conclusion. If an action would result in such an alteration or such burdens, a public entity shall take any other action that would not result in such an alteration or such burdens but would nevertheless ensure that individuals with disabilities receive the benefits or services provided by the public entity.

(b) Methods—(1) General. A public entity may comply with the requirements of this section through such means as redesign of equipment, reassignment of services to accessible buildings, assignment of aides to beneficiaries, home visits, delivery of services at alternate accessible sites, alteration of existing facilities and construction of new facilities, use of accessible rolling stock or other conveyances, or any other methods that result in making its services, programs, or activities readily accessible to and usable by individuals with disabilities. A public entity is not required to make structural changes in existing facilities where other methods are effective in achieving compliance with this section. A public entity, in making alterations to existing buildings, shall meet the accessibility requirements of § 35.151. In choosing among available methods for meeting the requirements of this section, a public entity shall give priority to those methods that offer services, programs, and activities to qualified

individuals with disabilities in the most integrated setting appropriate.

(2) Historic preservation programs. In meeting the requirements of § 35.150(a) in historic preservation programs, a public entity shall give priority to methods that provide physical access to individuals with disabilities. In cases where a physical alteration to an historic property is not required because of paragraph (a)(2) or (a)(3) of this section, alternative methods of achieving program accessibility include—

(i) Using audio-visual materials and devices to depict those portions of an historic property that cannot otherwise be made accessible;

(ii) Assigning persons to guide individuals with handicaps into or through portions of historic properties that cannot otherwise be made accessible; or

(iii) Adopting other innovative methods.

(c) Time period for compliance. Where structural changes in facilities are undertaken to comply with the obligations established under this section, such changes shall be made within three years of January 26, 1992, but in any event as expeditiously as possible.

(d) Transition plan. (1) In the event that structural changes to facilities will be undertaken to achieve program accessibility, a public entity that employs 50 or more persons shall develop, within six months of January 26, 1992, a transition plan setting forth the steps necessary to complete such changes. A public entity shall provide an opportunity to interested persons, including individuals with disabilities or organizations representing individuals with disabilities, to participate in the development of the transition plan by submitting comments. A copy of the transition plan shall be made available for public inspection.

(2) If a public entity has responsibility or authority over streets, roads, or walkways, its transition plan shall include a schedule for providing curb ramps or other sloped areas where pedestrian walks cross curbs, giving priority to walkways serving entities, covered by the Act, including State and local government offices and facilities, transportation, places of public accommodation, and employers, followed by walkways serving other areas.

(3) The plan shall, at a minimum—

(i) Identify physical obstacles in the public entity's facilities that limit the accessibility of its programs or activities to individuals with disabilities;

(ii) Describe in detail the methods that will be used to make the facilities accessible;

(iii) Specify the schedule for taking the steps necessary to achieve compliance with this section and, if the time period of the transition plan is longer than one year, identify steps that will be taken during each year of the transition period; and

(iv) Indicate the official responsible for implementation of the plan.

(4) If a public entity has already complied with the transition plan requirement of a Federal agency regulation implementing section 504 of the Rehabilitation Act of 1973, then the requirements of this paragraph (d) shall apply only to those policies and practices that were not included in the previous transition plan.

§ 35.151 New construction and alterations.

(a) Design and construction. Each facility or part of a facility constructed by, on behalf of, or for the use of a public entity shall be designed and constructed in such manner that the facility or part of the facility is readily accessible to and usable by individuals with disabilities, if the construction was commenced after January 26, 1992.

(b) Alteration. Each facility or part of a facility altered by, on behalf of, or for the use of a public entity in a manner that affects or could affect the usability of the facility or part of the facility shall, to the maximum extent feasible, be altered in such manner that the altered portion of the facility is readily accessible to and usable by individuals with disabilities, if the alteration was commenced after January 26, 1992.

(c) Accessibility standards. Design, construction, or alteration of facilities in conformance with the Uniform Federal Accessibility Standards (UFAS) (Appendix A to 41 CFR part 101–19.6) or with the Americans with Disabilities Act Accessibility Guidelines for Buildings and Facilities (ADAAG) (Appendix A to 28 CFR part 36) shall be deemed to comply with the requirements of this section with respect to those facilities, except that the elevator exemption contained at section 4.1.3(5) and section 4.1.6(1)(j) of ADAAG shall not apply. Departures from particular requirements of either standard by the use of other methods shall be permitted when it is clearly evident that equivalent access to the facility or part of the facility is thereby provided.

(d) Alterations: Historic properties. (1) Alterations to historic properties shall comply, to the maximum extent feasible, with section 4.1.7 of UFAS or section 4.1.7 of ADAAG.

(2) If it is not feasible to provide physical access to an historic property in a manner that will not threaten or destroy the historic significance of the building or facility, alternative methods of access shall be provided pursuant to the requirements of § 35.150.

(e) *Curb ramps.* (1) Newly constructed or altered streets, roads, and highways must contain curb ramps or other sloped areas at any intersection having curbs or other barriers to entry from a street level pedestrian walkway.

(2) Newly constructed or altered street level pedestrian walkways must contain curb ramps or other sloped areas at intersections to streets, roads, or highways.

§§ 35.152–35.159 [Reserved]

Subpart E—Communications

§ 35.160 General.

(a) A public entity shall take appropriate steps to ensure that communications with applicants, participants, and members of the public with disabilities are as effective as communications with others.

(b)(1) A public entity shall furnish appropriate auxiliary aids and services where necessary to afford an individual with a disability an equal opportunity to participate in, and enjoy the benefits of, a service, program, or activity conducted by a public entity.

(2) In determining what type of auxiliary aid and service is necessary, a public entity shall give primary consideration to the requests of the individual with disabilities.

§ 35.161 Telecommunication devices for the deaf (TDD's).

Where a public entity communicates by telephone with applicants and beneficiaries, TDD's or equally effective telecommunication systems shall be used to communicate with individuals with impaired hearing or speech.

§ 35.162 Telephone emergency services.

Telephone emergency services, including 911 services, shall provide direct access to individuals who use TDD's and computer modems.

§ 35.163 Information and signage.

(a) A public entity shall ensure that interested persons, including persons with impaired vision or hearing, can obtain information as to the existence and location of accessible services, activities, and facilities.

(b) A public entity shall provide signage at all inaccessible entrances to each of its facilities, directing users to an accessible entrance or to a location at which they can obtain information

about accessible facilities. The international symbol for accessibility shall be used at each accessible entrance of a facility.

§ 35.164 Duties.

This subpart does not require a public entity to take any action that it can demonstrate would result in a fundamental alteration in the nature of a service, program, or activity or in undue financial and administrative burdens. In those circumstances where personnel of the public entity believe that the proposed action would fundamentally alter the service, program, or activity or would result in undue financial and administrative burdens, a public entity has the burden of proving that compliance with this subpart would result in such alteration or burdens. The decision that compliance would result in such alteration or burdens must be made by the head of the public entity or his or her designee after considering all resources available for use in the funding and operation of the service, program, or activity and must be accompanied by a written statement of the reasons for reaching that conclusion. If an action required to comply with this subpart would result in such an alteration or such burdens, a public entity shall take any other action that would not result in such an alteration or such burdens but would nevertheless ensure that, to the maximum extent possible, individuals with disabilities receive the benefits or services provided by the public entity.

§§ 35.165–35.169 [Reserved]

Subpart F—Compliance Procedures

§ 35.170 Complaints.

(a) *Who may file.* An individual who believes that he or she or a specific class of individuals has been subjected to discrimination on the basis of disability by a public entity may, by himself or herself or by an authorized representative, file a complaint under this part.

(b) *Time for filing.* A complaint must be filed not later than 180 days from the date of the alleged discrimination, unless the time for filing is extended by the designated agency for good cause shown. A complaint is deemed to be filed under this section on the date it is first filed with any Federal agency.

(c) *Where to file.* An individual may file a complaint with any agency that he or she believes to be the appropriate agency designated under subpart G of this part, or with any agency that provides funding to the public entity that is the subject of the complaint, or with

the Department of Justice for referral as provided in § 35.171(a)(2).

§ 35.171 Acceptance of complaints.

(a) *Receipt of complaints.* (1)(i) Any Federal agency that receives a complaint of discrimination on the basis of disability by a public entity shall promptly review the complaint to determine whether it has jurisdiction over the complaint under section 504.

(ii) If the agency does not have section 504 jurisdiction, it shall promptly determine whether it is the designated agency under subpart G of this part responsible for complaints filed against that public entity.

(2)(i) If an agency other than the Department of Justice determines that it does not have section 504 jurisdiction and is not the designated agency, it shall promptly refer the complaint, and notify the complainant that it is referring the complaint to the Department of Justice.

(ii) When the Department of Justice receives a complaint for which it does not have jurisdiction under section 504 and is not the designated agency, it shall refer the complaint to an agency that does have jurisdiction under section 504 or to the appropriate agency designated in subpart G of this part or, in the case of an employment complaint that is also subject to title I of the Act, to the Equal Employment Opportunity Commission.

(3)(i) If the agency that receives a complaint has section 504 jurisdiction, it shall process the complaint according to its procedures for enforcing section 504.

(ii) If the agency that receives a complaint does not have section 504 jurisdiction, but is the designated agency, it shall process the complaint according to the procedures established by this subpart.

(b) *Employment complaints.* (1) If a complaint alleges employment discrimination subject to title I of the Act, and the agency has section 504 jurisdiction, the agency shall follow the procedures issued by the Department of Justice and the Equal Employment Opportunity Commission under section 107(b) of the Act.

(2) If a complaint alleges employment discrimination subject to title I of the Act, and the designated agency does not have section 504 jurisdiction, the agency shall refer the complaint to the Equal Employment Opportunity Commission for processing under title I of the Act.

(3) Complaints alleging employment discrimination subject to this part, but not to title I of the Act shall be processed in accordance with the procedures established by this subpart.

(c) *Complete complaints.* (1) A designated agency shall accept all complete complaints under this section and shall promptly notify the complainant and the public entity of the receipt and acceptance of the complaint.

(2) If the designated agency receives a complaint that is not complete, it shall notify the complainant and specify the additional information that is needed to make the complaint a complete complaint. If the complainant fails to complete the complaint, the designated agency shall close the complaint without prejudice.

§ 35.172 Resolution of complaints.

(a) The designated agency shall investigate each complete complaint, attempt informal resolution, and, if resolution is not achieved, issue to the complainant and the public entity a Letter of Findings that shall include—

(1) Findings of fact and conclusions of law;

(2) A description of a remedy for each violation found; and

(3) Notice of the rights available under paragraph (b) of this section.

(b) If the designated agency finds noncompliance, the procedures in §§ 35.173 and 35.174 shall be followed. At any time, the complainant may file a private suit pursuant to section 203 of the Act, whether or not the designated agency finds a violation.

§ 35.173 Voluntary compliance agreements.

(a) When the designated agency issues a noncompliance Letter of Findings, the designated agency shall—

(1) Notify the Assistant Attorney General by forwarding a copy of the Letter of Findings to the Assistant Attorney General; and

(2) Initiate negotiations with the public entity to secure compliance by voluntary means.

(b) Where the designated agency is able to secure voluntary compliance, the voluntary compliance agreement shall—

(1) Be in writing and signed by the parties;

(2) Address each cited violation;

(3) Specify the corrective or remedial action to be taken, within a stated period of time, to come into compliance;

(4) Provide assurance that discrimination will not recur; and

(5) Provide for enforcement by the Attorney General.

§ 35.174 Referral.

If the public entity declines to enter into voluntary compliance negotiations or if negotiations are unsuccessful, the designated agency shall refer the matter to the Attorney General with a recommendation for appropriate action.

§ 35.175 Attorney's fees.

In any action or administrative proceeding commenced pursuant to the Act or this part, the court or agency, in its discretion, may allow the prevailing party, other than the United States, a reasonable attorney's fee, including litigation expenses, and costs, and the United States shall be liable for the foregoing the same as a private individual.

§ 35.176 Alternative means of dispute resolution.

Where appropriate and to the extent authorized by law, the use of alternative means of dispute resolution, including settlement negotiations, conciliation, facilitation, mediation, factfinding, minitrials, and arbitration, is encouraged to resolve disputes arising under the Act and this part.

§ 35.177 Effect of unavailability of technical assistance.

A public entity shall not be excused from compliance with the requirements of this part because of any failure to receive technical assistance, including any failure in the development or dissemination of any technical assistance manual authorized by the Act.

§ 35.178 State immunity.

A State shall not be immune under the eleventh amendment to the Constitution of the United States from an action in Federal or State court of competent jurisdiction for a violation of this Act. In any action against a State for a violation of the requirements of this Act, remedies (including remedies both at law and in equity) are available for such a violation to the same extent as such remedies are available for such a violation in an action against any public or private entity other than a State.

§§ 35.179–35.189 [Reserved]

Subpart G—Designated Agencies

§ 35.190 Designated agencies.

(a) The Assistant Attorney General shall coordinate the compliance activities of Federal agencies with respect to State and local government components, and shall provide policy guidance and interpretations to designated agencies to ensure the consistent and effective implementation of the requirements of this part.

(b) The Federal agencies listed in paragraph (b) (1) through (8) of this section shall have responsibility for the implementation of subpart F of this part for components of State and local governments that exercise responsibilities, regulate, or administer services, programs, or activities in the following functional areas.

(1) *Department of Agriculture:* All programs, services, and regulatory activities relating to farming and the raising of livestock, including extension services.

(2) *Department of Education:* All programs, services, and regulatory activities relating to the operation of elementary and secondary education systems and institutions, institutions of higher education and vocational education (other than schools of medicine, dentistry, nursing, and other health-related schools), and libraries.

(3) *Department of Health and Human Services:* All programs, services, and regulatory activities relating to the provision of health care and social services, including schools of medicine, dentistry, nursing, and other health-related schools, the operation of health care and social service providers and institutions, including "grass-roots" and community services organizations and programs, and preschool and daycare programs.

(4) *Department of Housing and Urban Development:* All programs, services, and regulatory activities relating to state and local public housing, and housing assistance and referral.

(5) *Department of Interior:* All programs, services, and regulatory activities relating to lands and natural resources, including parks and recreation, water and waste management, environmental protection, energy, historic and cultural preservation, and museums.

(6) *Department of Justice:* All programs, services, and regulatory activities relating to law enforcement, public safety, and the administration of justice, including courts and correctional institutions; commerce and industry, including general economic development, banking and finance, consumer protection, insurance, and small business; planning, development, and regulation (unless assigned to other designated agencies); state and local government support services (e.g., audit, personnel, comptroller, administrative services); all other government functions not assigned to other designated agencies.

(7) *Department of Labor:* All programs, services, and regulatory activities relating to labor and the work force.

(8) *Department of Transportation:* All programs, services, and regulatory activities relating to transportation, including highways, public transportation, traffic management (non-

law enforcement), automobile licensing and inspection, and driver licensing.

(c) Responsibility for the implementation of subpart F of this part for components of State or local governments that exercise responsibilities, regulate, or administer services, programs, or activities relating to functions not assigned to specific designated agencies by paragraph (b) of this section may be assigned to other specific agencies by the Department of Justice.

(d) If two or more agencies have apparent responsibility over a complaint, the Assistant Attorney General shall determine which one of the agencies shall be the designated agency for purposes of that complaint.

§§ 35.191–35.999 [Reserved]

Appendix A to Part 35—Preamble to Regulation on Nondiscrimination on the Basis of Disability in State and Local Government Services (Published July 26, 1991)

Note: For the convenience of the reader, this appendix contains the text of the preamble to the final regulation on nondiscrimination on the basis of disability in State and local government services beginning at the heading "Section-by-Section Analysis" and ending before "List of Subjects in 28 CFR Part 35" (56 FR (INSERT FR PAGE CITATIONS); July 26, 1991).

Dated: July 17, 1991.

Dick Thornburgh,

Attorney General.

[FR Doc. 91–17368 Filed 7–25–91; 8:45 am]

BILLING CODE 4410-01-M

Equal Employment Opportunity Commission

29 CFR Part 1630
Equal Employment Opportunity for Individuals With Disabilities; Final Rule

29 CFR Parts 1602 and 1627
Recordkeeping and Reporting Under Title VII of the Civil Rights Act of 1964 and the Americans With Disabilities Act (ADA); Final Rule

Equal Employment Opportunity Commission

29 CFR Part 1630

Equal Employment Opportunity for Individuals With Disabilities

AGENCY: Equal Employment Opportunity Commission.
ACTION: Final rule.

SUMMARY: On July 26, 1990, the Americans With Disabilities Act (ADA) was signed into law. Section 106 of the ADA requires that the Equal Employment Opportunity Commission (EEOC) issue substantive regulations implementing title I (Employment) within one year of the date of enactment of the Act. Pursuant to this mandate, the Commission is publishing a new part 1630 to its regulations to implement title I and sections 3(2), 3(3), 501, 503, 506(e), 508, 510, and 511 of the ADA as those sections pertain to employment. New part 1630 prohibits discrimination against qualified individuals with disabilities in all aspects of employment.

EFFECTIVE DATE: July 26, 1992.

FOR FURTHER INFORMATION CONTACT: Elizabeth M. Thornton, Deputy Legal Counsel, (202) 663–4638 (voice), (202) 663–7026 (TDD) or Christopher G. Bell, Acting Associate Legal Counsel for Americans With Disabilities Act Services, (202) 663–4679 (voice), (202) 663–7026.

Copies of this final rule and interpretive appendix may be obtained by calling the Office of Communications and Legislative Affairs at (202) 663–4900. Copies in alternate formats may be obtained from the Office of Equal Employment Opportunity by calling (202) 663–4398 or (202) 663–4395 (voice) or (202) 663–4399 (TDD). The alternate formats available are: Large print, braille, electronic file on computer disk, and audio-tape.

SUPPLEMENTARY INFORMATION:

Rulemaking History

The Commission actively solicited and considered public comment in the development of part 1630. On August 1, 1990, the Commission published an advance notice of proposed rulemaking (ANPRM), 55 FR 31192, informing the public that the Commission had begun the process of developing substantive regulations pursuant to title I of the ADA and inviting comment from interested groups and individuals. The comment period ended on August 31, 1990. In response to the ANPRM, the Commission received 138 comments from various disability rights organizations, employer groups, and

individuals. Comments were also solicited at 62 ADA input meetings conducted by Commission field offices throughout the country. More than 2400 representatives from disability rights organizations and employer groups participated in these meetings.

On February 28, 1991, the Commission published a notice of proposed rulemaking (NPRM), 56 FR 8578, setting forth proposed part 1630 for public comment. The comment period ended April 29, 1991. In response to the NPRM, the Commission received 697 timely comments from interested groups and individuals. In many instances, a comment was submitted on behalf of several parties and represented the views of numerous groups, employers, or individuals with disabilities. The comments have been analyzed and considered in the development of this final rule.

Overview of Regulations

The format of part 1630 reflects congressional intent, as expressed in the legislative history, that the regulations implementing the employment provisions of the ADA be modeled on the regulations implementing section 504 of the Rehabilitation Act of 1973, as amended, 34 CFR part 104. Accordingly, in developing part 1630, the Commission has been guided by the section 504 regulations and the case law interpreting those regulations.

It is the intent of Congress that the regulations implementing the ADA be comprehensive and easily understood. Part 1630, therefore, defines terms not previously defined in the regulations implementing section 504 of the Rehabilitation Act, such as "substantially limits," "essential functions," and "reasonable accommodation." Of necessity, many of the determinations that may be required by this part must be made on a case-by-case basis. Where possible, part 1630 establishes parameters to serve as guidelines in such inquiries.

The Commission is also issuing interpretive guidance concurrently with the issuance of part 1630 in order to ensure that qualified individuals with disabilities understand their rights under this part and to facilitate and encourage compliance by covered entities. Therefore, part 1630 is accompanied by an appendix. This appendix represents the Commission's interpretation of the issues discussed, and the Commission will be guided by it when resolving charges of employment discrimination. The appendix addresses the major provisions of part 1630 and explains the major concepts of disability rights. Further, the appendix cites to the

authority, such as the legislative history of the ADA and case law interpreting section 504 of the Rehabilitation Act, that provides the basis and purpose of the rule and interpretative guidance.

More detailed guidance on specific issues will be forthcoming in the Commission's Compliance Manual. Several Compliance Manual sections and policy guidances on ADA issues are currently under development and are expected to be issued prior to the effective date of the Act. Among the issues to be addressed in depth are the theories of discrimination; definitions of disability and of qualified individual with a disability; reasonable accommodation and undue hardship, including the scope of reassignment; and pre-employment inquiries.

To assist us in the development of this guidance, the Commission requested comment in the NPRM from disability rights organizations, employers, unions, state agencies concerned with employment or workers compensation practices, and interested individuals on specific questions about insurance, workers' compensation, and collective bargaining agreements. Many commenters responded to these questions, and several commenters addressed other matters pertinent to these areas. The Commission has considered these comments in the development of the final rule and will continue to consider them as it develops further ADA guidance.

In the NPRM, the Commission raised questions about a number of insurance-related matters. Specifically, the Commission asked commenters to discuss risk assessment and classification, the relationship between "risk" and "cost," and whether employers should consider the effects that changes in insurance coverage will have on individuals with disabilities before making those changes. Many commenters provided information about insurance practices and explained some of the considerations that affect insurance decisions. In addition, some commenters discussed their experiences with insurance plans and coverage. The commenters presented a wide range of opinions on insurance-related matters, and the Commission will consider the comments as it continues to analyze these complex matters.

The Commission received a large number of comments concerning inquiries about an individual's workers' compensation history. Many employers asserted that such inquiries are job related and consistent with business necessity. Several individuals with disabilities and disability rights organizations, however, argued that such inquiries are prohibited pre-employment inquiries and are not job related and consistent with business necessity. The Commission has addressed this issue in the interpretive guidance accompanying § 1630.14(a) and will discuss the matter further in future guidance.

There was little controversy about the submission of medical information to workers' compensation offices. A number of employers and employer groups pointed out that the workers' compensation offices of many states request medical information in connection with the administration of second-injury funds. Further, they noted that the disclosure of medical information may be necessary to the defense of a workers' compensation claim. The Commission has responded to these comments by amending the interpretive guidance accompanying § 1630.14(b). This amendment, discussed below, notes that the submission of medical information to workers' compensation offices in accordance with state workers' compensation laws is not inconsistent with § 1630.14(b). The Commission will address this area in greater detail and will discuss other issues concerning workers' compensation matters in future guidances, including the policy guidance on pre-employment inquiries.

With respect to collective bargaining agreements, the Commission asked commenters to discuss the relationship between collective bargaining agreements and such matters as undue hardship, reassignment to a vacant position, the determination of what constitutes a "vacant" position, and the confidentiality requirements of the ADA. The comments that we received reflected a wide variety of views. For example, some commenters argued that it would always be an undue hardship for an employer to provide a reasonable accommodation that conflicted with the provisions of a collective bargaining agreement. Other commenters, however, argued that an accommodation's effect on an agreement should not be considered when assessing undue hardship. Similarly, some commenters stated that the appropriateness of reassignment to a vacant position should depend upon the provisions of a collective bargaining agreement while others asserted that an agreement cannot limit the right to reassignment. Many commenters discussed the relationship between an agreement's seniority provisions and an employer's reasonable accommodation obligations.

In response to comments, the Commission has amended § 1630.2(n)(3) to include "the terms of a collective bargaining agreement" in the types of evidence relevant to determining the essential functions of a position. The Commission has made a corresponding change to the interpretive guidance on § 1630.2(n)(3). In addition, the Commission has amended the interpretive guidance on § 1630.15(d) to note that the terms of a collective bargaining agreement may be relevant to determining whether an accommodation would pose an undue hardship on the operation of a covered entity's business.

The divergent views expressed in the public comments demonstrate the complexity of employment-related issues concerning insurance, workers' compensation, and collective bargaining agreement matters. These highly complex issues require extensive research and analysis and warrant further consideration. Accordingly, the Commission has decided to address the issues in depth in future Compliance Manual sections and policy guidances. The Commission will consider the public comments that it received in response to the NPRM as it develops further guidance on the application of title I of the ADA to these matters.

The Commission has also decided to address burdens-of-proof issues in future guidance documents, including the Compliance Manual section on the theories of discrimination. Many commenters discussed the allocation of the various burdens of proof under title I of the ADA and asked the Commission to clarify those burdens. The comments in this area addressed such matters as determining whether a person is a qualified individual with a disability, job relatedness and business necessity, and undue hardship. The Commission will consider these comments as it prepares further guidance in this area.

A discussion of other significant comments and an explanation of the changes made in part 1630 since publication of the NPRM follows.

Section-by-Section Analysis of Comments and Revisions

Section 1630.1 Purpose, Applicability, and Construction

The Commission has made a technical correction to § 1630.1(a) by adding section 506(e) to the list of statutory provisions implemented by this part. Section 506(e) of the ADA provides that the failure to receive technical assistance from the federal agencies that administer the ADA is not a

defense to failing to meet the obligations of title I.

Some commenters asked the Commission to note that the ADA does not preempt state claims, such as state tort claims, that confer greater remedies than are available under the ADA. The Commission has added a paragraph to that effect in the appendix discussion of §§ 1630.1 (b) and (c). This interpretation is consistent with the legislative history of the Act. See H.R. Rep. No. 485 part 3, 101st Cong., 2d Sess. 69–70 (1990) (hereinafter referred to as House Judiciary Report).

In addition, the Commission has made a technical amendment to the appendix discussion to note that the ADA does not automatically preempt medical standards or safety requirements established by Federal law or regulations. The Commission has also amended the discussion to refer to a direct threat that cannot be eliminated "or reduced" through reasonable accommodation. This language is consistent with the regulatory definition of direct threat. (See § 1630.2(r), below.)

Section 1630.2 Definitions

Section 1630.2(h) Physical or Mental Impairment

The Commission has amended the interpretive guidance accompanying § 1630.2(h) to note that the definition of the term "impairment" does not include characteristic predisposition to illness or disease.

In addition, the Commission has specifically noted in the interpretive guidance that pregnancy is not an impairment. This change responds to the numerous questions that the Commission has received concerning whether pregnancy is a disability covered by the ADA. Pregnancy, by itself, is not an impairment and is therefore not a disability.

Section 1630.2(j) Substantially Limits

The Commission has revised the interpretive guidance accompanying § 1630.2(j) to make clear that the determination of whether an impairment substantially limits one or more major life activities is to be made without regard to the availability of medicines, assistive devices, or other mitigating measures. This interpretation is consistent with the legislative history of the ADA. See S. Rep. No. 116, 101st Cong., 1st Sess. 23 (1989) (hereinafter referred to as Senate Report); H.R. Rep. No. 485 part 2, 101st Cong., 2d Sess. 52 (1990) (hereinafter referred to as House Labor Report); House Judiciary Report at 28. The Commission has also revised the examples in the third paragraph of this section's guidance. The examples now focus on the individual s capacity to perform major life activities rather than on the presence or absence of mitigating measures. These revisions respond to comments from disability rights groups, which were concerned that the discussion could be misconstrued to exclude from ADA coverage individuals with disabilities who function well because of assistive devices or other mitigating measures.

In an amendment to the paragraph concerning the factors to consider when determining whether an impairment is substantially limiting, the Commission has provided a second example of an impairment's "impact." This example notes that a traumatic head injury's affect on cognitive functions is the "impact" of that impairment.

Many commenters addressed the provisions concerning the definition of "substantially limits" with respect to the major life activity of working (§ 1630.2(j)(3)). Some employers generally supported the definition but argued that it should be applied narrowly. Other employers argued that the definition is too broad. Disability rights groups and individuals with disabilities, on the other hand, argued that the definition is too narrow, unduly limits coverage, and places an onerous burden on individuals seeking to establish that they are covered by the ADA. The Commission has responded to these comments by making a number of clarifications in this area.

The Commission has revised § 1630.2(j)(3)(ii) and the accompanying interpretive guidance to note that the listed factors "may" be considered when determining whether an individual is substantially limited in working. This revision clarifies that the factors are relevant to, but are not required elements of, a showing of a substantial limitation in working.

Disability rights groups asked the Commission to clarify that "substantially limited in working" applies only when an individual is not substantially limited in any other major life activity. In addition, several other commenters indicated confusion about whether and when the ability to work should be considered when assessing if an individual has a disability. In response to these comments, the Commission has amended the interpretive guidance by adding a new paragraph clarifying the circumstances under which one should determine whether an individual is substantially limited in the major life activity of working. This paragraph makes clear that a determination of whether an individual is substantially limited in the

ability to work should be made only when the individual is not disabled in any other major life activity. Thus, individuals need not establish that they are substantially limited in working if they already have established that they are, have a record of, or are regarded as being substantially limited in another major life activity.

The proposed interpretive guidance in this area provided an example concerning a surgeon with a slight hand impairment. Several commenters expressed concern about this example. Many of these comments indicated that the example confused, rather than clarified, the matter. The Commission, therefore, has deleted this example. To explain further the application of the "substantially limited in working" concept, the Commission has provided another example (concerning a commercial airline pilot) in the interpretive guidance.

In addition, the Commission has clarified that the terms "numbers and types of jobs" (see § 1630.2(j)(3)(ii)(B)) and "numbers and types of other jobs" (see § 1630.2(j)(3)(ii)(C)) do not require an onerous evidentiary showing.

In the proposed interpretive guidance Appendix, after the interpretive guidance accompanying § 1630.2(l), the Commission included a discussion entitled "Frequently Disabling Impairments." Many commenters expressed concern about this discussion. In response to these comments, and to avoid confusion, the Commission has revised the discussion and has deleted the list of frequently disabling impairments. The revised discussion now appears in the interpretive guidance accompanying § 1630.2(j).

Section 1630.2(l) Is Regarded as Having Such an Impairment

Section 1630.2(l)(3) has been changed to refer to "a substantially limiting impairment" rather than "such an impairment." This change clarifies that an individual meets the definition of the term "disability" when a covered entity treats the individual as having a substantially limiting impairment. That is, § 1630.2(l)(3) refers to any substantially limiting impairment, rather than just to one of the impairments described in §§ 1630.2(l) (1) or (2).

The proposed interpretive guidance on § 1630.2(l) stated that, when determining whether an individual is regarded as substantially limited in working, "it should be assumed that all similar employers would apply the same exclusionary qualification standard that the employer charged with discrimination has used." The Commission specifically requested

comment on this proposal, and many commenters addressed this issue. The Commission has decided to eliminate this assumption and to revise the interpretive guidance. The guidance now explains that an individual meets the "regarded as" part of the definition of disability if he or she can show that a covered entity made an employment decision because of a perception of a disability based on "myth, fear, or stereotype." This is consistent with the legislative history of the ADA. See House Judiciary Report at 30.

Section 1630.2(m) Qualified Individual With a Disability

Under the proposed part 1630, the first step in determining whether an individual with a disability is a qualified individual with a disability was to determine whether the individual "satisfies the requisite skill, experience and education requirements of the employment position" the individual holds or desires. Many employers and employer groups asserted that the proposed regulation unduly limited job prerequisites to skill, experience, and education requirements and did not permit employers to consider other job-related qualifications. To clarify that the reference to skill, experience, and education requirements was not intended to be an exhaustive list of permissible qualification requirements, the Commission has revised the phrase to include "skill, experience, education, and other job-related requirements." This revision recognizes that other types of job-related requirements may be relevant to determining whether an individual is qualified for a position.

Many individuals with disabilities and disability rights groups asked the Commission to emphasize that the determination of whether a person is a qualified individual with a disability must be made at the time of the employment action in question and cannot be based on speculation that the individual will become unable to perform the job in the future or may cause increased health insurance or workers' compensation costs. The Commission has amended the interpretive guidance on § 1630.2(m) to reflect this point. This guidance is consistent with the legislative history of the Act. See Senate Report at 26, House Labor Report at 55, 136; House Judiciary Report at 34, 71.

Section 1630.2(n) Essential Functions

Many employers and employer groups objected to the use of the terms "primary" and "intrinsic" in the definition of essential functions. To avoid confusion about the meanings of "primary" and "intrinsic," the Commission has deleted these terms from the definition. The final regulation defines essential functions as "fundamental job duties" and notes that essential functions do not include the marginal functions of a position.

The proposed interpretive guidance accompanying § 1630.2(n)(2)(ii) noted that one of the factors in determining whether a function is essential is the number of employees available to perform a job function or among whom the performance of that function can be distributed. The proposed guidance explained that "(t)his may be a factor either because the total number of employees is low, or because of the fluctuating demands of the business operations." Some employers and employer groups expressed concern that this language could be interpreted as requiring an assessment of whether a job function could be distributed among all employees in any job at any level. The Commission has amended the interpretive guidance on this factor to clarify that the factor refers only to distribution among "available" employees.

Section 1630.2(n)(3) lists several kinds of evidence that are relevant to determining whether a particular job function is essential. Some employers and unions asked the Commission to recognize that collective bargaining agreements may help to identify a position's essential functions. In response to these comments, the Commission has added "(t)he terms of a collective bargaining agreement" to the list. In addition, the Commission has amended the interpretive guidance to note specifically that this type of evidence is relevant to the determination of essential functions. This addition is consistent with the legislative history of the Act. See Senate Report at 32; House Labor Report at 63.

Proposed § 1630.2(n)(3) referred to the evidence on the list as evidence "that may be considered in determining whether a particular function is essential." The Commission has revised this section to refer to evidence "of" whether a particular function is essential. The Commission made this revision in response to concerns about the meaning of the phrase "may be considered." In that regard, some commenters questioned whether the phrase meant that some of the listed evidence might not be considered when determining whether a function is essential to a position. This revision clarifies that all of the types of evidence on the list, when available, are relevant

to the determination of a position's essential functions. As the final rule and interpretive guidance make clear, the list is not an exhaustive list of all types of relevant evidence. Other types of available evidence may also be relevant to the determination.

The Commission has amended the interpretive guidance concerning § 1630.2(n)(3)(ii) to make clear that covered entities are not required to develop and maintain written job descriptions. Such job descriptions are relevant to a determination of a position's essential functions, but they are not required by part 1630.

Several commenters suggested that the Commission establish a rebuttable presumption in favor of the employer's judgment concerning what functions are essential. The Commission has not done so. On that point, the Commission notes that the House Committee on the Judiciary specifically rejected an amendment that would have created such a presumption. See House Judiciary Report at 33–34.

The last paragraph of the interpretive guidance on § 1630.2(n) notes that the inquiry into what constitutes a position's essential functions is not intended to second guess an employer's business judgment regarding production standards, whether qualitative or quantitative. In response to several comments, the Commission has revised this paragraph to incorporate examples of qualitative production standards.

Section 1630.2(o)   Reasonable Accommodation

The Commission has deleted the reference to undue hardship from the definition of reasonable accommodation. This is a technical change reflecting that undue hardship is a defense to, rather than an aspect of, reasonable accommodation. As some commenters have noted, a defense to a term should not be part of the term's definition. Accordingly, we have separated the concept of undue hardship from the definition of reasonable accommodation. This change does not affect the obligations of employers or the rights of individuals with disabilities. Accordingly, a covered entity remains obligated to make reasonable accommodation to the known physical or mental limitations of an otherwise qualified individual with a disability unless to do so would impose an undue hardship on the operation of the covered entity's business. See § 1630.9.

With respect to § 1630.2(o)(1)(i), some commenters expressed confusion about the use of the phrase "qualified individual with a disability." In that

regard, they noted that the phrase has a specific definition under this part (see § 1630.2(m)) and questioned whether an individual must meet that definition to request an accommodation with regard to the application process. The Commission has substituted the phrase "qualified applicant with a disability" for "qualified individual with a disability." This change clarifies that an individual with a disability who requests a reasonable accommodation to participate in the application process must be eligible only with respect to the application process.

The Commission has modified § 1630.2(o)(1)(iii) to state that reasonable accommodation includes modifications or adjustments that enable employees with disabilities to enjoy benefits and privileges that are "equal" to (rather than "the same" as) the benefits and privileges that are enjoyed by other employees. This change clarifies that such modifications or adjustments must ensure that individuals with disabilities receive equal access to the benefits and privileges afforded to other employees but may not be able to ensure that the individuals receive the same results of those benefits and privileges or precisely the same benefits and privileges.

Many commenters discussed whether the provision of daily attendant care is a form of reasonable accommodation. Employers and employer groups asserted that reasonable accommodation does not include such assistance. Disability rights groups and individuals with disabilities, however, asserted that such assistance is a form of reasonable accommodation but that this part did not make that clear. To clarify the extent of the reasonable accommodation obligation with respect to daily attendant care, the Commission has amended the interpretive guidance on § 1630.2(o) to make clear that it may be a reasonable accommodation to provide personal assistants to help with specified duties related to the job.

The Commission also has amended the interpretive guidance to note that allowing an individual with a disability to provide and use equipment, aids, or services that an employer is not required to provide may also be a form of reasonable accommodation. Some individuals with disabilities and disability rights groups asked the Commission to make this clear.

The interpretive guidance points out that reasonable accommodation may include making non-work areas accessible to individuals with disabilities. Many commenters asked the Commission to include rest rooms in the examples of accessible areas that may be required as reasonable accommodations. In response to those comments, the Commission has added rest rooms to the examples.

In response to other comments, the Commission has added a paragraph to the guidance concerning job restructuring as a form of reasonable accommodation. The new paragraph notes that job restructuring may involve changing when or how an essential function is performed.

Several commenters asked the Commission to provide additional guidance concerning the reasonable accommodation of reassignment to a vacant position. Specifically, commenters asked the Commission to clarify how long an employer must wait for a vacancy to arise when considering reassignment and to explain whether the employer is required to maintain the salary of an individual who is reassigned from a higher-paying position to a lower-paying one. The Commission has amended the discussion of reassignment to refer to reassignment to a position that is vacant "within a reasonable amount of time * * * in light of the totality of the circumstances." In addition, the Commission has noted that an employer is not required to maintain the salaries of reassigned individuals with disabilities if it does not maintain the salaries of individuals who are not disabled.

Section 1630.2(p)   Undue Hardship

The Commission has substituted "facility" or "facilities" for "site." or "sites" in § 1630.2(p)(2) and has deleted the definition of the term "site" Many employers and employer groups expressed concern about the use and meaning of the term "site." The final regulation's use of the terms "facility" and "facilities" is consistent with the language of the statute.

The Commission has amended the last paragraph of the interpretive guidance accompanying § 1630.2(p) to note that, when the cost of a requested accommodation would result in an undue hardship and outside funding is not available, an individual with a disability should be given the option of paying the portion of the cost that constitutes an undue hardship. This amendment is consistent with the legislative history of the Act. See Senate Report at 36; House Labor Report at 69.

Several employers and employer groups asked the Commission to expand the list of factors to be considered when determining if an accommodation would impose an undue hardship on a covered entity by adding another factor: The

relationship of an accommodation's cost to the value of the position at issue, as measured by the compensation paid to the holder of the position. Congress, however, specifically rejected this type of factor. See House Judiciary Report at 41 (noting that the House Judiciary Committee rejected an amendment proposing that an accommodation costing more than ten percent of the employee's salary be treated as an undue hardship). The Commission, therefore, has not added this to the list.

Section 1630.2(q)   Qualification Standards

The Commission has deleted the reference to direct threat from the definition of qualification standards. This revision is consistent with the revisions the Commission has made to §§ 1630.10 and 1630.15(b). (See discussion below.)

Section 1630.2(r)   Direct Threat

Many disability rights groups and individuals with disabilities asserted that the definition of direct threat should not include a reference to the health or safety of the individual with a disability. They expressed concern that the reference to "risk to self" would result in direct threat determinations that are based on negative stereotypes and paternalistic views about what is best for individuals with disabilities. Alternatively, the commenters asked the Commission to clarify that any assessment of risk must be based on the individual's present condition and not on speculation about the individual's future condition. They also asked the Commission to specify evidence other than medical knowledge that may be relevant to the determination of direct threat.

The final regulation retains the reference to the health or safety of the individual with a disability. As the appendix notes, this is consistent with the legislative history of the ADA and the case law interpreting section 504 of the Rehabilitation Act.

To clarify the direct threat standard, the Commission has made four revisions to § 1630.2(r). First, the Commission has amended the first sentence of the definition of direct threat to refer to a significant risk of substantial harm that cannot be eliminated "or reduced" by reasonable accommodation. This amendment clarifies that the risk need not be eliminated entirely to fall below the direct threat definition; instead, the risk need only be reduced to the level at which there no longer exists a significant risk of substantial harm. In addition, the Commission has rephrased the second sentence of § 1630.2(r) to

clarify that an employer's direct threat standard must apply to all individuals, not just to individuals with disabilities. Further, the Commission has made clear that a direct threat determination must be based on "an individualized assessment of the individual's present ability to safely perform the essential functions of the job." This clarifies that a determination that employment of an individual would pose a direct threat must involve an individualized inquiry and must be based on the individual's current condition. In addition, the Commission has added "the imminence of the potential harm" to the list of factors to be considered when determining whether employment of an individual would pose a direct threat. This change clarifies that both the probability of harm and the imminence of harm are relevant to direct threat determinations. This definition of direct threat is consistent with the legislative history of the Act. See Senate Report at 27, House Labor Report at 56–57, 73–75, House Judiciary Report at 45–46.

Further, the Commission has amended the interpretive guidance on § 1630.2(r) to highlight the individualized nature of the direct threat assessment. In addition, the Commission has cited examples of evidence other than medical knowledge that may be relevant to determining whether employment of an individual would pose a direct threat.

Section 1630.3   Exceptions to the Definitions of "Disability" and "Qualified Individual With a Disability"

Many commenters asked the Commission to clarify that the term "rehabilitation program" includes self-help groups. In response to these comments, the Commission has amended the interpretive guidance in this area to include a reference to professionally recognized self-help programs.

The Commission has added a paragraph to the guidance on § 1630.3 to note that individuals who are not excluded under this provision from the definitions of the terms "disability" and "qualified individual with a disability" must still establish that they meet those definitions to be protected by part 1630. Several employers and employer groups asked the Commission to clarify that individuals are not automatically covered by the ADA simply because they do not fall into one of the exclusions listed in this section.

The proposed interpretive guidance on § 1630.3 noted that employers are entitled to seek reasonable assurances that an individual is not currently engaging in the illegal use of drugs. In that regard, the guidance stated, "It is essential that the individual offer evidence, such as a drug test, to prove that he or she is not currently engaging" in such use. Many commenters interpreted this guidance to require individuals to come forward with evidence even in the absence of a request by the employer. The Commission has revised the interpretive guidance to clarify that such evidence is required only upon request.

Section 1630.6   Contractual or Other Arrangements

The Commission has added a sentence to the first paragraph of the interpretive guidance on § 1630.6 to clarify that this section has no impact on whether one is a covered entity or employer as defined by § 1630.2.

The proposed interpretive guidance on contractual or other relationships noted that § 1630.6 applied to parties on either side of the relationship. To illustrate this point, the guidance stated that "a copier company would be required to ensure the provision of any reasonable accommodation necessary to enable its copier service representative with a disability to service a client's machine. Several employers objected to this example. In that respect, the commenters argued that the language of the example was too broad and could be interpreted as requiring employers to make all customers premises accessible. The Commission has revised the example to provide a clearer, more concrete indication of the scope of the reasonable accommodation obligations in this area.

In addition, the Commission has clarified the interpretive guidance by noting that the existence of a contractual relationship adds no new obligations "under this part."

Section 1630.8   Relationship or Association With an Individual With a Disability

The Commission has added the phrase "or otherwise discriminate against" to § 1630.8. This change clarifies that harassment or any other form of discrimination against a qualified individual because of the known disability of a person with whom the individual has a relationship or an association is also a prohibited form of discrimination.

The Commission has revised the first sentence of the interpretive guidance to refer to a person's relationship or association with an individual who has a "known" disability. This revision makes the language of the interpretive guidance consistent with the language of

the regulation. In addition, to reflect current, preferred terminology, the Commission has substituted the term "people who have AIDS" for the term "AIDS patients." Finally, the Commission has added a paragraph to clarify that this provision applies to discrimination in other employment privileges and benefits, such as health insurance benefits.

Section 1630.9   Not Making Reasonable Accommodation

Section 1630.9(c) provides that "(a) covered entity shall not be excused from the requirements of this part because of any failure to receive technical assistance * * *." Some employers asked the Commission to revise this section and to state that the failure to receive technical assistance is a defense to not providing reasonable accommodation. The Commission has not made the requested revision. Section 1630.9(c) is consistent with section 506(e) of the ADA, which states that the failure to receive technical assistance from the federal agencies that administer the ADA does not excuse a covered entity from compliance with the requirements of the Act.

The first paragraph of the interpretive guidance accompanying § 1630.9 notes that the reasonable accommodation obligation does not require employers to provide adjustments or modifications that are primarily for the personal use of the individual with a disability. The Commission has amended this guidance to clarify that employers may be required to provide items that are customarily personal-use items where the items are specifically designed or required to meet job-related needs.

In addition, the Commission has amended the interpretive guidance to clarify that there must be a nexus between an individual's disability and the need for accommodation. Thus, the guidance notes that an individual with a disability is "otherwise qualified" if he or she is qualified for the job except that, "because of the disability," the individual needs reasonable accommodation to perform the essential functions of the job. Similarly, the guidance notes that employers are required to accommodate only the physical or mental limitations "resulting from the disability" that are known to the employer.

In response to commenters' requests for clarification, the Commission has noted that employers may require individuals with disabilities to provide documentation of the need for reasonable accommodation when the need for a requested accommodation is not obvious.

In addition, the Commission has amended the last paragraph of the interpretive guidance on the "Process of Determining the Appropriate Reasonable Accommodation." This amendment clarifies that an employer must consider allowing an individual with a disability to provide his or her own accommodation if the individual wishes to do so. The employer, however, may not require the individual to provide the accommodation.

Section 1630.10   Qualification Standards, Tests, and Other Selection Criteria

The Commission has added the phrase "on the basis of disability" to § 1630.10(a) to clarify that a selection criterion that is not job related and consistent with business necessity violates this section only when it screens out an individual with a disability (or a class of individuals with disabilities) on the basis of disability. That is, there must be a nexus between the exclusion and the disability. A selection criterion that screens out an individual with a disability for reasons that are not related to the disability does not violate this section. The Commission has made similar changes to the interpretive guidance on this section.

Proposed § 1630.10(b) stated that a covered entity could use as a qualification standard the requirement that an individual not pose a direct threat to the health or safety of the individual or others. Many individuals with disabilities objected to the inclusion of the direct threat reference in this section and asked the Commission to clarify that the direct threat standard must be raised by the covered entity as a defense. In that regard, they specifically asked the Commission to move the direct threat provision from § 1630.10 (qualification standards) to § 1630.15 (defenses). The Commission has deleted the direct threat provision from § 1630.10 and has moved it to § 1630.15. This is consistent with section 103 of the ADA, which refers to defenses and states (in section 103(b)) that the term "qualification standards" may include a requirement that an individual not pose a direct threat.

Section 1630.11   Administration of Tests

The Commission has revised the interpretive guidance concerning § 1630.11 to clarify that a request for an alternative test format or other testing accommodation generally should be made prior to the administration of the test or as soon as the individual with a disability becomes aware of the need for accommodation. In addition, the Commission has amended the last paragraph of the guidance on this section to note that an employer can require a written test of an applicant with dyslexia if the ability to read is "the skill the test is designed to measure." This language is consistent with the regulatory language, which refers to the skills a test purports to measure.

Some commenters noted that certain tests are designed to measure the speed with which an applicant performs a function. In response to these comments, the Commission has amended the interpretive guidance to state that an employer may require an applicant to complete a test within a specified time frame if speed is one of the skills being tested.

In response to comments, the Commission has amended the interpretive guidance accompanying § 1630.14(a) to clarify that employers may invite applicants to request accommodations for taking tests. (See § 1630.14(a), below.)

Section 1630.12   Retaliation and Coercion

The Commission has amended § 1630.12 to clarify that this section also prohibits harassment.

Section 1630.13   Prohibited Medical Examinations and Inquiries

In response to the Commission's request for comment on certain workers' compensation matters, many commenters addressed whether a covered entity may ask applicants about their history of workers' compensation claims. Many employers and employer groups argued that an inquiry about an individual's workers' compensation history is job related and consistent with business necessity. Disability rights groups and individuals with disabilities, however, asserted that such an inquiry could disclose the existence of a disability. In response to comments and to clarify this matter, the Commission has amended the interpretive guidance accompanying § 1630.13(a). The amendment states that an employer may not inquire about an individual's workers' compensation history at the pre-offer stage.

The Commission has made a technical change to § 1630.13(b) by deleting the phrase "unless the examination or inquiry is shown to be job-related and consistent with business necessity" from the section. This change does not affect the substantive provisions of § 1630.13(b). The Commission has incorporated the job-relatedness and

business-necessity requirement into a new § 1630.14(c), which clarifies the scope of permissible examinations or inquiries of employees. (See § 1630.14(c), below.)

Section 1630.14   Medical Examinations and Inquiries Specifically Permitted

Section 1630.14(a)   Acceptable Pre-employment Inquiry

Proposed § 1630.14(a) stated that a covered entity may make pre-employment inquiries into an applicant's ability to perform job-related functions. The interpretive guidance accompanying this section noted that an employer may ask an individual whether he or she can perform a job function with or without reasonable accommodation.

Many employers asked the Commission to provide additional guidance in this area. Specifically, the commenters asked whether an employer may ask how an individual will perform a job function when the individual's known disability appears to interfere with or prevent performance of job-related functions. To clarify this matter, the Commission has amended § 1630.14(a) to state that a covered entity "may ask an applicant to describe or to demonstrate how, with or without reasonable accommodation, the applicant will be able to perform job-related functions." The Commission has amended the interpretive guidance accompanying § 1630.14(a) to reflect this change.

Many commenters asked the Commission to state that employers may inquire, before tests are taken, whether candidates will require any reasonable accommodations to take the tests. They asked the Commission to acknowledge that such inquiries constitute permissible pre-employment inquiries. In response to these comments, the Commission has added a new paragraph to the interpretive guidance on § 1630.14(a). This paragraph clarifies that employers may ask candidates to inform them of the need for reasonable accommodation within a reasonable time before the administration of the test and may request documentation verifying the need for accommodation.

The Commission has received many comments from law enforcement and other public safety agencies concerning the administration of physical agility tests. In response to those comments, the Commission has added a new paragraph clarifying that such tests are not medical examinations.

Many employers and employer groups have asked the Commission to discuss whether employers may invite applicants to self-identify as individuals

with disabilities. In that regard, many of the commenters noted that section 503 of the Rehabilitation Act imposes certain obligations on government contractors. The interpretive guidance accompanying § 1630.1(b) and (c) notes that "title I of the ADA would not be a defense to failing to collect information required to satisfy the affirmative action requirements of section 503 of the Rehabilitation Act." To reiterate this point, the Commission has amended the interpretive guidance accompanying § 1630.14(a) to note specifically that this section does not restrict employers from collecting information and inviting individuals to identify themselves as individuals with disabilities as required to satisfy the affirmative action requirements of section 503 of the Rehabilitation Act.

Section 1630.14(b)   Employment Entrance Examinations

Section 1630.14(b) has been amended to include the phrase "(and/or inquiry)" after references to medical examinations. Some commenters were concerned that the regulation as drafted prohibited covered entities from making any medical inquiries or administering questionnaires that did not constitute examinations. This change clarifies that the term "employment entrance examinations" includes medical inquiries as well as medical examinations.

Section 1630.14(b)(2) has been revised to state that the results of employment entrance examinations "shall not be used for any purpose inconsistent with this part." This language is consistent with the language used in § 1630.14(c)(2).

The second paragraph of the proposed interpretive guidance on this section referred to "relevant" physical and psychological criteria. Some commenters questioned the use of the term "relevant" and expressed concern about its meaning. The Commission has deleted this term from the paragraph.

Many commenters addressed the confidentiality provisions of this section. They noted that it may be necessary to disclose medical information in defense of workers' compensation claims or during the course of other legal proceedings. In addition, they pointed out that the workers' compensation offices of many states request such information for the administration of second-injury funds or for other administrative purposes.

The Commission has revised the last paragraph of the interpretive guidance on § 1630.14(b) to reflect that the information obtained during a permitted employment entrance examination or inquiry may be used only "in a manner not inconsistent with this part." In addition, the Commission has added language clarifying that it is permissible to submit the information to state workers' compensation offices.

Several commenters asked the Commission to clarify whether information obtained from employment entrance examinations and inquiries may be used for insurance purposes. In response to these comments, the Commission has noted in the interpretive guidance that such information may be used for insurance purposes described in § 1630.16(f).

Section 1630.14(c)   Examination of Employees

The Commission has added a new § 1630.14(c), Examination of employees, that clarifies the scope of permissible medical examinations and inquiries. Several employers and employer groups expressed concern that the proposed version of part 1630 did not make it clear that covered entities may require employee medical examinations, such as fitness-for-duty examinations, that are job related and consistent with business necessity. New § 1630.14(c) clarifies this by expressly permitting covered entities to require employee medical examinations and inquiries that are job related and consistent with business necessity. The information obtained from such examinations or inquiries must be treated as a confidential medical record. This section also incorporates the last sentence of proposed § 1630.14(c). The remainder of proposed § 1630.14(c) has become § 1630.14(d).

To comport with this technical change in the regulation, the Commission has made corresponding changes in the interpretive guidance. Thus, the Commission has moved the second paragraph of the proposed guidance on § 1630.13(b) to the guidance on § 1630.14(c). In addition, the Commission has reworded the paragraph to note that this provision permits (rather than does not prohibit) certain medical examinations and inquiries.

Some commenters asked the Commission to clarify whether employers may make inquiries or require medical examinations in connection with the reasonable accommodation process. The Commission has noted in the interpretive guidance that such inquiries and examinations are permissible when they are necessary to the reasonable accommodation process described in this part.

Section 1630.15   Defenses

The Commission has added a sentence to the interpretive guidance on § 1630.15(a) to clarify that the assertion that an insurance plan does not cover an individual's disability or that the disability would cause increased insurance or workers' compensation costs does not constitute a legitimate, nondiscriminatory reason for disparate treatment of an individual with a disability. This clarification, made in response to many comments from individuals with disabilities and disability rights groups, is consistent with the legislative history of the ADA. See Senate Report at 85; House Labor Report at 136; House Judiciary Report at 71.

The Commission has amended § 1630.15(b) by stating that the term "qualification standard" may include a requirement that an individual not pose a direct threat. As noted above, this is consistent with section 103 of the ADA and responds to many comments from individuals with disabilities.

The Commission has made a technical correction to § 1630.15(c) by changing the phrase "an individual or class of individuals with disabilities" to "an individual with a disability or a class of individuals with disabilities."

Several employers and employer groups asked the Commission to acknowledge that undue hardship considerations about reasonable accommodations at temporary work sites may be different from the considerations relevant to permanent work sites. In response to these comments, the Commission has amended the interpretive guidance on § 1630.15(d) to note that an accommodation that poses an undue hardship in a particular job setting, such as a temporary construction site, may not pose an undue hardship in another setting. This guidance is consistent with the legislative history of the ADA. See House Labor Report at 69–70; House Judiciary Report at 41–42.

The Commission also has amended the interpretive guidance to note that the terms of a collective bargaining agreement may be relevant to the determination of whether a requested accommodation would pose an undue hardship on the operation of a covered entity's business. This amendment, which responds to commenters' requests that the Commission recognize the relevancy of collective bargaining agreements, is consistent with the legislative history of the Act. See Senate Report at 32; House Labor Report at 63.

Section 1630.2(p)(2)(v) provides that the impact of an accommodation on the ability of other employees to perform their duties is one of the factors to be considered when determining whether the accommodation would impose an undue hardship on a covered entity. Many commenters addressed whether an accommodation's impact on the morale of other employees may be relevant to a determination of undue hardship. Some employers and employer groups asserted that a negative impact on employee morale should be considered an undue hardship. Disability rights groups and individuals with disabilities, however, argued that undue hardship determinations must not be based on the morale of other employees. It is the Commission's view that a negative effect on morale, by itself, is not sufficient to meet the undue hardship standard. The Commission has noted in the guidance on § 1630.15(d) that an employer cannot establish undue hardship by showing only that an accommodation would have a negative impact on employee morale.

Section 1630.16   Specific Activities Permitted

The Commission has revised the second sentence of the interpretive guidance on § 1630.16(b) to state that an employer may hold individuals with alcoholism and individuals who engage in the illegal use of drugs to the same performance and conduct standards to which it holds "all of its" other employees. In addition, the Commission has deleted the term "otherwise" from the third sentence of the guidance. These revisions clarify that employers may hold all employees, disabled (including those disabled by alcoholism or drug addiction) and nondisabled, to the same performance and conduct standards.

Many commenters asked the Commission to clarify that the drug testing provisions of § 1630.16(c) pertain only to tests to determine the illegal use of drugs. Accordingly, the Commission has amended § 1630.16(c)(1) to refer to the administration of "such" drug tests and § 1630.16(c)(3) to refer to information obtained from a "test to determine the illegal use of drugs." We have also made a change in the grammatical structure of the last sentence of § 1630.16(c)(1). We have made similar changes to the corresponding section of the interpretive guidance. In addition, the Commission has amended the interpretive guidance to state that such tests are neither encouraged, "authorized," nor prohibited. This amendment conforms the language of the guidance to the language of § 1630.16(c)(1).

The Commission has revised § 1630.16(e)(1) to refer to communicable diseases that "are" (rather than "may be") transmitted through the handling of food. Several commenters asked the Commission to make this technical change, which adopts the statutory language.

Several commenters also asked the Commission to conform the language of proposed § 1630.16(f) (1) and (2) to the language of sections 501(c) (1) and (2) of the Act. The Commission has made this change. Thus, § 1630.16(f) (1) and (2) now refer to risks that are "not inconsistent with State law."

Executive Order 12291 and Regulatory Flexibility Act

The Commission published a Preliminary Regulatory Impact Analysis on February 28, 1991 (56 FR 8578). Based on the Preliminary Regulatory Impact Analysis, the Commission certifies that this final rule will not have a significant economic impact on a substantial number of small business entities. The Commission is issuing this final rule at this time in the absence of a Final Regulatory Impact Analysis in order to meet the statutory deadline. The Commission's Preliminary Regulatory Impact Analysis was based upon existing data on the costs of reasonable accommodation. The Commission received few comments on this aspect of its rulemaking. Because of the complexity inherent in assessing the economic costs and benefits of this rule and the relative paucity of data on this issue, the Commission will further study the economic impact of the regulation and intends to issue a Final Regulatory Impact Analysis prior to January 1, 1992. As indicated above, the Preliminary Regulatory Impact Analysis was published on February 28, 1991 (56 FR 8578) for comment. The Commission will also provide a copy to the public upon request by calling the Commission's Office of Communications and Legislative Affairs at (202) 663-4900. Commenters are urged to provide additional information as to the costs and benefits associated with this rule. This will further facilitate the development of a Final Regulatory Impact Analysis. Comments must be received by September 26, 1991. Written comments should be submitted to Frances M. Hart, Executive Officer, Executive Secretariat, Equal Employment Opportunity Commission, 1801 "L" Street, NW., Washington, DC 20507.

As a convenience to commenters, the Executive Secretariat will accept public comments transmitted by facsimile ("FAX") machine. The telephone number of the FAX receiver is (202) 663-4114. (This is not a toll-free number). Only public comments of six or fewer pages will be accepted via FAX transmittal. This limitation is necessary in order to assure access to the equipment. Comments sent by FAX in excess of six pages will not be accepted. Receipt of FAX transmittals will not be acknowledged, except that the sender may request confirmation of receipt by calling the Executive Secretariat Staff at (202) 663-4078. (This is not a toll-free number).

Comments received will be available for public inspection in the EEOC Library, room 6502, by appointment only, from 9 a.m. to 5 p.m., Monday through Friday except legal holidays from October 15, 1991, until the Final Regulatory Impact Analysis is published. Persons who need assistance to review the comments will be provided with appropriate aids such as readers or print magnifiers. To schedule an appointment call (202) 663-4630 (voice), (202) 663-4630 (TDD).

List of Subjects in 29 CFR Part 1630

Equal employment opportunity, Handicapped, Individuals with disabilities.

For the Commission.

Evan J. Kemp, Jr.,
Chairman.

Accordingly, 29 CFR chapter XIV is amended by adding part 1630 to read as follows:

PART 1630—REGULATIONS TO IMPLEMENT THE EQUAL EMPLOYMENT PROVISIONS OF THE AMERICANS WITH DISABILITIES ACT

Sec.
1630.1 Purpose, applicability, and construction.
1630.2 Definitions.
1630.3 Exceptions to the definitions of "Disability" and "Qualified Individual with a Disability."
1630.4 Discrimination prohibited.
1630.5 Limiting, segregating, and classifying.
1630.6 Contractual or other arrangements.
1630.7 Standards, criteria, or methods of administration.
1630.8 Relationship or association with an individual with a disability.
1630.9 Not making reasonable accommodation.
1630.10 Qualification standards, tests, and other selection criteria.
1630.11 Administration of tests.
1630.12 Retaliation and coercion.
1630.13 Prohibited medical examinations and inquiries.
1630.14 Medical examinations and inquiries specifically permitted.
1630.15 Defenses.
1630.16 Specific activities permitted.

Appendix to Part 1630—Interpretive Guidance on Title I of the Americans with Disabilities Act

Authority: 42 U.S.C. 12116.

§ 1630.1 Purpose, applicability, and construction.

(a) *Purpose.* The purpose of this part is to implement title I of the Americans with Disabilities Act (42 U.S.C. 12101, *et seq.*) (ADA), requiring equal employment opportunities for qualified individuals with disabilities, and sections 3(2), 3(3), 501, 503, 506(e), 508, 510, and 511 of the ADA as those sections pertain to the employment of qualified individuals with disabilities.

(b) *Applicability.* This part applies to "covered entities" as defined at § 1630.2(b).

(c) *Construction.*—(1) *In general.* Except as otherwise provided in this part, this part does not apply a lesser standard than the standards applied under title V of the Rehabilitation Act of 1973 (29 U.S.C. 790–794a), or the regulations issued by Federal agencies pursuant to that title.

(2) *Relationship to other laws.* This part does not invalidate or limit the remedies, rights, and procedures of any Federal law or law of any State or political subdivision of any State or jurisdiction that provides greater or equal protection for the rights of individuals with disabilities than are afforded by this part.

§ 1630.2 Definitions.

(a) *Commission* means the Equal Employment Opportunity Commission established by section 705 of the Civil Rights Act of 1964 (42 U.S.C. 2000e–4).

(b) *Covered Entity* means an employer, employment agency, labor organization, or joint labor management committee.

(c) *Person, labor organization, employment agency, commerce and industry affecting commerce* shall have the same meaning given those terms in section 701 of the Civil Rights Act of 1964 (42 U.S.C. 2000e).

(d) *State* means each of the several States, the District of Columbia, the Commonwealth of Puerto Rico, Guam, American Samoa, the Virgin Islands, the Trust Territory of the Pacific Islands, and the Commonwealth of the Northern Mariana Islands.

(e) *Employer.*—(1) *In general.* The term employer means a person engaged in an industry affecting commerce who has 15 or more employees for each working day in each of 20 or more calendar weeks in the current or preceding calendar year, and any agent of such person, except that, from July 26,

1992 through July 25, 1994, an employer means a person engaged in an industry affecting commerce who has 25 or more employees for each working day in each of 20 or more calendar weeks in the current or preceding year and any agent of such person.

(2) *Exceptions*. The term employer does not include—

(i) The United States, a corporation wholly owned by the government of the United States, or an Indian tribe; or

(ii) A bona fide private membership club (other than a labor organization) that is exempt from taxation under section 501(c) of the Internal Revenue Code of 1986.

(f) *Employee* means an individual employed by an employer.

(g) *Disability* means, with respect to an individual—

(1) A physical or mental impairment that substantially limits one or more of the major life activities of such individual;

(2) A record of such an impairment; or

(3) being regarded as having such an impairment.

(See § 1630.3 for exceptions to this definition).

(h) *Physical or mental impairment* means:

(1) Any physiological disorder, or condition, cosmetic disfigurement, or anatomical loss affecting one or more of the following body systems: neurological, musculoskeletal, special sense organs, respiratory (including speech organs), cardiovascular, reproductive, digestive, genito-urinary, hemic and lymphatic, skin, and endocrine; or

(2) Any mental or psychological disorder, such as mental retardation, organic brain syndrome, emotional or mental illness, and specific learning disabilities.

(i) *Major Life Activities* means functions such as caring for oneself, performing manual tasks, walking, seeing, hearing, speaking, breathing, learning, and working.

(j) *Substantially limits*—(1) The term *substantially limits* means:

(i) Unable to perform a major life activity that the average person in the general population can perform; or

(ii) Significantly restricted as to the condition, manner or duration under which an individual can perform a particular major life activity as compared to the condition, manner, or duration under which the average person in the general population can perform that same major life activity.

(2) The following factors should be considered in determining whether an individual is substantially limited in a major life activity:

(i) The nature and severity of the impairment;

(ii) The duration or expected duration of the impairment; and

(iii) The permanent or long term impact, or the expected permanent or long term impact of or resulting from the impairment.

(3) With respect to the major life activity of *working*—

(i) The term *substantially limits* means significantly restricted in the ability to perform either a class of jobs or a broad range of jobs in various classes as compared to the average person having comparable training, skills and abilities. The inability to perform a single, particular job does not constitute a substantial limitation in the major life activity of working.

(ii) In addition to the factors listed in paragraph (j)(2) of this section, the following factors may be considered in determining whether an individual is substantially limited in the major life activity of "working":

(A) The geographical area to which the individual has reasonable access;

(B) The job from which the individual has been disqualified because of an impairment, and the number and types of jobs utilizing similar training, knowledge, skills or abilities, within that geographical area, from which the individual is also disqualified because of the impairment (class of jobs); and/or

(C) The job from which the individual has been disqualified because of an impairment, and the number and types of other jobs not utilizing similar training, knowledge, skills or abilities, within that geographical area, from which the individual is also disqualified because of the impairment (broad range of jobs in various classes).

(k) *Has a record of such impairment* means has a history of, or has been misclassified as having, a mental or physical impairment that substantially limits one or more major life activities.

(l) *Is regarded as having such an impairment* means:

(1) Has a physical or mental impairment that does not substantially limit major life activities but is treated by a covered entity as constituting such limitation;

(2) Has a physical or mental impairment that substantially limits major life activities only as a result of the attitudes of others toward such impairment; or

(3) Has none of the impairments defined in paragraphs (h) (1) or (2) of this section but is treated by a covered entity as having a substantially limiting impairment.

(m) *Qualified individual with a disability* means an individual with a disability who satisfies the requisite skill, experience, education and other job-related requirements of the employment position such individual holds or desires, and who, with or without reasonable accommodation, can perform the essential functions of such position. (See § 1630.3 for exceptions to this definition).

(n) *Essential functions.*—(1) *In general*. The term *essential functions* means the fundamental job duties of the employment position the individual with a disability holds or desires. The term "essential functions" does not include the marginal functions of the position.

(2) A job function may be considered essential for any of several reasons, including but not limited to the following:

(i) The function may be essential because the reason the position exists is to perform that function;

(ii) The function may be essential because of the limited number of employees available among whom the performance of that job function can be distributed; and/or

(iii) The function may be highly specialized so that the incumbent in the position is hired for his or her expertise or ability to perform the particular function.

(3) Evidence of whether a particular function is essential includes, but is not limited to:

(i) The employer's judgment as to which functions are essential;

(ii) Written job descriptions prepared before advertising or interviewing applicants for the job;

(iii) The amount of time spent on the job performing the function;

(iv) The consequences of not requiring the incumbent to perform the function;

(v) The terms of a collective bargaining agreement;

(vi) The work experience of past incumbents in the job; and/or

(vii) The current work experience of incumbents in similar jobs.

(o) *Reasonable accommodation.* (1) The term *reasonable accommodation* means:

(i) Modifications or adjustments to a job application process that enable a qualified applicant with a disability to be considered for the position such qualified applicant desires; or

(ii) Modifications or adjustments to the work environment, or to the manner or circumstances under which the position held or desired is customarily performed, that enable a qualified individual with a disability to perform the essential functions of that position; or

(iii) Modifications or adjustments that enable a covered entity's employee with a disability to enjoy equal benefits and privileges of employment as are enjoyed by its other similarly situated employees without disabilities.

(2) *Reasonable accommodation* may include but is not limited to:

(i) Making existing facilities used by employees readily accessible to and usable by individuals with disabilities; and

(ii) Job restructuring; part-time or modified work schedules; reassignment to a vacant position; acquisition or modifications of equipment or devices; appropriate adjustment or modifications of examinations, training materials, or policies; the provision of qualified readers or interpreters; and other similar accommodations for individuals with disabilities.

(3) To determine the appropriate reasonable accommodation it may be necessary for the covered entity to initiate an informal, interactive process with the qualified individual with a disability in need of the accommodation. This process should identify the precise limitations resulting from the disability and potential reasonable accommodations that could overcome those limitations.

(p) *Undue hardship*—(1) *In general.* Undue hardship means, with respect to the provision of an accommodation, significant difficulty or expense incurred by a covered entity, when considered in light of the factors set forth in paragraph (p)(2) of this section.

(2) *Factors to be considered.* In determining whether an accommodation would impose an undue hardship on a covered entity, factors to be considered include:

(i) The nature and net cost of the accommodation needed under this part, taking into consideration the availability of tax credits and deductions, and/or outside funding;

(ii) The overall financial resources of the facility or facilities involved in the provision of the reasonable accommodation, the number of persons employed at such facility, and the effect on expenses and resources;

(iii) The overall financial resources of the covered entity, the overall size of the business of the covered entity with respect to the number of its employees, and the number, type and location of its facilities;

(iv) The type of operation or operations of the covered entity, including the composition, structure and functions of the workforce of such entity, and the geographic separateness and administrative or fiscal relationship of the facility or facilities in question to the covered entity; and

(v) The impact of the accommodation upon the operation of the facility, including the impact on the ability of other employees to perform their duties and the impact on the facility's ability to conduct business.

(q) *Qualification standards* means the personal and professional attributes including the skill, experience, education, physical, medical, safety and other requirements established by a covered entity as requirements which an individual must meet in order to be eligible for the position held or desired.

(r) *Direct Threat* means a significant risk of substantial harm to the health or safety of the individual or others that cannot be eliminated or reduced by reasonable accommodation. The determination that an individual poses a "direct threat" shall be based on an individualized assessment of the individual's present ability to safely perform the essential functions of the job. This assessment shall be based on a reasonable medical judgment that relies on the most current medical knowledge and/or on the best available objective evidence. In determining whether an individual would pose a direct threat, the factors to be considered include:

(1) The duration of the risk;

(2) The nature and severity of the potential harm;

(3) The likelihood that the potential harm will occur; and

(4) The imminence of the potential harm.

§ 1630.3 **Exceptions to the definitions of "Disability" and "Qualified Individual with a Disability."**

(a) The terms *disability* and *qualified individual with a disability* do not include individuals currently engaging in the illegal use of drugs, when the covered entity acts on the basis of such use.

(1) *Drug* means a controlled substance, as defined in schedules I through V of Section 202 of the Controlled Substances Act (21 U.S.C 812)

(2) *Illegal use of drugs* means the use of drugs the possession or distribution of which is unlawful under the Controlled Substances Act, as periodically updated by the Food and Drug Administration. This term does not include the use of a drug taken under the supervision of a licensed health care professional, or other uses authorized by the Controlled Substances Act or other provisions of Federal law.

(b) However, the terms *disability* and *qualified* individual with a disability may not exclude an individual who:

(1) Has successfully completed a supervised drug rehabilitation program and is no longer engaging in the illegal use of drugs, or has otherwise been rehabilitated successfully and is no longer engaging in the illegal use of drugs; or

(2) Is participating in a supervised rehabilitation program and is no longer engaging in such use; or

(3) Is erroneously regarded as engaging in such use, but is not engaging in such use.

(c) It shall not be a violation of this part for a covered entity to adopt or administer reasonable policies or procedures, including but not limited to drug testing, designed to ensure that an individual described in paragraph (b) (1) or (2) of this section is no longer engaging in the illegal use of drugs. (See § 1630.16(c) Drug testing).

(d) *Disability* does not include:

(1) Transvestism, transsexualism, pedophilia, exhibitionism, voyeurism, gender identity disorders not resulting from physical impairments, or other sexual behavior disorders;

(2) Compulsive gambling, kleptomania, or pyromania; or

(3) Psychoactive substance use disorders resulting from current illegal use of drugs.

(e) *Homosexuality and bisexuality* are not impairments and so are not disabilities as defined in this part.

§ 1630.4 **Discrimination prohibited.**

It is unlawful for a covered entity to discriminate on the basis of disability against a qualified individual with a disability in regard to:

(a) Recruitment, advertising, and job application procedures;

(b) Hiring, upgrading, promotion, award of tenure, demotion, transfer, layoff, termination, right of return from layoff, and rehiring;

(c) Rates of pay or any other form of compensation and changes in compensation;

(d) Job assignments, job classifications, organizational structures, position descriptions, lines of progression, and seniority lists;

(e) Leaves of absence, sick leave, or any other leave;

(f) Fringe benefits available by virtue of employment, whether or not administered by the covered entity;

(g) Selection and financial support for training, including: apprenticeships, professional meetings, conferences and other related activities, and selection for leaves of absence to pursue training;

(h) Activities sponsored by a covered entity including social and recreational programs; and

(i) Any other term, condition, or privilege of employment.

The term *discrimination* includes, but is not limited to, the acts described in §§ 1630.5 through 1630.13 of this part.

§ 1630.5 Limiting segregating, and classifying.

It is unlawful for a covered entity to limit, segregate, or classify a job applicant or employee in a way that adversely affects his or her employment opportunities or status on the basis of disability.

§ 1630.6 Contractual or other arrangements.

(a) *In general.* It is unlawful for a covered entity to participate in a contractual or other arrangement or relationship that has the effect of subjecting the covered entity's own qualified applicant or employee with a disability to the discrimination prohibited by this part.

(b) *Contractual or other arrangement defined.* The phrase *contractual or other arrangement or relationship* includes, but is not limited to, a relationship with an employment or referral agency; labor union, including collective bargaining agreements; an organization providing fringe benefits to an employee of the covered entity; or an organization providing training and apprenticeship programs.

(c) *Application.* This section applies to a covered entity, with respect to its own applicants or employees, whether the entity offered the contract or initiated the relationship, or whether the entity accepted the contract or acceded to the relationship. A covered entity is not liable for the actions of the other party or parties to the contract which only affect that other party's employees or applicants.

§ 1630.7 Standards, criteria, or methods of administration.

It is unlawful for a covered entity to use standards, criteria, or methods of administration, which are not job-related and consistent with business necessity, and:

(a) That have the effect of discriminating on the basis of disability; or

(b) That perpetuate the discrimination of others who are subject to common administrative control.

§ 1630.8 Relationship or association with an individual with a disability.

It is unlawful for a covered entity to exclude or deny equal jobs or benefits to, or otherwise discriminate against, a qualified individual because of the known disability of an individual with whom the qualified individual is known to have a family, business, social or other relationship or association.

§ 1630.9 Not making reasonable accommodation.

(a) It is unlawful for a covered entity not to make reasonable accommodation to the known physical or mental limitations of an otherwise qualified applicant or employee with a disability, unless such covered entity can demonstrate that the accommodation would impose an undue hardship on the operation of its business.

(b) It is unlawful for a covered entity to deny employment opportunities to an otherwise qualified job applicant or employee with a disability based on the need of such covered entity to make reasonable accommodation to such individual's physical or mental impairments.

(c) A covered entity shall not be excused from the requirements of this part because of any failure to receive technical assistance authorized by section 506 of the ADA, including any failure in the development or dissemination of any technical assistance manual authorized by that Act.

(d) A qualified individual with a disability is not required to accept an accommodation, aid, service, opportunity or benefit which such qualified individual chooses not to accept. However, if such individual rejects a reasonable accommodation, aid, service, opportunity or benefit that is necessary to enable the individual to perform the essential functions of the position held or desired, and cannot, as a result of that rejection, perform the essential functions of the position, the individual will not be considered a qualified individual with a disability.

§ 1630.10 Qualification standards, tests, and other selection criteria.

It is unlawful for a covered entity to use qualification standards, employment tests or other selection criteria that screen out or tend to screen out an individual with a disability or a class of individuals with disabilities, on the basis of disability, unless the standard, test or other selection criteria, as used by the covered entity, is shown to be job-related for the position in question and is consistent with business necessity.

§ 1630.11 Administration of tests.

It is unlawful for a covered entity to fail to select and administer tests concerning employment in the most effective manner to ensure that, when a test is administered to a job applicant or employee who has a disability that impairs sensory, manual or speaking skills, the test results accurately reflect the skills, aptitude, or whatever other factor of the applicant or employee that the test purports to measure, rather than reflecting the impaired sensory, manual, or speaking skills of such employee or applicant (except where such skills are the factors that the test purports to measure).

§ 1630.12 Retaliation and coercion.

(a) *Retaliation.* It is unlawful to discriminate against any individual because that individual has opposed any act or practice made unlawful by this part or because that individual made a charge, testified, assisted, or participated in any manner in an investigation, proceeding, or hearing to enforce any provision contained in this part.

(b) *Coercion, interference or intimidation.* It is unlawful to coerce, intimidate, threaten, harass or interfere with any individual in the exercise or enjoyment of, or because that individual aided or encouraged any other individual in the exercise of, any right granted or protected by this part.

§ 1630.13 Prohibited medical examinations and inquiries.

(a) *Pre-employment examination or inquiry.* Except as permitted by § 1630.14, it is unlawful for a covered entity to conduct a medical examination of an applicant or to make inquiries as to whether an applicant is an individual with a disability or as to the nature or severity of such disability.

(b) *Examination or inquiry of employees.* Except as permitted by § 1630.14, it is unlawful for a covered entity to require a medical examination of an employee or to make inquiries as to whether an employee is an individual with a disability or as to the nature or severity of such disability.

§ 1630.14 Medical examinations and inquiries specifically permitted.

(a) *Acceptable pre-employment inquiry.* A covered entity may make pre-employment inquiries into the ability of an applicant to perform job-related functions, and/or may ask an applicant to describe or to demonstrate how, with or without reasonable accommodation, the applicant will be able to perform job-related functions.

(b) *Employment entrance examination.* A covered entity may require a medical examination (and/or inquiry) after making an offer of employment to a job applicant and before the applicant begins his or her employment duties, and may condition an offer of employment on the results of such examination (and/or inquiry), if all entering employees in the same job category are subjected to such an examination (and/or inquiry) regardless of disability.

(1) Information obtained under paragraph (b) of this section regarding the medical condition or history of the applicant shall be collected and maintained on separate forms and in separate medical files and be treated as a confidential medical record, except that:

(i) Supervisors and managers may be informed regarding necessary restrictions on the work or duties of the employee and necessary accommodations;

(ii) First aid and safety personnel may be informed, when appropriate, if the disability might require emergency treatment; and

(iii) Government officials investigating compliance with this part shall be provided relevant information on request.

(2) The results of such examination shall not be used for any purpose inconsistent with this part.

(3) Medical examinations conducted in accordance with this section do not have to be job-related and consistent with business necessity. However, if certain criteria are used to screen out an employee or employees with disabilities as a result of such an examination or inquiry, the exclusionary criteria must be job-related and consistent with business necessity, and performance of the essential job functions cannot be accomplished with reasonable accommodation as required in this part. (See § 1630.15(b) Defenses to charges of discriminatory application of selection criteria.)

(c) *Examination of employees.* A covered entity may require a medical examination (and/or inquiry) of an employee that is job-related and consistent with business necessity. A covered entity may make inquiries into the ability of an employee to perform job-related functions.

(1) Information obtained under paragraph (c) of this section regarding the medical condition or history of any employee shall be collected and maintained on separate forms and in separate medical files and be treated as a confidential medical record, except that:

(i) Supervisors and managers may be informed regarding necessary restrictions on the work or duties of the employee and necessary accommodations;

(ii) First aid and safety personnel may be informed, when appropriate, if the

disability might require emergency treatment; and

(iii) Government officials investigating compliance with this part shall be provided relevant information on request.

(2) Information obtained under paragraph (c) of this section regarding the medical condition or history of any employee shall not be used for any purpose inconsistent with this part.

(d) *Other acceptable examinations and inquiries.* A covered entity may conduct voluntary medical examinations and activities, including voluntary medical histories, which are part of an employee health program available to employees at the work site.

(1) Information obtained under paragraph (d) of this section regarding the medical condition or history of any employee shall be collected and maintained on separate forms and in separate medical files and be treated as a confidential medical record, except that:

(i) Supervisors and managers may be informed regarding necessary restrictions on the work or duties of the employee and necessary accommodations;

(ii) First aid and safety personnel may be informed, when appropriate, if the disability might require emergency treatment; and

(iii) Government officials investigating compliance with this part shall be provided relevant information on request.

(2) Information obtained under paragraph (d) of this section regarding the medical condition or history of any employee shall not be used for any purpose inconsistent with this part.

§ 1630.15 Defenses.

Defenses to an allegation of discrimination under this part may include, but are not limited to, the following:

(a) *Disparate treatment charges.* It may be a defense to a charge of disparate treatment brought under §§ 1630.4 through 1630.8 and 1630.11 through 1630.12 that the challenged action is justified by a legitimate, nondiscriminatory reason.

(b) *Charges of discriminatory application of selection criteria—*(1) *In general.* It may be a defense to a charge of discrimination, as described in § 1630.10, that an alleged application of qualification standards, tests, or selection criteria that screens out or tends to screen out or otherwise denies a job or benefit to an individual with a disability has been shown to be job-related and consistent with business necessity, and such performance cannot

be accomplished with reasonable accommodation, as required in this part.

(2) *Direct threat as a qualification standard.* The term "qualification standard" may include a requirement that an individual shall not pose a direct threat to the health or safety of the individual or others in the workplace. (See § 1630.2(r) defining direct threat.)

(c) *Other disparate impact charges.* It may be a defense to a charge of discrimination brought under this part that a uniformly applied standard, criterion, or policy has a disparate impact on an individual with a disability or a class of individuals with disabilities that the challenged standard, criterion or policy has been shown to be job-related and consistent with business necessity, and such performance cannot be accomplished with reasonable accommodation, as required in this part.

(d) *Charges of not making reasonable accommodation.* It may be a defense to a charge of discrimination, as described in § 1630.9, that a requested or necessary accommodation would impose an undue hardship on the operation of the covered entity's business.

(e) *Conflict with other federal laws.* It may be a defense to a charge of discrimination under this part that a challenged action is required or necessitated by another Federal law or regulation, or that another Federal law or regulation prohibits an action (including the provision of a particular reasonable accommodation) that would otherwise be required by this part.

(f) *Additional defenses.* It may be a defense to a charge of discrimination under this part that the alleged discriminatory action is specifically permitted by §§ 1630.14 or 1630.16.

§ 1630.16 Specific activities permitted.

(a) *Religious entities.* A religious corporation, association, educational institution, or society is permitted to give preference in employment to individuals of a particular religion to perform work connected with the carrying on by that corporation, association, educational institution, or society of its activities. A religious entity may require that all applicants and employees conform to the religious tenets of such organization. However, a religious entity may not discriminate against a qualified individual, who satisfies the permitted religious criteria, because of his or her disability.

(b) *Regulation of alcohol and drugs.* A covered entity:

(1) May prohibit the illegal use of drugs and the use of alcohol at the workplace by all employees;

(2) May require that employees not be under the influence of alcohol or be engaging in the illegal use of drugs at the workplace;

(3) May require that all employees behave in conformance with the requirements established under the Drug-Free Workplace Act of 1988 (41 U.S.C. 701 et seq.);

(4) May hold an employee who engages in the illegal use of drugs or who is an alcoholic to the same qualification standards for employment or job performance and behavior to which the entity holds its other employees, even if any unsatisfactory performance or behavior is related to the employee's drug use or alcoholism;

(5) May require that its employees employed in an industry subject to such regulations comply with the standards established in the regulations (if any) of the Departments of Defense and Transportation, and of the Nuclear Regulatory Commission, regarding alcohol and the illegal use of drugs; and

(6) May require that employees employed in sensitive positions comply with the regulations (if any) of the Departments of Defense and Transportation and of the Nuclear Regulatory Commission that apply to employment in sensitive positions subject to such regulations.

(c) *Drug testing*—(1) *General policy.* For purposes of this part, a test to determine the illegal use of drugs is not considered a medical examination. Thus, the administration of such drug tests by a covered entity to its job applicants or employees is not a violation of § 1630.13 of this part. However, this part does not encourage, prohibit, or authorize a covered entity to conduct drug tests of job applicants or employees to determine the illegal use of drugs or to make employment decisions based on such test results.

(2) *Transportation Employees.* This part does not encourage, prohibit, or authorize the otherwise lawful exercise by entities subject to the jurisdiction of the Department of Transportation of authority to:

(i) Test employees of entities in, and applicants for, positions involving safety sensitive duties for the illegal use of drugs or for on-duty impairment by alcohol; and

(ii) Remove from safety-sensitive positions persons who test positive for illegal use of drugs or on-duty impairment by alcohol pursuant to paragraph (c)(2)(i) of this section.

(3) *Confidentiality.* Any information regarding the medical condition or history of any employee or applicant obtained from a test to determine the illegal use of drugs, except information

regarding the illegal use of drugs, is subject to the requirements of § 1630.14(b) (2) and (3) of this part.

(d) *Regulation of smoking.* A covered entity may prohibit or impose restrictions on smoking in places of employment. Such restrictions do not violate any provision of this part.

(e) *Infectious and communicable diseases; food handling jobs*—(1) *In general.* Under title I of the ADA, section 103(d)(1), the Secretary of Health and Human Services is to prepare a list, to be updated annually, of infectious and communicable diseases which are transmitted through the handling of food. [Copies may be obtained from Center for Infectious Diseases, Centers for Disease Control, 1600 Clifton Road, NE., Mailstop C09, Atlanta, GA 30333.] If an individual with a disability is disabled by one of the infectious or communicable diseases included on this list, and if the risk of transmitting the disease associated with the handling of food cannot be eliminated by reasonable accommodation, a covered entity may refuse to assign or continue to assign such individual to a job involving food handling. However, if the individual with a disability is a current employee, the employer must consider whether he or she can be accommodated by reassignment to a vacant position not involving food handling.

(2) *Effect on state or other laws.* This part does not preempt, modify, or amend any State, county, or local law, ordinance or regulation applicable to food handling which:

(i) Is in accordance with the list, referred to in paragraph (e)(1) of this section, of infectious or communicable diseases and the modes of transmissibility published by the Secretary of Health and Human Services; and

(ii) Is designed to protect the public health from individuals who pose a significant risk to the health or safety of others, where that risk cannot be eliminated by reasonable accommodation.

(f) *Health insurance, life insurance, and other benefit plans*—(1) An insurer, hospital, or medical service company, health maintenance organization, or any agent or entity that administers benefit plans, or similar organizations may underwrite risks, classify risks, or administer such risks that are based on or not inconsistent with State law.

(2) A covered entity may establish, sponsor, observe or administer the terms of a bona fide benefit plan that are based on underwriting risks, classifying risks, or administering such risks that

are based on or not inconsistent with State law.

(3) A covered entity may establish, sponsor, observe, or administer the terms of a bona fide benefit plan that is not subject to State laws that regulate insurance.

(4) The activities described in paragraphs (f) (1), (2), and (3) of this section are permitted unless these activities are being used as a subterfuge to evade the purposes of this part.

Appendix to Part 1630—Interpretive Guidance on Title I of the Americans with Disabilities Act

Background

The ADA is a federal antidiscrimination statute designed to remove barriers which prevent qualified individuals with disabilities from enjoying the same employment opportunities that are available to persons without disabilities.

Like the Civil Rights Act of 1964 that prohibits discrimination on the bases of race, color, religion, national origin, and sex, the ADA seeks to ensure access to equal employment opportunities based on merit. It does not guarantee equal results, establish quotas, or require preferences favoring individuals with disabilities over those without disabilities.

However, while the Civil Rights Act of 1964 prohibits any consideration of personal characteristics such as race or national origin, the ADA necessarily takes a different approach. When an individual's disability creates a barrier to employment opportunities, the ADA requires employers to consider whether reasonable accommodation could remove the barrier.

The ADA thus establishes a process in which the employer must assess a disabled individual's ability to perform the essential functions of the specific job held or desired. While the ADA focuses on eradicating barriers, the ADA does not relieve a disabled employee or applicant from the obligation to perform the essential functions of the job. To the contrary, the ADA is intended to enable disabled persons to compete in the workplace based on the same performance standards and requirements that employers expect of persons who are not disabled.

However, where that individual's functional limitation impedes such job performance, an employer must take steps to reasonably accommodate, and thus help overcome the particular impediment, unless to do so would impose an undue hardship. Such accommodations usually take the form of adjustments to the way a job customarily is performed, or to the work environment itself.

This process of identifying whether, and to what extent, a reasonable accommodation is required should be flexible and involve both the employer and the individual with a disability. Of course, the determination of whether an individual is qualified for a particular position must necessarily be made on a case-by-case basis. No specific form of accommodation is guaranteed for all individuals with a particular disability.

Rather, an accommodation must be tailored to match the needs of the disabled individual with the needs of the job's essential functions.

This case-by-case approach is essential if qualified individuals of varying abilities are to receive equal opportunities to compete for an infinitely diverse range of jobs. For this reason, neither the ADA nor this part can supply the "correct" answer in advance for each employment decision concerning an individual with a disability. Instead, the ADA simply establishes parameters to guide employers in how to consider, and take into account, the disabling condition involved.

Introduction

The Equal Employment Opportunity Commission (the Commission or EEOC) is responsible for enforcement of title I of the Americans with Disabilities Act (ADA), 42 U.S.C. 12101 *et seq.* (1990), which prohibits employment discrimination on the basis of disability. The Commission believes that it is essential to issue interpretive guidance concurrently with the issuance of this part in order to ensure that qualified individuals with disabilities understand their rights under this part and to facilitate and encourage compliance by covered entities. This appendix represents the Commission's interpretation of the issues discussed, and the Commission will be guided by it when resolving charges of employment discrimination. The appendix addresses the major provisions of this part and explains the major concepts of disability rights.

The terms "employer" or "employer or other covered entity" are used interchangeably throughout the appendix to refer to all covered entities subject to the employment provisions of the ADA.

Section 1630.1 Purpose, Applicability and Construction

Section 1630.1(a) Purpose

The Americans with Disabilities Act was signed into law on July 26, 1990. It is an antidiscrimination statute that requires that individuals with disabilities be given the same consideration for employment that individuals without disabilities are given. An individual who is qualified for an employment opportunity cannot be denied that opportunity because of the fact that the individual is disabled. The purpose of title I and this part is to ensure that qualified individuals with disabilities are protected from discrimination on the basis of disability.

The ADA uses the term "disabilities" rather than the term "handicaps" used in the Rehabilitation Act of 1973, 29 U.S.C. 701–796. Substantively, these terms are equivalent. As noted by the House Committee on the Judiciary, "[t]he use of the term 'disabilities' instead of the term 'handicaps' reflects the desire of the Committee to use the most current terminology. It reflects the preference of persons with disabilities to use that term rather than 'handicapped' as used in previous laws, such as the Rehabilitation Act of 1973 * * *." H.R. Rep. No. 485 part 3, 101st Cong., 2d Sess. 26–27 (1990) [hereinafter House Judiciary Report]; see also S. Rep. No. 116, 101st Cong., 1st Sess. 21 (1989) [hereinafter Senate Report]; H.R. Rep. No. 485 part 2, 101st Cong., 2d Sess. 50–51 (1990) [hereinafter House Labor Report].

The use of the term "Americans" in the title of the ADA is not intended to imply that the Act only applies to United States citizens. Rather, the ADA protects all qualified individuals with disabilities, regardless of their citizenship status or nationality.

Section 1630.1(b) and (c) Applicability and Construction

Unless expressly stated otherwise, the standards applied in the ADA are not intended to be lesser than the standards applied under the Rehabilitation Act of 1973. The ADA does not preempt any Federal law, or any state or local law, that grants to individuals with disabilities protection greater than or equivalent to that provided by the ADA. This means that the existence of a lesser standard of protection to individuals with disabilities under the ADA will not provide a defense to failing to meet a higher standard under another law. Thus, for example, title I of the ADA would not be a defense to failing to collect information required to satisfy the affirmative action requirements of section 503 of the Rehabilitation Act. On the other hand, the existence of a lesser standard under another law will not provide a defense to failing to meet a higher standard under the ADA. See House Labor Report at 135; House Judiciary Report at 69–70.

This also means that an individual with a disability could choose to pursue claims under a state discrimination or tort law that does not confer greater substantive rights, or even confers fewer substantive rights, if the potential available remedies would be greater than those available under the ADA and this part. The ADA does not restrict an individual with a disability from pursuing such claims in addition to charges brought under this part. House Judiciary at 69–70.

The ADA does not automatically preempt medical standards or safety requirements established by Federal law or regulations. It does not preempt State, county, or local laws, ordinances or regulations that are consistent with this part, and are designed to protect the public health from individuals who pose a direct threat, that cannot be eliminated or reduced by reasonable accommodation, to the health or safety of others. However, the ADA does preempt inconsistent requirements established by state or local law for safety or security sensitive positions. See Senate Report at 27; House Labor Report at 57.

An employer allegedly in violation of this part cannot successfully defend its actions by relying on the obligation to comply with the requirements of any state or local law that imposes prohibitions or limitations on the eligibility of qualified individuals with disabilities to practice any occupation or profession. For example, suppose a municipality has an ordinance that prohibits individuals with tuberculosis from teaching school children. If an individual with dormant tuberculosis challenges a private school's refusal to hire him or her because of the tuberculosis, the private school would not be able to rely on the city ordinance as a defense under the ADA.

Sections 1630.2(a)–(f) Commission, Covered Entity, etc.

The definitions section of part 1630 includes several terms that are identical, or almost identical, to the terms found in title VII of the Civil Rights Act of 1964. Among these terms are "Commission," "Person," "State," and "Employer." These terms are to be given the same meaning under the ADA that they are given under title VII.

In general, the term "employee" has the same meaning that it is given under title VII. However, the ADA's definition of "employee" does not contain an exception, as does title VII, for elected officials and their personal staffs. It should be further noted that all state and local governments are covered by title II of the ADA whether or not they are also covered by this part. Title II, which is enforced by the Department of Justice, becomes effective on January 26, 1992. See 28 CFR part 35.

The term "covered entity" is not found in title VII. However, the title VII definitions of the entities included in the term "covered entity" (e.g., employer, employment agency, etc.) are applicable to the ADA.

Section 1630.2(g) Disability

In addition to the term "covered entity," there are several other terms that are unique to the ADA. The first of these is the term "disability." Congress adopted the definition of this term from the Rehabilitation Act definition of the term "individual with handicaps." By so doing, Congress intended that the relevant caselaw developed under the Rehabilitation Act be generally applicable to the term "disability" as used in the ADA. Senate Report at 21; House Labor Report at 50; House Judiciary Report at 27.

The definition of the term "disability" is divided into three parts. An individual must satisfy at least one of these parts in order to be considered an individual with a disability for purposes of this part. An individual is considered to have a "disability" if that individual either (1) has a physical or mental impairment which substantially limits one or more of that person's major life activities, (2) has a record of such an impairment, or (3) is regarded by the covered entity as having such an impairment. To understand the meaning of the term "disability," it is necessary to understand, as a preliminary matter, what is meant by the terms "physical or mental impairment," "major life activity," and "substantially limits." Each of these terms is discussed below.

Section 1630.2(h) Physical or Mental Impairment

This term adopts the definition of the term "physical or mental impairment" found in the regulations implementing section 504 of the Rehabilitation Act at 34 CFR part 104. It defines physical or mental impairment as any physiological disorder or condition, cosmetic disfigurement, or anatomical loss affecting one or more of several body systems, or any mental or psychological disorder.

The existence of an impairment is to be determined without regard to mitigating measures such as medicines, or assistive or prosthetic devices. See Senate Report at 23,

House Labor Report at 52, House Judiciary Report at 28. For example, an individual with epilepsy would be considered to have an impairment even if the symptoms of the disorder were completely controlled by medicine. Similarly, an individual with hearing loss would be considered to have an impairment even if the condition were correctable through the use of a hearing aid.

It is important to distinguish between conditions that are impairments and physical, psychological, environmental, cultural and economic characteristics that are not impairments. The definition of the term "impairment" does not include physical characteristics such as eye color, hair color, left-handedness, or height, weight or muscle tone that are within "normal" range and are not the result of a physiological disorder. The definition, likewise, does not include characteristic predisposition to illness or disease. Other conditions, such as pregnancy, that are not the result of a physiological disorder are also not impairments. Similarly, the definition does not include common personality traits such as poor judgment or a quick temper where these are not symptoms of a mental or psychological disorder. Environmental, cultural, or economic disadvantages such as poverty, lack of education or a prison record are not impairments. Advanced age, in and of itself, is also not an impairment. However, various medical conditions commonly associated with age, such as hearing loss, osteoporosis, or arthritis would constitute impairments within the meaning of this part. See Senate Report at 22–23; House Labor Report at 51–52; House Judiciary Report at 28–29.

Section 1630.2(i)   Major Life Activities

This term adopts the definition of the term "major life activities" found in the regulations implementing section 504 of the Rehabilitation Act at 34 CFR part 104. "Major life activities" are those basic activities that the average person in the general population can perform with little or no difficulty. Major life activities include caring for oneself, performing manual tasks, walking, seeing, hearing, speaking, breathing, learning, and working. This list is not exhaustive. For example, other major life activities include, but are not limited to, sitting, standing, lifting, reaching. See Senate Report at 22; House Labor Report at 52; House Judiciary Report at 28.

Section 1630.2(j)   Substantially Limits

Determining whether a physical or mental impairment exists is only the first step in determining whether or not an individual is disabled. Many impairments do not impact an individual's life to the degree that they constitute disabling impairments. An impairment rises to the level of disability if the impairment substantially limits one or more of the individual's major life activities. Multiple impairments that combine to substantially limit one or more of an individual's major life activities also constitute a disability.

The ADA and this part, like the Rehabilitation Act of 1973, do not attempt a "laundry list" of impairments that are "disabilities." The determination of whether

an individual has a disability is not necessarily based on the name or diagnosis of the impairment the person has, but rather on the effect of that impairment on the life of the individual. Some impairments may be disabling for particular individuals but not for others, depending on the stage of the disease or disorder, the presence of other impairments that combine to make the impairment disabling or any number of other factors.

Other impairments, however, such as HIV infection, are inherently substantially limiting.

On the other hand, temporary, non-chronic impairments of short duration, with little or no long term or permanent impact, are usually not disabilities. Such impairments may include, but are not limited to, broken limbs, sprained joints, concussions, appendicitis, and influenza. Similarly, except in rare circumstances, obesity is not considered a disabling impairment.

An impairment that prevents an individual from performing a major life activity substantially limits that major life activity. For example, an individual whose legs are paralyzed is substantially limited in the major life activity of walking because he or she is unable, due to the impairment, to perform that major life activity.

Alternatively, an impairment is substantially limiting if it significantly restricts the duration, manner or condition under which an individual can perform a particular major life activity as compared to the average person in the general population's ability to perform that same major life activity. Thus, for example, an individual who, because of an impairment, can only walk for very brief periods of time would be substantially limited in the major life activity of walking. An individual who uses artificial legs would likewise be substantially limited in the major life activity of walking because the individual is unable to walk without the aid of prosthetic devices. Similarly, a diabetic who without insulin would lapse into a coma would be substantially limited because the individual cannot perform major life activities without the aid of medication. See Senate Report at 23; House Labor Report at 52. It should be noted that the term "average person" is not intended to imply a precise mathematical "average."

Part 1630 notes several factors that should be considered in making the determination of whether an impairment is substantially limiting. These factors are (1) the nature and severity of the impairment, (2) the duration or expected duration of the impairment, and (3) the permanent or long term impact, or the expected permanent or long term impact of, or resulting from, the impairment. The term "duration," as used in this context, refers to the length of time an impairment persists, while the term "impact" refers to the residual effects of an impairment. Thus, for example, a broken leg that takes eight weeks to heal is an impairment of fairly short duration. However, if the broken leg heals improperly, the "impact" of the impairment would be the resulting permanent limp. Likewise, the effect on cognitive functions resulting from traumatic head injury would be the "impact" of that impairment.

The determination of whether an individual is substantially limited in a major life activity must be made on a case by case basis, without regard to mitigating measures such as medicines, or assistive or prosthetic devices. An individual is not substantially limited in a major life activity if the limitation, when viewed in light of the factors noted above, does not amount to a significant restriction when compared with the abilities of the average person. For example, an individual who had once been able to walk at an extraordinary speed would not be substantially limited in the major life activity of walking if, as a result of a physical impairment, he or she were only able to walk at an average speed, or even at moderately below average speed.

It is important to remember that the restriction on the performance of the major life activity must be the result of a condition that is an impairment. As noted earlier, advanced age, physical or personality characteristics, and environmental, cultural, and economic disadvantages are not impairments. Consequently, even if such factors substantially limit an individual's ability to perform a major life activity, this limitation will not constitute a disability. For example, an individual who is unable to read because he or she was never taught to read would not be an individual with a disability because lack of education is not an impairment. However, an individual who is unable to read because of dyslexia would be an individual with a disability because dyslexia, a learning disability, is an impairment.

If an individual is not substantially limited with respect to any other major life activity, the individual's ability to perform the major life activity of working should be considered. If an individual is substantially limited in any other major life activity, no determination should be made as to whether the individual is substantially limited in working. For example, if an individual is blind, *i.e.*, substantially limited in the major life activity of seeing, there is no need to determine whether the individual is also substantially limited in the major life activity of working. The determination of whether an individual is substantially limited in working must also be made on a case by case basis.

This part lists specific factors that may be used in making the determination of whether the limitation in working is "substantial." These factors are:

(1) The geographical area to which the individual has reasonable access;

(2) The job from which the individual has been disqualified because of an impairment, and the number and types of jobs utilizing similar training, knowledge, skills or abilities, within that geographical area, from which the individual is also disqualified because of the impairment (class of jobs); and/or

(3) The job from which the individual has been disqualified because of an impairment, and the number and types of other jobs not utilizing similar training, knowledge, skills or abilities, within that geographical area, from which the individual is also disqualified because of the impairment (broad range of jobs in various classes).

Thus, an individual is not substantially limited in working just because he or she is unable to perform a particular job for one employer, or because he or she is unable to perform a specialized job or profession requiring extraordinary skill, prowess or talent. For example, an individual who cannot be a commercial airline pilot because of a minor vision impairment, but who can be a commercial airline co-pilot or a pilot for a courier service, would not be substantially limited in the major life activity of working. Nor would a professional baseball pitcher who develops a bad elbow and can no longer throw a baseball be considered substantially limited in the major life activity of working. In both of these examples, the individuals are not substantially limited in the ability to perform any other major life activity and, with regard to the major life activity of working, are only unable to perform either a particular specialized job or a narrow range of jobs. See *Forrisi* v. *Bowen*, 794 F.2d 931 (4th Cir. 1986); *Jasany* v. *U.S. Postal Service*, 755 F.2d 1244 (6th Cir. 1985); *E.E. Black, Ltd.* v. *Marshall*, 497 F. Supp. 1088 (D. Hawaii 1980).

On the other hand, an individual does not have to be totally unable to work in order to be considered substantially limited in the major life activity of working. An individual is substantially limited in working if the individual is significantly restricted in the ability to perform a class of jobs or a broad range of jobs in various classes, when compared with the ability of the average person with comparable qualifications to perform those same jobs. For example, an individual who has a back condition that prevents the individual from performing any heavy labor job would be substantially limited in the major life activity of working because the individual's impairment eliminates his or her ability to perform a class of jobs. This would be so even if the individual were able to perform jobs in another class, e.g., the class of semi-skilled jobs. Similarly, suppose an individual has an allergy to a substance found in most high rise office buildings, but seldom found elsewhere, that makes breathing extremely difficult. Since this individual would be substantially limited in the ability to perform the broad range of jobs in various classes that are conducted in high rise office buildings within the geographical area to which he or she has reasonable access, he or she would be substantially limited in working.

The terms "number and types of jobs" and "number and types of other jobs," as used in the factors discussed above, are not intended to require an onerous evidentiary showing. Rather, the terms only require the presentation of evidence of general employment demographics and/or of recognized occupational classifications that indicate the approximate number of jobs (e.g., "few," "many," "most") from which an individual would be excluded because of an impairment.

If an individual has a "mental or physical impairment" that "substantially limits" his or her ability to perform one or more "major life activities," that individual will satisfy the first part of the regulatory definition of "disability" and will be considered an individual with a disability. An individual who satisfies this first part of the definition of the term "disability" is not required to demonstrate that he or she satisfies either of the other parts of the definition. However, if an individual is unable to satisfy this part of the definition, he or she may be able to satisfy one of the other parts of the definition.

Section 1630.2(k) Record of a Substantially Limiting Condition

The second part of the definition provides that an individual with a record of an impairment that substantially limits a major life activity is an individual with a disability. The intent of this provision, in part, is to ensure that people are not discriminated against because of a history of disability. For example, this provision protects former cancer patients from discrimination based on their prior medical history. This provision also ensures that individuals are not discriminated against because they have been misclassified as disabled. For example, individuals misclassified as learning disabled are protected from discrimination on the basis of that erroneous classification. Senate Report at 23; House Labor Report at 52–53; House Judiciary Report at 29.

This part of the definition is satisfied if a record relied on by an employer indicates that the individual has or has had a substantially limiting impairment. The impairment indicated in the record must be an impairment that would substantially limit one or more of the individual's major life activities. There are many types of records that could potentially contain this information, including but not limited to, education, medical, or employment records.

The fact that an individual has a record of being a disabled veteran, or of disability retirement, or is classified as disabled for other purposes does not guarantee that the individual will satisfy the definition of "disability" under part 1630. Other statutes, regulations and programs may have a definition of "disability" that is not the same as the definition set forth in the ADA and contained in part 1630. Accordingly, in order for an individual who has been classified in a record as "disabled" for some other purpose to be considered disabled for purposes of part 1630, the impairment indicated in the record must be a physical or mental impairment that substantially limits one or more of the individual's major life activities.

Section 1630.2(l) Regarded as Substantially Limited in a Major Life Activity

If an individual cannot satisfy either the first part of the definition of "disability" or the second "record of" part of the definition, he or she may be able to satisfy the third part of the definition. The third part of the definition provides that an individual who is regarded by an employer or other covered entity as having an impairment that substantially limits a major life activity is an individual with a disability.

There are three different ways in which an individual may satisfy the definition of "being regarded as having a disability":

(1) The individual may have an impairment which is not substantially limiting but is perceived by the employer or other covered entity as constituting a substantially limiting impairment;

(2) The individual may have an impairment which is only substantially limiting because of the attitudes of others toward the impairment; or

(3) The individual may have no impairment at all but is regarded by the employer or other covered entity as having a substantially limiting impairment.

Senate Report at 23; House Labor Report at 53; House Judiciary Report at 29.

An individual satisfies the first part of this definition if the individual has an impairment that is not substantially limiting, but the covered entity perceives the impairment as being substantially limiting. For example, suppose an employee has controlled high blood pressure that is not substantially limiting. If an employer reassigns the individual to less strenuous work because of unsubstantiated fears that the individual will suffer a heart attack if he or she continues to perform strenuous work, the employer would be regarding the individual as disabled.

An individual satisfies the second part of the "regarded as" definition if the individual has an impairment that is only substantially limiting because of the attitudes of others toward the condition. For example, an individual may have a prominent facial scar or disfigurement, or may have a condition that periodically causes an involuntary jerk of the head but does not limit the individual's major life activities. If an employer discriminates against such an individual because of the negative reactions of customers, the employer would be regarding the individual as disabled and acting on the basis of that perceived disability. See Senate Report at 24; House Labor Report at 53; House Judiciary Report at 30–31.

An individual satisfies the third part of the "regarded as" definition of "disability" if the employer or other covered entity erroneously believes the individual has a substantially limiting impairment that the individual actually does not have. This situation could occur, for example, if an employer discharged an employee in response to a rumor that the employee is infected with Human Immunodeficiency Virus (HIV). Even though the rumor is totally unfounded and the individual has no impairment at all, the individual is considered an individual with a disability because the employer perceived of this individual as being disabled. Thus, in this example, the employer, by discharging this employee, is discriminating on the basis of disability.

The rationale for the "regarded as" part of the definition of disability was articulated by the Supreme Court in the context of the Rehabilitation Act of 1973 in *School Board of Nassau County* v. *Arline*, 480 U.S. 273 (1987). The Court noted that, although an individual may have an impairment that does not in fact substantially limit a major life activity, the reaction of others may prove just as disabling. "Such an impairment might not diminish a person's physical or mental capabilities, but could nevertheless substantially limit that person's ability to work as a result of the negative reactions of others to the impairment." 480 U.S. at 283. The Court concluded that by including "regarded as" in the Rehabilitation Act's definition, "Congress acknowledged that society's accumulated myths and fears about disability and diseases are as handicapping as are the physical limitations that flow from actual impairment." 480 U.S. at 284.

An individual rejected from a job because of the "myths, fears and stereotypes" associated with disabilities would be covered under this part of the definition of disability, whether or not the employer's or other covered entity's perception were shared by others in the field and whether or not the individual's actual physical or mental condition would be considered a disability under the first or second part of this definition. As the legislative history notes, sociologists have identified common attitudinal barriers that frequently result in employers excluding individuals with disabilities. These include concerns regarding productivity, safety, insurance, liability, attendance, cost of accommodation and accessibility, workers' compensation costs, and acceptance by coworkers and customers.

Therefore, if an individual can show that an employer or other covered entity made an employment decision because of a perception of disability based on "myth, fear or stereotype," the individual will satisfy the "regarded as" part of the definition of disability. If the employer cannot articulate a non-discriminatory reason for the employment action, an inference that the employer is acting on the basis of "myth, fear or stereotype" can be drawn.

Section 1630.2(m)   Qualified Individual With a Disability

The ADA prohibits discrimination on the basis of disability against qualified individuals with disabilities. The determination of whether an individual with a disability is "qualified" should be made in two steps. The first step is to determine if the individual satisfies the prerequisites for the position, such as possessing the appropriate educational background, employment experience, skills, licenses, etc. For example, the first step in determining whether an accountant who is paraplegic is qualified for a certified public accountant (CPA) position is to examine the individual's credentials to determine whether the individual is a licensed CPA. This is sometimes referred to in the Rehabilitation Act caselaw as determining whether the individual is "otherwise qualified" for the position. See Senate Report at 33; House Labor Report at 64–65. (See § 1630.9 Not Making Reasonable Accommodation).

The second step is to determine whether or not the individual can perform the essential functions of the position held or desired, with or without reasonable accommodation. The purpose of this second step is to ensure that individuals with disabilities who can perform the essential functions of the position held or desired are not denied employment opportunities because they are not able to perform marginal functions of the position. House Labor Report at 55.

The determination of whether an individual with a disability is qualified is to be made at the time of the employment decision. This determination should be based on the capabilities of the individual with a disability

at the time of the employment decision, and should not be based on speculation that the employee may become unable in the future or may cause increased health insurance premiums or workers compensation costs.

Section 1630.2(n)   Essential Functions

The determination of which functions are essential may be critical to the determination of whether or not the individual with a disability is qualified. The essential functions are those functions that the individual who holds the position must be able to perform unaided or with the assistance of a reasonable accommodation.

The inquiry into whether a particular function is essential initially focuses on whether the employer actually requires employees in the position to perform the functions that the employer asserts are essential. For example, an employer may state that typing is an essential function of a position. If, in fact, the employer has never required any employee in that particular position to type, this will be evidence that typing is not actually an essential function of the position.

If the individual who holds the position is actually required to perform the function the employer asserts is an essential function, the inquiry will then center around whether removing the function would fundamentally alter that position. This determination of whether or not a particular function is essential will generally include one or more of the following factors listed in part 1630.

The first factor is whether the position exists to perform a particular function. For example, an individual may be hired to proofread documents. The ability to proofread the documents would then be an essential function, since this is the only reason the position exists.

The second factor in determining whether a function is essential is the number of other employees available to perform that job function or among whom the performance of that job function can be distributed. This may be a factor either because the total number of available employees is low, or because of the fluctuating demands of the business operation. For example, if an employer has a relatively small number of available employees for the volume of work to be performed, it may be necessary that each employee perform a multitude of different functions. Therefore, the performance of those functions by each employee becomes more critical and the options for reorganizing the work become more limited. In such a situation, functions that might not be essential if there were a larger staff may become essential because the staff size is small compared to the volume of work that has to be done. See *Treadwell* v. *Alexander*, 707 F.2d 473 (11th Cir. 1983).

A similar situation might occur in a larger work force if the workflow follows a cycle of heavy demand for labor intensive work followed by low demand periods. This type of workflow might also make the performance of each function during the peak periods more critical and might limit the employer's flexibility in reorganizing operating procedures. See *Dexler* v. *Tisch*, 660 F. Supp. 1418 (D. Conn. 1987).

The third factor is the degree of expertise or skill required to perform the function. In certain professions and highly skilled positions the employee is hired for his or her expertise or ability to perform the particular function. In such a situation, the performance of that specialized task would be an essential function.

Whether a particular function is essential is a factual determination that must be made on a case by case basis. In determining whether or not a particular function is essential, all relevant evidence should be considered. Part 1630 lists various types of evidence, such as an established job description, that should be considered in determining whether a particular function is essential. Since the list is not exhaustive, other relevant evidence may also be presented. Greater weight will not be granted to the types of evidence included on the list than to the types of evidence not listed.

Although part 1630 does not require employers to develop or maintain job descriptions, written job descriptions prepared before advertising or interviewing applicants for the job, as well as the employer's judgment as to what functions are essential are among the relevant evidence to be considered in determining whether a particular function is essential. The terms of a collective bargaining agreement are also relevant to the determination of whether a particular function is essential. The work experience of past employees in the job or of current employees in similar jobs is likewise relevant to the determination of whether a particular function is essential. See H.R. Conf. Rep. No. 101–596, 101st Cong., 2d Sess. 58 (1990) [hereinafter Conference Report]; House Judiciary Report at 33–34. See also *Hall* v. *U.S. Postal Service*, 857 F.2d 1073 (6th Cir. 1988).

The time spent performing the particular function may also be an indicator of whether that function is essential. For example, if an employee spends the vast majority of his or her time working at a cash register, this would be evidence that operating the cash register is an essential function. The consequences of failing to require the employee to perform the function may be another indicator of whether a particular function is essential. For example, although a firefighter may not regularly have to carry an unconscious adult out of a burning building, the consequence of failing to require the firefighter to be able to perform this function would be serious.

It is important to note that the inquiry into essential functions is not intended to second guess an employer's business judgment with regard to production standards, whether qualitative or quantitative, nor to require employers to lower such standards. (See § 1630.10 Qualification Standards, Tests and Other Selection Criteria). If an employer requires its typists to be able to accurately type 75 words per minute, it will not be called upon to explain why an inaccurate work product, or a typing speed of 65 words per minute, would not be adequate. Similarly, if a hotel requires its service workers to thoroughly clean 16 rooms per day, it will not have to explain why it requires thorough cleaning, or why it chose a 16 room rather than a 10 room requirement. However, if an employer does require accurate 75 word per minute typing or the thorough cleaning of 16 rooms, it will have to show that it actually imposes such requirements on its employees in fact, and not simply on paper. It should also be noted that, if it is alleged that the employer intentionally selected the particular level of production to exclude individuals with disabilities, the employer may have to offer a legitimate, nondiscriminatory reason for its selection.

Section 1630.2(o) Reasonable Accommodation

An individual is considered a "qualified individual with a disability" if the individual can perform the essential functions of the position held or desired with or without reasonable accommodation. In general, an accommodation is any change in the work environment or in the way things are customarily done that enables an individual with a disability to enjoy equal employment opportunities. There are three categories of reasonable accommodation. These are (1) accommodations that are required to ensure equal opportunity in the application process; (2) accommodations that enable the employer's employees with disabilities to perform the essential functions of the position held or desired; and (3) accommodations that enable the employer's employees with disabilities to enjoy equal benefits and privileges of employment as are enjoyed by employees without disabilities. It should be noted that nothing in this part prohibits employers or other covered entities from providing accommodations beyond those required by this part.

Part 1630 lists the examples, specified in title I of the ADA, of the most common types of accommodation that an employer or other covered entity may be required to provide. There are any number of other specific accommodations that may be appropriate for particular situations but are not specifically mentioned in this listing. This listing is not intended to be exhaustive of accommodation possibilities. For example, other accommodations could include permitting the use of accrued paid leave or providing additional unpaid leave for necessary treatment, making employer provided transportation accessible, and providing reserved parking spaces. Providing personal assistants, such as a page turner for an employee with no hands or a travel attendant to act as a sighted guide to assist a blind employee on occasional business trips, may also be a reasonable accommodation. Senate Report at 31; House Labor Report at 62; House Judiciary Report at 39.

It may also be a reasonable accommodation to permit an individual with a disability the opportunity to provide and utilize equipment, aids or services that an employer is not required to provide as a reasonable accommodation. For example, it would be a reasonable accommodation for an employer to permit an individual who is blind to use a guide dog at work, even though the employer would not be required to provide a guide dog for the employee.

The accommodations included on the list of reasonable accommodations are generally self explanatory. However, there are a few that require further explanation. One of these is the accommodation of making existing facilities used by employees readily accessible to, and usable by, individuals with disabilities. This accommodation includes both those areas that must be accessible for the employee to perform essential job functions, as well as non-work areas used by the employer's employees for other purposes. For example, accessible break rooms, lunch rooms, training rooms, restrooms etc., may be required as reasonable accommodations.

Another of the potential accommodations listed is "job restructuring." An employer or other covered entity may restructure a job by reallocating or redistributing nonessential, marginal job functions. For example, an employer may have two jobs, each of which entails the performance of a number of marginal functions. The employer hires a qualified individual with a disability who is able to perform some of the marginal functions of each job but not all of the marginal functions of either job. As an accommodation, the employer may redistribute the marginal functions so that all of the marginal functions that the qualified individual with a disability can perform are made a part of the position to be filled by the qualified individual with a disability. The remaining marginal functions that the individual with a disability cannot perform would then be transferred to the other position. See Senate Report at 31; House Labor Report at 62.

An employer or other covered entity is not required to reallocate essential functions. The essential functions are by definition those that the individual who holds the job would have to perform, with or without reasonable accommodation, in order to be considered qualified for the position. For example, suppose a security guard position requires the individual who holds the job to inspect identification cards. An employer would not have to provide an individual who is legally blind with an assistant to look at the identification cards for the legally blind employee. In this situation the assistant would be performing the job for the individual with a disability rather than assisting the individual to perform the job. See *Coleman* v. *Darden*, 595 F.2d 533 (10th Cir. 1979).

An employer or other covered entity may also restructure a job by altering when and/or how an essential function is performed. For example, an essential function customarily performed in the early morning hours may be rescheduled until later in the day as a reasonable accommodation to a disability that precludes performance of the function at the customary hour. Likewise, as a reasonable accommodation, an employee with a disability that inhibits the ability to write, may be permitted to computerize records that were customarily maintained manually.

Reassignment to a vacant position is also listed as a potential reasonable accommodation. In general, reassignment should be considered only when accommodation within the individual's current position would pose an undue hardship. Reassignment is not available to applicants. An applicant for a position must be qualified for, and be able to perform the essential functions of, the position sought with or without reasonable accommodation.

Reassignment may not be used to limit, segregate, or otherwise discriminate against employees with disabilities by forcing reassignments to undesirable positions or to designated offices or facilities. Employers should reassign the individual to an equivalent position, in terms of pay, status, etc., if the individual is qualified, and if the position is vacant within a reasonable amount of time. A "reasonable amount of time" should be determined in light of the totality of the circumstances. As an example, suppose there is no vacant position available at the time that an individual with a disability requests reassignment as a reasonable accommodation. The employer, however, knows that an equivalent position for which the individual is qualified, will become vacant next week. Under these circumstances, the employer should reassign the individual to the position when it becomes available.

An employer may reassign an individual to a lower graded position if there are no accommodations that would enable the employee to remain in the current position and there are no vacant equivalent positions for which the individual is qualified with or without reasonable accommodation. An employer, however, is not required to maintain the reassigned individual with a disability at the salary of the higher graded position if it does not so maintain reassigned employees who are not disabled. It should also be noted that an employer is not required to promote an individual with a disability as an accommodation. See Senate Report at 31–32; House Labor Report at 63.

The determination of which accommodation is appropriate in a particular situation involves a process in which the employer and employee identify the precise limitations imposed by the disability and explore potential accommodations that would overcome those limitations. This process is discussed more fully in § 1630.9 Not Making Reasonable Accommodation.

Section 1630.2(p) Undue Hardship

An employer or other covered entity is not required to provide an accommodation that will impose an undue hardship on the operation of the employer's or other covered entity's business. The term "undue hardship" means significant difficulty or expense in, or resulting from, the provision of the accommodation. The "undue hardship" provision takes into account the financial realities of the particular employer or other covered entity. However, the concept of undue hardship is not limited to financial difficulty. "Undue hardship" refers to any accommodation that would be unduly costly, extensive, substantial, or disruptive, or that would fundamentally alter the nature or operation of the business. See Senate Report at 35; House Labor Report at 67.

For example, suppose an individual with a disabling visual impairment that makes it extremely difficult to see in dim lighting applies for a position as a waiter in a nightclub and requests that the club be brightly lit as a reasonable accommodation. Although the individual may be able to perform the job in bright lighting, the nightclub will probably be able to demonstrate that that particular accommodation, though inexpensive, would impose an undue hardship if the bright lighting would destroy the ambience of the nightclub and/or make it difficult for the customers to see the stage show. The fact that that particular accommodation poses an undue hardship, however, only means that the employer is not required to provide that accommodation. If there is another accommodation that will not create an undue hardship, the employer would be required to provide the alternative accommodation.

An employer's claim that the cost of a particular accommodation will impose an undue hardship will be analyzed in light of the factors outlined in part 1630. In part, this analysis requires a determination of whose financial resources should be considered in deciding whether the accommodation is unduly costly. In some cases the financial resources of the employer or other covered entity in its entirety should be considered in determining whether the cost of an accommodation poses an undue hardship. In other cases, consideration of the financial resources of the employer or other covered entity as a whole may be inappropriate because it may not give an accurate picture of the financial resources available to the particular facility that will actually be required to provide the accommodation. See House Labor Report at 68–69; House Judiciary Report at 40–41; see also Conference Report at 56–57.

If the employer or other covered entity asserts that only the financial resources of the facility where the individual will be employed should be considered, part 1630 requires a factual determination of the relationship between the employer or other covered entity and the facility that will provide the accommodation. As an example, suppose that an independently owned fast food franchise that receives no money from the franchisor refuses to hire an individual with a hearing impairment because it asserts that it would be an undue hardship to provide an interpreter to enable the individual to participate in monthly staff meetings. Since the financial relationship between the franchisor and the franchise is limited to payment of an annual franchise fee, only the financial resources of the franchise would be considered in determining whether or not providing the accommodation would be an undue hardship. See House Labor Report at 68; House Judiciary Report at 40.

If the employer or other covered entity can show that the cost of the accommodation would impose an undue hardship, it would still be required to provide the accommodation if the funding is available from another source, e.g., a State vocational rehabilitation agency, or if Federal, State or local tax deductions or tax credits are available to offset the cost of the accommodation. If the employer or other covered entity receives, or is eligible to receive, monies from an external source that would pay the entire cost of the

accommodation, it cannot claim cost as an undue hardship. In the absence of such funding, the individual with a disability requesting the accommodation should be given the option of providing the accommodation or of paying that portion of the cost which constitutes the undue hardship on the operation of the business. To the extent that such monies pay or would pay for only part of the cost of the accommodation, only that portion of the cost of the accommodation that could not be recovered—the final net cost to the entity—may be considered in determining undue hardship. (See § 1630.9 Not Making Reasonable Accommodation). See Senate Report at 36; House Labor Report at 69.

Section 1630.2(r)   Direct Threat

An employer may require, as a qualification standard, that an individual not pose a direct threat to the health or safety of himself/herself or others. Like any other qualification standard, such a standard must apply to all applicants or employees and not just to individuals with disabilities. If, however, an individual poses a direct threat as a result of a disability, the employer must determine whether a reasonable accommodation would either eliminate the risk or reduce it to an acceptable level. If no accommodation exists that would either eliminate or reduce the risk, the employer may refuse to hire an applicant or may discharge an employee who poses a direct threat.

An employer, however, is not permitted to deny an employment opportunity to an individual with a disability merely because of a slightly increased risk. The risk can only be considered when it poses a significant risk, i.e., high probability, of substantial harm; a speculative or remote risk is insufficient. See Senate Report at 27; House Report Labor Report at 56–57; House Judiciary Report at 45.

Determining whether an individual poses a significant risk of substantial harm to others must be made on a case by case basis. The employer should identify the specific risk posed by the individual. For individuals with mental or emotional disabilities, the employer must identify the specific behavior on the part of the individual that would pose the direct threat. For individuals with physical disabilities, the employer must identify the aspect of the disability that would pose the direct threat. The employer should then consider the four factors listed in part 1630:

(1) The duration of the risk;
(2) The nature and severity of the potential harm;
(3) The likelihood that the potential harm will occur; and
(4) The imminence of the potential harm.

Such consideration must rely on objective, factual evidence—not on subjective perceptions, irrational fears, patronizing attitudes, or stereotypes—about the nature or effect of a particular disability, or of disability generally. See Senate Report at 27; House Labor Report at 56–57; House Judiciary Report at 45–46. See also Strathie v. Department of Transportation, 716 F.2d 227 (3d Cir. 1983). Relevant evidence may include input from the individual with a disability,

the experience of the individual with a disability in previous similar positions, and opinions of medical doctors, rehabilitation counselors, or physical therapists who have expertise in the disability involved and/or direct knowledge of the individual with the disability.

An employer is also permitted to require that an individual not pose a direct threat of harm to his or her own safety or health. If performing the particular functions of a job would result in a high probability of substantial harm to the individual, the employer could reject or discharge the individual unless a reasonable accommodation that would not cause an undue hardship would avert the harm. For example, an employer would not be required to hire an individual, disabled by narcolepsy, who frequently and unexpectedly loses consciousness for a carpentry job the essential functions of which require the use of power saws and other dangerous equipment, where no accommodation exists that will reduce or eliminate the risk.

The assessment that there exists a high probability of substantial harm to the individual, like the assessment that there exists a high probability of substantial harm to others, must be strictly based on valid medical analyses and/or on other objective evidence. This determination must be based on individualized factual data, using the factors discussed above, rather than on stereotypic or patronizing assumptions and must consider potential reasonable accommodations. Generalized fears about risks from the employment environment, such as exacerbation of the disability caused by stress, cannot be used by an employer to disqualify an individual with a disability. For example, a law firm could not reject an applicant with a history of disabling mental illness based on a generalized fear that the stress of trying to make partner might trigger a relapse of the individual's mental illness. Nor can generalized fears about risks to individuals with disabilities in the event of an evacuation or other emergency be used by an employer to disqualify an individual with a disability. See Senate Report at 56; House Labor Report at 73–74; House Judiciary Report at 45. See also Mantolete v. Bolger, 767 F.2d 1416 (9th Cir. 1985); Bentivegna v. U.S. Department of Labor, 694 F.2d 619 (9th Cir.1982).

Section 1630.3   Exceptions to the Definitions of "Disability" and "Qualified Individual with a Disability"

Section 1630.3 (a) through (c)   Illegal Use of Drugs

Part 1630 provides that an individual currently engaging in the illegal use of drugs is not an individual with a disability for purposes of this part when the employer or other covered entity acts on the basis of such use. Illegal use of drugs refers both to the use of unlawful drugs, such as cocaine, and to the unlawful use of prescription drugs.

Employers, for example, may discharge or deny employment to persons who illegally use drugs, on the basis of such use, without fear of being held liable for discrimination. The term "currently engaging" is not intended to be limited to the use of drugs on the day of, or within a matter of days or weeks before, the employment action in question. Rather, the provision is intended to apply to the illegal use of drugs that has occurred recently enough to indicate that the individual is actively engaged in such conduct. See Conference Report at 64.

Individuals who are erroneously perceived as engaging in the illegal use of drugs, but are not in fact illegally using drugs are not excluded from the definitions of the terms "disability" and "qualified individual with a disability." Individuals who are no longer illegally using drugs and who have either been rehabilitated successfully or are in the process of completing a rehabilitation program are, likewise, not excluded from the definitions of those terms. The term "rehabilitation program" refers to both in-patient and out-patient programs, as well as to appropriate employee assistance programs, professionally recognized self-help programs, such as Narcotics Anonymous, or other programs that provide professional (not necessarily medical) assistance and counseling for individuals who illegally use drugs. See Conference Report at 64; see also House Labor Report at 77; House Judiciary Report at 47.

It should be noted that this provision simply provides that certain individuals are not excluded from the definitions of "disability" and "qualified individual with a disability." Consequently, such individuals are still required to establish that they satisfy the requirements of these definitions in order to be protected by the ADA and this part. An individual erroneously regarded as illegally using drugs, for example, would have to show that he or she was regarded as a drug addict in order to demonstrate that he or she meets the definition of "disability" as defined in this part.

Employers are entitled to seek reasonable assurances that no illegal use of drugs is occurring or has occurred recently enough so that continuing use is a real and ongoing problem. The reasonable assurances that employers may ask applicants or employees to provide include evidence that the individual is participating in a drug treatment program and/or evidence, such as drug test results, to show that the individual is not currently engaging in the illegal use of drugs. An employer, such as a law enforcement agency, may also be able to impose a qualification standard that excludes individuals with a history of illegal use of drugs if it can show that the standard is job-related and consistent with business necessity. (See § 1630.10 Qualification Standards, Tests and Other Selection Criteria) See Conference Report at 64.

Section 1630.4   Discrimination Prohibited

This provision prohibits discrimination against a qualified individual with a disability in all aspects of the employment relationship. The range of employment decisions covered by this nondiscrimination mandate is to be construed in a manner consistent with the regulations implementing section 504 of the Rehabilitation Act of 1973.

Part 1630 is not intended to limit the ability of covered entities to choose and maintain a qualified workforce. Employers can continue to use job-related criteria to select qualified employees, and can continue to hire employees who can perform the essential functions of the job.

Section 1630.5   Limiting, Segregating and Classifying

This provision and the several provisions that follow describe various specific forms of discrimination that are included within the general prohibition of § 1630.4. Covered entities are prohibited from restricting the employment opportunities of qualified individuals with disabilities on the basis of stereotypes and myths about the individual's disability. Rather, the capabilities of qualified individuals with disabilities must be determined on an individualized, case by case basis. Covered entities are also prohibited from segregating qualified employees into separate work areas or into separate lines of advancement.

Thus, for example, it would be a violation of this part for an employer to limit the duties of an employee with a disability based on a presumption of what is best for an individual with such a disability, or on a presumption about the abilities of an individual with such a disability. It would be a violation of this part for an employer to adopt a separate track of job promotion or progression for employees with disabilities based on a presumption that employees with disabilities are uninterested in, or incapable of, performing particular jobs. Similarly, it would be a violation for an employer to assign or reassign (as a reasonable accommodation) employees with disabilities to one particular office or installation, or to require that employees with disabilities only use particular employer provided non-work facilities such as segregated break-rooms, lunch rooms, or lounges. It would also be a violation of this part to deny employment to an applicant or employee with a disability based on generalized fears about the safety of an individual with such a disability, or based on generalized assumptions about the absenteeism rate of an individual with such a disability.

In addition, it should also be noted that this part is intended to require that employees with disabilities be accorded equal access to whatever health insurance coverage the employer provides to other employees. This part does not, however, affect pre-existing condition clauses included in health insurance policies offered by employers. Consequently, employers may continue to offer policies that contain such clauses, even if they adversely affect individuals with disabilities, so long as the clauses are not used as a subterfuge to evade the purposes of this part.

So, for example, it would be permissible for an employer to offer an insurance policy that limits coverage for certain procedures or treatments to a specified number per year. Thus, if a health insurance plan provided coverage for five blood transfusions a year to all covered employees, it would not be discriminatory to offer this plan simply because a hemophiliac employee may require more than five blood transfusions annually.

However, it would not be permissible to limit or deny the hemophiliac employee coverage for other procedures, such as heart surgery or the setting of a broken leg, even though the plan would not have to provide coverage for the additional blood transfusions that may be involved in these procedures. Likewise, limits may be placed on reimbursements for certain procedures or on the types of drugs or procedures covered (e.g. limits on the number of permitted X-rays or non-coverage of experimental drugs or procedures), but that limitation must be applied equally to individuals with and without disabilities. See Senate Report at 28–29; House Labor Report at 58–59; House Judiciary Report at 36.

Leave policies or benefit plans that are uniformly applied do not violate this part simply because they do not address the special needs of every individual with a disability. Thus, for example, an employer that reduces the number of paid sick leave days that it will provide to all employees, or reduces the amount of medical insurance coverage that it will provide to all employees, is not in violation of this part, even if the benefits reduction has an impact on employees with disabilities in need of greater sick leave and medical coverage. Benefits reductions adopted for discriminatory reasons are in violation of this part. See *Alexander v. Choate*, 469 U.S. 287 (1985). See Senate Report at 85; House Labor Report at 137. (See also, the discussion at § 1630.16(f) Health Insurance, Life Insurance, and Other Benefit Plans).

Section 1630.6   Contractual or Other Arrangements

An employer or other covered entity may not do through a contractual or other relationship what it is prohibited from doing directly. This provision does not affect the determination of whether or not one is a "covered entity" or "employer" as defined in § 1630.2.

This provision only applies to situations where an employer or other covered entity has entered into a contractual relationship that has the effect of discriminating against its own employees or applicants with disabilities. Accordingly, it would be a violation for an employer to participate in a contractual relationship that results in discrimination against the employer's employees with disabilities in hiring, training, promotion, or in any other aspect of the employment relationship. This provision applies not to the employer or other covered entity intended for the contractual relationship to have the discriminatory effect. Part 1630 notes that this provision applies to parties on either side of the contractual or other relationship. This is intended to highlight that an employer whose employees provide services to others, like an employer whose employees receive services, must ensure that those employees are not discriminated against on the basis of disability. For example, a copier company whose service representative is a dwarf could be required to provide a stepstool, as a reasonable accommodation, to enable him to perform the necessary repairs. However, the employer would not be required, as a reasonable accommodation, to make structural changes to its customer s inaccessible premises.

The existence of the contractual relationship adds no new obligations under part 1630. The employer, therefore, is not liable through the contractual arrangement for any discrimination by the contractor against the contractors own employees or applicants, although the contractor, as an employer, may be liable for such discrimination.

An employer or other covered entity, on the other hand, cannot evade the obligations imposed by this part by engaging in a contractual or other relationship. For example, an employer cannot avoid its responsibility to make reasonable accommodation subject to the undue hardship limitation through a contractual arrangement. See Conference Report at 59; House Labor Report at 59–61; House Judiciary Report at 36–37.

To illustrate, assume that an employer is seeking to contract with a company to provide training for its employees. Any responsibilities of reasonable accommodation applicable to the employer in providing the training remain with that employer even if It contracts with another company for this service. Thus, if the training company were required to conduct the training at an inaccessible location, thereby making it impossible for an employee who uses a wheelchair to attend, the employer would have a duty to make reasonable accommodation unless to do so would impose an undue hardship. Under these circumstances, appropriate accommodations might include (1) having the training company identify accessible training sites and relocate the training program; (2) having the training company make the training site accessible; (3) directly making the training site accessible or providing the training company with the means by which to make the site accessible; (4) identifying and contracting with another training company that uses accessible sites; or (5) any other accommodation that would result in making the training available to the employee.

As another illustration, assume that instead of contracting with a training company, the employer contracts with a hotel to host a conference for its employees. The employer will have a duty to ascertain and ensure the accessibility of the hotel and its conference facilities. To fulfill this obligation the employer could, for example, inspect the hotel first-hand or ask a local disability group to inspect the hotel. Alternatively, the employer could ensure that the contract with the hotel specifies it will provide accessible guest rooms for those who need them and that all rooms to be used for the conference, including exhibit and meeting rooms, are accessible. If the hotel breaches this accessibility provision, the hotel may be liable to the employer, under a non-ADA breach of contract theory, for the cost of any accommodation needed to provide access to the hotel and conference, and for any other costs accrued by the employer. (In addition, the hotel may also be independently liable under title III of the ADA). However, this would not relieve the employer of its

responsibility under this part nor shield it from charges of discrimination by its own employees. See House Labor Report at 40; House Judiciary Report at 37.

Section 1630.8 Relationship or Association With an Individual With a Disability

This provision is intended to protect any qualified individual, whether or not that individual has a disability, from discrimination because that person is known to have an association or relationship with an individual who has a known disability. This protection is not limited to those who have a familial relationship with an individual with a disability.

To illustrate the scope of this provision. assume that a qualified applicant without a disability applies for a job and discloses to the employer that his or her spouse has a disability. The employer thereupon declines to hire the applicant because the employer believes that the applicant would have to miss work or frequently leave work early in order to care for the spouse. Such a refusal to hire would be prohibited by this provision. Similarly, this provision would prohibit an employer from discharging an employee because the employee does volunteer work with people who have AIDS, and the employer fears that the employee may contract the disease.

This provision also applies to other benefits and privileges of employment. For example, an employer that provides health insurance benefits to its employees for their dependents may not reduce the level of those benefits to an employee simply because that employee has a dependent with a disability. This is true even if the provision of such benefits would result in increased health insurance costs for the employer.

It should be noted, however, that an employer need not provide the applicant or employee without a disability with a reasonable accommodation because that duty only applies to qualified applicants or employees with disabilities. Thus, for example, an employee would not be entitled to a modified work schedule as an accommodation to enable the employee to care for a spouse with a disability. See Senate Report at 30; House Labor Report at 61–62; House Judiciary Report at 38–39.

Section 1630.9   Not Making Reasonable Accommodation

The obligation to make reasonable accommodation is a form of non-discrimination. It applies to all employment decisions and to the job application process. This obligation does not extend to the provision of adjustments or modifications that are primarily for the personal benefit of the individual with a disability. Thus, if an adjustment or modification is job-related. *e.g.* specifically assists the individual in performing the duties of a particular job, it will be considered a type of reasonable accommodation. On the other hand, if an adjustment or modification assists the individual throughout his or her daily activities, on and off the job, it will be considered a personal item that the employer is not required to provide. Accordingly, an employer would generally not be required to

provide an employee with a disability with a prosthetic limb, wheelchair. or eyeglasses. Nor would an employer have to provide as an accommodation any amenity or convenience that is not job-related. such as a private hot plate, hot pot or refrigerator that is not provided to employees without disabilities. See Senate Report at 31; House Labor Report at 62.

It should be noted, however, that the provision of such items may be required as a reasonable accommodation where such items are specifically designed or required to meet job-related rather than personal needs. An employer, for example, may have to provide an individual with a disabling visual impairment with eyeglasses specifically designed to enable the individual to use the office computer monitors, but that are not otherwise needed by the individual outside of the office.

The term "supported employment," which has been applied to a wide variety of programs to assist individuals with severe disabilities in both competitive and non-competitive employment, is not synonymous with reasonable accommodation. Examples of supported employment include modified training materials, restructuring essential functions to enable an individual to perform a job, or hiring an outside professional ("job coach") to assist in job training. Whether a particular form of assistance would be required as a reasonable accommodation must be determined on an individualized. case by case basis without regard to whether that assistance is referred to as "supported employment." For example, an employer, under certain circumstances, may be required to provide modified training materials or a temporary "job coach" to assist in the training of a qualified individual with a disability as a reasonable accommodation. However, an employer would not be required to restructure the essential functions of a position to fit the skills of an individual with a disability who is not otherwise qualified to perform the position, as is done in certain supported employment programs. See 34 CFR part 363. It should be noted that it would not be a violation of this part for an employer to provide any of these personal modifications or adjustments, or to engage in supported employment or similar rehabilitative programs.

The obligation to make reasonable accommodation applies to all services and programs provided in connection with employment, and to all non-work facilities provided or maintained by an employer for use by its employees. Accordingly, the obligation to accommodate is applicable to employer sponsored placement or counseling services, and to employer provided cafeterias, lounges, gymnasiums, auditoriums, transportation and the like.

The reasonable accommodation requirement is best understood as a means by which barriers to the equal employment opportunity of an individual with a disability are removed or alleviated. These barriers may, for example, be physical or structural obstacles that inhibit or prevent the access of an individual with a disability to job sites, facilities or equipment. Or they may be rigid work schedules that permit no flexibility as to when work is performed or when breaks may be taken, or inflexible job procedures that unduly limit the modes of communication that are used on the job, or the way in which particular tasks are accomplished.

The term "otherwise qualified" is intended to make clear that the obligation to make reasonable accommodation is owed only to an individual with a disability who is qualified within the meaning of § 1630.2(m) in that he or she satisfies all the skill, experience, education and other job-related selection criteria. An individual with a disability is "otherwise qualified," in other words, if he or she is qualified for a job, except that, because of the disability, he or she needs a reasonable accommodation to be able to perform the job's essential functions.

For example, if a law firm requires that all incoming lawyers have graduated from an accredited law school and have passed the bar examination, the law firm need not provide an accommodation to an individual with a visual impairment who has not met these selection criteria. That individual is not entitled to a reasonable accommodation because the individual is not "otherwise qualified" for the position.

On the other hand, if the individual has graduated from an accredited law school and passed the bar examination, the individual would be "otherwise qualified." The law firm would thus be required to provide a reasonable accommodation, such as a machine that magnifies print, to enable the individual to perform the essential functions of the attorney position, unless the necessary accommodation would impose an undue hardship on the law firm. See Senate Report at 33–34; House Labor Report at 64–65.

The reasonable accommodation that is required by this part should provide the qualified individual with a disability with an equal employment opportunity. Equal employment opportunity means an opportunity to attain the same level of performance, or to enjoy the same level of benefits and privileges of employment as are available to the average similarly situated employee without a disability. Thus, for example, an accommodation made to assist an employee with a disability in the performance of his or her job must be adequate to enable the individual to perform the essential functions of the relevant position. The accommodation, however, does not have to be the "best" accommodation possible, so long as it is sufficient to meet the job-related needs of the individual being accommodated. Accordingly, an employer would not have to provide an employee disabled by a back impairment with a state-of-the-art mechanical lifting device if it provided the employee with a less expensive or more readily available device that enabled the employee to perform the essential functions of the job. See Senate Report at 35; House Labor Report at 66; see also *Carter* v. *Bennett*, 840 F.2d 63 (DC Cir. 1988).

Employers are obligated to make reasonable accommodation only to the physical or mental limitations resulting from the disability of a qualified individual with a disability that is known to the employer.

Thus, an employer would not be expected to accommodate disabilities of which it is unaware. If an employee with a known disability is having difficulty performing his or her job, an employer may inquire whether the employee is in need of a reasonable accommodation. In general, however, it is the responsibility of the individual with a disability to inform the employer that an accommodation is needed. When the need for an accommodation is not obvious, an employer, before providing a reasonable accommodation, may require that the individual with a disability provide documentation of the need for accommodation.

See Senate Report at 34; House Labor Report at 65.

Process of Determining the Appropriate Reasonable Accommodation

Once a qualified individual with a disability has requested provision of a reasonable accommodation, the employer must make a reasonable effort to determine the appropriate accommodation. The appropriate reasonable accommodation is best determined through a flexible, interactive process that involves both the employer and the qualified individual with a disability. Although this process is described below in terms of accommodations that enable the individual with a disability to perform the essential functions of the position held or desired, it is equally applicable to accommodations involving the job application process, and to accommodations that enable the individual with a disability to enjoy equal benefits and privileges of employment. See Senate Report at 34–35; House Labor Report at 65–67.

When a qualified individual with a disability has requested a reasonable accommodation to assist in the performance of a job, the employer, using a problem solving approach, should:

(1) Analyze the particular job involved and determine its purpose and essential functions;

(2) Consult with the individual with a disability to ascertain the precise job-related limitations imposed by the individual's disability and how those limitations could be overcome with a reasonable accommodation;

(3) In consultation with the individual to be accommodated, identify potential accommodations and assess the effectiveness each would have in enabling the individual to perform the essential functions of the position; and

(4) Consider the preference of the individual to be accommodated and select and implement the accommodation that is most appropriate for both the employee and the employer.

In many instances, the appropriate reasonable accommodation may be so obvious to either or both the employer and the qualified individual with a disability that it may not be necessary to proceed in this step-by-step fashion. For example, if an employee who uses a wheelchair requests that his or her desk be placed on blocks to elevate the desktop above the arms of the wheelchair and the employer complies, an appropriate accommodation has been requested, identified, and provided without either the employee or employer being aware

of having engaged in any sort of "reasonable accommodation process."

However, in some instances neither the individual requesting the accommodation nor the employer can readily identify the appropriate accommodation. For example, the individual needing the accommodation may not know enough about the equipment used by the employer or the exact nature of the work site to suggest an appropriate accommodation. Likewise, the employer may not know enough about the individual's disability or the limitations that disability would impose on the performance of the job to suggest an appropriate accommodation. Under such circumstances, it may be necessary for the employer to initiate a more defined problem solving process, such as the step-by-step process described above, as part of its reasonable effort to identify the appropriate reasonable accommodation.

This process requires the individual assessment of both the particular job at issue, and the specific physical or mental limitations of the particular individual in need of reasonable accommodation. With regard to assessment of the job, "individual assessment" means analyzing the actual job duties and determining the true purpose or object of the job. Such an assessment is necessary to ascertain which job functions are the essential functions that an accommodation must enable an individual with a disability to perform.

After assessing the relevant job, the employer, in consultation with the individual requesting the accommodation, should make an assessment of the specific limitations imposed by the disability on the individual's performance of the job's essential functions. This assessment will make it possible to ascertain the precise barrier to the employment opportunity which, in turn, will make it possible to determine the accommodation(s) that could alleviate or remove that barrier.

If consultation with the individual in need of the accommodation still does not reveal potential appropriate accommodations, then the employer, as part of this process, may find that technical assistance is helpful in determining how to accommodate the particular individual in the specific situation. Such assistance could be sought from the Commission, from state or local rehabilitation agencies, or from disability constituent organizations. It should be noted, however, that, as provided in § 1630.9(c) of this part, the failure to obtain or receive technical assistance from the federal agencies that administer the ADA will not excuse the employer from its reasonable accommodation obligation.

Once potential accommodations have been identified, the employer should assess the effectiveness of each potential accommodation in assisting the individual in need of the accommodation in the performance of the essential functions of the position. If more than one of these accommodations will enable the individual to perform the essential functions or if the individual would prefer to provide his or her own accommodation, the preference of the individual with a disability should be given primary consideration. However, the employer providing the accommodation has the ultimate discretion to choose between effective accommodations, and may choose the less expensive accommodation or the accommodation that is easier for it to provide. It should also be noted that the individual's willingness to provide his or her own accommodation does not relieve the employer of the duty to provide the accommodation should the individual for any reason be unable or unwilling to continue to provide the accommodation.

Reasonable Accommodation Process Illustrated

The following example illustrates the informal reasonable accommodation process. Suppose a Sack Handler position requires that the employee pick up fifty pound sacks and carry them from the company loading dock to the storage room, and that a sack handler who is disabled by a back impairment requests a reasonable accommodation. Upon receiving the request, the employer analyzes the Sack Handler job and determines that the essential function and purpose of the job is not the requirement that the job holder physically lift and carry the sacks, but the requirement that the job holder cause the sack to move from the loading dock to the storage room.

The employer then meets with the sack handler to ascertain precisely the barrier posed by the individual's specific disability to the performance of the job's essential function of relocating the sacks. At this meeting the employer learns that the individual can, in fact, lift the sacks to waist level, but is prevented by his or her disability from carrying the sacks from the loading dock to the storage room. The employer and the individual agree that any of a number of potential accommodations, such as the provision of a dolly, hand truck, or cart, could enable the individual to transport the sacks that he or she has lifted.

Upon further consideration, however, it is determined that the provision of a cart is not a feasible effective option. No carts are currently available at the company, and those that can be purchased by the company are the wrong shape to hold many of the bulky and irregularly shaped sacks that must be moved. Both the dolly and the hand truck, on the other hand, appear to be effective options. Both are readily available to the company, and either will enable the individual to relocate the sacks that he or she has lifted. The sack handler indicates his or her preference for the dolly. In consideration of this expressed preference, and because the employer feels that the dolly will allow the individual to move more sacks at a time and so be more efficient than would a hand truck, the employer ultimately provides the sack handler with a dolly in fulfillment of the obligation to make reasonable accommodation.

Section 1630.9(b)

This provision states that an employer or other covered entity cannot prefer or select a qualified individual without a disability over an equally qualified individual with a disability merely because the individual with a disability will require a reasonable accommodation. In other words, an individual's need for an accommodation cannot enter into the employer's or other covered entity's decision regarding hiring, discharge, promotion, or other similar employment decisions, unless the accommodation would impose an undue hardship on the employer. See House Labor Report at 70.

Section 1630.9(d)

The purpose of this provision is to clarify that an employer or other covered entity may not compel a qualified individual with a disability to accept an accommodation, where that accommodation is neither requested nor needed by the individual. However, if a necessary reasonable accommodation is refused, the individual may not be considered qualified. For example, an individual with a visual impairment that restricts his or her field of vision but who is able to read unaided would not be required to accept a reader as an accommodation. However, if the individual were not able to read unaided and reading was an essential function of the job, the individual would not be qualified for the job if he or she refused a reasonable accommodation that would enable him or her to read. See Senate Report at 34; House Labor Report at 65; House Judiciary Report at 71–72.

Section 1630.10 Qualification Standards, Tests, and Other Selection Criteria

The purpose of this provision is to ensure that individuals with disabilities are not excluded from job opportunities unless they are actually unable to do the job. It is to ensure that there is a fit between job criteria and an applicant's (or employee's) actual ability to do the job. Accordingly, job criteria that even unintentionally screen out, or tend to screen out, an individual with a disability or a class of individuals with disabilities because of their disability may not be used unless the employer demonstrates that that criteria, as used by the employer, are job-related to the position to which they are being applied and are consistent with business necessity. The concept of "business necessity" has the same meaning as the concept of "business necessity" under section 504 of the Rehabilitation Act of 1973.

Selection criteria that exclude, or tend to exclude, an individual with a disability or a class of individuals with disabilities because of their disability but do not concern an essential function of the job would not be consistent with business necessity.

The use of selection criteria that are related to an essential function of the job may be consistent with business necessity. However, selection criteria that are related to an essential function of the job may not be used to exclude an individual with a disability if that individual could satisfy the criteria with the provision of a reasonable accommodation. Experience under a similar provision of the regulations implementing section 504 of the Rehabilitation Act indicates that challenges to selection criteria are, in fact, most often resolved by reasonable accommodation. It is therefore anticipated that challenges to selection criteria brought under this part will generally be resolved in a like manner.

This provision is applicable to all types of selection criteria, including safety requirements, vision or hearing requirements, walking requirements, lifting requirements, and employment tests. See Senate Report at 37–39; House Labor Report at 70–72; House Judiciary Report at 42. As previously noted, however, it is not the intent of this part to second guess an employer's business judgment with regard to production standards. (See section 1630.2(n) Essential Functions). Consequently, production standards will generally not be subject to a challenge under this provision.

The Uniform Guidelines on Employee Selection Procedures (UGESP) 29 CFR part 1607 do not apply to the Rehabilitation Act and are similarly inapplicable to this part.

Section 1630.11 Administration of Tests

The intent of this provision is to further emphasize that individuals with disabilities are not to be excluded from jobs that they can actually perform merely because a disability prevents them from taking a test, or negatively influences the results of a test, that is a prerequisite to the job. Read together with the reasonable accommodation requirement of section 1630.9, this provision requires that employment tests be administered to eligible applicants or employees with disabilities that impair sensory, manual, or speaking skills in formats that do not require the use of the impaired skill.

The employer or other covered entity is, generally, only required to provide such reasonable accommodation if it knows, prior to the administration of the test, that the individual is disabled and that the disability impairs sensory, manual or speaking skills. Thus, for example, it would be unlawful to administer a written employment test to an individual who has informed the employer, prior to the administration of the test, that he is disabled with dyslexia and unable to read. In such a case, as a reasonable accommodation and in accordance with this provision, an alternative oral test should be administered to that individual. By the same token, a written test may need to be substituted for an oral test if the applicant taking the test is an individual with a disability that impairs speaking skills or impairs the processing of auditory information.

Occasionally, an individual with a disability may not realize, prior to the administration of a test, that he or she will need an accommodation to take that particular test. In such a situation, the individual with a disability, upon becoming aware of the need for an accommodation, must so inform the employer or other covered entity. For example, suppose an individual with a disabling visual impairment does not request an accommodation for a written examination because he or she is usually able to take written tests with the aid of his or her own specially designed lens. When the test is distributed, the individual with a disability discovers that the lens is insufficient to distinguish the words of the test because of the unusually low color contrast between the paper and the ink, the individual would be entitled, at that point, to request an accommodation. The employer or other covered entity would, thereupon, have to provide a test with higher contrast, schedule a retest, or provide any other effective accommodation unless to do so would impose an undue hardship.

Other alternative or accessible test modes or formats include the administration of tests in large print or braille, or via a reader or sign interpreter. Where it is not possible to test in an alternative format, the employer may be required, as a reasonable accommodation, to evaluate the skill to be tested in another manner (e.g., through an interview, or through education license, or work experience requirements). An employer may also be required, as a reasonable accommodation, to allow more time to complete the test. In addition, the employer's obligation to make reasonable accommodation extends to ensuring that the test site is accessible. (See § 1630.9 Not Making Reasonable Accommodation) See Senate Report at 37–38; House Labor Report at 70–72; House Judiciary Report at 42; see also *Stutts* v. *Freeman*, 694 F.2d 666 (11th Cir. 1983); *Crane* v. *Dole*, 617 F. Supp. 156 (D.D.C. 1985).

This provision does not require that an employer offer every applicant his or her choice of test format. Rather, this provision only requires that an employer provide, upon advance request, alternative, accessible tests to individuals with disabilities that impair sensory, manual, or speaking skills needed to take the test.

This provision does not apply to employment tests that require the use of sensory, manual, or speaking skills where the tests are intended to measure those skills. Thus, an employer could require that an applicant with dyslexia take a written test for a particular position if the ability to read is the skill the test is designed to measure. Similarly, an employer could require that an applicant complete a test within established time frames if speed were one of the skills for which the applicant was being tested. However, the results of such a test could not be used to exclude an individual with a disability unless the skill was necessary to perform an essential function of the position and no reasonable accommodation was available to enable the individual to perform that function, or the necessary accommodation would impose an undue hardship.

Section 1630.13 Prohibited Medical Examinations and Inquiries

Section 1630.13(a) Pre-employment Examination or Inquiry

This provision makes clear that an employer cannot inquire as to whether an individual has a disability at the pre-offer stage of the selection process. Nor can an employer inquire at the pre-offer stage about an applicant's workers' compensation history.

Employers may ask questions that relate to the applicant's ability to perform job-related functions. However, these questions should not be phrased in terms of disability. An employer, for example, may ask whether the applicant has a driver's license, if driving is a job function, but may not ask whether the

applicant has a visual disability. Employers may ask about an applicant's ability to perform both essential and marginal job functions. Employers, though, may not refuse to hire an applicant with a disability because the applicant's disability prevents him or her from performing marginal functions. See Senate Report at 39; House Labor Report at 72–73; House Judiciary Report at 42–43.

Section 1630.14(b) Examination or Inquiry of Employees

The purpose of this provision is to prevent the administration to employees of medical tests or inquiries that do not serve a legitimate business purpose. For example, if an employee suddenly starts to use increased amounts of sick leave or starts to appear sickly, an employer could not require that employee to be tested for AIDS, HIV infection, or cancer unless the employer can demonstrate that such testing is job-related and consistent with business necessity. See Senate Report at 39; House Labor Report at 75; House Judiciary Report at 44.

Section 1630.14 Medical Examinations and Inquiries Specifically Permitted

Section 1630.14(a) Pre-employment Inquiry

Employers are permitted to make pre-employment inquiries into the ability of an applicant to perform job-related functions. This inquiry must be narrowly tailored. The employer may describe or demonstrate the job function and inquire whether or not the applicant can perform the function with or without reasonable accommodation. For example, an employer may explain that the job requires assembling small parts and ask if the individual will be able to perform that function, with or without reasonable accommodation. See Senate Report at 39; House Labor Report at 73; House Judiciary Report at 43.

An employer may also ask an applicant to describe or to demonstrate how, with or without reasonable accommodation, the applicant will be able to perform job-related functions. Such a request may be made of all applicants in the same job category regardless of disability. Such a request may also be made of an applicant whose known disability may interfere with or prevent the performance of a job-related function, whether or not the employer routinely makes such a request of all applicants in the job category. For example, an employer may ask an individual with one leg who applies for a position as a home washing machine repairman to demonstrate or to explain how, with or without reasonable accommodation, he would be able to transport himself and his tools down basement stairs. However, the employer may not inquire as to the nature or severity of the disability. Therefore, for example, the employer cannot ask how the individual lost the leg or whether the loss of the leg is indicative of an underlying impairment.

On the other hand, if the known disability of an applicant will not interfere with or prevent the performance of a job-related function, the employer may only request a description or demonstration by the applicant if it routinely makes such a request of all applicants in the same job category. So, for

example, it would not be permitted for an employer to request that an applicant with one leg demonstrate his ability to assemble small parts while seated at a table, if the employer does not routinely request that all applicants provide such a demonstration.

An employer that requires an applicant with a disability to demonstrate how he or she will perform a job-related function must either provide the reasonable accommodation the applicant needs to perform the function or permit the applicant to explain how, with the accommodation, he or she will perform the function. If the job-related function is not an essential function, the employer may not exclude the applicant with a disability because of the applicant's inability to perform that function. Rather, the employer must, as a reasonable accommodation, either provide an accommodation that will enable the individual to perform the function, transfer the function to another position, or exchange the function for one the applicant is able to perform.

An employer may not use an application form that lists a number of potentially disabling impairments and ask the applicant to check any of the impairments he or she may have. In addition, as noted above, an employer may not ask how a particular individual became disabled or the prognosis of the individual's disability. The employer is also prohibited from asking how often the individual will require leave for treatment or use leave as a result of incapacitation because of the disability. However, the employer may state the attendance requirements of the job and inquire whether the applicant can meet them.

An employer is permitted to ask, on a test announcement or application form, that individuals with disabilities who will require a reasonable accommodation in order to take the test so inform the employer within a reasonable established time period prior to the administration of the test. The employer may also request that documentation of the need for the accommodation accompany the request. Requested accommodations may include accessible testing sites, modified testing conditions and accessible test formats. (See § 1630.11 Administration of Tests).

Physical agility tests are not medical examinations and so may be given at any point in the application or employment process. Such tests must be given to all similarly situated applicants or employees regardless of disability. If such tests screen out or tend to screen out an individual with a disability or a class of individuals with disabilities, the employer would have to demonstrate that the test is job-related and consistent with business necessity and that performance cannot be achieved with reasonable accommodation. (See § 1630.9 Not Making Reasonable Accommodation: Process of Determining the Appropriate Reasonable Accommodation).

As previously noted, collecting information and inviting individuals to identify themselves as individuals with disabilities as required to satisfy the affirmative action requirements of Section 503 of the Rehabilitation Act is not restricted by this part. (See § 1630.1 (b) and (c) Applicability and Construction).

Section 1630.14(b) Employment Entrance Examination

An employer is permitted to require post-offer medical examinations before the employee actually starts working. The employer may condition the offer of employment on the results of the examination, provided that all entering employees in the same job category are subjected to such an examination, regardless of disability, and that the confidentiality requirements specified in this part are met.

This provision recognizes that in many industries, such as air transportation and construction, applicants for certain positions are chosen on the basis of many factors including physical and psychological criteria, some of which may be identified as a result of post-offer medical examinations given prior to entry on duty. Only those employees who meet the employer's physical and psychological criteria for the job, with or without reasonable accommodation, will be qualified to receive confirmed offers of employment and begin working.

Medical examinations permitted by this section are not required to be job-related and consistent with business necessity. However, if an employer withdraws an offer of employment because the medical examination reveals that the employee does not satisfy certain employment criteria, either the exclusionary criteria must not screen out or tend to screen out an individual with a disability or a class of individuals with disabilities, or they must be job-related and consistent with business necessity. As part of the showing that an exclusionary criteria is job-related and consistent with business necessity, the employer must also demonstrate that there is no reasonable accommodation that will enable the individual with a disability to perform the essential functions of the job. See Conference Report at 59–60; Senate Report at 39; House Labor Report at 73–74; House Judiciary Report at 43.

As an example, suppose an employer makes a conditional offer of employment to an applicant, and it is an essential function of the job that the incumbent be available to work every day for the next three months. An employment entrance examination then reveals that the applicant has a disabling impairment that, according to reasonable medical judgment that relies on the most current medical knowledge, will require treatment that will render the applicant unable to work for a portion of the three month period. Under these circumstances, the employer would be able to withdraw the employment offer without violating this part.

The information obtained in the course of a permitted entrance examination or inquiry is to be treated as a confidential medical record and may only be used in a manner not inconsistent with this part. State workers' compensation laws are not preempted by the ADA or this part. These laws require the collection of information from individuals for state administrative purposes that do not conflict with the ADA or this part. Consequently, employers or other covered entities may submit information to state workers' compensation offices or second injury funds in accordance with state workers' compensation laws without violating this part.

Consistent with this section and with § 1630.16(f) of this part, information obtained in the course of a permitted entrance examination or inquiry may be used for insurance purposes described in § 1630.16(f).

Section 1630.14(c) Examination of Employees

This provision permits employers to make inquiries or require medical examinations (fitness for duty exams) when there is a need to determine whether an employee is still able to perform the essential functions of his or her job. The provision permits employers or other covered entities to make inquiries or require medical examinations necessary to the reasonable accommodation process described in this part. This provision also permits periodic physicals to determine fitness for duty or other medical monitoring if such physicals or monitoring are required by medical standards or requirements established by Federal, state, or local law that are consistent with the ADA and this part (or in the case of a federal standard, with section 504 of the Rehabilitation Act) in that they are job-related and consistent with business necessity.

Such standards may include federal safety regulations that regulate bus and truck driver qualifications, as well as laws establishing medical requirements for pilots or other air transportation personnel. These standards also include health standards promulgated pursuant to the Occupational Safety and Health Act of 1970, the Federal Coal Mine Health and Safety Act of 1969, or other similar statutes that require that employees exposed to certain toxic and hazardous substances be medically monitored at specific intervals. See House Labor Report at 74–75.

The information obtained in the course of such examination or inquiries is to be treated as a confidential medical record and may only be used in a manner not inconsistent with this part.

Section 1630.14(d) Other Acceptable Examinations and Inquiries

Part 1630 permits voluntary medical examinations, including voluntary medical histories, as part of employee health programs. These programs often include, for example, medical screening for high blood pressure, weight control counseling, and cancer detection. Voluntary activities, such as blood pressure monitoring and the administering of prescription drugs, such as insulin, are also permitted. It should be noted, however, that the medical records developed in the course of such activities must be maintained in the confidential manner required by this part and must not be used for any purpose in violation of this part, such as limiting health insurance eligibility. House Labor Report at 75; House Judiciary Report at 43–44.

Section 1630.15 Defenses

The section on defenses in part 1630 is not intended to be exhaustive. However, it is intended to inform employers of some of the potential defenses available to a charge of discrimination under the ADA and this part.

Section 1630.15(a) Disparate Treatment Defenses

The "traditional" defense to a charge of disparate treatment under title VII, as expressed in *McDonnell Douglas Corp.* v. *Green*, 411 U.S. 792 (1973), *Texas Department of Community Affairs* v. *Burdine*, 450 U.S. 248 (1981), and their progeny, may be applicable to charges of disparate treatment brought under the ADA. See *Prewitt* v. *U.S. Postal Service*, 662 F.2d 292 (5th Cir. 1981). Disparate treatment means, with respect to title I of the ADA, that an individual was treated differently on the basis of his or her disability. For example, disparate treatment has occurred where an employer excludes an employee with a severe facial disfigurement from staff meetings because the employer does not like to look at the employee. The individual is being treated differently because of the employer's attitude towards his or her perceived disability. Disparate treatment has also occurred where an employer has a policy of not hiring individuals with AIDS regardless of the individuals' qualifications.

The crux of the defense to this type of charge is that the individual was treated differently not because of his or her disability but for a legitimate nondiscriminatory reason such as poor performance unrelated to the individual's disability. The fact that the individual's disability is not covered by the employer's current insurance plan or would cause the employer's insurance premiums or workers' compensation costs to increase, would not be a legitimate nondiscriminatory reason justifying disparate treatment of an individual with a disability. Senate Report at 85; House Labor Report at 136 and House Judiciary Report at 70. The defense of a legitimate nondiscriminatory reason is rebutted if the alleged nondiscriminatory reason is shown to be pretextual.

Section 1630.15 (b) and (c) Disparate Impact Defenses

Disparate impact means, with respect to title I of the ADA and this part, that uniformly applied criteria have an adverse impact on an individual with a disability or a disproportionately negative impact on a class of individuals with disabilities. Section 1630.15(b) clarifies that an employer may use selection criteria that have such a disparate impact, *i.e.*, that screen out or tend to screen out an individual with a disability or a class of individuals with disabilities only when they are job-related and consistent with business necessity.

For example, an employer interviews two candidates for a position, one of whom is blind. Both are equally qualified. The employer decides that while it is not essential to the job it would be convenient to have an employee who has a driver's license and so could occasionally be asked to run errands by car. The employer hires the individual who is sighted because this individual has a driver's license. This is an example of a uniformly applied criterion, having a driver's permit, that screens out an individual who has a disability that makes it impossible to obtain a driver's permit. The employer would, thus, have to show that this criterion is job-related and consistent with business necessity. See House Labor Report at 55.

However, even if the criterion is job-related and consistent with business necessity, an employer could not exclude an individual with a disability if the criterion could be met or job performance accomplished with a reasonable accommodation. For example, suppose an employer requires, as part of its application process, an interview that is job-related and consistent with business necessity. The employer would not be able to refuse to hire a hearing impaired applicant because he or she could not be interviewed. This is so because an interpreter could be provided as a reasonable accommodation that would allow the individual to be interviewed, and thus satisfy the selection criterion.

With regard to safety requirements that screen out or tend to screen out an individual with a disability or a class of individuals with disabilities, an employer must demonstrate that the requirement, as applied to the individual, satisfies the "direct threat" standard in § 1630.2(r) in order to show that the requirement is job-related and consistent with business necessity.

Section 1630.15(c) clarifies that there may be uniformly applied standards, criteria and policies not relating to selection that may also screen out or tend to screen out an individual with a disability or a class of individuals with disabilities. Like selection criteria that have a disparate impact, non-selection criteria having such an impact may also have to be job-related and consistent with business necessity, subject to consideration of reasonable accommodation.

It should be noted, however, that some uniformly applied employment policies or practices, such as leave policies, are not subject to challenge under the adverse impact theory. "No-leave" policies (e.g., no leave during the first six months of employment) are likewise not subject to challenge under the adverse impact theory. However, an employer, in spite of its "no-leave" policy, may, in appropriate circumstances, have to consider the provision of leave to an employee with a disability as a reasonable accommodation, unless the provision of leave would impose an undue hardship. See discussion at § 1630.5 Limiting, Segregating and Classifying, and § 1630.10 Qualification Standards, Tests, and Other Selection Criteria.

Section 1630.15(d) Defense to Not Making Reasonable Accommodation

An employer or other covered entity alleged to have discriminated because it did not make a reasonable accommodation, as required by this part, may offer as a defense that it would have been an undue hardship to make the accommodation.

It should be noted, however, that an employer cannot simply assert that a needed accommodation will cause it undue hardship, as defined in § 1630.2(p), and thereupon be relieved of the duty to provide accommodation. Rather, an employer will have to present evidence and demonstrate

that the accommodation will, in fact, cause it undue hardship. Whether a particular accommodation will impose an undue hardship for a particular employer is determined on a case by case basis. Consequently, an accommodation that poses an undue hardship for one employer at a particular time may not pose an undue hardship for another employer, or even for the same employer at another time. Likewise, an accommodation that poses an undue hardship for one employer in a particular job setting, such as a temporary construction worksite, may not pose an undue hardship for another employer, or even for the same employer at a permanent worksite. See House Judiciary Report at 42.

The concept of undue hardship that has evolved under Section 504 of the Rehabilitation Act and is embodied in this part is unlike the "undue hardship" defense associated with the provision of religious accommodation under title VII of the Civil Rights Act of 1964. To demonstrate undue hardship pursuant to the ADA and this part, an employer must show substantially more difficulty or expense than would be needed to satisfy the "de minimis" title VII standard of undue hardship. For example, to demonstrate that the cost of an accommodation poses an undue hardship, an employer would have to show that the cost is undue as compared to the employer's budget. Simply comparing the cost of the accommodation to the salary of the individual with a disability in need of the accommodation will not suffice. Moreover, even if it is determined that the cost of an accommodation would unduly burden an employer, the employer cannot avoid making the accommodation if the individual with a disability can arrange to cover that portion of the cost that rises to the undue hardship level, or can otherwise arrange to provide the accommodation. Under such circumstances, the necessary accommodation would no longer pose an undue hardship. See Senate Report at 36; House Labor Report at 68–69; House Judiciary Report at 40–41.

Excessive cost is only one of several possible bases upon which an employer might be able to demonstrate undue hardship. Alternatively, for example, an employer could demonstrate that the provision of a particular accommodation would be unduly disruptive to its other employees or to the functioning of its business. The terms of a collective bargaining agreement may be relevant to this determination. By way of illustration, an employer would likely be able to show undue hardship if the employer could show that the requested accommodation of the upward adjustment of the business' thermostat would result in it becoming unduly hot for its other employees, or for its patrons or customers. The employer would thus not have to provide this accommodation. However, if there were an alternate accommodation that would not result in undue hardship, the employer would have to provide that accommodation.

It should be noted, moreover, that the employer would not be able to show undue hardship if the disruption to its employees were the result of those employees fears or prejudices toward the individual's disability and not the result of the provision of the

accommodation. Nor would the employer be able to demonstrate undue hardship by showing that the provision of the accommodation has a negative impact on the morale of its other employees but not on the ability of these employees to perform their jobs.

Section 1630.15(e) Defense—Conflicting Federal Laws and Regulations

There are several Federal laws and regulations that address medical standards and safety requirements. If the alleged discriminatory action was taken in compliance with another Federal law or regulation, the employer may offer its obligation to comply with the conflicting standard as a defense. The employer's defense of a conflicting Federal requirement or regulation may be rebutted by a showing of pretext, or by showing that the Federal standard did not require the discriminatory action, or that there was a nonexclusionary means to comply with the standard that would not conflict with this part. See House Labor Report at 74.

Section 1630.16 Specific Activities Permitted

Section 1630.16(a) Religious Entities

Religious organizations are not exempt from title I of the ADA or this part. A religious corporation, association, educational institution, or society may give a preference in employment to individuals of the particular religion, and may require that applicants and employees conform to the religious tenets of the organization. However, a religious organization may not discriminate against an individual who satisfies the permitted religious criteria because that individual is disabled. The religious entity, in other words, is required to consider qualified individuals with disabilities who satisfy the permitted religious criteria on an equal basis with qualified individuals without disabilities who similarly satisfy the religious criteria. See Senate Report at 42; House Labor Report at 76–77; House Judiciary Report at 46.

Section 1630.16(b) Regulation of Alcohol and Drugs

This provision permits employers to establish or comply with certain standards regulating the use of drugs and alcohol in the workplace. It also allows employers to hold alcoholics and persons who engage in the illegal use of drugs to the same performance and conduct standards to which it holds all of its other employees. Individuals disabled by alcoholism are entitled to the same protections accorded other individuals with disabilities under this part. As noted above, individuals currently engaging in the illegal use of drugs are not individuals with disabilities for purposes of part 1630 when the employer acts on the basis of such use.

Section 1630.16(c) Drug Testing

This provision reflects title I's neutrality toward testing for the illegal use of drugs. Such drug tests are neither encouraged, authorized nor prohibited. The results of such drug tests may be used as a basis for disciplinary action. Tests for the illegal use of drugs are not considered medical examinations for purposes of this part. If the results reveal information about an individual's medical condition beyond whether the individual is currently engaging in the illegal use of drugs, this additional information is to be treated as a confidential medical record. For example, if a test for the illegal use of drugs reveals the presence of a controlled substance that has been lawfully prescribed for a particular medical condition, this information is to be treated as a confidential medical record. See House Labor Report at 79; House Judiciary Report at 47.

Section 1630.16(e) Infectious and Communicable Diseases; Food Handling Jobs

This provision addressing food handling jobs applies the "direct threat" analysis to the particular situation of accommodating individuals with infectious or communicable diseases that are transmitted through the handling of food. The Department of Health and Human Services is to prepare a list of infectious and communicable diseases that are transmitted through the handling of food. If an individual with a disability has one of the listed diseases and works in or applies for a position in food handling, the employer must determine whether there is a reasonable accommodation that will eliminate the risk of transmitting the disease through the handling of food. If there is an accommodation that will not pose an undue hardship, and that will prevent the transmission of the disease through the handling of food, the employer must provide the accommodation to the individual. The employer, under these circumstances, would not be permitted to discriminate against the individual because of the need to provide the reasonable accommodation and would be required to maintain the individual in the food handling job.

If no such reasonable accommodation is possible, the employer may refuse to assign, or to continue to assign the individual to a position involving food handling. This means that if such an individual is an applicant for a food handling position the employer is not required to hire the individual. However, if the individual is a current employee, the employer would be required to consider the accommodation of reassignment to a vacant position not involving food handling for which the individual is qualified. Conference Report at 61-63. (See § 1630.2(r) Direct Threat).

Section 1630.16(f) Health Insurance, Life Insurance, and Other Benefit Plans

This provision is a limited exemption that is only applicable to those who establish, sponsor, observe or administer benefit plans, such as health and life insurance plans. It does not apply to those who establish, sponsor, observe or administer plans not involving benefits, such as liability insurance plans.

The purpose of this provision is to permit the development and administration of benefit plans in accordance with accepted principles of risk assessment. This provision is not intended to disrupt the current regulatory structure for self-insured employers. These employers may establish,

sponsor, observe, or administer the terms of a bona fide benefit plan not subject to state laws that regulate insurance. This provision is also not intended to disrupt the current nature of insurance underwriting, or current insurance industry practices in sales, underwriting, pricing, administrative and other services, claims and similar insurance related activities based on classification of risks as regulated by the States.

The activities permitted by this provision do not violate part 1630 even if they result in limitations on individuals with disabilities, provided that these activities are not used as a subterfuge to evade the purposes of this part. Whether or not these activities are being used as a subterfuge is to be determined without regard to the date the insurance plan or employee benefit plan was adopted.

However, an employer or other covered entity cannot deny a qualified individual with a disability equal access to insurance or subject a qualified individual with a disability to different terms or conditions of insurance based on disability alone, if the disability does not pose increased risks. Part 1630 requires that decisions not based on risk classification be made in conformity with non-discrimination requirements. See Senate Report at 84-86; House Labor Report at 136-138; House Judiciary Report at 70-71. See the discussion of § 1630.5 Limiting, Segregating and Classifying.

[FR Doc. 91-17512 Filed 7-25-91; 8:45 am]

BILLING CODE 6750-06-M

EQUAL EMPLOYMENT OPPORTUNITY COMMISSION

29 CFR Parts 1602 and 1627

Recordkeeping and Reporting Under Title VII and the ADA

AGENCY: Equal Employment Opportunity Commission (EEOC).

ACTION: Final rule.

SUMMARY: This final rule is based on two separate Notices of Proposed Rulemaking (NPRM) published on February 13, 1989 (54 FR 6551), and March 5, 1991 (56 FR 9185). This final rule amends 29 CFR part 1602, EEOC's regulations on Recordkeeping and Reporting under title VII of the Civil Rights Act of 1964 (title VII), to add recordkeeping requirements under the Americans with Disabilities Act of 1990 (ADA). It increases the records retention period required in part 1602 for title VII and the ADA from 6 months to one year. The Commission also is adding a new subpart R to part 1602, 29 CFR 1602.56, that will clarify that the Commission has the authority to investigate persons to determine whether they comply with the reporting or recordkeeping requirements of part 1602. In addition, the Commission is making several minor changes to §§ 1602.7 and 1602.10.

The Commission also is deleting § 1602.14(b) of its title VII recordkeeping regulations, which provides that the § 1602 recordkeeping requirements do not apply to temporary or seasonal positions. Information regarding such employees now must be reported on Standard Form 100 on September 30 of each year, in the same fashion as information regarding permanent employees is reported. Similarly, the Commission is deleting §§ 1627.3(b) and 1627.4(a)(2) of the Age Discrimination in Employment Act recordkeeping regulations, which provide for a 90-day retention period for temporary positions, and is clarifying the mandatory nature of such recordkeeping. The Commission is not issuing a final rule on proposed § 1602.57 at this time.

EFFECTIVE DATE: August 26, 1991.

FOR FURTHER INFORMATION CONTACT: Thomas J. Schlageter, Acting Assistant Legal Counsel, Grace C. Karmiol, General Attorney, or Wendy Adams, General Attorney, at (202) 663-4669 (voice) or (202) 663-4399 (TDD).

SUPPLEMENTARY INFORMATION: The Commission received nine comments in response to the NPRM published in the March 5, 1991 Federal Register on Recordkeeping and Reporting under title VII and the ADA. The comments responded to the invitation in the preamble of the NPRM for comment on whether there should be a reporting requirement under the ADA, how the reported information should be used, and how it should be collected. Four comments recommended that there be a reporting requirement although one of them suggested that it be collected by sampling rather than universal reporting. Five comments opposed any new reporting requirements on the grounds of administrative burden. One of these suggested that no reporting requirement be imposed at this time, but that the need for reporting be reassessed at a later date. Another of these argued that if a reporting requirement is necessary, it should be accomplished by using the existing EEO-1 rather than a separate report, should be collected by both employer visual identification and employee self-identification, and should be used to monitor the impact of the ADA and to document utilization of persons with disabilities, not for affirmative action purposes. The Commission is continuing its consideration of possible reporting requirements under the ADA and will confer with the Department of Labor, and any other affected federal agency, to discuss whether a reporting requirement would be appropriate under the ADA. If it concludes that a reporting requirement may be appropriate, it will issue an NPRM.

The Commission received over 20 comments in response to the February 13, 1989 NPRM. While this preamble does not address each individual comment, it addresses the most significant issues raised in the comments. Current § 1602.7 concerns the filing of Standard Form 100, and has been interpreted in conjunction with the instructions accompanying the form. In order to clarify which of the employers that are subject to title VII must file the report, the Commission has incorporated some of the information that is contained in the instructions into § 1602.7.

Current § 1602.14 provides that personnel or employment records made or kept by an employer shall be preserved by the employer for a period of six months from the date of the making of the record or of the personnel action involved, whichever is later. This requirement was promulgated before title VII was amended in 1972 to change the time limit for filing a charge from 90 days to 180 days (or, in some instances, to 300 days). Requiring an employer or labor organization to maintain records for six months when the charge filing limit was 90 days ensured that all applicable records were kept. Due to the lengthening of the filing period, however, it no longer is true that employers or labor organizations necessarily will have retained records until the title VII filing period expires. Under the current regulation, an employer or labor organization may have already lawfully destroyed its employment records before it is notified that a charge has been filed. Moreover, a one year retention period for employers and labor organizations subject to title VII and the ADA will make the records retention period the same as that required by the Commission's regulations under the Age Discrimination in Employment Act, 29 U.S.C. 621 *et seq.* (ADEA), 29 CFR 1627.3(b)(1) and 1627.4(a)(1). This uniform retention period will simplify and clarify recordkeeping for employers who are also subject to the ADEA.

In order to promote efficiency and to eliminate confusion as to recordkeeping requirements regarding temporary and seasonal employees, the Commission is deleting § 1602.14(b) which provides that the part 1602 recordkeeping requirements do not apply to temporary or seasonal positions. Similarly, the Commission is deleting §§ 1627.3(b)(3) and 1627.4(a)(2) of the ADEA recordkeeping regulations, which

provide for a 90 day records retention period for temporary positions, and is clarifying the mandatory nature of such recordkeeping. These changes will require employers to retain records on all employees, permanent and temporary, for a one year period. They will, however, impose a new recordkeeping requirement only on the relatively few employers who are not subject to the recordkeeping provisions of the ADEA.

Section 709(c) of title VII, 42 U.S.C. 2000e–8(c), provides, *inter alia,* that any person who fails to maintain information as required by that subsection and by Commission regulations may, upon application of the Commission or the Attorney General in a case involving a government, governmental agency or political subdivision, be ordered to comply by the appropriate United States district court. At present, Commission regulations do not explicitly provide that the Commission may conduct an investigation when it has reason to believe an employer or other entity subject to title VII has failed to comply with the recordkeeping requirements of part 1602, as when, for example, an employer does not provide the required recordkeeping information to the Commission. The Commission is adding § 1602.56 to give clear notice of its authority to enforce section 709(c) of title VII. The addition of this section is consistent with the Commission's authority to issue suitable procedural regulations to carry out the provisions of title VII, 42 U.S.C. 2000e–12(a), and is an appropriate procedural mechanism for investigating apparent violations of those provisions.

The revisions to § 1602.7 change the annual Standard Form 100 reporting date from March 31 to September 30. By changing the reporting date the Commission also is changing the dates for which the information should be reported, i.e., from the three months preceding March 31, to the three months preceding September 30. Any employer that has received permission to use a different period for reporting may continue to use that approved period. The Commission has determined that this change will result in a reporting date that is less affected by the variation in seasonal employment, such as employment in the construction industry, than the present date and will provide employment figures which reflect annual average employment more closely than the present date does. This change will not affect the date by which employers must report VETS information to the United States

Department of Labor, as the VETS data and the Standard Form 100 data are processed separately. The revisions also change the address for obtaining necessary reporting supplies from "Jeffersonville, Indiana" to "the Commission or its delegate."

The revision to § 1602.10 deletes the reference to "section 4(c) of the instructions" and substitutes "section 5 of the instructions." The reference to the 100 employee jurisdictional test of section 701(b) of title VII is deleted since the number of employees required for an employer to be subject to title VII now is 15 or more. This change in no way affects the present Standard Form 100 reporting requirement of 100 or more employees that is set out in the instructions accompanying the form and now is made explicit in the regulation.

In order to provide a mechanism for those subject to the reporting requirements to seek a change in the reporting date or the date by which data should be reported, the Commission has revised § 1602.10 to permit employers to seek changes in those requirements. The Commission notes that retention of records for the period of one year will increase only minimally, if at all, the employer's cost of maintaining the records. Employers already are required to maintain the records for a period of six months. The cost of retaining the records for an additional six months will be minimal. Moreover, most employers subject to Title VII also are subject to the ADEA, which presently requires that these records be retained for a period of one year.

The Commission estimates that the changes to §§ 1602.14 and 1602.28(a) increasing the title VII records retention period from six months to one year will result in an increased recordkeeping burden on employers of approximately 9,000 burden hours annually. The Commission estimates that the changes in the title VII and ADEA recordkeeping requirements for employers with temporary employees will result in an increased recordkeeping burden of approximately 20,800 burden hours annually. The Commission believes that this increase in burden hours is *de minimis* and that the modifications will not have a significant impact on a substantial number of small employers. Further, the Commission believes that the above cited benefits of the modifications, by establishing a uniform period of recordkeeping for full time and part time employees under title VII, ADA and the ADEA, outweigh the minimal increase in recordkeeping burden hours on employers. For the above reasons, the regulatory change will simplify the recordkeeping requirements. The Commission also certifies under 5 U.S.C. 605(b), enacted by the Regulatory Flexibility Act (Pub. L. No. 96–354), that these modifications will not result in a significant economic impact on a substantial number of small employers and that a regulatory flexibility analysis therefore is not required.

List of Subjects in 29 CFR Parts 1602 and 1627

Equal employment opportunity, Reporting and recordkeeping requirements.

For the Commission.

Evan J. Kemp, Jr.,

Chairman.

Accordingly, 29 CFR parts 1602 and 1627 are amended as follows:

PART 1602—[AMENDED]

1. The heading for part 1602 is revised to read as follows:

PART 1602—RECORDKEEPING AND REPORTING REQUIREMENTS UNDER TITLE VII AND THE ADA

2. The authority citation for part 1602 is revised to read as follows:

Authority: 42 U.S.C. 2000e–8, 2000e–12; 44 U.S.C. 3501 et seq.; 42 U.S.C. 12117.

3. Section 1602.1 is revised to read as follows:

§ 1602.1 Purpose and scope.

Section 709 of title VII (42 U.S.C. 2000e) and section 107 of the Americans with Disabilities Act (ADA) (42 U.S.C. 12117) require the Commission to establish regulations pursuant to which employers, labor organizations, joint labor-management committees, and employment agencies subject to those Acts shall make and preserve certain records and shall furnish specified information to aid in the administration and enforcement of the Acts.

4. The heading for Subpart A is revised to read as follows:

Subpart A—General

§ 1602.1 [Amended]

5. Section 1602.1 is moved under subpart A.

§§ 1602.2–1602.6 [Removed]

6. Sections 1602.2–1602.6 are removed and reserved.

§ 1602.7 [Amended]

7. Section 1602.7 is amended by revising the first and last sentences to read as follows:

§ 1602.7 Requirement for filing of report.

On or before September 30 of each year, every employer that is subject to title VII of the Civil Rights Act of 1964, as amended, and that has 100 or more employees, shall file with the Commission or its delegate executed copies of Standard Form 100, as revised (otherwise known as "Employer Information Report EEO–1") in conformity with the directions set forth in the form and accompanying instructions. * * * Appropriate copies of Standard Form 100 in blank will be supplied to every employer known to the Commission to be subject to the reporting requirements, but it is the responsibility of all such employers to obtain necessary supplies of the form from the Commission or its delegate prior to the filing date.

8. Section 1602.10 is revised to read as follows:

§ 1602.10 Employer's exemption from reporting requirements.

If an employer claims that the preparation or filing of the report would create undue hardship, the employer may apply to the Commission for an exemption from the requirements set forth in this part, according to instruction 5. If an employer is engaged in activities for which the reporting unit criteria described in section 5 of the instructions are not readily adaptable, special reporting procedures may be required. If an employer seeks to change the date for filing its Standard Form 100 or seeks to change the period for which data are reported, an alternative reporting date or period may be permitted. In such instances, the employer should so advise the Commission by submitting to the Commission or its delegate a specific written proposal for an alternative reporting system prior to the date on which the report is due.

§ 1602.11 [Amended]

9. Section 1602.11 is amended as follows:

a. In the first sentence, after "purposes of title VII" insert "or the ADA".

b. In the second sentence, after "section 709(c of title VII" insert "or section 107 of the ADA".

§ 1602.12 [Amended]

10. Section 1602.12 is amended as follows:

a. In the first sentence, after "purposes of Title VII" insert "or the ADA".

b. In the second sentence, after "section 709(c)" insert "of Title VII, or section 107 of the ADA".

c. By revising the parenthetical at the end of the section to read as follows:

(Approved by the Office of Management and Budget under control number 3046–0040)

§ 1602.14 [Amended]

11. Section 1602.14(a) is amended as follows:

a. By removing the words "6 months" wherever they appear and replacing them with the words "one year".

b. In the first sentence, after "not necessarily limited to" insert "requests for reasonable accommodation,".

c. In the third sentence, after "under title VII" insert "or the ADA".

d. By revising the parenthetical at the end of the section to read as follows:

(Approved by the Office of Management and Budget under control number 3046–0040)

§ 1602.14 [Amended]

12. Section 1602.14 is amended by removing paragraph (b), by removing the designation from paragraph (a), and by revising the parenthetical at the end of the section to read as follows:

(Approved by the Office of Management and Budget under control number 3046–0040)

§ 1602.19 [Amended]

13. Section 1602.19 is amended as follows:

a. In the first sentence, after "purpose of Title VII" insert "or the ADA".

b. In the second sentence, after "section 709(c) of title VII" insert "or section 107 of the ADA".

§ 1602.21 [Amended]

14. Section 1602.21(b) is amended as follows:

a. In the first sentence, after "not necessarily limited to" insert "requests for reasonable accommodation,".

b. In the second sentence, after "under Title VII" insert "or the ADA".

§ 1602.26 [Amended]

15. Section 1602.26 is amended as follows:

a. In the first sentence, after "purposes of Title VII" insert "or the ADA".

b. In the second sentence, after "section 709(c)" insert "of Title VII or section 107 of the ADA".

§ 1602.28 [Amended]

16. Section 1602.28(a) is amended as follows:

a. By removing the words "6 months" wherever they appear and replacing them with the words "one year".

b. In the third sentence, after "under title VII" insert "or the ADA".

c. By revising the parenthetical at the end of the section to read as follows:

(Approved by the Office of Management and Budget under control number 3046–0040)

§ 1602.31 [Amended]

17. Section 1602.31 is amended as follows:

a. By removing paragraph (b) and the designation from paragraph (a).

b. In the first sentence, after "not necessarily limited to" insert "requests for reasonable accommodation,".

c. In the third sentence, after "under title VII" insert "or the ADA".

d. By revising the parenthetical at the end of the section to read as follows:

(Approved by the Office of Management and Budget under control number 3046–0040)

§ 1602.37 [Amended]

18. Section 1602.37 is amended as follows:

a. In the first sentence, after "purposes of title VII" insert "or the ADA".

b. In the second sentence, after "section 709(c) of title VII" insert "or section 107 of the ADA".

§ 1602.40 [Amended]

19. Section 1602.40 is amended as follows:

a. By removing paragraph (b) and the designation from paragraph (a).

b. In the first sentence, after "not necessarily limited to" insert "requests for reasonable accommodation,".

c. By revising the parenthetical at the end of the section to read as follows:

(Approved by the Office of Management and Budget under control number 3046–0040)

§ 1602.45 [Amended]

20. Section 1602.45 is amended as follows:

a. In the first sentence, after "purposes of title VII" insert "or the ADA".

b. In the second sentence, after "section 709(c) of title VII" insert "or section 107 of the ADA".

§ 1602.49 [Amended]

21. Section 1602.49 is amended as follows:

a. By removing paragraph (b) and redesignating paragraph (c) as new paragraph (b).

b. In the first sentence of paragraph (a), after "not necessarily limited to" insert "requests for reasonable accommodation,".

c. By revising the parenthetical at the end of the section to read as follows:

(Approved by the Office of Management and Budget under control number 3046–0040)

§ 1602.54 [Amended]

22. Section 1602.54 is amended as follows:

a. In the first sentence, after "purposes of title VII" insert "or the ADA".

b. In the second sentence, after "section 709(c) of title VII" insert "or section 107 of the ADA".

23. A new subpart R consisting of § 1602.56 is added, to read as follows:

Subpart R—Investigation of Reporting or Recordkeeping Violations

§ 1602.56 Investigation of reporting or recordkeeping violations.

When it has received an allegation, or has reason to believe, that a person has not complied with the reporting or recordkeeping requirements of this Part or of Part 1607 of this chapter, the Commission may conduct an investigation of the alleged failure to comply.

Part 1627—[Amended]

24. The authority citation for 29 CFR part 1627 continues to read as follows:

Authority: Sec. 7, 81 Stat. 804; 29 U.S.C. 626; sec. 11, 52 Stat. 1066; 29 U.S.C. 211; sec. 12, 29 U.S.C. 631, Pub. L. No. 99–592, 100 Stat. 3342; sec. 2, Reorg. Plan No. 1 of 1978, 43 FR 19807.

§ 1627.3 [Amended]

25. In § 1627.3, paragraph (b)(3) is removed and paragraph (b)(4) is redesignated as new paragraph (b)(3).

26. Newly designated § 1627.3(b)(3) is amended by removing the word "may" and replacing it with the word "shall" and by revising the words "paragraph (b) (1), (2), or (3)" to read "paragraph (b) (1) or (2)".

§ 1627.4 [Amended]

27. In § 1627.4, paragraph (a)(2) is removed and paragraph (a)(3) is redesignated as new paragraph (a)(2).

28. Newly designated § 1627.4(a)(2) is amended by removing the word "may" and replacing it with the word "shall" and by revising the words "paragraph (a) (1) or (2)" to read "paragraph (a)(1)".

§ 1627.5 [Amended]

29. Section 1627.5(c) is amended by removing the word "may" and replacing it with the word "shall".

[FR Doc. 91–17513 Filed 7–25–91; 8:45 am]
BILLING CODE 6750–06–M

in which it offers service, telecommunications relay services (TRS) for individuals with hearing or speech disabilities, not later than three years after the ADA's enactment date.

EFFECTIVE DATE: September 30, 1991.

FOR FURTHER INFORMATION CONTACT: Linda B. Dubroof, (202) 634–1808 (Voice) and (202) 634–1855 (TT).

SUPPLEMENTARY INFORMATION: This summarizes the Commission's R&O in the matter of Telecommunications Services for Individuals with Hearing and Speech Disabilities, and the Americans with Disabilities Act of 1990 (CC Docket 90–571, FCC 91–213 adopted July 11, 1991 and released July 26, 1991. The R&O and supporting file may be examined in the Commission's Public Reference Room, room 239, 1919 M Street, NW., Washington, DC, during business hours or purchased from the duplicating contractor, Downtown Copy Center. 1114 21st, NW., Washington, DC 20036, (202) 452–1422. The R&O also will be published in the FCC Record.

This proceeding was initiated by the Commission's Notice of Proposed Rulemaking (NPRM) in CC Docket 90–571, FCC 90–376. 5 FCC Rcd 7187 (1990). [55 FR 50037, December 4, 1990], which proposed amendments to parts 0 and 64 of its rules to implement title IV of the ADA. The ADA provides a clear national mandate for the elimination of discrimination against individuals with disabilities and ensures that the Commission play an active role in enforcing the standards established in title IV. The primary purpose of title IV is to further the Communications Act's goal of universal telecommunications services by ensuring that interstate and intrastate TRS are available nationwide. to the extent possible and in the most efficient manner, to individuals in the United States with hearing or speech disabilities.

In its NPRM, the Commission proposed minimum standards designed to implement the provisions of title IV. Interested parties were invited to offer alternative language, additional provisions, or any other suggestions that might foster the intent of Congress to bring functionally equivalent telecommunications services to individuals with hearing or speech disabilities. After reviewing the sixty-one comments and/or reply comments submitted by interested parties, the Commission has modified some of the proposed rules and fashioned a comprehensive set of rules which (a) set forth terminology and definitions; (b) prescribe operational, technical, and functional minimum standards required

FEDERAL COMMUNICATIONS COMMISSION

47 CFR Parts 0 and 64

[CC Docket No. 90–571; FCC 91–213]

Telecommunications Services for Hearing and Speech Disabled

AGENCY: Federal Communications Commission.

ACTION: Final rule.

SUMMARY: Part 0 of the rules of the Federal Communications Commission (Commission) governing "Commission Organization", 47 CFR part 0, and subpart F of part 64 titled "Furnishing of Customer Premises Equipment and Related Services Needed by Persons with Impaired Hearing, Speech, Vision or Mobility", 47 CFR 64, are amended as set forth in this Report and Order (R&O). The purpose of the R&O is to implement title IV of the Americans with Disabilities Act of 1990 (ADA) which amends title II of the Communications Act of 1934, as amended, by adding new section 225, amending existing section 711, and conforming sections 2(b) and 221(b). See Public Law 101–336, 104 Stat. 327, 366–69 (July 26, 1990). Title IV mandates that the Commission prescribe regulations to implement section 225 not later than one year after the ADA's enactment date of July 26, 1990, and requires each common carrier providing telephone voice transmission services to provide, throughout the area of all TRS providers; and (c) delineate the state certification process. The rules are made a part of this publication.

Request for Comments on Funding Mechanisms

The ADA mandates that the Commission prescribe regulations governing the jurisdictional separation of costs, and that costs caused by interstate TRS be recovered from all subscribers for every interstate service and costs caused by intrastate TRS be recovered from the intrastate jurisdiction. The majority of commenters concur that existing accounting and separations rules are adequate to deal with interstate relay services. In order to achieve the goals of the ADA without unnecessarily disrupting TRS as currently provided, the Commission finds that current separations rules are adequate. However, the record is not adequate to determine a specific cost recovery mechanism. Therefore, the Commission seeks specific proposals from interested parties on cost recovery to be submitted to the Common Carrier Bureau no later than 60 days from the release date of this R&O. Responses to these proposals shall be filed not later than 30 days thereafter. All proposals and other comments must reference CC Docket No. 90–571. In particular, parties should address various proposed funding mechanisms and both the advantages and disadvantages of each proposal, including relative administrative costs of various mechanisms, the likely relative costs that would be borne by various interstate carriers under each proposal, and the impact on quality, if any, of the proposals. The Commission notes that in this proceeding some commenters have argued that the costs associated with interstate relay services should be shared. These commenters must make a well reasoned showing that self-funding would be inappropriate. The Commission is also especially interested in learning about different possible funding mechanisms from the experiences of the states.

Final Regulatory Flexibility Analysis

Pursuant to the Regulatory Flexibility Act of 1980, 5 U.S.C. section 601, *et seq.*, the Commission's final analysis in this Report and Order is as follows:

I. Need and Purpose of This Action

This Report and Order amends the Commission's rules to require that each common carrier engaged in interstate and/or intrastate telephone voice transmission services shall, no later than July 26, 1993, provide telecommunications relay services

throughout the area in which it offers service. The rule amendments are required by the Americans with Disabilities Act of 1990, which, *inter alia*, adds section 225 to the communications Act of 1934, as amended, 47 U.S.C. 225. The rules are intended to ensure that interstate and intrastate telecommunications relay services are available, to the extent possible and in the most efficient manner, to persons in the United States with speech and/or hearing disabilities.

II. Summary of Issues Raised by the Public Comments in Response to the Initial Regulatory Flexibility Analysis

No comments were submitted in direct response to the Initial Regulatory Flexibility Analysis.

III. Significant Alternatives Considered

The notice of proposed rulemaking in this proceeding (55 FR 50037, December 4, 1990) offered several proposals and requested comments as well as the views of commenters on other possibilities. The Commission has considered all comments, and has adopted most of its proposals in addition to some alternatives recommended by commenters. The Commission considers this Report and Order to be the most reasonable course of action under the mandate of section 225 of the Communications Act.

Paperwork Reduction Act Statement

Average reporting burdens for the collections of information are estimated as follows:

State certification: Respondent burden for complying with the certification requirement is 160 hours per submission. Certification remains in effect for five years; one year prior to expiration of certification, a state may apply for renewal as prescribed in the Commission's rules.

Complaints: Five burden hours to file a complaint.

The foregoing estimates include the time for reviewing instructions, searching existing data sources, gathering and maintaining the data needed, and completing and reviewing the collections of information. Send comments regarding burden estimates or any other aspect of the collections of information, including suggestions for reducing the burdens, to the Federal Communications Commission, Office of Managing Director, Paperwork Reduction Project (3060–0463), Washington, DC 20554, and also to the Office of Management and Budget, Paperwork Reduction Project (3060–0463), Washington, DC 20503.

Ordering Clauses

Accordingly, It is Ordered, That, pursuant to sections 1, 4(i), 4(j), 201–205, 225 and 403 of the Communications Act of 1934, as amended, parts 0 and 64 of the Commission's Rules and Regulations *are amended* as set forth below, effective 60 days after publication in the **Federal Register.**

It is Further Ordered, That specific proposals from interested parties on cost recovery shall be submitted to the Common Carrier Bureau, referencing CC Docket No. 90–571, no later than 60 days from the release date of this Report and Order, and responses to these proposals shall be filed not later than 30 days thereafter.

It is Further Ordered, That authority is delegated to the Chief, Common Carrier Bureau to implement the state certification and complaint process provided in the rules adopted herein, and to review specific proposals on cost recovery mechanisms submitted by interested parties.

It is Further Ordered, That, pursuant to the requirements of section 604 of the Regulatory Flexibility Act, 5 U.S.C. 604, the Secretary shall: (a) Make copies of this Report and Order available to members of the public and (b) shall cause a summary of this Report and Order to be published in the **Federal Register** which shall include a statement describing how members of the public may obtain such copies. The Secretary shall also provide a copy of this Report and Order to each state utility commission.

List of Subjects

47 CFR Part 0

Organization and functions (Government agencies).

47 CFR Part 64

Communications common carriers. Individuals with hearing and speech disabilities, Telecommunications relay services.

Amended Rules

Parts 0 and 64 of the Commission's Rules and Regulations (chapter I of title 47 of the Code of Federal Regulations, parts 0 and 64) are amended as follows:

PART 0—COMMISSION ORGANIZATION

1. The authority citation for part 0 is revised to read as follows:

Authority: Sec. 5, 48 Stat. 1068, as amended; 47 U.S.C. 155, 225, unless otherwise noted.

2. Section 0.91 is amended by adding new paragraph (m) to read as follows:

§ 0.91 Functions of the Bureau.

* * * * *

(m) Acts upon matters involving telecommunications relay services complaints and certification.

PART 64—MISCELLANEOUS RULES RELATING TO COMMON CARRIERS

1. The authority citation for part 64 is revised to read as follows:

Authority: Section 4, 48 Stat. 1066, as amended; 47 U.S.C. 154, unless otherwise noted. Interpret or apply secs. 201, 218, 225, 48 Stat. 1070, as amended, 1077; 47 U.S.C. 201, 218, 225 unless otherwise noted.

2. Subpart F of part 64 (consisting of §§ 64.601–64.608) is revised in its entirety to read as follows:

Subpart F—Telecommunications Relay Services and Related Customer Premises Equipment for Persons With Disabilities

Sec.
64.601 Definitions.
64.602 Jurisdiction.
64.603 Provision of services.
64.604 Mandatory minimum standards.
64.605 State certification.
64.606 Furnishing related customer premises equipment.
64.607 Provision of hearing aid compatible telephones by exchange carriers.
64.608 Enforcement of related customer premises equipment rules.

Subpart F—Telecommunications Relay Services and Related Customer Premises Equipment for Persons With Disabilities

§ 64.601 Definitions.

As used in this subpart, the following definitions apply:

(1) American Sign Language (ASL): A visual language based on hand shape, position, movement, and orientation of the hands in relation to each other and the body.

(2) ASCII: An acronym for American Standard Code for Information Interexchange which employs an eight bit code and can operate at any standard transmission baud rate including 300, 1200, 2400, and higher.

(3) Baudot: A seven bit code, only five of which are information bits. Baudot is used by some text telephones to communicate with each other at a 45.5 baud rate.

(4) Common carrier or carrier: Any common carrier engaged in interstate communication by wire or radio as defined in section 3(h) of the Communications Act of 1934, as amended (the Act), and any common carrier engaged in intrastate communication by wire or radio,

notwithstanding sections 2(b) and 221(b) of the Act.

(5) Communications assistant (CA): A person who transliterates conversation from text to voice and from voice to text between two end users of TRS. CA supersedes the term "TDD operator."

(6) Hearing carry over (HCO): A reduced form of TRS where the person with the speech disability is able to listen to the other end user and, in reply, the CA speaks the text as typed by the person with the speech disability. The CA does not type any conversation.

(7) Telecommunications relay services (TRS): Telephone transmission services that provide the ability for an individual who has a hearing or speech disability to engage in communication by wire or radio with a hearing individual in a manner that is functionally equivalent to the ability of an individual who does not have a hearing or speech disability to communicate using voice communication services by wire or radio. Such term includes services that enable two-way communication between an individual who uses a text telephone or other nonvoice terminal device and an individual who does not use such a device. TRS supersedes the terms "dual party relay system," "message relay services," and "TDD Relay."

(8) Text telephone (TT): A machine that employs graphic communication in the transmission of coded signals through a wire or radio communication system. TT supersedes the term "TDD" or "telecommunications device for the deaf."

(9) Voice carry over (VCO): A reduced form of TRS where the person with the hearing disability is able to speak directly to the other end user. The CA types the response back to the person with the hearing disability. The CA does not voice the conversation.

§ 64.602 Jurisdiction.

Any violation of this subpart by any common carrier engaged in intrastate communication shall be subject to the same remedies, penalties, and procedures as are applicable to a violation of the Act by a common carrier engaged in interstate communication.

§ 64.603 Provision of services.

Each common carrier providing telephone voice transmission services shall provide, not later than July 26, 1993, in compliance with the regulations prescribed herein, throughout the area in which it offers services, telecommunications relay services, individually, through designees, through a competitively selected vendor, or in concert with other carriers. A common

carrier shall be considered to be in compliance with these regulations:

(a) With respect to intrastate telecommunications relay services in any state that does not have a certified program under § 64.605 and with respect to interstate telecommunications relay services, if such common carrier (or other entity through which the carrier is providing such relay services) is in compliance with § 64.604; or

(b) With respect to intrastate telecommunications relay services in any state that has a certified program under § 64.605 for such state, if such common carrier (or other entity through which the carrier is providing such relay services) is in compliance with the program certified under § 64.605 for such state.

§ 64.604 Mandatory minimum standards.

(a) Operational standards.

(1) Communications assistant (CA). TRS providers are responsible for requiring that CAs be sufficiently trained to effectively meet the specialized communications needs of individuals with hearing and speech disabilities; and that CAs have competent skills in typing, grammar, spelling, interpretation of typewritten ASL, and familiarity with hearing and speech disability cultures, languages and etiquette.

(2) Confidentiality and conversation content. Consistent with the obligations of common carrier operators, CAs are prohibited from disclosing the content of any relayed conversation regardless of content and from keeping records of the content of any conversation beyond the duration of a call. CAs are prohibited from intentionally altering a relayed conversation and must relay all conversation verbatim unless the relay user specifically requests summarization.

(3) Types of calls. Consistent with the obligations of common carrier operators, CAs are prohibited from refusing single or sequential calls or limiting the length of calls utilizing relay services. TRS shall be capable of handling any type of call normally provided by common carriers and the burden of proving the infeasibility of handling any type of call will be placed on the carriers. Providers of TRS are permitted to decline to complete a call because credit authorization is denied. CAs shall handle emergency calls in the same manner as they handle any other TRS calls.

(b) Technical standards.

(1) ASCII and Baudot. TRS shall be capable of communicating with ASCII and Baudot format, at any speed generally in use.

(2) Speed of answer. TRS shall include adequate staffing to provide callers with efficient access under projected calling volumes, so that the probability of a busy response due to CA unavailability shall be functionally equivalent to what a voice caller would experience in attempting to reach a party through the voice telephone network. TRS shall, except during network failure, answer 85% of all calls within 10 seconds and no more than 30 seconds shall elapse between receipt of dialing information and the dialing of the requested number.

(3) Equal access to interexchange carriers. TRS users shall have access to their chosen interexchange carrier through the TRS, and to all other operator services, to the same extent that such access is provided to voice users.

(4) TRS facilities. TRS shall operate every day, 24 hours a day. TRS shall have redundancy features functionally equivalent to the equipment in normal central offices, including uninterruptible power for emergency use. TRS shall transmit conversations between TT and voice callers in real time. Adequate network facilities shall be used in conjunction with TRS so that under projected calling volume the probability of a busy response due to loop trunk congestion shall be functionally equivalent to what a voice caller would experience in attempting to reach a party through the voice telephone network.

(5) Technology. No regulation set forth in this subpart is intended to discourage or impair the development of improved technology that fosters the availability of telecommunications to person with disabilities. VCO and HCO technology are required to be standard features of TRS.

(c) Functional standards.

(1) Enforcement. Subject to § 64.603, the Commission shall resolve any complaint alleging a violation of this section within 180 days after the complaint is filed.

(2) Public access to information. Carriers, through publication in their directories, periodic billing inserts, placement of TRS instructions in telephone directories, through directory assistance services, and incorporation of TT numbers in telephone directories, shall assure that callers in their service areas are aware of the availability and use of TRS.

(3) Rates. TRS users shall pay rates no greater than the rates paid for functionally equivalent voice communication services with respect to such factors as the duration of the call, the time of day, and the distance from the point of origination to the point of termination.

(4) Jurisdictional separation of costs.

(i) General. Where appropriate, costs of providing TRS shall be separated in accordance with the jurisdictional separation procedures and standards set forth in the Commission's regulations adopted pursuant to section 410 of the Communications Act of 1934, as amended.

(ii) Cost recovery. Costs caused by interstate TRS shall be recovered from all subscribers for every interstate service. Costs caused by intrastate TRS providers shall be recovered from the intrastate jurisdiction. In a state that has a certified program under § 64.605, the state agency providing TRS shall, through the state's regulatory agency, permit a common carrier to recover costs incurred in providing TRS by a method consistent with the requirements of this section.

(5) Complaints.

(i) Referral of complaint. If a complaint to the Commission alleges a violation of this subpart with respect to intrastate TRS within a state and certification of the program of such state under § 64.605 is in effect, the Commission shall refer such complaint to such state expeditiously.

(ii) Jurisdiction of Commission. After referring a complaint to a state under paragraph (c)(5)(i) of this section, or if a complaint is filed directly with a state, the Commission shall exercise jurisdiction over such complaint only if:

(A) final action under such state program has not been taken within:

(1) 180 days after the complaint is filed with such state; or

(2) a shorter period as prescribed by the regulations of such state; or

(B) the Commission determines that such state program is no longer qualified for certification under § 64.605.

(iii) Complaint procedures.

(A) Content. A complaint shall be in writing, addressed to the Federal Communications Commission, Common Carrier Bureau, TRS Complaints, Washington, DC 20554, or addressed to the appropriate state office, and shall contain:

(1) the name and address of the complainant,

(2) the name and address of the defendant against whom the complaint is made,

(3) a complete statement of the facts, including supporting data, where

available, showing that such defendant did or omitted to do anything in contravention of this subpart, and

(4) the relief sought.

(B) Amended complaints. An amended complaint setting forth transactions, occurrences or events which have happened since the filing of the original complaint and which relate to the original cause of action may be filed with the Commission.

(C) Number of copies. An original and two copies of all pleadings shall be filed.

(D) Service.

(1) Except where a complaint is referred to a state pursuant to § 64.604(c)(5)(i), or where a complaint is filed directly with a state, the Commission will serve on the named party a copy of any complaint or amended complaint filed with it, together with a notice of the filing of the complaint. Such notice shall call upon the defendant to satisfy or answer the complaint in writing within the time specified in said notice of complaint.

(2) All subsequent pleadings and briefs shall be served by the filing party on all other parties to the proceeding in accordance with the requirements of § 1.47 of this chapter. Proof of such service shall also be made in accordance with the requirements of said section.

(E) Answers to complaints and amended complaints. Any party upon whom a copy of a complaint or amended complaint is served under this subpart shall serve an answer within the time specified by the Commission in its notice of complaint. The answer shall advise the parties and the Commission fully and completely of the nature of the defense and shall respond specifically to all material allegations of the complaint. In cases involving allegations of harm, the answer shall indicate what action has been taken or is proposed to be taken to stop the occurrence of such harm. Collateral or immaterial issues shall be avoided in answers and every effort should be made to narrow the issues. Matters alleged as affirmative defenses shall be separately stated and numbered. Any defendant failing to file and serve an answer within the time and in the manner prescribed may be deemed in default.

(F) Replies to answers or amended answers. Within 10 days after service of an answer or an amended answer, a complainant may file and serve a reply which shall be responsive to matters contained in such answer or amended answer and shall not contain new matter. Failure to reply will not be deemed an admission of any allegation contained in such answer or amended answer.

(G) Defective pleadings. Any pleading filed in a complaint proceeding that is not in substantial conformity with the requirements of the applicable rules in this subpart may be dismissed.

§ 64.605 State certification.

(a) State documentation. Any state, through its office of the governor or other delegated executive office empowered to provide TRS, desiring to establish a state program under this section shall submit, not later than October 1, 1992, documentation to the Commission addressed to the Federal Communications Commission, Chief, Common Carrier Bureau, TRS Certification Program, Washington, DC 20554, and captioned "TRS State Certification Application." All documentation shall be submitted in narrative form, shall clearly describe the state program for implementing intrastate TRS, and the procedures and remedies for enforcing any requirements imposed by the state program. The Commission shall give public notice of states filing for certification including notification in the Federal Register.

(b) Requirements for certification. After review of state documentation, the Commission shall certify, by letter, or order, the state program if the Commission determines that the state certification documentation:

(1) Establishes that the state program meets or exceeds all operational, technical, and functional minimum standards contained in § 64.604;

(2) Establishes that the state program makes available adequate procedures and remedies for enforcing the requirements of the state program; and

(3) Where a state program exceeds the mandatory minimum standards contained in § 64.604, the state establishes that its program in no way conflicts with federal law.

(c) Certification period. State certification shall remain in effect for five years. One year prior to expiration of certification, a state may apply for renewal of its certification by filing documentation as prescribed by paragraphs (a) and (b) of this section.

(d) Method of funding. Except as provided in § 64.604, the Commission shall not refuse to certify a state program based solely on the method such state will implement for funding intrastate TRS, but funding mechanisms, if labeled, shall be labeled in a manner that promote national understanding of TRS and do not offend the public.

(e) Suspension or revocation of certification. The Commission may suspend or revoke such certification if,

after notice and opportunity for hearing, the Commission determines that such certification is no longer warranted. In a state whose program has been suspended or revoked, the Commission shall take such steps as may be necessary, consistent with this subpart, to ensure continuity of TRS.

§ 64.606 Furnishing related customer premises equipment.

(a) Any communications common carrier may provide, under tariff, customer premises equipment (other than hearing aid compatible telephones as defined in part 68 of this chapter, needed by persons with hearing, speech, vision or mobility disabilities. Such equipment may be provided to persons with those disabilities or to associations or institutions who require such equipment regularly to communicate with persons with disabilities. Examples of such equipment include, but are not limited to, artificial larynxes, bone conductor receivers and TTs.

(b) Any carrier which provides telecommunications devices for persons with hearing and/or speech disabilities, whether or not pursuant to tariff, shall respond to any inquiry concerning:

(1) The availability (including general price levels) of TTs using ASCII, Baudot, or both formats; and

(2) The compatibility of any TT with other such devices and computers.

§ 64.607 Provision of hearing aid compatible telephones by exchange carriers.

In the absence of alternative suppliers in an exchange area, an exchange carrier must provide a hearing aid compatible telephone, as defined in part 68 of this chapter, and provide related installation and maintenance services for such telephones on a detariffed basis to any customer with a hearing disability who requests such equipment or services.

§ 64.608 Enforcement of related customer premises equipment rules.

Enforcement of §§ 64.606 and 64.607 is delegated to those state public utility or public service commissions which adopt those sections and provide for their enforcement.

Federal Communications Commission.

William F. Caton,

Acting Secretary.

[FR Doc. 91-18153 Filed 7-31-91; 8:45 am]

BILLING CODE 6712-01-M

Resources on Employing Persons With Disabilities

NATIONAL RESOURCES

Alexander Graham Bell Association
  for the Deaf
3417 Volta Place, NW
Washington, DC 20007

American Association on Mental
  Deficiency
1719 Kalorama Road, NW
Washington, DC 20009

American Cleft Palate Educational
  Foundation
331 Salk Hall
University of Pittsburgh
Pittsburgh, PA 19380

American Council of the Blind
1010 Vermont Avenue, NW #1100
Washington, DC 20005

American Diabetes Association
1660 Duke Street
Alexandria, VA 22314

American Foundation for Blind
15 West 16 Street
New York, NY 10011

American Heart Association
7320 Greenville Avenue
Dallas, TX 75231

American Hospital Association
840 North Lake Shore Drive
Chicago, IL 60611

American Lung Association
1740 Broadway
New York, NY 10019

American Paralysis Association
PO Box 187
Short Hills, NJ 07078-0187

American Physical Therapy
  Association
1111 North Fairfax Street
Alexandria, VA 22314

Note: The information provided in this appendix was provided, in part, by The President's Committee on Employment of People with Disabilities, Suite 636, 1111 20th Street, NW, Washington, DC 20036.

Arthritis Foundation
1314 Sprint Street, NW
Atlanta, GA 30309

Association for Children and Adults
With Learning Disability
4156 Library Road
Pittsburgh, PA 15234

Association for Persons With Severe
Handicap
7010 Roosevelt Way, NE
Seattle, WA 98115

Association of Learning Disabled
Adults
PO Box 9722 Friendship Station
Washington, DC 20036

Blinded Veterans Association
477 H Street, NW
Washington, DC 20001

Bureau of Services for Visually
Impaired
5533 Southwyck Boulevard, Suite
101
Toledo, OH 43614-1537

Cooley's Anemia Foundation
105 East 22 Street, Suite 911
New York, NY 10010

Cornelia De Lange Syndrome
Foundation
60 Dyer Avenue
Collinsville, CT 06022

Council of Citizens With Low
Vision
1400 North Drake Road #218
Kalamazoo, MI 49007

Council on Developmental
Disability
PO Box 7851
Madison, WI 53707

Developmental Care Homes, Inc.
20105 Delaware
Reford, MI 48240

Disability Access Network
3131 Sycamore Road
DeKalb, IL 60115

Disability Rights Education and
Defense Fund
2212 Sixth Street
Berkeley, CA 94710

Disabled American Veterans
807 Maine Avenue, SW
Washington, DC 20024

Disabled But Able to Vote
2500 Q Street, NW #121
Washington, DC 20007

Disabled Citizens Alliance for
Independence
Box 675
Viburnum, MO 65566

Epilepsy Foundation of America
4351 Garden City Drive
Landover, MD 20785

Handicapped Organized Women
PO Box 35481
Charlotte, NC 28235

Hogg Foundation for Mental Health
PO Box 7998
Austin, TX 78712

League of Human Dignity
1701 P Street
Lincoln, NE 68508-1741

Mainstream, Inc.
PO Box 65183
Washington, DC 20035-5183

Muscular Dystrophy Association
810 Seventh Avenue
New York, NY 10019

National Amputation Foundation
12-45 150 Street
Whitestone, NY 11357

National Association of
  Rehabilitation Facilities
1910 Association Drive
Reston, VA 22091

National Association of the Deaf
814 Thayer Avenue
Silver Spring, MD 20910

National Association of the
  Physically Handicapped
76 Elm Street
London, OH 43140

National Ataxia Foundation
600 Twelve Oaks Center, #15500
Wayzata, MN 55391

National Center of Law and the
  Deaf
800 Florida Avenue, NE
Washington, DC 20002

National Center on Employment of
  the Deaf
One Lomb Memorial Drive
Rochester, NY 14623

National Council of Stutterers
PO Box 8171
Grand Rapids, MI 49508

National Council on Independent
  Living
2111 Wilson Boulevard #400
Arlington, VA 22201

National Council on the
  Handicapped
800 Independence Avenue, SW
  #814
Washington, DC 20591

National Federation of the Blind
1800 Johnson Street
Baltimore, MD 21230

National Handicapped Recreation
  Association
PO Box 33141, Farragut Station
Washington, DC 20033

National Handicapped Sports and
  Recreation Association
4405 East West Highway #603
Bethesda, MD 20814

National Head Injury Foundation
PO Box 567
Framingham, MA 01701

National Kidney Foundation
2 Park Avenue
New York, NY 10016

National Multiple Sclerosis Society
205 East 42 Street
New York, NY 10017

National Network Learning
  Disabled Adults
PO Box 2
East Texas State University
Commerce, TX 75428

National Organization on Disability
910 16 Street, NW Room 600
Washington, DC 20006

National Parkinson Institute
1501 NW 9 Avenue
Miami, FL 33136

National Society Children and
  Adults With Autism
1234 Massachusetts Avenue NW,
  #1017
Washington, DC 20005

National Spinal Cord Injury
  Association
600 West Cummings Park #2000
Woburn, MA 01801

National Stroke Association
300 East Hampton Avenue #240
Englewood, CO 80110

National Stuttering Project
1269 7 Avenue
San Francisco, CA 94122

National Tay-Sachs and Allied
  Diseases
92 Washington Avenue
Cedarhurst, NY 11516

National Technology Institute for
  the Deaf
Rochester Institute of Technology
1 Lomb Memorial Drive
Rochester, NY 14623-0887

National Tuberous Sclerosis
  Association
PO Box 612
Winfield, IL 60190

Orton Dyslexia Society
724 York Road
Baltimore, MD 21204

Paralyzed Veterans of America
801 18 Street, NW
Washington, DC 20006

Parkinson's Disease Foundation
640 West 168 Street
New York, NY 10032

Prader-Willi Syndrome Association
5515 Malibu Drive
Edina, MN 55436

Project With Industry
2001 Eye Street, NW
Washington, DC 20006

Research to Prevent Blindness
598 Madison Avenue
New York, NY 10022

Self Help for Hard Hearing People
7800 Wisconsin Avenue
Bethesda, MD 20814

Sensory Aids Foundation
399 Sherman Avenue
Palo Alto, CA 94306

Smith-Kettlewell Institute for Visual
  Sciences
2232 Webster Street
San Francisco, CA 94115

Society Rehabilitation for Facially
  Disfigured
550 First Avenue
New York, NY 10016

Spina Bifida Association of America
1700 Rockville Pike, Suite 540
Rockville, MD 20852

Tourette Syndrome Association
41-02 Bell Boulevard
Bayside, NY 11360

United Cerebral Palsy Association
1522 K Street, NW #1112
Washington, DC 20005

United Scleroderma Foundation
PO Box 350
Watsonville, CA 95007

Veterans of Foreign Wars
200 Maryland Avenue, NE
Washington, DC 20002

Wilson's Disease Association
PO Box 75324
Washington, DC 20013

STATE GOVERNORS' COMMITTEES

ALABAMA

Governor's Committee on
  Employment of People With
  Disabilities
Division of Rehabilitation Service
PO Box 11586
2129 East South Boulevard
Montgomery, AL 36111-0586
(205) 281-8780

ALASKA

Governor's Committee on
  Employment of People With
  Disabilities
3719 Arctic Boulevard
Anchorage, AK 99503
(907) 561-7325
(907) 562-7325 (FAX)

ARIZONA

Arizona Governor's Committee on
  Employment of the Handicapped
1535 West Jefferson
Special Education Unit
Phoenix, AZ 85007
(602) 542-3850

ARKANSAS

Governor's Commission on People
  With Disabilities
7th and Main Streets
PO Box 3781
Little Rock, AR 72203
(501) 682-6695

CALIFORNIA

California Governor's Committee
  for Employment of Disabled
  Persons
PO Box 826880, MIC 41
Sacramento, CA 94280-0001
(916) 323-2545 (Voice or TDD)
(916) 445-0764 (FAX)

COLORADO

Colorado Coalition for Persons
  With Disabilities
Employ Ability, Inc.
789 Sherman Street, Suit 520
Denver, CO 80203
(303) 863-0013 (messages)
(303) 861-2735 (TDD)

CONNECTICUT

Governor's Committee on
  Employment of People With
  Disabilities
Labor Department Building
200 Folly Brook Boulevard
Wethersfield, CT 06109
(203) 566-8061

DELAWARE

Governor's Committee on
  Employment of People With
  Disabilities
Delaware Elwyn Building
321 East 11 Street
Wilmington, DE 19801
(302) 571-3915
(302) 656-0375 (FAX)

DISTRICT OF COLUMBIA

Mayor's Committee on Persons
  With Disabilities
East Potomac Building, Room 1108
605 G Street, NW
Washington, DC 20001
(202) 727-0904

FLORIDA

Florida Governor's Alliance for the
  Employment of Disabled Citizens
Magnolia Park Place
345 South Magnolia Drive, Suite
  A-17
Tallahassee, FL 32301-2947
(904) 487-2222 (Voice)
(904) 487-0925 (TDD)
(904) 922-6936 (FAX)

GEORGIA

Governor's Committee on
  Employment of Handicapped
  Persons
Division of Rehabilitation Service
Field Services Section, Suite 718
878 Peachtree Street, NE
Atlanta, GA 30309
(404) 894-3936
(404) 853-9059 (FAX)

HAWAII

Commission on Persons With
  Disabilities
500 Ala Moana Boulevard
5 Waterfront Plaza, Room 210
Honolulu, HI 96813
(808) 548-7606
(808) 548-7795 (FAX)

IDAHO

Governor's Committee on
  Employment of People With
  Disabilities
Department of Employment
317 Main Street
Boise, ID 83735
(208) 334-6193

ILLINOIS

Liaison to the President's
  Committee on Employment of
  People With Disabilities
Department of Rehabilitative
  Services
100 West Randolph Street, Suite
  8-100
Chicago, IL 60601
(312) 814-2921 (Voice)
(312) 814-5000 (TDD)
(312) 814-2920 (Switchboard)
(312) 814-2923 (FAX)

INDIANA

Indiana State Commission for the
  Handicapped
1330 West Michigan Street
PO Box 1964
Indianapolis, IN 46206-1964
(317) 633-0288
(317) 633-0859 (TDD)

IOWA

Iowa Commission of Persons With
  Disabilities
Department of Human Rights
Lucas State Office Building
Des Moines, IA 50319
(515) 281-5969

KANSAS

Kansas Commission on Disability
  Concerns
1430 SW Topeka Avenue
Topeka, KS 66612-1877
(913) 296-1722 (Voice)
(913) 296-5044 (TDD)
(913) 296-4065 (FAX)

KENTUCKY

Kentucky Committee on
  Employment of People With
  Disabilities
600 West Cedar Street
Louisville, KY 40203
(502) 588-4073

LOUISIANA

Liaison to President's Committee
  on Employment of People With
  Disabilities
Louisiana Rehabilitation Services
PO Box 94371
Baton Rouge, LA 70804
(504) 342-2719

D-6

MAINE

Governor's Committee on
  Employment of the Handicapped
35 Anthony Avenue
Augusta, ME 04330
(207) 626-5307

MARYLAND

Governor's Committee on
  Employment of People With
  Disabilities
1 Market Center, Box 10
300 West Lexington Street
Baltimore, MD 21201
(301) 333-2263
(301) 333-3098 (TDD)
(301) 333-6674 (FAX)

MASSACHUSETTS

Governor's Committee on
  Employment of People With
  Disabilities
Department of Employment and
  Training Policy Office
19 Stanford Street, 4 Floor
Boston, MA 02114
(617) 727-1826

MICHIGAN

Michigan Commission on
  Handicapped Concerns
201 North Washington Avenue
PO Box 30015
Lansing, MI 48909
(517) 373-8397 (Voice/TDD)

MINNESOTA

Minnesota State Council on
  Disability
145 Metro Square Building
7th Place and Jackson Street
St. Paul, MN 55101
(612) 296-6785
(800) 652-9747 (Minnesota only)
(612) 296-5935 (FAX)

MISSISSIPPI

Governor's Office of Handicapped
  Services
Mississippi Department of
  Rehabilitation Services
PO Box 22806
Jackson, MS 39225-2806
(601) 354-6100
(800) 622-6052 (National)

MISSOURI

Governor's Committee on
  Employment of People With
  Disabilities
PO Box 1668
3315 West Truman Boulevard
Jefferson City, MO 65102
(314) 751-2600 (Voice/TTY)
(314) 751-4135 (FAX)

MONTANA

Governor's Committee on
  Employment of People With
  Disabilities
Personnel Division
Mitchell Building, Room 130
Helena, MT 59620
(406) 444-3871
(406) 444-3886

NEBRASKA

Governor's Committee on
  Employment of the Handicapped
Nebraska Job Service, Department
  of Labor
550 South 16 Street, Box 94600
Lincoln, NB 68509
(402) 475-8451

NEVADA

Governor's Committee on
  Employment of People With
  Disabilities
3100 Mill International, Suite 115
Reno, NV 89502
(702) 789-0366
(702) 789-0589 (FAX)

NEW HAMPSHIRE

Governor's Commission on
   Disability
57 Regional Drive
Concord, NH 03301
(603) 271-2773
(603) 271-2837 (FAX)

NEW JERSEY

NO COMMITTEE, but contact:
Division of Developmental
   Disabilities
2-98 East State Street
Trenton, NJ 08625
(609) 292-7824
   or:
New Jersey Department of Labor
CN-110
Trenton, NJ 08625
(609) 292-2323

NEW MEXICO

Governor's Committee on Concerns
   of the Handicapped
Lamy Building, Room 117
491 Old Santa Fe Trail
Santa Fe, NM 87503
(505) 827-6465

NEW YORK

New York State Advocate for the
   Disabled
One Empire State Plaza, Building 1,
   10 Floor
Albany, NY 12223
(518) 474-2825
(518) 473-6005 (FAX)

NORTH CAROLINA

Governor's Advocacy Council for
   Persons With Disabilities
1318 Dale Street, Suite 100
Raleigh, NC 27605-1275
(919) 733-9250 (Voice/TTY)
(919) 733-9173 (FAX)

NORTH DAKOTA

Governor's Committee on
   Employment of People With
   Disabilities
State Capitol Building, 3 Floor
600 East Boulevard Avenue, 3 Floor
Bismarck, ND 58505
(701) 224-2970
(701) 224-3000 (FAX)

OHIO

Ohio Governor's Council on People
   With Disabilities
400 East Campus View Boulevard
Columbus, OH 43235-4604
(614) 438-1393
(800) 282-4536 ext. 1391 (Ohio
   only)
(614) 438-1257 (FAX)

OKLAHOMA

Governor's Committee on
   Employment of the Handicapped
Office of Handicapped Concerns
4300 North Lincoln Boulevard,
   Suite 200
Oklahoma City, OK 73105
(405) 521-3756 (Voice/TDD)
(800) 522-8224 (Voice/TDD)
   (Oklahoma only)

OREGON

Oregon Disabilities Commission
1880 Lancaster, Suite 106
Salem, OR 97310
(503) 378-3142 (Voice)
(503) 378-3599 (TDD)

PENNSYLVANIA

Governor's Committee on
   Employment of People With
   Disabilities
Labor and Industry Building
7th and Forster Streets, Room 1315
Harrisburg, PA 17120
(717) 787-5232
(717) 783-5221 (FAX)

PUERTO RICO

Governor's Committee on
  Employment of the Handicapped
c/o VARO (27)
PO Box 354
Hato Rey, PR 00919
(809) 781-1318

RHODE ISLAND

Governor's Commission on the
  Handicapped
Building 51, 3 Floor
555 Valley Street
Providence, RI 02908-5686
(401) 277-3731 (Voice/TDD)

SOUTH CAROLINA

Governor's Committee on
  Employment of the Handicapped
SC Vocational Rehabilitation
  Department
1410 Boston Avenue
PO Box 15
West Columbia, SC 29171-0015
(803) 822-5324
(803) 822-5386 (FAX)

SOUTH DAKOTA

Governor's Advisory Committee on
  Employment of People With
  Disabilities
Department of Human Services
Kneip Building
700 Governors Drive
Pierre, SD 57501-2275
(605) 773-5990
(605) 773-4855 (FAX)

TENNESSEE

Governor's Committee on
  Employment of People With
  Disabilities
Division of Rehabilitation Services
Citizens Plaza Building, Room 1100
400 Deaderick Street
Nashville, TN 37219
(615) 741-2095
(615) 741-5644 (TDD)
(615) 741-4165 (FAX)

TEXAS

Governor's Committee for Disabled
  Persons
Brown–Heatly Office Building
4900 North Lamar
Austin, TX 75751-2316
(512) 483-4381
(512) 483-4245 (FAX)

UTAH

Governor's Committee on
  Employment of the Handicapped
120 North 200 West
PO Box 45500
Salt Lake City, UT 84103
(801) 538-4210
(801) 538-4192 (TDD)

VERMONT

Governor's Committee on
  Employment of People With
  Disabilities
DD Council
103 South Main Street
Waterbury, VT 05676
(802) 241-2612 (Voice/TDD)
(802) 244-8103 (FAX)

VIRGINIA

Board for the Rights of Virginians
  With Disabilities
James Monroe Building, 17 Floor
101 North 14 Street
Richmond, VA 23219
(804) 225-2042
(804) 225-3221 (FAX)

VIRGIN ISLANDS

Governor's Committee on
  Employment of the Handicapped
Department of Human Services
Barbel Plaza South
St. Thomas, VI 00802
(809) 774-0930 ext. 157
(809) 774-3466 (FAX)

WASHINGTON

Governor's Committee on
  Disability Issues and Employment
Employment Services Division
Employment Security Building,
  KG-11
212 Maple Park
Olympia, WA 98504
(206) 438-3168
(206) 438-3167 (TDD)
(206) 438-4014 (FAX)

WEST VIRGINIA

Liaison Director, Division of
  Rehabilitation Services
State Capitol Building
1900 West Washington Street, East
Charleston, WV 25305
(304) 766-4601
(304) 766-4671 (FAX)

WISCONSIN

Governor's Committee for People
  With Disabilities
131 West Wilson, Suite 1003
PO Box 7852
Madison, WI 53707
(608) 266-5378
(608) 267-2082 (TDD)
(608) 267-2147 (FAX)

WYOMING

Governor's Committee on
  Employment of the Handicapped
Herschler Building, Room 1102
Cheyenne, WY 82002
(307) 777-7191 (Voice/TDD)

Table of Cases

[References are to paragraphs (¶) and Appendix A (A).]

[References are to paragraphs (¶) and Appendix A (A).]

TABLE OF CASES

[References are to paragraphs (¶) and Appendix A (A).]

F

Fazzio Real Estate Co., Adams
v. .... 5.07[1] n.292
Ferguson v. US Department of
Commerce .... 2.07[13] n.415;
A.07[3]; A.08[4][b]
Fields v. Lyng .... 2.02[1][b] n.100;
2.02[3] n.164; 2.06[2][c] n.331;
A.04[8][a]; A.05[2][c]; A.05[3][a]
Fisher v. City of Tucson
.... 1.03[1][c][ii] n.115
Fitzgerald v. Green Valley Area
Educ. Agency ...... 2.07[1] n.363;
A.03[2][e]
Fletcher, Smith v. ... 2.02[1][a] n.69;
3.04[10] & n.32
Fong v. US Department of
Treasury ..... A.07[2]; A.08[4][a]
Forrisi v. Bowen .... 2.02[1][a];
2.02[1][b] & ns. 92, 95;
2.02[2][d][i] & ns. 141, 147;
2.02[2][d][ii] n.156; A.02[2][d]
Fowler v. Frank .... A.04[8][b]
Fowler, Lutter v. .... 2.07[13] n.412
Frank, Black v. ... 2.02 n.33; 2.07[5]
n.383; A.04[6][b]
Frank, Davis v. .... 2.06[2][c]
& n.329; A.03[2][a]
Frank, Fowler v. .... A.04[8][b]
Franklin v. Postal Serv. .. 2.02[1][b]
ns. 92, 98; A.05[2][b]
Freeman, Stutts v. .. 2.02[1][a] n.59;
2.10[2] & n.473; 2.10[3] n.485;
A.06[4]
Fremont Christian School, EEOC
v. 2.01 n.23
Frito-Lay, Inc., Rogers v.
.... 1.03[1][c][ii] n.115

G

GAF Corp., Redmond v.
.... 1.03[1][b][iii] n.88
Garbarczyk v. Board of Educ.
.... 2.15[3] n.648
Gardner v. Morris .. 2.02[1][b] n.90;
2.07[1] n.360

Gardner-Denver, Alexander v.
.... 2.18[2] n.663
Garrison v. District of
Columbia .... 2.14[2] n.627;
A.08[1]; A.08[3][c]
Gelman v. Department of Educ.
.... 1.03[1][c][ii] n.125
General Motors Corp., Doss v.
.... 2.02[2][c] n.135
General Servs. Admin., Thomas
v. .... 2.04 n.231; A.02[2][b];
A.05[2][a]
Gerben v. Holsclaw .. 2.02[1][a] n.74
Goldschmidt, Dopico v. ... 4.01 n.7;
5.01[4][a] n.8
Graves v. Women's Professional
Rodeo Ass'n 2.01 n.6
Greater Los Angeles Council on
Deafness v. Zolin ...... 2.02[1][a]
n.63; 3.04[1] n.3
Green, McDonnell Douglas Corp.
v. .... 2.05[2] n.234; 2.06[2][b][v]
n.328
Green Valley Area Educ. Agency,
Fitzgerald v. .... 2.07[1] n.363;
A.03[2][e]
Griggs v. Duke Power Co.
.... 2.05[4][a] & n.260
Guerriero v. Schultz ..... 2.02[1][b]
ns. 92, 101; A.05[3][f]
Guinn v. Bolger ... 2.02[2][b] n.127;
2.06[2][b][i] & n.316; 3.04[3]
& n.12; A.06[5]
Gurmankin v. Costanzo .. 2.02[1][a]
n.58; 3.04[2] n.7

H

Hall v. US Postal Serv.
...... 1.03[1][b][iii] n.89; 2.06[2]
n.297; 2.11 & ns. 500, 501
H&H Music Co., McGann v.
.... 2.15[3] n.647
Hardison, TVA v. 2.08 n.426
Harris v. Adams ... 2.06[2][c] n.331
Harris, Longoria v. ...... 2.02[2][b]
n.128

[References are to paragraphs (¶) and Appendix A (A).]

Texas Indus., Inc., Department of
  Labor, OFCCP v. .... 2.02 ns. 39,
  42; 2.02[1][a] n.56; 2.12[1]
  n.530; A.06[6][a]
Texas Instruments, Department of
  Labor v. .... 2.12[1] n.526
Thomas v. General Servs. Admin.
  .... 2.04 n.231; A.02[2][b];
  A.05[2][a]
Thornburgh, Nelson v. ... 2.08[2] &
  n.446; 4.01 n.7; A.03[2][f]
Thornhill v. Marsh ...... 2.02[1][a]
  n.56; 2.02[5] & ns. 212, 216;
  A.01[2]
Tillman v. Wheaton-Haven
  Recreation Ass'n 2.01 n.16;
  5.02[1][c] n.44
Tisch, Carter v. ..... 2.02[1][a] n.61;
  2.07[5] n.383; A.04[4][b];
  A.04[6][c]
Tisch, Dexler v. .... 2.02[1][a] n.72;
  2.06[2][a] n.306;
  2.12[1] n.522
Tisch, Dowden v. 2.04 n.230
Tisch, Shea v. ... 1.03[1][b][iii] n.92;
  2.02[1][b] n.91; 2.07[5] n.383;
  A.04[4][a]
Tisch, Wright v. ...... 2.07[5] n.345
Treadwell v. Alexander
  .... 1.03[1][b][iii] n.94; 2.02[1][a]
  n.67; 2.02[1][c] n.106;
  2.06[2][a] n.305; 2.06[2][b][i]
  n.317; 2.06[2][c] ns. 331,
  332; 3.04[4] n.14;
  A.04[5][b]; A.04[7];
  A.05[5][b]
Trimble v. Carlin ..... 2.07[1] n.353;
  2.07[2] n.375; 2.07[14] n.420;
  A.03[1]
Tudyman v. United Airlines
  ... 2.02[1][a] n.84; 2.02[2][d][i] &
  n.143; A.02[2][h]
TVA v. Hardison 2.08 n.426

U

United Airlines, Tudyman v.
  ... 2.02[1][a] n.84; 2.02[2][d][i] &
  n.143; A.02[2][h]

United Air Lines, Inc., Davis v.
  .... 1.03[1][c][ii] n.115
United Air Lines Inc., McMann v.
  .... 2.15[3] n.643
United Way of Erie County,
  Martin v. .... 2.01 ns. 9, 10
University of NC, Crawford v.
  ..... 2.02[1][a] n.63; 3.04[1] n.3
University of Tex., Camenisch v.
  ..... 2.02[1][a] n.63; 3.04[1] n.3
University of Wis., Anderson v.
  .... 2.06[2][b][v] n.328
Upshur v. Love ..... 2.02[1][a] n.58;
  3.04[2] n.7
US Department of Army, Rosiak
  v. ...... 2.07[1] n.360; A.04[5][a];
  A.05[5][a]
US Department of Commerce,
  Ferguson v. ...... 2.07[13] n.415;
  A.07[3]; A.08[4][b]
US Department of Justice, Rezza
  v. ... 2.02[1][b] n.93; 2.02[3] n.163
US Department of Labor,
  Bentivegna v. 2.02 n.39;
  2.02[1][a] n.55; 2.06[2][c]
  n.330; 2.12[2] & n.533; 3.04[6]
  n.21; 4.01 n.7
US Department of Labor, Cook
  v. .... 2.06[2][d] n.335
US Department of the Army,
  Rhone v. 2.02 n.35; 4.01 n.7
US Department of Transp., Crane
  v. .... 2.07[1] n.353
US Department of Treasury,
  Blackwell v. .... 2.02[3] n.170;
  A.07[1]
US Department of Treasury, Fong
  v. .... A.08[4][a]; A.07[2]
US District Ct. Cent. Dist. of Cal.,
  Chalk v. .... 2.07[1] & n.369; 2.11
  n.494; 5.04[1][b] n.104;
  A.01[1][a]
US General Servs. Admin, Adams
  v. ...... 2.11[3] n.516; A.02[2][a];
  A.05[4][a]
US Postal Serv., Boyd v.
  .... 1.03[1][c][ii] n.116
US Postal Serv., Carty v.
  .... 1.03[1][b][iii] n.95;
  2.07[5] n.383

Index

[References are to paragraphs (¶) and Appendix A (A).]

INDEX

[References are to paragraphs (¶) and Appendix A (A).]

INDEX

[References are to paragraphs (¶) and Appendix A (A).]

[References are to paragraphs (¶) and Appendix A (A).]

[References are to paragraphs (¶) and Appendix A (A).]

[References are to paragraphs (¶) and Appendix A (A).]

INDEX

[References are to paragraphs (¶) and Appendix A (A).]

Rehabilitation, illegal drug or alcohol use, 2.14, 2.14[1][a]

Relationship to disabled. *See* Associate of disabled, discrimination against

Relay services
See also Telecommunications
as ADA Title III auxiliary aid and service, 5.04[4][a]
FCC enforcement, 6.02[6]
interstate communication, 6.02[5][a]
intrastate communication, 6.02[5][b]
remedies and complaints, 6.02[5][c]
telecommunications access, 6.02[1][c], 6.02[4][c], 6.02[4][e]

Relief
disability discrimination, 2.18[1]
telecommunications access complaints, 6.02[5][c]
violation of ADA Title II, 4.02[2]

Religious organization
ADA Title III exemption, 5.02[1][c]
scope of ADA, 2.01

Remanufactured rail passenger cars commuter cars, 4.05[3][c]
private company in transportation business, 5.06[1][e][ii]

Removal of structural barrier. *See* Barrier removal

Residence, ADA Title III definition, 5.02[1][b][i]

Restaurant, as ADA Title III public accommodation, 5.02[1][b][i]

Restrooms, accessibility, 7.02

Restructuring job. *See* Job restructuring

Right of action. *See* Private right of action

S

Safe harbor, implementation of accommodation methods, 2.09[2]

Safety
equal access exception to ADA Title III, 5.04[1][b]
Federal Railroad Safety Act, 5.06[1][e][i]
negates reasonable accommodation, A.04[7]

Sarcoidosis, reasonable accommodation alternative, A.03[2][c]

Schedule modification. *See* Job schedule

Schizophrenia, as legitimate rejection grounds for foreign service, A.05[3][f]

School
as ADA Title III public accommodation, 5.02[1][b][i]
transportation, 4.04[2][e]

Scope, disproportionate, ADA Title III construction and alteration, 5.05[2][c]

Screening, pre-employment
See also Qualification standards
prohibited criteria, 2.10
burden of proof, 2.10[3]
business necessity, 2.10[1]
combination of tasks, 2.10[4]
test administration, 2.10[2]

Section 225, ADA Title IV
telecommunications access for hearing and speech impaired individuals
definitions, 6.02[1]
common carrier or carrier, 6.02[1][a]
relay services, 6.02[1][c]
telecommunications device for the deaf, 6.02[1][b]
enforcement, 6.02[5]
interstate communications, 6.02[5][a]
intrastate communications, 6.02[5][b]

[References are to paragraphs (¶) and Appendix A (A).]

[References are to paragraphs (¶) and Appendix A (A).]

INDEX